THE WORLD'S GREAT CLASSICS

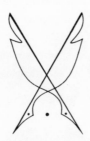

William Shakespeare

THE COMPLETE
HISTORIES

POEMS

Edited by GEORGE LYMAN KITTREDGE, Gurney Professor
of English Literature, Harvard University;
with an introduction by MICHAEL BENTHALL, Director of the
Old Vic Theatre, and a biography of the author by
EDWIN E. WILLOUGHBY of the Folger Shakespeare Library

THE KITTREDGE-PLAYERS EDITION
Illustrated with photographs of actual stage productions

Grolier
INCORPORATED
NEW YORK

Standard Book Number 7172-0000-0

PRINTED IN THE UNITED STATES OF AMERICA

Contents

HISTORIES

The Life and Death of King John	1
The Tragedy of King Richard the Second	35
The First Part of King Henry the Fourth	73
The Second Part of King Henry the Fourth	111
The Life of King Henry the Fifth	153
The First Part of King Henry the Sixth	195
The Second Part of King Henry the Sixth	233
The Third Part of King Henry the Sixth	275
The Tragedy of King Richard the Third	317
The Famous History of the Life of King Henry the Eighth	367

POEMS

Venus and Adonis	411
The Rape of Lucrece	428
Sonnets	451
A Lover's Complaint	480
The Passionate Pilgrim	484
The Phoenix and the Turtle	488

For a Glossary see THE COMPLETE COMEDIES

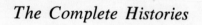

The Complete Histories

KING JOHN

'The Troublesome Raigne of Iohn King of England. . . . As it was (sundry times) publikely acted by the Queenes Maiesties Players' and 'The Second part of the troublesome Raigne of King Iohn. . . . As it was (sundry times) publikely acted by' the same were both published in 1591 as distinct quartos and republished together in 1611 and 1622. The title page of 1611 asserts that the whole was 'Written by W. Sh.' and that of 1622 spells the surname at full length. This ascription is unquestionably false. The author must remain anonymous. George Peele is a possible candidate, but the evidence in his favour is purely internal and not very impressive. The date of composition may be conjecturally put back two or three years before the publication in 1591. The short address in verse 'To the Gentlemen Readers,' prefixed to Part I, mentions *Tamburlaine* as having been received with applause. It sounds like a prologue, but may or may not have been written at the same time as the play. *Tamburlaine* dates from about 1587.

Shakespeare's play, THE LIFE AND DEATH OF KING JOHN, was first printed in the Folio of 1623, which is therefore our only authority for the text. Meres mentions it in 1598 among Shakespeare's tragedies (see p. 33, above). How much earlier it was written cannot be exactly determined. Shakespeare's son Hamnet died in August, 1596, and biographers are tempted to read his father's own grief in the passionate laments of Constance for Arthur. But that is reasoning in a circle, for nobody doubts that the greatest of all dramatists could have written these passages if he had never had a son. Still, 1596 is a reasonable date for KING JOHN. In any case, it is more likely to have preceded *Richard II* than to have followed it.

For his material Shakespeare went to *The Troublesome Reign* instead of working up a plot from Holinshed's *Chronicle*; but KING JOHN is a new play, not a revision. Like its predecessor it covers the whole of John's reign (1199–1216), and the order of events is the same, with a modicum of readjustment. That order quite warrantably sacrifices historical preciseness to dramatic effect. Chatillon's embassy is the invention of the older playwright. So is the episode of the Faulconbridge brothers, for which he may have taken a hint from the case of Dunois, the famous Bastard of Orleans, as recorded by Holinshed. Austria (in both plays) is a fusion (accidental or deliberate) of Duke Leopold, Richard Cœur-de-Lion's captor, who died in 1195, with Widomar Viscount of Limoges, killed, Holinshed says, by a bastard son of Richard to avenge his father, who met his death while besieging the viscount's castle.

Many incidents or whole episodes of *The Troublesome Reign* are dropped by Shakespeare. His omissions are : — Philip Faulconbridge's fruitless attempt to arrange for a duel with the Duke of Austria; his tearing the lion's skin from Austria's shoulders; his killing Austria in battle *coram populo*; the long scene in which he ransacks the chests of monk and nun and arrests Peter the prophet; the interview between Peter and King John in which the prophet interprets the omen of the five moons and tells the king that he shall lose his crown before high noon on Ascension Day; the very long scene on Ascension Day in which the king hears Peter reiterate his prophecy, is informed by

1

Hubert of Arthur's fatal fall, orders him to hang Peter forthwith, is told by Faulconbridge that the sentence has been carried out and also that Lewis (having been elected King of England by the peers) is expected to land at any moment, submits to Pandulph, and learns that the French fleet has actually been sighted off the coast of Kent; the scene at St. Edmondsbury, in which the English peers, despite the efforts of Faulconbridge, swear fealty to Lewis, and Lewis and the French nobles take an oath to put their English allies to death when the victory is won; the soliloquy of Thomas, a monk of Swinstead, in which he resolves to murder King John, and the interview between him and the Abbot, in which he discloses his purpose and is absolved; the poisoning of the king in a wassail cup and the death of the monk, who must, as 'taster,' drink first from the cup which he offers; the coronation of Henry III.

In most instances nothing is lost by these omissions, for the facts are made known to the audience in the course of the dialogue. Shakespeare has been censured, however, for nowhere revealing the poisoner's motive. Surely no such explanation was requisite. We have King John's orders to Faulconbridge (iii, 3, 7–11):

> See thou shake the bags
> Of hoarding abbots; set at liberty
> Imprison'd angels. The fat ribs of peace
> Must by the hungry now be fed upon.
> Use our commission in his utmost force.

And Faulconbridge has duly rendered his account (iv, 2, 141–142):

> How I have sped among the clergymen
> The sums I have collected shall express.

After that, the monk's motive might reasonably be taken for granted.

Most of the old play is in sonorous blank verse with occasional bits of competent prose. One scene exhibits a riotous mingle-mangle of rhyming measures — fourteeners, octosyllabics, and Skeltonical short lines — as well as a bit of prose dialogue. This is the comic scene (omitted by Shakespeare) in which Faulconbridge plunders the clergy.

In KING JOHN the language is Shakespeare's throughout, with occasional slight echoes of the older phraseology. He rewrites completely even those passages of which he keeps the substance. Compare with Faulconbridge's concluding speech in KING JOHN the similar valediction in the old play, which runs as follows:

> Thus England's peace begins in Henry's reign,
> And bloody wars are clos'd with happy league.
> Let England live but true within itself,
> And all the world can never wrong her state;
> Lewis, thou shalt be bravely shipp'd to France,
> For never Frenchman got of English ground
> The twentieth part that thou hast conquered.
> Dauphin, thy hand! To Worcester we will march.
> Lords all, lay hands to bear your sovereign
> With obsequies of honour to his grave.
> If England's peers and people join in one,
> Nor Pope, nor France, nor Spain can do them wrong.

2

THE LIFE AND DEATH OF
KING JOHN

[Dramatis Personæ.

King John.
Prince Henry, his son.
Arthur, Duke of Britain (Bretagne), son of the
King's elder brother, Geffrey.
The Earl of Pembroke.
The Earl of Essex.
The Earl of Salisbury.
The Lord Bigot.
Hubert de Burgh.
Robert Faulconbridge, son to Sir Robert Faulcon-
bridge.
Philip the Bastard, his half-brother.
James Gurney, servant to Lady Faulconbridge.
Peter of Pomfret, a prophet.
Philip, King of France.
Lewis, the Dauphin.

The Duke of Austria.
Cardinal Pandulph, the Pope's legate.
Melun, a French lord.
Chatillon, ambassador from France.

Queen Elinor, widow of King Henry II, and mother
to King John.
Constance, mother to Arthur.
Blanch of Spain, daughter to the King of Castile
and niece to King John.
Lady Faulconbridge, widow of Sir Robert Faulconbridge.

Lords, Citizens of Angiers, Sheriff, Heralds, Officers, Soldiers, Executioners, Messengers, Attendants.

SCENE. — Sometimes in England, sometimes in France.]

ACT I. Scene I. [King John's Palace.]

Enter King John, Queen Elinor, Pembroke,
Essex, and Salisbury, [and others,] with Chatillon of France.

K. John. Now say, Chatillon, what would
France with us?
Chat. Thus, after greeting, speaks the King
of France
In my behaviour to the majesty,
The borrowed majesty, of England here.
Eli. A strange beginning! 'Borrowed maj-
esty'? 5
K. John. Silence, good mother; hear the
embassy.
Chat. Philip of France, in right and true
behalf
Of thy deceased brother Geffrey's son,
Arthur Plantagenet, lays most lawful claim
To this fair island and the territories,
To Ireland, Poictiers, Anjou, Touraine, Maine,
Desiring thee to lay aside the sword
Which sways usurpingly these several titles
And put the same into young Arthur's hand,
Thy nephew and right royal sovereign. 15
K. John. What follows if we disallow of this?
Chat. The proud control of fierce and bloody
war,

To enforce these rights so forcibly withheld.
K. John. Here have we war for war and blood
for blood,
Controlment for controlment. So answer
France. 20
Chat. Then take my king's defiance from my
mouth,
The farthest limit of my embassy.
K. John. Bear mine to him, and so depart
in peace.
Be thou as lightning in the eyes of France;
For ere thou canst report I will be there, 25
The thunder of my cannon shall be heard.
So hence! Be thou the trumpet of our wrath
And sullen presage of your own decay.
An honourable conduct let him have;
Pembroke, look to't. Farewell, Chatillon. 30
Exeunt Chatillon and Pembroke.
Eli. What now, my son? Have I not ever
said
How that ambitious Constance would not cease
Till she had kindled France and all the
world
Upon the right and party of her son?
This might have been prevented and made
whole 35
With very easy arguments of love,

3

Which now the manage of two kingdoms must
With fearful bloody issue arbitrate.
K. John. Our strong possession and our
    right for us!
Eli. [*aside to K. John*] Your strong possession
much more than your right,   40
Or else it must go wrong with you and me.
So much my conscience whispers in your ear,
Which none but heaven and you and I shall
    hear.

Enter a *Sheriff.*

Essex. My liege, here is the strangest con-
    troversy
Come from the country to be judg'd by you 45
That e'er I heard. Shall I produce the men?
K. John. Let them approach.
                  [*Exit Sheriff.*]
Our abbeys and our priories shall pay
This expedition's charge.

Enter *Robert Faulconbridge* and *Philip* [his
    bastard brother].
          What men are you?
Phil. Your faithful subject I, a gentleman,
Born in Northamptonshire, and eldest son, 51
As I suppose, to Robert Faulconbridge,
A soldier by the honour-giving hand
Of Cœur-de-lion knighted in the field.
K. John. What art thou?   55
Rob. The son and heir to that same Faulcon-
    bridge.
K. John. Is that the elder, and art thou the
    heir?
You came not of one mother then, it seems.
Phil. Most certain of one mother, mighty
    king —
That is well known — and, as I think, one
    father;   60
But for the certain knowledge of that truth
I put you o'er to heaven and to my mother.
Of that I doubt, as all men's children may.
Eli. Out on thee, rude man! Thou dost
    shame thy mother
And wound her honour with this diffidence. 65
Phil. I, madam? No, I have no reason for
    it.
That is my brother's plea, and none of mine;
The which if he can prove, 'a pops me out
At least from fair five hundred pound a year.
Heaven guard my mother's honour and my
    land!   70
K. John. A good blunt fellow. Why, being
    younger born,
Doth he lay claim to thine inheritance?

Phil. I know not why, except to get the land;
But once he slander'd me with bastardy.
But whe'r I be as true begot or no,   75
That still I lay upon my mother's head;
But that I am as well begot, my liege
(Fair fall the bones that took the pains for me!),
Compare our faces and be judge yourself.
If old Sir Robert did beget us both   80
And were our father, and this son like him —
O old Sir Robert, father, on my knee
I give heaven thanks I was not like to thee!
K. John. Why, what a madcap hath heaven
    lent us here!   84
Eli. He hath a trick of Cœur-de-lion's face;
The accent of his tongue affecteth him.
Do you not read some tokens of my son
In the large composition of this man?
K. John. Mine eye hath well examined his
    parts   89
And finds them perfect Richard. Sirrah, speak,
What doth move you to claim your brother's
    land?
Phil. Because he hath a half-face, like my
    father.
With half that face would he have all my land.
A half-fac'd groat, five hundred pound a year!
Rob. My gracious liege, when that my father
    liv'd,   95
Your brother did employ my father much —
Phil. Well, sir, by this you cannot get my
    land.
Your tale must be how he employ'd my mother.
Rob. And once dispatch'd him in an embassy
To Germany, there with the Emperor   100
To treat of high affairs touching that time.
Th' advantage of his absence took the King
And in the meantime sojourn'd at my father's;
Where how he did prevail I shame to speak,
But truth is truth. Large lengths of seas and
    shores   105
Between my father and my mother lay,
As I have heard my father speak himself,
When this same lusty gentleman was got.
Upon his deathbed he by will bequeath'd
His lands to me, and took it on his death   110
That this, my mother's son, was none of his;
And if he were, he came into the world
Full fourteen weeks before the course of time.
Then, good my liege, let me have what is mine,
My father's land, as was my father's will.   115
K. John. Sirrah, your brother is legitimate.
Your father's wife did after wedlock bear him,
And if she did play false, the fault was hers;
Which fault lies on the hazards of all husbands
That marry wives. Tell me, how if my brother,

4

Who, as you say, took pains to get this son, 121
Had of your father claim'd this son for his?
In sooth, good friend, your father might have
    kept
This calf, bred from his cow, from all the world.
In sooth he might. Then, if he were my
    brother's,   125
My brother might not claim him; nor your
    father,
Being none of his, refuse him. This concludes:
My mother's son did get your father's heir;
Your father's heir must have your father's land.
  Rob. Shall then my father's will be of no
    force   130
To dispossess that child which is not his?
  Phil. Of no more force to dispossess me, sir,
Than was his will to get me, as I think.
  Eli. Whether hadst thou rather be a Faulcon-
    bridge,
And like thy brother, to enjoy thy land, 135
Or the reputed son of Cœur-de-lion,
Lord of thy presence and no land beside?
  Bast. Madam, an if my brother had my
    shape,
And I had his, Sir Robert his, like him;
And if my legs were two such riding rods, 140
My arms such eel-skins stuff'd, my face so thin
That in mine ear I durst not stick a rose
Lest men should say 'Look where three-
    farthings goes!'
And, to his shape, were heir to all this land —
Would I might never stir from off this place,
I would give it every foot to have this face! 146
I would not be Sir Nob in any case.
  Eli. I like thee well. Wilt thou forsake thy
    fortune,
Bequeath thy land to him, and follow me?
I am a soldier, and now bound to France. 150
  Bast. Brother, take you my land, I'll take
    my chance.
Your face hath got five hundred pound a year;
Yet sell your face for fivepence, and 'tis dear.
Madam, I'll follow you unto the death.
  Eli. Nay, I would have you go before me
    thither.   155
  Bast. Our country manners give our betters
    way.
  K. John. What is thy name?
  Bast. Philip, my liege, so is my name be-
    gun —
Philip, good old Sir Robert's wive's eldest son.
  K. John. From henceforth bear his name
    whose form thou bearest.   160
Kneel thou down Philip, but arise more great;
Arise Sir Richard and Plantagenet.

  Bast. Brother by th' mother's side, give me
    your hand!
My father gave me honour, yours gave land.
Now blessed be the hour, by night or day, 165
When I was got, Sir Robert was away!
  Eli. The very spirit of Plantagenet!
I am thy grandam, Richard. Call me so.
  Bast. Madam, by chance, but not by truth.
    What though?
Something about, a little from the right, 170
    In at the window, or else o'er the hatch.
Who dares not stir by day must walk by night;
    And have is have, however men do catch.
Near or far off, well won is still well shot,
And I am I, howe'er I was begot. 175
  K. John. Go, Faulconbridge; now hast thou
    thy desire:
A landless knight makes thee a landed squire.
Come, madam, and come, Richard; we must
    speed
For France, for France, for it is more than need.
  Bast. Brother, adieu. Good fortune come to
    thee!   180
For thou wast got i' th' way of honesty.
                 Exeunt all but Bastard.
A foot of honour better than I was,
But many a many foot of land the worse!
Well, now can I make any Joan a lady.
'Good den, Sir Richard!' 'God-a-mercy,
    fellow!'   185
And if his name be George, I'll call him Peter;
For new-made honour doth forget men's names:
'Tis too respective and too sociable
For your conversion. Now your traveller,
He and his toothpick at my worship's mess: 190
And when my knightly stomach is suffic'd,
Why, then I suck my teeth and catechize
My picked man of countries. 'My dear sir,'
Thus, leaning on mine elbow, I begin, 194
'I shall beseech you.' That is question now,
And then comes answer like an Absey-book:
'O sir,' says answer, 'at your best command,
At your employment, at your service, sir!'
'No, sir,' says question. 'I, sweet sir, at yours!'
And so, ere answer knows what question
    would —   200
Saving in dialogue of compliment,
And talking of the Alps and Apennines,
The Pyrenean and the river Po —
It draws toward supper in conclusion so.
But this is worshipful society 205
And fits the mounting spirit like myself;
For he is but a bastard to the time
That doth not smack of observation —
And so am I, whether I smack or no;

5

And not alone in habit and device, 210
Exterior form, outward accoutrement,
But from the inward motion to deliver
Sweet, sweet, sweet poison for the age's tooth;
Which, though I will not practise to deceive,
Yet, to avoid deceit, I mean to learn; 215
For it shall strew the footsteps of my rising.
But who comes in such haste in riding robes?
What woman post is this? Hath she no husband
That will take pains to blow a horn before her?

Enter Lady Faulconbridge and *James Gurney.*

O me! it is my mother. How now, good lady?
What brings you here to court so hastily? 221
Lady. Where is that slave, thy brother?
Where is he,
That holds in chase mine honour up and down?
Bast. My brother Robert? old Sir Robert's
son?
Colbrand the giant, that same mighty man? 225
Is it Sir Robert's son that you seek so?
Lady. Sir Robert's son? Ay, thou unrever-
end boy,
Sir Robert's son. Why scorn'st thou at Sir
Robert?
He is Sir Robert's son, and so art thou.
Bast. James Gurney, wilt thou give us leave
awhile? 230
Gur. Good leave, good Philip.
Bast. Philip? — sparrow! — James,
There's toys abroad. Anon I'll tell thee more.
Exit James.
Madam, I was not old Sir Robert's son;
Sir Robert might have eat his part in me
Upon Good Friday and ne'er broke his fast. 235
Sir Robert could do well: marry, to confess,
Could he get me? Sir Robert could not do it;
We know his handiwork. Therefore, good
mother,
To whom am I beholding for these limbs?
Sir Robert never holp to make this leg. 240
Lady. Hast thou conspired with thy brother
too,

That for thine own gain shouldst defend mine
honour?
What means this scorn, thou most untoward
knave?
Bast. Knight, knight, good mother, Basilisco-
like! 244
What! I am dubb'd; I have it on my shoulder.
But, mother, I am not Sir Robert's son;
I have disclaim'd Sir Robert and my land;
Legitimation, name, and all is gone.
Then, good my mother, let me know my father!
Some proper man, I hope. Who was it, mother?
Lady. Hast thou denied thyself a Faulcon-
bridge? 251
Bast. As faithfully as I deny the devil.
Lady. King Richard Cœur-de-lion was thy
father.
By long and vehement suit I was seduc'd 254
To make room for him in my husband's bed.
Heaven lay not my transgression to my charge!
Thou art the issue of my dear offence,
Which was so strongly urg'd past my defence.
Bast. Now, by this light, were I to get again,
Madam, I would not wish a better father. 260
Some sins do bear their privilege on earth,
And so doth yours. Your fault was not your
folly.
Needs must you lay your heart at his dispose,
Subjected tribute to commanding love,
Against whose fury and unmatched force 265
The awless lion could not wage the fight
Nor keep his princely heart from Richard's
hand.
He that perforce robs lions of their hearts
May easily win a woman's. Ay, my mother,
With all my heart I thank thee for my father!
Who lives and dares but say thou didst not well
When I was got, I'll send his soul to hell.
Come, lady, I will show thee to my kin;
And they shall say, when Richard me begot,
If thou hadst said him nay, it had been sin. 275
Who says it was, he lies; I say 'twas not.
Exeunt.

[ACT II. Scene I. *France. Before Angiers.*]

Enter, before Angiers, *Philip King of France,
Lewis [the] Dauphin, Constance, Arthur,* [with
Forces, at one door; at the other,] *Austria*
[with *Forces*].

France. Before Angiers well met, brave
Austria.
Arthur, that great forerunner of thy blood,

Richard, that robb'd the lion of his heart
And fought the holy wars in Palestine, 4
By this brave duke came early to his grave;
And, for amends to his posterity,
At our importance hither is he come
To spread his colours, boy, in thy behalf,
And to rebuke the usurpation
Of thy unnatural uncle, English John. 10

Embrace him, love him, give him welcome
hither.
Arth. God shall forgive you Cœur-de-lion's
death
The rather that you give his offspring life,
Shadowing their right under your wings of war.
I give you welcome with a powerless hand, 15
But with a heart full of unstained love.
Welcome before the gates of Angiers, Duke.
France. A noble boy! Who would not do thee
right?
Aust. Upon thy cheek lay I this zealous kiss
As seal to this indenture of my love: 20
That to my home I will no more return
Till Angiers and the right thou hast in France,
Together with that pale, that white-fac'd shore
Whose foot spurns back the ocean's roaring
tides
And coops from other lands her islanders — 25
Even till that England, hedg'd in with the
main,
That water-walled bulwark, still secure
And confident from foreign purposes —
Even till that utmost corner of the West
Salute thee for her king. Till then, fair boy, 30
Will I not think of home, but follow arms.
Const. O, take his mother's thanks, a widow's
thanks,
Till your strong hand shall help to give him
strength
To make a more requital to your love!
Aust. The peace of heaven is theirs that lift
their swords 35
In such a just and charitable war.
France. Well then, to work! Our cannon
shall be bent
Against the brows of this resisting town.
Call for our chiefest men of discipline,
To cull the plots of best advantages. 40
We'll lay before this town our royal bones,
Wade to the market place in Frenchmen's blood,
But we will make it subject to this boy.
Const. Stay for an answer to your embassy,
Lest unadvis'd you stain your swords with
blood. 45
My Lord Chatillon may from England bring
That right in peace which here we urge in war,
And then we shall repent each drop of blood
That hot rash haste so indirectly shed.

Enter Chatillon.

France. A wonder, lady! Lo, upon thy wish
Our messenger Chatillon is arriv'd! 51
What England says, say briefly, gentle lord.
We coldly pause for thee; Chatillon, speak.

Chat. Then turn your forces from this paltry
siege
And stir them up against a mightier task. 55
England, impatient of your just demands,
Hath put himself in arms. The adverse winds,
Whose leisure I have stay'd, have given him
time
To land his legions all as soon as I.
His marches are expedient to this town, 60
His forces strong, his soldiers confident.
With him along is come the mother queen,
An Ate stirring him to blood and strife;
With her her niece, the Lady Blanch of Spain;
With them a bastard of the King's deceas'd; 65
And all th' unsettled humours of the land,
Rash, inconsiderate, fiery voluntaries,
With ladies' faces and fierce dragons' spleens,
Have sold their fortunes at their native homes,
Bearing their birthrights proudly on their backs,
To make a hazard of new fortunes here. 71
In brief, a braver choice of dauntless spirits
Than now the English bottoms have waft o'er
Did never float upon the swelling tide
To do offence and scathe in Christendom. 75
               Drum beats.
The interruption of their churlish drums
Cuts off more circumstance. They are at hand,
To parley or to fight; therefore prepare.
France. How much unlook'd for is this ex-
pedition! 79
Aust. By how much unexpected, by so much
We must awake endeavour for defence;
For courage mounteth with occasion.
Let them be welcome then; we are prepar'd.

*Enter King of England, Bastard, Queen [Elinor],
Blanch, Pembroke, and others.*

K. John. Peace be to France, if France in
peace permit
Our just and lineal entrance to our own! 85
If not, bleed France, and peace ascend to
heaven,
Whiles we, God's wrathful agent, do correct
Their proud contempt that beats his peace to
heaven!
France. Peace be to England, if that war
return 89
From France to England, there to live in peace!
England we love, and for that England's sake
With burden of our armour here we sweat.
This toil of ours should be a work of thine;
But thou from loving England art so far 94
That thou hast underwrought his lawful king,
Cut off the sequence of posterity,
Outfaced infant state, and done a rape

7

Upon the maiden virtue of the crown.
Look here upon thy brother Geffrey's face!
These eyes, these brows, were moulded out of
his; 100
This little abstract doth contain that large
Which died in Geffrey, and the hand of time
Shall draw this brief into as huge a volume.
That Geffrey was thy elder brother born, 104
And this his son. England was Geffrey's right,
And this is Geffrey's. In the name of God,
How comes it then that thou art call'd a king
When living blood doth in these temples beat
Which owe the crown that thou o'ermasterest?
K. John. From whom hast thou this great
commission, France, 110
To draw my answer from thy articles?
France. From that supernal judge that stirs
good thoughts
In any breast of strong authority
To look into the blots and stains of right. 114
That judge hath made me guardian to this boy;
Under whose warrant I impeach thy wrong,
And by whose help I mean to chastise it.
K. John. Alack! thou dost usurp authority.
France. Excuse — it is to beat usurping
down. 119
Eli. Who is it thou dost call usurper, France?
Const. Let me make answer: thy usurping
son.
Eli. Out, insolent! Thy bastard shall be
King,
That thou mayst be a queen and check the
world!
Const. My bed was ever to thy son as true
As thine was to thy husband; and this boy 125
Liker in feature to his father Geffrey
Than thou and John in manners, being as like
As rain to water or devil to his dam.
My boy a bastard? By my soul, I think
His father never was so true begot! 130
It cannot be, an if thou wert his mother.
Eli. There's a good mother, boy, that blots
thy father!
Const. There's a good grandam, boy, that
would blot thee!
Aust. Peace!
Bast. Hear the crier.
Aust. What the devil art thou?
Bast. One that will play the devil, sir, with
you 135
An 'a may catch your hide and you alone.
You are the hare of whom the proverb goes,
Whose valour plucks dead lions by the beard.
I'll smoke your skin-coat an I catch you right.
Sirrah, look to't! I' faith I will, i' faith! 140

Blanch. O, well did he become that lion's
robe
That did disrobe the lion of that robe!
Bast. It lies as sightly on the back of him
As great Alcides' shows upon an ass. 144
But, ass, I'll take that burthen from your back
Or lay on that shall make your shoulders crack.
Aust. What cracker is this same that deafs
our ears
With this abundance of superfluous breath?
King Philip, determine what we shall do
straight.
France. Women and fools, break off your
conference. 150
King John, this is the very sum of all:
England and Ireland, Anjou, Touraine, Maine,
In right of Arthur do I claim of thee.
Wilt thou resign them and lay down thy arms?
K. John. My life as soon. I do defy thee,
France. 155
Arthur of Britain, yield thee to my hand,
And out of my dear love I'll give thee more
Than e'er the coward hand of France can win.
Submit thee, boy.
Eli. Come to thy grandam, child.
Const. Do, child! go to it grandam, child!
Give grandam kingdom, and it grandam will
Give it a plum, a cherry, and a fig.
There's a good grandam!
Arth. Good my mother, peace!
I would that I were low laid in my grave. 164
I am not worth this coil that's made for me.
Eli. His mother shames him so, poor boy
he weeps.
Const. Now shame upon you, whe'r she does
or no!
His grandam's wrongs, and not his mother's
shames,
Draws those heaven-moving pearls from his
poor eyes,
Which heaven shall take in nature of a fee. 170
Ay, with these crystal beads heaven shall be
brib'd
To do him justice and revenge on you.
Eli. Thou monstrous slanderer of heaven and
earth!
Const. Thou monstrous injurer of heaven
and earth,
Call not me slanderer! Thou and thine usurp
The dominations, royalties, and rights 176
Of this oppressed boy. This is thy eldest son's
son,
Infortunate in nothing but in thee.
Thy sins are visited in this poor child;
The canon of the law is laid on him, 180

8

Being but the second generation
Removed from thy sin-conceiving womb.
  K. John. Bedlam, have done!
  Const.   I have but this to say,
That he is not only plagued for her sin,
But God hath made her sin and her the plague
On this removed issue, plagu'd for her   186
And with her plague; her sin his injury,
Her injury the beadle to her sin;
All punish'd in the person of this child,
And all for her — a plague upon her!   190
  Eli. Thou unadvised scold, I can produce
A will that bars the title of thy son.
  Const. Ay, who doubts that? A will! a
    wicked will;
A woman's will; a cank'red grandam's will!
  France. Peace, lady! pause, or be more
    temperate.   195
It ill beseems this presence to cry aim
To these ill-tuned repetitions.
Some trumpet summon hither to the walls
These men of Angiers. Let us hear them speak
Whose title they admit, Arthur's or John's.   200

Trumpet sounds. Enter *Citizens* upon the walls.

  Citizen. Who is it that hath warn'd us to the
    walls?
  France. 'Tis France, for England.
  K. John.   England for itself.
You men of Angiers, and my loving subjects —
  France. You loving men of Angiers, Arthur's
    subjects,
Our trumpet call'd you to this gentle parle —
  K. John. For our advantage; therefore hear
    us first.   206
These flags of France that are advanced here
Before the eye and prospect of your town
Have hither march'd to your endamagement.
The cannons have their bowels full of wrath,
And ready mounted are they to spit forth   211
Their iron indignation 'gainst your walls.
All preparation for a bloody siege
And merciless proceeding by these French   214
Confronts your city's eyes, your winking gates;
And but for our approach, those sleeping stones
That as a waist doth girdle you about,
By the compulsion of their ordinance
By this time from their fixed beds of lime
Had been dishabited, and wide havoc made   220
For bloody power to rush upon your peace.
But on the sight of us your lawful king,
Who painfully with much expedient march
Have brought a countercheck before your gates,
To save unscratch'd your city's threat'ned
    cheeks —   225

Behold, the French amaz'd vouchsafe a parle;
And now, instead of bullets wrapp'd in fire
To make a shaking fever in your walls,
They shoot but calm words folded up in smoke,
To make a faithless error in your ears;   230
Which trust accordingly, kind citizens,
And let us in, your king, whose labour'd spirits,
Forwearied in this action of swift speed,
Crave harbourage within your city walls.
  France. When I have said, make answer to
    us both.   235
Lo, in this right hand, whose protection
Is most divinely vow'd upon the right
Of him it holds, stands young Plantagenet,
Son to the elder brother of this man,
And king o'er him and all that he enjoys.   240
For this downtrodden equity we tread
In warlike march these greens before your town,
Being no further enemy to you
Than the constraint of hospitable zeal
In the relief of this oppressed child   245
Religiously provokes. Be pleased then
To pay that duty which you truly owe
To him that owes it, namely, this young prince;
And then our arms, like to a muzzled bear,
Save in aspect, hath all offence seal'd up;   250
Our cannons' malice vainly shall be spent
Against th' invulnerable clouds of heaven;
And with a blessed and unvex'd retire,
With unhack'd swords and helmets all un-
    bruis'd,
We will bear home that lusty blood again   255
Which here we came to spout against your
    town,
And leave your children, wives, and you in
    peace.
But if you fondly pass our proffer'd offer,
'Tis not the roundure of your old-fac'd walls
Can hide you from our messengers of war,   260
Though all these English and their discipline
Were harbour'd in their rude circumference.
Then tell us, shall your city call us lord
In that behalf which we have challeng'd it?
Or shall we give the signal to our rage   265
And stalk in blood to our possession?
  Citizen. In brief, we are the King of Eng-
    land's subjects.
For him, and in his right, we hold this town.
  K. John. Acknowledge then the King, and
    let me in.
  Citizen. That can we not; but he that proves
    the King,   270
To him will we prove loyal. Till that time
Have we ramm'd up our gates against the
    world.

K. John. Doth not the crown of England prove the King?
And if not that, I bring you witnesses,
Twice fifteen thousand hearts of England's breed — 275
Bast. Bastards and else.
K. John. To verify our title with their lives.
France. As many and as well-born bloods as those —
Bast. Some bastards too.
France. Stand in his face to contradict his claim. 280
Citizen. Till you compound whose right is worthiest,
We for the worthiest hold the right from both.
K. John. Then God forgive the sin of all those souls
That to their everlasting residence,
Before the dew of evening fall, shall fleet 285
In dreadful trial of our kingdom's king!
France. Amen, amen! Mount, chevaliers! to arms!
Bast. Saint George that swing'd the dragon, and e'er since
Sits on his horseback at mine hostess' door,
Teach us some fence! [*To Austria*] Sirrah, were I at home, 290
At your den, sirrah, with your lioness,
I would set an ox-head to your lion's hide
And make a monster of you.
Aust.   Peace, no more!
Bast. O, tremble! for you hear the lion roar.
K. John. Up higher to the plain, where we'll set forth 295
In best appointment all our regiments.
Bast. Speed then to take advantage of the field.
France. It shall be so; and at the other hill
Command the rest to stand. God and our right!
Exeunt.

Here, after excursions, enter the *Herald of France*, with *Trumpets*, to the gates.

F. Her. You men of Angiers, open wide your gates 300
And let young Arthur, Duke of Britain, in,
Who by the hand of France this day hath made
Much work for tears in many an English mother
Whose sons lie scattered on the bleeding ground.
Many a widow's husband grovelling lies, 305
Coldly embracing the discoloured earth;
And victory with little loss doth play
Upon the dancing banners of the French,
Who are at hand, triumphantly display'd,
To enter conquerors and to proclaim 310
Arthur of Britain England's King and yours.

Enter *English Herald*, with *Trumpet.*

E. Her. Rejoice, you men of Angiers, ring your bells!
King John, your king and England's, doth approach,
Commander of this hot malicious day.
Their armours that march'd hence so silver-bright 315
Hither return all gilt with Frenchmen's blood.
There stuck no plume in any English crest
That is removed by a staff of France.
Our colours do return in those same hands'
That did display them when we first march'd forth; 320
And like a jolly troop of huntsmen come
Our lusty English, all with purpled hands,
Dy'd in the dying slaughter of their foes.
Open your gates, and give the victors way!
Citizen. Heralds, from off our tow'rs we might behold 325
From first to last the onset and retire
Of both your armies, whose equality
By our best eyes cannot be censured.
Blood hath bought blood, and blows have answer'd blows;
Strength match'd with strength, and power confronted power. 330
Both are alike, and both alike we like.
One must prove greatest. While they weigh so even,
We hold our town for neither; yet for both.

Enter the two *Kings*, with their *Powers*, at several doors.

K. John. France, hast thou·yet more blood to cast away?
Say, shall the current of our right run on? 335
Whose passage, vex'd with thy impediment,
Shall leave his native channel and o'erswell
With course disturb'd even thy confining shores,
Unless thou let his silver water keep
A peaceful progress to the ocean. 340
France. England, thou hast not sav'd one drop of blood
In this hot trial more than we of France;
Rather, lost more. And by this hand I swear,
That sways the earth this climate overlooks,
Before we will lay down our just-borne arms,
We'll put thee down, 'gainst whom these arms we bear, 346
Or add a royal number to the dead,

Gracing the scroll that tells of this war's loss
With slaughter coupled to the name of kings.
   Bast. Ha, majesty! how high thy glory
     tow'rs   350
When the rich blood of kings is set on fire!
O, now doth Death line his dead chaps with
     steel;
The swords of soldiers are his teeth, his fangs;
And now he feasts, mousing the flesh of men,
In undetermin'd differences of kings.   355
Why stand these royal fronts amazed thus?
Cry 'havoc,' kings. Back to the stained field,
You equal potents, fiery kindled spirits!
Then let confusion of one part confirm
The other's peace. Till then, blows, blood, and
     death!   360
   K. John. Whose party do the townsmen yet
     admit?
   France. Speak, citizens, for England. Who's
     your king?
   Citizen. The King of England, when we know
     the King.
   France. Know him in us that here hold up
     his right.
   K. John. In us that are our own great
     deputy   365
And bear possession of our person here,
Lord of our presence, Angiers, and of you.
   Citizen. A greater pow'r than we denies all
     this;
And till it be undoubted, we do lock   369
Our former scruple in our strong-barr'd gates;
King'd of our fears, until our fears, resolv'd,
Be by some certain king purg'd and depos'd.
   Bast. By heaven, these scroyles of Angiers
     flout you, kings,
And stand securely on their battlements,
As in a theatre, whence they gape and point 375
At your industrious scenes and acts of death.
Your royal presences be rul'd by me:
Do like the mutines of Jerusalem,
Be friends awhile, and both conjointly bend
Your sharpest deeds of malice on this town. 380
By east and west let France and England mount
Their battering cannon, charged to the mouths,
Till their soul-fearing clamours have brawl'd
     down
The flinty ribs of this contemptuous city.
I'd play incessantly upon these jades,   385
Even till unfenced desolation
Leave them as naked as the vulgar air.
That done, dissever your united strengths
And part your mingled colours once again,
Turn face to face and bloody point to point. 390
Then in a moment Fortune shall cull forth

Out of one side her happy minion,
To whom in favour she shall give the day
And kiss him with a glorious victory.   394
How like you this wild counsel, mighty states?
Smacks it not something of the policy?
   K. John. Now, by the sky that hangs above
     our heads,
I like it well. France, shall we knit our pow'rs
And lay this Angiers even with the ground;
Then after fight who shall be king of it?   400
   Bast. An if thou hast the mettle of a king,
Being wrong'd as we are by this peevish town,
Turn thou the mouth of thy artillery,
As we will ours, against these saucy walls;
And when that we have dash'd them to the
     ground,   405
Why, then defy each other, and pell-mell
Make work upon ourselves, for heaven or hell.
   France. Let it be so. Say, where will you
     assault?
   K. John. We from the west will send de-
     struction
Into this city's bosom.   410
   Aust. I from the north.
   France.   Our thunder from the south
Shall rain their drift of bullets on this town.
   Bast. [*aside*] O prudent discipline! From
     north to south!
Austria and France shoot in each other's mouth.
I'll stir them to it. — Come, away, away!   415
   Citizen. Hear us, great kings. Vouchsafe
     awhile to stay,
And I shall show you peace and fair-fac'd
     league,
Win you this city without stroke or wound,
Rescue those breathing lives to die in beds
That here come sacrifices for the field.   420
Persever not, but hear me, mighty kings!
   K. John. Speak on with favour; we are bent
     to hear.
   Citizen. That daughter there of Spain, the
     Lady Blanch,
Is niece to England. Look upon the years 424
Of Lewis the Dauphin and that lovely maid.
If lusty love should go in quest of beauty,
Where should he find it fairer than in Blanch?
If zealous love should go in search of virtue,
Where should he find it purer than in Blanch?
If love ambitious sought a match of birth, 430
Whose veins bound richer blood than Lady
     Blanch?
Such as she is, in beauty, virtue, birth,
Is the young Dauphin every way complete:
If not complete, I say, he is not she;
And she again wants nothing to name want, 435

If want it be not that she is not he.
He is the half part of a blessed man,
Left to be finished by such as she;
And she a fair divided excellence,
Whose fulness of perfection lies in him.   440
O, two such silver currents, when they join,
Do glorify the banks that bound them in;
And two such shores to two such streams made
    one,
Two such controlling bounds, shall you be,
    kings,
To these two princes, if you marry them.   445
This union shall do more than battery can
To our fast-closed gates; for at this match,
With swifter spleen than powder can enforce,
The mouth of passage shall we fling wide ope
And give you entrance; but without this match,
The sea enraged is not half so deaf,   451
Lions more confident, mountains and rocks
More free from motion — no, not Death him-
    self
In mortal fury half so peremptory
As we to keep this city.
    Bast.   Here's a 'Stay!'   455
That shakes the rotten carcass of old Death
Out of his rags! Here's a large mouth indeed,
That spits forth death, and mountains, rocks
    and seas;
Talks as familiarly of roaring lions
As maids of thirteen do of puppy-dogs!   460
What cannoneer begot this lusty blood?
He speaks plain cannon-fire and smoke and
    bounce;
He gives the bastinado with his tongue.
Our ears are cudgell'd; not a word of his
But buffets better than a fist of France.   465
Zounds! I was never so bethump'd with words
Since I first call'd my brother's father dad.
    Eli. Son, list to this conjunction, make this
    match;
Give with our niece a dowry large enough;
For by this knot thou shalt so surely tie   470
Thy now-unsur'd assurance to the crown
That yon green boy shall have no sun to ripe
The bloom that promiseth a mighty fruit.
I see a yielding in the looks of France.
Mark how they whisper. Urge them while
    their souls   475
Are capable of this ambition,
Lest zeal, now melted by the windy breath
Of soft petitions, pity, and remorse,
Cool and congeal again to what it was.
    Citizen. Why answer not the double Maj-
    esties   480
This friendly treaty of our threat'ned town?

France. Speak England first, that hath been
    forward first
To speak unto this city. What say you?
    K. John. If that the Dauphin there, thy
    princely son,
Can in this book of beauty read 'I love,'   485
Her dowry shall weigh equal with a queen;
For Anjou, and fair Touraine, Maine, Poictiers,
And all that we upon this side the sea
(Except this city now by us besieg'd)
Find liable to our crown and dignity,   490
Shall gild her bridal bed and make her rich
In titles, honours, and promotions,
As she in beauty, education, blood,
Holds hand with any princess of the world.
    France. What say'st thou, boy? Look in the
    lady's face.   495
    Dau. I do, my lord, and in her eye I find
A wonder, or a wondrous miracle —
The shadow of myself form'd in her eye;
Which, being but the shadow of your son,   499
Becomes a sun and makes your son a shadow.
I do protest I never lov'd myself
Till now infixed I beheld myself
Drawn in the flattering table of her eye.
                        Whispers with Blanch.
    Bast. [*aside*] Drawn in the flattering table of
    her eye,   504
Hang'd in the frowning wrinkle of her brow,
And quarter'd in her heart! He doth espy
Himself love's traitor. This is pity now
That hang'd and drawn and quarter'd there
    should be
In such a love so vile a lout as he.   509
    Blanch. My uncle's will in this respect is mine.
If he see aught in you that makes him like,
That anything he sees which moves his liking,
I can with ease translate it to my will;
Or if you will, to speak more properly,
I will enforce it eas'ly to my love.   515
Further I will not flatter you, my lord,
That all I see in you is worthy love
Than this — that nothing do I see in you,
Though churlish thoughts themselves should
    be your judge,
That I can find should merit any hate.   520
    K. John. What say these young ones? What
    say you, my niece?
    Blanch. That she is bound in honour still
    to do
What you in wisdom still vouchsafe to say.
    K. John. Speak then, Prince Dauphin. Can
    you love this lady?   524
    Dau. Nay, ask me if I can refrain from love,
For I do love her most unfeignedly.

K. John. Then do I give Volquessen, Tou-
raine, Maine,
Poictiers, and Anjou, these five provinces,
With her to thee; and this addition more,
Full thirty thousand marks of English coin. 530
Philip of France, if thou be pleas'd withal,
Command thy son and daughter to join hands.
    France. It likes us well. Young princes, close
    your hands.
    Aust. And your lips too; for I am well
    assur'd
That I did so when I was first assur'd.   535
    France. Now, citizens of Angiers, ope your
    gates,
Let in that amity which you have made;
For at Saint Mary's Chapel presently
The rites of marriage shall be solemniz'd.
Is not the Lady Constance in this troop?   540
I know she is not; for this match made up
Her presence would have interrupted much.
Where is she and her son? Tell me, who knows.
    Dau. She is sad and passionate at your
    Highness' tent.
    France. And, by my faith, this league that
    we have made   545
Will give her sadness very little cure.
Brother of England, how may we content
This widow lady? In her right we came,
Which we, God knows, have turn'd another
    way,
To our own vantage.
    K. John.   We will heal up all;   550
For we'll create young Arthur Duke of Britain
And Earl of Richmond, and this rich fair town
We make him lord of. Call the Lady Constance.
Some speedy messenger bid her repair
To our solemnity. I trust we shall,   555
If not fill up the measure of her will,
Yet in some measure satisfy her so
That we shall stop her exclamation.
Go we as well as haste will suffer us
To this unlook'd-for, unprepared pomp.   560
          Exeunt [all but the Bastard].

    Bast. Mad world! mad kings! mad com-
    position!
John, to stop Arthur's title in the whole,
Hath willingly departed with a part;
And France — whose armour conscience buck-
    led on,
Whom zeal and charity brought to the field   565
As God's own soldier — rounded in the ear
With that same purpose-changer, that sly devil,
That broker that still breaks the pate of faith,
That daily break-vow, he that wins of all,
Of kings, of beggars, old men, young men, maids,
Who, having no external thing to lose   571
But the word 'maid,' cheats the poor maid of
    that —
That smooth-fac'd gentleman, tickling Com-
    modity,
Commodity, the bias of the world —
The world, who of itself is peised well,   575
Made to run even upon even ground
Till this advantage, this vile drawing bias,
This sway of motion, this Commodity,
Makes it take head from all indifferency,
From all direction, purpose, course, intent —
And this same bias, this Commodity,   581
This bawd, this broker, this all-changing word,
Clapp'd on the outward eye of fickle France,
Hath drawn him from his own determin'd aid,
From a resolv'd and honourable war,   585
To a most base and vile-concluded peace.
And why rail I on this Commodity?
But for because he hath not woo'd me yet:
Not that I have the power to clutch my hand
When his fair angels would salute my palm,   590
But for my hand, as unattempted yet,
Like a poor beggar, raileth on the rich.
Well, whiles I am a beggar, I will rail
And say there is no sin but to be rich;
And being rich, my virtue then shall be   595
To say there is no vice but beggary.
Since kings break faith upon commodity,
Gain, be my lord, for I will worship thee!
                                        Exit.

[ACT III. Scene I. *France. The* French King's *tent.*]

Enter *Constance, Arthur,* and *Salisbury.*

    Const. Gone to be married? Gone to swear
    a peace?
False blood to false blood join'd! Gone to be
    friends?
Shall Lewis have Blanch, and Blanch those
    provinces?

It is not so! thou hast misspoke, misheard.
Be well advis'd, tell o'er thy tale again.   5
It cannot be; thou dost but say 'tis so.
I trust I may not trust thee, for thy word]
Is but the vain breath of a common man.
Believe me, I do not believe thee, man;
I have a king's oath to the contrary.   10
Thou shalt be punish'd for thus frighting me,

13

For I am sick, and capable of fears;
Oppress'd with wrongs, and therefore full of
fears;
A widow, husbandless, subject to fears;
A woman, naturally born to fears;   15
And though thou now confess thou didst but jest,
With my vex'd spirits I cannot take a truce,
But they will quake and tremble all this day.
What dost thou mean by shaking of thy head?
Why dost thou look so sadly on my son?   20
What means that hand upon that breast of
thine?
Why holds thine eye that lamentable rheum,
Like a proud river peering o'er his bounds?
Be these sad signs confirmers of thy words?
Then speak again — not all thy former tale, 25
But this one word, whether thy tale be true.
  Sal. As true as I believe you think them false
That give you cause to prove my saying true.
  Const. O, if thou teach me to believe this
sorrow,   29
Teach thou this sorrow how to make me die;
And let belief and life encounter so
As doth the fury of two desperate men
Which in the very meeting fall and die!
Lewis marry Blanch? O boy, then where art
thou?
France friend with England? What becomes
of me?   35
Fellow, be gone. I cannot brook thy sight;
This news hath made thee a most ugly man.
  Sal. What other harm have I, good lady,
done
But spoke the harm that is by others done?
  Const. Which harm within itself so heinous is
As it makes harmful all that speak of it.   41
  Arth. I do beseech you, madam, be content.
  Const. If thou that bid'st me be content
wert grim,
Ugly, and sland'rous to thy mother's womb,
Full of unpleasing blots and sightless stains, 45
Lame, foolish, crooked, swart, prodigious,
Patch'd with foul moles and eye-offending
marks,
I would not care, I then would be content,
For then I should not love thee — no, nor thou
Become thy great birth nor deserve a crown.
But thou art fair, and at thy birth, dear boy,
Nature and Fortune join'd to make thee great.
Of Nature's gifts thou mayst with lilies boast
And with the half-blown rose. But Fortune, O,
She is corrupted, chang'd, and won from thee!
Sh' adulterates hourly with thine uncle John,
And with her golden hand hath pluck'd on
France

To tread down fair respect of sovereignty,
And made his majesty the bawd to theirs.   59
France is a bawd to Fortune and King John —
That strumpet Fortune! that usurping John!
Tell me, thou fellow, is not France forsworn?
Envenom him with words; or get thee gone
And leave those woes alone which I alone
Am bound to underbear.
  Sal.   Pardon me, madam,
I may not go without you to the kings.   66
  Const. Thou mayst! thou shalt! I will not
go with thee.
I will instruct my sorrows to be proud;
For grief is proud, and makes his owner stoop
To me, and to the state of my great grief,   70
Let kings assemble; for my grief's so great
That no supporter but the huge firm earth
Can hold it up.   [*Seats herself on the ground.*]
Here I and sorrows sit;
Here is my throne, bid kings come bow to it.

Enter *King John, France, Dauphin, Blanch,
Elinor, Philip* [*the Bastard*], *Austria,* [and *Attendants*].

  France. 'Tis true, fair daughter, and this
blessed day   75
Ever in France shall be kept festival.
To solemnize this day the glorious sun
Stays in his course and plays the alchymist,
Turning with splendour of his precious eye
The meagre cloddy earth to glittering gold. 80
The yearly course that brings this day about
Shall never see it but a holiday.
  Const. [*rises*] A wicked day, and not a holy
day!
What hath this day deserv'd? what hath it done
That it in golden letters should be set   85
Among the high tides in the calendar?
Nay, rather turn this day out of the week,
This day of shame, oppression, perjury.
Or, if it must stand still, let wives with child
Pray that their burthens may not fall this day,
Lest that their hopes prodigiously be cross'd;
But on this day, let seamen fear no wrack;
No bargains break that are not this day made;
This day all things begun, come to ill end,
Yea, faith itself to hollow falsehood change! 95
  France. By heaven, lady, you shall have no
cause
To curse the fair proceedings of this day.
Have I not pawn'd to you my majesty?
  Const. You have beguil'd me with a counter-
feit
Resembling majesty, which, being touch'd and
tried,   100

Proves valueless. You are forsworn, forsworn!
You came in arms to spill mine enemies' blood,
But now in arms you strengthen it with yours.
The grappling vigour and rough frown of war
Is cold in amity and painted peace,   105
And our oppression hath made up this league.
Arm, arm, you heavens, against these perjur'd
    kings!
A widow cries; be husband to me, heavens!
Let not the hours of this ungodly day
Wear out the day in peace; but ere sunset 110
Set armed discord 'twixt these perjur'd kings!
Hear me, O, hear me!
    Aust.   Lady Constance, peace!
    Const. War! war! no peace! Peace is to me
    a war.
O Limoges! O Austria! thou dost shame
That bloody spoil. Thou slave, thou wretch,
    thou coward!   115
Thou little valiant, great in villany!
Thou ever strong upon the stronger side!
Thou Fortune's champion, that dost never fight
But when her humorous ladyship is by   119
To teach thee safety! Thou art perjur'd too,
And sooth'st up greatness. What a fool art thou,
A ramping fool, to brag and stamp and swear
Upon my party! Thou cold-blooded slave,
Hast thou not spoke like thunder on my side?
Been sworn my soldier, bidding me depend 125
Upon thy stars, thy fortune, and thy strength?
And dost thou now fall over to my foes?
Thou wear a lion's hide? Doff it for shame,
And hang a calve's-skin on those recreant limbs.
    Aust. O, that a man should speak those
    words to me!   130
    Bast. And hang a calve's-skin on those rec-
    reant limbs.
    Aust. Thou dar'st not say so, villain, for thy
    life.
    Bast. And hang a calve's-skin on those rec-
    reant limbs.
    K. John. We like not this; thou dost forget
    thyself.

                    Enter *Pandulph.*

    France. Here comes the holy legate of the
    Pope.   135
    Pand. Hail, you anointed deputies of heaven!
To thee, King John, my holy errand is.
I Pandulph, of fair Milan Cardinal,
And from Pope Innocent the legate here,
Do in his name religiously demand   140
Why thou against the Church, our holy mother,
So wilfully dost spurn, and force perforce
Keep Stephen Langton, chosen Archbishop

Of Canterbury, from that holy see.
This, in our foresaid holy father's name,   145
Pope Innocent, I do demand of thee.
    K. John. What earthly name to interroga-
    tories
Can task the free breath of a sacred king?
Thou canst not, Cardinal, devise a name
So slight, unworthy, and ridiculous   150
To charge me to an answer, as the Pope.
Tell him this tale, and from the mouth of
    England
Add thus much more, that no Italian priest
Shall tithe or toll in our dominions;   154
But as we, under heaven, are supreme head,
So, under Him that great supremacy,
Where we do reign, we will alone uphold,
Without th' assistance of a mortal hand.
So tell the Pope, all reverence set apart
To him and his usurp'd authority.   160
    France. Brother of England, you blaspheme
    in this.
    K. John. Though you and all the kings of
    Christendom
Are led so grossly by this meddling priest,
Dreading the curse that money may buy out,
And by the merit of vile gold, dross, dust, 165
Purchase corrupted pardon of a man,
Who in that sale sells pardon from himself —
Though you, and all the rest so grossly led,
This juggling witchcraft with revenue cherish,
Yet I alone, alone do me oppose   170
Against the Pope and count his friends my foes.
    Pand. Then by the lawful power that I have
Thou shalt stand curs'd and excommunicate,
And blessed shall he be that doth revolt
From his allegiance to an heretic,   175
And meritorious shall that hand be call'd,
Canonized, and worshipp'd as a saint,
That takes away by any secret course
Thy hateful life.
    Const.   O, lawful let it be   179
That I have room with Rome to curse awhile!
Good father Cardinal, cry thou amen
To my keen curses; for without my wrong
There is no tongue hath power to curse him
    right.
    Pand. There's law and warrant, lady, for
    my curse.
    Const. And for mine too! When law can do
    no right,   185
Let it be lawful that law bar no wrong.
Law cannot give my child his kingdom here,
For he that holds his kingdom holds the law.
Therefore, since law itself is perfect wrong, 189
How can the law forbid my tongue to curse?

Pand. Philip of France, on peril of a curse,
Let go the hand of that arch-heretic,
And raise the power of France upon his head
Unless he do submit himself to Rome.
 Eli. Look'st thou pale, France? Do not let
go thy hand. 195
 Const. Look to that, devil! lest that France
repent,
And by disjoining hands hell lose a soul.
 Aust. King Philip, listen to the Cardinal.
 Bast. And hang a calve's-skin on his recreant
limbs.
 Aust. Well, ruffian, I must pocket up these
wrongs, 200
Because —
 Bast. Your breeches best may carry them.
 K. John. Philip, what say'st thou to the
Cardinal?
 Const. What should he say, but as the
Cardinal?
 Dau. Bethink you, father; for the difference
Is purchase of a heavy curse from Rome 205
Or the light loss of England for a friend.
Forgo the easier.
 Blanch. That's the curse of Rome.
 Const. O Lewis, stand fast! The devil tempts
thee here
In likeness of a new untrimmed bride.
 Blanch. The Lady Constance speaks not
from her faith, 210
But from her need.
 Const. O, if thou grant my need,
Which only lives but by the death of faith,
That need must needs infer this principle —
That faith would live again by death of need!
O, then tread down my need, and faith mounts
up; 215
Keep my need up, and faith is trodden down!
 K. John. The King is mov'd and answers
not to this.
 Const. O, be remov'd from him, and answer
well!
 Aust. Do so, King Philip; hang no more in
doubt.
 Bast. Hang nothing but a calve's-skin, most
sweet lout. 220
 France. I am perplex'd and know not what
to say.
 Pand. What canst thou say but will perplex
thee more,
If thou stand excommunicate and curs'd?
 France. Good reverend father, make my
person yours 224
And tell me how you would bestow yourself.
This royal hand and mine are newly knit.

And the conjunction of our inward souls
Married in league, coupled, and link'd together
With all religious strength of sacred vows. 229
The latest breath that gave the sound of words
Was deep-sworn faith, peace, amity, true love
Between our kingdoms and our royal selves;
And even before this truce, but new before,
No longer than we well could wash our hands
To clap this royal bargain up of peace, 235
Heaven knows they were besmear'd and over-
stain'd
With slaughter's pencil, where revenge did paint
The fearful difference of incensed kings.
And shall these hands so lately purg'd of blood,
So newly join'd in love, so strong in both, 240
Unyoke this seizure and this kind regreet?
Play fast and loose with faith? so jest with
heaven,
Make such unconstant children of ourselves,
As now again to snatch our palm from palm,
Unswear faith sworn, and on the marriage bed
Of smiling peace to march a bloody host 246
And make a riot on the gentle brow
Of true sincerity? O holy sir,
My reverend father, let it not be so!
Out of your grace, devise, ordain, impose 250
Some gentle order, and then we shall be blest
To do your pleasure and continue friends.
 Pand. All form is formless, order orderless,
Save what is opposite to England's love.
Therefore, to arms! be champion of our
Church! 255
Or let the Church our mother breathe her curse,
A mother's curse, on her revolting son.
France, thou mayst hold a serpent by the
tongue,
A chafed lion by the mortal paw,
A fasting tiger safer by the tooth, 260
Than keep in peace that hand which thou dost
hold.
 France. I may disjoin my hand, but not my
faith.
 Pand. So mak'st thou faith an enemy to
faith,
And like a civil war set'st oath to oath,
Thy tongue against thy tongue. O, let thy vow
First made to heaven, first be to heaven per-
form'd, 266
That is, to be the champion of our Church!
What since thou swor'st is sworn against thyself
And may not be performed by thyself;
For that which thou hast sworn to do amiss 270
Is not amiss when it is truly done;
And being not done where doing tends to ill,
The truth is then most done, not doing it.

16

The better act of purposes mistook
Is to mistake again. Though indirect,   275
Yet indirection thereby grows direct,
And falsehood falsehood cures, as fire cools
    fire
Within the scorched veins of one new burn'd.
It is religion that doth make vows kept;
But thou hast sworn against religion,   280
By what thou swear'st against the thing thou
    swear'st,
And mak'st an oath the surety for thy truth
Against an oath. The truth thou art unsure
To swear, swears only not to be forsworn;
Else what a mockery should it be to swear! 285
But thou dost swear, only to be forsworn,
And most forsworn to keep what thou dost
    swear.
Therefore thy later vows against thy first
Is in thyself rebellion to thyself;
And better conquest never canst thou make 290
Than arm thy constant and thy nobler parts
Against these giddy loose suggestions;
Upon which better part our pray'rs come in,
If thou vouchsafe them. But if not, then know
The peril of our curses light on thee   295
So heavy as thou shalt not shake them off,
But in despair die under their black weight.
    Aust. Rebellion, flat rebellion!
    Bast.   Will't not be?
Will not a calve's-skin stop that mouth of
    thine?
    Dau. Father, to arms!
    Blanch.   Upon thy wedding day?
Against the blood that thou hast married?   301
What, shall our feast be kept with slaughtered
    men?
Shall braying trumpets and loud churlish drums,
Clamours of hell, be measures to our pomp?
O husband, hear me (ay, alack, how new   305
Is husband in my mouth!) even for that name
Which till this time my tongue did ne'er pro-
    nounce!
Upon my knee I beg, go not to arms
Against mine uncle.
    Const.   O, upon my knee,
Made hard with kneeling, I do pray to thee, 310
Thou virtuous Dauphin, alter not the doom
Forethought by heaven!
    Blanch. Now shall I see thy love. What
    motive may
Be stronger with thee than the name of wife?
    Const. That which upholdeth him that thee
    upholds,   315
His honour. O, thine honour, Lewis, thine
    honour!

    Dau. I muse your Majesty doth seem so cold
When such profound respects do pull you on.
    Pand. I will denounce a curse upon his head.
    France. Thou shalt not need. England, I
    will fall from thee.   320
    Const. O fair return of banish'd majesty!
    Eli. O foul revolt of French inconstancy!
    K. John. France, thou shalt rue this hour
    within this hour.
    Bast. Old Time the clock-setter, that bald
    sexton Time —
Is it as he will? Well then, France shall rue.
    Blanch. The sun's o'ercast with blood. Fair
    day, adieu!   326
Which is the side that I must go withal?
I am with both; each army hath a hand,
And in their rage, I having hold of both,
They whirl asunder and dismember me.   330
Husband, I cannot pray that thou mayst win;
Uncle, I needs must pray that thou mayst
    lose;
Father, I may not wish the fortune thine;
Grandam, I will not wish thy wishes thrive.
Whoever wins, on that side shall I lose: 335
Assured loss before the match be play'd!
    Dau. Lady, with me! With me thy fortune
    lies.
    Blanch. There where my fortune lives, there
    my life dies.
    K. John. Cousin, go draw our puissance
    together.
                             [*Exit Bastard.*]
France, I am burn'd up with inflaming wrath,
A rage whose heat hath this condition,   341
That nothing can allay — nothing but blood,
The blood, and dearest-valued blood, of France.
    France. Thy rage shall burn thee up, and
    thou shalt turn
To ashes, ere our blood shall quench that fire.
Look to thyself; thou art in jeopardy.   346
    K. John. No more than he that threats. To
    arms let's hie!   *Exeunt.*

Scene II. [*France.   Plains near Angiers.*]

Alarums, excursions. Enter *Bastard*, with
            Austria's head.

    Bast. Now, by my life, this day grows won-
    drous hot!
Some airy devil hovers in the sky
And pours down mischief. Austria's head lie
    there
While Philip breathes.

Enter [*King*] *John, Arthur, Hubert.*

K. John. Hubert, keep this boy. Philip,
make up! 5
My mother is assailed in our tent,
And ta'en, I fear.
Bast. My lord, I rescued her.
Her Highness is in safety, fear you not.
But on, my liege! for very little pains
Will bring this labour to an happy end. 10
Exeunt.

[Scene III. *France. Another part of
the plains.*]

Alarums, excursions, retreat. Enter [*King*] *John,
Elinor, Arthur, Bastard, Hubert, Lords.*

K. John. [*to Elinor*] So shall it be. Your
Grace shall stay behind,
So strongly guarded. [*To Arthur*] Cousin, look
not sad.
Thy grandam loves thee, and thy uncle will
As dear be to thee as thy father was.
Arth. O, this will make my mother die with
grief! 5
K. John. [*to Bastard*] Cousin, away for Eng-
land! Haste before;
And ere our coming see thou shake the bags
Of hoarding abbots; set at liberty
Imprison'd angels. The fat ribs of peace
Must by the hungry now be fed upon. 10
Use our commission in his utmost force.
Bast. Bell, book, and candle shall not drive
me back
When gold and silver becks me to come on.
I leave your Highness. Grandam, I will pray
(If ever I remember to be holy) 15
For your fair safety. So I kiss your hand.
Eli. Farewell, gentle cousin.
K. John. Coz, farewell.
[*Exit Bastard.*]
Eli. Come hither, little kinsman. Hark, a
word. [*Takes Arthur aside.*]
K. John. Come hither, Hubert. O my gentle
Hubert, 19
We owe thee much! Within this wall of flesh
There is a soul counts thee her creditor
And with advantage means to pay thy love;
And, my good friend, thy voluntary oath
Lives in this bosom, dearly cherished.
Give me thy hand. I had a thing to say, 25
But I will fit it with some better time.
By heaven, Hubert, I am almost asham'd
To say what good respect I have of thee.

Hub. I am much bounden to your Majesty.
K. John. Good friend, thou hast no cause to
say so yet, 30
But thou shalt have; and, creep time ne'er so
slow,
Yet it shall come for me to do thee good.
I had a thing to say; but let it go.
The sun is in the heaven, and the proud day,
Attended with the pleasures of the world, 35
Is all too wanton and too full of gauds
To give me audience. If the midnight bell
Did with his iron tongue and brazen mouth
Sound on into the drowsy ear of night; 39
If this same were a churchyard where we stand,
And thou possessed with a thousand wrongs;
Or if that surly spirit, melancholy,
Had bak'd thy blood and made it heavy, thick,
Which else runs tickling up and down the
veins, 44
Making that idiot, laughter, keep men's eyes
And strain their cheeks to idle merriment,
A passion hateful to my purposes;
Or if that thou couldst see me without eyes,
Hear me without thine ears, and make reply
Without a tongue, using conceit alone, 50
Without eyes, ears, and harmful sound of words:
Then, in despite of brooded watchful day,
I would into thy bosom pour my thoughts.
But, ah, I will not! Yet I love thee well,
And, by my troth, I think thou lov'st me
well. 55
Hub. So well that what you bid me under-
take,
Though that my death were adjunct to my act,
By heaven, I would do it!
K. John. Do not I know thou wouldst?
Good Hubert, Hubert, Hubert, throw thine eye
On yon young boy. I'll tell thee what, my
friend, 60
He is a very serpent in my way;
And wheresoe'er this foot of mine doth tread,
He lies before me. Dost thou understand me?
Thou art his keeper.
Hub. And I'll keep him so
That he shall not offend your Majesty.
K. John. Death. 65
Hub. My lord?
K. John. A grave.
Hub. He shall not live.
K. John. Enough.
I could be merry now. Hubert, I love thee.
Well, I'll not say what I intend for thee.
Remember. — Madam, fare you well.
I'll send those powers o'er to your Majesty. 70
Eli. My blessing go with thee!

18

K. John. [*To Arthur*] For England,
cousin! go.
Hubert shall be your man, attend on you
With all true duty. — On toward Calais, ho!
Exeunt.

Scene IV. [*France. The* French King's *tent.*]

Enter *France, Dauphin, Pandulph, Attendants.*

France. So by a roaring tempest on the flood
A whole armado of convicted sail
Is scattered and disjoin'd from fellowship.
Pand. Courage and comfort! All shall yet
go well.
France. What can go well when we have run
so ill? 5
Are we not beaten? Is not Angiers lost?
Arthur ta'en prisoner? divers dear friends
slain?
And bloody England into England gone,
O'erbearing interruption, spite of France?
Dau. What he hath won, that hath he for-
tified. 10
So hot a speed with such advice dispos'd,
Such temperate order in so fierce a course,
Doth want example. Who hath read or heard
Of any kindred action like to this?
France. Well could I bear that England had
this praise, 15
So we could find some pattern of our shame.

Enter *Constance.*

Look who comes here! a grave unto a soul,
Holding th' eternal spirit against her will
In the vile prison of afflicted breath.
I prithee, lady, go away with me. 20
Const. Lo now! now see the issue of your
peace!
France. Patience, good lady! comfort, gentle
Constance!
Const. No, I defy all counsel, all redress,
But that which ends all counsel, true redress.
Death, death, O amiable lovely death! 25
Thou odoriferous stench! sound rottenness!
Arise forth from the couch of lasting night,
Thou hate and terror to prosperity,
And I will kiss thy detestable bones,
And put my eyeballs in thy vaulty brows, 30
And ring these fingers with thy household
worms,
And stop this gap of breath with fulsome dust,
And be a carrion monster like thyself.

Come, grin on me, and I will think thou smil'st
And buss thee as thy wife. Misery's love, 35
O, come to me!
France. O fair affliction, peace!
Const. No, no, I will not, having breath to
cry.
O that my tongue were in the thunder's mouth!
Then with a passion would I shake the world
And rouse from sleep that fell anatomy 40
Which cannot hear a lady's feeble voice,
Which scorns a modern invocation.
Pand. Lady, you utter madness and not
sorrow.
Const. Thou art not holy to belie me so.
I am not mad. This hair I tear is mine; 45
My name is Constance; I was Geffrey's wife;
Young Arthur is my son, and he is lost.
I am not mad. I would to heaven I were!
For then 'tis like I should forget myself.
O, if I could, what grief should I forget! 50
Preach some philosophy to make me mad,
And thou shalt be canoniz'd, Cardinal;
For, being not mad, but sensible of grief,
My reasonable part produces reason
How I may be deliver'd of these woes 55
And teaches me to kill or hang myself.
If I were mad, I should forget my son,
Or madly think a babe of clouts were he.
I am not mad. Too well, too well I feel
The different plague of each calamity. 60
France. Bind up those tresses. O, what love
I note
In the fair multitude of those her hairs!
Where but by chance a silver drop hath fall'n,
Even to that drop ten thousand wiry friends
Do glue themselves in sociable grief, 65
Like true, inseparable, faithful loves,
Sticking together in calamity.
Const. To England, if you will.
France. Bind up your hairs.
Const. Yes, that I will! and wherefore will
I do it? 69
I tore them from their bonds and cried aloud
'O that these hands could so redeem my son
As they have given these hairs their liberty!'
But now I envy at their liberty
And will again commit them to their bonds,
Because my poor child is a prisoner. 75
And, father Cardinal, I have heard you say
That we shall see and know our friends in
heaven.
If that be true, I shall see my boy again;
For since the birth of Cain, the first male child,
To him that did but yesterday suspire, 80
There was not such a gracious creature born.

19

But now will canker-sorrow eat my bud
And chase the native beauty from his cheek,
And he will look as hollow as a ghost,
As dim and meagre as an ague's fit; 85
And so he'll die; and rising so again,
When I shall meet him in the court of heaven
I shall not know him. Therefore never, never
Must I behold my pretty Arthur more!

Pand. You hold too heinous a respect of
grief. 90

Const. He talks to me that never had a son.

France. You are as fond of grief as of your
child.

Const. Grief fills the room up of my absent
child:
Lies in his bed, walks up and down with me,
Puts on his pretty looks, repeats his words, 95
Remembers me of all his gracious parts,
Stuffs out his vacant garments with his form.
Then have I reason to be fond of grief?
Fare you well. Had you such a loss as I,
I could give better comfort than you do. 100
I will not keep this form upon my head
[Tears her hair.]
When there is such disorder in my wit.
O Lord! my boy, my Arthur, my fair son!
My life, my joy, my food, my all the world!
My widow-comfort, and my sorrows' cure! 105
Exit.

France. I fear some outrage, and I'll follow
her. *Exit.*

Dau. There's nothing in this world can make
me joy.
Life is as tedious as a twice-told tale
Vexing the dull ear of a drowsy man;
And bitter shame hath spoil'd the sweet world's
taste, 110
That it yields naught but shame and bitterness.

Pand. Before the curing of a strong disease,
Even in the instant of repair and health,
The fit is strongest. Evils that take leave
On their departure most of all show evil. 115
What have you lost by losing of this day?

Dau. All days of glory, joy, and happiness.

Pand. If you had won it, certainly you had.
No, no! When Fortune means to men most
good,
She looks upon them with a threat'ning eye.
'Tis strange to think how much King John
hath lost 121
In this which he accounts so clearly won.
Are not you griev'd that Arthur is his prisoner?

Dau. As heartily as he is glad he hath him.

Pand. Your mind is all as youthful as your
blood. 125

Now hear me speak with a prophetic spirit;
For even the breath of what I mean to speak
Shall blow each dust, each straw, each little rub,
Out of the path which shall directly lead
Thy foot to England's throne; and therefore
mark. 130
John hath seiz'd Arthur; and it cannot be
That, whiles warm life plays in that infant's
veins,
The misplac'd John should entertain an hour,
One minute, nay, one quiet breath of rest.
A sceptre snatch'd with an unruly hand 135
Must be as boisterously maintain'd as gain'd;
And he that stands upon a slipp'ry place
Makes nice of no vile hold to stay him up.
That John may stand, then Arthur needs must
fall.
So be it, for it cannot be but so. 140

Dau. But what shall I gain by young
Arthur's fall?

Pand. You, in the right of Lady Blanch your
wife,
May then make all the claim that Arthur did.

Dau. And lose it, life and all, as Arthur did.

Pand. How green you are and fresh in this
old world! 145
John lays you plots; the times conspire with
you;
For he that steeps his safety in true blood
Shall find but bloody safety and untrue.
This act so evilly borne shall cool the hearts
Of all his people and freeze up their zeal, 150
That none so small advantage shall step forth
To check his reign but they will cherish it;
No natural exhalation in the sky,
No scope of nature, no distemper'd day,
No common wind, no customed event, 155
But they will pluck away his natural cause
And call them meteors, prodigies, and signs,
Abortives, presages, and tongues of heaven,
Plainly denouncing vengeance upon John.

Dau. May be he will not touch young
Arthur's life, 160
But hold himself safe in his prisonment.

Pand. O, sir, when he shall hear of your
approach,
If that young Arthur be not gone already,
Even at that news he dies; and then the hearts
Of all his people shall revolt from him, 165
And kiss the lips of unacquainted change,
And pick strong matter of revolt and wrath
Out of the bloody fingers' ends of John.
Methinks I see this hurly all on foot.
And O, what better matter breeds for you 170
Than I have nam'd! The bastard Faulconbridge

Is now in England ransacking the Church,
Offending charity. If but a dozen French
Were there in arms, they would be as a call
To train ten thousand English to their side, 175
Or as a little snow, tumbled about,
Anon becomes a mountain. O noble Dauphin,
Go with me to the King. 'Tis wonderful

What may be wrought out of their discontent
Now that their souls are topful of offence. 180
For England go! I will whet on the King.
   Dau. Strong reasons make strange actions.
    Let us go.
If you say ay, the King will not say no.
                         Exeunt.

ACT IV. Scene I. [*England. A room in a castle.*]

Enter *Hubert* and *Executioners.*

   Hub. Heat me these irons hot, and look you
    stand
Within the arras. When I strike my foot
Upon the bosom of the ground, rush forth
And bind the boy which you shall find with me
Fast to the chair. Be heedful. Hence, and
    watch.   5
   Exec. I hope your warrant will bear out the
    deed.
   Hub. Uncleanly scruples! Fear not you.
    Look to't.
                [*Exeunt Executioners.*]
Young lad, come forth; I have to say with you.

Enter *Arthur.*

   Arth. Good morrow, Hubert.
   Hub.   Good morrow, little Prince.
   Arth. As little Prince, having so great a title
To be more prince, as may be. You are sad.
   Hub. Indeed I have been merrier.
   Arth.   Mercy on me!
Methinks nobody should be sad but I.
Yet I remember, when I was in France,
Young gentlemen would be as sad as night 15
Only for wantonness. By my christendom,
So I were out of prison and kept sheep,
I should be as merry as the day is long!
And so I would be here but that I doubt
My uncle practises more harm to me.   20
He is afraid of me, and I of him.
Is it my fault that I was Geffrey's son?
No indeed is't not! and I would to heaven
I were your son, so you would love me, Hubert.
   Hub. [*aside*] If I talk to him, with his inno-
    cent prate   25
He will awake my mercy, which lies dead.
Therefore I will be sudden and dispatch.
   Arth. Are you sick, Hubert? You look pale
    to-day.
In sooth I would you were a little sick,   29
That I might sit all night and watch with you.
I warrant I love you more than you do me.

   Hub. [*aside*] His words do take possession of
    my bosom. —
Read here, young Arthur.   [*Shows a paper.*]
          [*Aside*] How now, foolish rheum?
Turning dispiteous torture out of door?
I must be brief, lest resolution drop   35
Out at mine eyes in tender womanish tears. —
Can you not read it? Is it not fair writ?
   Arth. Too fairly, Hubert, for so foul effect!
Must you with hot irons burn out both mine
    eyes?
   Hub. Young boy, I must.
   Arth.   And will you?
   Hub.   And I will.
   Arth. Have you the heart? When your head
    did but ache,   41
I knit my handkercher about your brows
(The best I had; a princess wrought it me)
And I did never ask it you again;
And with my hand at midnight held your head;
And like the watchful minutes to the hour   46
Still and anon cheer'd up the heavy time,
Saying 'What lack you?' and 'Where lies your
    grief?'
Or 'What good love may I perform for you?'
Many a poor man's son would have lien still 50
And ne'er have spoke a loving word to you;
But you at your sick service had a prince.
Nay, you may think my love was crafty love
And call it cunning. Do, an if you will.
If heaven be pleas'd that you must use me ill,
Why, then you must. Will you put out mine
    eyes?   56
These eyes that never did nor never shall
So much as frown on you?
   Hub.   I have sworn to do it;
And with hot irons must I burn them out.
   Arth. Ah, none but in this iron age would
    do it!   60
The iron of itself, though heat redhot,
Approaching near these eyes, would drink my
    tears
And quench his fiery indignation
Even in the water of mine innocence;

Nay, after that, consume away in rust 65
But for containing fire to harm mine eyes.
Are you more stubborn-hard than hammer'd
  iron?
An if an angel should have come to me
And told me Hubert should put out mine eyes,
I would not have believ'd him — no tongue
  but Hubert's. 70
  Hub. [*stamps*] Come forth!

[Enter *Executioners*, with cord, irons, &c.]

Do as I bid you do.
  Arth. O, save me, Hubert, save me! My
  eyes are out
Even with the fierce looks of these bloody men.
  Hub. Give me the iron, I say, and bind him
  here. 75
  Arth. Alas, what need you be so boist'rous-
  rough?
I will not struggle, I will stand stone-still.
For heaven sake, Hubert, let me not be bound!
Nay, hear me, Hubert! Drive these men away,
And I will sit as quiet as a lamb; 80
I will not stir nor winch nor speak a word,
Nor look upon the iron angerly.
Thrust but these men away, and I'll forgive you,
Whatever torment you do put me to.
  Hub. Go stand within; let me alone with
  him. 85
  Exec. I am best pleas'd to be from such a
  deed. [*Exeunt Executioners.*]
  Arth. Alas, I then have chid away my friend!
He hath a stern look, but a gentle heart.
Let him come back, that his compassion may
Give life to yours.
  Hub. Come, boy, prepare yourself. 90
  Arth. Is there no remedy?
  Hub. None, but to lose your eyes.
  Arth. O heaven! that there were but a mote
  in yours,
A grain, a dust, a gnat, a wandering hair,
Any annoyance in that precious sense!
Then, feeling what small things are boisterous
  there, 95
Your vile intent must needs seem horrible.
  Hub. Is this your promise? Go to, hold your
  tongue.
  Arth. Hubert, the utterance of a brace of
  tongues
Must needs want pleading for a pair of eyes.
Let me not hold my tongue; let me not,
  Hubert! 100
Or, Hubert, if you will, cut out my tongue,
So I may keep mine eyes. O, spare mine eyes,
Though to no use but still to look on you!

Lo, by my troth, the instrument is cold
And would not harm me.
  Hub. I can heat it, boy. 105
  Arth. No, in good sooth! The fire is dead
  with grief,
Being create for comfort, to be us'd
In undeserv'd extremes. See else yourself!
There is no malice in this burning coal;
The breath of heaven hath blown his spirit out
And strew'd repentant ashes on his head. 111
  Hub. But with my breath I can revive it, boy.
  Arth. And if you do, you will but make it
  blush
And glow with shame of your proceedings,
  Hubert. 114
Nay, it perchance will sparkle in your eyes,
And, like a dog that is compell'd to fight,
Snatch at his master that doth tarre him on.
All things that you should use to do me wrong
Deny their office. Only you do lack
That mercy which fierce fire and iron extends,
Creatures of note for mercy-lacking uses. 121
  Hub. Well, see to live! I will not touch
  thine eyes
For all the treasure that thine uncle owes.
Yet am I sworn, and I did purpose, boy,
With this same very iron to burn them out. 125
  Arth. O, now you look like Hubert! All this
  while
You were disguised.
  Hub. Peace! no more! Adieu.
Your uncle must not know but you are dead.
I'll fill these dogged spies with false reports;
And, pretty child, sleep doubtless and secure
That Hubert, for the wealth of all the world,
Will not offend thee.
  Arth. O heaven! I thank you, Hubert.
  Hub. Silence! no more! Go closely in with
  me. 133
Much danger do I undergo for thee. *Exeunt.*

Scene II. [King John's *Palace.*]

Enter [*King*] *John, Pembroke, Salisbury,* and
  other *Lords.* [The *King* takes his state.]

  K. John. Here once again we sit, once again
  crown'd,
And look'd upon, I hope, with cheerful eyes.
  Pem. This once again, but that your High-
  ness pleas'd,
Was once superfluous. You were crown'd be-
  fore,
And that high royalty was ne'er pluck'd off, 5

The faiths of men ne'er stained with revolt;
Fresh expectation troubled not the land
With any long'd-for change or better state.
   Sal. Therefore, to be possess'd with double
     pomp,
To guard a title that was rich before,   10
To gild refined gold, to paint the lily,
To throw a perfume on the violet,
To smooth the ice, or add another hue
Unto the rainbow, or with taper light
To seek the beauteous eye of heaven to garnish,
Is wasteful and ridiculous excess.   16
   Pem. But that your royal pleasure must be
     done,
This act is as an ancient tale new told
And, in the last repeating, troublesome,
Being urged at a time unseasonable.   20
   Sal. In this the antique and well-noted face
Of plain old form is much disfigured,
And, like a shifted wind unto a sail,
It makes the course of thoughts to fetch about,
Startles and frights consideration,   25
Makes sound opinion sick, and truth suspected
For putting on so new a fashion'd robe.
   Pem. When workmen strive to do better
     than well,
They do confound their skill in covetousness;
And oftentimes excusing of a fault   30
Doth make the fault the worse by the excuse,
As patches set upon a little breach
Discredit more in hiding of the fault
Than did the fault before it was so patch'd.
   Sal. To this effect, before you were new
     crown'd,   35
We breath'd our counsel; but it pleas'd your
     Highness
To overbear it, and we are all well pleas'd,
Since all and every part of what we would
Doth make a stand at what your Highness will.
   K. John. Some reasons of this double coro-
     nation   40
I have possess'd you with, and think them
     strong;
And more, more strong (then lesser is my fear),
I shall indue you with. Meantime but ask
What you would have reform'd that is not well,
And well shall you perceive how willingly   45
I will both hear and grant you your requests.
   Pem. Then I — as one that am the tongue
     of these
To sound the purposes of all their hearts,
Both for myself and them, but chief of all,
Your safety, for the which myself and them   50
Bend their best studies — heartily request
Th' enfranchisement of Arthur, whose restraint

Doth move the murmuring lips of discontent
To break into this dangerous argument: —
If what in rest you have in right you hold,   55
Why then your fears, which (as they say) at-
     tend
The steps of wrong, should move you to mew up
Your tender kinsman, and to choke his days
With barbarous ignorance and deny his youth
The rich advantage of good exercise.   60
That the time's enemies may not have this
To grace occasions, let it be our suit
That you have bid us ask his liberty;
Which for our goods we do no further ask   64
Than whereupon our weal, on you depending,
Counts it your weal he have his liberty.

           Enter *Hubert.*

   K. John. Let it be so. I do commit his youth
To your direction. [*Talks with Hubert aside.*]
     Hubert, what news with you?
   Pem. This is the man should do the bloody
     deed;
He show'd his warrant to a friend of mine.   70
The image of a wicked heinous fault
Lives in his eye; that close aspect of his
Does show the mood of a much-troubled breast;
And I do fearfully believe 'tis done,
What we so fear'd he had a charge to do.   75
   Sal. The colour of the King doth come and go
Between his purpose and his conscience,
Like heralds 'twixt two dreadful battles set.
His passion is so ripe it needs must break.
   Pem. And when it breaks, I fear will issue
     thence   80
The foul corruption of a sweet child's death.
   K. John. We cannot hold mortality's strong
     hand.
Good lords, although my will to give is living,
The suit which you demand is gone and dead.
He tells us Arthur is deceas'd to-night.   85
   Sal. Indeed we fear'd his sickness was past
     cure.
   Pem. Indeed we heard how near his death
     he was
Before the child himself felt he was sick.
This must be answer'd, either here or hence.
   K. John. Why do you bend such solemn
     brows on me?   90
Think you I bear the shears of destiny?
Have I commandment on the pulse of life?
   Sal. It is apparent foul play, and 'tis shame
That greatness should so grossly offer it.
So thrive it in your game! and so farewell.   95
   Pem. Stay yet, Lord Salisbury. I'll go with
     thee

And find th' inheritance of this poor child,
His little kingdom of a forced grave.
That blood which ow'd the breadth of all this isle
Three foot of it doth hold — bad world the
    while!   100
This must not be thus borne; this will break out
To all our sorrows, and ere long I doubt.
               Exeunt [Lords].
K. John. They burn in indignation. I repent.

       Enter *Messenger.*

There is no sure foundation set on blood, 104
No certain life achiev'd by others' death. —
A fearful eye thou hast. Where is that blood
That I have seen inhabit in those cheeks?
So foul a sky clears not without a storm.
Pour down thy weather. How goes all in
    France?
  Mess. From France to England. Never such
    a pow'r   110
For any foreign preparation
Was levied in the body of a land.
The copy of your speed is learn'd by them;
For when you should be told they do prepare,
The tidings comes that they are all arriv'd. 115
  K. John. O, where hath our intelligence been
    drunk?
Where hath it slept? Where is my mother's care,
That such an army could be drawn in France
And she not hear of it?
  Mess.   My liege, her ear
Is stopp'd with dust. The first of April died 120
Your noble mother; and, as I hear, my lord,
The Lady Constance in a frenzy died
Three days before. But this from rumour's
    tongue
I idly heard; if true or false I know not.
  K. John. Withhold thy speed, dreadful
    Occasion!   125
O, make a league with me, till I have pleas'd
My discontented peers! What? mother dead?
How wildly then walks my estate in France!
Under whose conduct came those pow'rs of
    France   129
That thou for truth giv'st out are landed here?
  Mess. Under the Dauphin.

    Enter *Bastard* and *Peter of Pomfret.*

  K. John.   Thou hast made me giddy
With these ill tidings. — Now? What says the
    world
To your proceedings? Do not seek to stuff
My head with more ill news; for it is full. 134
  Bast. But if you be afeard to hear the worst,
Then let the worst, unheard, fall on your head!

  K. John. Bear with me, cousin, for I was
    amaz'd
Under the tide; but now I breathe again
Aloft the flood, and can give audience
To any tongue, speak it of what it will. 140
  Bast. How I have sped among the clergymen
The sums I have collected shall express.
But as I travell'd hither through the land,
I find the people strangely fantasied,
Possess'd with rumours, full of idle dreams, 145
Not knowing what they fear, but full of fear.
And here's a prophet that I brought with me
From forth the streets of Pomfret, whom I
    found
With many hundreds treading on his heels;
To whom he sung in rude harsh-sounding
    rhymes   150
That, ere the next Ascension Day at noon,
Your Highness should deliver up your crown.
  K. John. Thou idle dreamer, wherefore didst
    thou so?
  Peter. Foreknowing that the truth will fall
    out so.
  K. John. Hubert, away with him! imprison
    him,   155
And on that day at noon whereon he says
I shall yield up my crown, let him be hang'd.
Deliver him to safety, and return,
For I must use thee.
            [Exit Hubert with Peter.]
          O my gentle cousin, 159
Hear'st thou the news abroad, who are arriv'd?
  Bast. The French, my lord. Men's mouths
    are full of it.
Besides, I met Lord Bigot and Lord Salisbury
With eyes as red as new-enkindled fire,
And others more, going to seek the grave
Of Arthur, whom they say is kill'd to-night 165
On your suggestion.
  K. John.   Gentle kinsman, go
And thrust thyself into their companies.
I have a way to win their loves again.
Bring them before me.
  Bast.   I will seek them out.
  K. John. Nay, but make haste! the better
    foot before.   170
O, let me have no subject enemies
When adverse foreigners affright my towns
With dreadful pomp of stout invasion!
Be Mercury, set feathers to thy heels, 174
And fly (like thought) from them to me again.
  Bast. The spirit of the time shall teach me
    speed.   *Exit.*
  K. John. Spoke like a sprightful noble
    gentleman.

Michael Hordern in the sinister role of King John, usurper and murderer

THE LIFE AND DEATH
OF
KING JOHN

PHOTOGRAPHS BY ANGUS MCBEAN
PRODUCED BY THE OLD VIC COMPANY

"But thou art fair; and at thy birth, dear boy, Nature and Fortune join'd to make thee great." Constance takes pride in her son Arthur (Nicky Edmett), rightful heir to King Richard (*Act III, Scene I*)

Constance (Fay Compton), mother of Arthur

Richard Burton as Philip the Bastard, King John's adjutant and adviser

"Now, say, Chatillon, what would France with us?" In the play's opening scene, King John (*above*) receives Chatillon (David William), the French ambassador (*Act I, Scene I*)

"Why, being younger born, doth he lay claim to thine inheritance?" King John questions the Bastard. Because of Philip's illegitimacy, his younger brother, Robert Faulconbridge (Timothy Bateson), claimed the succession to his father's estate (*Act I, Scene I*)

Before the gates of Angiers, Arthur, accompanied by King Philip of France (William Squire) and the Dauphin (John Neville), greets the duke of Austria (Laurence Hardy), another of his allies (Act II, Scene I)

"Peace be to France." The French and English leaders meet before the gates of Angiers (Act II, Scene I)

"Thou unadvised scold, I can produce a will that bars the title of thy son." Queen Elinor (Viola Lyel) threatens to bar Constance's son from the throne (Act II, Scene I)

"Philip of France, on peril of a curse, let go the hand of that arch-heretic." Pandulph (Paul Daneman) announces the excommunication of King John and forbids the French king to support him (Act III, Scene I)

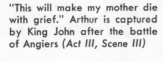

"Hang a calf's-skin on his recreant limbs." The Bastard provokes the duke of Austria by repeating the taunting remark of Constance (Act III, Scene I)

"This will make my mother die with grief." Arthur is captured by King John after the battle of Angiers (Act III, Scene III)

"He talks to me, that never had a son." The outburst of Constance when Pandulph rebukes her for excessive grief (Act III, Scene IV)

"I am much bounden to your Majesty." Assured of the loyalty of Hubert (Edgar Wreford), King John proceeds to give him the task of murdering Arthur (Act III, Scene III)

"Will you put out mine eyes?" Prince Arthur pleads for Hubert to be merciful (Act IV, Scene I)

"It is a damned and a bloody work." The Bastard comes upon the body of Arthur who has fallen to his death from the castle where he was imprisoned (*Act IV, Scene III*)

"According to the fair play of the world, let me have audience." The Bastard asks Pandulph for news of his intervention (*Act V, Scene II*)

"Strike up our drums, to find this danger out." The Dauphin and Philip the Bastard challenge each other on the eve of the battle of St. Edmundsbury (*Act V, Scene II*)

"I will not keep this form upon my head when there is such disorder in my wit." The terrible grief of Constance on being separated from her son Arthur (Act III, Scene IV)

'O cousin! thou art come to set mine eye." Poisoned by a monk, King John dies at Swinstead Abbey. The Bastard and Prince Henry (John Greenwood) attend upon the king in his last hours (Act V, Scene VII)

Go after him; for he perhaps shall need
Some messenger betwixt me and the peers,
And be thou he.
Mess.   With all my heart, my liege.
                                    [*Exit.*]
K. John. My mother dead?   181

Enter *Hubert.*

Hub. My lord, they say five moons were seen
     to-night;
Four fixed, and the fifth did whirl about
The other four in wondrous motion.
K. John. Five moons?
Hub.   Old men and beldames in the streets
Do prophesy upon it dangerously.   186
Young Arthur's death is common in their
     mouths;
And when they talk of him, they shake their
     heads
And whisper one another in the ear;   189
And he that speaks doth gripe the hearer's wrist,
Whilst he that hears makes fearful action
With wrinkled brows, with nods, with rolling
     eyes.
I saw a smith stand with his hammer, thus,
The whilst his iron did on the anvil cool, 194
With open mouth swallowing a tailor's news,
Who, with his shears and measure in his hand,
Standing on slippers, which his nimble haste
Had falsely thrust upon contrary feet,
Told of a many thousand warlike French
That were embattailed and rank'd in Kent. 200
Another lean unwash'd artificer
Cuts off his tale and talks of Arthur's death.
K. John. Why seek'st thou to possess me
     with these fears?
Why urgest thou so oft young Arthur's death?
Thy hand hath murd'red him. I had a mighty
     cause   205
To wish him dead, but thou hadst none to kill
     him.
Hub. No had, my lord? Why, did you not
     provoke me?
K. John. It is the curse of kings to be
     attended
By slaves that take their humours for a warrant
To break within the bloody house of life, 210
And on the winking of authority
To understand a law; to know the meaning
Of dangerous majesty when perchance it frowns
More upon humour than advis'd respect.
Hub. Here is your hand and seal for what
     I did.   215
K. John. O, when the last accompt 'twixt
     heaven and earth

Is to be made, then shall this hand and seal
Witness against us to damnation!
How oft the sight of means to do ill deeds
Make deeds ill done! Hadst not thou been by,
A fellow by the hand of nature mark'd,   221
Quoted, and sign'd to do a deed of shame,
This murther had not come into my mind;
But, taking note of thy abhorr'd aspect,
Finding thee fit for bloody villany,   225
Apt, liable to be employ'd in danger,
I faintly broke with thee of Arthur's death;
And thou, to be endeared to a king,
Made it no conscience to destroy a prince.
Hub. My lord —   230
K. John. Hadst thou but shook thy head or
     made a pause
When I spake darkly what I purposed,
Or turn'd an eye of doubt upon my face,
As bid me tell my tale in express words,
Deep shame had struck me dumb, made me
     break off,   235
And those thy fears might have wrought fears
     in me.
But thou didst understand me by my signs
And didst in signs again parley with sin;
Yea, without stop, didst let thy heart consent,
And consequently thy rude hand to act   240
The deed which both our tongues held vile to
     name.
Out of my sight, and never see me more!
My nobles leave me, and my state is brav'd,
Even at my gates, with ranks of foreign pow'rs.
Nay, in the body of this fleshly land,   245
This kingdom, this confine of blood and breath,
Hostility and civil tumult reigns
Between my conscience and my cousin's death.
Hub. Arm you against your other enemies;
I'll make a peace between your soul and you.
Young Arthur is alive. This hand of mine   251
Is yet a maiden and an innocent hand,
Not painted with the crimson spots of blood.
Within this bosom never ent'red yet   254
The dreadful motion of a murderous thought;
And you have slander'd nature in my form,
Which, howsoever rude exteriorly,
Is yet the cover of a fairer mind
Than to be butcher of an innocent child.
K. John. Doth Arthur live? O, haste thee
     to the peers!   260
Throw this report on their incensed rage
And make them tame to their obedience!
Forgive the comment that my passion made
Upon thy feature; for my rage was blind,
And foul imaginary eyes of blood   265
Presented thee more hideous than thou art.

O, answer not! but to my closet bring
The angry lords with all expedient haste!
I conjure thee but slowly; run more fast.
Exeunt.

Scene III. [*Before the castle.*]

*Enter Arthur on the walls, [disguised
as a shipboy].*

Arth. The wall is high, and yet will I leap
down.
Good ground, be pitiful and hurt me not!
There's few or none do know me; if they did,
This shipboy's semblance hath disguis'd me
quite.
I am afraid, and yet I'll venture it.   5
If I get down and do not break my limbs,
I'll find a thousand shifts to get away.
As good to die and go, as die and stay.
[*Leaps down.*]
O me! my uncle's spirit is in these stones.   9
Heaven take my soul, and England keep my
bones!   *Dies.*

Enter Pembroke, Salisbury, and Bigot.

Sal. Lords, I will meet him at Saint Ed-
mundsbury.
It is our safety, and we must embrace
This gentle offer of the perilous time.
Pem. Who brought that letter from the
Cardinal?   14
Sal. The Count Melun, a noble lord of France,
Whose private with me of the Dauphin's love
Is much more general than these lines import.
Big. To-morrow morning let us meet him
then.
Sal. Or rather then set forward; for 'twill be
Two long days' journey, lords, or ere we meet.

Enter Bastard.

Bast. Once more to-day well met, distem-
per'd lords!   21
The King by me requests your presence straight.
Sal. The King hath dispossess'd himself of us.
We will not line his thin bestained cloak
With our pure honours, nor attend the foot   25
That leaves the print of blood where'er it walks.
Return and tell him so. We know the worst.
Bast. Whate'er you think, good words I
think were best.
Sal. Our griefs, and not our manners, reason
now.   29
Bast. But there is little reason in your grief.
Therefore 'twere reason you had manners now.

Pem. Sir, sir, impatience hath his privilege.
Bast. 'Tis true — to hurt his master, no
man else.
Sal. This is the prison. What is he lies here?
Pem. O death, made proud with pure and
princely beauty!   35
The earth had not a hole to hide this deed.
Sal. Murther, as hating what himself hath
done,
Doth lay it open to urge on revenge.
Big. Or, when he doom'd this beauty to a
grave,
Found it too precious-princely for a grave.   40
Sal. Sir Richard, what think you? Have you
beheld,
Or have you read or heard, or could you think?
Or do you almost think, although you see,
That you do see? Could thought, without this
object,
Form such another? This is the very top,   45
The heightn, the crest, or crest unto the crest,
Of murther's arms. This is the bloodiest shame,
The wildest savagery, the vilest stroke
That ever wall-ey'd wrath or staring rage
Presented to the tears of soft remorse.   50
Pem. All murthers past do stand excus'd in
this;
And this, so sole and so unmatchable,
Shall give a holiness, a purity,
To the yet unbegotten sin of times,
And prove a deadly bloodshed but a jest,   55
Exampled by this heinous spectacle.
Bast. It is a damned and a bloody work,
The graceless action of a heavy hand,
If that it be the work of any hand.
Sal. If that it be the work of any hand?   60
We had a kind of light what would ensue.
It is the shameful work of Hubert's hand,
The practice and the purpose of the King;
From whose obedience I forbid my soul,
Kneeling before this ruin of sweet life,   65
And breathing to his breathless excellence
The incense of a vow, a holy vow,
Never to taste the pleasures of the world,
Never to be infected with delight
Nor conversant with ease and idleness,   70
Till I have set a glory to this hand
By giving it the worship of revenge.
Pem., Big. Our souls religiously confirm thy
words.

Enter Hubert.

Hub. Lords, I am hot with haste in seeking
you.
Arthur doth live; the King hath sent for you.   75

Sal. O, he is bold, and blushes not at death.
Avaunt, thou hateful villain, get thee gone!
   Hub. I am no villain.
   Sal.   Must I rob the law?
                         [Draws.]
   Bast. Your sword is bright, sir; put it up
again.
   Sal. Not till I sheathe it in a murtherer's
skin.   80
   Hub. Stand back, Lord Salisbury! stand
back, I say!
By heaven, I think my sword's as sharp as
yours.   *[Draws.]*
I would not have you, lord, forget yourself
Nor tempt the danger of my true defence,
Lest I, by marking of your rage, forget   85
Your worth, your greatness, and nobility.
   Big. Out, dunghill! Dar'st thou brave a
nobleman?
   Hub. Not for my life; but yet I dare defend
My innocent life against an emperor.
   Sal. Thou art a murtherer.
   Hub.   Do not prove me so. 90
Yet I am none! Whose tongue soe'er speaks
false,
Not truly speaks; who speaks not truly, lies.
   Pem. Cut him to pieces!
   Bast.   Keep the peace, I say.
   Sal. Stand by, or I shall gall you, Faulcon-
bridge.
   Bast. Thou wert better gall the devil, Salis-
bury.   95
If thou but frown on me, or stir thy foot,
Or teach thy hasty spleen to do me shame,
I'll strike thee dead. Put up thy sword betime,
Or I'll so maul you and your toasting iron 99
That you shall think the devil is come from hell.
   Big. What wilt thou do, renowned Faulcon-
bridge?
Second a villain and a murtherer?
   Hub. Lord Bigot, I am none.
   Big.   Who kill'd this prince?
   Hub. 'Tis not an hour since I left him well.
I honour'd him, I lov'd him, and will weep 105
My date of life out for his sweet live's loss.
   Sal. Trust not those cunning waters of his
eyes,
For villany is not without such rheum;
And he, long traded in it, makes it seem
Like rivers of remorse and innocency.   110
Away with me, all you whose souls abhor
Th' uncleanly savours of a slaughterhouse,
For I am stifled with this smell of sin.
   Big. Away toward Bury, to the Dauphin
there!

   Pem. There, tell the King, he may inquire
us out.   115
                       Exeunt Lords.
   Bast. Here's a good world! Knew you of
this fair work?
Beyond the infinite and boundless reach
Of mercy, if thou didst this deed of death,
Art thou damn'd, Hubert.
   Hub.   Do but hear me, sir!
   Bast. Ha! I'll tell thee what.   120
Thou'rt damn'd as black — nay, nothing is so
black!
Thou art more deep damn'd than Prince Lucifer.
There is not yet so ugly a fiend of hell
As thou shalt be, if thou didst kill this child.
   Hub. Upon my soul —
   Bast.   If thou didst but consent 125
To this most cruel act, do but despair;
And if thou want'st a cord, the smallest thread
That ever spider twisted from her womb
Will serve to strangle thee; a rush will be a
beam
To hang thee on. Or wouldst thou drown thy-
self,   130
Put but a little water in a spoon,
And it shall be as all the ocean,
Enough to stifle such a villain up.
I do suspect thee very grievously.
   Hub. If I in act, consent, or sin of thought 135
Be guilty of the stealing that sweet breath
Which was embounded in this beauteous clay,
Let hell want pains enough to torture me!
I left him well.
   Bast.   Go, bear him in thine arms.
I am amaz'd, methinks, and lose my way   140
Among the thorns and dangers of this world.
How easy dost thou take all England up!
From forth this morsel of dead royalty
The life, the right, and truth of all this realm
Is fled to heaven; and England now is left 145
To tug and scamble, and to part by th' teeth
The unowed interest of proud-swelling state.
Now for the bare-pick'd bone of majesty
Doth dogged war bristle his angry crest
And snarleth in the gentle eyes of peace.   150
Now powers from home and discontents at home
Meet in one line; and vast confusion waits,
As doth a raven on a sick-fall'n beast,
The imminent decay of wrested pomp.
Now happy he whose cloak and cincture can 155
Hold out this tempest! Bear away that child
And follow me with speed. I'll to the King.
A thousand businesses are brief in hand,
And heaven itself doth frown upon the land.
                         Exeunt.

Act V. Scene I. [King John's *Palace*.]

Enter King John and Pandulph, Attendants.

K. John. [*Gives the crown*] Thus have I
    yielded up into your hand
The circle of my glory.
Pand.   Take again
From this my hand, as holding of the Pope
Your sovereign greatness and authority.
              [*Gives back the crown.*]
K. John. Now keep your holy word: go
    meet the French,   5
And from his Holiness use all your power
To stop their marches fore we are inflam'd.
Our discontented counties do revolt;
Our people quarrel with obedience,
Swearing allegiance and the love of soul   10
To stranger blood, to foreign royalty.
This inundation of mistemp'red humour
Rests by you only to be qualified.
Then pause not; for the present time's so sick
That present med'cine must be minist'red   15
Or overthrow incurable ensues.
Pand. It was my breath that blew this tem-
    pest up,
Upon your stubborn usage of the Pope;
But since you are a gentle convertite,   19
My tongue shall hush again this storm of war
And make fair weather in your blust'ring land.
On this Ascension Day, remember well,
Upon your oath of service to the Pope,
Go I to make the French lay down their arms.
              Exit.
K. John. Is this Ascension Day? Did not
    the prophet   25
Say that before Ascension Day at noon
My crown I should give off? Even so I have.
I did suppose it should be on constraint;
But (heav'n be thank'd!) it is but voluntary.

       Enter Bastard.

Bast. All Kent hath yielded; nothing there
    holds out   30
But Dover Castle. London hath receiv'd,
Like a kind host, the Dauphin and his powers.
Your nobles will not hear you, but are gone
To offer service to your enemy;
And wild amazement hurries up and down   35
The little number of your doubtful friends.
K. John. Would not my lords return to me
    again
After they heard young Arthur was alive?

Bast. They found him dead and cast into
    the streets —
An empty casket where the jewel of life   40
By some damn'd hand was robb'd and ta'en
    away.
K. John. That villain Hubert told me he did
    live.
Bast. So, on my soul, he did, for aught he
    knew.
But wherefore do you droop? Why look you
    sad?
Be great in act, as you have been in thought.
Let not the world see fear and sad distrust   46
Govern the motion of a kingly eye.
Be stirring as the time; be fire with fire;
Threaten the threat'ner and outface the brow
Of bragging horror. So shall inferior eyes,   50
That borrow their behaviours from the great,
Grow great by your example and put on
The dauntless spirit of resolution.
Away, and glister like the god of war
When he intendeth to become the field.   55
Show boldness and aspiring confidence.
What, shall they seek the lion in his den,
And fright him there? and make him tremble
    there?
O, let it not be said! Forage, and run
To meet displeasure farther from the doors 60
And grapple with him ere he come so nigh.
K. John. The legate of the Pope hath been
    with me,
And I have made a happy peace with him,
And he hath promis'd to dismiss the powers
Led by the Dauphin.
Bast.   O inglorious league!   65
Shall we, upon the footing of our land,
Send fair-play orders and make compremise,
Insinuation, parley, and base truce
To arms invasive? Shall a beardless boy,
A cock'red silken wanton, brave our fields 70
And flesh his spirit in a warlike soil,
Mocking the air with colours idly spread,
And find no check? Let us, my liege, to arms.
Perchance the Cardinal cannot make your peace;
Or if he do, let it at least be said   75
They saw we had a purpose of defence.
K. John. Have thou the ordering of this
    present time.
Bast. Away, then, with good courage! Yet
    I know
Our party may well meet a prouder foe. *Exeunt.*

Scene II. [*Near St. Edmundsbury.
The* Dauphin's *camp.*]

Enter, in arms, *Dauphin, Salisbury, Melun,
Pembroke, Bigot, Soldiers.*

Dau. My Lord Melun, let this be copied out
And keep it safe for our remembrance.
Return the precedent to these lords again,
That, having our fair order written down,
Both they and we, perusing o'er these notes, 5
May know wherefore we took the sacrament
And keep our faiths firm and inviolable.
Sal. Upon our sides it never shall be broken.
And, noble Dauphin, albeit we swear
A voluntary zeal, an unurg'd faith, 10
To your proceedings, yet believe me, Prince,
I am not glad that such a sore of time
Should seek a plaster by contemn'd revolt
And heal the inveterate canker of one wound
By making many. O, it grieves my soul 15
That I must draw this metal from my side
To be a widow-maker! O, and there
Where honourable rescue and defence
Cries out upon the name of Salisbury!
But such is the infection of the time 20
That, for the health and physic of our right,
We cannot deal but with the very hand
Of stern injustice and confused wrong.
And is't not pity, O my grieved friends,
That we, the sons and children of this isle, 25
Were born to see so sad an hour as this,
Wherein we step after a stranger, march
Upon her gentle bosom, and fill up
Her enemies' ranks (I must withdraw and weep
Upon the spot of this enforced cause) 30
To grace the gentry of a land remote
And follow unacquainted colours here?
What, here? O nation, that thou couldst re-
move!
That Neptune's arms, who clippeth thee about,
Would bear thee from the knowledge of thy-
self
And gripple thee unto a pagan shore, 36
Where these two Christian armies might com-
bine
The blood of malice in a vein of league,
And not to spend it so unneighbourly! 39
Dau. A noble temper dost thou show in this,
And great affections wrestling in thy bosom
Doth make an earthquake of nobility.
O, what a noble combat hast thou fought
Between compulsion and a brave respect!
Let me wipe off this honourable dew 45
That silverly doth progress on thy cheeks.

My heart hath melted at a lady's tears,
Being an ordinary inundation;
But this effusion of such manly drops, 49
This show'r, blown up by tempest of the soul,
Startles mine eyes and makes me more amaz'd
Than had I seen the vaulty top of heaven
Figur'd quite o'er with burning meteors.
Lift up thy brow, renowned Salisbury, 54
And with a great heart heave away this storm.
Commend these waters to those baby eyes
That never saw the giant world enrag'd,
Nor met with fortune other than at feasts,
Full of warm blood, of mirth, of gossipping.
Come, come! for thou shalt thrust thy hand
as deep 60
Into the purse of rich prosperity
As Lewis himself. So, nobles, shall you all
That knit your sinews to the strength of mine.

Enter *Pandulph.*

And even there, methinks an angel spake.
Look where the holy legate comes apace, 65
To give us warrant from the hand of heaven
And on our actions set the name of right
With holy breath.
Pand.   Hail, noble Prince of France!
The next is this: King John hath reconcil'd
Himself to Rome; his spirit is come in, 70
That so stood out against the holy Church,
The great metropolis and see of Rome.
Therefore thy threat'ning colours now wind up
And tame the savage spirit of wild war,
That, like a lion fostered up at hand, 75
It may lie gently at the foot of peace
And be no further harmful than in show.
Dau. Your Grace shall pardon me, I will not
back.
I am too high-born to be propertied,
To be a secondary at control, 80
Or useful servingman and instrument
To any sovereign state throughout the world.
Your breath first kindled the dead coal of
wars
Between this chastis'd kingdom and myself 84
And brought in matter that should feed this
fire;
And now 'tis far too huge to be blown out
With that same weak wind which enkindled
it.
You taught me how to know the face of right,
Acquainted me with interest to this land,
Yea, thrust this enterprise into my heart; 90
And come ye now to tell me John hath made
His peace with Rome? What is that peace
to me?

I, by the honour of my marriage bed,
After young Arthur claim this land for mine;
And, now it is half conquer'd, must I back 95
Because that John hath made his peace with
    Rome?
Am I Rome's slave? What penny hath Rome
    borne,
What men provided, what munition sent
To underprop this action? Is't not I
That undergo this charge? Who else but I, 100
And such as to my claim are liable,
Sweat in this business and maintain this
    war?
Have I not heard these islanders shout out
'Vive le roi!' as I have bank'd their towns?
Have I not here the best cards for the game 105
To win this easy match, play'd for a crown?
And shall I now give o'er the yielded set?
No, no! on my soul, it never shall be said!
    Pand. You look but on the outside of this
    work.
    Dau. Outside or inside, I will not return 110
Till my attempt so much be glorified
As to my ample hope was promised
Before I drew this gallant head of war,
And cull'd these fiery spirits from the world
To outlook conquest, and to win renown 115
Even in the jaws of danger and of death.
                        [*Trumpet sounds.*]
What lusty trumpet thus doth summon us?

        Enter *Bastard*, [attended].

    Bast. According to the fair play of the world,
Let me have audience. I am sent to speak.
My holy Lord of Milan, from the King 120
I come to learn how you have dealt for him;
And as you answer, I do know the scope
And warrant limited unto my tongue.
    Pand. The Dauphin is too wilful-opposite
And will not temporize with my entreaties. 125
He flatly says he'll not lay down his arms.
    Bast. By all the blood that ever fury
    breath'd,
The youth says well! Now hear our English
    King,
For thus his royalty doth speak in me:
He is prepar'd — and reason too he should; 130
This apish and unmannerly approach,
This harness'd masque and unadvised revel,
This unhair'd sauciness and boyish troop,
The King doth smile at, and is well prepar'd
To whip this dwarfish war, these pygmy arms,
From out the circle of his territories. 136
That hand which had the strength, even at
    your door,

To cudgel you and make you take the hatch,
To dive like buckets in concealed wells,
To crouch in litter of your stable planks, 140
To lie like pawns lock'd up in chests and
    trunks,
To hug with swine, to seek sweet safety out
In vaults and prisons, and to thrill and shake
Even at the crying of your nation's crow,
Thinking his voice an armed Englishman — 145
Shall that victorious hand be feebled here
That in your chambers gave you chastise-
    ment?
No! Know the gallant monarch is in arms
And like an eagle o'er his aery tow'rs 149
To souse annoyance that comes near his
    nest.
And you degenerate, you ingrate revolts,
You bloody Neroes, ripping up the womb
Of your dear Mother England, blush for shame!
For your own ladies, and pale-visag'd maids,
Like Amazons, come tripping after drums, 155
Their thimbles into armed gauntlets change,
Their neelds to lances, and their gentle hearts
To fierce and bloody inclination.
    Dau. There end thy brave, and turn thy face
    in peace. 159
We grant thou canst outscold us. Fare thee
    well.
We hold our time too precious to be spent
With such a brabbler.
    Pand.   Give me leave to speak.
    Bast. No, I will speak.
    Dau.   We will attend to neither.
Strike up the drums, and let the tongue of
    war
Plead for our interest and our being here. 165
    Bast. Indeed, your drums, being beaten, will
    cry out;
And so shall you, being beaten. Do but start
An echo with the clamour of thy drum,
And even at hand a drum is ready brac'd
That shall reverberate all, as loud as thine. 170
Sound but another, and another shall,
As loud as thine, rattle the welkin's ear
And mock the deep-mouth'd thunder; for at
    hand
(Not trusting to this halting legate here,
Whom he hath us'd rather for sport than need)
Is warlike John; and in his forehead sits 176
A bare-ribb'd death, whose office is this day
To feast upon whole thousands of the French.
    Dau. Strike up our drums to find this danger
    out.
    Bast. And thou shalt find it, Dauphin; do
    not doubt.   *Exeunt.*

Scene III. [*Near Saint Edmundsbury.
A field of battle.*]

Alarums. Enter [*King*] *John* and *Hubert.*

K. John. How goes the day with us? O, tell
me, Hubert.
Hub. Badly, I fear. How fares your Majesty?
K. John. This fever that hath troubled me
so long
Lies heavy on me. O, my heart is sick!

Enter a *Messenger.*

Mess. My lord, your valiant kinsman, Faul-
conbridge,   5
Desires your Majesty to leave the field
And send him word by me which way you go.
K. John. Tell him toward Swinstead, to the
abbey there.
Mess. Be of good comfort; for the great
supply
That was expected by the Dauphin here   10
Are wrack'd three nights ago on Goodwin Sands.
This news was brought to Richard but even now.
The French fight coldly, and retire themselves.
K. John. Ay me, this tyrant fever burns me
up   14
And will not let me welcome this good news!
Set on toward Swinstead. To my litter straight.
Weakness possesseth me, and I am faint.
                                    Exeunt.

Scene IV. [*Another part of the field.*]

Enter *Salisbury, Pembroke,* and *Bigot.*

Sal. I did not think the King so stor'd with
friends.
Pem. Up once again! put spirit in the French.
If they miscarry, we miscarry too.
Sal. That misbegotten devil, Faulconbridge,
In spite of spite, alone upholds the day.   5
Pem. They say King John, sore sick, hath
left the field.

Enter *Melun* wounded.

Mel. Lead me to the revolts of England here.
Sal. When we were happy we had other
names.
Pem. It is the Count Melun.
Sal.   Wounded to death.
Mel. Fly, noble English; you are bought
and sold!   10
Unthread the rude eye of rebellion

And welcome home again discarded faith.
Seek out King John, and fall before his feet;
For if the French be lords of this loud day,   14
He means to recompense the pains you take
By cutting off your heads. Thus hath he sworn,
And I with him, and many moe with me,
Upon the altar at Saint Edmundsbury,
Even on that altar where we swore to you
Dear amity and everlasting love.   20
Sal. May this be possible? May this be true?
Mel. Have I not hideous death within my
view,
Retaining but a quantity of life,
Which bleeds away, even as a form of wax
Resolveth from his figure 'gainst the fire?   25
What in the world should make me now deceive,
Since I must lose the use of all deceit?
Why should I then be false, since it is true
That I must die here, and live hence, by truth?
I say again, if Lewis do win the day,   30
He is forsworn if e'er those eyes of yours
Behold another day break in the East;
But even this night, whose black contagious
breath
Already smokes about the burning crest
Of the old, feeble, and day-wearied sun —   35
Even this ill night, your breathing shall expire,
Paying the fine of rated treachery
Even with a treacherous fine of all your lives,
If Lewis by your assistance win the day.
Commend me to one Hubert, with your king.
The love of him, and this respect besides,   41
For that my grandsire was an Englishman,
Awakes my conscience to confess all this.
In lieu whereof I pray you bear me hence   44
From forth the noise and rumour of the field,
Where I may think the remnant of my thoughts
In peace, and part this body and my soul
With contemplation and devout desires.
Sal. We do believe thee; and beshrew my soul
But I do love the favour and the form   50
Of this most fair occasion, by the which
We will untread the steps of damned flight
And, like a bated and retired flood,
Leaving our rankness and irregular course,
Stoop low within those bounds we have o'er-
look'd   55
And calmly run on in obedience
Even to our ocean, to our great King John.
My arm shall give thee help to bear thee hence,
For I do see the cruel pangs of death
Right in thine eye. Away, my friends! New
flight!   60
And happy newness, that intends old right!
                      Exeunt, [*leading off Melun*].

Scene V. [*The French camp.*]

Enter *Dauphin* and his *Train.*

Dau. The sun of heaven, methought, was
  loath to set,
But stay'd and made the western welkin blush,
When English measure backward their own
  ground
In faint retire. O, bravely came we off
When with a volley of our needless shot,   5
After such bloody toil, we bid good night
And wound our tott'ring colours clearly up,
Last in the field and almost lords of it!

Enter a *Messenger.*

Mess. Where is my prince, the Dauphin?
Dau.   Here. What news?
Mess. The Count Melun is slain. The Eng-
  lish lords   10
By his persuasion are again fall'n off,
And your supply, which you have wish'd so
  long,
Are cast away and sunk on Goodwin Sands.
Dau. Ah, foul shrewd news! Beshrew thy
  very heart!
I did not think to be so sad to-night   15
As this hath made me. Who was he that
  said
King John did fly an hour or two before
The stumbling night did part our weary
  pow'rs?
Mess. Whoever spoke it, it is true, my
  lord.
Dau. Well; keep good quarter and good
  care to-night.   20
The day shall not be up so soon as I
To try the fair adventure of to-morrow. *Exeunt.*

Scene VI. [*An open place near Swinstead Abbey.*]

Enter *Bastard* and *Hubert,* severally.

Hub. Who's there? Speak, ho! speak quickly,
  or I shoot!
Bast. A friend. What art thou?
Hub.   Of the part of England.
Bast. Whither dost thou go?
Hub. What's that to thee? Why may not I
  demand
Of thine affairs as well as thou of mine?   5
Bast. Hubert, I think.

Hub.   Thou hast a perfect thought.
I will upon all hazards well believe
Thou art my friend that know'st my tongue so
  well.
Who art thou?
Bast.   Who thou wilt; and if thou please,
Thou mayst befriend me so much as to think   10
I come one way of the Plantagenets.
Hub. Unkind remembrance! thou and eye-
  less night
Have done me shame. Brave soldier, pardon
  me
That any accent breaking from thy tongue
Should scape the true acquaintance of mine
  ear.   15
Bast. Come, come! Sans compliment, what
  news abroad?
Hub. Why, here walk I in the black brow of
  night
To find you out.
Bast.   Brief then! and what's the news?
Hub. O my sweet sir, news fitting to the
  night,
Black, fearful, comfortless, and horrible.   20
Bast. Show me the very wound of this ill
  news.
I am no woman; I'll not swound at it.
Hub. The King, I fear, is poison'd by a
  monk.
I left him almost speechless, and broke out
To acquaint you with this evil, that you might
The better arm you to the sudden time   26
Than if you had at leisure known of this.
Bast. How did he take it? Who did taste
  to him?
Hub. A monk, I tell you, a resolved villain,
Whose bowels suddenly burst out. The King
Yet speaks and peradventure may recover.   31
Bast. Who didst thou leave to tend his
  Majesty?
Hub. Why, know you not? The lords are
  all come back,
And brought Prince Henry in their company,
At whose request the King hath pardon'd
  them,   35
And they are all about his Majesty.
Bast. Withhold thine indignation, mighty
  heaven,
And tempt us not to bear above our power!
I'll tell thee, Hubert, half my power this night,
Passing these flats, are taken by the tide;   40
These Lincoln Washes have devoured them;
Myself, well mounted, hardly have escap'd.
Away before! conduct me to the King;
I doubt he will be dead or ere I come. *Exeunt.*

Scene VII. [*The orchard of Swinstead
                Abbey.*]

Enter *Prince Henry, Salisbury*, and *Bigot.*

Hen. It is too late. The life of all his blood
Is touch'd corruptibly; and his pure brain
(Which some suppose the soul's frail dwelling
        house)
Doth, by the idle comments that it makes,
Foretell the ending of mortality.   5

            Enter *Pembroke.*

Pem. His Highness yet doth speak, and holds
        belief
That, being brought into the open air,
It would allay the burning quality
Of that fell poison which assaileth him.
    Hen. Let him be brought into the orchard
        here.   10
                                    [*Exit Bigot.*]
Doth he still rage?
    Pem.   He is more patient
Than when you left him. Even now he sung.
    Hen. O vanity of sickness! Fierce extremes
In their continuance will not feel themselves.
Death, having prey'd upon the outward parts,
Leaves them insensible; and his siege is now   16
Against the mind, the which he pricks and
        wounds
With many legions of strange fantasies,
Which, in their throng and press to that last
        hold,
Confound themselves. 'Tis strange that death
        should sing!   20
I am the cygnet to this pale faint swan
Who chants a doleful hymn to his own death
And from the organ-pipe of frailty sings
His soul and body to their lasting rest.
    Sal. Be of good comfort, Prince; for you are
        born   25
To set a form upon that indigest
Which he hath left so shapeless and so rude.

[*King*] *John* brought in [by *Attendants, Bigot*
        accompanying him].

    K. John. Ay, marry, now my soul hath elbow
        room.
It would not out at windows nor at doors.
There is so hot a summer in my bosom   30
That all my bowels crumble up to dust.
I am a scribbled form drawn with a pen
Upon a parchment, and against this fire
Do I shrink up.
    Hen.   How fares your Majesty?

    K. John. Poison'd, ill fare! dead, forsook,
        cast off!   35
And none of you will bid the winter come
To thrust his icy fingers in my maw,
Nor let my kingdom's rivers take their course
Through my burn'd bosom, nor entreat the
        North   39
To make his bleak winds kiss my parched lips
And comfort me with cold. I do not ask you
        much;
I beg cold comfort; and you are so strait
And so ingrateful you deny me that.
    Hen. O that there were some virtue in my
        tears
That might relieve you!
    K. John.   The salt in them is hot.
Within me is a hell, and there the poison   46
Is, as a fiend, confin'd to tyrannize
On unreprievable condemned blood.

            Enter *Bastard.*

    Bast. O, I am scalded with my violent mo-
        tion
And spleen of speed to see your Majesty!   50
    K. John. O cousin, thou art come to set mine
        eye!
The tackle of my heart is crack'd and burnt,
And all the shrouds wherewith my life should
        sail
Are turned to one thread, one little hair.
My heart hath one poor string to stay it by,   55
Which holds but till thy news be uttered;
And then all this thou seest is but a clod,
And module of confounded royalty.
    Bast. The Dauphin is preparing hitherward,
Where God he knows how we shall answer him;
For in a night the best part of my pow'r,   61
As I upon advantage did remove,
Were in the Washes all unwarily
Devoured by the unexpected flood.
                                    [*King John dies.*]
    Sal. You breathe these dead news in as dead
        an ear.   65
My liege! my lord! But now a king, now thus!
    Hen. Even so must I run on, and even so
        stop.
What surety of the world, what hope, what
        stay,
When this was now a king, and now is clay?
    Bast. Art thou gone so? I do but stay behind
To do the office for thee of revenge,   71
And then my soul shall wait on thee to heaven,
As it on earth hath been thy servant still.
Now, now, you stars that move in your right
        spheres,

33

Where be your pow'rs? Show now your mended
    faiths,   75
And instantly return with me again
To push destruction and perpetual shame
Out of the weak door of our fainting land.
Straight let us seek, or straight we shall be
    sought.
The Dauphin rages at our very heels.   80
    Sal. It seems you know not, then, so much
    as we.
The Cardinal Pandulph is within at rest,
Who half an hour since came from the Dauphin,
And brings from him such offers of our peace
As we with honour and respect may take,   85
With purpose presently to leave this war.
    Bast. He will the rather do it when he
    sees
Ourselves well sinewed to our defence.
    Sal. Nay, it is in a manner done already;
For many carriages he hath dispatch'd   90
To the seaside, and put his cause and quarrel
To the disposing of the Cardinal;
With whom yourself, myself, and other lords,
If you think meet, this afternoon will post
To consummate this business happily.   95
    Bast. Let it be so; and you, my noble Prince,

With other princes that may best be spar'd,
Shall wait upon your father's funeral.
    Hen. At Worcester must his body be in-
    terr'd,
For so he will'd it.
    Bast.   Thither shall it then;   100
And happily may your sweet self put on
The lineal state and glory of the land!
To whom with all submission, on my knee,
I do bequeath my faithful services
And true subjection everlastingly.   105
    Sal. And the like tender of our love we make,
To rest without a spot for evermore.
    Hen. I have a kind soul that would give you
    thanks,
And knows not how to do it but with tears. 109
    Bast. O, let us pay the time but needful woe,
Since it hath been beforehand with our griefs.
This England never did, nor never shall,
Lie at the proud foot of a conqueror
But when it first did help to wound itself.
Now these her princes are come home again, 115
Come the three corners of the world in arms,
And we shall shock them. Naught shall make
    us rue
If England to itself do rest but true. *Exeunt.*

RICHARD THE SECOND

For RICHARD THE SECOND the First Quarto (1597) furnishes a good text, which, except for the abdication scene (iv, 1, 154–318), is the basis of the present edition. Later quartos date from 1598 (two), 1608, and 1615, each being set up from its immediate predecessor. For the First Folio a copy of the Fifth Quarto (1615) seems to have been used. The abdication scene was published for the first time in the Fourth Quarto (1608). Its omission from the earlier Quartos was probably due to official censorship or to the publishers' fear of prosecution. At all events, it was manifestly present in the drama as originally written. The Quarto text is defective and corrupt in the abdication scene, but the Folio affords most of the necessary corrections.

Style and blank verse put RICHARD THE SECOND close to the time of *King John*. Which came first is doubtful, but *King John* is probably the older; for it would have been more natural for Shakespeare to pass on to *Henry IV* after writing RICHARD THE SECOND than to turn back two hundred years for his next historical subject. This consideration outweighs the argument that, since RICHARD THE SECOND belongs to the so-called 'lyrical group' and *King John* does not, RICHARD THE SECOND must be the earlier, inasmuch as Shakespeare would never have returned to his lyrical manner after he had once abandoned it. But Shakespeare was surely capable of lyricism at any period, and, though he dropped this manner in *King John*, there is no reason why he should not have resumed it under the compulsion of a theme so essentially lyrical as the character and misfortunes of King Richard. If, as is possible, he had written *A Midsummer Night's Dream* in the interval, the lyric manner of RICHARD THE SECOND may well have been influenced thereby. Reasonable dates, then, are 1594 for *King John*, early in 1595 for *A Midsummer Night's Dream*, and late in 1595 or early in 1596 for RICHARD THE SECOND.

Parallels between RICHARD THE SECOND and Samuel Daniel's poem on *The Civil Wars* have been cited as evidence for 1595 as a date for the play, but these prove nothing. Quite as elusive is the testimony of a letter written by Sir Edward Hoby on December 7, 1595, to invite Sir Robert Cecil to his house in Canon Row, Westminster, on the 9th, 'where as late as it shal please you a gate for your supper shal be open: & K. Richard present him selfe to your vewe.' If Hoby was referring to a dramatic entertainment (as may or may not be the case), nothing proves that he had Shakespeare's play in mind, for there were other dramas in existence dealing with the same reign; nor is it certain that some *Richard the Third* was not the piece in question.

For his historical materials Shakespeare used the second edition of Holinshed's *Chronicle* (1587). Perhaps he took a hint now and then from other easily accessible books. The pretty story about 'roan Barbary,' for instance (v, 5, 76 ff.), may have been suggested by what is told about the king's greyhound by Froissart, whom Shakespeare doubtless knew in Berners's translation. Froissart is mentioned in *1 Henry VI*, i, 2, 29. The garden scene (iii, 4) and the parting of Richard and his queen (v, 1) are Shakespeare's own. The time covered by the action is so short that no such chronological vagaries are to be expected as we have noted in *King John* (p. 471). The play opens on April 29, 1398; on September 16, Bolingbroke and Mowbray met in the lists at Coventry and were banished; Bolingbroke landed at Ravenspurgh in June or July, 1399; King Richard was deposed on September 30 in the same year and was murdered at Pomfret Castle in January, 1400.

The connection of RICHARD THE SECOND with Essex's rebellion in 1601 is a matter of curious interest but has no literary significance, except as showing the popularity of the play. When Essex was tried in 1600 for his acts in Ireland, his fondness for this play was part of the evidence against him; and RICHARD THE SECOND was played at the Globe, at the instance of his partisans, on the day before the outbreak.

Because RICHARD THE SECOND does not maintain an absolutely uniform standard of excellence in style and metre, critics have suspected that Shakespeare utilized some lost play on the subject and kept fragments of the old text without change. There is not much to be said in favour of any such theory.

Though RICHARD THE SECOND is not Marlowesque in style, Shakespeare was undoubtedly influenced bv Marlowe's *Edward II* in his choice of a subject; and there is more or less resemblance between his Richard and Marlowe's Edward. Both are weak, impulsive, and self-willed, and both are governed by unworthy favourites. But Marlowe's king is worse than frivolous; he is frankly despicable. He has neither the poetic nature nor the imaginative intensity of Shakespeare's Richard. There is no comparison between the plays in the matter of pathos and emotional sway.

THE TRAGEDY OF
KING RICHARD THE SECOND

[Dramatis Personæ.

King Richard II.
John of Gaunt, Duke of Lancaster, ⎱ uncles to the
Edmund of Langley, Duke of York, ⎰ King.
Henry, surnamed *Bolingbroke*, Duke of Hereford,
   son to *John of Gaunt* afterwards *King Henry IV.*
Duke of Aumerle, son to the *Duke of York.*
Thomas Mowbray, Duke of Norfolk.
Duke of Surrey.
Earl of Salisbury.
Lord Berkeley.
Bushy, ⎱
Bagot, ⎰ servants to *King Richard.*
Green, ⎰
Earl of Northumberland.
Henry Percy, surnamed *Hotspur*, his son.
Lord Ross.

Lord Willoughby.
Lord Fitzwater.
Bishop of Carlisle.
Abbot of Westminster.
Lord Marshal.
Sir Stephen Scroop.
Sir Pierce of Exton.
Captain of a band of Welshmen.
Two Gardeners.

Queen to *King Richard.*
Duchess of York.
Duchess of Gloucester.
Ladies attending on the *Queen.*

Lords, Heralds, Officers, Soldiers, Keeper, Messenger, Groom, and other Attendants.

SCENE. — *England and Wales.*]

ACT I. Scene I. [*London. The Palace.*]

Enter *King Richard, John of Gaunt*, with
   other *Nobles* and *Attendants.*

King. Old John of Gaunt, time-honoured
   Lancaster,
Hast thou, according to thy oath and band,
Brought hither Henry Hereford, thy bold son,
Here to make good the boist'rous late appeal,
Which then our leisure would not let us hear, 5
Against the Duke of Norfolk, Thomas Mowbray?
Gaunt. I have, my liege.
King. Tell me, moreover, hast thou sounded
   him
If he appeal the Duke on ancient malice,
Or worthily, as a good subject should, 10
On some known ground of treachery in him?
Gaunt. As near as I could sift him on that
   argument,
On some apparent danger seen in him
Aim'd at your Highness, no inveterate malice.
King. Then call them to our presence.
                  [*Exit Attendant.*]
               Face to face,
And frowning brow to brow, ourselves will hear
The accuser and the accused freely speak.

High-stomach'd are they both and full of ire,
In rage deaf as the sea, hasty as fire.

Enter *Bolingbroke* and *Mowbray.*

Boling. Many years of happy days befall 20
My gracious sovereign, my most loving liege!
Mowb. Each day still better other's happiness
Until the heavens, envying earth's good hap,
Add an immortal title to your crown!
King. We thank you both. Yet one but
   flatters us, 25
As well appeareth by the cause you come —
Namely, to appeal each other of high treason.
Cousin of Hereford, what dost thou object
Against the Duke of Norfolk, Thomas Mowbray?
Boling. First — heaven be the record to my
   speech! — 30
In the devotion of a subject's love,
Tend'ring the precious safety of my prince
And free from other misbegotten hate,
Come I appellant to this princely presence.
Now, Thomas Mowbray, do I turn to thee, 35
And mark my greeting well; for what I speak
My body shall make good upon this earth

37

Or my divine soul answer it in heaven.
Thou art a traitor and a miscreant,
Too good to be so, and too bad to live,   40
Since the more fair and crystal is the sky,
The uglier seem the clouds that in it fly.
Once more, the more to aggravate the note,
With a foul traitor's name stuff I thy throat
And wish (so please my sovereign), ere I move,
What my tongue speaks my right-drawn sword
    may prove.   46
Mowb. Let not my cold words here accuse
    my zeal.
'Tis not the trial of a woman's war,
The bitter clamour of two eager tongues,
Can arbitrate this cause betwixt us twain;   50
The blood is hot that must be cool'd for this.
Yet can I not of such tame patience boast
As to be hush'd and naught at all to say.
First, the fair reverence of your Highness curbs
    me   54
From giving reins and spurs to my free speech,
Which else would post until it had return'd
These terms of treason doubled down his throat.
Setting aside his high blood's royalty,
And let him be no kinsman to my liege,
I do defy him and I spit at him,   60
Call him a slanderous coward and a villain;
Which to maintain, I would allow him odds
And meet him, were I tied to run afoot
Even to the frozen ridges of the Alps,
Or any other ground inhabitable   65
Where ever Englishman durst set his foot.
Meantime let this defend my loyalty —
By all my hopes, most falsely doth he lie.
    Boling. Pale trembling coward, there I throw
    my gage,
Disclaiming here the kinred of the King,   70
And lay aside my high blood's royalty,
Which fear, not reverence, makes thee to except.
If guilty dread have left thee so much strength
As to take up mine honour's pawn, then stoop.
By that and all the rites of knighthood else,   75
Will I make good against thee, arm to arm,
What I have spoke or thou canst worse de-
    vise.
Mowb. I take it up; and by that sword I
    swear
Which gently laid my knighthood on my
    shoulder,
I'll answer thee in any fair degree   80
Or chivalrous design of knightly trial;
And when I mount, alive may I not light
If I be traitor or unjustly fight!
    King. What doth our cousin lay to Mow-
    bray's charge?

It must be great that can inherit us   85
So much as of a thought of ill in him.
    Boling. Look, what I speak, my life shall
    prove it true —
That Mowbray hath receiv'd eight thousand
    nobles
In name of lendings for your Highness' soldiers,
The which he hath detain'd for lewd employ-
    ments,   90
Like a false traitor and injurious villain.
Besides I say, and will in battle prove —
Or here, or elsewhere to the furthest verge
That ever was survey'd by English eye —
That all the treasons for these eighteen years
Complotted and contrived in this land   96
Fetch from false Mowbray their first head and
    spring.
Further I say, and further will maintain
Upon his bad life to make all this good,
That he did plot the Duke of Gloucester's
    death,   100
Suggest his soon-believing adversaries,
And consequently, like a traitor coward,
Sluic'd out his innocent soul through streams
    of blood;
Which blood, like sacrificing Abel's, cries,   104
Even from the tongueless caverns of the earth,
To me for justice and rough chastisement;
And, by the glorious worth of my descent,
This arm shall do it, or this life be spent.
    King. How high a pitch his resolution soars!
Thomas of Norfolk, what say'st thou to this?
    Mowb. O, let my sovereign turn away his
    face   111
And bid his ears a little while be deaf,
Till I have told this slander of his blood
How God and good men hate so foul a liar!
    King. Mowbray, impartial are our eyes and
    ears.   115
Were he my brother, nay, my kingdom's heir,
As he is but my father's brother's son,
Now by my sceptre's awe I make a vow,
Such neighbour nearness to our sacred blood
Should nothing privilege him nor partialize 120
The unstooping firmness of my upright soul.
He is our subject, Mowbray; so art thou:
Free speech and fearless I to thee allow.
    Mowb. Then, Bolingbroke, as low as to thy
    heart
Through the false passage of thy throat, thou
    liest!   125
Three parts of that receipt I had for Calais
Disburs'd I duly to his Highness' soldiers.
The other part reserv'd I by consent,
For that my sovereign liege was in my debt

38

Upon remainder of a dear account   130
Since last I went to France to fetch his queen.
Now swallow down that lie! For Gloucester's
   death,
I slew him not, but, to my own disgrace,
Neglected my sworn duty in that case.
For you, my noble Lord of Lancaster,   135
The honourable father to my foe,
Once did I lay an ambush for your life —
A trespass that doth vex my grieved soul;
But ere I last receiv'd the sacrament,
I did confess it and exactly begg'd   140
Your Grace's pardon, and I hope I had it.
This is my fault. As for the rest appeal'd,
It issues from the rancour of a villain,
A recreant and most degenerate traitor;
Which in myself I boldly will defend,   145
And interchangeably hurl down my gage
Upon this overweening traitor's foot
To prove myself a loyal gentleman
Even in the best blood chamber'd in his bosom.
In haste whereof most heartily I pray   150
Your Highness to assign our trial day.
   King. Wrath-kindled gentlemen, be rul'd
   by me;
Let's purge this choler without letting blood.
This we prescribe, though no physician;
Deep malice makes too deep incision.   155
Forget, forgive; conclude and be agreed;
Our doctors say this is no month to bleed.
Good uncle, let this end where it begun;
We'll calm the Duke of Norfolk, you your son.
   Gaunt. To be a make-peace shall become
   my age.   160
Throw down, my son, the Duke of Norfolk's
   gage.
   King. And, Norfolk, throw down his.
   Gaunt.   When, Harry? when?
Obedience bids I should not bid again.
   King. Norfolk, throw down, we bid. There
   is no boot.
   Mowb. Myself I throw, dread sovereign, at
   thy foot.   165
My life thou shalt command, but not my
   shame.
The one my duty owes; but my fair name,
Despite of death that lives upon my grave,
To dark dishonour's use thou shalt not have.
I am disgrac'd, impeach'd, and baffled here;
Pierc'd to the soul with slander's venom'd spear,
The which no balm can cure but his heart-
   blood
Which breath'd this poison.
   King.   Rage must be withstood.
Give me his gage. Lions make leopards tame.

   Mowb. Yea, but not change his spots! Take
   but my shame,   175
And I resign my gage. My dear dear lord,
The purest treasure mortal times afford
Is spotless reputation. That away,
Men are but gilded loam or painted clay.
A jewel in a ten times barr'd-up chest   180
Is a bold spirit in a loyal breast.
Mine honour is my life. Both grow in one;
Take honour from me, and my life is done.
Then, dear my liege, mine honour let me try;
In that I live, and for that will I die.   185
   King. Cousin, throw up your gage. Do you
   begin.
   Boling. O, God defend my soul from such
   deep sin!
Shall I seem crestfallen in my father's sight?
Or with pale beggar-fear impeach my height
Before this outdar'd dastard? Ere my tongue
Shall wound my honour with such feeble wrong
Or sound so base a parle, my teeth shall tear
The slavish motive of recanting fear
And spit it bleeding in his high disgrace, 194
Where shame doth harbour, even in Mowbray's
   face.   *Exit Gaunt.*
   King. We were not born to sue, but to
   command;
Which since we cannot do to make you friends,
Be ready, as your lives shall answer it,
At Coventry upon Saint Lambert's day.   199
There shall your swords and lances arbitrate
The swelling difference of your settled hate:
Since we cannot atone you, we shall see
Justice design the victor's chivalry.
Lord Marshal, command our officers-at-arms
Be ready to direct these home alarms. *Exeunt.*

Scene II. [*London. The* Duke of
Lancaster's *Palace.*]

Enter *John of Gaunt* with the *Duchess
of Gloucester.*

   Gaunt. Alas, the part I had in Woodstock's
   blood
Doth more solicit me than your exclaims
To stir against the butchers of his life!
But since correction lieth in those hands
Which made the fault that we cannot correct, 5
Put we our quarrel to the will of heaven,
Who, when they see the hours ripe on earth,
Will rain hot vengeance on offenders' heads.
   Duch. Finds brotherhood in thee no sharper
   spur?

39

Hath love in thy old blood no living fire?   10
Edward's seven sons, whereof thyself art one,
Were as seven vials of his sacred blood,
Or seven fair branches springing from one root.
Some of those seven are dried by nature's
    course,   14
Some of those branches by the Destinies cut;
But Thomas, my dear lord, my life, my
    Gloucester,
One vial full of Edward's sacred blood,
One flourishing branch of his most royal root,
Is crack'd, and all the precious liquor spilt,
Is hack'd down, and his summer leaves all
    faded,   20
By envy's hand and murder's bloody axe.
Ah, Gaunt, his blood was thine! That bed,
    that womb,
That metal, that self mould that fashioned thee,
Made him a man; and though thou livest and
    breathest,   24
Yet art thou slain in him. Thou dost consent
In some large measure to thy father's death
In that thou seest thy wretched brother die,
Who was the model of thy father's life.
Call it not patience, Gaunt; it is despair.
In suff'ring thus thy brother to be slaught'red
Thou showest the naked pathway to thy life, 31
Teaching stern murder how to butcher thee.
That which in mean men we entitle patience
Is pale cold cowardice in noble breasts.
What shall I say? To safeguard thine own life
The best way is to venge my Gloucester's
    death.   36
    Gaunt. God's is the quarrel; for God's sub-
    stitute,
His deputy anointed in his sight,
Hath caus'd his death; the which if wrong-
    fully,
Let heaven revenge; for I may never lift   40
An angry arm against his minister.
    Duch. Where then, alas, may I complain
    myself?
    Gaunt. To God, the widow's champion and
    defence.
    Duch. Why then, I will. Farewell, old
    Gaunt.
Thou goest to Coventry, there to behold   45
Our cousin Hereford and fell Mowbray fight.
O, sit my husband's wrongs on Hereford's
    spear,
That it may enter butcher Mowbray's breast!
Or, if misfortune miss the first career,
Be Mowbray's sins so heavy in his bosom   50
That they may break his foaming courser's
    back

And throw the rider headlong in the lists,
A caitiff recreant to my cousin Hereford!
Farewell, old Gaunt. Thy sometimes brother's
    wife   54
With her companion, Grief, must end her life.
    Gaunt. Sister, farewell; I must to Coventry.
As much good stay with thee as go with me!
    Duch. Yet one word more! Grief boundeth
    where it falls,
Not with the empty hollowness, but weight.
I take my leave before I have begun,   60
For sorrow ends not when it seemeth done.
Commend me to thy brother, Edmund York.
Lo, this is all. Nay, yet depart not so!
Though this be all, do not so quickly go.
I shall remember more. Bid him—ah, what?—
With all good speed at Plashy visit me.   66
Alack, and what shall good old York there see
But empty lodgings and unfurnish'd walls,
Unpeopled offices, untrodden stones?
And what hear there for welcome but my
    groans?   70
Therefore commend me — let him not come
    there
To seek out sorrow that dwells everywhere.
Desolate, desolate will I hence and die!
The last leave of thee takes my weeping eye.
                          Exeunt.

Scene III. [*The lists at Coventry.*]

Enter *Lord Marshal* and the *Duke Aumerle.*

    Mar. My Lord Aumerle, is Harry Hereford
    arm'd?
    Aum. Yea, at all points, and longs to enter in.
    Mar. The Duke of Norfolk, sprightfully and
    bold,
Stays but the summons of the appellant's
    trumpet.
    Aum. Why, then the champions are pre-
    par'd, and stay   5
For nothing but his Majesty's approach.

The trumpets sound and the King *enters with
his Nobles,* Gaunt, Bushy, Bagot, Green, *and
others. When they are set, enter* Mowbray the
Duke of Norfolk *in arms, defendant, and* Herald.

    King. Marshal, demand of yonder champion
The cause of his arrival here in arms.
Ask him his name and orderly proceed
To swear him in the justice of his cause.   10
    Mar. In God's name and the King's, say
    who thou art,

And why thou comest thus knightly clad in
arms;
Against what man thou com'st, and what thy
quarrel.
Speak truly on thy knighthood and thy oath,
As so defend thee heaven and thy valour! 15
Mowb. My name is Thomas Mowbray, Duke
of Norfolk,
Who hither come engaged by my oath
(Which God defend a knight should violate!)
Both to defend my loyalty and truth
To God, my King, and his succeeding issue 20
Against the Duke of Hereford that appeals
me;
And, by the grace of God and this mine arm,
To prove him, in defending of myself,
A traitor to my God, my King, and me;
And as I truly fight, defend me heaven! 25

The trumpets sound. Enter [*Bolingbroke*], *Duke
of Hereford*, appellant, in armour, and *Herald.*

King. Marshal, ask yonder knight in arms
Both who he is and why he cometh hither
Thus plated in habiliments of war;
And formally, according to our law,
Depose him in the justice of his cause. 30
Mar. What is thy name? and wherefore
com'st thou hither,
Before King Richard in his royal lists?
Against whom comest thou? and what's thy
quarrel?
Speak like a true knight, so defend thee heaven!
Boling. Harry of Hereford, Lancaster, and
Derby 35
Am I, who ready here do stand in arms
To prove, by God's grace and my body's valour
In lists on Thomas Mowbray, Duke of Norfolk,
That he is a traitor, foul and dangerous,
To God of heaven, King Richard, and to me;
And as I truly fight, defend me heaven! 41
Mar. On pain of death, no person be so bold
Or daring-hardy as to touch the lists,
Except the Marshal and such officers
Appointed to direct these fair designs. 45
Boling. Lord Marshal, let me kiss my sov-
ereign's hand
And bow my knee before his Majesty;
For Mowbray and myself are like two men
That vow a long and weary pilgrimage.
Then let us take a ceremonious leave 50
And loving farewell of our several friends.
Mar. The appellant in all duty greets your
Highness
And craves to kiss your hand and take his
leave.

King. We will descend and fold him in our
arms.
Cousin of Hereford, as thy cause is right, 55
So be thy fortune in this royal fight!
Farewell, my blood; which if to-day thou shed,
Lament we may, but not revenge thee dead.
Boling. O, let no noble eye profane a tear
For me, if I be gor'd with Mowbray's spear. 60
As confident as is the falcon's flight
Against a bird, do I with Mowbray fight.
My loving lord, I take my leave of you;
Of you, my noble cousin, Lord Aumerle;
Not sick, although I have to do with death, 65
But lusty, young, and cheerly drawing breath.
Lo, as at English feasts, so I regreet
The daintiest last, to make the end most sweet.
O thou, the earthly author of my blood,
Whose youthful spirit, in me regenerate, 70
Doth with a twofold vigour lift me up
To reach at victory above my head,
Add proof unto mine armour with thy prayers,
And with thy blessings steel my lance's point,
That it may enter Mowbray's waxen coat 75
And furbish new the name of John o' Gaunt
Even in the lusty haviour of his son.
Gaunt. God in thy good cause make thee
prosperous!
Be swift like lightning in the execution
And let thy blows, doubly redoubled, 80
Fall like amazing thunder on the casque
Of thy adverse pernicious enemy.
Rouse up thy youthful blood; be valiant and
live.
Boling. Mine innocency and Saint George to
thrive! 84
Mowb. However God or fortune cast my
lot,
There lives or dies, true to King Richard's
throne,
A loyal, just, and upright gentleman.
Never did captive with a freer heart
Cast off his chains of bondage and embrace
His golden uncontroll'd enfranchisement, 90
More than my dancing soul doth celebrate
This feast of battle with mine adversary.
Most mighty liege, and my companion peers,
Take from my mouth the wish of happy years.
As gentle and as jocund as to jest 95
Go I to fight. Truth hath a quiet breast.
King. Farewell, my lord. Securely I espy
Virtue with valour couched in thine eye.
Order the trial, Marshal, and begin.
Mar. Harry of Hereford, Lancaster, and
Derby, 100
Receive thy lance, and God defend the right!

41

Boling. Strong as a tower in hope, I cry
     amen.
Mar. [*to an Officer*] Go bear this lance to
     Thomas, Duke of Norfolk.
1. Herald. Harry of Hereford, Lancaster, and
     Derby
Stands here for God, his sovereign, and himself,
On pain to be found false and recreant,   106
To prove the Duke of Norfolk, Thomas Mow-
     bray,
A traitor to his God, his King, and him,
And dares him to set forward to the fight.
2. Herald. Here standeth Thomas Mowbray,
     Duke of Norfolk,   110
On pain to be found false and recreant,
Both to defend himself and to approve
Henry of Hereford, Lancaster, and Derby
To God, his sovereign, and to him disloyal,
Courageously and with a free desire   115
Attending but the signal to begin.
Mar. Sound trumpets, and set forward com-
     batants.
                         A charge sounded.
Stay! The King hath thrown his warder down.
King. Let them lay by their helmets and
     their spears
And both return back to their chairs again.   120
Withdraw with us; and let the trumpets sound
While we return these dukes what we decree.
                         A long flourish.
Draw near,
And list what with our Council we have done.
For that our kingdom's earth should not be
     soil'd   125
With that dear blood which it hath fostered;
And for our eyes do hate the dire aspect
Of civil wounds plough'd up with neighbours'
     sword;
And for we think the eagle-winged pride
Of sky-aspiring and ambitious thoughts   130
With rival-hating envy set on you
To wake our peace, which in our country's
     cradle
Draws the sweet infant breath of gentle sleep;
Which so rous'd up with boist'rous untun'd
     drums,
With harsh-resounding trumpets' dreadful bray
And grating shock of wrathful iron arms,   136
Might from our quiet confines fright fair peace
And make us wade even in our kinred's blood:
Therefore we banish you our territories.
You, cousin Hereford, upon pain of life,   140
Till twice five summers have enrich'd our fields
Shall not regreet our fair dominions
But tread the stranger paths of banishment.

Boling. Your will be done. This must my
     comfort be —
That sun that warms you here shall shine on me,
And those his golden beams to you here lent 146
Shall point on me and gild my banishment.
King. Norfolk, for thee remains a heavier
     doom,
Which I with some unwillingness pronounce ·
The sly-slow hours shall not determinate   150
The dateless limit of thy dear exile.
The hopeless word of 'never to return'
Breathe I against thee, upon pain of life.
Mowb. A heavy sentence, my most sovereign
     liege,
And all unlook'd for from your Highness'
     mouth.   155
A dearer merit, not so deep a maim
As to be cast forth in the common air,
Have I deserved at your Highness' hands.
The language I have learnt these forty years,
My native English, now I must forgo;   160
And now my tongue's use is to me no more
Than an unstringed viol or a harp,
Or like a cunning instrument cas'd up
Or, being open, put into his hands
That knows no touch to tune the harmony. 165
Within my mouth you have enjail'd my tongue,
Doubly portcullis'd with my teeth and lips;
And dull, unfeeling, barren ignorance
Is made my jailer to attend on me.
I am too old to fawn upon a nurse,   170
Too far in years to be a pupil now.
What is thy sentence then but speechless death,
Which robs my tongue from breathing native
     breath?
King. It boots thee not to be compassionate.
After our sentence plaining comes too late. 175
Mowb. Then thus I turn me from my coun-
     try's light
To dwell in solemn shades of endless night.
King. Return again and take an oath with
     thee.
Lay on our royal sword your banish'd hands;
Swear by the duty that you owe to God   180
(Our part therein we banish with yourselves)
To keep the oath that we administer:
You never shall, so help you truth and God,
Embrace each other's love in banishment;
Nor never look upon each other's face;   185
Nor never write, regreet, nor reconcile
This low'ring tempest of your home-bred hate;
Nor never by advised purpose meet
To plot, contrive, or complot any ill
'Gainst us, our state, our subjects, or our land.
Boling. I swear.   191

Mowb. And I, to keep all this.

Boling. Norfolk, so far as to mine enemy:
By this time, had the King permitted us,
One of our souls had wand'red in the air,   195
Banish'd this frail sepulchre of our flesh,
As now our flesh is banish'd from this land.
Confess thy treasons ere thou fly the realm.
Since thou hast far to go, bear not along
The clogging burthen of a guilty soul.   200

Mowb. No, Bolingbroke. If ever I were
traitor,
My name be blotted from the book of life
And I from heaven banish'd as from hence!
But what thou art, God, thou, and I do know;
And all too soon, I fear, the King shall rue.   205
Farewell, my liege. Now no way can I stray.
Save back to England, all the world's my way.
Exit.

King. Uncle, even in the glasses of thine eyes
I see thy grieved heart. Thy sad aspect
Hath from the number of his banish'd years
Pluck'd four away. [*To Bolingbroke*] Six frozen
winters spent,   211
Return with welcome home from banishment.

Boling. How long a time lies in one little
word!
Four lagging winters and four wanton springs
End in a word, such is the breath of kings.   215

Gaunt. I thank my liege that in regard of me
He shortens four years of my son's exile.
But little vantage shall I reap thereby;
For ere the six years that he hath to spend
Can change their moons and bring their times
about,   220
My oil-dried lamp and time-bewasted light
Shall be extinct with age and endless night,
My inch of taper will be burnt and done,
And blindfold death not let me see my son.

King. Why, uncle, thou hast many years to
live.   225

Gaunt. But not a minute, King, that thou
canst give.
Shorten my days thou canst with sullen sorrow
And pluck nights from me, but not lend a
morrow.
Thou canst help time to furrow me with age,
But stop no wrinkle in his pilgrimage.   230
Thy word is current with him for my death,
But dead, thy kingdom cannot buy my breath.

King. Thy son is banish'd upon good advice,
Whereto thy tongue a party-verdict gave.   234
Why at our justice seem'st thou then to low'r?

Gaunt. Things sweet to taste prove in digestion sour.
You urg'd me as a judge; but I had rather

You would have bid me argue like a father.
O, had it been a stranger, not my child,
To smooth his fault I should have been more
mild.   240
A partial slander sought I to avoid,
And in the sentence my own life destroy'd.
Alas, I look'd when some of you should say
I was too strict to make mine own away;
But you gave leave to my unwilling tongue   245
Against my will to do myself this wrong.

King. Cousin, farewell; and, uncle, bid him
so.
Six years we banish him, and he shall go.
Flourish. Exit [King with his Train].

Aum. Cousin, farewell. What presence must
not know,
From where you do remain let paper show.   250

Mar. My lord, no leave take I; for I will
ride,
As far as land will let me, by your side.

Gaunt. O, to what purpose dost thou hoard
thy words
That thou returnest no greeting to thy friends?

Boling. I have too few to take my leave of
you,   255
When the tongue's office should be prodigal
To breathe the abundant dolour of the heart.

Gaunt. Thy grief is but thy absence for a
time.

Boling. Joy absent, grief is present for that
time.

Gaunt. What is six winters? They are
quickly gone.   260

Boling. To men in joy; but grief makes one
hour ten.

Gaunt. Call it a travel that thou tak'st for
pleasure.

Boling. My heart will sigh when I miscall
it so,
Which finds it an enforced pilgrimage.   264

Gaunt. The sullen passage of thy weary steps
Esteem as foil wherein thou art to set
The precious jewel of thy home return.

Boling. Nay, rather every tedious stride I
make
Will but remember me what a deal of world
I wander from the jewels that I love.   270
Must I not serve a long apprenticehood
To foreign passages and, in the end,
Having my freedom, boast of nothing else
But that I was a journeyman to grief?

Gaunt. All places that the eye of heaven
visits   275
Are to a wise man ports and happy havens.
Teach thy necessity to reason thus:

There is no virtue like necessity.
Think not the King did banish thee,
But thou the King. Woe doth the heavier
    sit   280
Where it perceives it is but faintly borne.
Go, say I sent thee forth to purchase honour,
And not, the King exil'd thee; or suppose
Devouring pestilence hangs in our air
And thou art flying to a fresher clime.   285
Look, what thy soul holds dear, imagine it
To lie that way thou goest, not whence thou
    com'st.
Suppose the singing birds musicians,
The grass whereon thou tread'st the presence
    strow'd,   289
The flowers fair ladies, and thy steps no more
Than a delightful measure or a dance;
For gnarling sorrow hath less power to bite
The man that mocks at it and sets it light.
    Boling. O, who can hold a fire in his hand
By thinking on the frosty Caucasus?   295
Or cloy the hungry edge of appetite
By bare imagination of a feast?
Or wallow naked in December snow
By thinking on fantastic summer's heat?
O, no! The apprehension of the good   300
Gives but the greater feeling to the worse.
Fell sorrow's tooth doth never rankle more
Than when he bites, but lanceth not the sore.
    Gaunt. Come, come, my son, I'll bring thee
    on thy way.   304
Had I thy youth and cause, I would not stay.
    Boling. Then, England's ground, farewell;
    sweet soil, adieu,
My mother, and my nurse, that bears me yet!
Where'er I wander, boast of this I can,
Though banish'd, yet a trueborn English man.
                                                    Exeunt.

Scene IV. [*London. The court.*]

Enter the *King*, with *Green* and *Bagot*, at one
    door, and the *Lord Aumerle* at another.

    King. We did observe. Cousin Aumerle,
How far brought you high Hereford on his way?
    Aum. I brought high Hereford, if you call
    him so,
But to the next high way, and there I left him.
    King. And say, what store of parting tears
    were shed?   5
    Aum. Faith, none for me; except the north-
    east wind,
Which then blew bitterly against our faces,

Awak'd the sleeping rheum, and so by chance
Did grace our hollow parting with a tear.
    King. What said our cousin when you
    parted with him?   10
    Aum. 'Farewell!'
And, for my heart disdained that my tongue
Should so profane the word, that taught me
    craft
To counterfeit oppression of such grief   14
That words seem'd buried in my sorrow's grave.
Marry, would the word 'farewell' have length-
    'ned hours
And added years to his short banishment,
He should have had a volume of farewells,
But since it would not, he had none of me.
    King. He is our cousin, cousin; but 'tis
    doubt,   20
When time shall call him home from banish-
    ment,
Whether our kinsman come to see his friends.
Ourself and Bushy, Bagot here, and Green
Observ'd his courtship to the common people;
How he did seem to dive into their hearts   25
With humble and familiar courtesy;
What reverence he did throw away on slaves,
Wooing poor craftsmen with the craft of smiles
And patient underbearing of his fortune,
As 'twere to banish their affects with him.   30
Off goes his bonnet to an oyster-wench;
A brace of draymen bid God speed him well
And had the tribute of his supple knee,
With 'Thanks, my countrymen, my loving
    friends';
As were our England in reversion his,   35
And he our subjects' next degree in hope.
    Green. Well, he is gone, and with him go
    these thoughts!
Now for the rebels which stand out in Ireland,
Expedient manage must be made, my liege,
Ere further leisure yield them further means 40
For their advantage and your Highness' loss.
    King. We will ourself in person to this war;
And, for our coffers, with too great a court
And liberal largess, are grown somewhat light,
We are enforc'd to farm our royal realm,   45
The revenue whereof shall furnish us
For our affairs in hand. If that come short,
Our substitutes at home shall have blank
    charters,
Whereto, when they shall know what men are
    rich,
They shall subscribe them for large sums of
    gold   50
And send them after to supply our wants,
For we will make for Ireland presently.

Enter *Bushy*.

Bushy, what news?

  Bushy. Old John of Gaunt is grievous sick,
    my lord,
Suddenly taken, and hath sent post-haste   55
To entreat your Majesty to visit him.
  King. Where lies he?
  Bushy. At Ely House.

  King. Now put it, God, in the physician's
    mind
To help him to his grave immediately!   60
The lining of his coffers shall make coats
To deck our soldiers for these Irish wars.
Come, gentlemen, let's all go visit him.
Pray God we may make haste, and come too
  late!
  All. Amen.   *Exeunt.*

ACT II. Scene I. [*London. Ely House.*]

Enter *John of Gaunt*, sick, with the
Duke of York &c.

  Gaunt. Will the King come, that I may
    breathe my last
In wholesome counsel to his unstaid youth?
  York. Vex not yourself nor strive not with
    your breath,
For all in vain comes counsel to his ear.
  Gaunt. O, but they say the tongues of dying
    men   5
Enforce attention like deep harmony.
Where words are scarce, they are seldom spent
  in vain,
For they breathe truth that breathe their words
  in pain.
He that no more must say is listened more
  Than they whom youth and ease have taught
    to glose.   10
More are men's ends mark'd than their lives
  before.
  The setting sun, and music at the close,
As the last taste of sweets, is sweetest last,
Writ in remembrance more than things long
  past.
Though Richard my live's counsel would not
  hear,   15
My death's sad tale may yet undeaf his ear.
  York. No; it is stopp'd with other flattering
    sounds,
As praises, of whose taste the wise are fond,
Lascivious metres, to whose venom sound
The open ear of youth doth always listen;   20
Report of fashions in proud Italy,
Whose manners still our tardy apish nation
Limps after in base imitation.
Where doth the world thrust forth a vanity
(So it be new, there's no respect how vile)   25
That is not quickly buzz'd into his ears?
Then all too late comes counsel to be heard
Where will doth mutiny with wit's regard.
Direct not him whose way himself will choose.

'Tis breath thou lack'st, and that breath wilt
  thou lose.   30
  Gaunt. Methinks I am a prophet new in-
    spir'd
And thus, expiring, do foretell of him:
His rash fierce blaze of riot cannot last,
For violent fires soon burn out themselves;
Small show'rs last long, but sudden storms are
  short;   35
He tires betimes that spurs too fast betimes;
With eager feeding food doth choke the feeder;
Light vanity, insatiate cormorant,
Consuming means, soon preys upon itself.   39
This royal throne of kings, this scept'red isle,
This earth of majesty, this seat of Mars,
This other Eden, demi-paradise,
This fortress built by Nature for herself
Against infection and the hand of war,
This happy breed of men, this little world,   45
This precious stone set in the silver sea,
Which serves it in the office of a wall,
Or as a moat defensive to a house,
Against the envy of less happier lands;
This blessed plot, this earth, this realm, this
  England,   50
This nurse, this teeming womb of royal kings,
Fear'd by their breed and famous by their birth,
Renowned for their deeds as far from home,
For Christian service and true chivalry,
As is the sepulchre in stubborn Jewry   55
Of the world's ransom, blessed Mary's son;
This land of such dear souls, this dear dear
  land,
Dear for her reputation through the world,
Is now leas'd out (I die pronouncing it)
Like to a tenement or pelting farm.   60
England, bound in with the triumphant sea,
Whose rocky shore beats back the envious siege
Of wat'ry Neptune, is now bound in with shame,
With inky blots and rotten parchment bonds.
That England that was wont to conquer others
Hath made a shameful conquest of itself.   66

Ah, would the scandal vanish with my life,
How happy then were my ensuing death!

Enter *King, Queen, Aumerle, Bushy, Green,*
    Bagot, Ross, and *Willoughby.*

York. The King is come. Deal mildly with
    his youth;
For young hot colts, being rag'd, do rage the
    more.   70
    Queen. How fares our noble uncle Lancaster?
    King. What comfort, man? How is't with
    aged Gaunt?
    Gaunt. O, how that name befits my com-
    position!
Old Gaunt indeed, and gaunt in being old.
Within me grief hath kept a tedious fast;   75
And who abstains from meat that is not
    gaunt?
For sleeping England long time have I watch'd;
Watching breeds leanness, leanness is all gaunt.
The pleasure that some fathers feed upon   79
Is my strict fast—I mean my children's looks—
And therein fasting hast thou made me gaunt.
Gaunt am I for the grave, gaunt as a grave,
Whose hollow womb inherits naught but bones.
    King. Can sick men play so nicely with their
    names?
    Gaunt. No, misery makes sport to mock it-
    self.   85
Since thou dost seek to kill my name in me,
I mock my name, great King, to flatter thee.
    King. Should dying men flatter with those
    that live?
    Gaunt. No, no! men living flatter those that
    die.
    King. Thou, now a-dying, say'st thou flat-
    terest me.   90
    Gaunt. O, no! thou diest, though I the
    sicker be.
    King. I am in health, I breathe, and see
    thee ill.
    Gaunt. Now, he that made me knows I see
    thee ill;
Ill in myself to see, and in thee seeing ill.
Thy deathbed is no lesser than thy land,   95
Wherein thou liest in reputation sick;
And thou, too careless patient as thou art,
Committ'st thy anointed body to the cure
Of those physicians that first wounded thee.
A thousand flatterers sit within thy crown,   100
Whose compass is no bigger than thy head;
And yet, incaged in so small a verge,
The waste is no whit lesser than thy land.
O, had thy grandsire, with a prophet's eye,
Seen how his son's son should destroy his sons,

From forth thy reach he would have laid thy
    shame,   106
Deposing thee before thou wert possess'd,
Which art possess'd now to depose thyself.
Why, cousin, wert thou regent of the world,
It were a shame to let this land by lease;   110
But, for thy world enjoying but this land,
Is it not more than shame to shame it so?
Landlord of England art thou now, not King.
Thy state of law is bondslave to the law,
And thou —
    King.   A lunatic lean-witted fool,   115
Presuming on an ague's privilege,
Dar'st with thy frozen admonition
Make pale our cheek, chasing the royal blood
With fury from his native residence.
Now, by my seat's right royal majesty,   120
Wert thou not brother to great Edward's son,
This tongue that runs so roundly in thy head
Should run thy head from thy unreverent
    shoulders.
    Gaunt. O, spare me not, my brother Ed-
    ward's son,
For that I was his father Edward's son!   125
That blood already, like the pelican,
Hast thou tapp'd out and drunkenly carous'd.
My brother Gloucester, plain well-meaning soul
(Whom fair befall in heaven 'mongst happy
    souls!),
May be a precedent and witness good   130
That thou respect'st not spilling Edward's
    blood.
Join with the present sickness that I have,
And thy unkindness be like crooked age,
To crop at once a too long withered flower.
Live in thy shame, but die not shame with thee!
These words hereafter thy tormenters be!   136
Convey me to my bed, then to my grave.
Love they to live that love and honour have.
                Exit [borne off by Attendants].
    King. And let them die that age and sullens
    have;   139
For both hast thou, and both become the grave.
    York. I do beseech your Majesty, impute his
    words
To wayward sickliness and age in him.
He loves you, on my life, and holds you dear
As Harry Duke of Hereford, were he here.
    King. Right, you say true! As Hereford's
    love, so his;   145
As theirs, so mine; and all be as it is!

Enter *Northumberland.*

North. My liege, old Gaunt commends him
to your Majesty.

King. What says he?
North.   Nay, nothing; all is said.
His tongue is now a stringless instrument;
Words, life, and all, old Lancaster hath spent.
  York. Be York the next that must be bank-
    rout so!   151
Though death be poor, it ends a mortal woe.
  King. The ripest fruit first falls, and so
    doth he;
His time is spent, our pilgrimage must be.
So much for that. Now for our Irish wars.   155
We must supplant those rough rug-headed
    kerns,
Which live like venom where no venom else
But only they have privilege to live.
And, for these great affairs do ask some charge,
Towards our assistance we do seize to us   160
The plate, coin, revenues, and moveables
Whereof our uncle Gaunt did stand possess'd.
  York. How long shall I be patient? Ah, how
    long
Shall tender duty make me suffer wrong?
Not Gloucester's death, nor Hereford's banish-
    ment,   165
Nor Gaunt's rebukes, nor England's private
    wrongs,
Nor the prevention of poor Bolingbroke
About his marriage, nor my own disgrace,
Have ever made me sour my patient cheek
Or bend one wrinkle on my sovereign's face.
I am the last of noble Edward's sons,   171
Of whom thy father, Prince of Wales, was first.
In war was never lion rag'd more fierce,
In peace was never gentle lamb more mild,
Than was that young and princely gentleman.
His face thou hast, for even so look'd he,   176
Accomplish'd with the number of thy hours;
But when he frown'd, it was against the French
And not against his friends. His noble hand
Did win what he did spend, and spent not that
Which his triumphant father's hand had won.
His hands were guilty of no kinred blood,
But bloody with the enemies of his kin.
O Richard! York is too far gone with grief,
Or else he never would compare between.   185
  King. Why, uncle, what's the matter?
  York.   O my liege,
Pardon me, if you please; if not, I, pleas'd
Not to be pardoned, am content withal.
Seek you to seize and gripe into your hands
The royalties and rights of banish'd Hereford?
Is not Gaunt dead? and doth not Hereford
    live?   191
Was not Gaunt just? and is not Harry true?
Did not the one deserve to have an heir?

Is not his heir a well-deserving son?
Take Hereford's rights away, and take from
    Time   195
His charters and his customary rights;
Let not to-morrow then ensue to-day;
Be not thyself — for how art thou a king
But by fair sequence and succession?
Now, afore God (God forbid I say true!),   200
If you do wrongfully seize Hereford's rights,
Call in the letters patents that he hath
By his attorneys general to sue
His livery, and deny his off'red homage,   204
You pluck a thousand dangers on your head,
You lose a thousand well-disposed hearts,
And prick my tender patience to those thoughts
Which honour and allegiance cannot think.
  King. Think what you will, we seize into our
    hands   209
His plate, his goods, his money, and his lands.
  York. I'll not be by the while. My liege,
    farewell.
What will ensue hereof there's none can tell;
But by bad courses may be understood
That their events can never fall out good. *Exit.*
  King. Go, Bushy, to the Earl of Wiltshire
    straight.   215
Bid him repair to us to Ely House
To see this business. To-morrow next
We will for Ireland; and 'tis time, I trow.
And we create, in absence of ourself,
Our uncle York Lord Governor of England;
For he is just and always lov'd us well.   221
Come on, our queen. To-morrow must we part.
Be merry, for our time of stay is short.
      Flourish. Exeunt. Manent Northumber-
                land, Willoughby, and Ross.
  North. Well, lords, the Duke of Lancaster is
    dead.
  Ross. And living too; for now his son is
    Duke.   225
  Wil. Barely in title, not in revenues.
  North. Richly in both, if justice had her right.
  Ross. My heart is great; but it must break
    with silence,
Ere 't be disburdened with a liberal tongue.
  North. Nay, speak thy mind; and let him
    ne'er speak more   230
That speaks thy words again to do thee harm!
  Wil. Tends that thou wouldst speak to the
    Duke of Hereford?
If it be so, out with it boldly, man!
Quick is mine ear to hear of good towards him.
  Ross. No good at all that I can do for him;
Unless you call it good to pity him,   236
Bereft and gelded of his patrimony.

North. Now, afore God, 'tis shame such
    wrongs are borne
In him a royal prince and many moe
Of noble blood in this declining land.   240
The King is not himself, but basely led
By flatterers; and what they will inform,
Merely in hate, 'gainst any of us all,
That will the King severely prosecute
'Gainst us, our lives, our children, and our
    heirs.   245
    Ross. The commons hath he pill'd with
    grievous taxes
And quite lost their hearts; the nobles hath
    he fin'd
For ancient quarrels and quite lost their hearts.
    Wil. And daily new exactions are devis'd,
As blanks, benevolences, and I wot not what;
But what, a God's name, doth become of this?
    North. Wars have not wasted it, for warr'd
    he hath not,
But basely yielded upon compromise
That which his noble ancestors achiev'd with
    blows.   254
More hath he spent in peace than they in wars.
    Ross. The Earl of Wiltshire hath the realm
    in farm.
    Wil. The King's grown bankrout, like a
    broken man.
    North. Reproach and dissolution hangeth
    over him.
    Ross. He hath not money for these Irish
    wars,
His burthenous taxations notwithstanding, 260
But by the robbing of the banish'd Duke.
    North. His noble kinsman. Most degenerate
    king!
But, lords, we hear this fearful tempest sing,
Yet seek no shelter to avoid the storm.
We see the wind sit sore upon our sails, 265
And yet we strike not, but securely perish.
    Ross. We see the very wrack that we must
    suffer,
And unavoided is the danger now
For suffering so the causes of our wrack.
    North. Not so. Even through the hollow
    eyes of death   270
I spy life peering; but I dare not say
How near the tidings of our comfort is.
    Wil. Nay, let us share thy thoughts as thou
    dost ours.
    Ross. Be confident to speak, Northumber-
    land.
We three are but thyself, and speaking so, 275
Thy words are but as thoughts. Therefore be
    bold.

    North. Then thus: I have from Le Port
    Blanc, a bay
In Britain, receiv'd intelligence
That Harry Duke of Hereford, Rainold Lord
    Cobham,
. . . .   280
That late broke from the Duke of Exeter,
His brother, Archbishop late of Canterbury,
Sir Thomas Erpingham, Sir John Ramston,
Sir John Norbery, Sir Robert Waterton, and
    Francis Quoint,   284
All these well furnish'd by the Duke of Britain
With eight tall ships, three thousand men of
    war,
Are making hither with all due expedience
And shortly mean to touch our northern shore.
Perhaps they had ere this, but that they stay
The first departing of the King for Ireland. 290
If then we shall shake off our slavish yoke,
Imp out our drooping country's broken wing,
Redeem from broking pawn the blemish'd
    crown,
Wipe off the dust that hides our sceptre's gilt,
And make high majesty look like itself, 295
Away with me in post to Ravenspurgh;
But if you faint, as fearing to do so,
Stay and be secret, and myself will go.
    Ross. To horse, to horse! Urge doubts to
    them that fear.
    Wil. Hold out my horse, and I will first be
    there.   300
                Exeunt.

Scene II. [*Windsor Castle.*]

Enter the *Queen, Bushy, Bagot.*

    Bushy. Madam, your Majesty is too much
    sad.
You promis'd, when you parted with the King,
To lay aside life-harming heaviness
And entertain a cheerful disposition.
    Queen. To please the King, I did; to please
    myself,   5
I cannot do it. Yet I know no cause
Why I should welcome such a guest as grief
Save bidding farewell to so sweet a guest
As my sweet Richard. Yet again, methinks,
Some unborn sorrow, ripe in fortune's womb, 10
Is coming towards me, and my inward soul
With nothing trembles. At something it grieves
More than with parting from my lord the King.
    Bushy. Each substance of a grief hath twenty
    shadows,

Which shows like grief itself, but is not so; 15
For sorrow's eye, glazed with blinding tears,
Divides one thing entire to many objects,
Like perspectives, which rightly gaz'd upon,
Show nothing but confusion — ey'd awry,
Distinguish form. So your sweet Majesty, 20
Looking awry upon your lord's departure,
Find shapes of grief more than himself to wail,
Which, look'd on as it is, is naught but shadows
Of what it is not. Then, thrice-gracious Queen,
More than your lord's departure weep not.
　　More's not seen; 25
Or if it be, 'tis with false sorrow's eye,
Which for things true weeps things imaginary.
　　Queen. It may be so; but yet my inward
　　　soul
Persuades me it is otherwise. Howe'er it be,
I cannot but be sad — so heavy sad — 30
As, though in thinking on no thought I think,
Makes me with heavy nothing faint and shrink.
　　Bushy. 'Tis nothing but conceit, my gracious
　　　lady.
　　Queen. 'Tis nothing less. Conceit is still
　　　deriv'd
From some forefather grief. Mine is not so, 35
For nothing hath begot my something grief,
Or something hath the nothing that I grieve.
'Tis in reversion that I do possess;
But what it is that is not yet known what,
I cannot name. 'Tis nameless woe, I wot. 40

Enter *Green.*

　　Green. God save your Majesty! and well
　　　met, gentlemen.
I hope the King is not yet shipp'd for Ireland.
　　Queen. Why hopest thou so? 'Tis better
　　　hope he is;
For his designs crave haste, his haste good hope;
Then wherefore dost thou hope he is not
　　　shipp'd? 45
　　Green. That he, our hope, might have re-
　　　tir'd his power
And driven into despair an enemy's hope
Who strongly hath set footing in this land.
The banish'd Bolingbroke repeals himself
And with uplifted arms is safe arriv'd 50
At Ravenspurgh.
　　Queen. 　　　　Now God in heaven forbid!
　　Green. Ah, madam, 'tis too true; and that is
　　　worse,
The Lord Northumberland, his son young
　　Henry Percy,
The Lords of Ross, Beaumond, and Willoughby,
With all their powerful friends, are fled to
　　him. 55

　　Bushy. Why have you not proclaim'd North-
　　umberland
And all the rest revolted faction traitors?
　　Green. We have; whereupon the Earl of
　　　Worcester
Hath broken his staff, resign'd his stewardship,
And all the household servants fled with him
　　to Bolingbroke. 60
　　Queen. So, Green, thou art the midwife to
　　　my woe,
And Bolingbroke my sorrow's dismal heir.
Now hath my soul brought forth her prodigy;
And I, a gasping new-deliver'd mother,
Have woe to woe, sorrow to sorrow join'd. 65
　　Bushy. Despair not, madam.
　　Queen. 　　　　　Who shall hinder me?
I will despair, and be at enmity
With cozening Hope. He is a flatterer,
A parasite, a keeper-back of Death,
Who gently would dissolve the bands of life, 70
Which false hope lingers in extremity.

Enter *York.*

　　Green. Here comes the Duke of York.
　　Queen. With signs of war about his aged neck.
O, full of careful business are his looks. 74
Uncle, for God's sake, speak comfortable words!
　　York. Should I do so, I should belie my
　　　thoughts.
Comfort's in heaven, and we are on the earth,
Where nothing lives but crosses, cares, and grief.
Your husband, he is gone to save far off,
Whilst others come to make him lose at home.
Here am I left to underprop his land, 81
Who, weak with age, cannot support myself.
Now comes the sick hour that his surfeit made;
Now shall he try his friends that flatter'd him.

Enter a *Servingman.*

　　Serv. My lord, your son was gone before I
　　　came. 85
　　York. He was? Why, so! Go all which way
　　　it will!
The nobles they are fled, the commons they are
　　cold
And will, I fear, revolt on Hereford's side.
Sirrah, get thee to Plashy to my sister Glouces-
　　ter; 89
Bid her send me presently a thousand pound.
Hold, take my ring.
　　Serv. My lord, I had forgot to tell your
　　　lordship
To-day, as I came by, I called there —
But I shall grieve you to report the rest.
　　York. What is't, knave? 95

Serv. An hour before I came the Duchess
died.
York. God for his mercy! what a tide of woes
Comes rushing on this woful land at once!
I know not what to do. I would to God
(So my untruth had not provok'd him to it) 100
The King had cut off my head with my broth-
er's.
What, are there no posts dispatch'd for Ireland?
How shall we do for money for these wars?
Come, sister — cousin I would say — pray par-
don me. —
Go, fellow, get thee home, provide some carts
And bring away the armour that is there. 106
[*Exit Servingman.*]
Gentlemen, will you go muster men? If I
Know how or which way to order these affairs,
Thus thrust disorderly into my hands,
Never believe me. Both are my kinsmen. 110
Th' one is my sovereign, whom both my oath
And duty bids defend; t' other again
Is my kinsman, whom the King hath wrong'd,
Whom conscience and my kinred bids to right.
Well, somewhat we must do. Come, cousin, I'll
Dispose of you. 116
Gentlemen, go muster up your men,
And meet me presently at Berkeley Castle.
I should to Plashy too,
But time will not permit. All is uneven, 120
And everything is left at six and seven.
Exeunt Duke, Queen.
Bushy. The wind sits fair for news to go for
Ireland,
But none returns. For us to levy power
Proportionable to the enemy
Is all unpossible. 125
Green. Besides, our nearness to the King in
love
Is near the hate of those love not the King.
Bagot. And that's the wavering commons;
for their love
Lies in their purses, and whoso empties them,
By so much fills their hearts with deadly hate.
Bushy. Wherein the King stands generally
condemn'd. 131
Bagot. If judgment lie in them, then so do we,
Because we ever have been near the King.
Green. Well, I will for refuge straight to
Bristow Castle.
The Earl of Wiltshire is already there. 135
Bushy. Thither will I with you; for little
office
The hateful commons will perform for us,
Except like curs to tear us all to pieces.
Will you go along with us?

Bagot. No; I will to Ireland to his Majesty.
Farewell. If heart's presages be not vain, 141
We three here part that ne'er shall meet again.
Bushy. That's as York thrives to beat back
Bolingbroke.
Green. Alas, poor Duke! The task he under-
takes
Is numb'ring sands and drinking oceans dry.
Where one on his side fights, thousands will fly.
Bagot. Farewell at once — for once, for all,
and ever.
Bushy. Well, we may meet again.
Bagot.   I fear me, never.
Exeunt.

Scene III. [*The wilds in Gloucestershire.*]

Enter [*Bolingbroke*] *the Duke of Hereford,*
and *Northumberland.*

Boling. How far is it, my lord, to Berkeley
now?
North. Believe me, noble lord,
I am a stranger here in Gloucestershire.
These high wild hills and rough uneven ways
Draws out our miles and makes them weari-
some; 5
And yet your fair discourse hath been as sugar,
Making the hard way sweet and delectable.
But I bethink me what a weary way
From Ravenspurgh to Cotshall will be found
In Ross and Willoughby, wanting your company,
Which, I protest, hath very much beguil'd 11
The tediousness and process of my travel;
But theirs is sweet'ned with the hope to have
The present benefit which I possess;
And hope to joy is little less in joy 15
Than hope enjoy'd. By this the weary lords
Shall make their way seem short, as mine hath
done
By sight of what I have, your noble company.
Boling. Of much less value is my company
Than your good words. But who comes here?

Enter *Harry Percy.*

North. It is my son, young Harry Percy,
Sent from my brother Worcester, whencesoever.
Harry, how fares your uncle?
Percy. I had thought, my lord, to have
learn'd his health of you.
North. Why, is he not with the Queen? 25
Percy. No, my good lord; he hath forsook
the court,
Broken his staff of office, and dispers'd
The household of the King.

North.   What was his reason?
He was not so resolv'd when last we spake to-
gether.
Percy. Because your lordship was proclaimed
traitor.   30
But he, my lord, is gone to Ravenspurgh
To offer service to the Duke of Hereford;
And sent me over by Berkeley to discover
What power the Duke of York had levied there;
Then with directions to repair to Ravenspurgh.
North. Have you forgot the Duke of Here-
ford, boy?   36
Percy. No, my good lord, for that is not for-
got
Which ne'er I did remember. To my knowledge,
I never in my life did look on him.
North. Then learn to know him now. This
is the Duke.   40
Percy. My gracious lord, I tender you my
service,
Such as it is, being tender, raw, and young;
Which elder days shall ripen and confirm
To more approved service and desert.
Boling. I thank thee, gentle Percy; and be
sure   45
I count myself in nothing else so happy
As in a soul rememb'ring my good friends;
And, as my fortune ripens with thy love,
It shall be still thy true love's recompense.
My heart this covenant makes, my hand thus
seals it.   50
North. How far is it to Berkeley? and what
stir
Keeps good old York there with his men of war?
Percy. There stands the castle by yon tuft
of trees,
Mann'd with three hundred men, as I have
heard;
And in it are the Lords of York, Berkeley, and
Seymour,   55
None else of name and noble estimate.

Enter *Ross* and *Willoughby.*

North. Here come the Lords of Ross and
Willoughby,
Bloody with spurring, fiery red with haste.
Boling. Welcome, my lords. I wot your love
pursues
A banish'd traitor. All my treasury   60
Is yet but unfelt thanks, which, more enrich'd,
Shall be your love and labour's recompense.
Ross. Your prèsence makes us rich, most
noble lord.
Wil. And far surmounts our labour to at-
tain it.

Boling. Evermore thanks, the exchequer of
the poor,   65
Which, till my infant fortune comes to years,
Stands for my bounty. But who comes here?

Enter *Berkeley.*

North. It is my Lord of Berkeley, as I guess.
Berk. My Lord of Hereford, my message is
to you.
Boling. My lord, my answer is — 'to Lan-
caster';   70
And I am come to seek that name in England;
And I must find that title in your tongue
Before I make reply to aught you say.
Berk. Mistake me not, my lord. 'Tis not
my meaning
To rase one title of your honour out.   75
To you, my lord, I come (what lord you will)
From the most gracious Regent of this land,
The Duke of York, to know what pricks you on
To take advantage of the absent time   79
And fright our native peace with self-born arms.

Enter *York* [attended].

Boling. I shall not need transport my words
by you;
Here comes his Grace in person. My noble
uncle! [*Kneels.*]
York. Show me thy humble heart, and not
thy knee,
Whose duty is deceivable and false.
Boling. My gracious uncle!   85
York. Tut, tut!
Grace me no grace, nor uncle me no uncle.
I am no traitor's uncle, and that word 'grace'
In an ungracious mouth is but profane.
Why have those banish'd and forbidden legs 90
Dar'd once to touch a dust of England's
ground?
But then more why? — why have they dar'd
to march
So many miles upon her peaceful bosom,
Frighting her pale-fac'd villages with war
And ostentation of despised arms?   95
Com'st thou because the anointed King is hence?
Why, foolish boy, the King is left behind,
And in my loyal bosom lies his power.
Were I but now lord of such hot youth
As when brave Gaunt thy father and myself 100
Rescued the Black Prince, that young Mars of
men,
From forth the ranks of many thousand French,
O, then how quickly should this arm of mine,
Now prisoner to the palsy, chastise thee
And minister correction to thy fault!   105

51

Boling. My gracious uncle, let me know my
    fault;
On what condition stands it and wherein?
    York. Even in condition of the worst degree,
In gross rebellion and detested treason.
Thou art a banish'd man; and here art come,
Before the expiration of thy time,   111
In braving arms against thy sovereign.
    Boling. As I was banish'd, I was banish'd
    Hereford;
But as I come, I come for Lancaster.
And, noble uncle, I beseech your Grace   115
Look on my wrongs with an indifferent eye.
You are my father, for methinks in you
I see old Gaunt alive. O, then, my father,
Will you permit that I shall stand condemn'd
A wandering vagabond, my rights and royalties
Pluck'd from my arms perforce, and given away
To upstart unthrifts? Wherefore was I born?
If that my cousin king be King of England,
It must be granted I am Duke of Lancaster.
You have a son, Aumerle, my noble cousin. 125
Had you first died, and he been thus trod down,
He should have found his uncle Gaunt a father
To rouse his wrongs and chase them to the bay.
I am denied to sue my livery here,
And yet my letters patents give me leave. 130
My father's goods are all distrain'd and sold;
And these, and all, are all amiss employ'd.
What would you have me do? I am a subject,
And I challenge law. Attorneys are denied me,
And therefore personally I lay my claim   135
To my inheritance of free descent.
    North. The noble Duke hath been too much
    abus'd.
    Ross. It stands your Grace upon to do him
    right.
    Wil. Base men by his endowments are made
    great.
    York. My lords of England, let me tell you
    this: 140
I have had feeling of my cousin's wrongs,
And labour'd all I could to do him right;
But in this kind to come, in braving arms,
Be his own carver and cut out his way
To find out right with wrong — it may not be;
And you that do abet him in this kind   146
Cherish rebellion and are rebels all.
    North. The noble Duke hath sworn his com-
    ing is
But for his own; and for the right of that
We all have strongly sworn to give him aid; 150
And let him never see joy that breaks that oath!
    York. Well, well, I see the issue of these arms.
I cannot mend it, I must needs confess,

Because my power is weak and all ill left;
But if I could, by him that gave me life,   155
I would attach you all and make you stoop
Unto the sovereign mercy of the King;
But since I cannot, be it known to you
I do remain as neuter. So fare you well —
Unless you please to enter in the castle   160
And there repose you for this night.
    Boling. An offer, uncle, that we will accept;
But we must win your Grace to go with us
To Bristow Castle, which they say is held
By Bushy, Bagot, and their complices,   165
The caterpillars of the commonwealth,
Which I have sworn to weed and pluck away.
    York. It may be I will go with you; but yet
    I'll pause,
For I am loath to break our country's laws.
Nor friends nor foes, to me welcome you are. 170
Things past redress are now with me past care.
    Exeunt.

Scene IV. [*A camp in Wales.*]

Enter *Earl of Salisbury* and a *Welsh Captain.*
    Welsh. My Lord of Salisbury, we have stay'd
    ten days
And hardly kept our countrymen together,
And yet we hear no tidings from the King.
Therefore we will disperse ourselves. Farewell.
    Sal. Stay yet another day, thou trusty Welsh-
    man.   5
The King reposeth all his confidence in thee.
    Welsh. 'Tis thought the King is dead. We
    will not stay.
The bay trees in our country all are wither'd,
And meteors fright the fixed stars of heaven;
The pale-fac'd moon looks bloody on the earth,
And lean-look'd prophets whisper fearful
    change;
Rich men look sad, and ruffians dance and leap —
The one in fear to lose what they enjoy,
The other to enjoy by rage and war.   14
These signs forerun the death or fall of kings.
Farewell. Our countrymen are gone and fled,
As well assur'd Richard their king is dead.
    Exit.
    Sal. Ah, Richard! with the eyes of heavy
    mind,
I see thy glory, like a shooting star,
Fall to the base earth from the firmament. 20
Thy sun sets weeping in the lowly West,
Witnessing storms to come, woe, and unrest;
Thy friends are fled to wait upon thy foes,
And crossly to thy good all fortune goes. *Exit.*

ACT III. Scene I. [Bolingbroke's *camp at Bristol.*]

Enter *Bolingbroke Duke of Hereford, York, Northumberland, Ross, Percy, Willoughby*, with *Bushy* and *Green* prisoners.

Boling. Bring forth these men.
Bushy and Green, I will not vex your souls
(Since presently your souls must part your
    bodies)
With too much urging your pernicious lives,
For 'twere no charity; yet, to wash your blood
From off my hands, here in the view of men   6
I will unfold some causes of your deaths.
You have misled a prince, a royal king,
A happy gentleman in blood and lineaments,
By you unhappied and disfigured clean.   10
You have in manner with your sinful hours
Made a divorce betwixt his queen and him,
Broke the possession of a royal bed,
And stain'd the beauty of a fair queen's cheeks
With tears drawn from her eyes by your foul
    wrongs.   15
Myself — a prince by fortune of my birth,
Near to the King in blood, and near in love
Till you did make him misinterpret me —
Have stoop'd my neck under your injuries
And sigh'd my English breath in foreign clouds,
Eating the bitter bread of banishment,   21
Whilst you have fed upon my signories,
Dispark'd my parks and fell'd my forest woods,
From my own windows torn my household
    coat,
Ras'd out my imprese, leaving me no sign,   25
Save men's opinions and my living blood,
To show the world I am a gentleman.
This and much more, much more than twice
    all this,
Condemns you to the death. See them deliv-
    ered over
To execution and the hand of death.   30
Bushy. More welcome is the stroke of death
    to me
Than Bolingbroke to England. Lords, farewell.
Green. My comfort is that heaven will take
    our souls
And plague injustice with the pains of hell.
Boling. My Lord Northumberland, see them
    dispatch'd.   35
    [*Exeunt Northumberland and others, with
        the prisoners.*]
Uncle, you say the Queen is at your house.
For God's sake, fairly let her be entreated.

Tell her I send to her my kind commends;
Take special care my greetings be delivered.
York. A gentleman of mine I have dispatch'd
With letters of your love to her at large.   41
Boling. Thanks, gentle uncle. Come, lords,
    away,
To fight with Glendower and his complices.
Awhile to work, and after holiday.   *Exeunt.*

Scene II. [*The coast of Wales. A
castle in view.*]

Drums. Flourish and Colours. Enter *the King,
Aumerle,* [*the Bishop of*] *Carlisle,* and *Soldiers.*

King. Barkloughly Castle call they this at
    hand?
Aum. Yea, my lord. How brooks your Grace
    the air
After your late tossing on the breaking seas?
King. Needs must I like it well. I weep for
    joy
To stand upon my kingdom once again.   5
Dear earth, I do salute thee with my hand,
Though rebels wound thee with their horses'
    hoofs.
As a long-parted mother with her child
Plays fondly with her tears and smiles in
    meeting,
So weeping, smiling, greet I thee, my earth,   10
And do thee favours with my royal hands.
Feed not thy sovereign's foe, my gentle earth,
Nor with thy sweets comfort his ravenous
    sense;
But let thy spiders that suck up thy venom,
And heavy-gaited toads, lie in their way,   15
Doing annoyance to the treacherous feet
Which with usurping steps do trample thee.
Yield stinging nettles to mine enemies;
And when they from thy bosom pluck a flower,
Guard it, I pray thee, with a lurking adder   20
Whose double tongue may with a mortal touch
Throw death upon thy sovereign's enemies.
Mock not my senseless conjuration, lords.
This earth shall have a feeling, and these stones
Prove armed soldiers ere her native king   25
Shall falter under foul rebellion's arms.
Car. Fear not, my lord. That Power that
    made you king
Hath power to keep you king in spite of all.

53

The means that heaven yields must be em-
brac'd,
And not neglected; else, if heaven would,   30
And we will not, heaven's offer we refuse,
The proffered means of succour and redress.
    Aum. He means, my lord, that we are too
remiss,
Whilst Bolingbroke, through our security,
Grows strong and great in substance and in
power.   35
    King. Discomfortable cousin! know'st thou
not
That when the searching eye of heaven is hid
Behind the globe, that lights the lower world,
Then thieves and robbers range abroad unseen
In murthers and in outrage boldly here;   40
But when from under this terrestrial ball
He fires the proud tops of the Eastern pines
And darts his light through every guilty hole,
Then murthers, treasons, and detested sins,
The cloak of night being pluck'd from off their
backs,   45
Stand bare and naked, trembling at themselves?
So when this thief, this traitor Bolingbroke,
Who all this while hath revell'd in the night
Whilst we were wand'ring with the Antipodes,
Shall see us rising in our throne, the East,   50
His treasons will sit blushing in his face,
Not able to endure the sight of day,
But self-affrighted tremble at his sin.
Not all the water in the rough rude sea
Can wash the balm off from an anointed
king.
The breath of worldly men cannot depose   56
The deputy elected by the Lord.
For every man that Bolingbroke hath press'd
To lift shrewd steel against our golden crown,
God for his Richard hath in heavenly pay   60
A glorious angel. Then, if angels fight,
Weak men must fall; for heaven still guards
the right.

Enter *Salisbury.*

Welcome, my lord. How far off lies your power?
    Sal. Nor near nor farther off, my gracious
lord,
Than this weak arm. Discomfort guides my
tongue   65
And bids me speak of nothing but despair.
One day too late, I fear me, noble lord,
Hath clouded all thy happy days on earth.
O, call back yesterday, bid time return,
And thou shalt have twelve thousand fighting
men!   70
To-day, to-day, unhappy day too late,

O'erthrows thy joys, friends, fortune, and thy
state;
For all the Welshmen, hearing thou wert dead,
Are gone to Bolingbroke, dispers'd, and fled.
    Aum. Comfort, my liege. Why looks your
Grace so pale?   75
    King. But now the blood of twenty thousand
men
Did triumph in my face, and they are fled;
And, till so much blood thither come again,
Have I not reason to look pale and dead?
All souls that will be safe, fly from my side; 80
For time hath set a blot upon my pride.
    Aum. Comfort, my liege. Remember who
you are.
    King. I had forgot myself. Am I not King?
Awake, thou coward majesty! thou sleepest.
Is not the King's name twenty thousand
names?   85
Arm, arm, my name! A puny subject strikes
At thy great glory. Look not to the ground,
Ye favourites of a king. Are we not high?
High be our thoughts. I know my uncle York
Hath power enough to serve our turn. But
who comes here?   90

Enter *Scroop.*

    Scroop. More health and happiness betide
my liege
Than can my care-tun'd tongue deliver him!
    King. Mine ear is open and my heart pre-
par'd.
The worst is worldly loss thou canst unfold.
Say, is my kingdom lost? Why, 'twas my care;
And what loss is it to be rid of care?   95
Strives Bolingbroke to be as great as we?
Greater he shall not be; if he serve God,
We'll serve him too, and be his fellow so.
Revolt our subjects? That we cannot mend;
They break their faith to God as well as us. 101
Cry woe, destruction, ruin, and decay:
The worst is death, and death will have his day.
    Scroop. Glad am I that your Highness is so
arm'd
To bear the tidings of calamity.   105
Like an unseasonable stormy day
Which makes the silver rivers drown their
shores
As if the world were all dissolv'd to tears,
So high above his limits swells the rage
Of Bolingbroke, covering your fearful land 110
With hard bright steel, and hearts harder than
steel.
White-beards have arm'd their thin and hairless
scalps

Against thy majesty. Boys with women's
  voices
Strive to speak big, and clap their female joints
In stiff unwieldy arms against thy crown. 115
Thy very beadsmen learn to bend their bows
Of double-fatal yew against thy state.
Yea, distaff-women manage rusty bills
Against thy seat. Both young and old rebel,
And all goes worse than I have power to tell.
  King. Too well, too well thou tell'st a tale
  so ill. 121
Where is the Earl of Wiltshire? Where is
  Bagot?
What is become of Bushy? Where is Green?
That they have let the dangerous enemy
Measure our confines with such peaceful steps?
If we prevail, their heads shall pay for it. 126
I warrant they have made peace with Boling-
  broke.
  Scroop. Peace have they made with him in-
  deed, my lord.
  King. O villains, vipers, damn'd without re-
  demption!
Dogs easily won to fawn on any man! 130
Snakes in my heart-blood warm'd that sting
  my heart!
Three Judases, each one thrice worse than
  Judas!
Would they make peace? Terrible hell make
  war
Upon their spotted souls for this offence!
  Scroop. Sweet love, I see, changing his prop-
  erty, 135
Turns to the sourest and most deadly hate.
Again uncurse their souls. Their peace is made
With heads, and not with hands. Those whom
  you curse
Have felt the worst of death's destroying wound
And lie full low, grav'd in the hollow ground.
  Aum. Is Bushy, Green, and the Earl of
  Wiltshire dead? 141
  Scroop. Ay, all of them at Bristow lost their
  heads.
  Aum. Where is the Duke my father with his
  power?
  King. No matter where. Of comfort no man
  speak!
Let's talk of graves, of worms, and epitaphs, 145
Make dust our paper, and with rainy eyes
Write sorrow on the bosom of the earth.
Let's choose executors and talk of wills.
And yet not so — for what can we bequeath,
Save our deposed bodies to the ground? 150
Our lands, our lives, and all are Bolingbroke's,
And nothing can we call our own but death

And that small model of the barren earth
Which serves as paste and cover to our bones.
For God's sake let us sit upon the ground 155
And tell sad stories of the death of kings!
How some have been depos'd, some slain in war,
Some haunted by the ghosts they have depos'd,
Some poisoned by their wives, some sleeping
  kill'd —
All murthered; for within the hollow crown 160
That rounds the mortal temples of a king
Keeps Death his court; and there the antic sits,
Scoffing his state and grinning at his pomp;
Allowing him a breath, a little scene,
To monarchize, be fear'd, and kill with looks;
Infusing him with self and vain conceit, 166
As if this flesh which walls about our life
Were brass impregnable; and humour'd thus,
Comes at the last, and with a little pin
Bores through his castle wall, and farewell
  king! 170
Cover your heads, and mock not flesh and blood
With solemn reverence. Throw away respect,
Tradition, form, and ceremonious duty;
For you have but mistook me all this while.
I live with bread like you, feel want, taste grief,
Need friends. Subjected thus, 176
How can you say to me I am a king?
  Car. My lord, wise men ne'er sit and wail
  their woes,
But presently prevent the ways to wail. 179
To fear the foe, since fear oppresseth strength,
Gives, in your weakness, strength unto your foe,
And so your follies fight against yourself.
Fear, and be slain — no worse can come to fight;
And fight and die is death destroying death,
Where fearing dying pays death servile breath.
  Aum. My father hath a power. Inquire of
  him, 186
And learn to make a body of a limb.
  King. Thou chid'st me well. Proud Boling-
  broke, I come
To change blows with thee for our day of doom.
This ague fit of fear is overblown. 190
An easy task it is to win our own.
Say, Scroop, where lies our uncle with his power?
Speak sweetly, man, although thy looks be sour.
  Scroop. Men judge by the complexion of the
  sky
The state and inclination of the day; 195
So may you by my dull and heavy eye:
My tongue hath but a heavier tale to say.
I play the torturer, by small and small
To lengthen out the worst that must be spoken.
Your uncle York is join'd with Bolingbroke,
And all your Northern castles yielded up, 201

And all your Southern gentlemen in arms
Upon his party.
   King.   Thou hast said enough.
[*To Aumerle*] Beshrew thee, cousin, which
   didst lead me forth
Of that sweet way I was in to despair!   205
What say you now? What comfort have we
   now?
By heaven, I'll hate him everlastingly
That bids me be of comfort any more.
Go to Flint Castle. There I'll pine away;
A king, woe's slave, shall kingly woe obey.   210
That power I have, discharge; and let them go
To ear the land that hath some hope to grow,
For I have none. Let no man speak again
To alter this, for counsel is but vain.
   Aum. My liege, one word.
   King.   He does me double wrong
That wounds me with the flatteries of his
   tongue.   216
Discharge my followers. Let them hence away,
From Richard's night to Bolingbroke's fair day.
                        Exeunt.

Scene III. [*Wales. Before Flint Castle.*]

Enter, with *Drum* and *Colours, Bolingbroke,
York, Northumberland, Attendants,* [and *Soldiers*].

   Boling. So that by this intelligence we learn
The Welshmen are dispers'd, and Salisbury
Is gone to meet the King, who lately landed
With some few private friends upon this coast.
   North. The news is very fair and good, my
   lord.   5
Richard not far from hence hath hid his head.
   York. It would beseem the Lord Northum-
   berland
To say 'King Richard.' Alack the heavy day
When such a sacred king should hide his head!
   North. Your Grace mistakes. Only to be
   brief,   10
Left I his title out.
   York.   The time hath been,
Would you have been so brief with him, he
   would
Have been so brief with you to shorten you,
For taking so the head, your whole head's
   length.
   Boling. Mistake not, uncle, further than you
   should.   15
   York. Take not, good cousin, further than
   you should,

Lest you mistake. The heavens are over our
   heads.
   Boling. I know it, uncle, and oppose not
   myself
Against their will. But who comes here?

              Enter *Percy.*

Welcome, Harry. What, will not this castle
   yield?   20
   Percy. The castle royally is mann'd, my lord,
Against thy entrance.
   Boling. Royally?
Why, it contains no king?
   Percy.   Yes, my good lord,
It doth contain a king. King Richard lies   25
Within the limits of yon lime and stone;
And with him are the Lord Aumerle, Lord
   Salisbury,
Sir Stephen Scroop, besides a clergyman
Of holy reverence — who, I cannot learn.
   North. O, belike it is the Bishop of Carlisle.
   Boling. Noble lords,   31
Go to the rude ribs of that ancient castle;
Through brazen trumpet send the breath of
   parley
Into his ruin'd ears, and thus deliver:
Henry Bolingbroke   35
On both his knees doth kiss King Richard's
   hand
And sends allegiance and true faith of heart
To his most royal person; hither come
Even at his feet to lay my arms and power,
Provided that my banishment repeal'd   40
And lands restor'd again be freely granted.
If not, I'll use the advantage of my power,
And lay the summer's dust with show'rs of
   blood
Rain'd from the wounds of slaughtered Eng-
   lishmen;
The which, how far off from the mind of Boling-
   broke   45
It is, such crimson tempest should bedrench
The fresh green lap of fair King Richard's land,
My stooping duty tenderly shall show.
Go signify as much, while here we march
Upon the grassy carpet of this plain.   50
Let's march without the noise of threat'ning
   drum,
That from this castle's tattered battlements
Our fair appointments may be well perus'd.
Methinks King Richard and myself should
   meet
With no less terror than the elements   55
Of fire and water when their thund'ring shock
At meeting tears the cloudy cheeks of heaven.

THE TRAGEDY OF KING RICHARD II

PHOTOGRAPHS BY ANGUS MCBEAN
PRODUCED BY TENNENT PRODUCTIONS LTD.

Paul Scofield as the weak and tragic Richard II

Queen to Richard II, played by Joy Parker

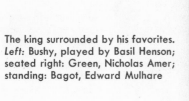

The king surrounded by his favorites. *Left:* Bushy, played by Basil Henson; seated right: Green, Nicholas Amer; standing: Bagot, Edward Mulhare

"Look, what I speak, my life shall prove it true." Richard's cousin Henry Bolingbroke (Eric Porter) points accusingly at Mowbray, the Duke of Norfolk (Paul Daneman) (Act I, Scene I)

Before the lists near Coventry—where there is to be a trial by combat between Bolingbroke and Mowbray—Richard speaks to his cousin: "As thy cause is right, so be thy fortune in this royal fight!" (Act I, Scene III)

An instant before the adversaries cross lances, Richard halts the trial. He then banishes Mowbray from his territories for life; his cousin for ten years (Act I, Scene III)

"This happy breed of men, this little world, this precious stone set in the silver sea." So had the aged John of Gaunt (Herbert Lomas) apostrophized on England. Dying, he is visited by the King and Queen (Act II, Scene I)

Bagot, Green, and Bushy attempt to cheer a woeful Queen (Act II, Scene II). The King—having seized the dead Gaunt's property, claiming need of the revenue for wars—has gone to Ireland

"For God's sake, let us sit upon the ground and tell sad stories of the death of kings." Aumerle (Leo Ciceri) and the Bishop of Carlisle (Paul Daneman) look on as the King pities himself (Act III, Scene II). Bolingbroke, Gaunt's rightful heir, has broken exile

Returned from Ireland to Wales, Richard takes refuge from Bolingbroke's forces in Flint Castle (Act III, Scene III)

"Tell Bolingbroke ... that every stride he makes upon my land is dangerous treason" (Act III, Scene III)

Richard surrenders his sword to the Earl of Northumberland (Brewster Mason), who has joined Bolingbroke's army (Act III, Scene III)

"I give this heavy weight from off my head."
In Westminster Hall, London, Richard resigns
his crown to Bolingbroke (Act IV, Scene I)

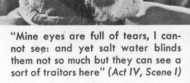

"Mine eyes are full of tears, I cannot see: and yet salt water blinds them not so much but they can see a sort of traitors here" (Act IV, Scene I)

"God save King Henry, unking'd Richard says, and send him many years of sunshine days! What more remains?" (Act IV, Scene I)

"And must we be divided? must we part?" Under Northumberland's watchful gaze, Richard bids farewell to his Queen. "Ay, hand from hand, my love, and heart from heart" (Act V, Scene I)

"We make woe wanton with this fond delay: once more, adieu; the rest let sorrow say" (Act V, Scene I)

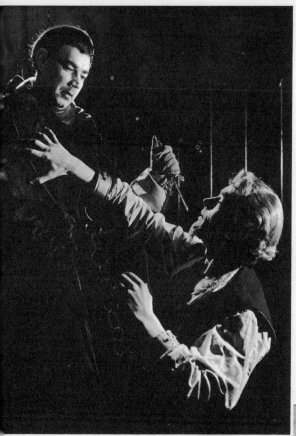

Sir Pierce of Exton (Paul Hardwick), on a hint from the new king, murders the deposed and imprisoned Richard II (*Act V, Scene V*)

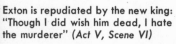

Exton is repudiated by the new king: "Though I did wish him dead, I hate the murderer" (*Act V, Scene VI*)

Henry, surnamed Bolingbroke, son to John of Gaunt, now Henry IV

Be he the fire, I'll be the yielding water;
The rage be his, whilst on the earth I rain
My waters — on the earth, and not on him. 60
March on, and mark King Richard how he looks.

Parle without, and answer within; then a flourish.
Enter, on the walls, [King] Richard, [the Bishop
of] Carlisle, Aumerle, Scroop, Salisbury.

See, see, King Richard doth himself appear,
As doth the blushing discontented sun
From out the fiery portal of the East
When he perceives the envious clouds are bent
To dim his glory and to stain the track   66
Of his bright passage to the Occident.
    York. Yet looks he like a king. Behold, his
        eye,
As bright as is the eagle's, lightens forth
Controlling majesty. Alack, alack, for woe, 70
That any harm should stain so fair a show!
    King. [*to Northumberland*] We are amaz'd;
        and thus long have we stood
To watch the fearful bending of thy knee,
Because we thought ourself thy lawful king.
And if we be, how dare thy joints forget   75
To pay their awful duty to our presence?
If we be not, show us the hand of God
That hath dismiss'd us from our stewardship;
For well we know no hand of blood and bone
Can gripe the sacred handle of our sceptre, 80
Unless he do profane, steal, or usurp.
And though you think that all, as you have
        done,
Have torn their souls by turning them from us
And we are barren and bereft of friends,
Yet know, my master, God omnipotent,   85
Is mustering in his clouds on our behalf
Armies of pestilence, and they shall strike
Your children yet unborn and unbegot
That lift your vassal hands against my head
And threat the glory of my precious crown. 90
Tell Bolingbroke, for yon methinks he stands,
That every stride he makes upon my land
Is dangerous treason. He is come to open
The purple testament of bleeding war.
But ere the crown he looks for live in peace, 95
Ten thousand bloody crowns of mothers' sons
Shall ill become the flower of England's face,
Change the complexion of her maid-pale peace
To scarlet indignation, and bedew   99
Her pastures' grass with faithful English blood.
    North. The King of Heaven forbid our lord
        the King
Should so with civil and uncivil arms
Be rush'd upon! Thy thrice-noble cousin
Harry Bolingbroke doth humbly kiss thy hand:

And by the honourable tomb he swears   105
That stands upon your royal grandsire's bones,
And by the royalties of both your bloods
(Currents that spring from one most gracious
        head),
And by the buried hand of warlike Gaunt,
And by the worth and honour of himself,   110
Comprising all that may be sworn or said,
His coming hither hath no further scope
Than for his lineal royalties, and to beg
Enfranchisement immediate on his knees;
Which on thy royal party granted once,   115
His glittering arms he will commend to rust,
His barbed steeds to stables, and his heart
To faithful service of your Majesty.
This swears he, as he is a prince, is just;
And as I am a gentleman, I credit him.   120
    King. Northumberland, say thus the King
        returns:
His noble cousin is right welcome hither;
And all the number of his fair demands
Shall be accomplish'd without contradiction.
With all the gracious utterance thou hast 125
Speak to his gentle hearing kind commends.
[*To Aumerle*] We do debase ourselves, cousin,
        do we not,
To look so poorly and to speak so fair?
Shall we call back Northumberland and send
Defiance to the traitor, and so die?   130
    Aum. No, good my lord. Let's fight with
        gentle words
Till time lend friends, and friends their helpful
        swords.
    King. O God, O God! that e'er this tongue
        of mine
That laid the sentence of dread banishment
On yon proud man, should take it off again 135
With words of sooth! O that I were as great
As is my grief, or lesser than my name!
Or that I could forget what I have been!
Or not remember what I must be now!
Swell'st thou, proud heart? I'll give thee scope
        to beat,   140
Since foes have scope to beat both thee and me.
    Aum. Northumberland comes back from
        Bolingbroke.
    King. What must the King do now? Must
        he submit?
The King shall do it. Must he be depos'd?
The King shall be contented. Must he lose 145
The name of king? A God's name, let it go!
I'll give my jewels for a set of beads,
My gorgeous palace for a hermitage,
My gay apparel for an almsman's gown,
My figur'd goblets for a dish of wood,   150

My sceptre for a palmer's walking staff,
My subjects for a pair of carved saints,
And my large kingdom for a little grave,
A little little grave, an obscure grave;
Or I'll be buried in the king's highway,   155
Some way of common trade, where subjects'
    feet
May hourly trample on their sovereign's head;
For on my heart they tread now whilst I live,
And buried once, why not upon my head?
Aumerle, thou weep'st, my tender-hearted
    cousin!   160
We'll make foul weather with despised tears;
Our sighs and they shall lodge the summer corn
And make a dearth in this revolting land.
Or shall we play the wantons with our woes
And make some pretty match with shedding
    tears?   165
As thus — to drop them still upon one place
Till they have fretted us a pair of graves
Within the earth; and therein laid — there
    lies
Two kinsmen digg'd their graves with weeping
    eyes.
Would not this ill do well? Well, well, I see   170
I talk but idly, and you laugh at me.
Most mighty prince, my Lord Northumberland,
What says King Bolingbroke? Will his Majesty
Give Richard leave to live till Richard die?
You make a leg, and Bolingbroke says ay.   175
North. My lord, in the base court he doth
    attend
To speak with you, may it please you to come
    down.
King. Down, down I come, like glist'ring
    Phaëton,
Wanting the manage of unruly jades.
In the base court? Base court, where kings
    grow base,   180
To come at traitors' calls and do them grace!
In the base court? Come down? Down court!
    down king!
For night owls shriek where mounting larks
    should sing.   [*Exeunt from above.*]
Boling. What says his Majesty?
North.   Sorrow and grief of heart
Makes him speak fondly, like a frantic man.
Yet he is come.   186

[*Enter King Richard attended, below.*]

Boling. Stand all apart
And show fair duty to his Majesty.
                              He kneels down.
My gracious lord —

King. Fair cousin, you debase your princely
    knee   190
To make the base earth proud with kissing it.
Me rather had my heart might feel your love
Than my unpleas'd eye see your courtesy.
Up, cousin, up! Your heart is up, I know,
Thus high at least [*touches his own head*], although your knee be low.   195
Boling. [*rises*] My gracious lord, I come but
    for mine own.
King. Your own is yours, and I am yours,
    and all.
Boling. So far be mine, my most redoubted
    lord,
As my true service shall deserve your love.
King. Well you deserve. They well deserve
    to have   200
That know the strong'st and surest way to get.
Uncle, give me your hand. Nay, dry your eyes.
Tears show their love, but want their remedies.
Cousin, I am too young to be your father,
Though you are old enough to be my heir.   205
What you will have, I'll give, and willing too;
For do we must what force will have us do.
Set on towards London. Cousin, is it so?
Boling. Yea, my good lord.
King.   Then I must not say no.
                         Flourish. Exeunt.

Scene IV. [*Langley. The* Duke of
    York's *garden.*]

Enter the *Queen* with two *Ladies,*
    her *Attendants.*

Queen. What sport shall we devise here in
    this garden
To drive away the heavy thought of care?
Lady. Madam, we'll play at bowls.
Queen. 'Twill make me think the world is
    full of rubs
And that my fortune runs against the bias.   5
Lady. Madam, we'll dance.
Queen. My legs can keep no measure in
    delight
When my poor heart no measure keeps in grief.
Therefore no dancing, girl; some other sport.
Lady. Madam, we'll tell tales.   10
Queen. Of sorrow or of joy?
Lady.   Of either, madam.
Queen. Of neither, girl;
For if of joy, being altogether wanting,
It doth remember me the more of sorrow;
Or if of grief, being altogether had,   15

It adds more sorrow to my want of joy;
For what I have I need not to repeat,
And what I want it boots not to complain.
   Lady. Madam, I'll sing.
   Queen.   'Tis well that thou hast cause;
But thou shouldst please me better, wouldst
    thou weep.   20
   Lady. I could weep, madam, would it do
    you good.
   Queen. And I could sing, would weeping do
    me good,
And never borrow any tear of thee.

     Enter a *Gardener* and two *Servants.*

But stay, here come the gardeners.
Let's step into the shadow of these trees.   25
My wretchedness unto a row of pins,
They will talk of state, for every one doth
   so
Against a change: woe is forerun with woe.
           [*Queen and Ladies step aside.*]
   Gard. Go bind thou up yon dangling apri-
    cocks,
Which, like unruly children, make their sire 30
Stoop with oppression of their prodigal weight.
Give some supportance to the bending twigs.
Go thou and, like an executioner,
Cut off the heads of too fast growing sprays
That look too lofty in our commonwealth.   35
All must be even in our government.
You thus employ'd, I will go root away
The noisome weeds which without profit suck
The soil's fertility from wholesome flowers.
   Man. Why should we, in the compass of a
    pale,   40
Keep law and form and due proportion,
Showing, as in a model, our firm estate,
When our sea-walled garden, the whole land,
Is full of weeds, her fairest flowers chok'd
   up,   44
Her fruit trees all unprun'd, her hedges ruin'd,
Her knots disordered, and her wholesome herbs
Swarming with caterpillars?
   Gard.   Hold thy peace.
He that hath suffer'd this disordered spring
Hath now himself met with the fall of leaf.
The weeds which his broad-spreading leaves
   did shelter,   50
That seem'd in eating him to hold him up,
Are pluck'd up root and all by Bolingbroke —
I mean the Earl of Wiltshire, Bushy, Green.
   Man. What, are they dead?
   Gard.   They are; and Bolingbroke
Hath seiz'd the wasteful King. O, what pity
   is it   55

That he had not so trimm'd and dress'd his
   land
As we this garden! We at time of year
Do wound the bark, the skin of our fruit trees,
Lest, being over-proud in sap and blood,
With too much riches it confound itself.   60
Had he done so to great and growing men,
They might have liv'd to bear, and he to
   taste
Their fruits of duty. Superfluous branches
We lop away, that bearing boughs may live.
Had he done so, himself had borne the crown,
Which waste of idle hours hath quite thrown
   down.   66
   Man. What, think you the King shall be
    depos'd?
   Gard. Depress'd he is already, and depos'd
'Tis doubt he will be. Letters came last night
To a dear friend of the good Duke of York's 70
That tell black tidings.
   Queen. O, I am press'd to death through want
    of speaking!   [*Comes forward.*]
Thou old Adam's likeness, set to dress this
   garden,
How dares thy harsh rude tongue sound this
   unpleasing news?   74
What Eve, what serpent, hath suggested thee
To make a second fall of cursed man?
Why dost thou say King Richard is depos'd?
Dar'st thou, thou little better thing than earth,
Divine his downfall? Say, where, when, and
   how
Cam'st thou by this ill tidings? Speak, thou
   wretch!   80
   Gard. Pardon me, madam. Little joy have I
To breathe this news; yet what I say is true.
King Richard, he is in the mighty hold
Of Bolingbroke. Their fortunes both are
   weigh'd.
In your lord's scale is nothing but himself, 85
And some few vanities that make him light;
But in the balance of great Bolingbroke,
Besides himself, are all the English peers,
And with that odds he weighs King Richard
   down.
Post you to London, and you will find it so. 90
I speak no more than every one doth know.
   Queen. Nimble mischance, that art so light
    of foot,
Doth not thy embassage belong to me,
And am I last that knows it? O, thou thinkest
To serve me last, that I may longest keep 95
Thy sorrow in my breast. Come, ladies, go
To meet at London London's king in woe.
What, was I born to this, that my sad look

Should grace the triumph of great Bolingbroke?
Gard'ner, for telling me these news of woe, 100
Pray God the plants thou graft'st may never
    grow.   *Exit [with Ladies].*
  Gard. Poor Queen, so that thy state might
  be no worse,

I would my skill were subject to thy curse!
Here did she fall a tear; here in this place
I'll set a bank of rue, sour herb of grace. 105
Rue, even for ruth, here shortly shall be seen,
In the remembrance of a weeping queen.
                   Exeunt.

ACT IV. Scene I. [*Westminster Hall.*]

Enter, as to the Parliament, *Bolingbroke, Aumerle, Northumberland, Percy, Fitzwater, Surrey,* [and another *Lord, the Bishop of*] *Carlisle, Abbot of Westminster, Herald; Officers* and *Bagot.*

  Boling. Call forth Bagot.
          [*Officers bring him forward.*]
Now, Bagot, freely speak thy mind,
What thou dost know of noble Gloucester's
  death;
Who wrought it with the King, and who per-
  form'd
The bloody office of his timeless end.   5
  Bagot. Then set before my face the Lord
  Aumerle.
  Boling. Cousin, stand forth, and look upon
  that man.
  Bagot. My Lord Aumerle, I know your dar-
  ing tongue
Scorns to unsay what once it hath deliver'd.
In that dead time when Gloucester's death was
  plotted,   10
I heard you say, 'Is not my arm of length,
That reacheth from the restful English court
As far as Calais to mine uncle's head?'
Amongst much other talk that very time
I heard you say that you had rather refuse 15
The offer of an hundred thousand crowns
Than Bolingbroke's return to England;
Adding withal, how blest this land would be
In this your cousin's death.
  Aum.   Princes and noble lords,
What answer shall I make to this base man? 20
Shall I so much dishonour my fair stars
On equal terms to give him chastisement?
Either I must, or have mine honour soil'd
With the attainder of his slanderous lips.
There is my gage, the manual seal of death 25
That marks thee out for hell. I say thou
  liest,
And will maintain what thou hast said is false
In thy heart-blood, though being all too base
To stain the temper of my knightly sword.
  Boling. Bagot, forbear; thou shalt not take
  it up.   30

  Aum. Excepting one, I would he were the
  best
In all this presence that hath mov'd me so.
  Fitz. If that thy valour stand on sympathy,
There is my gage, Aumerle, in gage to thine.
By that fair sun which shows me where thou
  stand'st,   35
I heard thee say, and vauntingly thou spak'st
  it,
That thou wert cause of noble Gloucester's
  death.
If thou deniest it twenty times, thou liest,
And I will turn thy falsehood to thy heart,
Where it was forged, with my rapier's point. 40
  Aum. Thou dar'st not, coward, live to see
  that day.
  Fitz. Now, by my soul, I would it were this
  hour.
  Aum. Fitzwater, thou art damn'd to hell
  for this.
  Percy. Aumerle, thou liest. His honour is as
  true
In this appeal as thou art all unjust;   45
And that thou art so, there I throw my gage
To prove it on thee to the extremest point
Of mortal breathing. Seize it if thou dar'st.
  Aum. And if I do not, may my hands rot off
And never brandish more revengeful steel   50
Over the glittering helmet of my foe!
  Another Lord. I task thee to the like, for-
  sworn Aumerle;
And spur thee on with full as many lies
As may be holloa'd in thy treacherous ear
From sun to sun. There is my honour's pawn.
Engage it to the trial, if thou dar'st.   56
  Aum. Who sets me else? By heaven, I'll
  throw at all!
I have a thousand spirits in one breast
To answer twenty thousand such as you.
  Surrey. My Lord Fitzwater, I do remember
  well   60
The very time Aumerle and you did talk.
  Fitz. 'Tis very true. You were in presence
  then,
And you can witness with me this is true.

Surrey. As false, by heaven, as heaven itself
  is true!
Fitz. Surrey, thou liest.
  Surrey.   Dishonourable boy!
That lie shall lie so heavy on my sword   66
That it shall render vengeance and revenge
Till thou the lie-giver and that lie do lie
In earth as quiet as thy father's skull.
In proof whereof there is my honour's pawn.
Engage it to the trial if thou dar'st.   71
  Fitz. How fondly dost thou spur a forward
    horse!
If I dare eat, or drink, or breathe, or live,
I dare meet Surrey in a wilderness,
And spit upon him whilst I say he lies,   75
And lies, and lies. There is my bond of faith
To tie thee to my strong correction.
As I intend to thrive in this new world,
Aumerle is guilty of my true appeal.
Besides, I heard the banish'd Norfolk say   80
That thou, Aumerle, didst send two of thy men
To execute the noble Duke at Calais.
  Aum. Some honest Christian trust me with
    a gage
That Norfolk lies. Here do I throw down this,
If he may be repeal'd to try his honour.   85
  Boling. These differences shall all rest under
    gage
Till Norfolk be repeal'd. Repeal'd he shall be
And, though mine enemy, restor'd again
To all his lands and signories. When he's re-
    turn'd,
Against Aumerle we will enforce his trial.   90
  Car. That honourable day shall ne'er be
    seen.
Many a time hath banish'd Norfolk fought
For Jesu Christ in glorious Christian field,
Streaming the ensign of the Christian cross
Against black pagans, Turks, and Saracens;   95
And, toil'd with works of war, retir'd himself
To Italy; and there, at Venice, gave
His body to that pleasant country's earth
And his pure soul unto his captain, Christ,   99
Under whose colours he had fought so long.
  Boling. Why, Bishop, is Norfolk dead?
  Car. As surely as I live, my lord.
  Boling. Sweet peace conduct his sweet soul
    to the bosom
Of good old Abraham! Lords appellants,
Your differences shall all rest under gage   105
Till we assign you to your days of trial.

      Enter *York* [attended].

  York. Great Duke of Lancaster, I come to
    thee

From plume-pluck'd Richard, who with willing
  soul
Adopts thee heir and his high sceptre yields
To the possession of thy royal hand.   110
Ascend his throne, descending now from him,
And long live Henry, fourth of that name!
  Boling. In God's name I'll ascend the regal
    throne.
  Car. Marry, God forbid!
Worst in this royal presence may I speak,   115
Yet best beseeming me to speak the truth
Would God that any in this noble presence
Were enough noble to be upright judge
Of noble Richard! then true noblesse would
Learn him forbearance from so foul a wrong.
What subject can give sentence on his king?
And who sits here that is not Richard's subject?
Thieves are not judg'd but they are by to hear,
Although apparent guilt be seen in them;
And shall the figure of God's majesty,   125
His captain, steward, deputy elect,
Anointed, crowned, planted many years,
Be judg'd by subject and inferior breath,
And he himself not present? O, forfend it God
That, in a Christian climate, souls refin'd   130
Should show so heinous, black, obscene a deed!
I speak to subjects, and a subject speaks,
Stirr'd up by God, thus boldly for his king.
My Lord of Hereford here, whom you call king,
Is a foul traitor to proud Hereford's king;   135
And if you crown him, let me prophesy,
The blood of English shall manure the ground
And future ages groan for this foul act;
Peace shall go sleep with Turks and infidels,
And in this seat of peace tumultuous wars   140
Shall kin with kin and kind with kind confound;
Disorder, horror, fear, and mutiny
Shall here inhabit, and this land be call'd
The field of Golgotha and dead men's skulls.
O, if you raise this house against this house,   145
It will the wofullest division prove
That ever fell upon this cursed earth.
Prevent it, resist it, let it not be so,
Lest child, child's children cry against you woe:
  North. Well have you argued, sir; and for
    your pains   150
Of capital treason we arrest you here.
My Lord of Westminster, be it your charge
To keep him safely till his day of trial.
May it please you, lords, to grant the com-
    mons' suit.
  Boling. Fetch hither Richard, that in com-
    mon view   155
He may surrender. So we shall proceed
Without suspicion.

York.   I will be his conduct. *Exit.*
Boling. Lords, you that here are under our
          arrest,
Procure your sureties for your days of answer.
Little are we beholding to your love,   160
And little look'd for at your helping hands.

Enter *Richard* and *York*, [with *Officers* bearing
          the crown, &c.].

Rich. Alack, why am I sent for to a king
Before I have shook off the regal thoughts
Wherewith I reign'd? I hardly yet have learn'd
To insinuate, flatter, bow, and bend my limbs.
Give sorrow leave awhile to tutor me   166
To this submission. Yet I well remember
The favours of these men. Were they not mine?
Did they not sometime cry 'All hail!' to me?
So Judas did to Christ; but he, in twelve,   170
Found truth in all but one; I, in twelve thou-
          sand none.
God save the King! Will no man say amen?
Am I both priest and clerk? Well then, amen!
God save the King! although I be not he;
And yet amen, if heaven do think him me.   175
To do what service am I sent for hither?
York. To do that office of thine own good will
Which tired majesty did make thee offer —
The resignation of thy state and crown
To Henry Bolingbroke.   180
Rich. Give me the crown. Here, cousin,
          seize the crown.
Here, cousin,
On this side my hand, and on that side yours.
Now is this golden crown like a deep well
That owes two buckets, filling one another,   185
The emptier ever dancing in the air,
The other down, unseen, and full of water.
That bucket down and full of tears am I,
Drinking my griefs whilst you mount up on
          high.
Boling. I thought you had been willing to
          resign.   190
Rich. My crown I am, but still my griefs are
          mine.
You may my glories and my state depose,
But not my griefs. Still am I king of those.
Boling. Part of your cares you give me with
          your crown.
Rich. Your cares set up do not pluck my
          cares down.   195
My care is loss of care, by old care done;
Your care is gain of care, by new care won.
The cares I give I have, though given away;
They tend the crown, yet still with me they
          stay.

Boling. Are you contented to resign the
          crown?   200
Rich. Ay, no; no, ay; for I must nothing be;
Therefore no no, for I resign to thee.
Now mark me how I will undo myself.
I give this heavy weight from off my head
And this unwieldy sceptre from my hand,   205
The pride of kingly sway from out my heart.
With mine own tears I wash away my balm,
With mine own hands I give away my crown,
With mine own tongue deny my sacred state,
With mine own breath release all duty's rites.
All pomp and majesty I do forswear;   211
My manors, rents, revenues I forgo;
My acts, decrees, and statutes I deny.
God pardon all oaths that are broke to me!
God keep all vows unbroke that swear to thee!
Make me, that nothing have, with nothing
          griev'd,   216
And thou with all pleas'd, that hast all achiev'd!
Long mayst thou live in Richard's seat to sit,
And soon lie Richard in an earthy pit!   219
God save King Harry, unking'd Richard says,
And send him many years of sunshine days!
What more remains?
North.   No more, but that you read
These accusations and these grievous crimes
Committed by your person and your followers
Against the state and profit of this land,   225
That, by confessing them, the souls of men
May deem that you are worthily depos'd.
Rich. Must I do so? and must I ravel out
My weav'd-up folly? Gentle Northumberland,
If thy offences were upon record,   230
Would it not shame thee in so fair a troop
To read a lecture of them? If thou wouldst,
There shouldst thou find one heinous article,
Containing the deposing of a king
And cracking the strong warrant of an oath,
Mark'd with a blot, damn'd in the book of
          heaven.   236
Nay, all of you that stand and look upon
Whilst that my wretchedness doth bait myself,
Though some of you, with Pilate, wash your
          hands,
Showing an outward pity, yet you Pilates   240
Have here deliver'd me to my sour cross,
And water cannot wash away your sin.
North. My lord, dispatch. Read o'er these
          articles.
Rich. Mine eyes are full of tears; I cannot
          see.
And yet salt water blinds them not so much   245
But they can see a sort of traitors here.
Nay, if I turn mine eyes upon myself,

I find myself a traitor with the rest;
For I have given here my soul's consent
To undeck the pompous body of a king;   250
Made glory base, and sovereignty a slave,
Proud majesty a subject, state a peasant.
   North. My lord —
   Rich. No lord of thine, thou haught insulting
      man,   254
Nor no man's lord. I have no name, no title —
No, not that name was given me at the font —
But 'tis usurp'd. Alack the heavy day,
That I have worn so many winters out
And know not now what name to call myself!
O that I were a mockery king of snow,   260
Standing before the sun of Bolingbroke
To melt myself away in water drops!
Good king, great king, and yet not greatly good,
An if my word be sterling yet in England,
Let it command a mirror hither straight,   265
That it may show me what a face I have
Since it is bankrout of his majesty.
   Boling. Go some of you and fetch a looking
      glass.   [*Exit an Attendant.*]
   North. Read o'er this paper while the glass
      doth come.
   Rich. Fiend, thou torments me ere I come
      to hell!   270
   Boling. Urge it no more, my Lord Northum-
      berland.
   North. The commons will not then be satis-
      fied.
   Rich. They shall be satisfied. I'll read
      enough
When I do see the very book indeed   274
Where all my sins are writ, and that's myself.

           Enter *one with a glass.*

Give me the glass, and therein will I read.
No deeper wrinkles yet? Hath sorrow struck
So many blows upon this face of mine
And made no deeper wounds? O flattering
      glass,
Like to my followers in prosperity,   280
Thou dost beguile me! Was this face the face
That every day under his household roof
Did keep ten thousand men? Was this the face
That like the sun did make beholders wink?
Was this the face that fac'd so many follies   285
And was at last outfac'd by Bolingbroke?
A brittle glory shineth in this face.
As brittle as the glory is the face,
           [*Dashes the glass to the floor.*]
For there it is, crack'd in a hundred shivers.
Mark, silent king, the moral of this sport —   290
How soon my sorrow hath destroy'd my face.

   Boling. The shadow of your sorrow hath
      destroy'd
The shadow of your face.
   Rich.   Say that again.
The shadow of my sorrow? Ha! let's see!
'Tis very true: my grief lies all within;   295
And these external manners of laments
Are merely shadows to the unseen grief
That swells with silence in the tortured soul.
There lies the substance; and I thank thee,
      king,
For thy great bounty that not only giv'st   300
Me cause to wail, but teachest me the way
How to lament the cause. I'll beg one boon,
And then be gone and trouble you no more.
Shall I obtain it?
   Boling.   Name it, fair cousin.
   Rich. Fair cousin? I am greater than a king;
For when I was a king, my flatterers   306
Were then but subjects; being now a subject,
I have a king here to my flatterer.
Being so great, I have no need to beg.
   Boling. Yet ask.   310
   Rich. And shall I have?
   Boling. You shall.
   Rich. Then give me leave to go.
   Boling. Whither?
   Rich. Whither you will, so I were from your
      sights.   315
   Boling. Go some of you, convey him to the
      Tower.
   Rich. O, good! Convey? Conveyers are
      you all,
That rise thus nimbly by a true king's fall.
      [*Exit Richard, with some Lords and a Guard.*]
   Boling. On Wednesday next we solemnly set
      down   319
Our coronation. Lords, prepare yourselves.
      Exeunt. Manent [*the Abbot of*] *Westminster,*
           [*the Bishop of*] *Carlisle, Aumerle.*
   Abbot. A woful pageant have we here beheld.
   Car. The woe's to come. The children yet
      unborn
Shall feel this day as sharp to them as thorn.
   Aum. You holy clergymen, is there no plot
To rid the realm of this pernicious blot?   325
   Abbot. My lord,
Before I freely speak my mind herein,
You shall not only take the sacrament
To bury mine intents, but also to effect
Whatever I shall happen to devise.   330
I see your brows are full of discontent,
Your hearts of sorrow, and your eyes of tears.
Come home with me to supper. I will lay
A plot shall show us all a merry day. *Exeunt.*

Act V. Scene I. [*London. A street leading to the Tower.*]

Enter the *Queen* with *Ladies*, her *Attendants*.

Queen. This way the King will come. This
 is the way
To Julius Cæsar's ill-erected tower,
To whose flint bosom my condemned lord
Is doom'd a prisoner by proud Bolingbroke.
Here let us rest, if this rebellious earth   5
Have any resting for her true king's queen.

   Enter *Richard* and *Guard.*

But soft, but see, or rather do not see,
My fair rose wither. Yet look up, behold,
That you in pity may dissolve to dew   9
And wash him fresh again with true-love tears.
Ah, thou the model where old Troy did stand,
Thou map of honour, thou King Richard's
 tomb,
And not King Richard! Thou most beauteous
 inn,
Why should hard-favour'd grief be lodg'd in thee
When triumph is become an alehouse guest?
 Rich. Join not with grief, fair woman, do
 not so,   16
To make my end too sudden. Learn, good soul,
To think our former state a happy dream;
From which awak'd, the truth of what we are
Shows us but this. I am sworn brother, sweet,
To grim Necessity, and he and I   21
Will keep a league till death. Hie thee to
 France
And cloister thee in some religious house.
Our holy lives must win a new world's crown,
Which our profane hours here have stricken
 down.   25
 Queen. What, is my Richard both in shape
 and mind
Transform'd and weak'ned? Hath Bolingbroke
 depos'd
Thine intellect? Hath he been in thy heart?
The lion dying thrusteth forth his paw   29
And wounds the earth, if nothing else, with rage
To be o'erpow'r'd; and wilt thou pupil-like
Take thy correction, mildly kiss the rod,
And fawn on rage with base humility,
Which art a lion and the king of beasts?
 Rich. A king of beasts indeed! If aught but
 beasts,   35
I had been still a happy king of men.
Good sometime queen, prepare thee hence for
 France.

Think I am dead, and that even here thou
 takest,
As from my deathbed, thy last living leave.
In winter's tedious nights sit by the fire   40
With good old folks, and let them tell thee tales
Of woful ages long ago betid;
And ere thou bid good-night, to quite their
 griefs
Tell thou the lamentable tale of me,
And send the hearers weeping to their beds.   45
For why, the senseless brands will sympathize
The heavy accent of thy moving tongue
And in compassion weep the fire out;
And some will mourn in ashes, some coal-black,
For the deposing of a rightful king.   50

   Enter *Northumberland* [attended].

 North. My lord, the mind of Bolingbroke is
 chang'd.
You must to Pomfret, not unto the Tower.
And, madam, there is order ta'en for you:
With all swift speed you must away to France.
 Rich. Northumberland, thou ladder where-
 withal   55
The mounting Bolingbroke ascends my throne,
The time shall not be many hours of age
More than it is, ere foul sin gathering head
Shall break into corruption. Thou shalt think,
Though he divide the realm and give thee half,
It is too little, helping him to all.   61
And he shall think that thou, which know'st
 the way
To plant unrightful kings, wilt know again,
Being ne'er so little urg'd, another way,
To pluck him headlong from the usurped
 throne.   65
The love of wicked men converts to fear;
That fear to hate, and hate turns one or both
To worthy danger and deserved death.
 North. My guilt be on my head, and there
 an end!
Take leave and part, for you must part forth-
 with.   70
 Rich. Doubly divorc'd! Bad men, you vi-
 olate
A twofold marriage — 'twixt my crown and me,
And then betwixt me and my married wife.
Let me unkiss the oath 'twixt thee and me;
And yet not so, for with a kiss 'twas made.   75
Part us, Northumberland — I towards the
 North,

Where shivering cold and sickness pines the
    clime;
My wife to France, from whence, set forth in
    pomp,
She came adorned hither like sweet May,
Sent back like Hallowmas or short'st of day. 80
    Queen. And must we be divided? Must we
        part?
    Rich. Ay, hand from hand, my love, and
        heart from heart.
    Queen. Banish us both, and send the King
        with me.
    North. That were some love, but little policy.
    Queen. Then whither he goes, thither let
        me go.   85
    Rich. So two, together weeping, make one
        woe.
Weep thou for me in France, I for thee here.
Better far off than near be ne'er the near.
Go, count thy way with sighs; I mine with
    groans.
    Queen. So longest way shall have the longest
        moans.   90
    Rich. Twice for one step I'll groan, the way
        being short,
And piece the way out with a heavy heart.
Come, come, in wooing sorrow let's be brief,
Since, wedding it, there is such length in grief.
One kiss shall stop our mouths, and dumbly
    part.   95
Thus give I mine, and thus take I thy heart.
    Queen. Give me mine own again. 'Twere no
        good part
To take on me to keep and kill thy heart.
So, now I have mine own again, be gone,
That I may strive to kill it with a groan.   100
    Rich. We make woe wanton with this fond
        delay.
Once more adieu! The rest let sorrow say.
                                Exeunt.

Scene II. [*London. The* Duke of York's *Palace.*]

Enter *Duke of York* and the *Duchess.*

    Duch. My lord, you told me you would tell
        the rest,
When weeping made you break the story off
Of our two cousins' coming into London.
    York. Where did I leave?
    Duch.   At that sad stop, my lord,
Where rude misgoverned hands from windows'
    tops   5

Threw dust and rubbish on King Richard's
    head.
    York. Then, as I said, the Duke, great
        Bolingbroke,
Mounted upon a hot and fiery steed
Which his aspiring rider seem'd to know,   9
With slow but stately pace kept on his course,
Whilst all tongues cried 'God save thee,
    Bolingbroke!'
You would have thought the very windows
    spake,
So many greedy looks of young and old
Through casements darted their desiring eyes
Upon his visage; and that all the walls   15
With painted imagery had said at once
'Jesu preserve thee! Welcome, Bolingbroke!'
Whilst he, from the one side to the other turn-
    ing,
Bareheaded, lower than his proud steed's neck,
Bespake them thus, 'I thank you, countrymen.'
And thus still doing, thus he pass'd along. 21
    Duch. Alack, poor Richard! Where rode he
        the whilst?
    York. As in a theatre the eyes of men,
After a well-grac'd actor leaves the stage,
Are idly bent on him that enters next,   25
Thinking his prattle to be tedious,
Even so, or with much more contempt, men's
    eyes
Did scowl on gentle Richard. No man cried
    'God save him!'
No joyful tongue gave him his welcome home,
But dust was thrown upon his sacred head; 30
Which with such gentle sorrow he shook off,
His face still combating with tears and smiles
(The badges of his grief and patience),
That, had not God for some strong purpose
    steel'd
The hearts of men, they must perforce have
    melted   35
And barbarism itself have pitied him.
But heaven hath a hand in these events,
To whose high will we bound our calm contents.
To Bolingbroke are we sworn subjects now,
Whose state and honour I for aye allow.   40

Enter *Aumerle.*

    Duch. Here comes my son Aumerle.
    York.   Aumerle that was;
But that is lost for being Richard's friend,
And, madam, you must call him Rutland now.
I am in parliament pledge for his truth
And lasting fealty to the new-made king   45
    Duch. Welcome, my son. Who are the
        violets now

That strew the green lap of the new-come
　　spring?
　Aum. Madam, I know not, nor I greatly
　　care not.
God knows I had as lief be none as one.
　York. Well, bear you well in this new spring
　　of time,　　　　　　　　　　　　　　50
Lest you be cropp'd before you come to prime.
What news from Oxford? Do these justs and
　　triumphs hold?
　Aum. For aught I know, my lord, they do.
　York. You will be there, I know.
　Aum. If God prevent not, I purpose so.　55
　York. What seal is that that hangs without
　　thy bosom?
Yea, look'st thou pale? Let me see the writing.
　Aum. My lord, 'tis nothing.
　York.　　　　No matter then who see it.
I will be satisfied; let me see the writing.
　Aum. I do beseech your Grace to pardon
　　me.
It is a matter of small consequence　　　61
Which for some reasons I would not have seen.
　York. Which for some reasons, sir, I mean
　　to see.
I fear, I fear —
　Duch.　　　What should you fear?
'Tis nothing but some bond that he is ent'red
　　into ·　　　　　　　　　　　　　　　65
For gay apparel 'gainst the triumph day.
　York. Bound to himself? What doth he
　　with a bond
That he is bound to? Wife, thou art a fool.
Boy, let me see the writing.
　Aum. I do beseech you pardon me. I may
　　not show it.　　　　　　　　　　　　70
　York. I will be satisfied. Let me see it, I
　　say.
　　He plucks it out of his bosom and reads it.
Treason, foul treason! Villain! traitor! slave!
　Duch. What is the matter, my lord?
　York. Ho! who is within there?

　　　　　　[Enter a *Servant.*]
　　　　　　　　　　　　Saddle my horse.
God for his mercy, what treachery is here!　75
　Duch. Why, what is it, my lord?
　York. Give me my boots, I say. Saddle my
　　horse.
　　　　　　　　　　　　[*Exit Servant.*]
Now, by mine honour, by my life, by my
　　troth,
I will appeach the villain.
　Duch.　　　　　What is the matter?
　York. Peace, foolish woman.　　　　80

　Duch. I will not peace. What is the matter,
　　Aumerle?
　Aum. Good mother, be content. It is no
　　more
Than my poor life must answer.
　Duch.　　　　　Thy life answer?
　York. Bring me my boots! I will unto the
　　King.

　　　His *Man* enters with his boots.

　Duch. Strike him, Aumerle. Poor boy, thou
　　art amaz'd. —　　　　　　　　　　85
Hence, villain! Never more come in my sight.
　York. Give me my boots, I say!
　　　　　　　[*Servant does so and exit.*]
　Duch. Why, York, what wilt thou do?
Wilt thou not hide the trespass of thine own?
Have we more sons? or are we like to have?　90
Is not my teeming date drunk up with time?
And wilt thou pluck my fair son from mine
　　age
And rob me of a happy mother's name?
Is he not like thee? Is he not thine own?
　York. Thou fond mad woman,　　　　95
Wilt thou conceal this dark conspiracy?
A dozen of them here have ta'en the sacra-
　　ment,
And interchangeably set down their hands,
To kill the King at Oxford.
　Duch.　　　　　He shall be none;
We'll keep him here. Then what is that to
　　him?
　York. Away, fond woman! Were he twenty
　　times　　　　　　　　　　　　　101
My son, I would appeach him.
　Duch.　　　　Hadst thou groan'd for him
As I have done, thou wouldst be more pitiful.
But now I know thy mind. Thou dost suspect
That I have been disloyal to thy bed　　105
And that he is a bastard, not thy son.
Sweet York, sweet husband, be not of that mind!
He is as like thee as a man may be,
Not like to me, or any of my kin,
And yet I love him.
　York.　　　Make way, unruly woman!
　　　　　　　　　　　　　　　　Exit.
　Duch. After, Aumerle! Mount thee upon
　　his horse,　　　　　　　　　　　111
Spur post and get before him to the King,
And beg thy pardon ere he do accuse thee.
I'll not be long behind. Though I be old,
I doubt not but to ride as fast as York;　115
And never will I rise up from the ground
Till Bolingbroke have pardon'd thee. Away,
　　be gone!　　　　　　　　　　　*Exeunt.*

Scene III. [*Windsor Castle.*]

Enter *King* [*Henry*], *Percy*, and other *Lords*.

King H. Can no man tell me of my unthrifty
  son?
'Tis full three months since I did see him
  last.
If any plague hang over us, 'tis he.
I would to God, my lords, he might be
  found.
Inquire at London, 'mongst the taverns there,
For there, they say, he daily doth frequent,   6
With unrestrained loose companions,
Even such, they say, as stand in narrow lanes
And beat our watch and rob our passengers,
Which he, young wanton and effeminate boy,
Takes on the point of honour to support   11
So dissolute a crew.
  Percy. My lord, some two days since I saw
    the Prince
And told him of those triumphs held at Ox-
  ford.
King H. And what said the gallant?   15
Percy. His answer was, he would unto the
  stews,
And from the common'st creature pluck a glove
And wear it as a favour, and with that
He would unhorse the lustiest challenger.
  King H. As dissolute as desperate! Yet
    through both   20
I see some sparks of better hope, which elder
  years
May happily bring forth. But who comes here?

Enter *Aumerle*, amazed.

Aum. Where is the King?
  King H. What means our cousin, that he
    stares and looks
So wildly?
  Aum. God save your Grace! I do beseech
    your Majesty   26
To have some conference with your Grace alone.
  King H. Withdraw yourselves and leave us
    here alone.
                           [*Exeunt Percy and Lords.*]
What is the matter with our cousin now?
  Aum. For ever may my knees grow to the
    earth,   [*Kneels.*]
My tongue cleave to the roof within my mouth,
Unless a pardon ere I rise or speak.
  King H. Intended, or committed, was this
    fault?
If on the first, how heinous e'er it be,
To win thy after-love I pardon thee.   35

Aum. Then give me leave that I may turn
  the key,
That no man enter till my tale be done.
  King H. Have thy desire.

[*Aumerle locks the door.*] *The Duke of York
    knocks at the door and crieth.*

York. (*within*) My liege, beware! look to
  thyself!
Thou hast a traitor in thy presence there.   40
  King H. Villain, I'll make thee safe. [*Draws.*]
  Aum. Stay thy revengeful hand; thou hast
    no cause to fear.
  York. (*within*) Open the door, secure fool-
    hardy king!
Shall I for love speak treason to thy face?
Open the door, or I will break it open!   45

Enter *York.*

King H. What is the matter, uncle? Speak.
Recover breath; tell us how near is danger,
That we may arm us to encounter it.
  York. Peruse this writing here, and thou
    shalt know
The treason that my haste forbids me show.   50
  Aum. Remember, as thou read'st, thy prom-
    ise pass'd.
I do repent me. Read not my name there.
My heart is not confederate with my hand.
  York. It was, villain, ere thy hand did set
    it down.
I tore it from the traitor's bosom, King.   55
Fear, and not love, begets his penitence.
Forget to pity him, lest thy pity prove
A serpent that will sting thee to the heart.
  King H. O heinous, strong, and bold con-
    spiracy!
O loyal father of a treacherous son!   60
Thou sheer, immaculate, and silver fountain,
From whence this stream through muddy pas-
  sages
Hath held his current and defil'd himself!
Thy overflow of good converts to bad,
And thy abundant goodness shall excuse   65
This deadly blot in thy digressing son.
  York. So shall my virtue be his vice's
    bawd,
And he shall spend mine honour with his
  shame,
As thriftless sons their scraping father's gold.
Mine honour lives when his dishonour dies,   70
Or my sham'd life in his dishonour lies.
Thou kill'st me in his life; giving him breath,
The traitor lives, the true man's put to death.

Duch. (*within*) What ho, my liege! For
God's sake let me in!
King H. What shrill-voic'd suppliant makes
this eager cry?   75
Duch. (*within*) A woman, and thy aunt,
great King. 'Tis I.
Speak with me, pity me, open the door!
A beggar begs that never begg'd before.
King H. Our scene is alt'red from a serious
thing,
And now chang'd to 'The Beggar and the King.'
My dangerous cousin, let your mother in.   81
I know she is come to pray for your foul sin.
York. If thou do pardon, whosoever pray,
More sins for this forgiveness prosper may.
This fest'red joint cut off, the rest rest sound;
This let alone will all the rest confound.   86

Enter *Duchess.*

Duch. O King, believe not this hard-hearted
man!
Love loving not itself, none other can.
York. Thou frantic woman, what dost thou
make here?
Shall thy old dugs once more a traitor rear? 90
Duch. Sweet York, be patient. Hear me,
gentle liege.   [*Kneels.*]
King H. Rise up, good aunt.
Duch.   Not yet, I thee beseech.
For ever will I walk upon my knees,
And never see day that the happy sees,
'Till thou give joy, until thou bid me joy   95
By pardoning Rutland, my transgressing boy.
Aum. Unto my mother's prayers I bend my
knee.   [*Kneels.*]
York. Against them both my true joints
bended be.   [*Kneels.*]
Ill mayst thou thrive if thou grant any grace!
Duch. Pleads he in earnest? Look upon his
face.   100
His eyes do drop no tears, his prayers are in jest;
His words come from his mouth, ours from our
breast.
He prays but faintly and would be denied;
We pray with heart and soul and all beside:
His weary joints would gladly rise, I know; 105
Our knees shall kneel till to the ground they
grow.
His prayers are full of false hypocrisy;
Ours of true zeal and deep integrity.
Our prayers do outpray his; then let them have
That mercy which true prayer ought to have.
King H. Good aunt, stand up.
Duch.   Nay, do not say 'stand up.'
Say 'pardon' first, and afterwards 'stand up.'

An if I were thy nurse, thy tongue to teach,
'Pardon' should be the first word of thy speech.
I never long'd to hear a word till now.   115
Say 'pardon,' King; let pity teach thee how.
The word is short, but not so short as sweet;
No word like 'pardon' for kings' mouths so
meet.
York. Speak it in French, King. Say 'Par-
donne moi.'
Duch. Dost thou teach pardon pardon to
destroy?   120
Ah, my sour husband, my hard-hearted lord,
That sets the word itself against the word!
Speak 'pardon' as 'tis current in our land;
The chopping French we do not understand.
Thine eye begins to speak, set thy tongue there;
Or in thy piteous heart plant thou thine ear, 126
That hearing how our plaints and prayers do
pierce,
Pity may move thee 'pardon' to rehearse.
King H. Good aunt, stand up.
Duch.   I do not sue to stand.
Pardon is all the suit I have in hand.   130
King H. I pardon him as God shall pardon
me.
Duch. O happy vantage of a kneeling knee!
Yet am I sick for fear. Speak it again.
Twice saying 'pardon' doth not pardon twain,
But makes one pardon strong.
King H.   With all my heart 135
I pardon him.
Duch.   A god on earth thou art. [*Rises.*]
King H. But for our trusty brother-in-law
and the Abbot,
With all the rest of that consorted crew,
Destruction straight shall dog them at the
heels.
Good uncle, help to order several powers,   140
To Oxford, or where'er these traitors are.
They shall not live within this world, I swear,
But I will have them, if I once know where.
Uncle, farewell; and, cousin, adieu.
Your mother well hath pray'd, and prove you
true.   145
Duch. Come, my old son. I pray God make
thee new.   *Exeunt.*

[Scene IV. *Windsor Castle.*]

Enter *Sir Pierce Exton* and *Servant.*

Exton. Didst thou not mark the King, what
words he spake?
'Have I no friend will rid me of this living fear?'
Was it not so?

Man.   These were his very words.
Exton. 'Have I no friend?' quoth he. He
  spake it twice
And urg'd it twice together, did he not?   5
Man. He did.
Exton. And speaking it, he wishtly look'd on
  me,
As who should say, 'I would thou wert the
  man
That would divorce this terror from my heart!'
Meaning the king at Pomfret. Come, let's go.
I am the King's friend, and will rid his foe. 11
                        Exeunt.

Scene V. [*Pomfret Castle.*]

Enter *Richard*, alone.

Rich. I have been studying how I may com-
  pare
This prison where I live unto the world;
And, for because the world is populous,
And here is not a creature but myself,
I cannot do it. Yet I'll hammer it out.   5
My brain I'll prove the female to my soul,
My soul the father; and these two beget
A generation of still-breeding thoughts;
And these same thoughts people this little world,
In humours like the people of this world,   10
For no thought is contented. The better sort,
As thoughts of things divine, are intermix'd
With scruples, and do set the word itself
Against the word:
As thus, 'Come, little ones,' and then again, 15
'It is as hard to come as for a camel
To thread the postern of a small needle's eye.'
Thoughts tending to ambition, they do plot
Unlikely wonders — how these vain weak nails
May tear a passage through the flinty ribs   20
Of this hard world, my ragged prison walls;
And, for they cannot, die in their own pride.
Thoughts tending to content flatter themselves
That they are not the first of fortune's slaves,
Nor shall not be the last; like seely beggars   25
Who, sitting in the stocks, refuge their shame,
That many have, and others must sit there.
And in this thought they find a kind of ease,
Bearing their own misfortunes on the back
Of such as have before endur'd the like.   30
Thus play I in one person many people,
And none contented. Sometimes am I king:
Then treasons make me wish myself a beggar,
And so I am. Then crushing penury
Persuades me I was better when a king;   35

Then am I king'd again; and by-and-by
Think that I am unking'd by Bolingbroke,
And straight am nothing. But whate'er I be,
Nor I, nor any man that but man is,
With nothing shall be pleas'd till he be eas'd 40
With being nothing.   *The music plays.*
                  Music do I hear?
Ha, ha! keep time. How sour sweet music is
When time is broke and no proportion kept!
So is it in the music of men's lives.
And here have I the daintiness of ear   45
To check time broke in a disordered string;
But, for the concord of my state and time,
Had not an ear to hear my true time broke.
I wasted time, and now doth time waste me;
For now hath time made me his numb'ring
  clock: 50
My thoughts are minutes; and with sighs they
  jar
Their watches on unto mine eyes, the outward
  watch,
Whereto my finger, like a dial's point,
Is pointing still, in cleansing them from tears.
Now, sir, the sounds that tell what hour it is 55
Are clamorous groans, that strike upon my
  heart,
Which is the bell. So sighs and tears and
  groans
Show minutes, times, and hours. But my time
Runs posting on in Bolingbroke's proud joy,
While I stand fooling here, his Jack o' th'
  clock.
This music mads me. Let it sound no more; 61
For though it have holp madmen to their wits,
In me it seems it will make wise men mad.
Yet blessing on his heart that gives it me!
For 'tis a sign of love, and love to Richard 65
Is a strange brooch in this all-hating world.

Enter a *Groom* of the stable.

Groom. Hail, royal prince!
Rich.   Thanks, noble peer.
The cheapest of us is ten groats too dear.
What art thou? and how comest thou hither,
Where no man never comes but that sad dog 70
That brings me food to make misfortune live?
Groom. I was a poor groom of thy stable,
  King,
When thou wert king; who, travelling towards
  York,
With much ado, at length, have gotten leave
To look upon my sometimes royal master's face.
O, how it ern'd my heart when I beheld,   76
In London streets, that coronation day,
When Bolingbroke rode on roan Barbary,

That horse that thou so often hast bestrid,
That horse that I so carefully have dress'd! 80
Rich. Rode he on Barbary? Tell me, gentle
friend,
How went he under him?
Groom. So proudly as if he had disdain'd
the ground.
Rich. So proud that Bolingbroke was on his
back!
That jade hath eat bread from my royal hand;
This hand hath made him proud with clapping
him. 86
Would he not stumble? would he not fall
down
(Since pride must have a fall) and break the
neck
Of that proud man that did usurp his back?
Forgiveness, horse! Why do I rail on thee, 90
Since thou, created to be aw'd by man,
Wast born to bear? I was not made a horse;
And yet I bear a burthen like an ass,
Spurr'd, gall'd and tir'd by jauncing Boling-
broke.

Enter *Keeper*, with a dish.

Keeper. Fellow, give place. Here is no
longer stay. 95
Rich. If thou love me, 'tis time thou wert
away.
Groom. What my tongue dares not, that my
heart shall say. *Exit.*
Keeper. My lord, will't please you to fall
to?
Rich. Taste of it first, as thou art wont to
do.
Keeper. My lord, I dare not. Sir Pierce of
Exton, 100
Who lately came from the King, commands the
contrary.
Rich. The devil take Henry of Lancaster,
and thee!
Patience is stale, and I am weary of it.
[*Beats the Keeper.*]
Keeper. Help, help, help!

Exton and *Servants*, the Murderers, rush in.

Rich. How now! What means death in this
rude assault? 105
Villain, thy own hand yields thy death's instrument.
[*Snatches a weapon from a Servant and kills
him.*]
Go thou and fill another room in hell.
[*Kills another.*] Here Exton strikes him
down.

That hand shall burn in never-quenching fire
That staggers thus my person. Exton, thy
fierce hand
Hath with the King's blood stain'd the King's
own land. 110
Mount, mount, my soul! thy seat is up on high;
Whilst my gross flesh sinks downward, here to
die. [*Dies.*]
Exton. As full of valour as of royal blood.
Both have I spill'd. O, would the deed were
good!
For now the devil, that told me I did well, 115
Says that this deed is chronicled in hell.
This dead king to the living king I'll bear.
Take hence the rest, and give them burial here.
Exeunt.

Scene VI. [*Windsor Castle.*]

Flourish. Enter *Bolingbroke* [as *King*], the
Duke of York, with other *Lords*, and *Attendants.*

King. Kind uncle York, the latest news we
hear
Is that the rebels have consum'd with fire
Our town of Ciceter in Gloucestershire;
But whether they be ta'en or slain we hear not.

Enter *Northumberland.*

Welcome, my lord. What is the news? 5
North. First, to thy sacred state wish I all
happiness.
The next news is, I have to London sent
The heads of Oxford, Salisbury, Blunt, and
Kent.
The manner of their taking may appear
At large discoursed in this paper here. 10
King. We thank thee, gentle Percy, for thy
pains
And to thy worth will add right worthy gains.

Enter *Lord Fitzwater.*

Fitz. My lord, I have from Oxford sent to
London
The heads of Brocas and Sir Bennet Seely,
Two of the dangerous consorted traitors 15
That sought at Oxford thy dire overthrow.
King. Thy pains, Fitzwater, shall not be
forgot.
Right noble is thy merit, well I wot.

Enter *Henry Percy* and [the *Bishop of*] *Carlisle.*

Percy. The grand conspirator, Abbot of
Westminster,
With clog of conscience and sour melancholy 20

Hath yielded up his body to the grave;
But here is Carlisle living, to abide
Thy kingly doom and sentence of his pride.
   King. Carlisle, this is your doom:
Choose out some secret place, some reverend
      room,   25
More than thou hast, and with it joy thy life.
So, as thou liv'st in peace, die free from strife;
For though mine enemy thou hast ever been,
High sparks of honour in thee have I seen.

Enter Exton, with [Attendants bearing] a coffin.

   Exton. Great King, within this coffin I
      present   30
Thy buried fear. Herein all breathless lies
The mightiest of thy greatest enemies,
Richard of Bordeaux, by me hither brought.
   King. Exton, I thank thee not; for thou
      hast wrought
A deed of slander, with thy fatal hand,   35
Upon my head and all this famous land.

   Exton. From your own mouth, my lord, did
      I this deed.
   King. They love not poison that do poison
      need,
Nor do I thee. Though I did wish him dead,
I hate the murtherer, love him murthered.   40
The guilt of conscience take thou for thy
      labour,
But neither my good word nor princely favour.
With Cain go wander thorough shades of night,
And never show thy head by day nor light.
Lords, I protest my soul is full of woe   45
That blood should sprinkle me to make me
      grow.
Come, mourn with me for what I do lament,
And put on sullen black incontinent.
I'll make a voyage to the Holy Land
To wash this blood off from my guilty hand. 50
March sadly after. Grace my mournings here
In weeping after this untimely bier.
                                        Exeunt.

THE FIRST PART OF KING HENRY THE FOURTH

PART I OF HENRY THE FOURTH was entered in the Stationers' Register on February 25, 1598, as 'The historye of Henry the IIIIth . . . with the conceipted mirthe of Sir John Falstoff,' and the First Quarto (our authority for the text) came out in the same year. Meres, before October 19, 1598, mentions 'Henry the 4' among Shakespeare's excellent tragedies. Perhaps he means to include both Parts under that title; but his evidence is ambiguous. The Second Part must have followed the First rather promptly, and doubtless with no other drama intervening. For *Part I* we may fix upon 1597, and for *Part II* upon 1598, without risk of serious error. Jonson mentions Justice Silence in his *Every Man out of his Humour*, which was acted in 1599.

PART I is manifestly later than *Richard the Second*. The connection between them is close. Bolingbroke's character, well intimated in *Richard the Second*, is so developed in the later play that he becomes, as King Henry, one of the most baffling of all Shakespeare's complex creatures. He is genuinely patriotic. He had the good of his country at heart, and not merely personal advantage, when he deposed King Richard. His anxiety about his dissolute son is not paternal only: it is largely due to his fear of what will happen to England if another Harry shows himself another Richard in instability and tyrannical license. And so, profound dissembler as he is, he actually lays bare his own dissimulation in admonishing his son (iii, 2):

> And then I stole all courtesy from heaven
> And dress'd myself in such humility
> That I did pluck allegiance from men's hearts,
> Loud shouts and salutations from their mouths,
> Even in the presence of the crowned king.

This whole speech would be almost cynical, were it not for the passionate intensity which submerges the cynicism of its outspokenness. It looks back to King Richard's account of Bolingbroke's 'courtship of the common people' (i, 4, 20 ff.) and to York's description of his triumphal progress after his return from banishment (v, 2).

Prince Hal does not appear in *Richard the Second*, but his riotous conduct and his companionship with highwaymen are deplored by his father in v, 3, where Hotspur's scorn of him, so hotly uttered in 1 HENRY IV (i, 3, 230 ff.), comes out by implication in his answer to King Henry's question. Before he began PART I, Shakespeare had somewhat modified his former conception of the Prince's character. In *Richard the Second* he is called 'as dissolute as desperate.' In 1 HENRY IV, on the contrary, he is neither desperate nor, in the full sense of the word, dissolute. His riots are mere frolics. He does not get drunk and is never involved in any scandal with a woman. Shakespeare, indeed, is so much concerned to guard against misconception on the part of the audience, that he deliberately renounces dramatic propriety in the famous soliloquy at the end of i, 2. This is, in effect, the author's explanation — a kind of chorus — and should be so understood. It is not the expression of the Prince's actual motive in upholding 'the unyoked humour' of his riotous comrades. It amounts to a mere statement of the fact in the third person:

'When this Prince turns over a new leaf, he will be all the more admired for the contrast.'

For historical materials in HENRY THE FOURTH, as in *Richard the Second*, Shakespeare went to the second edition of Holinshed (1587). The events in PART I all come within the limits of almost exactly a year. Sir Edmund Mortimer (whom Shakespeare, like Holinshed, confuses with the Earl of March) was taken prisoner by Glendower on June 22, 1402; the defeat of the Scots at Homildon followed on September 14; on July 21, 1403, Hotspur was killed in the Battle of Shrewsbury — no one knows by whom; Worcester and Vernon were executed two days later. Henry IV was born in 1367; Prince Hal in 1387. Hotspur was quite as old as the King — indeed, a little older. Shakespeare has so reduced his age that he is 'not more in debt to years' than the Prince. Thus the contrast is made dramatically possible.

Shakespeare owes much to Holinshed for facts and ideas; little for phraseology. A typical instance is Hotspur's famous speech before the battle (v, 2, 82 ff.): 'O, gentlemen, the time of life is short!' Holinshed reports it thus:

This daie shall either bring vs all to aduauncement & honor, or else, if it shall chance vs to be ouercome, shall deliuer vs from the kings spitefull malice and cruell disdaine: for plaieng the men (as we ought to doo), better it is to die in battell for the commonwealths cause, than through cowardlike feare to prolong life which after shall be taken from vs, by sentence of the enimie.

For the riotous behaviour of Hal and his companions Shakespeare found suggestions in Holinshed and Stow; but more noteworthy are the curious details that he derived from the old play of *The Famous Victories of Henry the Fifth*. This he used for both Parts of HENRY THE FOURTH. In the old play, for instance, when the Prince promises Ned that he shall be Chief Justice, Ned replies, 'By gogs wounds, ile be the brauest Lord chiefe Iustice That euer was in England' (cf. I, i, 2, 72); Derick tickles his nose with a straw to make it bleed (cf. I, ii, 4, 340); the Prince's resort is 'the olde Tauerne in Eastcheape'; there is a comic scene of conscription (cf. II, iii, 2), and so on.

When Shakespeare wrote the FIRST PART OF HENRY THE FOURTH he gave to the character whom we know as Falstaff the name of Sir John Oldcastle, which he took from *The Famous Victories of Henry the Fifth*. This he changed to Falstaff before the play was printed. Traces of the change appear in the text of both parts. In *Part I*, the Prince calls him 'my old lad of the castle' (i, 2, 47); and one line (ii, 2, 115), though not unmetrical as it stands, would be more regular if 'Oldcastle' were read instead of 'Falstaff.' In *Part II*, a speech of Falstaff's (i, 2, 137) is still marked *Old.* in the Quarto of 1600; the Epilogue expressly declares that 'Oldcastle died a martyr, and this is not the man.' The historical Sir John Oldcastle (called Lord Cobham in his wife's right) was executed for heresy in 1417. The Cobham family was powerful in Shakespeare's time and no doubt protested against the profanation of what to them was a sacred name. For a substitute, Shakespeare went back to *1 Henry VI*, in which one Sir John Fastolfe plays a coward's part, and borrowed the name, with a shift of letters. Perhaps this choice of name suggested itself because the Prince accuses Oldcastle-Falstaff of cowardice in ii, 4, after the robbers have been robbed; but Falstaff is not a coward in fact, though traditional interpretation has heedlessly taken the Prince's practical joke as if it justified the accusation.

74

THE FIRST PART OF
KING HENRY THE FOURTH

[Dramatis Personæ.

King Henry the Fourth.
Henry, Prince of Wales, ⎫
Prince John of Lancaster, ⎬ sons to the *King.*
Earl of Westmoreland.
Sir Walter Blunt.
Thomas Percy, Earl of Worcester.
Henry Percy, Earl of Northumberland.
Henry Percy, surnamed *Hotspur,* his son.
Edmund Mortimer, Earl of March.
Richard Scroop Archbishop of York.
Archibald, Earl of Douglas.
Owen Glendower.
Sir Richard Vernon.
Sir John Falstaff.

Sir Michael, a friend to the *Archbishop of York.*
Poins.
Gadshill.
Peto.
Bardolph.

Lady Percy, wife to *Hotspur,* and sister to *Mortimer.*
Lady Mortimer, daughter to *Glendower,* and wife to *Mortimer.*
Mistress Quickly, hostess of the Boar's Head in Eastcheap.

Lords, Officers, Sheriff, Vintner, Chamberlain, Drawers, two Carriers, Travellers, and Attendants.

SCENE. — *England and Wales.*]

ACT I. Scene I. [*London. The Palace.*]

Enter the *King, Lord John of Lancaster, Earl of Westmoreland,* [*Sir Walter Blunt,*] with others.

King. So shaken as we are, so wan with care,
Find we a time for frighted peace to pant
And breathe short-winded accents of new broils
To be commenc'd in stronds afar remote.
No more the thirsty entrance of this soil   5
Shall daub her lips with her own children's blood.
No more shall trenching war channel her fields,
Nor bruise her flow'rets with the armed hoofs
Of hostile paces. Those opposed eyes   9
Which, like the meteors of a troubled heaven,
All of one nature, of one substance bred,
Did lately meet in the intestine shock
And furious close of civil butchery,
Shall now in mutual well-beseeming ranks
March all one way and be no more oppos'd   15
Against acquaintance, kindred, and allies.
The edge of war, like an ill-sheathed knife,
No more shall cut his master. Therefore, friends,
As far as to the sepulchre of Christ —   19
Whose soldier now, under whose blessed cross
We are impressed and engag'd to fight —
Forthwith a power of English shall we levy,
Whose arms were moulded in their mother's womb
To chase these pagans in those holy fields
Over whose acres walk'd those blessed feet   25
Which fourteen hundred years ago were nail'd
For our advantage on the bitter cross.
But this our purpose now is twelvemonth old,
And bootless 'tis to tell you we will go.   29
Therefore we meet not now. Then let me hear
Of you, my gentle cousin Westmoreland,
What yesternight our Council did decree
In forwarding this dear expedience.
West. My liege, this haste was hot in question
And many limits of the charge set down   35
But yesternight; when all athwart there came
A post from Wales, loaden with heavy news;
Whose worst was that the noble Mortimer,
Leading the men of Herefordshire to fight
Against the irregular and wild Glendower,   40
Was by the rude hands of that Welshman taken,
A thousand of his people butchered;
Upon whose dead corpse there was such misuse,
Such beastly shameless transformation,
By those Welshwomen done as may not be   45
Without much shame retold or spoken of.

75

King. It seems then that the tidings of this broil
Brake off our business for the Holy Land.
　West. This, match'd with other, did, my gracious lord;
For more uneven and unwelcome news　50
Came from the North, and thus it did import:
On Holy-rood Day the gallant Hotspur there,
Young Harry Percy, and brave Archibald,
That ever-valiant and approved Scot,
At Holmedon met,　55
Where they did spend a sad and bloody hour;
As by discharge of their artillery
And shape of likelihood the news was told;
For he that brought them, in the very heat
And pride of their contention did take horse,　60
Uncertain of the issue any way.
　King. Here is a dear, a true-industrious friend,
Sir Walter Blunt, new lighted from his horse,
Stain'd with the variation of each soil
Betwixt that Holmedon and this seat of ours,
And he hath brought us smooth and welcome news.　66
The Earl of Douglas is discomfited;
Ten thousand bold Scots, two-and-twenty knights,
Balk'd in their own blood did Sir Walter see
On Holmedon's plains. Of prisoners, Hotspur took　70
Mordake Earl of Fife and eldest son
To beaten Douglas, and the Earl of Athol,
Of Murray, Angus, and Menteith.
And is not this an honourable spoil?
A gallant prize? Ha, cousin, is it not?　75
　West. In faith,
It is a conquest for a prince to boast of.
　King. Yea, there thou mak'st me sad, and mak'st me sin
In envy that my Lord Northumberland
Should be the father to so blest a son —　80
A son who is the theme of honour's tongue,
Amongst a grove the very straightest plant;
Who is sweet Fortune's minion and her pride;
Whilst I, by looking on the praise of him,
See riot and dishonour stain the brow　85
Of my young Harry. O that it could be prov'd
That some night-tripping fairy had exchang'd
In cradle clothes our children where they lay,
And call'd mine Percy, his Plantagenet!
Then would I have his Harry, and he mine.　90
But let him from my thoughts. What think you, coz,
Of this young Percy's pride? The prisoners
Which he in this adventure hath surpris'd

To his own use he keeps, and sends me word
I shall have none but Mordake Earl of Fife.
　West. This is his uncle's teaching, this is Worcester,　96
Malevolent to you in all aspects,
Which makes him prune himself and bristle up
The crest of youth against your dignity.
　King. But I have sent for him to answer this;　100
And for this cause awhile we must neglect
Our holy purpose to Jerusalem.
Cousin, on Wednesday next our council we
Will hold at Windsor. So inform the lords;
But come yourself with speed to us again;　105
For more is to be said and to be done
Than out of anger can be uttered.
　West. I will, my liege.　*Exeunt.*

Scene II. [*London. An apartment of the* Prince's.]

Enter *Prince of Wales* and *Sir John Falstaff.*

　Fal. Now, Hal, what time of day is it, lad?
　Prince. Thou art so fat-witted with drinking of old sack, and unbuttoning thee after supper, and sleeping upon benches after noon, that thou hast forgotten to demand that truly which thou wouldest truly know. What a devil hast thou to do with the time of the day? Unless hours were cups of sack, and minutes capons, and clocks the tongues of bawds, and dials the signs of leaping houses, and the blessed sun himself a fair hot wench in flame-coloured taffeta, I see no reason why thou shouldst be so superfluous to demand the time of the day.　13
　Fal. Indeed you come near me now, Hal; for we that take purses go by the moon and the seven stars, and not by Phœbus, he, that wand'ring knight so fair. And I prithee, sweet wag, when thou art king, as, God save thy Grace — Majesty I should say, for grace thou wilt have none —　20
　Prince. What, none?
　Fal. No, by my troth; not so much as will serve to be prologue to an egg and butter.
　Prince. Well, how then? Come, roundly, roundly.　25
　Fal. Marry, then, sweet wag, when thou art king, let not us that are squires of the night's body be called thieves of the day's beauty. Let us be Diana's Foresters, Gentlemen of the Shade, Minions of the Moon; and let men say we be men of good government, being governed

as the sea is. by our noble and chaste mistress the moon, under whose countenance we steal.

Prince. Thou sayest well, and it holds well too; for the fortune of us that are the moon's men doth ebb and flow like the sea, being governed, as the sea is, by the moon. As, for proof now: a purse of gold most resolutely snatch'd on Monday night and most dissolutely spent on Tuesday morning; got with swearing 'Lay by,' and spent with crying 'Bring in'; now in as low an ebb as the foot of the ladder, and by-and-by in as high a flow as the ridge of the gallows.

Fal. By the Lord, thou say'st true, lad — and is not my hostess of the tavern a most sweet wench?   46

Prince. As the honey of Hybla, my old lad of the castle — and is not a buff jerkin a most sweet robe of durance?   49

Fal. How now, how now, mad wag? What, in thy quips and thy quiddities? What a plague have I to do with a buff jerkin?

Prince. Why, what a pox have I to do with my hostess of the tavern?   54

Fal. Well, thou hast call'd her to a reckoning many a time and oft.

Prince. Did I ever call for thee to pay thy part?   58

Fal. No; I'll give thee thy due, thou hast paid all there.

Prince. Yea, and elsewhere, so far as my coin would stretch; and where it would not, I have used my credit.   63

Fal. Yea, and so us'd it that, were it not here apparent that thou art heir apparent — But I prithee, sweet wag, shall there be gallows standing in England when thou art king? and resolution thus fubb'd as it is with the rusty curb of old father antic the law? Do not thou, when thou art king, hang a thief.   70

Prince. No; thou shalt.

Fal. Shall I? O rare! By the Lord, I'll be a brave judge.

Prince. Thou judgest false already. I mean, thou shalt have the hanging of the thieves and so become a rare hangman.   76

Fal. Well, Hal, well; and in some sort it jumps with my humour as well as waiting in the court, I can tell you.

Prince. For obtaining of suits?   80

Fal. Yea, for obtaining of suits, whereof the hangman hath no lean wardrobe. 'Sblood, I am as melancholy as a gib-cat or a lugg'd bear.

Prince. Or an old lion, or a lover's lute.

Fal. Yea, or the drone of a Lincolnshire bagpipe.   86

Prince. What sayest thou to a hare, or the melancholy of Moor Ditch?

Fal. Thou hast the most unsavoury similes, and art indeed the most comparative, rascalliest, sweet young prince. But, Hal, I prithee trouble me no more with vanity. I would to God thou and I knew where a commodity of good names were to be bought. An old lord of the Council rated me the other day in the street about you, sir, but I mark'd him not; and yet he talk'd very wisely, but I regarded him not; and yet he talk'd wisely, and in the street too.

Prince. Thou didst well; for wisdom cries out in the streets, and no man regards it.   100

Fal. O, thou hast damnable iteration, and art indeed able to corrupt a saint. Thou hast done much harm upon me, Hal — God forgive thee for it! Before I knew thee, Hal, I knew nothing; and now am I, if a man should speak truly, little better than one of the wicked. I must give over this life, and I will give it over! By the Lord, an I do not, I am a villain! I'll be damn'd for never a king's son in Christendom.

Prince. Where shall we take a purse tomorrow, Jack?   111

Fal. Zounds, where thou wilt, lad! I'll make one. An I do not, call me villain and baffle me.

Prince. I see a good amendment of life in thee — from praying to purse-taking.   115

Fal. Why, Hal, 'tis my vocation, Hal. 'Tis no sin for a man to labour in his vocation.

Enter *Poins.*

Poins! Now shall we know if Gadshill have set a match. O, if men were to be saved by merit, what hole in hell were hot enough for him? This is the most omnipotent villain that ever cried 'Stand!' to a true man.   122

Prince. Good morrow, Ned.

Poins. Good morrow, sweet Hal. What says Monsieur Remorse? What says Sir John Sack and Sugar? Jack, how agrees the devil and thee about thy soul, that thou soldest him on Good Friday last for a cup of Madeira and a cold capon's leg?   129

Prince. Sir John stands to his word, the devil shall have his bargain; for he was never yet a breaker of proverbs. He will give the devil his due.

Poins. Then art thou damn'd for keeping thy word with the devil.   135

Prince. Else he had been damn'd for cozening the devil.

Poins. But, my lads, my lads, to-morrow morning, by four o'clock early, at Gadshill! There are pilgrims going to Canterbury with rich offerings, and traders riding to London with fat purses. I have vizards for you all; you have horses for yourselves. Gadshill lies to-night in Rochester. I have bespoke supper to-morrow night in Eastcheap. We may do it as secure as sleep. If you will go, I will stuff your purses full of crowns; if you will not, tarry at home and be hang'd!

Fal. Hear ye, Yedward: if I tarry at home and go not, I'll hang you for going. 150

Poins. You will, chops?

Fal. Hal, wilt thou make one?

Prince. Who, I rob? I a thief? Not I, by my faith. 154

Fal. There's neither honesty, manhood, nor good fellowship in thee, nor thou cam'st not of the blood royal if thou darest not stand for ten shillings.

Prince. Well then, once in my days I'll be a madcap. 160

Fal. Why, that's well said.

Prince. Well, come what will, I'll tarry at home.

Fal. By the Lord, I'll be a traitor then, when thou art king. 165

Prince. I care not.

Poins. Sir John, I prithee, leave the Prince and me alone. I will lay him down such reasons for this adventure that he shall go. 169

Fal. Well, God give thee the spirit of persuasion and him the ears of profiting, that what thou speakest may move and what he hears may be believed, that the true prince may (for recreation sake) prove a false thief; for the poor abuses of the time want countenance. Farewell; you shall find me in Eastcheap. 176

Prince. Farewell, thou latter spring! farewell, All-hallown summer!

[*Exit Falstaff.*]

Poins. Now, my good sweet honey lord, ride with us to-morrow. I have a jest to execute that I cannot manage alone. Falstaff, Bardolph, Peto, and Gadshill shall rob those men that we have already waylaid; yourself and I will not be there; and when they have the booty, if you and I do not rob them, cut this head off from my shoulders. 186

Prince. How shall we part with them in setting forth?

Poins. Why, we will set forth before or after them and appoint them a place of meeting, wherein it is at our pleasure to fail; and then will they adventure upon the exploit themselves; which they shall have no sooner achieved, but we'll set upon them. 194

Prince. Yea, but 'tis like that they will know us by our horses, by our habits, and by every other appointment, to be ourselves.

Poins. Tut! our horses they shall not see — I'll tie them in the wood; our vizards we will change after we leave them; and, sirrah, I have cases of buckram for the nonce, to immask our noted outward garments.

Prince. Yea, but I doubt they will be too hard for us. 204

Poins. Well, for two of them, I know them to be as true-bred cowards as ever turn'd back; and for the third, if he fight longer than he sees reason, I'll forswear arms. The virtue of this jest will be the incomprehensible lies that this same fat rogue will tell us when we meet at supper: how thirty, at least, he fought with; what wards, what blows, what extremities he endured; and in the reproof of this lies the jest. 214

Prince. Well, I'll go with thee. Provide us all things necessary and meet me to-night in Eastcheap. There I'll sup. Farewell.

Poins. Farewell, my lord. *Exit.*

Prince. I know you all, and will awhile uphold
The unyok'd humour of your idleness. 220
Yet herein will I imitate the sun,
Who doth permit the base contagious clouds
To smother up his beauty from the world,
That, when he please again to be himself, 224
Being wanted, he may be more wond'red at
By breaking through the foul and ugly mists
Of vapours that did seem to strangle him.
If all the year were playing holidays,
To sport would be as tedious as to work;
But when they seldom come, they wish'd-for come, 230
And nothing pleaseth but rare accidents.
So, when this loose behaviour I throw off
And pay the debt I never promised,
By how much better than my word I am,
By so much shall I falsify men's hopes; 235
And, like bright metal on a sullen ground,
My reformation, glitt'ring o'er my fault,
Shall show more goodly and attract more eyes
Than that which hath no foil to set it off.
I'll so offend to make offence a skill, 240
Redeeming time when men think least I will.
Exit.

Scene III. [*London. The Palace.*]

Enter the *King, Northumberland, Worcester,
Hotspur, Sir Walter Blunt,* with others.

King. My blood hath been too cold and
  temperate,
Unapt to stir at these indignities,
And you have found me, for accordingly
You tread upon my patience; but be sure
I will from henceforth rather be myself,   5
Mighty and to be fear'd, than my condition,
Which hath been smooth as oil, soft as young
  down,
And therefore lost that title of respect
Which the proud soul ne'er pays but to the
  proud.
  Wor. Our house, my sovereign liege, little
  deserves   10
The scourge of greatness to be us'd on it —
And that same greatness too which our own
  hands
Have holp to make so portly.
  North. My lord —   14
  King. Worcester, get thee gone; for I do see
Danger and disobedience in thine eye.
O, sir, your presence is too bold and peremp-
  tory,
And majesty might never yet endure
The moody frontier of a servant brow.   19
You have good leave to leave us. When we need
Your use and counsel, we shall send for you.
                    Exit Worcester.
You were about to speak.
  North.   Yea, my good lord.
Those prisoners in your Highness' name de-
  manded
Which Harry Percy here at Holmedon took,
Were, as he says, not with such strength denied
As is delivered to your Majesty.   26
Either envy, therefore, or misprision
Is guilty of this fault, and not my son.
  Hot. My liege, I did deny no prisoners.
But I remember, when the fight was done,   30
When I was dry with rage and extreme toil,
Breathless and faint, leaning upon my sword,
Came there a certain lord, neat and trimly
  dress'd,
Fresh as a bridegroom; and his chin new
  reap'd
Show'd like a stubble land at harvest home.   35
He was perfumed like a milliner,
And 'twixt his finger and his thumb he held
A pouncet box, which ever and anon
He gave his nose, and took't away again;   39

Who therewith angry, when it next came there,
Took it in snuff; and still he smil'd and talk'd;
And as the soldiers bore dead bodies by,
He call'd them untaught knaves, unmannerly,
To bring a slovenly unhandsome corse
Betwixt the wind and his nobility.   45
With many holiday and lady terms
He questioned me, amongst the rest demanded
My prisoners in your Majesty's behalf.
I then, all smarting with my wounds being cold,
To be so pest'red with a popingay,   50
Out of my grief and my impatience,
Answer'd neglectingly, I know not what —
He should, or he should not; for he made me
  mad
To see him shine so brisk, and smell so sweet,
And talk so like a waiting gentlewoman   55
Of guns and drums and wounds — God save
  the mark! —
And telling me the sovereignest thing on earth
Was parmacity for an inward bruise;
And that it was great pity, so it was,
This villanous saltpetre should be digg'd   60
Out of the bowels of the harmless earth,
Which many a good tall fellow had destroy'd
So cowardly; and but for these vile guns,
He would himself have been a soldier.
This bald unjointed chat of his, my lord,   65
I answered indirectly, as I said,
And I beseech you, let not his report
Come current for an accusation
Betwixt my love and your high majesty.
  Blunt. The circumstance considered, good
  my lord,   70
Whate'er Lord Harry Percy then had said
To such a person, and in such a place,
At such a time, with all the rest retold,
May reasonably die, and never rise
To do him wrong, or any way impeach   75
What then he said, so he unsay it now.
  King. Why, yet he doth deny his prisoners,
But with proviso and exception,
That we at our own charge shall ransom straight
His brother-in-law, the foolish Mortimer;   80
Who, on my soul, hath wilfully betray'd
The lives of those that he did lead to fight
Against that great magician, damn'd Glen-
  dower,
Whose daughter, as we hear, the Earl of March
Hath lately married. Shall our coffers, then,   85
Be emptied to redeem a traitor home?
Shall we buy treason? and indent with fears
When they have lost and forfeited themselves?
No, on the barren mountains let him starve!
For I shall never hold that man my friend   90

Whose tongue shall ask me for one penny cost
To ransom home revolted Mortimer.
　Hot. Revolted Mortimer?
He never did fall off, my sovereign liege,　94
But by the chance of war. To prove that true
Needs no more but one tongue for all those
　　wounds,
Those mouthed wounds, which valiantly he took
When on the gentle Severn's sedgy bank,
In single opposition hand to hand,
He did confound the best part of an hour　100
In changing hardiment with great Glendower.
Three times they breath'd, and three times did
　　they drink,
Upon agreement, of swift Severn's flood;
Who then, affrighted with their bloody looks,
Ran fearfully among the trembling reeds　105
And hid his crisp head in the hollow bank,
Bloodstained with these valiant combatants.
Never did base and rotten policy
Colour her working with such deadly wounds;
Nor never could the noble Mortimer　110
Receive so many, and all willingly.
Then let not him be slandered with revolt.
　King. Thou dost belie him, Percy, thou dost
　　belie him!
He never did encounter with Glendower.
I tell thee　115
He durst as well have met the devil alone
As Owen Glendower for an enemy.
Art thou not asham'd? But, sirrah, henceforth
Let me not hear you speak of Mortimer.
Send me your prisoners with the speediest
　　means,　120
Or you shall hear in such a kind from me
As will displease you. My Lord Northumber-
　　land,
We license your departure with your son. —
Send us your prisoners, or you will hear of it.
　　　　Exeunt King, [Blunt, and Train].
　Hot. An if the devil come and roar for them,
I will not send them. I will after straight　126
And tell him so; for I will ease my heart,
Albeit I make a hazard of my head.
　North. What, drunk with choler? Stay, and
　　pause awhile.
Here comes your uncle.

　　　　　Enter *Worcester.*

　Hot.　　　　Speak of Mortimer?　130
Zounds, I will speak of him, and let my soul
Want mercy if I do not join with him!
Yea, on his part I'll empty all these veins,
And shed my dear blood drop by drop in the
　　dust,

But I will lift the downtrod Mortimer　135
As high in the air as this unthankful king,
As this ingrate and cank'red Bolingbroke.
　North. Brother, the King hath made your
　　nephew mad.
　Wor. Who struck this heat up after I was
　　gone?　139
　Hot. He will (forsooth) have all my prisoners;
And when I urg'd the ransom once again
Of my wive's brother, then his cheek look'd
　　pale,
And on my face he turn'd an eye of death,
Trembling even at the name of Mortimer.
　Wor. I cannot blame him. Was not he pro-
　　claim'd　145
By Richard that dead is, the next of blood?
　North. He was; I heard the proclamation.
And then it was when the unhappy King
(Whose wrongs in us God pardon!) did set forth
Upon his Irish expedition;　150
From whence he intercepted did return
To be depos'd, and shortly murdered.
　Wor. And for whose death we in the world's
　　wide mouth
Live scandaliz'd and foully spoken of.
　Hot. But soft, I pray you. Did King Richard
　　then　155
Proclaim my brother Edmund Mortimer
Heir to the crown?
　North.　　　　He did; myself did hear it.
　Hot. Nay, then I cannot blame his cousin
　　king,
That wish'd him on the barren mountains
　　starve.
But shall it be that you, that set the crown　160
Upon the head of this forgetful man,
And for his sake wear the detested blot
Of murtherous subornation — shall it be
That you a world of curses undergo,
Being the agents or base second means,　165
The cords, the ladder, or the hangman rather?
O, pardon me that I descend so low
To show the line and the predicament
Wherein you range under this subtile king!
Shall it for shame be spoken in these days,　170
Or fill up chronicles in time to come,
That men of your nobility and power
Did gage them both in an unjust behalf
(As both of you, God pardon it! have done)
To put down Richard, that sweet lovely rose,
And plant this thorn, this canker, Bolingbroke?
And shall it in more shame be further spoken
That you are fool'd, discarded, and shook off
By him for whom these shames ye underwent?
No! yet time serves wherein you may redeem

Your banish'd honours and restore yourselves
Into the good thoughts of the world again;
Revenge the jeering and disdain'd contempt
Of this proud king, who studies day and night
To answer all the debt he owes to you   185
Even with the bloody payment of your deaths.
Therefore I say —
 Wor.   Peace, cousin, say no more;
And now I will unclasp a secret book,
And to your quick-conceiving discontents
I'll read you matter deep and dangerous,   190
As full of peril and adventurous spirit
As to o'erwalk a current roaring loud
On the unsteadfast footing of a spear.
 Hot. If he fall in, good night, or sink or
  swim!
Send danger from the east unto the west,   195
So honour cross it from the north to south,
And let them grapple. O, the blood more stirs
To rouse a lion than to start a hare!
 North. Imagination of some great exploit
Drives him beyond the bounds of patience. 200
 Hot. By heaven, methinks it were an easy
  leap
To pluck bright honour from the pale-fac'd
  moon,
Or dive into the bottom of the deep,
Where fadom line could never touch the ground,
And pluck up drowned honour by the locks,
So he that doth redeem her thence might wear
Without corrival all her dignities;
But out upon this half-fac'd fellowship!
 Wor. He apprehends a world of figures here,
But not the form of what he should attend. 210
Good cousin, give me audience for a while.
 Hot. I cry you mercy.
 Wor.   Those same noble Scots
That are your prisoners —
 Hot.   I'll keep them all.
By God, he shall not have a Scot of them!   214
No, if a Scot would save his soul, he shall not.
I'll keep them, by this hand!
 Wor.   You start away.
And lend no ear unto my purposes.
Those prisoners you shall keep.
 Hot.   Nay, I will! That's flat!
He said he would not ransom Mortimer,
Forbade my tongue to speak of Mortimer,   220
But I will find him when he lies asleep,
And in his ear I'll holloa 'Mortimer.'
Nay;
I'll have a starling shall be taught to speak
Nothing but 'Mortimer,' and give it him   225
To keep his anger still in motion.
 Wor. Hear you, cousin, a word.

 Hot. All studies here I solemnly defy
Save how to gall and pinch this Bolingbroke;
And that same sword-and-buckler Prince of
  Wales —   230
But that I think his father loves him not
And would be glad he met with some mischance,
I would have him poisoned with a pot of ale.
 Wor. Farewell, kinsman. I will talk to you
When you are better temper'd to attend.   235
 North. Why, what a wasp-stung and impa-
  tient fool
Art thou to break into this woman's mood,
Tying thine ear to no tongue but thine own!
 Hot. Why, look you, I am whipp'd and
  scourg'd with rods,
Nettled, and stung with pismires when I hear
Of this vile politician, Bolingbroke.   241
In Richard's time — what do you call the
  place? —
A plague upon it! it is in Gloucestershire —
'Twas where the madcap Duke his uncle kept —
His uncle York — where I first bow'd my knee
Unto this king of smiles, this Bolingbroke —
'Sblood!
When you and he came back from Ravens-
  purgh —
 North. At Berkeley Castle.
 Hot. You say true.   250
Why, what a candy deal of courtesy
This fawning greyhound then did proffer me!
Look, 'when his infant fortune came to age,'
And 'gentle Harry Percy,' and 'kind cousin' —
O, the devil take such cozeners! — God forgive
  me!   255
Good uncle, tell your tale, for I have done.
 Wor. Nay, if you have not, to it again.
We will stay your leisure.
 Hot.   I have done, i' faith.
 Wor. Then once more to your Scottish pris-
  oners.   259
Deliver them up without their ransom straight,
And make the Douglas' son your only mean
For powers in Scotland; which, for divers
  reasons
Which I shall send you written, be assur'd
Will easily be granted. [*To Northumberland*]
  You, my lord,
Your son in Scotland being thus employ'd,   265
Shall secretly into the bosom creep
Of that same noble prelate well-belov'd,
The Archbishop.
 Hot. Of York, is it not?
 Wor. True; who bears hard   270
His brother's death at Bristow, the Lord Scroop.
I speak not this in estimation,

As what I think might be, but what I know
Is ruminated, plotted, and set down,
And only stays but to behold the face   275
Of that occasion that shall bring it on.
  Hot. I smell it. Upon my life, it will do
    well.
  North. Before the game is afoot thou still
    let'st slip.
  Hot. Why, it cannot choose but be a noble
    plot.   279
And then the power of Scotland and of York
To join with Mortimer, ha?
  Wor.   And so they shall.
  Hot. In faith, it is exceedingly well aim'd.
  Wor. And 'tis no little reason bids us speed,
To save our heads by raising of a head;
For, bear ourselves as even as we can,   285
The King will always think him in our debt,
And think we think ourselves unsatisfied,

Till he hath found a time to pay us home.
And see already how he doth begin
To make us strangers to his looks of love.   290
  Hot. He does, he does! We'll be reveng'd on
    him.
  Wor. Cousin, farewell. No further go in this
Than I by letters shall direct your course.
When time is ripe, which will be suddenly,
I'll steal to Glendower and Lord Mortimer,
Where you and Douglas, and our pow'rs at
    once,
As I will fashion it, shall happily meet,
To bear our fortunes in our own strong arms,
Which now we hold at much uncertainty.
  North. Farewell, good brother. We shall
    thrive, I trust.   300
  Hot. Uncle, adieu. O, let the hours be short
Till fields and blows and groans applaud our
    sport!   *Exeunt.*

ACT II. Scene I. [*Rochester. An inn yard.*]

Enter a *Carrier* with a lantern in his hand.

  1. Car. Heigh-ho! an it be not four by the
day, I'll be hang'd. Charles' wain is over the
new chimney, and yet our horse not pack'd. —
What, ostler!
  Ost. [*within*] Anon, anon.   5
  1. Car. I prithee, Tom, beat Cut's saddle,
put a few flocks in the point. Poor jade is
wrung in the withers out of all cess.

Enter another *Carrier.*

  2. Car. Peas and beans are as dank here as a
dog, and that is the next way to give poor jades
the bots. This house is turned upside down
since Robin Ostler died.   12
  1. Car. Poor fellow never joyed since the
price of oats rose. It was the death of him.
  2. Car. I think this be the most villanous
house in all London road for fleas. I am stung
like a tench.   17
  1. Car. Like a tench? By the mass, there is
ne'er a king christen could be better bit than I
have been since the first cock.   20
  2. Car. Why, they will allow us ne'er a jordan, and then we leak in your chimney, and
your chamber-lye breeds fleas like a loach.
  1. Car. What, ostler! come away and be
hang'd! come away!   25
  2. Car. I have a gammon of bacon and two
razes of ginger, to be delivered as far as Charing
Cross.
  1. Car. God's body! the turkeys in my pan-

nier are quite starved. What, ostler! A plague
on thee! hast thou never an eye in thy head?
Canst not hear? An 'twere not as good deed as
drink to break the pate on thee, I am a very
villain. Come, and be hang'd! Hast no faith
in thee?   35

Enter *Gadshill.*

  Gads. Good morrow, carriers. What's
o'clock?
  1. Car. I think it be two o'clock.
  Gads. I prithee lend me thy lantern to see my
gelding in the stable.   39
  1. Car. Nay, by God, soft! I know a trick
worth two of that, i' faith.
  Gads. I pray thee lend me thine.
  2. Car. Ay, when? canst tell? Lend me thy
lantern, quoth he? Marry, I'll see thee hang'd
first!   45
  Gads. Sirrah carrier, what time do you mean
to come to London?
  2. Car. Time enough to go to bed with a
candle, I warrant thee. Come, neighbour
Mugs, we'll call up the gentlemen. They will
along with company, for they have great
charge.   *Exeunt* [*Carriers*].
  Gads. What, ho! chamberlain!   52

Enter *Chamberlain.*

  Cham. At hand, quoth pickpurse.
  Gads. That's even as fair as — 'at hand,
quoth the chamberlain'; for thou variest no

more from picking of purses than giving direction doth from labouring: thou layest the plot how.   57

Cham. Good morrow, Master Gadshill. It holds current that I told you yesternight. There's a franklin in the Wild of Kent hath brought three hundred marks with him in gold. I heard him tell it to one of his company last night at supper — a kind of auditor; one that hath abundance of charge too, God knows what. They are up already and call for eggs and butter. They will away presently.   66

Gads. Sirrah, if they meet not with Saint Nicholas' clerks, I'll give thee this neck.

Cham. No, I'll none of it. I pray thee keep that for the hangman; for I know thou worshippest Saint Nicholas as truly as a man of falsehood may.   72

Gads. What talkest thou to me of the hangman? If I hang, I'll make a fat pair of gallows; for if I hang, old Sir John hangs with me, and thou knowest he is no starveling. Tut! there are other Troyans that thou dream'st not of, the which for sport sake are content to do the profession some grace; that would (if matters should be look'd into) for their own credit sake make all whole. I am joined with no foot landrakers, no long-staff sixpenny strikers, none of these mad mustachio purple-hued maltworms; but with nobility and tranquillity, burgomasters and great oneyers, such as can hold in, such as will strike sooner than speak, and speak sooner than drink, and drink sooner than pray; and yet, zounds, I lie; for they pray continually to their saint, the commonwealth, or rather, not pray to her, but prey on her, for they ride up and down on her and make her their boots.   91

Cham. What, the commonwealth their boots? Will she hold out water in foul way?

Gads. She will, she will! Justice hath liquor'd her. We steal as in a castle, cocksure. We have the receipt of fernseed, we walk invisible.

Cham. Nay, by my faith, I think you are more beholding to the night than to fernseed for your walking invisible.   99

Gads. Give me thy hand. Thou shalt have a share in our purchase, as I am a true man.

Cham. Nay, rather let me have it, as you are a false thief.

Gads. Go to; 'homo' is a common name to all men. Bid the ostler bring my gelding out of the stable. Farewell, you muddy knave.   106

Exeunt.

Scene II. [*The highway near Gadshill.*]

Enter *Prince* and *Poins.*

Poins. Come, shelter, shelter! I have remov'd Falstaff's horse, and he frets like a gumm'd velvet.

Prince. Stand close.   [*They step aside.*]

Enter *Falstaff.*

Fal. Poins! Poins, and be hang'd! Poins!

Prince. [*comes forward*] Peace, ye fat-kidney'd rascal! What a brawling dost thou keep!

Fal. Where's Poins, Hal?   7

Prince. He is walk'd up to the top of the hill. I'll go seek him.   [*Steps aside.*]

Fal. I am accurs'd to rob in that thief's company. The rascal hath removed my horse and tied him I know not where. If I travel but four foot by the squire further afoot, I shall break my wind. Well, I doubt not but to die a fair death for all this, if I scape hanging for killing that rogue. I have forsworn his company hourly any time this two-and-twenty years, and yet I am bewitch'd with the rogue's company. If the rascal have not given me medicines to make me love him, I'll be hang'd. It could not be else. I have drunk medicines. Poins! Hal! A plague upon you both! Bardolph! Peto! I'll starve ere I'll rob a foot further. An 'twere not as good a deed as drink to turn true man and to leave these rogues, I am the veriest varlet that ever chewed with a tooth. Eight yards of uneven ground is threescore and ten miles afoot with me, and the stony-hearted villains know it well enough. A plague upon it when thieves cannot be true one to another! (*They whistle.*) Whew! A plague upon you all! Give me my horse, you rogues! give me my horse and be hang'd!   32

Prince. [*comes forward*] Peace, ye fat-guts! Lie down, lay thine ear close to the ground, and list if thou canst hear the tread of travellers.

Fal. Have you any levers to lift me up again, being down? 'Sblood, I'll not bear mine own flesh so far afoot again for all the coin in thy father's exchequer. What a plague mean ye to colt me thus?   40

Prince. Thou liest; thou art not colted, thou art uncolted.

Fal. I prithee, good Prince Hal, help me to my horse, good king's son.   44

Prince. Out, ye rogue! Shall I be your ostler?

Fal. Go hang thyself in thine own heir-apparent garters! If I be ta'en, I'll peach for

this. An I have not ballads made on you all,
and sung to filthy tunes, let a cup of sack be my
poison. When a jest is so forward — and afoot
too — I hate it.   50

Enter *Gadshill*, [*Bardolph* and *Peto* with him].

Gads. Stand!
Fal. So I do, against my will.
Poins. [*comes forward*] O, 'tis our setter. I
know his voice. Bardolph, what news?   54
Bar. Case ye, case ye! On with your vizards!
There's money of the King's coming down the
hill; 'tis going to the King's exchequer.
Fal. You lie, ye rogue! 'Tis going to the
King's tavern.
Gads. There's enough to make us all.   60
Fal. To be hang'd.
Prince. Sirs, you four shall front them in the
narrow lane; Ned Poins and I will walk lower.
If they scape from your encounter, then they
light on us.   65
Peto. How many be there of them?
Gads. Some eight or ten.
Fal. Zounds, will they not rob us?
Prince. What, a coward, Sir John Paunch?
Fal. Indeed, I am not John of Gaunt, your
grandfather; but yet no coward, Hal.   71
Prince. Well, we leave that to the proof.
Poins. Sirrah Jack, thy horse stands behind
the hedge. When thou need'st him, there thou
shalt find him. Farewell and stand fast.   75
Fal. Now cannot I strike him, if I should be
hang'd.
Prince. [*aside to Poins*] Ned, where are our
disguises?
Poins. [*aside to Prince*] Here, hard by.
Stand close.   [*Exeunt Prince and Poins.*]
Fal. Now, my masters, happy man be his
dole, say I. Every man to his business.   81

Enter the *Travellers*.

Traveller. Come, neighbour.
The boy shall lead our horses down the hill;
We'll walk afoot awhile and ease our legs.
Thieves. Stand!   85
Traveller. Jesus bless us!
Fal. Strike! down with them! cut the vil-
lains' throats! Ah, whoreson caterpillars! ba-
con-fed knaves! they hate us youth. Down
with them! fleece them!   90
Traveller. O, we are undone, both we and
ours for ever!
Fal. Hang ye, gorbellied knaves, are ye un-
done? No, ye fat chuffs; I would your store
were here! On, bacons, on! What, ye knaves!

young men must live. You are grandjurors,
are ye? We'll jure ye, faith!   97
Here they rob and bind them. Exeunt.

Enter the *Prince* and *Poins* [in buckram suits].

Prince. The thieves have bound the true
men. Now could thou and I rob the thieves
and go merrily to London, it would be argument for a week, laughter for a month, and a
good jest for ever.   102
Poins. Stand close! I hear them coming.
                              [*They stand aside.*]

Enter the *Thieves* again.

Fal. Come, my masters, let us share, and
then to horse before day. An the Prince and
Poins be not two arrant cowards, there's no
equity stirring. There's no more valour in that
Poins than in a wild duck.   108

Prince. Your money! } ⎧ As they are sharing,
Poins. Villains!   } ⎜ the Prince and Poins
                           ⎜ set upon them. They
                           ⎨ all run away, and
                           ⎜ Falstaff, after a blow
                           ⎜ or two, runs away
                           ⎜ too, leaving the booty
                           ⎩ behind them.

Prince. Got with much ease. Now merrily
to horse.   111
The thieves are scattered, and possess'd with
fear
So strongly that they dare not meet each other.
Each takes his fellow for an officer.
Away, good Ned. Falstaff sweats to death 115
And lards the lean earth as he walks along.
Were't not for laughing, I should pity him.
Poins. How the rogue roar'd!   *Exeunt.*

Scene III. [*Warkworth Castle.*]

Enter *Hotspur* solus, reading a letter.

Hot. 'But, for mine own part, my lord, I
could be well contented to be there, in respect
of the love I bear your house.' He could be contented — why is he not then? In respect of the
love he bears our house! He shows in this he
loves his own barn better than he loves our
house. Let me see some more. 'The purpose
you undertake is dangerous' — Why, that's
certain! 'Tis dangerous to take a cold, to sleep,
to drink; but I tell you, my lord fool, out of
this nettle, danger, we pluck this flower, safety.
'The purpose you undertake is dangerous, the
friends you have named uncertain, the time

itself unsorted, and your whole plot too light
for the counterpoise of so great an opposition.'
Say you so, say you so? I say unto you again,
you are a shallow, cowardly hind, and you lie.
What a lack-brain is this! By the Lord, our
plot is a good plot as ever was laid; our friends
true and constant: a good plot, good friends,
and full of expectation; an excellent plot, very
good friends. What a frosty-spirited rogue is
this! Why, my Lord of York commends the
plot and the general course of the action.
Zounds, an I were now by this rascal, I could
brain him with his lady's fan. Is there not my
father, my uncle, and myself; Lord Edmund
Mortimer, my Lord of York, and Owen Glendower? Is there not, besides, the Douglas?
Have I not all their letters to meet me in arms
by the ninth of the next month, and are they
not some of them set forward already? What a
pagan rascal is this! an infidel! Ha! you shall
see now, in very sincerity of fear and cold heart
will he to the King and lay open all our proceedings. O, I could divide myself and go to buffets
for moving such a dish of skim milk with so
honourable an action! Hang him, let him tell
the King! we are prepared. I will set forward
to-night.   38

Enter his *Lady.*

How now, Kate? I must leave you within
   these two hours.
   Lady. O my good lord, why are you thus
      alone?
For what offence have I this fortnight been
A banish'd woman from my Harry's bed?
Tell me, sweet lord, what is't that takes from
   thee
Thy stomach, pleasure, and thy golden sleep?
Why dost thou bend thine eyes upon the earth,
And start so often when thou sit'st alone?   46
Why hast thou lost the fresh blood in thy cheeks
And given my treasures and my rights of thee
To thick-ey'd musing and curs'd melancholy?
In thy faint slumbers I by thee have watch'd,
And heard thee murmur tales of iron wars,   51
Speak terms of manage to thy bounding steed,
Cry 'Courage! to the field!' And thou hast
   talk'd
Of sallies and retires, of trenches, tents,
Of palisadoes, frontiers, parapets,   55
Of basilisks, of cannon, culverin,
Of prisoners' ransom, and of soldiers slain,
And all the currents of a heady fight.
Thy spirit within thee hath been so at war,
And thus hath so bestirr'd thee in thy sleep, 60

That beads of sweat have stood upon thy brow
Like bubbles in a late-disturbed stream,
And in thy face strange motions have appear'd,
Such as we see when men restrain their breath
On some great sudden hest. O, what portents
   are these?   65
Some heavy business hath my lord in hand,
And I must know it, else he loves me not.
   Hot. What, ho!

      [Enter a *Servant.*]
               Is Gilliams with the packet gone?
   Serv. He is, my lord, an hour ago.
   Hot. Hath Butler brought those horses from
      the sheriff?   70
   Serv. One horse, my lord, he brought even
      now.
   Hot. What horse? A roan, a crop-ear, is it
      not?
   Serv. It is, my lord.
   Hot.   That roan shall be my throne.
Well, I will back him straight. O esperance!
Bid Butler lead him forth into the park.   75
                              [*Exit Servant.*]
   Lady. But hear you, my lord.
   Hot. What say'st thou, my lady?
   Lady. What is it carries you away?
   Hot. Why, my horse, my love — my horse!
   Lady. Out, you mad-headed ape!   80
A weasel hath not such a deal of spleen
As you are toss'd with. In faith,
I'll know your business, Harry; that I will!
I fear my brother Mortimer doth stir
About his title and hath sent for you   85
To line his enterprise; but if you go —
   Hot. So far afoot, I shall be weary, love.
   Lady. Come, come, you paraquito, answer
      me
Directly unto this question that I ask.
In faith, I'll break thy little finger, Harry, 90
An if thou wilt not tell me all things true.
   Hot. Away,
Away, you trifler! Love? I love thee not;
I care not for thee, Kate. This is no world
To play with mammets and to tilt with lips. 95
We must have bloody noses and crack'd crowns,
And pass them current too. Gods me, my
   horse!
What say'st thou, Kate? What wouldst thou
   have with me?
   Lady. Do you not love me? do you not
      indeed?
Well, do not then; for since you love me not,
I will not love myself. Do you not love me? 101
Nay, tell me if you speak in jest or no.

Hot. Come, wilt thou see me ride?
And when I am a-horseback, I will swear
I love thee infinitely. But hark you, Kate: 105
I must not have you henceforth question me
Whither I go, nor reason whereabout.
Whither I must, I must; and to conclude,
This evening must I leave you, gentle Kate.
I know you wise; but yet no farther wise 110
Than Harry Percy's wife; constant you are,
But yet a woman; and for secrecy,
No lady closer, for I well believe
Thou wilt not utter what thou dost not know,
And so far will I trust thee, gentle Kate. 115
Lady. How? so far?
Hot. Not an inch further. But hark you,
Kate:
Whither I go, thither shall you go too;
To-day will I set forth, to-morrow you. 119
Will this content you, Kate?
Lady. It must of force. *Exeunt.*

Scene IV. [*Eastcheap. The Boar's Head Tavern.*]

Enter *Prince* and *Poins.*

Prince. Ned, prithee come out of that fat-room and lend me thy hand to laugh a little.
Poins. Where hast been, Hal?
Prince. With three or four loggerheads amongst three or fourscore hogsheads. I have sounded the very bass-string of humility. Sirrah, I am sworn brother to a leash of drawers and can call them all by their christen names, as Tom, Dick, and Francis. They take it already upon their salvation that, though I be but Prince of Wales, yet I am the king of courtesy; and tell me flatly I am no proud Jack like Falstaff, but a Corinthian, a lad of mettle, a good boy (by the Lord, so they call me!), and when I am King of England I shall command all the good lads in Eastcheap. They call drinking deep, dying scarlet; and when you breathe in your watering, they cry 'hem!' and bid you play it off. To conclude, I am so good a proficient in one quarter of an hour that I can drink with any tinker in his own language during my life. I tell thee, Ned, thou hast lost much honour that thou wert not with me in this action. But, sweet Ned — to sweeten which name of Ned, I give thee this pennyworth of sugar, clapp'd even now into my hand by an under-skinker, one that never spake other English in his life than 'Eight

shillings and sixpence,' and 'You are welcome,' with this shrill addition, 'Anon, anon, sir! Score a pint of bastard in the Half-moon,' or so — but, Ned, to drive away the time till Falstaff come, I prithee do thou stand in some by-room while I question my puny drawer to what end he gave me the sugar; and do thou never leave calling 'Francis!' that his tale to me may be nothing but 'Anon!' Step aside, and I'll show thee a precedent. 37
Poins. Francis!
Prince. Thou art perfect.
Poins. Francis! [*Exit Poins.*]

Enter [*Francis,* a] Drawer.

Fran. Anon, anon, sir. — Look down into the Pomgarnet, Ralph.
Prince. Come hither, Francis.
Fran. My lord?
Prince. How long hast thou to serve, Francis? 45
Fran. Forsooth, five years, and as much as to —
Poins. [*within*] Francis!
Fran. Anon, anon, sir. 49
Prince. Five year! by'r Lady, a long lease for the clinking of pewter. But, Francis, darest thou be so valiant as to play the coward with thy indenture and show it a fair pair of heels and run from it? 54
Fran. O Lord, sir, I'll be sworn upon all the books in England I could find in my heart —
Poins. [*within*] Francis!
Fran. Anon, anon, sir.
Prince. How old art thou, Francis?
Fran. Let me see. About Michaelmas next I shall be — 61
Poins. [*within*] Francis!
Fran. Anon, sir. Pray stay a little, my lord.
Prince. Nay, but hark you, Francis. For the sugar thou gavest me — 'twas a penny-worth, was't not? 66
Fran. O Lord! I would it had been two!
Prince. I will give thee for it a thousand pound. Ask me when thou wilt, and thou shalt have it. 70
Poins. [*within*] Francis!
Fran. Anon, anon.
Prince. Anon, Francis? No, Francis; but to-morrow, Francis; or, Francis, a Thursday; or indeed, Francis, when thou wilt. But Francis — 75
Fran. My lord?
Prince. Wilt thou rob this leathern-jerkin, crystal-button, not-pated, agate-ring, puke-

stocking, caddis-garter, smooth-tongue, Span-
ish-pouch —   80
Fran. O Lord, sir, who do you mean?
Prince. Why then, your brown bastard is
your only drink; for look you, Francis, your
white canvas doublet will sully. In Barbary,
sir, it cannot come to so much.   85
Fran. What, sir?
Poins. [*within*] Francis!
Prince. Away, you rogue! Dost thou not
hear them call?   89
*Here they both call him. The Drawer stands
amazed, not knowing which way to go.*

Enter *Vintner*.

Vint. What, stand'st thou still, and hear'st
such a calling? Look to the guests within.
[*Exit Francis.*] My lord, old Sir John, with half-
a-dozen more, are at the door. Shall I let
them in?   94
Prince. Let them alone awhile, and then
open the door. [*Exit Vintner.*] Poins!
Poins. [*within*] Anon, anon, sir.

Enter *Poins*.

Prince. Sirrah, Falstaff and the rest of the
thieves are at the door. Shall we be merry? 99
Poins. As merry as crickets, my lad. But
hark ye; what cunning match have you made
with this jest of the drawer? Come, what's
the issue?
Prince. I am now of all humours that have
showed themselves humours since the old days
of goodman Adam to the pupil age of this
present twelve o'clock at midnight.   107

[Enter *Francis*.]

What's o'clock, Francis?
Fran. Anon, anon, sir.   [*Exit.*]
Prince. That ever this fellow should have
fewer words than a parrot, and yet the son of
a woman! His industry is upstairs and down-
stairs, his eloquence the parcel of a reckoning.
I am not yet of Percy's mind, the Hotspur of
the North; he that kills me some six or seven
dozen of Scots at a breakfast, washes his
hands, and says to his wife, 'Fie upon this
quiet life! I want work.' 'O my sweet Harry,'
says she, 'how many hast thou kill'd to-day?'
'Give my roan horse a drench,' says he, and
answers 'Some fourteen,' an hour after, 'a
trifle, a trifle.' I prithee call in Falstaff. I'll
play Percy, and that damn'd brawn shall play
Dame Mortimer his wife. 'Rivo!' says the
drunkard. Call in ribs, call in tallow.   125

Enter *Falstaff*, [*Gadshill, Bardolph,* and *Peto;
Francis* follows with wine].

Poins. Welcome, Jack. Where hast thou
been?
Fal. A plague of all cowards, I say, and a
vengeance too! Marry and amen! Give me a
cup of sack, boy. Ere I lead this life long,
I'll sew nether-stocks, and mend them and foot
them too. A plague of all cowards! Give me
a cup of sack, rogue. Is there no virtue extant?
He drinketh.
Prince. Didst thou never see Titan kiss a
dish of butter? Pitiful-hearted butter, that
melted at the sweet tale of the sun! If thou
didst, then behold that compound.   136
Fal. You rogue, here's lime in this sack too!
There is nothing but roguery to be found in
villanous man. Yet a coward is worse than a
cup of sack with lime in it — a villanous coward! Go thy ways, old Jack, die when thou
wilt; if manhood, good manhood, be not forgot upon the face of the earth, then am I a
shotten herring. There lives not three good men
unhang'd in England; and one of them is fat,
and grows old. God help the while! A bad
world, I say. I would I were a weaver; I could
sing psalms or anything. A plague of all cowards I say still!
Prince. How now, woolsack? What mutter
you?   149
Fal. A king's son! If I do not beat thee
out of thy kingdom with a dagger of lath and
drive all thy subjects afore thee like a flock of
wild geese, I'll never wear hair on my face more.
You Prince of Wales?
Prince. Why, you whoreson round man,
what's the matter?   156
Fal. Are not you a coward? Answer me to
that — and Poins there?
Poins. Zounds, ye fat paunch, an ye call
me coward, by the Lord, I'll stab thee.   160
Fal. I call thee coward? I'll see thee damn'd
ere I call thee coward, but I would give a
thousand pound I could run as fast as thou
canst. You are straight enough in the shoulders; you care not who sees your back. Call
you that backing of your friends? A plague
upon such backing! Give me them that will
face me. Give me a cup of sack. I am a rogue
if I drunk to-day.
Prince. O villain! thy lips are scarce wip'd
since thou drunk'st last.   171
Fal. All is one for that. (*He drinketh.*) A
plague of all cowards still say I.

Prince. What's the matter?   174

Fal. What's the matter? There be four of us here have ta'en a thousand pound this day morning.

Prince. Where is it, Jack? Where is it?

Fal. Where is it? Taken from us it is. A hundred upon poor four of us!   18θ

Prince. What, a hundred, man?

Fal. I am a rogue if I were not at half-sword with a dozen of them two hours together. I have scap'd by miracle. I am eight times thrust through the doublet, four through the hose; ı v buckler cut through and through; my sword hack'd like a handsaw — ecce signum! I never dealt better since I was a man. All would not do. A plague of all cowards! Let them speak. If they speak more or less than ᵗruth, they are villains and the sons of darkness.

Prince. Speak, sirs. How was it?

Gads. We four set upon some dozen —

Fal. Sixteen at least, my lord.

Gads. And bound them.   195

Peto. No, no, they were not bound.

Fal. You rogue, they were bound, every man of them, or I am a Jew else — an Ebrew Jew.

Gads. As we were sharing, some six or seven fresh men set upon us —   200

Fal. And unbound the rest, and then come in the other.

Prince. What, fought you with them all?

Fal. All? I know not what you call all, but if I fought not with fifty of them, I am a bunch of radish! If there were not two or three and fifty upon poor old Jack, then am I no two-legg'd creature.

Prince. Pray God you have not murd'red some of them.   210

Fal. Nay, that's past praying for. I have pepper'd two of them. Two I am sure I have paid, two rogues in buckram suits. I tell thee what, Hal — if I tell thee a lie, spit in my face, call me horse. Thou knowest my old ward. Here I lay, and thus I bore my point. Four rogues in buckram let drive at me.

Prince. What, four? Thou saidst but two even now.

Fal. Four, Hal. I told thee four.   220

Poins. Ay, ay, he said four.

Fal. These four came all afront and mainly thrust at me. I made me no more ado but took all their seven points in my target, thus.

Prince. Seven? Why, there were but four even now.   226

Fal. In buckram?

Poins. Ay, four, in buckram suits.

Fal. Seven, by these hilts, or I am a villain else.   230

Prince. [*aside to Poins*] Prithee let him alone. We shall have more anon.

Fal. Dost thou hear me, Hal?

Prince. Ay, and mark thee too, Jack.

Fal. Do so, for it is worth the list'ning to. These nine in buckram that I told thee of —

Prince. So, two more already.

Fal. Their points being broken —

Poins. Down fell their hose.   239

Fal. Began to give me ground; but I followed me close, came in, foot and hand, and with a thought seven of the eleven I paid.

Prince. O monstrous! Eleven buckram men grown out of two!   244

Fal. But, as the devil would have it, three misbegotten knaves in Kendal green came at my back and let drive at me; for it was so dark, Hal, that thou couldst not see thy hand.

Prince. These lies are like their father that begets them — gross as a mountain, open, palpable. Why, thou clay-brain'd guts, thou knotty-pated fool, thou whoreson obscene greasy tallow-catch —

Fal. What, art thou mad? art thou mad? Is not the truth the truth?   255

Prince. Why, how couldst thou know these men in Kendal green when it was so dark thou couldst not see thy hand? Come, tell us your reason. What sayest thou to this?   259

Poins. Come, your reason, Jack, your reason.

Fal. What, upon compulsion? Zounds, an I were at the strappado or all the racks in the world, I would not tell you on compulsion. Give you a reason on compulsion? If reasons were as plentiful as blackberries, I would give no man a reason upon compulsion, I.   266

Prince. I'll be no longer guilty of this sin; this sanguine coward, this bed-presser, this horseback-breaker, this huge hill of flesh — 269

Fal. 'Sblood, you starveling, you elf-skin, you dried neat's-tongue, you bull's pizzle, you stockfish — O for breath to utter what is like thee! — you tailor's yard, you sheath, you bowcase, you vile standing tuck!   274

Prince. Well, breathe awhile, and then to it again; and when thou hast tired thyself in base comparisons, hear me speak but this.

Poins. Mark, Jack.   278

Prince. We two saw you four set on four, and bound them and were masters of their wealth. Mark now how a plain tale shall put you down. Then did we two set on you four and, with a word, outfac'd you from your prize, and have it

Falstaff (Paul Rogers), enthroned, chides Prince Hal (Robert Hardy) for his antics

HENRY IV
PART ONE

PHOTOGRAPHS BY HOUSTON ROGERS
PRODUCED BY THE OLD VIC COMPANY

Henry Percy, surnamed Hotspur, son to the Earl of Northumberland. Outspoken, manly, easily provoked, and eager "To pluck bright honour from the pale-fac'd moon" (*Act I, Scene III*). His rebuke from Henry IV leads him to think of war

Hotspur (John Neville), rebuked for not surrendering prisoners (*Act I, Scene III*). *Left to right:* Hotspur; Northumberland (Laurence Hardy); the king; Blunt (Daniel Thorndike)

Engaged in banter, Falstaff justi-
fies purse-taking to an attentive
Prince. "Why, Hal, 'tis my vocation, Hal; 'tis no sin for a man to
labour in his vocation"
(Act I, Scene II)

Hotspur's wife (Ann Todd), unaware of his plans for rebellion,
seeks to discover the cause of
her husband's unrest. "I must
know it, else he loves me not"
(Act II, Scene III)

Amoral, irrepressible, cunning, crafty, witty, and fat, Falstaff is jestingly characterized by his friend, Prince Hal, as "That villanous abominable misleader of youth" (Act II, Scene IV)

Lady Mortimer (Virginia McKenna), the wife of Edmund Mortimer, brother-in-law to Hotspur. An additional injury was felt by Hotspur in his interview with the king when Mortimer was accused of treason (Act I, Scene III)

"The hope and expectation of thy time is ruin'd, and the soul of every man prophetically do forethink thy fall." Henry IV (Eric Porter) to his son (Act III, Scene II)

Slow to forsake completely his former companions and way of life, the Prince rejoins the carefree Falstaff at the Boar's Head Tavern (Act III, Scene III)

The Welsh rebel and dreamer, Owen Glendower, calls on the musicians to accompany his daughter, Lady Mortimer, as she sings a Welsh song (*Act III, Scene I*)

The rebels, Worcester (Paul Daneman), Mortimer (Anthony White), Hotspur, and Glendower (Meredith Edwards), plot to divide a country they have not yet won (Act III, Scene I)

The king's camp near Shrewsbury before the battle with the rebels (Act V, Scene I). The king, his sons—Prince Hal at his right, John of Lancaster (Alan Dobie) at his left— and his followers in an act of dedication

"Two stars keep not their motion in one sphere." Prince Henry slays Hotspur (Act V, Scene IV)

Henry, Prince of Wales, reformed. "So, when this loose behaviour throw off . . . my reformation, glittering o'er my fault, shall show more goodly" (Act I, Scene II)

yea, and can show it you here in the house. And, Falstaff, you carried your guts away as nimbly, with as quick dexterity, and roar'd for mercy, and still run and roar'd, as ever I heard bullcalf. What a slave art thou to hack thy sword as thou hast done, and then say it was in fight! What trick, what device, what starting hole canst thou now find out to hide thee from this open and apparent shame?

Poins. Come, let's hear, Jack. What trick hast thou now? 294

Fal. By the Lord, I knew ye as well as he that made ye. Why, hear you, my masters. Was it for me to kill the heir apparent? Should I turn upon the true prince? Why, thou knowest I am as valiant as Hercules; but beware instinct. The lion will not touch the true prince. Instinct is a great matter. I was now a coward on instinct. I shall think the better of myself, and thee, during my life — I for a valiant lion, and thou for a true prince. But, by the Lord, lads, I am glad you have the money. Hostess, clap to the doors. Watch to-night, pray to-morrow. Gallants, lads, boys, hearts of gold, all the titles of good fellowship come to you! What, shall we be merry? Shall we have a play extempore? 309

Prince. Content — and the argument shall be thy running away.

Fal. Ah, no more of that, Hal, an thou lovest me!

Enter *Hostess.*

Host. O Jesu, my lord the Prince! 314

Prince. How now, my lady the hostess? What say'st thou to me?

Host. Marry, my lord, there is a nobleman of the court at door would speak with you. He says he comes from your father. 319

Prince. Give him as much as will make him a royal man, and send him back again to my mother.

Fal. What manner of man is he?

Host. An old man.

Fal. What doth gravity out of his bed at midnight? Shall I give him his answer? 326

Prince. Prithee do, Jack.

Fal. Faith, and I'll send him packing.

Exit.

Prince. Now, sirs. By'r lady, you fought fair; so did you, Peto; so did you, Bardolph. You are lions too, you ran away upon instinct, you will not touch the true prince; no — fie!

Bard. Faith, I ran when I saw others run.

Prince. Tell me now in earnest, how came Falstaff's sword so hack'd? 335

Peto. Why, he hack'd it with his dagger, and said he would swear truth out of England but he would make you believe it was done in fight, and persuaded us to do the like. 339

Bard. Yea, and to tickle our noses with speargrass to make them bleed, and then to beslubber our garments with it and swear it was the blood of true men. I did that I did not this seven year before — I blush'd to hear his monstrous devices. 344

Prince. O villain! thou stolest a cup of sack eighteen years ago and wert taken with the manner, and ever since thou hast blush'd extempore. Thou hadst fire and sword on thy side, and yet thou ran'st away. What instinct hadst thou for it? 350

Bard. My lord, do you see these meteors? Do you behold these exhalations?

Prince. I do.

Bard. What think you they portend?

Prince. Hot livers and cold purses. 355

Bard. Choler, my lord, if rightly taken.

Prince. No, if rightly taken, halter.

Enter *Falstaff.*

Here comes lean Jack; here comes bare-bone. How now, my sweet creature of bombast? How long is't ago, Jack, since thou sawest thine own knee? 361

Fal. My own knee? When I was about thy years, Hal, I was not an eagle's talent in the waist; I could have crept into any alderman's thumb-ring. A plague of sighing and grief! It blows a man up like a bladder. There's villanous news abroad. Here was Sir John Bracy from your father. You must to the court in the morning. That same mad fellow of the North, Percy, and he of Wales that gave Amamon the bastinado, and made Lucifer cuckold, and swore the devil his true liegeman upon the cross of a Welsh hook — what a plague call you him?

Poins. O, Glendower. 374

Fal. Owen, Owen — the same; and his son-in-law Mortimer, and old Northumberland, and that sprightly Scot of Scots, Douglas, that runs a-horseback up a hill perpendicular —

Prince. He that rides at high speed and with his pistol kills a sparrow flying. 380

Fal. You have hit it.

Prince. So did he never the sparrow.

Fal. Well, that rascal hath good metal in him; he will not run. 384

Prince. Why, what a rascal art thou then, to praise him so for running!

Fal. A-horseback, ye cuckoo! but afoot he will not budge a foot.

Prince. Yes, Jack, upon instinct.   389

Fal. I grant ye, upon instinct. Well, he is there too, and one Mordake, and a thousand bluecaps more. Worcester is stol'n away to-night; thy father's beard is turn'd white with the news; you may buy land now as cheap as stinking mack'rel.   395

Prince. Why then, it is like, if there come a hot June, and this civil buffeting hold, we shall buy maidenheads as they buy hobnails, by the hundreds.   399

Fal. By the mass, lad, thou sayest true; it is like we shall have good trading that way. But tell me, Hal, art not thou horrible afeard? Thou being heir apparent, could the world pick thee out three such enemies again as that fiend Douglas, that spirit Percy, and that devil Glendower? Art thou not horribly afraid? Doth not thy blood thrill at it?   407

Prince. Not a whit, i' faith. I lack some of thy instinct.

Fal. Well, thou wilt be horribly chid to-morrow when thou comest to thy father. If thou love me, practise an answer.   412

Prince. Do thou stand for my father and examine me upon the particulars of my life.

Fal. Shall I? Content. This chair shall be my state, this dagger my sceptre, and this cushion my crown.   417

Prince. Thy state is taken for a join'd-stool, thy golden sceptre for a leaden dagger, and thy precious rich crown for a pitiful bald crown.

Fal. Well, an the fire of grace be not quite out of thee, now shalt thou be moved. Give me a cup of sack to make my eyes look red, that it may be thought I have wept; for I must speak in passion, and I will do it in King Cambyses' vein.   426

Prince. Well, here is my leg.

Fal. And here is my speech. Stand aside, nobility.   429

Host. O Jesu, this is excellent sport, i' faith!

Fal. Weep not, sweet queen, for trickling tears are vain.

Host. O, the Father, how he holds his countenance!

Fal. For God's sake, lords, convey my tristful queen!   434

For tears do stop the floodgates of her eyes.

Host. O Jesu, he doth it as like one of these harlotry players as ever I see!

Fal. Peace, good pintpot. Peace, good tickle-brain. — Harry, I do not only marvel where thou spendest thy time, but also how thou art accompanied. For though the camomile, the more it is trodden on, the faster it grows, yet youth, the more it is wasted, the sooner it wears. That thou art my son I have partly thy mother's word, partly my own opinion, but chiefly a villanous trick of thine eye and a foolish hanging of thy nether lip that doth warrant me. If then thou be son to me, here lies the point: why, being son to me, art thou so pointed at? Shall the blessed sun of heaven prove a micher and eat blackberries? A question not to be ask'd. Shall the son of England prove a thief and take purses? A question to be ask'd. There is a thing, Harry, which thou hast often heard of, and it is known to many in our land by the name of pitch. This pitch, as ancient writers do report, doth defile; so doth the company thou keepest. For, Harry, now I do not speak to thee in drink, but in tears; not in pleasure, but in passion; not in words only, but in woes also: and yet there is a virtuous man whom I have often noted in thy company, but I know not his name.   461

Prince. What manner of man, an it like your Majesty?

Fal. A goodly portly man, i' faith, and a corpulent; of a cheerful look, a pleasing eye, and a most noble carriage; and, as I think, his age some fifty, or, by'r Lady, inclining to threescore; and now I remember me, his name is Falstaff. If that man should be lewdly given, he deceiveth me; for, Harry, I see virtue in his looks. If then the tree may be known by the fruit, as the fruit by the tree, then, peremptorily I speak it, there is virtue in that Falstaff. Him keep with, the rest banish. And tell me now, thou naughty varlet, tell me where hast thou been this month?   475

Prince. Dost thou speak like a king? Do thou stand for me, and I'll play my father.

Fal. Depose me? If thou dost it half so gravely, so majestically, both in word and matter, hang me up by the heels for a rabbit-sucker or a poulter's hare.   481

Prince. Well, here I am set.

Fal. And here I stand. Judge, my masters.

Prince. Now, Harry, whence come you?

Fal. My noble lord, from Eastcheap.   485

Prince. The complaints I hear of thee are grievous.

Fal. 'Sblood, my lord, they are false! Nay, I'll tickle ye for a young prince, i' faith.   489

Prince. Swearest thou, ungracious boy? Henceforth ne'er look on me. Thou art violently carried away from grace. There is a devil haunts thee in the likeness of an old fat man; a tun of man is thy companion. Why dost thou converse with that trunk of humours, that bolting hutch of beastliness, that swoll'n parcel of dropsies, that huge bombard of sack, that stuff'd cloakbag of guts, that roasted Manningtree ox with the pudding in his belly, that reverend vice, that grey iniquity, that father ruffian, that vanity in years? Wherein is he good, but to taste sack and drink it? wherein neat and cleanly, but to carve a capon and eat it? wherein cunning, but in craft? wherein crafty, but in villany? wherein villanous, but in all things? wherein worthy, but in nothing?   505

Fal. I would your Grace would take me with you. Whom means your Grace?

Prince. That villanous abominable misleader of youth, Falstaff, that old white-bearded Satan.

Fal. My lord, the man I know.   510

Prince. I know thou dost.

Fal. But to say I know more harm in him than in myself were to say more than I know. That he is old (the more the pity) his white hairs do witness it; but that he is (saving your reverence) a whoremaster, that I utterly deny. If sack and sugar be a fault, God help the wicked! If to be old and merry be a sin, then many an old host that I know is damn'd. If to be fat be to be hated, then Pharaoh's lean kine are to be loved. No, my good lord. Banish Peto, banish Bardolph, banish Poins; but for sweet Jack Falstaff, kind Jack Falstaff, true Jack Falstaff, valiant Jack Falstaff, and therefore more valiant being, as he is, old Jack Falstaff, banish not him thy Harry's company, banish not him thy Harry's company. Banish plump Jack, and banish all the world!   527

Prince. I do, I will.   [*A knocking heard.*]
      [*Exeunt Hostess, Francis, and Bardolph.*]

Enter *Bardolph*, running.

Bard. O, my lord, my lord! the sheriff with a most monstrous watch is at the door.   530

Fal. Out, ye rogue! Play out the play. I have much to say in the behalf of that Falstaff.

Enter the *Hostess.*

Host. O Jesu, my lord, my lord!

Prince. Heigh, heigh, the devil rides upon a fiddlestick! What's the matter?   535

Host. The sheriff and all the watch are at the door. They are come to search the house. Shall I let them in?

Fal. Dost thou hear, Hal? Never call a true piece of gold a counterfeit. Thou art essentially mad without seeming so.   541

Prince. And thou a natural coward without instinct.

Fal. I deny your major. If you will deny the sheriff, so; if not, let him enter. If I become not a cart as well as another man, a plague on my bringing up! I hope I shall as soon be strangled with a halter as another.

Prince. Go hide thee behind the arras. The rest walk up above. Now, my masters, for a true face and good conscience.   551

Fal. Both which I have had; but their date is out, and therefore I'll hide me.   *Exit.*

Prince. Call in the sheriff.
      [*Exeunt. Manent the Prince and Peto.*]

Enter *Sheriff* and the *Carrier.*

Now, Master Sheriff, what is your will with me?

Sher. First, pardon me, my lord. A hue and cry   556
Hath followed certain men unto this house.

Prince. What men?

Sher. One of them is well known, my gracious lord —
A gross fat man.

Carrier.   As fat as butter.   560

Prince. The man, I do assure you, is not here,
For I myself at this time have employ'd him.
And, sheriff, I will engage my word to thee
That I will by to-morrow dinner time
Send him to answer thee, or any man,   565
For anything he shall be charg'd withal;
And so let me entreat you leave the house.

Sher. I will, my lord. There are two gentlemen
Have in this robbery lost three hundred marks.

Prince. It may be so. If he have robb'd these men,   570
He shall be answerable; and so farewell.

Sher. Good night, my noble lord.

Prince. I think it is good morrow, is it not?

Sher. Indeed, my lord, I think it be two o'clock.   *Exit* [*with Carrier*].

Prince. This oily rascal is known as well as Paul's. Go call him forth.   576

Peto. Falstaff! Fast asleep behind the arras, and snorting like a horse.

Prince. Hark how hard he fetches breath.
Search his pockets.   580
He searcheth his pockets and findeth certain
papers.
What hast thou found?
Peto. Nothing but papers, my lord.
Prince. Let's see what they be. Read them.

Peto. [*reads*] 'Item, A capon . . ii s. ii d.
Item, Sauce . . . iiii d.
Item, Sack two gallons v s. viii d.
Item, Anchovies and
    Sack after supper . ii s. vi d.
Item, Bread . . ob.'

Prince. O monstrous! but one halfpenny-
worth of bread to this intolerable deal of sack!
What there is else, keep close; we'll read it at
more advantage. There let him sleep till day.
I'll to the court in the morning. We must all
to the wars, and thy place shall be honourable.
I'll procure this fat rogue a charge of foot;
and I know his death will be a march of twelve
score. The money shall be paid back again
with advantage. Be with me betimes in the
morning, and so good morrow, Peto.   601
Peto. Good morrow, good my lord.
                                        Exeunt.

Act III. Scene I. [*Bangor. The Archdeacon's house.*]

Enter *Hotspur, Worcester, Lord Mortimer,*
    Owen Glendower.

Mort. These promises are fair, the parties
    sure,
And our induction full of prosperous hope.
Hot. Lord Mortimer, and cousin Glendower,
Will you sit down?
And uncle Worcester. A plague upon it!   5
I have forgot the map.
Glend.   No, here it is.
Sit, cousin Percy; sit, good cousin Hotspur,
For by that name as oft as Lancaster
Doth speak of you, his cheek looks pale, and
    with
A rising sigh he wisheth you in heaven.   10
Hot. And you in hell, as oft as he hears
Owen Glendower spoke of.
Glend. I cannot blame him. At my nativity
The front of heaven was full of fiery shapes
Of burning cressets, and at my birth   15
The frame and huge foundation of the earth
Shak'd like a coward.
Hot. Why, so it would have done at the same
season, if your mother's cat had but kitten'd,
though yourself had never been born.   20
Glend. I say the earth did shake when I was
    born.
Hot. And I say the earth was not of my mind,
If you suppose as fearing you it shook.
Glend. The heavens were all on fire, the
    earth did tremble.
Hot. O, then the earth shook to see the heav-
    ens on fire,   25
And not in fear of your nativity.
Diseased nature oftentimes breaks forth
In strange eruptions; oft the teeming earth
Is with a kind of colic pinch'd and vex'd

By the imprisoning of unruly wind   30
Within her womb, which, for enlargement striv-
    ing,
Shakes the old beldame earth and topples down
Steeples and mossgrown towers. At your birth
Our grandam earth, having this distemp'rature,
In passion shook.
Glend.   Cousin, of many men   35
I do not bear these crossings. Give me leave
To tell you once again that at my birth
The front of heaven was full of fiery shapes,
The goats ran from the mountains, and the
    herds
Were strangely clamorous to the frighted fields.
These signs have mark'd me extraordinary,   41
And all the courses of my life do show
I am not in the roll of common men.
Where is he living, clipp'd in with the sea
That chides the banks of England, Scotland,
    Wales,   45
Which calls me pupil or hath read to me?
And bring him out that is but woman's son
Can trace me in the tedious ways of art
And hold me pace in deep experiments.
Hot. I think there's no man speaks better
Welsh. I'll to dinner.   51
Mort. Peace, cousin Percy; you will make
    him mad.
Glend. I can call spirits from the vasty
    deep.
Hot. Why, so can I, or so can any man;
But will they come when you do call for
    them?   55
Glend. Why, I can teach you, cousin, to
    command
The devil.
Hot. And I can teach thee, coz, to shame the
    devil —

By telling truth. Tell truth and shame the
   devil.
If thou have power to raise him, bring him
   hither,   60
And I'll be sworn I have power to shame him
   hence.
O, while you live, tell truth and shame the devil!
   Mort. Come, come, no more of this unprofit-
   able chat.
   Glend. Three times hath Henry Bolingbroke
   made head
Against my power; thrice from the banks of
   Wye   65
And sandy-bottom'd Severn have I sent him
Bootless home and weather-beaten back.
   Hot. Home without boots, and in foul
   weather too?
How scapes he agues, in the devil's name?
   Glend. Come, here's the map. Shall we di-
   vide our right   70
According to our threefold order ta'en?
   Mort. The Archdeacon hath divided it
Into three limits very equally.
England, from Trent and Severn hitherto,
By south and east is to my part assign'd;   75
All westward, Wales beyond the Severn shore,
And all the fertile land within that bound,
To Owen Glendower; and, dear coz, to you
The remnant northward lying off from Trent.
And our indentures tripartite are drawn;   80
Which being sealed interchangeably
(A business that this night may execute),
To-morrow, cousin Percy, you and I
And my good Lord of Worcester will set forth
To meet your father and the Scottish power,   85
As is appointed us, at Shrewsbury.
My father Glendower is not ready yet,
Nor shall we need his help these fourteen days.
[*To Glend.*] Within that space you may have
   drawn together
Your tenants, friends, and neighbouring gentle-
   men.   90
   Glend. A shorter time shall send me to you,
   lords;
And in my conduct shall your ladies come,
From whom you now must steal and take no
   leave,
For there will be a world of water shed
Upon the parting of your wives and you.   95
   Hot. Methinks my moiety, north from Bur-
   ton here,
In quantity equals not one of yours.
See how this river comes me cranking in
And cuts me from the best of all my land
A huge half-moon, a monstrous cantle out.   100

I'll have the current in this place damm'd up,
And here the smug and silver Trent shall run
In a new channel fair and evenly.
It shall not wind with such a deep indent
To rob me of so rich a bottom here.   105
   Glend. Not wind? It shall, it must! You see
   it doth.
   Mort. Yea, but
Mark how he bears his course, and runs me up
With like advantage on the other side,
Gelding the opposed continent as much   110
As on the other side it takes from you.
   Wor. Yea, but a little charge will trench him
   here
And on this north side win this cape of land:
And then he runs straight and even.   114
   Hot. I'll have it so. A little charge will do it.
   Glend. I will not have it alt'red.
   Hot.   Will not you?
   Glend. No, nor you shall not.
   Hot.   Who shall say me nay?
   Glend. Why, that will I.
   Hot. Let me not understand you then; speak
   it in Welsh.   120
   Glend. I can speak English, lord, as well as
   you;
For I was train'd up in the English court,
Where, being but young, I framed to the harp
Many an English ditty lovely well,
And gave the tongue a helpful ornament —   125
A virtue that was never seen in you.
   Hot. Marry,
And I am glad of it with all my heart!
I had rather be a kitten and cry mew   129
Than one of these same metre ballet-mongers.
I had rather hear a brazen canstick turn'd
Or a dry wheel grate on the axletree,
And that would set my teeth nothing on edge,
Nothing so much as mincing poetry.
'Tis like the forc'd gait of a shuffling nag.   135
   Glend. Come, you shall have Trent turn'd.
   Hot. I do not care. I'll give thrice so much
   land
To any well-deserving friend;
But in the way of bargain, mark ye me,
I'll cavil on the ninth part of a hair.   140
Are the indentures drawn? Shall we be gone?
   Glend. The moon shines fair; you may away
   by night.
I'll haste the writer, and withal
Break with your wives of your departure hence.
I am afraid my daughter will run mad,   145
So much she doteth on her Mortimer.   *Exit*
   Mort. Fie, cousin Percy! how you cross my
   father!

Hot. I cannot choose. Sometime he angers me
With telling me of the moldwarp and the ant,
Of the dreamer Merlin and his prophecies, 150
And of a dragon and a finless fish,
A clip-wing'd griffin and a moulten raven,
A couching lion and a ramping cat,
And such a deal of skimble-skamble stuff 154
As puts me from my faith. I tell you what —
He held me last night at least nine hours
In reckoning up the several devils' names
That were his lackeys. I cried 'hum,' and 'Well, go to!'
But mark'd him not a word. O, he is as tedious
As a tired horse, a railing wife; 160
Worse than a smoky house. I had rather live
With cheese and garlic in a windmill far
Than feed on cates and have him talk to me
In any summer house in Christendom. 164
Mort. In faith, he is a worthy gentleman,
Exceedingly well read, and profited
In strange concealments, valiant as a lion,
And wondrous affable, and as bountiful
As mines of India. Shall I tell you, cousin?
He holds your temper in a high respect 170
And curbs himself even of his natural scope
When you come 'cross his humour. Faith, he does.
I warrant you that man is not alive
Might so have tempted him as you have done
Without the taste of danger and reproof. 175
But do not use it oft, let me entreat you.
Wor. In faith, my lord, you are too wilful-blame,
And since your coming hither have done enough
To put him quite besides his patience.
You must needs learn, lord, to amend this fault.
Though sometimes it show greatness, courage, blood — 181
And that's the dearest grace it renders you —
Yet oftentimes it doth present harsh rage,
Defect of manners, want of government,
Pride, haughtiness, opinion, and disdain; 185
The least of which haunting a nobleman
Loseth men's hearts, and leaves behind a stain
Upon the beauty of all parts besides,
Beguiling them of commendation.
Hot. Well, I am school'd. Good manners be your speed! 190
Here come our wives, and let us take our leave.

Enter *Glendower* with the *Ladies.*

Mort. This is the deadly spite that angers me —
My wife can speak no English, I no Welsh.

Glend. My daughter weeps; she will not part with you;
She'll be a soldier too, she'll to the wars. 195
Mort. Good father, tell her that she and my aunt Percy
Shall follow in your conduct speedily.

Glendower speaks to her in Welsh, and she answers him in the same.

Glend. She is desperate here. A peevish self-will'd harlotry,
One that no persuasion can do good upon.

The Lady speaks in Welsh.

Mort. I understand thy looks. That pretty Welsh 200
Which thou pourest down from these swelling heavens
I am too perfect in; and, but for shame,
In such a parley should I answer thee.

The Lady again in Welsh.

I understand thy kisses, and thou mine,
And that's a feeling disputation. 205
But I will never be a truant, love,
Till I have learnt thy language; for thy tongue
Makes Welsh as sweet as ditties highly penn'd,
Sung by a fair queen in a summer's bow'r,
With ravishing division, to her lute. 210
Glend. Nay, if you melt, then will she run mad.

The Lady speaks again in Welsh.

Mort. O, I am ignorance itself in this!
Glend. She bids you on the wanton rushes lay you down
And rest your gentle head upon her lap,
And she will sing the song that pleaseth you 215
And on your eyelids crown the god of sleep,
Charming your blood with pleasing heaviness,
Making such difference 'twixt wake and sleep
As is the difference betwixt day and night 219
The hour before the heavenly-harness'd team
Begins his golden progress in the East.
Mort. With all my heart I'll sit and hear her sing.
By that time will our book, I think, be drawn.
Glend.   Do so,
And those musicians that shall play to you
Hang in the air a thousand leagues from hence, 225
And straight they shall be here. Sit, and attend.
Hot. Come, Kate, thou art perfect in lying down. Come, quick, quick, that I may lay my head in thy lap. 229
Lady. Go, ye giddy goose.

The music plays.

Hot. Now I perceive the devil understands Welsh;

94

And 'tis no marvel, he is so humorous.
By'r Lady, he is a good musician.

Lady P. Then should you be nothing but musical; for you are altogether govern'd by humours. Lie still, ye thief, and hear the lady sing
in Welsh.   237

Hot. I had rather hear Lady, my brach, howl
in Irish.

Lady P. Wouldst thou have thy head broken?

Hot. No.   241

Lady P. Then be still.

Hot. Neither! 'Tis a woman's fault.

Lady P. Now God help thee!

Hot. To the Welsh lady's bed.   245

Lady P. What's that?

Hot. Peace! she sings.
            Here the Lady sings a Welsh song.
Come, Kate, I'll have your song too.

Lady P. Not mine, in good sooth.   249

Hot. Not yours, in good sooth? Heart! you
swear like a comfit-maker's wife. 'Not you, in
good sooth!' and 'as true as I live!' and 'as God
shall mend me!' and 'as sure as day!'   253
And givest such sarcenet surety for thy oaths
As if thou ne'er walk'st further than Finsbury.
Swear me, Kate, like a lady as thou art,
A good mouth-filling oath; and leave 'in
      sooth'
And such protest of pepper gingerbread
To velvet guards and Sunday citizens.
Come, sing.   260

Lady P. I will not sing.

Hot. 'Tis the next way to turn tailor or
be redbreast-teacher. An the indentures be
drawn, I'll away within these two hours; and
so come in when ye will.   *Exit.*

Glend. Come, come, Lord Mortimer. You
are as slow
As hot Lord Percy is on fire to go.
By this our book is drawn; we'll but seal,
And then to horse immediately.

Mort.   With all my heart.   269
                                    Exeunt.

Scene II. [*London. The Palace.*]

Enter the *King, Prince of Wales,* and others.

King. Lords, give us leave. The Prince of
Wales and I
Must have some private conference; but be
      near at hand,
For we shall presently have need of you.
                            Exeunt Lords.

I know not whether God will have it so,
For some displeasing service I have done,   5
That, in his secret doom, out of my blood
He'll breed revengement and a scourge for me;
But thou dost in thy passages of life
Make me believe that thou art only mark'd
For the hot vengeance and the rod of heaven
To punish my misreadings. Tell me else,   1i
Could such inordinate and low desires,
Such poor, such bare, such lewd, such mean
      attempts,
Such barren pleasures, rude society,
As thou art match'd withal and grafted to,   15
Accompany the greatness of thy blood
And hold their level with thy princely heart?

Prince. So please your Majesty, I would I
      could
Quit all offences with as clear excuse
As well as I am doubtless I can purge   20
Myself of many I am charg'd withal.
Yet such extenuation let me beg
As, in reproof of many tales devis'd,
Which oft the ear of greatness needs must hear
By smiling pickthanks and base newsmongers,
I may, for some things true wherein my youth
Hath faulty wand'red and irregular,
Find pardon on my true submission.

King. God pardon thee! Yet let me wonder,
      Harry,
At thy affections, which do hold a wing   30
Quite from the flight of all thy ancestors.
Thy place in Council thou hast rudely lost,
Which by thy younger brother is supplied,
And art almost an alien to the hearts
Of all the court and princes of my blood.   35
The hope and expectation of thy time
Is ruin'd, and the soul of every man
Prophetically do forethink thy fall.
Had I so lavish of my presence been,
So common-hackney'd in the eyes of men,   40
So stale and cheap to vulgar company,
Opinion, that did help me to the crown,
Had still kept loyal to possession
And left me in reputeless banishment,
A fellow of no mark nor likelihood.   45
By being seldom seen, I could not stir
But, like a comet, I was wond'red at;
That men would tell their children, 'This is he!'
Others would say, 'Where? Which is Boling-
      broke?'
And then I stole all courtesy from heaven,   50
And dress'd myself in such humility
That I did pluck allegiance from men's hearts,
Loud shouts and salutations from their mouths
Even in the presence of the crowned King.

Thus did I keep my person fresh and new,   55
My presence, like a robe pontifical,
Ne'er seen but wond'red at; and so my state,
Seldom but sumptuous, show'd like a feast
And won by rareness such solemnity.
The skipping King, he ambled up and down   60
With shallow jesters and rash bavin wits,
Soon kindled and soon burnt; carded his state;
Mingled his royalty with cap'ring fools;
Had his great name profaned with their scorns
And gave his countenance, against his name,
To laugh at gibing boys and stand the push
Of every beardless vain comparative;
Grew a companion to the common streets,
Enfeoff'd himself to popularity;
That, being daily swallowed by men's eyes,   70
They surfeited with honey and began
To loathe the taste of sweetness, whereof a little
More than a little is by much too much.
So, when he had occasion to be seen,
He was but as the cuckoo is in June,   75
Heard, not regarded — seen, but with such eyes
As, sick and blunted with community,
Afford no extraordinary gaze,
Such as is bent on sunlike majesty
When it shines seldom in admiring eyes;   80
But rather drows'd and hung their eyelids down,
Slept in his face, and rend'red such aspect
As cloudy men use to their adversaries,
Being with his presence glutted, gorg'd, and full.
And in that very line, Harry, standest thou;
For thou hast lost thy princely privilege   86
With vile participation. Not an eye
But is aweary of thy common sight,
Save mine, which hath desir'd to see thee more;
Which now doth that I would not have it do —
Make blind itself with foolish tenderness.   91
    Prince. I shall hereafter, my thrice-gracious lord,
Be more myself.
    King.   For all the world,
As thou art to this hour, was Richard then
When I from France set foot at Ravenspurgh;
And even as I was then is Percy now.   96
Now, by my sceptre, and my soul to boot,
He hath more worthy interest to the state
Than thou, the shadow of succession;
For of no right, nor colour like to right,   100
He doth fill fields with harness in the realm,
Turns head against the lion's armed jaws,
And, being no more in debt to years than thou,
Leads ancient lords and reverend bishops on
To bloody battles and to bruising arms.   105

What never-dying honour hath he got
Against renowmed Douglas! whose high deeds,
Whose hot incursions and great name in arms
Holds from all soldiers chief majority
And military title capital   110
Through all the kingdoms that acknowledge
    Christ.
Thrice hath this Hotspur, Mars in swathling clothes,
This infant warrior, in his enterprises
Discomfited great Douglas; ta'en him once,
Enlarged him, and made a friend of him,   115
To fill the mouth of deep defiance up
And shake the peace and safety of our throne.
And what say you to this? Percy, Northumberland,
The Archbishop's Grace of York, Douglas, Mortimer
Capitulate against us and are up.   120
But wherefore do I tell these news to thee?
Why, Harry, do I tell thee of my foes,
Which art my nearest and dearest enemy?
Thou that art like enough, through vassal fear,
Base inclination, and the start of spleen,   125
To fight against me under Percy's pay,
To dog his heels and curtsy at his frowns,
To show how much thou art degenerate.
    Prince. Do not think so. You shall not find
    it so.   129
And God forgive them that so much have sway'd
Your Majesty's good thoughts away from me!
I will redeem all this on Percy's head
And, in the closing of some glorious day,
Be bold to tell you that I am your son,
When I will wear a garment all of blood,   135
And stain my favours in a bloody mask,
Which, wash'd away, shall scour my shame with it.
And that shall be the day, whene'er it lights,
That this same child of honour and renown,
This gallant Hotspur, this all-praised knight,
And your unthought-of Harry chance to meet.
For every honour sitting on his helm,
Would they were multitudes, and on my head
My shames redoubled! For the time will come
That I shall make this Northern youth exchange   145
His glorious deeds for my indignities.
Percy is but my factor, good my lord,
To engross up glorious deeds on my behalf;
And I will call him to so strict account
That he shall render every glory up,   150
Yea, even the slightest worship of his time,
Or I will tear the reckoning from his heart.
This in the name of God I promise here;

The which if he be pleas'd I shall perform,
I do beseech your Majesty may salve   155
The long-grown wounds of my intemperance.
If not, the end of life cancels all bands,
And I will die a hundred thousand deaths
Ere break the smallest parcel of this vow.
  King. A hundred thousand rebels die in this!
Thou shalt have charge and sovereign trust
    herein.   161

                  Enter Blunt.

How now, good Blunt? Thy looks are full of
    speed.
  Blunt. So hath the business that I come to
speak of.
Lord Mortimer of Scotland hath sent word
That Douglas and the English rebels met   165
The eleventh of this month at Shrewsbury.
A mighty and a fearful head they are,
If promises be kept on every hand,
As ever off'red foul play in a state.
  King. The Earl of Westmoreland set forth
    to-day;   170
With him my son, Lord John of Lancaster;
For this advertisement is five days old.
On Wednesday next, Harry, you shall set for-
    ward;
On Thursday we ourselves will march. Our
    meeting   174
Is Bridgenorth; and, Harry, you shall march
Through Gloucestershire; by which account,
Our business valued, some twelve days hence
Our general forces at Bridgenorth shall meet.
Our hands are full of business. Let's away.
Advantage feeds him fat while men delay.   180
                                     Exeunt.

Scene III. [*Eastcheap. The Boar's Head Tavern.*]

Enter *Falstaff* and *Bardolph.*

  Fal. Bardolph, am I not fall'n away vilely
since this last action? Do I not bate? Do I not
dwindle? Why, my skin hangs about me like an
old lady's loose gown! I am withered like an old
apple John. Well, I'll repent, and that suddenly,
while I am in some liking. I shall be out of heart
shortly, and then I shall have no strength to repent. An I have not forgotten what the inside
of a church is made of, I am a peppercorn, a
brewer's horse. The inside of a church! Company, villanous company, hath been the spoil
of me.   12

  Bard. Sir John, you are so fretful you cannot
live long.
  Fal. Why, there is it! Come, sing me a
bawdy song; make me merry. I was as virtu-
ously given as a gentleman need to be, virtuous
enough: swore little, dic'd not above seven
times a week, went to a bawdy house not above
once in a quarter — of an hour, paid money
that I borrowed — three or four times, lived
well, and in good compass; and now I live out
of all order, out of all compass.
  Bard. Why, you are so fat, Sir John, that you
must needs be out of all compass — out of all
reasonable compass, Sir John.   26
  Fal. Do thou amend thy face, and I'll amend
my life. Thou art our admiral, thou bearest the
lantern in the poop — but 'tis in the nose of
thee. Thou art the Knight of the Burning
Lamp.   30
  Bard. Why, Sir John, my face does you no
harm.
  Fal. No, I'll be sworn. I make as good use of
it as many a man doth of a death's-head or a
memento mori. I never see thy face but I think
upon hellfire and Dives that lived in purple; for
there he is in his robes, burning, burning. If
thou wert any way given to virtue, I would
swear by thy face; my oath should be 'By this
fire, that's God's angel.' But thou art altogether given over, and wert indeed, but for the
light in thy face, the son of utter darkness.
When thou ran'st up Gadshill in the night to
catch my horse, if I did not think thou hadst
been an ignis fatuus or a ball of wildfire, there's
no purchase in money. O, thou art a perpetual
triumph, an everlasting bonfire-light! Thou
hast saved me a thousand marks in links and
torches, walking with thee in the night betwixt
tavern and tavern; but the sack that thou hast
drunk me would have bought me lights as good
cheap at the dearest chandler's in Europe. I
have maintained that salamander of yours with
fire any time this two-and-thirty years. God
reward me for it!   55
  Bard. 'Sblood, I would my face were in your
belly!
  Fal. God-a-mercy! so should I be sure to be
heart-burn'd.

Enter *Hostess.*

How now, Dame Partlet the hen? Have you
enquir'd yet who pick'd my pocket?   61
  Host. Why, Sir John, what do you think, Sir
John? Do you think I keep thieves in my
house? I have search'd, I have enquired, so has

my husband, man by man, boy by boy, servant by servant. The tithe of a hair was never lost in my house before. 67

Fal. Ye lie, hostess. Bardolph was shav'd and lost many a hair, and I'll be sworn my pocket was pick'd. Go to, you are a woman, go!

Host. Who, I? No; I defy thee! God's light, I was never call'd so in mine own house before! 72

Fal. Go to, I know you well enough.

Host. No, Sir John; you do not know me, Sir John. I know you, Sir John. You owe me money, Sir John, and now you pick a quarrel to beguile me of it. I bought you a dozen of shirts to your back. 78

Fal. Dowlas, filthy dowlas! I have given them away to bakers' wives; they have made bolters of them. 81

Host. Now, as I am a true woman, holland of eight shillings an ell. You owe money here besides, Sir John, for your diet and by-drinkings, and money lent you, four-and-twenty pound.

Fal. He had his part of it; let him pay. 87

Host. He? Alas, he is poor; he hath nothing.

Fal. How? Poor? Look upon his face. What call you rich? Let them coin his nose, let them coin his cheeks. I'll not pay a denier. What, will you make a younker of me? Shall I not take mine ease in mine inn but I shall have my pocket pick'd? I have lost a seal-ring of my grandfather's worth forty mark. 95

Host. O Jesu, I have heard the Prince tell him, I know not how oft, that that ring was copper!

Fal. How? the Prince is a Jack, a sneak-cup. 'Sblood, an he were here, I would cudgel him like a dog if he would say so. 101

Enter the *Prince* [and *Poins*], marching; and *Falstaff* meets them, playing upon his truncheon like a fife.

How now, lad? Is the wind in that door, i' faith? Must we all march?

Bard. Yea, two and two, Newgate fashion.

Host. My lord, I pray you hear me. 105

Prince. What say'st thou, Mistress Quickly? How doth thy husband? I love him well; he is an honest man.

Host. Good my lord, hear me.

Fal. Prithee let her alone and list to me. 110

Prince. What say'st thou, Jack?

Fal. The other night I fell asleep here behind the arras and had my pocket pick'd. This house is turn'd bawdy house; they pick pockets.

Prince. What didst thou lose, Jack? 115

Fal. Wilt thou believe me, Hal? Three or four bonds of forty pound apiece and a seal-ring of my grandfather's.

Prince. A trifle, some eightpenny matter.

Host. So I told him, my lord, and I said I heard your Grace say so; and, my lord, he speaks most vilely of you, like a foul-mouth'd man as he is, and said he would cudgel you.

Prince. What! he did not? 124

Host. There's neither faith, truth, nor womanhood in me else.

Fal. There's no more faith in thee than in a stewed prune, nor no more truth in thee than in a drawn fox; and for womanhood, Maid Marian may be the deputy's wife of the ward to thee. Go, you thing, go! 131

Host. Say, what thing? what thing?

Fal. What thing? Why, a thing to thank God on. 134

Host. I am no thing to thank God on, I would thou shouldst know it! I am an honest man's wife, and, setting thy knighthood aside, thou art a knave to call me so.

Fal. Setting thy womanhood aside, thou art a beast to say otherwise. 140

Host. Say, what beast, thou knave, thou?

Fal. What beast? Why, an otter.

Prince. An otter, Sir John? Why an otter?

Fal. Why, she's neither fish nor flesh; a man knows not where to have her. 145

Host. Thou art an unjust man in saying so. Thou or any man knows where to have me, thou knave, thou!

Prince. Thou say'st true, hostess, and he slanders thee most grossly. 150

Host. So he doth you, my lord, and said this other day you ought him a thousand pound.

Prince. Sirrah, do I owe you a thousand pound? 154

Fal. A thousand pound, Hal? A million! Thy love is worth a million; thou owest me thy love.

Host. Nay, my lord, he call'd you Jack and said he would cudgel you.

Fal. Did I, Bardolph? 160

Bard. Indeed, Sir John, you said so.

Fal. Yea, if he said my ring was copper.

Prince. I say 'tis copper. Darest thou be as good as thy word now? 164

Fal. Why, Hal, thou knowest, as thou art but man, I dare; but as thou art Prince, I fear thee as I fear the roaring of the lion's whelp.

Prince. And why not as the lion? 168

Fal. The King himself is to be feared as the lion. Dost thou think I'll fear thee as I fear thy father? Nay, an I do, I pray God my girdle break. 171

Prince. O, if it should, how would thy guts fall about thy knees! But, sirrah, there's no room for faith, truth, nor honesty in this bosom of thine. It is all fill'd up with guts and midriff. Charge an honest woman with picking thy pocket? Why, thou whoreson, impudent, emboss'd rascal, if there were anything in thy pocket but tavern reckonings, memorandums of bawdy houses, and one poor pennyworth of sugar candy to make thee long-winded — if thy pocket were enrich'd with any other injuries but these, I am a villain. And yet you will stand to it; you will not pocket up wrong. Art thou not ashamed? 184

Fal. Dost thou hear, Hal? Thou knowest in the state of innocency Adam fell; and what should poor Jack Falstaff do in the days of villany? Thou seest I have more flesh than another man, and therefore more frailty. You confess then, you pick'd my pocket? 190

Prince. It appears so by the story.

Fal. Hostess, I forgive thee. Go make ready breakfast. Love thy husband, look to thy servants, cherish thy guests. Thou shalt find me tractable to any honest reason. Thou seest I am pacified. — Still? — Nay, prithee be gone. (*Exit Hostess.*) Now, Hal, to the news at court. For the robbery, lad — how is that answered?

Prince. O my sweet beef, I must still be good angel to thee. The money is paid back again.

Fal. O, I do not like that paying back! 'Tis a double labour.

Prince. I am good friends with my father, and may do anything. 204

Fal. Rob me the exchequer the first thing thou doest, and do it with unwash'd hands too.

Bard. Do, my lord.

Prince. I have procured thee, Jack, a charge of foot. 209

Fal. I would it had been of horse. Where shall I find one that can steal well? O for a fine thief of the age of two-and-twenty or thereabouts! I am heinously unprovided. Well, God be thanked for these rebels. They offend none but the virtuous. I laud them, I praise them.

Prince. Bardolph! 216

Bard. My lord?

Prince. Go bear this letter to Lord John of Lancaster,
To my brother John; this to my Lord of Westmoreland. 219
[*Exit Bardolph.*]
Go, Poins, to horse, to horse; for thou and I
Have thirty miles to ride yet ere dinner time.
[*Exit Poins.*]
Jack, meet me to-morrow in the Temple Hall
At two o'clock in the afternoon.
There shalt thou know thy charge, and there receive
Money and order for their furniture. 225
The land is burning; Percy stands on high;
And either they or we must lower lie. [*Exit.*]

Fal. Rare words! brave world! Hostess, my breakfast, come.
O, I could wish this tavern were my drum! 229
Exit.

ACT IV. Scene I. [*The rebel camp near Shrewsbury.*]

Enter *Harry Hotspur, Worcester,* and *Douglas.*

Hot. Well said, my noble Scot. If speaking truth
In this fine age were not thought flattery,
Such attribution should the Douglas have
As not a soldier of this season's stamp
Should go so general current through the world.
By God, I cannot flatter, I defy 6
The tongues of soothers! but a braver place
In my heart's love hath no man than yourself.
Nay, task me to my word; approve me, lord.

Doug. Thou art the king of honour. 10
No man so potent breathes upon the ground
But I will beard him.

Enter *one with letters.*

Hot. Do so, and 'tis well.—
What letters hast thou there? — I can but thank you.

Messenger. These letters come from your father.

Hot. Letters from him? Why comes he not himself? 15

Mess. He cannot come, my lord; he is grievous sick.

Hot. Zounds! how has he the leisure to be sick
In such a justling time? Who leads his power?
Under whose government come they along?

Mess. His letters bears his mind, not I, my
　　lord.　　　　　　　　　　　　　　　　20
Wor. I prithee tell me, doth he keep his bed?
Mess. He did, my lord, four days ere I set
　　forth,
And at the time of my departure thence
He was much fear'd by his physicians.
　　Wor. I would the state of time had first
　　been whole　　　　　　　　　　　　　25
Ere he by sickness had been visited.
His health was never better worth than now.
　　Hot. Sick now? droop now? This sickness
　　doth infect
The very lifeblood of our enterprise.
'Tis catching hither, even to our camp.　　30
He writes me here that inward sickness —
And that his friends by deputation could not
So soon be drawn; nor did he think it meet
To lay so dangerous and dear a trust
On any soul remov'd but on his own.　　35
Yet doth he give us bold advertisement,
That with our small conjunction we should on,
To see how fortune is dispos'd to us;
For, as he writes, there is no quailing now,
Because the King is certainly possess'd　　40
Of all our purposes. What say you to it?
　　Wor. Your father's sickness is a maim to us.
　　Hot. A perilous gash, a very limb lopp'd off.
And yet, in faith, it is not! His present want
Seems more than we shall find it. Were it good
To set the exact wealth of all our states　　46
All at one cast? to set so rich a main
On the nice hazard of one doubtful hour?
It were not good; for therein should we read
The very bottom and the soul of hope,　　50
The very list, the very utmost bound
Of all our fortunes.
　　Doug.　　　　　Faith, and so we should;
Where now remains a sweet reversion.
We may boldly spend upon the hope of what
Is to come in.　　　　　　　　　　　55
A comfort of retirement lives in this.
　　Hot. A rendezvous, a home to fly unto,
If that the devil and mischance look big
Upon the maidenhead of our affairs.
　　Wor. But yet I would your father had been
　　here.　　　　　　　　　　　　　　60
The quality and hair of our attempt
Brooks no division. It will be thought
By some that know not why he is away,
That wisdom, loyalty, and mere dislike
Of our proceedings kept the Earl from hence.
And think how such an apprehension　　66
May turn the tide of fearful faction
And breed a kind of question in our cause.

For well you know we of the off'ring side
Must keep aloof from strict arbitrement,　　70
And stop all sight-holes, every loop from whence
The eye of reason may pry in upon us.
This absence of your father's draws a curtain
That shows the ignorant a kind of fear
Before not dreamt of.
　　Hot.　　　　　You strain too far.　　75
I rather of his absence make this use:
It lends a lustre and more great opinion,
A larger dare to our great enterprise,
Than if the Earl were here; for men must think,
If we, without his help, can make a head　　80
To push against a kingdom, with his help
We shall o'erturn it topsy-turvy down.
Yet all goes well; yet all our joints are whole.
　　Doug. As heart can think. There is not such
　　a word
Spoke of in Scotland as this term of fear.　　85

Enter *Sir Richard Vernon.*

　　Hot. My cousin Vernon! welcome, by my
　　soul.
　　Ver. Pray God my news be worth a welcome,
　　lord.
The Earl of Westmoreland, seven thousand
　　strong,
Is marching hitherwards; with him Prince
　　John.
　　Hot. No harm. What more?
　　Ver.　　　　　And further, I have learn'd　90
The King himself in person is set forth,
Or hitherwards intended speedily,
With strong and mighty preparation.
　　Hot. He shall be welcome too. Where is his
　　son,
The nimble-footed madcap Prince of Wales,　95
And his comrades, that daff'd the world aside
And bid it pass?
　　Ver.　　　　All furnish'd, all in arms;
All plum'd like estridges that with the wind
Bated like eagles having lately bath'd;
Glittering in golden coats like images;　　100
As full of spirit as the month of May
And gorgeous as the sun at midsummer;
Wanton as youthful goats, wild as young bulls.
I saw young Harry with his beaver on,
His cushes on his thighs, gallantly arm'd,　105
Rise from the ground like feathered Mercury,
And vaulted with such ease into his seat
As if an angel dropp'd down from the clouds
To turn and wind a fiery Pegasus
And witch the world with noble horsemanship.
　　Hot. No more, no more! Worse than the sun
　　in March,　　　　　　　　　　　　111

This praise doth nourish agues. Let them come.
They come like sacrifices in their trim,
And to the fire-ey'd maid of smoky war
All hot and bleeding will we offer them.   115
The mailed Mars shall on his altar sit
Up to the ears in blood. I am on fire
To hear this rich reprisal is so nigh,
And yet not ours. Come, let me taste my horse,
Who is to bear me like a thunderbolt   120
Against the bosom of the Prince of Wales.
Harry to Harry shall, hot horse to horse,
Meet, and ne'er part till one drop down a corse.
O that Glendower were come!

Ver.   There is more news.
I learn'd in Worcester, as I rode along,   125
He cannot draw his power this fourteen days.

Doug. That's the worst tidings that I hear
of yet.

Wor. Ay, by my faith, that bears a frosty
sound.

Hot. What may the King's whole battle
reach unto?

Ver. To thirty thousand.

Hot.   Forty let it be.   130
My father and Glendower being both away,
The powers of us may serve so great a day.
Come, let us take a muster speedily.
Doomsday is near. Die all, die merrily.

Doug. Talk not of dying. I am out of fear
Of death or death's hand for this one half-year.
                                        Exeunt.

Scene II. [*A public road near Coventry.*]

Enter *Falstaff* and *Bardolph.*

Fal. Bardolph, get thee before to Coventry;
fill me a bottle of sack. Our soldiers shall march
through. We'll to Sutton Co'fil' to-night.

Bard. Will you give me money, Captain?

Fal. Lay out, lay out.   5

Bard. This bottle makes an angel.

Fal. An if it do, take it for thy labour; an
if it make twenty, take them all; I'll answer
the coinage. Bid my lieutenant Peto meet me
at town's end.   10

Bard. I will, Captain. Farewell.   *Exit.*

Fal. If I be not ashamed of my soldiers, I
am a sous'd gurnet. I have misused the King's
press damnably. I have got, in exchange of a
hundred and fifty soldiers, three hundred and
odd pounds. I press me none but good house-
holders, yeomen's sons; inquire me out contracted bachelors, such as had been ask'd twice
on the banes — such a commodity of warm

slaves as had as lieve hear the devil as a drum;
such as fear the report of a caliver worse than
a struck fowl or a hurt wild duck. I press'd
me none but such toasts-and-butter, with hearts
in their bellies no bigger than pins' heads, and
they have bought out their services; and now
my whole charge consists of ancients, corporals,
lieutenants, gentlemen of companies — slaves
as ragged as Lazarus in the painted cloth,
where the glutton's dogs licked his sores; and
such as indeed were never soldiers, but discarded unjust servingmen, younger sons to
younger brothers, revolted tapsters, and ostlers
trade-fall'n; the cankers of a calm world and
a long peace; ten times more dishonourable
ragged than an old fac'd ancient; and such
have I to fill up the rooms of them that have
bought out their services that you would think
that I had a hundred and fifty tattered Prodi-
gals lately come from swine-keeping, from eating draff and husks. A mad fellow met me on
the way, and told me I had unloaded all the
gibbets and press'd the dead bodies. No eye
hath seen such scarecrows. I'll not march
through Coventry with them, that's flat. Nay,
and the villains march wide betwixt the legs,
as if they had gyves on; for indeed I had the
most of them out of prison. There's but a
shirt and a half in all my company; and the
half-shirt is two napkins tack'd together and
thrown over the shoulders like a herald's coat
without sleeves; and the shirt, to say the
truth, stol'n from my host at Saint Alban's, or
the red-nose innkeeper of Daventry. But that's
all one; they'll find linen enough on every
hedge.   52

Enter the *Prince* and the *Lord of Westmoreland.*

Prince. How now, blown Jack? How now,
quilt?

Fal. What, Hal? How now, mad wag?
What a devil dost thou in Warwickshire? My
good Lord of Westmoreland, I cry you mercy.
I thought your honour had already been at
Shrewsbury.   59

West. Faith, Sir John, 'tis more than time
that I were there, and you too; but my powers
are there already. The King, I can tell you,
looks for us all. We must away all, to-night.

Fal. Tut, never fear me. I am as vigilant
as a cat to steal cream.   65

Prince. I think, to steal cream indeed, for
thy theft hath already made thee butter. But
tell me, Jack, whose fellows are these that come
after?

Fal. Mine, Hal, mine.   69
Prince. I did never see such pitiful rascals.
Fal. Tut, tut! good enough to toss; food
for powder, food for powder. They'll fill a pit
as well as better. Tush, man, mortal men,
mortal men.
West. Ay, but, Sir John, methinks they are
exceeding poor and bare — too beggarly.   75
Fal. Faith, for their poverty, I know not
where they had that; and for their bareness,
I am sure they never learn'd that of me.
Prince. No, I'll be sworn, unless you call
three fingers on the ribs bare. But, sirrah,
make haste. Percy is already in the field.   81
                                            Exit.
Fal. What, is the King encamp'd?
West. He is, Sir John. I fear we shall stay
too long.   [*Exit.*]
Fal. Well,
To the latter end of a fray and the beginning of
a feast   85
Fits a dull fighter and a keen guest.   *Exit.*

Scene III. [*The rebel camp near Shrewsbury.*]

Enter *Hotspur, Worcester, Douglas, Vernon.*

Hot. We'll fight with him to-night.
Wor.   It may not be.
Doug. You give him then advantage.
Ver.   Not a whit.
Hot. Why say you so? Looks he not for
supply?
Ver. So do we.
Hot.   His is certain, ours is doubtful.
Wor. Good cousin, be advis'd; stir not
to-night.   5
Ver. Do not, my lord.
Doug.   You do not counsel well.
You speak it out of fear and cold heart.
Ver. Do me no slander, Douglas. By my
life —
And I dare well maintain it with my life —
If well-respected honour bid me on,   10
I hold as little counsel with weak fear
As you, my lord, or any Scot that this day lives.
Let it be seen to-morrow in the battle
Which of us fears.
Doug.   Yea, or to-night.
Ver.   Content.
Hot. To-night, say I.   15
Ver. Come, come, it may not be. I wonder
much,
Being men of such great leading as you are,

That you foresee not what impediments
Drag back our expedition. Certain horse
Of my cousin Vernon's are not yet come up. 20
Your uncle Worcester's horse came but to-day;
And now their pride and mettle is asleep,
Their courage with hard labour tame and dull,
That not a horse is half the half of himself.
Hot. So are the horses of the enemy,   25
In general journey-bated and brought low.
The better part of ours are full of rest.
Wor. The number of the King exceedeth ours.
For God's sake, cousin, stay till all come in.

The trumpet sounds a parley.

Enter *Sir Walter Blunt.*

Blunt. I come with gracious offers from the
King,   30
If you vouchsafe me hearing and respect.
Hot. Welcome, Sir Walter Blunt, and would
to God
You were of our determination!
Some of us love you well; and even those some
Envy your great deservings and good name,   35
Because you are not of our quality,
But stand against us like an enemy.
Blunt. And God defend but still I should
stand so,
So long as out of limit and true rule
You stand against anointed majesty!   40
But to my charge. The King hath sent to know
The nature of your griefs; and whereupon
You conjure from the breast of civil peace
Such bold hostility, teaching his duteous land
Audacious cruelty. If that the King   45
Have any way your good deserts forgot,
Which he confesseth to be manifold,
He bids you name your griefs, and with all speed
You shall have your desires with interest,
And pardon absolute for yourself and these   50
Herein misled by your suggestion.
Hot. The King is kind; and well we know
the King
Knows at what time to promise, when to pay.
My father and my uncle and myself
Did give him that same royalty he wears;   55
And when he was not six-and-twenty strong,
Sick in the world's regard, wretched and low,
A poor unminded outlaw sneaking home,
My father gave him welcome to the shore;
And when he heard him swear and vow to God
He came but to be Duke of Lancaster,   61
To sue his livery and beg his peace,
With tears of innocency and terms of zeal,
My father, in kind heart and pity mov'd,

Swore him assistance, and perform'd it too. 65
Now when the lords and barons of the realm
Perceiv'd Northumberland did lean to him,
The more and less came in with cap and knee;
Met him in boroughs, cities, villages,
Attended him on bridges, stood in lanes, 70
Laid gifts before him, proffer'd him their oaths,
Gave him their heirs as pages, followed him
Even at the heels in golden multitudes.
He presently, as greatness knows itself,
Steps me a little higher than his vow 75
Made to my father, while his blood was poor,
Upon the naked shore at Ravenspurgh;
And now, forsooth, takes on him to reform
Some certain edicts and some strait decrees
That lie too heavy on the commonwealth; 80
Cries out upon abuses, seems to weep
Over his country's wrongs; and by this face,
This seeming brow of justice, did he win
The hearts of all that he did angle for;
Proceeded further — cut me off the heads 85
Of all the favourites that the absent King
In deputation left behind him here
When he was personal in the Irish war.
    Blunt. Tut! I came not to hear this.
    Hot.   Then to the point.
In short time after he depos'd the King; 90
Soon after that depriv'd him of his life;
And in the neck of that task'd the whole state;
To make that worse, suff'red his kinsman March
(Who is, if every owner were well plac'd,
Indeed his king) to be engag'd in Wales, 95
There without ransom to lie forfeited;
Disgrac'd me in my happy victories,
Sought to entrap me by intelligence;
Rated mine uncle from the Council board;
In rage dismiss'd my father from the court; 100
Broke oath on oath, committed wrong on
    wrong;
And in conclusion drove us to seek out
This head of safety, and withal to pry
Into his title, the which we find
Too indirect for long continuance. 105
    Blunt. Shall I return this answer to the King?
    Hot. Not so, Sir Walter. We'll withdraw
    awhile.
Go to the King; and let there be impawn'd
Some surety for a safe return again,
And in the morning early shall mine uncle 110
Bring him our purposes; and so farewell.
    Blunt. I would you would accept of grace
    and love.
    Hot. And may be so we shall.
    Blunt.   Pray God you do.
                                    Exeunt.

Scene IV. [*York. The* Archbishop's
                    Palace.]

Enter the *Archbishop of York* and *Sir Michael.*
    Arch. Hie, good Sir Michael; bear this
    sealed brief
With winged haste to the Lord Marshal;
This to my cousin Scroop; and all the rest
To whom they are directed. If you knew
How much they do import, you would make
    haste. 5
    Sir M. My good lord,
I guess their tenour.
    Arch.   Like enough you do.
To-morrow, good Sir Michael, is a day
Wherein the fortune of ten thousand men 9
Must bide the touch; for, sir, at Shrewsbury,
As I am truly given to understand,
The King with mighty and quick-raised power
Meets with Lord Harry; and I fear, Sir
    Michael,
What with the sickness of Northumberland,
Whose power was in the first proportion, 15
And what with Owen Glendower's absence
    thence,
Who with them was a rated sinew too
And comes not in, overrul'd by prophecies —
I fear the power of Percy is too weak
To wage an instant trial with the King. 20
    Sir M. Why, my good lord, you need not fear;
There is Douglas and Lord Mortimer.
    Arch. No, Mortimer is not there.
    Sir M. But there is Mordake, Vernon, Lord
    Harry Percy, 24
And there is my Lord of Worcester, and a head
Of gallant warriors, noble gentlemen.
    Arch. And so there is; but yet the King
    hath drawn
The special head of all the land together —
The Prince of Wales, Lord John of Lancaster,
The noble Westmoreland and warlike Blunt,
And many moe corrivals and dear men 31
Of estimation and command in arms.
    Sir M. Doubt not, my lord, they shall be
    well oppos'd.
    Arch. I hope no less, yet needful 'tis to fear;
And, to prevent the worst, Sir Michael, speed.
For if Lord Percy thrive not, ere the King 36
Dismiss his power, he means to visit us,
For he hath heard of our confederacy,
And 'tis but wisdom to make strong against him.
Therefore make haste. I must go write again
To other friends; and so farewell, Sir Michael.
                                    Exeunt.

Act V. Scene I. [*The* King's *camp near Shrewsbury.*]

*Enter the King, Prince of Wales, Lord John of
Lancaster, Sir Walter Blunt, Falstaff.*

King. How bloodily the sun begins to peer
Above yon busky hill! The day looks pale
At his distemp'rature.
 Prince.   The southern wind
Doth play the trumpet to his purposes
And by his hollow whistling in the leaves 5
Foretells a tempest and a blust'ring day.
 King. Then with the losers let it sympathize,
For nothing can seem foul to those that win.

The trumpet sounds. Enter *Worcester*
[*and Vernon*].

How now, my Lord of Worcester? 'Tis not well
That you and I should meet upon such terms
As now we meet. You have deceiv'd our trust
And made us doff our easy robes of peace
To crush our old limbs in ungentle steel.
This is not well, my lord; this is not well.
What say you to it? Will you again unknit 15
This churlish knot of all-abhorred war,
And move in that obedient orb again
Where you did give a fair and natural light,
And be no more an exhal'd meteor,
A prodigy of fear, and a portent 20
Of broached mischief to the unborn times?
 Wor. Hear me, my liege.
For mine own part, I could be well content
To entertain the lag-end of my life
With quiet hours; for I do protest 25
I have not sought the day of this dislike.
 King. You have not sought it! How comes
  it then?
 Fal. Rebellion lay in his way, and he found it.
 Prince. Peace, chewet, peace!
 Wor. It pleas'd your Majesty to turn your
  looks 30
Of favour from myself and all our house;
And yet I must remember you, my lord,
We were the first and dearest of your friends.
For you my staff of office did I break 34
In Richard's time, and posted day and night
To meet you on the way and kiss your hand
When yet you were in place and in account
Nothing so strong and fortunate as I.
It was myself, my brother, and his son 39
That brought you home and boldly did outdare
The dangers of the time. You swore to us,
And you did swear that oath at Doncaster,

That you did nothing purpose 'gainst the state,
Nor claim no further than your new-fall'n right,
The seat of Gaunt, dukedom of Lancaster. 45
To this we swore our aid. But in short space
It rain'd down fortune show'ring on your head,
And such a flood of greatness fell on you —
What with our help, what with the absent King,
What with the injuries of a wanton time, 50
The seeming sufferances that you had borne,
And the contrarious winds that held the King
So long in his unlucky Irish wars
That all in England did repute him dead —
And from this swarm of fair advantages 55
You took occasion to be quickly woo'd
To gripe the general sway into your hand;
Forgot your oath to us at Doncaster;
And, being fed by us, you us'd us so
As that ungentle gull, the cuckoo's bird, 60
Useth the sparrow — did oppress our nest;
Grew by our feeding to so great a bulk
That even our love durst not come near your
  sight
For fear of swallowing; but with nimble wing
We were enforc'd for safety sake to fly 65
Out of your sight and raise this present head;
Whereby we stand opposed by such means
As you yourself have forg'd against yourself
By unkind usage, dangerous countenance,
And violation of all faith and troth 70
Sworn to us in your younger enterprise.
 King. These things, indeed, you have ar-
  ticulate,
Proclaim'd at market crosses, read in churches,
To face the garment of rebellion 74
With some fine colour that may please the eye
Of fickle changelings and poor discontents,
Which gape and rub the elbow at the news
Of hurlyburly innovation.
And never yet did insurrection want
Such water colours to impaint his cause, 80
Nor moody beggars, starving for a time
Of pell-mell havoc and confusion.
 Prince. In both our armies there is many a
  soul
Shall pay full dearly for this encounter,
If once they join in trial. Tell your nephew 85
The Prince of Wales doth join with all the world
In praise of Henry Percy. By my hopes,
This present enterprise set off his head,
I do not think a braver gentleman,
More active-valiant or more valiant-young, 90

104

More daring or more bold, is now alive
To grace this latter age with noble deeds.
For my part, I may speak it to my shame,
I have a truant been to chivalry;
And so I hear he doth account me too.   95
Yet this before my father's Majesty —
I am content that he shall take the odds
Of his great name and estimation,
And will, to save the blood on either side,
Try fortune with him in a single fight.   100
    King. And, Prince of Wales, so dare we venture thee,
Albeit considerations infinite
Do make against it. No, good Worcester, no!
We love our people well; even those we love
That are misled upon your cousin's part;   105
And, will they take the offer of our grace,
Both he, and they, and you, yea, every man
Shall be my friend again, and I'll be his.
So tell your cousin, and bring me word
What he will do. But if he will not yield,   110
Rebuke and dread correction wait on us,
And they shall do their office. So be gone.
We will not now be troubled with reply.
We offer fair; take it advisedly.   114
        Exit Worcester [with Vernon].
    Prince. It will not be accepted, on my life.
The Douglas and the Hotspur both together
Are confident against the world in arms.
    King. Hence, therefore, every leader to his charge;
For, on their answer, will we set on them,
And God befriend us as our cause is just!   120
        Exeunt. Manent Prince, Falstaff.
    Fal. Hal, if thou see me down in the battle
and bestride me, so! 'Tis a point of friendship.
    Prince. Nothing but a Colossus can do thee
that friendship. Say thy prayers, and farewell.
    Fal. I would 'twere bedtime, Hal, and all
well.   126
    Prince. Why, thou owest God a death.
        [Exit.]
    Fal. 'Tis not due yet. I would be loath to
pay him before his day. What need I be so forward with him that calls not on me? Well, 'tis
no matter; honour pricks me on. Yea, but how
if honour prick me off when I come on? How
then? Can honour set to a leg? No. Or an
arm? No. Or take away the grief of a wound?
No. Honour hath no skill in surgery then? No.
What is honour? A word. What is that word
honour? Air. A trim reckoning! Who hath it?
He that died a Wednesday. Doth he feel it?
No. Doth he hear it? No. 'Tis insensible
then? Yea, to the dead. But will it not live

with the living? No. Why? Detraction will
not suffer it. Therefore I'll none of it. Honour
is a mere scutcheon — and so ends my catechism.   *Exit.*

Scene II. [*The rebel camp.*]

Enter Worcester and Sir Richard Vernon.

    Wor. O no, my nephew must not know, Sir Richard,
The liberal and kind offer of the King.
    Ver. 'Twere best he did.
    Wor.   Then are we all undone.
It is not possible, it cannot be,
The King should keep his word in loving us.   5
He will suspect us still and find a time
To punish this offence in other faults.
Suspicion all our lives shall be stuck full of eyes;
For treason is but trusted like the fox,
Who, ne'er so tame, so cherish'd and lock'd up,
Will have a wild trick of his ancestors.   11
Look how we can, or sad or merrily,
Interpretation will misquote our looks,
And we shall feed like oxen at a stall,
The better cherish'd, still the nearer death.   15
My nephew's trespass may be well forgot;
It hath the excuse of youth and heat of blood,
And an adopted name of privilege —
A hare-brain'd Hotspur, govern'd by a spleen.
All his offences live upon my head   20
And on his father's. We did train him on;
And, his corruption being ta'en from us,
We, as the spring of all, shall pay for all.
Therefore, good cousin, let not Harry know,
In any case, the offer of the King.   25

Enter Hotspur [and Douglas].

    Ver. Deliver what you will, I'll say 'tis so.
Here comes your cousin.
    Hot.   My uncle is return'd.
Deliver up my Lord of Westmoreland.
Uncle, what news?   30
    Wor. The King will bid you battle presently.
    Doug. Defy him by the Lord of Westmoreland.
    Hot. Lord Douglas, go you and tell him so.
    Doug. Marry, and shall, and very willingly.
        Exit.
    Wor. There is no seeming mercy in the King.
    Hot. Did you beg any? God forbid!   36
    Wor. I told him gently of our grievances,
Of his oath-breaking; which he mended thus,
By now forswearing that he is forsworn.

He calls us rebels, traitors, and will scourge 40
With haughty arms this hateful name in us.

Enter *Douglas.*

Doug. Arm, gentlemen! to arms! for I have
thrown
A brave defiance in King Henry's teeth,
And Westmoreland, that was engag'd, did
bear it; 44
Which cannot choose but bring him quickly on.
Wor. The Prince of Wales stepp'd forth be-
fore the King
And, nephew, challeng'd you to single fight.
Hot. O, would the quarrel lay upon our
heads,
And that no man might draw short breath to-
day 49
But I and Harry Monmouth! Tell me, tell me,
How show'd his tasking? Seem'd it in con-
tempt?
Ver. No, by my soul. I never in my life
Did hear a challenge urg'd more modestly,
Unless a brother should a brother dare
To gentle exercise and proof of arms. 55
He gave you all the duties of a man;
Trimm'd up your praises with a princely tongue;
Spoke your deservings like a chronicle;
Making you ever better than his praise
By still dispraising praise valued with you; 60
And, which became him like a prince indeed,
He made a blushing cital of himself,
And chid his truant youth with such a grace
As if he mast'red there a double spirit
Of teaching and of learning instantly. 65
There did he pause; but let me tell the world,
If he outlive the envy of this day,
England did never owe so sweet a hope,
So much misconstrued in his wantonness.
Hot. Cousin, I think thou art enamoured 70
Upon his follies. Never did I hear
Of any prince so wild a libertine.
But be he as he will, yet once ere night
I will embrace him with a soldier's arm,
That he shall shrink under my courtesy. 75
Arm, arm with speed! and, fellows, soldiers,
friends,
Better consider what you have to do
Than I, that have not well the gift of tongue,
Can lift your blood up with persuasion.

Enter a *Messenger.*

Mess. My lord, here are letters for you. 80
Hot. I cannot read them now. —
O gentlemen, the time of life is short!
To spend that shortness basely were too long

If life did ride upon a dial's point,
Still ending at the arrival of an hour. 85
An if we live, we live to tread on kings;
If die, brave death, when princes die with us!
Now for our consciences, the arms are fair,
When the intent of bearing them is just.

Enter another *Messenger.*

Mess. My lord, prepare. The King comes
on apace. 90
Hot. I thank him that he cuts me from my
tale,
For I profess not talking. Only this —
Let each man do his best; and here draw I
A sword whose temper I intend to stain
With the best blood that I can meet withal 95
In the adventure of this perilous day.
Now, Esperance! Percy! and set on.
Sound all the lofty instruments of war,
And by that music let us all embrace;
For, heaven to earth, some of us never shall 100
A second time do such a courtesy.

Here they embrace. The trumpets sound.
[Exeunt.]

[Scene III. *Plain between the camps.*]

The *King* enters with his *Power.* Alarum to
the battle. Then enter *Douglas* and *Sir Walter*
Blunt.

Blunt. What is thy name, that in the battle
thus
Thou crossest me? What honour dost thou seek
Upon my head?
Doug. Know then my name is Douglas,
And I do haunt thee in the battle thus
Because some tell me that thou art a king. 5
Blunt. They tell thee true.
Doug. The Lord of Stafford dear to-day
hath bought
Thy likeness; for instead of thee, King Harry,
This sword hath ended him. So shall it thee,
Unless thou yield thee as my prisoner. 10
Blunt. I was not born a yielder, thou proud
Scot;
And thou shalt find a king that will revenge
Lord Stafford's death.

They fight. Douglas kills Blunt.
Then enter Hotspur.

Hot. O Douglas, hadst thou fought at
Holmedon thus,
I never had triumph'd upon a Scot. 15

Doug. All's done, all's won. Here breathless
   lies the King.
Hot. Where?
Doug. Here.
Hot. This, Douglas? No. I know this face
   full well.
A gallant knight he was, his name was Blunt;
Semblably furnish'd like the King himself. 21
Doug. A fool go with thy soul, whither it goes!
A borrowed title hast thou bought too dear:
Why didst thou tell me that thou wert a king?
Hot. The King hath many marching in his
   coats. 25
Doug. Now, by my sword, I will kill all his
   coats;
I'll murder all his wardrop, piece by piece,
Until I meet the King.
Hot.   Up and away!
Our soldiers stand full fairly for the day. 29
                                   Exeunt.

   Alarum. Enter *Falstaff* solus.

Fal. Though I could scape shot-free at London, I fear the shot here. Here's no scoring
but upon the pate. Soft! who are you? Sir
Walter Blunt. There's honour for you! Here's
no vanity! I am as hot as molten lead, and as
heavy too. God keep lead out of me! I need
no more weight than mine own bowels. I have
led my rag-of-muffins where they are pepper'd.
There's not three of my hundred and fifty left
alive; and they are for the town's end, to beg
during life. But who comes here? 40

   Enter the *Prince.*

Prince. What, stand'st thou idle here? Lend
   me thy sword.
Many a nobleman lies stark and stiff
Under the hoofs of vaunting enemies,
Whose deaths are yet unreveng'd. I prithee
Lend me thy sword. 44
Fal. O Hal, I prithee give me leave to breathe
awhile. Turk Gregory never did such deeds in
arms as I have done this day. I have paid
Percy; I have made him sure.
Prince. He is indeed, and living to kill thee.
I prithee lend me thy sword. 50
Fal. Nay, before God, Hal, if Percy be alive,
thou get'st not my sword; but take my pistol,
if thou wilt.
Prince. Give it me. What, is it in the case?
Fal. Ay, Hal. 'Tis hot, 'tis hot. There's
that will sack a city. 56
   *The Prince draws it out and finds it to be a
                         bottle of sack.*

Prince. What, is it a time to jest and dally
now?   *He throws the bottle at him. Exit.*
Fal. Well, if Percy be alive, I'll pierce him.
If he do come in my way, so; if he do not, if I
come in his willingly, let him make a carbonado
of me. I like not such grinning honour as Sir
Walter hath. Give me life; which if I can
save, so; if not, honour comes unlook'd for,
and there's an end.   *Exit.*

   Scene IV. [*Another part of the field.*]

Alarum. Excursions. Enter the *King*, the
*Prince, Lord John of Lancaster, Earl of West-
                 moreland.*

King. I prithee,
Harry, withdraw thyself; thou bleedest too
   much.
Lord John of Lancaster, go you with him.
John. Not I, my lord, unless I did bleed too.
Prince. I do beseech your Majesty make up,
Lest your retirement do amaze your friends. 6
King. I will do so.
My Lord of Westmoreland, lead him to his tent.
West. Come, my lord, I'll lead you to your
   tent.
Prince. Lead me, my lord? I do not need
   your help; 10
And God forbid a shallow scratch should drive
The Prince of Wales from such a field as this,
Where stain'd nobility lies trodden on,
And rebels' arms triumph in massacres!
John. We breathe too long. Come, cousin
   Westmoreland, 15
Our duty this way lies. For God's sake, come.
   [*Exeunt Prince John and Westmoreland.*]
Prince. By God, thou hast deceiv'd me,
   Lancaster!
I did not think thee lord of such a spirit.
Before, I lov'd thee as a brother, John;
But now, I do respect thee as my soul. 20
King. I saw him hold Lord Percy at the point
With lustier maintenance than I did look for
Of such an ungrown warrior.
Prince.   O, this boy
Lends mettle to us all!   *Exit.*

   Enter *Douglas.*

Doug. Another king? They grow like Hy-
   dra's heads. 25
I am the Douglas, fatal to all those
That wear those colours on them. What art
   thou
That counterfeit'st the person of a king?

King. The King himself, who, Douglas, grieves at heart
So many of his shadows thou hast met, 30
And not the very King. I have two boys
Seek Percy and thyself about the field;
But, seeing thou fall'st on me so luckily,
I will assay thee. So defend thyself. 34
Doug. I fear thou art another counterfeit;
And yet, in faith, thou bearest thee like a king.
But mine I am sure thou art, whoe'er thou be,
And thus I win thee.

They fight. The King being in danger, enter Prince of Wales.

Prince. Hold up thy head, vile Scot, or thou art like
Never to hold it up again! The spirits 40
Of valiant Shirley, Stafford, Blunt are in my arms.
It is the Prince of Wales that threatens thee,
Who never promiseth but he means to pay.
They fight. Douglas flieth.
Cheerly, my lord. How fares your Grace? 45
Sir Nicholas Gawsey hath for succour sent,
And so hath Clifton. I'll to Clifton straight.
King. Stay and breathe awhile.
Thou hast redeem'd thy lost opinion,
And show'd thou mak'st some tender of my life,
In this fair rescue thou hast brought to me. 50
Prince. O God! they did me too much injury
That ever said I heark'ned for your death.
If it were so, I might have let alone
The insulting hand of Douglas over you, 54
Which would have been as speedy in your end
As all the poisonous potions in the world,
And sav'd the treacherous labour of your son.
King. Make up to Clifton; I'll to Sir Nicholas Gawsey. *Exit.*

Enter *Hotspur.*

Hot. If I mistake not, thou art Harry Monmouth.
Prince. Thou speak'st as if I would deny my name. 60
Hot. My name is Harry Percy.
Prince. Why, then I see
A very valiant rebel of the name.
I am the Prince of Wales; and think not, Percy,
To share with me in glory any more. 64
Two stars keep not their motion in one sphere,
Nor can one England brook a double reign
Of Harry Percy and the Prince of Wales.

Hot. Nor shall it, Harry; for the hour is come
To end the one of us; and would to God 69
Thy name in arms were now as great as mine!
Prince. I'll make it greater ere I part from thee,
And all the budding honours on thy crest
I'll crop to make a garland for my head.
Hot. I can no longer brook thy vanities.
They fight.

Enter *Falstaff.*

Fal. Well said, Hal! to it, Hal! Nay, you shall find no boy's play here, I can tell you. 76

Enter *Douglas. He fighteth with Falstaff, who falls down as if he were dead. [Exit Douglas.] The Prince killeth Percy.*

Hot. O Harry, thou hast robb'd me of my youth!
I better brook the loss of brittle life
Than those proud titles thou hast won of me.
They wound my thoughts worse than thy sword my flesh. 80
But thoughts the slaves of life, and life time's fool,
And time, that takes survey of all the world,
Must have a stop. O, I could prophesy,
But that the earthy and cold hand of death 84
Lies on my tongue. No, Percy, thou art dust,
And food for — *[Dies.]*
Prince. For worms, brave Percy. Fare thee well, great heart!
Ill-weav'd ambition, how much art thou shrunk!
When that this body did contain a spirit,
A kingdom for it was too small a bound; 90
But now two paces of the vilest earth
Is room enough. This earth that bears thee dead
Bears not alive so stout a gentleman.
If thou wert sensible of courtesy,
I should not make so dear a show of zeal. 95
But let my favours hide thy mangled face;
And, even in thy behalf, I'll thank myself
For doing these fair rites of tenderness.
Adieu, and take thy praise with thee to heaven!
Thy ignominy sleep with thee in the grave,
But not rememb'red in thy epitaph! 101
He spieth Falstaff on the ground.
What, old acquaintance? Could not all this flesh
Keep in a little life? Poor Jack, farewell!
I could have better spar'd a better man.
O, I should have a heavy miss of thee 105
If I were much in love with vanity!

Death hath not struck so fat a deer to-day,
Though many dearer, in this bloody fray.
Embowell'd will I see thee by-and-by;   109
Till then in blood by noble Percy lie.   *Exit.*

Falstaff riseth up.

Fal. Embowell'd? If thou embowel me to-day, I'll give you leave to powder me and eat me too to-morrow. 'Sblood, 'twas time to counterfeit, or that hot termagant Scot had paid me scot and lot too. Counterfeit? I lie; I am no counterfeit. To die is to be a counterfeit; for he is but the counterfeit of a man who hath not the life of a man; but to counterfeit dying when a man thereby liveth, is to be no counterfeit, but the true and perfect image of life indeed. The better part of valour is discretion; in the which better part I have saved my life. Zounds, I am afraid of this gunpowder Percy, though he be dead. How if he should counterfeit too, and rise? By my faith, I am afraid he would prove the better counterfeit. Therefore I'll make him sure; yea, and I'll swear I kill'd him. Why may not he rise as well as I? Nothing confutes me but eyes, and nobody sees me. Therefore, sirrah [*stabs him*], with a new wound in your thigh, come you along with me.   132

He takes up Hotspur on his back. Enter
Prince, and *John of Lancaster.*

Prince. Come, brother John; full bravely hast thou flesh'd
Thy maiden sword.
John.   But, soft! whom have we here?
Did you not tell me this fat man was dead?
Prince. I did; I saw him dead,   136
Breathless and bleeding on the ground. Art thou alive,
Or is it fantasy that plays upon our eyesight?
I prithee speak. We will not trust our eyes
Without our ears. Thou art not what thou seem'st.   140
Fal. No, that's certain! I am not a double man; but if I be not Jack Falstaff, then am I a Jack. There is Percy. If your father will do me any honour, so; if not, let him kill the next Percy himself. I look to be either earl or duke, I can assure you.   146
Prince. Why, Percy I kill'd myself, and saw thee dead!
Fal. Didst thou? Lord, Lord, how this world is given to lying! I grant you I was down, and out of breath, and so was he; but we rose

both at an instant and fought a long hour by Shrewsbury clock. If I may be believ'd, so; if not, let them that should reward valour bear the sin upon their own heads. I'll take it upon my death, I gave him this wound in the thigh. If the man were alive and would deny it, zounds! I would make him eat a piece of my sword.
John. This is the strangest tale that ever I heard.
Prince. This is the strangest fellow, brother John.   159
Come, bring your luggage nobly on your back.
For my part, if a lie may do thee grace,
I'll gild it with the happiest terms I have.
                              A retreat is sounded.
The trumpet sounds retreat; the day is ours.
Come, brother, let's to the highest of the field,
To see what friends are living, who are dead.
         Exeunt [*Prince Henry and Prince John*].
Fal. I'll follow, as they say, for reward. He that rewards me, God reward him! If I do grow great, I'll grow less; for I'll purge, and leave sack, and live cleanly, as a nobleman should do.   *Exit* [*bearing off the body*].

Scene V. [*Another part of the field.*]

The trumpets sound. Enter the *King, Prince of Wales, Lord John of Lancaster, Earl of Westmoreland,* with *Worcester* and *Vernon* prisoners.

King. Thus ever did rebellion find rebuke.
Ill-spirited Worcester! did not we send grace,
Pardon, and terms of love to all of you?
And wouldst thou turn our offers contrary?
Misuse the tenour of thy kinsman's trust?
Three knights upon our party slain to-day,
A noble earl, and many a creature else
Had been alive this hour,
If like a Christian thou hadst truly borne
Betwixt our armies true intelligence.   10
Wor. What I have done my safety urg'd me to;
And I embrace this fortune patiently,
Since not to be avoided it falls on me.
King. Bear Worcester to the death, and Vernon too;
Other offenders we will pause upon.   15
         Exeunt Worcester and Vernon, [*guarded*].
How goes the field?
Prince. The noble Scot, Lord Douglas, when he saw

The fortune of the day quite turn'd from
    him,
The noble Percy slain, and all his men
Upon the foot of fear, fled with the rest;   20
And falling from a hill, he was so bruis'd
That the pursuers took him. At my tent
The Douglas is, and I beseech your Grace
I may dispose of him.
   King.   With all my heart.
   Prince. Then, brother John of Lancaster, to
    you   25
This honourable bounty shall belong.
Go to the Douglas and deliver him
Up to his pleasure, ransomless and free.
His valour shown upon our crests to-day   29
Hath taught us how to cherish such high
    deeds,
Even in the bosom of our adversaries.

   John. I thank your Grace for this high
    courtesy,
Which I shall give away immediately.
   King. Then this remains, that we divide our
    power.   34
You, son John, and my cousin Westmoreland,
Towards York shall bend you with your dearest
    speed
To meet Northumberland and the prelate
    Scroop,
Who, as we hear, are busily in arms.
Myself and you, son Harry, will towards Wales
To fight with Glendower and the Earl of March.
Rebellion in this land shall lose his sway,   41
Meeting the check of such another day;
And since this business so fair is done,
Let us not leave till all our own be won.
                         Exeunt.

THE SECOND PART OF KING HENRY THE FOURTH

THE SECOND PART OF KING HENRY THE FOURTH was entered in the Stationers' Register on August 23, 1600, and the Quarto appeared in the same year.

The title page reads like a table of contents: 'The Second part of Henrie the fourth, continuing to his death, and coronation of Henrie the fift. With the humours of sir Iohn Falstaffe, and swaggering Pistoll. As it hath been sundrie times publikely acted by the right honourable, the Lord Chamberlaine his seruants. Written by William Shakespeare.'

PART I ends with the King's victory over Hotspur at Shrewsbury (July 21, 1403) and the closing speech is to all intents and purposes an announcement that a continuation may be expected. Doubtless Shakespeare began to write the SECOND PART soon after he finished the FIRST. As dates, 1597 for *Part I* and 1598 for *Part II* are probable.

Between the two plays there is only the interval needed to carry the news to Hotspur's father, the Earl of Northumberland. In the first scene of PART II the tidings reach the Earl's castle at Warkworth. In the same scene we learn that the Archbishop of York has raised an army against the King and that 'more and less do flock to follow him.' In fact, the Archbishop's rebellion occurred in May and June, 1405, almost two years after the Battle of Shrewsbury. PART II ends with the coronation of Henry V, which took place on April 9, 1413.

For most of the text the Quarto is the basis, but the Folio supplies several passages that the Quarto lacks. Important omissions in the Quarto are i, 1, 166–179, 189–209; i, 3, 21–24, 36–55, 85 (second part)–108; ii, 3, 23–45 (first part); iv, 1, 55–79, 103 (second part)–139. All these passages undoubtedly stood in the original text.

Some of the cuts were heedlessly made. Thus, when Morton's speech (i, 1, 187–209) is reduced to the first two lines (187–188), it has no meaning and Northumberland's reply becomes unintelligible. In such cases the printer may have misunderstood deletions in his copy. Sometimes the cut seems to have a special reason. Thus the omission of i, 1, 166–179, spares Northumberland reproaches that sound rather unfeeling. Cf. also lines 32–45, a part of the cut (ii, 3, 23–45) in Lady Percy's long speech. The excision of iv, 1, 55–79, may be due to a feeling (perhaps on the censor's part) that these lines sounded too much like a justification of Essex. His trial took place in June, 1600, and he was not completely set at liberty until August, the very month in which the First Quarto was entered in the Register. The Folio omits a few short passages, amounting in the aggregate to about forty lines.

Oldcastle, not Falstaff, was in the original text, as the accidental retention of *Old.* by the Quarto in one speech heading (i, 2, 137) proves. This is corrected to *Fal.* in the Folio. The Epilogue, in announcing *Henry V* as in prospect, calls attention to the change of name: 'If you be not too much cloy'd with fat meat, our humble author will continue the story, with Sir John in it, and make you merry with fair Katherine of France; where for anything I know, Falstaff shall die of a sweat, unless already 'a be kill'd with your hard opinions; for Oldcastle died a martyr, and this is not the man.' See p. 544, above.

For material Shakespeare drew upon Holinshed, as heretofore, and seems to have consulted Stow. He also made liberal use of *The Famous Victories* (see p. 544). The anecdote of the attack upon the Chief Justice illustrates his procedure. Holinshed says that the Prince struck the Chief Justice with his fist; in *The Famous Victories* he gives him a box on the ear; in Sir Thomas Elyot's *Governour* (1531), copied by Stow, he threatens violence but commits no assault. In the old play the scene is dramatized. Shakespeare, suppressing the action, has the Justice describe the affair in defending his own conduct (v, 2): '[You] struck me in my very seat of judgment.' His speech echoes a phrase of the old play; but neither the old play nor Holinshed records the words that King Henry used in praising the sternness of the judge and the obedience of his son. These are found in Elyot (whom Stow copies). Shakespeare makes Henry V quote them (v, 2, 107–112):

> So shall I live to speak my father's words:
> 'Happy am I that have a man so bold
> That dares do justice on my proper son;
> And not less happy, having such a son
> That would deliver up his greatness so
> Into the hands of justice.'

In Elyot, Henry IV exclaims:

> O mercifull god, how moche am I, aboue all other men, bounde to your infinite goodnes! specially for that ye haue gyuen me a iuge who feareth nat to ministre iustice, and also a sonne who can suffre semblably and obey iustice!

The conscription scene (iii, 2) takes a hint or two from *The Famous Victories*.

The scene of Falstaff's humiliation (v, 5) was also suggested by the old play. Jockey and Ned and Tom, the Prince's roistering companions, have been present at the coronation and accost the king in the street as he comes out 'with the Archbishop and the Lord of Oxford.' He repulses them and speaks their sentence: 'Not vpon pain of death to approach my presence by ten miles space, then if I heare wel of you, it may be I wil do somewhat for you.' There is no such incident in Holinshed, who simply records the fact that, 'whereas aforetime he had made himselfe a companion vnto misrulie mates of dissolute order and life, he now banished them all from his presence (but not vnrewarded, or else vnpreferred); inhibiting them vpon a great paine, not once to approch, lodge, or soiourne within ten miles of his court or presence.' As Shakespeare has adjusted the situation, the young king's severity, which sentimentalists deplore, is stern necessity. There stands Falstaff, stained with travel and sweating with eagerness — a tun of man. Behind him is Pistol, that 'roaring devil i' th' old play' — tall, stalwart, and long-haired, with the ferocious swagger of the professional bully. By Falstaff's side is Bardolph, with his face 'all bubukles and whelks and knobs and flames o' fire.' And there too is Justice Shallow — a starveling figure of comic dignity, like a hermit's staff with a head. 'God save thy Grace, King Hal, my royal Hal!' Falstaff, infatuated, has doomed himself. There is no answer possible but King Henry's:

> 'I know thee not, old man. Fall to thy prayers.
> How ill white hairs become a fool and jester!'

THE SECOND PART OF
KING HENRY THE FOURTH

The Actors' Names.

Rumour, the Presenter.

King Henry the Fourth.
Prince Henry, afterwards crowned King Henry the
  Fifth.
Prince John of Lancaster, ⎫ sons to Henry IV and
Humphrey of Gloucester, ⎬ brethren to Henry V.
Thomas of Clarence, ⎭
[Earl of] Northumberland, ⎫
[Richard Scroop,] the Arch- ⎪
  bishop of York, ⎪
[Lord] Mowbray, ⎪ opposites against
[Lord] Hastings, ⎬ King Henry the
Lord Bardolph, ⎪ Fourth.
Travers, ⎫ [retainers of North- ⎪
Morton, ⎭ umberland,] ⎪
[Sir John] Colevile, ⎭
[Earl of] Warwick, ⎫
[Earl of] Westmoreland, ⎪
[Earl of] Surrey, ⎪
Gower, ⎬ of the King's party.
Harcourt, ⎪
[Blunt,] ⎪
Lord Chief Justice, ⎭
[A servant of the Chief Justice.]

[Sir John] Falstaff, ⎫
Poins, ⎪
Bardolph, ⎪
Pistol, ⎬ irregular humourists.
Peto, ⎪
Page [to Falstaff], ⎭
[Robert] Shallow, ⎫ both country Justices.
Silence, ⎭
Davy, servant to Shallow.
Fang and Snare, two Sergeants.
[Ralph] Mouldy, ⎫
[Simon] Shadow, ⎪
[Thomas] Wart, ⎬ country soldiers [or recruits].
[Francis] Feeble, ⎪
[Peter] Bullcalf, ⎭

Northumberland's Wife.
[Lady Percy,] Percy's widow.
Hostess Quickly, [of the Boar's Head tavern, East-
  cheap].
Doll Tearsheet.

[Lords and Attendants; a Porter;] Drawers,
  Beadles, Grooms, [Servants; a Dancer as]
  Epilogue.

[SCENE. — England.]

INDUCTION. [Warkworth. Before Northumberland's Castle.]

Enter Rumour, painted full of tongues.

Open your ears, for which of you will stop
The vent of hearing when loud Rumour
  speaks?
I from the Orient to the drooping West,
Making the wind my posthorse, still unfold
The acts commenced on this ball of earth. 5
Upon my tongues continual slanders ride,
The which in every language I pronounce,
Stuffing the ears of men with false reports.
I speak of peace while covert enmity, 9
Under the smile of safety, wounds the world.
And who but Rumour, who but only I,
Make fearful musters and prepar'd defence,
Whiles the big year, swol'n with some other
  grief,
Is thought with child by the stern tyrant
  War,
And no such matter? Rumour is a pipe 15

Blown by surmises, jealousies, conjectures;
And of so easy and so plain a stop
That the blunt monster with uncounted heads,
The still-discordant wav'ring multitude,
Can play upon it. But what need I thus 20
My well-known body to anatomize
Among my household? Why is Rumour here?
I run before King Harry's victory,
Who, in a bloody field by Shrewsbury,
Hath beaten down young Hotspur and his
  troops, 25
Quenching the flame of bold rebellion
Even with the rebels' blood. But what mean I
To speak so true at first? My office is
To noise abroad that Harry Monmouth fell
Under the wrath of noble Hotspur's sword, 30
And that the King before the Douglas' rage
Stoop'd his anointed head as low as death.
This have I rumour'd through the peasant
  towns

Between that royal field of Shrewsbury
And this worm-eaten hold of ragged stone, 35
Where Hotspur's father, old Northumberland,
Lies crafty-sick. The posts come tiring on,
And not a man of them brings other news

Than they have learnt of me. From Rumour's
tongues 39
They bring smooth comforts false, worse than
true wrongs. *Exit.*

ACT I. Scene I. [*Warkworth. Before* Northumberland's *Castle.*]

Enter the *Lord Bardolph.*

L. Bard. Who keeps the gate here, ho?

Enter the *Porter.*

Where is the Earl?
Port. What shall I say you are?
L. Bard. Tell thou the Earl
That the Lord Bardolph doth attend him here.
Port. His lordship is walk'd forth into the
orchard. 4
Please it your honour knock but at the gate,
And he himself will answer.

Enter the *Earl of Northumberland.*

L. Bard. Here comes the Earl.
[*Exit Porter.*]
North. What news, Lord Bardolph? Every
minute now
Should be the father of some stratagem.
The times are wild. Contention, like a horse
Full of high feeding, madly hath broke loose
And bears down all before him.
L. Bard. Noble Earl, 11
I bring you certain news from Shrewsbury.
North. Good, an God will!
L. Bard. As good as heart can wish.
The King is almost wounded to the death;
And, in the fortune of my lord your son, 15
Prince Harry slain outright; and both the
Blunts
Kill'd by the hand of Douglas; young Prince
John
And Westmoreland and Stafford fled the field;
And Harry Monmouth's brawn, the hulk Sir
John,
Is prisoner to your son. O, such a day, 20
So fought, so followed, and so fairly won,
Came not till now to dignify the times,
Since Cæsar's fortunes!
North. How is this deriv'd?
Saw you the field? Came you from Shrews-
bury?
L. Bard. I spake with one, my lord, that
came from thence, 25
A gentleman well bred and of good name,
That freely rend'red me these news for true.

Enter *Travers.*

North. Here comes my servant Travers,
whom I sent
On Tuesday last to listen after news.
L. Bard. My lord, I overrode him on the way,
And he is furnish'd with no certainties
More than he haply may retail from me.
North. Now, Travers, what good tidings
comes with you?
Tra. My lord, Sir John Umfrevile turn'd me
back 34
With joyful tidings and, being better hors'd,
Outrode me. After him came spurring hard
A gentleman, almost forspent with speed,
That stopp'd by me to breathe his bloodied
horse.
He ask'd the way to Chester, and of him
I did demand what news from Shrewsbury. 40
He told me that rebellion had bad luck
And that young Harry Percy's spur was cold.
With that he gave his able horse the head
And, bending forward, struck his armed heels
Against the panting sides of his poor jade 45
Up to the rowel-head; and starting so,
He seem'd in running to devour the way,
Staying no longer question.
North. Ha! Again.
Said he young Harry Percy's spur was cold?
Of Hotspur, Coldspur? that rebellion 50
Had met ill luck?
L. Bard. My lord, I'll tell you what:
If my young lord your son have not the day,
Upon mine honour, for a silken point
I'll give my barony. Never talk of it.
North. Why should that gentleman that rode
by Travers 55
Give then such instances of loss?
L. Bard. Who? he?
He was some hilding fellow that had stol'n
The horse he rode on and, upon my life,
Spoke at a venture. Look, here comes more
news.

Enter *Morton.*

North. Yea, this man's brow, like to a title-
leaf, 60

Foretells the nature of a tragic volume.
So looks the strond whereon the imperious flood
Hath left a witness'd usurpation.
Say, Morton, didst thou come from Shrews-
    bury?   64
  Mor. I ran from Shrewsbury, my noble lord,
Where hateful death put on his ugliest mask
To fright our party.
  North.   How doth my son and brother?
Thou tremblest, and the whiteness in thy cheek
Is apter than thy tongue to tell thy errand.
Even such a man, so faint, so spiritless,   70
So dull, so dead in look, so woe-begone,
Drew Priam's curtain in the dead of night
And would have told him half his Troy was
    burnt;
But Priam found the fire ere he his tongue,
And I my Percy's death ere thou report'st it.
This thou wouldst say, 'Your son did thus and
    thus;   76
Your brother thus; so fought the noble
    Douglas' —
Stopping my greedy ear with their bold deeds;
But in the end, to stop my ear indeed,
Thou hast a sigh to blow away this praise,   80
Ending with 'Brother, son, and all are dead.'
  Mor. Douglas is living, and your brother yet;
But for my lord your son —
  North.   Why, he is dead!
See what a ready tongue suspicion hath!   84
He that but fears the thing he would not know
Hath by instinct knowledge from others' eyes
That what he fear'd is chanced. Yet speak,
    Morton.
Tell thou an earl his divination lies,
And I will take it as a sweet disgrace   89
And make thee rich for doing me such wrong.
  Mor. You are too great to be by me gainsaid.
Your spirit is too true, your fears too certain.
  North. Yet for all this, say not that Percy's
    dead.
I see a strange confession in thine eye.   94
Thou shak'st thy head and hold'st it fear or sin
To speak a truth. If he be slain, say so.
The tongue offends not that reports his death;
And he doth sin that doth belie the dead,
Not he which says the dead is not alive.
Yet the first bringer of unwelcome news   100
Hath but a losing office, and his tongue
Sounds ever after as a sullen bell,
Remem'bred tolling a departing friend.
  L. Bard. I cannot think, my lord, your son
    is dead.   104
  Mor. I am sorry I should force you to believe
That which I would to God I had not seen!

But these mine eyes saw him in bloody state,
Rend'ring faint quittance, wearied and out-
    breath'd,
To Harry Monmouth; whose swift wrath beat
    down
The never-daunted Percy to the earth,   110
From whence with life he never more sprung up.
In few, his death (whose spirit lent a fire
Even to the dullest peasant in his camp)
Being bruited once, took fire and heat away
From the best-temper'd courage in his troops;
For from his metal was his party steel'd,   116
Which once in him abated, all the rest
Turn'd on themselves, like dull and heavy lead;
And as the thing that's heavy in itself
Upon enforcement flies with greatest speed,   120
So did our men, heavy in Hotspur's loss,
Lend to this weight such lightness with their
    fear
That arrows fled not swifter toward their aim
Than did our soldiers, aiming at their safety,
Fly from the field. Then was the noble Wor-
    cester   125
Too soon ta'en prisoner, and that furious Scot,
The bloody Douglas, whose well-labouring
    sword
Had three times slain th' appearance of the
    King,
Gan vail his stomach and did grace the shame
Of those that turn'd their backs, and in his
    flight,
Stumbling in fear, was took. The sum of all   131
Is that the King hath won, and hath sent out
A speedy power to encounter you, my lord,
Under the conduct of young Lancaster
And Westmoreland. This is the news at full.
  North. For this I shall have time enough to
    mourn.   136
In poison there is physic, and these news,
Having been well, that would have made me
    sick,
Being sick, have in some measure made me
    well;
And as the wretch whose fever-weak'ned joints,
Like strengthless hinges, buckle under life,
Impatient of his fit, breaks like a fire
Out of his keeper's arms, even so my limbs,
Weakened with grief, being now enrag'd with
    grief,
Are thrice themselves. Hence, therefore, thou
    nice crutch!   145
A scaly gauntlet now, with joints of steel,
Must glove this hand; and hence, thou sickly
    coif!
Thou art a guard too wanton for the head

Which princes, flesh'd with conquest, aim to hit.
Now bind my brows with iron, and approach
The ragged'st hour that time and spite dare
    bring   151
To frown upon th' enrag'd Northumberland!
Let heaven kiss earth! Now let not Nature's
    hand
Keep the wild flood confin'd! Let order die!
And let this world no longer be a stage   155
To feed contention in a ling'ring act;
But let one spirit of the first-born Cain
Reign in all bosoms, that, each heart being set
On bloody courses, the rude scene may end,
And darkness be the burier of the dead!   160
   Tra. This strained passion doth you wrong,
    my lord.
   L. Bard. Sweet Earl, divorce not wisdom
from your honour.
   Mor. The lives of all your loving complices
Lean on your health; the which, if you give o'er
To stormy passion, must perforce decay.   165
You cast th' event of war, my noble lord,
And summ'd the accompt of chance before you
    said,
'Let us make head.' It was your presurmise
That, in the dole of blows, your son might drop.
You knew he walk'd o'er perils on an edge, 170
More likely to fall in than to get o'er.
You were advis'd his flesh was capable
Of wounds and scars, and that his forward
    spirit
Would lift him where most trade of danger
    rang'd.   174
Yet did you say 'Go forth,' and none of this,
Though strongly apprehended, could restrain
The stiff-borne action. What hath, then, be-
    fall'n,
Or what hath this bold enterprise brought forth,
More than that being which was like to be?
   L. Bard. We all that are engaged to this loss
Knew that we ventured on such dangerous seas
That if we wrought out life, 'twas ten to one;
And yet we ventur'd, for the gain propos'd
Chok'd the respect of likely peril fear'd;
And since we are o'erset, venture again.   185
Come, we will all put forth, body and goods.
   Mor. 'Tis more than time. And, my most
    noble lord,
I hear for certain, and dare speak the truth:
The gentle Archbishop of York is up
With well-appointed pow'rs. He is a man   190
Who with a double surety binds his followers.
My lord your son had only but the corpse,
But shadows and the shows of men, to fight;
For that same word 'rebellion' did divide

The action of their bodies from their souls; 195
And they did fight with queasiness, constrain'd,
As men drink potions; that their weapons only
Seem'd on our side, but for their spirits and
    souls,
This word 'rebellion' it had froze them up,
As fish are in a pond. But now the Bishop 200
Turns insurrection to religion.
Suppos'd sincere, and holy in his thoughts,
He's follow'd both with body and with mind;
And doth enlarge his rising with the blood
Of fair King Richard, scrap'd from Pomfret
    stones;   205
Derives from heaven his quarrel and his cause;
Tells them he doth bestride a bleeding land,
Gasping for life under great Bolingbroke;
And more and less do flock to follow him.
   North. I knew of this before; but, to speak
    truth,   210
This present grief had wip'd it from my mind.
Go in with me; and counsel every man
The aptest way for safety and revenge.
Get posts and letters, and make friends with
    speed —
Never so few, and never yet more need. *Exeunt.*

Scene II. [*London. A street.*]

Enter *Sir John Falstaff*, with his *Page* bearing
his sword and buckler.

   Fal. Sirrah, you giant, what says the doctor
to my water?
   Page. He said, sir, the water itself was a
good healthy water; but, for the party that
owed it, he might have moe diseases than he
knew for.   6
   Fal. Men of all sorts take a pride to gird
at me. The brain of this foolish-compounded
clay, man, is not able to invent anything that
intends to laughter, more than I invent or is
invented on me. I am not only witty in myself, but the cause that wit is in other men. I
do here walk before thee like a sow that hath
overwhelm'd all her litter but one. If the
Prince put thee into my service for any other
reason than to set me off, why then I have no
judgment. Thou whoreson mandrake, thou art
fitter to be worn in my cap than to wait at
my heels. I was never manned with an agate
till now; but I will inset you neither in gold
nor silver, but in vile apparel, and send you
back again to your master for a jewel — the
juvenal, the Prince your master, whose chin is

not yet fledge. I will sooner have a beard grow in the palm of my hand than he shall get one off his cheek; and yet he will not stick to say his face is a face-royal! God may finish it when he will; 'tis not a hair amiss yet. He may keep it still at a face-royal, for a barber shall never earn sixpence out of it; and yet he'll be crowing as if he had writ man ever since his father was a bachelor. He may keep his own grace, but he's almost out of mine, I can assure him. What said Master Dommelton about the satin for my short cloak and my slops?   34

Page. He said, sir, you should procure him better assurance than Bardolph. He would not take his band and yours. He liked not the security.   38

Fal. Let him be damn'd like the glutton! Pray God his tongue be hotter! A whoreson Achitophel! a rascally yea-forsooth knave! to bear a gentleman in hand, and then stand upon security! The whoreson smooth-pates do now wear nothing but high shoes, and bunches of keys at their girdles; and if a man is through with them in honest taking-up, then they must stand upon security. I had as live they would put ratsbane in my mouth as offer to stop it with security. I look'd 'a should have sent me two-and-twenty yards of satin, as I am a true knight, and he sends me security. Well, he may sleep in security; for he hath the horn of abundance, and the lightness of his wife shines through it; and yet cannot he see, though he have his own lanthorn to light him. Where's Bardolph?   55

Page. He's gone into Smithfield to buy your worship a horse.

Fal. I bought him in Paul's, and he'll buy me a horse in Smithfield. An I could get me but a wife in the stews, I were mann'd, hors'd, and wiv'd.   61

Enter *Lord Chief Justice and Servant.*

Page. Sir, here comes the nobleman that committed the Prince for striking him about Bardolph.

Fal. Wait close. I will not see him.   65

Just. What's he that goes there?

Serv. Falstaff, an't please your lordship.

Just. He that was in question for the rob-b'ry?   69

Serv. He, my lord; but he hath since done good service at Shrewsbury, and, as I hear, is now going with some charge to the Lord John of Lancaster.

Just. What, to York? Call him back again.

Serv. Sir John Falstaff!   76

Fal. Boy, tell him I am deaf.

Page. You must speak louder. My master is deaf.

Just. I am sure he is, to the hearing of anything good. Go pluck him by the elbow. I must speak with him.

Serv. Sir John!   83

Fal. What? A young knave, and begging? Is there not wars? Is there not employment? Doth not the King lack subjects? Do not the rebels need soldiers? Though it be a shame to be on any side but one, it is worse shame to beg than to be on the worst side, were it worse than the name of rebellion can tell how to make it.

Serv. You mistake me, sir.   91

Fal. Why, sir, did I say you were an honest man? Setting my knighthood and my soldiership aside, I had lied in my throat if I had said so.   94

Serv. I pray you, sir, then set your knighthood and your soldiership aside, and give me leave to tell you you lie in your throat if you say I am any other than an honest man.

Fal. I give thee leave to tell me so? I lay aside that which grows to me? If thou get'st any leave of me, hang me; if thou tak'st leave, thou wert better be hang'd. You hunt counter. Hence! avaunt!

Serv. Sir, my lord would speak with you.

Just. Sir John Falstaff, a word with you.   105

Fal. My good lord! God give your lordship good time of day! I am glad to see your lordship abroad. I heard say your lordship was sick. I hope your lordship goes abroad by advice. Your lordship, though not clean past your youth, hath yet some smack of age in you, some relish of the saltness of time; and I most humbly beseech your lordship to have a reverend care of your health.

Just. Sir John, I sent for you before your expedition to Shrewsbury.   116

Fal. An't please your lordship, I hear his Majesty is return'd with some discomfort from Wales.

Just. I talk not of his Majesty. You would not come when I sent for you.   121

Fal. And I hear, moreover, his Highness is fall'n into this same whoreson apoplexy.

Just. Well, God mend him! I pray you let me speak with you.   125

Fal. This apoplexy, as I take it, is a kind of lethargy, an't please your lordship; a kind of sleeping in the blood, a whoreson tingling.

Just. What tell you me of it? Be it as it is.

Fal. It hath it original from much grief, from study and perturbation of the brain. I have read the cause of his effects in Galen. It is a kind of deafness. 134

Just. I think you are fall'n into the disease, for you hear not what I say to you.

Fal. Very well, my lord, very well. Rather, an't please you, it is the disease of not list'ning, the malady of not marking, that I am troubled withal. 140

Just. To punish you by the heels would amend the attention of your ears, and I care not if I do become your physician.

Fal. I am as poor as Job, my lord, but not so patient. Your lordship may minister the potion of imprisonment to me in respect of poverty; but how I should be your patient to follow your prescriptions, the wise may make some dram of a scruple, or indeed a scruple itself.

Just. I sent for you when there were matters against you for your life, to come speak with me.

Fal. As I was then advis'd by my learned counsel in the laws of this land service, I did not come. 155

Just. Well, the truth is, Sir John, you live in great infamy.

Fal. He that buckles himself in my belt cannot live in less.

Just. Your means are very slender, and your waste is great. 161

Fal. I would it were otherwise. I would my means were greater and my waist slenderer.

Just. You have misled the youthful prince.

Fal. The young prince hath misled me. I am the fellow with the great belly, and he my dog. 166

Just. Well, I am loath to gall a new-heal'd wound. Your day's service at Shrewsbury hath a little gilded over your night's exploit on Gadshill. You may thank th' unquiet time for your quiet o'erposting that action. 171

Fal. My lord —

Just. But since all is well, keep it so. Wake not a sleeping wolf.

Fal. To wake a wolf is as bad as smell a fox.

Just. What! you are as a candle, the better part burnt out.

Fal. A wassail candle, my lord; all tallow. If I did say of wax, my growth would approve the truth. 181

Just. There is not a white hair on your face but should have his effect of gravity.

Fal. His effect of gravy, gravy, gravy.

Just. You follow the young prince up and down, like his ill angel. 186

Fal. Not so, my lord. Your ill angel is light, but I hope he that looks upon me will take me without weighing. And yet, in some respects, I grant, I cannot go. I cannot tell. Virtue is of so little regard in these costermonger's times that true valour is turn'd berod; pregnancy is made a tapster, and his quick wit wasted in giving reckonings. All the other gifts appertinent to man, as the malice of this age shapes them, are not worth a gooseberry. You that are old consider not the capacities of us that are young. You do measure the heat of our livers with the bitterness of your galls; and we that are in the vaward of our youth, I must confess, are wags too. 200

Just. Do you set down your name in the scroll of youth, that are written down old with all the characters of age? Have you not a moist eye, a dry hand, a yellow cheek, a white beard, a decreasing leg, an increasing belly? Is not your voice broken, your wind short, your chin double, your wit single, and every part about you blasted with antiquity? And will you yet call yourself young? Fie, fie, fie, Sir John! 209

Fal. My lord, I was born about three of the clock in the afternoon, with a white head and something a round belly. For my voice, I have lost it with halloaing, and singing of anthems. To approve my youth further, I will not. The truth is, I am only old in judgment and understanding; and he that will caper with me for a thousand marks, let him lend me the money, and have at him. For the box of the ear that the Prince gave you, he gave it like a rude prince, and you took it like a sensible lord. I have check'd him for it, and the young lion repents — marry, not in ashes and sackcloth, but in new silk and old sack. 222

Just. Well, God send the Prince a better companion!

Fal. God send the companion a better Prince! I cannot rid my hands of him. 226

Just. Well, the King hath sever'd you and Prince Harry. I hear you are going with Lord John of Lancaster against the Archbishop and the Earl of Northumberland. 230

Fal. Yea, I thank your pretty sweet wit for it! But look you pray, all you that kiss my Lady Peace at home, that our armies join not in a hot day; for, by the Lord, I take but two shirts out with me, and I mean not to sweat extraordinarily. If it be a hot day, and I brandish anything but a bottle, I would I might never spit white again! There is not a dangerous action can peep out his head but I am thrust upon it. Well, I cannot last ever; but it was alway yet the trick of our English nation, if they have a good thing, to make it too common. If ye will needs say I am an old man, you should give me rest. I would to God my name were not so terrible to the enemy as it is. I were better to be eaten to death with a rust than to be scoured to nothing with perpetual motion.

Just. Well, be honest, be honest; and God bless your expedition!   249

Fal. Will your lordship lend me a thousand pound to furnish me forth?

Just. Not a penny, not a penny! You are too impatient to bear crosses. Fare you well. Commend me to my cousin Westmoreland.

                [*Exeunt Chief Justice and Servant.*]

Fal. If I do, fillip me with a three-man beetle! A man can no more separate age and covetousness than 'a can part young limbs and lechery; but the gout galls the one, and the pox pinches the other; and so both the degrees prevent my curses. Boy!   260

Page. Sir?

Fal. What money is in my purse?

Page. Seven groats and twopence.

Fal. I can get no remedy against this consumption of the purse. Borrowing only lingers and lingers it out, but the disease is incurable. Go bear this letter to my Lord of Lancaster; this to the Prince; this to the Earl of Westmoreland; and this to old Mistress Ursula, whom I have weekly sworn to marry since I perceiv'd the first white hair on my chin. About it! You know where to find me. [*Exit Page.*] A pox of this gout! or, a gout of this pox! for the one or the other plays the rogue with my great toe. 'Tis no matter if I do halt. I have the wars for my colour, and my pension shall seem the more reasonable. A good wit will make use of anything. I will turn diseases to commodity.   *Exit.*

Scene III. [*York. The Archbishop's Palace.*]

Enter the *Archbishop, Thomas Mowbray (Earl Marshal)*, the *Lords Hastings* and *Bardolph.*

Arch. Thus have you heard our cause and known our means;
And, my most noble friends, I pray you all
Speak plainly your opinions of our hopes.
And first, Lord Marshal, what say you to it?

Mowb. I well allow the occasion of our arms,

But gladly would be better satisfied   6
How in our means we should advance ourselves
To look with forehead bold and big enough
Upon the power and puissance of the King.   9

Hast. Our present musters grow upon the file
To five-and-twenty thousand men of choice;
And our supplies live largely in the hope
Of great Northumberland, whose bosom burns
With an incensed fire of injuries.

L. Bard. The question then, Lord Hastings,
        standeth thus: 15
Whether our present five-and-twenty thousand
May hold up head without Northumberland.

Hast. With him, we may.

L. Bard.   Yea, marry, there's the point!
But if without him we be thought too feeble,
My judgment is we should not step too far 20
Till we had his assistance by the hand;
For, in a theme so bloody-fac'd as this,
Conjecture, expectation, and surmise
Of aids incertain should not be admitted.

Arch. 'Tis very true, Lord Bardolph; for
        indeed   25
It was young Hotspur's case at Shrewsbury.

L. Bard. It was, my lord; who lin'd himself
        with hope,
Eating the air on promise of supply,
Flatt'ring himself in project of a power   29
Much smaller than the smallest of his thoughts,
And so, with great imagination,
Proper to madmen, led his powers to death
And, winking, leapt into destruction.

Hast. But, by your leave, it never yet did hurt
To lay down likelihoods and forms of hope.

L. Bard. Yes, in this present quality of war,
Indeed, the instant action. A cause on foot
Lives so in hope as in an early spring
We see th' appearing buds, which to prove fruit
Hope gives not so much warrant as despair 40
That frosts will bite them. When we mean to
        build,
We first survey the plot, then draw the model;
And when we see the figure of the house,
Then must we rate the cost of the erection,
Which if we find outweighs ability,   45
What do we then but draw anew the model
In fewer offices, or at least desist
To build at all? Much more, in this great
        work —
Which is (almost) to pluck a kingdom down
And set another up — should we survey   50
The plot of situation and the model,
Consent upon a sure foundation,
Question surveyors, know our own estate,
How able such a work to undergo.

To weigh against his opposite; or else   55
We fortify in paper and in figures,
Using the names of men instead of men,
Like one that draws the model of a house
Beyond his power to build it, who (half
  through)
Gives o'er, and leaves his part-created cost   60
A naked subject to the weeping clouds
And waste for churlish winter's tyranny.
  Hast. Grant that our hopes (yet likely of
    fair birth)
Should be stillborn, and that we now possess'd
The utmost man of expectation,   65
I think we are so a body strong enough,
Even as we are, to equal with the King.
  L. Bard. What, is the King but five-and-
    twenty thousand?
  Hast. To us no more; nay, not so much,
    Lord Bardolph.
For his divisions, as the times do brawl,   70
Are in three heads: one power against the
    French
And one against Glendower; perforce a third
Must take up us. So is the unfirm King
In three divided, and his coffers sound
With hollow poverty and emptiness.   75
  Arch. That he should draw his several
    strengths together
And come against us in full puissance
Need not be dreaded.
  Hast.   If he should do so,
To French and Welsh he leaves his back un-
    arm'd,   79
They baying him at the heels. Never fear that.
  L. Bard. Who is it like should lead his forces
    hither?
  Hast. The Duke of Lancaster and Westmore-
    land;

Against the Welsh, himself and Harry Mon-
    mouth;
But who is substituted 'gainst the French,
I have no certain notice.
  Arch.   Let us on,   85
And publish the occasion of our arms.
The commonwealth is sick of their own choice;
Their over-greedy love hath surfeited.
An habitation giddy and unsure
Hath he that buildeth on the vulgar heart.   90
O thou fond Many! with what loud applause
Didst thou beat heaven with blessing Boling-
    broke
Before he was what thou wouldst have him be!
And being now trimm'd in thine own desires,
Thou (beastly feeder) art so full of him   95
That thou provok'st thyself to cast him up.
So, so (thou common dog) didst thou disgorge
Thy glutton bosom of the royal Richard;
And now thou wouldst eat thy dead vomit up,
And howl'st to find it. What trust is in these
    times?   100
They that, when Richard liv'd, would have him
    die
Are now become enamour'd on his grave.
Thou that threw'st dust upon his goodly head
When through proud London he came sighing
    on
After th' admired heels of Bolingbroke,   105
Criest now, 'O earth, yield us that king again,
And take thou this!' O thoughts of men
    accurs'd!
Past, and to come, seems best; things present,
    worst.
  Mowb. Shall we go draw our numbers and
    set on?   109
  Hast. We are time's subjects, and time bids
    be gone.   *Exeunt.*

ACT II. Scene I. [*London. A street.*]

Enter *Hostess* of the Tavern, with two *Officers*
    (*Fang* and *Snare*) [and *Fang's Boy*].

  Host. Master Fang, have you ent'red the
action?
  Fang. It is ent'red.
  Host. Where's your yeoman? Is't a lusty
yeoman? Will 'a stand to't?   5
  Fang. Sirrah, where's Snare?
  Host. O Lord, ay! good Master Snare.
  Snare. Here, here.
  Fang. Snare, we must arrest Sir John
Falstaff.

  Host. Yea, good Master Snare. I have
ent'red him and all.   11
  Snare. It may chance cost some of us our
lives, for he will stab.
  Host. Alas the day! take heed of him. He
stabb'd me in mine own house most beastly, in
good faith! 'A cares not what mischief he does,
if his weapon be out. He will foin like any devil;
he will spare neither man, woman, nor child.
  Fang. If I can close with him, I care not for
his thrust.
  Host. No, nor I neither. I'll be at your
elbow.   22

Henry, Prince of Wales (Robert Hardy), and a companion, Poins (Michael Bates)

HENRY IV
PART TWO

PHOTOGRAPHS BY HOUSTON ROGERS
PRODUCED BY THE OLD VIC COMPANY

Pistol (John Neville), Justice Shallow (Paul Daneman), and Sir John Falstaff (Paul Rogers)

Falstaff's toast: "I would to God my name were not so terrible to the enemy" (Act I, Scene II)

A forgetful Falstaff is reproached by Mistress Quickly (Rachel Roberts) (Act II, Scene I)

Pistol shocks Mistress Quickly, hostess at the Boar's Head Tavern (Act II, Scene IV)

"Saturn and Venus this year in conjunction! What says the almanack to that?" Doll Tearsheet (Gwen Cherrell) grants the aging Falstaff a kiss (*Act II, Scene IV*)

Doll suits action to her words: "Thou abominable damned cheater, art thou not ashamed to be called captain?" (*Act II, Scene IV*)

The braggadocio, Pistol. "Fear we broadsides? no, let the fiend give fire" (*Act II, Scene IV*)

With Silence (Meredith Edwards), Bardolph (Ronald Fraser), and Falstaff looking on, Justice Shallow demonstrates the handling of the musket to Falstaff's motley, ragged band of new recruits for King Henry's army (*Act III, Scene III*)

Left: John of Lancaster (Alan Dobie, center), by an act of treachery overcomes the rebels (*Act IV, Scene II*). To Lancaster's left stands the Archbishop of York (Daniel Thorndike)

Right: Lady Percy (Ann Todd), widow of Hotspur. "... And never shall have length of life enough to rain upon remembrance with mine eyes ... for recordation of my noble husband" (*Act II, Scene III*)

Westmoreland (John Wood), Warwick (Donald Moffat), Prince Hal, and Clarence (Clifford

"I know thee not, old man: fall to thy prayers." Prince Hal, now Henry V, shuns Falstaff (*Act V, Scene V*)

Williams) before the stricken King (Eric Porter). Behind the King, Gloucester (Nicholas Amer); right, Lancaster (*Act IV, Scene V*)

"How ill white hairs become a fool and jester! I have long dream'd of such a man, so surfeit-swell'd, so old and so profane; but, being awak'd, I do despise my dream." Thus does Henry V reject the friend of his immaturity (*Act V, Scene V*)

The King to the King-to-be: "Therefore, my Harry, be it thy course to busy giddy minds with foreign quarrels" (*Act IV, Scene III*)

Fang. An I but fist him once! An 'a come but within my vice!   24

Host. I am undone by his going. I warrant you he's an infinitive thing upon my score. Good Master Fang, hold him sure. Good Master Snare, let him not scape. 'A comes continuantly to Pie Corner (saving your manhoods) to buy a saddle, and he is indited to dinner to the Lubber's Head in Lumbert Street, to Master Smooth's the silkman. I pray you, since my exion is ent'red, and my case so openly known to the world, let him be brought in to his answer. A hundred mark is a long one for a poor lone woman to bear; and I have borne, and borne, and borne; and have been fubb'd off, and fubb'd off, and fubb'd off, from this day to that day, that it is a shame to be thought on. There is no honesty in such dealing, unless a woman should be made an ass and a beast, to bear every knave's wrong.   41

Enter *Sir John [Falstaff]* and *Bardolph* and the *Boy.*

Yonder he comes! and that arrant malmseynose knave Bardolph with him! Do your offices, do your offices! Master Fang and Master Snare, do me, do me, do me your offices!   45

Fal. How now? Whose mare's dead? What's the matter?

Fang. Sir John, I arrest you at the suit of Mistress Quickly.   49

Fal. Away, varlets! Draw, Bardolph! Cut me off the villain's head! Throw the quean in the channel!

Host. Throw me in the channel? I'll throw thee in the channel! Wilt thou? wilt thou, thou bastardly rogue? Murder, murder! Ah, thou honeysuckle villain! wilt thou kill God's officers and the King's? Ah, thou honeyseed rogue! thou art a honeyseed, a man-queller and a woman-queller.

Fal. Keep them off, Bardolph.   60

Fang. A rescue! a rescue!

Host. Good people, bring a rescue or two. Thou wo't, wo't thou? Thou wo't, wo't ta? Do, do, thou rogue! do, thou hempseed!

Fal. Away, you scullion! you rampallian! you fustilarian! I'll tickle your catastrophe.

Enter *Lord Chief Justice* and his *men.*

Just. What is the matter? Keep the peace here, ho!

Host. Good my lord, be good to me! I beseech you stand to me!   70

Just. How now, Sir John? What are you brawling here?

Doth this become your place, your time, and business?

You should have been well on your way to York.

Stand from him, fellow. Wherefore hang'st upon him?   74

Host. O my most worshipful lord! an't please your Grace, I am a poor widow of Eastcheap, and he is arrested at my suit.

Just. For what sum?   78

Host. It is more than for some, my lord; it is for all — all I have. He hath eaten me out of house and home; he hath put all my substance into that fat belly of his. But I will have some of it out again, or I will ride thee a-nights like the mare.

Fal. I think I am as like to ride the mare, if I have any vantage of ground to get up.   85

Just. How comes this, Sir John? Fie! what man of good temper would endure this tempest of exclamation? Are you not ashamed to enforce a poor widow to so rough a course to come by her own?   90

Fal. What is the gross sum that I owe thee?

Host. Marry, if thou wert an honest man, thyself and the money too! Thou didst swear to me upon a parcel-gilt goblet, sitting in my Dolphin chamber, at the round table by a sea-coal fire, upon Wednesday in Wheeson week, when the Prince broke thy head for liking his father to a singing man of Windsor — thou didst swear to me then, as I was washing thy wound, to marry me and make me my lady thy wife. Canst thou deny it? Did not goodwife Keech, the butcher's wife, come in then and call me gossip Quickly? coming in to borrow a mess of vinegar, telling us she had a good dish of prawns, whereby thou didst desire to eat some, whereby I told thee they were ill for a green wound? And didst thou not, when she was gone down stairs, desire me to be no more so familiarity with such poor people, saying thus ere long they should call me madam? And didst thou not kiss me, and bid me fetch thee thirty shillings? I put thee now to thy book-oath. Deny it if thou canst.   112

Fal. My lord, this is a poor mad soul; and she says, up and down the town, that her eldest son is like you. She hath been in good case, and the truth is, poverty hath distracted her. But for these foolish officers, I beseech you I may have redress against them.   118

Just. Sir John, Sir John, I am well acquainted with your manner of wrenching the true cause the false way. It is not a confident brow, nor the throng of words that come with such more than impudent sauciness from you, can thrust me from a level consideration. You have, as it appears to me, practis'd upon the easy-yielding spirit of this woman, and made her serve your uses both in purse and in person.

Host. Yea, in truth, my lord.   128

Just. Pray thee peace. Pay her the debt you owe her, and unpay the villany you have done her. The one you may do with sterling money, and the other with current repentance.

Fal. My lord, I will not undergo this sneap without reply. You call honourable boldness impudent sauciness. If a man will make curtsy and say nothing, he is virtuous. No, my lord, my humble duty rememb'red, I will not be your suitor. I say to you I do desire deliverance from these officers, being upon hasty employment in the King's affairs.   140

Just. You speak as having power to do wrong. But answer in th' effect of your reputation, and satisfy the poor woman.

Fal. Come hither, hostess.
                              [*Takes her aside.*]

Enter *Master Gower* (a Messenger).

Just. Now, Master Gower, what news?   145

Gow. The King, my lord, and Harry Prince of Wales
Are near at hand. The rest the paper tells.
                              [*Gives a letter.*]

Fal. As I am a gentleman!

Host. Faith, you said so before.

Fal. As I am a gentleman! Come, no more words of it.   151

Host. By this heav'nly ground I tread on, I must be fain to pawn both my plate and the tapestry of my dining chambers.

Fal. Glasses, glasses is the only drinking; and for thy walls, a pretty slight drollery, or the story of the Prodigal, or the German Hunting in waterwork, is worth a thousand of these bed-hangers and these fly-bitten tapestries. Let it be ten pound, if thou canst. Come, an 'twere not for thy humours, there's not a better wench in England. Go wash thy face and draw the action. Come, thou must not be in this humour with me. Dost not know me? Come, come, I know thou wast set on to this.   165

Host. Pray thee, Sir John, let it be but twenty nobles. I' faith, I am loath to pawn my plate, so God save me, la!

Fal. Let it alone. I'll make other shift
You'll be a fool still.   17

Host. Well, you shall have it, though I pawn my gown. I hope you'll come to supper. You'll pay me all together?

Fal. Will I live? [*To Bardolph*] Go with her with her! Hook on, hook on.   175

Host. Will you have Doll Tearsheet meet you at supper?

Fal. No more words. Let's have her.

Exeunt Hostess, [Bardolph,] Officers, [and Boy]

Just. I have heard better news.

Fal. What's the news, my lord?   18

Just. Where lay the King to-night?

Gow. At Basingstoke, my lord.

Fal. I hope, my lord, all's well. What is th news, my lord?

Just. Come all his forces back?   18

Gow. No; fifteen hundred foot, five hundred horse
Are march'd up to my Lord of Lancaster
Against Northumberland and the Archbishop

Fal. Comes the King back from Wales, m noble lord?   18

Just. You shall have letters of me presently Come, go along with me, good Master Gower

Fal. My lord!

Just. What's the matter?

Fal. Master Gower, shall I entreat you with me to dinner?   19

Gow. I must wait upon my good lord here I thank you, good Sir John.

Just. Sir John, you loiter here too long, bein you are to take soldiers up in counties as you go.   20

Fal. Will you sup with me, Master Gower

Just. What foolish master taught you thes manners, Sir John?

Fal. Master Gower, if they become me not he was a fool that taught them me. This is th right fencing grace, my lord — tap for tap, an so part fair.   20

Just. Now, the Lord lighten thee! thou ar a great fool.   *Exeunt*

Scene II. [*London. Another street.*]

Enter *Prince Henry* and *Poins.*

Prince. Before God, I am exceeding weary

Poins. Is't come to that? I had though weariness durst not have attach'd one of s high blood.

Prince. Faith, it does me, though it discolours the complexion of my greatness to acknowledge it. Doth it not show vilely in me to desire small beer?   8

Poins. Why, a prince should not be so loosely studied as to remember so weak a composition.

Prince. Belike then my appetite was not princely got; for, by my troth, I do now remember the poor creature, small beer. But indeed these humble considerations make me out of love with my greatness. What a disgrace is it to me to remember thy name! or to know thy face to-morrow! or to take note how many pair of silk stockings thou hast, — viz., these, and those that were thy peach-colour'd ones! or to bear the inventory of thy shirts — as, one for superfluity and another for use! But that the tennis-court-keeper knows better than I; for it is a low ebb of linen with thee when thou keepest not racket there; as thou hast not done a great while, because the rest of thy low countries have made a shift to eat up thy holland; and God knows whether those that bawl out the ruins of thy linen shall inherit his kingdom; but the midwives say the children are not in the fault; whereupon the world increases, and kinreds are mightily strengthened.   30

Poins. How ill it follows, after you have laboured so hard, you should talk so idly! Tell me, how many good young princes would do so, their fathers being so sick as yours at this time is?

Prince. Shall I tell thee one thing, Poins?   35

Poins. Yes, faith; and let it be an excellent good thing.

Prince. It shall serve among wits of no higher breeding than thine.

Poins. Go to! I stand the push of your one thing that you will tell.   41

Prince. Marry, I tell thee it is not meet that I should be sad now my father is sick; albeit I could tell to thee (as to one it pleases me, for fault of a better, to call my friend) I could be sad, and sad indeed too.   46

Poins. Very hardly, upon such a subject.

Prince. By this hand, thou thinkest me as far in the devil's book as thou and Falstaff for obduracy and persistency. Let the end try the man. But I tell thee, my heart bleeds inwardly that my father is so sick; and keeping such vile company as thou art hath in reason taken from me all ostentation of sorrow.

Poins. The reason?   55

Prince. What wouldst thou think of me if I should weep?

Poins. I would think thee a most princely hypocrite.   59

Prince. It would be every man's thought, and thou art a blessed fellow to think as every man thinks. Never a man's thought in the world keeps the roadway better than thine. Every man would think me an hypocrite indeed. And what accites your most worshipful thought to think so?   65

Poins. Why, because you have been so lewd and so much engraffed to Falstaff.

Prince. And to thee.

Poins. By this light, I am well spoke on; I can hear it with mine own ears. The worst that they can say of me is, that I am a second brother, and that I am a proper fellow of my hands; and those two things I confess I cannot help. By the mass, here comes Bardolph.   74

Enter *Bardolph* and *Page.*

Prince. And the boy that I gave Falstaff. 'A had him from me Christian, and look if the fat villain have not transform'd him ape.

Bard. God save your Grace!   78

Prince. And yours, most noble Bardolph!

Bard. [*to the Page*] Come, you virtuous ass, you bashful fool, must you be blushing? Wherefore blush you now? What a maidenly man-at-arms are you become! Is't such a matter to get a pottle-pot's maidenhead?   84

Page. 'A calls me e'en now, my lord, through a red lattice, and I could discern no part of his face from the window. At last I spied his eyes, and methought he had made two holes in the alewife's new petticoat, and so peep'd through.

Prince. Has not the boy profited?   90

Bard. Away, you whoreson upright rabbit, away!

Page. Away, you rascally Althæa's dream, away!   94

Prince. Instruct us, boy. What dream, boy?

Page. Marry, my lord, Althæa dreamt she was delivered of a firebrand, and therefore I call him her dream.

Prince. A crown's worth of good interpretation. There 'tis, boy.   100

Poins. O that this good blossom could be kept from cankers! Well, there is sixpence to preserve thee.

Bard. An you do not make him be hang'd among you, the gallows shall have wrong. 105

Prince. And how doth thy master, Bardolph?

Bard. Well, my lord. He heard of your Grace's coming to town. There's a letter for you.

Poins. Deliver'd with good respect! And how doth the Martlemas, your master?   110

Bard. In bodily health, sir.

Poins. Marry, the immortal part needs a physician. But that moves not him; though that be sick, it dies not.

Prince. I do allow this wen to be as familiar with me as my dog; and he holds his place, for look you how he writes.   117

Poins. [*reads*] 'John Falstaff, knight'— Every man must know that as oft as he has occasion to name himself; even like those that are kin to the King; for they never prick their finger but they say, 'There's some of the King's blood spilt.' 'How comes that?' says he that takes upon him not to conceive. The answer is as ready as a borrower's cap: 'I am the King's poor cousin, sir.'   126

Prince. Nay, they will be kin to us, or they will fetch it from Japhet. But to the letter!

Poins. [*reads*] 'Sir John Falstaff, knight, to the son of the King, nearest his father, Harry Prince of Wales, greeting.' Why, this is a certificate.   132

Prince. Peace!

Poins. [*reads*] 'I will imitate the honourable Romans in brevity.' He sure means brevity in breath — short-winded. 'I commend me to thee, I commend thee, and I leave thee. Be not too familiar with Poins, for he misuses thy favours so much that he swears thou art to marry his sister Nell. Repent at idle times as thou mayst; and so farewell.   141

'Thine, by yea and no (which is as much as to say, as thou usest him), JACK FAL-STAFF with my familiars, JOHN with my brothers and sisters, and SIR JOHN with all Europe.'

My lord, I'll steep this letter in sack and make him eat it.

Prince. That's to make him eat twenty of his words. But do you use me thus, Ned? Must I marry your sister?   151

Poins. God send the wench no worse fortune! but I never said so.

Prince. Well, thus we play the fools with the time, and the spirits of the wise sit in the clouds and mock us. Is your master here in London?

Bard. Yea, my lord.

Prince. Where sups he? Doth the old boar feed in the old frank?   160

Bard. At the old place, my lord, in East-cheap.

Prince. What company?

Page. Ephesians, my lord, of the old church.

Prince. Sup any women with him?   165

Page. None, my lord, but old Mistress Quickly and Mistress Doll Tearsheet.

Prince. What pagan may that be?

Page. A proper gentlewoman, sir, and a kinswoman of my master's.   170

Prince. Even such kin as the parish heifers are to the town bull. Shall we steal upon them, Ned, at supper?

Poins. I am your shadow, my lord; I'll follow you.   175

Prince. Sirrah, you boy, and Bardolph, no word to your master that I am yet come to town. There's for your silence. [*Gives money.*]

Bard. I have no tongue, sir.   179

Page. And for mine, sir, I will govern it.

Prince. Fare you well, go. [*Exeunt Bardolph and Boy.*] This Doll Tearsheet should be some road.

Poins. I warrant you, as common as the way between Saint Alban's and London.   185

Prince. How might we see Falstaff bestow himself to-night in his true colours, and not ourselves be seen?

Poins. Put on two leathern jerkins and aprons and wait upon him at his table as drawers.   191

Prince. From a god to a bull? A heavy descension! It was Jove's case. From a prince to a prentice? A low transformation! That shall be mine; for in everything the purpose must weigh with the folly. Follow me, Ned. *Exeunt.*

Scene III. [*Warkworth. Before the Castle.*]

Enter *Northumberland*, his *Wife*, and the *Wife* to *Harry Percy*.

North. I pray thee, loving wife, and gentle
        daughter,
Give even way unto my rough affairs.
Put not you on the visage of the times
And be, like them, to Percy troublesome.

Wife. I have given over, I will speak no
        more.   5
Do what you will; your wisdom be your guide.

North. Alas, sweet wife, my honour is at
        pawn;
And but my going, nothing can redeem it.

Lady Percy. O, yet, for God's sake, go not to
        these wars!   9

The time was, father, that you broke your word
When you were more endear'd to it than now;
When your own Percy, when my heart's dear
 Harry
Threw many a northward look to see his father
Bring up his powers; but he did long in vain.
Who then persuaded you to stay at home? 15
There were two honours lost, yours and your
 son's.
For yours, the God of heaven brighten it!
For his, it stuck upon him as the sun
In the grey vault of heaven, and by his light
Did all the chivalry of England move 20
To do brave acts. He was indeed the glass
Wherein the noble youth did dress themselves.
He had no legs that practis'd not his gait;
And speaking thick (which nature made his
 blemish)
Became the accents of the valiant; 25
For those that could speak low and tardily
Would turn their own perfection to abuse
To seem like him; so that in speech, in gait,
In diet, in affections of delight,
In military rules, humours of blood, 30
He was the mark and glass, copy and book,
That fashion'd others. And him — O wondrous
 him!
O miracle of men! — him did you leave —
Second to none, unseconded by you —
To look upon the hideous god of war 35
In disadvantage, to abide a field
Where nothing but the sound of Hotspur's
 name
Did seem defensible. So you left him.
Never, O never, do his ghost the wrong
To hold your honour more precise and nice 40
With others than with him! Let them alone.
The Marshal and the Archbishop are strong.
Had my sweet Harry had but half their
 numbers,
To-day might I, hanging on Hotspur's neck,
Have talk'd of Monmouth's grave.
 North.   Beshrew your heart. 45
Fair daughter! you do draw my spirits from
 me
With new lamenting ancient oversights.
But I must go and meet with danger there,
Or it will seek me in another place
And find me worse provided.
 Wife.   O, fly to Scotland, 50
Till that the nobles and the armed commons
Have of their puissance made a little taste.
 Lady Percy. If they get ground and vantage
of the King,
Then join you with them like a rib of steel,

To make strength stronger; but, for all our
 loves, 55
First let them try themselves. So did your son;
He was so suff'red; so came I a widow,
And never shall have length of life enough
To rain upon remembrance with mine eyes, 59
That it may grow and sprout as high as heaven,
For recordation to my noble husband.
 North. Come, come, go in with me. 'Tis
 with my mind
As with the tide swell'd up unto his height,
That makes a still-stand, running neither way.
Fain would I go to meet the Archbishop, 65
But many thousand reasons hold me back.
I will resolve for Scotland. There am I,
Till time and vantage crave my company.
        Exeunt.

Scene IV. [*London. The Boar's Head Tavern in Eastcheap.*]

Enter two *Drawers.*

1. Draw. What the devil hast thou brought
there? apple Johns? Thou knowest Sir John
cannot endure an apple John.
 2. Draw. Mass, thou say'st true. The
Prince once set a dish of apple Johns before him
and told him there were five more Sir Johns,
and, putting off his hat, said, 'I will now take
my leave of these six dry, round, old, withered
knights.' It ang'red him to the heart. But he
hath forgot that. 10
 1. Draw. Why then, cover and set them
down; and see if thou canst find out Sneak's
noise. Mistress Tearsheet would fain hear some
music. Dispatch! The room where they supp'd
is too hot; they'll come in straight. 15
 2. Draw. Sirrah, here will be the Prince and
Master Poins anon; and they will put on two
of our jerkins and aprons, and Sir John must
not know of it. Bardolph hath brought word.
 1. Draw. By the mass, here will be old utis!
It will be an excellent stratagem.] 22
 2. Draw. I'll see if I can find out Sneak.
        Exit.

Enter *Mistress Quickly* (*Hostess*) and *Doll Tearsheet.*

Host. I' faith, sweetheart, methinks now you
are in an excellent good temperality. Your
pulsidge beats as extraordinarily as heart would
desire; and your colour, I warrant you, is as
red as any rose, in good truth, la. But, i' faith,

you have drunk too much canaries; and that's a marvellous searching wine, and it perfumes the blood ere one can say 'What's this?' How do you now? 32

Doll. Better than I was. Hem.

Host. Why, that's well said! A good heart's worth gold. Lo, here comes Sir John. 35

Enter *Sir John Falstaff.*

Fal. [*sings*] 'When Arthur first in court' — Empty the jordan. [*Exit First Drawer.*]—[*Sings*] 'And was a worthy king.' — How now, Mistress Doll?

Host. Sick of a calm; yea, good faith. 40

Fal. So is all her sect. An they be once in a calm, they are sick.

Doll. A pox damn you, you muddy rascal! Is that all the comfort you give me?

Fal. You make fat rascals, Mistress Doll. 45

Doll. I make them? Gluttony and diseases make them. I make them not.

Fal. If the cook help to make the gluttony, you help to make the diseases, Doll. We catch of you, Doll; we catch of you. Grant that, my poor virtue, grant that. 51

Doll. Yea, joy — our chains and our jewels.

Fal. 'Your brooches, pearls, and ouches.' For to serve bravely is to come halting off: you know, to come off the breach with his pike bent bravely, and to surgery bravely; to venture upon the charg'd chambers bravely —

Doll. Hang yourself, you muddy conger, hang yourself! 59

Host. By my troth, this is the old fashion! You two never meet but you fall to some discord. You are both, i' good truth, as rheumatic as two dry toasts. You cannot one bear with another's confirmities. What the goodyere! One must bear, and that must be you. You are the weaker vessel, as they say, the emptier vessel. 66

Doll. Can a weak empty vessel bear such a huge full hogshead? There's a whole merchant's venture of Bordeaux stuff in him. You have not seen a hulk better stuff'd in the hold. Come, I'll be friends with thee, Jack. Thou art going to the wars; and whether I shall ever see thee again or no, there is nobody cares.

Enter *Drawer.*

Draw. Sir, Ancient Pistol's below, and would speak with you. 75

Doll. Hang him, swaggering rascal! let him not come hither. It is the foul-mouth'dst rogue in England.

Host. If he swagger, let him not come here. No, by my faith! I must live among my neighbours. I'll no swaggerers. I am in good name and fame with the very best. Shut the door! There comes no swaggerers here. I have not liv'd all this while to have swaggering now. Shut the door, I pray you. 85

Fal. Dost thou hear, hostess?

Host. Pray ye pacify yourself, Sir John. There comes no swaggerers here.

Fal. Dost thou hear? It is mine ancient.

Host. Tilly-fally, Sir John, ne'er tell me! Your ancient swagg'rer comes not in my doors. I was before Master Tisick, the debuty, t'other day; and, as he said to me — 'twas no longer ago than Wednesday last i' good faith — 'Neighbour Quickly,' says he—Master Dumbe, our minister, was by then — 'Neighbour Quickly,' says he, 'receive those that are civil, for,' said he, 'you are in an ill name.' Now 'a said so, I can tell whereupon. 'For,' says he, 'you are an honest woman, and well thought on; therefore take heed what guests you receive. Receive,' says he, 'no swaggering companions.' There comes none here! You would bless you to hear what he said. No! I'll no swagg'rers. 104

Fal. He's no swagg'rer, hostess — a tame cheater, i' faith. You may stroke him as gently as a puppy greyhound. He'll not swagger with a Barbary hen if her feathers turn back in any show of resistance. Call him up, drawer. 109

[*Exit Drawer.*]

Host. Cheater call you him? I will bar no honest man my house, nor no cheater; but I do not love swaggering. By my troth, I am the worse when one says 'swagger.' Feel, masters, how I shake. Look you, I warrant you.

Doll. So you do, hostess. 115

Host. Do I? Yea, in very truth, do I, an 'twere an aspen leaf. I cannot abide swagg'rers.

Enter *Ancient Pistol* and *Bardolph* and *Boy.*

Pist. God save you, Sir John! 119

Fal. Welcome, Ancient Pistol. Here, Pistol, I charge you with a cup of sack. Do you discharge upon mine hostess.

Pist. I will discharge upon her, Sir John, with two bullets.

Fal. She is pistol-proof, sir. You shall hardly offend her. 126

Host. Come, I'll drink no proofs nor no bullets. I'll drink no more than will do me good, for no man's pleasure, I.

126

Pist. Then to you, Mistress Dorothy! I will charge you.   131

Doll. Charge me? I scorn you, scurvy companion. What! you poor, base, rascally, cheating, lack-linen mate! Away, you mouldy rogue, away! I am meat for your master.   135

Pist. I know you, Mistress Dorothy.

Doll. Away, you cutpurse rascal! You filthy bung, away! By this wine, I'll thrust my knife in your mouldy chaps an you play the saucy cuttle with me. Away, you bottle-ale rascal! you basket-hilt stale juggler, you! Since when, I pray you, sir? God's light, with two points on your shoulder? Much!

Pist. God let me not live but I will murther your ruff for this.   145

Fal. No more, Pistol. I would not have you go off here. Discharge yourself of our company, Pistol.

Host. No, good Captain Pistol! not here, sweet Captain.   150

Doll. Captain? Thou abominable damn'd cheater, art thou not ashamed to be called Captain? An captains were of my mind, they would truncheon you out for taking their names upon you before you have earn'd them. You a captain? You slave, for what? For tearing a poor whore's ruff in a bawdy house! He a captain? Hang him, rogue! he lives upon mouldy stew'd prunes and dried cakes. A captain? God's light! these villains will make the word as odious as the word 'occupy,' which was an excellent good word before it was ill sorted. Therefore captains had need look to't.

Bard. Pray thee go down, good Ancient.

Fal. Hark thee hither, Mistress Doll.   165

Pist. Not I! I tell thee what, Corporal Bardolph, I could tear her. I'll be reveng'd of her.

Boy. Pray thee go down.

Pist. I'll see her damn'd first! to Pluto's damned lake, by this hand, to th' infernal deep, with Erebus and tortures vile also! Hold hook and line, say I. Down! down, dogs! down, faitors! Have we not Hiren here?

Host. Good Captain Peesell, be quiet. 'Tis very late, i' faith. I beseek you now, aggravate your choler.   176

Pist. These be good humours indeed. Shall packhorses,
And hollow pamper'd jades of Asia,
Which cannot go but thirty mile a day,
Compare with Cæsars, and with Cannibals, 180
And Troyan Greeks? Nay, rather damn them with

King Cerberus and let the welkin roar!
Shall we fall foul for toys?

Host. By my troth, Captain, these are very bitter words.   185

Bard. Be gone, good Ancient. This will grow to a brawl anon.

Pist. Die men like dogs! Give crowns like pins! Have we not Hiren here?   189

Host. O' my word, Captain, there's none such here. What the goodyere! Do you think I would deny her? For God's sake, be quiet.

Pist. Then feed, and be fat, my fair Calipolis. Come, give 's some sack.   194
'Si fortune me tormente, sperato me contento.'
Fear we broadsides? No, let the fiend give fire!
Give me some sack; and, sweetheart, lie thou there.   [*Lays down his sword.*]
Come we to full points here, and are et-ceteras nothing?

Fal. Pistol, I would be quiet.

Pist. Sweet knight, I kiss thy neaf. What! we have seen the Seven Stars.   201

Doll. For God's sake, thrust him down stairs! I cannot endure such a fustian rascal.

Pist. Thrust him down stairs? Know we not Galloway nags?   205

Fal. Quoit him down, Bardolph, like a shove-groat shilling. Nay, an 'a do nothing but speak nothing, 'a shall be nothing here.

Bard. Come, get you down stairs.   209

Pist. What? shall we have incision? Shall we imbrue?   [*Snatches up his sword.*]
Then death rock me asleep, abridge my doleful days!
Why then, let grievous, ghastly, gaping wounds
Untwine the Sisters Three! Come, Atropos, I say!

Host. Here's goodly stuff toward!

Fal. Give me my rapier, boy.   215

Doll. I pray thee, Jack, I pray thee do not draw.

Fal. Get you down stairs.
                    [*Draws and drives Pistol out.*]

Host. Here's a goodly tumult! I'll forswear keeping house afore I'll be in these tirrits and frights. So! Murder, I warrant now. Alas, alas! Put up your naked weapons, put up your naked weapons.
                    [*Exeunt Pistol and Bardolph.*]

Doll. I pray thee, Jack, be quiet; the rascal's gone. Ah, you whoreson little valiant villain, you!   226

Host. Are you not hurt i' th' groin? Methought 'a made a shrewd thrust at your belly.

127

[Enter *Bardolph.*]

Fal. Have you turn'd him out o' doors?

Bard. Yea, sir. The rascal's drunk. You have hurt him, sir, i' th' shoulder.   231

Fal. A rascal! to brave me?

Doll. Ah, you sweet little rogue, you! Alas, poor ape, how thou sweat'st! Come, let me wipe thy face. Come on, you whoreson chops. Ah, rogue! i' faith, I love thee. Thou art as valorous as Hector of Troy, worth five of Agamemnon, and ten times better than the Nine Worthies. Ah, villain!

Fal. A rascally slave! I will toss the rogue in a blanket.   241

Doll. Do, an thou dar'st for thy heart. An thou dost, I'll canvass thee between a pair of sheets.

Enter *Music.*

Page. The music is come, sir.   245

Fal. Let them play. Play, sirs. Sit on my knee, Doll. A rascal bragging slave! The rogue fled from me like quicksilver.

Doll. I' faith, and thou follow'dst him like a church. Thou whoreson little tidy Bartholomew boar-pig, when wilt thou leave fighting a-days and foining a-nights, and begin to patch up thine old body for heaven?

Enter, [behind,] *Prince* and *Poins* disguis'd [as *Drawers*].

Fal. Peace, good Doll! Do not speak like a death's-head. Do not bid me remember mine end.   255

Doll. Sirrah, what humour's the Prince of?

Fal. A good shallow young fellow. 'A would have made a good pantler; 'a would 'a' chipp'd bread well.

Doll. They say Poins has a good wit.   260

Fal. He a good wit? Hang him, baboon! His wit's as thick as Tewksbury mustard. There's no more conceit in him than is in a mallet.

Doll. Why does the Prince love him so then?

Fal. Because their legs are both of a bigness, and 'a plays at quoits well, and eats conger and fennel, and drinks off candles' ends for flapdragons, and rides the wild mare with the boys, and jumps upon join'd-stools, and swears with a good grace, and wears his boots very smooth like unto the sign of the Leg, and breeds no bate with telling of discreet stories, and such other gambol faculties 'a has that show a weak mind and an able body, for the which the Prince admits him; for the Prince

himself is such another. The weight of a hair will turn scales between their avoirdupois.

Prince. Would not this nave of a wheel have his ears cut off?   279

Poins. Let's beat him before his whore.

Prince. Look, whe'r the wither'd elder hath not his poll claw'd like a parrot.

Poins. Is it not strange that desire should so many years outlive performance?

Fal. Kiss me, Doll.   285

Prince. Saturn and Venus this year in conjunction? What says th' almanac to that?

Poins. And look whether the fiery Trigon, his man, be not lisping to his master's old tables, his notebook, his counsel-keeper.   290

Fal. Thou dost give me flattering busses.

Doll. By my troth, I kiss thee with a most constant heart.

Fal. I am old, I am old.

Doll. I love thee better than I love e'er a scurvy young boy of them all.   296

Fal. What stuff wilt have a kirtle of? I shall receive money a Thursday. Shalt have a cap to-morrow. A merry song, come. It grows late; we'll to bed. Thou't forget me when I am gone.

Doll. By my troth, thou't set me a-weeping an thou say'st so. Prove that ever I dress myself handsome till thy return. Well, hearken o' th' end.

Fal. Some sack, Francis.   305

Prince, Poins. Anon, anon, sir.

Fal. Ha! a bastard son of the King's? And art not thou Poins his brother?

Prince. Why, thou globe of sinful continents, what a life dost thou lead!   310

Fal. A better than thou. I am a gentleman; thou art a drawer.

Prince. Very true, sir; and I come to draw you out by the ears.   314

Host. O, the Lord preserve thy good Grace! By my troth, welcome to London. Now the Lord bless that sweet face of thine! O Jesu, are you come from Wales?   318

Fal. Thou whoreson mad compound of majesty, by this light flesh and corrupt blood, thou art welcome.   [*Lays his hand upon Doll.*]

Doll. How, you fat fool? I scorn you.

Poins. My lord, he will drive you out of your revenge, and turn all to a merriment, if you take not the heat.   325

Prince. You whoreson candle-mine, you, how vilely did you speak of me even now before this honest, virtuous, civil gentlewoman!

Host. God's blessing of your good heart! and so she is, by my troth.   330

128

Fal. Didst thou hear me?

Prince. Yea; and you knew me, as you did when you ran away by Gadshill. You knew I was at your back, and spoke it on purpose to try my patience.   335

Fal. No, no, no! not so. I did not think thou wast within hearing.

Prince. I shall drive you then to confess the wilful abuse, and then I know how to handle you.

Fal. No abuse, Hal, o' mine honour! no abuse.   340

Prince. Not — to dispraise me, and call me pantler, and bread-chipper, and I know not what?

Fal. No abuse, Hal.

Poins. No abuse?   344

Fal. No abuse, Ned, i' th' world! honest Ned, none. I disprais'd him before the wicked, that the wicked might not fall in love with him; in which doing, I have done the part of a careful friend and a true subject, and thy father is to give me thanks for it. No abuse, Hal. None, Ned, none. No, faith, boys, none.   351

Prince. See now whether pure fear and entire cowardice doth not make thee wrong this virtuous gentlewoman to close with us? Is she of the wicked? Is thine hostess here of the wicked? or is thy boy of the wicked? or honest Bardolph, whose zeal burns in his nose, of the wicked?

Poins. Answer, thou dead elm, answer.   358

Fal. The fiend hath prick'd down Bardolph irrecoverable; and his face is Lucifer's privy kitchen, where he doth nothing but roast maltworms. For the boy, there is a good angel about him; but the devil outbids him too.

Prince. For the women?   364

Fal. For one of them, she's in hell already, and burns poor souls. For th' other, I owe her money; and whether she be damn'd for that, I know not.

Host. No, I warrant you.   369

Fal. No, I think thou art not; I think thou art quit for that. Marry, there is another indictment upon thee, for suffering flesh to be eaten in thy house contrary to the law, for the which I think thou wilt howl.   374

Host. All vict'lers do so. What's a joint of mutton or two in a whole Lent?

Prince. You, gentlewoman —

Doll. What says your Grace?

Fal. His grace says that which his flesh rebels against.   380

Peto knocks at door.

Host. Who knocks so loud at door? Look to th' door there, Francis.

Enter *Peto.*

Prince. Peto, how now? What news?

Peto. The King your father is at Westminster;   384
And there are twenty weak and wearied posts
Come from the North; and as I came along,
I met and overtook a dozen captains,
Bareheaded, sweating, knocking at the taverns,
And asking every one for Sir John Falstaff.

Prince. By heaven, Poins, I feel me much to blame   390
So idly to profane the precious time,
When tempest of commotion, like the South,
Borne with black vapour, doth begin to melt
And drop upon our bare unarmed heads.
Give me my sword and cloak. Falstaff, good night.   395
Exeunt Prince, Poins, [Peto, and Bardolph].

Fal. Now comes in the sweetest morsel of the night, and we must hence and leave it unpick'd. [*Knocking within.*] More knocking at the door?

[Enter *Bardolph.*]

How now? What's the matter?   400

Bard. You must away to court, sir, presently.
A dozen captains stay at door for you.

Fal. [*to the Page*] Pay the musicians, sirrah. — Farewell, hostess; farewell, Doll. You see, my good wenches, how men of merit are sought after. The undeserver may sleep, when the man of action is call'd on. Farewell, good wenches. If I be not sent away post, I will see you again ere I go.

Doll. I cannot speak. If my heart be not ready to burst! — Well, sweet Jack, have a care of thyself.   410

Fal. Farewell, farewell.

Exit [with Bardolph].

Host. Well, fare thee well. I have known thee these twenty-nine years, come peascod-time; but an honester and truer-hearted man — Well, fare thee well.   415

Bard. [*within*] Mistress Tearsheet!

Host. What's the matter?

Bard. [*within*] Bid Mistress Tearsheet come to my master.   419

Host. O, run, Doll, run! run, good Doll! come. (*She comes blubber'd.*) Yea, will you come, Doll?   *Exeunt.*

ACT III. Scene I. [*Westminster. The Palace.*]

Enter the *King* in his nightgown, with a *Page.*

King. Go call the Earls of Surrey and of
Warwick;
But ere they come, bid them o'erread these
letters
And well consider of them. Make good speed.
Exit [*Page*].
How many thousand of my poorest subjects
Are at this hour asleep! O sleep, O gentle sleep!
Nature's soft nurse, how have I frighted thee,
That thou no more wilt weigh my eyelids down
And steep my senses in forgetfulness?
Why rather, sleep, liest thou in smoky cribs,
Upon uneasy pallets stretching thee,   10
And hush'd with buzzing night-flies to thy
slumber,
Than in the perfum'd chambers of the great,
Under the canopies of costly state,
And lull'd with sound of sweetest melody?   15
O thou dull god, why liest thou with the vile
In loathsome beds, and leav'st the kingly couch
A watchcase or a common 'larum-bell?
Wilt thou upon the high and giddy mast
Seel up the shipboy's eyes, and rock his brains   20
In cradle of the rude imperious surge,
And in the visitation of the winds,
Who take the ruffian billows by the top,
Curling their monstrous heads, and hanging
them
With deaf'ning clamour in the slippery clouds,
That with the hurly death itself awakes?   25
Canst thou, O partial sleep, give thy repose
To the wet seaboy in an hour so rude,
And in the calmest and most stillest night,
With all appliances and means to boot,
Deny it to a king? Then, happy low, lie down!
Uneasy lies the head that wears a crown.   31

Enter *Warwick* and *Surrey.*

War. Many good morrows to your Majesty!
King. Is it good morrow, lords?
War. 'Tis one o'clock, and past.
King. Why then, good morrow to you all,
my lords.   35
Have you read o'er the letters that I sent you?
War. We have, my liege.
King. Then you perceive the body of our
kingdom,
How foul it is; what rank diseases grow,
And with what danger, near the heart of it.   40

War. It is but as a body yet distempered,
Which to his former strength may be restor'd
With good advice and little medicine.
My Lord Northumberland will soon be cool'd.
King. O God, that one might read the book
of fate,   45
And see the revolution of the times
Make mountains level, and the continent,
Weary of solid firmness, melt itself
Into the sea! and other times to see
The beachy girdle of the ocean   50
Too wide for Neptune's hips; how chances
mock,
And changes fill the cup of alteration
With divers liquors! O, if this were seen,
The happiest youth, viewing his progress
through,
What perils past, what crosses to ensue,   55
Would shut the book and sit him down and die
'Tis not ten years gone
Since Richard and Northumberland, great
friends,
Did feast together, and in two years after   59
Were they at wars. It is but eight years since
This Percy was the man nearest my soul,
Who like a brother toil'd in my affairs
And laid his love and life under my foot;
Yea, for my sake, even to the eyes of Richard
Gave him defiance. But which of you was by —
[*To Warwick*] You, cousin Nevil, as I may re-
member —   66
When Richard, with his eye brimful of tears,
Then check'd and rated by Northumberland,
Did speak these words, now prov'd a prophecy?
'Northumberland, thou ladder by the which   70
My cousin Bolingbroke ascends my throne —'
Though then, God knows, I had no such intent,
But that necessity so bow'd the state
That I and greatness were compell'd to kiss —
'The time shall come,' thus did he follow it,   75
'The time will come that foul sin, gathering
head,
Shall break into corruption': so went on,
Foretelling this same time's condition
And the division of our amity.   79
War. There is a history in all men's lives,
Figuring the nature of the times deceas'd;
The which observ'd, a man may prophesy,
With a near aim, of the main chance of things
As yet not come to life, which in their seeds
And weak beginnings lie intreasured.   85

Such things become the hatch and brood of time.
And by the necessary form of this
King Richard might create a perfect guess
That great Northumberland, then false to him,
Would of that seed grow to a greater falseness,
Which should not find a ground to root upon
Unless on you.

King.   Are these things then necessities?
Then let us meet them like necessities!
And that same word even now cries out on us.
They say the Bishop and Northumberland 95
Are fifty thousand strong.

War.   It cannot be, my lord.
Rumour doth double, like the voice and echo,
The numbers of the fear'd. Please it your
     Grace
To go to bed. Upon my soul, my lord, 99
The powers that you already have sent forth
Shall bring this prize in very easily.
To comfort you the more, I have receiv'd
A certain instance that Glendower is dead.
Your Majesty hath been this fortnight ill, 104
And these unseasoned hours perforce must add
Unto your sickness.

King.   I will take your counsel.
And were these inward wars once out of hand.
We would, dear lords, unto the Holy Land.
                                   Exeunt.

Scene II. [*Before* Justice Shallow's
     house in Gloucestershire.]

Enter *Justice Shallow* and *Justice Silence* [meeting]; *Mouldy, Shadow, Wart, Feeble, Bullcalf,*
[*and Servants,* behind].

Shal. Come on, come on, come on, sir. Give
me your hand, sir; give me your hand, sir.
An early stirrer, by the rood. And how doth
my good cousin Silence?

Sil. Good morrow, good cousin Shallow. 5

Shal. And how doth my cousin your bedfellow? and your fairest daughter and mine,
my goddaughter Ellen?

Sil. Alas, a black woosel, cousin Shallow! 9

Shal. By yea and no, sir, I dare say my
cousin William is become a good scholar. He
is at Oxford still, is he not?

Sil. Indeed, sir, to my cost.

Shal. 'A must, then, to the Inns o' Court
shortly. I was once of Clement's Inn, where I
think they will talk of mad Shallow yet. 16

Sil. You were call'd 'lusty Shallow' then,
cousin.

Shal. By the mass, I was call'd anything!
and I would have done anything indeed too,
and roundly too. There was I, and little John
Doit of Staffordshire, and black George Barnes,
and Francis Pickbone, and Will Squele, a
Cotsole man — you had not four such swinge-
bucklers in all the Inns o' Court again. And I
may say to you, we knew where the bona robas
were and had the best of them all at commandment. Then was Jack Falstaff, now Sir John,
a boy, and page to Thomas Mowbray, Duke of
Norfolk.

Sil. This Sir John, cousin, that comes hither
anon about soldiers? 31

Shal. The same Sir John, the very same. I
see him break Skogan's head at the court gate
when 'a was a crack not thus high; and the
very same day did I fight with one Samson
Stockfish, a fruiterer, behind Gray's Inn. Jesu,
Jesu, the mad days that I have spent! And to
see how many of my old acquaintance are dead!

Sil. We shall all follow, cousin. 39

Shal. Certain, 'tis certain; very sure, very
sure. Death, as the Psalmist saith, is certain
to all; all shall die. How a good yoke of bul-
locks at Stamford fair?

Sil. By my troth, I was not there.

Shal. Death is certain. Is old Dooble of
your town living yet? 46

Sil. Dead, sir.

Shal. Jesu, Jesu, dead! 'A drew a good bow
— and dead! 'A shot a fine shoot. John o'
Gaunt loved him well and betted much money
on his head. Dead! 'A would have clapp'd i'
th' clout at twelve score, and carried you a
forehand shaft a fourteen and fourteen and
a half, that it would have done a man's heart
good to see. How a score of ewes now? 55

Sil. Thereafter as they be. A score of good
ewes may be worth ten pounds.

Shal. And is old Dooble dead?

Sil. Here come two of Sir John Falstaff's
men, as I think. 60

Enter *Bardolph*, and *one with him.*

Bard. Good morrow, honest gentlemen. I
beseech you, which is Justice Shallow?

Shal. I am Robert Shallow, sir, a poor esquire of this county, and one of the King's
justices of the peace. What is your good pleasure with me? 65

Bard. My captain, sir, commends him to
you — my captain, Sir John Falstaff, a tall
gentleman, by heaven, and a most gallant
leader.

Shal. He greets me well, sir. I knew him a good backsword man. How doth the good knight? May I ask how my lady his wife doth?

Bard. Sir, pardon; a soldier is better accommodated than with a wife.   73

Shal. It is well said, in faith, sir; and it is well said indeed too. 'Better accommodated!' It is good; yea indeed is it. Good phrases are surely, and ever were, very commendable. 'Accommodated!' It comes of *accommodo.* Very good; a good phrase.   79

Bard. Pardon me, sir; I have heard the word. 'Phrase' call you it? By this good day, I know not the phrase; but I will maintain the word with my sword to be a soldier-like word and a word of exceeding good command, by heaven. Accommodated: that is, when a man is, as they say, accommodated; or when a man is, being, whereby 'a may be thought to be accommodated — which is an excellent thing.

Enter *Sir John Falstaff.*

Shal. It is very just. Look, here comes good Sir John. Give me your good hand, give me your worship's good hand. By my troth, you like well, and bear your years very well. Welcome, good Sir John.   93

Fal. I am glad to see you well, good Master Robert Shallow. Master Surecard, as I think?

Shal. No, Sir John. It is my cousin Silence, in commission with me.

Fal. Good Master Silence, it well befits you should be of the peace.

Sil. Your good worship is welcome.   100

Fal. Fie! this is hot weather. Gentlemen, have you provided me here half a dozen sufficient men?

Shal. Marry have we, sir. Will you sit?

Fal. Let me see them, I beseech you.   105

Shal. Where's the roll? Where's the roll? Where's the roll? Let me see, let me see, let me see. So, so, so, so, so — so, so. Yea, marry, sir. Ralph Mouldy! Let them appear as I call; let them do so, let them do so. Let me see. Where is Mouldy?   111

Moul. Here, an it please you.

Shal. What think you, Sir John? A good-limb'd fellow, young, strong, and of good friends.

Fal. Is thy name Mouldy?   115

Moul. Yea, an't please you.

Fal. 'Tis the more time thou wert us'd.

Shal. Ha, ha, ha! Most excellent, i' faith! Things that are mouldy lack use. Very singular good! In faith, well said, Sir John, very well said.

Fal. Prick him.   121

Moul. I was prick'd well enough before, an you could have let me alone. My old dame will be undone now for one to do her husbandry and her drudgery. You need not to have prick'd me. There are other men fitter to go out than I.

Fal. Go to! peace, Mouldy; you shall go. Mouldy, it is time you were spent.

Moul. Spent?   129

Shal. Peace, fellow, peace; stand aside. Know you where you are? For th' other, Sir John. Let me see. Simon Shadow!

Fal. Yea, marry, let me have him to sit under. He's like to be a cold soldier.

Shal. Where's Shadow?   135

Shad. Here, sir.

Fal. Shadow, whose son art thou?

Shad. My mother's son, sir.

Fal. Thy mother's son! Like enough; and thy father's shadow. So the son of the female is the shadow of the male. It is often so indeed; but much of the father's substance!   142

Shal. Do you like him, Sir John?

Fal. Shadow will serve for summer. Prick him; for we have a number of shadows to fill up the muster book.   146

Shal. Thomas Wart!

Fal. Where's he?

Wart. Here, sir.

Fal. Is thy name Wart?   150

Wart. Yea, sir.

Fal. Thou art a very ragged wart.

Shal. Shall I prick him, Sir John?

Fal. It were superfluous; for his apparel is built upon his back, and the whole frame stands upon pins. Prick him no more.   156

Shal. Ha, ha, ha! You can do it, sir; you can do it! I commend you well. Francis Feeble!

Fee. Here, sir.

Fal. What trade art thou, Feeble?   160

Fee. A woman's tailor, sir.

Shal. Shall I prick him, sir?

Fal. You may; but if he had been a man's tailor, he'd 'a' prick'd you. Wilt thou make as many holes in an enemy's battle as thou hast done in a woman's petticoat?   166

Fee. I will do my good will, sir. You can have no more.

Fal. Well said, good woman's tailor! Well said, courageous Feeble! Thou wilt be as valiant as the wrathful dove or most magnanimous mouse. Prick the woman's tailor well, Master Shallow; deep, Master Shallow.

Fee. I would Wart might have gone, sir. 174

Fal. I would thou wert a man's tailor, that thou mightst mend him and make him fit to go. I cannot put him to a private soldier that is the leader of so many thousands. Let that suffice, most forcible Feeble.

Fee. It shall suffice, sir.   180

Fal. I am bound to thee, reverend Feeble. Who is next?

Shal. Peter Bullcalf o' th' green!

Fal. Yea, marry, let's see Bullcalf.

Bull. Here, sir.   185

Fal. Fore God, a likely fellow! Come, prick me Bullcalf till he roar again.

Bull. O Lord! good my Lord Captain —

Fal. What, dost thou roar before thou art prick'd?   190

Bull. O Lord, sir! I am a diseased man.

Fal. What disease hast thou?

Bull. A whoreson cold, sir, a cough, sir, which I caught with ringing in the King's affairs upon his coronation day, sir.   195

Fal. Come, thou shalt go to the wars in a gown. We will have away thy cold; and I will take such order that thy friends shall ring for thee. Is here all?   199

Shal. Here is two more call'd than your number. You must have but four here, sir; and so I pray you go in with me to dinner.

Fal. Come, I will go drink with you, but I cannot tarry dinner. I am glad to see you, by my troth, Master Shallow.   205

Shal. O Sir John, do you remember since we lay all night in the windmill in Saint George's Field?

Fal. No more of that, good Master Shallow! No more of that!

Shal. Ha, 'twas a merry night. And is Jane Nightwork alive?   211

Fal. She lives, Master Shallow.

Shal. She never could away with me.

Fal. Never, never. She would always say she could not abide Master Shallow.   215

Shal. By the mass, I could anger her to th' heart. She was then a bona roba. Doth she hold her own well?

Fal. Old, old, Master Shallow.   219

Shal. Nay, she must be old; she cannot choose but be old; certain she's old; and had Robin Nightwork by old Nightwork before I came to Clement's Inn.

Sil. That's fifty-five year ago.   224

Shal. Ha, cousin Silence, that thou hadst seen that that this knight and I have seen! Ha, Sir John, said I well?

Fal. We have heard the chimes at midnight, Master Shallow.   229

Shal. That we have, that we have, that we have! In faith, Sir John, we have. Our watchword was 'Hem, boys!' Come, let's to dinner; come, let's to dinner. Jesus, the days that we have seen! Come, come.   234

Exeunt [Falstaff and the Justices].

Bull. Good Master Corporate Bardolph, stand my friend, and here's four Harry tenshillings in French crowns for you. In very truth, sir, I had as live be hang'd, sir, as go. And yet, for mine own part, sir, I do not care; but rather because I am unwilling and, for mine own part, have a desire to stay with my friends. Else, sir, I did not care, for mine own part, so much.   242

Bard. Go to; stand aside.

Moul. And, good Master Corporal Captain, for my dame's sake stand my friend. She has nobody to do anything about her when I am gone, and she is old and cannot help herself. You shall have forty, sir.

Bard. Go to; stand aside.   249

Fee. By my troth, I care not. A man can die but once; we owe God a death. I'll ne'er bear a base mind. An't be my destiny, so; an't be not, so. No man 's too good to serve 's prince; and let it go which way it will, he that dies this year is quit for the next.   255

Bard. Well said. Th'art a good fellow.

Fee. Faith, I'll bear no base mind.

Enter *Falstaff* and the *Justices.*

Fal. Come, sir, which men shall I have?

Shal. Four of which you please.   259

Bard. Sir, a word with you. I have three pound to free Mouldy and Bullcalf.

Fal. Go to; well.

Shal. Come, Sir John, which four will you have?

Fal. Do you choose for me.   265

Shal. Marry, then, Mouldy, Bullcalf, Feeble, and Shadow.

Fal. Mouldy and Bullcalf: for you, Mouldy, stay at home till you are past service; and for your part, Bullcalf, grow till you come unto it. I will none of you.   271

Shal. Sir John, Sir John, do not yourself wrong. They are your likeliest men, and I would have you serv'd with the best.   274

Fal. Will you tell me, Master Shallow, how to choose a man? Care I for the limb, the thews, the stature, bulk, and big assemblance of a man? Give me the spirit, Master Shallow.

Here's Wart. You see what a ragged appearance it is. 'A shall charge you and discharge you with the motion of a pewterer's hammer, come off and on swifter than he that gibbets on the brewer's bucket. And this same half-fac'd fellow, Shadow — give me this man. He presents no mark to the enemy; the foeman may with as great aim level at the edge of a penknife. And for a retreat — how swiftly will this Feeble, the woman's tailor, run off! O, give me the spare men and spare me the great ones. Put me a caliver into Wart's hand, Bardolph.   290

Bard. Hold, Wart, traverse. Thas, thas, thas!

Fal. Come, manage me your caliver. So; very well! go to; very good, exceeding good. O, give me always a little, lean, old, chopt, bald shot. Well said, i' faith, Wart. Th'art a good scab. Hold, there's a tester for thee.   296

Shal. He is not his craft's master; he doth not do it right. I remember at Mile-end Green, when I lay at Clement's Inn, — I was then Sir Dagonet in Arthur's Show, — there was a little quiver fellow, and 'a would manage you his piece thus; and 'a would about and about, and come you in and come you in. 'Rah, tah, tah!' would 'a say; 'Bounce!' would 'a say; and away again would 'a go, and again would 'a come. I shall ne'er see such a fellow.   306

Fal. These fellows will do well, Master Shallow. God keep you, Master Silence. I will not use many words with you. Fare you well, gentlemen both. I thank you. I must a dozen mile to-night. Bardolph, give the soldiers coats.

Shal. Sir John, the Lord bless you! God prosper your affairs! God send us peace! At your return visit our house; let our old acquaintance be renewed. Peradventure I will with ye to the court.   316

Fal. Fore God, I would you would, Master Shallow.

Shal. Go to; I have spoke at a word. God keep you!   320

Fal. Fare you well, gentle gentlemen. (*Exeunt [Shallow and Silence].*) On, Bardolph; lead the men away. [*Exeunt all but Falstaff.*] As I return, I will fetch off these justices. I do see the bottom of Justice Shallow. Lord, Lord, how subject we old men are to this vice of lying! This same starv'd justice hath done nothing but prate to me of the wildness of his youth and the feats he hath done about Turnbull Street; and every third word a lie, duer paid to the hearer than the Turk's tribute. I do remember him at Clement's Inn, like a man made after supper of a cheese paring. When 'a was naked, he was for all the world like a fork'd radish, with a head fantastically carved upon it with a knife; 'a was so forlorn that his dimensions to any thick sight were invincible. 'A was the very genius of famine; yet lecherous as a monkey, and the whores call'd him 'mandrake.' 'A came ever in the rearward of the fashion, and sung those tunes to the overscutch'd huswives that he heard the carmen whistle, and sware they were his Fancies or his Good-nights. And now is this Vice's dagger become a squire, and talks as familiarly of John o' Gaunt as if he had been sworn brother to him; and I'll be sworn 'a ne'er saw him but once in the Tilt Yard, and then he burst his head for crowding among the marshal's men. I saw it, and told John o' Gaunt he beat his own name; for you might have thrust him and all his apparel into an eel-skin; the case of a treble hautboy was a mansion for him, a court; and now has he land and beeves. Well, I'll be acquainted with him, if I return; and 't shall go hard but I'll make him a philosopher's two stones to me. If the young dace be a bait for the old pike, I see no reason in the law of nature but I may snap at him. Let time shape, and there an end.   *Exit.*

ACT IV. Scene I. [*Gaultree Forest in Yorkshire.*]

Enter the *Archbishop [of York], Mowbray, [Lord] Bardolph, Hastings,* within the Forest of Gaultree.

Arch. What is this forest call'd?

Hast. 'Tis Gaultree Forest, an't shall please your Grace.

Arch. Here stand, my lords, and send discoverers forth
To know the numbers of our enemies.

Hast. We have sent forth already.

Arch.   'Tis well done. 5
My friends, and brethren in these great affairs,
I must acquaint you that I have receiv'd
New-dated letters from Northumberland,
Their cold intent, tenure, and substance thus:
Here doth he wish his person, with such powers
As might hold sortance with his quality,   11
The which he could not levy; whereupon
He is retir'd, to ripe his growing fortunes,

To Scotland; and concludes in hearty prayers
That your attempts may overlive the hazard
And fearful meeting of their opposite.   16
  Mowb. Thus do the hopes we have in him
    touch ground
And dash themselves to pieces.

Enter Messenger.

  Hast.   Now, what news?
  Mess. West of this forest, scarcely off a mile,
In goodly form comes on the enemy;   20
And by the ground they hide, I judge their
    number
Upon or near the rate of thirty thousand.
  Mowb. The just proportion that we gave
    them out.
Let us sway on and face them in the field.

Enter Westmoreland.

  Arch. What well-appointed leader fronts us
    here?   25
  Mowb. I think it is my Lord of Westmore-
    land.
  West. Health and fair greeting from our
    general,
The prince, Lord John and Duke of Lancaster.
  Arch. Say on, my Lord of Westmoreland, in
    peace.
What doth concern your coming?
  West.   Then, my lord,   30
Unto your Grace do I in chief address
The substance of my speech. If that rebellion
Came like itself, in base and abject routs,
Led on by bloody youth, guarded with rags,
And countenanc'd by boys and beggary —   35
I say, if damn'd commotion so appear'd,
In his true, native, and most proper shape,
You, reverend Father, and these noble lords
Had not been here to dress the ugly form
Of base and bloody insurrection   40
With your fair honours. You, Lord Archbishop,
Whose see is by a civil peace maintain'd,
Whose beard the silver hand of peace hath
    touch'd,
Whose learning and good letters peace hath
    tutor'd,
Whose white investments figure innocence,   45
The dove and very blessed spirit of peace —
Wherefore do you so ill translate yourself
Out of the speech of peace, that bears such
    grace,
Into the harsh and boist'rous tongue of war;
Turning your books to graves, your ink to
    blood,   50

Your pens to lances, and your tongue divine
To a loud trumpet and a point of war?
  Arch. Wherefore do I this? So the question
    stands.
Briefly to this end: we are all diseas'd
And with our surfeiting and wanton hours   55
Have brought ourselves into a burning fever,
And we must bleed for it; of which disease
Our late King, Richard, being infected, died.
But, my most noble Lord of Westmoreland,
I take not on me here as a physician;   60
Nor do I, as an enemy to peace,
Troop in the throngs of military men;
But rather show awhile like fearful war
To diet rank minds, sick of happiness,   64
And purge th' obstructions which begin to stop
Our very veins of life. Hear me more plainly.
I have in equal balance justly weigh'd
What wrongs our arms may do, what wrongs
    we suffer,
And find our griefs heavier than our offences.
We see which way the stream of time doth
    run,
And are enforc'd from our most quiet there   71
By the rough torrent of occasion;
And have the summary of all our griefs,
When time shall serve, to show in articles,
Which long ere this we offer'd to the King   75
And might by no suit gain our audience.
When we are wrong'd, and would unfold our
    griefs,
We are denied access unto his person
Even by those men that most have done us
    wrong.
The dangers of the days but newly gone,   80
Whose memory is written on the earth
With yet-appearing blood, and the examples
Of every minute's instance (present now)
Hath put us in these ill-beseeming arms;
Not to break peace, or any branch of it,   85
But to establish here a peace indeed,
Concurring both in name and quality.
  West. When ever yet was your appeal
    denied?
Wherein have you been galled by the King?
What peer hath been suborn'd to grate on you?
That you should seal this lawless bloody book
Of forg'd rebellion with a seal divine
And consecrate commotion's bitter edge?
  Arch. My brother general, the common-
    wealth,
To brother born an household cruelty,   95
I make my quarrel in particular.
  West. There is no need of any such redress;
Or if there were, it not belongs to you.

Mowb. Why not to him in part, and to us
all
That feel the bruises of the days before   100
And suffer the condition of these times
To lay a heavy and unequal hand
Upon our honours?
    West.   O, my good Lord Mowbray,
Construe the times to their necessities,
And you shall say, indeed, it is the time,   105
And not the King, that doth you injuries.
Yet, for your part, it not appears to me,
Either from the King, or in the present time,
That you should have an inch of any ground
To build a grief on. Were you not restor'd   110
To all the Duke of Norfolk's signiories,
Your noble and right well-rememb'red father's?
    Mowb. What thing, in honour, had my father
lost
That need to be reviv'd and breath'd in me?
The King that lov'd him, as the state stood
then,   115
Was force perforce compell'd to banish him;
And when that Henry Bolingbroke and he —
Being mounted and both roused in their seats,
Their neighing coursers daring of the spur,
Their armed staves in charge, their beavers
down,   120
Their eyes of fire sparkling through sights of
steel,
And the loud trumpet blowing them together —
Then, then, when there was nothing could have
stay'd
My father from the breast of Bolingbroke,
O, when the King did throw his warder down,
His own life hung upon the staff he threw.
Then threw he down himself, and all their
lives
That by indictment and by dint of sword
Have since miscarried under Bolingbroke.
    West. You speak, Lord Mowbray, now you
know not what.   130
The Earl of Hereford was reputed then
In England the most valiant gentleman.
Who knows on whom fortune would then have
smil'd?
But if your father had been victor there,
He ne'er had borne it out of Coventry;   135
For all the country, in a general voice,
Cried hate upon him; and all their prayers and
love
Were set on Hereford, whom they doted on,
And bless'd and grac'd, indeed, more than the
King.
But this is mere digression from my purpose.   140
Here come I from our princely general

To know your griefs; to tell you from his Grace
That he will give you audience, and wherein
It shall appear that your demands are just,
You shall enjoy them, everything set off   145
That might so much as think you enemies.
    Mowb. But he hath forc'd us to compel this
offer;
And it proceeds from policy, not love.
    West. Mowbray, you overween to take it
so.
This offer comes from mercy, not from fear;   150
For, lo! within a ken our army lies —
Upon mine honour, all too confident
To give admittance to a thought of fear.
Our battle is more full of names than yours,
Our men more perfect in the use of arms,   155
Our armour all as strong, our cause the best:
Then reason will our hearts should be as good.
Say you not, then, our offer is compell'd.
    Mowb. Well, by my will we shall admit no
parley.
    West. That argues but the shame of your
offence.   160
A rotten case abides no handling.
    Hast. Hath the Prince John a full commis-
sion,
In very ample virtue of his father,
To hear and absolutely to determine
Of what conditions we shall stand upon?   165
    West. That is intended in the general's name.
I muse you make so slight a question.
    Arch. Then take, my Lord of Westmoreland,
this schedule,
For this contains our general grievances.
Each several article herein redress'd,   170
All members of our cause, both here and hence,
That are ensinewed to this action
Acquitted by a true substantial form,
And present execution of our wills
To us and to our purposes confin'd —   175
We come within our awful banks again
And knit our powers to the arm of peace.
    West. This will I show the general. Please
you, lords,
In sight of both our battles we may meet;
And either end in peace (which God so frame!)
Or to the place of diff'rence call the swords   181
Which must decide it.
    Arch.   My lord, we will do so.
                  Exit Westmoreland.
    Mowb. There is a thing within my bosom
tells me
That no conditions of our peace can stand.
    Hast. Fear you not that. If we can make
our peace   185

Upon such large terms and so absolute
As our conditions shall consist upon,
Our peace shall stand as firm as rocky moun-
tains.

   Mowb. Yea, but our valuation shall be such
That every slight and false-derived cause, 190
Yea, every idle, nice, and wanton reason,
Shall to the King taste of this action;
That, were our royal faiths martyrs in love,
We shall be winnow'd with so rough a wind
That even our corn shall seem as light as chaff,
And good from bad find no partition. 196

   Arch. No, no, my lord. Note this: the King
    is weary
Of dainty and such picking grievances;
For he hath found, to end one doubt by death
Revives two greater in the heirs of life; 200
And therefore will he wipe his tables clean,
And keep no telltale to his memory
That may repeat and history his loss
To new remembrance. For full well he knows
He cannot so precisely weed this land 205
As his misdoubts present occasion.
His foes are so enrooted with his friends
That, plucking to unfix an enemy,
He doth unfasten so and shake a friend;
So that this land, like an offensive wife 210
That hath enrag'd him on to offer strokes,
As he is striking, holds his infant up,
And hangs resolv'd correction in the arm
That was uprear'd to execution.

   Hast. Besides, the King hath wasted all his
    rods 215
On late offenders, that he now doth lack
The very instruments of chastisement;
So that his power, like to a fangless lion,
May offer, but not hold.

   Arch.   'Tis very true;
And therefore be assur'd, my good Lord Mar-
    shal, 220
If we do now make our atonement well,
Our peace will, like a broken limb united,
Grow stronger for the breaking.

   Mowb.   Be it so.
Here is return'd my Lord of Westmoreland.

          Enter Westmoreland.

   West. The Prince is here at hand. Pleaseth
    your lordship 225
To meet his Grace just distance 'tween our
    armies.

   Mowb. Your Grace of York, in God's name,
    then, set forward.

   Arch. Before, and greet his Grace. My lord,
    we come.   *[Exeunt.]*

[Scene II. *Another part of Gaultree
          Forest.*]

  Enter *Prince John* [*of Lancaster*] *and his Army,*
[*with Westmoreland; meeting the Archbishop,
    Mowbray, Hastings,* and *Officers*].

   John. You are well encount'red here, my
    cousin Mowbray.
Good day to you, gentle Lord Archbishop;
And so to you, Lord Hastings, and to all.
My Lord of York, it better show'd with you
When that your flock, assembled by the bell, 5
Encircled you to hear with reverence
Your exposition on the holy text
Than now to see you here an iron man,
Cheering a rout of rebels with your drum,
Turning the word to sword, and life to death.
That man that sits within a monarch's heart 11
And ripens in the sunshine of his favour,
Would he abuse the countenance of the king,
Alack, what mischiefs might be set abroach
In shadow of such greatness! With you, Lord
    Bishop, 15
It is even so. Who hath not heard it spoken
How deep you were within the books of God?
To us the speaker in his parliament;
To us th' imagin'd voice of God himself;
The very opener and intelligencer 20
Between the grace, the sanctities of heaven
And our dull workings. O, who shall believe
But you misuse the reverence of your place,
Employ the countenance and grace of heav'n,
As a false favourite doth his prince's name, 25
In deeds dishonourable? You have ta'en up,
Under the counterfeited zeal of God,
The subjects of his substitute, my father,
And both against the peace of heaven and
    him
Have here upswarm'd them.

   Arch.   Good my Lord of Lancaster, 30
I am not here against your father's peace;
But, as I told my Lord of Westmoreland,
The time misord'red doth, in common sense,
Crowd us and crush us to this monstrous form
To hold our safety up. I sent your Grace 35
The parcels and particulars of our grief,
The which hath been with scorn shov'd from
    the court,
Whereon this Hydra son of war is born;
Whose dangerous eyes may well be charm'd
    asleep 39
With grant of our most just and right desires,
And true obedience, of this madness cur'd,
Stoop tamely to the foot of majesty.

Mowb. If not, we ready are to try our for-
tunes
To the last man.
   Hast.   And though we here fall down,
We have supplies to second our attempt.   45
If they miscarry, theirs shall second them;
And so success of mischief shall be born,
And heir from heir shall hold this quarrel up
Whiles England shall have generation.
   John. You are too shallow, Hastings, much
too shallow   50
To sound the bottom of the after-times.
   West. Pleaseth your Grace to answer them
directly,
How far forth you do like their articles.
   John. I like them all and do allow them
well,
And swear here, by the honour of my blood,   55
My father's purposes have been mistook,
And some about him have too lavishly
Wrested his meaning and authority.
My lord, these griefs shall be with speed re-
dress'd;
Upon my soul, they shall. If this may please
you,   60
Discharge your powers unto their several coun-
ties,
As we will ours; and here. between the armies,
Let's drink together friendly and embrace,
That all their eyes may bear those tokens home
Of our restored love and amity.   65
   Arch. I take your princely word for these
redresses.
   John. I give it you and will maintain my
word;
And thereupon I drink unto your Grace.
                              [*Drinks.*]
   Hast. [*to an Officer*] Go, Captain, and deliver
to the army
This news of peace. Let them have pay, and
part.   70
I know it will well please them. Hie thee,
Captain.
                          Exit [*Officer*].
   Arch. To you, my noble Lord of Westmore-
land.   [*Drinks.*]
   West. I pledge your Grace [*drinks*]; and,
if you knew what pains
I have bestowed to breed this present peace,
You would drink freely; but my love to ye   75
Shall show itself more openly hereafter.
   Arch. I do not doubt you.
   West.   I am glad of it.
Health to my lord and gentle cousin Mowbray.
                              [*Drinks.*]

   Mowb. You wish me health in very happy
season,
For I am on the sudden something ill.   80
   Arch. Against ill chances men are ever merry,
But heaviness foreruns the good event.
   West. Therefore be merry, coz; since sudden
sorrow
Serves to say thus, 'Some good thing comes to-
morrow.'
   Arch. Believe me, I am passing light in spirit.
   Mowb. So much the worse, if your own rule
be true.   86
                          Shout [*within*].
   John. The word of peace is rend'red. Hark
how they shout!
   Mowb. This had been cheerful after victory.
   Arch. A peace is of the nature of a conquest;
For then both parties nobly are subdu'd,   90
And neither party loser.
   John.   Go, my lord,
And let our army be discharged too.
                  Exit [*Westmoreland*].
And, good my lord, so please you, let our trains
March by us, that we may peruse the men
We should have cop'd withal.
   Arch.   Go, good Lord Hastings,   95
And ere they be dismiss'd, let them march by.
                          Exit [*Hastings*].
   John. I trust, lords, we shall lie to-night
together.

                Enter *Westmoreland*.

Now, cousin, wherefore stands our army still?
   West. The leaders, having charge from you
to stand,
Will not go off until they hear you speak.   100
   John. They know their duties.

                  Enter *Hastings*.

   Hast. My lord, our army is dispers'd already.
Like youthful steers unyok'd, they take their
courses
East, west, north, south; or, like a school
broke up,
Each hurries toward his home and sporting
place.   105
   West. Good tidings, my Lord Hastings; for
the which
I do arrest thee, traitor, of high treason;
And you, Lord Archbishop; and you, Lord
Mowbray,
Of capital treason I attach you both.
   Mowb. Is this proceeding just and honour-
able?   110
   West. Is your assembly so?

Arch. Will you thus break your faith?
John.   I pawn'd thee none:
I promis'd you redress of these same grievances
Whereof you did complain; which, by mine
        honour,
I will perform with a most Christian care. 115
But for you rebels — look to taste the due
Meet for rebellion and such acts as yours.
Most shallowly did you these arms commence,
Fondly brought here, and foolishly sent hence.
Strike up our drums, pursue the scatt'red stray.
God, and not we, hath safely fought to-day.
Some guard these traitors to the block of death,
Treason's true bed and yielder-up of breath.
                                Exeunt.

[Scene III. *Another part of the Gaultree
            Forest.*]

Alarum; excursions. Enter *Falstaff* and
            Colevile, [meeting].

Fal. What's your name, sir? Of what con-
dition are you and of what place, I pray?
Cole. I am a knight, sir, and my name is
Colevile of the Dale.   4
Fal. Well then, Colevile is your name, a
knight is your degree, and your place the Dale.
Colevile shall be still your name, a traitor your
degree, and the dungeon your place — a place
deep enough. So shall you be still Colevile of
the Dale.   10
Cole. Are you not Sir John Falstaff?
Fal. As good a man as he, sir, whoe'er I am.
Do ye yield, sir, or shall I sweat for you? If I do
sweat, they are the drops of thy lovers, and they
weep for thy death. Therefore rouse up fear
and trembling and do observance to my mercy.
Cole. I think you are Sir John Falstaff, and
in that thought yield me.   19
Fal. I have a whole school of tongues in this
belly of mine, and not a tongue of them all
speaks any other word but my name. An I had
but a belly of any indifferency, I were simply
the most active fellow in Europe. My womb,
my womb, my womb undoes me! Here comes
our general.   26

Enter *Prince John, Westmoreland,* [*Blunt,*]
            and the rest.

John. The heat is past; follow no further
now.
Call in the powers, good cousin Westmoreland.
                        [*Exit Westmoreland.*]

Now, Falstaff, where have you been all this
        while?
When everything is ended, then you come. 30
These tardy tricks of yours will, on my life,
One time or other break some gallows' back.
Fal. I would be sorry, my lord, but it should
be thus. I never knew yet but rebuke and check
was the reward of valour. Do you think me a
swallow, an arrow, or a bullet? Have I in my
poor and old motion the expedition of thought?
I have speeded hither with the very extremest
inch of possibility; I have found'red ninescore
and odd posts; and here, travel-tainted as I
am, have, in my pure and immaculate valour,
taken Sir John Colevile of the Dale, a most
furious knight and valorous enemy. But what
of that? He saw me, and yielded; that I may
justly say with the hook-nos'd fellow of Rome
— I came, saw, and overcame.   46
John. It was more of his courtesy than your
deserving.
Fal. I know not. Here he is, and here I yield
him. And I beseech your Grace let it be book'd
with the rest of this day's deeds; or, by the
Lord, I will have it in a particular ballad else,
with mine own picture on the top on't, Colevile
kissing my foot; to the which course if I be enforc'd, if you do not all show like gilt twopences
to me, and I in the clear sky of fame o'ershine
you as much as the full moon doth the cinders
of the element, which show like pins' heads to
her, believe not the word of the noble. There-
fore let me have right, and let desert mount. 61
John. Thine's too heavy to mount.
Fal. Let it shine then.
John. Thine's too thick to shine.
Fal. Let it do something, my good lord, that
may do me good, and call it what you will. 66
John. Is thy name Colevile?
Cole. It is, my lord.
John. A famous rebel art thou, Colevile.
Fal. And a famous true subject took him. 70
Cole. I am, my lord, but as my betters are,
That led me hither. Had they been rul'd by me,
You should have won them dearer than you
        have.
Fal. I know not how they sold themselves;
but thou, like a kind fellow, gavest thyself
away gratis, and I thank thee for thee.   76

Enter *Westmoreland.*

John. Now, have you left pursuit?
West. Retreat is made and execution stay'd.
John. Send Colevile, with his confederates,
To York, to present execution.   80

Blunt, lead him hence and see you guard him
    sure.   *Exit [Blunt] with Colevile.*
And now dispatch we toward the court, my
    lords.
I hear the King my father is sore sick.
Our news shall go before us to his Majesty,
Which, cousin, you shall bear to comfort him,
And we with sober speed will follow you.   86
    Fal. My lord, I beseech you give me leave
    to go
Through Gloucestershire; and when you come
    to court,
Stand my good lord, pray, in your good report.
    John. Fare you well, Falstaff. I, in my
    condition,   90
Shall better speak of you than you deserve.
                  Exeunt [all but Falstaff].
    Fal. I would you had but the wit. 'Twere
better than your dukedom. Good faith, this
same young sober-blooded boy doth not love
me; nor a man cannot make him laugh. But
that's no marvel; he drinks no wine. There's
never none of these demure boys come to any
proof; for thin drink doth so over-cool their
blood, and making many fish-meals, that they
fall into a kind of male greensickness; and then,
when they marry, they get wenches. They are
generally fools and cowards — which some of us
should be too, but for inflammation. A good
sherris sack hath a twofold operation in it. It
ascends me into the brain; dries me there all
the foolish and dull and crudy vapours which
environ it; makes it apprehensive, quick, for-
getive, full of nimble, fiery, and delectable
shapes; which delivered o'er to the voice, the
tongue, which is the birth, becomes excellent
wit. The second property of your excellent
sherris is the warming of the blood; which before (cold and settled) left the liver white and
pale, which is the badge of pusillanimity and
cowardice; but the sherris warms it and makes
it course from the inwards to the parts extremes. It illumineth the face, which, as a
beacon, gives warning to all the rest of this
little kingdom, man, to arm; and then the
vital commoners and inland petty spirits muster
me all to their captain, the heart; who, great
and puff'd up with this retinue, doth any deed
of courage. And this valour comes of sherris:
so that skill in the weapon is nothing without
sack, for that sets it awork; and learning a mere
hoard of gold kept by a devil, till sack com-
mences it and sets it in act and use. Hereof
comes it that Prince Harry is valiant; for the
cold blood he did naturally inherit of his father,

he hath, like lean, sterile, and bare land, ma-
nured, husbanded, and till'd with excellent endeavour of drinking good and good store of fertile sherris, that he is become very hot and
valiant. If I had a thousand sons, the first hu-
mane principle I would teach them should be to
forswear thin potations and to addict themselves to sack.   135

                Enter Bardolph.

How now, Bardolph?
    Bard. The army is discharged all and gone.
    Fal. Let them go. I'll through Gloucester-
shire, and there will I visit Master Robert
Shallow, Esquire. I have him already temp'ring
between my finger and my thumb, and shortly
will I seal with him. Come away.   *Exeunt.*

Scene IV. [*Westminster. The Jerusalem
               Chamber.*]

Enter the *King, Warwick, Thomas Duke of
Clarence, Humphrey of Gloucester,* [and others].
    King. Now, lords, if God doth give success-
    ful end
To this debate that bleedeth at our doors,
We will our youth lead on to higher fields
And draw no swords but what are sanctified.
Our navy is address'd, our power collected,   5
Our substitutes in absence well invested,
And everything lies level to our wish.
Only we want a little personal strength;
And pause us till these rebels, now afoot,
Come underneath the yoke of government.   10
    War. Both which we doubt not but your
    Majesty
Shall soon enjoy.
    King.   Humphrey, my son of Gloucester,
Where is the Prince your brother?
    Glouc. I think he's gone to hunt, my lord, at
    Windsor.
    King. And how accompanied?
    Glouc.   I do not know, my lord.   15
    King. Is not his brother Thomas of Clarence
    with him?
    Glouc. No, my good lord; he is in presence
    here.
    Clar. What would my lord and father?
    King. Nothing but well to thee, Thomas of
    Clarence.
How chance thou art not with the Prince thy
    brother?   20
He loves thee, and thou dost neglect him,
    Thomas.

Thou hast a better place in his affection
Than all thy brothers. Cherish it, my boy,
And noble offices thou mayst effect
Of mediation, after I am dead,   25
Between his greatness and thy other brethren.
Therefore omit him not; blunt not his love,
Nor lose the good advantage of his grace
By seeming cold, or careless of his will;
For he is gracious, if he be observ'd;   30
He hath a tear for pity, and a hand
Open as day for melting charity.
Yet notwithstanding, being incens'd, he's flint;
As humorous as winter, and as sudden
As flaws congealed in the spring of day.   35
His temper, therefore, must be well observ'd.
Chide him for faults, and do it reverently,
When you perceive his blood inclin'd to mirth;
But being moody, give him line and scope
Till that his passions, like a whale on ground,
Confound themselves with working. Learn
this, Thomas,   41
And thou shalt prove a shelter to thy friends;
A hoop of gold to bind thy brothers in,
That the united vessel of their blood,
Mingled with venom of suggestion   45
(As, force perforce, the age will pour it in),
Shall never leak, though it do work as strong
As aconitum or rash gunpowder.
  Clar. I shall observe him with all care and
    love.
  King. Why art thou not at Windsor with
    him, Thomas?   50
  Clar. He is not there to-day; he dines in
    London.
  King. And how accompanied? Canst thou
    tell that?
  Clar. With Poins and other his continual
    followers.
  King. Most subject is the fattest soil to
    weeds;
And he, the noble image of my youth,   55
Is overspread with them. Therefore my grief
Stretches itself beyond the hour of death.
The blood weeps from my heart when I do
    shape,
In forms imaginary, th' unguided days
And rotten times that you shall look upon   60
When I am sleeping with my ancestors.
For when his headstrong riot hath no curb,
When rage and hot blood are his counsellors,
When means and lavish manners meet together,
O, with what wings shall his affections fly   65
Towards fronting peril and oppos'd decay!
  War. My gracious lord, you look beyond
    him quite.

The Prince but studies his companions
Like a strange tongue, wherein, to gain the
    language,
'Tis needful that the most immodest word   70
Be look'd upon and learnt; which once attain'd,
Your Highness knows, comes to no further use
But to be known and hated. So, like gross
    terms,
The Prince will, in the perfectness of time,
Cast off his followers; and their memory   75
Shall as a pattern or a measure live
By which his Grace must mete the lives of
    others,
Turning past evils to advantages.
  King. 'Tis seldom when the bee doth leave
    her comb
In the dead carrion.

                Enter Westmoreland.

                Who's here? Westmoreland?   80
  West. Health to my sovereign, and new hap-
    piness
Added to that that I am to deliver!
Prince John, your son, doth kiss your Grace's
    hand.
Mowbray, the Bishop Scroop, Hastings, and all
Are brought to the correction of your law.   85
There is not now a rebel's sword unsheath'd,
But Peace puts forth her olive everywhere.
The manner how this action hath been borne
Here at more leisure may your Highness read,
With every course in his particular.   90
  King. O Westmoreland, thou art a summer
    bird,
Which ever in the haunch of winter sings
The lifting-up of day.

                Enter Harcourt.

                Look, here's more news.
  Har. From enemies heaven keep your
    Majesty;
And when they stand against you, may they fall
As those that I am come to tell you of!   96
The Earl Northumberland and the Lord Bar-
    dolph,
With a great power of English and of Scots,
Are by the shrieve of Yorkshire overthrown.
The manner and true order of the fight   100
This packet, please it you, contains at large.
  King. And wherefore should these good news
    make me sick?
Will Fortune never come with both hands full,
But write her fair words still in foulest letters?
She either gives a stomach, and no food   105
(Such are the poor, in health), or else a feast,

And takes away the stomach — such are the
rich
That have abundance and enjoy it not.
I should rejoice now at this happy news;
And now my sight fails and my brain is
giddy.
O me! come near me. Now I am much ill. 111
Glouc. Comfort your Majesty!
Clar. O my royal father!
West. My sovereign lord, cheer up yourself,
look up.
War. Be patient, Princes. You do know
these fits 114
Are with his Highness very ordinary.
Stand from him, give him air; he'll straight be
well.
Clar. No, no! he cannot long hold out these
pangs.
Th' incessant care and labour of his mind
Hath wrought the mure that should confine it
in
So thin that life looks through, and will break
out. 120
Glouc. The people fear me, for they do ob-
serve
Unfather'd heirs and loathly births of nature.
The seasons change their manners, as the year
Had found some months asleep, and leapt them
over.
Clar. The river hath thrice flow'd, no ebb
between; 125
And the old folk, Time's doting chronicles,
Say it did so a little time before
That our great-grandsire, Edward, sick'd and
died.
War. Speak lower, Princes, for the King
recovers.
Glouc. This apoplexy will certain be his end.
King. I pray you take me up, and bear me
hence 131
Into some other chamber. Softly, pray.
[*Exeunt.*]

[Scene V. *Westminster. Another chamber
in the Palace.*]

[The *King* on a bed, *Clarence, Gloucester,
Warwick*, and others attending.]

King. Let there be no noise made, my gentle
friends,
Unless some dull and favourable hand
Will whisper music to my weary spirit.
War. Call for the music in the other room.

King. Set me the crown upon my pillow here.
Clar. His eye is hollow, and he changes much.
War. Less noise, less noise!

Enter *Prince Henry.*

Prince. Who saw the Duke of Clarence?
Clar. I am here, brother, full of heaviness.
Prince. How now? Rain within doors, and
none abroad?
How doth the King? 10
Glouc. Exceeding ill.
Prince. Heard he the good news yet?
Tell it him.
Glouc. He alter'd much upon the hearing it.
Prince. If he be sick
With joy, he'll recover without physic. 15
War. Not so much noise, my lords. Sweet
Prince, speak low.
The King your father is dispos'd to sleep.
Clar. Let us withdraw into the other room.
War. Will't please your Grace to go along
with us? 19
Prince. No, I will sit and watch here by the
King. [*Exeunt all but the Prince.*]
Why doth the crown lie there upon his pillow,
Being so troublesome a bedfellow?
O polish'd perturbation! golden care!
That keep'st the ports of slumber open wide
To many a watchful night! Sleep with it now!
Yet not so sound and half so deeply sweet 26
As he whose brow, with homely biggen bound,
Snores out the watch of night. O majesty!
When thou dost pinch thy bearer, thou dost sit
Like a rich armour worn in heat of day, 30
That scalds with safety. By his gates of breath
There lies a dowlny feather which stirs not.
Did he suspire, that light and weightless dowln
Perforce must move. My gracious lord! my
father!
This sleep is sound indeed. This is a sleep 35
That from this golden rigoll hath divorc'd
So many English kings. Thy due from me
Is tears and heavy sorrows of the blood,
Which nature, love, and filial tenderness
Shall, O dear father, pay thee plenteously. 40
My due from thee is this imperial crown,
Which, as immediate from thy place and blood,
Derives itself to me. Lo, where it sits —
[*Puts it on.*]
Which God shall guard; and put the world's
whole strength
Into one giant arm, it shall not force 45
This lineal honour from me. This from thee
Will I to mine leave, as 'tis left to me. *Exit.*
King. Warwick! Gloucester! Clarence!

Enter *Warwick, Gloucester, Clarence.*

Clar. Doth the King call?
War. What would your Majesty? How
fares your Grace? 50
King. Why did you leave me here alone, my
lords?
Clar. We left the Prince my brother here,
my liege,
Who undertook to sit and watch by you.
King. The Prince of Wales? Where is he?
Let me see him.
He is not here. 55
War. This door is open; he is gone this way.
Glouc. He came not through the chamber
where we stay'd.
King. Where is the crown? Who took it
from my pillow?
War. When we withdrew, my liege, we left
it here.
King. The Prince hath ta'en it hence. Go
seek him out. 60
Is he so hasty that he doth suppose
My sleep my death?
Find him, my Lord of Warwick; chide him
hither.
[*Exit Warwick.*]
This part of his conjoins with my disease
And helps to end me. See, sons, what things
you are! 65
How quickly nature falls into revolt
When gold becomes her object!
For this the foolish over-careful fathers
Have broke their sleep with thoughts, their
brains with care,
Their bones with industry; 70
For this they have engrossed and pil'd up
The cank'red heaps of strange-achieved gold;
For this they have been thoughtful to invest
Their sons with arts and martial exercises:
When, like the bee, tolling from every flower 75
The virtuous sweets,
Our thighs pack'd with wax, our mouths with
honey,
We bring it to the hive, and, like the bees,
Are murd'red for our pains. This bitter taste
Yields his engrossments to the ending father. 80

Enter *Warwick.*

Now where is he that will not stay so long
Till his friend sickness hath determin'd me?
War. My lord, I found the Prince in the
next room,
Washing with kindly tears his gentle cheeks,
With such a deep demeanour in great sorrow 85

That tyranny, which never quaff'd but blood
Would, by beholding him, have wash'd his knife
With gentle eye-drops. He is coming hither.
King. But wherefore did he take away the
crown?

Enter *Prince Henry.*

Lo where he comes. Come hither to me, Harry.
Depart the chamber, leave us here alone. 91
Exeunt [all but the King and the Prince].
Prince. I never thought to hear you speak
again.
King. Thy wish was father, Harry, to that
thought.
I stay too long bv thee, I weary thee.
Dost thou so hunger for mine empty chair 95
That thou wilt needs invest thee with my
honours
Before thy hour be ripe? O foolish youth!
Thou seek'st the greatness that will overwhelm
thee.
Stay but a little; for my cloud of dignity
Is held from falling with so weak a wind 100
That it will quickly drop; my day is dim.
Thou hast stol'n that which, after some few
hours,
Were thine without offence; and at my death
Thou hast seal'd up my expectation.
Thy life did manifest thou lov'dst me not, 105
And thou wilt have me die assur'd of it.
Thou hid'st a thousand daggers in thy thoughts,
Which thou hast whetted on thy stony heart
To stab at half an hour of my life. 109
What, canst thou not forbear me half an hour?
Then get thee gone and dig my grave thyself,
And bid the merry bells ring to thine ear,
That thou art crowned, not that I am dead.
Let all the tears that should bedew my hearse
Be drops of balm to sanctify thy head. 115
Only compound me with forgotten dust;
Give that which gave thee life unto the worms.
Pluck down my officers, break my decrees;
For now a time is come to mock at form.
Harry the Fifth is crown'd. Up, vanity! 120
Down, royal state! All you sage counsellors,
hence!
And to the English court assemble now,
From every region, apes of idleness!
Now, neighbour confines, purge you of your
scum. 124
Have you a ruffian that will swear, drink, dance,
Revel the night, rob, murder, and commit
The oldest sins the newest kind of ways?
Be happy, he will trouble you no more!
England shall double gild his treble guilt; 129

143

England shall give him office, honour, might;
For the Fifth Harry from curb'd license plucks
The muzzle of restraint, and the wild dog
Shall flesh his tooth on every innocent.
O my poor kingdom, sick with civil blows!
When that my care could not withhold thy
    riots,   135
What wilt thou do when riot is thy care?
O, thou wilt be a wilderness again,
Peopled with wolves, thy old inhabitants!
    Prince. O, pardon me, my liege! But for
    my tears,
The moist impediments unto my speech,   140
I had forestall'd this dear and deep rebuke,
Ere you with grief had spoke and I had heard
The course of it so far. There is your crown;
And he that wears the crown immortally
Long guard it yours! [*Kneels.*] If I affect it
    more   145
Than as your honour and as your renown,
Let me no more from this obedience rise
Which my most inward true and duteous spirit
Teacheth — this prostrate and exterior bend-
    ing!
[*Rises.*] God witness with me, when I here came
    in,   150
And found no course of breath within your
    Majesty,
How cold it struck my heart! If I do feign,
O, let me in my present wildness die,
And never live to show th' incredulous world
The noble change that I have purposed!   155
Coming to look on you, thinking you dead —
And dead almost, my liege, to think you were —
I spake unto this crown as having sense,
And thus upbraided it: 'The care on thee de-
    pending
Hath fed upon the body of my father.   160
Therefore thou best of gold art worst of gold.
Other, less fine in carat, is more precious,
Preserving life in med'cine potable;
But thou, most fine, most honour'd, most re-
    nown'd,
Hast eat thy bearer up.' Thus, my most royal
    liege,   165
Accusing it, I put it on my head,
To try with it (as with an enemy
That had before my face murdered my father)
The quarrel of a true inheritor.
But if it did infect my blood with joy   170
Or swell my thoughts to any strain of pride,
If any rebel or vain spirit of mine
Did with the least affection of a welcome
Give entertainment to the might of it,
Let God for ever keep it from my head   175

And make me as the poorest vassal is
That doth with awe and terror kneel to it!
    King. O my son,
God put it in thy mind to take it hence,
That thou mightst win the more thy father's
    love,   180
Pleading so wisely in excuse of it!
Come hither, Harry, sit thou by my bed,
And hear, I think, the very latest counsel
That ever I shall breathe. God knows, my
    son,
By what bypaths and indirect crook'd ways 185
I met this crown; and I myself know well
How troublesome it sat upon my head.
To thee it shall descend with better quiet,
Better opinion, better confirmation;
For all the soil of the achievement goes   190
With me into the earth. It seem'd in me
But as an honour snatch'd with boist'rous
    hand;
And I had many living to upbraid
My gain of it by their assistances;   194
Which daily grew to quarrel and to bloodshed,
Wounding supposed peace. All these bold fears
Thou seest with peril I have answered;
For all my reign hath been but as a scene
Acting that argument. And now my death
Changes the mood; for what in me was pur-
    chas'd,   200
Falls upon thee in a more fairer sort;
So thou the garland wear'st successively.
Yet, though thou stand'st more sure than I
    could do,
Thou art not firm enough, since griefs are green;
And all my friends, which thou must make thy
    friends,   205
Have but their stings and teeth newly ta'en
    out;
By whose fell working I was first advanc'd,
And by whose power I well might lodge a fear
To be again displac'd; which to avoid,
I cut them off, and had a purpose now   210
To lead out many to the Holy Land,
Lest rest and lying still might make them look
Too near unto my state. Therefore, my Harry,
Be it thy course to busy giddy minds
With foreign quarrels, that action, hence borne
    out,   215
May waste the memory of the former days.
More would I, but my lungs are wasted so
That strength of speech is utterly denied me.
How I came by the crown, O God forgive,
And grant it may with thee in true peace live!
    Prince. My gracious liege,   221
You won it, wore it, kept it, gave it me;

Then plain and right must my possession be;
Which I with more than with a common
    pain
'Gainst all the world will rightfully maintain.

Enter Lord John of Lancaster and Warwick.

King. Look, look, here comes my John of
    Lancaster.   226
John. Health, peace, and happiness to my
    royal father!
King. Thou bring'st me happiness and peace,
    son John;
But health, alack, with youthful wings is
    flown

From this bare wither'd trunk. Upon thy sight,
My worldly business makes a period.   231
Where is my Lord of Warwick?
    Prince.   My Lord of Warwick!
King. Doth any name particular belong
Unto the lodging where I first did swound?
War. 'Tis call'd Jerusalem, my noble lord.
King. Laud be to God! Even there my life
    must end.   236
It hath been prophesied to me many years,
I should not die but in Jerusalem;
Which vainly I suppos'd the Holy Land.
But bear me to that chamber; there I'll lie. 240
In that Jerusalem shall Harry die.   *Exeunt.*

ACT V. Scene I. [*Gloucestershire.* Shallow's *house.*]

Enter Shallow, Falstaff, Bardolph, and Page.

Shal. By cock and pie, sir, you shall not
away to-night. What, Davy, I say!
Fal. You must excuse me, Master Robert
Shallow.   4
Shal. I will not excuse you; you shall not be
excus'd; excuses shall not be admitted; there
is no excuse shall serve; you shall not be excus'd. Why, Davy!

Enter Davy.

Davy. Here, sir.   9
Shal. Davy, Davy, Davy, Davy; let me see,
Davy; let me see, Davy; let me see — Yea,
marry, William Cook! bid him come hither.
Sir John, you shall not be excus'd.
Davy. Marry, sir, thus: those precepts cannot be served. And again, sir — shall we sow
the headland with wheat?   16
Shal. With red wheat, Davy. But for William Cook — Are there no young pigeons?
Davy. Yes, sir. Here is now the smith's note
for shoeing and plough-irons.   20
Shal. Let it be cast and paid. Sir John, you
shall not be excus'd.
Davy. Now, sir, a new link to the bucket
must needs be had; and, sir, do you mean to
stop any of William's wages about the sack he
lost the other day at Hinckley fair?   26
Shal. 'A shall answer it. Some pigeons,
Davy, a couple of short-legg'd hens, a joint of
mutton, and any pretty little tiny kickshaws,
tell William Cook.   30
Davy. Doth the man of war stay all night,
sir?

Shal. Yea, Davy, I will use him well. A
friend i' th' court is better than a penny in
purse. Use his men well, Davy; for they are
arrant knaves and will backbite.   36
Davy. No worse than they are backbitten,
sir; for they have marvail's foul linen.
Shal. Well conceited, Davy. About thy
business, Davy.   40
Davy. I beseech you, sir, to countenance
William Visor of Woncot against Clement
Perkes o' th' hill.
Shal. There is many complaints, Davy,
against that Visor. That Visor is an arrant
knave, on my knowledge.   46
Davy. I grant your worship that he is a
knave, sir; but yet God forbid, sir, but a
knave should have some countenance at his
friend's request! An honest man, sir, is able to
speak for himself when a knave is not. I have
serv'd your worship truly, sir, this eight years;
and if I cannot once or twice in a quarter bear
out a knave against an honest man, I have but
a very little credit with your worship. The
knave is mine honest friend, sir. Therefore, I
beseech you, let him be countenanc'd.   57
Shal. Go to. I say he shall have no wrong.
Look about, Davy. [*Exit Davy.*] Where are
you, Sir John? Come, come, come, off with
your boots. Give me your hand, Master
Bardolph.   62
Bard. I am glad to see your worship.
Shal. I thank thee with all my heart, kind
Master Bardolph. [*To the Page*] And welcome,
my tall fellow. — Come, Sir John.   66
Fal. I'll follow you, good Master Robert
Shallow. [*Exit Shallow.*] Bardolph, look to our
horses. [*Exeunt Bardolph and Page.*] If I were

sawed into quantities, I should make four dozen of such bearded hermits' staves as Master Shallow. It is a wonderful thing to see the semblable coherence of his men's spirits and his. They, by observing of him, do bear themselves like foolish justices; he, by conversing with them, is turned into a justice-like servingman. Their spirits are so married in conjunction with the participation of society that they flock together in consent, like so many wild geese. If I had a suit to Master Shallow, I would humour his men with the imputation of being near their master; if to his men, I would curry with Master Shallow that no man could better command his servants. It is certain that either wise bearing or ignorant carriage is caught, as men take diseases, one of another. Therefore let men take heed of their company. I will devise matter enough out of this Shallow to keep Prince Harry in continual laughter the wearing-out of six fashions, which is four terms, or two actions; and 'a shall laugh without intervallums. O, it is much that a lie with a slight oath, and a jest with a sad brow, will do with a fellow that never had the ache in his shoulders! O, you shall see him laugh till his face be like a wet cloak ill laid up!   95

Shal. [*within*] Sir John!

Fal. I come, Master Shallow. I come, Master Shallow.   *Exit.*

Scene II. [*Westminster. The Palace.*]

Enter *Warwick* and the *Lord Chief Justice*, [meeting].

War. How now, my Lord Chief Justice? Whither away?

Just. How doth the King?

War. Exceeding well; his cares are now all ended.

Just. I hope, not dead.

War.   He's walk'd the way of nature,
And, to our purposes, he lives no more.   5

Just. I would his Majesty had call'd me with him.
The service that I truly did his life
Hath left me open to all injuries.

War. Indeed I think the young King loves you not.

Just. I know he doth not, and do arm myself
To welcome the condition of the time,   11
Which cannot look more hideously upon me
Than I have drawn it in my fantasy.

Enter *John of Lancaster, Thomas* [*of Clarence*], and *Humphrey* [*of Gloucester*, with *Westmoreland* and others].

War. Here come the heavy issue of dead Harry.
O that the living Harry had the temper   15
Of him, the worst of these three gentlemen!
How many nobles then should hold their places
That must strike sail to spirits of vile sort!

Just. O God, I fear all will be overturn'd!

John. Good morrow, cousin Warwick, good morrow.   20

Glouc., Clar. Good morrow, cousin.

John. We meet like men that had forgot to speak.

War. We do remember; but our argument
Is all too heavy to admit much talk.

John. Well, peace be with him that hath made us heavy!   25

Just. Peace be with us, lest we be heavier!

Glouc. O, good my lord, you have lost a friend indeed!
And I dare swear you borrow not that face
Of seeming sorrow — it is sure your own.

John. Though no man be assur'd what grace to find,   30
You stand in coldest expectation.
I am the sorrier. Would 'twere otherwise.

Clar. Well, you must now speak Sir John Falstaff fair;
Which swims against your stream of quality.

Just. Sweet Princes, what I did, I did in honour,   35
Led by th' impartial conduct of my soul;
And never shall you see that I will beg
A ragged and forestall'd remission.
If truth and upright innocency fail me,
I'll to the King my master that is dead   40
And tell him who hath sent me after him.

Enter the *Prince*, [now *King Henry the Fifth*, attended].

War. Here comes the Prince.

Just. Good morrow, and God save your Majesty!

Prince. This new and gorgeous garment, majesty,
Sits not so easy on me as you think.   45
Brothers, you mix your sadness with some fear.
This is the English, not the Turkish court;
Not Amurath an Amurath succeeds,
But Harry Harry. Yet be sad, good brothers,
For, by my faith, it very well becomes you.   50

Sorrow so royally in you appears
That I will deeply put the fashion on
And wear it in my heart. Why then, be sad;
But entertain no more of it, good brothers,
Than a joint burden laid upon us all.   55
For me, by heaven, I bid you be assur'd
I'll be your father and your brother too.
Let me but bear your love, I'll bear your
     cares.
Yet weep that Harry's dead, and so will I;
But Harry lives, that shall convert those tears,
By number, into hours of happiness.   61
  Brothers. We hope no otherwise from your
     Majesty.
  Prince. You all look strangely on me; and
     you most.
You are, I think, assur'd I love you not.   64
  Just. I am assur'd, if I be measur'd rightly,
Your Majesty hath no just cause to hate
     me.
  Prince. No?
How might a prince of my great hopes forget
So great indignities you laid upon me?   69
What? rate, rebuke, and roughly send to prison
Th' immediate heir of England! Was this easy?
May this be wash'd in Lethe and forgotten?
  Just. I then did use the person of your
     father;
The image of his power lay then in me;
And in th' administration of his law,   75
Whiles I was busy for the commonwealth,
Your Highness pleased to forget my place,
The majesty and power of law and justice,
The image of the King whom I presented,
And struck me in my very seat of judgment;
Whereon, as an offender to your father,   81
I gave bold way to my authority
And did commit you. If the deed were ill,
Be you contented, wearing now the garland,
To have a son set your decrees at naught,   85
To pluck down justice from your awful bench,
To trip the course of law, and blunt the
     sword
That guards the peace and safety of your per-
     son;
Nay, more, to spurn at your most royal image
And mock your workings in a second body.   90
Question your royal thoughts, make the case
     yours;
Be now the father, and propose a son;
Hear your own dignity so much profan'd,
See your most dreadful laws so loosely slighted,
Behold yourself so by a son disdain'd;   95
And then imagine me taking your part
And, in your power, so silencing your son.

After this cold considerance, sentence me;
And, as you are a king, speak in your state
What I have done that misbecame my place,
My person, or my liege's sovereignty.   101
  Prince. You are right, Justice, and you
     weigh this well.
Therefore still bear the balance and the sword;
And I do wish your honours may increase
Till you do live to see a son of mine   105
Offend you, and obey you, as I did.
So shall I live to speak my father's words:
'Happy am I that have a man so bold
That dares do justice on my proper son;
And not less happy, having such a son   110
That would deliver up his greatness so
Into the hands of justice.' You did commit
     me;
For which I do commit into your hand
Th' unstained sword that you have us'd to
     bear,
With this remembrance, that you use the same
With the like bold, just, and impartial spirit 116
As you have done 'gainst me. There is my
     hand.
You shall be as a father to my youth;
My voice shall sound as you do prompt mine
     ear,
And I will stoop and humble my intents   120
To your well-practis'd wise directions.
And, Princes all, believe me, I beseech you:
My father is gone wild into his grave;
For in his tomb lie my affections,
And with his spirit sadly I survive,   125
To mock the expectation of the world,
To frustrate prophecies, and to rase out
Rotten opinion, who hath writ me down
After my seeming. The tide of blood in me
Hath proudly flow'd in vanity till now.   130
Now doth it turn and ebb back to the sea,
Where it shall mingle with the state of floods
And flow henceforth in formal majesty.
Now call we our high court of parliament;
And let us choose such limbs of noble counsel
That the great body of our state may go   136
In equal rank with the best-govern'd nation;
That war, or peace, or both at once, may be
As things acquainted and familiar to us;
In which you, father, shall have foremost hand.
Our coronation done, we will accite,   141
As I before rememb'red, all our state;
And (God consigning to my good intents)
No prince nor peer shall have just cause to
     say,
'God shorten Harry's happy life one day!'   145
                                   Exeunt.

Scene III. [*Gloucestershire. Shallow's
garden.*]

*Enter Sir John Falstaff, Shallow, Silence, Davy,
Bardolph, Page.*

Shal. Nay, you shall see my orchard, where,
in an arbour, we will eat a last year's pippin
of mine own graffing, with a dish of caraways
and so forth. Come, cousin Silence. And then
to bed.   5
Fal. Fore God, you have here a goodly dwell-
ing and a rich.
Shal. Barren, barren, barren! beggars all,
beggars all, Sir John! Marry, good air. Spread,
Davy; spread, Davy. Well said, Davy.   10
Fal. This Davy serves you for good uses. He
is your servingman and your husband.
Shal. A good varlet, a good varlet, a very
good varlet, Sir John. By the mass, I have
drunk too much sack at supper. A good varlet.
Now sit down, now sit down. Come, cousin.
Sil. Ah, sirrah! quoth-a — we shall

[*Sings.*]

Do nothing but eat and make good cheer
And praise God for the merry year,
When flesh is cheap and females dear,   20
And lusty lads roam here and there
            So merrily,
And ever among so merrily.

Fal. There's a merry heart! Good Master
Silence, I'll give you a health for that anon.
Shal. Give Master Bardolph some wine,
Davy.   27
Davy. Sweet sir, sit; I'll be with you anon.
Most sweet sir, sit. Master page, good master
page, sit. Proface! What you want in meat,
we'll have in drink. But you must bear; the
heart's all.   [*Exit.*]
Shal. Be merry, Master Bardolph; and, my
little soldier there, be merry.
Sil. [*sings*]

Be merry, be merry, my wife has all,   35
For women are shrows, both short and tall.
'Tis merry in hall when beards wag all,
    And welcome merry Shrovetide!
Be merry, be merry.

Fal. I did not think Master Silence had been
a man of this metal.   41
Sil. Who, I? I have been merry twice and
once ere now.

Enter Davy.

Davy. [*To Bardolph*] There's a dish of leather-
coats for you.
Shal. Davy!   45
Davy. Your worship? [*To Bardolph*] I'll be
with you straight. — A cup of wine, sir?
Sil. [*sings*]

A cup of wine that's brisk and fine,
And drink unto the leman mine,
    And a merry heart lives long-a.   50

Fal. Well said, Master Silence.
Sil. An we shall be merry, now comes in the
sweet o' th' night.
Fal. Health and long life to you, Master
Silence!   55
Sil. [*sings*]

Fill the cup, and let it come!
I'll pledge you a mile to th' bottom.

Shal. Honest Bardolph, welcome! If thou
want'st anything and wilt not call, beshrew thy
heart. [*To the Page*] Welcome, my little tiny
thief, and welcome indeed too!—I'll drink to
Master Bardolph, and to all the cabileros about
London.
Davy. I hope to see London once ere I die.
Bard. An I might see you there, Davy! 65
Shal. By the mass, you'll crack a quart to-
gether. Ha, will you not, Master Bardolph?
Bard. Yea, sir, in a pottle-pot.
Shal. By God's liggens, I thank thee. The
knave will stick by thee, I can assure thee that.
'A will not out; 'a is true-bred.   71
Bard. And I'll stick by him, sir.
Shal. Why, there spoke a king! Lack noth-
ing; be merry. (*One knocks at door.*) Look
who's at door there, ho! Who knocks?   75
                                            [*Exit Davy.*]
Fal. Why, now you have done me right.
[*To Silence, who has just drunk a bumper.*]

Sil. [*sings*] Do me right
            And dub me knight.
                Samingo!

Is't not so?   80
Fal. 'Tis so.
Sil. Is't so? Why then, say an old man can
do somewhat.

[*Enter Davy.*]

Davy. An't please your worship, there's one
Pistol come from the court with news.   85
Fal. From the court? Let him come in.

Enter *Pistol*.

How now, Pistol?

Pist. Sir John, God save you!

Fal. What wind blew you hither, Pistol?

Pist. Not the ill wind which blows no man
to good.

Sweet knight, thou art now one of the greatest men in this realm.

Sil. By'r Lady, I think 'a be, but goodman
Puff of Barson.

Pist. Puff?   95

Puff i' thy teeth, most recreant coward base!
Sir John, I am thy Pistol and thy friend,
And helter-skelter have I rode to thee;
And tidings do I bring, and lucky joys,
And golden times, and happy news of price. 100

Fal. I pray thee now deliver them like a
man of this world.

Pist. A foutra for the world and worldlings
base!

I speak of Africa and golden joys.

Fal. O base Assyrian knight, what is thy
news?   105

Let King Cophetua know the truth thereof.

Sil. [*sings*] And Robin Hood, Scarlet, and
John.

Pist. Shall dunghill curs confront the Heli-
cons?

And shall good news be baffled?

Then, Pistol, lay thy head in Furies' lap. 110

Shal. Honest, gentleman I know not your
breeding.

Pist. Why then, lament therefore.

Shal. Give me pardon, sir. If, sir, you come
with news from the court, I take it there's but
two ways — either to utter them, or conceal them.
I am, sir, under the King, in some authority.

Pist. Under which king, Besonian? Speak,
or die!

Shal. Under King Harry.

Pist.   Harry the Fourth — or Fifth?

Shal. Harry the Fourth.

Pist.   A foutra for thine office! 120

Sir John, thy tender lambkin now is King.
Harry the Fifth's the man. I speak the truth.
When Pistol lies, do this, and fig me, like
The bragging Spaniard.

Fal. What, is the old king dead?   125

Pist. As nail in door. The things I speak are
just.

Fal. Away, Bardolph! saddle my horse.
Master Robert Shallow, choose what office
thou wilt in the land, 'tis thine. Pistol, I will
double-charge thee with dignities.

Bard. O joyful day!   131

I would not take a knighthood for my fortune.

Pist. What, I do bring good news?

Fal. Carry Master Silence to bed. Master
Shallow, my Lord Shallow, be what thou wilt:
I am Fortune's steward. Get on thy boots;
we'll ride all night. O sweet Pistol! Away,
Bardolph! [*Exit Bardolph.*] Come, Pistol, utter
more to me; and withal devise something to do
thyself good. Boot, boot, Master Shallow! I
know the young king is sick for me. Let us take
any man's horses; the laws of England are at
my commandment. Blessed are they that have
been my friends, and woe to my Lord Chief
Justice!   144

Pist. Let vultures vile seize on his lungs also!
'Where is the life that late I led?' say they.
Why, here it is! welcome these pleasant days!
Exeunt.

Scene IV. [*London. A street.*]

Enter *Hostess Quickly, Doll Tearsheet,* and
Beadles.

Host. No, thou arrant knave! I would to
God that I might die, that I might have thee
hang'd. Thou hast drawn my shoulder out of
joint.

Officer. The constables have delivered her
over to me; and she shall have whipping cheer
enough, I warrant her. There hath been a man
or two lately kill'd about her.   7

Doll. Nuthook, nuthook, you lie! Come on!
I'll tell thee what, thou damn'd tripe-visag'd
rascal, an the child I now go with do miscarry,
thou wert better thou hadst struck thy mother,
thou paper-fac'd villain.   12

Host. O the Lord, that Sir John were come!
He would make this a bloody day to somebody!
But I pray God the fruit of her womb mis-
carry!

Officer. If it do, you shall have a dozen of
cushions again; you have but eleven now.
Come, I charge you both go with me; for the
man is dead that you and Pistol beat amongst
you.   19

Doll. I'll tell you what, you thin man in a
censer, I will have you as soundly swing'd for
this! You blue-bottle rogue, you filthy famish'd correctioner, if you be not swing'd, I'll
forswear half-kirtles.

Officer. Come, come, you she knight-errant,
come.   26

Host. O God, that right should thus over-
come might! Well, of sufferance comes ease.
Doll. Come, you rogue, come! Bring me to
a justice.   30
Host. Ay, come, you starv'd bloodhound!
Doll. Goodman Death, goodman Bones!
Host. Thou atomy thou!
Doll. Come, you thin thing! Come, you
rascal!   34
Officer. Very well.   *Exeunt.*

Scene V. [*A public place near Westminster
Abbey.*]

Enter three *Grooms*, strewers of rushes.

1. Groom. More rushes, more rushes!
2. Groom. The trumpets have sounded twice.
3. Groom. 'Twill be two o'clock ere they
come from the coronation. Dispatch, dispatch.
                                         Exeunt.

*Trumpets sound and the King and his Train pass
over the stage. After them enter Falstaff, Shallow,
Pistol, Bardolph,* and the *Boy.*

Fal. Stand here by me, Master Robert Shallow. I will make the King do you grace. I will
leer upon him as 'a comes by; and do but mark
the countenance that he will give me.
Pist. God bless thy lungs, good knight.   9
Fal. Come here, Pistol, stand behind me!
[*To Shallow*] O, if I had had time to have made
new liveries, I would have bestowed the thou-
sand pound I borrowed of you. But 'tis no mat-
ter. This poor show doth better; this doth
infer the zeal I had to see him.   15
Shal. It doth so.
Fal. It shows my earnestness of affection —
Shal. It doth so.
Fal. My devotion —
Shal. It doth, it doth, it doth.   20
Fal. As it were, to ride day and night; and
not to deliberate, not to remember, not to have
patience to shift me —
Shal. It is best, certain.   24
Fal. But to stand stained with travel and
sweating with desire to see him, thinking of
nothing else, putting all affairs else in oblivion,
as if there were nothing else to be done but to
see him.   29
Pist. 'Tis 'semper idem,' for 'absque hoc
nihil est.' 'Tis all in every part.
Shal. 'Tis so indeed.

Pist. My knight, I will inflame thy noble
liver
And make thee rage.
Thy Doll, and Helen of thy noble thoughts, 35
Is in base durance and contagious prison,
Hal'd thither
By most mechanical and dirty hand.
Rouse up revenge from ebon den with fell
Alecto's snake,   39
For Doll is in. Pistol speaks naught but truth.
Fal. I will deliver her.
          [*Shouts within.*] *The trumpets sound.*
Pist. There roar'd the sea, and trumpet
clangor sounds.

Enter the *King* and his *Train, Lord Chief
Justice* [among them].

Fal. God save thy Grace, King Hal, my
royal Hal!
Pist. The heavens thee guard and keep, most
royal imp of fame!   46
Fal. God save thee, my sweet boy!
King. My Lord Chief Justice, speak to that
vain man.
Just. Have you your wits? Know you what
'tis you speak?
Fal. My king! my Jove! I speak to thee,
my heart!   50
King. I know thee not, old man. Fall to thy
prayers.
How ill white hairs become a fool and jester!
I have long dreamt of such a kind of man,
So surfeit-swell'd, so old, and so profane;
But being awak'd, I do despise my dream.   55
Make less thy body, hence, and more thy grace;
Leave gormandizing. Know the grave doth
gape
For thee thrice wider than for other men.
Reply not to me with a fool-born jest.
Presume not that I am the thing I was;   60
For God doth know (so shall the world per-
ceive)
That I have turn'd away my former self;
So will I those that kept me company.
When thou dost hear I am as I have been,   64
Approach me, and thou shalt be as thou wast,
The tutor and the feeder of my riots.
Till then I banish thee, on pain of death,
As I have done the rest of my misleaders,
Not to come near our person by ten mile.
For competence of life I will allow you,   70
That lack of means enforce you not to evil;
And, as we hear you do reform yourselves,
We will, according to your strengths and qual-
ities,

Give you advancement. Be it your charge, my lord,
To see perform'd the tenure of our word.   75
Set on.   *Exit King [with his Train].*
    Fal. Master Shallow, I owe you a thousand pound.
    Shal. Yea, marry, Sir John; which I beseech you to let me have home with me.   80
    Fal. That can hardly be, Master Shallow. Do not you grieve at this. I shall be sent for in private to him. Look you, he must seem thus to the world. Fear not your advancements. I will be the man yet that shall make you great.
    Shal. I cannot well perceive how, unless you should give me your doublet and stuff me out with straw. I beseech you, good Sir John, let me have five hundred of my thousand.   89
    Fal. Sir, I will be as good as my word. This that you heard was but a colour.
    Shal. A colour that I fear you will die in, Sir John.
    Fal. Fear no colours! Go with me to dinner. Come, Lieutenant Pistol; come, Bardolph. I shall be sent for soon at night.   96

    Enter [*Chief*] *Justice* and *Prince John,*
              [with *Officers*].

    Just. Go carry Sir John Falstaff to the Fleet. Take all his company along with him.
    Fal. My lord, my lord —
    Just. I cannot now speak; I will hear you soon.   100
Take them away.
    Pist. 'Si fortuna me tormenta, spero contenta.'
    Exeunt. Manent Lancaster and Chief Justice.
    John. I like this fair proceeding of the King's. He hath intent his wonted followers
Shall all be very well provided for;   105
But all are banish'd till their conversations
Appear more wise and modest to the world.
    Just. And so they are.
    John. The King hath call'd his parliament, my lord.
    Just. He hath.   110
    John. I will lay odds that, ere this year expire,

We bear our civil swords and native fire
As far as France. I heard a bird so sing,
Whose music, to my thinking, pleas'd the King.
Come, will you hence?   *Exeunt.*

EPILOGUE.

[SPOKEN BY A *Dancer*.]

First my fear; then my cursy; last my speech. My fear, is your displeasure; my cursy, my duty; and my speech, to beg your pardons. If you look for a good speech now, you undo me; for what I have to say is of mine own making; and what indeed I should say will, I doubt, prove mine own marring. But to the purpose, and so to the venture. Be it known to you (as it is very well) I was lately here in the end of a displeasing play, to pray your patience for it and to promise you a better. I meant indeed to pay you with this; which, if like an ill venture it come unluckily home, I break, and you my gentle creditors lose. Here I promis'd you I would be, and here I commit my body to your mercies. Bate me some, and I will pay you some, and, as most debtors do, promise you infinitely.   17

If my tongue cannot entreat you to acquit me, will you command me to use my legs? And yet that were but light payment — to dance out of your debt. But a good conscience will make any possible satisfaction, and so would I. All the gentlewomen here have forgiven me. If the gentlemen will not, then the gentlemen do not agree with the gentlewomen, which was never seen before in such an assembly.   26

One word more, I beseech you. If you be not too much cloy'd with fat meat, our humble author will continue the story, with Sir John in it, and make you merry with fair Katherine of France; where, for anything I know, Falstaff shall die of a sweat, unless already 'a be kill'd with your hard opinions; for Oldcastle died a martyr, and this is not the man. My tongue is weary. When my legs are too, I will bid you good night; and so kneel down before you — but, indeed, to pray for the Queen.   37

KING HENRY THE FIFTH

HENRY THE FIFTH is mentioned in the Stationers' Register on August 4, 1600, and the formal entry, by Thomas Pavyer, comes ten days later. The First Quarto (1600) offers a garbled text of a drastically cut-down version. The Second Quarto (1602) was printed from the First; and so, apparently, was the Third, which, though dated 1608, was in fact published in 1619. The First Folio contains the play in its full and authentic form. Bad as it is, the First Quarto enables one to correct a good many of the Folio's misprints. Three lines not found in the Folio appear to be genuine and are supplied from the Quarto in the present text (ii, 1, 110–111; iv, 3, 48). The most famous of all Shakespearean emendations is Theobald's correction of the Folio reading 'and a Table of greene fields' (ii, 3, 17), which makes no sense, to 'and 'a babbled of green fields.' The Quartos omit the words.

The proper division into acts is shown by the Chorus in each case. In the Quarto (which omits the speeches of the Chorus) there is no division. The Folio marks the acts, but in some instances erroneously.

The date of HENRY THE FIFTH is fixed with unusual exactness by the reference to Essex in the Chorus to Act V:

> Were now the general of our gracious Empress
> (As in good time he may) from Ireland coming,
> Bringing rebellion broached on his sword,
> How many would the peaceful city quit
> To welcome him!

Essex left London on March 27, 1599, reached Dublin in April, and, returning from a campaign which was a complete fiasco, arrived at London on September 28 in the same year. Meres, in his *Palladis Tamia*, published in the autumn of 1598, mentions *Henry the Fourth*, but not HENRY THE FIFTH. The play is promised in the Epilogue to *Henry the Fourth, Part II*.

For history Shakespeare relies for the most part on Holinshed's *Chronicle*. *The Famous Victories of Henry the Fifth* includes most of the reign, ending with the betrothal to Katherine of France, which took place on May 21, 1420. From this old play Shakespeare took hints for the action and he sometimes echoes its phrases. Thus, in the famous anecdote of the tennis balls (i, 2, 234 ff.), the king's eloquent reply to the Dauphin's insulting message is quite original; but there are traces of both Holinshed and the old play. In the play we have: 'My lord prince Dolphin is very pleasant with me: but tel him, that in steed of balles of leather, we wil tose him balles of brasse and yron, yea such balles as neuer were tost in France, the proudest tennis court shall rue it. . . . Therfore get thee hence, and tel him thy message quickly, least I be there before thee: away priest, be gone.' In Holinshed: 'The K[ing] wrote to him, [the Dauphin,] that yer ought long, he would tosse him some London balles that perchance should shake the walles of the best court in France.'

The French nobles are not well treated by Shakespeare. Their rather vulgar frivolity is distasteful to the modern reader, who looks at the situation impartially, and not with the eyes of a patriotic Elizabethan. Holinshed tells us simply that the French, confident of victory, 'made great triumph; for the capteins had determined before how to diuide the spoile, and the soldiers the night before had plaid the Englishmen at dice.' The old play dramatizes Holinshed. It brings in three soldiers and a drummer playing at dice and speaking broken English; also a captain who has 'set three or foure chaire makers a worke, to make a new disguised chaire to set that womanly King of England in, that all the people may laugh and scoffe at him.' Yet he pities the 'poore English scabs': 'Why, take an English man out of his warme bed and his stale drinke, but one moneth, and alas what wil become of him? But giue the Frenchman a Reddish roote, and he wil liue with it all the dayes of his life.' (Cf. iii, 7, 93, 158 ff.; iv, Chorus, 17–22.) Alençon is of much the same opinion in *1 Henry VI*, i, 2, 9–12:

> They want their porridge and their fat bull-beeves.
> Either they must be dieted like mules
> And have their provender tied to their mouths,
> Or piteous they will look, like drowned mice.

The way in which Shakespeare picked up phrases is well illustrated in the Prologue:

> Then should the warlike Harry, like himself,
> Assume the port of Mars, and at his heels
> (Leash'd in, like hounds) should famine, sword, and fire
> Crouch for employment.

In Holinshed King Henry uses a similar figure in reply to an ambassador from the besieged citizens of Rouen: 'He declared that the goddesse of battell, called *Bellona*, had three handmaidens, euer of necessitie attending vpon her, as blood, fire, and famine.' Cf. also the exhortation of the Archbishop of Canterbury (i, 2, 131): 'With blood and sword and fire to win your right.' Canterbury's long address in explanation of King Henry's title to the crown of France (i, 2, 35–100) is simply versified from Holinshed, with only such slight changes as are needed to transfer prose into blank verse. Indeed, Shakespeare found in Holinshed's prose four or five lines which he could take over as verse without the change of a word. This illustrates the fallacy of any argument based on the discovery of so-called 'verse fossils' in prose passages.

The Quarto omits the Prologue and all other speeches of the Chorus. Some of these furnish historical information that the audience cannot do without. Incidentally, they are interesting documents in the history of dramatic criticism. They express, over and over again, the doctrine of the voluntary subjection of our minds to the illusion of the stage (as opposed to dramatic deception) — a principle which a succession of eminent critics arrived at by a long course of study and debate, and which Schlegel and Coleridge are often thought to have finally worked out.

The character of Henry V in this play is inconsistent with the character of the Prince in *Henry the Fourth*. The difference is not moral, but mental. The Prince has a brilliant intellect that works with flashing rapidity; King Henry's mind is not inferior, but it is of another order: it is strong and sure, but does not scintillate. No such mental transformation could result from a reform in manners and morals. The inconsistency is, of course, in no sense a fault in Shakespeare's portrayal. He was quite at liberty to give different accounts of the same personage in different plays. For the intensely religious nature of King Henry, Shakespeare had ample justification in Holinshed, and he has emphasized it throughout, so that the conquest of France becomes to all intents and purposes a holy war.

THE LIFE OF
KING HENRY the FIFTH

[Dramatis Personæ.

Chorus.

King Henry the Fifth.
Duke of Gloucester, } brothers to the *King.*
Duke of Bedford,
Duke of Exeter, uncle to the *King.*
Duke of York, cousin to the *King.*
Earl of Salisbury.
Earl of Westmoreland.
Earl of Warwick.
Archbishop of Canterbury.
Bishop of Ely.
Earl of Cambridge.
Lord Scroop.
Sir Thomas Grey.
Sir Thomas Erpingham,
Gower, an English captain, } officers in *King*
Fluellen, a Welsh captain, } *Henry's* army.
Macmorris, an Irish captain,
Jamy, a Scottish captain,
John Bates,
Alexander Court, } soldiers in the same.
Michael Williams,
Pistol.
Nym.

Bardolph.
Boy.
A Herald.

Charles the Sixth, King of France.
Lewis, the Dauphin.
Duke of Burgundy.
Duke of Orleans.
Duke of Bourbon.
The Constable of France.
Rambures,
Grandpré, } French lords.
Beaumont,
Governor of Harfleur.
Montjoy, a French herald.
Ambassadors to the *King of England*

Isabel, Queen of France.
Katherine, daughter to *Charles* and *Isabel.*
Alice, a lady attending on her.
Hostess of the Boar's Head tavern in Eastcheap
(formerly *Mistress Quickly,* now married to
Pistol).

Lords, Ladies, Officers, Soldiers, Citizens, Messengers, and Attendants.

SCENE. — *England and France.*]

Enter *Prologue.*

O for a Muse of fire, that would ascend
The brightest heaven of invention,
A kingdom for a stage, princes to act,
And monarchs to behold the swelling scene!
Then should the warlike Harry, like himself, 5
Assume the port of Mars, and at his heels
(Leash'd in, like hounds) should famine, sword,
    and fire
Crouch for employment. But pardon, gentles
    all,
The flat unraised spirits that have dar'd
On this unworthy scaffold to bring forth 10
So great an object. Can this cockpit hold
The vasty fields of France? Or may we
    cram
Within this wooden O the very casques
That did affright the air at Agincourt?
O, pardon! since a crooked figure may 15
Attest in little place a million,

And let us, ciphers to this great accompt,
On your imaginary forces work.
Suppose within the girdle of these walls
Are now confin'd two mighty monarchies, 20
Whose high-upreared and abutting fronts
The perilous narrow ocean parts asunder.
Piece out our imperfections with your thoughts :
Into a thousand parts divide one man
And make imaginary puissance. 25
Think, when we talk of horses, that you see
    them
Printing their proud hoofs i' th' receiving
    earth.
For 'tis your thoughts that now must deck our
    kings,
Carry them here and there, jumping o'er times,
Turning th' accomplishment of many years 30
Into an hourglass ; for the which supply,
Admit me Chorus to this history,
Who, Prologue-like, your humble patience pray,
Gently to hear, kindly to judge our play. *Exit.*

ACT I. Scene I. [*London. An antechamber in the* King's *Palace.*]

Enter the two *Bishops* — [*the Archbishop*]
 of Canterbury and [*the Bishop of*] *Ely.*

Cant. My lord, I'll tell you, that self bill is
 urg'd
Which in th' eleventh year of the last king's
 reign
Was like, and had indeed against us pass'd
But that the scambling and unquiet time
Did push it out of farther question.   5
 Ely. But how, my lord, shall we resist it now?
 Cant. It must be thought on. If it pass
 against us,
We lose the better half of our possession;
For all the temporal lands which men devout
By testament have given to the Church   10
Would they strip from us; being valu'd thus —
As much as would maintain, to the King's hon-
 our,
Full fifteen earls and fifteen hundred knights,
Six thousand and two hundred good esquires,
And, to relief of lazars and weak age,   15
Of indigent faint souls, past corporal toil,
A hundred almshouses right well supplied;
And to the coffers of the King beside,
A thousand pounds by th' year. Thus runs
 the bill.
 Ely. This would drink deep.
 Cant.   'Twould drink the cup and all. 20
 Ely. But what prevention?
 Cant. The King is full of grace and fair re-
 gard.
 Ely. And a true lover of the holy Church.
 Cant. The courses of his youth promis'd it
 not.
The breath no sooner left his father's body   25
But that his wildness, mortified in him,
Seem'd to die too. Yea, at that very moment
Consideration like an angel came
And whipp'd th' offending Adam out of him,
Leaving his body as a paradise   30
T' envelop and contain celestial spirits.
Never was such a sudden scholar made;
Never came reformation in a flood
With such a heady currance scouring faults;
Nor never hydra-headed wilfulness   35
So soon did lose his seat, and all at once,
As in this king.
 Ely.   We are blessed in the change.
 Cant. Hear him but reason in divinity,
And, all-admiring, with an inward wish

You would desire the King were made a prel-
 ate;   40
Hear him debate of commonwealth affairs,
You would say it hath been all in all his study;
List his discourse of war, and you shall hear
A fearful battle rend'red you in music;
Turn him to any cause of policy,   45
The Gordian knot of it he will unloose,
Familiar as his garter; that, when he speaks,
The air, a charter'd libertine, is still,
And the mute wonder lurketh in men's ears
To steal his sweet and honey'd sentences; 50
So that the art and practic part of life
Must be the mistress to this theoric;
Which is a wonder how his Grace should glean
 it,
Since his addiction was to courses vain,
His companies unletter'd, rude, and shallow, 55
His hours fill'd up with riots, banquets, sports;
And never noted in him any study,
Any retirement, any sequestration
From open haunts and popularity.
 Ely. The strawberry grows underneath the
 nettle,   60
And wholesome berries thrive and ripen best
Neighbour'd by fruit of baser quality;
And so the Prince obscur'd his contemplation
Under the veil of wildness, which (no doubt)
Grew like the summer grass, fastest by night,
Unseen, yet crescive in his faculty.   66
 Cant. It must be so; for miracles are ceas'd,
And therefore we must needs admit the means
How things are perfected.
 Ely.   But, my good lord,
How now for mitigation of this bill   70
Urg'd by the commons? Doth his Majesty
Incline to it, or no?
 Cant.   He seems indifferent;
Or rather swaying more upon our part
Than cherishing th' exhibiters against us;
For I have made an offer to his Majesty — 75
Upon our spiritual Convocation,
And in regard of causes now in hand,
Which I have open'd to his Grace at large,
As touching France — to give a greater sum
Than ever at one time the clergy yet   80
Did to his predecessors part withal.
 Ely. How did this offer seem receiv'd, my
 lord?
 Cant. With good acceptance of his Majesty;
Save that there was not time enough to hear,

As I perceiv'd his Grace would fain have done,
The severals and unhidden passages   86
Of his true titles to some certain dukedoms,
And generally to the crown and seat of France,
Deriv'd from Edward, his great-grandfather.
  Ely. What was th' impediment that broke
    this off?   90
  Cant. The French ambassador upon that
    instant
Crav'd audience; and the hour I think is come
To give him hearing. Is it four o'clock?
  Ely. It is.
  Cant. Then go we in to know his embassy,
Which I could with a ready guess declare
Before the Frenchman speak a word of it.
  Ely. I'll wait upon you, and I long to hear it.
                                       Exeunt.

[Scene II. *London. The presence
    chamber in the Palace.*]

Enter the *King*, *Humphrey* [*Duke of Gloucester*],
Bedford, *Clarence*, *Warwick*, *Westmoreland*, and
Exeter, [with *Attendants*].

  King. Where is my gracious Lord of Can-
    terbury?
  Exe. Not here in presence.
  King.   Send for him, good uncle.
  West. Shall we call in th' ambassador, my
    liege?
  King. Not yet, my cousin. We would be
    resolv'd,
Before we hear him, of some things of weight, 5
That task our thoughts, concerning us and
    France.

Enter two *Bishops* — [the *Archbishop of
    Canterbury* and the *Bishop of Ely*].

  Cant. God and his angels guard your sacred
    throne
And make you long become it!
  King.   Sure we thank you.
My learned lord, we pray you to proceed
And justly and religiously unfold   10
Why the Law Salique, that they have in France,
Or should or should not bar us in our claim.
And God forbid, my dear and faithful lord,
That you should fashion, wrest, or bow your
    reading,
Or nicely charge your understanding soul   15
With opening titles miscreate whose right
Suits not in native colours with the truth;
For God doth know how many, now in health,

Shall drop their blood in approbation
Of what your reverence shall incite us to.   20
Therefore take heed how you impawn our per-
    son,
How you awake our sleeping sword of war.
We charge you in the name of God, take heed;
For never two such kingdoms did contend
Without much fall of blood, whose guiltless
    drops   25
Are every one a woe, a sore complaint
'Gainst him whose wrong gives edge unto the
    swords
That make such waste in brief mortality.
Under this conjuration speak, my lord;
For we will hear, note, and believe in heart 30
That what you speak is in your conscience
    wash'd
As pure as sin with baptism.
  Cant. Then hear me, gracious sovereign, and
    you peers,
That owe yourselves, your lives, and services
To this imperial throne. There is no bar   35
To make against your Highness' claim to
    France
But this which they produce from Pharamond:
'In terram Salicam mulieres ne succadant';
'No woman shall succeed in Salique land.'
Which Salique land the French unjustly gloze
To be the realm of France, and Pharamond   41
The founder of this law and female bar.
Yet their own authors faithfully affirm
That the land Salique is in Germany,
Between the floods of Sala and of Elbe;   45
Where Charles the Great, having subdu'd the
    Saxons,
There left behind and settled certain French;
Who, holding in disdain the German women
For some dishonest manners of their life,
Establish'd then this law: to wit, no female 50
Should be inheritrix in Salique land;
Which Salique (as I said) 'twixt Elbe and Sala
Is at this day in Germany call'd Meisen.
Then doth it well appear the Salique Law
Was not devised for the realm of France;   55
Nor did the French possess the Salique land
Until four hundred one and twenty years
After defunction of King Pharamond,
Idly suppos'd the founder of this law,
Who died within the year of our redemption   60
Four hundred twenty-six; and Charles the
    Great
Subdu'd the Saxons, and did seat the French
Beyond the river Sala, in the year
Eight hundred five. Besides, their writers say,
King Pepin, which deposed Childeric,   65

Did, as heir general, being descended
Of Blithild, which was daughter to King
    Clothair,
Make claim and title to the crown of France.
Hugh Capet also — who usurp'd the crown
Of Charles the Duke of Lorraine, sole heir male
Of the true line and stock of Charles the
    Great —   71
To fine his title with some shows of truth,
Though in pure truth it was corrupt and naught,
Convey'd himself as heir to th' Lady Lingare,
Daughter to Charlemain, who was the son   75
To Lewis the Emperor, and Lewis the son
Of Charles the Great. Also King Lewis the
    Tenth,
Who was sole heir to the usurper Capet,
Could not keep quiet in his conscience,
Wearing the crown of France, till satisfied   80
That fair Queen Isabel, his grandmother,
Was lineal of the Lady Ermengare,
Daughter to Charles the foresaid Duke of Lor-
    raine;
By the which marriage the line of Charles the
    Great
Was reunited to the crown of France.   85
So that, as clear as is the summer's sun,
King Pepin's title and Hugh Capet's claim,
King Lewis his satisfaction, all appear
To hold in right and title of the female.
So do the kings of France unto this day,   90
Howbeit they would hold up this Salique Law
To bar your Highness claiming from the female,
And rather choose to hide them in a net
Than amply to imbare their crooked titles
Usurp'd from you and your progenitors.   95
    King. May I with right and conscience make
    this claim?
    Cant. The sin upon my head, dread sov-
    ereign!
For in the Book of Numbers is it writ:
When the man dies, let the inheritance
Descend unto the daughter. Gracious lord,   100
Stand for your own, unwind your bloody flag,
Look back into your mighty ancestors;
Go, my dread lord, to your great-grandsire's
    tomb,
From whom you claim; invoke his warlike
    spirit,
And your great-uncle's, Edward the Black
    Prince,   105
Who on the French ground play'd a tragedy,
Making defeat on the full power of France,
Whiles his most mighty father on a hill
Stood smiling to behold his lion's whelp
Forage in blood of French nobility.   110

O noble English, that could entertain
With half their forces the full pride of France
And let another half stand laughing by,
All out of work and cold for action!
    Ely. Awake remembrance of these valiant
    dead   115
And with your puissant arm renew their feats.
You are their heir; you sit upon their throne;
The blood and courage that renowned them
Runs in your veins; and my thrice-puissant
    liege
Is in the very May-morn of his youth,   120
Ripe for exploits and mighty enterprises.
    Exe. Your brother kings and monarchs of
    the earth
Do all expect that you should rouse yourself,
As did the former lions of your blood.
    West. They know your Grace hath cause
    and means and might;   125
So hath your Highness. Never king of England
Had nobles richer and more loyal subjects,
Whose hearts have left their bodies here in
    England
And lie pavilion'd in the fields of France.
    Cant. O, let their bodies follow, my dear
    liege,   130
With blood and sword and fire, to win your
    right!
In aid whereof we of the spiritualty
Will raise your Highness such a mighty sum
As never did the clergy at one time
Bring in to any of your ancestors.   135
    King. We must not only arm t' invade the
    French,
But lay down our proportions to defend
Against the Scot, who will make road upon us
With all advantages.
    Cant. They of those marches, gracious sov-
    ereign,   140
Shall be a wall sufficient to defend
Our inland from the pilfering borderers.
    King. We do not mean the coursing snatch-
    ers only,
But fear the main intendment of the Scot,
Who hath been still a giddy neighbour to us;
For you shall read that my great-grandfather
Never went with his forces into France
But that the Scot on his unfurnish'd kingdom
Came pouring like the tide into a breach,
With ample and brim fulness of his force,   150
Galling the gleaned land with hot assays,
Girding with grievous siege castles and towns;
That England, being empty of defence,
Hath shook and trembled at th' ill neighbour-
    hood.

Cant. She hath been then more fear'd than
   harm'd, my liege;   155
For hear her but exampled by herself:
When all her chivalry hath been in France,
And she a mourning widow of her nobles,
She hath herself not only well defended
But taken and impounded as a stray   160
The King of Scots; whom she did send to
   France
To fill King Edward's fame with prisoner kings,
And make her chronicle as rich with praise
As is the ooze and bottom of the sea
With sunken wrack and sumless treasuries. 165
West. But there's a saying very old and
   true —
     'If that you will France win,
     Then with Scotland first begin.'
For once the eagle (England) being in prey,
To her unguarded nest the weasel (Scot)   170
Comes sneaking, and so sucks her princely eggs,
Playing the mouse in absence of the cat,
To spoil and havoc more than she can eat.
Exe. It follows then, the cat must stay at
   home.
Yet that is but a curst necessity,   175
Since we have locks to safeguard necessaries,
And pretty traps to catch the petty thieves,
While that the armed hand doth fight abroad,
Th' advised head defends itself at home;
For government, though high, and low, and
   lower,   180
Put into parts, doth keep in one consent,
Congreeing in a full and natural close,
Like music.
Cant. True! Therefore doth heaven divide
The state of man in divers functions,
Setting endeavour in continual motion;   185
To which is fixed as an aim or butt
Obedience; for so work the honeybees,
Creatures that by a rule in nature teach
The act of order to a peopled kingdom.
They have a king, and officers of sorts,   190
Where some like magistrates correct at home,
Others like merchants venture trade abroad,
Others like soldiers armed in their stings
Make boot upon the summer's velvet buds,
Which pillage they with merry march bring
   home   195
To the tent-royal of their emperor,
Who, busied in his majesty, surveys
The singing masons building roofs of gold,
The civil citizens kneading up the honey,
The poor mechanic porters crowding in   200
Their heavy burthens at his narrow gate,
The sad-ey'd justice, with his surly hum,

Delivering o'er to executors pale
The lazy yawning drone. I this infer,
That many things having full reference   205
To one consent may work contrariously,
As many arrows loosed several ways
Come to one mark, as many ways meet in one
   town,
As many fresh streams meet in one salt sea,
As many lines close in the dial's centre;   210
So may a thousand actions, once afoot,
End in one purpose, and be all well borne
Without defeat. Therefore to France, my liege!
Divide your happy England into four,
Whereof take you one quarter into France, 215
And you withal shall make all Gallia shake.
If we, with thrice such powers left at home,
Cannot defend our own doors from the dog,
Let us be worried, and our nation lose
The name of hardiness and policy.   220
King. Call in the messengers sent from the
   Dauphin.

               [Exeunt some Attendants.]
Now are we well resolv'd, and by God's help
And yours, the noble sinews of our power,
France being ours, we'll bend it to our awe,
Or break it all to pieces. Or there we'll sit, 225
Ruling in large and ample empery
O'er France and all her (almost) kingly duke-
   doms,
Or lay these bones in an unworthy urn,
Tombless, with no remembrance over them.
Either our history shall with full mouth   230
Speak freely of our acts, or else our grave,
Like Turkish mute, shall have a tongueless
   mouth,
Not worshipp'd with a waxen epitaph.

   Enter *Ambassadors* of France, [attended].

Now are we well prepar'd to know the pleasure
Of our fair cousin Dauphin; for we hear   235
Your greeting is from him, not from the King.
Ambassador. May't please your Majesty to
   give us leave
Freely to render what we have in charge;
Or shall we sparingly show you far off
The Dauphin's meaning, and our embassy? 240
King. We are no tyrant, but a Christian
   king,
Unto whose grace our passion is as subject
As are our wretches fett'red in our prisons.
Therefore with frank and with uncurbed plain-
   ness
Tell us the Dauphin's mind.
Ambassador.   Thus then, in few: 245
Your Highness, lately sending into France.

Did claim some certain dukedoms, in the right
Of your great predecessor, King Edward the
Third.
In answer of which claim, the Prince our master
Says that you savour too much of your youth,
And bids you be advis'd. There's naught in
France 251
That can be with a nimble galliard won;
You cannot revel into dukedoms there.
He therefore sends you, meeter for your spirit,
This tun of treasure; and, in lieu of this, 255
Desires you let the dukedoms that you claim
Hear no more of you. This the Dauphin speaks.
King. What treasure, uncle?
Exe. Tennis balls, my liege.
King. We are glad the Dauphin is so pleas-
ant with us.
His present and your pains we thank you for.
When we have match'd our rackets to these
balls, 261
We will in France (by God's grace) play a set
Shall strike his father's crown into the hazard.
Tell him he hath made a match with such a
wrangler
That all the courts of France will be disturb'd
With chases. And we understand him well, 266
How he comes o'er us with our wilder days,
Not measuring what use we made of them.
We never valu'd this poor seat of England,
And therefore, living hence, did give ourself 270
To barbarous license; as 'tis ever common
That men are merriest when they are from
home.
But tell the Dauphin I will keep my state,
Be like a king, and show my sail of greatness,
When I do rouse me in my throne of France.
For that I have laid by my majesty 276
And plodded like a man for working days.
But I will rise there with so full a glory
That I will dazzle all the eyes of France,

Yea, strike the Dauphin blind to look on us. 280
And tell the pleasant Prince this mock of his
Hath turn'd his balls to gunstones, and his soul
Shall stand sore charged for the wasteful venge-
ance
That shall fly with them; for many a thousand
widows
Shall this his mock mock out of their dear
husbands, 285
Mock mothers from their sons, mock castles
down;
And some are yet ungotten and unborn
That shall have cause to curse the Dauphin's
scorn.
But this lies all within the will of God,
To whom I do appeal, and in whose name, 290
Tell you the Dauphin, I am coming on,
To venge me as I may and to put forth
My rightful hand in a well-hallow'd cause.
So get you hence in peace. And tell the
Dauphin
His jest will savour but of shallow wit 295
When thousands weep more than did laugh at it.
Convey them with safe conduct. Fare you well.
Exeunt Ambassadors.
Exe. This was a merry message.
King. We hope to make the sender blush at
it.
Therefore, my lords, omit no happy hour 300
That may give furth'rance to our expedition;
For we have now no thought in us but France,
Save those to God, that run before our business.
Therefore let our proportions for these wars
Be soon collected, and all things thought upon
That may with reasonable swiftness add 306
More feathers to our wings; for, God before,
We'll chide this Dauphin at his father's door.
Therefore let every man now task his thought
That this fair action may on foot be brought.
Exeunt.

[ACT II.]

Flourish. Enter *Chorus.*

Now all the youth of England are on fire,
And silken dalliance in the wardrobe lies.
Now thrive the armourers, and honour's thought
Reigns solely in the breast of every man.
They sell the pasture now to buy the horse, 5
Following the mirror of all Christian kings
With winged heels, as English Mercuries.
For now sits Expectation in the air
And hides a sword, from hilts unto the point,

With crowns imperial, crowns, and coronets 10
Promis'd to Harry and his followers.
The French, advis'd by good intelligence
Of this most dreadful preparation,
Shake in their fear and with pale policy
Seek to divert the English purposes. 15
O England! model to thy inward greatness,
Like little body with a mighty heart,
What mightst thou do that honour would thee
do,
Were all thy children kind and natural!

160

But see thy fault! France hath in thee found
out   20
A nest of hollow bosoms, which he fills
With treacherous crowns; and three corrupted
men —
One, Richard Earl of Cambridge, and the sec-
ond,
Henry Lord Scroop of Masham, and the third,
Sir Thomas Grey, knight, of Northumberland—
Have, for the gilt of France (O guilt indeed!)
Confirm'd conspiracy with fearful France,
And by their hands this grace of kings must die,
If hell and treason hold their promises,
Ere he take ship for France, and in Southamp-
ton.   30
Linger your patience on, and well digest
Th' abuse of distance. Force a play!
The sum is paid, the traitors are agreed,
The King is set from London, and the scene
Is now transported, gentles, to Southampton.
There is the playhouse now, there must you
sit,   36
And thence to France shall we convey you safe
And bring you back, charming the narrow seas
To give you gentle pass; for, if we may,
We'll not offend one stomach with our play.   40
But, till the King come forth, and not till then,
Unto Southampton do we shift our scene. *Exit.*

[Scene I. *London. A street.*]

Enter *Corporal Nym* and *Lieutenant Bardolph.*

Bard. Well met, Corporal Nym.
Nym. Good morrow, Lieutenant Bardolph.
Bard. What, are Ancient Pistol and you
friends yet?   4
Nym. For my part, I care not. I say little;
but when time shall serve, there shall be smiles
— but that shall be as it may. I dare not
fight; but I will wink and hold out mine iron.
It is a simple one; but what though? It will
toast cheese, and it will endure cold as another
man's sword will — and there's an end.   11
Bard. I will bestow a breakfast to make you
friends, and we'll be all three sworn brothers
to France. Let't be so, good Corporal Nym.
Nym. Faith, I will live so long as I may,
that's the certain of it; and when I cannot live
any longer, I will do as I may. That is my
rest, that is the rendezvous of it.
Bard. It is certain, Corporal, that he is married to Nell Quickly, and certainly she did you
wrong, for you were troth-plight to her.   21

Nym. I cannot tell. Things must be as
they may. Men may sleep, and they may have
their throats about them at that time, and
some say knives have edges. It must be as it
may. Though patience be a tired mare, yet
she will plod. There must be conclusions.
Well, I cannot tell.   27

Enter *Pistol* and *Hostess Quickly.*

Bard. Here comes Ancient Pistol and his
wife. Good Corporal, be patient here. How
now, mine host Pistol?   30
Pist. Base tyke, call'st thou me host?
Now by this hand I swear I scorn the term;
Nor shall my Nell keep lodgers!
Host. No, by my troth, not long; for we
cannot lodge and board a dozen or fourteen
gentlewomen that live honestly by the prick
of their needles but it will be thought we keep
a bawdy house straight. [*Nym and Pistol
draw.*] O well-a-day, Lady, if he be not drawn
now! We shall see wilful adultery and murther
committed.   40
Bard. Good Lieutenant — good Corporal —
offer nothing here.
Nym. Pish!
Pist. Pish for thee, Iceland dog! thou prick-
ear'd cur of Iceland!
Host. Good Corporal Nym, show thy valour,
and put up your sword.   46
Nym. Will you shog off? I would have you
solus.
Pist. 'Solus,' egregrious dog? O viper vile!
The 'solus' in thy most mervailous face!   50
The 'solus' in thy teeth, and in thy throat,
And in thy hateful lungs, yea, in thy maw,
perdy!
And, which is worse, within thy nasty mouth!
I do retort the 'solus' in thy bowels;
For I can take, and Pistol's cock is up,   55
And flashing fire will follow.
Nym. I am not Barbason; you cannot con-
jure me. I have an humour to knock you in-
differently well. If you grow foul with me,
Pistol, I will scour you with my rapier, as I
may, in fair terms. If you would walk off, I
would prick your guts a little in good terms, as
I may, and that's the humour of it.
Pist. O braggard vile, and damned furious
wight,
The grave doth gape, and doting death is near.
Therefore exhale!   66
Bard. Hear me, hear me what I say! He
that strikes the first stroke, I'll run him up to
the hilts, as I am a soldier.   [*Draws.*]

161

Pist. An oath of mickle might, and fury
shall abate.   70
> [*Pistol and Nym sheathe their swords.*]

Give me thy fist, thy forefoot to me give.
Thy spirits are most tall.

Nym. I will cut thy throat one time or other
in fair terms. That is the humour of it.

Pist. Couple a gorge!   75
That is the word. I thee defy again.
O hound of Crete, think'st thou my spouse to
get?
No; to the spital go,
And from the powd'ring tub of infamy
Fetch forth the lazar kite of Cressid's kind,   80
Doll Tearsheet, she by name, and her espouse.
I have, and I will hold, the quondam Quickly
For the only she; and — pauca, there's enough.
Go to!   84

Enter the *Boy*.

Boy. Mine host Pistol, you must come to
my master — and you, hostess. He is very
sick and would to bed. Good Bardolph, put
thy face between his sheets and do the office
of a warming pan. Faith, he's very ill.

Bard. Away, you rogue!   90

Host. By my troth, he'll yield the crow a
pudding one of these days. The King has kill'd
his heart. Good husband, come home presently.
> *Exit* [*with Boy*].

Bard. Come, shall I make you two friends?
We must to France together. Why the devil
should we keep knives to cut one another's
throats?   96

Pist. Let floods o'erswell, and fiends for food
howl on!

Nym. You'll pay me the eight shillings I won
of you at betting?

Pist. Base is the slave that pays.   100

Nym. That now I will have. That's the
humour of it.

Pist. As manhood shall compound. Push
home.   *They draw.*

Bard. By this sword, he that makes the first
thrust, I'll kill him! By this sword, I will.   105
> [*Draws.*]

Pist. 'Sword' is an oath, and oaths must
have their course.   [*Sheathes his sword.*]

Bard. Corporal Nym, an thou wilt be friends,
be friends; an thou wilt not, why then be enemies with me too. Prithee put up.

Nym. I shall have my eight shillings I won
of you at betting?   111

Pist. A noble shalt thou have, and present
pay;

And liquor likewise will I give to thee,
And friendship shall combine, and brotherhood.
I'll live by Nym, and Nym shall live by me.   115
Is not this just? For I shall sutler be
Unto the camp, and profits will accrue.
Give me thy hand.
> [*Nym sheathes his sword.*]

Nym. I shall have my noble?

Pist. In cash, most justly paid.   120

Nym. Well then, that's the humour of't.
> [*They shake hands.*]

Enter *Hostess*.

Host. As ever you came of women, come in
quickly to Sir John. Ah, poor heart! he is so
shak'd of a burning quotidian tertian that it is
most lamentable to behold. Sweet men, come
to him.   126

Nym. The King hath run bad humours on
the knight; that's the even of it.

Pist. Nym, thou hast spoke the right.
His heart is fracted and corroborate.   130

Nym. The King is a good king, but it must
be as it may. He passes some humours and
careers.

Pist. Let us condole the knight; for, lamb-
kins, we will live.   *Exeunt.*

[Scene II. *Southampton. A council chamber.*]

Enter *Exeter, Bedford*, and *Westmoreland*.

Bed. Fore God, his Grace is bold to trust
these traitors.

Exe. They shall be apprehended by-and-by.

West. How smooth and even they do bear
themselves,
As if allegiance in their bosoms sat,
Crowned with faith and constant loyalty!   5

Bed. The King hath note of all that they
intend,
By interception which they dream not of.

Exe. Nay, but the man that was his bed-
fellow,
Whom he hath dull'd and cloy'd with gracious
favours —
That he should, for a foreign purse, so sell   10
His sovereign's life to death and treachery!

Sound trumpets. Enter the *King, Scroop, Cambridge*, and *Grey*, [*Lords*, and *Attendants*].

King. Now sits the wind fair, and we will
aboard.

My Lord of Cambridge, and my kind Lord of
Masham,
And you, my gentle knight, give me your
thoughts.
Think you not that the pow'rs we bear with us
Will cut their passage through the force of
France,   16
Doing the execution and the act
For which we have in head assembled them?
  Scroop. No doubt, my liege, if each man do
his best.
  King. I doubt not that, since we are well
persuaded   20
We carry not a heart with us from hence
That grows not in a fair consent with ours,
Nor leave not one behind that doth not wish
Success and conquest to attend on us.
  Cam. Never was monarch better fear'd and
lov'd   25
Than is your Majesty. There's not, I think,
a subject
That sits in heart-grief and uneasiness
Under the sweet shade of your government.
  Grey. True. Those that were your father's
enemies
Have steep'd their galls in honey and do serve
you   30
With hearts create of duty and of zeal.
  King. We therefore have great cause of
thankfulness,
And shall forget the office of our hand
Sooner than quittance of desert and merit
According to the weight and worthiness.   35
  Scroop. So service shall with steeled sinews
toil,
And labour shall refresh itself with hope,
To do your Grace incessant services.
  King. We judge no less. Uncle of Exeter,
Enlarge the man committed yesterday   40
That rail'd against our person. We consider
It was excess of wine that set him on,
And on his more advice, we pardon him.   43
  Scroop. That's mercy, but too much security.
Let him be punish'd, sovereign, lest example
Breed (by his sufferance) more of such a kind.
  King. O, let us yet be merciful!
  Cam. So may your Highness, and yet punish
too.
  Grey. Sir,
You show great mercy if you give him life 50
After the taste of much correction.
  King. Alas, your too much love and care of
me
Are heavy orisons 'gainst this poor wretch!
If little faults proceeding on distemper

Shall not be wink'd at, how shall we stretch our
eye   55
When capital crimes, chew'd, swallow'd, and
digested,
Appear before us? We'll yet enlarge that man,
Though Cambridge, Scroop, and Grey, in their
dear care
And tender preservation of our person,
Would have him punish'd. And now to our
French causes.   60
Who are the late commissioners?
  Cam. I one, my lord.
Your Highness bade me ask for it to-day.
  Scroop. So did you me, my liege.
  Grey. And I, my royal sovereign.   65
  King. Then, Richard Earl of Cambridge,
there is yours;
There yours, Lord Scroop of Masham; and,
Sir Knight,
Grey of Northumberland, this same is yours.
Read them, and know I know your worthiness.
My Lord of Westmoreland, and uncle Exeter,
We will aboard to-night. — Why how now,
gentlemen?   71
What see you in those papers that you lose
So much complexion? — Look ye, how they
change!
Their cheeks are paper. — Why, what read you
there   74
That hath so cowarded and chas'd your blood
Out of appearance?
  Cam.   I do confess my fault,
And do submit me to your Highness' mercy.
  Grey, Scroop. To which we all appeal.
  King. The mercy that was quick in us but
late,   79
By your own counsel is suppress'd and kill'd.
You must not dare (for shame) to talk of mercy;
For your own reasons turn into your bosoms
As dogs upon their masters, worrying you.
See you, my princes and my noble peers,
These English monsters! My Lord of Cam-
bridge here —   85
You know how apt our love was to accord
To furnish him with all appertinents
Belonging to his honour; and this man
Hath, for a few light crowns, lightly conspir'd
And sworn unto the practices of France   90
To kill us here in Hampton; to the which
This knight, no less for bounty bound to us
Than Cambridge is, hath likewise sworn. But
O,
What shall I say to thee, Lord Scroop, thou
cruel,
Ingrateful, savage, and inhuman creature? 95

Thou that didst bear the key of all my counsels,
That knew'st the very bottom of my soul,
That (almost) mightst have coin'd me into gold,
Wouldst thou have practis'd on me for thy
   use —
May it be possible that foreign hire   100
Could out of thee extract one spark of evil
That might annoy my finger? 'Tis so strange
That, though the truth of it stands off as gross
As black and white, my eye will scarcely see it.
Treason and murther ever kept together,   105
As two yoke-devils sworn to either's purpose,
Working so grossly in a natural cause
That admiration did not whoop at them;
But thou ('gainst all proportion) didst bring in
Wonder to wait on treason and on murther;
And whatsoever cunning fiend it was   111
That wrought upon thee so preposterously
Hath got the voice in hell for excellence.
All other devils that suggest by treasons
Do botch and bungle up damnation   115
With patches, colours, and with forms being
   fetch'd
From glist'ring semblances of piety;
But he that temper'd thee bade thee stand up,
Gave thee no instance why thou shouldst do
   treason,   119
Unless to dub thee with the name of traitor.
If that same demon that hath gull'd thee thus
Should with his lion gait walk the whole world,
He might return to vasty Tartar back
And tell the legions, 'I can never win
A soul so easy as that Englishman's.'   125
O, how hast thou with jealousy infected
The sweetness of affiance! Show men dutiful?
Why, so didst thou. Seem they grave and
   learned?
Why, so didst thou. Come they of noble family?
Why, so didst thou. Seem they religious?   130
Why, so didst thou. Or are they spare in diet,
Free from gross passion or of mirth or anger,
Constant in spirit, not swerving with the blood,
Garnish'd and deck'd in modest complement,
Not working with the eye without the ear,   135
And but in purged judgment trusting neither?
Such and so finely bolted didst thou seem;
And thus thy fall hath left a kind of blot
To mark the full-fraught man and best indu'd
With some suspicion. I will weep for thee;   140
For this revolt of thine, methinks, is like
Another fall of man. Their faults are open.
Arrest them to the answer of the law;
And God acquit them of their practices!
   Exe. I arrest thee of high treason by the
name of Richard Earl of Cambridge.   146

I arrest thee of high treason by the name of
Henry Lord Scroop of Masham.
I arrest thee of high treason by the name of
Thomas Grey, knight, of Northumberland.   150
   Scroop. Our purposes God justly hath dis-
   cover'd,
And I repent my fault more than my death,
Which I beseech your Highness to forgive,
Although my body pay the price of it.
   Cam. For me, the gold of France did not
   seduce,   155
Although I did admit it as a motive
The sooner to effect what I intended.
But God be thanked for prevention,
Which I in sufferance heartily will rejoice,
Beseeching God, and you, to pardon me.   160
   Grey. Never did faithful subject more rejoice
At the discovery of most dangerous treason
Than I do at this hour joy o'er myself,
Prevented from a damned enterprise.   164
My fault, but not my body, pardon, sovereign.
   King. God quit you in his mercy! Hear your
   sentence.
You have conspir'd against our royal person,
Join'd with an enemy proclaim'd, and from his
   coffers
Receiv'd the golden earnest of our death;
Wherein you would have sold your king to
   slaughter,   170
His princes and his peers to servitude,
His subjects to oppression and contempt,
And his whole kingdom into desolation.
Touching our person, seek we no revenge,   174
But we our kingdom's safety must so tender,
Whose ruin you have sought, that to her laws
We do deliver you. Get you therefore hence
(Poor miserable wretches) to your death;
The taste whereof God of his mercy give   179
You patience to endure, and true repentance
Of all your dear offences! Bear them hence.
   Exeunt [Cambridge, Scroop, and Grey,
           guarded].
Now, lords, for France; the enterprise whereof
Shall be to you as us, like glorious.
We doubt not of a fair and lucky war,   184
Since God so graciously hath brought to light
This dangerous treason, lurking in our way
To hinder our beginnings. We doubt not now
But every rub is smoothed on our way.
Then, forth, dear countrymen. Let us deliver
Our puissance into the hand of God,   190
Putting it straight in expedition.
Cheerly to sea; the signs of war advance.
No king of England, if not King of France!
                  Flourish. Exeunt.

[Scene III. *London. Before the Boar's
Head Tavern, Eastcheap.*]

Enter *Pistol, Nym, Bardolph, Boy,* and *Hostess.*

Host. Prithee, honey-sweet husband, let me
bring thee to Staines.
Pist. No; for my manly heart doth ern.
Bardolph, be blithe; Nym, rouse thy vaunting
veins;
Boy, bristle thy courage up; for Falstaff he is
dead,   5
And we must ern therefore.
Bard. Would I were with him, wheresome'er
he is, either in heaven or in hell!
Host. Nay sure, he's not in hell! He's in
Arthur's bosom, if ever man went to Arthur's
bosom. 'A made a finer end, and went away an
it had been any christom child. 'A parted ev'n
just between twelve and one, ev'n at the turning
o' th' tide. For after I saw him fumble with the
sheets, and play with flowers, and smile upon
his fingers' ends, I knew there was but one way;
for his nose was as sharp as a pen, and 'a babbled of green fields. 'How now, Sir John?'
quoth I. 'What, man? be o' good cheer.' So 'a
cried out 'God, God, God!' three or four times.
Now I, to comfort him, bid him 'a should not
think of God; I hop'd there was no need to
trouble himself with any such thoughts yet. So
'a bade me lay more clothes on his feet. I put
my hand into the bed and felt them, and they
were as cold as any stone. Then I felt to his
knees, and so upward and upward, and all was
as cold as any stone.
Nym. They say he cried out of sack.
Host. Ay, that 'a did.   30
Bard. And of women.
Host. Nay, that 'a did not.
Boy. Yes, that 'a did, and said they were
devils incarnate.   34
Host. 'A could never abide carnation; 'twas
a colour he never lik'd.
Boy. 'A said once the devil would have him
about women.
Host. 'A did in some sort, indeed, handle
women; but then he was rheumatic, and talk'd
of the Whore of Babylon.   41
Boy. Do you not remember 'a saw a flea
stick upon Bardolph's nose, and 'a said it was
a black soul burning in hellfire?   44
Bard. Well, the fuel is gone that maintain'd
that fire. That's all the riches I got in his
service.

Nym. Shall we shog? The King will be gone
from Southampton.
Pist. Come, let's away. My love, give me
thy lips.
Look to my chattels and my moveables.   50
Let senses rule. The word is 'Pitch and pay.'
Trust none;
For oaths are straws, men's faiths are wafer-
cakes,
And Hold-fast is the only dog, my duck.
Therefore Caveto be thy counsellor.   55
Go, clear thy crystals. Yoke-fellows in arms,
Let us to France, like horse-leeches, my boys,
To suck, to suck, the very blood to suck!
Boy. And that's but unwholesome food, they
say.   60
Pist. Touch her soft mouth, and march.
Bard. Farewell, hostess.   [*Kisses her.*]
Nym. I cannot kiss, that is the humour of it;
but adieu!
Pist. Let housewifery appear. Keep close, I
thee command.
Host. Farewell! adieu!   *Exeunt.*

[Scene IV. *France.* The French King's
Palace.]

Flourish. Enter the *French King,* the *Dauphin,*
the *Dukes of Berri* and *Britain,* [the *Constable,*
and others].

King. Thus comes the English with full
power upon us,
And more than carefully it us concerns
To answer royally in our defences.
Therefore the Dukes of Berri and Britain,
Of Brabant and of Orleans, shall make forth,   5
And you, Prince Dauphin, with all swift dis-
patch,
To line and new repair our towns of war
With men of courage and with means defend-
ant;
For England his approaches makes as fierce
As waters to the sucking of a gulf.   10
It fits us then to be as provident
As fear may teach us out of late examples
Left by the fatal and neglected English
Upon our fields.
Dau.   My most redoubted father,
It is most meet we arm us 'gainst the foe;   15
For peace itself should not so dull a kingdom
(Though war nor no known quarrel were in
question)
But that defences, musters, preparations

Should be maintain'd, assembled, and collected,
As were a war in expectation.   20
Therefore I say 'tis meet we all go forth
To view the sick and feeble parts of France;
And let us do it with no show of fear —
No, with no more than if we heard that Eng-
land
Were busied with a Whitsun morris dance; 25
For, my good liege, she is so idly king'd,
Her sceptre so fantastically borne,
By a vain, giddy, shallow, humorous youth,
That fear attends her not.
    Con.   O peace, Prince Dauphin!
You are too much mistaken in this king.   30
Question your Grace the late ambassadors,
With what great state he heard their embassy,
How well supplied with noble counsellors,
How modest in exception, and withal
How terrible in constant resolution,   35
And you shall find his vanities forespent
Were but the outside of the Roman Brutus,
Covering discretion with a coat of folly;
As gardeners do with ordure hide those roots
That shall first spring and be most delicate. 40
    Dau. Well, 'tis not so, my Lord High Con-
stable!
But though we think it so, it is no matter.
In cases of defence 'tis best to weigh
The enemy more mighty than he seems.
So the proportions of defence are fill'd;   45
Which of a weak and niggardly projection
Doth, like a miser, spoil his coat with scanting
A little cloth.
    King.   Think we King Harry strong;
And, princes, look you strongly arm to meet
him.   49
The kindred of him hath been flesh'd upon
us;
And he is bred out of that bloody strain
That haunted us in our familiar paths.
Witness our too much memorable shame
When Cressy battle fatally was struck,
And all our princes captiv'd, by the hand   55
Of that black name, Edward, Black Prince of
Wales;
Whiles that his mountain sire — on mountain
standing,
Up in the air, crown'd with the golden sun —
Saw his heroical seed, and smil'd to see him,
Mangle the work of nature, and deface   60
The patterns that by God and by French
fathers
Had twenty years been made. This is a stem
Of that victorious stock; and let us fear
The native mightiness and fate of him.

Enter a *Messenger*.

    Mess. Ambassadors from Harry King of
England   65
Do crave admittance to your Majesty.
    King. We'll give them present audience. Go,
and bring them.
        [*Exeunt Messenger and certain Lords.*]
You see this chase is hotly followed, friends.
    Dau. Turn head, and stop pursuit; for
coward dogs
Most spend their mouths when what they seem
to threaten   70
Runs far before them. Good my sovereign,
Take up the English short, and let them know
Of what a monarchy you are the head.
Self-love, my liege, is not so vile a sin
As self-neglecting.

Enter [*Lords*, with] *Exeter* [and *Train*].

    King.   From our brother England? 75
    Exe. From him, and thus he greets your
Majesty:
He wills you, in the name of God Almighty,
That you devest yourself, and lay apart
The borrowed glories that by gift of heaven,
By law of nature and of nations, 'longs   80
To him and to his heirs — namely, the crown
And all wide-stretched honours that pertain
By custom, and the ordinance of times,
Unto the crown of France. That you may know
'Tis no sinister nor no awkward claim,   85
Pick'd from the wormholes of long-vanish'd
days,
Nor from the dust of old oblivion rak'd,
He sends you this most memorable line,
                              [*Gives a paper.*]
In every branch truly demonstrative;
Willing you overlook this pedigree;   90
And when you find him evenly deriv'd
From his most fam'd of famous ancestors,
Edward the Third, he bids you then resign
Your crown and kingdom, indirectly held
From him, the native and true challenger.   95
    King. Or else what follows?
    Exe. Bloody constraint; for if you hide the
crown
Even in your hearts, there will he rake for it.
Therefore in fiery tempest is he coming,
In thunder and in earthquake, like a Jove; 100
That, if requiring fail, he will compel;
And bids you, in the bowels of the Lord,
Deliver up the crown, and to take mercy
On the poor souls for whom this hungry war
Opens his vasty jaws; and on your head   105

Turns he the widows' tears, the orphans' cries,
The dead men's blood, the pining maidens'
      groans,
For husbands, fathers, and betrothed lovers
That shall be swallowed in this controversy.
This is his claim, his threat'ning, and my mes-
      sage;   110
Unless the Dauphin be in presence here,
To whom expressly I bring greeting too.
  King. For us, we will consider of this further.
To-morrow shall you bear our full intent
Back to our brother England.
  Dau.   For the Dauphin,   115
I stand here for him. What to him from
      England?
  Exe. Scorn and defiance, slight regard, con-
      tempt,
And anything that may not misbecome
The mighty sender, doth he prize you at.
Thus says my king: An if your father's High-
      ness   120
Do not, in grant of all demands at large,
Sweeten the bitter mock you sent his Majesty,
He'll call you to so hot an answer of it
That caves and womby vaultages of France
Shall chide your trespass, and return your
      mock   125
In second accent of his ordinance.

  Dau. Say, if my father render fair return,
It is against my will; for I desire
Nothing but odds with England. To that end,
As matching to his youth and vanity,   130
I did present him with the Paris balls.
  Exe. He'll make your Paris Louvre shake
      for it,
Were it the mistress court of mighty Europe;
And be assur'd you'll find a difference,
As we his subjects have in wonder found,   135
Between the promise of his greener days
And these he masters now. Now he weighs
      time
Even to the utmost grain. That you shall
      read
In your own losses, if he stay in France.
  King. To-morrow shall you know our mind
      at full.   140
  Exe. Dispatch us with all speed, lest that
      our king
Come here himself to question our delay;
For he is footed in this land already.
  King. You shall be soon dispatch'd with fair
      conditions.
A night is but small breath and little pause 145
To answer matters of this consequence.
                              Flourish. Exeunt.

ACT III.

Enter *Chorus.*

Thus with imagin'd wing our swift scene flies,
In motion of no less celerity
Than that of thought. Suppose that you have
      seen
The well-appointed King at Hampton pier
Embark his royalty; and his brave fleet   5
With silken streamers the young Phœbus fan-
      ning.
Play with your fancies; and in them behold
Upon the hempen tackle shipboys climbing;
Hear the shrill whistle, which doth order give
To sounds confus'd; behold the threaden sails,
Borne with th' invisible and creeping wind, 11
Draw the huge bottoms through the furrowed
      sea,
Breasting the lofty surge. O, do but think
You stand upon the rivage and behold
A city on th' inconstant billows dancing;
For so appears this fleet majestical,
Holding due course to Harflew. Follow, follow!
Grapple your minds to sternage of this navy,

And leave your England as dead midnight still,
Guarded with grandsires, babies, and old
      women,   20
Either past or not arriv'd to pith and puissance;
For who is he whose chin is but enrich'd
With one appearing hair that will not follow
These cull'd and choice-drawn cavaliers to
      France?
Work, work your thoughts, and therein see a
      siege.   25
Behold the ordinance on their carriages,
With fatal mouths gaping on girded Harflew.
Suppose th' ambassador from the French comes
      back;
Tells Harry that the King doth offer him   29
Katherine his daughter, and with her to dowry
Some petty and unprofitable dukedoms.
The offer likes not; and the nimble gunner
With linstock now the devilish cannon touches.
                    Alarum, and chambers go off.
And down goes all before them. Still be kind,
And eke out our performance with your mind.
                                          Exit.

[Scene I. *France.   Before Harfleur.*]

Alarum. Enter the *King, Exeter, Bedford,* and *Gloucester,* [with *Soldiers* carrying] scaling ladders at Harflew.

King. Once more unto the breach, dear friends, once more;
Or close the wall up with our English dead!
In peace there's nothing so becomes a man
As modest stillness and humility;
But when the blast of war blows in our ears, 5
Then imitate the action of the tiger:
Stiffen the sinews, summon up the blood,
Disguise fair nature with hard-favour'd rage;
Then lend the eye a terrible aspect;
Let it pry through the portage of the head 10
Like the brass cannon; let the brow o'erwhelm it
As fearfully as doth a galled rock
O'erhang and jutty his confounded base,
Swill'd with the wild and wasteful ocean. 14
Now set the teeth and stretch the nostril wide,
Hold hard the breath and bend up every spirit
To his full height! On, on, you noble English,
Whose blood is fet from fathers of war-proof!
Fathers that like so many Alexanders 19
Have in these parts from morn till even fought,
And sheath'd their swords for lack of argument.
Dishonour not your mothers; now attest
That those whom you call'd fathers did beget you!
Be copy now to men of grosser blood
And teach them how to war! And you, good yeomen, 25
Whose limbs were made in England, show us here
The mettle of your pasture. Let us swear
That you are worth your breeding; which I doubt not,
For there is none of you so mean and base
That hath not noble lustre in your eyes. 30
I see you stand like greyhounds in the slips,
Straining upon the start. The game's afoot!
Follow your spirit; and upon this charge
Cry 'God for Harry! England and Saint George!'
[*Exeunt.*] *Alarum, and chambers go off.*

[Scene II.   *Before Harfleur.*]

Enter *Nym, Bardolph, Pistol,* and *Boy.*

Bard. On, on, on, on. on! to the breach, to the breach!

Nym. Pray thee, Corporal, stay. The knocks are too hot; and, for mine own part, I have not a case of lives. The humour of it is too hot; that is the very plain-song of it. 6
Pist. The plain-song is most just; for humours do abound.

Knocks go and come; God's vassals drop and die;
    And sword and shield
        In bloody field 10
    Doth win immortal fame.

Boy. Would I were in an alehouse in London! I would give all my fame for a pot of ale and safety.
Pist. And I: 15

If wishes would prevail with me,
My purpose should not fail with me,
    But thither would I hie.
Boy. As duly, but not as truly,
    As bird doth sing on bough. 20

Enter *Fluellen.*

Flu. Up to the breach, you dogs! Avaunt, you cullions!   [*Drives them forward.*]
Pist. Be merciful, great duke, to men of mould!
Abate thy rage, abate thy manly rage,
Abate thy rage, great duke! 25
Good bawcock, bate thy rage! Use lenity, sweet chuck!
Nym. These be good humours. Your honour wins bad humours.
Exeunt [all but Boy].
Boy. As young as I am, I have observ'd these three swashers. I am boy to them all three; but all they three, though they would serve me, could not be man to me; for indeed three such antics do not amount to a man. For Bardolph, he is white-liver'd and red-fac'd; by the means whereof 'a faces it out, but fights not. For Pistol, he hath a killing tongue and a quiet sword; by the means whereof 'a breaks words and keeps whole weapons. For Nym, he hath heard that men of few words are the best men, and therefore he scorns to say his prayers, lest 'a should be thought a coward; but his few bad words are match'd with as few good deeds, for 'a never broke any man's head but his own, and that was against a post when he was drunk. They will steal anything, and call it purchase. Bardolph stole a lute-case, bore it twelve leagues, and sold it for three halfpence. Nym and Bardolph are sworn brothers in filching, and in Calais they stole a fire-shovel. I knew by that piece of service the men would carry

coals. They would have me as familiar with men's pockets as their gloves or their hand-kerchers; which makes much against my man-hood, if I should take from another's pocket to put into mine; for it is plain pocketing up of wrongs. I must leave them and seek some better service. Their villany goes against my weak stomach, and therefore I must cast it up. *Exit.*

Enter *Gower* [and *Fluellen*].

Gow. Captain Fluellen, you must come presently to the mines. The Duke of Gloucester would speak with you.   60
Flu. To the mines? Tell you the Duke, it is not so good to come to the mines; for look you, the mines is not according to the disci-plines of the war. The concavities of it is not sufficient; for look you, th' athversary, you may discuss unto the Duke, look you, is digt himself four yard under the countermines. By Cheshu, I think 'a will plow up all, if there is not better directions.   68
Gow. The Duke of Gloucester, to whom the order of the siege is given, is altogether directed by an Irishman, a very valiant gentleman, i' faith.   71
Flu. It is Captain Macmorris, is it not?
Gow. I think it be.
Flu. By Cheshu, he is an ass, as in the world! I will verify as much in his beard. He has no more directions in the true disciplines of the wars, look you, of the Roman disciplines, than is a puppy-dog.

Enter *Macmorris* and *Captain Jamy.*

Gow. Here 'a comes, and the Scots captain, Captain Jamy, with him.   80
Flu. Captain Jamy is a marvellous falorous gentleman, that is certain, and of great expe-dition and knowledge in th' aunchiant wars, upon my particular knowledge of his direc-tions. By Cheshu, he will maintain his argu-ment as well as any military man in the world in the disciplines of the pristine wars of the Romans.
Jamy. I say gud day, Captain Fluellen.
Flu. God-den to your worship, good Captain James.   90
Gow. How now, Captain Macmorris? Have you quit the mines? Have the pioners given o'er?
Mac. By Chrish, la, tish ill done! The work ish give over, the trumpet sound the retreat. By my hand I swear, and my father's soul, the

work ish ill done! It ish give over. I would have blowed up the town, so Chrish save me la! in an hour. O, tish ill done! tish ill done! By my hand, tish ill done!   99
Flu. Captain Macmorris, I beseech you now, will you voutsafe me, look you, a few disputa-tions with you, as partly touching or concern-ing the disciplines of the war, the Roman wars? In the way of argument, look you, and friendly communication, partly to satisfy my opinion, and partly for the satisfaction, look you, of my mind — as touching the direction of the mili-tary discipline, that is the point.   108
Jamy. It sall be vary gud, gud feith, gud Captens bath, and I sall quit you with gud leve, as I may pick occasion. That sall I, mary.
Mac. It is no time to discourse, so Chrish save me! The day is hot, and the weather, and the wars, and the King, and the Dukes. It is no time to discourse. The town is beseech'd, and the trompet call us to the breach, and we talk, and, be Chrish, do nothing. 'Tis shame for us all. So God sa' me, 'tis shame to stand still, it is shame, by my hand! and there is throats to be cut, and works to be done, and there ish nothing done, so Chrish sa' me, la!
Jamy. By the mess, ere theise eyes of mine take themselves to slomber, ay'll de gud service, or ay'll lig i' th' grund for it! ay, or go to death! And ay'll pay't as valorously as I may, that sall I suerly do, that is the breff and the long. Mary, I wad full fain heard some question 'tween you tway.
Flu. Captain Macmorris, I think, look you, under your correction, there is not many of your nation —   131
Mac. Of my nation? What ish my nation? Ish a villain, and a basterd, and a knave, and a rascal. What ish my nation? Who talks of my nation?   135
Flu. Look you, if you take the matter other-wise than is meant, Captain Macmorris, per-adventure I shall think you do not use me with that affability as in discretion you ought to use me, look you, being as good a man as yourself, both in the disciplines of war, and in the deriva-tion of my birth, and in other particularities.
Mac. I do not know you so good a man as myself. So Chrish save me, I will cut off your head!   145
Gow. Gentlemen both, you will mistake each other.
Jamy. Ah, that's a foul fault!
                                A parley [*sounded*].
Gow. The town sounds a parley.   149

Flu. Captain Macmorris, when there is more better oportunity to be required, look you, I will be so bold as to tell you I know the disciplines of war; and there is an end. *Exeunt.*

[Scene III. *Before the gates of Harfleur.*]

[Enter the *Governor* and some *Citizens* on the walls.] Enter *King* [*Henry*] and all his *Train* before the gates.

King. How yet resolves the Governor of the town?
This is the latest parle we will admit.
Therefore to our best mercy give yourselves,
Or, like to men proud of destruction,
Defy us to our worst; for, as I am a soldier, 5
A name that in my thoughts becomes me best,
If I begin the batt'ry once again,
I will not leave the half-achieved Harflew
Till in her ashes she lie buried.
The gates of mercy shall be all shut up, 10
And the flesh'd soldier, rough and hard of heart,
In liberty of bloody hand shall range
With conscience wide as hell, mowing like grass
Your fresh fair virgins and your flow'ring infants.
What is it then to me if impious war, 15
Array'd in flames like to the prince of fiends,
Do with his smirch'd complexion all fell feats
Enlink'd to waste and desolation?
What is't to me, when you yourselves are cause,
If your pure maidens fall into the hand 20
Of hot and forcing violation?
What rein can hold licentious wickedness
When down the hill he holds his fierce career?
We may as bootless spend our vain command
Upon th' enraged soldiers in their spoil 25
As send precepts to the Leviathan
To come ashore. Therefore, you men of Harflew,
Take pity of your town and of your people
Whiles yet my soldiers are in my command,
Whiles yet the cool and temperate wind of grace
O'erblows the filthy and contagious clouds 31
Of heady murther, spoil, and villany.
If not — why, in a moment look to see
The blind and bloody soldier with foul hand
Defile the locks of your shrill-shrieking daughters; 35
Your fathers taken by the silver beards,
And their most reverend heads dash'd to the walls;
Your naked infants spitted upon pikes,

Whiles the mad mothers with their howls confus'd
Do break the clouds, as did the wives of Jewry
At Herod's bloody-hunting slaughtermen. 41
What say you? Will you yield, and this avoid?
Or, guilty in defence, be thus destroy'd?
Gov. Our expectation hath this day an end.
The Dauphin, whom of succours we entreated,
Returns us that his powers are yet not ready
To raise so great a siege. Therefore, dread king,
We yield our town and lives to thy soft mercy.
Enter our gates, dispose of us and ours,
For we no longer are defensible. 50
King. Open your gates. [*Exit Governor.*]
Come, uncle Exeter,
Go you and enter Harflew; there remain
And fortify it strongly 'gainst the French.
Use mercy to them all. For us, dear uncle,
The winter coming on, and sickness growing
Upon our soldiers, we will retire to Calais. 56
To-night in Harflew will we be your guest;
To-morrow for the march are we addrest.
Flourish, and enter the town.

[Scene IV. *Rouen. The* French King's *Palace.*]

Enter *Katherine* and [*Alice*,] an old *Gentlewoman.*

Kath. Alice, tu as esté en Angleterre, et tu parles bien le langage.
Alice. Un peu, madame.
Kath. Je te prie m'enseignez; il faut que j'apprenne à parler. Comment appelez-vous la main en Anglois? 6
Alice. La main? Elle est appelée 'de hand.'
Kath. 'De hand.' Et les doigts?
Alice. Les doigts? Ma foi, j'oublie les doigts; mais je me souviendrai. Les doigts? Je pense qu'ils sont appelés 'de fingres'; oui, 'de fingres.' 11
Kath. La main, 'de hand'; les doigts, 'de fingres.' Je pense que je suis le bon escolier; j'ai gagné deux mots d'Anglois vistement. Comment appelez-vous les ongles? 15
Alice. Les ongles? Nous les appelons 'de nails.'
Kath. 'De nails.' Escoutez; dites-moi, si je parle bien: 'de hand, de fingres,' et 'de nails.'
Alice. C'est bien dict, madame; il est fort bon Anglois. 20
Kath. Dites-moi l'Anglois pour le bras.
Alice. 'De arm,' madame.

Kath. Et le coude.
Alice. 'D' elbow.'   24
Kath. 'D' elbow.' Je m'en fais la répétition
de tous les mots que vous m'avez appris dès
à présent.
Alice. Il est trop difficile, madame, comme
je pense.   29
Kath. Excusez-moi, Alice ; escoutez : 'd' hand,
de fingres, de nails, d' arma, de bilbow.'
Alice. 'D' elbow,' madame.
Kath. O Seigneur Dieu, je m'en oublie !
'D' elbow.' Comment appelez-vous le col ?
Alice. 'De nick,' madame.   35
Kath. 'De nick.' Et le menton ?
Alice. 'De chin.'
Kath. 'De sin.' Le col, 'de nick' ; le menton,
'de sin.'   39
Alice. Oui. Sauf vostre honneur, en vérité,
vous prononcez les mots aussi droict que les
natifs d'Angleterre.
Kath. Je ne doute point d'apprendre, par la
grace de Dieu, et en peu de temps.   44
Alice. N'avez-vous pas déjà oublié ce que je
vous ai enseigné ?
Kath. Non, je réciterai à vous promptement :
'd' hand, de fingres, de mails' —
Alice. 'De nails,' madame.
Kath. 'De nails, de arm, de ilbow.'   50
Alice. Sauf vostre honneur, 'd' elbow.'
Kath. Ainsi dis-je ; 'd' elbow, de nick,' et 'de
sin.' Comment appelez-vous le pied et la robe ?
Alice. 'De foot,' madame ; et 'de coun.'   54
Kath. 'De foot et de coun !' O Seigneur Dieu !
ce sont mots de son mauvais, corruptible, gros,
et impudique, et non pour les dames d'honneur
d'user : je ne voudrois prononcer ces mots
devant les seigneurs de France pour tout le
monde. Foh ! 'le foot' et 'le coun' ! Néantmoins, je réciterai une autre fois ma leçon en-
semble : 'd' hand, de fingres, de nails, d' arm,
d' elbow, de nick, de sin, de foot, de coun.'
Alice. Excellent, madame !   64
Kath. C'est assez pour une fois : allons-nous
à diner.   *Exeunt.*

[Scene V. *Rouen. The Palace.*]

Enter the *King of France*, the *Dauphin, Bourbon*, the *Constable of France*, and others.

King. 'Tis certain he hath pass'd the river
Somme.
Con. And if he be not fought withal, my lord,
Let us not live in France ; let us quit all
And give our vineyards to a barbarous people.

Dau. O Dieu vivant ! Shall a few sprays
of us,   5
The emptying of our fathers' luxury,
Our scions, put in wild and savage stock,
Spirt up so suddenly into the clouds
And overlook their grafters ?
Bour. Normans, but bastard Normans, Nor-
man bastards !   10
Mort de ma vie ! if they march along
Unfought withal, but I will sell my dukedom
To buy a slobb'ry and a dirty farm
In that nook-shotten isle of Albion.
Con. Dieu de batailles ! whence have they
this mettle ?   15
Is not their climate foggy, raw, and dull,
On whom, as in despite, the sun looks pale,
Killing their fruit with frowns ? Can sodden
water,
A drench for sur-rein'd jades, their barley broth,
Decoct their cold blood to such valiant heat ?
And shall our quick blood, spirited with wine,
Seem frosty ? O, for honour of our land,
Let us not hang like roping icicles
Upon our houses' thatch, whiles a more frosty
people
Sweat drops of gallant youth in our rich
fields —   25
'Poor' we may call them in their native lords !
Dau. By faith and honour,
Our madams mock at us and plainly say
Our mettle is bred out, and they will give
Their bodies to the lust of English youth   30
To new-store France with bastard warriors.
Bour. They bid us to the English dancing
schools
And teach lavoltas high and swift corantos,
Saying our grace is only in our heels
And that we are most lofty runaways.   35
King. Where is Montjoy the herald ? Speed
him hence ;
Let him greet England with our sharp defiance.
Up, princes ! and, with spirit of honour edged,
More sharper than your swords, hie to the field.
Charles Delabreth, High Constable of France,
You Dukes of Orleans, Bourbon, and of Berri,
Alençon, Brabant, Bar, and Burgundy ;
Jaques Chatillon, Rambures, Vaudemont,
Beaumont, Grandpré, Roussi, and Fauconberg,
Foix, Lestrale, Bouciqualt, and Charolois, 45
High dukes, great princes, barons, lords, and
knights,
For your great seats now quit you of great
shames.
Bar Harry England, that sweeps through our land
With pennons painted in the blood of Harflew.

Rush on his host as doth the melted snow 50
Upon the valleys whose low vassal seat
The Alps doth spit and void his rheum upon.
Go down upon him — you have power enough—
And in a captive chariot into Roan
Bring him our prisoner.
 Con.   This becomes the great. 55
Sorry am I his numbers are so few,
His soldiers sick and famish'd in their march;
For I am sure, when he shall see our army,
He'll drop his heart into the sink of fear
And, for achievement, offer us his ransom. 60
 King. Therefore, Lord Constable, haste on
 Montjoy,
And let him say to England that we send
To know what willing ransom he will give.
Prince Dauphin, you shall stay with us in Roan.
 Dau. Not so, I do beseech your Majesty. 65
 King. Be patient, for you shall remain with
 us.
Now forth, Lord Constable and princes all,
And quickly bring us word of England's fall.
           Exeunt.

[Scene VI. *The English camp in Picardy.*]

Enter *Captains*, English and Welsh — *Gower*
    and *Fluellen.*

 Gow. How now, Captain Fluellen? Come
you from the bridge?
 Flu. I assure you there is very excellent
services committed at the bridge.
 Gow. Is the Duke of Exeter safe? 5
 Flu. The Duke of Exeter is as magnanimous
as Agamemnon, and a man that I love and honour with my soul, and my heart, and my duty,
and my live, and my living, and my uttermost
power. He is not — God be praised and
plessed! — any hurt in the world, but keeps
the pridge most valiantly, with excellent discipline. There is an aunchient lieutenant there
at the pridge, I think in my very conscience he
is as valiant a man as Mark Anthony, and he is
a man of no estimation in the world, but I did
see him do as gallant service.
 Gow. What do you call him?
 Flu. He is call'd Aunchient Pistol.
 Gow. I know him not. 20

    Enter *Pistol.*

 Flu. Here is the man.
 Pist. Captain, I thee beseech to do me fa-
vours.
The Duke of Exeter doth love thee well.

 Flu. Ay, I praise God; and I have merited
some love at his hands. 25
 Pist. Bardolph, a soldier firm and sound of
 heart,
And of buxom valour, hath by cruel fate,
And giddy Fortune's furious fickle wheel —
That goddess blind, 30
That stands upon the rolling restless stone —
 Flu. By your patience, Aunchient Pistol.
Fortune is painted plind, with a muffler afore
her eyes, to signify to you that Fortune is plind;
and she is painted also with a wheel, to signify
to you, which is the moral of it, that she is
turning and inconstant, and mutability, and
variation; and her foot, look you, is fixed upon
a spherical stone, which rolls, and rolls, and
rolls. In good truth, the poet makes a most ex-
cellent description of it. Fortune is an excellent
moral. 40
 Pist. Fortune is Bardolph's foe, and frowns
on him;
For he hath stol'n a pax, and hanged must 'a
 be —
A damned death!
Let gallows gape for dog; let man go free,
And let not hemp his windpipe suffocate. 45
But Exeter hath given the doom of death
For pax of little price.
Therefore, go speak — the Duke will hear thy
 voice;
And let not Bardolph's vital thread be cut
With edge of penny cord and vile reproach. 50
Speak, Captain, for his life, and I will thee
 requite.
 Flu. Aunchient Pistol, I do partly under-
stand your meaning.
 Pist. Why then, rejoice therefore! 54
 Flu. Certainly, aunchient, it is not a thing to
rejoice at; for if, look you, he were my brother,
I would desire the Duke to use his good pleasure
and put him to execution; for discipline ought
to be used.
 Pist. Die and be damn'd! and figo for thy
 friendship! 60
 Flu. It is well.
 Pist. The fig of Spain!   *Exit.*
 Flu. Very good.
 Gow. Why, this is an arrant counterfeit rascal! I remember him now — a bawd, a cutpurse. 65
 Flu. I'll assure you, 'a utt'red as prave words
at the pridge as you shall see in a summer's
day. But it is very well. What he has spoke
to me, that is well, I warrant you, when time
is serve. 69

Gow. Why, 'tis a gull, a fool, a rogue, that now and then goes to the wars to grace himself, at his return into London, under the form of a soldier. And such fellows are perfect in the great commanders' names, and they will learn you by rote where services were done: — at such and such a sconce, at such a breach, at such a convoy; who came off bravely, who was shot, who disgrac'd, what terms the enemy stood on; and this they con perfectly in the phrase of war, which they trick up with new-tuned oaths; and what a beard of the General's cut and a horrid suit of the camp will do among foaming bottles and ale-wash'd wits is wonderful to be thought on. But you must learn to know such slanders of the age, or else you may be marvellously mistook.   85

Flu. I tell you what, Captain Gower, I do perceive he is not the man that he would gladly make show to the world he is. If I find a hole in his coat, I will tell him my mind. [*Drum within.*] Hark you, the King is coming, and I must speak with him from the pridge.   91

Drum and colours. Enter the *King* and his
     poor *Soldiers*, [and *Gloucester*].

God pless your Majesty!

King. How now, Fluellen? Cam'st thou from the bridge?

Flu. Ay, so please your Majesty. The Duke of Exeter has very gallantly maintain'd the pridge; the French is gone off, look you, and there is gallant and most prave passages. Marry, th' athversary was have possession of the pridge, but he is enforced to retire, and the Duke of Exeter is master of the pridge. I can tell your Majesty, the Duke is a prave man.   101

King. What men have you lost, Fluellen?

Flu. The perdition of th' athversary hath been very great, reasonable great. Marry, for my part, I think the Duke hath lost never a man but one that is like to be executed for robbing a church — one Bardolph, if your Majesty know the man. His face is all bubukles and whelks, and knobs, and flames o' fire, and his lips blows at his nose, and it is like a coal of fire, sometimes plue and sometimes red; but his nose is executed, and his fire's out.   112

King. We would have all such offenders so cut off. And we give express charge that in our marches through the country there be nothing compell'd from the villages, nothing taken but paid for; none of the French upbraided or abused in disdainful language; for when lenity and cruelty play for a kingdom, the gentler gamester is the soonest winner.   120

Tucket. Enter *Montjoy.*

Mont. You know me by my habit.

King. Well then, I know thee. What shall I know of thee?

Mont. My master's mind.

King. Unfold it.   124

Mont. Thus says my king: — Say thou to Harry of England: Though we seem'd dead, we did but sleep. Advantage is a better soldier than rashness. Tell him we could have rebuk'd him at Harflew, but that we thought not good to bruise an injury till it were full ripe. Now we speak upon our cue, and our voice is imperial. England shall repent his folly, see his weakness, and admire our sufferance. Bid him therefore consider of his ransom, which must proportion the losses we have borne, the subjects we have lost, the disgrace we have digested; which in weight to re-answer, his pettiness would bow under. For our losses, his exchequer is too poor; for th' effusion of our blood, the muster of his kingdom too faint a number; and for our disgrace, his own person kneeling at our feet but a weak and worthless satisfaction. To this add defiance; and tell him for conclusion, he hath betrayed his followers, whose condemnation is pronounc'd. So far my king and master; so much my office.   145

King. What is thy name? I know thy quality.

Mont. Montjoy.

King. Thou dost thy office fairly. Turn thee back,
And tell thy king I do not seek him now,
But could be willing to march on to Calais 150
Without impeachment: for, to say the sooth,
Though 'tis no wisdom to confess so much
Unto an enemy of craft and vantage,
My people are with sickness much enfeebled,
My numbers lessen'd, and those few I have,
Almost no better than so many French;   156
Who when they were in health, I tell thee, herald,
I thought upon one pair of English legs
Did march three Frenchmen. Yet forgive me, God,   159
That I do brag thus! This your air of France
Hath blown that vice in me. I must repent.
Go therefore tell thy master here I am;
My ransom is this frail and worthless trunk;
My army but a weak and sickly guard;

173

Yet, God before, tell him we will come on, 165
Though France himself and such another
    neighbour
Stand in our way. There's for thy labour,
    Montjoy.   [*Gives a purse.*]
Go bid thy master well advise himself:
If we may pass, we will; if we be hind'red,
We shall your tawny ground with your red
    blood   170
Discolour; and so, Montjoy, fare you well.
The sum of all our answer is but this:
We would not seek a battle, as we are,
Nor, as we are, we say we will not shun it.
So tell your master.   175
    Mont. I shall deliver so. Thanks to your
    Highness.   [*Exit.*]
    Glouc. I hope they will not come upon us
    now.
    King. We are in God's hand, brother, not
    in theirs.
March to the bridge. It now draws toward
    night.
Beyond the river we'll encamp ourselves, 180
And on to-morrow bid them march away.
        Exeunt.

[Scene VII. *The French camp, near
    Agincourt.*]

Enter the *Constable of France,* the *Lord Rambures, Orleans, Dauphin,* with others.

    Con. Tut! I have the best armour of the
world. Would it were day!
    Orl. You have an excellent armour; but let
my horse have his due.
    Con. It is the best horse of Europe.   5
    Orl. Will it never be morning?
    Dau. My Lord of Orleans, and my Lord
High Constable, you talk of horse and armour?
    Orl. You are as well provided of both as any
prince in the world.   10
    Dau. What a long night is this! I will not
change my horse with any that treads but on
four pasterns. Ça, ha! he bounds from the
earth, as if his entrails were hairs; le cheval
volant, the Pegasus, avec les narines de feu!
When I bestride him, I soar, I am a hawk. He
trots the air. The earth sings when he touches
it. The basest horn of his hoof is more musical
than the pipe of Hermes.
    Orl. He's of the colour of the nutmeg.   20
    Dau. And of the heat of the ginger. It is a
beast for Perseus: he is pure air and fire; and

the dull elements of earth and water never appear in him, but only in patient stillness while
his rider mounts him. He is indeed a horse, and
all other jades you may call beasts.   26
    Con. Indeed, my lord, it is a most absolute
and excellent horse.
    Dau. It is the prince of palfreys. His neigh
is like the bidding of a monarch, and his countenance enforces homage.   31
    Orl. No more, cousin.
    Dau. Nay, the man hath no wit that cannot,
from the rising of the lark to the lodging of the
lamb, vary deserved praise on my palfrey. It
is a theme as fluent as the sea. Turn the
sands into eloquent tongues, and my horse
is argument for them all. 'Tis a subject for a
sovereign to reason on, and for a sovereign's
sovereign to ride on; and for the world, familiar to us and unknown, to lay apart their
particular functions and wonder at him. I once
writ a sonnet in his praise and began thus,
'Wonder of nature!'
    Orl. I have heard a sonnet begin so to one's
mistress.   45
    Dau. Then did they imitate that which I
compos'd to my courser, for my horse is my
mistress.
    Orl. Your mistress bears well.
    Dau. Me well, which is the prescript praise
and perfection of a good and particular mistress.
    Con. Nay, for methought yesterday your
mistress shrewdly shook your back.
    Dau. So perhaps did yours.
    Con. Mine was not bridled.   54
    Dau. O, then belike she was old and gentle,
and you rode like a kern of Ireland, your
French hose off, and in your strait strossers.
    Con. You have good judgment in horse-
manship.   59
    Dau. Be warn'd by me then. They that ride
so, and ride not warily, fall into foul bogs. I
had rather have my horse to my mistress.
    Con. I had as live have my mistress a
jade.
    Dau. I tell thee, Constable, my mistress
wears his own hair.   65
    Con. I could make as true a boast as that, if
I had a sow to my mistress.
    Dau. 'Le chien est retourné à son propre
vomissement, et la truie lavée au bourbier.'
Thou mak'st use of anything.   70
    Con. Yet do I not use my horse for my mis-
tress, or any such proverb so little kin to the
purpose.

Ram. My Lord Constable, the armour that I saw in your tent to-night — are those stars or suns upon it?   75

Con. Stars, my lord.

Dau. Some of them will fall to-morrow, I hope.

Con. And yet my sky shall not want.

Dau. That may be, for you bear a many superfluously, and 'twere more honour some were away.   81

Con. Ev'n as your horse bears your praises, who would trot as well, were some of your brags dismounted.   84

Dau. Would I were able to load him with his desert! Will it never be day? I will trot to-morrow a mile, and my way shall be paved with English faces.

Con. I will not say so, for fear I should be fac'd out of my way; but I would it were morning, for I would fain be about the ears of the English.   92

Ram. Who will go to hazard with me for twenty prisoners?

Con. You must first go yourself to hazard ere you have them.   96

Dau. 'Tis midnight; I'll go arm myself.

                                          Exit.

Orl. The Dauphin longs for morning.

Ram. He longs to eat the English.

Con. I think he will eat all he kills.   100

Orl. By the white hand of my lady, he's a gallant prince.

Con. Swear by her foot, that she may tread out the oath

Orl. He is simply the most active gentleman of France.   106

Con. Doing is activity, and he will still be doing.

Orl. He never did harm, that I heard of.

Con. Nor will do none to-morrow. He will keep that good name still.   111

Orl. I know him to be valiant.

Con. I was told that by one that knows him better than you.

Orl. What's he?   115

Con. Marry, he told me so himself, and he said he car'd not who knew it.

Orl. He needs not; it is no hidden virtue in him.   119

Con. By my faith, sir, but it is! Never anybody saw it but his lackey. 'Tis a hooded valour; and when it appears, it will bate.

Orl. Ill will never said well.

Con. I will cap that proverb with 'There is flattery in friendship.'   125

Orl. And I will take up that with 'Give the devil his due.'

Con. Well plac'd! There stands your friend for the devil. Have at the very eye of that proverb with 'A pox of the devil!'   130

Orl. You are the better at proverbs, by how much 'a fool's bolt is soon shot.'

Con. You have shot over.

Orl. 'Tis not the first time you were overshot.

                  Enter a *Messenger.*

Mess. My Lord High Constable, the English lie within fifteen hundred paces of your tents.

Con. Who hath measur'd the ground?

Mess. The Lord Grandpré.   138

Con. A valiant and most expert gentleman. Would it were day! Alas, poor Harry of England! He longs not for the dawning, as we do.

Orl. What a wretched and peevish fellow is this King of England, to mope with his fat-brain'd followers so far out of his knowledge!

Con. If the English had any apprehension, they would run away.   146

Orl. That they lack; for if their heads had any intellectual armour, they could never wear such heavy headpieces.

Ram. That island of England breeds very valiant creatures. Their mastiffs are of unmatchable courage.   152

Orl. Foolish curs, that run winking into the mouth of a Russian bear and have their heads crush'd like rotten apples! You may as well say that's a valiant flea that dare eat his breakfast on the lip of a lion.   157

Con. Just, just! and the men do sympathize with the mastiffs in robustious and rough coming on, leaving their wits with their wives; and then give them great meals of beef and iron and steel, they will eat like wolves and fight like devils.   162

Orl. Ay, but these English are shrowdly out of beef.

Con. Then shall we find to-morrow they have only stomachs to eat and none to fight. Now is it time to arm. Come, shall we about it?   167

Orl. It is now two o'clock; but let me see — by ten

We shall have each a hundred Englishmen.

                                       Exeunt.

Chorus.

Now entertain conjecture of a time
When creeping murmur and the poring dark
Fills the wide vessel of the universe.
From camp to camp, through the foul womb
    of night,
The hum of either army stilly sounds,   5
That the fix'd sentinels almost receive
The secret whispers of each other's watch.
Fire answers fire, and through their paly
    flames
Each battle sees the other's umber'd face.
Steed threatens steed, in high and boastful
    neighs   10
Piercing the night's dull ear; and from the
    tents
The armourers accomplishing the knights,
With busy hammers closing rivets up,
Give dreadful note of preparation.
The country cocks do crow, the clocks do
    toll   15
And the third hour of drowsy morning name.
Proud of their numbers and secure in soul,
The confident and over-lusty French
Do the low-rated English play at dice;
And chide the cripple tardy-gaited night   20
Who like a foul and ugly witch doth limp
So tediously away. The poor condemned
    English,
Like sacrifices, by their watchful fires
Sit patiently and inly ruminate   24
The morning's danger; and their gesture sad,
Investing lank-lean cheeks and war-worn coats,
Presenteth them unto the gazing moon
So many horrid ghosts. O, now, who will be-
    hold
The royal captain of this ruin'd band
Walking from watch to watch, from tent to
    tent,   30
Let him cry 'Praise and glory on his head!'
For forth he goes and visits all his host,
Bids them good morrow with a modest smile
And calls them brothers, friends, and country-
    men.
Upon his royal face there is no note   35
How dread an army hath enrounded him;
Nor doth he dedicate one jot of colour
Unto the weary and all-watched night,
But freshly looks, and overbears attaint   39
With cheerful semblance and sweet majesty;
That every wretch, pining and pale before,
Beholding him, plucks comfort from his looks.
A largess universal, like the sun,
His liberal eye doth give to every one,   44
Thawing cold fear. Then, mean and gentle all,
Behold, as may unworthiness define,
A little touch of Harry in the night.
And so our scene must to the battle fly;
Where (O for pity!) we shall much disgrace
With four or five most vile and ragged foils, 50
Right ill-dispos'd in brawl ridiculous,
The name of Agincourt. Yet sit and see,
Minding true things by what their mock'ries be.
                                        Exit.

[Scene I. *France. The English camp
            at Agincourt.*]

Enter the *King, Bedford,* and *Gloucester.*

King. Gloucester, 'tis true that we are in
    great danger;
The greater therefore should our courage be.
Good morrow, brother Bedford. God Almighty!
There is some soul of goodness in things evil,
Would men observingly distil it out;   5
For our bad neighbour makes us early stirrers,
Which is both healthful, and good husbandry.
Besides, they are our outward consciences,
And preachers to us all, admonishing
That we should dress us fairly for our end. 10
Thus may we gather honey from the weed
And make a moral of the devil himself.

Enter *Erpingham.*

Good morrow, old Sir Thomas Erpingham.
A good soft pillow for that good white head
Were better than a churlish turf of France. 15
Erp. Not so, my liege. This lodging likes
    me better,
Since I may say 'Now lie I like a king.'
King. 'Tis good for men to love their present
    pains
Upon example: so the spirit is eas'd;   19
And when the mind is quick'ned, out of doubt
The organs, though defunct and dead before,
Break up their drowsy grave and newly move
With casted slough and fresh legerity.
Lend me thy cloak, Sir Thomas. Brothers
    both,

176

Commend me to the princes in our camp; 25
Do my good morrow to them, and anon
Desire them all to my pavilion.

Glouc. We shall, my liege.

Erp. Shall I attend your Grace?

King.   No, my good knight.
Go with my brothers to my lords of England.
I and my bosom must debate awhile, 31
And then I would no other company.

Erp. The Lord in heaven bless thee, noble
Harry!

Exeunt [all but the King].

King. God-a-mercy, old heart! thou speak'st
cheerfully.

Enter *Pistol.*

Pist. Qui va là? 35

King. A friend.

Pist. Discuss unto me, art thou officer;
Or art thou base, common, and popular?

King. I am a gentleman of a company.

Pist. Trail'st thou the puissant pike? 40

King. Even so. What are you?

Pist. As good a gentleman as the Emperor.

King. Then you are a better than the
King.

Pist. The King's a bawcock, and a heart of
gold,
A lad of life, an imp of fame, 45
Of parents good, of fist most valiant.
I kiss his dirty shoe, and from heartstring
I love the lovely bully. What is thy name?

King. Harry le Roy.

Pist. Le Roy? A Cornish name. Art thou
of Cornish crew? 50

King. No, I am a Welshman.

Pist. Know'st thou Fluellen?

King. Yes.

Pist. Tell him I'll knock his leek about his
pate
Upon Saint Davy's day. 55

King. Do not you wear your dagger in your
cap that day, lest he knock that about yours.

Pist. Art thou his friend?

King. And his kinsman too.

Pist. The figo for thee then! 60

King. I thank you. God be with you!

Pist. My name is Pistol call'd.

Exit. Manet King.

King. It sorts well with your fierceness.

Enter *Fluellen* and *Gower.*

Gow. Captain Fluellen! 64

Flu. So! in the name of Jesu Christ, speak
lower. It is the greatest admiration in the universal world, when the true and aunchient pre-
rogatifes and laws of the wars is not kept. If you
would take the pains but to examine the wars of
Pompey the Great, you shall find, I warrant
you, that there is no tiddle taddle nor pibble
pabble in Pompey's camp. I warrant you, you
shall find the ceremonies of the wars, and the
cares of it, and the forms of it, and the sobriety
of it, and the modesty of it, to be otherwise. 75

Gow. Why, the enemy is loud; you hear him
all night.

Flu. If the enemy is an ass and a fool and a
prating coxcomb, is it meet, think you, that we
should also, look you, be an ass and a fool and
a prating coxcomb? In your own conscience
now? 81

Gow. I will speak lower.

Flu. I pray you and beseech you that you
will.

Exeunt [Gower and Fluellen].

King. Though it appear a little out of
fashion, 85
There is much care and valour in this Welshman.

Enter three Soldiers, *John Bates, Alexander
Court,* and *Michael Williams.*

Court. Brother John Bates, is not that the
morning which breaks yonder?

Bates. I think it be; but we have no great
cause to desire the approach of day. 90

Will. We see yonder the beginning of the
day, but I think we shall never see the end of it.
Who goes there?

King. A friend.

Will. Under what captain serve you? 95

King. Under Sir Thomas Erpingham.

Will. A good old commander and a most kind
gentleman. I pray you, what thinks he of our
estate? 99

King. Even as men wrack'd upon a sand,
that look to be wash'd off the next tide.

Bates. He hath not told his thought to the
King?

King. No; nor is it not meet he should. For
though I speak it to you, I think the King is but
a man, as I am. The violet smells to him as it
doth to me; the element shows to him as it doth
to me; all his senses have but human conditions. His ceremonies laid by, in his nakedness
he appears but a man; and though his affections are higher mounted than ours, yet, when
they stoop, they stoop with the like wing.
Therefore, when he sees reason of fears, as we
do, his fears, out of doubt, be of the same relish

177

as ours are. Yet, in reason, no man should possess him with any appearance of fear, lest he, by showing it, should dishearten his army. 117

Bates. He may show what outward courage he will; but I believe, as cold a night as 'tis, he could wish himself in Thames up to the neck; and so I would he were, and I by him, at all adventures, so we were quit here. 122

King. By my troth, I will speak my conscience of the King: I think he would not wish himself anywhere but where he is.

Bates. Then I would he were here alone. So should he be sure to be ransomed, and a many poor men's lives saved. 128

King. I dare say you love him not so ill to wish him here alone, howsoever you speak this to feel other men's minds. Methinks I could not die anywhere so contented as in the King's company, his cause being just and his quarrel honourable.

Will. That's more than we know. 135

Bates. Ay, or more than we should seek after; for we know enough if we know we are the King's subjects. If his cause be wrong, our obedience to the King wipes the crime of it out of us. 139

Will. But if the cause be not good, the King himself hath a heavy reckoning to make when all those legs and arms and heads, chopp'd off in a battle, shall join together at the latter day and cry all 'We died at such a place!' some swearing, some crying for a surgeon, some upon their wives left poor behind them, some upon the debts they owe, some upon their children rawly left. I am afeard there are few die well that die in a battle; for how can they charitably dispose of anything when blood is their argument? Now, if these men do not die well, it will be a black matter for the King that led them to it; who to disobey were against all proportion of subjection. 153

King. So, if a son that is by his father sent about merchandise do sinfully miscarry upon the sea, the imputation of his wickedness, by your rule, should be imposed upon his father that sent him; or if a servant, under his master's command transporting a sum of money, be assailed by robbers and die in many irreconcil'd iniquities, you may call the business of the master the author of the servant's damnation. But this is not so. The King is not bound to answer the particular endings of his soldiers, the father of his son, nor the master of his servant; for they purpose not their death when they purpose their services. Besides, there is no king, be

his cause never so spotless, if it come to the arbitrement of swords, can try it out with all unspotted soldiers. Some (peradventure) have on them the guilt of premeditated and contrived murther; some, of beguiling virgins with the broken seals of perjury; some, making the wars their bulwark, that have before gored the gentle bosom of peace with pillage and robbery. Now, if these men have defeated the law and outrun native punishment, though they can outstrip men, they have no wings to fly from God. War is his beadle, war is his vengeance; so that here men are punish'd for before-breach of the King's laws in now the King's quarrel. Where they feared the death, they have borne life away; and where they would be safe, they perish. Then if they die unprovided, no more is the King guilty of their damnation than he was before guilty of those impieties for the which they are now visited. Every subject's duty is the King's, but every subject's soul is his own. Therefore should every soldier in the wars do as every sick man in his bed — wash every mote out of his conscience; and dying so, death is to him advantage; or not dying, the time was blessedly lost wherein such preparation was gained; and in him that escapes, it were not sin to think that, making God so free an offer, he let him outlive that day to see his greatness and to teach others how they should prepare. 196

Will. 'Tis certain, every man that dies ill, the ill upon his own head — the King is not to answer it.

Bates. I do not desire he should answer for me, and yet I determine to fight lustily for him.

King. I myself heard the King say he would not be ransom'd. 203

Will. Ay, he said so, to make us fight cheerfully; but when our throats are cut, he may be ransom'd, and we ne'er the wiser.

King. If I live to see it, I will never trust his word after. 208

Will. You pay him then! That's a perilous shot out of an elder-gun that a poor and a private displeasure can do against a monarch! You may as well go about to turn the sun to ice with fanning in his face with a peacock's feather. You'll never trust his word after! Come, 'tis a foolish saying. 215

King. Your reproof is something too round. I should be angry with you if the time were convenient.

Will. Let it be a quarrel between us if you live. 220

King. I embrace it.

Will. How shall I know thee again?

King. Give me any gage of thine, and I will wear it in my bonnet. Then, if ever thou dar'st acknowledge it, I will make it my quarrel.

Will. Here's my glove. Give me another of thine.   227

King. There.

Will. This will I also wear in my cap. If ever thou come to me and say, after to-morrow, 'This is my glove,' by this hand, I will take thee a box on the ear.   232

King. If ever I live to see it, I will challenge it.

Will. Thou dar'st as well be hang'd.

King. Well, I will do it, though I take thee in the King's company.

Will. Keep thy word. Fare thee well.

Bates. Be friends, you English fools, be friends! We have French quarrels enow, if you could tell how to reckon.   241

King. Indeed the French may lay twenty French crowns to one they will beat us, for they bear them on their shoulders; but it is no English treason to cut French crowns, and to-morrow the King himself will be a clipper. 246

Exeunt Soldiers.

Upon the King! Let us our lives, our souls, Our debts, our careful wives, Our children, and our sins, lay on the King! We must bear all. O hard condition,   250 Twin-born with greatness, subject to the breath Of every fool, whose sense no more can feel But his own wringing! What infinite heart's-ease Must kings neglect that private men enjoy! And what have kings that privates have not too,   255 Save ceremony, save general ceremony? And what art thou, thou idol Ceremony? What kind of god art thou, that suffer'st more Of mortal griefs than do thy worshippers? What are thy rents? What are thy comings-in?   260 O Ceremony, show me but thy worth! What is thy soul of adoration? Art thou aught else but place, degree, and form, Creating awe and fear in other men? Wherein thou art less happy being fear'd   265 Than they in fearing. What drink'st thou oft, instead of homage sweet, But poison'd flattery? O, be sick, great greatness,

And bid thy ceremony give thee cure! Think'st thou the fiery fever will go out   270 With titles blown from adulation? Will it give place to flexure and low bending? Canst thou, when thou command'st the beggar's knee, Command the health of it? No, thou proud dream,   274 That play'st so subtilly with a king's repose. I am a king that find thee; and I know 'Tis not the balm, the sceptre, and the ball, The sword, the mace, the crown imperial, The intertissued robe of gold and pearl, The farced title running fore the king,   280 The throne he sits on, nor the tide of pomp That beats upon the high shore of this world — No, not all these, thrice-gorgeous ceremony, Not all these, laid in bed majestical, Can sleep so soundly as the wretched slave, 285 Who, with a body fill'd, and vacant mind, Gets him to rest, cramm'd with distressful bread; Never sees horrid night, the child of hell; But like a lackey, from the rise to set, Sweats in the eye of Phœbus, and all night 290 Sleeps in Elysium; next day after dawn, Doth rise and help Hyperion to his horse; And follows so the ever-running year With profitable labour to his grave; And but for ceremony, such a wretch,   296 Winding up days with toil and nights with sleep, Had the forehand and vantage of a king. The slave, a member of the country's peace, Enjoys it; but in gross brain little wots What watch the king keeps to maintain the peace,   300 Whose hours the peasant best advantages.

Enter Erpingham.

Erp. My lord, your nobles, jealous of your absence, Seek through your camp to find you.

King.   Good old knight, Collect them all together at my tent. I'll be before thee.

Erp.   I shall do't, my lord. *Exit.*

King. O God of battles, steel my soldiers' hearts,   306 Possess them not with fear! Take from them now The sense of reck'ning, if th' opposed numbers Pluck their hearts from them. Not to-day, O Lord, O, not to-day, think not upon the fault   310

My father made in compassing the crown!
I Richard's body have interred new;
And on it have bestowed more contrite tears
Than from it issued forced drops of blood.
Five hundred poor I have in yearly pay,   315
Who twice a day their wither'd hands hold up
Toward heaven, to pardon blood; and I have
built
Two chantries, where the sad and solemn priests
Sing still for Richard's soul. More will I do!
Though all that I can do is nothing worth,   320
Since that my penitence comes after all,
Imploring pardon.

Enter *Gloucester*.

Glouc. My liege!
King. My brother Gloucester's voice? Ay.
I know thy errand; I will go with thee.   325
The day, my friends, and all things stay for me.
                                           Exeunt.

[Scene II. *The French camp.*]

Enter the *Dauphin, Orleans, Rambures*, and *Beaumont*.

Orl. The sun doth gild our armour. Up, my
lords!
Dau. Montez à cheval! My horse! Varlet,
laquais! Ha!
Orl. O brave spirit!
Dau. Via! les eaux et la terre—
Orl. Rien puis? L'air et le feu.   5
Dau. Ciel! cousin Orleans.

Enter *Constable*.

Now, my Lord Constable?
Con. Hark how our steeds for present service
neigh!
Dau. Mount them and make incision in their
hides,
That their hot blood may spin in English
eyes   10
And dout them with superfluous courage, ha!
Ram. What, will you have them weep our
horses' blood?
How shall we then behold their natural tears?

Enter *Messenger*.

Mess. The English are embattail'd, you
French peers.
Con. To horse, you gallant princes! straight
to horse!   15
Do but behold yond poor and starved band,

And your fair show shall suck away their souls,
Leaving them but the shales and husks of
men.
There is not work enough for all our hands,   19
Scarce blood enough in all their sickly veins
To give each naked curtleaxe a stain
That our French gallants shall to-day draw out
And sheathe for lack of sport. Let us but blow
on them,
The vapour of our valour will o'erturn them.
'Tis positive 'gainst all exceptions, lords,   25
That our superfluous lackeys and our peasants,
Who in unnecessary action swarm
About our squares of battle, were enow
To purge this field of such a hilding foe,
Though we upon this mountain's basis by   30
Took stand for idle speculation:
But that our honours must not. What's to say?
A very little little let us do,
And all is done. Then let the trumpets sound
The tucket sonance and the note to mount;   35
For our approach shall so much dare the field
That England shall couch down in fear and
yield.

Enter *Grandpré*.

Grand. Why do you stay so long, my lords
of France?
Yond island carrions, desperate of their bones,
Ill-favouredly become the morning field.   40
Their ragged curtains poorly are let loose,
And our air shakes them passing scornfully.
Big Mars seems bankrout in their beggar'd
host
And faintly through a rusty beaver peeps.
The horsemen sit like fixed candlesticks   45
With torch-staves in their hand; and their
poor jades
Lob down their heads, dropping the hides and
hips,
The gum down roping from their pale-dead
eyes,
And in their pale dull mouths the gimmal'd bit
Lies foul with chaw'd grass, still and motionless;
And their executors, the knavish crows,   51
Fly o'er them, all impatient for their hour.
Description cannot suit itself in words
To demonstrate the life of such a battle
In life so liveless as it shows itself.   55
Con. They have said their prayers, and they
stay for death.
Dau. Shall we go send them dinners and
fresh suits
And give their fasting horses provender,
And after fight with them?   59

Con. I stay but for my guidon. To the field!
I will the banner from a trumpet take
And use it for my haste. Come, come away!
The sun is high, and we outwear the day.
                                    Exeunt.

[Scene III. *The English camp.*]

Enter *Gloucester, Bedford, Exeter, Erpingham*
with all his host, *Salisbury,* and *Westmoreland.*

Glouc. Where is the King?

Bed. The King himself is rode to view their
battle.

West. Of fighting men they have full threescore thousand.

Exe. There's five to one; besides, they all
are fresh.

Sal. God's arm strike with us! 'Tis a fearful
odds.   5
God b' wi' you, princes all; I'll to my charge.
If we no more meet till we meet in heaven,
Then joyfully, my noble Lord of Bedford,
My dear Lord Gloucester, and my good Lord
Exeter,
And my kind kinsman, warriors all, adieu!   10

Bed. Farewell, good Salisbury, and good luck
go with thee!

Exe. Farewell, kind lord. Fight valiantly
to-day;
And yet I do thee wrong to mind thee of it,
For thou art fram'd of the firm truth of valour.
                             [*Exit Salisbury.*]

Bed. He is as full of valour as of kindness,
Princely in both.

Enter the *King.*

West.   O that we now had here   16
But one ten thousand of those men in England
That do no work to-day!

King.   What's he that wishes so?
My cousin Westmoreland? No, my fair cousin.
If we are mark'd to die, we are enow   20
To do our country loss; and if to live,
The fewer men, the greater share of honour.
God's will! I pray thee wish not one man more.
By Jove, I am not covetous for gold,
Nor care I who doth feed upon my cost;   25
It yearns me not if men my garments wear;
Such outward things dwell not in my desires:
But if it be a sin to covet honour,
I am the most offending soul alive.
No, faith, my coz, wish not a man from
England.   30

God's peace! I would not lose so great an
honour
As one man more methinks would share from me
For the best hope I have. O, do not wish one
more!
Rather proclaim it, Westmoreland, through my
host,   34
That he which hath no stomach to this fight,
Let him depart; his passport shall be made,
And crowns for convoy put into his purse.
We would not die in that man's company
That fears his fellowship to die with us.
This day is call'd the Feast of Crispian.   40
He that outlives this day, and comes safe home,
Will stand a-tiptoe when this day is nam'd
And rouse him at the name of Crispian.
He that shall live this day, and see old age,
Will yearly on the vigil feast his neighbours 45
And say 'To-morrow is Saint Crispian.'
Then will he strip his sleeve and show his scars,
And say 'These wounds I had on Crispin's day.'
Old men forget; yet all shall be forgot,
But he'll remember, with advantages,   50
What feats he did that day. Then shall our
names,
Familiar in his mouth as household words —
Harry the King, Bedford and Exeter,
Warwick and Talbot, Salisbury and Glouces-
ter —   54
Be in their flowing cups freshly rememb'red.
This story shall the good man teach his son;
And Crispin Crispian shall ne'er go by,
From this day to the ending of the world,
But we in it shall be remembered —   59
We few, we happy few, we band of brothers;
For he to-day that sheds his blood with me
Shall be my brother. Be he ne'er so vile,
This day shall gentle his condition;
And gentlemen in England now abed
Shall think themselves accurs'd they were not
here,   65
And hold their manhoods cheap whiles any
speaks
That fought with us upon Saint Crispin's day.

Enter *Salisbury.*

Sal. My sovereign lord, bestow yourself with
speed.
The French are bravely in their battles set
And will with all expedience charge on us.   70

King. All things are ready, if our minds be so.

West. Perish the man whose mind is backward now!

King. Thou dost not wish more help from
England, coz?

West. God's will, my liege! would you and
I alone, 74
Without more help, could fight this royal battle!
King. Why, now thou hast unwish'd five
thousand men!
Which likes me better than to wish us one.
You know your places. God be with you all!

Tucket. Enter *Montjoy.*

Mont. Once more I come to know of thee,
King Harry,
If for thy ransom thou wilt now compound, 80
Before thy most assured overthrow;
For certainly thou art so near the gulf
Thou needs must be englutted. Besides, in
mercy,
The Constable desires thee thou wilt mind
Thy followers of repentance, that their souls 85
May make a peaceful and a sweet retire
From all these fields, where (wretches!) their
poor bodies
Must lie and fester.
King. Who hath sent thee now?
Mont. The Constable of France.
King. I pray thee bear my former answer
back: 90
Bid them achieve me, and then sell my bones.
Good God! why should they mock poor fellows
thus?
The man that once did sell the lion's skin
While the beast liv'd, was kill'd with hunting
him.
A many of our bodies shall no doubt 95
Find native graves; upon the which, I trust,
Shall witness live in brass of this day's work;
And those that leave their valiant bones in
France,
Dying like men, though buried in your dunghills,
They shall be fam'd; for there the sun shall
greet them 100
And draw their honours reeking up to heaven,
Leaving their earthly parts to choke your clime,
The smell whereof shall breed a plague in
France.
Mark then abounding valour in our English,
That, being dead, like to the bullet's grazing,
Break out into a second course of mischief, 106
Killing in relapse of mortality.
Let me speak proudly. Tell the Constable
We are but warriors for the working day.
Our gayness and our gilt are all besmirch'd 110
With rainy marching in the painful field.
There's not a piece of feather in our host —
Good argument, I hope, we will not fly —
And time hath worn us into slovenry.

But, by the mass, our hearts are in the trim;
And my poor soldiers tell me, yet ere night 116
They'll be in fresher robes, or they will pluck
The gay new coats o'er the French soldiers'
heads
And turn them out of service. If they do this
(As, if God please, they shall), my ransom then
Will soon be levied. Herald, save thou thy
labour. 121
Come thou no more for ransom, gentle herald.
They shall have none, I swear, but these my
joints;
Which if they have as I will leave 'em them,
Shall yield them little, tell the Constable. 125
Mont. I shall, King Harry. And so fare
thee well.
Thou never shalt hear herald any more. *Exit.*
King. I fear thou wilt once more come again
for ransom.

Enter *York.*

York. My lord, most humbly on my knee
I beg
The leading of the vaward. 130
King. Take it, brave York. Now, soldiers,
march away;
And how thou pleasest, God, dispose the day!
Exeunt.

[Scene IV. *The field of battle.*]

Alarum. Excursions. Enter *Pistol, French
Soldier, Boy.*

Pist. Yield, cur!
French. Je pense que vous estes le gentil-
homme de bonne qualité.
Pist. Quality! Callino custore me! Art thou
a gentleman? What is thy name? Discuss.
French. O Seigneur Dieu! 6
Pist. O Signieur Dew should be a gentle-
man.
Perpend my words, O Signieur Dew, and mark.
O Signieur Dew, thou diest on point of fox,
Except, O signieur, thou do give to me 10
Egregious ransom.
French. O, prenez miséricorde! ayez pitié
de moi!
Pist. Moy shall not serve. I will have forty
moys;
Or I will fetch thy rim out at thy throat 15
In drops of crimson blood.
French. Est-il impossible d'eschapper la force
de ton bras?

182

Pist. Brass, cur?
Thou damned and luxurious mountain goat, 20
Offer'st me brass?
French. O, pardonnez-moi!
Pist. Say'st thou me so? Is that a ton of
moys?
Come hither, boy; ask me this slave in French
What is his name. 25
Boy. Escoutez. Comment estes-vous appelé?
French. Monsieur le Fer.
Boy. He says his name is Master Fer.
Pist. Master Fer? I'll fer him, and firk him,
and ferret him! Discuss the same in French
unto him. 31
Boy. I do not know the French for 'fer,' and
'ferret,' and 'firk.'
Pist. Bid him prepare, for I will cut his
throat.
French. Que dit-il, monsieur? 35
Boy. Il me commande à vous dire que vous
faites vous prest; car ce soldat ici est disposé
tout à cette heure de couper vostre gorge.
Pist. Owy, cuppele gorge, permafoy!
Peasant, unless thou give me crowns, brave
crowns; 40
Or mangled shalt thou be by this my sword.
French. O, je vous supplie, pour l'amour de
Dieu, me pardonner! Je suis gentilhomme de
bonne maison. Gardez ma vie, et je vous don-
nerai deux cents escus. 45
Pist. What are his words?
Boy. He prays you to save his life. He is a
gentleman of a good house, and for his ransom
he will give you two hundred crowns.
Pist. Tell him my fury shall abate, and I 50
The crowns will take.
French. Petit monsieur, que dit-il?
Boy. Encore qu'il est contre son jurement de
pardonner aucun prisonnier, néantmoins, pour
les escus que vous l'avez promis, il est content
de vous donner la liberté, le franchisement. 56
French. Sur mes genoux je vous donne mille
remercimens; et je m'estime heureux que je
suis tombé entre les mains d'un chevalier, je
pense, le plus brave, vaillant, et très-distingué
seigneur d'Angleterre. 61
Pist. Expound unto me, boy.
Boy. He gives you, upon his knees, a thousand thanks; and he esteems himself happy
that he hath fall'n into the hands of one (as he
thinks) the most brave, valorous, and thrice-
worthy signieur of England. 67
Pist. As I suck blood, I will some mercy
show!
Follow me, cur. [*Exit.*]

Boy. Suivez-vous le grand Capitaine. [*Exit
French Soldier.*] I did never know so full a voice
issue from so empty a heart; but the saying is
true, 'The empty vessel makes the greatest
sound.' Bardolph and Nym had ten times more
valour than this roaring devil i' th' old play that
every one may pare his nails with a wooden dagger; and they are both hang'd; and so would
this be, if he durst steal anything adventur-
ously. I must stay with the lackeys with the
luggage of our camp. The French might have a
good prey of us, if he knew of it; for there is
none to guard it but boys. *Exit.*

[Scene V. *Another part of the field of
battle.*]

Enter *Constable, Orleans, Bourbon, Dauphin,*
and *Rambures.*

Con. O diable!
Orl. O Seigneur! le jour est perdu, tout est
perdu!
Dau. Mort de ma vie! all is confounded,
all!
Reproach and everlasting shame 4
Sits mocking in our plumes.
                    A short alarum.
O méchante fortune! Do not run away.
Con. Why, all our ranks are broke.
Dau. O perdurable shame! Let's stab our-
selves.
Be these the wretches that we play'd at dice
for?
Orl. Is this the king we sent to for his
ransom?
Bour. Shame, and eternal shame! nothing
but shame! 10
Let's die in honour. Once more back again!
And he that will not follow Bourbon now,
Let him go hence, and with his cap in hand
Like a base pander hold the chamber door
Whilst by a slave, no gentler than my dog, 15
His fairest daughter is contaminated.
Con. Disorder, that hath spoil'd us, friend
us now!
Let us on heaps go offer up our lives.
Orl. We are enow yet living in the field
To smother up the English in our throngs, 20
If any order might be thought upon.
Bour. The devil take order now! I'll to the
throng.
Let life be short; else shame will be too long.
                    Exeunt.

[Scene VI. *Another part of the field.*]

Alarum. Enter the *King* and his *Train,*
[*Exeter,* and others,] with *Prisoners.*

King. Well have we done, thrice-valiant
countrymen;
But all's not done, yet keep the French the
field.

Exe. The Duke of York commends him to
your Majesty.

King. Lives he, good uncle? Thrice within
this hour
I saw him down; thrice up again and fighting.
From helmet to the spur all blood he was.   6

Exe. In which array, brave soldier, doth he
lie,
Larding the plain; and by his bloody side,
Yoke-fellow to his honour-owing wounds,
The noble Earl of Suffolk also lies.   10
Suffolk first died; and York, all haggled over,
Comes to him, where in gore he lay insteep'd,
And takes him by the beard, kisses the gashes
That bloodily did yawn upon his face,   14
And cries aloud, 'Tarry, dear cousin Suffolk!
My soul shall thine keep company to heaven.
Tarry, sweet soul, for mine, then fly abreast;
As in this glorious and well-foughten field
We kept together in our chivalry!'
Upon these words I came and cheer'd him
up.   20
He smil'd me in the face, raught me his
hand,
And, with a feeble gripe, says 'Dear my lord,
Commend my service to my sovereign.'
So did he turn, and over Suffolk's neck
He threw his wounded arm and kiss'd his
lips;   25
And so, espous'd to death, with blood he
seal'd
A testament of noble-ending love.
The pretty and sweet manner of it forc'd
Those waters from me which I would have
stopp'd;
But I had not so much of man in me,   30
And all my mother came into mine eyes
And gave me up to tears.

King.   I blame you not;
For, hearing this, I must perforce compound
With mistful eyes, or they will issue too.
Alarum.
But hark! what new alarum is this same?   35
The French have reinforc'd their scatter'd men.
Then every soldier kill his prisoners!
Give the word through.   *Exeunt.*

[Scene VII. *Another part of the field.*]

Enter *Fluellen* and *Gower.*

Flu. Kill the poys and the luggage? 'Tis
expressly against the law of arms. 'Tis as arrant
a piece of knavery, mark you now, as can be
offert. In your conscience, now, is it not?   4

Gow. 'Tis certain there's not a boy left alive;
and the cowardly rascals that ran from the battle ha' done this slaughter. Besides, they have
burned and carried away all that was in the
King's tent; wherefore the King most worthily
hath caus'd every soldier to cut his prisoner's
throat. O, 'tis a gallant king!   11

Flu. Ay, he was porn at Monmouth, Captain Gower. What call you the town's name
where Alexander the Pig was born?

Gow. Alexander the Great.   15

Flu. Why, I pray you, is not 'pig' great?
The pig, or the great, or the mighty, or the
huge, or the magnanimous are all one reckonings, save the phrase is a little variations.

Gow. I think Alexander the Great was born
in Macedon. His father was called Philip of
Macedon, as I take it.   22

Flu. I think it is in Macedon where Alexander is porn. I tell you, Captain, if you look in
the maps of the orld, I warrant you sall find, in
the comparisons between Macedon and Monmouth, that the situations, look you, is both
alike. There is a river in Macedon, and there is
also moreover a river at Monmouth. It is call'd
Wye at Monmouth; but it is out of my prains
what is the name of the other river. But 'tis all
one; 'tis alike as my fingers is to my fingers,
and there is salmons in both. If you mark
Alexander's life well, Harry of Monmouth's life
is come after it indifferent well; for there is figures in all things. Alexander, God knows and
you know, in his rages, and his furies, and his
wraths, and his cholers, and his moods, and his
displeasures, and his indignations, and also
being a little intoxicates in his prains, did, in his
ales and his angers, look you, kill his best
friend, Cleitus.   41

Gow. Our King is not like him in that. He
never kill'd any of his friends.

Flu. It is not well done, mark you now, to
take the tales out of my mouth ere it is made
and finished. I speak but in the figures and
comparisons of it. As Alexander kill'd his friend
Cleitus, being in his ales and his cups, so also
Harry Monmouth, being in his right wits and
his good judgments, turn'd away the fat knight

THE LIFE
OF
KING HENRY V

PHOTOGRAPHS BY JOHN VICKERS
PRODUCED BY THE OLD VIC COMPANY

Alec Clunes in the role of Henry V,
bluff, valorous king of England

"O God! thy arm was here." Henry
gives thanks after his victory at
Agincourt (*Act IV, Scene VIII*)

Dorothy Tutin as Katharine of France

Henry V, Katharine's English suitor

Exeter (Mark Dignam), King Henry's uncle

Paul Rogers as the Dauphin, the French prince

Right: William Devlin playing
Fluellen, an officer in Henry's army

Below: The comic Pistol (Robert
Eddison), Nell Quickly's husband

Above: Henry V, valiant leader of the English

Right: Chorus (Roger
Livesey) sets the scenes

The French ambassador (Douglas Campbell) delivers his taunt to King Henry (*Act I, Scene II*)

"His nose was as sharp as a pen, and a' babbled of green fields." Mistress Quickly (Nuna Davey) describes the death of Falstaff to his followers (*Act II, Scene III*)

"Come, let's away. My love, give me thy lips." Pistol kisses his wife as he leaves for the army (*Act II, Scene III*)

"Com'st thou again for ransom?" The English king jokingly challenges Montjoy (James Wellman), the French herald (*Act IV, Scene VII*)

Henry has Exeter arrest three of his lords for treason (Act II, Scene II)

"So Chrish save me, I will cut off your head." The Irish captain, Macmorris (Anthony van Bridge), threatens the Welshman, Fluellen (Act III, Scene II)

Below: "Once more unto the breach." Henry exhorts his men before Harfleur (Act III, Scene I)

"I think the king is but a man, as I am." His men fail to recognize Henry as he goes among them in disguise on the eve of battle (Act IV, Scene I)

"We few, we happy few, we band of brothers." Henry speaks to his followers before Agincourt (*Act IV, Scene III*)

"I was not angry since came to France." The king is outraged to find the French have murdered the scullions in the English camp (*Act IV, Scene VII*)

Exeter delivers Henry's ultimatum to the king of France (*Act II, Scene IV*)

"I pray you, fall to." The Welshman Fluellen turns on the mocking Pistol and forces him to eat a leek, emblem of Saint David, patron of Wales (*Act V, Scene I*)

The Dauphin boasts of his horse's prowess (Act III, Scene VII)

Katharine of France with her ladies. *Right Center:* Pauline Jameson as her attendant Alice

'God, the best maker of all marriages, combine your hearts in one." Isabel (Dorothy Green) blesses the union of Katharine and Henry (Act V, Scene II)

"By mine honour, in true English I love thee, Kate." Henry finally abandons his attempts to woo the Princess Katharine in her tongue (Act V, Scene II)

"You have witchcraft in your lips, Kate." Henry's wooing becomes eloquent and poetic (Act V, Scene II)

"You and I cannot be confined within the weak list of a country's fashion." Henry kisses Katharine in spite of protests (Act V, Scene II)

with the great belly doublet. He was full of
ests, and gipes, and knaveries, and mocks. I
ave forgot his name.

Gow. Sir John Falstaff.   54

Flu. That is he. I'll tell you there is good
men porn at Monmouth.

Gow. Here comes his Majesty.

Alarum. Enter *King Harry, [Warwick,
Gloucester, Exeter,* and others,] with *Prisoners. Flourish.*

King. I was not angry since I came to France
Until this instant. Take a trumpet, herald;
Ride thou unto the horsemen on yond hill.   60
If they will fight with us, bid them come down,
Or void the field. They do offend our sight.
If they'll do neither, we will come to them
And make them skirr away as swift as stones
Enforced from the old Assyrian slings.   65
Besides, we'll cut the throats of those we have;
And not a man of them that we shall take
Shall taste our mercy. Go and tell them so.

Enter *Montjoy [the Herald].*

Exe. Here comes the herald of the French,
my liege.

Glouc. His eyes are humbler than they us'd
to be.   70

King. How now? What means this, herald?
Know'st thou not
That I have fin'd these bones of mine for ran-
som?
Com'st thou again for ransom?

Herald.   No, great King.
I come to thee for charitable license
That we may wander o'er this bloody field   75
To look our dead, and then to bury them;
To sort our nobles from our common men;
For many of our princes (woe the while!)
Lie drown'd and soak'd in mercenary blood;
To do our vulgar drench their peasant limbs 80
In blood of princes; and the wounded steeds
Fret fetlock-deep in gore and with wild rage
Yerk out their armed heels at their dead masters,
Killing them twice. O, give us leave, great King,
To view the field in safety and dispose   85
Of their dead bodies!

King.   I tell thee truly, herald,
I know not if the day be ours or no;
For yet a many of your horsemen peer
And gallop o'er the field.

Herald.   The day is yours.

King. Praised be God and not our strength
for it!   90
What is this castle call'd that stands hard by?

Herald. They call it Agincourt.

King. Then call we this the field of Agincourt,
Fought on the day of Crispin Crispianus.   94

Flu. Your grandfather of famous memory,
an't please your Majesty, and your great-
uncle Edward the Plack Prince of Wales, as I
have read in the chronicles, fought a most prave
pattle here in France.

King. They did, Fluellen.   100

Flu. Your Majesty says very true. If your
Majesties is remem'bred of it, the Welshmen
did good service in a garden where leeks did
grow, wearing leeks in their Monmouth caps;
which your Majesty know to this hour is an
honourable badge of the service; and I do believe your Majesty takes no scorn to wear the
leek upon Saint Tavy's day.   108

King. I wear it for a memorable honour;
For I am Welsh, you know, good countryman.

Flu. All the water in Wye cannot wash your
Majesty's Welsh plood out of your pody, I can
tell you that. God pless it and preserve it, as
long as it pleases his grace, and his majesty too!

King. Thanks, good my countryman.   115

Flu. By Jeshu, I am your Majesty's countryman, I care not who know it! I will confess it to
all the orld. I need not to be ashamed of your
Majesty, praised be God, so long as your Majesty is an honest man.   120

King. God keep me so!

Enter *Williams.*

                          Our heralds go with him.
Bring me just notice of the numbers dead
On both our parts.

              [*Exeunt Heralds with Montjoy.*]
                      Call yonder fellow hither.

Exe. Soldier, you must come to the King.

King. Soldier, why wear'st thou that glove
in thy cap?

Will. An't please your Majesty, 'tis the gage
of one that I should fight withal, if he be alive.

King. An Englishman?   129

Will. An't please your Majesty, a rascal that
swagger'd with me last night; who, if 'a live
and ever dare to challenge this glove, I have
sworn to take him a box o' th' ear; or if I can
see my glove in his cap, which he swore, as he
was a soldier, he would wear (if alive), I will
strike it out soundly.   136

King. What think you, Captain Fluellen?
Is it fit this soldier keep his oath?

Flu. He is a craven and a villain else, an't
please your Majesty, in my conscience.   140

185

King. It may be his enemy is a gentleman of great sort, quite from the answer of his degree.

Flu. Though he be as good a gentleman as the devil is, as Lucifer and Belzebub himself, it is necessary, look your Grace, that he keep his vow and his oath. If he be perjur'd, see you now, his reputation is as arrant a villain and a Jacksauce as ever his black shoe trod upon God's ground and his earth, in my conscience, la!   150

King. Then keep thy vow, sirrah, when thou meet'st the fellow.

Will. So I will, my liege, as I live.

King. Who serv'st thou under?

Will. Under Captain Gower, my liege.   155

Flu. Gower is a good captain and is good knowledge and literatured in the wars.

King. Call him hither to me, soldier.

Will. I will, my liege.   *Exit.*

King. Here, Fluellen; wear thou this favour for me and stick it in thy cap. When Alençon and myself were down together, I pluck'd this glove from his helm. If any man challenge this, he is a friend to Alençon and an enemy to our person. If thou encounter any such, apprehend him, an thou dost me love.   166

Flu. Your Grace doo's me as great honours as can be desir'd in the hearts of his subjects. I would fain see the man, that has but two legs, that shall find himself aggrief'd at this glove, that is all. But I would fain see it once, an please God of his grace that I might see.   172

King. Know'st thou Gower?

Flu. He is my dear friend, an please you.

King. Pray thee go seek him and bring him to my tent.   176

Flu. I will fetch him.   *Exit.*

King. My Lord of Warwick, and my brother Gloucester,

Follow Fluellen closely at the heels.
The glove which I have given him for a favour   180
May haply purchase him a box o' th' ear;
It is the soldier's. I by bargain should
Wear it myself. Follow, good cousin War-
wick.
If that the soldier strike him — as I judge
By his blunt bearing, he will keep his word —
Some sudden mischief may arise of it;   186
For I do know Fluellen valiant,
And, touch'd with choler, hot as gunpowder,
And quickly will return an injury.
Follow, and see there be no harm between
them.   190
Go you with me, uncle of Exeter.   *Exeunt.*

[Scene VIII. *Before* King Henry's
pavilion.]

Enter *Gower* and *Williams.*

Will. I warrant it is to knight you, Captain

Enter *Fluellen.*

Flu. God's will and his pleasure, Captain, beseech you now, come apace to the King There is more good toward you peradventure than is in your knowledge to dream of.

Will. Sir, know you this glove?

Flu. Know the glove? I know the glove is a glove.

Will. I know this; and thus I challenge it
                                                Strikes him

Flu. 'Sblood! an arrant traitor as any 's in the universal world, or in France, or in England

Gow. How now, sir? You villain!

Will. Do you think I'll be forsworn?

Flu. Stand away, Captain Gower. I will give treason his payment into plows, I warrant you.   1

Will. I am no traitor.

Flu. That's a lie in thy throat. I charge you in his Majesty's name apprehend him. He's a friend of the Duke Alençon's.

Enter *Warwick* and *Gloucester.*

War. How now, how now? What's the matter?   2

Flu. My Lord of Warwick, here is (praised be God for it!) a most contagious treason come to light, look you, as you shall desire in a summer's day. Here is his Majesty.

Enter *King* and *Exeter.*

King. How now? What's the matter?   2

Flu. My liege, here is a villain and a traitor that, look your Grace, has struck the glove which your Majesty is take out of the helmet of Alençon.

Will. My liege, this was my glove, here is the fellow of it; and he that I gave it to in change promis'd to wear it in his cap. I promis'd to strike him if he did. I met this man with my glove in his cap, and I have been as good a my word.   3

Flu. Your Majesty hear now, saving your Majesty's manhood, what an arrant, rascally beggarly, lousy knave it is! I hope your Majesty is pear me testimony and witness, and will avouchment, that this is the glove of Alençon that your Majesty is give me, in your conscience, now.   4

King. Give me thy glove, soldier. Look, here
is the fellow of it.
'Twas I indeed thou promised'st to strike;
And thou hast given me most bitter terms. 44
Flu. An please your Majesty, let his neck
answer for it, if there is any martial law in the
world.
King. How canst thou make me satisfaction?
Will. All offences, my lord, come from the
heart. Never came any from mine that might
offend your Majesty. 51
King. It was ourself thou didst abuse.
Will. Your Majesty came not like yourself.
You appear'd to me but as a common man;
witness the night, your garments, your lowli-
ness. And what your Highness suffer'd under
that shape, I beseech you take it for your own
fault, and not mine; for had you been as I took
you for, I made no offence. Therefore I beseech
your Highness pardon me. 60
King. Here, uncle Exeter, fill this glove with
crowns
And give it to this fellow. Keep it, fellow,
And wear it for an honour in thy cap
Till I do challenge it. Give him the crowns;
And, Captain, you must needs be friends with
him. 65
Flu. By this day and this light, the fellow has
mettle enough in his belly. Hold, there is twelve
pence for you; and I pray you to serve God,
and keep you out of prawls, and prabbles, and
quarrels, and dissensions, and, I warrant you it
is the better for you. 71
Will. I will none of your money.
Flu. It is with a good will. I can tell you it
will serve you to mend your shoes. Come,
wherefore should you be so pashful? Your
shoes is not so good. 'Tis a good silling, I warrant you, or I will change it. 77

Enter [an English] *Herald.*

King. Now, herald, are the dead numb'red?
Her. Here is the number of the slaught'red
French.   [*Gives a paper.*]
King. What prisoners of good sort are taken,
uncle? 80
Exe. Charles Duke of Orleans, nephew to the
King;
John Duke of Bourbon and Lord Bouciqualt:
Of other lords and barons, knights and squires,
Full fifteen hundred, besides common men.
King. This note doth tell me of ten thousand
French 85
That in the field lie slain. Of princes, in this
number,

And nobles bearing banners, there lie dead
One hundred twenty-six; added to these,
Of knights, esquires, and gallant gentlemen,
Eight thousand and four hundred; of the
which, 90
Five hundred were but yesterday dubb'd
knights;
So that in these ten thousand they have lost
There are but sixteen hundred mercenaries;
The rest are princes, barons, lords, knights,
squires,
And gentlemen of blood and quality. 95
The names of those their nobles that lie dead:
Charles Delabreth, High Constable of France;
Jaques of Chatillon, Admiral of France;
The master of the crossbows, Lord Rambures;
Great Master of France, the brave Sir Guichard
Dauphin; 100
John Duke of Alençon; Anthony Duke of Bra-
bant,
The brother to the Duke of Burgundy;
And Edward Duke of Bar; of lusty earls,
Grandpré and Roussi, Fauconberg and Foix,
Beaumont and Marle, Vaudemont and Lestrale.
Here was a royal fellowship of death! 106
Where is the number of our English dead?
                    [*Herald gives another paper.*]
Edward the Duke of York, the Earl of Suffolk,
Sir Richard Ketly, Davy Gam, Esquire;
None else of name; and of all other men 110
But five-and-twenty. O God, thy arm was here!
And not to us, but to thy arm alone,
Ascribe we all! When, without stratagem,
But in plain shock and even play of battle,
Was ever known so great and little loss 115
On one part and on th' other? Take it, God,
For it is only thine!
Exe.   'Tis wonderful!
King. Come, go we in procession to the
village;
And be it death proclaimed through our host
To boast of this, or take that praise from God
Which is his only. 121
Flu. Is it not lawful, an please your Majesty,
to tell how many is kill'd?
King. Yes, Captain; but with this acknowl-
edgment,
That God fought for us. 125
Flu. Yes, my conscience, he did us great good.
King. Do we all holy rites.
Let there be sung 'Non nobis' and 'Te Deum,'
The dead with charity enclos'd in clay,
And then to Calais; and to England then; 130
Where ne'er from France arriv'd more happy
men.   *Exeunt.*

Enter *Chorus*.

Vouchsafe to those that have not read the
story
That I may prompt them; and of such as
have,
I humbly pray them to admit th' excuse
Of time, of numbers, and due course of things
Which cannot in their huge and proper life   5
Be here presented. Now we bear the King
Toward Calais. Grant him there. There seen,
Heave him away upon your winged thoughts
Athwart the sea. Behold, the English beach
Pales in the flood with men, with wives and
boys,   10
Whose shouts and claps outvoice the deep-
mouth'd sea,
Which, like a mighty whiffler fore the King,
Seems to prepare his way. So let him land,
And solemnly see him set on to London.
So swift a pace hath thought that even now 15
You may imagine him upon Blackheath;
Where that his lords desire him to have borne
His bruised helmet and his bended sword
Before him through the city. He forbids it,
Being free from vainness and self-glorious pride;
Giving full trophy, signal, and ostent   21
Quite from himself to God. But now behold,
In the quick forge and working house of thought,
How London doth pour out her citizens!   24
The Mayor and all his brethren in best sort —
Like to the senators of th' antique Rome,
With the plebeians swarming at their heels —
Go forth and fetch their conqu'ring Cæsar in;
As, by a lower but loving likelihood,   29
Were now the general of our gracious Empress
(As in good time he may) from Ireland coming,
Bringing rebellion broached on his sword,
How many would the peaceful city quit
To welcome him! Much more, and much more
cause,
Did they this Harry. Now in London place
him;   35
As yet the lamentation of the French
Invites the King of England's stay at home;
The Emperor's coming in behalf of France
To order peace between them; and omit
All the occurrences, whatever chanc'd,   40
Till Harry's back-return again to France.
There must we bring him; and myself have
play'd

The interim, by rememb'ring you 'tis past.
Then brook abridgment; and your eyes ad
vance,   4
After your thoughts, straight back again t
France.   *Exi*

[Scene I. *France. The English camp.*]

Enter *Fluellen* and *Gower*.

Gow. Nay, that's right. But why wear yo
your leek to-day? Saint Davy's day is past.
Flu. There is occasions and causes why an
wherefore in all things. I will tell you ass m
friend, Captain Gower. The rascally, scauld
beggarly, lousy, pragging knave, Pistol –
which you and yourself and all the world kno
to be no petter than a fellow, look you now, o
no merits — he is come to me and prings m
pread and salt yesterday, look you, and bid m
eat my leek. It was in a place where I could no
breed no contention with him; but I will be s
bold as to wear it in my cap till I see him onc
again, and then I will tell him a little piece o
my desires.

Enter *Pistol*.

Gow. Why, here he comes, swelling like
turkey cock.   1
Flu. 'Tis no matter for his swellings nor hi
turkey cocks. God pless you, Aunchient Pistol
you scurvy, lousy knave, God pless you!
Pist. Ha! art thou bedlam? Dost tho
thirst, base Troyan,   2
To have me fold up Parca's fatal web?
Hence! I am qualmish at the smell of leek.
Flu. I peseech you heartily, scurvy, lous
knave, at my desires, and my requests, and m
petitions, to eat, look you, this leek. Because
look you, you do not love it, nor your affection
and your appetites and your disgestions doo'
not agree with it, I would desire you to eat it
Pist. Not for Cadwallader and all his goat
Flu. There is one goat for you. (*Strikes him.*
Will you be so good, scauld knave, as eat it?
Pist. Base Troyan, thou shalt die!   3
Flu. You say very true, scauld knave, whe
God's will is. I will desire you to live in th
meantime, and eat your victuals. Come, the
is sauce for it. [*Strikes him.*] You call'd m

yesterday mountain-squire; but I will make
you to-day a squire of low degree. I pray you
all to. If you can mock a leek, you can eat
a leek.   39
  Gow. Enough, Captain. You have aston-
ish'd him.
  Flu. I say I will make him eat some part of
my leek, or I will peat his pate four days. —
Bite, I pray you. It is good for your green
wound and your ploody coxcomb.   45
  Pist. Must I bite?
  Flu. Yes, certainly, and out of doubt, and
out of question too, and ambiguities.
  Pist. By this leek, I will most horribly re-
venge! I eat, and yet, I swear —   50
  Flu. Eat, I pray you. Will you have some
more sauce to your leek? There is not enough
leek to swear by.
  Pist. Quiet thy cudgel. Thou dost see I eat.
  Flu. Much good do you, scauld knave,
heartily. Nay, pray you throw none away.
The skin is good for your broken coxcomb.
When you take occasions to see leeks hereafter,
I pray you mock at 'em; that is all.
  Pist. Good.   60
  Flu. Ay, leeks is good. Hold you, there is a
groat to heal your pate.
  Pist. Me a groat?
  Flu. Yes, verily and in truth, you shall take
it; or I have another leek in my pocket, which
you shall eat.   66
  Pist. I take thy groat in earnest of revenge.
  Flu. If I owe you anything, I will pay you in
cudgels. You shall be a woodmonger and buy
nothing of me but cudgels. God b' wi' you, and
keep you, and heal your pate.   *Exit.*
  Pist. All hell shall stir for this!   72
  Gow. Go, go. You are a counterfeit cowardly
knave. Will you mock at an ancient tradition,
begun upon an honourable respect and worn as
a memorable trophy of predeceased valour, and
dare not avouch in your deeds any of your
words? I have seen you gleeking and galling at
this gentleman twice or thrice. You thought,
because he could not speak English in the native garb, he could not therefore handle an
English cudgel. You find it otherwise; and
henceforth let a Welsh correction teach you a
good English condition. Fare ye well.   *Exit.*
  Pist. Doth Fortune play the huswife with
  me now?   85
News have I, that my Nell is dead i' th' spital
Of malady of France;
And there my rendezvous is quite cut off.
Old I do wax, and from my weary limbs   89

Honour is cudgell'd. Well, bawd will I turn,
And something lean to cutpurse of quick hand.
To England will I steal, and there I'll steal;
And patches will I get unto these cudgell'd
  scars
And swear I got them in the Gallia wars. *Exit.*

[Scene II. *France. The* French King's
          Palace.]

Enter, at one door, *King Henry, Exeter, Bedford,*
[*Gloucester,*] *Warwick,* [*Westmoreland,*] and other
Lords; at another, *Queen Isabel,* the [*French*]
King, the *Duke of Burgundy,* [the *Princess
Katherine, Alice,*] and other *French.*

  King H. Peace to this meeting, wherefore we
  are met!
Unto our brother France and to our sister
Health and fair time of day. Joy and good
  wishes
To our most fair and princely cousin Katherine.
And as a branch and member of this royalty, 5
By whom this great assembly is contriv'd,
We do salute you, Duke of Burgundy.
And, princes French, and peers, health to you
  all!
  France. Right joyous are we to behold your
  face,
Most worthy brother England. Fairly met. 10
So are you, princes English, every one.
  Queen. So happy be the issue, brother
  England,
Of this good day and of this gracious meeting
As we are now glad to behold your eyes — 14
Your eyes which hitherto have borne in them,
Against the French that met them in their bent,
The fatal balls of murthering basilisks.
The venom of such looks, we fairly hope,
Have lost their quality, and that this day 19
Shall change all griefs and quarrels into love.
  King H. To cry amen to that, thus we ap-
  pear.
  Queen. You English princes all, I do salute
  you.
  Burg. My duty to you both, on equal love,
Great Kings of France and England! That I
  have labour'd
With all my wits, my pains, and strong en-
  deavours   25
To bring your most imperial Majesties
Unto this bar and royal interview,
Your mightiness on both parts best can witness.
Since, then, my office hath so far prevail'd

That, face to face and royal eye to eye,   30
You have congreeted, let it not disgrace me
If I demand, before this royal view,
What rub or what impediment there is
Why that the naked, poor, and mangled Peace,
Dear nurse of arts, plenty, and joyful births,
Should not, in this best garden of the world,
Our fertile France, put up her lovely visage.
Alas, she hath from France too long been
    chas'd!
And all her husbandry doth lie on heaps,
Corrupting in it own fertility.   40
Her vine, the merry cheerer of the heart,
Unpruned dies; her hedges even-pleach'd,
Like prisoners wildly overgrown with hair,
Put forth disorder'd twigs; her fallow leas
The darnel, hemlock, and rank fumitory   45
Doth root upon, while that the coulter rusts
That should deracinate such savagery.
The even mead, that erst brought sweetly forth
The freckled cowslip, burnet, and green clover,
Wanting the scythe, all uncorrected, rank,   50
Conceives by idleness and nothing teems
But hateful docks, rough thistles, kecksies,
    burrs,
Losing both beauty and utility.
And as our vineyards, fallows, meads, and
    hedges,   54
Defective in their natures, grow to wildness,
Even so our houses and ourselves and children
Have lost, or do not learn for want of time,
The sciences that should become our country;
But grow like savages — as soldiers will,
That nothing do but meditate on blood —   60
To swearing and stern looks, defus'd attire,
And everything that seems unnatural.
Which to reduce into our former favour
You are assembled; and my speech entreats
That I may know the let why gentle Peace   65
Should not expel these inconveniences
And bless us with her former qualities.
    King H. If, Duke of Burgundy, you would
        the peace
Whose want gives growth to th' imperfections
Which you have cited, you must buy that peace
With full accord to all our just demands;   71
Whose tenures and particular effects
You have, enschedul'd briefly, in your hands.
    Burg. The King hath heard them; to the
        which as yet
There is no answer made.
    King H.   Well then, the peace,   75
Which you before so urg'd, lies in his answer.
    France. I have but with a cursorary eye
O'erglanc'd the articles. Pleaseth your Grace

To appoint some of your Council presently
To sit with us once more, with better heed   80
To resurvey them, we will suddenly
Pass our accept and peremptory answer.
    King H. Brother, we shall. Go, uncle
        Exeter,
And brother Clarence, and you, brother
        Gloucester,   84
Warwick, and Huntingdon — go with the King
And take with you free power to ratify,
Augment, or alter, as your wisdoms best
Shall see advantageable for our dignity,
Anything in or out of our demands;   89
And we'll consign thereto. Will you, fair sis-
        ter,   90
Go with the princes or stay here with us?
    Queen. Our gracious brother, I will go with
        them.
Happily a woman's voice may do some good
When articles too nicely urg'd be stood on.
    King H. Yet leave our cousin Katherine here
        with us.   95
She is our capital demand, compris'd
Within the fore-rank of our articles.
    Queen. She hath good leave.
        Exeunt. Manent King Henry, Katherine,
                and the Gentlewoman [Alice]
    King H.   Fair Katherine, and most fair
Will you vouchsafe to teach a soldier terms
Such as will enter at a lady's ear   100
And plead his love suit to her gentle heart?
    Kath. Your Majesty shall mock at me. I
cannot speak your England.
    King H. O fair Katherine, if you will love me
soundly with your French heart, I will be glad
to hear you confess it brokenly with your
English tongue. Do you like me, Kate?   107
    Kath. Pardonnez-moi, I cannot tell vat is
'like me.'
    King H. An angel is like you, Kate, and you
are like an angel.   111
    Kath. Que dit-il? Que je suis semblable à
les anges?
    Alice. Oui, vraiment, sauf vostre grâce, ainsi
dit-il.
    King H. I said so, dear Katherine, and I
must not blush to affirm it.   117
    Kath. O bon Dieu! les langues des hommes
sont pleines de tromperies.
    King H. What says she, fair one? that the
tongues of men are full of deceits?   121
    Alice. Oui, dat de tongues of de mans is be
full of deceits. Dat is de Princesse.
    King H. The Princess is the better English-
woman. I' faith, Kate, my wooing is fit for thy

understanding. I am glad thou canst speak no better English; for if thou couldst, thou wouldst find me such a plain king that thou wouldst think I had sold my farm to buy my crown. I know no ways to mince it in love but directly to say 'I love you.' Then, if you urge me farther than to say, 'Do you in faith?' I wear out my suit. Give me your answer; i' faith, do! and so clap hands and a bargain. How say you, lady?

Kath. Sauf vostre honneur, me understand well.   136

King H. Marry, if you would put me to verses or to dance for your sake, Kate, why, you undid me. For the one I have neither words nor measure; and for the other I have no strength in measure, yet a reasonable measure in strength. If I could win a lady at leapfrog, or by vaulting into my saddle with my armour on my back, under the correction of bragging be it spoken, I should quickly leap into a wife. Or if I might buffet for my love, or bound my horse for her favours, I could lay on like a butcher and sit like a jackanapes, never off. But, before God, Kate, I cannot look greenly nor gasp out my eloquence, nor I have no cunning in protestation; only downright oaths, which I never use till urg'd, nor never break for urging. If thou canst love a fellow of this temper, Kate, whose face is not worth sunburning, that never looks in his glass for love of anything he sees there, let thine eye be thy cook. I speak to thee plain soldier. If thou canst love me for this, take me; if not, to say to thee that I shall die, is true — but for thy love, by the Lord, no; yet I love thee too. And while thou liv'st, dear Kate, take a fellow of plain and uncoined constancy; for he perforce must do thee right, because he hath not the gift to woo in other places. For these fellows of infinite tongue that can rhyme themselves into ladies' favours, they do always reason themselves out again. What! A speaker is but a prater; a rhyme is but a ballad. A good leg will fall, a straight back will stoop, a black beard will turn white, a curl'd pate will grow bald, a fair face will wither, a full eye will wax hollow; but a good heart, Kate, is the sun and the moon; or rather, the sun, and not the moon, for it shines bright and never changes, but keeps his course truly. If thou would have such a one, take me; and take me, take a soldier; take a soldier, take a king. And what say'st thou then to my love? Speak, my fair — and fairly, I pray thee.

Kath. Is it possible dat I sould love de ennemie of France?   179

King H. No, it is not possible you should love the enemy of France, Kate; but in loving me you should love the friend of France; for I love France so well that I will not part with a village of it — I will have it all mine. And, Kate, when France is mine and I am yours, then yours is France and you are mine.   186

Kath. I cannot tell vat is dat.

King H. No, Kate? I will tell thee in French; which I am sure will hang upon my tongue like a new-married wife about her husband's neck, hardly to be shook off. Quand j'ai la possession de France, et quand vous avez la possession de moi (Let me see, what then? Saint Denis be my speed!), donc vostre est France et vous estes mienne. It is as easy for me, Kate, to conquer the kingdom as to speak so much more French. I shall never move thee in French, unless it be to laugh at me.   198

Kath. Sauf vostre honneur, le François que vous parlez, il est meilleur que l'Anglois lequel je parle.

King H. No, faith, is't not, Kate. But thy speaking of my tongue, and I thine, most trulyfalsely, must needs be granted to be much at one. But, Kate, dost thou understand thus much English? Canst thou love me?   206

Kath. I cannot tell.

King H. Can any of your neighbours tell, Kate? I'll ask them. Come, I know thou lovest me; and at night when you come into your closet, you'll question this gentlewoman about me; and I know, Kate, you will to her dispraise those parts in me that you love with your heart; but, good Kate, mock me mercifully; the rather, gentle Princess, because I love thee cruelly. If ever thou beest mine, Kate — as I have a saving faith within me tells me thou shalt — I get thee with scambling, and thou must therefore needs prove a good soldierbreeder. Shall not thou and I, between Saint Denis and Saint George, compound a boy, half French, half English, that shall go to Constantinople and take the Turk by the beard? Shall we not? What say'st thou, my fair flower-de-luce?

Kath. I do not know dat.   225

King H. No; 'tis hereafter to know, but now to promise. Do but now promise, Kate, you will endeavour for your French part of such a boy; and for my English moiety take the word of a king and a bachelor. How answer you, la plus belle Katherine du monde, mon très-cher et devin déesse?   232

Kath. Your Majestee ave fausse French enough to deceive de most sage damoisell dat is en France. 235

King H. Now, fie upon my false French! By mine honour in true English, I love thee, Kate; by which honour I dare not swear thou lovest me; yet my blood begins to flatter me that thou dost, notwithstanding the poor and untempering effect of my visage. Now beshrew my father's ambition! He was thinking of civil wars when he got me; therefore was I created with a stubborn outside, with an aspect of iron, that, when I come to woo ladies, I fright them. But in faith, Kate, the elder I wax, the better I shall appear. My comfort is, that old age, that ill layer-up of beauty, can do no more spoil upon my face. Thou hast me, if thou hast me, at the worst; and thou shalt wear me, if thou wear me, better and better; and therefore tell me, most fair Katherine, will you have me? Put off your maiden blushes; avouch the thoughts of your heart with the looks of an empress; take me by the hand, and say 'Harry of England, I am thine!' which word thou shalt no sooner bless mine ear withal but I will tell thee aloud 'England is thine, Ireland is thine, France is thine, and Henry Plantagenet is thine'; who, though I speak it before his face, if he be not fellow with the best king, thou shalt find the best king of good fellows. Come, your answer in broken music! for thy voice is music and thy English broken; therefore, queen of all Katherines, break thy mind to me in broken English. Wilt thou have me? 266

Kath. Dat is as it sall please de roi mon père.

King H. Nay, it will please him well, Kate. It shall please him, Kate.

Kath. Den it sall also content me. 270

King H. Upon that I kiss your hand and I call you my queen.

Kath. Laissez, mon seigneur, laissez, laissez! Ma foi, je ne veux point que vous abaissiez vostre grandeur en baisant la main d'une de vostre Seigneurie indigne serviteur. Excusez-moi, je vous supplie, mon très-puissant seigneur.

King H. Then I will kiss your lips, Kate.

Kath. Les dames et demoiselles pour estre baisées devant leur noces, il n'est pas la coutume de France. 281

King H. Madam my interpreter, what says she?

Alice. Dat it is not be de fashon pour de ladies of France — I cannot tell vat is 'baiser' en Anglish. 286

King H. To kiss.

Alice. Your Majestee entendre bettre que moi.

King H. It is not a fashion for the maids in France to kiss before they are married, would she say? 291

Alice. Oui, vraiment.

King H. O Kate, nice customs cursy to great kings. Dear Kate, you and I cannot be confin'd within the weak list of a country's fashion. We are the makers of manners, Kate; and the liberty that follows our places stops the mouth of all find-faults, as I will do yours for upholding the nice fashion of your country in denying me a kiss. Therefore patiently, and yielding. [*Kisses her.*] You have witchcraft in your lips, Kate. There is more eloquence in a sugar touch of them than in the tongues of the French Council, and they should sooner persuade Harry of England than a general petition of monarchs. Here comes your father. 306

Enter the *French Power* and the *English Lords.*

Burg. God save your Majesty! My royal cousin,
Teach you our princess English?

King H. I would have her learn, my fair cousin, how perfectly I love her, and that is good English. 311

Burg. Is she not apt?

King H. Our tongue is rough, coz, and my condition is not smooth; so that, having neither the voice nor the heart of flattery about me, I cannot so conjure up the spirit of love in her that he will appear in his true likeness. 317

Burg. Pardon the frankness of my mirth if I answer you for that. If you would conjure in her, you must make a circle; if conjure up love in her in his true likeness, he must appear naked and blind. Can you blame her then, being a maid yet ros'd over with the virgin crimson of modesty, if she deny the appearance of a naked blind boy in her naked seeing self? It were, my lord, a hard condition for a maid to consign to.

King H. Yet they do wink and yield, as love is blind and enforces.

Burg. They are then excus'd, my lord, when they see not what they do. 330

King H. Then, good my lord, teach your cousin to consent winking.

Burg. I will wink on her to consent, my lord, if you will teach her to know my meaning; for maids well summer'd and warm kept are like flies at Bartholomew-tide, blind, though they have their eyes; and then they will endure

handling which before would not abide looking on.   338

King H. This moral ties me over to time and
a hot summer; and so I shall catch the fly, your
cousin, in the latter end, and she must be
blind too.

Burg. As love is, my lord, before it loves.

King H. It is so; and you may, some of you,
thank love for my blindness, who cannot see
many a fair French city for one fair French
maid that stands in my way.   346

France. Yes, my lord, you see them perspec-
tively — the cities turn'd into a maid; for they
are all girdled with maiden walls that war hath
never ent'red.   350

King H. Shall Kate be my wife?

France. So please you.

King H. I am content, so the maiden cities
you talk of may wait on her. So the maid that
stood in the way for my wish shall show me the
way to my will.   356

France. We have consented to all terms of
reason.

King H. Is't so, my lords of England?

West. The King hath granted every article:
His daughter first; and in sequel, all,   361
According to their firm proposed natures.

Exe. Only he hath not yet subscribed this:
Where your Majesty demands that the King of
France, having any occasion to write for matter
of grant, shall name your Highness in this form
and with this addition, in French, 'Nostre très-
cher fils Henri, Roi d'Angleterre, héritier de
France'; and thus in Latin, 'Praecarissimus
filius noster Henricus, Rex Angliae et haeres
Franciae.'   370

France. Nor this I have not, brother, so
denied
But your request shall make me let it pass.

King H. I pray you then, in love and dear
alliance,
Let that one article rank with the rest,
And thereupon give me your daughter.   375

France. Take her, fair son, and from her
blood raise up
Issue to me, that the contending kingdoms
Of France and England, whose very shores look
pale
With envy of each other's happiness,
May cease their hatred; and this dear con-
junction   380
Plant neighbourhood and Christianlike accord
In their sweet bosoms, that never war advance
His bleeding sword 'twixt England and fair
France.

Lords. Amen!

King H. Now, welcome, Kate; and bear me
witness all   385
That here I kiss her as my sovereign queen.
                                        Flourish.

Queen. God, the best maker of all marriages,
Combine your hearts in one, your realms in
one!
As man and wife, being two, are one in love,
So be there 'twixt your kingdoms such a spousal
That never may ill office, or fell jealousy,   391
Which troubles oft the bed of blessed marriage,
Thrust in between the paction of these king-
doms
To make divorce of their incorporate league;
That English may as French, French English-
men,   395
Receive each other! God speak this Amen!

All. Amen!

King H. Prepare we for our marriage; on
which day,
My Lord of Burgundy, we'll take your oath,
And all the peers', for surety of our leagues.
Then shall I swear to Kate, and you to me,
And may our oaths well kept and prosp'rous be!
                                  Sennet. Exeunt.

[EPILOGUE.]

Enter *Chorus*.

Thus far, with rough and all-unable pen,
  Our bending author hath pursu'd the story,
In little room confining mighty men,
  Mangling by starts the full course of their
  glory.
Small time; but in that small, most greatly
  lived   5
  This Star of England. Fortune made his
  sword;
By which the world's best garden he achieved,
  And of it left his son imperial lord.
Henry the Sixth, in infant bands crown'd King
  Of France and England, did this king suc-
  ceed;   10
Whose state so many had the managing
  That they lost France and made his England
  bleed;
Which oft our stage hath shown; and for their
  sake
In your fair minds let this acceptance take.
                                        [*Exit.*]

For The First Part of King Henry the Sixth the Folio of 1623 is our only authority. The play shows great variety in style and manner, as well as in metre. There is no agreement as to the authorship, but the usual opinion is that Shakespeare's share was small. It seems to be a reworking of one or more older plays. In such a process some scenes might be kept and others replaced by fresh matter covering the same ground, while still others were merely revised. That there were more stages than one in the process is also possible.

In its present form the play might well be called the Tragedy of Talbot. His career is the framework of the structure. The scheme is the struggle of Talbot and Joan, in which he represents the forces of England and righteousness; she the forces of France and demonic malice. Their first encounter is at Orleans, where they fight hand-to-hand (i, 5). A second encounter is at Rouen, where Joan is on the walls and Talbot below (iii, 2). After the battle in which Talbot and his son are killed, Joan exults over their bodies (iv, 7). Finally, Joan is captured by York and condemned to death (v, 3-4). On all but one of these occasions Joan's dealing with devils is emphasized by the English, and immediately before her capture her fiends are actually brought upon the stage and desert her. All these incidents are set forth in a style which marks them as the work of a single author. The scenes in which they occur, and other scenes intimately connected, are by some regarded as too poor to be Shakespeare's and as probably survivals of the old play. One theory is that this play (including almost everything in the Folio text except the undoubtedly Shakespearean scenes) was put together in 1592. If so, it must be the drama mentioned by Nashe in *Pierce Penilesse* (1592): 'How would it have ioyed braue Talbot (the terror of the French) to thinke that after he had lyne two hundred yeares in his Tombe, hee should triumphe againe on the Stage, and haue his bones newe embalmed with the teares of ten thousand spectators at least (at seuerall times) who, in the Tragedian that represents his person, imagine they behold him fresh bleeding.' Nashe seems to be referring to the 'Harey the VI' which Henslowe records as a new play produced on March 3, 1592.

The 1592 play must have included all or most of the Talbot scenes, either in substantially their present form or in some form which that supersedes. How far it drew from lost predecessors is debatable. It is also uncertain whether or not Shakespeare had a hand in its composition. Much of the material that deals with affairs in England is good enough to be his work in 1592, when he was still under the influence of Marlowe, to whom, indeed, a good deal of the Folio text is often ascribed. Greene and Peele have also been suggested as authors in part.

Undoubtedly Shakespearean are the Temple Garden scene (ii, 4) and that in which Talbot summons Bordeaux (iv, 2). One theory is that these were written by Shakespeare in 1594, or later, for a revival of the three plays on Henry VI. Such a revival is probable enough. It may be plausibly inferred from the language of the Epilogue to *Henry the Fifth*. Meres, in 1598, mentions neither *Henry V* nor Henry VI. Perhaps the revival took place in that year, but later than the date on which he wrote (before October 19). The Mortimer scene (ii, 5) and the rhyming Talbot scenes (in Act iv) may also be

Shakespeare's work. The last act of the 1592 play must have ended with the fourth scene, which makes a good formal conclusion. The fifth scene was obviously added to lead up to the *Second Part*. Who wrote it we cannot tell, but it may well enough be Shakespeare's.

For most of the facts the author or authors went to Holinshed or Halle. The play begins with the funeral of Henry V in 1422 and ends in 1444 with the arrangements for the marriage of Henry VI. Chronology is handled with the utmost freedom. For instance, Joan, who was put to death in 1431, takes part in the battle in which Talbot lost his life in 1453.

Much of the play is unhistorical. Purely fictitious are Talbot's capture of Orleans after Joan had forced the English to raise the siege (ii, 1); the romantic episode of Talbot and the Duchess of Auvergne (ii, 2, 34–60; ii, 3); the scene in the Temple Garden (ii, 4); the interview between Richard Plantagenet and Mortimer in the Tower, followed by Mortimer's death (ii, 5); Joan's capture of Rouen and Talbot's recovery of the town on the same day (iii, 2); Fastolfe's cowardice on this occasion (iii, 2); Joan's persuading Burgundy to abandon his English allegiance (iii, 3); Talbot's interview with the French general at Bordeaux (iv, 2); the whole imbroglio between York and Somerset as to the relief of Talbot (iv, 3–4); the wooing of Margaret by Suffolk (v, 3, 45 ff.).

The episode of Talbot and the Duchess is somehow related to an ancient and very popular romance of which Solomon, Don Ramiro II of Leon, and the Bastard of Bouillon appear as the hero in different versions. The substance of the romance was doubtless known to the Elizabethans as an anecdote which might attach itself to any favourite hero. At all events, the tale was current in Scotland in the eighteenth century as the ballad of *John Thomson and the Turk* (Child, No. 266).

On the whole, it seems likely that Shakespeare was the author, at one time or other, of much more of the text than critics admit. Reluctance to make him responsible for the offensive passages concerning Joan of Arc has tempted skepticism, perhaps unduly. The Duke of Bedford, in 1434, termed Joan 'a disciple and limb of the fiend . . . that used false enchantments and sorcery.' She was believed to have been trained by hags of her neighbourhood, which (so the articles of accusation aver) was infamous of old for such practices. The opinion of Shakespeare's day is well illustrated by Cotta, an enlightened physician, skeptical about witchcraft, who refers to her, in 1616, as 'that infamous woman.' Holinshed tells of her association with wicked spirits, says she was 'fullie possest of the feend,' and approves her execution. He likewise repeats the slanderous tale of her attempt to prolong her life by pleading pregnancy. Cauchon, the Bishop of Beauvais, was her judge, and it was not until 1456, twenty-five years after her death, that the proceedings were annulled. In 1909 Joan was beatified, and canonized in 1919. Shakespeare, or whoever it was that wrote the scenes that we find so shocking, could not be expected to criticize the historians whom he consulted. It is enough that he made the Dauphin prophesy: 'Joan la Pucelle shall be France's saint.'

THE FIRST PART OF
KING HENRY THE SIXTH

[Dramatis Personæ.

King Henry the Sixth.
Duke of Gloucester, uncle to the *King*, and Protector.
Duke of Bedford, uncle to the *King*, and Regent of France.
Thomas Beaufort, Duke of Exeter, great-uncle to the *King*.
Henry Beaufort, great-uncle to the *King*, Bishop of Winchester, and afterwards Cardinal.
John Beaufort, Earl of Somerset, afterwards Duke.
Richard Plantagenet, son of Richard late Earl of Cambridge, afterwards Duke of York.
Earl of Warwick.
Earl of Salisbury.
Earl of Suffolk.
Lord Talbot, afterwards Earl of Shrewsbury.
John Talbot, his son.
Edmund Mortimer, Earl of March.
Sir John Fastolfe.
Sir William Lucy.
Sir William Glansdale.
Sir Thomas Gargrave.
Mayor of London.
Woodvile, Lieutenant of the Tower.
Vernon, of the White Rose or York faction.
Basset, of the Red Rose or Lancaster faction.

A Lawyer.
Mortimer's Keepers.

Charles, Dauphin, and afterwards King, of France.
Reignier, Duke of Anjou, and titular King of Naples.
Duke of Burgundy.
Duke of Alençon.
Bastard of Orleans.
Governor of Paris.
Master Gunner of Orleans, and his Son.
General of the French forces in Bordeaux.
A French Sergeant.
A Porter.
An old Shepherd, father to *Joan la Pucelle*.

Margaret, daughter to *Reignier*, afterwards married to *King Henry*.
Countess of Auvergne.
Joan la Pucelle, commonly called *Joan of Arc*.

Fiends appearing to *La Pucelle*.

Lords, Warders of the Tower, Heralds, Officers, Soldiers, Messengers, and several Attendants both on the English and the French.

SCENE. — *Partly in England, partly in France.*]

ACT I. Scene I. [*Westminster Abbey.*]

Dead march. Enter the *Funeral of King Henry the Fifth*, attended on by the *Duke of Bedford* (Regent of France), the *Duke of Gloucester* (Protector), the *Duke of Exeter*, [the *Earl of*] *Warwick*, the *Bishop of Winchester*, and the *Duke of Somerset*, [with *Heralds*, etc.].

Bed. Hung be the heavens with black, yield day to night!
Comets, importing change of times and states,
Brandish your crystal tresses in the sky
And with them scourge the bad revolting stars
That have consented unto Henry's death — 5
King Henry the Fifth, too famous to live long!
England ne'er lost a king of so much worth.
Glou. England ne'er had a king until his time.
Virtue he had, deserving to command;
His brandish'd sword did blind men with his beams · 10

His arms spread wider than a dragon's wings;
His sparkling eyes, replete with wrathful fire,
More dazzled and drove back his enemies
Than midday sun fierce bent against their faces.
What should I say? His deeds exceed all speech.
He ne'er lift up his hand but conquered. 16
Exe. We mourn in black. Why mourn we not in blood?
Henry is dead and never shall revive.
Upon a wooden coffin we attend,
And death's dishonourable victory 20
We with our stately presence glorify,
Like captives bound to a triumphant car.
What? Shall we curse the planets of mishap
That plotted thus our glory's overthrow?
Or shall we think the subtile-witted French 25
Conjurers and sorcerers, that, afraid of him,
By magic verses have contriv'd his end?

197

Win. He was a king bless'd of the King of
    Kings.
Unto the French the dreadful judgment day
So dreadful will not be as was his sight.   30
The battles of the Lord of Hosts he fought;
The church's prayers made him so prosperous.
   Glou. The Church? Where is it? Had not
    churchmen pray'd,
His thread of life had not so soon decay'd.
None do you like but an effeminate prince 35
Whom like a schoolboy you may overawe.
   Win. Gloucester, whate'er we like, thou art
    Protector
And lookest to command the prince and realm.
Thy wife is proud. She holdeth thee in awe
More than God or religious churchmen may.
   Glou. Name not religion, for thou lov'st the
    flesh,   41
And ne'er throughout the year to church thou
    go'st,
Except it be to pray against thy foes.
   Bed. Cease, cease these jars, and rest your
    minds in peace!
Let's to the altar. Heralds, wait on us.   45
Instead of gold we'll offer up our arms,
Since arms avail not, now that Henry's dead.
Posterity, await for wretched years,
When at their mothers' moist eyes babes shall
    suck,
Our isle be made a marish of salt tears,   50
And none but women left to wail the dead.
Henry the Fifth, thy ghost I invocate:
Prosper this realm, keep it from civil broils!
Combat with adverse planets in the heavens!
A far more glorious star thy soul will make 55
Than Julius Cæsar or bright —

Enter a Messenger.

   Mess. My honourable lords, health to you
    all!
Sad tidings bring I to you out of France,
Of loss, of slaughter, and discomfiture.
Guyenne, Champagne, Rheims, Orleans,   60
Paris, Guysors, Poictiers, are all quite lost.
   Bed. What say'st thou, man, before dead
    Henry's corse?
Speak softly, or the loss of those great towns
Will make him burst his lead and rise from
    death.   64
   Glou. Is Paris lost? Is Roan yielded up?
If Henry were recall'd to life again,
These news would cause him once more yield
    the ghost.
   Exe. How were they lost? What treachery
    was us'd?

   Mess. No treachery, but want of men and
    money.
Amongst the soldiers this is muttered,   70
That here you maintain several factions,
And whilst a field should be dispatch'd and
    fought,
You are disputing of your generals.
One would have ling'ring wars, with little cost;
Another would fly swift, but wanteth wings;
A third thinks, without expense at all,   76
By guileful fair words peace may be obtain'd.
Awake, awake, English nobility!
Let not sloth dim your honours new begot.
Cropp'd are the flower-de-luces in your arms;
Of England's coat one half is cut away. [*Exit.*
   Exe. Were our tears wanting to this funeral,
These tidings would call forth their flowing
    tides.
   Bed. Me they concern; Regent I am of
    France.   84
Give me my steeled coat! I'll fight for France.
Away with these disgraceful wailing robes!
Wounds will I lend the French, instead of eyes,
To weep their intermissive miseries.

Enter to them another Messenger.

   Mess. Lords, view these letters, full of bad
    mischance.
France is revolted from the English quite, 90
Except some petty towns of no import.
The Dauphin Charles is crowned king in
    Rheims;
The Bastard of Orleans with him is join'd;
Reignier, Duke of Anjou, doth take his part;
The Duke of Alençon flieth to his side.   *Exit.*
   Exe. The Dauphin crowned king? All fly
    to him?   96
O, whither shall we fly from this reproach?
   Glou. We will not fly, but to our enemies'
    throats!
Bedford, if thou be slack, I'll fight it out.
   Bed. Gloucester, why doubt'st thou of my
    forwardness?   100
An army have I muster'd in my thoughts,
Wherewith already France is overrun.

Enter another Messenger.

   Mess. My gracious lords, to add to your
    laments,
Wherewith you now bedew King Henry's
    hearse,
I must inform you of a dismal fight   105
Betwixt the stout Lord Talbot and the French.
   Win. What? Wherein Talbot overcame, is't
    so?

Mess. O, no! wherein Lord Talbot was o'er-
   thrown.
The circumstance I'll tell you more at large.
The tenth of August last this dreadful lord, 110
Retiring from the siege of Orleans,
Having full scarce six thousand in his troop,
By three-and-twenty thousand of the French
Was round encompassed and set upon.
No leisure had he to enrank his men; 115
He wanted pikes to set before his archers;
Instead whereof, sharp stakes pluck'd out of
   hedges
They pitched in the ground confusedly
To keep the horsemen off from breaking in.
More than three hours the fight continued, 120
Where valiant Talbot above human thought
Enacted wonders with his sword and lance.
Hundreds he sent to hell, and none durst stand
   him;
Here, there, and everywhere enrag'd he slew.
The French exclaim'd the devil was in arms;
All the whole army stood agaz'd on him. 126
His soldiers, spying his undaunted spirit,
'A Talbot! a Talbot!' cried out amain
And rush'd into the bowels of the battle.
Here had the conquest fully been seal'd up 130
If Sir John Fastolfe had not play'd the coward.
He, being in the vaward, plac'd behind
With purpose to relieve and follow them,
Cowardly fled, not having struck one stroke.
Hence grew the general wrack and massacre.
Enclosed were they with their enemies. 136
A base Walloon, to win the Dauphin's grace,
Thrust Talbot with a spear into the back,
Whom all France with their chief assembled
   strength
Durst not presume to look once in the face. 140
   Bed. Is Talbot slain? Then I will slay my-
   self
For living idly here in pomp and ease
Whilst such a worthy leader, wanting aid,
Unto his dastard foemen is betray'd.
   Mess. O, no, he lives, but is took prisoner,
And Lord Scales with him, and Lord Hunger-
   ford; 146
Most of the rest slaughter'd or took likewise.
   Bed. His ransom there is none but I shall
   pay.
I'll hale the Dauphin headlong from his throne;
His crown shall be the ransom of my friend.
Four of their lords I'll change for one of ours.
Farewell, my masters; to my task will I.
Bonfires in France forthwith I am to make
To keep our great Saint George's feast withal.
Ten thousand soldiers with me I will take, 155

Whose bloody deeds shall make all Europe
   quake.
   Mess. So you had need; for Orleans is be-
   sieg'd;
The English army is grown weak and faint;
The Earl of Salisbury craveth supply
And hardly keeps his men from mutiny, 160
Since they, so few, watch such a multitude.
                           [Exit.]
   Exe. Remember, lords, your oaths to Henry
   sworn,
Either to quell the Dauphin utterly
Or bring him in obedience to your yoke.
   Bed. I do remember it, and here take my
   leave 165
To go about my preparation.   *Exit.*
   Glou. I'll to the Tower with all the haste
   I can
To view th' artillery and munition,
And then I will proclaim young Henry king.
                           Exit.
   Exe. To Eltham will I, where the young
   King is, 170
Being ordain'd his special governor,
And for his safety there I'll best devise. *Exit.*
   Win. Each hath his place and function to
   attend:
I am left out; for me nothing remains.
But long I will not be Jack out of office! 175
The King from Eltham I intend to steal
And sit at chiefest stern of public weal. *Exit.*
[Curtain drawn to shut off the bier and Attendants.]

   [Scene II. *France. Before Orleans.*]

Sound a flourish. Enter *Charles [the Dauphin],
Alençon,* and *Reignier,* marching with *Drum*
        and *Soldiers.*

   Char. Mars his true moving, even as in the
   heavens
So in the earth, to this day is not known.
Late did he shine upon the English side;
Now we are victors, upon us he smiles.
What towns of any moment but we have? 5
At pleasure here we lie, near Orleans;
Otherwhiles the famish'd English, like pale
   ghosts,
Faintly besiege us one hour in a month.
   Alen. They want their porridge and their fat
   bull-beeves.
Either they must be dieted like mules 10
And have their provender tied to their mouths
Or piteous they will look, like drowned mice.

Reig. Let's raise the siege. Why live we
idly here?
Talbot is taken, whom we wont to fear.
Remaineth none but mad-brain'd Salisbury, 15
And he may well in fretting spend his gall;
Nor men nor money hath he to make war.
   Char. Sound, sound alarum! We will rush
on them.
Now for the honour of the forlorn French!
Him I forgive my death that killeth me   20
When he sees me go back one foot or fly.
                         Exeunt.

*Here alarum. They are beaten back by the English
with great loss. Enter Charles, Alençon, and
              Reignier.*

   Char. Who ever saw the like? What men
have I!
Dogs! cowards! dastards! I would ne'er have
fled
But that they left me 'midst my enemies.
   Reig. Salisbury is a desperate homicide; 25
He fighteth as one weary of his life.
The other lords, like lions wanting food,
Do rush upon us as their hungry prey.
   Alen. Froissart, a countryman of ours,
records
England all Olivers and Rowlands bred   30
During the time Edward the Third did reign.
More truly now may this be verified;
For none but Samsons and Goliases
It sendeth forth to skirmish. One to ten?
Lean raw-bon'd rascals — who would e'er
suppose   35
They had such courage and audacity?
   Char. Let's leave this town; for they are
harebrain'd slaves,
And hunger will enforce them to be more eager.
Of old I know them. Rather with their teeth
The walls they'll tear down than forsake the
siege.   40
   Reig. I think by some odd gimmors or device
Their arms are set, like clocks, still to strike on.
Else ne'er could they hold out so as they do.
By my consent, we'll even let them alone.
   Alen. Be it so.   45

      Enter the *Bastard of Orleans.*

   Bast. Where's the Prince Dauphin? I have
news for him.
   Dauph. Bastard of Orleans, thrice welcome
to us.
   Bast. Methinks your looks are sad, your
cheer appall'd.
Hath the late overthrow wrought this offence?

Be not dismay'd, for succour is at hand.   50
A holy maid hither with me I bring
Which by a vision sent to her from heaven
Ordained is to raise this tedious siege
And drive the English forth the bounds of
France.
The spirit of deep prophecy she hath,   55
Exceeding the nine Sibyls of old Rome:
What's past and what's to come she can descry.
Speak, shall I call her in? Believe my words,
For they are certain and unfallible.
   Dauph. Go, call her in. [*Exit Bastard.*] But
first, to try her skill,   60
Reignier, stand thou as Dauphin in my place:
Question her proudly; let thy looks be stern.
By this means shall we sound what skill she
hath.   [*Steps back.*]

    Enter *Joan Pucelle* [and *Bastard*].

   Reig. Fair maid, is't thou wilt do these won-
drous feats?
   Puc. Reignier, is't thou that thinkest to be-
guile me?   65
Where is the Dauphin? Come, come from be-
hind.
I know thee well, though never seen before.
Be not amaz'd; there's nothing hid from me.
In private will I talk with thee apart.   !69
Stand back, you lords, and give us leave awhile.
   Reig. She takes upon her bravely at first
dash.
   Puc. Dauphin, I am by birth a shepherd's
daughter,
My wit untrain'd in any kind of art.
Heaven and our Lady gracious hath it pleas'd
To shine on my contemptible estate.   75
Lo, whilst I waited on my tender lambs
And to sun's parching heat display'd my cheeks,
God's Mother deigned to appear to me,
And in a vision full of majesty
Will'd me to leave my base vocation   80
And free my country from calamity;
Her aid she promis'd and assur'd success.
In complete glory she reveal'd herself;
And whereas I was black and swart before, 84
With those clear rays which she infus'd on me
That beauty am I blest with which you see.
Ask me what question thou canst possible,
And I will answer unpremeditated.
My courage try by combat, if thou dar'st,
And thou shalt find that I exceed my sex.   90
Resolve on this: thou shalt be fortunate
If thou receive me for thy warlike mate.
   Dauph. Thou hast astonish'd me with thy
high terms.

Only this proof I'll of thy valour make:
In single combat thou shalt buckle with me, 95
And if thou vanquishest, thy words are true;
Otherwise I renounce all confidence.

Puc. I am prepar'd. Here is my keen-edg'd
sword,
Deck'd with five flower-de-luces on each side,
The which at Touraine in Saint Katherine's
churchyard 100
Out of a great deal of old iron I chose forth.

Dauph. Then come, a God's name! I fear
no woman.

Puc. And while I live, I'll ne'er fly from a
man.

Here they fight, and Joan la Pucelle overcomes.

Dauph. Stay, stay thy hands! Thou art an
Amazon
And fightest with the sword of Deborah. 105

Puc. Christ's Mother helps me, else I were
too weak.

Dauph. Whoe'er helps thee, 'tis thou that
must help me!
Impatiently I burn with thy desire;
My heart and hands thou hast at once subdu'd.
Excellent Pucelle, if thy name be so, 110
Let me thy servant and not sovereign be.
'Tis the French Dauphin sueth to thee thus.

Puc. I must not yield to any rites of love,
For my profession's sacred from above. 114
When I have chased all thy foes from hence,
Then will I think upon a recompense.

Dauph. Meantime look gracious on thy
prostrate thrall.

Reig. My lord, methinks, is very long in talk.

Alen. Doubtless he shrives this woman to
her smock; 119
Else ne'er could he so long protract his speech.

Reig. Shall we disturb him, since he keeps
no mean?

Alen. He may mean more than we poor men
do know.
These women are shrewd tempters with their
tongues.

Reig. My lord, where are you? What devise you on?
Shall we give o'er Orleans, or no? 125

Puc. Why, no, I say! Distrustful recreants,
Fight till the last gasp. I will be your guard.

Dauph. What she says, I'll confirm. We'll
fight it out.

Puc. Assign'd am I to be the English scourge.
This night the siege assuredly I'll raise. 130
Expect Saint Martin's summer, halcyon days,
Since I have entered into these wars.

Glory is like a circle in the water,
Which never ceaseth to enlarge itself 134
Till by broad spreading it disperse to naught.
With Henry's death the English circle ends;
Dispersed are the glories it included.
Now am I like that proud insulting ship
Which Cæsar and his fortune bare at once.

Dauph. Was Mahomet inspired with a dove?
Thou with an eagle art inspired then! 141
Helen, the mother of great Constantine,
Nor yet Saint Philip's daughters, were like
thee.
Bright star of Venus, fall'n down on the earth,
How may I reverently worship thee enough?

Alen. Leave off delays and let us raise the
siege. 146

Reig. Woman, do what thou canst to save
our honours.
Drive them from Orleans and be immortaliz'd.

Dauph. Presently we'll try. Come, let's
away about it.
No prophet will I trust if she prove false. 150
Exeunt.

[Scene III. *London. Before the Tower
gates.*]

Enter *Gloucester*, with his *Servingmen*
[in blue coats].

Glou. I am come to survey the Tower this
day.
Since Henry's death I fear there is convey-
ance.
Where be these warders that they wait not
here?
Open the gates! 'Tis Gloucester that calls.
[*Servingmen knock.*]

1. Warder. [*within*] Who's there that knocks
so imperiously? 5

Glouc.'s 1. Man. It is the noble Duke of
Gloucester.

2. Warder. [*within*] Whoe'er he be, you may
not be let in.

1. Man. Villains, answer you so the Lord
Protector?

1. Warder. [*within*] The Lord protect him!
So we answer him.
We do no otherwise than we are will'd. 10

Glou. Who willed you? or whose will stands
but mine?
There's none Protector of the realm but I.
Break up the gates! I'll be your warrantize.
Shall I be flouted thus by dunghill grooms?

*Gloucester's men rush at the Tower gates, and
Woodvile the Lieutenant speaks within.*

Wood. What noise is this? What traitors
    have we here?   15
Glou. Lieutenant, is it you whose voice I
    hear?
Open the gates. Here's Gloucester that would
    enter.
Wood. Have patience, noble Duke. I may
    not open;
The Cardinal of Winchester forbids.
From him I have express commandëment   20
That thou nor none of thine shall be let in.
Glou. Faint-hearted Woodvile, prizest him
    fore me?
Arrogant Winchester, that haughty prelate,
Whom Henry, our late sovereign, ne'er could
    brook?
Thou art no friend to God or to the King. 25
Open the gates, or I'll shut thee out shortly.
Servingmen. Open the gates unto the Lord
    Protector!
Or we'll burst them open if that you come not
    quickly.

Enter to the Protector *at the Tower gates*
Winchester, *and his* Men *in tawny coats.*

Win. How now, ambitious Humphrey?
    What means this?
Glou. Peel'd priest, dost thou command me
    to be shut out?   30
Win. I do, thou most usurping Proditor,
And not Protector of the King or realm.
Glou. Stand back, thou manifest conspirator,
Thou that contrivedst to murther our dead lord,
Thou that giv'st whores indulgences to sin. 35
I'll canvass thee in thy broad cardinal's hat
If thou proceed in this thy insolence.
Win. Nay, stand thou back! I will not budge
    a foot.
This be Damascus, be thou cursed Cain,
To slay thy brother Abel, if thou wilt.   40
Glou. I will not slay thee, but I'll drive thee
    back.
Thy scarlet robes as a child's bearing cloth
I'll use to carry thee out of this place.
Win. Do what thou dar'st! I beard thee to
    thy face.
Glou. What? Am I dar'd, and bearded to
    my face?   45
Draw, men, for all this privileged place.
Blue-coats to tawny-coats! Priest, beware your
    beard.
I mean to tug it and to cuff you soundly

Under my feet I stamp thy cardinal's hat.
In spite of Pope or dignities of Church,   50
Here by the cheeks I'll drag thee up and down.
Win. Gloucester, thou wilt answer this be-
    fore the Pope.
Glou. Winchester goose! I cry a rope! a rope!
Now beat them hence. Why do you let them stay?
Thee I'll chase hence, thou wolf in sheep's array.
Out, tawny-coats! Out, scarlet hypocrite!   56

Here Gloucester's Men *beat out the* Cardinal's
Men; *and enter in the hurly-burly the* Mayor
of London and his Officers.

May. Fie, lords, that you, being supreme
    magistrates,
Thus contumeliously should break the peace!
Glou. Peace, Mayor! Thou know'st little of
    my wrongs.   59
Here's Beaufort, that regards nor God nor king,
Hath here distrain'd the Tower to his use.
Win. Here's Gloucester, a foe to citizens,
One that still motions war and never peace,
O'ercharging your free purses with large fines,
That seeks to overthrow religion   65
Because he is Protector of the realm,
And would have armour here out of the Tower
To crown himself king and suppress the Prince.
Glou. I will not answer thee with words, but
    blows.   *Here they skirmish again.*
May. Naught rests for me in this tumultuous
    strife   70
But to make open proclamation.
Come, officer; as loud as e'er thou canst.

[The Officer] cries [out, reading the proclamation]:

    All manner of men assembled here in arms this
day against God's peace and the King's, we charge
and command you, in his Highness' name, to repair to your several dwelling places, and not to
wear, handle, or use any sword, weapon, or dagger
henceforward, upon pain of death.

Glou. Cardinal, I'll be no breaker of the law;
But we shall meet and break our minds at large.
Win. Gloucester, we'll meet to thy cost, be
    sure: 82
Thy heart-blood I will have for this day's work.
May. I'll call for clubs if you will not away.
This cardinal's more haughty than the devil.
Glou. Mayor, farewell. Thou dost but what
    thou mayst.   86
Win. Abominable Gloucester, guard thy
    head;
For I intend to have it ere long.
    *Exeunt [Gloucester and Winchester with their
                                    Servingmen].*

May. See the coast clear'd, and then we will
 depart.
Good God, these nobles should such stomachs
 bear!   90
I myself fight not once in forty year. *Exeunt.*

[Scene IV. *Orleans.*]

Enter [on the walls] the *Master Gunner*
 of Orleans and his *Boy.*

M. Gun. Sirrah, thou know'st how Orleans
 is besieg'd
And how the English have the suburbs won.
Boy. Father, I know, and oft have shot at
 them,
Howe'er unfortunate I miss'd my aim.
M. Gun. But now thou shalt not. Be thou
 rul'd by me.   5
Chief master gunner am I of this town;
Something I must do to procure me grace.
The Prince's espials have informed me
How the English, in the suburbs close in-
 trench'd,
Wont through a secret grate of iron bars   10
In yonder tower to overpeer the city,
And thence discover how with most advantage
They may vex us with shot or with assault.
To intercept this inconvenience
A piece of ordnance 'gainst it I have plac'd, 15
And even these three days have I watch'd,
If I could see them.
Now do thou watch, for I can stay no longer.
If thou spy'st any, run and bring me word,
And thou shalt find me at the Governor's.   20
                                        Exit.
Boy. Father, I warrant you; take you no
 care.
I'll never trouble you if I may spy them. *Exit.*

Enter *Salisbury* and *Talbot* on the turrets, with
[*Sir William Glansdale, Sir Thomas Gargrave,*
 and] others.

Sal. Talbot, my life, my joy, again return'd?
How wert thou handled being prisoner,   24
Or by what means got'st thou to be releas'd?
Discourse, I prithee, on this turret's top.
Tal. The Duke of Bedford had a prisoner
Call'd the brave Lord Ponton de Santrailles;
For him was I exchang'd and ransomed.
But with a baser man-of-arms by far   30
Once in contempt they would have barter'd me;
Which I disdaining scorn'd, and craved death
Rather than I would be so vile esteem'd.

In fine, redeem'd I was as I desir'd.
But, O, the treacherous Fastolfe wounds my
 heart!   35
Whom with my bare fists I would execute
If I now had him brought into my power.
Sal. Yet tell'st thou not how thou wert en-
 tertain'd.
Tal. With scoffs and scorns and contumeli-
 ous taunts
In open market place produc'd they me   40
To be a public spectacle to all.
'Here,' said they, 'is the terror of the French,
The scarecrow that affrights our children so.'
Then broke I from the officers that led me
And with my nails digg'd stones out of the
 ground   45
To hurl at the beholders of my shame.
My grisly countenance made others fly;
None durst come near for fear of sudden death.
In iron walls they deem'd me not secure;
So great fear of my name 'mongst them was
 spread   50
That they suppos'd I could rend bars of steel
And spurn in pieces posts of adamant.
Wherefore a guard of chosen shot I had
That walk'd about me every minute while;
And if I did but stir out of my bed,   55
Ready they were to shoot me to the heart.

Enter the *Boy* with a linstock.

Sal. I grieve to hear what torments you
 endur'd,
But we will be reveng'd sufficiently.
Now it is supper time in Orleans.   59
Here, through this secret grate, I count each one
And view the Frenchmen how they fortify.
Let us look in; the sight will much delight thee.
Sir Thomas Gargrave and Sir William Glans-
 dale,
Let me have your express opinions   64
Where is best place to make our batt'ry next.
Gar. I think at the north gate, for there
 stand lords.
Glan. And I here, at the bulwark of the
 bridge.
Tal. For aught I see, this city must be
 famish'd
Or with light skirmishes enfeebled.
      Here they shoot, and Salisbury [and Gar-
                        grave] fall down.
Sal. O Lord have mercy on us, wretched
 sinners!   70
Gar. O Lord have mercy on me, woful man!
Tal. What chance is this that suddenly hath
 cross'd us?

Speak, Salisbury; at least, if thou canst speak.
How far'st thou, mirror of all martial men? 74
One of thy eyes and thy cheek's side struck
off?
Accursed tower! Accursed fatal hand
That hath contriv'd this woful tragedy!
In thirteen battles Salisbury o'ercame;
Henry the Fifth he first train'd to the wars;
Whilst any trump did sound or drum struck
up   80
His sword did ne'er leave striking in the
field.
Yet liv'st thou, Salisbury? Though thy speech
doth fail,
One eye thou hast to look to heaven for
grace.
The sun with one eye vieweth all the world.
Heaven, be thou gracious to none alive   85
If Salisbury wants mercy at thy hands!
Bear hence his body; I will help to bury it.
Sir Thomas Gargrave, hast thou any life?
Speak unto Talbot. Nay, look up to him.
Salisbury, cheer thy spirit with this comfort, 90
Thou shalt not die whiles —
He beckons with his hand and smiles on me,
As who should say 'When I am dead and
gone,
Remember to avenge me on the French.'
Plantagenet, I will, and like thee, Nero,   95
Play on the lute, beholding the towns burn.
Wretched shall France be only in my name.
   Here an alarum, and it thunders and lightens.
What stir is this? What tumult's in the
heavens?
Whence cometh this alarum and the noise?

Enter a *Messenger.*

Mess. My lord, my lord, the French have
   gather'd head!   100
The Dauphin, with one Joan la Pucelle join'd,
A holy prophetess new risen up,
Is come with a great power to raise the siege.
   Here Salisbury lifteth himself up and groans.
Tal. Hear, hear, how dying Salisbury doth
   groan!
It irks his heart he cannot be reveng'd.   105
Frenchmen, I'll be a Salisbury to you.
Pucelle or Pussel, Dolphin or Dogfish,
Your hearts I'll stamp out with my horse's
heels
And make a quagmire of your mingled brains.
Convey me Salisbury into his tent,   110
And then we'll try what these dastard French-
men dare.
   Alarum. Exeunt [with the bodies].

[Scene V. *Before Orleans.*]

*Here an alarum again, and Talbot pursueth the
Dauphin and driveth him.* Then enter *Joan la
Pucelle,* driving Englishmen before her [and
exit]. Then enter *Talbot.*

Tal. Where is my strength, my valour, and
   my force?
Our English troops retire, I cannot stay them;
A woman clad in armour chaseth them.

Enter *Pucelle.*

Here, here she comes. I'll have a bout with
   thee.
Devil or devil's dam, I'll conjure thee.   5
Blood will I draw on thee — thou art a witch —
And straightway give thy soul to him thou
serv'st.
Puc. Come, come, 'tis only I that must dis-
   grace thee.   *Here they fight.*
Tal. Heavens, can you suffer hell so to
   prevail?
My breast I'll burst with straining of my
courage   10
And from my shoulders crack my arms asunder
But I will chastise this high-minded strumpet.
            They fight again.
Puc. Talbot, farewell; thy hour is not yet
come.
I must go victual Orleans forthwith.

A short alarum. Then enter the town
         with *Soldiers.*

O'ertake me if thou canst! I scorn thy strength.
Go, go, cheer up thy hungry starved men.   16
Help Salisbury to make his testament.
This day is ours, as many more shall be. *Exit.*
Tal. My thoughts are whirled like a potter's
wheel;
I know not where I am nor what I do.   20
A witch by fear, not force, like Hannibal,
Drives back our troops and conquers as she lists.
So bees with smoke and doves with noisome
stench
Are from their hives and houses driven away.
They call'd us, for our fierceness, English dogs;
Now, like to whelps, we crying run away.   26
                A short alarum.
Hark, countrymen! Either renew the fight
Or tear the lions out of England's coat,
Renounce your soil, give sheep in lions' stead.
Sheep run not half so treacherous from the wolf,
Or horse or oxen from the leopard,   31

As you fly from your oft-subdued slaves.
Alarum. Here another skirmish.
It will not be. Retire into your trenches.
You all consented unto Salisbury's death,
For none would strike a stroke in his revenge.
Pucelle is ent'red into Orleans   36
In spite of us or aught that we could do.
O, would I were to die with Salisbury!
The shame hereof will make me hide my head.
Exit.
Alarum. Retreat.

[Scene VI. *Orleans.*]

Flourish. Enter, on the walls, *Pucelle, Dauphin, Reignier, Alençon,* and *Soldiers.*

Puc. Advance our waving colours on the walls;
Rescu'd is Orleans from the English.
Thus Joan la Pucelle hath perform'd her word.
Dauph. Divinest creature, Astræa's daughter,
How shall I honour thee for this success?   5
Thy promises are like Adonis' gardens,
That one day bloom'd and fruitful were the next.
France, triumph in thy glorious prophetess!

Recover'd is the town of Orleans.
More blessed hap did ne'er befall our state. 10
Reig. Why ring not out the bells aloud
throughout the town?
Dauphin, command the citizens make bonfires
And feast and banquet in the open streets
To celebrate the joy that God hath given us.
Alen. All France will be replete with mirth
and joy   15
When they shall hear how we have play'd the
men.
Dauph. 'Tis Joan, not we, by whom the day
is won;
For which I will divide my crown with her,
And all the priests and friars in my realm
Shall in procession sing her endless praise.   20
A statelier pyramis to her I'll rear
Than Rhodope's of Memphis ever was.
In memory of her, when she is dead,
Her ashes, in an urn more precious
Than the rich-jewell'd coffer of Darius,   25
Transported shall be at high festivals
Before the kings and queens of France.
No longer on Saint Denis will we cry,
But Joan la Pucelle shall be France's saint.
Come in, and let us banquet royally   30
After this golden day of victory.
Flourish. Exeunt.

ACT II. Scene I. [*Orleans.*]

Enter a [*French*] *Sergeant of a Band,*
with two *Sentinels.*

Serg. Sirs, take your places and be vigilant.
If any noise or soldier you perceive
Near to the walls, by some apparent sign
Let us have knowledge at the court of guard.
Sentinel. Sergeant, you shall. [*Exit Sergeant.*] Thus are poor servitors,   5
When others sleep upon their quiet beds,
Constrain'd to watch in darkness, rain, and
cold.

Enter *Talbot, Bedford,* and *Burgundy,* [and *Forces,*] with scaling ladders, their *Drums* beating a dead march.

Tal. Lord Regent, and redoubted Burgundy,
By whose approach the regions of Artois,
Wallon, and Picardy are friends to us,   10
This happy night the Frenchmen are secure,
Having all day carous'd and banqueted.
Embrace we then this opportunity,
As fitting best to quittance their deceit,
Contriv'd by art and baleful sorcery.   15

Bed. Coward of France! How much he
wrongs his fame,
Despairing of his own arm's fortitude,
To join with witches and the help of hell!
Bur. Traitors have never other company.
But what's that Pucelle whom they term so
pure?   20
Tal. A maid, they say.
Bed.   A maid? and be so martial?
Bur. Pray God she prove not masculine ere
long,
If underneath the standard of the French
She carry armour as she hath begun.
Tal. Well, let them practise and converse
with spirits.   25
God is our fortress, in whose conquering name
Let us resolve to scale their flinty bulwarks.
Bed. Ascend, brave Talbot. We will follow
thee.
Tal. Not all together. Better far, I guess,
That we do make our entrance several ways; 3C
That, if it chance the one of us do fail,
The other yet may rise against their force.

205

Bed. Agreed. I'll to yond corner.
Bur.   And I to this.
Tal. And here will Talbot mount, or make
his grave.
Now, Salisbury, for thee, and for the right   35
Of English Henry! Shall this night appear
How much in duty I am bound to both.
Sentinel. Arm! arm! The enemy doth make
assault!

[*The English scale the walls.*] *Cry:*
'Saint George! a Talbot!'

The French leap o'er the walls in their shirts.
Enter, several ways, *Bastard [of Orleans], Alençon, Reignier,* half ready and half unready.

Alen. How now, my lords? What, all un-
ready so?
Bast. Unready? Ay, and glad we scap'd so
well.   40
Reig. 'Twas time, I trow, to wake and leave
our beds,
Hearing alarums at our chamber doors.
Alen. Of all exploits since first I follow'd
arms
Ne'er heard I of a warlike enterprise
More venturous or desperate than this.   45
Bast. I think this Talbot be a fiend of hell.
Reig. If not of hell, the heavens sure favour
him.
Alen. Here cometh Charles. I marvel how
he sped.

Enter *Charles* [the *Dauphin*] and *Joan.*

Bast. Tut! holy Joan was his defensive
guard.
Char. Is this thy cunning, thou deceitful
dame?   50
Didst thou at first, to flatter us withal,
Make us partakers of a little gain
That now our loss might be ten times so much?
Joan. Wherefore is Charles impatient with
his friend?
At all times will you have my power alike?   55
Sleeping or waking must I still prevail,
Or will you blame and lay the fault on me?
Improvident soldiers, had your watch been
good,
This sudden mischief never could have fall'n!
Char. Duke of Alençon, this was your de-
fault   60
That, being captain of the watch to-night,
Did look no better to that weighty charge.
Alen. Had all your quarters been as safely
kept

As that whereof I had the government,
We had not been thus shamefully surpris'd.   65
Bast. Mine was secure.
Reig.   And so was mine, my lord.
Char. And for myself, most part of all this
night
Within her quarter and mine own precinct
I was employ'd in passing to and fro
About relieving of the sentinels.   70
Then how or which way should they first break
in?
Joan. Question, my lords, no further of the
case,
How or which way. 'Tis sure they found some
place
But weakly guarded, where the breach was
made.
And now there rests no other shift but this — 75
To gather our soldiers, scatter'd and dispers'd,
And lay new platforms to endamage them.

Alarum. Enter a *Soldier,* crying 'A Talbot! a
Talbot!' *They fly, leaving their clothes behind.*

Sold. I'll be so bold to take what they have
left.
The cry of 'Talbot' serves me for a sword;
For I have loaden me with many spoils,   80
Using no other weapon but his name.   *Exit.*

[Scene II. *Orleans. Within the town.*]

Enter *Talbot, Bedford, Burgundy,* [a *Captain,
and others*].

Bed. The day begins to break and night is
fled,
Whose pitchy mantle overveil'd the earth.
Here sound retreat and cease our hot pursuit.
                                Retreat [sounded].
Tal. Bring forth the body of old Salisbury
And here advance it in the market place,   5
The middle centre of this cursed town.
Now have I paid my vow unto his soul:
For every drop of blood was drawn from him
There hath at least five Frenchmen died to-
night.
And that hereafter ages may behold   10
What ruin happened in revenge of him,
Within their chiefest temple I'll erect
A tomb, wherein his corpse shall be interr'd;
Upon the which, that every one may read,
Shall be engrav'd the sack of Orleans,   15
The treacherous manner of his mournful death,
And what a terror he had been to France.

But, lords, in all our bloody massacre,
I muse we met not with the Dauphin's Grace,
His new-come champion, virtuous Joan of Arc,
Nor any of his false confederates.   21
  Bed. 'Tis thought, Lord Talbot, when the
        fight began,
Rous'd on the sudden from their drowsy beds,
They did amongst the troops of armed men
Leap o'er the walls for refuge in the field.   25
  Bur. Myself, as far as I could well discern
For smoke and dusky vapours of the night,
Am sure I scar'd the Dauphin and his trull,
When arm in arm they both came swifty run-
        ning,
Like to a pair of loving turtledoves   30
That could not live asunder day or night.
After that things are set in order here,
We'll follow them with all the power we have.

          Enter a *Messenger*.

  Mess. All hail, my lords! Which of this
        princely train
Call ye the warlike Talbot, for his acts   35
So much applauded through the realm of
        France?
  Tal. Here is the Talbot. Who would speak
        with him?
  Mess. The virtuous lady, Countess of
        Auvergne,
With modesty admiring thy renown,
By me entreats, great lord, thou wouldst vouch-
        safe   40
To visit her poor castle where she lies,
That she may boast she hath beheld the man
Whose glory fills the world with loud report.
  Bur. Is it even so? Nay, then I see our wars
Will turn unto a peaceful comic sport,   45
When ladies crave to be encount'red with.
You may not, my lord, despise her gentle suit.
  Tal. Ne'er trust me then; for when a world
        of men
Could not prevail with all their oratory,
Yet hath a woman's kindness overrul'd;   50
And therefore tell her I return great thanks
And in submission will attend on her.
Will not your honours bear me company?
  Bed. No, truly! 'tis more than manners will;
And I have heard it said, unbidden guests   55
Are often welcomest when they are gone.
  Tal. Well then, alone (since there's no remedy)
I mean to prove this lady's courtesy.
Come hither, Captain. (*Whispers.*) You per-
        ceive my mind?
  Capt. I do, my lord, and mean accordingly.
                                           Exeunt

          [Scene III. *Auvergne. The Castle of
                  the* Countess.]

          Enter *Countess* [and her *Porter*].

  Count. Porter, remember what I gave in
        charge,
And when you have done so, bring the keys to
        me.
  Port. Madam, I will.   *Exit.*
  Count. The plot is laid. If all things fall out
        right,
I shall as famous be by this exploit   5
As Scythian Tomyris by Cyrus' death.
Great is the rumour of this dreadful knight,
And his achievements of no less account.
Fain would mine eyes be witness with mine ears,
To give their censure of these rare reports.   10

          Enter *Messenger* and *Talbot*.

  Mess. Madam,
According as your ladyship desir'd,
By message crav'd, so is Lord Talbot come.
  Count. And he is welcome. What? Is this
        the man?
  Mess. Madam, it is.
  Count. Is this the scourge of France?   15
Is this the Talbot, so much fear'd abroad
That with his name the mothers still their
        babes?
I see report is fabulous and false.
I thought I should have seen some Hercules,
A second Hector, for his grim aspect   20
And large proportion of his strong-knit limbs.
Alas, this is a child, a silly dwarf!
It cannot be this weak and writhled shrimp
Should strike such terror to his enemies.
  Tal. Madam, I have been bold to trouble
        you;   25
But since your ladyship is not at leisure,
I'll sort some other time to visit you. [*Going.*]
  Count. What means he now? Go ask him
        whither he goes.
  Mess. Stay, my Lord Talbot; for my lady
        craves
To know the cause of your abrupt departure. 30
  Tal. Marry, for that she's in a wrong belief,
I go to certify her Talbot's here.

          Enter *Porter* with keys.

  Count. If thou be he, then art thou prisoner.
  Tal. Prisoner? to whom?
  Count.   To me, bloodthirsty lord!
And for that cause I train'd thee to my house. 35
Long time thy shadow hath been thrall to me,

For in my gallery thy picture hangs;
But now the substance shall endure the like,
And I will chain these legs and arms of thine
That hast by tyranny these many years   40
Wasted our country, slain our citizens,
And sent our sons and husbands captivate.
  Tal. Ha, ha, ha!
  Count. Laughest thou, wretch? Thy mirth
shall turn to moan.
  Tal. I laugh to see your ladyship so fond 45
To think that you have aught but Talbot's
shadow
Whereon to practise your severity.
  Count. Why? Art not thou the man?
  Tal.   I am indeed.
  Count. Then have I substance too.
  Tal. No, no! I am but shadow of myself. 50
You are deceiv'd, my substance is not here;
For what you see is but the smallest part
And least proportion of humanity.
I tell you, madam, were the whole frame here,
It is of such a spacious lofty pitch   55
Your roof were not sufficient to contain't.
  Count. This is a riddling merchant for the
nonce!
He will be here, and yet he is not here.
How can these contrarieties agree?
  Tal. That will I show you presently.   60

*Winds his horn. Drums strike up. A peal of
    ordinance. Enter Soldiers.*

How say you, madam? Are you now persuaded
That Talbot is but shadow of himself?
These are his substance, sinews, arms, and
strength,
With which he yoketh your rebellious necks,
Razeth your cities, and subverts your towns 65
And in a moment makes them desolate.
  Count. Victorious Talbot, pardon my abuse!
I find thou art no less than fame hath bruited,
And more than may be gathered by thy
shape.
Let my presumption not provoke thy wrath, 70
For I am sorry that with reverence
I did not entertain thee as thou art.
  Tal. Be not dismay'd, fair lady, nor mis-
conster
The mind of Talbot as you did mistake
The outward composition of his body.   75
What you have done hath not offended me;
Nor other satisfaction do I crave
But only, with your patience, that we may
Taste of your wine and see what cates you
have;
For soldiers' stomachs always serve them well.

  Count. With all my heart, and think me
honoured   81
To feast so great a warrior in my house.
                    Exeunt.

[Scene IV. *London. The Temple Garden.*]

Enter *Richard Plantagenet, Warwick, Somerset,
Pole [Earl of Suffolk, Vernon,] and others.*
  Rich. Great lords and gentlemen, what
means this silence?
Dare no man answer in a case of truth?
  Suf. Within the Temple Hall we were too
loud.
The Garden here is more convenient.
  Rich. Then say at once if I maintain'd the
truth;   5
Or else was wrangling Somerset in th' error?
  Suf. Faith, I have been a truant in the law
And never yet could frame my will to it,
And therefore frame the law unto my will.
  Som. Judge you, my Lord of Warwick, then
between us.   10
  War. Between two hawks, which flies the
higher pitch —
Between two dogs, which hath the deeper
mouth —
Between two blades, which bears the better
temper —
Between two horses, which doth bear him
best —
Between two girls, which hath the merriest
eye —   15
I have perhaps some shallow spirit of judg-
ment;
But in these nice sharp quillets of the law,
Good faith, I am no wiser than a daw.
  Rich. Tut, tut! here is a mannerly forbear-
ance.
The truth appears so naked on my side   20
That any purblind eye may find it out.
  Som. And on my side it is so well apparell'd,
So clear, so shining, and so evident,
That it will glimmer through a blind man's eye.
  Rich. Since you are tongue-tied and so loath
to speak,   25
In dumb significants proclaim your thoughts.
Let him that is a true-born gentleman
And stands upon the honour of his birth,
If he suppose that I have pleaded truth,   29
From off this brier pluck a white rose with me.
  Som. Let him that is no coward nor no
flatterer,

But dare maintain the party of the truth,
Pluck a red rose from off this thorn with me.
  War. I love no colours, and without all colour
Of base insinuating flattery   35
I pluck this white rose with Plantagenet.
  Suf. I pluck this red rose with young Somerset,
And say withal I think he held the right.
  Ver. Stay, lords and gentlemen, and pluck no more
Till you conclude that he upon whose side 40
The fewest roses are cropp'd from the tree
Shall yield the other in the right opinion.
  Som. Good Master Vernon, it is well objected.
If I have fewest, I subscribe in silence.
  Rich. And I.   45
  Ver. Then for the truth and plainness of the case
I pluck this pale and maiden blossom here,
Giving my verdict on the white rose side.
  Som. Prick not your finger as you pluck it off,
Lest, bleeding, you do paint the white rose red
And fall on my side so against your will. 51
  Ver. If I, my lord, for my opinion bleed,
Opinion shall be surgeon to my hurt
And keep me on the side where still I am.
  Som. Well, well, come on! Who else? 55
  Lawyer. [*to Somerset*] Unless my study and my books be false,
The argument you held was wrong in you;
In sign whereof I pluck a white rose too.
  Rich. Now, Somerset, where is your argument? 59
  Som. Here in my scabbard, meditating that
Shall dye your white rose in a bloody red.
  Rich. Meantime your cheeks do counterfeit our roses;
For pale they look with fear, as witnessing
The truth on our side.
  Som.   No, Plantagenet!
'Tis not for fear, but anger, that thy cheeks 65
Blush for pure shame to counterfeit our roses,
And yet thy tongue will not confess thy error.
  Rich. Hath not thy rose a canker, Somerset?
  Som. Hath not thy rose a thorn, Plantagenet?
  Rich. Ay, sharp and piercing, to maintain his truth, 70
Whiles thy consuming canker eats his falsehood.
  Som. Well, I'll find friends to wear my bleeding roses,
That shall maintain what I have said is true
Where false Plantagenet dare not be seen.
  Rich. Now by this maiden blossom in my hand, 75
I scorn thee and thy faction, peevish boy!
  Suf. Turn not thy scorns this way, Plantagenet.
  Rich. Proud Pole, I will, and scorn both him and thee.
  Suf. I'll turn my part thereof into thy throat.
  Som. Away, away, good William de la Pole!
We grace the yeoman by conversing with him.
  War. Now, by God's will, thou wrong'st him, Somerset!
His grandfather was Lionel Duke of Clarence,
Third son to the third Edward, King of England. 84
Spring crestless yeomen from so deep a root?
  Rich. He bears him on the place's privilege,
Or durst not for his craven heart say thus.
  Som. By him that made me, I'll maintain my words
On any plot of ground in Christendom! 89
Was not thy father, Richard Earl of Cambridge,
For treason executed in our late king's days?
And by his treason stand'st not thou attainted,
Corrupted, and exempt from ancient gentry?
His trespass yet lives guilty in thy blood,
And till thou be restor'd thou art a yeoman. 95
  Rich. My father was attached, not attainted;
Condemn'd to die for treason, but no traitor;
And that I'll prove on better men than Somerset,
Were growing time once ripened to my will.
For your partaker Pole, and you yourself, 100
I'll note you in my book of memory
To scourge you for this apprehension.
Look to it well and say you are well warn'd.
  Som. Ah, thou shalt find us ready for thee still; 104
And know us by these colours for thy foes,
For these my friends in spite of thee shall wear.
  Rich. And, by my soul, this pale and angry rose,
As cognizance of my blood-drinking hate,
Will I for ever, and my faction, wear
Until it wither with me to my grave 110
Or flourish to the height of my degree.
  Suf. Go forward, and be chok'd with thy ambition!
And so farewell until I meet thee next.   *Exit*
  Som. Have with thee, Pole. Farewell, ambitious Richard.   *Exit.*
  Rich. How I am brav'd and must perforce endure it! 115
  War. This blot that they object against your house

Shall be wip'd out in the next parliament,
Call'd for the truce of Winchester and Glouces-
ter;
And if thou be not then created York,
I will not live to be accounted Warwick. 120
Meantime, in signal of my love to thee,
Against proud Somerset and William Pole
Will I upon thy party wear this rose;
And here I prophesy : this brawl to-day 124
Grown to this faction in the Temple Garden
Shall send, between the Red Rose and the
White,
A thousand souls to death and deadly night.
  Rich. Good Master Vernon, I am bound to
    you
That you on my behalf would pluck a flower.
  Ver. In your behalf still will I wear the same.
  Lawyer. And so will I.   131
  Rich. Thanks, gentle sir.
Come, let us four to dinner. I dare say
This quarrel will drink blood another day.
                              Exeunt.

[Scene V. *The Tower of London.*]

Enter *Mortimer,* brought in a chair, and *Jailers.*

  Mor. Kind keepers of my weak decaying age,
Let dying Mortimer here rest himself.
Even like a man new haled from the rack,
So fare my limbs with long imprisonment; 4
And these grey locks, the pursuivants of death,
Nestor-like aged in an age of care,
Argue the end of Edmund Mortimer.
These eyes, like lamps whose wasting oil is
    spent,
Wax dim, as drawing to their exigent;
Weak shoulders, overborne with burthening
    grief,   10
And pithless arms, like to a withered vine
That droops his sapless branches to the ground.
Yet are these feet (whose strengthless stay is
    numb,
Unable to support this lump of clay)
Swift-winged with desire to get a grave, 15
As witting I no other comfort have.
But tell me, keeper, will my nephew come?
  Keeper. Richard Plantagenet, my lord, will
    come.
We sent unto the Temple, unto his chamber,
And answer was return'd that he will come. 20
  Mor. Enough. My soul shall then be satis-
fied.
Poor gentleman! his wrong doth equal mine.

Since Henry Monmouth first began to reign
Before whose glory I was great in arms,
This loathsome sequestration have I had; 25
And even since then hath Richard been ob-
    scur'd,
Depriv'd of honour and inheritance.
But now the arbitrator of despairs,
Just Death, kind umpire of men's miseries,
With sweet enlargement doth dismiss me hence.
I would his troubles likewise were expir'd, 31
That so he might recover what was lost.

           Enter *Richard* [*Plantagenet*].

  Keeper. My lord, your loving nephew now
    is come.
  Mor. Richard Plantagenet, friend, is he
    come?
  Rich. Ay, noble uncle, thus ignobly us'd, 35
Your nephew, late despised Richard, comes.
  Mor. Direct mine arms I may embrace his
    neck
And in his bosom spend my latter gasp.
O, tell me when my lips do touch his cheeks,
That I may kindly give one fainting kiss! 40
And now declare, sweet stem from York's great
    stock,
Why didst thou say of late thou wert despis'd?
  Rich. First lean thine aged back against
    mine arm,
And in that ease I'll tell thee my disease.
This day in argument upon a case 45
Some words there grew 'twixt Somerset and me;
Among which terms he us'd his lavish tongue
And did upbraid me with my father's death;
Which obloquy set bars before my tongue,
Else with the like I had requited him. 50
Therefore, good uncle, for my father's sake,
In honour of a true Plantagenet,
And for alliance sake, declare the cause
My father, Earl of Cambridge, lost his head.
  Mor. That cause, fair nephew, that im-
    prison'd me   55
And hath detain'd me all my flow'ring youth
Within a loathsome dungeon, there to pine,
Was cursed instrument of his decease.
  Rich. Discover more at large what cause
    that was,
For I am ignorant and cannot guess. 60
  Mor. I will, if that my fading breath permit
And death approach not ere my tale be done.
Henry the Fourth, grandfather to this king,
Depos'd his nephew Richard, Edward's son.
The first-begotten and the lawful heir 65
Of Edward king, the third of that descent;
During whose reign, the Percies of the North,

Finding his usurpation most unjust,
Endeavour'd my advancement to the throne.
The reason mov'd these warlike lords to this 70
Was for that (young King Richard thus re-
    mov'd,
Leaving no heir begotten of his body)
I was the next by birth and parentage;
For by my mother I derived am
From Lionel Duke of Clarence, third son 75
To King Edward the Third; whereas he
From John of Gaunt doth bring his pedigree,
Being but fourth of that heroic line.
But mark! As in this haughty great attempt
They laboured to plant the rightful heir, 80
I lost my liberty, and they their lives.
Long after this, when Henry the Fifth
(Succeeding his father Bolingbroke) did reign,
Thy father, Earl of Cambridge, then deriv'd
From famous Edmund Langley, Duke of York,
Marrying my sister that thy mother was, 86
Again, in pity of my hard distress,
Levied an army, weening to redeem
And have install'd me in the diadem;
But, as the rest, so fell that noble earl, 90
And was beheaded. Thus the Mortimers,
In whom the title rested, were suppress'd.
   Rich. Of which, my lord, your Honour is the
    last.
   Mor. True, and thou seest that I no issue
    have, 94
And that my fainting words do warrant death.
Thou art my heir. The rest I wish thee
    gather;
But yet be wary in thy studious care.
   Rich. Thy grave admonishments prevail
    with me.

But yet methinks my father's execution
Was nothing less than bloody tyranny. 100
   Mor. With silence, nephew, be thou politic.
Strong fixed is the house of Lancaster
And like a mountain, not to be remov'd.
But now thy uncle is removing hence,
As princes do their courts when they are cloy'd
With long continuance in a settled place. 106
   Rich. O uncle, would some part of my young
    years
Might but redeem the passage of your age!
   Mor. Thou dost then wrong me, as that
    slaughterer doth 109
Which giveth many wounds when one will kill.
Mourn not, except thou sorrow for my good;
Only give order for my funeral.
And so farewell, and fair be all thy hopes,
And prosperous be thy life in peace and war!
                           Dies.
   Rich. And peace, no war, befall thy parting
    soul! 115
In prison hast thou spent a pilgrimage
And like a hermit overpass'd thy days.
Well, I will lock his counsel in my breast,
And what I do imagine, let that rest.
Keepers, convey him hence, and I myself 120
Will see his burial better than his life.
    Exeunt [*Jailers, with Mortimer's body*].
Here dies the dusky torch of Mortimer,
Chok'd with ambition of the meaner sort.
And for those wrongs, those bitter injuries,
Which Somerset hath offer'd to my house 125
I doubt not but with honour to redress;
And therefore haste I to the parliament,
Either to be restored to my blood
Or make my ill th' advantage of my good. *Exit.*

ACT III. Scene I. [*London. The Parliament House.*]

Flourish. Enter *King, Exeter, Gloucester, Win-*
chester, Warwick, Somerset, Suffolk, Richard
Plantagenet, [*and others*]. *Gloucester offers to put*
up a bill. *Winchester snatches it, tears it.*

   Win. Com'st thou with deep premeditated
    lines?
With written pamphlets studiously devis'd?
Humphrey of Gloucester, if thou canst accuse
Or aught intend'st to lay unto my charge,
Do it without invention, suddenly, 5
As I with sudden and extemporal speech
Purpose to answer what thou canst object.
   Glou. Presumptuous priest, this place com-
    mands my patience,

Or thou shouldst find thou hast dishonour'd me.
Think not, although in writing I preferr'd 10
The manner of thy vile outrageous crimes,
That therefore I have forg'd, or am not able
Verbatim to rehearse the method of my pen.
No, prelate! Such is thy audacious wickedness,
Thy lewd, pestiferous, and dissentious pranks,
As very infants prattle of thy pride. 16
Thou art a most pernicious usurer;
Froward by nature, enemy to peace,
Lascivious, wanton, more than well beseems
A man of thy profession and degree. 20
And for thy treachery, what's more manifest?
In that thou laid'st a trap to take my life
As well at London Bridge as at the Tower.

Beside, I fear me, if thy thoughts were sifted,
The King thy sovereign is not quite exempt 25
From envious malice of thy swelling heart.
  Win. Gloucester, I do defy thee. Lords, vouchsafe
To give me hearing what I shall reply.
If I were covetous, ambitious, or perverse,
As he will have me — how am I so poor? 30
Or how haps it I seek not to advance
Or raise myself, but keep my wonted calling?
And for dissension, who preferreth peace
More than I do, except I be provok'd?
No, my good lords, it is not that offends; 35
It is not that that hath incens'd the Duke.
It is because no one should sway but he,
No one but he should be about the King;
And that engenders thunder in his breast
And makes him roar these accusations forth. 40
But he shall know I am as good —
  Glou.   As good?
Thou bastard of my grandfather!
  Win. Ay, lordly sir! For what are you, I pray,
But one imperious in another's throne?
  Glou. Am I not Protector, saucy priest? 45
  Win. And am not I a prelate of the Church?
  Glou. Yes, as an outlaw in a castle keeps
And useth it to patronage his theft.
  Win. Unreverent Gloucester.
  Glou.   Thou art reverent
Touching thy spiritual function, not thy life. 50
  Win. Rome shall remedy this.
  War.   Roam thither then!
  Som. My lord, it were your duty to forbear.
  War. Ay, see the Bishop be not overborne.
  Som. Methinks my lord should be religious
And know the office that belongs to such. 55
  War. Methinks his lordship should be humbler.
It fitteth not a prelate so to plead.
  Som. Yes, when his holy state is touch'd so near.
  War. State holy, or unhallow'd, what of that?
Is not his Grace Protector to the King? 60
  Rich. [*aside*] Plantagenet, I see, must hold his tongue,
Lest it be said 'Speak, sirrah, when you should!
Must your bold verdict enter talk with lords?'
Else would I have a fling at Winchester.
  King. Uncles of Gloucester and of Winchester, 65
The special watchmen of our English weal,
I would prevail, if prayers might prevail,
To join your hearts in love and amity.

O, what a scandal is it to our crown
That two such noble peers as ye should jar! 70
Believe me, lords, my tender years can tell
Civil dissension is a viperous worm
That gnaws the bowels of the commonwealth.

  A noise within, 'Down with the Tawny Coats!'

  King. What tumult's this?
  War.   An uproar, I dare warrant,
Begun through malice of the Bishop's men. 75

  A noise again [*within*], 'Stones! stones!'

  Enter *Mayor* [*of London*, attended].

  May. O my good lords, and virtuous Henry,
Pity the city of London, pity us!
The Bishop and the Duke of Gloucester's men,
Forbidden late to carry any weapon,
Have fill'd their pockets full of pebble stones 80
And, banding themselves in contrary parts,
Do pelt so fast at one another's pate
That many have their giddy brains knock'd out.
Our windows are broke down in every street
And we, for fear, compell'd to shut our shops. 85

Enter in skirmish [*Servingmen of Gloucester and Winchester*] with bloody pates.

  King. We charge you, on allegiance to ourself,
To hold your slaught'ring hands and keep the peace.
Pray, uncle Gloucester, mitigate this strife.
  1. Serv. Nay, if we be forbidden stones, we'll fall to it with our teeth. 90
  2. Serv. Do what ye dare, we are as resolute.
                    Skirmish again.
  Glou. You of my household, leave this peevish broil
And set this unaccustom'd fight aside.
  3. Serv. My lord, we know your Grace to be a man
Just and upright, and for your royal birth 95
Inferior to none but to his Majesty;
And ere that we will suffer such a prince,
So kind a father of the commonweal,
To be disgraced by an inkhorn mate,
We and our wives and children all will fight 100
And have our bodies slaught'red by thy foes.
  1. Serv. Ay, and the very parings of our nails
Shall pitch a field when we are dead.
                    Begin again.
  Glou.   Stay, stay, I say!
And if you love me, as you say you do,
Let me persuade you to forbear awhile. 105
  King. O, how this discord doth afflict my soul!
Can you, my Lord of Winchester, behold

My sighs and tears and will not once relent?
Who should be pitiful if you be not?
Or who should study to prefer a peace   110
If holy churchmen take delight in broils?
  War. Yield, my Lord Protector! yield,
    Winchester!
Except you mean with obstinate repulse
To slay your sovereign and destroy the realm.
You see what mischief, and what murther too,
Hath been enacted through your enmity.   116
Then be at peace, except ye thirst for blood.
  Win. He shall submit, or I will never yield.
  Glou. Compassion on the King commands
    me stoop,
Or I would see his heart out ere the priest   120
Should ever get that privilege of me.
  War. Behold, my Lord of Winchester, the
    Duke
Hath banish'd moody discontented fury,
As by his smoothed brows it doth appear.
Why look you still so stern and tragical?   125
  Glou. Here, Winchester, I offer thee my hand.
  King. Fie, uncle Beaufort! I have heard you
    preach
That malice was a great and grievous sin;
And will not you maintain the thing you teach,
But prove a chief offender in the same?   130
  War. [*aside*] Sweet King! The Bishop hath
    a kindly gird. —
For shame, my Lord of Winchester, relent!
What, shall a child instruct you what to do?
  Win. Well, Duke of Gloucester, I will yield
    to thee.
Love for thy love and hand for hand I give.   135
  Glou. [*aside*] Ay, but I fear me with a hollow
    heart! —
See here, my friends and loving countrymen:
This token serveth for a flag of truce
Betwixt ourselves and all our followers.
So help me God as I dissemble not!   140
  Win. [*aside*] So help me God as I intend it
    not!
  King. O loving uncle, kind Duke of Glouces-
    ter,
How joyful am I made by this contract!
Away, my masters! Trouble us no more,
But join in friendship, as your lords have
    done.   145
  1. Serv. Content. I'll to the surgeon's.
  2. Serv.   And so will I.
  3. Serv. And I will see what physic the tavern
    affords.
            Exeunt [*Servingmen, Mayor, &c.*].
  War. Accept this scroll most gracious sov-
    ereign,

Which in the right of Richard Plantagenet
We do exhibit to your Majesty.   150
  Glou. Well urg'd, my Lord of Warwick; for,
    sweet prince,
An if your Grace mark every circumstance,
You have great reason to do Richard right,
Especially for those occasions
At Eltham Place I told your Majesty.   155
  King. And those occasions, uncle, were of
    force.
Therefore, my loving lords, our pleasure is
That Richard be restored to his blood.
  War. Let Richard be restored to his blood.
So shall his father's wrongs be recompens'd.
  Win. As will the rest, so willeth Winchester.
  King. If Richard will be true, not that alone
But all the whole inheritance I give
That doth belong unto the house of York,
From whence you spring by lineal descent.   165
  Rich. Thy humble servant vows obedience
And humble service till the point of death.
  King. Stoop then and set your knee against
    my foot,
And in reguerdon of that duty done
I gird thee with the valiant sword of York.   170
Rise, Richard, like a true Plantagenet,
And rise created princely Duke of York.
  Rich. And so thrive Richard as thy foes may
    fall!
And as my duty springs, so perish they   174
That grudge one thought against your Majesty!
  All. Welcome, high prince, the mighty Duke
    of York!
  Som. [*aside*] Perish, base prince, ignoble
    Duke of York!
  Glou. Now will it best avail your Majesty
To cross the seas and to be crown'd in France.
The presence of a king engenders love   180
Amongst his subjects and his loyal friends,
As it disanimates his enemies.
  King. When Gloucester says the word, King
    Henry goes,
For friendly counsel cuts off many foes.   184
  Glou. Your ships already are in readiness.
          Sennet. Flourish. Exeunt. Manet Exeter.
  Exe. Ay, we may march in England or in
    France,
Not seeing what is likely to ensue.
This late dissension grown betwixt the peers
Burns under feigned ashes of forg'd love
And will at last break out into a flame.   190
As fest'red members rot but by degree
Till bones and flesh and sinews fall away,
So will this base and envious discord breed.
And now I fear that fatal prophecy   194

Which in the time of Henry nam'd the Fifth
Was in the mouth of every sucking babe:
That Henry born at Monmouth should win all
And Henry born at Windsor should lose all;
Which is so plain that Exeter doth wish
His days may finish ere that hapless time. 200
Exit.

Scene II. [*Before Rouen.*]

Enter *Pucelle* disguis'd, with four *Soldiers*
[dressed like *Countrymen*] with sacks upon
their backs.

Puc. These are the city gates, the gates of
Roan,
Through which our policy must make a breach.
Take heed, be wary how you place your words;
Talk like the vulgar sort of marketmen
That come to gather money for their corn. 5
If we have entrance, as I hope we shall,
And that we find the slothful watch but weak,
I'll by a sign give notice to our friends,
That Charles the Dauphin may encounter them.
Soldier. Our sacks shall be a mean to sack
the city, 10
And we be lords and rulers over Roan.
Therefore we'll knock. *Knock.*
Watch. [*within*] Qui est là?
Puc. Paysans, pauvres gens de France, 14
Poor market folks that come to sell their corn.
Watch. Enter, go in; the market bell is rung.
Puc. Now, Roan, I'll shake thy bulwarks to
the ground. *Exeunt.*

Enter *Charles, Bastard, Alençon,* [*Reignier,*
and *Soldiers*].

Char. Saint Denis bless this happy strata-
gem,
And once again we'll sleep secure in Roan.
Bast. Here ent'red Pucelle and her prac-
tisants. 20
Now she is there, how will she specify
Where is the best and safest passage in?
Reig. By thrusting out a torch from yonder
tower,
Which, once discern'd, shows that her meaning
is, 24
No way to that (for weakness) which she ent'red.

Enter *Pucelle* on the top, thrusting out a torch
burning.

Puc. Behold, this is the happy wedding torch
That joineth Roan unto her countrymen,
But burning fatal to the Talbonites.

Bast. See, noble Charles, the beacon of our
friend.
The burning torch in yonder turret stands. 30
Char. Now shine it like a comet of revenge,
A prophet to the fall of all our foes!
Reig. Defer no time; delays have dangerous
ends.
Enter and cry 'The Dauphin!' presently,
And then do execution on the watch. 35
*Alarum. [They enter the town. Exit Pucelle
above.]*

*An Alarum. [Enter, from the town,] Talbot
[and English Soldiers] in an excursion.*

Tal. France, thou shalt rue this treason with
thy tears
If Talbot but survive thy treachery.
Pucelle, that witch, that damned sorceress,
Hath wrought this hellish mischief unawares,
That hardly we escap'd the pride of France. 40
Exeunt.

*An Alarum. Excursions. Bedford brought in
sick in a chair. Enter Talbot and Burgundy
without; within, Pucelle, Charles, Bastard,
[Alençon,] and Reignier on the walls.*

Puc. Good morrow, gallants! Want ye corn
for bread?
I think the Duke of Burgundy will fast
Before he'll buy again at such a rate.
'Twas full of darnel. Do you like the taste?
Bur. Scoff on, vile fiend and shameless
courtesan! 45
I trust ere long to choke thee with thine
own
And make thee curse the harvest of that corn.
Char. Your Grace may starve, perhaps, be-
fore that time.
Bed. O, let no words, but deeds, revenge
this treason!
Puc. What will you do, good greybeard?
break a lance 50
And run a-tilt at death within a chair?
Tal. Foul fiend of France and hag of all
despite,
Encompass'd with thy lustful paramours,
Becomes it thee to taunt his valiant age
And twit with cowardice a man half dead? 55
Damsel, I'll have a bout with you again,
Or else let Talbot perish with this shame.
Puc. Are ye so hot, sir? Yet, Pucelle, hold
thy peace.
If Talbot do but thunder, rain will follow.
*They [i.e. Talbot, Bedford, and Burgundy]
whisper together in counsel.*

God speed the parliament! Who shall be the
    Speaker?   60
  Tal. Dare ye come forth and meet us in the
    field?
  Puc. Belike your lordship takes us then for
    fools,
To try if that our own be ours or no.
  Tal. I speak not to that railing Hecate,
But unto thee, Alençon, and the rest.   65
Will ye, like soldiers, come and fight it out?
  Alen. Signior, no.
  Tal. Signior, hang! Base muleters of France!
Like peasant footboys do they keep the walls
And dare not take up arms like gentlemen. 70
  Puc. Away, captains! Let's get us from the
    walls,
For Talbot means no goodness by his looks.
God b'uy, my lord! We came but to tell you
That we are here.
    Exeunt [Pucelle and the French] from the
                           walls.
  Tal. And there will we be too ere it be long,
Or else reproach be Talbot's greatest fame! 76
Vow, Burgundy, by honour of thy house,
Prick'd on by public wrongs sustain'd in France,
Either to get the town again or die;
And I, as sure as English Henry lives   80
And as his father here was conqueror,
As sure as in this late betrayed town
Great Cœur-de-lion's heart was buried —
So sure I swear to get the town or die.
  Bur. My vows are equal partners with thy
    vows.   85
  Tal. But, ere we go, regard this dying prince,
The valiant Duke of Bedford. Come, my lord,
We will bestow you in some better place,
Fitter for sickness and for crazy age.   89
  Bed. Lord Talbot, do not so dishonour me.
Here will I sit, before the walls of Roan,
And will be partner of your weal or woe.
  Bur. Courageous Bedford, let us now per-
    suade you.
  Bed. Not to be gone from hence; for once
    I read
That stout Pendragon in his litter sick   95
Came to the field and vanquished his foes.
Methinks I should revive the soldiers' hearts,
Because I ever found them as myself.
  Tal. Undaunted spirit in a dying breast!
Then be it so. Heavens keep old Bedford safe!
And now no more ado, brave Burgundy,   101
But gather we our forces out of hand
And set upon our boasting enemy.
    Exeunt [to the assault all but Bedford and
                         Attendants].

    An Alarum. Excursions. Enter *Sir John*
        Fastolfe and a *Captain.*

  Capt. Whither away, Sir John Fastolfe, in
    such haste?
  Fast. Whither away? To save myself by
    flight.   105
We are like to have the overthrow again.
  Capt. What? Will you fly and leave Lord
    Talbot?
  Fast.   Ay!
All the Talbots in the world, to save my life.
                                 Exit.
  Capt. Cowardly knight, ill fortune follow
    thee!   *Exit.*

    Retreat. Excursions. Pucelle, Alençon, *and*
                Charles fly.

  Bed. Now, quiet soul, depart when heaven
    please,   110
For I have seen our enemies' overthrow.
What is the trust or strength of foolish man?
They that of late were daring with their scoffs
Are glad and fain by flight to save themselves.
    Bedford dies and is carried in by two in his
                          chair.

    An Alarum. Enter *Talbot, Burgundy,* and
        the rest.

  Tal. Lost and recovered in a day again!
This is a double honour, Burgundy.   116
Yet heavens have glory for this victory!
  Bur. Warlike and martial Talbot, Burgundy
Enshrines thee in his heart and there erects
Thy noble deeds as valour's monuments.   120
  Tal. Thanks, gentle Duke. But where is
    Pucelle now?
I think her old familiar is asleep.
Now where's the Bastard's braves and Charles
    his glikes?
What, all amort? Roan hangs her head for grief
That such a valiant company are fled.   125
Now will we take some order in the town,
Placing therein some expert officers,
And then depart to Paris to the King,
For there young Henry with his nobles lie.
  Bur. What wills Lord Talbot pleaseth Bur-
    gundy.   130
  Tal. But yet, before we go, let's not forget
The noble Duke of Bedford, late deceas'd,
But see his exequies fulfill'd in Roan.
A braver soldier never couched lance,
A gentler heart did never sway in court.   135
But kings and mightiest potentates must die,
For that's the end of human misery.   *Exeunt.*

Scene III. [*The plains near Rouen.*]

Enter *Charles, Bastard, Alençon, Pucelle,*
[*and Soldiers*].

Puc. Dismay not, princes, at this accident,
Nor grieve that Roan is so recovered.
Care is no cure, but rather corrosive,
For things that are not to be remedied.
Let frantic Talbot triumph for a while   5
And like a peacock sweep along his tail;
We'll pull his plumes and take away his train,
If Dauphin and the rest will be but rul'd.
Char. We have been guided by thee hitherto
And of thy cunning had no diffidence.   10
One sudden foil shall never breed distrust.
Bast. Search out thy wit for secret policies,
And we will make thee famous through the
world.
Alen. We'll set thy statue in some holy place
And have thee reverenc'd like a blessed saint. 15
Employ thee then, sweet virgin, for our good.
Puc. Then thus it must be; this doth Joan
devise:
By fair persuasions, mix'd with sug'red words,
We will entice the Duke of Burgundy
To leave the Talbot and to follow us.   20
Char. Ay, marry, sweeting, if we could do
that,
France were no place for Henry's warriors,
Nor should that nation boast it so with us,
But be extirped from our provinces.
Alen. For ever should they be expuls'd from
France   25
And not have title of an earldom here.
Puc. Your Honours shall perceive how I will
work
To bring this matter to the wished end.
                    Drum sounds afar off.
Hark! by the sound of drum you may per-
ceive
Their powers are marching unto Paris-ward. 30

Here sound an English march. [Enter, and pass
over at a distance, *Talbot* and his *Troops.*]

There goes the Talbot, with his colours spread,
And all the troops of English after him.

French march. [Enter the *Duke of Burgundy*
and his *Troops.*]

Now in the rearward comes the Duke and his.
Fortune in favour makes him lag behind.
Summon a parley; we will talk with him.   35
                    Trumpets sound a parley.
Char. A parley with the Duke of Burgundy!

Bur. Who craves a parley with the Bur-
gundy?
Puc. The princely Charles of France, thy
countryman.
Bur. What say'st thou, Charles? for I am
marching hence.
Char. Speak, Pucelle, and enchant him with
thy words.   40
Puc. Brave Burgundy, undoubted hope of
France,
Stay, let thy humble handmaid speak to thee!
Bur. Speak on; but be not over-tedious.
Puc. Look on thy country, look on fertile
France,
And see the cities and the towns defac'd   45
By wasting ruin of the cruel foe,
As looks the mother on her lowly babe
When death doth close his tender dying eyes.
See, see the pining malady of France!   49
Behold the wounds, the most unnatural wounds,
Which thou thyself hast given her woful breast!
O, turn thy edged sword another way;
Strike those that hurt, and hurt not those that
help!
One drop of blood drawn from thy country's
bosom
Should grieve thee more than streams of foreign
gore.   55
Return thee therefore with a flood of tears
And wash away thy country's stained spots.
Bur. [*aside*] Either she hath bewitch'd me
with her words,
Or nature makes me suddenly relent.
Puc. Besides, all French and France ex-
claims on thee,   60
Doubting thy birth and lawful progeny.
Who join'st thou with but with a lordly nation
That will not trust thee but for profit's sake?
When Talbot hath set footing once in France
And fashion'd thee that instrument of ill,   65
Who then but English Henry will be lord,
And thou be thrust out like a fugitive?
Call we to mind — and mark but this for proof:
Was not the Duke of Orleans thy foe?
And was he not in England prisoner?   70
But when they heard he was thine enemy,
They set him free without his ransom paid,
In spite of Burgundy and all his friends.
See then, thou fight'st against thy countrymen
And join'st with them will be thy slaughtermen.
Come, come, return! Return, thou wandering
lord!   76
Charles and the rest will take thee in their arms.
Bur. [*aside*] I am vanquished! These haughty
words of hers

216

HENRY VI
PART ONE

PHOTOGRAPHS BY LISEL HAAS
PRODUCED BY THE BIRMINGHAM
REPERTORY THEATRE

"God save King Henry, of that name the sixth." In Paris, Henry Beaufort, Bishop of Winchester (Alfred Burke), sets the crown upon the head of Henry (Jack May) (*Act IV, Scene I*)

"Henry the Sixth, in infant bands crown'd King of France and England ... whose state so many had the managing, that they lost France and made his England bleed" (*Henry the Fifth: Act V, Scene II*)

Gloucester (Edgar Wreford), the king's uncle and protector, withdraws from Henry's presence to leave for France. His long-time rival, Winchester, through bribery now a Cardinal, glares balefully at right (Act V, Scene I)

The leader of the English, Lord Talbot (Alan Bridges), taunts the shepherd maid of France, Joan la Pucelle (Nancie Jackson), before one of the gates of Orleans: "Blood will I draw on thee, thou art a witch" (Act I, Scene V)

Once rescued by his father, Talbot's son (John Greenwood) later leaves his father's side and is killed by the French. "Come, come, and lay him in his father's arms: my spirit can no longer bear these harms. Soldiers, adieu! I have what I would have" (Act IV, Scene VII)

The French, led by Joan la Pucelle, famous as Joan of Arc, arrive in time to hear Talbot's last words over the body of his son: "Now my old arms are young John Talbot's grave." Then he too dies (Act IV, Scene VII)

"Fond man! remember that thou hast a wife; then how can Margaret be thy paramour?" In an aside, Suffolk (Richard Pasco) reasons with himself after taking captive Margaret of Anjou (Rosalind Boxall) (Act V, Scene III)

"My ancient incantations are too weak, and hell too strong for me to buckle with: now, France, thy glory droopeth to the dust." Deserted by the "familiars" who had appeared to her, Joan is captured by the English under York (Act V, Scene III)

Richard Plantagenet, Duke of York (John Arnatt), addresses his captive: "Damsel of France, I think I have you fast: unchain your spirits now with spelling charms, and try if they can gain your liberty" (Act V, Scene III)

"First, let me tell you whom you have condemn'd: not me begotten of a shepherd swain, but issu'd from the progeny of kings; virtuous and holy; chosen from above, by inspiration of celestial grace, to work exceeding miracles on earth." Joan's futile plea (Act V, Scene IV)

Have batt'red me like roaring cannon-shot
And made me almost yield upon my knees. —
Forgive me, country, and sweet countrymen!
And, lords, accept this hearty kind embrace.
My forces and my power of men are yours.
So farewell, Talbot! I'll no longer trust thee.
   Puc. Done like a Frenchman — [*aside*]
      turn and turn again!   85
   Char. Welcome, brave Duke! Thy friend-
      ship makes us fresh.
   Bast. And doth beget new courage in our
      breasts.
   Alen. Pucelle hath bravely play'd her part
      in this
And doth deserve a coronet of gold.
   Char. Now let us on, my lords, and join our
      powers,   90
And seek how we may prejudice the foe.
                                          Exeunt.

Scene IV. [*Paris. The Palace.*]

Enter the *King, Gloucester, Winchester,* [*Richard
Duke of*] *York, Suffolk, Somerset, Warwick,
Exeter,* [*Vernon, Basset,* and others]. To them,
      with his *Soldiers, Talbot.*

   Tal. My gracious prince, and honourable
      peers,
Hearing of your arrival in this realm,
I have awhile given truce unto my wars
To do my duty to my sovereign;
In sign whereof this arm that hath reclaim'd 5
To your obedience fifty fortresses,
Twelve cities, and seven walled towns of
      strength,
Beside five hundred prisoners of esteem,
Lets fall his sword before your Highness' feet
                                          [*Kneels.*]
And with submissive loyalty of heart   10
Ascribes the glory of his conquest got
First to my God and next unto your Grace.

   King. Is this the Lord Talbot, uncle Glouces-
      ter,
That hath so long been resident in France?
   Glou. Yes, if it please your Majesty, my liege.
   King. Welcome, brave captain and victo-
      rious lord!   16
When I was young (as yet I am not old)
I do remember how my father said
A stouter champion never handled sword.
Long since we were resolved of your truth, 20
Your faithful service, and your toil in war;
Yet never have you tasted our reward
Or been reguerdon'd with so much as thanks,
Because till now we never saw your face.
Therefore stand up, and for these good deserts
We here create you Earl of Shrewsbury,   26
And in our coronation take your place.
      *Sennet. Flourish. Exeunt. Manent Vernon
                                      and Basset.*
   Ver. Now, sir, to you, that were so hot at sea,
Disgracing of these colours that I wear
In honour of my noble Lord of York —   30
Dar'st thou maintain the former words thou
      spak'st?
   Bas. Yes, sir, as well as you dare patronage
The envious barking of your saucy tongue
Against my lord the Duke of Somerset.
   Ver. Sirrah, thy lord I honour as he is.   35
   Bas. Why, what is he? As good a man as
      York.
   Ver. Hark ye! Not so. In witness take ye
      that.   *Strikes him.*
   Bas. Villain, thou knowest the law of arms
      is such
That whoso draws a sword, 'tis present death,
Or else this blow should broach thy dearest blood.
But I'll unto his Majesty and crave
I may have liberty to venge this wrong,
When thou shalt see I'll meet thee to thy cost.
   Ver. Well, miscreant, I'll be there as soon as
      you,   44
And after meet you, sooner than you would.
                                          Exeunt.

ACT IV. Scene I. [*Paris. A room of state in the Palace.*]

Enter *King, Gloucester, Winchester, York, Suffolk, Somerset, Warwick, Talbot, Exeter,* and
      Governor [*of Paris*].

   Glou. Lord Bishop, set the crown upon his
      head.
   Win. God save King Henry, of that name
      the Sixth!

   Glou. Now, Governor of Paris, take your
      oath,   [*Governor kneels.*]
That you elect no other king but him,
Esteem none friends but such as are his friends,
And none your foes but such as shall pretend 6
Malicious practices against his state.
This shall ye do, so help you righteous God!
                        [*Governor rises and retires.*]

Enter *Fastolfe.*

Fast. My gracious sovereign, as I rode from
Calais
To haste unto your coronation,   10
A letter was deliver'd to my hands,
Writ to your Grace from th' Duke of Burgundy.
                                    [*Presents it.*]

Tal. Shame to the Duke of Burgundy and
thee!
I vow'd, base knight, when I did meet thee next
To tear the Garter from thy craven's leg,   15
                                    [*Plucks it off.*]
Which I have done, because, unworthily,
Thou wast installed in that high degree.
Pardon me, princely Henry, and the rest.
This dastard, at the battle of Patay,
When, but in all, I was six thousand strong 20
And that the French were almost ten to one,
Before we met or that a stroke was given,
Like to a trusty squire did run away;
In which assault we lost twelve hundred men.
Myself and divers gentlemen beside   25
Were there surpris'd and taken prisoners.
Then judge, great lords, if I have done amiss,
Or whether that such cowards ought to wear
This ornament of knighthood — yea or no?

Glou. To say the truth, this fact was in-
famous,   30
And ill beseeming any common man;
Much more a knight, a captain, and a leader.

Tal. When first this order was ordain'd, my
lords,
Knights of the Garter were of noble birth,
Valiant and virtuous, full of haughty courage,
Such as were grown to credit by the wars;   36
Not fearing death nor shrinking for distress,
But always resolute in most extremes.
He then that is not furnish'd in this sort
Doth but usurp the sacred name of knight,   40
Profaning this most honourable order,
And should (if I were worthy to be judge)
Be quite degraded, like a hedge-born swain
That doth presume to boast of gentle blood.

King. Stain to thy countrymen, thou hear'st
thy doom!   45
Be packing therefore, thou that wast a knight.
Henceforth we banish thee on pain of death.
                                    [*Exit Fastolfe.*]
And now, my Lord Protector, view the letter
Sent from our uncle Duke of Burgundy.

Glou. What means his Grace that he hath
chang'd his style?   50
                            [*Views the superscription.*]
No more but plain and bluntly 'To the King'?

Hath he forgot he is his sovereign?
Or doth this churlish superscription
Pretend some alteration in good will?
What's here? [*Reads*] 'I have, upon especia
cause,   5
Mov'd with compassion of my country's wrac
Together with the pitiful complaints
Of such as your oppression feeds upon,
Forsaken your pernicious faction
And join'd with Charles, the rightful King ¢
France.'   ¢
O monstrous treachery! Can this be so?
That in alliance, amity, and oaths
There should be found such false dissemblin
guile?

King. What? Doth my uncle Burgund
revolt?

Glou. He doth, my lord, and is become you
foe.   ¢

King. Is that the worst this letter doth cor
tain?

Glou. It is the worst, and all, my lord, h
writes.

King. Why, then Lord Talbot there sha
talk with him
And give him chastisement for this abuse.   ¢
How say you, my lord? Are you not content

Tal. Content, my liege? Yes. But that
am prevented,
I should have begg'd I might have been em
ploy'd.

King. Then gather strength and march unt
him straight.
Let him perceive how ill we brook his treaso
And what offence it is to flout his friends.   7

Tal. I go, my lord, in heart desiring still
You may behold confusion of your foes.
                                           [*Exit*

Enter *Vernon* and *Basset.*

Ver. Grant me the combat, gracious sove
eign!

Bas. And me, my lord — grant me the con
bat too!

York. This is my servant. Hear him, nob¹
prince!   8

Som. And this is mine. Sweet Henry, fa
vour him!

King. Be patient, lords, and give them leav
to speak.
Say, gentlemen, what makes you thus exclaim
And wherefore crave you combat? or wit
whom?

Ver. With him, my lord, for he hath don
me wrong.   8

Bas. And I with him, for he hath done me
wrong.

King. What is that wrong whereof you both
complain?
First let me know, and then I'll answer you.

Bas. Crossing the sea from England into
France,
This fellow here with envious carping tongue
Upbraided me about the rose I wear,   91
Saying the sanguine colour of the leaves
Did represent my master's blushing cheeks
When stubbornly he did repugn the truth
About a certain question in the law   95
Argu'd betwixt the Duke of York and him —
With other vile and ignominious terms;
In confutation of which rude reproach,
And in defence of my lord's worthiness,
I crave the benefit of law of arms.   100

Ver. And that is my petition, noble lord.
For though he seem with forged quaint con-
ceit
To set a gloss upon his bold intent,
Yet know, my lord, I was provok'd by him,
And he first took exceptions at this badge, 105
Pronouncing that the paleness of this flower
Bewray'd the faintness of my master's heart.

York. Will not this malice, Somerset, be left?

Som. Your private grudge, my Lord of York,
will out,
Though ne'er so cunningly you smother it.   110

King. Good Lord, what madness rules in
brainsick men
When for so slight and frivolous a cause
Such factious emulations shall arise!
Good cousins both, of York and Somerset,
Quiet yourselves, I pray, and be at peace.   115

York. Let this dissension first be tried by
fight,
And then your Highness shall command a peace.

Som. The quarrel toucheth none but us
alone.
Betwixt ourselves let us decide it then.

York. There is my pledge. Accept it,
Somerset.   120

Ver. Nay, let it rest where it began at first.

Bas. Confirm it so, mine honourable lord.

Glou. Confirm it so? Confounded be your
strife!
And perish ye with your audacious prate!
Presumptuous vassals, are you not asham'd
With this immodest clamorous outrage   126
To trouble and disturb the King and us?
And you, my lords, methinks you do not well
To bear with their perverse objections;
Much less to take occasion from their mouths

To raise a mutiny betwixt yourselves.   131
Let me persuade you take a better course.

Exe. It grieves his Highness. Good my lords,
be friends.

King. Come hither you that would be com-
batants.
Henceforth I charge you, as you love our
favour,   135
Quite to forget this quarrel and the cause.
And you, my lords — remember where we are,
In France, amongst a fickle wavering nation.
If they perceive dissension in our looks
And that within ourselves we disagree,   140
How will their grudging stomachs be provok'd
To wilful disobedience, and rebel!
Beside, what infamy will there arise
When foreign princes shall be certified
That for a toy, a thing of no regard,   145
King Henry's peers and chief nobility
Destroy'd themselves and lost the realm of
France!
O, think upon the conquest of my father,
My tender years, and let us not forgo
That for a trifle that was bought with blood!
Let me be umpire in this doubtful strife.   151
I see no reason, if I wear this rose,
                        [*Puts on a red rose.*]
That any one should therefore be suspicious
I more incline to Somerset than York.
Both are my kinsmen, and I love them both.
As well they may upbraid me with my crown
Because (forsooth) the King of Scots is crown'd!
But your discretions better can persuade
Than I am able to instruct or teach;
And therefore, as we hither came in peace,   160
So let us still continue peace and love.
Cousin of York, we institute your Grace
To be our Regent in these parts of France;
And, good my Lord of Somerset, unite   164
Your troops of horsemen with his bands of foot;
And like true subjects, sons of your progeni-
tors,
Go cheerfully together and digest
Your angry choler on your enemies.
Ourself, my Lord Protector, and the rest,
After some respite will return to Calais;   170
From thence to England, where I hope ere long
To be presented, by your victories,
With Charles, Alençon, and that traitorous
rout.
        Flourish. Exeunt. Manent York, Warwick,
                                Exeter, Vernon.

War. My Lord of York, I promise you, the
King
Prettily, methought, did play the orator.   175

York. And so he did; but yet I like it not,
In that he wears the badge of Somerset.
  War. Tush, that was but his fancy. Blame
    him not!
I dare presume, sweet prince, he thought no
    harm.
  York. An if I wist he did — But let it rest;
Other affairs must now be managed.   181
                    Exeunt. Manet Exeter.
  Exe. Well didst thou, Richard, to suppress
    thy voice;
For, had the passions of thy heart burst out,
I fear we should have seen decipher'd there
More rancorous spite, more furious raging
    broils,   185
Than yet can be imagin'd or suppos'd.
But howsoe'er, no simple man that sees
This jarring discord of nobility,
This shouldering of each other in the court,
This factious bandying of their favourites, 190
But that it doth presage some ill event.
'Tis much when sceptres are in children's hands,
But more when envy breeds unkind division.
There comes the ruin, there begins confusion.
                                        Exit.

[Scene II.]

Enter *Talbot*, with *Trump* and *Drum*
before Bordeaux.

  Tal. Go to the gates of Bordeaux, trumpeter.
Summon their general unto the wall.

[*Trumpet*] *sounds* [*a parley*]. Enter [the *Captain*] *General* [*of the French*, and others], aloft.

English John Talbot, Captains, calls you forth,
Servant in arms to Harry King of England;
And thus he would: Open your city gates,   5
Be humble to us, call my sovereign yours
And do him homage as obedient subjects,
And I'll withdraw me and my bloody power;
But if you frown upon this proffer'd peace,
You tempt the fury of my three attendants, 10
Lean famine, quartering steel, and climbing
    fire,
Who in a moment even with the earth
Shall lay your stately and air-braving towers,
If you forsake the offer of their love.
  Capt. Thou ominous and fearful owl of
    death,   15
Our nation's terror and their bloody scourge,
The period of thy tyranny approacheth!
On us thou canst not enter but by death;

For I protest we are well fortified
And strong enough to issue out and fight. 20
If thou retire, the Dauphin, well appointed,
Stands with the snares of war to tangle thee.
On either hand thee there are squadrons pitch'd
To wall thee from the liberty of flight;
And no way canst thou turn thee for redress 25
But death doth front thee with apparent spoil
And pale destruction meets thee in the face.
Ten thousand French have ta'en the sacrament
To rive their dangerous artillery
Upon no Christian soul but English Talbot. 30
Lo, there thou stand'st, a breathing valiant
    man
Of an invincible unconquer'd spirit!
This is the latest glory of thy praise
That I thy enemy due thee withal;
For ere the glass that now begins to run   35
Finish the process of his sandy hour,
These eyes that see thee now well-coloured
Shall see thee withered, bloody, pale, and dead.
                                Drum afar off.
Hark! hark! The Dauphin's drum, a warning
    bell,
Sings heavy music to thy timorous soul;   40
And mine shall ring thy dire departure out.
                          Exit [*with his men*].
  Tal. He fables not; I hear the enemy.
Out, some light horsemen, and peruse their
    wings.
O, negligent and heedless discipline!
How are we park'd and bounded in a pale,   45
A little herd of England's timorous deer,
Maz'd with a yelping kennel of French curs!
If we be English deer, be then in blood;
Not rascal-like, to fall down with a pinch, 49
But rather, moody-mad and desperate stags,
Turn on the bloody hounds with heads of steel
And make the cowards stand aloof at bay.
Sell every man his life as dear as mine,
And they shall find dear deer of us, my friends.
God and Saint George, Talbot and England's
    right,   55
Prosper our colours in this dangerous fight!
                                    [*Exeunt.*]

[Scene III. *Plains in Gascony.*]

Enter a *Messenger* that meets *York.* Enter
York, with *Trumpet* and many *Soldiers*.

  York. Are not the speedy scouts return'd
    again
That dogg'd the mighty army of the Dauphin?

Mess. They are return'd, my lord, and give
it out
That he is march'd to Bordeaux with his power
To fight with Talbot. As he march'd along, 5
By your espials were discovered
Two mightier troops than that the Dauphin led,
Which join'd with him and made their march
for Bordeaux.
York. A plague upon that villain Somerset
That thus delays my promised supply 10
Of horsemen that were levied for this siege!
Renowned Talbot doth expect my aid,
And I am louted by a traitor villain
And cannot help the noble chevalier.
God comfort him in this necessity! 15
If he miscarry, farewell wars in France.

Enter [Sir William Lucy,] another Messenger.

Lucy. Thou princely leader of our English
strength,
Never so needful on the earth of France,
Spur to the rescue of the noble Talbot,
Who now is girdled with a waist of iron 20
And hemm'd about with grim destruction.
To Bordeaux, warlike Duke! to Bordeaux,
York!
Else farewell Talbot, France, and England's
honour.
York. O God, that Somerset, who in proud
heart
Doth stop my cornets, were in Talbot's place!
So should we save a valiant gentleman 26
By forfeiting a traitor and a coward.
Mad ire and wrathful fury makes me weep
That thus we die while remiss traitors sleep.
Lucy. O, send some succour to the distress'd
lord! 30
York. He dies, we lose; I break my warlike
word;
We mourn, France smiles; we lose, they daily
get;
All long of this vile traitor Somerset.
Lucy. Then God take mercy on brave Tal-
bot's soul
And on his son, young John, who two hours
since 35
I met in travel toward his warlike father!
This seven years did not Talbot see his son,
And now they meet where both their lives are
done.
York. Alas, what joy shall noble Talbot have
To bid his young son welcome to his grave? 40
Away! Vexation almost stops my breath
That sund'red friends greet in the hour of death.
Lucy, farewell. No more my fortune can

But curse the cause I cannot aid the man.
Maine, Blois, Poictiers, and Tours are won
away, 45
Long all of Somerset and his delay.
                    Exit [with Soldiers].
Lucy. Thus, while the vulture of sedition
Feeds in the bosom of such great commanders,
Sleeping neglection doth betray to loss
The conquest of our scarce-cold conqueror, 50
That ever-living man of memory,
Henry the Fifth. Whiles they each other cross,
Lives, honours, lands, and all hurry to loss.
                    [Exit.]

[Scene IV. *Other plains in Gascony.*]

*Enter Somerset, with his Army, [a Captain of
Talbot's with him].*

Som. It is too late; I cannot send them now.
This expedition was by York and Talbot
Too rashly plotted. All our general force
Might with a sally of the very town
Be buckled with. The over-daring Talbot 5
Hath sullied all his gloss of former honour
By this unheedful, desperate, wild adventure.
York set him on to fight, and die in shame,
That, Talbot dead, great York might bear the
name.

[*Enter Sir William Lucy.*]

Capt. Here is Sir William Lucy, who with
me 10
Set from our o'ermatch'd forces forth for aid.
Som. How now, Sir William? Whither were
you sent?
Lucy. Whither, my lord? From bought and
sold Lord Talbot,
Who, ring'd about with bold adversity,
Cries out for noble York and Somerset 15
To beat assailing death from his weak legions;
And whiles the honourable captain there
Drops bloody sweat from his war-wearied limbs,
And, in advantage ling'ring, looks for rescue,
You, his false hopes, the trust of England's
honour, 20
Keep off aloof with worthless emulation.
Let not your private discord keep away
The levied succours that should lend him aid,
While he, renowned noble gentleman,
Yield up his life unto a world of odds. 25
Orleans the Bastard, Charles, Burgundy,
Alençon, Reignier compass him about,
And Talbot perisheth by your default.

221

Som. York set him on; York should have
sent him aid.
Lucy. And York as fast upon your Grace
exclaims,   30
Swearing that you withhold his levied host,
Collected for this expedition.
   Som. York lies. He might have sent and had
the horse.
I owe him little duty, and less love,
And take foul scorn to fawn on him by send-
ing.   35
   Lucy. The fraud of England, not the force of
France,
Hath now entrapp'd the noble-minded Talbot.
Never to England shall he bear his life,
But dies betray'd to fortune by your strife.
   Som. Come, go! I will dispatch the horse-
men straight;   40
Within six hours they will be at his aid.
   Lucy. Too late comes rescue. He is ta'en or
slain;
For fly he could not, if he would have fled;
And fly would Talbot never, though he
might.
   Som. If he be dead, brave Talbot, then
adieu!   45
   Lucy. His fame lives in the world, his shame
in you.   *Exeunt.*

[Scene V. *The English camp near
Bordeaux.*]

Enter *Talbot* and [*John*] his son.

   Tal. O young John Talbot, I did send for
thee
To tutor thee in stratagems of war,
That Talbot's name might be in thee reviv'd
When sapless age and weak unable limbs
Should bring thy father to his drooping chair. 5
But O malignant and ill-boding stars!
Now thou art come unto a feast of death,
A terrible and unavoided danger.
Therefore, dear boy, mount on my swiftest
horse,
And I'll direct thee how thou shalt escape   10
By sudden flight. Come, dally not, be gone!
   John. Is my name Talbot? and am I your
son?
And shall I fly? O, if you love my mother,
Dishonour not her honourable name
To make a bastard and a slave of me!   15
The world will say he is not Talbot's blood
That basely fled when noble Talbot stood.

   Tal. Fly, to revenge my death if I be slain.
   John. He that flies so will ne'er return
again.
   Tal. If we both stay, we both are sure to
die.   2
   John. Then let me stay, and, father, do you
fly.
Your loss is great, so your regard should be;
My worth unknown, no loss is known in me.
Upon my death the French can little boast;
In yours they will, in you all hopes are lost. 2
Flight cannot stain the honour you have
won;
But mine it will, that no exploit have done.
You fled for vantage, every one will swear;
But if I bow, they'll say it was for fear.
There is no hope that ever I will stay   3
If the first hour I shrink and run away.
Here on my knee I beg mortality
Rather than life preserv'd with infamy.
   Tal. Shall all thy mother's hopes lie in one
tomb?
   John. Ay, rather than I'll shame my mother's
womb.   3
   Tal. Upon my blessing I command thee go.
   John. To fight I will, but not to fly the
foe.
   Tal. Part of thy father may be sav'd in
thee.
   John. No part of him but will be shame in
me.
   Tal. Thou never hadst renown, nor canst
not lose it.   4
   John. Yes, your renowned name. Shall
flight abuse it?
   Tal. Thy father's charge shall clear thee from
that stain.
   John. You cannot witness for me, being
slain.
If death be so apparent, then both fly.
   Tal. And leave my followers here to fight
and die?   45
My age was never tainted with such shame.
   John. And shall my youth be guilty of such
blame?
No more can I be severed from your side
Than can yourself yourself in twain divide.
Stay, go, do what you will — the like do I;   50
For live I will not if my father die.
   Tal. Then here I take my leave of thee, fair
son,
Born to eclipse thy life this afternoon.
Come, side by side together live and die,   54
And soul with soul from France to heaven fly!
                                               Exeunt.

[Scene VI. *A field of battle.*]

*Alarum. Excursions, wherein Talbot's Son
is hemm'd about and Talbot rescues him.*

Tal. Saint George and victory! Fight,
   soldiers, fight!
The Regent hath with Talbot broke his word
And left us to the rage of France his sword.
Where is John Talbot? Pause, and take thy
   breath.
I gave thee life and rescu'd thee from death.   5
John. O twice my father, twice am I thy
   son!
The life thou gav'st me first was lost and
   done
Till with thy warlike sword, despite of fate,
To my determin'd time thou gav'st new date.
Tal. When from the Dauphin's crest thy
   sword struck fire,   10
It warm'd thy father's heart with proud de-
   sire
Of bold-fac'd victory. Then leaden age,
Quicken'd with youthful spleen and warlike
   rage,
Beat down Alençon, Orleans, Burgundy,
And from the pride of Gallia rescued thee.   15
The ireful Bastard Orleans, that drew blood
From thee, my boy, and had the maidenhood
Of thy first fight, I soon encountered,
And interchanging blows, I quickly shed
Some of his bastard blood; and in disgrace   20
Bespoke him thus: 'Contaminated, base,
And misbegotten blood I spill of thine,
Mean and right poor, for that pure blood of
   mine
Which thou didst force from Talbot, my brave
   boy.
Here, purposing the Bastard to destroy,   25
Came in strong rescue. Speak, thy father's care.
Art thou not weary, John? How dost thou
   fare?
Wilt thou yet leave the battle, boy, and fly,
Now thou art seal'd the son of chivalry?
Fly, to revenge my death when I am dead.   30
The help of one stands me in little stead.
O, too much folly is it, well I wot,
To hazard all our lives in one small boat!
If I to-day die not with Frenchmen's rage,
To-morrow I shall die with mickle age.   35
By me they nothing gain an if I stay;
'Tis but the short'ning of my life one day.
In thee thy mother dies, our household's name,
My death's revenge, thy youth, and England's
   fame.

All these, and more, we hazard by thy stay;   40
All these are sav'd if thou wilt fly away.
   John. The sword of Orleans hath not made
   me smart;
These words of yours draw lifeblood from my
   heart.
On that advantage, bought with such a shame,
To save a paltry life and slay bright fame,   45
Before young Talbot from old Talbot fly,
The coward horse that bears me fall and die!
And like me to the peasant boys of France,
To be shame's scorn and subject of mischance!
Surely, by all the glory you have won,   50
An if I fly, I am not Talbot's son.
Then talk no more of flight! It is no boot.
If son to Talbot, die at Talbot's foot.
   Tal. Then follow thou thy desp'rate sire of
   Crete,
Thou Icarus. Thy life to me is sweet.   55
If thou wilt fight, fight by thy father's side;
And, commendable prov'd, let's die in pride.
                                        Exeunt.

[Scene VII. *Another part of the field.*]

Alarum. Excursions. Enter old *Talbot*, led.

   Tal. Where is my other life? Mine own is
   gone.
O, where's young Talbot? Where is valiant
   John?
Triumphant death, smear'd with captivity,
Young Talbot's valour makes me smile at thee.
When he perceiv'd me shrink and on my knee,   5
His bloody sword he brandish'd over me
And like a hungry lion did commence
Rough deeds of rage and stern impatience;
But when my angry guardant stood alone,
Tend'ring my ruin and assail'd of none,   10
Dizzy-ey'd fury and great rage of heart
Suddenly made him from my side to start
Into the clust'ring battle of the French;
And in that sea of blood my boy did drench
His over-mounting spirit; and there died   15
My Icarus, my blossom, in his pride.

   Enter [*Soldiers*] with *John Talbot*, borne.

   Servant. O my dear lord, lo where your son is
   borne!
   Tal. Thou antic Death, which laugh'st us
   here to scorn,
Anon, from thy insulting tyranny,
Coupled in bonds of perpetuity,   20
Two Talbots, winged through the lither sky,

223

In thy despite shall scape mortality.
O thou whose wounds become hard-favoured
death,
Speak to thy father ere thou yield thy breath!
Brave Death by speaking, whether he will or
no.   25
Imagine him a Frenchman, and thy foe.
Poor boy! he smiles, methinks, as who should
say,
'Had Death been French, then Death had died
to-day.'
Come, come, and lay him in his father's arms!
My spirit can no longer bear these harms.   30
Soldiers, adieu! I have what I would have,
Now my old arms are young John Talbot's
grave.   *Dies.*

Enter *Charles, Alençon, Burgundy, Bastard,*
     and *Pucelle.*

Char. Had York and Somerset brought
  rescue in,
We should have found a bloody day of this.
Bast. How the young whelp of Talbot's, rag-
  ing wood,   35
Did flesh his puny sword in Frenchmen's blood!
Puc. Once I encount'red him and thus I
  said,
'Thou maiden youth, be vanquish'd by a maid.'
But with a proud majestical high scorn
He answer'd thus, 'Young Talbot was not born
To be the pillage of a giglot wench.'   41
So, rushing in the bowels of the French,
He left me proudly, as unworthy fight.
Bur. Doubtless he would have made a noble
  knight.
See where he lies inhearsed in the arms   45
Of the most bloody nurser of his harms.
Bast. Hew them to pieces! hack their bones
  asunder
Whose life was England's glory, Gallia's
  wonder!
Char. O, no, forbear! For that which we
  have fled
During the life, let us not wrong it dead.   50

Enter *Lucy,* [attended; a *French Herald*
     preceding].

Lucy. Herald, conduct me to the Dauphin's
  tent,
To know who hath obtain'd the glory of the
  day.
Char. On what submissive message art thou
  sent?
Lucy. Submission, Dauphin? 'Tis a mere
  French word.   54

We English warriors wot not what it means.
I come to know what prisoners thou hast ta'en
And to survey the bodies of the dead.
Char. For prisoners ask'st thou? Hell our
  prison is.
But tell me whom thou seek'st.   59
Lucy. Where is the great Alcides of the field,
Valiant Lord Talbot, Earl of Shrewsbury,
Created for his rare success in arms
Great Earl of Washford, Waterford, and
  Valence,
Lord Talbot of Goodrig and Urchinfield,
Lord Strange of Blackmere, Lord Verdun of
  Alton,   65
Lord Cromwell of Wingfield, Lord Furnival of
  Sheffield,
The thrice-victorious Lord of Falconbridge,
Knight of the noble order of Saint George,
Worthy Saint Michael, and the Golden Fleece,
Great Marshal to Henry the Sixth   70
Of all his wars within the realm of France?
Puc. Here is a silly-stately style indeed!
The Turk, that two-and-fifty kingdoms hath,
Writes not so tedious a style as this.   74
Him that thou magnifi'st with all these titles,
Stinking and flyblown lies here at our feet.
Lucy. Is Talbot slain, the Frenchmen's only
  scourge,
Your kingdom's terror and black Nemesis?
O, were mine eyeballs into bullets turn'd,
That I in rage might shoot them at your
  faces!   80
O that I could but call these dead to life!
It were enough to fright the realm of France.
Were but his picture left amongst you here,
It would amaze the proudest of you all.
Give me their bodies, that I may bear them
  hence   85
And give them burial as beseems their worth.
Puc. I think this upstart is old Talbot's
  ghost,
He speaks with such a proud commanding
  spirit.
For God's sake, let him have them! To keep
  them here,
They would but stink and putrefy the air.   90
Char. Go take their bodies hence.
Lucy. I'll bear them hence; but from their
  ashes shall be rear'd
A phœnix that shall make all France afeard.
Char. So we be rid of them, do with them
  what thou wilt.
And now to Paris in this conquering vein!   95
All will be ours, now bloody Talbot's slain.
                                        Exeunt.

[ACT V.] Scene [I. *London. The Palace.*]

Sennet. Enter *King, Gloucester,* and *Exeter.*

King. Have you perus'd the letters from
  the Pope,
The Emperor, and the Earl of Armagnac?
  Glou. I have, my lord, and their intent is
  this:
They humbly sue unto your Excellence
To have a godly peace concluded of   5
Between the realms of England and of France.
  King. How doth your Grace affect their
  motion?
  Glou. Well, my good lord, and as the only
  means
To stop effusion of our Christian blood
And stablish quietness on every side.   10
  King. Ay, marry, uncle; for I always thought
It was both impious and unnatural
That such immanity and bloody strife
Should reign among professors of one faith.
  Glou. Beside, my lord, the sooner to effect 15
And surer bind this knot of amity,
The Earl of Armagnac, near knit to Charles,
A man of great authority in France,
Proffers his only daughter to your Grace   19
In marriage, with a large and sumptuous dowry.
  King. Marriage, uncle? Alas! my years are
  young,
And fitter is my study and my books
Than wanton dalliance with a paramour.
Yet, call th' ambassadors; and as you please,
So let them have their answers every one. 25
I shall be well content with any choice
Tends to God's glory and my country's weal.

Enter *Winchester* [in Cardinal's habit] and
  three *Ambassadors*, [one a *Papal Legate*].

  Exe. [*aside*] What, is my Lord of Winchester
  install'd,
And call'd unto a cardinal's degree?
Then I perceive that will be verified   30
Henry the Fifth did sometime prophesy —
'If once he come to be a cardinal,
He'll make his cap coequal with the crown.'
  King. My Lords Ambassadors, your several
  suits
Have been consider'd and debated on.   35
Your purpose is both good and reasonable,
And therefore are we certainly resolv'd
To draw conditions of a friendly peace,
Which by my Lord of Winchester we mean
Shall be transported presently to France. 40

  Glou. And for the proffer of my lord your
  master,
I have inform'd his Highness so at large
As, liking of the lady's virtuous gifts,
Her beauty, and the value of her dower, 44
He doth intend she shall be England's Queen.
  King. In argument and proof of which
  contract
Bear her this jewel, pledge of my affection.
And so, my Lord Protector, see them guarded
And safely brought to Dover, where inshipp'd
Commit them to the fortune of the sea. 50
    Exeunt [*all but Winchester and the Legate*].
  Win. Stay, my Lord Legate. You shall first
  receive
The sum of money which I promised
Should be delivered to his Holiness
For clothing me in these grave ornaments.
  Legate. I will attend upon your lordship's
  leisure.   [*Steps aside.*]
  Win. Now Winchester will not submit, I
  trow,   56
Or be inferior to the proudest peer.
Humphrey of Gloucester, thou shalt well per-
  ceive
That neither in birth or for authority
The Bishop will be overborne by thee. 60
I'll either make thee stoop and bend thy knee
Or sack this country with a mutiny. *Exeunt.*

Scene [II. *France. Plains in Anjou.*]

Enter *Charles, Burgundy, Alençon, Bastard,*
  Reignier, and *Joan.*

  Char. These news, my lords, may cheer our
  drooping spirits:
'Tis said the stout Parisians do revolt
And turn again unto the warlike French.
  Alen. Then march to Paris, royal Charles of
  France,
And keep not back your powers in dalliance. 5
  Puc. Peace be amongst them if they turn
  to us;
Else ruin combat with their palaces!

Enter *Scout.*

  Scout. Success unto our valiant general
And happiness to his accomplices!
  Char. What tidings send our scouts? I
  prithee speak.   10

Scout. The English army, that divided was
Into two parties, is now conjoin'd in one
And means to give you battle presently.
  Char. Somewhat too sudden, sirs, the warn-
    ing is,
But we will presently provide for them.   15
  Bur. I trust the ghost of Talbot is not there.
Now he is gone, my lord, you need not fear.
  Puc. Of all base passions fear is most ac-
    curs'd.
Command the conquest, Charles, it shall be
    thine,
Let Henry fret and all the world repine.   20
  Char. Then on, my lords; and France be
    fortunate!   *Exeunt.*

[Scene III. *Before Angiers.*]

Alarum. Excursions. Enter *Joan la Pucelle.*
  Puc. The Regent conquers and the French-
    men fly.
Now help, ye charming spells and periapts;
And ye choice spirits that admonish me,
And give me signs of future accidents.
                                  Thunder.
You speedy helpers that are substitutes   5
Under the lordly Monarch of the North,
Appear and aid me in this enterprise!

Enter *Fiends.*

This speedy and quick appearance argues proof
Of your accustom'd diligence to me.
Now, ye familiar spirits that are cull'd   10
Out of the powerful legions under earth,
Help me this once, that France may get the
    field.   *They walk, and speak not.*
O, hold me not with silence over-long!
Where I was wont to feed you with my blood,
I'll lop a member off and give it you   15
In earnest of a further benefit,
So you do condescend to help me now.
                          They hang their heads.
No hope to have redress? My body shall
Pay recompense if you will grant my suit.
                          They shake their heads.
Cannot my body nor blood-sacrifice   20
Entreat you to your wonted furtherance?
Then take my soul — my body, soul, and all,
Before that England give the French the foil.
                                  They depart.
See, they forsake me! Now the time is come
That France must vail her lofty-plumed crest
And let her head fall into England's lap.   26
My ancient incantations are too weak,

And hell too strong for me to buckle with.
Now, France, thy glory droopeth to the dust.
                                      Exit.

Excursions. [Enter *French* and *English,* fight-
ing.] *Burgundy* and *York* fight hand to hand.
  French fly. [*La Pucelle* is taken.]
  York. Damsel of France, I think I have you
    fast.   30
Unchain your spirits now with spelling charms
And try if they can gain your liberty.
A goodly prize, fit for the devil's grace!
See how the ugly witch doth bend her brows
As if, with Circe, she would change my shape!
  Puc. Chang'd to a worser shape thou canst
    not be.   36
  York. O, Charles the Dauphin is a proper
    man!
No shape but his can please your dainty eye.
  Puc. A plaguing mischief light on Charles
    and thee!
And may ye both be suddenly surpris'd   40
By bloody hands in sleeping on your beds!
  York. Fell banning hag, enchantress, hold
    thy tongue!
  Puc. I prithee give me leave to curse awhile.
  York. Curse, miscreant, when thou comest
    to the stake.   *Exeunt.*

Alarum. Enter *Suffolk,* with *Margaret* in
            his hand.

  Suf. Be what thou wilt, thou art my prisoner.
                              Gazes on her.
O fairest beauty, do not fear nor fly!   46
For I will touch thee but with reverent hands;
I kiss these fingers for eternal peace
And lay them gently on thy tender side.
Who art thou? Say, that I may honour thee.
  Mar. Margaret my name, and daughter to
    a king,   51
The King of Naples, whosoe'er thou art.
  Suf. An earl I am and Suffolk am I call'd.
Be not offended, nature's miracle,
Thou art allotted to be ta'en by me.   55
So doth the swan her downy cygnets save,
Keeping them prisoner underneath her wings.
Yet, if this servile usage once offend,
Go and be free again as Suffolk's friend.   59
                                She is going.
O, stay! [*Aside*] I have no power to let her pass;
My hand would free her, but my heart says no.
As plays the sun upon the glassy streams,
Twinkling another counterfeited beam,
So seems this gorgeous beauty to mine eyes.
Fain would I woo her, yet I dare not speak.   65

I'll call for pen and ink and write my mind.
Fie, de la Pole! disable not thyself.
Hast not a tongue? Is she not here thy prisoner?
Wilt thou be daunted at a woman's sight?
Ay, beauty's princely majesty is such   70
Confounds the tongue and makes the senses
rough.
  Mar. Say, Earl of Suffolk, if thy name be so,
What ransom must I pay before I pass?
For I perceive I am thy prisoner.
  Suf. How canst thou tell she will deny thy
suit   75
Before thou make a trial of her love?
  Mar. Why speak'st thou not? What ransom
must I pay?
  Suf. She's beautiful, and therefore to be
woo'd;
She is a woman, therefore to be won.
  Mar. Wilt thou accept of ransom — yea or
no?   80
  Suf. Fond man, remember that thou hast a
wife.
Then how can Margaret be thy paramour?
  Mar. I were best to leave him, for he will not
hear.
  Suf. There all is marr'd; there lies a cooling
card.
  Mar. He talks at randon. Sure the man is
mad.   85
  Suf. And yet a dispensation may be had.
  Mar. And yet I would that you would an-
swer me.
  Suf. I'll win this Lady Margaret. For
whom?
Why, for my king. Tush, that's a wooden thing!
  Mar. He talks of wood. It is some carpenter.
  Suf. Yet so my fancy may be satisfied   91
And peace established between these realms.
But there remains a scruple in that too;
For though her father be the King of Naples,
Duke of Anjou and Maine, yet is he poor,   95
And our nobility will scorn the match.
  Mar. Hear ye, Captain? Are you not at
leisure?
  Suf. It shall be so, disdain they ne'er so
much.
Henry is youthful and will quickly yield. —
Madam, I have a secret to reveal.   100
  Mar. What though I be enthrall'd? He
seems a knight
And will not any way dishonour me.
  Suf. Lady, vouchsafe to listen what I say.
  Mar. Perhaps I shall be rescu'd by the
French,
And then I need not crave his courtesy.   105

  Suf. Sweet madam, give me hearing in a
cause —
  Mar. Tush, women have been captivate ere
now.
  Suf. Lady, wherefore talk you so?
  Mar. I cry you mercy, 'tis but Quid for
Quo.
  Suf. Say, gentle Princess, would you not
suppose   110
Your bondage happy, to be made a queen?
  Mar. To be a queen in bondage is more vile
Than is a slave in base servility;
For princes should be free.
  Suf.   And so shall you,
If happy England's royal king be free.   115
  Mar. Why, what concerns his freedom unto
me?
  Suf. I'll undertake to make thee Henry's
queen,
To put a golden sceptre in thy hand
And set a precious crown upon thy head,
If thou wilt condescend to be my —
  Mar.   What?   120
  Suf. His love.
  Mar. I am unworthy to be Henry's wife.
  Suf. No, gentle madam. I unworthy am
To woo so fair a dame to be his wife
And have no portion in the choice myself.   125
How say you, madam? Are ye so content?
  Mar. An if my father please, I am content.
  Suf. Then call our captains and our colours
forth!
And, madam, at your father's castle walls
We'll crave a parley to confer with him.   130

Sound [a parley]. Enter Reignier on the walls.
See, Reignier, see, thy daughter prisoner!
  Reig. To whom?
  Suf.   To me.
  Reig.   Suffolk, what remedy?
I am a soldier, and unapt to weep
Or to exclaim on fortune's fickleness.
  Suf. Yes, there is remedy enough, my lord.
Consent, and for thy honour give consent,   136
Thy daughter shall be wedded to my king,
Whom I with pain have woo'd and won thereto;
And this her easy-held imprisonment
Hath gain'd thy daughter princely liberty.   140
  Reig. Speaks Suffolk as he thinks?
  Suf.   Fair Margaret knows
That Suffolk doth not flatter, face, or feign.
  Reig. Upon thy princely warrant I descend
To give thee answer of thy just demand.
  Suf. And here I will expect thy coming.   145
                       [Exit Reignier.]

Trumpets sound. Enter *Reignier* [below].

Reig. Welcome, brave Earl, into our terri-
tories.
Command in Anjou what your Honour pleases.
Suf. Thanks, Reignier, happy for so sweet a
child,
Fit to be made companion with a king.   149
What answer makes your Grace unto my suit?
Reig. Since thou dost deign to woo her little
worth
To be the princely bride of such a lord,
Upon condition I may quietly
Enjoy mine own, the counties Maine and Anjou,
Free from oppression or the stroke of war,   155
My daughter shall be Henry's, if he please.
Suf. That is her ransom. I deliver her,
And those two counties I will undertake
Your Grace shall well and quietly enjoy.
Reig. And I again, in Henry's royal name, 160
As deputy unto that gracious king,
Give thee her hand for sign of plighted faith.
Suf. Reignier of France, I give thee kingly
thanks,
Because this is in traffic of a king.
[*Aside*] And yet methinks I could be well con-
tent   165
To be mine own attorney in this case. —
I'll over then to England with this news
And make this marriage to be solemniz'd.
So, farewell, Reignier. Set this diamond safe
In golden palaces, as it becomes.   170
Reig. I do embrace thee as I would embrace
The Christian prince King Henry, were he here.
Mar. Farewell, my lord. Good wishes, praise,
and prayers
Shall Suffolk ever have of Margaret.
                              She is going.
Suf. Farewell, sweet madam. But hark you,
Margaret —   175
No princely commendations to my king?
Mar. Such commendations as becomes a
maid,
A virgin, and his servant, say to him.
Suf. Words sweetly plac'd and modestly
directed.
But, madam, I must trouble you again —   180
No loving token to his Majesty?
Mar. Yes, my good lord: a pure unspotted
heart,
Never yet taint with love, I send the King.
Suf. And this withal.   *Kiss her.*
Mar. That for thyself. I will not so presume
To send such peevish tokens to a king.   186
          [*Exeunt Reignier and Margaret.*]

Suf. O, wert thou for myself! But, Suffolk,
stay.
Thou mayst not wander in that labyrinth;
There Minotaurs and ugly treasons lurk.
Solicit Henry with her wondrous praise.   190
Bethink thee on her virtues that surmount,
And natural graces that extinguish art;
Repeat their semblance often on the seas,
That, when thou com'st to kneel at Henry's
feet,
Thou mayst bereave him of his wits with
wonder.   *Exit.*

[Scene IV. *Camp of the* Duke of York
in Anjou.]

Enter *York, Warwick, Shepherd, Pucelle*
[guarded].

York. Bring forth that sorceress condemn'd
to burn.
Shep. Ah, Joan, this kills thy father's heart
outright!
Have I sought every country far and near,
And, now it is my chance to find thee out,
Must I behold thy timeless cruel death?   5
Ah, Joan, sweet daughter Joan, I'll die with
thee!
Puc. Decrepit miser! base ignoble wretch!
I am descended of a gentler blood.
Thou art no father nor no friend of mine.
Shep. Out, out! My lords, an please you,
'tis not so.   10
I did beget her, all the parish knows.
Her mother liveth yet, can testify
She was the first fruit of my bach'lorship.
War. Graceless! wilt thou deny thy parent-
age?
York. This argues what her kind of life hath
been,   15
Wicked and vile; and so her death concludes.
Shep. Fie, Joan, that thou wilt be so obstacle!
God knows thou art a collop of my flesh,
And for thy sake have I shed many a tear.
Deny me not, I prithee, gentle Joan.   20
Puc. Peasant, avaunt! You have suborn'd
this man,
Of purpose to obscure my noble birth.
Shep. 'Tis true, I gave a noble to the priest
The morn that I was wedded to her mother.
Kneel down and take my blessing, good my
girl.   25
Wilt thou not stoop? Now cursed be the time
Of thy nativity! I would the milk

Thy mother gave thee when thou suck'dst her
  breast
Had been a little ratsbane for thy sake!
Or else, when thou didst keep my lambs
  afield,
I wish some ravenous wolf had eaten thee! 31
Dost thou deny thy father, cursed drab?
O, burn her, burn her! Hanging is too good.
                                Exit.
  York. Take her away; for she hath liv'd too
  long,
To fill the world with vicious qualities. 35
  Puc. First let me tell you whom you have
  condemn'd:
Not one begotten of a shepherd swain,
But issued from the progeny of kings,
Virtuous and holy, chosen from above
By inspiration of celestial grace 40
To work exceeding miracles on earth.
I never had to do with wicked spirits;
But you, that are polluted with your lusts,
Stain'd with the guiltless blood of innocents,
Corrupt and tainted with a thousand vices — 45
Because you want the grace that others have,
You judge it straight a thing impossible
To compass wonders but by help of devils.
No, misconceived! Joan of Arc hath been
A virgin from her tender infancy, 50
Chaste and immaculate in very thought,
Whose maiden blood, thus rigorously effus'd,
Will cry for vengeance at the gates of heaven.
  York. Ay, ay. Away with her to execution!
  War. And hark ye, sirs. Because she is a
  maid, 55
Spare for no fagots, let there be enow.
Place barrels of pitch upon the fatal stake,
That so her torture may be shortened.
  Puc. Will nothing turn your unrelenting
  hearts?
Then, Joan, discover thine infirmity, 60
That warranteth by law to be thy privilege.
I am with child, ye bloody homicides,
Murther not then the fruit within my womb,
Although ye hale me to a violent death.
  York. Now heaven forfend! The holy maid
  with child? 65
  War. The greatest miracle that e'er ye
  wrought.
Is all your strict preciseness come to this?
  York. She and the Dauphin have been jug-
  gling.
I did imagine what would be her refuge.
  War. Well, go to! We'll have no bastards
  live, 70
Especially since Charles must father it.

  Puc. You are deceiv'd. My child is none of
  his.
It was Alençon that enjoy'd my love.
  York. Alençon! that notorious Machiavel?
It dies, an if it had a thousand lives. 75
  Puc. O, give me leave! I have deluded you.
'Twas neither Charles nor yet the duke I
  nam'd,
But Reignier, King of Naples, that prevail'd.
  War. A married man! That's most intoler-
  able.
  York. Why, here's a girl! I think she knows
  not well 80
(There were so many) whom she may accuse.
  War. It's sign she hath been liberal and free.
  York. And yet, forsooth, she is a virgin pure!
Strumpet, thy words condemn thy brat and
  thee.
Use no entreaty, for it is in vain. 85
  Puc. Then lead me hence; with whom I
  leave my curse.
May never glorious sun reflex his beams
Upon the country where you make abode;
But darkness and the gloomy shade of death
Environ you, till mischief and despair 90
Drive you to break your necks or hang your-
  selves!   *Exit [guarded].*
  York. Break thou in pieces and consume to
  ashes,
Thou foul accursed minister of hell!

    Enter *Cardinal [Beaufort,* attended].

  Car. Lord Regent, I do greet your Excellence
With letters of commission from the King. 95
For know, my lords, the states of Christendom,
Mov'd with remorse of these outrageous broils,
Have earnestly implor'd a general peace
Betwixt our nation and the aspiring French;
And here at hand the Dauphin and his train
Approacheth, to confer about some matter. 101
  York. Is all our travail turn'd to this effect?
After the slaughter of so many peers,
So many captains, gentlemen, and soldiers,
That in this quarrel have been overthrown 105
And sold their bodies for their country's benefit,
Shall we at last conclude effeminate peace?
Have we not lost most part of all the towns
By treason, falsehood, and by treachery
Our great progenitors had conquered? 110
O, Warwick, Warwick! I foresee with grief
The utter loss of all the realm of France.
  War. Be patient, York. If we conclude a
  peace,
It shall be with such strict and severe covenants
As little shall the Frenchmen gain thereby. 115

Enter *Charles, Alençon, Bastard, Reignier,*
[and others].

Char. Since, lords of England, it is thus
agreed
That peaceful truce shall be proclaim'd in
France,
We come to be informed by yourselves
What the conditions of that league must be.

York. Speak, Winchester; for boiling choler
chokes   120
The hollow passage of my poison'd voice
By sight of these our baleful enemies.

Car. Charles, and the rest, it is enacted thus:
That, in regard King Henry gives consent,
Of mere compassion and of lenity,   125
To ease your country of distressful war
And suffer you to breathe in fruitful peace,
You, shall become true liegemen to his crown;
And, Charles, upon condition thou wilt swear
To pay him tribute and submit thyself,   130
Thou shalt be plac'd as viceroy under him
And still enjoy thy regal dignity.

Alen. Must he be then as shadow of himself?
Adorn his temples with a coronet,
And yet, in substance and authority,   135
Retain but privilege of a private man?
This proffer is absurd and reasonless.

Char. 'Tis known already that I am pos-
sess'd
With more than half the Gallian territories
And therein reverenc'd for their lawful king.
Shall I, for lucre of the rest unvanquish'd,   141
Detract so much from that prerogative
As to be call'd but viceroy of the whole?
No, Lord Ambassador. I'll rather keep
That which I have than, coveting for more,   145
Be cast from possibility of all.

York. Insulting Charles, hast thou by secret
means
Us'd intercession to obtain a league,
And, now the matter grows to compremise,
Stand'st thou aloof upon comparison?   150
Either accept the title thou usurp'st,
Of benefit proceeding from our king
And not of any challenge of desert,
Or we will plague thee with incessant wars.

Reig. [*aside to Charles*] My lord, you do not
well in obstinacy   155
To cavil in the course of this contract.
If once it be neglected, ten to one
We shall not find like opportunity.

Alen. [*aside to Charles*] To say the truth, it
is your policy
To save your subjects from such massacre   160

And ruthless slaughters as are daily seen
By our proceeding in hostility;
And therefore take this compact of a truce,
Although you break it when your pleasure
serves.

War. How say'st thou, Charles? Shall our
condition stand?   165

Char. It shall;
Only reserv'd, you claim no interest
In any of our towns of garrison.

York. Then swear allegiance to his Majesty:
As thou art knight, never to disobey   170
Nor be rebellious to the crown of England —
Thou, nor thy nobles, to the crown of England.
[*Charles and the rest give tokens of fealty.*]
So, now dismiss your army when ye please,
Hang up your ensigns, let your drums be still,
For here we entertain a solemn peace.   175
Exeunt.

[Scene V. *London. The Palace.*]

Enter *Suffolk*, in conference with the *King;*
Gloucester and *Exeter.*

King. Your wondrous rare description, noble
Earl,
Of beauteous Margaret hath astonish'd me.
Her virtues, graced with external gifts,
Do breed love's settled passions in my heart;
And like as rigour of tempestuous gusts   5
Provokes the mightiest hulk against the tide,
So am I driven by breath of her renown
Either to suffer shipwrack or arrive
Where I may have fruition of her love.

Suf. Tush, my good lord! This superficial
tale   10
Is but a preface of her worthy praise.
The chief perfections of that lovely dame
(Had I sufficient skill to utter them)
Would make a volume of enticing lines
Able to ravish any dull conceit;   15
And, which is more, she is not so divine,
So full replete with choice of all delights,
But with as humble lowliness of mind
She is content to be at your command;   19
Command, I mean, of virtuous chaste intents,
To love and honour Henry as her lord.

King. And otherwise will Henry ne'er pre-
sume.
Therefore, my Lord Protector, give consent
That Marg'ret may be England's royal Queen.

Glou. So should I give consent to flatter sin.
You know, my lord, your Highness is betroth'd

230

Unto another lady of esteem.
How shall we then dispense with that contract
And not deface your honour with reproach?

 Suf. As doth a ruler with unlawful oaths, 30
Or one that at a triumph, having vow'd
To try his strength, forsaketh yet the lists
By reason of his adversary's odds.
A poor earl's daughter is unequal odds, 34
And therefore may be broke without offence.

 Glou. Why, what, I pray, is Margaret more
  than that?
Her father is no better than an earl,
Although in glorious titles he excel.

 Suf. Yes, my lord, her father is a king,
The King of Naples and Jerusalem, 40
And of such great authority in France
As his alliance will confirm our peace
And keep the Frenchmen in allegiance.

 Glou. And so the Earl of Armagnac may do,
Because he is near kinsman unto Charles. 45

 Exe. Beside, his wealth doth warrant a liberal dower,
Where Reignier sooner will receive than give.

 Suf. A dow'r, my lords? Disgrace not so
  your king
That he should be so abject, base, and poor
To choose for wealth and not for perfect love!
Henry is able to enrich his queen, 51
And not to seek a queen to make him rich.
So worthless peasants bargain for their wives,
As marketmen for oxen, sheep, or horse.
Marriage is a matter of more worth 55
Than to be dealt in by attorneyship.
Not whom we will, but whom his Grace affects,
Must be companion of his nuptial bed.
And therefore, lords, since he affects her most,
It most of all these reasons bindeth us 60
In our opinions she should be preferr'd;
For what is wedlock forced but a hell,
An age of discord and continual strife?
Whereas the contrary bringeth bliss
And is a pattern of celestial peace. 65
Whom should we match with Henry, being a
 king,
But Margaret, that is daughter to a king?
Her peerless feature, joined with her birth,
Approves her fit for none but for a king.

Her valiant courage and undaunted spirit 70
(More than in women commonly is seen)
Will answer our hope in issue of a king;
For Henry, son unto a conqueror,
Is likely to beget more conquerors
If with a lady of so high resolve 75
As is fair Margaret he be link'd in love.
Then yield, my lords, and here conclude with
 me
That Margaret shall be Queen, and none but
 she.

 King. Whether it be through force of your
 report,
My noble Lord of Suffolk, or for that 80
My tender youth was never yet attaint
With any passion of inflaming love,
I cannot tell; but this I am assur'd,
I feel such sharp dissension in my breast,
Such fierce alarums both of hope and fear, 85
As I am sick with working of my thoughts.
Take, therefore, shipping; post, my lord, to
 France;
Agree to any covenants, and procure
That Lady Margaret do vouchsafe to come
To cross the seas to England and be crown'd
King Henry's faithful and anointed queen. 91
For your expenses and sufficient charge,
Among the people gather up a tenth.
Be gone, I say; for till you do return
I rest perplexed with a thousand cares. 95
And you, good uncle, banish all offence.
If you do censure me by what you were,
Not what you are, I know it will excuse
This sudden execution of my will.
And so conduct me where, from company, 100
I may revolve and ruminate my grief. *Exit.*

 Glou. Ay, grief, I fear me, both at first and
  last! *Exit Gloucester [with Exeter].*

 Suf. Thus Suffolk hath prevail'd; and thus
 he goes,
As did the youthful Paris once to Greece,
With hope to find the like event in love 105
But prosper better than the Troyan did.
Margaret shall now be Queen, and rule the
 King;
But I will rule both her, the King, and realm.
          Exit.

The Second Part of King Henry the Sixth

'The First part of the Contention betwixt the two famous Houses of Yorke and Lancaster, with the death of the good Duke Humphrey: And the banishment and death of the Duke of Suffolke, and the Tragicall end of the proud Cardinall of Winchester, with the notable Rebellion of Iacke Cade' was published as a quarto in 1594 and again in 1600. This is an imperfect form of The Second Part of King Henry the Sixth. In 1595 appeared 'The true Tragedie of Richard Duke of Yorke,' which is an imperfect form of *Part III*. In 1619 *The First Part of the Contention* and *The True Tragedie* came out together as 'The Whole Contention betweene the two Famous Houses, Lancaster and Yorke . . . Diuided into two Parts. . . . Written by William Shakespeare, Gent.' For the text of The Second Part of King Henry the Sixth our only authority is the Folio of 1623. The relation of this Part II to *The First Part of the Contention* is a matter of debate. There are three possibilities: *The First Part of the Contention* may be Shakespeare's own work in an earlier form than Henry the Sixth, Part II; it may be the work of some other dramatist which Shakespeare rewrote with extensive additions; it may be merely an abbreviated and garbled text of Shakespeare's Part II. On the whole, this third hypothesis seems to explain the phenomena most satisfactorily. Demonstration is impossible, but we may tentatively accept the Folio text of Part II as Shakespeare's in its entirety. Many scholars, however, maintain that *The First Part of the Contention* is Marlowe's, except for the Cade scenes, which show a comic spirit quite foreign to his genius and are sometimes credited to Greene. These, even in the form that they have in *The Contention*, are often ascribed to Shakespeare. For the rest, Shakespeare's work in his Part II (except for minutiæ in revision) would, on this hypothesis, be limited to those portions of Part II that are lacking in *The Contention*.

The text of *The First Part of the Contention* is in a deplorable state. Not to speak of other corruptions, the blank verse limps continually and sometimes lapses into prose, or into a halting mixture of prose and metre. A flagrant instance is the pedigree which York expounds to support his claim to the throne (cf. *2 Henry VI*, ii, 2), in which facts and metre are equally disordered. The Quarto of 1619 amends the genealogy but makes no attempt to restore the verse. Many differences between *The Contention* and Part II are due to omissions in the Quarto text that may well be cuts made to shorten the play for acting.

The Second Part of King Henry VI contains all the material of *The First Part of the Contention*, arranged in substantially the same order. Most of the lines in *The Contention* appear also in 2 Henry VI in some shape or other, — rarely word for word, often with but slight variation, frequently in what looks like paraphrase. An instance of close verbal agreement, line for line, may be seen in iii, 2, 188–229. Instances of considerable variation are the conjuring scene (i, 4, 1–43) and the last two scenes of Act v. In none of them, however, is there any inconsistency in substance. The concluding speech is identical in *The First Part of the Contention* and in Shakespeare's Part II. His Part II is longer than *The First Part of the Contention* by about a third, and the additional passages are among the best in the play. See, for examples, iii, 1, 15–27, 199–220, 241–281, 360–373; iii, 2, 76–81, 87–121, 254–269 (cf. *As You Like It*, iv, 3, 105–114), 360–366; iv, 1, 1–7, 77–105; v, 1, 6–11, 149–191; v, 2, 19–61. The Cade scenes are much better in PART II than in *The Contention* and are credited to Shakespeare by an almost unanimous vote.

With due allowance for the badness of the Quarto text, the style and metre of *The First Part of the Contention*, as well as the dramatic method and the characters of the *dramatis personæ*, undoubtedly accord with what we know of Marlowe's work. But Marlowe exercised a strong influence upon Shakespeare in the period to which KING HENRY THE SIXTH belongs, and some of the admittedly Shakespearean portions of PART II are quite as much like Marlowe as anything in *The Contention*. That Shakespeare actually collaborated with Marlowe and Greene, or with either of them, is altogether unlikely.

For PART II OF HENRY THE SIXTH a probable date is 1590 or 1591. It is, at all events, earlier than PART I. If there was a revival in 1594 or later (see p. 665), the Folio text may be the result of some slight revision by the author.

For facts Shakespeare relied upon Holinshed or Halle, whom for this period Holinshed paraphrases. The episode of the feigned miracle, with Simpcox's discomfiture, is worked up from a story that Sir Thomas More had heard his father tell. More records it in his *Dialogue of the Worship of Images*, and Richard Grafton copied it from More. Of course Shakespeare knew Grafton's *Chronicle*. The action of the play begins in 1445 with Margaret's arrival from France and closes with York's victory at St. Albans ten years later. Chronology is adjusted to suit the dramatist's convenience. Thus young Richard (afterwards Richard III) distinguishes himself in the battle, though in fact he was then less than three years old.

THE SECOND PART OF
KING HENRY THE SIXTH

[Dramatis Personæ.

King Henry the Sixth.
Humphrey, Duke of Gloucester, his uncle.
Cardinal Beaufort, Bishop of Winchester, great-
   uncle to the *King.*
Richard Plantagenet, Duke of York.
Edward and *Richard,* his sons.
Duke of Somerset.
Duke of Suffolk.
Duke of Buckingham.
Lord Clifford.
Young Clifford, his son.
Earl of Salisbury.
Earl of Warwick.
Lord Scales.
Lord Say.
Sir Humphrey Stafford.
William Stafford, his brother.
Sir John Stanley.
Vaux.
Matthew Goffe.
A Lieutenant, a Shipmaster, a Master's Mate, and
   Walter Whitmore.
Two Gentlemen, prisoners with *Suffolk.*

Alexander Iden, a Kentish gentleman.
John Hume and *John Southwell,* two priests.
Roger Bolingbroke, a conjurer.
Thomas Horner, an armourer.
Peter, his man.
Clerk of Chatham.
Mayor of Saint Alban's.
Saunder Simpcox, an impostor.
Jack Cade, a rebel.
George Bevis, John Holland, Dick the butcher,
   Smith the weaver, *Michael,* &c., his followers.
Two Murderers.

Margaret, Queen to *King Henry.*
Eleanor, Duchess of Gloucester.
Margery Jourdain, a witch.
Wife to *Simpcox.*

Lords, Ladies, and Attendants, Petitioners, Aldermen, a Herald, a Beadle, a Sheriff, Officers, Citizens, Prentices, Falconers, Guards, Soldiers,
   Messengers, &c.

A Spirit.

SCENE. — *England.*]

ACT I. Scene I. [*London. The Palace.*]

Flourish of trumpets; then hautboys. Enter
*King, Duke Humphrey of Gloucester, Salisbury,
Warwick,* and *Cardinal Beaufort* on the one
side; *the Queen, Suffolk, York, Somerset,* and
   Buckingham, on the other.

Suf. As by your high imperial Majesty
I had in charge at my depart for France,
As procurator to your Excellence,
To marry Princess Margaret for your Grace,
So, in the famous ancient city Tours,   5
In presence of the Kings of France and Sicil,
The Dukes of Orleans, Calaber, Bretagne, and
   Alençon,
Seven earls, twelve barons, and twenty reverend
   bishops,
I have perform'd my task and was espous'd;
And humbly now upon my bended knee,   10
In sight of England and her lordly peers,
Deliver up my title in the Queen

To your most gracious hands, that are the sub-
   stance
Of that great shadow I did represent:
The happiest gift that ever marquess gave,   15
The fairest queen that ever king receiv'd.
   King. Suffolk, arise. Welcome, Queen Mar-
   garet.
I can express no kinder sign of love
Than this kind kiss. O Lord, that lends me life,
Lend me a heart replete with thankfulness!   20
For thou hast given me in this beauteous face
A world of earthly blessings to my soul,
If sympathy of love unite our thoughts.
   Queen. Great King of England and my gra-
   cious lord,
The mutual conference that my mind hath had,   25
By day, by night, waking and in my dreams,
In courtly company or at my beads,
With you, mine alderliefest sovereign,
Makes me the bolder to salute my king

235

With ruder terms, such as my wit affords   30
And over-joy of heart doth minister.
　King. Her sight did ravish, but her grace in
　　speech,
Her words yclad with wisdom's majesty,
Makes me from wond'ring fall to weeping joys,
Such is the fulness of my heart's content.   35
Lords, with one cheerful voice welcome my love.
　All. (*kneel*) Long live Queen Margaret, Eng-
　　land's happiness!
　Queen. We thank you all.   *Flourish.*
　Suf. My Lord Protector, so it please your
　　Grace,
Here are the articles of contracted peace   40
Between our sovereign and the French king
　　Charles,
For eighteen months concluded by consent.

　Glou. (*reads*) '*Inprimis*, It is agreed between
the French king Charles and William de la Pole,
Marquess of Suffolk, ambassador for Henry King
of England, that the said Henry shall espouse the
Lady Margaret, daughter unto Reignier King of
Naples, Sicilia, and Jerusalem, and crown her
Queen of England ere the thirtieth of May next
ensuing.
　Item, that the duchy of Anjou and the county of
Maine shall be released and delivered to the King
her father' —   52
　　　　　　Duke Humphrey lets it fall.

　King. Uncle, how now?
　Glou.　　　　　Pardon me, gracious lord.
Some sudden qualm hath struck me at the heart,
And dimm'd mine eyes that I can read no
　　further.   55
　King. Uncle of Winchester, I pray read on.

　Car. [*reads*] '*Item*, It is further agreed between
them that the duchies of Anjou and Maine shall be
released and delivered over to the King her father,
and she sent over of the King of England's own
proper cost and charges, without having any
dowry.'   62

　King. They please us well. Lord Marquess,
　　kneel down.
We here create thee the first Duke of Suffolk
And girt thee with the sword. Cousin of York.
We here discharge your Grace from being
　　Regent   66
I' th' parts of France till term of eighteen
　　months
Be full expir'd. Thanks, uncle Winchester,
Gloucester, York, Buckingham, Somerset,
Salisbury, and Warwick.   70
We thank you all for this great favour done
In entertainment to my princely queen.

Come, let us in, and with all speed provide
To see her coronation be perform'd.
　　　Exeunt King, Queen, and Suffolk. Manent
　　　　　　　　　　　　　　the rest.
　Glou. Brave peers of England, pillars of the
　　state,   75
To you Duke Humphrey must unload his
　　grief —
Your grief, the common grief of all the land.
What? Did my brother Henry spend his youth,
His valour, coin, and people in the wars?
Did he so often lodge in open field,   80
In winter's cold and summer's parching heat,
To conquer France, his true inheritance?
And did my brother Bedford toil his wits
To keep by policy what Henry got?   84
Have you yourselves, Somerset, Buckingham,
Brave York, Salisbury, and victorious Warwick,
Receiv'd deep scars in France and Normandy?
Or hath mine uncle Beaufort and myself,
With all the learned Council of the realm,
Studied so long, sat in the Council House   90
Early and late, debating to and fro
How France and Frenchmen might be kept in
　　awe?
And was his Highness in his infancy
Crowned in Paris in despite of foes?   94
And shall these labours and these honours die?
Shall Henry's conquest, Bedford's vigilance,
Your deeds of war, and all our counsel die?
O peers of England, shameful is this league!
Fatal this marriage, cancelling your fame,
Blotting your names from books of memory, 100
Rasing the characters of your renown,
Defacing monuments of conquer'd France,
Undoing all as all had never been!
　Car. Nephew, what means this passionate
　　discourse,
This peroration with such circumstance?   105
For France, 'tis ours; and we will keep it still.
　Glou. Ay, uncle, we will keep it if we can;
But now it is impossible we should.
Suffolk, the new-made duke that rules the roast,
Hath given the duchy of Anjou, and Maine 110
Unto the poor King Reignier, whose large style
Agrees not with the leanness of his purse.
　Sal. Now, by the death of him that died for
　　all,   113
These counties were the keys of Normandy!
But wherefore weeps Warwick, my valiant son?
　War. For grief that they are past recovery;
For, were there hope to conquer them again,
My sword should shed hot blood, mine eyes no
　　tears.
Anjou and Maine? Myself did win them both;

Those provinces these arms of mine did con-
quer;   120
And are the cities that I got with wounds
Deliver'd up again with peaceful words?
Mort Dieu!

York. For Suffolk's duke, may he be suffocate,
That dims the honour of this warlike isle!   125
France should have torn and rent my very
heart
Before I would have yielded to this league.
I never read but England's kings have had
Large sums of gold and dowries with their wives,
And our King Henry gives away his own   130
To match with her that brings no vantages.

Hum. A proper jest, and never heard before,
That Suffolk should demand a whole fifteenth
For costs and charges in transporting her!
She should have stay'd in France, and starv'd in
France,   135
Before —

Car. My Lord of Gloucester, now ye grow
too hot.
It was the pleasure of my lord the King.

Hum. My Lord of Winchester, I know your
mind.
'Tis not my speeches that you do mislike,   140
But 'tis my presence that doth trouble ye.
Rancour will out. Proud prelate, in thy face
I see thy fury. If I longer stay,
We shall begin our ancient bickerings.   144
Lordings, farewell; and say, when I am gone,
I prophesied, France will be lost ere long. *Exit.*

Car. So, there goes our Protector in a rage.
'Tis known to you he is mine enemy;
Nay more, an enemy unto you all,
And no great friend, I fear me, to the King.   150
Consider, lords, he is the next of blood
And heir apparent to the English crown.
Had Henry got an empire by his marriage
And all the wealthy kingdoms of the West,
There's reason he should be displeas'd at it.   155
Look to it, lords. Let not his smoothing words
Bewitch your hearts; be wise and circumspect.
What though the common people favour him,
Calling him 'Humphrey, the good Duke of
Gloucester,'   159
Clapping their hands and crying with loud voice
'Jesu maintain your royal Excellence!'
With 'God preserve the good Duke Humphrey!'
I fear me, lords, for all this flattering gloss,
He will be found a dangerous Protector.

Buck. Why should he then protect our
sovereign,   165
He being of age to govern of himself?
Cousin of Somerset, join you with me,

And all together with the Duke of Suffolk,
We'll quickly hoise Duke Humphrey from his
seat.

Car. This weighty business will not brook
delay.   170
I'll to the Duke of Suffolk presently.   *Exit.*

Som. Cousin of Buckingham, though Hum-
phrey's pride
And greatness of his place be grief to us,
Yet let us watch the haughty Cardinal.
His insolence is more intolerable   175
Than all the princes in the land beside.
If Gloucester be displac'd, he'll be Protector.

Buck. Or thou or I, Somerset, will be Protec-
tor
Despite Duke Humphrey or the Cardinal.   179
Exeunt Buckingham and Somerset.

Sal. Pride went before, ambition follows him.
While these do labour for their own preferment,
Behooves it us to labour for the realm.
I never saw but Humphrey Duke of Gloucester
Did bear him like a noble gentleman.
Oft have I seen the haughty Cardinal,   185
More like a soldier than a man o' th' church,
As stout and proud as he were lord of all,
Swear like a ruffian and demean himself
Unlike the ruler of a commonweal.
Warwick my son, the comfort of my age,   190
Thy deeds, thy plainness, and thy housekeeping
Hath won the greatest favour of the commons,
Excepting none but good Duke Humphrey.
And, brother York, thy acts in Ireland
In bringing them to civil discipline,   195
Thy late exploits done in the heart of France
When thou wert Regent for our sovereign,
Have made thee fear'd and honour'd of the
people.
Join we together for the public good,
In what we can to bridle and suppress   200
The pride of Suffolk and the Cardinal
With Somerset's and Buckingham's ambition;
And, as we may, cherish Duke Humphrey's
deeds
While they do tend the profit of the land.

War. So God help Warwick as he loves the
land   205
And common profit of his country!

York. [*aside*] And so says York, for he hath
greatest cause.

Sal. Then let's make haste away, and look
unto the main.

War. Unto the main? O father, Maine is
lost!
That Maine which by main force Warwick did
win,   210

And would have kept so long as breath did last.
Main chance, father, you meant; but I meant
    Maine,
Which I will win from France, or else be slain.
    Exeunt Warwick and Salisbury. Manet
                          York.
  York. Anjou and Maine are given to the
    French,
Paris is lost, the state of Normandy   215
Stands on a tickle point now they are gone.
Suffolk concluded on the articles,
The peers agreed, and Henry was well pleas'd
To change two dukedoms for a duke's fair
    daughter.   219
I cannot blame them all. What is't to them?
'Tis thine they give away, and not their own.
Pirates may make cheap pennyworths of their
    pillage,
And purchase friends, and give to courtesans,
Still revelling like lords till all be gone,
While as the silly owner of the goods   225
Weeps over them and wrings his hapless hands
And shakes his head and trembling stands aloof
While all is shar'd and all is borne away,
Ready to starve and dare not touch his own.
So York must sit and fret and bite his tongue
While his own lands are bargain'd for and sold.
Methinks the realms of England, France, and
    Ireland
Bear that proportion to my flesh and blood
As did the fatal brand Althæa burnt
Unto the prince's heart of Calydon.   235
Anjou and Maine both given unto the French?
Cold news for me! for I had hope of France,
Even as I have of fertile England's soil.
A day will come when York shall claim his own;
And therefore I will take the Nevils' parts, 240
And make a show of love to proud Duke
    Humphrey,
And when I spy advantage, claim the crown,
For that's the golden mark I seek to hit.
Nor shall proud Lancaster usurp my right,
Nor hold the sceptre in his childish fist, 245
Nor wear the diadem upon his head,
Whose churchlike humours fits not for a crown.
Then, York, be still awhile, till time do serve:
Watch thou and wake when others be asleep,
To pry into the secrets of the state, 250
Till Henry, surfeiting in joys of love,
With his new bride and England's dear-bought
    queen,
And Humphrey with the peers be fall'n at jars.
Then will I raise aloft the milk-white rose,
With whose sweet smell the air shall be per-
    fum'd,   255

And in my standard bear the arms of York
To grapple with the house of Lancaster;
And force perforce I'll make him yield the crown
Whose bookish rule hath pull'd fair England
    down.   *Exit.*

[Scene II. *London. The* Duke of
    Gloucester's *house.*]

Enter *Duke Humphrey and his wife Eleanor.*
  Elean. Why droops my lord, like over-
    ripen'd corn
Hanging the head at Ceres' plenteous load?
Why doth the great Duke Humphrey knit his
    brows,
As frowning at the favours of the world?
Why are thine eyes fix'd to the sullen earth, 5
Gazing on that which seems to dim thy sight?
What seest thou there? King Henry's diadem,
Enchas'd with all the honours of the world?
If so, gaze on, and grovel on thy face,
Until thy head be circled with the same.   10
Put forth thy hand, reach at the glorious gold.
What, is't too short? I'll lengthen it with
    mine;
And having both together heav'd it up,
We'll both together lift our heads to heaven
And never more abase our sight so low   15
As to vouchsafe one glance unto the ground.
  Hum. O Nell, sweet Nell, if thou dost love
    thy lord,
Banish the canker of ambitious thoughts!
And may that thought, when I imagine ill 19
Against my king and nephew, virtuous Henry,
Be my last breathing in this mortal world!
My troublous dream this night doth make me
    sad.
  Elean. What dream'd my lord? Tell me,
    and I'll requite it
With sweet rehearsal of my morning's dream.
  Hum. Methought this staff, mine office-
    badge in court,   25
Was broke in twain; by whom I have forgot,
But as I think, it was by th' Cardinal;
And on the pieces of the broken wand
Were plac'd the heads of Edmund Duke of
    Somerset   29
And William de la Pole, first Duke of Suffolk.
This was my dream. What it doth bode, God
    knows.
  Elean. Tut, this was nothing but an argu-
    ment
That he that breaks a stick of Gloucester's
    grove

Shall lose his head for his presumption.   34
But list to me, my Humphrey, my sweet duke.
Methought I sat in seat of majesty
In the cathedral church of Westminster
And in that chair where kings and queens are
    crown'd;
Where Henry and Dame Margaret kneel'd to me
And on my head did set the diadem.   40
   Hum. Nay, Eleanor, then must I chide
    outright.
Presumptuous dame, ill-nurtur'd Eleanor!
Art thou not second woman in the realm,
And the Protector's wife, belov'd of him?   44
Hast thou not worldly pleasure at command
Above the reach or compass of thy thought?
And wilt thou still be hammering treachery
To tumble down thy husband and thyself
From top of honour to disgrace's feet?
Away from me, and let me hear no more!   50
   Elean. What, what, my lord? Are you so
    choleric
With Eleanor for telling but her dream?
Next time I'll keep my dreams unto myself
And not be check'd.   54
   Hum. Nay, be not angry. I am pleas'd again.

       Enter *Messenger.*

   Mess. My Lord Protector, 'tis his Highness'
    pleasure
You do prepare to ride unto Saint Alban's,
Where as the King and Queen do mean to hawk.
   Hum. I go. Come, Nell — thou wilt ride
    with us?
   Elean. Yes, my good lord, I'll follow pres-
    ently.   60
      Exit Humphrey [with Messenger].
Follow I must; I cannot go before
While Gloucester bears this base and humble
    mind.
Were I a man, a duke, and next of blood,
I would remove these tedious stumbling blocks
And smooth my way upon their headless necks;
And being a woman, I will not be slack   66
To play my part in Fortune's pageant.
Where are you there? Sir John! Nay, fear
    not, man.
We are alone; here's none but thee and I.

       Enter *Hume.*

   Hume. Jesus preserve your Royal Majesty!
   Elean. What say'st thou? Majesty? I am
    but Grace.   71
   Hume. But by the grace of God and Hume's
    advice
Your Grace's title shall be multiplied.

   Elean. What say'st thou, man? Hast thou
    as yet conferr'd
With Margery Jourdain, the cunning witch,   75
With Roger Bolingbroke, the conjurer?
And will they undertake to do me good?
   Hume. This they have promised, to show
    your Highness
A spirit rais'd from depth of underground
That shall make answer to such questions   80
As by your Grace shall be propounded him.
   Elean. It is enough. I'll think upon the
    questions.
When from Saint Alban's we do make return
We'll see these things effected to the full.
Here, Hume, take this reward. Make merry,
    man,   85
With thy confederates in this weighty cause.
         Exit.
   Hume. Hume must make merry with the
    Duchess' gold.
Marry, and shall! But, how now, Sir John
    Hume?
Seal up your lips and give no words but mum;
The business asketh silent secrecy.   90
Dame Eleanor gives gold to bring the witch;
Gold cannot come amiss, were she a devil.
Yet have I gold flies from another coast:
I dare not say, from the rich Cardinal
And from the great and new-made Duke of
    Suffolk;   95
Yet I do find it so; for, to be plain,
They (knowing Dame Eleanor's aspiring hu-
    mour)
Have hired me to undermine the Duchess
And buzz these conjurations in her brain.
They say, 'A crafty knave does need no
    broker';   100
Yet am I Suffolk and the Cardinal's broker.
Hume, if you take not heed, you shall go near
To call them both a pair of crafty knaves.
Well, so it stands; and thus, I fear, at last
Hume's knavery will be the Duchess' wrack
And her attainture will be Humphrey's fall.
Sort how it will, I shall have gold for all. *Exit.*

     [Scene III. *London. The Palace.*]

Enter three or four *Petitioners,* the *Armourer's*
      Man (Peter) being one.

   1. Petit. My masters, let's stand close. My
Lord Protector will come this way by-and-by,
and then we may deliver our supplications in
the quill.   4

2. Petit. Marry, the Lord protect him, for he's a good man, Jesu bless him!

Enter *Suffolk* and *Queen.*

1. Petit. Here 'a comes, methinks, and the Queen with him. I'll be the first, sure.

2. Petit. Come back, fool. This is the Duke of Suffolk and not my Lord Protector.   10

Suf. How now, fellow? Wouldst anything with me?

1. Petit. I pray, my lord, pardon me. I took ye for my Lord Protector.   14

Queen. [*reads*] 'To my Lord Protector'? Are your supplications to his lordship? Let me see them. What is thine?

1. Petit. Mine is, an't please your Grace, against John Goodman, my Lord Cardinal's man, for keeping my house and lands, and wife and all, from me.   21

Suf. Thy wife too? That's some wrong indeed. What's yours? What's here? [*Reads*] Against the Duke of Suffolk, for enclosing the commons of Melford.' How now, sir knave?

2. Petit. Alas, sir, I am but a poor petitioner of our whole township.

Peter. [*presents his petition*] Against my master, Thomas Horner, for saying that the Duke of York was rightful heir to the crown.   30

Queen. What say'st thou? Did the Duke of York say he was rightful heir to the crown?

Peter. That my master was? No, forsooth! My master said that he was, and that the King was an usurper.   35

Suf. Who is there?

Enter *Servant.*

Take this fellow in and send for his master with a pursuivant presently. We'll hear more of your matter before the King.

Exit [*Servant with Peter*].

Queen. And as for you that love to be protected   40
Under the wings of our Protector's grace,
Begin your suits anew and sue to him.

Tear the supplication.

Away, base cullions! Suffolk, let them go.

All. Come, let's be gone.   *Exeunt.*

Queen. My Lord of Suffolk, say, is this the guise,   45
Is this the fashion in the court of England?
Is this the government of Britain's isle,
And this the royalty of Albion's king?
What, shall King Henry be a pupil still,
Under the surly Gloucester's governance?   50
Am I a queen in title and in style

And must be made a subject to a duke?
I tell thee, Pole, when in the city Tours
Thou ran'st a-tilt in honour of my love
And stol'st away the ladies' hearts of France,
I thought King Henry had resembled thee   56
In courage, courtship, and proportion;
But all his mind is bent to holiness,
To number Ave-Maries on his beads;
His champions are the prophets and apostles,
His weapons holy saws of sacred writ;   61
His study is his tiltyard, and his loves
Are brazen images of canonized saints.
I would the college of the Cardinals
Would choose him Pope and carry him to Rome
And set the triple crown upon his head!   66
That were a state fit for his holiness.

Suf. Madam, be patient. As I was cause
Your Highness came to England, so will I
In England work your Grace's full content.   70

Queen. Beside the haughty Protector, have we Beaufort
The imperious churchman, Somerset, Buckingham,
And grumbling York; and not the least of these
But can do more in England than the King.

Suf. And he of these that can do most of all
Cannot do more in England than the Nevils.
Salisbury and Warwick are no simple peers.

Queen. Not all these lords do vex me half so much
As that proud dame, the Lord Protector's wife.
She sweeps it through the court with troops of ladies,   80
More like an empress than Duke Humphrey's wife.
Strangers in court do take her for the Queen.
She bears a duke's revenues on her back,
And in her heart she scorns our poverty.
Shall I not live to be aveng'd on her?   85
Contemptuous base-born callot as she is,
She vaunted 'mongst her minions t'other day,
The very train of her worst wearing gown
Was better worth than all my father's lands
Till Suffolk gave two dukedoms for his daughter.

Suf. Madam, myself have lim'd a bush for her,   91
And plac'd a choir of such enticing birds
That she will light to listen to their lays
And never mount to trouble you again.
So let her rest. And, madam, list to me,   95
For I am bold to counsel you in this:
Although we fancy not the Cardinal,
Yet must we join with him and with the lords
Till we have brought Duke Humphrey in disgrace.

As for the Duke of York, this late complaint
Will make but little for his benefit.   101
So one by one we'll weed them all at last,
And you yourself shall steer the happy helm.

Sound a sennet. Enter the *King, Duke Humphrey, Cardinal [Beaufort], Buckingham, York, Somerset, Salisbury, Warwick,* and the *Duchess [of Gloucester].*

King. For my part, noble lords, I care not
which:
Or Somerset or York, all's one to me.   105
  York. If York have ill demean'd himself in
France,
Then let him be denay'd the regentship.
  Som. If Somerset be unworthy of the place,
Let York be Regent; I will yield to him.
  War. Whether your Grace be worthy, yea
or no,   110
Dispute not that. York is the worthier.
  Car. Ambitious Warwick, let thy betters
speak!
  War. The Cardinal's not my better in the
field.
  Buck. All in this presence are thy betters,
Warwick.   114
  War. Warwick may live to be the best of all.
  Sal. Peace, son! and show some reason,
Buckingham,
Why Somerset should be preferr'd in this.
  Queen. Because the King forsooth will have
it so.
  Hum. Madam, the King is old enough himself
To give his censure. These are no women's
matters.   120
  Queen. If he be old enough, what needs your
Grace
To be Protector of his Excellence?
  Hum. Madam, I am Protector of the realm,
And at his pleasure will resign my place.   124
  Suf. Resign it then and leave thine insolence.
Since thou wert king (as who is king but thou?)
The commonwealth hath daily run to wrack,
The Dauphin hath prevail'd beyond the seas,
And all the peers and nobles of the realm
Have been as bondmen to thy sovereignty.   130
  Car. The commons hast thou rack'd; the
clergy's bags
Are lank and lean with thy extortions.
  Som. Thy sumptuous buildings and thy
wive's attire
Have cost a mass of public treasury.
  Buck. Thy cruelty in execution   135
Upon offenders hath exceeded law,
And left thee to the mercy of the law.

  Queen. Thy sale of offices and towns in
France —
If they were known, as the suspect is great —
Would make thee quickly hop without thy
head.   140
  Exit Humphrey. [*The Queen drops her fan.*]
Give me my fan! What, minion, can ye not?
          She gives the Duchess a box on the ear.
I cry you mercy, madam. Was it you?
  Duch. Was't I? Yea, I it was, proud French-
woman!
Could I come near your beauty with my nails,
I would set my ten commandments in your face.
  King. Sweet aunt, be quiet. 'Twas against
her will.   146
  Duch. Against her will, good King? Look
to't in time!
She'll hamper thee and dandle thee like a baby.
Though in this place most master wear no
breeches,   149
She shall not strike Dame Eleanor unreveng'd.
                                               Exit.
  Buck. Lord Cardinal, I will follow Eleanor,
And listen after Humphrey, how he proceeds.
She's tickled now; her fume needs no spurs,
She'll gallop far enough to her destruction.
                                               Exit.

          Enter [*Duke*] Humphrey.

  Hum. Now, lords, my choler being over-
blown   155
With walking once about the quadrangle,
I come to talk of commonwealth affairs.
As for your spiteful false objections,
Prove them, and I lie open to the law;
But God in mercy so deal with my soul   160
As I in duty love my king and country!
But to the matter that we have in hand:
I say, my sovereign, York is meetest man
To be your Regent in the realm of France.
  Suf. Before we make election, give me leave
To show some reason, of no little force,   166
That York is most unmeet of any man.
  York. I'll tell thee, Suffolk, why I am un-
meet:
First, for I cannot flatter thee in pride;
Next, if I be appointed for the place,   170
My Lord of Somerset will keep me here
Without discharge, money, or furniture
Till France be won into the Dauphin's hands.
Last time I danc'd attendance on his will
Till Paris was besieg'd, famish'd, and lost.   175
  War. That can I witness; and a fouler fact
Did never traitor in the land commit.
  Suf. Peace, headstrong Warwick!

War. Image of pride, why should I hold my
peace? 179

Enter [*Horner*] *the Armourer.* and his
Man [*Peter*, guarded].

Suf. Because here is a man accus'd of treason.
Pray God the Duke of York excuse himself!
York. Doth any one accuse York for a
traitor?
King. What mean'st thou, Suffolk? Tell me,
what are these?
Suf. Please it your Majesty, this is the man
That doth accuse his master of high treason.
His words were these: that Richard Duke of
York 186
Was rightful heir unto the English crown
And that your Majesty was an usurper.
King. Say, man, were these thy words? 189
Arm. An't shall please your Majesty, I never
said nor thought any such matter. God is my
witness, I am falsely accus'd by the villain.
Peter. By these ten bones, my lords, he did
speak them to me in the garret one night, as we
were scouring my Lord of York's armour. 195
York. Base dunghill villain and mechanical,
I'll have thy head for this thy traitor's speech.
I do beseech your royal Majesty,
Let him have all the rigour of the law. 199
Arm. Alas, my lord, hang me if ever I spake
the words! My accuser is my prentice; and
when I did correct him for his fault the other
day, he did vow upon his knees he would be
even with me. I have good witness of this.
Therefore I beseech your Majesty, do not cast
away an honest man for a villain's accusation.
King. Uncle, what shall we say to this in
law?
Hum. This is my doom, my lord, if I may
judge:
Let Somerset be Regent o'er the French,
Because in York this breeds suspicion; 210
And let these have a day appointed them
For single combat in convenient place,
For he hath witness of his servant's malice.
This is the law, and this Duke Humphrey's
doom. 214
King. Then be it so. My Lord of Somerset,
We make your Grace Regent over the French.
Som. I humbly thank your royal Majesty.
Arm. And I accept the combat willingly.
Peter. Alas, my lord, I cannot fight! For
God's sake pity my case! The spite of man pre-
vaileth against me. O Lord have mercy upon
me! I shall never be able to fight a blow. O
Lord, my heart!

Hum. Sirrah, or you must fight or else be
hang'd.
King. Away with them to prison! and the
day 225
Of combat shall be the last of the next month.
Come, Somerset, we'll see thee sent away.
Flourish. Exeunt.

[Scene IV. *London.* Gloucester's *garden.*]

Enter *Margery Jourdain* the *Witch*, the two
Priests [*Hume* and *Southwell*], and *Bolingbroke.*

Hume. Come, my masters. The Duchess, I
tell you, expects performance of your promises.
Boling. Master Hume, we are therefore provided. Will her ladyship behold and hear our
exorcisms? 5
Hume. Ay, what else? Fear you not her
courage.
Boling. I have heard her reported to be a
woman of an invincible spirit. But it shall be
convenient, Master Hume, that you be by her
aloft while we be busy below; and so I pray you
go in God's name, and leave us. (*Exit Hume.*)
Mother Jourdain, be you prostrate and grovel
on the earth. John Southwell, read you, and let
us to our work. 15

Enter [*Duchess*] *Eleanor* aloft, [followed
by *Hume*].

Elean. Well said, my masters, and welcome
all. To this gear, the sooner the better.
Boling. Patience, good lady; wizards know
their times.
Deep night, dark night, the silent of the night,
The time of night when Troy was set on fire;
The time when screech owls cry and bandogs
howl 21
And spirits walk and ghosts break up their
graves —
That time best fits the work we have in hand.
Madam, sit you and fear not. Whom we
raise,
We will make fast within a hallow'd verge. 25

*Here do the ceremonies belonging, and make the
circle. Bolingbroke or Southwell reads:* 'Con-
iuro te,' &c. *It thunders and lightens terribly;
then the Spirit riseth.*

Spirit. Adsum.
Witch. Asmath,
By the eternal God, whose name and power
Thou tremblest at, answer that I shall ask;

For till thou speak thou shalt not pass from
  hence.　　　　　　　　　　　　　　　30
  Spirit. Ask what thou wilt. That I had said
  and done!
  Boling. [*reads*] 'First of the King: what
  shall of him become?'
  Spirit. The duke yet lives that Henry shall
  depose;
But him outlive, and die a violent death.
  [*As the Spirit speaks, Southwell writes the
  answer.*]
  Boling. 'What fates await the Duke of
  Suffolk?'　　　　　　　　　　　　35
  Spirit. By water shall he die and take his end.
  Boling. 'What shall befall the Duke of
  Somerset?'
  Spirit. Let him shun castles.
Safer shall he be upon the sandy plains
Than where castles mounted stand.　　40
Have done, for more I hardly can endure.
  Boling. Descend to darkness and the burn-
  ing lake!
False fiend, avoid!
　　　　Thunder and lightning. Exit Spirit.

Enter the *Duke of York* and the *Duke of Buckingham*, with their *Guard*, and break in.

  York. Lay hands upon these traitors and
  their trash.
Beldam, I think we watch'd you at an inch.　45
What, madam, are you there? The King and
  commonweal
Are deeply indebted for this piece of pains.
My Lord Protector will, I doubt it not,
See you well guerdon'd for these good deserts.
  Elean. Not half so bad as thine to England's
  king,　　　　　　　　　　　　　　50
Injurious Duke, that threatest where's no cause.
  Buck. True, madam, none at all. What call
  you this?　　　　[*Shows her the paper.*]
Away with them! Let them be clapp'd up close

And kept asunder. You, madam, shall with us.
Stafford, take her to thee.　　　　　55
We'll see your trinkets here all forthcoming.
All away!
　　Exeunt [*above, Duchess and Hume, guarded;
　　below, Witch, Southwell, and Bolingbroke,
　　guarded*].
  York. Lord Buckingham, methinks you
  watch'd her well.
A pretty plot, well chosen to build upon!　59
Now pray, my lord, let's see the devil's writ.
What have we here?　　　　　*Reads.*
'The duke yet lives that Henry shall depose;
But him outlive, and die a violent death.'
Why, this is just
'Aio te, Aeacida, Romanos vincere posse.'　65
Well, to the rest:
'Tell me, what fate awaits the Duke of Suffolk?
By water shall he die and take his end.
What shall betide the Duke of Somerset?
Let him shun castles.　　　　　70
Safer shall he be upon the sandy plains
Than where castles mounted stand.'
Come, come, my lords! These oracles
Are hardly attain'd and hardly understood.
The King is now in progress towards Saint
  Alban's,　　　　　　　　　　　　75
With him the husband of this lovely lady.
Thither goes these news as fast as horse can
  carry them —
A sorry breakfast for my Lord Protector.
  Buck. Your Grace shall give me leave, my
  Lord of York,
To be the post, in hope of his reward.　　80
  York. At your pleasure, my good lord.
  Who's within there, ho?

　　　　　Enter a *Servingman.*

Invite my Lords of Salisbury and Warwick
To sup with me to-morrow night. Away!
　　　　　　　　　　　　Exeunt.

　　　[ACT II. Scene I. *Saint Alban's.*]

Enter the *King, Queen, Protector* [*Gloucester*],
Cardinal, and *Suffolk*, with *Falconers* halloaing.

  Queen. Believe me, lords, for flying at the
  brook
I saw not better sport these seven years' day.
Yet, by your leave, the wind was very high,
And, ten to one, old Joan had not gone out.
  King. But what a point, my lord, your falcon
  made,　　　　　　　　　　　　5

And what a pitch she flew above the rest!
To see how God in all his creatures works!
Yea, man and birds are fain of climbing
  high.
  Suf. No marvel, an it like your Majesty,
My Lord Protector's hawks do tow'r so well.　10
They know their master loves to be aloft
And bears his thoughts above his falcon's pitch.
  Glouc. My lord, 'tis but a base ignoble mind
That mounts no higher than a bird can soar.

Car. I thought as much. He would be above
the clouds.   15
Glou. Ay, my Lord Cardinal, how think you
by that?
Were it not good your Grace could fly to
heaven?
King. The treasury of everlasting joy.
Car. Thy heaven is on earth; thine eyes and
thoughts
Beat on a crown, the treasure of thy heart, 20
Pernicious Protector, dangerous peer,
That smooth'st it so with King and common-
weal!
Glou. What, Cardinal, is your priesthood
grown peremptory?
'Tantaene animis coelestibus irae?'
Churchmen so hot? Good uncle, hide such
malice;   25
For with such holiness well can you do it.
Suf. No malice, sir; no more than well
becomes
So good a quarrel and so bad a peer.
Glou. As who, my lord?
Suf.   Why, as you, my lord,
An't like your lordly Lord's Protectorship. 30
Glou. Why, Suffolk, England knows thine
insolence.
Queen. And thy ambition, Gloucester.
King.   I prithee, peace,
Good Queen, and whet not on these furious
peers;
For blessed are the peacemakers on earth. 35
Car. Let me be blessed for the peace I make
Against this proud Protector with my sword!
Glou. [*aside to Cardinal*] Faith, holy uncle,
would 'twere come to that!
Car. [*aside to Gloucester*] Marry, when thou
dar'st.
Glou. [*aside to Cardinal*] Make up no factious
numbers for the matter;   40
In thine own person answer thy abuse.
Car. [*aside to Gloucester*] Ay, where thou
dar'st not peep; and if thou dar'st,
This evening on the east side of the grove.
King. How now, my lords?
Car.   Believe me, cousin Gloucester,
Had not your man put up the fowl so suddenly,
We had had more sport — [*Aside to Gloucester*]
Come with thy two-hand sword.   46
Glou. True, uncle.
Car. [*aside to Gloucester*] Are ye advis'd?
The east side of the grove.
Glou. [*aside to Cardinal*] Cardinal, I am with
you.
King.   Why, how now, uncle Gloucester?

Glou. Talking of hawking; nothing else, my
lord.   50
[*Aside to Cardinal*] Now, by God's Mother,
priest, I'll shave your crown for this,
Or all my fence shall fail.
Car. [*aside to Gloucester*] Medice, teipsum.
Protector, see to't well; protect yourself.
King. The winds grow high; so do your
stomachs, lords.   55
How irksome is this music to my heart!
When such strings jar, what hope of harmony?
I pray, my lords, let me compound this strife.

Enter *one crying* 'A miracle!'

Glou. What means this noise?
Fellow, what miracle dost thou proclaim?   60
One. A miracle! a miracle!
Suf. Come to the King and tell him what
miracle.
One. Forsooth, a blind man at Saint Alban's
shrine
Within this half hour hath receiv'd his sight —
A man that ne'er saw in his life before.   65
King. Now God be prais'd that to believing
souls
Gives light in darkness, comfort in despair!

Enter the *Mayor of Saint Alban's* and his
Brethren, bearing the man, [*Simpcox*,] between
two in a chair, [*Simpcox's Wife* and a *crowd of
Townsmen* following].

Car. Here comes the townsmen on procession
To present your Highness with the man.
King. Great is his comfort in this earthly
vale,   70
Although by his sight his sin be multiplied.
Glou. Stand by, my masters. Bring him near
the King;
His Highness' pleasure is to talk with him.
King. Good fellow, tell us here the circum-
stance,
That we for thee may glorify the Lord.   75
What, hast thou been long blind, and now
restor'd?
Simp. Born blind, an't please your Grace.
Wife. Ay indeed was he.
Suf. What woman is this?
Wife. His wife, an't like your worship.   80
Glou. Hadst thou been his mother, thou
couldst have better told.
King. Where wert thou born?
Simp. At Berwick in the North, an't like
your Grace.
King. Poor soul, God's goodness hath been
great to thee!

Let never day nor night unhallowed pass, 85
But still remember what the Lord hath done.

Queen. Tell me, good fellow, cam'st thou
  here by chance,
Or of devotion, to this holy shrine?

Simp. God knows, of pure devotion, being
  call'd
A hundred times and oft'ner in my sleep 90
By good Saint Alban, who said 'Simpcox,
  come;
Come offer at my shrine and I will help thee.'

Wife. Most true, forsooth! and many time
  and oft
Myself have heard a voice to call him so.

Car. What, art thou lame?

Simp.   Ay, God Almighty help me! 95

Suf. How cam'st thou so?

Simp.   A fall off of a tree.

Wife. A plum tree, master.

Glou.   How long hast thou been blind?

Simp. O, born so, master!

Glou.   What, and wouldst climb a tree?

Simp. But that in all my life, when I was a
  youth.

Wife. Too true, and bought his climbing
  very dear.   100

Glou. Mass, thou lov'dst plums well, that
  wouldst venture so.

Simp. Alas, good master, my wife desir'd
  some damsons
And made me climb, with danger of my life.

Glou. A subtile knave! But yet it shall not
  serve.
Let me see thine eyes. Wink now. Now open
  them.   105
In my opinion yet thou seest not well.

Simp. Yes, master, clear as day, I thank God
  and Saint Alban.

Glou. Say'st thou me so? What colour is
  this cloak of?

Simp. Red, master; red as blood.   110

Glou. Why, that's well said. What colour is
  my gown of?

Simp. Black, forsooth; coal-black, as jet.

King. Why then, thou know'st what colour
  jet is of?

Suf. And yet, I think, jet did he never see.

Glou. But cloaks and gowns before this day
  a many.   115

Wife. Never before this day in all his life.

Glou. Tell me, sirrah, what's my name?

Simp. Alas, master, I know not.

Glou. What's his name?

Simp. I know not.   120

Glou. Nor his?

Simp. No indeed, master.

Glou. What's thine own name?

Simp. Saunder Simpcox, an if it please you,
  master.   125

Glou. Then, Saunder, sit there, the lying'st
  knave in Christendom. If thou hadst been born
blind, thou mightst as well have known all our
names as thus to name the several colours we do
wear. Sight may distinguish of colours; but
suddenly to nominate them all, it is impossible.
My lords, Saint Alban here hath done a miracle;
and would ye not think his cunning to be great
that could restore this cripple to his legs again?

Simp. O master, that you could!   135

Glou. My masters of Saint Alban's, have you
not beadles in your town, and things call'd
whips?

Mayor. Yes, my lord, if it please your Grace.

Glou. Then send for one presently.   140

Mayor. Sirrah, go fetch the beadle hither
  straight.   *Exit [an Attendant].*

Glou. Now fetch me a stool hither by-and-by.
[*A stool brought.*] Now, sirrah, if you mean to
save yourself from whipping, leap me over this
stool and run away.

Simp. Alas, master, I am not able to stand
  alone!   145
You go about to torture me in vain.

Enter a *Beadle* with whips.

Glou. Well, sir, we must have you find your
legs. Sirrah beadle, whip him till he leap over
that same stool.

Bead. I will, my lord. Come on, sirrah. Off
with your doublet quickly.   151

Simp. Alas, master, what shall I do? I am
not able to stand.

  *After the Beadle hath hit him once, he leaps
    over the stool and runs away; and they
    follow and cry 'A miracle!'*

King. O God, seest thou this, and bearest so
long?

Queen. It made me laugh to see the villain
run.   155

Glou. Follow the knave, and take this drab
away.

Wife. Alas, sir, we did it for pure need!

Glou. Let them be whipp'd through every
market town till they come to Berwick, from
whence they came.   160

      Exeunt Mayor, [Beadle, Wife, &c.].

Car. Duke Humphrey has done a miracle
to-day.

Suf. True; made the lame to leap and fly
away.

Glou. But you have done more miracles
than I;
You made in a day, my lord, whole towns to fly.

Enter *Buckingham.*

King. What tidings with our cousin Buck-
ingham? 165
Buck. Such as my heart doth tremble to
unfold.
A sort of naughty persons, lewdly bent,
Under the countenance and confederacy
Of Lady Eleanor, the Protector's wife,
The ringleader and head of all this rout, 170
Have practis'd dangerously against your state,
Dealing with witches and with conjurers,
Whom we have apprehended in the fact,
Raising up wicked spirits from underground,
Demanding of King Henry's life and death 175
And other of your Highness' Privy Council,
As more at large your Grace shall understand.
Car. And so, my Lord Protector, by this
means
Your lady is forthcoming yet at London.
This news, I think, hath turn'd your weapon's
edge. 180
'Tis like, my lord, you will not keep your
hour.
Glou. Ambitious churchman, leave to afflict
my heart.
Sorrow and grief have vanquish'd all my
powers;
And, vanquish'd as I am, I yield to thee
Or to the meanest groom. 185
King. O God, what mischiefs work the
wicked ones,
Heaping confusion on their own heads thereby!
Queen. Gloucester, see here the taincture of
thy nest;
And look thyself be faultless, thou wert best.
Glou. Madam, for myself, to heaven I do
appeal, 190
How I have lov'd my king and commonweal;
And for my wife, I know not how it stands.
Sorry I am to hear what I have heard.
Noble she is; but if she have forgot
Honour and virtue and convers'd with such 195
As, like to pitch, defile nobility,
I banish her my bed and company
And give her as a prey to law and shame
That hath dishonoured Gloucester's honest
name.
King. Well, for this night we will repose us
here. 200
To-morrow toward London back again
To look into this business thoroughly

And call these foul offenders to their answers
And poise the cause in justice' equal scales,
Whose beam stands sure, whose rightful cause
prevails. *Flourish. Exeunt.*

[Scene II. *London. The* Duke of
York's *garden.*]

Enter *York, Salisbury,* and *Warwick.*

York. Now, my good Lords of Salisbury and
Warwick,
Our simple supper ended, give me leave
In this close walk to satisfy myself
In craving your opinion of my title,
Which is infallible, to England's crown. 5
Sal. My lord, I long to hear it at full.
War. Sweet York, begin; and if thy claim
be good,
The Nevils are thy subjects to command.
York. Then thus: 9
Edward the Third, my lords, had seven sons:
The first, Edward the Black Prince, Prince of
Wales;
The second, William of Hatfield; and the third,
Lionel Duke of Clarence; next to whom
Was John of Gaunt, the Duke of Lancaster;
The fifth was Edmund Langley, Duke of York;
The sixth was Thomas of Woodstock, Duke of
Gloucester; 16
William of Windsor was the seventh and last.
Edward the Black Prince died before his father
And left behind him Richard, his only son,
Who after Edward the Third's death reign'd as
king 20
Till Henry Bolingbroke, Duke of Lancaster,
The eldest son and heir of John of Gaunt,
Crown'd by the name of Henry the Fourth,
Seiz'd on the realm, depos'd the rightful king,
Sent his poor queen to France, from whence
she came, 25
And him to Pomfret, where, as all you know,
Harmless Richard was murthered traitorously.
War. Father, the Duke hath told the truth.
Thus got the house of Lancaster the crown.
York. Which now they hold by force, and
not by right; 30
For Richard, the first son's heir, being dead,
The issue of the next son should have reign'd.
Sal. But William of Hatfield died without
an heir.
York. The third son, Duke of Clarence, from
whose line
I claim the crown, had issue. Philip, a daughter,

Who married Edmund Mortimer, Earl of
   March.   36
Edmund had issue, Roger Earl of March;
Roger had issue, Edmund, Anne, and Eleanor.
   Sal. This Edmund in the reign of Boling-
broke,
As I have read, laid claim unto the crown;   40
And, but for Owen Glendower, had been king,
Who kept him in captivity till he died.
But to the rest.
   York.   His eldest sister, Anne,
My mother, being heir unto the crown,
Married Richard Earl of Cambridge, who was
   son   45
To Edmund Langley, Edward the Third's fifth
   son.
By her I claim the kingdom. She was heir
To Roger Earl of March, who was the son
Of Edmund Mortimer, who married Philip,
Sole daughter unto Lionel Duke of Clarence.
So, if the issue of the elder son   51
Succeed before the younger, I am King.
   War. What plain proceeding is more plain
   than this?
Henry doth claim the crown from John of
   Gaunt,
The fourth son; York claims it from the third.
Till Lionel's issue fails, his should not reign. 56
It fails not yet, but flourishes in thee
And in thy sons, fair slips of such a stock.
Then, father Salisbury, kneel we together,
And in this private plot be we the first   60
That shall salute our rightful sovereign
With honour of his birthright to the crown.
   Both. Long live our sovereign Richard,
   England's King!
   York. We thank you, lords. But I am not
   your king
Till I be crown'd and that my sword be stain'd
With heart-blood of the house of Lancaster. 66
And that's not suddenly to be perform'd,
But with advice and silent secrecy.
Do you as I do in these dangerous days:
Wink at the Duke of Suffolk's insolence,   70
At Beaufort's pride, at Somerset's ambition,
At Buckingham and all the crew of them,
Till they have snar'd the shepherd of the flock
That virtuous prince, the good Duke Hum-
   phrey.   74
'Tis that they seek; and they in seeking that
Shall find their deaths, if York can prophesy.
   Sal. My lord, break we off. We know your
   mind at full.
   War. My heart assures me that the Earl of
   Warwick

Shall one day make the Duke of York a
   king.   79
   York. And, Nevil, this I do assure myself,
Richard shall live to make the Earl of Warwick
The greatest man in England but the King.
                                         Exeunt.

[Scene III. *London. A hall of justice.*]

Sound trumpets. Enter the *King* and *State,* [i.e.
the *Queen, Gloucester, York, Suffolk,* and *Salisbury,*] with *Guard,* to banish the *Duchess.*
[Enter, guarded, the *Duchess of Gloucester,
Margery Jourdain, Hume, Southwell,* and *Bolingbroke.*]

   King. Stand forth, Dame Eleanor Cobham,
   Gloucester's wife.
In sight of God and us your guilt is great.
Receive the sentence of the law for sins
Such as by God's book are adjudg'd to death.
[*To Jourdain and the others*] You four, from
   hence to prison back again;   5
From thence unto the place of execution. —
The witch in Smithfield shall be burn'd to ashes,
And you three shall be strangled on the gal-
   lows. —
[*To the Duchess*] You, madam, for you are more
   nobly born,
Despoiled of your honour in your life,   10
Shall, after three days' open penance done,
Live in your country here in banishment
With Sir John Stanley in the Isle of Man.
   Elean. Welcome is banishment! Welcome
   were my death!
   Glou. Eleanor, the law, thou seest, hath
   judged thee.   15
I cannot justify whom the law condemns.
   Exeunt [*the Duchess and the other prisoners,
                                         guarded*].
Mine eyes are full of tears, my heart of grief.
Ah, Humphrey, this dishonour in thine age
Will bring thy head with sorrow to the ground!
I beseech your Majesty give me leave to go. 20
Sorrow would solace, and mine age would ease.
   King. Stay, Humphrey Duke of Gloucester.
   Ere thou go,
Give up thy staff. Henry will to himself
Protector be; and God shall be my hope,   24
My stay, my guide, and lanthorn to my feet.
And go in peace, Humphrey, no less belov'd
Than when thou wert Protector to thy king.
   Queen. I see no reason why a king of years
Should be to be protected like a child.   29

God and King Henry govern England's helm!
Give up your staff, sir, and the King his
　realm.
　Glou. My staff? Here, noble Henry, is my
　staff.
As willingly do I the same resign
As e'er thy father Henry made it mine;
And even as willingly at thy feet I leave it 35
As others would ambitiously receive it.
Farewell, good King. When I am dead and
　gone,
May honourable peace attend thy throne!
　　　　　　　　　　　　　　　　Exit.
　Queen. Why, now is Henry king, and Mar-
　garet queen,
And Humphrey Duke of Gloucester scarce
　himself,　　　　　　　　　　　　　40
That bears so shrewd a maim: two pulls at
　once —
His lady banish'd, and a limb lopp'd off.
This staff of honour raught, there let it
　stand
Where it best fits to be, in Henry's hand.
　Suf. Thus droops this lofty pine and hangs
　his sprays;　　　　　　　　　　　45
Thus Eleanor's pride dies in her youngest
　days.
　York. Lords, let him go. Please it your
　Majesty,
This is the day appointed for the combat;
And ready are the appellant and defendant,
The armourer and his man, to enter the
　lists,　　　　　　　　　　　　　50
So please your Highness to behold the fight.
　Queen. Ay, good my lord; for purposely
　therefore
Left I the court, to see this quarrel tried.
　King. A God's name see the lists and all
　things fit.
Here let them end it, and God defend the
　right!　　　　　　　　　　　　55
　York. I never saw a fellow worse bestead
Or more afraid to fight than is the appellant,
The servant of this armourer, my lords.

Enter at one door, the *Armourer* [*Horner*] and
his *Neighbours*, drinking to him so much that he
is drunk; and he enters with a *Drum* before
him, and his staff with a sandbag fastened to
it; and, at the other door, his *Man* [*Peter*],
with a *Drum* and sandbag, and *Prentices
　　　　drinking to him.*

　1. Neigh. Here, neighbour Horner, I drink to
you in a cup of sack; and fear not, neighbour,
you shall do well enough.　　　　　61

　2. Neigh. And here, neighbour, here's a cup
of charneco.
　3. Neigh. And here's a pot of good double-
beer, neighbour. Drink, and fear not your man.
　Arm. Let it come, i' faith, and I'll pledge you
all; and a fig for Peter!
　1. Pren. Here, Peter, I drink to thee; and be
not afraid.　　　　　　　　　　　69
　2 Pren. Be merry, Peter, and fear not thy
master. Fight for credit of the prentices.
　Peter. I thank you all. Drink, and pray for
me, I pray you; for I think I have taken my
last draught in this world. Here, Robin, an if
I die, I give thee my apron: and, Will, thou
shalt have my hammer; and here, Tom, take
all the money that I have. O Lord bless me,
I pray God! for I am never able to deal with
my master, he hath learnt so much fence
already.　　　　　　　　　　　79
　Sal. Come, leave your drinking and fall to
blows. Sirrah, what's thy name?
　Peter. Peter, forsooth.
　Sal. Peter? What more?
　Peter. Thump.　　　　　　　　　84
　Sal. Thump? Then see thou thump thy
master well.
　Arm. Masters, I am come hither, as it were,
upon my man's instigation, to prove him a
knave and myself an honest man; and touching
the Duke of York, I will take my death I never
meant him any ill, nor the King, nor the Queen;
and therefore, Peter, have at thee with a downright blow!
　York. Dispatch. This knave's tongue begins
　to double.
Sound, trumpets, alarum to the combatants! 95
　*Alarum. They fight, and Peter strikes him
　　　　　　　　　　　　　　　　down.*
　Arm. Hold, Peter, hold! I confess, I confess
treason.　　　　　　　　　　　　*Dies.*
　York. Take away his weapon. Fellow, thank
God, and the good wine in thy master's
way.　　　　　　　　　　　　　99
　Peter. O God, have I overcome mine enemies
in this presence? O Peter, thou hast prevail'd
in right!
　King. Go, take hence that traitor from our
　sight,
For by his death we do perceive his guilt,
And God in justice hath reveal'd to us　105
The truth and innocence of this poor fellow,
Which he had thought to have murther'd
　wrongfully.
Come, fellow, follow us for thy reward.
　　　　　　　　　Sound a flourish. Exeunt.

Unable to wed her for himself, Suffolk acts as procurator and delivers Margaret of Anjou to the court as queen to Henry. In dismay, Gloucester reads the marriage-treaty (*Act I, Scene I*)

HENRY VI
PART TWO

Suspecting treachery, the commons demand Suffolk's death (*Act III, Scene II*)

The Duchess of Gloucester (Hazel Hughes) is cautioned by her husband to "banish the canker of ambitious thoughts" (Act I, Scene II)

Sword in hand, the Duke of York (Peter Neil) tells the Earls of Warwick (John York) and Salisbury (Robert Webber; seated) of his claim to the crown of England and gains their support (Act II, Scene II)

In a hall of justice—the king present—an apprentice and his master settle their dispute by single combat (Act II, Scene III)

Desiring to be queen, the Duchess of Gloucester resorts to sorcery. She is arrested and made to do public penance (Act II, Scene IV)

"So bad a death argues a monstrous life." The evil Cardinal (Paul Daneman), taken suddenly ill, dies (Act III, Scene III)

The Queen bids farewell to Suffolk (Alfred Burke) after Henry, at the insistence of the commons, has banished him (Act III, Scene II)

Sir Humphrey Stafford (Frederick Treves) defies the rabble of Jack Cade (Paul Daneman) (Act IV, Scene II). Cade has been encouraged by the rebellious Duke of York to provoke trouble in England

"Thou hast most traitor-
ously corrupted the youth
of the realm in erecting a
grammar-school." Cade
baits Lord Say (Eric Jones)
before having him be-
headed (*Act IV, Scene VII*)

"Thy hand is made to grasp a palmer's staff, and not to grace an awful
princely sceptre." York openly defies the king (*Act V, Scene I*)

Lord Clifford (Philip Whibley), leader of the
king's forces, is slain by York (*Act V, Scene II*)

A victorious York rejoices: "The king is fled to
London . . . Let us pursue" (*Act V, Scene III*)

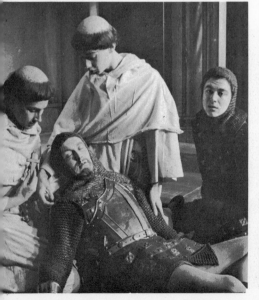

[Scene IV. *London. A street.*]

Enter *Duke Humphrey* [*of Gloucester*] *and his*
       Men in mourning cloaks.

Glou. Thus sometimes hath the brightest
       day a cloud,
And after summer evermore succeeds
Barren winter with his wrathful nipping cold.
So cares and joys abound, as seasons fleet.
Sirs, what's o'clock?
    Servant.   Ten, my lord.   5
Glou. Ten is the hour that was appointed me
To watch the coming of my punish'd duchess.
Uneath may she endure the flinty streets
To tread them with her tender-feeling feet.
Sweet Nell, ill can thy noble mind abrook   10
The abject people gazing on thy face,
With envious looks laughing at thy shame,
That erst did follow thy proud chariot wheels
When thou didst ride in triumpn through the
       streets.
But, soft! I think she comes, and I'll prepare
My tear-stain'd eyes to see her miseries.   16

Enter the *Duchess* barefoot in a white sheet,
       with papers pinned upon her back] and a taper
       burning in her hand; with the *Sheriff* and *Offi-*
       cers; *Sir John Stanley.*

   Servant. So please your Grace, we'll take her
       from the sheriff.
   Glou. No, stir not for your lives! Let her
       pass by.
   Elean. Come you, my lord, to see my open
       shame?
Now thou dost penance too. Look how they
       gaze!   20
See how the giddy multitude do point
And nod their heads and throw their eyes on
       thee!
Ah, Gloucester, hide thee from their hateful
       looks,
And in thy closet pent up, rue my shame   24
And ban thine enemies, both mine and thine!
   Glou. Be patient, gentle Nell; forget this
       grief.
   Elean. Ah, Gloucester, teach me to forget
       myself!
For, whilst I think I am thy married wife
And thou a prince, Protector of this land,
Methinks I should not thus be led along,   30
Mail'd up in shame, with papers on my back,
And follow'd with a rabble that rejoice
To see my tears and hear my deep-fet groans.
The ruthless flint doth cut my tender feet;

And when I start, the envious people laugh   35
And bid me be advised how I tread.
Ah, Humphrey, can I bear this shameful yoke?
Trowest thou that e'er I'll look upon the world
Or count them happy that enjoy the sun?
No! Dark shall be my light, and night my day;
To think upon my pomp shall be my hell.   41
Sometime I'll say, I am Duke Humphrey's wife,
And he a prince, and ruler of the land;
Yet so he rul'd, and such a prince he was,
As he stood by whilst I, his forlorn duchess,   45
Was made a wonder and a pointing stock
To every idle rascal follower.
But be thou mild and blush not at my shame,
Nor stir at nothing till the axe of death
Hang over thee, as sure it shortly will.   50
For Suffolk — he that can do all in all
With her that hateth thee and hates us all —
And York and impious Beaufort, that false
       priest,
Have all lim'd bushes to betray thy wings,
And, fly thou how thou canst, they'll tangle
       thee.   55
But fear not thou until thy foot be snar'd,
Nor never seek prevention of thy foes.
   Glou. Ah, Nell, forbear! Thou aimest all
       awry.
I must offend before I be attainted;
And had I twenty times so many foes,   60
And each of them had twenty times their power,
All these could not procure me any scathe
So long as I am loyal, true, and crimeless.
Wouldst have me rescue thee from this re-
       proach?
Why, yet thy scandal were not wip'd away,   65
But I in danger for the breach of law!
Thy greatest help is quiet, gentle Nell.
I pray thee sort thy heart to patience;
These few days' wonder will be quickly worn.

Enter a *Herald.*

   Her. I summon your Grace to his Majesty's
       parliament,   70
Holden at Bury the first of this next month.
   Glou. And my consent ne'er ask'd herein
       before?
This is close dealing. Well, I will be there.
                              Exit Herald.
My Nell, I take my leave. And, Master Sheriff,
Let not her penance exceed the King's com-
       mission.   75
   Sheriff. An't please your Grace, here my
       commission stays,
And Sir John Stanley is appointed now
To take her with him to the Isle of Man.

Glou. Must you, Sir John, protect my lady here?

Stanley. So am I given in charge, may't please your Grace.   80

Glou. Entreat her not the worse in that I pray
You use her well. The world may laugh again,
And I may live to do you kindness if
You do it her; and so, Sir John, farewell.

Elean. What, gone, my lord, and bid me not farewell?   85

Glou. Witness my tears, I cannot stay to speak.

Exeunt Gloucester and his Men.

Elean. Art thou gone too? All comfort go with thee!
For none abides with me. My joy is death —
Death, at whose name I oft have been afeard,
Because I wish'd this world's eternity.   90
Stanley, I prithee go, and take me hence;
I care not whither, for I beg no favour.
Only convey me where thou art commanded.

Stanley. Why, madam, that is to the Isle of Man,
There to be us'd according to your state.   95

Elean. That's bad enough, for I am but reproach!
And shall I then be us'd reproachfully?

Stanley. Like to a duchess and Duke Humphrey's lady —
According to that state you shall be us'd.

Elean. Sheriff, farewell, and better than I fare,   100
Although thou hast been conduct of my shame.

Sheriff. It is my office; and, madam, pardon me.

Elean. Ay, ay, farewell; thy office is discharg'd.
Come, Stanley, shall we go?

Stanley. Madam, your penance done, throw off this sheet,   105
And go we to attire you for our journey.

Elean. My shame will not be shifted with my sheet.
No! it will hang upon my richest robes
And show itself, attire me how I can.
Go, lead the way; I long to see my prison.   110

Exeunt

[ACT III. Scene I. *The Abbey at Bury St. Edmund's.*]

Sound a sennet. Enter *King, Queen, Cardinal, Suffolk, York, Buckingham, Salisbury,* and *Warwick,* to the Parliament.

King. I muse my Lord of Gloucester is not come.
'Tis not his wont to be the hindmost man,
Whate'er occasion keeps him from us now.

Queen. Can you not see? or will ye not observe
The strangeness of his alter'd countenance — 5
With what a majesty he bears himself;
How insolent of late he is become,
How proud, how peremptory, and unlike himself?
We know the time since he was mild and affable,
And if we did but glance a far-off look,   10
Immediately he was upon his knee,
That all the court admir'd him for submission;
But meet him now and, be it in the morn,
When every one will give the time of day,
He knits his brow and shows an angry eye   15
And passeth by with stiff unbowed knee,
Disdaining duty that to us belongs.
Small curs are not regarded when they grin,
But great men tremble when the lion roars,
And Humphrey is no little man in England.   20
First note that he is near you in descent,
And should you fall, he is the next will mount.
Me seemeth then it is no policy,
Respecting what a rancorous mind he bears
And his advantage following your decease,   25
That he should come about your royal person
Or be admitted to your Highness' Council.
By flattery hath he won the commons' hearts
And when he please to make commotion,
'Tis to be fear'd they all will follow him.   30
Now 'tis the spring, and weeds are shallow-rooted.
Suffer them now, and they'll o'ergrow the garden
And choke the herbs for want of husbandry.
The reverent care I bear unto my lord
Made me collect these dangers in the Duke.   35
If it be fond, call it a woman's fear;
Which fear if better reasons can supplant,
I will subscribe and say I wrong'd the Duke.
My Lords of Suffolk, Buckingham, and York
Reprove my allegation if you can,   40
Or else conclude my words effectual.

Suf. Well hath your Highness seen into this duke:

nd, had I first been put to speak my mind,
   think I should have told your Grace's tale.
The Duchess by his subornation,   45
Jpon my life, began her devilish practices;
Jr if he were not privy to those faults,
Yet by reputing of his high descent —
As next the King he was successive heir,
And such high vaunts of his nobility—   50
Did instigate the bedlam brainsick Duchess
By wicked means to frame our sovereign's fall.
Smooth runs the water where the brook is deep,
And in his simple show he harbours treason.
The fox barks not when he would steal the lamb.
No, no, my sovereign! Gloucester is a man   56
Unsounded yet and full of deep deceit.
   Car. Did he not, contrary to form of law,
Devise strange deaths for small offences done?
   York. And did he not in his protectorship 60
Levy great sums of money through the realm
For soldiers' pay in France, and never sent
   it?
By means whereof the towns each day revolted.
   Buck. Tut, these are petty faults to faults
   unknown
Which time will bring to light in smooth Duke
   Humphrey.   65
   King. My lords at once, the care you have
   of us,
To mow down thorns that would annoy our
   foot,
Is worthy praise; but, shall I speak my con-
   science,
Our kinsman Gloucester is as innocent
From meaning treason to our royal person   70
As is the sucking lamb or harmless dove.
The Duke is virtuous, mild, and too well-given
To dream on evil or to work my downfall.
   Queen. Ah, what's more dangerous than this
   fond affiance?
Seems he a dove? His feathers are but bor-
   row'd,   75
For he's disposed as the hateful raven.
Is he a lamb? His skin is surely lent him,
For he's inclin'd as is the ravenous wolf.
Who cannot steal a shape that means deceit?
Take heed, my lord. The welfare of us all   80
Hangs on the cutting short that fraudful man.

Enter *Somerset.*

   Som. All health unto my gracious sovereign!
   King. Welcome, Lord Somerset. What news
   from France?
   Som. That all your interest in those ter-
   ritories
Is utterly bereft you. All is lost.   85

   King. Cold news, Lord Somerset! but God's
   will be done.
   York. [*aside*] Cold news for me! for I had
   hope of France
As firmly as I hope for fertile England.
Thus are my blossoms blasted in the bud,
And caterpillars eat my leaves away;   90
But I will remedy this gear ere long
Or sell my title for a glorious grave.

Enter *Gloucester.*

   Glou. All happiness unto my lord the King!
Pardon, my liege, that I have stay'd so long.
   Suf. Nay, Gloucester, know that thou art
   come too soon   95
Unless thou wert more loyal than thou art.
I do arrest thee of high treason here.
   Glou. Well, Suffolk, thou shalt not see me
   blush
Nor change my countenance for this arrest.
A heart unspotted is not easily daunted.   100
The purest spring is not so free from mud
As I am clear from treason to my sovereign.
Who can accuse me? Wherein am I guilty?
   York. 'Tis thought, my lord, that you took
   bribes of France
And, being Protector, stay'd the soldiers' pay,
By means whereof his Highness hath lost
   France.   106
   Glou. Is it but thought so? What are they
   that think it?
I never robb'd the soldiers of their pay
Nor ever had one penny bribe from France.
So help me God as I have watch'd the night —
Ay, night by night — in studying good for
   England!   111
That doit that e'er I wrested from the King,
Or any groat I hoarded to my use,
Be brought against me at my trial day!   114
No! Many a pound of mine own proper store,
Because I would not tax the needy commons,
Have I dispursed to the garrisons,
And never ask'd for restitution.
   Car. It serves you well, my lord, to say so
   much.
   Glou. I say no more than truth, so help me
   God!   120
   York. In your protectorship you did devise
Strange tortures for offenders, never heard of,
That England was defam'd by tyranny.
   Glou. Why, 'tis well known that, whiles I
   was Protector,
Pity was all the fault that was in me;   125
For I should melt at an offender's tears
And lowly words were ransom for their fault.

Unless it were a bloody murtherer,
Or foul felonious thief that fleec'd poor pas-
    sengers,
I never gave them condign punishment.   130
Murther indeed, that bloody sin, I tortur'd
Above the felon or what trespass else.
    Suf. My lord, these faults are easy, quickly
    answer'd ;
But mightier crimes are laid unto your charge,
Whereof you cannot easily purge yourself.   135
I do arrest you in his Highness' name
And here commit you to my Lord Cardinal
To keep until your further time of trial.
    King. My Lord of Gloucester, 'tis my spe-
    cial hope   139
That you will clear yourself from all suspect.
My conscience tells me you are innocent.
    Glou. Ah, gracious lord, these days are dan-
    gerous !
Virtue is chok'd with foul ambition
And charity chas'd hence by rancour's hand ;
Foul subornation is predominant   145
And equity exil'd your Highness' land.
I know their complot is to have my life ;
And if my death might make this island happy
And prove the period of their tyranny,
I would expend it with all willingness.   150
But mine is made the prologue to their play ;
For thousands more, that yet suspect no peril,
Will not conclude their plotted tragedy.
Beaufort's red sparkling eyes blab his heart's
    malice   154
And Suffolk's cloudy brow his stormy hate ;
Sharp Buckingham unburthens with his tongue
The envious load that lies upon his heart ;
And dogged York, that reaches at the moon,
Whose overweening arm I have pluck'd back,
By false accuse doth level at my life ;   160
And you, my sovereign lady, with the rest,
Causeless have laid disgraces on my head
And with your best endeavour have stirr'd up
My liefest liege to be mine enemy.   164
Ay, all of you have laid your heads together —
Myself had notice of your conventicles —
And all to make away my guiltless life.
I shall not want false witness to condemn me
Nor store of treasons to augment my guilt.
The ancient proverb will be well effected —
'A staff is quickly found to beat a dog.'   171
    Car. My liege, his railing is intolerable.
If those that care to keep your royal person
From treason's secret knife and traitor's rage
Be thus upbraided, chid, and rated at,   175
And the offender granted scope of speech,
'Twill make them cool in zeal unto your Grace.

    Suf. Hath he not twit our sovereign lady here
With ignominious words, though clerkly
    couch'd,
As if she had suborned some to swear   180
False allegations to o'erthrow his state?
    Queen. But I can give the loser leave to
    chide.
    Glou. Far truer spoke than meant ! I lose
    indeed.
Beshrew the winners, for they play'd me false
And well such losers may have leave to speak
    Buck. He'll wrest the sense and hold us here
    all day.   186
Lord Cardinal, he is your prisoner.
    Car. Sirs, take away the Duke and guard
    him sure.
    Glou. Ah, thus King Henry throws away his
    crutch
Before his legs be firm to bear his body.   190
Thus is the shepherd beaten from thy side,
And wolves are gnarling who shall gnaw thee
    first.
Ah that my fear were false ! ah that it were !
For, good King Henry, thy decay I fear.
                         Exit [guarded].
    King. My lords, what to your wisdoms
    seemeth best   195
Do or undo, as if ourself were here.
    Queen. What, will your Highness leave the
    parliament?
    King. Ay, Margaret. My heart is drown'd
    with grief,
Whose flood begins to flow within mine eyes ;
My body round engirt with misery —   200
For what's more miserable than discontent?
Ah, uncle Humphrey, in thy face I see
The map of honour, truth, and loyalty ;
And yet, good Humphrey, is the hour to come
That e'er I prov'd thee false or fear'd thy faith.
What low'ring star now envies thy estate   206
That these great lords and Margaret our queen
Do seek subversion of thy harmless life?
Thou never didst them wrong nor no man
    wrong !
And as the butcher takes away the calf   210
And binds the wretch and beats it when it
    strays,
Bearing it to the bloody slaughterhouse,
Even so remorseless have they borne him hence ;
And as the dam runs lowing up and down,   214
Looking the way her harmless young one went,
And can do naught but wail her darling's loss
Even so myself bewails good Gloucester's case
With sad unhelpful tears, and with dimm'd eyes
Look after him and cannot do him good,

So mighty are his vowed enemies.   220
His fortunes I will weep, and 'twixt each groan
Say 'Who's a traitor? Gloucester he is none.'
    Exeunt [all but Queen, Cardinal, Suffolk,
            York, and Somerset].
  Queen. Free lords, cold snow melts with the
    sun's hot beams.
Henry my lord is cold in great affairs,
Too full of foolish pity; and Gloucester's show
Beguiles him as the mournful crocodile   226
With sorrow snares relenting passengers,
Or as the snake, roll'd in a flow'ring bank,
With shining checker'd slough, doth sting a
    child
That for the beauty thinks it excellent.   230
Believe me, lords, were none more wise than I —
And yet herein I judge mine own wit good —
This Gloucester should be quickly rid the world,
To rid us from the fear we have of him.   234
  Car. That he should die is worthy policy;
But yet we want a colour for his death.
Tis meet he be condemn'd by course of law.
  Suf. But, in my mind, that were no policy.
The King will labour still to save his life,
The commons haply rise to save his life;   240
And yet we have but trivial argument,
More than mistrust, that shows him worthy
    death.
  York. So that, by this, you would not have
    him die.
  Suf. Ah, York, no man alive so fain as I!
  York. 'Tis York that hath more reason for
    his death.   245
But, my Lord Cardinal, and you, my Lord of
    Suffolk,
Say as you think and speak it from your souls:
Were't not all one an empty eagle were set
To guard the chicken from a hungry kite
As place Duke Humphrey for the King's Pro-
    tector?   250
  Queen. So the poor chicken should be sure
    of death.
  Suf. Madam, 'tis true; and were't not mad-
    ness then
To make the fox surveyor of the fold?
Who being accus'd a crafty murtherer,
His guilt should be but idly posted over   255
Because his purpose is not executed.
No! Let him die in that he is a fox,
By nature prov'd an enemy to the flock,
Before his chaps be stain'd with crimson blood,
As Humphrey, prov'd by reasons, to my liege.
And do not stand on quillets how to slay him.
Be it by gins, by snares, by subtlety,   262
Sleeping or waking, 'tis no matter how,

So he be dead; for that is good deceit
Which mates him first that first intends deceit.
  Queen. Thrice-noble Suffolk, 'tis resolutely
    spoke.   266
  Suf. Not resolute, except so much were done,
For things are often spoke and seldom meant;
But that my heart accordeth with my tongue,
Seeing the deed is meritorious,   270
And to preserve my sovereign from his foe,
Say but the word, and I will be his priest.
  Car. But I would have him dead, my Lord
    of Suffolk,
Ere you can take due orders for a priest.
Say you consent and censure well the deed,   275
And I'll provide his executioner,
I tender so the safety of my liege.
  Suf. Here is my hand, the deed is worthy
    doing.
  Queen. And so say I.
  York. And I. And now we three have spoken
    it,   280
It skills not greatly who impugns our doom.

            Enter a *Post.*

  Post. Great lords, from Ireland am I come
    amain
To signify that rebels there are up
And put the Englishmen unto the sword.
Send succours, lords, and stop the rage betime,
Before the wound do grow uncurable;   286
For, being green, there is great hope of help.
  Car. A breach that craves a quick expedient
    stop!
What counsel give you in this weighty cause?
  York. That Somerset be sent as Regent
    thither.   290
'Tis meet that lucky ruler be employ'd;
Witness the fortune he hath had in France.
  Som. If York with all his far-fet policy
Had been the Regent there instead of me,   294
He never would have stay'd in France so long.
  York. No, not to lose it all, as thou hast
    done.
I rather would have lost my life betimes
Than bring a burthen of dishonour home
By staying there so long till all were lost.
Show me one scar character'd on thy skin.   300
Men's flesh preserv'd so whole do seldom win.
  Queen. Nay then, this spark will prove a
    raging fire
If wind and fuel be brought to feed it with.
No more, good York! Sweet Somerset, be still!
Thy fortune, York, hadst thou been Regent
    there,   305
Might happily have prov'd far worse than his.

York. What, worse than naught? Nay, then
  a shame take all!
Som. And, in the number, thee that wishest
  shame!
Car. My Lord of York, try what your for-
  tune is.
Th' uncivil kerns of Ireland are in arms   310
And temper clay with blood of Englishmen.
To Ireland will you lead a band of men,
Collected choicely, from each county some,
And try your hap against the Irishmen?   314
York. I will, my lord, so please his Majesty.
Suf. Why, our authority is his consent,
And what we do establish he confirms.
Then, noble York, take thou this task in hand.
York. I am content. Provide me soldiers,
  lords,
Whiles I take order for mine own affairs.   320
Suf. A charge, Lord York, that I will see
  perform'd.
But now return we to the false Duke Hum-
  phrey.
Car. No more of him; for I will deal with
  him
That henceforth he shall trouble us no more.
And so break off; the day is almost spent.   325
Lord Suffolk, you and I must talk of that event.
York. My Lord of Suffolk, within fourteen
  days
At Bristow I expect my soldiers,
For there I'll ship them all for Ireland.   329
Suf. I'll see it truly done, my Lord of York.
                    Exeunt. Manet York.
York. Now, York, or never, steel thy fear-
  ful thoughts
And change misdoubt to resolution.
Be that thou hop'st to be; or what thou art
Resign to death: it is not worth th' enjoying.
Let pale-fac'd fear keep with the mean-born
  man   335
And find no harbour in a royal heart.
Faster than springtime show'rs comes thought
  on thought,
And not a thought but thinks on dignity.
My brain, more busy than the labouring spider,
Weaves tedious snares to trap mine enemies.
Well, nobles, well! 'tis politicly done   341
To send me packing with a host of men.
I fear me you but warm the starved snake,
Who, cherish'd in your breasts, will sting your
  hearts.   344
'Twas men I lack'd, and you will give them me.
I take it kindly. Yet be well assur'd
You put sharp weapons in a madman's hands.
Whiles I in Ireland nourish a mighty band,

I will stir up in England some black storm   349
Shall blow ten thousand souls to heaven or hell;
And this fell tempest shall not cease to rage
Until the golden circuit on my head,
Like to the glorious sun's transparent beams,
Do calm the fury of this mad-bred flaw.
And for a minister of my intent   355
I have seduc'd a headstrong Kentishman,
John Cade of Ashford,
To make commotion, as full well he can,
Under the title of John Mortimer.
In Ireland have I seen this stubborn Cade   360
Oppose himself against a troop of kerns,
And fought so long till that his thighs with darts
Were almost like a sharp-quill'd porpentine;
And in the end being rescued, I have seen
Him caper upright like a wild Morisco,   365
Shaking the bloody darts as he his bells.
Full often, like a shag-hair'd crafty kern,
Hath he conversed with the enemy
And undiscover'd come to me again
And given me notice of their villanies.   370
This devil here shall be my substitute;
For that John Mortimer which now is dead
In face, in gait, in speech, he doth resemble.
By this I shall perceive the commons' mind,
How they affect the house and claim of York.
Say he be taken, rack'd, and tortured;   376
I know no pain they can inflict upon him
Will make him say I mov'd him to those arms.
Say that he thrive, as 'tis great like he will;
Why, then from Ireland come I with my
  strength   380
And reap the harvest which that rascal sow'd;
For, Humphrey being dead, as he shall be,
And Henry put apart, the next for me!   *Exit.*

[Scene II. *Bury St. Edmund's. A
          room of state.*]

Enter *two or three* running over the stage,
  from the murther of *Duke Humphrey.*

1. Mur. Run to my Lord of Suffolk. Let
  him know
We have dispatch'd the Duke, as he commanded.
2. Mur. O that it were to do! What have we
  done?
Didst ever hear a man so penitent?

          Enter *Suffolk.*

1. Mur. Here comes my lord.   5
Suf. Now, sirs, have you dispatch'd this
  thing?

1. Mur. Ay, my good lord; he's dead.

Suf. Why, that's well said. Go, get you to my house.

will reward you for this venturous deed. 9
The King and all the peers are here at hand.
Have you laid fair the bed? Is all things well,
According as I gave directions?

1. Mur. 'Tis, my good lord.

Suf. Away! be gone!

Exeunt Murtherers.

Sound trumpets. Enter the *King*, the *Queen*, *Cardinal*, *Somerset*, with *Attendants.*

King. Go call our uncle to our presence straight. 15
Say we intend to try his Grace to-day,
If he be guilty, as 'tis published.

Suf. I'll call him presently, my noble lord.
Exit.

King. Lords, take your places; and I pray you all 19
Proceed no straiter 'gainst our uncle Gloucester
Than from true evidence, of good esteem,
He be approv'd in practice culpable.

Queen. God forbid any malice should prevail
That faultless may condemn a nobleman!
Pray God he may acquit him of suspicion. 25

King. I thank thee, Meg. These words content me much.

Enter *Suffolk.*

How now? Why look'st thou pale? Why tremblest thou?
Where is our uncle? What's the matter, Suffolk?

Suf. Dead in his bed, my lord! Gloucester is dead.

Queen. Marry, God forfend! 30

Car. God's secret judgment! I did dream to-night
The Duke was dumb and could not speak a word. *King sounds.*

Queen. How fares my lord? Help, lords! The King is dead.

Som. Rear up his body; wring him by the nose.

Queen. Run, go! help, help! O Henry, ope thine eyes! 35

Suf. He doth revive again. Madam, be patient.

King. O heavenly God!

Queen.   How fares my gracious lord?

Suf. Comfort, my sovereign! Gracious Henry, comfort!

King. What, doth my Lord of Suffolk comfort me?
Came he right now to sing a raven's note 40
Whose dismal tune bereft my vital pow'rs,
And thinks he that the chirping of a wren,
By crying comfort from a hollow breast,
Can chase away the first-conceived sound?
Hide not thy poison with such sug'red words.
Lay not thy hands on me. Forbear, I say! 46
Their touch affrights me as a serpent's sting.
Thou baleful messenger, out of my sight!
Upon thy eyeballs murderous tyranny
Sits in grim majesty, to fright the world. 50
Look not upon me, for thine eyes are wounding.
Yet do not go away. Come, basilisk,
And kill the innocent gazer with thy sight;
For in the shade of death I shall find joy —
In life but double death, now Gloucester's dead.

Queen. Why do you rate my Lord of Suffolk thus? 56
Although the Duke was enemy to him,
Yet he most Christianlike laments his death;
And for myself, foe as he was to me,
Might liquid tears or heart-offending groans 60
Or blood-consuming sighs recall his life,
I would be blind with weeping, sick with groans,
Look pale as primrose with blood-drinking sighs,
And all to have the noble Duke alive. 64
What know I how the world may deem of me?
For it is known we were but hollow friends.
It may be judg'd I made the Duke away;
So shall my name with slander's tongue be wounded
And princes' courts be fill'd with my reproach.
This get I by his death. Ay me unhappy, 70
To be a queen, and crown'd with infamy!

King. Ah, woe is me for Gloucester, wretched man!

Queen. Be woe for me, more wretched than he is!
What, dost thou turn away, and hide thy face?
I am no loathsome leper. Look on me. 75
What? Art thou like the adder waxen deaf?
Be poisonous too, and kill thy forlorn queen.
Is all thy comfort shut in Gloucester's tomb?
Why, then Dame Margaret was ne'er thy joy.
Erect his statuë and worship it, 80
And make my image but an alehouse sign.
Was I for this nigh wrack'd upon the sea
And twice by awkward wind from England's bank
Drove back again unto my native clime?
What boded this but well-forewarning wind 85
Did seem to say 'Seek not a scorpion's nest

255

Nor set no footing on this unkind shore'?
What did I then but curs'd the gentle gusts
And he that loos'd them forth their brazen
     caves,
And bid them blow towards England's blessed
     shore   90
Or turn our stern upon a dreadful rock?
Yet Æolus would not be a murtherer,
But left that hateful office unto thee.
The pretty vaulting sea refus'd to drown me,
Knowing that thou wouldst have me drown'd
     on shore   95
With tears as salt as sea through thy un-
     kindness.
The splitting rocks cow'r'd in the sinking sands
And would not dash me with their ragged sides,
Because thy flinty heart, more hard than they,
Might in thy palace perish Margaret.   100
As far as I could ken thy chalky cliffs,
When from thy shore the tempest beat us back,
I stood upon the hatches in the storm;
And when the dusky sky began to rob
My earnest-gaping sight of thy land's view,
I took a costly jewel from my neck,   106
A heart it was, bound in with diamonds,
And threw it towards thy land. The sea re-
     ceiv'd it,
And so I wish'd thy body might my heart;   109
And even with this I lost fair England's view,
And bid mine eyes be packing with my heart,
And call'd them blind and dusky spectacles
For losing ken of Albion's wished coast.
How often have I tempted Suffolk's tongue
(The agent of thy foul inconstancy)   115
To sit and witch me as Ascanius did
When he to madding Dido would unfold
His father's acts commenc'd in burning Troy!
Am I not witch'd like her? or thou not false
     like him?
Ay me, I can no more! Die, Margaret!   120
For Henry weeps that thou dost live so long.

Noise within. Enter *Warwick, Salisbury,*
          and many *Commons.*

War. It is reported, mighty sovereign,
That good Duke Humphrey traitorously is
     murd'red
By Suffolk and the Cardinal Beaufort's means.
The commons, like an angry hive of bees   125
That want their leader, scatter up and down
And care not who they sting in his revenge.
Myself have calm'd their spleenful mutiny
Until they hear the order of his death.
     King. That he is dead, good Warwick, 'tis
     too true;   130

But how he died God knows, not Henry.
Enter his chamber, view his breathless corpse,
And comment then upon his sudden death.
     War. That shall I do, my liege. Stay,
     Salisbury,
With the rude multitude till I return.   135
     [*Exit.*] *Exit Salisbury* [*with the Commons*].
     King. O thou that judgest all things, stay
     my thoughts —
My thoughts, that labour to persuade my soul
Some violent hands were laid on Humphrey's
     life!
If my suspect be false, forgive me, God;
For judgment only doth belong to thee.   140
Fain would I go to chafe his paly lips
With twenty thousand kisses and to drain
Upon his face an ocean of salt tears,
To tell my love unto his dumb deaf trunk,
And with my fingers feel his hand unfeeling.
But all in vain are these mean obsequies;   146

Bed put forth [*with the body.* Enter *Warwick*].

And to survey his dead and earthy image,
What were it but to make my sorrow greater?
     War. Come hither, gracious sovereign, view
     this body.
     King. That is to see how deep my grave is
     made;   150
For with his soul fled all my worldly solace,
And seeing him, I see my life in death.
     War. As surely as my soul intends to live
With that dread King that took our state upon
     him
To free us from his Father's wrathful curse,
I do believe that violent hands were laid   156
Upon the life of this thrice-famed duke.
     Suf. A dreadful oath, sworn with a solemn
     tongue!
What instance gives Lord Warwick for his vow?
     War. See how the blood is settled in his face.
Oft have I seen a timely-parted ghost,   161
Of ashy semblance, meagre, pale, and bloodless,
Being all descended to the labouring heart,
Who, in the conflict that it holds with death,
Attracts the same for aidance 'gainst the enemy,
Which with the heart there cools, and ne'er
     returneth   166
To blush and beautify the cheek again.
But see, his face is black and full of blood;
His eyeballs further out than when he liv'd,
Staring full ghastly, like a strangled man;   170
His hair uprear'd, his nostrils stretch'd with
     struggling;
His hands abroad display'd, as one that grasp'd
And tugg'd for life and was by strength subdu'd.

Look, on the sheets his hair, you see, is sticking;
His well-proportion'd beard made rough and
    rugged,   175
Like to the summer's corn by tempest lodg'd.
It cannot be but he was murd'red here.
The least of all these signs were probable.
  Suf. Why, Warwick, who should do the
    Duke to death?
Myself and Beaufort had him in protection,
And we, I hope, sir, are no murtherers.   181
  War. But both of you were vow'd Duke
    Humphrey's foes,
And you (forsooth) had the good Duke to keep.
'Tis like you would not feast him like a friend,
And 'tis well seen he found an enemy.   185
  Queen. Then you belike suspect these noble-
    men
As guilty of Duke Humphrey's timeless death.
  War. Who finds the heifer dead, and bleeding
    fresh,
And sees fast-by a butcher with an axe,
But will suspect 'twas he that made the
    slaughter?   190
Who finds the partridge in the puttock's nest
But may imagine how the bird was dead,
Although the kite soar with unbloodied beak?
Even so suspicious is this tragedy.
  Queen. Are you the butcher, Suffolk?
    Where's your knife?   195
Is Beaufort term'd a kite? Where are his
    talons?
  Suf. I wear no knife to slaughter sleeping
    men;
But here's a vengeful sword, rusted with ease,
That shall be scoured in his rancorous heart
That slanders me with murther's crimson
    badge.   200
Say, if thou dar'st, proud Lord of Warwick-
    shire,
That I am faulty in Duke Humphrey's death.
    Exeunt Cardinal, [*Somerset, and others*].
  War. What dares not Warwick, if false
    Suffolk dare him?
  Queen. He dares not calm his contumelious
    spirit,
Nor cease to be an arrogant controller,   205
Though Suffolk dare him twenty thousand
    times.
  War. Madam, be still. With reverence may
    I say;
For every word you speak in his behalf
Is slander to your royal dignity.
  Suf. Blunt-witted lord, ignoble in demean-
    our!   210
If ever lady wrong'd her lord so much,

Thy mother took into her blameful bed
Some stern untutor'd churl, and noble stock
Was graft with crab-tree slip, whose fruit thou
    art,
And never of the Nevils' noble race.   215
  War. But that the guilt of murther bucklers
    thee,
And I should rob the deathsman of his fee,
Quitting thee thereby of ten thousand shames,
And that my sovereign's presence makes me
    mild,   219
I would, false murd'rous coward, on thy knee
Make thee beg pardon for thy passed speech
And say it was thy mother that thou meant'st,
That thou thyself wast born in bastardy;
And after all this fearful homage done,
Give thee thy hire, and send thy soul to hell,
Pernicious bloodsucker of sleeping men!   226
  Suf. Thou shalt be waking while I shed thy
    blood,
If from this presence thou dar'st go with me.
  War. Away even now, or I will drag thee
    hence!   229
Unworthy though thou art, I'll cope with thee
And do some service to Duke Humphrey's
    ghost.   *Exeunt Suffolk and Warwick.*
  King. What stronger breastplate than a
    heart untainted?
Thrice is he arm'd that hath his quarrel just,
And he but naked, though lock'd up in steel,
Whose conscience with injustice is corrupted.
    A noise within.
  Queen. What noise is this?   236

Enter *Suffolk* and *Warwick*, with their
weapons drawn.

  King. Why, how now, lords? your wrathful
    weapons drawn
Here in our presence? Dare you be so bold?
Why, what tumultuous clamour have we here?
  Suf. The trait'rous Warwick, with the men
    of Bury,   240
Set all upon me, mighty sovereign.

Enter *Salisbury.*

  Sal. [*to the Commons, who are within*] Sirs,
    stand apart. The King shall know your
    mind. —
Dread lord, the commons send you word by me,
Unless false Suffolk straight be done to death
Or banished fair England's territories,   245
They will by violence tear him from your palace
And torture him with grievous ling'ring death.
They say, by him the good Duke Humphrey
    died;

They say, in him they fear your Highness'
   death;
And mere instinct of love and loyalty —   250
Free from a stubborn opposite intent,
As being thought to contradict your liking —
Makes them thus forward in his banishment.
They say, in care of your most royal person,
That if your Highness should intend to sleep
And charge that no man should disturb your
   rest   256
In pain of your dislike or pain of death,
Yet, notwithstanding such a strait edict,
Were there a serpent seen with forked tongue
That slily glided towards your Majesty,   260
It were but necessary you were wak'd,
Lest, being suffer'd in that harmful slumber,
The mortal worm might make the sleep eternal.
And therefore do they cry, though you forbid,
That they will guard you, whe'r you will or
   no,   265
From such fell serpents as false Suffolk is;
With whose envenomed and fatal sting
Your loving uncle, twenty times his worth,
They say is shamefully bereft of life.
Commons. (*within*) An answer from the King,
   my Lord of Salisbury!   270
Suf. 'Tis like the commons, rude unpolish'd
   hinds,
Could send such message to their sovereign!
But you, my lord, were glad to be employ'd,
To show how quaint an orator you are.
But all the honour Salisbury hath won   275
Is, that he was the lord ambassador
Sent from a sort of tinkers to the King.
Commons. (*within*) An answer from the King,
   or we will all break in!
King. Go, Salisbury, and tell them all from
   me
I thank them for their tender loving care;   280
And had I not been cited so by them,
Yet did I purpose as they do entreat.
For sure my thoughts do hourly prophesy
Mischance unto my state by Suffolk's means;
And therefore by his majesty I swear   285
Whose far unworthy deputy I am,
He shall not breathe infection in this air
But three days longer, on the pain of death.
                Exit Salisbury.
Queen. O Henry, let me plead for gentle
   Suffolk!
King. Ungentle queen, to call him gentle
   Suffolk!   290
No more, I say. If thou dost plead for him,
Thou wilt but add increase unto my wrath.
Had I but said, I would have kept my word;

But when I swear, it is irrevocable. —
If after three days' space thou here be'st found
On any ground that I am ruler of,   296
The world shall not be ransom for thy life. —
Come, Warwick, come, good Warwick, go with
   me;
I have great matters to impart to thee.
          Exeunt all but Queen and Suffolk.
Queen. Mischance and sorrow go along with
   you!   300
Heart's discontent and sour affliction
Be playfellows to keep you company!
There's two of you; the devil make a third,
And threefold vengeance tend upon your steps!
Suf. Cease, gentle queen, these execrations
And let thy Suffolk take his heavy leave.   306
Queen. Fie, coward woman and soft-hearted
   wretch!
Hast thou not spirit to curse thine enemy?
Suf. A plague upon them! Wherefore should
   I curse them?
Would curses kill as doth the mandrake's groan,
I would invent as bitter searching terms,   311
As curst, as harsh, and horrible to hear,
Deliver'd strongly through my fixed teeth,
With full as many signs of deadly hate,
As lean-fac'd Envy in her loathsome cave.   315
My tongue should stumble in mine earnest
   words,
Mine eyes should sparkle like the beaten flint,
Mine hair be fix'd an end, as one distract;
Ay, every joint should seem to curse and ban;
And even now my burthen'd heart would break
Should I not curse them. Poison be their drink!
Gall, worse than gall, the daintiest that they
   taste!   322
Their sweetest shade a grove of cypress trees!
Their chiefest prospect murd'ring basilisks!
Their softest touch as smart as lizards' stings!
Their music frightful as the serpent's hiss,   326
And boding screech owls make the consort full!
All the foul terrors in dark-seated hell —
Queen. Enough, sweet Suffolk. Thou tor-
   ment'st thyself;
And these dread curses, like the sun 'gainst
   glass,   330
Or like an overcharged gun, recoil
And turn the force of them upon thyself.
Suf. You bade me ban, and will you bid me
   leave?
Now by the ground that I am banish'd from,
Well could I curse away a winter's night,   335
Though standing naked on a mountain top
Where biting cold would never let grass grow,
And think it but a minute spent in sport.

Queen. O, let me entreat thee cease! Give
  me thy hand,
That I may dew it with my mournful tears;
Nor let the rain of heaven wet this place   341
To wash away my woful monuments.
O, could this kiss be printed in thy hand,
               [*Kisses his hand.*]
That thou mightst think upon these by the
  seal
Through whom a thousand sighs are breath'd
  for thee!   345
So get thee gone, that I may know my grief!
'Tis but surmis'd whiles thou art standing by,
As one that surfeits, thinking on a want.
I will repeal thee or, be well assur'd,
Adventure to be banished myself;   350
And banished I am, if but from thee.
Go, speak not to me. Even now be gone!
O, go not yet! Even thus two friends con-
  demn'd
Embrace, and kiss, and take ten thousand
  leaves,
Loather a hundred times to part than die.   355
Yet now farewell, and farewell life with thee!
  Suf. Thus is poor Suffolk ten times banished,
Once by the King and three times thrice by
  thee.
'Tis not the land I care for, wert thou thence.
A wilderness is populous enough,   360
So Suffolk had thy heavenly company;
For where thou art, there is the world itself
With every several pleasure in the world;
And where thou art not, desolation.
I can no more. Live thou to joy thy life;   365
Myself no joy in naught, but that thou liv'st.

            Enter *Vaux.*

  Queen. Whither goes Vaux so fast? What
  news, I prithee?
  Vaux. To signify unto his Majesty
That Cardinal Beaufort is at point of death;
For suddenly a grievous sickness took him   370
That makes him gasp and stare and catch the
  air,
Blaspheming God and cursing men on earth.
Sometime he talks as if Duke Humphrey's
  ghost
Were by his side; sometime he calls the King
And whispers to his pillow, as to him,   375
The secrets of his overcharged soul;
And I am sent to tell his Majesty
That even now he cries aloud for him.
  Queen. Go tell this heavy message to the
  King.
                  Exit Vaux.

Ay me! What is this world? What news are
  these!   380
But wherefore grieve I at an hour's poor loss,
Omitting Suffolk's exile, my soul's treasure?
Why only, Suffolk, mourn I not for thee,
And with the southern clouds contend in tears—
Theirs for the earth's increase, mine for my
  sorrows?   385
Now get thee hence. The King thou know'st
  is coming.
If thou be found by me, thou art but dead.
  Suf. If I depart from thee, I cannot live;
And in thy sight to die, what were it else
But like a pleasant slumber in thy lap?   390
Here could I breathe my soul into the air,
As mild and gentle as the cradle-babe
Dying with mother's dug between its lips;
Where, from thy sight, I should be raging mad
And cry out for thee to close up mine eyes,   395
To have thee with thy lips to stop my mouth.
So shouldst thou either turn my flying soul,
Or I should breathe it so into thy body,
And then it liv'd in sweet Elysium.
To die by thee were but to die in jest;   400
From thee to die were torture more than death.
O, let me stay, befall what may befall!
  Queen. Away! Though parting be a fretful
  corrosive,
It is applied to a deathful wound.
To France, sweet Suffolk! Let me hear from
  thee;   405
For wheresoe'er thou art in this world's globe,
I'll have an Iris that shall find thee out.
  Suf. I go.
  Queen.   And take my heart with thee.
  Suf. A jewel, lock'd into the wofull'st cask
That ever did contain a thing of worth.   410
Even as a splitted bark, so sunder we.
This way fall I to death.
  Queen.   This way for me.
               Exeunt [*severally*].

  [Scene III. *London.* Cardinal Beau-
       fort's *bedchamber.*]

Enter the *King, Salisbury,* and *Warwick,* to the
            Cardinal in bed.

  King. How fares my lord? Speak, Beaufort,
  to thy sovereign.
  Car. If thou be'st Death, I'll give thee Eng-
  land's treasure,
Enough to purchase such another island,
So thou wilt let me live and feel no pain.

King. Ah, what a sign it is of evil life 5
Where death's approach is seen so terrible!
War. Beaufort, it is thy sovereign speaks to
thee.
Car. Bring me unto my trial when you will.
Died he not in his bed? Where should he die?
Can I make men live, whe'r they will or no? 10
O, torture me no more! I will confess.
Alive again? Then show me where he is.
I'll give a thousand pound to look upon him.
He hath no eyes; the dust hath blinded them.
Comb down his hair. Look, look! it stands
upright, 15
Like lime-twigs set to catch my winged soul!
Give me some drink, and bid the apothecary
Bring the strong poison that I bought of him.
King. O thou eternal Mover of the heavens,
Look with a gentle eye upon this wretch! 20

O, beat away the busy meddling fiend
That lays strong siege unto this wretch's soul,
And from his bosom purge this black despair!
War. See how the pangs of death do make
him grin!
Sal. Disturb him not; let him pass peace-
ably. 25
King. Peace to his soul, if God's good pleas-
ure be!
Lord Card'nal, if thou think'st on heaven's
bliss,
Hold up thy hand, make signal of thy hope.
He dies and makes no sign. O God, forgive him!
War. So bad a death argues a monstrous life.
King. Forbear to judge, for we are sinners
all.
Close up his eyes and draw the curtain close,
And let us all to meditation. *Exeunt.*

[ACT IV. Scene I. *Kent, the seashore.*]

Alarum. Fight at sea. Ordnance goes off.

Enter *Lieutenant*, a *Shipmaster* and his *Mate*,
and *Walter Whitmore*, [with *Sailors*]; *Suffolk*
and others [as prisoners].

Lieut. The gaudy, blabbing, and remorseful
day
Is crept into the bosom of the sea;
And now loud-howling wolves arouse the jades
That drag the tragic melancholy night,
Who with their drowsy, slow, and flagging
wings 5
Cleep dead men's graves, and from their misty
jaws
Breathe foul contagious darkness in the air.
Therefore bring forth the soldiers of our prize;
For, whilst our pinnace anchors in the Downs,
Here shall they make their ransom on the sand
Or with their blood stain this discoloured shore.
Master, this prisoner freely give I thee;
And thou that art his mate, make boot of this;
The other, Walter Whitmore, is thy share.
1. Gent. What is my ransom, master? Let
me know. 15
Mast. A thousand crowns, or else lay down
your head.
Mate. And so much shall you give, or off
goes yours.
Lieut. What, think you much to pay two
thousand crowns,
And bear the name and port of gentlemen?
Cut both the villains' throats; for die you
shall! 20

The lives of those which we have lost in fight
Be counterpois'd with such a petty sum!
1. Gent. I'll give it, sir; and therefore spare
my life.
2. Gent. And so will I, and write home for it
straight.
Whit. I lost mine eye in laying the prize
aboard, 25
[*To Suffolk*] And therefore to revenge it shalt
thou die;
And so should these, if I might have my will.
Lieut. Be not so rash. Take ransom, let him
live.
Suf. Look on my George; I am a gentle-
man.
Rate me at what thou wilt, thou shalt be paid.
Whit. And so am I. My name is Walter
Whitmore. 31
How now? Why starts thou? What, doth
death affright?
Suf. Thy name affrights me, in whose sound
is death.
A cunning man did calculate my birth
And told me that by Water I should die. 35
Yet let not this make thee be bloody-minded.
Thy name is Gaultier, being rightly sounded.
Whit. Gaultier or Walter, which it is I care
not.
Never yet did base dishonour blur our name
But with our sword we wip'd away the blot; 40
Therefore, when merchantlike I sell revenge,
Broke be my sword, my arms torn and defac'd,
And I proclaim'd a coward through the world!

260

Suf. Stay, Whitmore; for thy prisoner is a prince,
The Duke of Suffolk, William de la Pole.   45
Whit. The Duke of Suffolk muffled up in rags?
Suf. Ay, but these rags are no part of the Duke.
Jove sometime went disguis'd, and why not I?
Lieut. But Jove was never slain, as thou shalt be.
Suf. Obscure and lowly swain, King Henry's blood,   50
The honourable blood of Lancaster,
Must not be shed by such a jaded groom.
Hast thou not kiss'd thy hand and held my stirrup?
Bare-headed plodded by my footcloth mule,
And thought thee happy when I shook my head?   55
How often hast thou waited at my cup,
Fed from my trencher, kneel'd down at the board,
When I have feasted with Queen Margaret!
Remember it, and let it make thee crestfall'n,
Ay, and allay this thy abortive pride.   60
How in our voiding lobby hast thou stood
And duly waited for my coming forth!
This hand of mine hath writ in thy behalf,
And therefore shall it charm thy riotous tongue.
Whit. Speak, Captain, shall I stab the forlorn swain?   65
Lieut. First let my words stab him, as he hath me.
Suf. Base slave, thy words are blunt, and so art thou.
Lieut. Convey him hence, and on our longboat's side
Strike off his head.
Suf.   Thou dar'st not, for thy own!
Lieut. Yes, Pole?
Suf.   Pole?
Lieut.   Pool? Sir Pool? Lord!   70
Ay, kennel, puddle, sink! whose filth and dirt
Troubles the silver spring where England drinks.
Now will I dam up this thy yawning mouth
For swallowing the treasure of the realm.
Thy lips that kiss'd the Queen shall sweep the ground;   75
And thou that smil'dst at good Duke Humphrey's death
Against the senseless winds shalt grin in vain,
Who in contempt shall hiss at thee again.
And wedded be thou to the hags of hell
For daring to affy a mighty lord   80
Unto the daughter of a worthless king,

Having neither subject, wealth, nor diadem.
By devilish policy art thou grown great,
And, like ambitious Sylla, overgorg'd   84
With gobbets of thy mother's bleeding heart.
By thee Anjou and Maine were sold to France;
The false revolting Normans thorough thee
Disdain to call us lord, and Picardy
Hath slain their governors, surpris'd our forts,
And sent the ragged soldiers wounded home.
The princely Warwick and the Nevils all,   91
Whose dreadful swords were never drawn in vain,
As hating thee, are rising up in arms;
And now the house of York, thrust from the crown
By shameful murther of a guiltless king   95
And lofty, proud, encroaching tyranny,
Burns with revenging fire, whose hopeful colours
Advance our half-fac'd sun, striving to shine,
Under the which is writ 'Invitis nubibus.'
The commons here in Kent are up in arms,   100
And to conclude, reproach and beggary
Is crept into the palace of our king,
And all by thee. Away! convey him hence.
Suf. O that I were a god, to shoot forth thunder
Upon these paltry, servile, abject drudges!   105
Small things make base men proud. This villain here,
Being captain of a pinnace, threatens more
Than Bargulus, the strong Illyrian pirate.
Drones suck not eagles' blood but rob beehives.
It is impossible that I should die   110
By such a lowly vassal as thyself.
Thy words move rage and not remorse in me.
I go of message from the Queen to France.
I charge thee waft me safely 'cross the Channel.
Lieut. Walter!   115
Whit. Come, Suffolk, I must waft thee to thy death.
Suf. Gelidus timor occupat artus. It is thee I fear.
Whit. Thou shalt have cause to fear before I leave thee.
What, are ye daunted now? Now will ye stoop?
1. Gent. My gracious lord, entreat him, speak him fair.   120
Suf. Suffolk's imperial tongue is stern and rough,
Us'd to command, untaught to plead for favour.
Far be it we should honour such as these
With humble suit. No, rather let my head
Stoop to the block than these knees bow to any

Save to the God of heaven and to my king;
And sooner dance upon a bloody pole
Than stand uncover'd to the vulgar groom.
True nobility is exempt from fear.
More can I bear than you dare execute.   130
   Lieut. Hale him away and let him talk no
more.
   Suf. Come, soldiers, show what cruelty ye
can,
That this my death may never be forgot!
Great men oft die by vile bezonians.
A Roman sworder and banditto slave   135
Murder'd sweet Tully; Brutus' bastard hand
Stabb'd Julius Cæsar; savage islanders
Pompey the Great; and Suffolk dies by pirates.
       Exit Walter [Whitmore] with Suffolk.
   Lieut. And as for these whose ransom we
have set,
It is our pleasure one of them depart.   140
Therefore come you with us, and let him go.
       Exeunt Lieutenant and the rest. Manet the
                      First Gentleman.

   Enter *Walter [Whitmore]* with the body
            [of *Suffolk*].

   Whit. There let his head and liveless body
lie
Until the Queen his mistress bury it.   *Exit.*
   1. Gent. O barbarous and bloody spectacle!
His body will I bear unto the King.   145
If he revenge it not, yet will his friends;
So will the Queen, that living held him dear.
              [*Exit with the body.*]

[Scene II. *Blackheath.*]

Enter [*George*] *Bevis* and *John Holland.*

   Bevis. Come and get thee a sword, though
made of a lath. They have been up these two
days.
   Hol. They have the more need to sleep now
then.   4
   Bevis. I tell thee Jack Cade the clothier
means to dress the commonwealth and turn it
and set a new nap upon it.
   Hol. So he had need, for 'tis threadbare.
Well, I say it was never merry world in England
since gentlemen came up.   10
   Bevis. O miserable age! Virtue is not regarded in handicraftsmen.
   Hol. The nobility think scorn to go in leather
aprons.   14

   Bevis. Nay, more, the King's Council are no
good workmen.
   Hol. True; and yet it is said, 'Labour in thy
vocation'; which is as much to say as 'Let the
magistrates be labouring men'; and therefore
should we be magistrates.   20
   Bevis. Thou hast hit it; for there's no better
sign of a brave mind than a hard hand.
   Hol. I see them! I see them! There's Best's
son, the tanner of Wingham —
   Bevis. He shall have the skins of our enemies
to make dog's leather of.   26
   Hol. And Dick the butcher —
   Bevis. Then is sin struck down like an ox and
iniquity's throat cut like a calf.
   Hol. And Smith the weaver.   30
   Bevis. Argo, their thread of life is spun.
   Hol. Come, come, let's fall in with them.

   Drum. Enter *Cade, Dick Butcher, Smith* the
   Weaver, and a *Sawyer,* with *infinite numbers.*

   Cade. We, John Cade, so term'd of our sup-
posed father —   34
   Butch. [*aside*] Or rather, of stealing a cade
of herrings.
   Cade. For our enemies shall fall before us —
inspired with the spirit of putting down kings
and princes — Command silence.
   Butch. Silence!   40
   Cade. My father was a Mortimer —
   Butch. [*aside*] He was an honest man and a
good bricklayer.
   Cade. My mother a Plantagenet —
   Butch. [*aside*] I knew her well. She was a
midwife.
   Cade. My wife descended of the Lacies.
   Butch. [*aside*] She was indeed a pedlar's
daughter and sold many laces.   49
   Weav. [*aside*] But now of late, not able to
travel with her furr'd pack, she washes bucks
here at home.
   Cade. Therefore am I of an honourable
house.
   Butch. [*aside*] Ay, by my faith, the field is
honourable and there was he born, under a
hedge; for his father had never a house but
the cage.   56
   Cade. Valiant I am.
   Weav. [*aside*] 'A must needs, for beggary is
valiant.
   Cade. I am able to endure much.   60
   Butch. [*aside*] No question of that; for I
have seen him whipp'd three market days
together.
   Cade. I fear neither sword nor fire.

Weav. [*aside*] He need not fear the sword, for his coat is of proof. 65

Butch. [*aside*] But methinks he should stand in fear of fire, being burnt i' th' hand for stealing of sheep.

Cade. Be brave then, for your captain is brave and vows reformation. There shall be in England seven halfpenny loaves sold for a penny; the three-hoop'd pot shall have ten hoops, and I will make it felony to drink small beer. All the realm shall be in common, and in Cheapside shall my palfrey go to grass; and when I am king, as king I will be — 76

All. God save your Majesty!

Cade. I thank you, good people. There shall be no money; all shall eat and drink on my score; and I will apparel them all in one livery, that they may agree like brothers and worship me their lord. 82

Butch. The first thing we do, let's kill all the lawyers.

Cade. Nay, that I mean to do. Is not this a lamentable thing, that of the skin of an innocent lamb should be made parchment? that parchment, being scribbled o'er, should undo a man? Some say the bee stings; but I say 'tis the bee's wax; for I did but seal once to a thing, and I was never mine own man since. How now? Who's there? 91

Enter a *Clerk* [as prisoner].

Weav. The clerk of Chatham. He can write and read and cast accompt.

Cade. O monstrous! 94

Weav. We took him setting of boys' copies.

Cade. Here's a villain!

Weav. Has a book in his pocket with red letters in't.

Cade. Nay, then he is a conjurer. 99

Butch. Nay, he can make obligations and write court-hand.

Cade. I am sorry for't. The man is a proper man, of mine honour. Unless I find him guilty, he shall not die. Come hither, sirrah, I must examine thee. What is thy name? 105

Clerk. Emanuel.

Butch. They use to write it on the top of letters. 'Twill go hard with you.

Cade. Let me alone. Dost thou use to write thy name? or hast thou a mark to thyself, like an honest plain-dealing man? 111

Clerk. Sir, I thank God, I have been so well brought up that I can write my name.

All. He hath confess'd! Away with him! He's a villain and a traitor! 115

Cade. Away with him, I say! Hang him with his pen and inkhorn about his neck.

Exit one with the Clerk.

Enter *Michael.*

Mich. Where's our general?

Cade. Here I am, thou particular fellow. 119

Mich. Fly, fly, fly! Sir Humphrey Stafford and his brother are hard by, with the King's forces.

Cade. Stand, villain, stand, or I'll fell thee down! He shall be encount'red with a man as good as himself. He is but a knight, is 'a? 125

Mich. No.

Cade. To equal him, I will make myself a knight presently. [*Kneels.*] Rise up Sir John Mortimer. [*Rises.*] Now have at him!

Enter *Sir Humphrey Stafford* and his brother [*William*], with *Drum* and *Soldiers.*

Staf. Rebellious hinds, the filth and scum of Kent, 130
Mark'd for the gallows! Lay your weapons down;
Home to your cottages; forsake this groom.
The King is merciful, if you revolt.

Bro. But angry, wrathful, and inclin'd to blood,
If you go forward. Therefore yield or die. 135

Cade. As for these silken-coated slaves, I pass not.
It is to you, good people, that I speak,
O'er whom (in time to come) I hope to reign;
For I am rightful heir unto the crown.

Staf. Villain, thy father was a plasterer, 140
And thou thyself a shearman, art thou not?

Cade. And Adam was a gardener.

Bro. And what of that?

Cade. Marry, this: Edmund Mortimer, Earl of March,
Married the Duke of Clarence' daughter, did he not? 145

Staf. Ay, sir.

Cade. By her he had two children at one birth.

Bro. That's false.

Cade. Ay, there's the question. But I say 'tis true.
The elder of them, being put to nurse, 150
Was by a beggar woman stol'n away
And, ignorant of his birth and parentage,
Became a bricklayer when he came to age.
His son am I. Deny it if you can.

Butch. Nay, 'tis too true. Therefore he shall be king. 155

263

Weav. Sir, he made a chimney in my father's house, and the bricks are alive at this day to testify it. Therefore deny it not.

Staf. And will you credit this base drudge's words
That speaks he knows not what?   160
All. Ay, marry, will we. Therefore get ye gone.
Bro. Jack Cade, the Duke of York hath taught you this.
Cade. [*aside*] He lies, for I invented it myself. —
Go to, sirrah, tell the King from me that, for his father's sake, Henry the Fifth (in whose time boys went to span-counter for French crowns), I am content he shall reign, but I'll be Protector over him.   168
Butch. And furthermore we'll have the Lord Say's head for selling the dukedom of Maine.
Cade. And good reason; for thereby is England main'd and fain to go with a staff, but that my puissance holds it up. Fellow kings, I tell you that that Lord Say hath gelded the commonwealth and made it an eunuch; and more than that, he can speak French, and therefore he is a traitor.   177
Staf. O gross and miserable ignorance!
Cade. Nay, answer, if you can. The Frenchmen are our enemies. Go to then, I ask but this: Can he that speaks with the tongue of an enemy be a good counsellor, or no?   182
All. No, no! and therefore we'll have his head.
Bro. Well, seeing gentle words will not prevail,
Assail them with the army of the King.   185
Staf. Herald, away; and throughout every town
Proclaim them traitors that are up with Cade;
That those which fly before the battle ends
May, even in their wives' and children's sight,
Be hang'd up for example at their doors;   190
And you that be the King's friends, follow me.
Exeunt [*the two Staffords and Soldiers*].
Cade. And you that love the commons, follow me.
Now show yourselves men! 'Tis for liberty.
We will not leave one lord, one gentleman.
Spare none but such as go in clouted shoon,   196
For they are thrifty honest men and such
As would (but that they dare not) take our parts.
Butch. They are all in order and march toward us.
Cade. But then are we in order when we are most out of order. Come, march forward!   200
Exeunt.

[Scene III. *Another part of Blackheath.*]

Alarums to the fight, wherein both the Staffords are slain. Enter Cade and the rest.

Cade. Where's Dick, the butcher of Ashford?
Butch. Here, sir.
Cade. They fell before thee like sheep and oxen, and thou behavedst thyself as if thou hadst been in thine own slaughterhouse. Therefore thus will I reward thee: the Lent shall be as long again as it is, and thou shalt have a license to kill for a hundred lacking one a week.
Butch. I desire no more.   10
Cade. And, to speak truth, thou deserv'st no less. This monument of the victory will I bear [*puts on Sir Humphrey's brigandine*]; and the bodies shall be dragg'd at my horse heels till I do come to London, where we will have the mayor's sword borne before us.   16
Butch. If we mean to thrive and do good, break open the jails and let out the prisoners.
Cade. Fear not that, I warrant thee. Come, let's march towards London.   *Exeunt.*

[Scene IV. *London. The Palace.*]

Enter the King, with a supplication, and the Queen with Suffolk's head; the Duke of Buckingham and the Lord Say.

Queen. Oft have I heard that grief softens the mind
And makes it fearful and degenerate.
Think therefore on revenge and cease to weep.
But who can cease to weep, and look on this?
Here may his head lie on my throbbing breast;
But where's the body that I should embrace?
Buck. What answer makes your Grace to the rebels' supplication?
King. I'll send some holy bishop to entreat;
For God forbid so many simple souls   10
Should perish by the sword! And I myself,
Rather than bloody war shall cut them short,
Will parley with Jack Cade their general.
But stay, I'll read it over once again.
Queen. Ah, barbarous villains! Hath this lovely face   15
Rul'd like a wandering planet over me,
And could it not enforce them to relent
That were unworthy to behold the same?
King. Lord Say, Jack Cade hath sworn to have thy head.

Say. Ay, but I hope your Highness shall have
his.   20
King. How now, madam?
Still lamenting and mourning for Suffolk's
death?
I fear me, love, if that I had been dead,
Thou wouldest not have mourn'd so much
for me.
Queen. No, my love, I should not mourn, but
die for thee.   25

Enter a *Messenger*.

King. How now? What news? Why com'st
thou in such haste?
Mess. The rebels are in Southwark. Fly,
my lord!
Jack Cade proclaims himself Lord Mortimer,
Descended from the Duke of Clarence' house,
And calls your Grace usurper openly   30
And vows to crown himself in Westminster.
His army is a ragged multitude
Of hinds and peasants, rude and merciless.
Sir Humphrey Stafford and his brother's death
Hath given them heart and courage to proceed.
All scholars, lawyers, courtiers, gentlemen, 36
They call false caterpillars and intend their
death.
King. O graceless men! they know not what
they do.
Buck. My gracious lord, retire to Killing-
worth
Until a power be rais'd to put them down.   40
Queen. Ah, were the Duke of Suffolk now
alive,
These Kentish rebels would be soon appeas'd.
King. Lord Say, the traitors hate thee;
Therefore away with us to Killingworth.
Say. So might your Grace's person be in
danger.   45
The sight of me is odious in their eyes;
And therefore in this city will I stay
And live alone as secret as I may.

Enter another *Messenger*.

Mess. Jack Cade hath gotten London
Bridge;
The citizens fly and forsake their houses;   50
The rascal people, thirsting after prey,
Join with the traitor, and they jointly swear
To spoil the city and your royal court.
Buck. Then linger not, my lord. Away, take
horse!
King. Come, Margaret. God, our hope, will
succour us.   55

Queen. My hope is gone now Suffolk is
deceas'd.
King. [*to Lord Say*] Farewell, my lord. Trust
not the Kentish rebels.
Buck. Trust nobody, for fear you be be-
tray'd.
Say. The trust I have is in mine innocence,
And therefore am I bold and resolute.   60
Exeunt.

[Scene V. *London. The Tower.*]

Enter *Lord Scales* upon the Tower, walking.
Then enter *two or three Citizens* below.

Scales. How now? Is Jack Cade slain?
1. Cit. No, my lord, nor likely to be slain;
for they have won the Bridge, killing all those
that withstand them. The Lord Mayor craves
aid of your honour from the Tower to defend
the city from the rebels.   6
Scales. Such aid as I can spare you shall
command,
But I am troubled here with them myself;
The rebels have assay'd to win the Tower.
But get you to Smithfield and gather head,   10
And thither I will send you Matthew Goffe.
Fight for your king, your country, and your
lives;
And so farewell, for I must hence again.
Exeunt.

[Scene VI. *London. Cannon Street.*]

Enter *Jack Cade* and the rest, and strikes his
staff on London Stone.

Cade. Now is Mortimer lord of this city.
And here, sitting upon London Stone, I charge
and command that, of the city's cost, the pissing
conduit run nothing but claret wine this first
year of our reign. And now henceforward it
shall be treason for any that calls me other
than Lord Mortimer.   7

Enter a *Soldier*, running.

Sold. Jack Cade! Jack Cade!
Cade. Knock him down there.
They kill him.
Weav. If this fellow be wise, he'll never call
ye Jack Cade more. I think he hath a very fair
warning.

Butch. My lord, there's an army gathered together in Smithfield.   14
Cade. Come then, let's go fight with them. But first go and set London Bridge on fire, and, if you can, burn down the Tower too. Come, let's away.   *Exeunt omnes.*

[Scene VII. *London. Smithfield.*]

Alarums. Matthew Goffe is slain, and all the rest [of the loyal forces]. Then enter *Jack Cade* with his *Company.*

Cade. So, sirs. Now go some and pull down the Savoy; others to th' Inns of Court. Down with them all!
Butch. I have a suit unto your lordship.
Cade. Be it a lordship, thou shalt have it for that word.   6
Butch. Only that the laws of England may come out of your mouth.
Hol. [*aside*] Mass, 'twill be sore law then; for he was thrust in the mouth with a spear, and 'tis not whole yet.   11
Weav. [*aside*] Nay, John, it will be stinking law; for his breath stinks with eating toasted cheese.
Cade. I have thought upon it; it shall be so. Away, burn all the records of the realm! My mouth shall be the parliament of England.
Hol. [*aside*] Then we are like to have biting statutes, unless his teeth be pull'd out.
Cade. And henceforward all things shall be in common.   21

Enter a *Messenger.*

Mess. My lord, a prize, a prize! Here's the Lord Say, which sold the towns in France; he that made us pay one-and-twenty fifteens, and one shilling to the pound, the last subsidy.   25

Enter *George* [*Bevis*], with the *Lord Say.*

Cade. Well, he shall be beheaded for it ten times. Ah, thou say, thou serge, nay, thou buckram lord! now art thou within point-blank of our jurisdiction regal. What canst thou an-swer to my Majesty for giving up of Normandy unto Mounsieur Basimecu, the Dauphin of France? Be it known unto thee by these pres-ence, even the presence of Lord Mortimer, that I am the besom that must sweep the court clean of such filth as thou art. Thou hast most traitorously corrupted the youth of the realm in erecting a grammar school; and whereas, be-fore, our forefathers had no other books but the score and the tally, thou hast caused printing to be us'd, and, contrary to the King, his crown and dignity, thou hast built a paper mill. It will be proved to thy face that thou hast men about thee that usually talk of a noun and a verb and such abominable words as no Chris-tian ear can endure to hear. Thou hast ap-pointed justices of peace, to call poor men be-fore them about matters they were not able to answer. Moreover, thou hast put them in prison, and because they could not read, thou hast hang'd them, when, indeed, only for that cause they have been most worthy to live. Thou dost ride in a footcloth, dost thou not?
Say. What of that?
Cade. Marry, thou ought'st not to let thy horse wear a cloak when honester men than thou go in their hose and doublets.   56
Butch. And work in their shirt too; as my-self, for example, that am a butcher.
Say. You men of Kent —
Butch. What say you of Kent?   60
Say. Nothing but this — 'tis 'bona terra, mala gens.'
Cade. Away with him, away with him! He speaks Latin.
Say. Hear me but speak, and bear me where you will.
Kent, in the Commentaries Cæsar writ,   65
Is term'd the civil'st place of all this isle.
Sweet is the country, because full of riches;
The people liberal, valiant, active, wealthy,
Which makes me hope you are not void of pity.
I sold not Maine, I lost not Normandy;   70
Yet to recover them would lose my life.
Justice with favour have I always done;
Prayers and tears have mov'd me, gifts could never.
When have I aught exacted at your hands   74
But to maintain the King, the realm, and you?
Large gifts have I bestow'd on learned clerks,
Because my book preferr'd me to the King;
And, seeing ignorance is the curse of God,
Knowledge the wing wherewith we fly to heaven,
Unless you be possess'd with devilish spirits,
You cannot but forbear to murther me.   81
This tongue hath parley'd unto foreign kings
For your behoof.
Cade. Tut! when struck'st thou one blow in the field?   85
Say. Great men have reaching hands. Oft have I struck
Those that I never saw, and struck them dead.
Bevis. O monstrous coward! What, to come behind folks?

Say. These cheeks are pale for watching for
    your good.   90
Cade. Give him a box o' th' ear, and that will
make 'em red again.
Say. Long sitting to determine poor men's
    causes
Hath made me full of sickness and diseases.
Cade. Ye shall have a hempen caudle then,
and the help of hatchet.   96
Butch. Why dost thou quiver, man?
Say. It is the palsy, and not fear, provokes
me.
Cade. Nay, he nods at us, as who should say,
'I'll be even with you.' I'll see if his head will
stand steadier on a pole or no. Take him away
and behead him.   102
Say. Tell me: wherein have I offended
    most?
Have I affected wealth or honour? Speak.
Are my chests fill'd up with extorted gold?   105
Is my apparel sumptuous to behold?
Whom have I injur'd, that ye seek my
    death?
These hands are free from guiltless blood-
    shedding,
This breast from harbouring foul deceitful
    thoughts.
O, let me live!   110
Cade. [*aside*] I feel remorse in myself with
his words; but I'll bridle it. He shall die, an
it be but for pleading so well for his life. —
Away with him! he has a familiar under his
tongue; he speaks not a God's name. Go,
take him away, I say, and strike off his head
presently; and then break into his son-in-law's
house, Sir James Cromer, and strike off his
head, and bring them both upon two poles
hither.
All. It shall be done.   120
Say. Ah, countrymen! If when you make
your pray'rs,
God should be so obdurate as yourselves,
How would it fare with your departed souls?
And therefore yet relent, and save my life.
Cade. Away with him, and do as I command
ye!   *Exeunt some with Lord Say.*
The proudest peer in the realm shall not wear a
head on his shoulders unless he pay me tribute.
There shall not a maid be married but she shall
pay to me her maidenhead ere they have it.
Men shall hold of me *in capite*; and we charge
and command that their wives be as free as
heart can wish or tongue can tell.   133
Butch. My lord, when shall we go to Cheapside and take up commodities upon our bills?

Cade. Marry, presently.   136
All. O brave!

Enter *one, with the heads.*

Cade. But is not this braver? Let them kiss
one another, for they lov'd well when they were
alive. Now part them again, lest they consult
about the giving up of some more towns in
France. Soldiers, defer the spoil of the city
until night; for with these borne before us instead of maces will we ride through the streets,
and at every corner have them kiss. Away! 145
                                            Exeunt.

[Scene VIII. *Southwark.*]

Alarum and Retreat. Enter again *Cade*
and all his *rabblement.*

Cade. Up Fish Street! down Saint Magnus
Corner! Kill and knock down! Throw them
into Thames! (*Sound a parley.*) What noise is
this I hear? Dare any be so bold to sound retreat or parley when I command them kill?   5

Enter *Buckingham* and *Old Clifford.*

Buck. Ay, here they be that dare and will
    disturb thee.
Know, Cade, we come ambassadors from the
    King
Unto the commons, whom thou hast misled;
And here pronounce free pardon to them all
That will forsake thee and go home in peace.
Clif. What say ye, countrymen? Will ye
    relent   11
And yield to mercy whilst 'tis offered you,
Or let a rebel lead you to your deaths?
Who loves the King, and will embrace his
    pardon,
Fling up his cap and say 'God save his Maj-
    esty!'   15
Who hateth him and honours not his father,
Henry the Fifth, that made all France to
    quake,
Shake he his weapon at us and pass by.
All. God save the King! God save the King.
Cade. What, Buckingham and Clifford, are
ye so brave? And you, base peasants, do ye be-
lieve them? Will you needs be hang'd with
your pardons about your necks? Hath my
sword therefore broke through London gates,
that you should leave me at the White Hart in
Southwark? I thought ye would never have
given out these arms till you had recovered your

ancient freedom. But you are all recreants and
dastards and delight to live in slavery to the
nobility. Let them break your backs with
burthens, take your houses over your heads,
ravish your wives and daughters before your
faces. For me, I will make shift for one; and so
God's curse light upon you all!   34

All. We'll follow Cade! We'll follow Cade!

Clif. Is Cade the son of Henry the Fifth
That thus you do exclaim you'll go with
   him?
Will he conduct you through the heart of
   France
And make the meanest of you earls and
   dukes?
Alas, he hath no home, no place to fly to;   40
Nor knows he how to live but by the spoil,
Unless by robbing of your friends and us.
Were't not a shame that whilst you live at
   jar
The fearful French, whom you late vanquished,
Should make a start o'er seas and vanquish you?
Methinks already in this civil broil   46
I see them lording it in London streets,
Crying 'Villiago!' unto all they meet.
Better ten thousand base-born Cades miscarry
Than you should stoop unto a Frenchman's
   mercy.   50
To France, to France, and get what you have
   lost!
Spare England, for it is your native coast.
Henry hath money, you are strong and manly;
God on our side, doubt not of victory.

All. A Clifford! a Clifford! We'll follow the
King and Clifford.   56

Cade. Was ever feather so lightly blown to
and fro as this multitude? The name of Henry
the Fifth hales them to an hundred mischiefs
and makes them leave me desolate. I see them
lay their heads together to surprise me. My
sword make way for me, for here is no staying.
In despite of the devils and hell, have through
the very middest of you! and heavens and honour be witness that no want of resolution in me,
but only my followers' base and ignominious
treasons, makes me betake me to my heels.   67
                                        Exit.

Buck. What, is he fled? Go some, and follow
   him;
And he that brings his head unto the King
Shall have a thousand crowns for his reward.
                              Exeunt some of them.
Follow me, soldiers. We'll devise a mean   71
To reconcile you all unto the King.
                                   Exeunt omnes.

[Scene IX. *Killingworth Castle.*]

Sound trumpets. Enter *King, Queen,* and
         Somerset, on the terrace.

King. Was ever king that joy'd an earthly
   throne
And could command no more content than I?
No sooner was I crept out of my cradle
But I was made a king, at nine months old.
Was never subject long'd to be a king   5
As I do long and wish to be a subject.

     Enter *Buckingham* and [*Old*] *Clifford.*

Buck. Health and glad tidings to your Majesty!

King. Why, Buckingham, is the traitor Cade
   surpris'd?
Or is he but retir'd to make him strong?

Enter [*below*] *Multitudes,* with halters about
            their necks.

Clif. He is fled, my lord, and all his powers
   do yield,   10
And humbly thus, with halters on their necks,
Expect your Highness' doom of life or death.

King. Then, heaven, set ope thy everlasting
   gates
To entertain my vows of thanks and praise!
Soldiers, this day have you redeem'd your lives
And show'd how well you love your prince and
   country.   16
Continue still in this so good a mind,
And Henry, though he be infortunate,
Assure yourselves, will never be unkind.
And so, with thanks, and pardon to you all, 20
I do dismiss you to your several countries.

All. God save the King! God save the King!

          Enter a *Messenger.*

Mess. Please it your Grace to be advertised
The Duke of York is newly come from Ireland
And with a puissant and a mighty power   25
Of gallowglasses and stout kerns
Is marching hitherward in proud array,
And still proclaimeth, as he comes along,
His arms are only to remove from thee
The Duke of Somerset, whom he terms a
   traitor.   30

King. Thus stands my state, 'twixt Cade
   and York distress'd;
Like to a ship that, having scap'd a tempest,
Is straightway calm'd, and boarded with a
   pirate.
But now is Cade driven back, his men dispers'd,

And now is York in arms to second him.   35
I pray thee, Buckingham, go and meet him,
And ask him what's the reason of these arms.
Tell him I'll send Duke Edmund to the Tower;
And, Somerset, we will commit thee thither
Until his army be dismiss'd from him.   40

   Som. My lord,
I'll yield myself to prison willingly,
Or unto death, to do my country good.

   King. In any case, be not too rough in terms,
For he is fierce and cannot brook hard language.

   Buck. I will, my lord, and doubt not so to
     deal   46
As all things shall redound unto your good.

   King. Come, wife, let's in, and learn to
     govern better;
For yet may England curse my wretched reign.
     Flourish. Exeunt.

[Scene X. *Kent.* Iden's *garden.*]

Enter *Cade.*

   Cade. Fie on ambitions! Fie on myself, that
have a sword and yet am ready to famish!
These five days have I hid me in these woods
and durst not peep out, for all the country is
laid for me; but now am I so hungry that, if I
might have a lease of my life for a thousand
years, I could stay no longer. Wherefore, on a
brick wall have I climb'd into this garden, to
see if I can eat grass, or pick a sallet another
while, which is not amiss to cool a man's stomach this hot weather. And I think this word
'sallet' was born to do me good; for many a
time, but for a sallet, my brainpan had been
cleft with a brown bill; and many a time, when
I have been dry, and bravely marching, it hath
serv'd me instead of a quart pot to drink in;
and now the word 'sallet' must serve me to
feed on.   17

Enter *Iden.*

   Iden. Lord, who would live turmoiled in the
     court
And may enjoy such quiet walks as these?
This small inheritance my father left me   20
Contenteth me, and worth a monarchy.
I seek not to wax great by others' waning,
Or gather wealth, I care not with what envy.
Sufficeth that I have maintains my state   24
And sends the poor well pleased from my gate.

   Cade. Here's the lord of the soil come to seize
me for a stray, for entering his fee simple without leave. Ah, villain, thou wilt betray me and

get a thousand crowns of the King by carrying
my head to him; but I'll make thee eat iron
like an ostridge and swallow my sword like a
great pin ere thou and I part.

   Iden. Why, rude companion, whatsoe'er
     thou be,
I know thee not. Why then should I betray
     thee?
Is't not enough to break into my garden   35
And like a thief to come to rob my grounds,
Climbing my walls in spite of me the owner,
But thou wilt brave me with these saucy terms?

   Cade. Brave thee? Ay, by the best blood
that ever was broach'd, and beard thee too!
Look on me well. I have eat no meat these five
days; yet, come thou and thy five men, and if
I do not leave you all as dead as a doornail, I
pray God I may never eat grass more.

   Iden. Nay, it shall ne'er be said, while
     England stands,   45
That Alexander Iden, an esquire of Kent,
Took odds to combat a poor famish'd man.
Oppose thy steadfast-gazing eyes to mine;
See if thou canst outface me with thy looks.
Set limb to limb, and thou art far the lesser;
Thy hand is but a finger to my fist,   51
Thy leg a stick compared with this truncheon;
My foot shall fight with all the strength thou
     hast;
And if mine arm be heaved in the air,
Thy grave is digg'd already in the earth.   55
As for words, whose greatness answers words,
Let this my sword report what speech forbears.

   Cade. By my valour, the most complete
champion that ever I heard! Steel, if thou turn
the edge, or cut not out the burly-bon'd clown
in chines of beef ere thou sleep in thy sheath, I
beseech God on my knees thou mayst be turn'd
to hobnails. (*Here they fight. Cade falls.*) O, I
am slain! Famine and no other hath slain me.
Let ten thousand devils come against me, and
give me but the ten meals I have lost, and I'd
defy them all. Wither, garden, and be henceforth a burying place to all that do dwell in this
house, because the unconquered soul of Cade
is fled.   70

   Iden. Is't Cade that I have slain, that mon-
     strous traitor?
Sword, I will hallow thee for this thy deed
And hang thee o'er my tomb when I am dead.
Ne'er shall this blood be wiped from thy point,
But thou shalt wear it as a herald's coat,   75
To emblaze the honour that thy master got.

   Cade. Iden, farewell, and be proud of thy
victory. Tell Kent from me, she hath lost her

best man, and exhort all the world to be cowards; for I, that never feared any, am vanquished by famine, not by valour.   *Dies.*

   Iden. How much thou wrong'st me, heaven be my judge.   82
Die, damned wretch, the curse of her that bare thee!
And as I thrust thy body in with my sword,

So wish I, I might thrust thy soul to hell!   85
Hence will I drag thee headlong by the heels
Unto a dunghill, which shall be thy grave,
And there cut off thy most ungracious head,
Which I will bear in triumph to the King,
Leaving thy trunk for crows to feed upon.   90
                    Exit.

[ACT V. Scene I. *Fields between Dartford and Blackheath.*]

Enter *York* and his army of *Irish*, with *Drum* and *Colours*.

   York. From Ireland thus comes York to claim his right
And pluck the crown from feeble Henry's head.
Ring bells aloud, burn bonfires clear and bright,
To entertain great England's lawful king.
Ah, Sancta Maiestas! who would not buy thee dear?   5
Let them obey that know not how to rule;
This hand was made to handle naught but gold.
I cannot give due action to my words
Except a sword or sceptre balance it.
A sceptre shall it have, have I a soul,   10
On which I'll to e the fleur-de-luce of France.

      Enter *Buckingham.*

[*Aside*] Whom have we here? Buckingham, to disturb me?
The King hath sent him sure. I must dissemble.
   Buck. York, if thou meanest well, I greet thee well.
   York. Humphrey of Buckingham, I accept thy greeting.   15
Art thou a messenger or come of pleasure?
   Buck. A messenger from Henry, our dread liege,
To know the reason of these arms in peace;
Or why thou, being a subject as I am,
Against thy oath and true allegiance sworn   20
Should raise so great a power without his leave,
Or dare to bring thy force so near the court.
   York. [*aside*] Scarce can I speak, my choler is so great.
O, I could hew up rocks and fight with flint,
I am so angry at these abject terms;   25
And now, like Ajax Telamonius,
On sheep or oxen could I spend my fury!
I am far better born than is the King,
More like a king, more kingly in my thoughts.
But I must make fair weather yet a while,   30
Till Henry be more weak, and I more strong. —
Buckingham, I prithee pardon me

That I have given no answer all this while.
My mind was troubled with deep melancholy.
The cause why I have brought this army hither
Is to remove proud Somerset from the King,   36
Seditious to his Grace and to the state.
   Buck. That is too much presumption on thy part.
But if thy arms be to no other end,
The King hath yielded unto thy demand.   40
The Duke of Somerset is in the Tower.
   York. Upon thine honour, is he prisoner?
   Buck. Upon mine honour, he is prisoner.
   York. Then, Buckingham, I do dismiss my pow'rs.   44
Soldiers, I thank you all. Disperse yourselves.
Meet me to-morrow in Saint George's Field,
You shall have pay and everything you wish.
And let my sovereign, virtuous Henry,
Command my eldest son, nay, all my sons,
As pledges of my fealty and love.   50
I'll send them all as willing as I live.
Lands, goods, horse, armour, anything I have
Is his to use, so Somerset may die.
              Exeunt Soldiers.
   Buck. York, I commend this kind submission.
We twain will go into his Highness' tent.   55

    Enter *King* and *Attendants.*

   King. Buckingham, doth York intend no harm to us
That thus he marcheth with thee arm in arm?
   York. In all submission and humility
York doth present himself unto your Highness.
   King. Then what intends these forces thou dost bring?   60
   York. To heave the traitor Somerset from hence
And fight against that monstrous rebel Cade,
Who since I heard to be discomfited.

    Enter *Iden*, with *Cade's* head.

   Iden. If one so rude and of so mean condition
May pass into the presence of a king,   65

Lo, I present your Grace a traitor's head,
The head of Cade, whom I in combat slew.
   King. The head of Cade? Great God, how
     just art thou!
O, let me view his visage, being dead,
That living wrought me such exceeding trouble.
Tell me, my friend, art thou the man that slew
   him?   71
   Iden. I was, an't like your Majesty.
   King. How art thou call'd, and what is thy
     degree?
   Iden. Alexander Iden, that's my name;
A poor esquire of Kent that loves his king. 75
   Buck. So please it you, my lord, 'twere not
     amiss
He were created knight for his good service.
   King. Iden, kneel down. [*He kneels.*] Rise
     up a knight.   [*He rises.*]
We give thee for reward a thousand marks,
And will that thou henceforth attend on us. 80
   Iden. May Iden live to merit such a bounty,
And never live but true unto his liege!

Enter *Queen* and *Somerset.*

   King. See, Buckingham! Somerset comes
     with th' Queen.
Go bid her hide him quickly from the Duke.
   Queen. For thousand Yorks he shall not hide
     his head,   85
But boldly stand and front him to his face.
   York. How now? Is Somerset at liberty?
Then, York, unloose thy long-imprisoned
   thoughts
And let thy tongue be equal with thy heart.
Shall I endure the sight of Somerset? 90
False king, why hast thou broken faith with
   me,
Knowing how hardly I can brook abuse?
King did I call thee? No! thou art not King,
Not fit to govern and rule multitudes,
Which dar'st not, no, nor canst not rule a
   traitor.   95
That head of thine doth not become a crown;
Thy hand is made to grasp a palmer's staff
And not to grace an awful princely sceptre.
That gold must round engirt these brows of
   mine,
Whose smile and frown, like to Achilles' spear,
Is able with the change to kill and cure. 101
Here is a hand to hold a sceptre up
And with the same to act controlling laws.
Give place. By heaven, thou shalt rule no more
O'er him whom heaven created for thy ruler.
   Som. O monstrous traitor! I arrest thee,
   York,   106

Of capital treason 'gainst the King and crown.
Obey, audacious traitor; kneel for grace.
   York. Wouldst have me kneel? First let me
     ask of these
If they can brook I bow a knee to man. 110
Sirrah, call in my sons to be my bail.
                 [*Exit an Attendant.*]
I know, ere they will have me go to ward,
They'll pawn their swords for my enfranchise-
   ment.
   Queen. Call hither Clifford. Bid him come
     amain
To say if that the bastard boys of York 115
Shall be the surety for their traitor father.
                [*Exit Buckingham.*]
   York. O blood-bespotted Neapolitan,
Outcast of Naples, England's bloody scourge!
The sons of York, thy betters in their birth,
Shall be their father's bail; and bane to those
That for my surety will refuse the boys! 121

Enter *Edward* and *Richard* [*Plantagenet*].

See where they come. I'll warrant they'll make
   it good.

Enter *Clifford* and his *Son.*

   Queen. And here comes Clifford to deny
     their bail.
   Clif. Health and all happiness to my lord
     the King!   *Kneels.*
   York. I thank thee, Clifford. Say, what news
     with thee?   125
Nay, do not fright us with an angry look.
We are thy sovereign, Clifford, kneel again.
For thy mistaking so, we pardon thee.
   Clif. This is my king, York, I do not mistake;
But thou mistak'st me much to think I do. 130
To Bedlam with him! Is the man grown mad?
   King. Ay, Clifford. A bedlam and ambitious
     humour
Makes him oppose himself against his king.
   Clif. He is a traitor; let him to the Tower,
And chop away that factious pate of his. 135
   Queen. He is arrested, but will not obey.
His sons, he says, shall give their words for him.
   York. Will you not, sons?
   Edw. Ay, noble father, if our words will
     serve.
   Rich. And if words will not, then our weap-
     ons shall.   140
   Clif. Why, what a brood of traitors have we
     here!
   York. Look in a glass and call thy image so.
I am thy king, and thou a false-heart traitor.
Call hither to the stake my two brave bears,

That with the very shaking of their chains 145
They may astonish these fell-lurking curs.
Bid Salisbury and Warwick come to me.

[Exit an Attendant.]

Enter the *Earls of Warwick* and *Salisbury.*

Clif. Are these thy bears? We'll bait thy
    bears to death
And manacle the berard in their chains 149
If thou dar'st bring them to the baiting place.
Rich. Oft have I seen a hot o'erweening cur
Run back and bite because he was withheld,
Who, being suffer'd, with the bear's fell paw
Hath clapp'd his tail between his legs and cried;
And such a piece of service will you do 155
If you oppose yourselves to match Lord
    Warwick.
Clif. Hence, heap of wrath, foul indigested
    lump,
As crooked in thy manners as thy shape!
York. Nay, we shall heat you thoroughly
    anon.
Clif. Take heed lest by your heat you burn
    yourselves. 160
King. Why Warwick, hath thy knee forgot
    to bow?
Old Salisbury, shame to thy silver hair,
Thou mad misleader of thy brainsick son!
What, wilt thou on thy deathbed play the
    ruffian
And seek for sorrow with thy spectacles? 165
O, where is faith? O, where is loyalty?
If it be banish'd from the frosty head,
Where shall it find a harbour in the earth?
Wilt thou go dig a grave to find out war,
And stain thine honourable age with blood?
Why art thou old, and want'st experience? 171
Or wherefore dost abuse it if thou hast it?
For shame! In duty bend thy knee to me,
That bows unto the grave with mickle age.
Sal. My lord, I have considered with myself
The title of this most renowned duke 176
And, in my conscience, do repute his Grace
The rightful heir to England's royal seat.
King. Hast thou not sworn allegiance unto
    me?
Sal. I have. 180
King. Canst thou dispense with heaven for
    such an oath?
Sal. It is great sin to swear unto a sin,
But greater sin to keep a sinful oath.
Who can be bound by any solemn vow
To do a murd'rous deed, to rob a man, 185
To force a spotless virgin's chastity,
To reave the orphan of his patrimony,

To wring the widow from her custom'd right,
And have no other reason for this wrong
But that he was bound by a solemn oath? 190
Queen. A subtle traitor needs no sophister.
King. Call Buckingham and bid him arm
    himself.
York. Call Buckingham and all the friends
    thou hast,
I am resolv'd for death or dignity.
Clif. The first I warrant thee, if dreams
    prove true. 195
War. You were best to go to bed and dream
    again
To keep thee from the tempest of the field.
Clif. I am resolv'd to bear a greater storm
Than any thou canst conjure up to-day;
And that I'll write upon thy burgonet, 200
Might I but know thee by thy household badge.
War. Now, by my father's badge, old Nevil's
    crest,
The rampant bear chain'd to the ragged staff,
This day I'll wear aloft my burgonet,
As on a mountain top the cedar shows, 205
That keeps his leaves in spite of any storm,
Even to affright thee with the view thereof.
Clif. And from thy burgonet I'll rend thy bear
And tread it under foot with all contempt,
Despite the berard that protects the bear. 210
Young Clif. And so to arms, victorious father,
To quell the rebels and their complices!
Rich. Fie! charity, for shame! Speak not in
    spite,
For you shall sup with Jesu Christ to-night.
Young Clif. Foul stigmatic, that's more than
    thou canst tell. 215
Rich. If not in heaven, you'll surely sup in
    hell. *Exeunt [severally].*

[Scene II. *Saint Alban's.*]

Alarums to the battle. Enter *Warwick.*

War. Clifford of Cumberland, 'tis Warwick
    calls!
And if thou dost not hide thee from the bear,
Now, when the angry trumpet sounds alarum
And dead men's cries do fill the empty air, 4
Clifford, I say, come forth and fight with me!
Proud Northern lord, Clifford of Cumberland,
Warwick is hoarse with calling thee to arms.

Enter *York.*

How now, my noble lord? What, all afoot?
York. The deadly-handed Clifford slew my
    steed; 9

But match to match I have encount'red him
And made a prey for carrion kites and crows
Even of the bonny beast he lov'd so well.

Enter [Old] Clifford.

War. Of one or both of us the time is come.
York. Hold, Warwick, seek thee out some
    other chase,
For I myself must hunt this deer to death.   15
War. Then nobly, York! 'Tis for a crown
    thou fight'st.
As I intend, Clifford, to thrive to-day,
It grieves my soul to leave thee unassail'd.
                                            Exit.
Clif. What seest thou in me, York? Why
    dost thou pause?
York. With thy brave bearing should I be
    in love   20
But that thou art so fast mine enemy.
Clif. Nor should thy prowess want praise
    and esteem
But that 'tis shown ignobly and in treason.
York. So let it help me now against thy
    sword
As I in justice and true right express it!   25
Clif. My soul and body on the action both!
York. A dreadful lay! Address thee in-
    stantly.   *They fight and York kills Clifford.*
Clif. La fin couronne les œuvres.   [*Dies.*]
York. Thus war hath given thee peace, for
    thou art still.
Peace with his soul, heaven, if it be thy will! 30
                                            Exit.

Enter Young Clifford.

Clif. Shame and confusion! All is on the
    rout.
Fear frames disorder, and disorder wounds
Where it should guard. O war, thou son of hell,
Whom angry heavens do make their minister,
Throw in the frozen bosoms of our part   35
Hot coals of vengeance! Let no soldier fly.
He that is truly dedicate to war
Hath no self-love; nor he that loves himself
Hath not essentially, but by circumstance,   39
The name of valour.   [*Sees his father's body.*]
    O, let the vile world end
And the premised flames of the last day
Knit earth and heaven together!
Now let the general trumpet blow his blast,
Particularities and petty sounds
To cease! Wast thou ordain'd, dear father,   45
To lose thy youth in peace and to achieve
The silver livery of advised age,
And in thy reverence and thy chair-days thus

To die in ruffian battle? Even at this sight
My heart is turn'd to stone; and while 'tis
    mine,   50
It shall be stony. York not our old men spares;
No more will I their babes. Tears virginal
Shall be to me even as the dew to fire;
And beauty, that the tyrant oft reclaims,
Shall to my flaming wrath be oil and flax.   55
Henceforth I will not have to do with pity.
Meet I an infant of the house of York,
Into as many gobbets will I cut it
As wild Medea young Absyrtus did.
In cruelty will I seek out my fame.   60
Come, thou new ruin of old Clifford's house.
As did Æneas old Anchises bear,
So bear I thee upon my manly shoulders;
But then Æneas bare a living load,
Nothing so heavy as these woes of mine.   65
                                [*Exit with the body.*]

Enter Richard and Somerset to fight. [Somerset
    is killed.]

Rich. So lie thou there!
For underneath an alehouse' paltry sign,
The Castle in Saint Alban's, Somerset
Hath made the wizard famous in his death.
Sword, hold thy temper. Heart, be wrathful
    still.   70
Priests pray for enemies, but princes kill.
                                            Exit.

Fight. Excursions. Enter King, Queen,
    and others.

Queen. Away, my lord! You are slow. For
    shame, away!
King. Can we outrun the heavens? Good
    Margaret, stay.
Queen. What are you made of? You'll nor
    fight nor fly.
Now is it manhood, wisdom, and defence   75
To give the enemy way, and to secure us
By what we can, which can no more but fly.
                                    Alarum afar off.
If you be ta'en, we then should see the bottom
Of all our fortunes; but if we haply scape   79
(As well we may, if not through your neglect),
We shall to London get, where you are lov'd,
And where this breach now in our fortunes made
May readily be stopp'd.

Enter [Young] Clifford.

Clif. But that my heart's on future mischief
    set,
I would speak blasphemy ere bid you fly!   85
But fly you must. Uncurable discomfite

273

Reigns in the hearts of all our present parts.
Away, for your relief! and we will live
To see their day and them our fortune give.
Away, my lord, away!   *Exeunt.*

[Scene III. *Field near Saint Alban's.*]

Alarum. Retreat. Enter *York, Richard, Warwick,* and *Soldiers,* with *Drum* and *Colours.*

York. Old Salisbury, who can report of him,
That winter lion, who in rage forgets
Aged contusions and all brush of time
And, like a gallant in the brow of youth,
Repairs him with occasion? This happy day 5
Is not itself, nor have we won one foot,
If Salisbury be lost.
    Rich.   My noble father,
Three times to-day I holp him to his horse,
Three times bestrid him, thrice I led him off,
Persuaded him from any further act;   10
But still where danger was, still there I met
    him;
And like rich hangings in a homely house,
So was his will in his old feeble body.
But, noble as he is, look where he comes.

Enter *Salisbury.*

Sal. Now, by my sword, well hast thou
    fought to-day!   15
By th' mass, so did we all! I thank you,
    Richard.
God knows how long it is I have to live;
And it hath pleas'd him that three times to-day
You have defended me from imminent death.
Well, lords, we have not got that which we have.
'Tis not enough our foes are this time fled, 21
Being opposites of such repairing nature.
    York. I know our safety is to follow them;
For, as I hear, the King is fled to London
To call a present court of parliament.   25
Let us pursue him ere the writs go forth.
What says Lord Warwick? Shall we after
    them?
    War. After them? Nay, before them, if we
    can!
Now, by my faith, lords, 'twas a glorious day.
Saint Alban's battle, won by famous York, 30
Shall be eterniz'd in all age to come.
Sound drums and trumpets, and to London all;
And more such days as these to us befall!
                            Exeunt.

THE THIRD PART OF KING HENRY THE SIXTH

THE THIRD PART OF KING HENRY THE SIXTH bears the same relation to *The True Tragedie of Richard Duke of Yorke* that the *Second Part* bears to *The First Part of the Contention*, and the theories discussed in the Introduction to *Part II* are all applicable to the present play (see p. 703). As before, we may accept the Folio version, which is the sole authority for the text, as entirely Shakespeare's work. The Quarto of *The True Tragedie* is, then, a reduced and imperfect form of Shakespeare's play, and not an older drama from which Shakespeare elaborated his PART III.

The so-called First Quarto of *The True Tragedie* (really an octavo) appeared in 1595, the Second Quarto in 1600, and the Quarto of 1619 (*The Whole Contention*) includes both *The First Part of the Contention* and *The True Tragedie*.

The True Tragedie covers the same ground as Shakespeare's PART III, but is only two-thirds as long. Material and arrangement are substantially identical, and differences in phraseology are less striking than in the case of PART II and *The Contention*. In the opening scene the text is almost literally identical, verse for verse and word for word, until Queen Margaret enters — that is, for about two hundred lines. Both texts close with a typical concluding speech in which they disagree in only a single word.

For specimens of the additional matter in PART III compare i, 1, 215–229; i, 2, 28–34; ii, 5, 20–54; iii, 1, 72–96; iii, 2, 164–181; iii, 3, 4–43; iv, 3, 1–22; iv, 6, 3–36, 77–102; v, 4, 1–43. In some instances, the lack of the passage in *The True Tragedie* is manifestly due to a cut; in some, the Quarto shows slight traces of the Folio text; in others, it partly fills the gap with other lines.

PART III plunges *in medias res*. Abundant expository matter follows at once. The Battle of St. Albans (May 22, 1455) is fused with the Yorkist victory at Northampton (July 10, 1460), and the opening scene in the Parliament House (October, 1460) is made to follow the battle with only the interval required to reach London. The crown is assured to Henry for life, but the title is to pass to Richard of York and his heirs. Civil war follows, and the Battle of Wakefield is won by the King's party (December 30). As a matter of history, York fell in the battle; but Halle (copied by Holinshed) relates an alternative story, according to which he was taken alive and 'in derision caused to stand upon a molehill.' This is dramatized in i, 4.

Act ii takes us through the Battle of Towton (March, 1461). The famous scene (ii, 5) in which a son who has killed his father appears, and a father who has killed his son, was suggested by a sentence in Halle: 'This conflict was in maner vnnaturall, for in it the sonne fought agaynst the father, the brother agaynst the brother, the nephew against the uncle, and the tenaunt agaynst his lord.' King Henry flees to Scotland. The coronation of Edward IV (June 28, 1461) is assumed to take place between the acts.

In the first scene of Act iii, Henry, having returned in disguise, is arrested (1465). An interlude is now provided by King Edward's wooing of Lady Grey (iii, 2). The marriage took place on May Day, 1464. Scene iii condenses history in defiance of dates: Queen Margaret's reception by the French king (1462), Warwick's negotiations for Edward's marriage with the

275

Lady Bona (1464) — frustrated by the marriage of Edward and Lady Grey — and his return with French forces (1470) to reinstate Henry, are brought together.

Act iv dramatizes Warwick's military operations of 1470 and the restoration of King Henry. The capture of Edward (iv, 3) actually took place in the campaign of 1469, and he escaped in October of that year. In 1470 he was not captured but fled to the Continent (iv, 6, 78 ff.) on hearing of Warwick's approach. Henry's release from the Tower (October, 1470) is dramatized in scene 6. King Henry's prophecy about young Richmond (iv, 6, 68–76) was suggested by a passage in Halle-Holinshed.

From Act iv, scene 7, to the end the order of events agrees well enough with the historical record. Edward's return (March 14, 1471) and the Battle of Barnet (April 14), in which Warwick is killed, decide the fate of the Lancastrians (iv, 7–8; v, 1–5). Henry has been captured in the interval (iv, 8) and sent to the Tower. The Battle of Tewkesbury (May 4) results in the capture of Queen Margaret and young Prince Edward (v, 4–5). The murder of the Prince follows immediately. Holinshed writes (on Halle's authority) that, on being asked by the king 'how he durst so presumptuouslie enter into his realme with banner displaied,' he replied boldly: 'To recouer my father's kingdome and heritage, from his father and grandfather to him, and from him after him to me, lineallie descended' (v, 5, 14 ff.), whereupon he was 'suddenlie murthered' by Clarence, Richard, Dorset, and Hastings. King Henry died in the Tower soon after — no one knows under what circumstances; but Shakespeare is justified by 'constant fame' in making Richard of Gloucester his murderer (v, 6). The closing scene of the play is imaginary. It is supposed to occur soon after King Henry's death.

From this review it appears that THE THIRD PART OF KING HENRY THE SIXTH is quite intelligible in and for itself. It required no *Part I* or *Part II* to make it clear to any audience.

The association of Marlowe and Greene with the three plays on Henry VI seems to owe its origin to a misunderstanding of a passage in Robert Greene's *Groatsworth of Wit*. Addressing three playwrights of his acquaintance, Greene bids them put no trust in actors — 'painted monsters' — 'puppets that spake from our mouths' — 'anticks garnisht in our colours.' 'Trust them not: for there is an vpstart Crow, beautified with our feathers, that with his *Tygers hart wrapt in a Players hyde*, supposes he is as well able to bombast out a blanke verse as the best of you: and beeing an absolute *Iohannes fac totum*, is in his owne conceit the onely Shake-scene in a countrey.' He adjures the three to abandon play-writing for 'more profitable courses.' One of the persons addressed was undoubtedly Marlowe. 'Shake-scene' is obviously Shakespeare. All this has been taken as an assertion that Shakespeare had stolen literary matter from Marlowe and Greene to use in his HENRY THE SIXTH. But no charge of plagiarism is involved. Greene despises those speaking puppets, the actors, because they owe their fame to the mere declamation of other men's verses; and one of these puppets has even presumed to write plays of his own, and thinks he can make as good blank verse as the best of us.

Greene was writing shortly before September, 1592. The italicized line parodies 3 HENRY VI, i, 4, 137. His evidence suffices to put PART III as early as that year. A reasonable date is 1591.

THE THIRD PART OF
KING HENRY THE SIXTH

[Dramatis Personae.

King Henry the Sixth.
Edward, Prince of Wales, his son.
Lewis XI, King of France.
Duke of Somerset.
Duke of Exeter.
Earl of Oxford.
Earl of Northumberland.
Earl of Westmoreland.
Lord Clifford.
Richard Plantagenet, Duke of York.
Edward, Earl of March, afterwards
   King Edward IV,
Edmund, Earl of Rutland,   his sons.
George, afterwards Duke of Clarence,
Richard, afterwards Duke of Gloucester,
Duke of Norfolk.
Marquess of Montague.
Earl of Warwick.
Earl of Pembroke.
Lord Hastings.
Lord Stafford.
Sir John Mortimer, uncles to Richard, Duke of
Sir Hugh Mortimer,   York.

Henry, young Earl of Richmond.
Lord Rivers, brother to Lady Grey.
Sir William Stanley.
Sir John Montgomery.
Sir John Somervile.
Tutor to Rutland.
Mayor of York and Aldermen.
Mayor of Coventry.
Lieutenant of the Tower.
A Nobleman.
Two Keepers (Sinklo and Humphrey).
A Son that has killed his father.
A Father that has killed his son.
The French Admiral.

Queen Margaret.
Lady Grey, a widow, afterwards Queen to Edward IV.
Bona, sister to the French Queen.

Soldiers, Attendants, Messengers, Watchmen, a Huntsman.

SCENE. — England and France.]

ACT I. Scene I. [London. The Parliament House.]

Alarum. Enter Plantagenet Duke of York, Edward, Richard, Norfolk, Montague, Warwick, and Soldiers.

War. I wonder how the King escap'd our
   hands.
York. While we pursu'd the horsemen of the
   North,
He slily stole away and left his men;
Whereat the great Lord of Northumberland,
Whose warlike ears could never brook retreat,   5
Cheer'd up the drooping army, and himself,
Lord Clifford, and Lord Stafford, all abreast,
Charg'd our main battle's front and, breaking in,
Were by the swords of common soldiers slain.
Edw. Lord Stafford's father, Duke of Buckingham,   10
Is either slain or wounded dangerous;

I cleft his beaver with a downright blow.
That this is true, father, behold his blood.
     [Shows his bloody sword.]
Mont. And, brother, here's the Earl of Wiltshire's blood,
Whom I encount'red as the battles join'd.   15
Rich. Speak thou for me, and tell them what
   I did.   [Throws down Somerset's head.]
York. Richard hath best deserv'd of all my
   sons.
But is your Grace dead, my Lord of Somerset?
Norf. Such hap have all the line of John of
   Gaunt!
Rich. Thus do I hope to shake King Henry's
   head.   20
War. And so do I. Victorious Prince of
   York,
Before I see thee seated in that throne
Which now the house of Lancaster usurps,
I vow by heaven these eyes shall never close.

This is the palace of the fearful King   25
And this the regal seat. Possess it, York;
For this is thine, and not King Henry's heirs'.
  York. Assist me then, sweet Warwick, and
I will;
For hither we have broken in by force.
  Norf. We'll all assist you. He that flies
shall die.   30
  York. Thanks, gentle Norfolk. Stay by me,
my lords;
And, soldiers, stay, and lodge by me this night.
          They go up.
  War. And when the King comes, offer him
no violence
Unless he seek to thrust you out perforce.
          [*The Soldiers stand back.*]
  York. The Queen this day here holds her
parliament,   35
But little thinks we shall be of her council.
By words or blows here let us win our right.
  Rich. Arm'd as we are, let's stay within this
house.
  War. The bloody parliament shall this be
call'd
Unless Plantagenet, Duke of York, be King 40
And bashful Henry depos'd, whose cowardice
Hath made us bywords to our enemies.
  York. Then leave me not, my lords. Be
resolute.
I mean to take possession of my right.
  War. Neither the King, nor he that loves
him best,   45
The proudest he that holds up Lancaster,
Dares stir a wing if Warwick shake his bells.
I'll plant Plantagenet, root him up who dares.
Resolve thee, Richard; claim the English
crown.   [*York seats himself in the throne.*]

Flourish. Enter *King Henry, Clifford, Northumberland, Westmoreland, Exeter,* and the rest.

  K. Hen. My lords, look where the sturdy
rebel sits,   50
Even in the chair of state! Belike he means,
Back'd by the power of Warwick, that false
peer,
To aspire unto the crown and reign as king.
Earl of Northumberland, he slew thy father,
And thine, Lord Clifford, and you both have
vow'd revenge   55
On him, his sons, his favourites, and his friends.
  North. If I be not, heavens be reveng'd on
me!
  Clif. The hope thereof makes Clifford mourn
in steel.

  West. What, shall we suffer this? Let's
pluck him down.   59
My heart for anger burns. I cannot brook it.
  K. Hen. Be patient, gentle Earl of West-
moreland.
  Clif. Patience is for poltroons, such as he.
He durst not sit there, had your father liv'd.
My gracious lord, here in the parliament
Let us assail the family of York.   65
  North. Well hast thou spoken, cousin. Be
it so.
  K. Hen. Ah, know you not the city favours
them
And they have troops of soldiers at their beck?
  Exe. But when the Duke is slain, they'll
quickly fly.
  K. Hen. Far be the thought of this from
Henry's heart,   70
To make a shambles of the Parliament House!
Cousin of Exeter, frowns, words, and threats
Shall be the war that Henry means to use.
Thou factious Duke of York, descend my
throne
And kneel for grace and mercy at my feet. 75
I am thy sovereign.
  York.   Thou art deceiv'd. I am thine.
  Exe. For shame! come down. He made thee
Duke of York.
  York. It was my inheritance, as the earldom
was.
  Exe. Thy father was a traitor to the crown.
  War. Exeter, thou art a traitor to the crown
In following this usurping Henry.   81
  Clif. Whom should he follow but his natural
king?
  War. True, Clifford; and that's Richard
Duke of York.
  K. Hen. And shall I stand, and thou sit in
my throne?
  York. It must and shall be so. Content
thyself.   85
  War. Be Duke of Lancaster; let him be
King.
  West. He is both King and Duke of Lan-
caster,
And that the Lord of Westmoreland shall
maintain.
  War. And Warwick shall disprove it. You
forget
That we are those which chas'd you from the
field   90
And slew your fathers and with colours spread
March'd through the city to the palace gates.
  North. Yes, Warwick, I remember it to my
grief;

And, by his soul, thou and thy house shall
  rue it.
  West. Plantagenet, of thee and these thy
  sons,   95
Thy kinsmen, and thy friends, I'll have more
  lives
Than drops of blood were in my father's veins.
  Clif. Urge it no more; lest that instead of
  words
I send thee, Warwick, such a messenger
As shall revenge his death before I stir.   100
  War. Poor Clifford! how I scorn his worth-
  less threats!
  York. Will you we show our title to the
  crown?
If not, our swords shall plead it in the field.
  K. Hen. What title hast thou, traitor, to the
  crown?
Thy father was, as thou art, Duke of York;
Thy grandfather, Roger Mortimer, Earl of
  March.   106
I am the son of Henry the Fifth,
Who made the Dauphin and the French to
  stoop
And seiz'd upon their towns and provinces.
  War. Talk not of France, sith thou hast lost
  it all.   110
  K. Hen. The Lord Protector lost it, and
  not I.
When I was crown'd I was but nine months
  old.
  Rich. You are old enough now, and yet me-
  thinks you lose.
Father, tear the crown from the usurper's head.
  Edw. Sweet father, do so. Set it on your
  head.   115
  Mont. [*to York*] Good brother, as thou lov'st
  and honourest arms,
Let's fight it out and not stand cavilling thus.
  Rich. Sound drums and trumpets, and the
  King will fly.
  York. Sons, peace!
  K. Hen. Peace thou! and give King Henry
  leave to speak.   120
  War. Plantagenet shall speak first. Hear
  him, lords,
And be you silent and attentive too,
For he that interrupts him shall not live.
  K. Hen. Think'st thou that I will leave my
  kingly throne,
Wherein my grandsire and my father sat? 125
No! First shall war unpeople this my realm;
Ay, and their colours, often borne in France,
And now in England to our heart's great sor-
  row,

Shall be my winding sheet. Why faint you,
  lords?
My title's good, and better far than his.   130
  War. Prove it, Henry, and thou shalt be
  King.
  K. Hen. Henry the Fourth by conquest got
  the crown.
  York. 'Twas by rebellion against his king.
  K. Hen. [*aside*] I know not what to say; my
  title's weak. —
Tell me, may not a king adopt an heir?   135
  York. What then?
  K. Hen. An if he may, then am I lawful
  king;
For Richard, in the view of many lords,
Resign'd the crown to Henry the Fourth,
Whose heir my father was, and I am his.   140
  York. He rose against him, being his sover-
  eign,
And made him to resign his crown perforce.
  War. Suppose, my lords, he did it uncon-
  strain'd,
Think you 'twere prejudicial to his crown?
  Exe. No; for he could not so resign his
  crown   145
But that the next heir should succeed and
  reign.
  K. Hen. Art thou against us, Duke of Exeter?
  Exe. His is the right, and therefore pardon
  me.
  York. Why whisper you, my lords, and an-
  swer not?
  Exe. My conscience tells me he is lawful
  king.   150
  K. Hen. [*aside*] All will revolt from me and
  turn to him.
  North. Plantagenet, for all the claim thou
  lay'st,
Think not that Henry shall be so depos'd.
  War. Depos'd he shall be, in despite of all.
  North. Thou art deceiv'd. 'Tis not thy
  Southern power   155
Of Essex, Norfolk, Suffolk, nor of Kent,
Which makes thee thus presumptuous and
  proud,
Can set the Duke up in despite of me.
  Clif. King Henry, be thy title right or
  wrong,
Lord Clifford vows to fight in thy defence. 160
May that ground gape and swallow me alive
Where I shall kneel to him that slew my father!
  K. Hen. O Clifford, how thy words revive
  my heart!
  York. Henry of Lancaster, resign thy crown.
What mutter you or what conspire you, lords?

War. Do right unto this princely Duke of
York,   166
Or I will fill the house with armed men
And over the chair of state, where now he sits,
Write up his title with usurping blood.
   *He stamps with his foot, and the Soldiers
        show themselves.*
K. Hen. My Lord of Warwick, hear me but
one word.   170
Let me for this my lifetime reign as king.
York. Confirm the crown to me and to mine
heirs
And thou shalt reign in quiet while thou liv'st.
K. Hen. I am content. Richard Plantagenet,
Enjoy the kingdom after my decease.   175
Clif. What wrong is this unto the Prince
your son!
War. What good is this to England and
himself!
West. Base, fearful, and despairing Henry!
Clif. How hast thou injur'd both thyself
and us!   179
West. I cannot stay to hear these articles.
North. Nor I.
Clif. Come, cousin, let us tell the Queen
these news.
West. Farewell, faint-hearted and degenerate
king,
In whose cold blood no spark of honour bides.
North. Be thou a prey unto the house of
York   185
And die in bands for this unmanly deed!
Clif. In dreadful war mayst thou be over-
come
Or live in peace abandon'd and despis'd!
   [*Exeunt Northumberland, Clifford, and
        Westmoreland.*]
War. Turn this way, Henry, and regard
them not.
Exe. They seek revenge and therefore will
not yield.   190
K. Hen. Ah, Exeter!
War.   Why should you sigh, my lord?
K. Hen. Not for myself, Lord Warwick, but
my son,
Whom I unnaturally shall disinherit.
But be it as it may. [*To York.*] I here entail
The crown to thee and to thine heirs for ever,
Conditionally that here thou take an oath   196
To cease this civil war, and whilst I live
To honour me as thy king and sovereign,
And neither by treason nor hostility
To seek to put me down and reign thyself.   200
York. This oath I willingly take, and will
perform.   [*Comes from the throne.*]

War. Long live King Henry! Plantagenet,
embrace him.
K. Hen. And long live thou, and these thy
forward sons!
York. Now York and Lancaster are recon-
cil'd.
Exe. Accurs'd be he that seeks to make them
foes!   205
   Sennet. Here they come down.
York. Farewell, my gracious lord. I'll to my
castle.
War. And I'll keep London with my soldiers.
Norf. And I to Norfolk with my followers.
Mont. And I unto the sea, from whence I
came.
   *Exeunt York and his Sons, [Warwick, Nor-
   folk, Montague, with their Soldiers, and
   Attendants].*
K. Hen. And I with grief and sorrow to the
court.   210

Enter the *Queen [Margaret]* and [*Edward*]
Prince [of Wales].

Exe. Here comes the Queen, whose looks
bewray her anger.
I'll steal away.
K. Hen.   Exeter, so will I.
Queen. Nay, go not from me. I will follow
thee.
K. Hen. Be patient, gentle queen, and I will
stay.   214
Queen. Who can be patient in such extremes?
Ah, wretched man! Would I had died a
maid
And never seen thee, never borne thee son,
Seeing thou hast prov'd so unnatural a father!
Hath he deserv'd to lose his birthright thus?
Hadst thou but lov'd him half so well as I,   220
Or felt that pain which I did for him once,
Or nourish'd him as I did with my blood,
Thou wouldst have left thy dearest heart-blood
there
Rather than have made that savage duke thine
heir
And disinherited thine only son.   225
Prince. Father, you cannot disinherit me.
If you be King, why should not I succeed?
K. Hen. Pardon me, Margaret. Pardon me,
sweet son.
The Earl of Warwick and the Duke enforc'd
me.
Queen. Enforc'd thee? Art thou King, and
wilt be forc'd?   230
I shame to hear thee speak. Ah, timorous
wretch!

HENRY VI

PART THREE

PHOTOGRAPHS BY LISEL HAAS
PRODUCED BY THE BIRMINGHAM
REPERTORY THEATRE

Henry VI (Jack May). Wishing to live a simple, peaceful life, he weakly promises the throne to the Duke of York when he shall die on condition "that here thou take an oath to cease this civil war" (Act I, Scene I)

The remorseless Margaret, Queen to Henry VI (Rosalind Boxall). "Ah! timorous wretch; thou hast undone thyself, thy son, and me ... And yet shalt thou be safe? such safety finds the trembling lamb environed with wolves" (Act I, Scene I)

The widowed Lady Grey as played by Christine Finn

The proud-hearted kingmaker, Warwick (Edgar Wreford)

Richard (Paul Daneman), son of the Duke of York, later the Duke of Gloucester: "I'll make my heaven to dream upon the crown"

York rises to answer the king's charge of usurpation. "Henry of Lancaster, resign thy crown. What mutter you, or what conspire you, lords?" (Act I, Scene I)

Backed by his sons and Warwick, York listens from the throne as King Henry speaks: "My lords, look where the sturdy rebel sits, even in the chair of state!" (Act I, Scene I)

Warwick joins in the pledge to honor Henry as King, yet has already prophetically observed that "Neither the king, nor he that loves him best ... dares stir a wing if Warwick shake his bells" (Act I, Scene I)

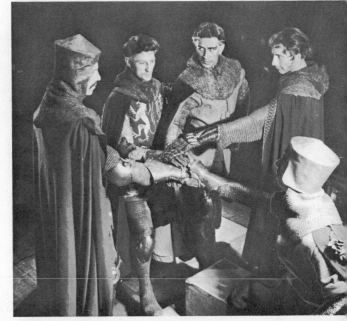

Richard to his father: "For a kingdom any oath may be broken; I would break a thousand oaths to reign one year" (Act I, Scene II)

Captured in a battle near Wakefield, York is taunted by the queen as she places a paper crown upon his head. "A crown for York! and, lords, bow low to him." Moments later he is slain and then beheaded (Act I, Scene IV)

The murdered York's son, Edward (Basil Henson), hurls a challenge: "Now, perjud'd Henry, wilt thou kneel for grace, and set thy diadem upon my head; or bide the mortal fortune of the field?" (Act II, Scene II)

Crook-back Richard exults over the body of the man who killed his father (Act II, Scene VI)

With Henry deposed, the widowed Lady Grey comes to the palace to beg the new king, Edward IV, to restore her husband's estates to her. Edward, in turn, advances a proposal of his own: "To tell thee plain, I aim to lie with thee" (Act III, Scene II)

At the French court, Margaret and Warwick press conflicting petitions on Lewis XI (Redmond Phillips). Warwick's request is about to be granted when word arrives that Edward has married Lady Grey. This news prompts Warwick to denounce Edward and reconcile himself with Margaret (Act III, Scene III)

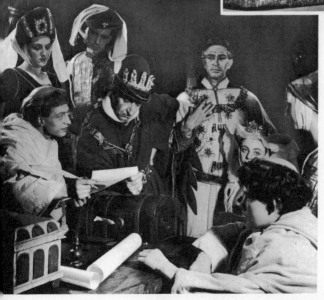

The king of France, alluding to forces which he is sending with Warwick and Margaret, bids a messenger "Tell false Edward ... that Lewis of France is sending over masquers to revel it with him and his new bride" (Act III, Scene III)

The invading forces surprise Edward in his camp (Act IV, Scene III)

Warwick tells Edward that "Henry now shall wear the English crown, and be true king indeed, thou but the shadow" (Act IV, Scene III)

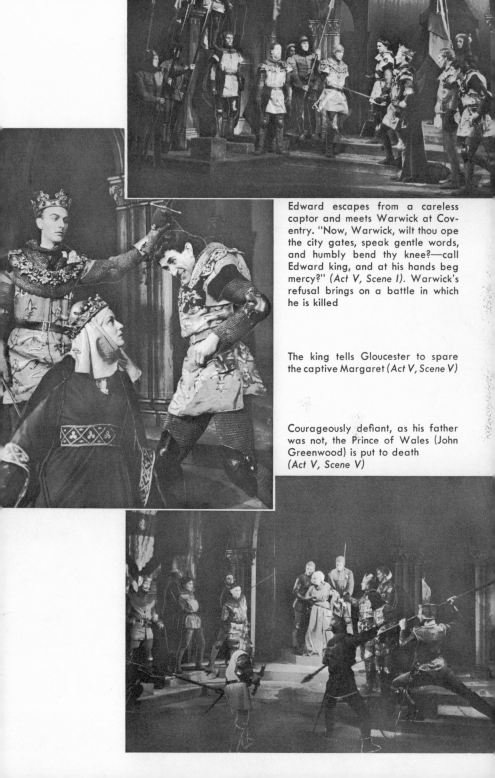

Edward escapes from a careless captor and meets Warwick at Coventry. "Now, Warwick, wilt thou ope the city gates, speak gentle words, and humbly bend thy knee?—call Edward king, and at his hands beg mercy?" (*Act V, Scene I*). Warwick's refusal brings on a battle in which he is killed

The king tells Gloucester to spare the captive Margaret (*Act V, Scene V*)

Courageously defiant, as his father was not, the Prince of Wales (John Greenwood) is put to death (*Act V, Scene V*)

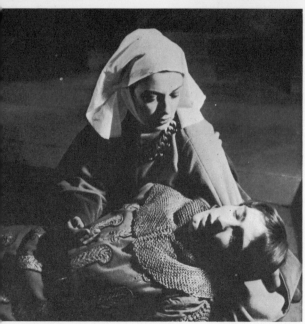

Margaret, the prince's mother, mourns his death. "No, no, my heart will burst, an if I speak: and I will speak, that so my heart may burst" (*Act V, Scene V*)

Having murdered Henry VI and thus made his brother Edward's claim to the throne secure, Richard bides his time. "This shoulder was ordain'd so thick to heave; and heave it shall some weight, or break my back"
(*Act V, Scene VII*)

Thou hast undone thyself, thy son, and me,
And giv'n unto the house of York such head
As thou shalt reign but by their sufferance.
To entail him and his heirs unto the crown,
What is it but to make thy sepulchre   236
And creep into it far before thy time?
Warwick is Chancellor and the lord of Calais;
Stern Falconbridge commands the narrow seas;
The Duke is made Protector of the realm;   240
And yet shalt thou be safe? Such safety
   finds
The trembling lamb environed with wolves.
Had I been there, which am a silly woman,
The soldiers should have toss'd me on their
   pikes
Before I would have granted to that act.   245
But thou preferr'st thy life before thine honour;
And seeing thou dost, I here divorce myself
Both from thy table, Henry, and thy bed
Until that act of parliament be repeal'd
Whereby my son is disinherited.   250
The Northern lords, that have forsworn thy
   colours,
Will follow mine, if once they see them spread;
And spread they shall be, to thy foul dis-
   grace
And utter ruin of the house of York.   254
Thus do I leave thee. Come, son, let's away.
Our army is ready. Come, we'll after them.
   K. Hen. Stay, gentle Margaret, and hear me
   speak.
   Queen. Thou hast spoke too much already.
   Get thee gone.
   K. Hen. Gentle son Edward, thou wilt stay
   with me?
   Queen. Ay, to be murther'd by his enemies!
   Prince. When I return with victory from the
   field   261
I'll see your Grace. Till then I'll follow her.
   Queen. Come, son, away. We may not linger
   thus.
     [*Exeunt Queen Margaret and the Prince.*]
   K. Hen. Poor queen! How love to me and
   to her son   264
Hath made her break out into terms of rage!
Reveng'd may she be on that hateful duke,
Whose haughty spirit, winged with desire,
Will cost my crown and like an empty eagle
Tire on the flesh of me and of my son!
The loss of those three lords torments my
   heart.   270
I'll write unto them and entreat them fair.
Come, cousin, you shall be the messenger.
   Exe. And I, I hope, shall reconcile them all.
                       Exeunt.

[Scene II. *Sandal Castle, near Wakefield,*
             in Yorkshire.]

    Enter *Richard, Edward,* and *Montague.*
   Rich. Brother, though I be youngest, give
   me leave.
   Edw. No, I can better play the orator.
   Mont. But I have reasons strong and forcible.

       Enter the *Duke of York.*
   York. Why, how now, sons and brother? at
   a strife?
What is your quarrel? How began it first?   5
   Edw. No quarrel, but a slight contention.
   York. About what?
   Rich. About that which concerns your Grace
   and us —
The crown of England, father, which is yours.
   York. Mine, boy? Not till King Henry be
   dead.   10
   Rich. Your right depends not on his life or
   death.
   Edw. Now you are heir; therefore enjoy it
   now.
By giving the house of Lancaster leave to
   breathe,
It will outrun you, father, in the end.
   York. I took an oath that he should quietly
   reign.   15
   Edw. But for a kingdom any oath may be
   broken.
I would break a thousand oaths to reign one
   year.
   Rich. No. God forbid your Grace should be
   forsworn!
   York. I shall be, if I claim by open war.
   Rich. I'll prove the contrary if you'll hear
   me speak.   20
   York. Thou canst not, son. It is impossible.
   Rich. An oath is of no moment, being not
   took
Before a true and lawful magistrate
That hath authority over him that swears.
Henry had none, but did usurp the place.   25
Then, seeing 'twas he that made you to de-
   pose,
Your oath, my lord, is vain and frivolous.
Therefore, to arms! And, father, do but think
How sweet a thing it is to wear a crown,
Within whose circuit is Elysium   30
And all that poets feign of bliss and joy.
Why do we linger thus? I cannot rest
Until the white rose that I wear be dy'd
Even in the lukewarm blood of Henry's heart.

York. Richard, enough. I will be King or
die!   35
Brother, thou shalt to London presently
And whet on Warwick to this enterprise.
Thou, Richard, shalt to the Duke of Norfolk
And tell him privily of our intent.
You, Edward, shall unto my Lord Cobham, 40
With whom the Kentishmen will willingly rise.
In them I trust; for they are soldiers,
Witty, courteous, liberal, full of spirit.
While you are thus employ'd, what resteth more
But that I seek occasion how to rise,   45
And yet the King not privy to my drift,
Nor any of the house of Lancaster?

Enter *Gabriel* (a *Messenger*).

But stay! What news? Why com'st thou in
such post?
Gabr. The Queen with all the Northern earls
and lords
Intend here to besiege you in your castle. 50
She is hard by with twenty thousand men;
And therefore fortify your hold, my lord.
York. Ay, with my sword! What? Think'st
thou that we fear them?
Edward and Richard, you shall stay with me;
My brother Montague shall post to London.
Let noble Warwick, Cobham, and the rest, 56
Whom we have left protectors of the King,
With pow'rful policy strengthen themselves
And trust not simple Henry nor his oaths.
Mont. Brother, I go. I'll win them; fear it
not;   60
And thus most humbly I do take my leave.
Exit.

Enter *Sir John Mortimer* and *Sir Hugh,*
his *Brother.*

York. Sir John and Sir Hugh Mortimer, mine
uncles!
You are come to Sandal in a happy hour.
The army of the Queen mean to besiege us.
John. She shall not need; we'll meet her in
the field.   65
York. What, with five thousand men?
Rich. Ay, with five hundred, father, for a
need!
A woman's general. What should we fear?
A march afar off.
Edw. I hear their drums. Let's set our men
in order   69
And issue forth and bid them battle straight.
York. Five men to twenty! Though the odds
be great,
I doubt not, uncle, of our victory.

Many a battle have I won in France
When as the enemy hath been ten to one. 7
Why should I not now have the like success?
Alarum. Exeunt

[Scene III. *Field of battle between
Sandal Castle and Wakefield.*]

Alarums. Enter *Rutland* and his *Tutor.*

Rut. Ah, whither shall I fly to scape their
hands?
Ah, tutor, look where bloody Clifford comes!

Enter *Clifford* [and *Soldiers*].

Clif. Chaplain, away! Thy priesthood save
thy life.
As for the brat of this accursed duke,
Whose father slew my father, he shall die. *
Tutor. And I, my lord, will bear him com
pany.
Clif. Soldiers, away with him!
Tutor. Ah, Clifford, murther not this inno-
cent child,
Lest thou be hated both of God and man!
Exit [*dragged off by Soldiers*]
Clif. How now? Is he dead already? Or is
it fear   1
That makes him close his eyes? I'll open them
Rut. So looks the pent-up lion o'er the wretch
That trembles under his devouring paws;
And so he walks, insulting o'er his prey,
And so he comes, to rend his limbs asunder. 1
Ah, gentle Clifford, kill me with thy sword
And not with such a cruel threat'ning look!
Sweet Clifford, hear me speak before I die!
I am too mean a subject for thy wrath.
Be thou reveng'd on men and let me live. 2
Clif. In vain thou speak'st, poor boy! My
father's blood
Hath stopp'd the passage where thy word
should enter.
Rut. Then let my father's blood open i
again.
He is a man, and, Clifford, cope with him.
Clif. Had I thy brethren here, their lives and
thine   2
Were not revenge sufficient for me.
No, if I digg'd up thy forefathers' graves
And hung their rotten coffins up in chains,
It could not slake mine ire nor ease my heart
The sight of any of the house of York   3
Is as a Fury to torment my soul;
And till I root out their accursed line

282

And leave not one alive, I live in hell.
Therefore —   34
  Rut. O, let me pray before I take my death!
To thee I pray. Sweet Clifford, pity me!
  Clif. Such pity as my rapier's point affords.
  Rut. I never did thee harm. Why wilt thou
slay me?
  Clif. Thy father hath.
  Rut.   But 'twas ere I was born.
Thou hast one son. For his sake pity me!   40
Lest in revenge thereof, sith God is just,
He be as miserably slain as I.
Ah, let me live in prison all my days;
And when I give occasion of offence,
Then let me die, for now thou hast no cause.
  Clif. No cause?   46
Thy father slew my father. Therefore die.
                  [*Stabs him.*]
  Rut. Di faciant laudis summa sit ista tuae!
                    [*Dies.*]
  Clif. Plantagenet, I come, Plantagenet!
And this thy son's blood cleaving to my blade
Shall rust upon my weapon till thy blood, 51
Congeal'd with this, do make me wipe off both.
                     Exit.

[Scene IV. *Another part of the field.*]

Alarum. Enter *Richard Duke of York.*

  York. The army of the Queen hath got the
field.
My uncles both are slain in rescuing me,
And all my followers to the eager foe
Turn back and fly, like ships before the wind
Or lambs pursu'd by hunger-starved wolves. 5
My sons — God knows what hath bechanced
them;
But this I know, they have demean'd themselves
Like men born to renown by life or death.
Three times did Richard make a lane to me
And thrice cried 'Courage, father! fight it out!'
And full as oft came Edward to my side   11
With purple falchion, painted to the hilt
In blood of those that had encount'red him.
And when the hardiest warriors did retire,
Richard cried 'Charge! and give no foot of
ground!'   15
And cried 'A crown, or else a glorious tomb!
A sceptre, or an earthly sepulchre!'
With this we charg'd again; but out alas!
We bodg'd again, as I have seen a swan
With bootless labour swim against the tide 20
And spend her **strength** with overmatching
waves.   *A short alarum within.*

Ah, hark! The fatal followers do pursue,
And I am faint and cannot fly their fury;
And were I strong, I would not shun their fury.
The sands are numb'red that makes up my life.
Here must I stay and here my life must end. 26

Enter the *Queen [Margaret], Clifford, Northumberland,* the young *Prince,* and *Soldiers.*

Come, bloody Clifford, rough Northumberland,
I dare your quenchless fury to more rage.
I am your butt and I abide your shot.
  North. Yield to our mercy, proud Plantag-
enet.   30
  Clif. Ay, to such mercy as his ruthless arm
With downright payment show'd unto my
father.
Now Phaëton hath tumbled from his car
And made an evening at the noontide prick.
  York. My ashes, as the phœnix, may bring
forth   35
A bird that will revenge upon you all;
And in that hope I throw mine eyes to heaven,
Scorning whate'er you can afflict me with.
Why come you not? What? multitudes, and
fear?
  Clif. So cowards fight when they can fly no
further;   40
So doves do peck the falcon's piercing talons;
So desperate thieves, all hopeless of their lives,
Breathe out invectives 'gainst the officers.
  York. O Clifford, but bethink thee once
again,   44
And in thy thought o'errun my former time;
And, if thou canst for blushing, view this face,
And bite thy tongue that slanders him with
cowardice
Whose frown hath made thee faint and fly ere
this.
  Clif. I will not bandy with thee word for
word,   49
But buckle with thee blows, twice two for one.
  Queen. Hold, valiant Clifford! For a thou-
sand causes
I would prolong awhile the traitor's life.
Wrath makes him deaf. Speak thou, North-
umberland.
  North. Hold, Clifford! Do not honour him
so much   54
To prick thy finger, though to wound his heart.
What valour were it, when a cur doth grin,
For one to thrust his hand between his teeth
When he might spurn him with his foot away?
It is war's prize to take all vantages;
And ten to one is no impeach of valour.   60
      [*They lay hands on York, who struggles.*]

Clif. Ay, ay, so strives the woodcock with
the gin.
North. So doth the cony struggle in the net.
York. So triumph thieves upon their con-
quer'd booty;
So true men yield, with robbers so o'ermatch'd.
North. What would your Grace have done
unto him now? 65
Queen. Brave warriors, Clifford and North-
umberland,
Come, make him stand upon this molehill here
That raught at mountains with outstretched
arms,
Yet parted but the shadow with his hand.
What, was it you that would be England's
king? 70
Was't you that revell'd in our parliament
And made a preachment of your high descent?
Where are your mess of sons to back you now?
The wanton Edward, and the lusty George?
And where's that valiant crookback prodigy,
Dicky your boy, that with his grumbling voice
Was wont to cheer his dad in mutinies?
Or, with the rest, where is your darling Rut-
land?
Look, York! I stain'd this napkin with the
blood 79
That valiant Clifford with his rapier's point
Made issue from the bosom of the boy;
And if thine eyes can water for his death,
I give thee this to dry thy cheeks withal.
Alas, poor York! but that I hate thee deadly,
I should lament thy miserable state. 85
I prithee grieve, to make me merry, York.
What? hath thy fiery heart so parch'd thine
entrails
That not a tear can fall for Rutland's death?
Why art thou patient, man? Thou shouldst
be mad; 89
And I to make thee mad do mock thee thus.
Stamp, rave, and fret, that I may sing and
dance.
Thou wouldst be fee'd, I see, to make me sport.
York cannot speak unless he wear a crown.
A crown for York! and, lords, bow low to him.
Hold you his hands whilst I do set it on. 95
[*Puts a paper crown on his head.*]
Ay, marry, sir, now looks he like a king!
Ay, this is he that took King Henry's chair
And this is he was his adopted heir.
But how is it that great Plantagenet 99
Is crown'd so soon, and broke his solemn oath?
As I bethink me, you should not be King
Till our King Henry had shook hands with
death.

And will you pale your head in Henry's glory
And rob his temples of the diadem
Now in his life, against your holy oath? 105
O, 'tis a fault too too unpardonable!
Off with the crown, and with the crown his
head!
And whilst we breathe, take time to do him
dead.
Clif. That is my office, for my father's sake.
Queen. Nay, stay. Let's hear the orisons he
makes. 110
York. She-wolf of France, but worse than
wolves of France,
Whose tongue more poisons than the adder's
tooth!
How ill-beseeming is it in thy sex
To triumph like an Amazonian trull
Upon their woes whom fortune captivates! 115
But that thy face is vizard-like, unchanging,
Made impudent with use of evil deeds,
I would assay, proud queen, to make thee blush.
To tell thee whence thou cam'st, of whom
deriv'd,
Were shame enough to shame thee, wert thou
not shameless. 120
Thy father bears the type of King of Naples,
Of both the Sicils and Jerusalem,
Yet not so wealthy as an English yeoman.
Hath that poor monarch taught thee to insult?
It needs not nor it boots thee not, proud queen,
Unless the adage must be verified, 126
That beggars mounted run their horse to death.
'Tis beauty that doth oft make women proud;
But God he knows thy share thereof is small.
'Tis virtue that doth make them most admir'd;
The contrary doth make thee wond'red at. 131
'Tis government that makes them seem divine;
The want thereof makes thee abominable.
Thou art as opposite to every good
As the Antipodes are unto us 135
Or as the South to the Septentrion.
O tiger's heart wrapp'd in a woman's hide!
How couldst thou drain the lifeblood of the
child,
To bid the father wipe his eyes withal,
And yet be seen to bear a woman's face? 140
Women are soft, mild, pitiful, and flexible;
Thou stern, obdurate, flinty, rough, remorseless.
Bid'st thou me rage? Why, now thou hast thy
wish.
Wouldst have me weep? Why, now thou hast
thy will.
For raging wind blows up incessant showers,
And when the rage allays the rain begins. 146
These tears are my sweet Rutland's obsequies,

And every drop cries vengeance for his death
'Gainst thee, fell Clifford, and thee, false
    Frenchwoman.
    North. Beshrew me but his passion moves
    me so   150
That hardly can I check my eyes from tears.
    York. That face of his the hungry cannibals
Would not have touch'd, would not have
    stain'd with blood;
But you are more inhuman, more inexorable —
O, ten times more! — than tigers of Hyrcania.
See, ruthless queen, a hapless father's tears.
This cloth thou dipp'dst in blood of my sweet
    boy,
And I with tears do wash the blood away.
Keep thou the napkin and go boast of this;
And if thou tell'st the heavy story right,   160
Upon my soul, the hearers will shed tears.
Yea, even my foes will shed fast-falling tears
And say 'Alas, it was a piteous deed!'
There, take the crown, and with the crown my
    curse;
And in thy need such comfort come to thee   165

As now I reap at thy too cruel hand!
Hard-hearted Clifford, take me from the world.
My soul to heaven, my blood upon your heads!
    North. Had he been slaughterman to all my
    kin,
I should not for my life but weep with him   170
To see how inly sorrow gripes his soul.
    Queen. What, weeping-ripe, my Lord North-
    umberland?
Think but upon the wrong he did us all
And that will quickly dry thy melting tears.
    Clif. Here's for my oath! here's for my
    father's death!   [*Stabs him.*]
    Queen. And here's to right our gentle-
    hearted king!   [*Stabs him.*]
    York. Open thy gate of mercy, gracious
    God!   177
My soul flies through these wounds to seek out
    thee.   [*Dies.*]
    Queen. Off with his head and set it on York
    gates!
So York may overlook the town of York.   180
                        Flourish. Exeunt.

[ACT II. Scene I. *A plain near Mortimer's Cross in Herefordshire.*]

A march. Enter *Edward, Richard,* and
        their *Power.*

    Edw. I wonder how our princely father
        scap'd,
Or whether he be scap'd away or no
From Clifford's and Northumberland's pursuit.
Had he been ta'en, we should have heard the
    news;
Had he been slain, we should have heard the
    news;   5
Or had he scap'd, methinks we should have
    heard
The happy tidings of his good escape.
How fares my brother? Why is he so sad?
    Rich. I cannot joy until I be resolv'd
Where our right valiant father is become.   10
I saw him in the battle range about
And watch'd him how he singled Clifford forth.
Methought he bore him in the thickest troop
As doth a lion in a herd of neat,
Or as a bear encompass'd round with dogs,   15
Who having pinch'd a few and made them
    cry,
The rest stand all aloof and bark at him.
So far'd our father with his enemies;
So fled his enemies my warlike father.
Methinks 'tis prize enough to be his son.   20

See how the morning opes her golden gates
And takes her farewell of the glorious sun!
How well resembles it the prime of youth,
Trimm'd like a younker prancing to his love!
    Edw. Dazzle mine eyes, or do I see three
    suns?   25
    Rich. Three glorious suns, each one a per-
    fect sun,
Not separated with the racking clouds,
But sever'd in a pale clear-shining sky.
See, see! They join, embrace, and seem to
    kiss,
As if they vow'd some league inviolable.   30
Now are they but one lamp, one light, one
    sun.
In this the heaven figures some event.
    Edw. 'Tis wondrous strange, the like yet
    never heard of.
I think it cites us, brother, to the field,
That we, the sons of brave Plantagenet,   35
Each one already blazing by our meeds,
Should notwithstanding join our lights together
And overshine the earth, as this the world.
Whate'er it bodes, henceforward will I bear
Upon my target three fair-shining suns.   40
    Rich. Nay, bear three daughters. By your
    leave I speak it,
You love the breeder better than the male.

285

Enter *one blowing*.

But what art thou whose heavy looks foretell
Some dreadful story hanging on thy tongue?
 Messenger. Ah, one that was a woful looker-
  on   45
When as the noble Duke of York was slain,
Your princely father and my loving lord!
 Edw. O, speak no more, for I have heard too
  much!
 Rich. Say how he died, for I will hear it all.
 Messenger. Environed he was with many
  foes,   50
And stood against them as the hope of Troy
Against the Greeks that would have ent'red
  Troy.
But Hercules himself must yield to odds;
And many strokes, though with a little axe,
Hews down and fells the hardest-timber'd oak.
By many hands your father was subdu'd,   56
But only slaught'red by the ireful arm
Of unrelenting Clifford and the Queen,
Who crown'd the gracious Duke in high despite,
Laugh'd in his face, and when with grief he
  wept,   60
The ruthless Queen gave him, to dry his cheeks,
A napkin steeped in the harmless blood
Of sweet young Rutland, by rough Clifford
  slain;
And after many scorns, many foul taunts,   64
They took his head and on the gates of York
They set the same; and there it doth remain,
The saddest spectacle that e'er I view'd.
 Edw. Sweet Duke of York, our prop to lean
  upon,
Now thou art gone, we have no staff, no stay!
O Clifford, boist'rous Clifford, thou hast slain
The flow'r of Europe for his chivalry;   71
And treacherously hast thou vanquish'd him,
For hand to hand he would have vanquish'd
  thee!
Now my soul's palace is become a prison.
Ah, would she break from hence, that this my
  body   75
Might in the ground be closed up in rest!
For never henceforth shall I joy again;
Never, O never, shall I see more joy.
 Rich. I cannot weep, for all my body's
  moisture
Scarce serves to quench my furnace-burning
  heart;   80
Nor can my tongue unload my heart's great
  burthen,
For selfsame wind that I should speak withal
Is kindling coals that fires all my breast

And burns me up with flames that tears would
  quench.
To weep is to make less the depth of grief. 85
Tears, then, for babes; blows and revenge for
  me!
Richard, I bear thy name; I'll venge thy death
Or die renowned by attempting it.
 Edw. His name that valiant duke hath left
  with thee;
His dukedom and his chair with me is left. 90
 Rich. Nay, if thou be that princely eagle's
  bird,
Show thy descent by gazing 'gainst the sun;
For chair and dukedom, throne and kingdom
  say,
Either that is thine, or else thou wert not his.

 March. Enter *Warwick, Marquess Montague,*
    and their *Army*.

 War. How now, fair lords! What fare?
  What news abroad?   95
 Rich. Great Lord of Warwick, if we should
  recompt
Our baleful news and at each word's deliverance
Stab poniards in our flesh till all were told,
The words would add more anguish than the
  wounds.
O valiant lord, the Duke of York is slain! 100
 Edw. O Warwick, Warwick! that Plan-
  tagenet
Which held thee dearly as his soul's redemption
Is by the stern Lord Clifford done to death.
 War. Ten days ago I drown'd these news
  in tears;   104
And now, to add more measure to your woes,
I come to tell you things sith then befall'n.
After the bloody fray at Wakefield fought,
Where your brave father breath'd his latest
  gasp,
Tidings, as swiftly as the posts could run,
Were brought me of your loss and his depart.
I, then in London, keeper of the King,   111
Muster'd my soldiers, gathered flocks of friends,
And very well appointed, as I thought,
March'd toward Saint Alban's to intercept the
  Queen,
Bearing the King in my behalf along;   115
For by my scouts I was advertised
That she was coming with a full intent
To dash our late decree in parliament
Touching King Henry's oath and your succes-
  sion.   119
Short tale to make, we at Saint Alban's met,
Our battles join'd, and both sides fiercely
  fought;

But whether 'twas the coldness of the King,
Who look'd full gently on his warlike queen,
That robb'd my soldiers of their heated spleen,
Or whether 'twas report of her success,   125
Or more than common fear of Clifford's rigour,
Who thunders to his captives blood and death,
I cannot judge; but to conclude with truth,
Their weapons like to lightning came and went;
Our soldiers', like the night owl's lazy flight
Or like an idle thresher with a flail,   131
Fell gently down, as if they struck their friends.
I cheer'd them up with justice of our cause,
With promise of high pay and great rewards;
But all in vain; they had no heart to fight,
And we (in them) no hope to win the day;   136
So that we fled: the King unto the Queen;
Lord George your brother, Norfolk, and my-
self,
In haste, post-haste, are come to join with
you;
For in the marches here we heard you were,
Making another head to fight again.   141
   Edw. Where is the Duke of Norfolk, gentle
Warwick?
And when came George from Burgundy to
England?
   War. Some six miles off the Duke is with
his power;
And for your brother, he was lately sent   145
From your kind aunt, Duchess of Burgundy,
With aid of soldiers to this needful war.
   Rich. 'Twas odds belike when valiant War-
wick fled.
Oft have I heard his praises in pursuit,
But ne'er till now his scandal of retire.   150
   War. Nor now my scandal, Richard, dost
thou hear;
For thou shalt know this strong right hand of
mine
Can pluck the diadem from faint Henry's head
And wring the awful sceptre from his fist,
Were he as famous and as bold in war   155
As he is fam'd for mildness, peace, and prayer.
   Rich. I know it well, Lord Warwick. Blame
me not.
'Tis love I bear thy glories makes me speak.
But in this troublous time what's to be done?
Shall we go throw away our coats of steel   160
And wrap our bodies in black mourning gowns,
Numb'ring our Ave-Maries with our beads?
Or shall we on the helmets of our foes
Tell our devotion with revengeful arms?
If for the last, say 'Ay,' and to it, lords!   165
   War. Why, therefore Warwick came to seek
you out.

And therefore comes my brother Montague.
Attend me, lords. The proud insulting Queen,
With Clifford and the haught Northumber-
land,
And of their feather many moe proud birds,   170
Have wrought the easy-melting King like
wax.
He swore consent to your succession,
His oath enrolled in the parliament;
And now to London all the crew are gone,
To frustrate both his oath, and what beside   175
May make against the house of Lancaster.
Their power, I think, is thirty thousand strong.
Now if the help of Norfolk and myself
With all the friends that thou, brave Earl of
March,   179
Amongst the loving Welshmen canst procure,
Will but amount to five-and-twenty thousand,
Why, via! to London will we march amain,
And once again bestride our foaming steeds,
And once again cry 'Charge!' upon our foes,
But never once again turn back and fly.   185
   Rich. Ay, now methinks I hear great War-
wick speak.
Ne'er may he live to see a sunshine day
That cries, 'Retire!' if Warwick bid him stay.
   Edw. Lord Warwick, on thy shoulder will
I lean,   189
And when thou fail'st (as God forbid the hour!)
Must Edward fall, which peril heaven forfend!
   War. No longer Earl of March, but Duke of
York.
The next degree is England's royal throne;
For King of England shalt thou be proclaim'd
In every borough as we pass along;   195
And he that throws not up his cap for joy
Shall for the fault make forfeit of his head.
King Edward, valiant Richard, Montague,
Stay we no longer, dreaming of renown,
But sound the trumpets and about our task!
   Rich. Then, Clifford, were thy heart as hard
as steel,   201
As thou hast shown it flinty by thy deeds,
I come to pierce it or to give thee mine.
   Edw. Then strike up drums. God and Saint
George for us!

         Enter a *Messenger.*

   War. How now? What news?   205
   Mess. The Duke of Norfolk sends you word
by me
The Queen is coming with a puissant host,
And craves your company for speedy counsel.
   War. Why, then it sorts. Brave warriors,
let's away.   *Exeunt omnes.*

[Scene II. *Before York.*]

Flourish. Enter the *King*, the *Queen* [*Margaret*], *Clifford*, *Northumberland*, and *young Prince*, with *Drum* and *Trumpets*.

Queen. Welcome, my lord, to this brave town of York.
Yonder's the head of that arch-enemy
That sought to be encompass'd with your crown.
Doth not the object cheer your heart, my lord?
K. Hen. Ay, as the rocks cheer them that fear their wrack.   5
To see this sight it irks my very soul.
Withhold revenge, dear God! 'Tis not my fault,
Nor wittingly have I infring'd my vow.
Clif. My gracious liege, this too much lenity
And harmful pity must be laid aside.   10
To whom do lions cast their gentle looks?
Not to the beast that would usurp their den.
Whose hand is that the forest bear doth lick?
Not his that spoils her young before her face.
Who scapes the lurking serpent's mortal sting?
Not he that sets his foot upon her back.   15
The smallest worm will turn, being trodden on,
And doves will peck in safeguard of their brood.
Ambitious York did level at thy crown,
Thou smiling while he knit his angry brows. 20
He, but a duke, would have his son a king
And raise his issue like a loving sire;
Thou, being a king, blest with a goodly son,
Didst yield consent to disinherit him,
Which argued thee a most unloving father.   25
Unreasonable creatures feed their young;
And though man's face be fearful to their eyes,
Yet, in protection of their tender ones,
Who hath not seen them, even with those wings
Which sometime they have us'd in fearful flight,
Make war with him that climb'd unto their nest,   31
Offering their own lives in their young's defence?
For shame, my liege! Make them your precedent!
Were it not pity that this goodly boy
Should lose his birthright by his father's fault
And long hereafter say unto his child,   36
'What my great-grandfather and grandsire got
My careless father fondly gave away'?
Ah, what a shame were this! Look on the boy,
And let his manly face, which promiseth   40

Successful fortune, steel thy melting heart
To hold thine own and leave thine own with him.
K. Hen. Full well hath Clifford play'd the orator,
Inferring arguments of mighty force.
But, Clifford, tell me, didst thou never hear 45
That things ill got had ever bad success?
And happy always was it for that son
Whose father for his hoarding went to hell?
I'll leave my son my virtuous deeds behind,
And would my father had left me no more!   50
For all the rest is held at such a rate
As brings a thousandfold more care to keep
Than in possession any jot of pleasure.
Ah, cousin York, would thy best friends did know   54
How it doth grieve me that thy head is here!
Queen. My lord, cheer up your spirits. Our foes are nigh,
And this soft courage makes your followers faint.
You promis'd knighthood to our forward son.
Unsheathe your sword and dub him presently.
Edward, kneel down.   60
K. Hen. Edward Plantagenet, arise a knight,
And learn this lesson: Draw thy sword in right.
Prince. My gracious father, by your kingly leave,
I'll draw it as apparent to the crown
And in that quarrel use it to the death.   65
Clif. Why, that is spoken like a toward prince.

Enter a *Messenger.*

Mess. Royal commanders, be in readiness;
For with a band of thirty thousand men
Comes Warwick, backing of the Duke of York,
And in the towns, as they do march along,   70
Proclaims him King, and many fly to him.
Darraign your battle, for they are at hand.
Clif. I would your Highness would depart the field.
The Queen hath best success when you are absent.
Queen. Ay, good my lord, and leave us to our fortune.   75
K. Hen. Why, that's my fortune too. Therefore I'll stay.
North. Be it with resolution, then, to fight.
Prince. My royal father, cheer these noble lords
And hearten those that fight in your defence.
Unsheathe your sword, good father. Cry 'Saint George!'   80

March. Enter *Edward, Warwick, Richard, Clarence, Norfolk, Montague,* and *Soldiers.*

Edw. Now, perjur'd Henry, wilt thou kneel
for grace
And set thy diadem upon my head,
Or bide the mortal fortune of the field?
Queen. Go rate thy minions, proud insulting
boy!
Becomes it thee to be thus bold in terms   85
Before thy sovereign and thy lawful king?
Edw. I am his king, and he should bow his
knee.
I was adopted heir by his consent;
Since when, his oath is broke; for, as I hear,
You that are King, though he do wear the
crown,   90
Have caus'd him by new act of parliament
To blot out me and put his own son in.
Clif. And reason too!
Who should succeed the father but the son?
Rich. Are you there, butcher? O, I cannot
speak!   95
Clif. Ay, Crookback, here I stand to answer
thee,
Or any he, the proudest of thy sort.
Rich. 'Twas you that kill'd young Rutland,
was it not?
Clif. Ay, and old York, and yet not satis-
fied.
Rich. For God's sake, lords, give signal to
the fight.   100
War. What say'st thou, Henry? Wilt thou
yield the crown?
Queen. Why, how now, long-tongu'd War-
wick? Dare you speak?
When you and I met at Saint Alban's last,
Your legs did better service than your hands.
War. Then 'twas my turn to fly, and now
'tis thine.   105
Clif. You said so much before, and yet you
fled.
War. 'Twas not your valour, Clifford, drove
me thence.
North. No, nor your manhood that durst
make you stay.
Rich. Northumberland, I hold thee rever-
ently.   109
Break off the parley, for scarce I can refrain
The execution of my big-swol'n heart
Upon that Clifford, that cruel child-killer.
Clif. I slew thy father. Call'st thou him a
child?
Rich. Ay, like a dastard and a treacherous
coward,   114

As thou didst kill our tender brother Rutland!
But ere sun set I'll make thee curse the deed.
K. Hen. Have done with words, my lords,
and hear me speak.
Queen. Defy them then, or else hold close
thy lips.
K. Hen. I prithee give no limits to my
tongue.
I am a king, and privileg'd to speak.   120
Clif. My liege, the wound that bred this
meeting here
Cannot be cur'd by words. Therefore be still.
Rich. Then, executioner, unsheathe thy
sword.
By him that made us all, I am resolv'd   124
That Clifford's manhood lies upon his tongue.
Edw. Say, Henry, shall I have my right,
or no?
A thousand men have broke their fasts to-day
That ne'er shall dine unless thou yield the
crown.
War. If thou deny, their blood upon thy
head!
For York in justice puts his armour on.   130
Prince. If that be right which Warwick says
is right,
There is no wrong, but everything is right.
Rich. Whoever got thee, there thy mother
stands;
For well I wot thou hast thy mother's tongue.
Queen. But thou art neither like thy sire
nor dam,   135
But like a foul misshapen stigmatic,
Mark'd by the Destinies to be avoided,
As venom toads or lizards' dreadful stings.
Rich. Iron of Naples, hid with English gilt,
Whose father bears the title of a king   140
(As if a channel should be call'd the sea),
Sham'st thou not, knowing whence thou art
extraught,
To let thy tongue detect thy base-born heart?
Edw. A wisp of straw were worth a thousand
crowns,   144
To make this shameless callet know herself.
Helen of Greece was fairer far than thou,
Although thy husband may be Menelaus;
And ne'er was Agamemnon's brother wrong'd
By that false woman as this king by thee.
His father revell'd in the heart of France, 150
And tam'd the King, and made the Dauphin
stoop;
And had he match'd according to his state,
He might have kept that glory to this day;
But when he took a beggar to his bed   154
And grac'd thy poor sire with his bridal day,

Even then that sunshine brew'd a show'r for
  him
That wash'd his father's fortunes forth of
  France
And heap'd sedition on his crown at home.
For what hath broach'd this tumult but thy
  pride?   159
Hadst thou been meek, our title still had slept,
And we, in pity of the gentle King,
Had slipp'd our claim until another age.
  Clar. But when we saw our sunshine made
    thy spring
And that thy summer bred us no increase,
We set the axe to thy usurping root;   165
And though the edge hath something hit our-
  selves,
Yet know thou, since we have begun to strike,
We'll never leave till we have hewn thee down
Or bath'd thy growing with our heated bloods.
  Edw. And in this resolution I defy thee, 170
Not willing any longer conference,
Since thou deniest the gentle King to speak.
Sound trumpets! Let our bloody colours wave!
And either victory, or else a grave!
  Queen. Stay, Edward.   175
  Edw. No, wrangling woman, we'll no longer
    stay.
These words will cost ten thousand lives this
  day.   *Exeunt omnes.*

[Scene III. *A field of battle between Towton
  and Saxton, in Yorkshire.*]

Alarum. Excursions. Enter *Warwick.*

  War. Forspent with toil, as runners with a
    race,
I lay me down a little while to breathe;
For strokes receiv'd and many blows repaid
Have robb'd my strong-knit sinews of their
  strength,
And spite of spite needs must I rest awhile. 5

Enter *Edward*, running.

  Edw. Smile, gentle heaven! or strike, un-
    gentle death!
For this world frowns, and Edward's sun is
  clouded.
  War. How now, my lord? What hap?
    What hope of good?

Enter *Clarence.*

  Clar. Our hap is loss, our hope but sad
    despair!

Our ranks are broke and ruin follows us. 10
What counsel give you? Whither shall we fly?
  Edw. Bootless is flight. They follow us with
    wings,
And weak we are and cannot shun pursuit.

Enter *Richard.*

  Rich. Ah, Warwick, why hast thou with-
    drawn thyself?
Thy brother's blood the thirsty earth hath
  drunk,   15
Broach'd with the steely point of Clifford's
  lance;
And in the very pangs of death he cried,
Like to a dismal clangor heard from far,
'Warwick, revenge! Brother, revenge my
  death!'
So, underneath the belly of their steeds, 20
That stain'd their fetlocks in his smoking blood,
The noble gentleman gave up the ghost.
  War. Then let the earth be drunken with
    our blood!
I'll kill my horse, because I will not fly. 24
Why stand we like soft-hearted women here,
Wailing our losses, whiles the foe doth rage,
And look upon, as if the tragedy
Were play'd in jest by counterfeiting actors?
Here on my knee I vow to God above
I'll never pause again, never stand still, 30
Till either death hath clos'd these eyes of mine
Or fortune given me measure of revenge.
  Edw. O Warwick, I do bend my knee with
    thine
And in this vow do chain my soul to thine! 34
And ere my knee rise from the earth's cold face,
I throw my hands, mine eyes, my heart to thee,
Thou setter up and plucker down of kings,
Beseeching thee (if with thy will it stands)
That to my foes this body must be prey, 39
Yet that thy brazen gates of heaven may ope
And give sweet passage to my sinful soul!
Now, lords, take leave until we meet again,
Where'er it be, in heaven or in earth.
  Rich. Brother, give me thy hand; and,
    gentle Warwick,
Let me embrace thee in my weary arms. 45
I, that did never weep, now melt with woe
That winter should cut off our springtime so.
  War. Away, away! Once more, sweet lords,
    farewell.
  Clar. Yet let us all together to our troops,
And give them leave to fly that will not stay,
And call them pillars that will stand to us; 51
And, if we thrive, promise them such rewards
As victors wear at the Olympian games.

This may plant courage in their quailing
   breasts;
For yet is hope of life and victory.   55
Forslow no longer! Make we hence amain!
                          Exeunt.

[Scene IV. *Another part of the field.*]

Excursions. Enter *Richard* and *Clifford.*

Rich. Now, Clifford, I have singled thee
   alone.
Suppose this arm is for the Duke of York,
And this for Rutland — both bound to revenge,
Wert thou environ'd with a brazen wall.

Clif. Now, Richard, I am with thee here
   alone.   5
This is the hand that stabb'd thy father York,
And this the hand that slew thy brother Rut-
   land;
And here's the heart that triumphs in their
   death
And cheers these hands that slew thy sire and
   brother
To execute the like upon thyself.   10
And so have at thee!

They fight. Warwick comes. Clifford flies.

Rich. Nay, Warwick, single out some other
   chase,
For I myself will hunt this wolf to death.
                          Exeunt.

[Scene V. *Another part of the field.*]

Alarum. Enter *King Henry* alone.

K. Hen. This battle fares like to the morn-
   ing's war,
When dying clouds contend with growing light,
What time the shepherd, blowing of his nails,
Can neither call it perfect day nor night.
Now sways it this way, like a mighty sea   5
Forc'd by the tide to combat with the wind;
Now sways it that way, like the selfsame sea
Forc'd to retire by fury of the wind.
Sometime the flood prevails, and then the wind;
Now one the better, then another best;   10
Both tugging to be victors, breast to breast,
Yet neither conqueror nor conquered.
So is the equal poise of this fell war.
Here on this molehill will I sit me down.
To whom God will, there be the victory!   15

For Margaret my queen, and Clifford too,
Have chid me from the battle, swearing both
They prosper best of all when I am thence.
Would I were dead, if God's good will were so!
For what is in this world but grief and woe?
O God! methinks it were a happy life   21
To be no better than a homely swain;
To sit upon a hill, as I do now,
To carve out dials quaintly, point by point,
Thereby to see the minutes how they run —
How many makes the hour full complete,   26
How many hours brings about the day,
How many days will finish up the year,
How many years a mortal man may live;
When this is known, then to divide the times —
So many hours must I tend my flock,   31
So many hours must I take my rest,
So many hours must I contemplate,
So many hours must I sport myself;
So many days my ewes have been with young,
So many weeks ere the poor fools will ean,   36
So many months ere I shall shear the fleece.
So minutes, hours, days, weeks, months, and
   years,
Pass'd over to the end they were created,
Would bring white hairs unto a quiet grave,
Ah, what a life were this! how sweet! how
   lovely!   41
Gives not the hawthorn bush a sweeter shade
To shepherds looking on their silly sheep
Than doth a rich embroider'd canopy
To kings that fear their subjects' treachery?
O yes, it doth! a thousandfold it doth!   46
And to conclude, the shepherd's homely curds,
His cold thin drink out of his leather bottle,
His wonted sleep under a fresh tree's shade,
All which secure and sweetly he enjoys,   50
Is far beyond a prince's delicates,
His viands sparkling in a golden cup,
His body couched in a curious bed,
When care, mistrust, and treason waits on him.

Alarum. Enter a *Son* that hath kill'd his Father,
   at one door, [dragging in the body].

Son. Ill blows the wind that profits nobody.
This man whom hand to hand I slew in fight   56
May be possessed with some store of crowns;
And I that, haply, take them from him now
May yet, ere night, yield both my life and them
To some man else, as this dead man doth me.
Who's this? O God! It is my father's face,   61
Whom in this conflict I, unawares, have kill'd.
O heavy times, begetting such events!
From London by the King was I press'd forth;
My father, being the Earl of Warwick's man,

Came on the part of York, press'd by his
 master;   66
And I, who at his hands receiv'd my life,
Have by my hands of life bereaved him.
Pardon me, God! I knew not what I did.
And pardon, father, for I knew not thee! 70
My tears shall wipe away these bloody marks;
And no more words till they have flow'd their
 fill.
 K. Hen. O piteous spectacle! O bloody
 times!
Whiles lions war and battle for their dens,
Poor harmless lambs abide their enmity. 75
Weep, wretched man! I'll aid thee tear for
 tear;
And let our hearts and eyes, like civil war,
Be blind with tears and break o'ercharg'd with
 grief.

*Enter, at another door, a Father that hath
kill'd his Son, bearing of his Son['s body].*

 Father. Thou that so stoutly hast resisted
 me,
Give me thy gold, if thou hast any gold; 80
For I have bought it with an hundred blows.
But let me see. Is this our foeman's face?
Ah, no, no, no! It is mine only son!
Ah, boy, if any life be left in thee,
Throw up thine eye! See, see what show'rs
 arise,   85
Blown with the windy tempest of my heart
Upon thy wounds, that kills mine eye and heart!
O, pity, God, this miserable age!
What stratagems, how fell, how butcherly,
Erroneous, mutinous, and unnatural, 90
This deadly quarrel daily doth beget!
O boy! thy father gave thee life too soon,
And hath bereft thee of thy life too late.
 K. Hen. Woe above woe! grief more than
 common grief!
O that my death would stay these ruthful
 deeds!   95
O, pity, pity, gentle heaven, pity!
The red rose and the white are on his face,
The fatal colours of our striving houses.
The one his purple blood right well resembles;
The other his pale cheeks, methinks, presenteth.
Wither one rose, and let the other flourish! 101
If you contend, a thousand lives must wither.
 Son. How will my mother for a father's
 death
Take on with me, and ne'er be satisfied!
 Father. How will my wife for slaughter of
 my son   105
Shed seas of tears, and ne'er be satisfied!

 K. Hen. How will the country for these
 woful chances
Misthink the King, and not be satisfied!
 Son. Was ever son so ru'd a father's death?
 Father. Was ever father so bemoan'd his son?
 K. Hen. Was ever king so griev'd for sub-
 ject's woe?   111
Much is your sorrow; mine ten times so much.
 Son. I'll bear thee hence, where I may weep
 my fill.   *Exit [with the body].*
 Father. These arms of mine shall be thy
 winding sheet;   114
My heart, sweet boy, shall be thy sepulchre,
For from my heart thine image ne'er shall go.
My sighing breast shall be thy funeral bell;
And so obsequious will thy father be,
Even for the loss of thee, having no more,
As Priam was for all his valiant sons. 120
I'll bear thee hence, and let them fight that will,
For I have murthered where I should not kill.
         Exit [with the body].
 K. Hen. Sad-hearted men, much overgone
 with care,
Here sits a king more woful than you are.

*Alarums. Excursions. Enter the Queen
[Margaret], the Prince, and Exeter.*

 Prince. Fly, father, fly! for all your friends
 are fled   125
And Warwick rages like a chafed bull.
Away! for death doth hold us in pursuit.
 Queen. Mount you, my lord. Towards Ber-
 wick post amain.
Edward and Richard, like a brace of greyhounds
Having the fearful flying hare in sight, 130
With fiery eyes, sparkling for very wrath,
And bloody steel grasp'd in their ireful hands,
Are at our backs; and therefore hence amain!
 Exe. Away! for vengeance comes along with
 them.
Nay, stay not to expostulate; make speed! 135
Or else come after. I'll away before.
 K. Hen. Nay, take me with thee, good sweet
 Exeter.
Not that I fear to stay, but love to go
Whither the Queen intends. Forward, away!
          Exeunt.

[Scene VI. *Another part of the field.*]

A loud alarum. Enter Clifford, wounded.

 Clif. Here burns my candle out; ay, here
 it dies,
Which, whiles it lasted, gave King Henry light.

O Lancaster! I fear thy overthrow
More than my body's parting with my soul.
My love and fear glu'd many friends to thee, 5
And now I fall, the tough commixture melts,
Impairing Henry, strength'ning misproud York.
The common people swarm like summer flies;
And whither fly the gnats but to the sun?
And who shines now but Henry's enemies? 10
O Phœbus, hadst thou never given consent
That Phaëton should check thy fiery steeds,
Thy burning car never had scorch'd the earth!
And, Henry, hadst thou sway'd as kings
      should do,
Or as thy father and his father did, 15
Giving no ground unto the house of York,
They never then had sprung like summer flies;
I and ten thousand in this luckless realm
Had left no mourning widows for our death,
And thou this day hadst kept thy chair in
      peace. 20
For what doth cherish weeds but gentle air?
And what makes robbers bold but too much
      lenity?
Bootless are plaints and cureless are my
      wounds;
No way to fly, nor strength to hold out flight; 25
The foe is merciless and will not pity,
For at their hands I have deserv'd no pity.
The air hath got into my deadly wounds
And much effuse of blood doth make me faint.
Come, York and Richard, Warwick and the
      rest. 29
I stabb'd your fathers' bosoms; split my
      breast.   [*Faints.*]

Alarum and retreat. Enter *Edward, Warwick,*
Richard, Montague, and *Clarence,* and *Soldiers.*

  Edw. Now breathe we, lords. Good fortune
      bids us pause
And smooth the frowns of war with peaceful
      looks.
Some troops pursue the bloody-minded Queen
That led calm Henry, though he were a king,
As doth a sail, fill'd with a fretting gust, 35
Command an argosy to stem the waves.
But think you, lords, that Clifford fled with
      them?
  War. No, 'tis impossible he should escape;
For, though before his face I speak the words,
Your brother Richard mark'd him for the
      grave; 40
And wheresoe'er he is, he's surely dead.
                    Clifford groans and dies.
  Edw. Whose soul is that which takes her
      heavy leave?

  Rich. A deadly groan, like life and death's
      departing.
  Edw. See who it is; and now the battle's
      ended,
If friend or foe, let him be gently us'd. 45
  Rich. Revoke that doom of mercy, for 'tis
      Clifford,
Who not contented that he lopp'd the branch
In hewing Rutland when his leaves put forth,
But set his murth'ring knife unto the root
From whence that tender spray did sweetly
      spring: 50
I mean our princely father, Duke of York.
  War. From off the gates of York fetch down
      the head,
Your father's head, which Clifford placed there;
Instead whereof let this supply the room.
Measure for measure must be answered. 55
  Edw. Bring forth that fatal screech owl to
      our house,
That nothing sung but death to us and ours.
Now death shall stop his dismal threat'ning
      sound
And his ill-boding tongue no more shall speak.
  War. I think his understanding is bereft. 60
Speak, Clifford, dost thou know who speaks to
      thee?
Dark cloudy death o'ershades his beams of
      life,
And he nor sees, nor hears us what we say.
  Rich. O, would he did! and so, perhaps, he
      doth.
'Tis but his policy to counterfeit, 65
Because he would avoid such bitter taunts
Which in the time of death he gave our father.
  Clar. If so thou think'st, vex him with eager
      words.
  Rich. Clifford, ask mercy, and obtain no
      grace. 69
  Edw. Clifford, repent in bootless penitence.
  War. Clifford, devise excuses for thy faults.
  Clar. While we devise fell tortures for thy
      faults.
  Rich. Thou didst love York, and I am son
      to York.
  Edw. Thou pitied'st Rutland; I will pity
      thee.
  Clar. Where's Captain Margaret, to fence
      you now? 75
  War. They mock thee, Clifford. Swear as
      thou wast wont.
  Rich. What, not an oath? Nay, then the
      world goes hard
When Clifford cannot spare his friends an oath.
I know by that he's dead; and, by my soul,

If this right hand would buy two hours' life,
That I (in all despite) might rail at him,   81
This hand should chop it off, and with the
   issuing blood
Stifle the villain whose unstanched thirst
York and young Rutland could not satisfy.

War. Ay, but he's dead. Off with the trai-
   tor's head   85
And rear it in the place your father's stands.
And now to London with triumphant march,
There to be crowned England's royal King;
From whence shall Warwick cut the sea to
   France
And ask the Lady Bona for thy queen.   90
So shalt thou sinew both these lands together;
And, having France thy friend, thou shalt not
   dread
The scatt'red foe that hopes to rise again;
For though they cannot greatly sting to hurt,

Yet look to have them buzz to offend thine ears.
First will I see the coronation,   96
And then to Brittany I'll cross the sea
To effect this marriage, so it please my lord.

Edw. Even as thou wilt, sweet Warwick, let
   it be;
For in thy shoulder do I build my seat,   100
And never will I undertake the thing
Wherein thy counsel and consent is wanting.
Richard, I will create thee Duke of Gloucester;
And George, of Clarence. Warwick, as ourself,
Shall do and undo as him pleaseth best.   105

Rich. Let me be Duke of Clarence, George
   of Gloucester;
For Gloucester's dukedom is too ominous.

War. Tut, that's a foolish observation!
Richard, be Duke of Gloucester. Now to
   London   109
To see these honours in possession.   *Exeunt.*

[ACT III. Scene I. *A forest in the North of England.*]

Enter *Sinklo* and *Humfrey* (two *Keepers*) with
   crossbows in their hands.

Sink. Under this thick-grown brake we'll
   shroud ourselves,
For through this laund anon the deer will come,
And in this covert will we make our stand,
Culling the principal of all the deer.

Hum. I'll stay above the hill, so both may
   shoot.   5

Sink. That cannot be; the noise of thy
   crossbow
Will scare the herd, and so my shoot is lost.
Here stand we both and aim we at the best;
And, for the time shall not seem tedious,
I'll tell thee what befell me on a day   10
In this self place where now we mean to stand.

Hum. Here comes a man. Let's stay till he
   be past.

Enter *King Henry*, disguis'd, with a
prayer book.

K. Hen. From Scotland am I stol'n, even of
   pure love,
To greet mine own land with my wishful sight.
No, Harry, Harry, 'tis no land of thine!   15
Thy place is fill'd, thy sceptre wrung from thee,
Thy balm wash'd off wherewith thou wast
   anointed.
No bending knee will call thee Cæsar now,
No humble suitors press to speak for right:
No, not a man comes for redress of thee;   20
For how can I help them, and not myself?

Sink. Ay, here's a deer whose skin's a
   keeper's fee!
This is the quondam king. Let's seize upon
   him.

K. Hen. Let me embrace thee, sour adversity,
For wise men say it is the wisest course.   25

Hum. Why linger we? Let us lay hands
   upon him.

Sink. Forbear awhile. We'll hear a little
   more.

K. Hen. My queen and son are gone to
   France for aid;
And, as I hear, the great commanding Warwick
Is thither gone to crave the French king's sister
To wife for Edward. If this news be true,   31
Poor queen and son, your labour is but lost;
For Warwick is a subtle orator
And Lewis a prince soon won with moving
   words.
By this account, then, Margaret may win him;
For she's a woman to be pitied much.   36
Her sighs will make a batt'ry in his breast;
Her tears will pierce into a marble heart;
The tiger will be mild whiles she doth mourn,
And Nero will be tainted with remorse   40
To hear and see her plaints, her brinish tears.
Ay, but she's come to beg; Warwick, to give;
She on his left side, craving aid for Henry;
He on his right, asking a wife for Edward.
She weeps, and says her Henry is depos'd;   45
He smiles, and says his Edward is install'd;

That she (poor wretch) for grief can speak no
    more,
Whiles Warwick tells his title, smooths the
    wrong,
Inferreth arguments of mighty strength,
And in conclusion wins the king from her   50
With promise of his sister, and what else,
To strengthen and support King Edward's
    place.
O Margaret, thus 'twill be! and thou (poor
    soul)
Art then forsaken, as thou went'st forlorn!
  Hum. Say, what art thou that talk'st of
    kings and queens?   55
  K. Hen. More than I seem, and less than I
    was born to:
A man at least, for less I should not be;
And men may talk of kings, and why not I?
  Hum. Ay, but thou talk'st as if thou wert a
    king.
  K. Hen. Why, so I am (in mind), and that's
    enough.   60
  Hum. But if thou be a king, where is thy
    crown?
  K. Hen. My crown is in my heart, not on
    my head;
Not deck'd with diamonds and Indian stones,
Nor to be seen. My crown is call'd content;
A crown it is that seldom kings enjoy.   65
  Hum. Well, if you be a king crown'd with
    content,
Your crown content and you must be contented
To go along with us; for, as we think,
You are the king King Edward hath depos'd;
And we his subjects, sworn in all allegiance, 70
Will apprehend you as his enemy.
  K. Hen. But did you never swear, and break
    an oath?
  Hum. No, never such an oath; nor will not
    now.
  K. Hen. Where did you dwell when I was
    King of England?
  Hum. Here in this country where we now
    remain.   75
  K. Hen. I was anointed king at nine months
    old;
My father and my grandfather were kings;
And you were sworn true subjects unto me;
And tell me then, have you not broke your
    oaths?
  Sink. No;   80
For we were subjects but while you were king.
  K. Hen. Why, am I dead? Do I not breathe
    a man?
Ah, simple men, you know not what you swear!

Look, as I blow this feather from my face
And as the air blows it to me again,   85
Obeying with my wind when I do blow
And yielding to another when it blows,
Commanded always by the greater gust —
Such is the lightness of you common men.   89
But do not break your oaths; for of that sin
My mild entreaty shall not make you guilty.
Go where you will, the King shall be com-
    manded;
And be you kings. Command, and I'll obey.
  Sink. We are true subjects to the king, King
    Edward.
  K. Hen. So would you be again to Henry 95
If he were seated as King Edward is.
  Sink. We charge you, in God's name and
    the King's,
To go with us unto the officers.
  K. Hen. In God's name, lead. Your king's
    name be obey'd;   99
And what God will, that let your king perform;
And what he will, I humbly yield unto.
                    Exeunt.

[Scene II. *London. The Palace.*]

Enter *King Edward,* [*Richard of*] *Gloucester,*
    Clarence, Lady Grey [*a widow*].

  K. Edw. Brother of Gloucester, at Saint
    Alban's field
This lady's husband, Sir Richard Grey, was
    slain,
His lands then seiz'd on by the conqueror.
Her suit is now to repossess those lands;
Which we in justice cannot well deny,   5
Because in quarrel of the house of York
The worthy gentleman did lose his life.
  Rich. Your Highness shall do well to grant
    her suit.
It were dishonour to deny it her.
  K. Edw. It were no less; but yet I'll make
    a pause.   10
  Rich. [*aside to Clarence*] Yea, is it so?
I see the lady hath a thing to grant
Before the King will grant her humble suit.
  Clar. [*aside to Richard*] He knows the game.
    How true he keeps the wind!
  Rich. [*aside to Clarence*] Silence!   15
  K. Edw. Widow, we will consider of your
    suit;
And come some other time to know our mind
  Widow. Right gracious lord, I cannot brook
    delay.

May it please your Highness to resolve me now,
And what your pleasure is shall satisfy me. 20
Rich. [*aside*] Ay, widow? Then I'll warrant
you all your lands
An if what pleases him shall pleasure you.
Fight closer or, good faith, you'll catch a blow.
Clar. [*aside to Richard*] I fear her not, unless
she chance to fall.
Rich. [*aside to Clarence*] God forbid that!
for he'll take vantages. 25
K. Edw. How many children hast thou,
widow? Tell me.
Clar. [*aside to Richard*] I think he means to
beg a child of her.
Rich. [*aside to Clarence*] Nay, whip me then!
He'll rather give her two.
Widow. Three, my most gracious lord.
Rich. [*aside*] You shall have four if you'll be
rul'd by him. 30
K. Edw. 'Twere pity they should lose their
father's lands.
Widow. Be pitiful, dread lord, and grant it
then.
K. Edw. Lords, give us leave. I'll try this
widow's wit.
Rich. [*aside*] Ay, good leave have you; for
you will have leave 34
Till youth take leave and leave you to the
crutch. [*Retires with Clarence.*]
K. Edw. Now tell me, madam, do you love
your children?
Widow. Ay, full as dearly as I love myself.
K. Edw. And would you not do much to do
them good?
Widow. To do them good I would sustain
some harm.
K. Edw. Then get your husband's lands, to
do them good. 40
Widow. Therefore I came unto your Majesty.
K. Edw. I'll tell you how these lands are to
be got.
Widow. So shall you bind me to your Highness' service.
K. Edw. What service wilt thou do me if I
give them?
Widow. What you command that rests in
me to do. 45
K. Edw. But you will take exceptions to my
boon.
Widow. No, gracious lord, except I cannot
do it.
K. Edw. Ay, but thou canst do what I mean
to ask.
Widow. Why, then I will do what your Grace
commands.

Rich. [*aside to Clarence*] He plies her hard,
and much rain wears the marble. 50
Clar. [*aside to Richard*] As red as fire? Nay
then, her wax must melt.
Widow. Why stops my lord? Shall I not
hear my task?
K. Edw. An easy task. 'Tis but to love a
king.
Widow. That's soon perform'd, because I am
a subject.
K. Edw. Why then, thy husband's lands I
freely give thee. 55
Widow. I take my leave with many thousand
thanks.
Rich. [*aside to Clarence*] The match is made.
She seals it with a cursy.
K. Edw. But stay thee. 'Tis the fruits of
love I mean.
Widow. The fruits of love I mean, my loving
liege. 59
K. Edw. Ay, but, I fear me, in another sense.
What love, think'st thou, I sue so much to get?
Widow. My love till death, my humble
thanks, my prayers;
That love which virtue begs and virtue grants.
K. Edw. No, by my troth, I did not mean
such love.
Widow. Why, then you mean not as I
thought you did. 65
K. Edw. But now you partly may perceive
my mind.
Widow. My mind will never grant what I
perceive
Your Highness aims at, if I aim aright.
K. Edw. To tell thee plain, I aim to lie with
thee.
Widow. To tell you plain, I had rather lie in
prison. 70
K. Edw. Why, then thou shalt not have thy
husband's lands.
Widow. Why, then mine honesty shall be my
dower;
For by that loss I will not purchase them.
K. Edw. Therein thou wrong'st thy children
mightily.
Widow. Herein your Highness wrongs both
them and me. 75
But, mighty lord, this merry inclination
Accords not with the sadness of my suit.
Please you dismiss me, either with ay or no.
K. Edw. Ay, if thou wilt say ay to my request;
No, if thou dost say no to my demand. 80
Widow. Then, no, my lord. My suit is at
an end.

Rich. [*aside to Clarence*] The widow likes him
    not ; she knits her brows.
Clar. [*aside to Richard*] He is the bluntest
    wooer in Christendom.
K. Edw. [*aside*] Her looks do argue her re-
    plete with modesty ;
Her words do show her wit incomparable ;   85
All her perfections challenge sovereignty.
One way or other, she is for a king ;
And she shall be my love, or else my queen. —
Say that King Edward take thee for his queen ?
Widow. 'Tis better said than done, my gra-
    cious lord.   90
I am a subject fit to jest withal,
But far unfit to be a sovereign.
K. Edw. Sweet widow, by my state I swear
    to thee
I speak no more than what my soul intends ;
And that is, to enjoy thee for my love.   95
Widow. And that is more than I will yield
    unto.
I know I am too mean to be your queen,
And yet too good to be your concubine.
K. Edw. You cavil, widow. I did mean my
    queen.
Widow. 'Twill grieve your Grace my sons
    should call you father.   100
K. Edw. No more than when my daughters
    call thee mother.
Thou art a widow, and thou hast some chil-
    dren ;
And, by God's Mother, I, being but a bachelor,
Have other some. Why, 'tis a happy thing
To be the father unto many sons.   105
Answer no more, for thou shalt be my queen.
Rich. [*aside to Clarence*] The ghostly father
    now hath done his shrift.
Clar. [*aside to Richard*] When he was made
    a shriver, 'twas for shift.
K. Edw. Brothers, you muse what chat we
    two have had.
Rich. The widow likes it not, for she looks
    very sad.   110
K. Edw. You'ld think it strange if I should
    marry her.
Clar. To who, my lord ?
K. Edw.   Why, Clarence, to myself.
Rich. That would be ten days' wonder at the
    least.
Clar. That's a day longer than a wonder
    lasts.   114
Rich. By so much is the wonder in extremes.
K. Edw. Well, jest on, brothers. I can tell
    you both
Her suit is granted for her husband's lands.

Enter a *Nobleman*.

Nob. My gracious lord, Henry your foe is
    taken
And brought as prisoner to your palace gate.
K. Edw. See that he be convey'd unto the
    Tower.   120
And go we, brothers, to the man that took him
To question of his apprehension.
Widow, go you along. Lords, use her hon-
    ourably.   *Exeunt. Manet Richard.*
Rich. Ay, Edward will use women hon-
    ourably !   124
Would he were wasted, marrow, bones, and all,
That from his loins no hopeful branch may
    spring
To cross me from the golden time I look for !
And yet, between my soul's desire and me —
The lustful Edward's title buried —   129
Is Clarence, Henry, and his son young Edward,
And all the unlook'd-for issue of their bodies,
To take their rooms ere I can place myself.
A cold premeditation for my purpose !
Why, then I do but dream on sovereignty,
Like one that stands upon a promontory   135
And spies a far-off shore where he would tread,
Wishing his foot were equal with his eye,
And chides the sea that sunders him from
    thence,
Saying he'll lade it dry to have his way :
So do I wish the crown, being so far off ;   140
And so I chide the means that keeps me from it,
And so, I say, I'll cut the causes off,
Flattering me with impossibilities.
My eye's too quick, my heart o'erweens too
    much,   144
Unless my hand and strength could equal them.
Well, say there is no kingdom then for Richard :
What other pleasure can the world afford ?
I'll make my heaven in a lady's lap
And deck my body in gay ornaments
And witch sweet ladies with my words and
    looks.   150
O miserable thought ! and more unlikely
Than to accomplish twenty golden crowns !
Why, love forswore me in my mother's womb ;
And, for I should not deal in her soft laws, 154
She did corrupt frail nature with some bribe
To shrink mine arm up like a wither'd shrub ;
To make an envious mountain on my back,
Where sits deformity to mock my body ;
To shape my legs of an unequal size ;
To disproportion me in every part,   160
Like to a chaos, or an unlick'd bear-whelp,
That carries no impression like the dam.

And am I then a man to be belov'd?
O monstrous fault to harbour such a thought!
Then, since this earth affords no joy to me 165
But to command, to check, to o'erbear such
As are of better person than myself,
I'll make my heaven to dream upon the crown
And, whiles I live, t' account this world but hell
Until my misshap'd trunk that bears this head
Be round impaled with a glorious crown. 171
And yet I know not how to get the crown,
For many lives stand between me and home;
And I — like one lost in a thorny wood,
That rents the thorns and is rent with the
thorns, 175
Seeking a way and straying from the way,
Not knowing how to find the open air
But toiling desperately to find it out —
Torment myself to catch the English crown;
And from that torment I will free myself 180
Or hew my way out with a bloody axe.
Why, I can smile, and murther whiles I smile,
And cry 'Content!' to that which grieves my
heart,
And wet my cheeks with artifi̇cial tears,
And frame my face to all occasions. 185
I'll drown more sailors than the mermaid shall;
I'll slay more gazers than the basilisk;
I'll play the orator as well as Nestor,
Deceive more slily than Ulysses could,
And, like a Sinon, take another Troy. 190
I can add colours to the chameleon,
Change shapes with Proteus for advantages,
And set the murtherous Machiavel to school.
Can I do this, and cannot get a crown?
Tut, were it farther off, I'll pluck it down. 195
Exit.

[Scene III. *France. The* King's *Palace.*]

Flourish. Enter *Lewis the French King,* his
sister *Bona,* his *Admiral,* call'd *Bourbon; Prince
Edward, Queen Margaret,* and the *Earl of Oxford. Lewis* sits, and riseth up again.

Lewis. Fair Queen of England, worthy Mar-
garet,
Sit down with us. It ill befits thy state
And birth that thou shouldst stand while Lewis
doth sit.
Marg. No, mighty King of France. Now
Margaret 4
Must strike her sail, and learn awhile to serve
Where kings command. I was, I must confess,
Great Albion's Queen in former golden days;
But now mischance hath trod my title down

And with dishonour laid me on the ground,
Where I must take like seat unto my fortune
And to my humble seat conform myself. 11
Lewis. Why, say, fair queen, whence springs
this deep despair?
Marg. From such a cause as fills mine eyes
with tears
And stops my tongue, while heart is drown'd in
cares.
Lewis. Whate'er it be, be thou still like
thyself, 15
And sit thee by our side. (*Seats her by him.*)
Yield not thy neck
To fortune's yoke, but let thy dauntless mind
Still ride in triumph over all mischance.
Be plain, Queen Margaret, and tell thy grief.
It shall be eas'd if France can yield relief. 20
Marg. Those gracious words revive my
drooping thoughts
And give my tongue-tied sorrows leave to
speak.
Now therefore be it known to noble Lewis
That Henry, sole possessor of my love,
Is, of a king, become a banish'd man 25
And forc'd to live in Scotland a forlorn;
While proud ambitious Edward Duke of York
Usurps the regal title and the seat
Of England's true anointed lawful King.
This is the cause that I, poor Margaret, 30
With this my son, Prince Edward, Henry's heir,
Am come to crave thy just and lawful aid;
And if thou fail us, all our hope is done.
Scotland hath will to help, but cannot help;
Our people and our peers are both misled, 35
Our treasure seiz'd, our soldiers put to flight,
And (as thou seest) ourselves in heavy plight.
Lewis. Renowned queen, with patience calm
the storm
While we bethink a means to break it off.
Marg. The more we stay, the stronger grows
our foe. 40
Lewis. The more I stay, the more I'll suc-
cour thee.
Marg. O, but impatience waiteth on true
sorrow.
And see where comes the breeder of my sorrow!

Enter *Warwick.*

Lewis. What's he approacheth boldly to our
presence?
Marg. Our Earl of Warwick, Edward's greatest friend. 45
Lewis. Welcome, brave Warwick! What
brings thee to France?
He descends. She ariseth.

298

Marg. [*aside*] Ay, now begins a second storm
   to rise;
For this is he that moves both wind and tide.
  War. From worthy Edward, King of Albion,
My lord and sovereign and thy vowed friend,
I come, in kindness and unfeigned love,   51
First to do greetings to thy royal person,
And then to crave a league of amity,
And lastly to confirm that amity
With nuptial knot, if thou vouchsafe to grant
That virtuous Lady Bona, thy fair sister,   56
To England's King in lawful marriage.
  Marg. [*aside*] If that go forward, Henry's
   hope is done.
  War. (*speaking to Bona*) And, gracious
   madam, in our king's behalf,   59
I am commanded, with your leave and favour,
Humbly to kiss your hand, and with my tongue
To tell the passion of my sovereign's heart;
Where fame, late ent'ring at his heedful ears,
Hath plac'd thy beauty's image and thy virtue.
  Marg. King Lewis, and Lady Bona, hear me
   speak   65
Before you answer Warwick. His demand
Springs not from Edward's well-meant honest
   love,
But from deceit, bred by necessity;
For how can tyrants safely govern home
Unless abroad they purchase great alliance?   70
To prove him tyrant this reason may suffice,
That Henry liveth still; but were he dead,
Yet here Prince Edward stands, King Henry's
   son.
Look, therefore, Lewis, that by this league and
   marriage   74
Thou draw not on thy danger and dishonour;
For though usurpers sway the rule awhile,
Yet heav'ns are just and time suppresseth
   wrongs.
  War. Injurious Margaret!
  Prince Edw.   And why not Queen?
  War. Because thy father Henry did usurp,
And thou no more art Prince than she is
   Queen.   80
  Oxf. Then Warwick disannuls great John of
   Gaunt,
Which did subdue the greatest part of Spain;
And after John of Gaunt, Henry the Fourth,
Whose wisdom was a mirror to the wisest;
And after that wise prince, Henry the Fifth,
Who by his prowess conquered all France.   86
From these our Henry lineally descends.
  War. Oxford, how haps it in this smooth
   discourse
You told not how Henry the Sixth hath lost

All that which Henry the Fifth had gotten?
Methinks these peers of France should smile
   at that.   91
But for the rest: you tell a pedigree
Of threescore and two years — a silly time
To make prescription for a kingdom's worth.
  Oxf. Why, Warwick, canst thou speak
   against thy liege,   95
Whom thou obeyed'st thirty and six years,
And not bewray thy treason with a blush?
  War. Can Oxford, that did ever fence the
   right,
Now buckler falsehood with a pedigree?
For shame! Leave Henry and call Edward
   king.   100
  Oxf. Call him my king by whose injurious
   doom
My elder brother, the Lord Aubrey Vere,
Was done to death? and more than so, my
   father,
Even in the downfall of his mellow'd years,
When nature brought him to the door of death?
No, Warwick, no! While life upholds this arm,
This arm upholds the house of Lancaster.
  War. And I the house of York.
  Lewis. Queen Margaret, Prince Edward, and
   Oxford,
Vouchsafe at our request to stand aside   110
While I use further conference with Warwick.
               They stand aloof.
  Marg. Heavens grant that Warwick's words
   bewitch him not!
  Lewis. Now, Warwick, tell me, even upon
   thy conscience,
Is Edward your true king? For I were loath
To link with him that were not lawful chosen.
  War. Thereon I pawn my credit and mine
   honour.   116
  Lewis. But is he gracious in the people's eye?
  War. The more that Henry was unfortunate.
  Lewis. Then further: all dissembling set
   aside,
Tell me for truth the measure of his love   120
Unto our sister Bona.
  War.   Such it seems
As may beseem a monarch like himself.
Myself have often heard him say and swear
That this his love was an eternal plant,
Whereof the root was fix'd in virtue's ground,
The leaves and fruit maintain'd with beauty's
   sun,   126
Exempt from envy, but not from disdain,
Unless the Lady Bona quit his pain.
  Lewis. Now, sister, let us hear your firm
   resolve.

Bona. Your grant, or your denial, shall be
mine.   130
(*Speaks to Warwick.*) Yet I confess that often
ere this day,
When I have heard your king's desert re-
counted,
Mine ear hath tempted judgment to desire.
    Lewis. Then, Warwick, thus: our sister
shall be Edward's,
And now forthwith shall articles be drawn   135
Touching the jointure that your king must
make,
Which with her dowry shall be counterpois'd.
Draw near, Queen Margaret, and be a witness
That Bona shall be wife to the English king.
    Prince Edw. To Edward, but not to the
English king.   140
    Marg. Deceitful Warwick, it was thy device
By this alliance to make void my suit!
Before thy coming Lewis was Henry's friend.
    Lewis. And still is friend to him, and Mar-
garet.
But if your title to the crown be weak,   145
As may appear by Edward's good success,
Then 'tis but reason that I be releas'd
From giving aid which late I promised.
Yet shall you have all kindness at my hand
That your estate requires and mine can yield.
    War. Henry now lives in Scotland at his ease,
Where having nothing, nothing can he lose.
And as for you yourself, our quondam queen,
You have a father able to maintain you,
And better 'twere you troubled him than
France.   155
    Marg. Peace, impudent and shameless War-
wick! peace,
Proud setter up and puller down of kings!
I will not hence till with my talk and tears
(Both full of truth) I make King Lewis be-
hold   159
Thy sly conveyance and thy lord's false love;
For both of you are birds of selfsame feather.
                        Post blowing a horn within.
    Lewis. Warwick, this is some post to us or
thee.

                    Enter the *Post.*

    Post. (*speaks to Warwick*) My Lord Ambas-
sador, these letters are for you,
Sent from your brother, Marquess Montague;
(*To Lewis*) These from our king unto your
Majesty;   165
(*To Margaret*) And, madam, these for you:
from whom I know not.
                        They all read their letters.

    Oxf. I like it well that our fair queen and
mistress
Smiles at her news, while Warwick frowns at
his.
    Prince Edw. Nay, mark how Lewis stamps
as he were nettled.
I hope all's for the best.   170
    Lewis. Warwick, what are thy news? and
yours, fair queen?
    Marg. Mine such as fill my heart with un-
hop'd joys.
    War. Mine full of sorrow and heart's dis-
content.
    Lewis. What? Has your king married the
Lady Grey?
And now, to soothe your forgery and his,   175
Sends me a paper to persuade me patience?
Is this th' alliance that he seeks with France?
Dare he presume to scorn us in this manner?
    Marg. I told your Majesty as much before.
This proveth Edward's love and Warwick's
honesty.   180
    War. King Lewis, I here protest in sight of
heaven
And by the hope I have of heavenly bliss
That I am clear from this misdeed of Ed-
ward's —
No more my king, for he dishonours me,
But most himself, if he could see his shame.
Did I forget that by the House of York   186
My father came untimely to his death?
Did I let pass th' abuse done to my niece?
Did I impale him with the regal crown?
Did I put Henry from his native right?   190
And am I guerdon'd at the last with shame?
Shame on himself! for my desert is honour;
And to repair my honour, lost for him,
I here renounce him and return to Henry.
My noble queen, let former grudges pass,   195
And henceforth I am thy true servitor.
I will revenge his wrong to Lady Bona
And replant Henry in his former state.
    Marg. Warwick, these words have turn'd my
hate to love,
And I forgive and quite forget old faults   200
And joy that thou becom'st King Henry's
friend.
    War. So much his friend, ay, his unfeigned
friend,
That, if King Lewis vouchsafe to furnish us
With some few bands of chosen soldiers,
I'll undertake to land them on our coast   205
And force the tyrant from his seat by war.
'Tis not his new-made bride shall succour him!
And as for Clarence, as my letters tell me,

He's very likely now to fall from him
For matching more for wanton lust than
  honour   210
Or than for strength and safety of our country.
  Bona. Dear brother, how shall Bona be
  reveng'd
But by thy help to this distressed queen?
  Marg. Renowned prince, how shall poor
  Henry live
Unless thou rescue him from foul despair? 215
  Bona. My quarrel and this English queen's
  are one.
  War. And mine, fair Lady Bona, joins with
  yours.
  Lewis. And mine with hers and thine and
  Margaret's.
Therefore, at last, I firmly am resolv'd
You shall have aid.   220
  Marg. Let me give humble thanks for all at
  once.
  Lewis. Then, England's messenger, return
  in post
And tell false Edward, thy supposed king,
That Lewis of France is sending over mas-
  quers
To revel it with him and his new bride. 225
Thou seest what's past. Go fear thy king
  withal.
  Bona. Tell him, in hope he'll prove a widower
  shortly,
I'll wear the willow garland for his sake.
  Marg. Tell him my mourning weeds are laid
  aside
And I am ready to put armour on.   230
  War. Tell him from me that he hath done
  me wrong
And therefore I'll uncrown him ere't be long.
There's thy reward. [*Gives a purse.*] Be gone.
                            Exit Post.

  Lewis.   But, Warwick.
Thou and Oxford, with five thousand men,
Shall cross the seas and bid false Edward
  battle;   235
And as occasion serves, this noble queen
And prince shall follow with a fresh supply.
Yet, ere thou go, but answer me one doubt:
What pledge have we of thy firm loyalty? 239
  War. This shall assure my constant loyalty,
That if our queen and this young prince agree,
I'll join mine eldest daughter, and my joy,
To him forthwith in holy wedlock bands.
  Marg. Yes, I agree, and thank you for your
  motion.
Son Edward, she is fair and virtuous.   245
Therefore delay not; give thy hand to Warwick
And, with thy hand, thy faith irrevocable
That only Warwick's daughter shall be thine.
  Prince Edw. Yes, I accept her, for she well
  deserves it,   249
And here to pledge my vow I give my hand.
                He gives his hand to Warwick.
  Lewis. Why stay we now? These soldiers
  shall be levied,
And thou, Lord Bourbon, our High Admiral,
Shalt waft them over with our royal fleet.
I long till Edward fall by war's mischance 254
For mocking marriage with a dame of France.
                Exeunt. Manet Warwick.
  War. I came from Edward as ambassador,
But I return his sworn and mortal foe.
Matter of marriage was the charge he gave me,
But dreadful war shall answer his demand.
Had he none else to make a stale but me? 260
Then none but I shall turn his jest to sorrow.
I was the chief that rais'd him to the crown
And I'll be chief to bring him down again;
Not that I pity Henry's misery,   264
But seek revenge on Edward's mockery. *Exit.*

    [ACT IV. Scene I. *London. The Palace.*]

    Enter *Richard, Clarence, Somerset, and
          Montague.*

  Rich. Now tell me, brother Clarence, what
  think you
Of this new marriage with the Lady Grey?
Hath not our brother made a worthy choice?
  Clar. Alas, you know 'tis far from hence to
  France!   4
How could he stay till Warwick made return?
  Som. My lords, forbear this talk. Here
  comes the King.

Flourish. Enter *King Edward,* [attended,] *Lady
Grey* [as *Queen*], *Pembroke, Stafford, Hastings.*
Four stand on one side and four on the other.

  Rich. And his well-chosen bride.
  Clar. I mind to tell him plainly what I
  think.
  K. Edw. Now, brother of Clarence, how like
  you our choice,
That you stand pensive, as half malecontent?
  Clar. As well as Lewis of France or the Earl
  of Warwick,   11

                         301

Which are so weak of courage and in judgment
That they'll take no offence at our abuse.

  K. Edw. Suppose they take offence without
  a cause:

They are but Lewis and Warwick; I am
Edward,   15
Your king and Warwick's, and must have my
will.

  Rich. And you shall have your will, because
our king.

Yet hasty marriage seldom proveth well.

  K. Edw. Yea, brother Richard, are you offended too?

  Rich. Not I.   20
No, God forbid that I should wish them sever'd
Whom God hath join'd together! Ay, and
'twere pity
To sunder them that yoke so well together.

  K. Edw. Setting your scorns and your mislike aside,

Tell me some reason why the Lady Grey 25
Should not become my wife and England's
Queen.

And you too, Somerset, and Montague,
Speak freely what you think.

  Clar. Then this is mine opinion, that King
Lewis

Becomes your enemy for mocking him 30
About the marriage of the Lady Bona.

  Rich. And Warwick, doing what you gave
in charge,

Is now dishonoured by this new marriage.

  K. Edw. What if both Lewis and Warwick
be appeas'd

By such invention as I can devise? 35

  Mont. Yet, to have join'd with France in
such alliance

Would more have strength'ned this our commonwealth

'Gainst foreign storms than any home-bred
marriage.

  Hast. Why, knows not Montague that of
itself

England is safe, if true within itself? 40

  Mont. Yes, but the safer when 'tis back'd
with France.

  Hast. 'Tis better using France than trusting
France.

Let us be back'd with God, and with the seas,
Which he hath giv'n for fence impregnable,
And with their helps only defend ourselves. 45
In them and in ourselves our safety lies.

  Clar. For this one speech Lord Hastings well
deserves

To have the heir of the Lord Hungerford.

  K. Edw. Ay, what of that? It was my will
and grant, 49
And for this once my will shall stand for law.

  Rich. And yet methinks your Grace hath
not done well

To give the heir and daughter of Lord Scales
Unto the brother of your loving bride.
She better would have fitted me or Clarence;
But in your bride you bury brotherhood. 55

  Clar. Or else you would not have bestow'd
the heir

Of the Lord Bonville on your new wive's son
And leave your brothers to go speed elsewhere.

  K. Edw. Alas, poor Clarence! Is it for a wife
That thou are malecontent? I will provide
thee. 60

  Clar. In choosing for yourself you show'd
your judgment,

Which being shallow, you shall give me leave
To play the broker in mine own behalf;
And to that end I shortly mind to leave you.

  K. Edw. Leave me or tarry, Edward will be
King 65
And not be tied unto his brother's will.

  Lady Grey. My lords, before it pleas'd his
Majesty

To raise my state to title of a queen,
Do me but right, and you must all confess
That I was not ignoble of descent, 70
And meaner than myself have had like fortune.
But as this title honours me and mine,
So your dislikes, to whom I would be pleasing,
Doth cloud my joys with danger and with
sorrow.

  K. Edw. My love, forbear to fawn upon
their frowns. 75
What danger or what sorrow can befall thee
So long as Edward is thy constant friend
And their true sovereign, whom they must
obey?
Nay, whom they shall obey, and love thee too,
Unless they seek for hatred at my hands; 80
Which if they do, yet will I keep thee safe,
And they shall feel the vengeance of my wrath.

  Rich. [*aside*] I hear; yet say not much, but
think the more.

Enter a Post.

  K. Edw. Now, messenger, what letters or
what news
From France? 85

  Post. My sovereign liege, no letters, and
few words,
But such as I, without your special pardon,
Dare not relate.

302

K. Edw. Go to, we pardon thee. Therefore, in brief,
Tell me their words as near as thou canst guess them.   90
What answer makes King Lewis unto our letters?
Post. At my depart these were his very words:
'Go tell false Edward, thy supposed king,
That Lewis of France is sending over masquers
To revel it with him and his new bride.'   95
K. Edw. Is Lewis so brave? Belike he thinks me Henry.
But what said Lady Bona to my marriage?
Post. These were her words, utt'red with mild disdain:
'Tell him, in hope he'll prove a widower shortly,
I'll wear the willow garland for his sake.'   100
K. Edw. I blame not her. She could say little less.
She had the wrong. But what said Henry's queen?
For I have heard that she was there in place.
Post. 'Tell him,' quoth she, 'my mourning weeds are done
And I am ready to put armour on.'   105
K. Edw. Belike she minds to play the Amazon.
But what said Warwick to these injuries?
Post. He, more incens'd against your Majesty
Than all the rest, discharg'd me with these words:
'Tell him from me that he hath done me wrong,   110
And therefore I'll uncrown him ere't be long.'
K. Edw. Ha! durst the traitor breathe out so proud words?
Well, I will arm me, being thus forewarn'd.
They shall have wars and pay for their presumption.   114
But say, is Warwick friends with Margaret?
Post. Ay, gracious sovereign. They are so link'd in friendship
That young Prince Edward marries Warwick's daughter.
Clar. Belike the elder; Clarence will have the younger.
Now, brother king, farewell, and sit you fast;
For I will hence to Warwick's other daughter,
That, though I want a kingdom, yet in marriage   121
I may not prove inferior to yourself.
You that love me and Warwick, follow me.
    Exit Clarence, and Somerset follows.

Rich. [*aside*] Not I.
My thoughts aim at a further matter. I   125
Stay not for the love of Edward but the crown.
K. Edw. Clarence and Somerset both gone to Warwick?
Yet am I arm'd against the worst can happen;
And haste is needful in this desp'rate case.
Pembroke and Stafford, you in our behalf   130
Go levy men and make prepare for war.
They are already, or quickly will be landed.
Myself in person will straight follow you.
    Exeunt Pembroke and Stafford.
But ere I go, Hastings and Montague,   134
Resolve my doubt. You twain, of all the rest,
Are near to Warwick by blood and by alliance.
Tell me if you love Warwick more than me.
If it be so, then both depart to him;
I rather wish you foes than hollow friends.
But if you mind to hold your true obedience,
Give me assurance with some friendly vow,   141
That I may never have you in suspect.
Mont. So God help Montague as he proves true!
Hast. And Hastings as he favours Edward's cause!
K. Edw. Now, brother Richard, will you stand by us?   145
Rich. Ay, in despite of all that shall withstand you.
K. Edw. Why, so! then am I sure of victory.
Now therefore let us hence, and lose no hour
Till we meet Warwick with his foreign pow'r.
    Exeunt.

[Scene II. *A plain in Warwickshire.*]

Enter *Warwick* and *Oxford* in England with
    French Soldiers.

War. Trust me, my lord, all hitherto goes well.
The common people by numbers swarm to us.

Enter *Clarence* and *Somerset.*

But see where Somerset and Clarence comes!
Speak suddenly, my lords, are we all friends?
Clar. Fear not that, my lord.   5
War. Then, gentle Clarence, welcome unto Warwick;
And welcome, Somerset. I hold it cowardice
To rest mistrustful where a noble heart
Hath pawn'd an open hand in sign of love.
Else might I think that Clarence, Edward's brother.   10

Were but a feigned friend to our proceedings.
But welcome, sweet Clarence. My daughter
   shall be thine.
And now what rests but, in night's coverture,
Thy brother being carelessly encamp'd,
His soldiers lurking in the towns about,   15
And but attended by a simple guard,
We may surprise and take him at our pleasure?
Our scouts have found the adventure very easy;
That as Ulysses and stout Diomede
With sleight and manhood stole to Rhesus' tents
And brought from thence the Thracian fatal
   steeds,   21
So we, well cover'd with the night's black
   mantle,
At unawares may beat down Edward's guard
And seize himself. I say not, slaughter him,
For I intend but only to surprise him.   25
You that will follow me to this attempt,
Applaud the name of Henry with your leader.
                 They all cry 'Henry!'
Why then, let's on our way in silent sort.
For Warwick and his friends, God and Saint
   George!   *Exeunt.*

[Scene III. Edward's *camp, near Warwick.*]

Enter three *Watchmen*, to guard the *King's* tent.

1. Watch. Come on, my masters. Each man
   take his stand.
The King by this is set him down to sleep.
2. Watch. What, will he not to bed?
1. Watch. Why, no; for he hath made a
   solemn vow
Never to lie and take his natural rest   5
Till Warwick or himself be quite suppress'd.
2. Watch. To-morrow then belike shall be
   the day,
If Warwick be so near as men report.
3. Watch. But say, I pray, what nobleman
   is that   9
That with the King here resteth in his tent?
1. Watch. 'Tis the Lord Hastings, the King's
   chiefest friend.
3. Watch. O, is it so? But why commands
   the King
That his chief followers lodge in towns about
   him,
While he himself keeps in the cold field?
2. Watch. 'Tis the more honour, because
   more dangerous.   15
3. Watch. Ay, but give me worship and
   quietness.

I like it better than a dangerous honour.
If Warwick knew in what estate he stands,
'Tis to be doubted he would waken him.
   1. Watch. Unless our halberds did shut up
      his passage.   20
   2. Watch. Ay! wherefore else guard we his
      royal tent
But to defend his person from night-foes?

Enter *Warwick, Clarence, Oxford, Somerset,*
   and *French Soldiers*, silent all.

   War. This is his tent; and see where stand
      his guard.
Courage, my masters! Honour now or never!
But follow me, and Edward shall be ours.   25
   1. Watch. Who goes there?
   2. Watch. Stay, or thou diest!
      Warwick and the rest cry all 'Warwick!
      Warwick!' *and set upon the Guard, who
      fly, crying* 'Arm! arm!' *Warwick and the
      rest following them.*

The *Drum* playing and *Trumpet* sounding, enter *Warwick, Somerset,* and the rest, bringing
the *King* out in his gown, sitting in a chair.
   Richard and *Hastings* fly over the stage.

   Som. What are they that fly there?
   War. Richard and Hastings. Let them go.
      Here is the Duke.
   K. Edw. The Duke? Why, Warwick, when
      we parted last   30
Thou call'dst me King.
   War.   Ay, but the case is alter'd.
When you disgrac'd me in my embassade,
Then I degraded you from being King,
And come now to create you Duke of York.
Alas, how should you govern any kingdom   35
That know not how to use ambassadors,
Nor how to be contented with one wife,
Nor how to use your brothers brotherly,
Nor how to study for the people's welfare,
Nor how to shroud yourself from enemies?   40
   K. Edw. Yea, brother of Clarence, art thou
      here too?
Nay, then I see that Edward needs must down.
Yet, Warwick, in despite of all mischance,
Of thee thyself, and all thy complices,
Edward will always bear himself as King.   45
Though Fortune's malice overthrow my state,
My mind exceeds the compass of her wheel.
   War. Then, for his mind, be Edward Eng-
      land's King;   *Takes off his crown.*
But Henry now shall wear the English crown
And be true king indeed, thou but the shadow.
My Lord of Somerset, at my request   51

See that forthwith Duke Edward be convey'd
Unto my brother, Archbishop of York.
When I have fought with Pembroke and his
  fellows,
I'll follow you and tell what answer   55
Lewis and the Lady Bona send to him.
Now for a while farewell, good Duke of York.
                    They lead him out forcibly.
  K. Edw. What fates impose, that men must
    needs abide;
It boots not to resist both wind and tide.
    Exeunt [*King Edward, guarded, and Som-
                                        erset*].
  Oxf. What now remains, my lords, for us to
    do   60
But march to London with our soldiers?
  War. Ay, that's the first thing that we have
    to do,
To free King Henry from imprisonment
And see him seated in the regal throne.
                                    Exeunt.

[Scene IV. *London. The Palace.*]

¡Enter *Rivers* and *Lady Grey* [as *Queen*].
  Riv. Madam, what makes you in this sud-
    den change?
  Grey. Why, brother Rivers, are you yet to
    learn
What late misfortune is befall'n King Edward?
  Riv. What? loss of some pitch'd battle
    against Warwick?   4
  Grey. No, but the loss of his own royal person.
  Riv. Then is my sovereign slain?
  Grey. Ay, almost slain, for he is taken
    prisoner,
Either betray'd by falsehood of his guard
Or by his foe surpris'd at unawares;
And, as I further have to understand,   10
Is new committed to the Bishop of York,
Fell Warwick's brother, and by that our foe.
  Riv. These news, I must confess, are full of
    grief.
Yet, gracious madam, bear it as you may;
Warwick may lose, that now hath won the day.
  Grey. Till then fair hope must hinder live's
    decay.   16
And I the rather wean me from despair
For love of Edward's offspring in my womb.
This is it that makes me bridle passion
And bear with mildness my misfortune's cross.
Ay, ay, for this I draw in many a tear   21
And stop the rising of bloodsucking sighs,

Lest with my sighs or tears I blast or drown
King Edward's fruit, true heir to th' English
  crown.
  Riv. But, madam, where is Warwick then
    become?   25
  Grey. I am inform'd that he comes towards
    London
To set the crown once more on Henry's head.
Guess thou the rest. King Edward's friends
  must down.
But, to prevent the tyrant's violence
(For trust not him that hath once broken faith)
I'll hence forthwith unto the sanctuary,   31
To save, at least, the heir of Edward's right.
There shall I rest secure from force and fraud.
Come, therefore, let us fly while we may fly.
If Warwick take us, we are sure to die.   35
                                    Exeunt.

[Scene V. *A park near Middleham
              Castle in Yorkshire.*]

Enter *Richard, Lord Hastings,* and *Sir
              William Stanley.*

  Rich. Now, my Lord Hastings and Sir Wil-
    liam Stanley,
Leave off to wonder why I drew you hither
Into this chiefest thicket of the park.
Thus stands the case: you know our king, my
    brother,   4
Is prisoner to the Bishop here, at whose hands
He hath good usage and great liberty;
And often, but attended with weak guard,
Comes hunting this way to disport himself.
I have advertis'd him by secret means
That if about this hour he make this way   10
Under the colour of his usual game,
He shall here find his friends with horse and
    men
To set him free from his captivity.

Enter *King Edward* and a *Huntsman* with him.

  Hunt. This way, my lord, for this way lies
    the game.
  K. Edw. Nay, this way, man! See where the
    huntsmen stand.   15
Now, brother of Gloucester, Lord Hastings,
    and the rest,
Stand you thus close to steal the Bishop's deer?
  Rich. Brother, the time and case requireth
    haste.
Your horse stands ready at the park corner.
  K. Edw. But whither shall we then?   20

Hast. To Lynn, my lord, and ship from thence to Flanders.

Rich. Well guess'd, believe me; for that was my meaning.

K. Edw. Stanley, I will requite thy forwardness.

Rich. But wherefore stay we? 'Tis no time to talk.

K. Edw. Huntsman, what say'st thou? Wilt thou go along?   25

Hunt. Better do so than tarry and be hang'd.

Rich. Come then, away. Let's ha' no more ado.

K. Edw. Bishop, farewell. Shield thee from Warwick's frown

And pray that I may repossess the crown.

Exeunt.

[Scene VI. *London. The Tower.*]

Flourish. Enter *King Henry the Sixth, Clarence, Warwick, Somerset,* young *Henry Earl of Richmond, Oxford, Montague,* and *Lieutenant* [*of the Tower*].

K. Hen. Master Lieutenant, now that God and friends

Have shaken Edward from the regal seat

And turn'd my captive state to liberty,

My fear to hope, my sorrows unto joys,

At our enlargement what are thy due fees? 5

Lieut. Subjects may challenge nothing of their sov'reigns;

But if an humble prayer may prevail,

I then crave pardon of your Majesty.

K. Hen. For what, Lieutenant? for well using me?

Nay, be thou sure I'll well requite thy kindness   10

For that it made my imprisonment a pleasure;

Ay, such a pleasure as incaged birds

Conceive when, after many moody thoughts,

At last by notes of household harmony

They quite forget their loss of liberty. 15

But, Warwick, after God, thou set'st me free,

And chiefly therefore I thank God and thee;

He was the author, thou the instrument.

Therefore, that I may conquer fortune's spite

By living low, where fortune cannot hurt me,

And that the people of this blessed land 21

May not be punish'd with my thwarting stars,

Warwick, although my head still wear the crown,

I here resign my government to thee,

For thou art fortunate in all thy deeds. 25

War. Your Grace hath still been fam'd for virtuous,

And now may seem as wise as virtuous

By spying and avoiding fortune's malice,

For few men rightly temper with the stars.

Yet in this one thing let me blame your Grace,   30

For choosing me when Clarence is in place.

Clar. No, Warwick, thou art worthy of the sway,

To whom the heav'ns in thy nativity

Adjudg'd an olive branch and laurel crown,

As likely to be blest in peace and war; 35

And therefore I yield thee my free consent.

War. And I choose Clarence only for Protector.

K. Hen. Warwick and Clarence, give me both your hands.

Now join your hands, and with your hands your hearts,

That no dissension hinder government. 40

I make you both Protectors of this land,

While I myself will lead a private life

And in devotion spend my latter days,

To sin's rebuke and my Creator's praise.

War. What answers Clarence to his sovereign's will?   45

Clar. That he consents, if Warwick yield consent,

For on thy fortune I repose myself.

War. Why then, though loath, yet must I be content.

We'll yoke together, like a double shadow

To Henry's body, and supply his place; 50

I mean, in bearing weight of government,

While he enjoys the honour and his ease.

And, Clarence, now then it is more than needful

Forthwith that Edward be pronounc'd a traitor

And all his lands and goods be confiscate. 55

Clar. What else? And that succession be determin'd.

War. Ay, therein Clarence shall not want his part.

K. Hen. But with the first of all your chief affairs,

Let me entreat (for I command no more) 59

That Margaret your queen and my son Edward

Be sent for, to return from France with speed;

For till I see them here, by doubtful fear

My joy of liberty is half eclips'd.

Clar. It shall be done, my sovereign, with all speed.

K. Hen. My Lord of Somerset, what youth
  is that   65
Of whom you seem to have so tender care?
  Som. My liege, it is young Henry, Earl of
  Richmond.
  K. Hen. Come hither, England's hope.
           Lays his hand on his head.
           If secret powers
Suggest but truth to my divining thoughts,
This pretty lad will prove our country's bliss.
His looks are full of peaceful majesty,   71
His head by nature fram'd to wear a crown,
His hand to wield a sceptre, and himself
Likely in time to bless a regal throne.
Make much of him, my lords; for this is he 75
Must help you more than you are hurt by me.

        Enter a *Post.*

War. What news, my friend?
Post. That Edward is escaped from your
  brother
And fled, as he hears since, to Burgundy.
  War. Unsavoury news! But how made he
  escape?   80
Post. He was convey'd by Richard Duke of
  Gloucester
And the Lord Hastings, who attended him
In secret ambush on the forest side
And from the Bishop's huntsmen rescu'd him;
For hunting was his daily exercise.   85
  War. My brother was too careless of his
  charge.
But let us hence, my sovereign, to provide
A salve for any sore that may betide.
    Exeunt. Manent Somerset, Richmond, and
                  Oxford.
  Som. My lord, I like not of this flight of
  Edward's,
For doubtless Burgundy will yield him help 90
And we shall have more wars before 't be long.
As Henry's late presaging prophecy
Did glad my heart with hope of this young
  Richmond,
So doth my heart misgive me, in these con-
  flicts
What may befall him, to his harm and ours. 95
Therefore, Lord Oxford, to prevent the worst,
Forthwith we'll send him hence to Brittany
Till storms be past of civil enmity.
  Oxf. Ay, for if Edward repossess the crown,
'Tis like that Richmond with the rest shall
  down.   100
  Som. It shall be so; he shall to Brittany.
Come therefore, let's about it speedily.
                    Exeunt.

[Scene VII. *Before York.*]

Flourish. Enter [*King*] *Edward, Richard,*
    Hastings, and *Soldiers.*

K. Edw. Now, brother Richard, Lord Has-
  tings, and the rest,
Yet thus far Fortune maketh us amends
And says that once more I shall interchange
My waned state for Henry's regal crown.   4
Well have we pass'd and now repass'd the seas
And brought desired help from Burgundy.
What then remains, we being thus arriv'd
From Ravenspurgh haven before the gates of
  York,
But that we enter, as into our dukedom?
  Rich. The gates made fast? Brother, I like
  not this!   10
For many men that stumble at the threshold
Are well foretold that danger lurks within.
  K. Edw. Tush, man, abodements must not
  now affright us!
By fair or foul means we must enter in,
For hither will our friends repair to us.   15
  Hast. My liege, I'll knock once more to
  summon them.

    Enter, on the walls, the *Mayor of York*
        and his *Brethren.*

  May. My lords, we were forewarned of your
  coming
And shut the gates for safety of ourselves;
For now we owe allegiance unto Henry.
  K. Edw. But, Master Mayor, if Henry be
  your king,   20
Yet Edward at the least is Duke of York.
  May. True, my good lord. I know you for
  no less
  K. Edw. Why, and I challenge nothing but
  my dukedom,
As being well content with that alone.
  Rich. [*aside*] But when the fox hath once
  got in his nose,   25
He'll soon find means to make the body follow.
  Hast. Why, Master Mayor, why stand you
  in a doubt?
Open the gates. We are King Henry's friends.
  May. Ay, say you so? The gates shall then
  be opened.
        He descends [*with the Aldermen*].
  Rich. A wise stout captain, and soon per-
  suaded!   30
  Hast. The good old man would fain that all
  were well,
So twere not long of him; but being ent'red,

I doubt not, I, but we shall soon persuade
Both him and all his brothers unto reason.

Enter the *Mayor* and two *Aldermen* [below].

K. Edw. So, Master Mayor. These gates
must not be shut   35
But in the night or in the time of war.
What, fear not, man, but yield me up the keys;
                                Takes his keys.
For Edward will defend the town and thee
And all those friends that deign to follow me.

March. Enter *Montgomery* with *Drum*
and *Soldiers.*

Rich. Brother, this is Sir John Montgomery,
Our trusty friend, unless I be deceiv'd.   41
K. Edw. Welcome, Sir John! But why come
you in arms?
Mont. To help King Edward in his time of
storm,
As every loyal subject ought to do.
K. Edw. Thanks, good Montgomery. But
we now forget   45
Our title to the crown and only claim
Our dukedom till God please to send the rest.
Mont. Then fare you well, for I will hence
again.
I came to serve a king and not a duke.
Drummer, strike up, and let us march away.
                        The Drum begins to march.
K. Edw. Nay, stay, Sir John, awhile, and
we'll debate   51
By what safe means the crown may be re-
cover'd.
Mont. What talk you of debating? In few
words,
If you'll not here proclaim yourself our king,
I'll leave you to your fortune and be gone 55
To keep them back that come to succour
you.
Why shall we fight, if you pretend no title?
Rich. Why, brother, wherefore stand you on
nice points?
K. Edw. When we grow stronger, then we'll
make our claim;
Till then 'tis wisdom to conceal our meaning.
Hast. Away with scrupulous wit! Now arms
must rule.   61
Rich. And fearless minds climb soonest unto
crowns.
Brother, we will proclaim you out of hand;
The bruit thereof will bring you many friends;
K. Edw. Then be it as you will; for 'tis my
right,   65
And Henry but usurps the diadem.

Mont. Ay, now my sovereign speaketh like
himself
And now will I be Edward's champion.
Hast. Sound trumpet. Edward shall be here
proclaim'd.   69
Come, fellow soldier, make thou proclamation.
        [*Gives him a paper.*] *Flourish. Sound.*
Soldier. [*reads*] 'Edward the Fourth, by the
grace of God, King of England and France, and
Lord of Ireland, &c.'
Mont. And whosoe'er gainsays King Ed-
ward's right,
By this I challenge him to single fight.   75
                        Throws down his gauntlet.
All. Long live Edward the Fourth!
K. Edw. Thanks, brave Montgomery, and
thanks unto you all.
If fortune serve me, I'll requite this kindness.
Now for this night let's harbour here in York,
And when the morning sun shall raise his car
Above the border of this horizon,   81
We'll forward towards Warwick and his mates;
For well I wot that Henry is no soldier.
Ah, froward Clarence, how evil it beseems thee
To flatter Henry and forsake thy brother! 85
Yet, as we may, we'll meet both thee and
Warwick.
Come on, brave soldiers. Doubt not of the day,
And that once gotten, doubt not of large pay.
                                                Exeunt.

[Scene VIII. *London. The* Bishop
of London's *Palace.*]

Flourish. Enter the *King* [*Henry*], *Warwick,*
Montague, Clarence, Oxford, [and *Exeter*].

War. What counsel, lords? Edward from
Belgia,
With hasty Germans and blunt Hollanders,
Hath pass'd in safety through the narrow seas
And with his troops doth march amain to
London,
And many giddy people flock to him.   5
Oxf. Let's levy men and beat him back
again.
Clar. A little fire is quickly trodden out,
Which, being suffer'd, rivers cannot quench.
War. In Warwickshire I have true-hearted
friends,
Not mutinous in peace, yet bold in war.   10
Those will I muster up; and thou, son Clarence,
Shalt stir up in Suffolk, Norfolk, and in Kent
The knights and gentlemen to come with thee.

Thou, brother Montague, in Buckingham,
Northampton, and in Leicestershire shalt find
Men well inclin'd to hear what thou com-
  mand'st.   16
And thou, brave Oxford, wondrous well belov'd,
In Oxfordshire shalt muster up thy friends.
My sovereign, with the loving citizens,
Like to his island girt in with the ocean   20
Or modest Dian circled with her nymphs,
Shall rest in London till we come to him.
Fair lords, take leave and stand not to reply.
Farewell, my sovereign.
  K. Hen. Farewell, my Hector and my Troy's
  true hope.   25
  Clar. In sign of truth I kiss your Highness'
  hand.
  K. Hen. Well-minded Clarence, be thou for-
  tunate!
  Mont. Comfort, my lord! and so I take my
  leave.
  Oxf. [*kisses Henry's hand*] And thus I seal
  my truth and bid adieu.
  K. Hen. Sweet Oxford, and my loving Mon-
  tague,   30
And all at once, once more a happy farewell!
  War. Farewell, sweet lords. Let's meet at
  Coventry.
    Exeunt [all but King Henry and Exeter].
  K. Hen. Here at the palace will I rest awhile.
Cousin of Exeter, what thinks your lordship?
Methinks the power that Edward hath in field
Should not be able to encounter mine.   36
  Exe. The doubt is that he will seduce the
  rest.
  K. Hen. That's not my fear. My meed hath
  got me fame.
I have not stopp'd mine ears to their demands
Nor posted off their suits with slow delays. 40

My pity hath been balm to heal their wounds,
My mildness hath allay'd their swelling griefs,
My mercy dried their water-flowing tears.
I have not been desirous of their wealth
Nor much oppress'd them with great subsidies,
Nor forward of revenge, though they much
  err'd.   46
Then why should they love Edward more than
  me?
No, Exeter, these graces challenge grace;
And when the lion fawns upon the lamb,
The lamb will never cease to follow him.   50
  Shout within, 'A Lancaster! A Lancaster!'
  Exe. Hark, hark, my lord! what shouts are
  these?

  Enter [*King*] *Edward* and his *Soldiers,* [with
    Richard].

  K. Edw. Seize on the shamefac'd Henry,
  bear him hence,
And once again proclaim us King of England.
You are the fount that makes small brooks to
  flow.
Now stops thy spring; my sea shall suck them
  dry   55
And swell so much the higher by their ebb.
Hence with him to the Tower. Let him not
  speak.
    Exeunt [some] with King Henry.
And, lords, towards Coventry bend we our
  course,
Where peremptory Warwick now remains.
The sun shines hot, and if we use delay,   60
Cold biting winter mars our hop'd-for hay.
  Rich. Away betimes, before his forces join,
And take the great-grown traitor unawares.
Brave warriors, march amain towards Cov-
  entry.   *Exeunt.*

[ACT V. Scene I. *Coventry.*]

Enter *Warwick,* the *Mayor of Coventry,* two
  Messengers, and others, upon the walls.

  War. Where is the post that came from
  valiant Oxford?
How far hence is thy lord, mine honest fellow?
  1. Mess. By this at Dunsmore, marching
  hitherward.
  War. How far off is our brother Montague?
Where is the post that came from Montague?
  2. Mess. By this at Daintry, with a puissant
  troop.   6

  Enter [*Sir John*] *Somervile.*

  War. Say, Somervile, what says my loving
  son?
And by thy guess how nigh is Clarence now?
  Som. At Southam I did leave him with his
  forces
And do expect him here some two hours hence.
    [*Drum heard.*]
  War. Then Clarence is at hand. I hear his
  drum.   11
  Som. It is not his, my lord. Here Southam
  lies.

The drum your Honour hears marcheth from
Warwick.

War. Who should that be? Belike unlook'd-
for friends.

Som. They are at hand, and you shall quickly
know.   15

March. Flourish. Enter [*King*] *Edward,
Richard,* and *Soldiers.*

K. Edw. Go, trumpet, to the walls, and
sound a parle.

Rich. See how the surly Warwick mans the
wall!

War. O unbid spite! Is sportful Edward
come?

Where slept our scouts or how are they seduc'd
That we could hear no news of his repair?   20

K. Edw. Now, Warwick, wilt thou ope the
city gates,
Speak gentle words, and humbly bend thy knee,
Call Edward king, and at his hands beg mercy?
And he shall pardon thee these outrages.

War. Nay rather, wilt thou draw thy forces
hence.   25
Confess who set thee up and pluck'd thee down,
Call Warwick patron, and be penitent?
And thou shalt still remain the Duke of York.

Rich. I thought at least he would have said
'the King';
Or did he make the jest against his will?   30

War. Is not a dukedom, sir, a goodly gift?

Rich. Ay, by my faith, for a poor earl to give!
I'll do thee service for so good a gift.

War. 'Twas I that gave the kingdom to thy
brother.

K. Edw. Why, then 'tis mine, if but by Warwick's gift.   35

War. Thou art no Atlas for so great a weight;
And, weakling, Warwick takes his gift again,
And Henry is my king, Warwick his subject.

K. Edw. But Warwick's king is Edward's
prisoner;
And, gallant Warwick, do but answer this: 40
What is the body when the head is off?

Rich. Alas that Warwick had no more fore-
cast,
But, whiles he thought to steal the single ten,
The king was slily finger'd from the deck!
You left poor Henry at the Bishop's palace   45
And ten to one you'll meet him in the Tower.

K. Edw. 'Tis even so. Yet you are Warwick
still.

Rich. Come, Warwick, take the time. Kneel
down, kneel down!
Nay, when? Strike now, or else the iron cools.

War. I had rather chop this hand off at a
blow   50
And with the other fling it at thy face
Than bear so low a sail to strike to thee.

K. Edw. Sail how thou canst, have wind and
tide thy friend,
This hand, fast wound about thy coal-black
hair,   54
Shall, whiles thy head is warm and new cut off,
Write in the dust this sentence with thy blood:
'Wind-changing Warwick now can change no
more.'

Enter *Oxford,* with *Drum* and *Colours.*

War. O cheerful colours! See where Oxford
comes!

Oxf. Oxford, Oxford, for Lancaster!
                    [*He and his Forces enter the city.*]

Rich. The gates are open; let us enter too.

K. Edw. So other foes may set upon our
backs.   61
Stand we in good array, for they no doubt
Will issue out again and bid us battle.
If not, the city being but of small defence,
We'll quickly rouse the traitors in the same.

War. O, welcome, Oxford! for we want thy
help.   66

Enter *Montague,* with *Drum* and *Colours.*

Mont. Montague, Montague, for Lancaster!
                    [*He and his Forces enter the city.*]

Rich. Thou and thy brother both shall buy
this treason
Even with the dearest blood your bodies bear.

K. Edw. The harder match'd, the greater
victory!   70
My mind presageth happy gain and conquest.

Enter *Somerset,* with *Drum* and *Colours.*

Som. Somerset, Somerset, for Lancaster!
                    [*He and his Forces enter the city.*]

Rich. Two of thy name, both Dukes of
Somerset,
Have sold their lives unto the house of York;
And thou shalt be the third, if this sword hold.

Enter *Clarence,* with *Drum* and *Colours.*

War. And lo where George of Clarence
sweeps along,   76
Of force enough to bid his brother battle;
With whom an upright zeal to right prevails
More than the nature of a brother's love!
Come, Clarence, come! Thou wilt, if Warwick
call.   80

Clar. Father of Warwick, know you what
this means?

   Takes his red rose out of his hat.

Look here, I throw my infamy at thee.
I will not ruinate my father's house,
Who gave his blood to lime the stones together,
And set up Lancaster. Why, trowest thou,
 Warwick,   85
That Clarence is so harsh, so blunt, unnatural,
To bend the fatal instruments of war
Against his brother and his lawful king?
Perhaps thou wilt object my holy oath.
To keep that oath were more impiety 90
Than Jephtha when he sacrific'd his daughter.
I am so sorry for my trespass made
That, to deserve well at my brother's hands,
I here proclaim myself thy mortal foe;
With resolution, wheresoe'er I meet thee 95
(As I will meet thee if thou stir abroad),
To plague thee for thy foul misleading me.
And so, proud-hearted Warwick, I defy thee
And to my brother turn my blushing cheeks.
Pardon me, Edward! I will make amends; 100
And, Richard, do not frown upon my faults,
For I will henceforth be no more unconstant.
 K. Edw. Now welcome more, and ten times
  more belov'd,
Than if thou never hadst deserv'd our hate.
 Rich. Welcome, good Clarence! This is
  brotherlike.   105
War. O passing traitor, perjur'd and unjust!
 K. Edw. What, Warwick, wilt thou leave the
  town and fight?
Or shall we beat the stones about thine ears?
 War. Alas, I am not coop'd here for de-
  fence!
I will away towards Barnet presently 110
And bid thee battle, Edward, if thou dar'st.
 K. Edw. Yes, Warwick, Edward dares and
  leads the way.
Lords, to the field. Saint George and victory!
  Exeunt [King Edward and his Company].
  March. Warwick and his Company fol-
  lows.

[Scene II. *A field of battle near Barnet.*]

Alarum and excursions. Enter [*King*] *Edward*,
 bringing forth *Warwick* wounded.

 K. Edw. So, lie thou there! Die thou, and
  die our fear!
For Warwick was a bug that fear'd us all.
Now, Montague, sit fast. I seek for thee,

That Warwick's bones may keep thine com-
 pany.   *Exit.*
 War. Ah, who is nigh? Come to me, friend
  or foe,   5
And tell me who is victor, York or Warwick.
Why ask I that? My mangled body shows,
My blood, my want of strength, my sick heart
 shows,
That I must yield my body to the earth
And, by my fall, the conquest to my foe. 10
Thus yields the cedar to the axe's edge,
Whose arms gave shelter to the princely eagle,
Under whose shade the ramping lion slept,
Whose top-branch overpeer'd Jove's spreading
 tree
And kept low shrubs from winter's pow'rful
 wind.   15
These eyes, that now are dimm'd with death's
 black veil,
Have been as piercing as the midday sun
To search the secret treasons of the world.
The wrinkles in my brows, now fill'd with
 blood,
Were lik'ned oft to kingly sepulchres; 20
For who liv'd king but I could dig his grave?
And who durst smile when Warwick bent his
 brow?
Lo now my glory smear'd in dust and blood!
My parks, my walks, my manors that I had,
Even now forsake me; and of all my lands 25
Is nothing left me but my body's length!
Why, what is pomp, rule, reign, but earth and
 dust?
And, live we how we can, yet die we must.

   Enter *Oxford* and *Somerset.*

 Som. Ah, Warwick, Warwick, wert thou as
  we are,
We might recover all our loss again! 30
The Queen from France hath brought a puis-
 sant power.
Even now we heard the news. Ah, couldst
 thou fly!
 War. Why, then I would not fly. Ah,
  Montague,
If thou be there, sweet brother, take my
 hand
And with thy lips keep in my soul awhile! 35
Thou lov'st me not; for, brother, if thou
 didst,
Thy tears would wash this cold congealed blood
That glues my lips and will not let me speak.
Come quickly, Montague, or I am dead.
 Som. Ah, Warwick! Montague hath breath'd
  his last,   40

And to the latest gasp cried out for Warwick
And said 'Commend me to my valiant brother.'
And more he would have said, and more he
  spoke,
Which sounded like a clamour in a vault,   44
That mought not be distinguish'd; but at last
I well might hear, delivered with a groan,
'O, farewell, Warwick!'
  War. Sweet rest his soul! Fly, lords, and
  save yourselves;
For Warwick bids you all farewell, to meet in
  heaven.   *Dies.*
  Oxf. Away, away, to meet the Queen's great
  power!   50
    Here they bear away his body. Exeunt.

[Scene III. *Another part of the field.*]

Flourish. Enter *King Edward* in triumph;
  with *Richard, Clarence,* and the rest.

  K. Edw. Thus far our fortune keeps an up-
  ward course
And we are grac'd with wreaths of victory;
But in the midst of this bright-shining day
I spy a black, suspicious, threat'ning cloud
That will encounter with our glorious sun   5
Ere he attain his easeful western bed.
I mean, my lords, those powers that the
  Queen
Hath rais'd in Gallia have arriv'd our coast
And, as we hear, march on to fight with us.
  Clar. A little gale will soon disperse that
  cloud   10
And blow it to the source from whence it
  came.
Thy very beams will dry those vapours up,
For every cloud engenders not a storm.
  Rich. The Queen is valued thirty thousand
  strong,
And Somerset, with Oxford, fled to her.   15
If she have time to breathe, be well assur'd
Her faction will be full as strong as ours.
  K. Edw. We are advertis'd by our loving
  friends
That they do hold their course toward Tewks-
  bury.
We, having now the best at Barnet field,   20
Will thither straight, for willingness rids way;
And as we march our strength will be aug-
  mented
In every county as we go along.
Strike up the drum. Cry 'Courage!' and away.
          Exeunt.

[Scene IV. *Plains near Tewksbury.*]

Flourish. March. Enter the *Queen [Margaret],*
young Prince Edward, Somerset, Oxford, and
      Soldiers.

  Queen. Great lords, wise men ne'er sit and
  wail their loss
But cheerly seek how to redress their harms.
What though the mast be now blown overboard,
The cable broke, the holding anchor lost,
And half our sailors swallow'd in the flood?   5
Yet lives our pilot still. Is't meet that he
Should leave the helm and, like a fearful lad,
With tearful eyes add water to the sea
And give more strength to that which hath too
  much,   9
Whiles, in his moan, the ship splits on the rock,
Which industry and courage might have sav'd?
Ah, what a shame! ah, what a fault were this
Say Warwick was our anchor. What of that?
And Montague our topmast. What of him?
Our slaught'red friends the tackles. What of
  these?   15
Why, is not Oxford here, another anchor?
And Somerset, another goodly mast?
The friends of France our shrouds and tack-
  lings?
And, though unskilful, why not Ned and I
For once allow'd the skilful pilot's charge?   20
We will not from the helm, to sit and weep,
But keep our course (though the rough wind
  say no)
From shelves and rocks that threaten us with
  wrack.
As good to chide the waves as speak them fair.
And what is Edward but a ruthless sea?   25
What Clarence but a quicksand of deceit?
And Richard but a ragged fatal rock?
All these the enemies to our poor bark.
Say you can swim — alas, 'tis but a while!
Tread on the sand — why, there you quickly
  sink!   30
Bestride the rock — the tide will wash you off,
Or else you famish: that's a threefold death.
This speak I, lords, to let you understand,
If case some one of you would fly from us,
That there's no hop'd-for mercy with the
  brothers   35
More than with ruthless waves, with sands and
  rocks.
Why, courage then! What cannot be avoided
'Twere childish weakness to lament or fear.
  Prince. Methinks a woman of this valiant
  spirit

Should, if a coward heard her speak these words,   40
Infuse his breast with magnanimity
And make him, naked, foil a man-at-arms.
I speak not this as doubting any here;
For did I but suspect a fearful man,
He should have leave to go away betimes,   45
Lest in our need he might infect another
And make him of like spirit to himself.
If any such be here (as God forbid!),
Let him depart before we need his help.
    Oxf. Women and children of so high a courage,   50
And warriors faint? Why, 'twere perpetual shame.
O brave young Prince! Thy famous grandfather
Doth live again in thee. Long mayst thou live
To bear his image and renew his glories!
    Som. And he that will not fight for such a hope,   55
Go home to bed, and, like the owl by day,
If he arise, be mock'd and wond'red at.
    Queen. Thanks, gentle Somerset. Sweet Oxford, thanks.
    Prince. And take his thanks that yet hath nothing else.

                Enter a *Messenger.*

    Mess. Prepare you, lords; for Edward is at hand,   60
Ready to fight. Therefore be resolute.
    Oxf. I thought no less. It is his policy
To haste thus fast, to find us unprovided.
    Som. But he's deceiv'd; we are in readiness.
    Queen. This cheers my heart, to see your forwardness.   65
    Oxf. Here pitch our battle; hence we will not budge.

Flourish and march. Enter, *King Edward,
    Richard, Clarence,* and *Soldiers.*

    K. Edw. Brave followers, yonder stands the thorny wood
Which, by the heavens' assistance and your strength,
Must by the roots be hewn up yet ere night.
I need not add more fuel to your fire,   70
For well I wot ye blaze to burn them out.
Give signal to the fight, and to it, lords!
    Queen. Lords, knights, and gentlemen, what I should say
My tears gainsay; for every word I speak,
Ye see I drink the water of mine eyes.   75

Therefore, no more but this: Henry, your sovereign,
Is prisoner to the foe, his state usurp'd,
His realm a slaughterhouse, his subjects slain,
His statutes cancell'd, and his treasure spent;
And yonder is the wolf that makes this spoil.
You fight in justice. Then, in God's name, lords,   81
Be valiant and give signal to the fight.
    Alarum. Retreat. Excursions. Exeunt.

        [Scene V. *Another part of the field.*]

Flourish. Enter [*King*] *Edward, Richard, Clarence,* [*Soldiers*; with] *Queen* [*Margaret*], *Oxford, Somerset* [as prisoners].

    K. Edw. Now here a period of tumultuous broils!
Away with Oxford to Hames Castle straight.
For Somerset, off with his guilty head!
Go bear them hence. I will not hear them speak.
    Oxf. For my part, I'll not trouble thee with words.   5
    Som. Nor I, but stoop with patience to my fortune.
        Exeunt [*Oxford and Somerset, guarded*].
    Queen. So part we sadly in this troublous world
To meet with joy in sweet Jerusalem.
    K. Edw. Is proclamation made that who finds Edward
Shall have a high reward, and he his life?   10
    Rich. It is. And lo where youthful Edward comes!

    Enter [*Soldiers,* with] the *Prince* [*Edward*].

    K. Edw. Bring forth the gallant; let us hear him speak.
What? Can so young a thorn begin to prick?
Edward, what satisfaction canst thou make   14
For bearing arms, for stirring up my subjects,
And all the trouble thou hast turn'd me to?
    Prince. Speak like a subject, proud ambitious York!
Suppose that I am now my father's mouth;
Resign thy chair, and where I stand kneel thou,
Whilst I propose the selfsame words to thee   20
Which, traitor, thou wouldst have me answer to.
    Queen. Ah, that thy father had been so resolv'd!
    Rich. That you might still have worn the petticoat

                    313

And ne'er have stol'n the breech from Lan-
caster.   24
Prince. Let Æsop fable in a winter's night.
His currish riddles sorts not with this place.
Rich. By heaven, brat, I'll plague ye for that
word.
Queen. Ay, thou wast born to be a plague
to men.
Rich. For God's sake take away this captive
scold!
Prince. Nay, take away this scolding crook-
back rather.   30
K. Edw. Peace, wilful boy, or I will charm
your tongue.
Clar. Untutor'd lad, thou art too malapert.
Prince. I know my duty; you are all un-
dutiful.
Lascivious Edward, and thou perjur'd George,
And thou misshapen Dick, I tell ye all   35
I am your better, traitors as ye are,
And thou usurp'st my father's right and mine.
K. Edw. Take that, the likeness of this railer
here!   *Stabs him.*
Rich. Sprawl'st thou? Take that, to end
thy agony.   *Richard stabs him.*
Clar. And there's for twitting me with per-
jury!   *Clarence stabs him.*
Queen. O, kill me too!   41
Rich. Marry, and shall!   *Offers to kill her.*
K. Edw. Hold, Richard, hold; for we have
done too much.
Rich. Why should she live to fill the world
with words?
K. Edw. What? Doth she swoon? Use
means for her recovery.   45
Rich. Clarence, excuse me to the King my
brother.
I'll hence to London on a serious matter;
Ere ye come there, be sure to hear some news.
Clar. What? what?   49
Rich. The Tower, the Tower!   *Exit.*
Queen. O Ned, sweet Ned, speak to thy
mother, boy!
Canst thou not speak? O traitors! murtherers!
They that stabb'd Cæsar shed no blood at all,
Did not offend, nor were not worthy blame,
If this foul deed were by, to equal it.   55
He was a man; this (in respect) a child,
And men ne'er spend their fury on a child.
What's worse than murtherer, that I may name
it?
No, no, my heart will burst an if I speak!
And I will speak, that so my heart may burst.
Butchers and villains, bloody cannibals,   61
How sweet a plant have you untimely cropp'd!

You have no children, butchers! If you had,
The thought of them would have stirr'd up
remorse;
But if you ever chance to have a child,   65
Look in his youth to have him so cut off
As, deathsmen, you have rid this sweet young
prince!
K. Edw. Away with her! Go bear her hence
perforce!
Queen. Nay, never bear me hence! Dis-
patch me here.
Here sheathe thy sword, I'll pardon thee my
death.   70
What, wilt thou not? Then, Clarence, do it
thou.
Clar. By heaven, I will not do thee so much
ease.
Queen. Good Clarence, do! Sweet Clarence
do thou do it!
Clar. Didst thou not hear me swear I would
not do it?
Queen. Ay, but thou usest to forswear thy-
self.   75
'Twas sin before, but now 'tis charity.
What, wilt thou not? Where is that devil's
butcher,
Hard-favour'd Richard? Richard, where art
thou?
Thou art not here. Murther is thy almsdeed.
Petitioners for blood thou ne'er put'st back.
K. Edw. Away, I say. I charge ye bear her
hence.   81
Queen. So come to you and yours as to this
prince!   *Exit [led out]*
K. Edw. Where's Richard gone?
Clar. To London, all in post; and, as I guess,
To make a bloody supper in the Tower.   85
K. Edw. He's sudden if a thing comes in his
head.
Now march we hence, discharge the common
sort
With pay and thanks, and let's away to London
And see our gentle queen how well she fares.
By this, I hope, she hath a son for me.   90
                                            Exeunt.

[Scene VI. *London. The Tower.*]

Enter *Henry the Sixth* and *Richard*, with
the *Lieutenant*, on the walls.

Rich. Good day, my lord. What, at your
book so hard?
K. Hen. Ay, my good lord — 'my lord'
should say rather.

Tis sin to flatter. 'Good' was little better.
'Good Gloucester' and 'good devil' were alike,
And both preposterous. Therefore, not 'good
    lord.'   5

Rich. Sirrah, leave us to ourselves; we must
confer.
                            [*Exit Lieutenant.*]

K. Hen. So flies the reckless shepherd from
    the wolf;
So first the harmless sheep doth yield his fleece,
And next his throat unto the butcher's knife.
What scene of death hath Roscius now to act?

Rich. Suspicion always haunts the guilty
    mind;   11
The thief doth fear each bush an officer.

K. Hen. The bird that hath been limed in a
    bush
With trembling wings misdoubteth every bush;
And I, the hapless male to one sweet bird,   15
Have now the fatal object in my eye
Where my poor young was lim'd, was caught,
    and kill'd.

Rich. Why, what a peevish fool was that of
    Crete
That taught his son the office of a fowl!   19
And yet, for all his wings, the fool was drown'd.

K. Hen. I, Dædalus; my poor boy, Icarus;
Thy father, Minos, that denied our course;
The sun that sear'd the wings of my sweet
    boy,
Thy brother Edward; and thyself, the sea
Whose envious gulf did swallow up his life.   25
Ah, kill me with thy weapon, not with words!
My breast can better brook thy dagger's point
Than can my ears that tragic history.
But wherefore dost thou come? Is't for my
    life?   29

Rich. Think'st thou I am an executioner?

K. Hen. A persecutor I am sure thou art.
If murthering innocents be executing,
Why, then thou art an executioner.

Rich. Thy son I kill'd for his presumption.

K. Hen. Hadst thou been kill'd when first
    thou didst presume,   35
Thou hadst not liv'd to kill a son of mine.
And thus I prophesy, that many a thousand
Which now mistrust no parcel of my fear,
And many an old man's sigh and many a
    widow's,   39
And many an orphan's water-standing eye —
Men for their sons, wives for their husbands,
And orphans for their parents' timeless death —
Shall rue the hour that ever thou wast born.
The owl shriek'd at thy birth, an evil sign;
The night crow cried, aboding luckless time;

Dogs howl'd and hideous tempest shook down
    trees;   46
The raven rook'd her on the chimney's top,
And chatt'ring pies in dismal discord sung.
Thy mother felt more than a mother's pain,
And yet brought forth less than a mother's
    hope,   50
To wit, an indigested and deformed lump,
Not like the fruit of such a goodly tree.
Teeth hadst thou in thy head when thou wast
    born,
To signify thou cam'st to bite the world;
And, if the rest be true which I have heard,   55
Thou cam'st —

Rich. I'll hear no more. Die, prophet, in
    thy speech.   *Stabs him.*
For this (amongst the rest) was I ordain'd.

K. Hen. Ay, and for much more slaughter
    after this.
O, God forgive my sins and pardon thee!   60
                                        Dies.

Rich. What? Will the aspiring blood of
    Lancaster
Sink in the ground? I thought it would have
    mounted.
See how my sword weeps for the poor King's
    death!
O may such purple tears be alway shed
From those that wish the downfall of our
    house!   65
If any spark of life be yet remaining,
Down, down to hell, and say I sent thee
    thither!   *Stabs him again.*
I, that have neither pity, love, nor fear.
Indeed 'tis true that Henry told me of;
For I have often heard my mother say   70
I came into the world with my legs forward.
Had I not reason, think ye, to make haste
And seek their ruin that usurp'd our right?
The midwife wonder'd, and the women cried
'O, Jesus bless us! He is born with teeth!'   75
And so I was; which plainly signified
That I should snarl and bite and play the dog.
Then, since the heavens have shap'd my body
    so,
Let hell make crook'd my mind to answer it.
I have no brother, I am like no brother;   80
And this word 'love,' which greybeards call
    divine,
Be resident in men like one another,
And not in me! I am myself alone.
Clarence, beware. Thou keep'st me from the
    light;
But I will sort a pitchy day for thee;   85
For I will buzz abroad such prophecies

That Edward shall be fearful of his life;
And then, to purge his fear, I'll be thy death.
King Henry and the Prince his son are gone.
Clarence, thy turn is next, and then the rest,
Counting myself but bad till I be best.   91
I'll throw thy body in another room
And triumph, Henry, in thy day of doom.
                              Exit [with the body].

[Scene VII. *London. The Palace.*]

Flourish. Enter *King Edward, Queen Elizabeth,
Clarence, Richard, Hastings, Nurse* (with the
young Prince), and *Attendants.*

  K. Edw. Once more we sit in England's royal
throne,
Repurchas'd with the blood of enemies.
What valiant foemen, like to autumn's corn,
Have we mow'd down in tops of all their pride!
Three Dukes of Somerset, threefold renown'd
For hardly and undoubted champions;   6
Two Cliffords, as the father and the son;
And two Northumberlands — two braver men
Ne'er spurr'd their coursers at the trumpet's
sound;
With them, the two brave bears, Warwick and
Montague,   10
That in their chains fetter'd the kingly lion
And made the forest tremble when they roar'd.
Thus have we swept suspicion from our seat
And made our footstool of security.
Come hither, Bess, and let me kiss my boy. 15
Young Ned, for thee thine uncles and myself
Have in our armours watch'd the winter's night,
Went all afoot in summer's scalding heat,
That thou mightst repossess the crown in peace;
And of our labours thou shalt reap the gain. 20

  Rich. [*aside*] I'll blast his harvest, if your
head were laid;
For yet I am not look'd on in the world.
This shoulder was ordain'd so thick to heave,
And heave it shall some weight or break my
back.
Work thou the way, and thou shalt execute. 25
  K. Edw. Clarence and Gloucester, love my
lovely queen,
And kiss your princely nephew, brothers both.
  Clar. The duty that I owe unto your
Majesty
I seal upon the lips of this sweet babe.
  Queen. Thanks, noble Clarence; worthy
brother, thanks.   30
  Rich. And that I love the tree from whence
thou sprang'st
Witness the loving kiss I give the fruit.
[*Aside*] To say the truth, so Judas kiss'd his
master
And cried 'All hail!' when as he meant all harm
  K. Edw. Now am I seated as my soul de-
lights,   35
Having my country's peace and brothers' loves.
  Clar. What will your Grace have done with
Margaret?
Reignier, her father, to the King of France
Hath pawn'd the Sicils and Jerusalem,   39
And hither have they sent it for her ransom.
  K. Edw. Away with her, and waft her hence
to France!
And now what rests but that we spend the
time
With stately triumphs, mirthful comic shows,
Such as befits the pleasure of the court?
Sound drums and trumpets! Farewell sour
annoy!   45
For here I hope begins our lasting joy.
                              Exeunt omnes

316

RICHARD THE THIRD was entered in the Stationers' Register on October 20, 1597, and the First Quarto came out in that year: 'The Tragedy of King Richard the third. . . . As it hath beene lately Acted by the Right honourable the Lord Chamberlaine his seruants' — Shakespeare's company. No author's name is mentioned in the title page or elsewhere. Five other quartos were published (1598, 1602, 1605, 1612, 1622) before the Folio of 1623, and all of them ascribe the play to 'William Shake-speare' or 'William Shakespeare.' The textual differences among the quartos are of no moment. In contents, the First Quarto and the Folio agree in the main; but the Quarto has about forty lines that the Folio lacks, and the Folio has about two hundred and thirty that are not found in the Quarto. For the text, the Folio is the authority, but most of the missing lines are undoubtedly genuine and are supplied from the Quarto. The only considerable omission in the Folio consists of lines 101–118 in iv, 2.

Apart from misprints, the Quarto text differs from that of the Folio in an infinity of little matters of expression. Many of the differences consist in the mere substitution of a synonym: as, for example, 'spie' (Quarto) for 'see' (i, 1, 26), 'holes' for 'wounds' (i, 2, 11), 'euils' for 'Crimes' (76), 'bloudy' for 'murd'rous' (94), 'slew' (137) for 'kill'd.' In some cases the Quarto reading has been adopted in many modern editions and has become so consecrated by usage that one finds it hard to be conscientious and accept the Folio text. Thus, in Clarence's dream, 'that grim ferriman' may seem better than 'that sowre Ferry-man' (i, 4, 46), but 'sowre' is probably what Shakespeare wrote. The connotation of words — what we may call their atmosphere — changes from age to age; and 'sour' was a more poetical adjective in Shakespeare's time than it is to-day.

Some critics regard the Quarto text as Shakespeare's first draft and take the Folio text for his (or another's) revision; but there is little to be said for such a theory. The First Quarto may have been printed from a carelessly made copy of Shakespeare's manuscript. In general, its readings are not authoritative when they disagree with the Folio, though now and then they enable us to correct a Folio misprint.

In *The Second Part of King Henry the Sixth* Richard fights valiantly at the Battle of St. Albans (May 22, 1455), though in fact he was less than three years old at the time (v, 2, 66 ff.; v, 3). His character is worked out with care in the *Third Part of King Henry the Sixth*. His main characteristics appear when he urges his father to repudiate his oath (i, 2, 18 ff.). His words express not alone his conscious delight in the arts of the sophist and his restless ferocity, but that imperious spirit which makes him a Marlovian character — his passionate love of sovereign power:

> And, father, do but think
> How sweet a thing it is to wear a crown,
> Within whose circuit is Elysium
> And all that poets feign of bliss and joy.
> Why do we linger thus? I cannot rest
> Until the white rose that I wear be dy'd
> Even in the lukewarm blood of Henry's heart.

His valour is emphasized from the outset, even by Queen Margaret (i, 4, 75 ff.):

> That valiant crookback prodigy,
> Dicky your boy, that with his grumbling voice
> Was wont to cheer his dad in mutinies.

Two fine soliloquies (iii, 2, 124 ff.; v, 6, 68 ff.), in which Shakespeare out-Marlowes Marlowe, develop the hints already given. They look forward to the tragedy of RICHARD THE THIRD, and indeed may almost be said to announce it as in preparation. Their connection with the soliloquy with which the play begins is obvious. 'I am determined to prove a villain' echoes Richard's self-analysis in *Part III*, in which he declares that he can 'set the murtherous Machiavel to school' (iii, 2, 193).

Richard, then, may be termed Shakespeare's dramatic interpretation of the Machiavellian villain — a type whose general features were already well settled in the Elizabethan mind. Comparison with Marlowe's *Jew of Malta* is inevitable. There Machiavel speaks the Prologue and registers Barabas as a disciple of his school. That Shakespeare was strongly influenced by Marlowe in this period is certain; and that is enough to account for those features of the present play and its immediate predecessors that have tempted critics, with no sound arguments to support them, to contend that Marlowe had some hand in *Henry the Sixth* and RICHARD THE THIRD.

As to date, the close connection with *3 Henry VI* suggests that RICHARD THE THIRD followed that play almost immediately. If we refer *Part III* to 1591, RICHARD THE THIRD may well be dated 1592. There is no direct evidence to the contrary.

For material, Shakespeare went to Holinshed, who for this reign uses Sir Thomas More's life of Richard III and Halle's *Chronicle*. The play covers the period from the funeral of Henry VI (1471) to the defeat and death of Richard on Bosworth field (August 22, 1485). Historical time is condensed. The murder of Clarence, which in Shakespeare comes soon after the funeral, took place in 1478. King Edward's death (ii, 2) occurred on April 9, 1483. The coronation of Richard followed on July 6. The wooing of Lady Anne, which interrupts King Henry's funeral procession (i, 2), is imaginary.

Richardus Tertius, a Latin drama by Thomas Legge, was performed at Cambridge in 1580. The anonymous *True Tragedie of Richard the Third*, printed in 1594, may or may not be older than Shakespeare's play. Neither can be regarded as a source for his KING RICHARD THE THIRD.

Colley Cibber's adaptation of RICHARD THE THIRD was first acted in 1700 at Drury Lane and held the stage for more than a hundred and fifty years. At least two of Richard's lines in Cibber's play have become proverbial and are often quoted as Shakespeare's: — 'Off with his head — so much for Buckingham!' (iv, 3) and 'Conscience avaunt, Richard's himself again!' (v, 3).

THE TRAGEDY OF
KING RICHARD THE THIRD

[Dramatis Personæ.

King Edward the Fourth.

Edward, Prince of Wales, afterwards King Edward V,
Richard, Duke of York, } sons to the King.

George, Duke of Clarence,
Richard, Duke of Gloucester, afterwards King Richard III, } brothers to the King.

A young Son of Clarence.

Henry, Earl of Richmond, afterwards King Henry VII.

Cardinal Bourchier, Archbishop of Canterbury.
Thomas Rotherham, Archbishop of York.
John Morton, Bishop of Ely.
Duke of Buckingham.
Duke of Norfolk.
Earl of Surrey, his son.
Earl Rivers, brother to Queen Elizabeth.
Marquess of Dorset and Lord Grey, her sons.
Earl of Oxford.
Lord Hastings.
Lord Stanley (also styled Earl of Derby).
Lord Lovel.
Sir Thomas Vaughan.
Sir Richard Ratcliff.
Sir William Catesby.
Sir James Tyrrel.

Sir James Blunt.
Sir Walter Herbert.
Sir Robert Brakenbury, Lieutenant of the Tower.
Keeper in the Tower.
Sir William Brandon.
Christopher Urswick, a priest.
Lord Mayor of London.
Sheriff of Wiltshire.
Tressel and Berkeley, gentlemen attending on Lady Anne.

Elizabeth, Queen to King Edward IV.
Margaret, widow of King Henry VI.
Duchess of York, mother to King Edward IV.
Lady Anne, widow of Edward, Prince of Wales, son to King Henry VI; afterwards married to Richard, Duke of Gloucester.
A young Daughter of Clarence (Lady Margaret Plantagenet).

Ghosts of Richard's victims.

Lords, Gentlemen, and other Attendants; a Pursuivant, a Page, a Scrivener, a Priest, Bishops, Citizens, Aldermen, Councillors, Murderers, Messengers, Soldiers, &c.

SCENE. — England.]

ACT I. Scene I. [*London. A street.*]

Enter *Richard Duke of Gloucester* solus.

Rich. Now is the winter of our discontent
Made glorious summer by this sun of York,
And all the clouds that low'rd upon our house
In the deep bosom of the ocean buried.
Now are our brows bound with victorious wreaths,   5
Our bruised arms hung up for monuments,
Our stern alarums chang'd to merry meetings,
Our dreadful marches to delightful measures.
Grim-visag'd War hath smooth'd his wrinkled front,   9
And now, instead of mounting barbed steeds
To fright the souls of fearful adversaries,
He capers nimbly in a lady's chamber
To the lascivious pleasing of a lute.
But I, that am not shap'd for sportive tricks

Nor made to court an amorous looking glass;
I, that am rudely stamp'd, and want love's majesty   16
To strut before a wanton ambling nymph;
I, that am curtail'd of this fair proportion,
Cheated of feature by dissembling Nature,
Deform'd, unfinish'd, sent before my time   20
Into this breathing world, scarce half made up,
And that so lamely and unfashionable
That dogs bark at me as I halt by them —
Why, I, in this weak piping time of peace,
Have no delight to pass away the time,   25
Unless to see my shadow in the sun
And descant on mine own deformity.
And therefore, since I cannot prove a lover
To entertain these fair well-spoken days,
I am determined to prove a villain   30
And hate the idle pleasures of these days.

319

Plots have I laid, inductions dangerous.
By drunken prophecies, libels, and dreams,
To set my brother Clarence and the King
In deadly hate the one against the other; 35
And if King Edward be as true and just
As I am subtle, false, and treacherous,
This day should Clarence closely be mew'd up
About a prophecy which says that G
Of Edward's heirs the murtherer shall be. 40
Dive, thoughts, down to my soul! Here Clarence comes.

Enter Clarence guarded, and Brakenbury.

Brother, good day. What means this armed guard
That waits upon your Grace?
  Clar.   His Majesty,
Tend'ring my person's safety, hath appointed
This conduct to convey me to the Tower. 45
  Rich. Upon what cause?
  Clar.   Because my name is George.
  Rich. Alack, my lord, that fault is none of yours!
He should for that commit your godfathers.
O, belike his Majesty hath some intent 49
That you should be new christ'ned in the Tower.
But what's the matter, Clarence? May I know?
  Clar. Yea, Richard, when I know; for I protest
As yet I do not. But, as I can learn,
He hearkens after prophecies and dreams,
And from the cross-row plucks the letter G, 55
And says a wizard told him that by G
His issue disinherited should be;
And, for my name of George begins with G,
It follows in his thought that I am he. 59
These (as I learn) and such-like toys as these
Have mov'd his Highness to commit me now.
  Rich. Why, this it is when men are rul'd by women!
'Tis not the King that sends you to the Tower;
My Lady Grey his wife, Clarence, 'tis she
That tempts him to this harsh extremity. 65
Was it not she, and that good man of worship,
Anthony Woodville, her brother there,
That made him send Lord Hastings to the Tower,
From whence this present day he is deliver'd?
We are not safe, Clarence; we are not safe. 70
  Clar. By heaven, I think there is no man secure
But the Queen's kindred, and night-walking heralds
That trudge betwixt the King and Mistress Shore.

Heard you not what an humble suppliant
Lord Hastings was to her for his delivery? 75
  Rich. Humbly complaining to her deity
Got my Lord Chamberlain his liberty.
I'll tell you what —I think it is our way,
If we will keep in favour with the King,
To be her men and wear her livery. 80
The jealous o'erworn widow and herself,
Since that our brother dubb'd them gentlewomen,
Are mighty gossips in our monarchy.
  Brak. I beseech your Graces both to pardon me.
His Majesty hath straitly given in charge 85
That no man shall have private conference
(Of what degree soever) with your brother.
  Rich. Even so, an't please your worship. Brakenbury,
You may partake of anything we say. 89
We speak no treason, man. We say the King
Is wise and virtuous, and his noble queen
Well struck in years, fair, and not jealous.
We say that Shore's wife hath a pretty foot,
A cherry lip, a bonny eye, a passing pleasing tongue;
And that the Queen's kindred are made gentlefolks. 95
How say you, sir? Can you deny all this?
  Brak. With this, my lord, myself have naught to do.
  Rich. Naught to do with Mistress Shore? I tell thee, fellow,
He that doth naught with her (excepting one)
Were best to do it secretly alone. 100
  Brak. What one, my lord?
  Rich. Her husband, knave. Wouldst thou betray me?
  Brak. I beseech your Grace to pardon me, and withal
Forbear your conference with the noble Duke.
  Clar. We know thy charge, Brakenbury, and will obey. 105
  Rich. We are the Queen's abjects, and must obey.
Brother, farewell. I will unto the King;
And whatsoe'er you will employ me in,
Were it to call King Edward's widow sister,
I will perform it to enfranchise you. 110
Meantime, this deep disgrace in brotherhood
Touches me deeper than you can imagine.
  Clar. I know it pleaseth neither of us well.
  Rich. Well, your imprisonment shall not be long:
I will deliver you, or else lie for you. 115
Meantime, have patience.

Clar.   I must perforce. Farewell.
Exit Clarence, [with Brakenbury and Guard].
Rich. Go tread the path that thou shalt ne'er
return,
Simple plain Clarence! I do love thee so
That I will shortly send thy soul to heaven,
If heaven will take the present at our hands.
But who comes here? The new-delivered Has-
tings?   121

Enter *Lord Hastings.*

Hast. Good time of day unto my gracious
lord.
Rich. As much unto my good Lord Cham-
berlain.
Well are you welcome to this open air.
How hath your lordship brook'd imprisonment?
Hast. With patience, noble lord, as prisoners
must;   126
But I shall live, my lord, to give them thanks
That were the cause of my imprisonment.
Rich. No doubt, no doubt; and so shall
Clarence too,
For they that were your enemies are his   130
And have prevail'd as much on him as you.
Hast. More pity that the eagle should be
mew'd,
While kites and buzzards prey at liberty.
Rich. What news abroad?
Hast. No news so bad abroad as this at home:
The King is sickly, weak, and melancholy, 136
And his physicians fear him mightily.
Rich. Now, by Saint Paul, that news is bad
indeed!
O, he hath kept an evil diet long
And overmuch consum'd his royal person. 140
'Tis very grievous to be thought upon.
Where is he? In his bed?
Hast. He is.
Rich. Go you before, and I will follow you.
Exit Hastings.
He cannot live, I hope, and must not die 145
Till George be pack'd with posthorse up to
heaven.
I'll in, to urge his hatred more to Clarence
With lies well steel'd with weighty arguments;
And, if I fail not in my deep intent,
Clarence hath not another day to live.   150
Which done, God take King Edward to his
mercy
And leave the world for me to bustle in!
For then I'll marry Warwick's youngest
daughter.
What though I kill'd her husband and her
father?   154

The readiest way to make the wench amends
Is to become her husband and her father;
The which will I — not all so much for love
As for another secret close intent
By marrying her which I must reach unto.
But yet I run before my horse to market: 160
Clarence still breathes; Edward still lives and
reigns;
When they are gone, then must I count my
gains.   *Exit.*

Scene II. [*London. Another street.*]

Enter the corse of *Henry the Sixth*, with *Halberds* to guard it, [with them *Tressel* and
Berkeley]; *Lady Anne* being the mourner.

Anne. Set down, set down your honourable
load,
If honour may be shrouded in a hearse,
Whilst I awhile obsequiously lament
Th' untimely fall of virtuous Lancaster.
[*The Bearers set down the coffin.*]
Poor key-cold figure of a holy king,   5
Pale ashes of the house of Lancaster,
Thou bloodless remnant of that royal blood,
Be it lawful that I invocate thy ghost
To hear the lamentations of poor Anne,
Wife to thy Edward, to thy slaught'red son 10
Stabb'd by the selfsame hand that made these
wounds!
Lo, in these windows that let forth thy life
I pour the helpless balm of my poor eyes.
O, cursed be the hand that made these holes!
Cursed the heart that had the heart to do it!
Cursed the blood that let this blood from hence!
More direful hap betide that hated wretch
That makes us wretched by the death of thee
Than I can wish to wolves — to spiders, toads,
Or any creeping venom'd thing that lives! 20
If ever he have child, abortive be it,
Prodigious, and untimely brought to light,
Whose ugly and unnatural aspect
May fright the hopeful mother at the view,
And that be heir to his unhappiness!   25
If ever he have wife, let her be made
More miserable by the death of him
Than I am made by my young lord and thee!
Come, now towards Chertsey with your holy
load,
Taken from Paul's to be interred there;   30
And still as you are weary of this weight,
Rest you whiles I lament King Henry's corse.
[*The Bearers take up the coffin.*]

321

Enter *Richard Duke of Gloucester.*

Rich. Stay, you that bear the corse, and set
it down.

Anne. What black magician conjures up this
fiend

To stop devoted charitable deeds? 35

Rich. Villains, set down the corse, or, by
Saint Paul,

I'll make a corse of him that disobeys!

Gent. My lord, stand back, and let the coffin
pass.

Rich. Unmanner'd dog, stand thou when I
command! 39

Advance thy halberd higher than my breast,

Or, by Saint Paul, I'll strike thee to my foot

And spurn upon thee, beggar, for thy boldness.

[*The Bearers set down the coffin.*]

Anne. What, do you tremble? Are you all
afraid?

Alas, I blame you not, for you are mortal,

And mortal eyes cannot endure the devil. 45

Avaunt, thou dreadful minister of hell!

Thou hadst but power over his mortal body;

His soul thou canst not have. Therefore, be
gone.

Rich. Sweet saint, for charity, be not so
curst.

Anne. Foul devil, for God's sake hence, and
trouble us not! 50

For thou hast made the happy earth thy hell,

Fill'd it with cursing cries and deep exclaims.

If thou delight to view thy heinous deeds,

Behold this pattern of thy butcheries. 54

O gentlemen, see, see! Dead Henry's wounds

Open their congeal'd mouths and bleed afresh!

Blush, blush, thou lump of foul deformity;

For 'tis thy presence that exhales this blood

From cold and empty veins where no blood
dwells.

Thy deed inhuman and unnatural 60

Provokes this deluge most unnatural.

O God, which this blood mad'st, revenge his
death!

O earth, which this blood drink'st, revenge his
death!

Either, heav'n, with lightning strike the murth'rer dead; 64

Or, earth, gape open wide and eat him quick,

As thou dost swallow up this good king's blood

Which his hell-govern'd arm hath butchered!

Rich. Lady, you know no rules of charity,

Which renders good for bad, blessings for curses.

Anne. Villain, thou know'st no law of God
nor man. 70

No beast so fierce but knows some touch of
pity.

Rich. But I know none, and therefore am
no beast.

Anne. O wonderful, when devils tell the
truth!

Rich. More wonderful, when angels are so
angry.

Vouchsafe, divine perfection of a woman, 75

Of these supposed crimes to give me leave

By circumstance but to acquit myself.

Anne. Vouchsafe, defus'd infection of a man,

For these known evils, but to give me leave

By circumstance to curse thy cursed self. 80

Rich. Fairer than tongue can name thee, let
me have

Some patient leisure to excuse myself.

Anne. Fouler than heart can think thee, thou
canst make

No excuse current but to hang thyself.

Rich. By such despair I should accuse myself.

Anne. And by despairing shalt thou stand
excus'd 86

For doing worthy vengeance on thyself

That didst unworthy slaughter upon others.

Rich. Say that I slew them not?

Anne.　　　　　Then say they were not slain.

But dead they are, and, devilish slave, by thee.

Rich. I did not kill your husband.

Anne.　　　　　Why, then he is alive.

Rich. Nay, he is dead, and slain by Edward's
hand.

Anne. In thy foul throat thou liest! Queen
Margaret saw

Thy murd'rous falchion smoking in his blood;

The which thou once didst bend against her
breast, 95

But that thy brothers beat aside the point.

Rich. I was provoked by her sland'rous
tongue

That laid their guilt upon my guiltless shoulders.

Anne. Thou wast provoked by thy bloody
mind 99

That never dream'st on aught but butcheries.

Didst thou not kill this king?

Rich.　　　　　I grant ye.

Anne. Dost grant me, hedgehog? Then God
grant me too

Thou mayst be damned for that wicked deed!

O, he was gentle, mild, and virtuous!

Rich. The better for the King of Heaven,
that hath him. 105

Anne. He is in heaven, where thou shalt
never come.

Rich. Let him thank me, that holp to send
  him thither;
For he was fitter for that place than earth.
Anne. And thou unfit for any place, but hell.
Rich. Yes, one place else, if you will hear me
  name it.   110
Anne. Some dungeon.
Rich.   Your bedchamber.
Anne. Ill rest betide the chamber where thou
  liest!
Rich. So will it, madam, till I lie with you.
Anne. I hope so.
Rich.   I know so. But, gentle Lady Anne,
To leave this keen encounter of our wits   115
And fall something into a slower method —
Is not the causer of the timeless deaths
Of these Plantagenets, Henry and Edward,
As blameful as the executioner?
Anne. Thou wast the cause and most ac-
  curs'd effect.   120
Rich. Your beauty was the cause of that
  effect —
Your beauty, that did haunt me in my sleep
To undertake the death of all the world,
So I might live one hour in your sweet bosom.
Anne. If I thought that, I tell thee, homicide,
These nails should rent that beauty from my
  cheeks.   126
Rich. These eyes could not endure that
  beauty's wrack;
You should not blemish it, if I stood by.
As all the world is cheered by the sun,
So I by that. It is my day, my life.   130
Anne. Black night o'ershade thy day, and
  death thy life!
Rich. Curse not thyself, fair creature! Thou
  art both.
Anne. I would I were, to be reveng'd on thee.
Rich. It is a quarrel most unnatural,
To be reveng'd on him that loveth thee.   135
Anne. It is a quarrel just and reasonable,
To be reveng'd on him that kill'd my husband.
Rich. He that bereft thee, lady, of thy
  husband,
Did it to help thee to a better husband.
Anne. His better doth not breathe upon the
  earth.   140
Rich. He lives that loves thee better than
  he could.
Anne. Name him.
Rich.   Plantagenet.
Anne.   Why, that was he.
Rich. The selfsame name, but one of better
  nature.
Anne. Where is he?

Rich.   Here. (*She spitteth at him.*)
  Why dost thou spit at me?
Anne. Would it were mortal poison for thy
  sake!   145
Rich. Never came poison from so sweet a
  place.
Anne. Never hung poison on a fouler toad.
Out of my sight! Thou dost infect mine eyes.
Rich. Thine eyes, sweet lady, have infected
  mine.
Anne. Would they were basilisks, to strike
  thee dead!   150
Rich. I would they were, that I might die
  at once;
For now they kill me with a living death.
Those eyes of thine from mine have drawn salt
  tears,
Sham'd their aspects with store of childish
  drops —   154
These eyes, which never shed remorseful tear.
No, when my father York and Edward wept
To hear the piteous moan that Rutland made
When black-fac'd Clifford shook his sword at
  him;
Nor when thy warlike father, like a child,
Told the sad story of my father's death   160
And twenty times made pause to sob and weep,
That all the standers-by had wet their cheeks
Like trees bedash'd with rain — in that sad
  time
My manly eyes did scorn an humble tear;
And what these sorrows could not thence exhale,
Thy beauty hath, and made them blind with
  weeping.   166
I never sued to friend nor enemy;
My tongue could never learn sweet smoothing
  word;
But, now thy beauty is propos'd my fee,
My proud heart sues, and prompts my tongue
  to speak.   170
               She looks scornfully at him.
Teach not thy lip such scorn; for it was made
For kissing, lady, not for such contempt.
If thy revengeful heart cannot forgive,
Lo, here I lend thee this sharp-pointed sword,
Which if thou please to hide in this true breast
And let the soul forth that adoreth thee,   176
I lay it naked to the deadly stroke
And humbly beg the death upon my knee.
    He [*kneels and*] *lays his breast open. She*
                  offers at it with his sword.
Nay, do not pause; for I did kill King Henry —
But 'twas thy beauty that provoked me.   180
Nay, now dispatch. 'Twas I that stabb'd
  young Edward —

But 'twas thy heavenly face that set me on.
She falls the sword.
Take up the sword again, or take up me.
    Anne. Arise, dissembler. Though I wish
thy death,
I will not be thy executioner. 185
    Rich. Then bid me kill myself, and I will
do it.   [*Rises, and takes up his sword.*]
    Anne. I have already.
    Rich.   That was in thy rage.
Speak it again, and even with the word
This hand, which for thy love did kill thy love,
Shall for thy love kill a far truer love. 190
To both their deaths shalt thou be accessary.
    Anne. I would I knew thy heart.
    Rich. 'Tis figur'd in my tongue.
    Anne. I fear me both are false.
    Rich. Then never man was true. 195
    Anne. Well, well, put up your sword.
    Rich. Say then my peace is made.
    Anne. That shalt thou know hereafter.
    Rich. But shall I live in hope?
    Anne. All men, I hope, live so. 200
    Rich. Vouchsafe to wear this ring.
    Anne. To take is not to give.
                  [*Puts on the ring.*]
    Rich. Look how my ring encompasseth thy
finger,
Even so thy breast encloseth my poor heart.
Wear both of them, for both of them are thine.
And if thy poor devoted servant may 206
But beg one favour at thy gracious hand,
Thou dost confirm his happiness for ever.
    Anne. What is it?
    Rich. That it may please you leave these
sad designs 210
To him that hath most cause to be a mourner,
And presently repair to Crosby House;
Where — after I have solemnly interr'd
At Chertsey monast'ry this noble king
And wet his grave with my repentant tears 215
I will with all expedient duty see you.
For divers unknown reasons I beseech you,
Grant me this boon.
    Anne. With all my heart; and much it joys
me too
To see you are become so penitent. 220
Tressel and Berkeley, go along with me.
    Rich. Bid me farewell.
    Anne.   'Tis more than you deserve;
But since you teach me how to flatter you,
Imagine I have said farewell already.
    Exeunt two, [*Tressel and Berkeley,*] *with*
Anne.
    Rich. Sirs, take up the corse.

    Gent.   Towards Chertsey, noble lord? 225
    Rich. No, to White Friars. There attend my
coming.   *Exeunt. Manet Gloucester.*
Was ever woman in this humour woo'd?
Was ever woman in this humour won?
I'll have her, but I will not keep her long.
What? I that kill'd her husband and his father
To take her in her heart's extremest hate, 231
With curses in her mouth, tears in her eyes,
The bleeding witness of my hatred by,
Having God, her conscience, and these bars
against me,
And I no friends to back my suit withal 235
But the plain devil and dissembling looks?
And yet to win her — all the world to nothing?
Ha!
Hath she forgot already that brave prince,
Edward, her lord, whom I, some three months
since, 240
Stabb'd in my angry mood at Tewksbury?
A sweeter and a lovelier gentleman —
Fram'd in the prodigality of nature,
Young, valiant, wise, and (no doubt) right
    loyal —
The spacious world cannot again afford; 245
And will she yet abase her eyes on me,
That cropp'd the golden prime of this sweet
    prince
And made her widow to a woful bed?
On me, whose all not equals Edward's moiety?
On me, that halt and am misshapen thus? 250
My dukedom to a beggarly denier,
I do mistake my person all this while!
Upon my life, she finds (although I cannot)
Myself to be a marv'llous proper man.
I'll be at charges for a looking glass 255
And entertain a score or two of tailors
To study fashions to adorn my body.
Since I am crept in favour with myself,
I will maintain it with some little cost.
But first I'll turn yon fellow in his grave, 260
And then return lamenting to my love.
Shine out, fair sun, till I have bought a glass,
That I may see my shadow as I pass.   *Exit.*

Scene III. [*London. The Palace.*]

Enter Queen [*Elizabeth*], *Lord Rivers,* and
Lord Grey.

    Riv. Have patience, madam. There's no
doubt his Majesty
Will soon recover his accustom'd health.
    Grey. In that you brook it ill, it makes him
worse.

324

Therefore for God's sake entertain good com-
   fort   4
And cheer his Grace with quick and merry eyes.
  Queen. If he were dead, what would betide
    on me?
  Grey. No other harm but loss of such a
    lord.
  Queen. The loss of such a lord includes all
    harms.
  Grey. The heavens have bless'd you with a
    goodly son
To be your comforter when he is gone.   10
  Queen. Ah, he is young; and his minority
Is put unto the trust of Richard Gloucester,
A man that loves not me, nor none of you.
  Riv. Is it concluded he shall be Protector?
  Queen. It is determin'd, not concluded yet;
But so it must be if the King miscarry.   16

    Enter *Buckingham* and *Derby.*

  Grey. Here come the lords of Buckingham
    and Derby.
  Buck. Good time of day unto your royal
    Grace!
  Der. God make your Majesty joyful, as you
    have been!
  Queen. The Countess Richmond, good my
    Lord of Derby,   20
To your good prayer will scarcely say amen.
Yet, Derby, notwithstanding she's your wife
And loves not me, be you, good lord, assur'd
I hate not you for her proud arrogance.   24
  Der. I do beseech you, either not believe
The envious slanders of her false accusers;
Or, if she be accus'd on true report,
Bear with her weakness, which I think proceeds
From wayward sickness, and no grounded
    malice.
  Queen. Saw you the King to-day, my Lord
    of Derby?   30
  Der. But now the Duke of Buckingham
    and I
Are come from visiting his Majesty.
  Queen. What likelihood of his amendment,
    lords?
  Buck. Madam, good hope. His Grace speaks
    cheerfully.
  Queen. God grant him health! Did you
    confer with him?   35
  Buck. Ay, madam. He desires to make atone-
    ment
Between the Duke of Gloucester and your
    brothers,
And between them and my Lord Chamberlain,
And sent to warn them to his royal presence.

  Queen. Would all were well! but that will
    never be.   40
I fear our happiness is at the height.

    Enter *Richard,* [*Hastings,* and *Dorset*].

  Rich. They do me wrong, and I will not
    endure it!
Who is it that complains unto the King
That I (forsooth) am stern, and love them not?
By holy Paul, they love his Grace but lightly
That fill his ears with such dissentious rumours.
Because I cannot flatter and look fair,
Smile in men's faces, smooth, deceive, and cog,
Duck with French nods and apish courtesy,
I must be held a rancorous enemy.   50
Cannot a plain man live and think no harm
But thus his simple truth must be abus'd
With silken, sly, insinuating Jacks?
  Grey. To whom in all this presence speaks
    your Grace?
  Rich. To thee that hast nor honesty nor
    grace.   55
When have I injur'd thee? when done thee
    wrong?
Or thee? or thee? or any of your faction?
A plague upon you all! His royal Grace
(Whom God preserve better than you would
    wish!)
Cannot be quiet scarce a breathing while   60
But you must trouble him with lewd complaints.
  Queen. Brother of Gloucester, you mistake
    the matter.
The King, on his own royal disposition,
And not provok'd by any suitor else,
Aiming (belike) at your interior hatred,   65
That in your outward action shows itself
Against my children, brothers, and myself,
Makes him to send, that thereby he may gather
The ground of your ill will and so remove it.
  Rich. I cannot tell. The world is grown so
    bad   70
That wrens make prey where eagles dare not
    perch.
Since every Jack became a gentleman,
There's many a gentle person made a Jack.
  Queen. Come, come, we know your meaning,
    brother Gloucester: 74
You envy my advancement and my friends'.
God grant we never may have need of you!
  Rich. Meantime, God grants that I have
    need of you.
Our brother is imprison'd by your means,
Myself disgrac'd, and the nobility
Held in contempt, while great promotions   80
Are daily given to ennoble those

That scarce, some two days since, were worth
    a noble.
    Queen. By Him that rais'd me to this careful
    height
From that contented hap which I enjoy'd,
I never did incense his Majesty   85
Against the Duke of Clarence, but have been
An earnest advocate to plead for him.
My lord, you do me shameful injury
Falsely to draw me in these vile suspects.
    Rich. You may deny that you were not the
    mean   90
Of my Lord Hastings' late imprisonment.
    Riv. She may, my lord, for —
    Rich. She may, Lord Rivers? Why, who
    knows not so?
She may do more, sir, than denying that :
She may help you to many fair preferments, 95
And then deny her aiding hand therein
And lay those honours on your high desert.
What may she not? She may — ay marry
    may she —
    Riv. What marry may she?
    Rich. What marry may she? Marry with a
    king,   100
A bachelor and a handsome stripling too.
Iwis your grandam had a worser match.
    Queen. My Lord of Gloucester, I have too
    long borne
Your blunt upbraidings and your bitter scoffs.
By heaven, I will acquaint his Majesty   105
Of those gross taunts that oft I have endur'd.
I had rather be a country servant maid
Than a great queen with this condition,
To be so baited, scorn'd, and stormed at.   109

    Enter old *Queen Margaret*, [behind].

Small joy have I in being England's Queen.
    Q. Marg. [*aside*] And less'ned be that small,
    God I beseech him!
Thy honour, state, and seat is due to me.
    Rich. What? Threat you me with telling of
    the King?
Tell him, and spare not. Look, what I have said
I will avouch't in presence of the King.   115
I dare adventure to be sent to th' Tower.
'Tis time to speak : my pains are quite forgot.
    Q. Marg. [*aside*] Out, devil! I do remember
    them too well.
Thou kill'dst my husband Henry in the Tower,
And Edward, my poor son, at Tewksbury.   120
    Rich. Ere you were Queen, ay, or your hus-
    band King,
I was a packhorse in his great affairs ;
A weeder-out of his proud adversaries,

A liberal rewarder of his friends.
To royalize his blood I spent mine own.   125
    Q. Marg. [*aside*] Ay, and much better blood
    than his or thine.
    Rich. In all which time you and your hus-
    band Grey
Were factious for the house of Lancaster.
And, Rivers, so were you. Was not your hus-
    band   129
In Margaret's battle at Saint Alban's slain?
Let me put in your minds, if you forget,
What you have been ere this, and what you are;
Withal, what I have been, and what I am.
    Q. Marg. [*aside*] A murth'rous villain, and so
    still thou art.
    Rich. Poor Clarence did forsake his father
    Warwick ;   135
Ay, and forswore himself (which Jesu par-
    don!) —
    Q. Marg. [*aside*] Which God revenge!
    Rich. To fight on Edward's party for the
    crown ;
And for his meed, poor lord, he is mewed up.
I would to God my heart were flint like Ed-
    ward's,   140
Or Edward's soft and pitiful like mine.
I am too childish-foolish for this world.
    Q. Marg. [*aside*] Hie thee to hell for shame,
    and leave this world,
Thou cacodemon! There thy kingdom is.
    Riv. My Lord of Gloucester, in those busy
    days   145
Which here you urge to prove us enemies,
We follow'd then our lord, our sovereign king.
So should we you, if you should be our king.
    Rich. If I should be? I had rather be a
    pedlar.   149
Far be it from my heart, the thought thereof!
    Queen. As little joy, my lord, as you suppose
You should enjoy, were you this country's
    king —
As little joy may you suppose in me
That I enjoy, being the queen thereof.
    Q. Marg. [*aside*] As little joy enjoys the
    queen thereof ;   155
For I am she, and altogether joyless.
I can no longer hold me patient.
                [*Comes forward.*]
Hear me, you wrangling pirates, that fall out
In sharing that which you have pill'd from me!
Which of you trembles not that looks on me?
If not that I am Queen, you bow like sub-
    jects,   161
Yet that, by you depos'd, you quake like rebels?
Ah, gentle villain, do not turn away!

326

Rich. Foul wrinkled witch, what mak'st thou
in my sight?

Q. Marg. But repetition of what thou hast
marr'd.   165

That will I make before I let thee go.

Rich. Wert thou not banished on pain of
death?

Q. Marg. I was; but I do find more pain in
banishment

Than death can yield me here by my abode.

A husband and a son thou ow'st to me —   170

And thou a kingdom — all of you allegiance.

This sorrow that I have, by right is yours,

And all the pleasures you usurp are mine.

Rich. The curse my noble father laid on thee

When thou didst crown his warlike brows with
paper   175

And with thy scorns drew'st rivers from his eyes

And then, to dry them, gav'st the Duke a clout

Steep'd in the faultless blood of pretty Rutland —

His curses then, from bitterness of soul   179

Denounc'd against thee, are all fall'n upon thee;

And God, not we, hath plagu'd thy bloody deed.

Queen. So just is God, to right the innocent.

Hast. O, 'twas the foulest deed to slay that
babe

And the most merciless that e'er was heard of!

Riv. Tyrants themselves wept when it was
reported.   185

Dor. No man but prophesied revenge for it.

Buck. Northumberland, then present, wept
to see it.

Q. Marg. What? Were you snarling all before I came,

Ready to catch each other by the throat,

And turn you all your hatred now on me?   190

Did York's dread curse prevail so much with
heaven

That Henry's death, my lovely Edward's death,

Their kingdom's loss, my woful banishment,

Should all but answer for that peevish brat?

Can curses pierce the clouds and enter heaven?

Why then, give way, dull clouds, to my quick
curses!   196

Though not by war, by surfeit die your king,

As ours by murther to make him a king!

Edward thy son, that now is Prince of Wales,

For Edward our son, that was Prince of Wales,

Die in his youth by like untimely violence! 201

Thyself a queen, for me that was a queen,

Outlive thy glory, like my wretched self!

Long mayst thou live to wail thy children's
death

And see another, as I see thee now,   205

Deck'd in thy rights as thou art stall'd in mine!

Long die thy happy days before thy death,

And, after many length'ned hours of grief,

Die neither mother, wife, nor England's Queen!

Rivers and Dorset, you were standers-by,   210

And so wast thou, Lord Hastings, when my son

Was stabb'd with bloody daggers. God I pray
him

That none of you may live his natural age,

But by some unlook'd accident cut off!

Rich. Have done thy charm, thou hateful
wither'd hag!   215

Q. Marg. And leave out thee? Stay, dog, for
thou shalt hear me.

If heaven have any grievous plague in store

Exceeding those that I can wish upon thee,

O let them keep it till thy sins be ripe,

And then hurl down their indignation   220

On thee, the troubler of the poor world's peace!

The worm of conscience still begnaw thy soul!

Thy friends suspect for traitors while thou liv'st,

And take deep traitors for thy dearest friends!

No sleep close up that deadly eye of thine,   225

Unless it be while some tormenting dream

Affrights thee with a hell of ugly devils!

Thou elvish-mark'd, abortive, rooting hog!

Thou that wast seal'd in thy nativity

The slave of nature and the son of hell!   230

Thou slander of thy heavy mother's womb!

Thou loathed issue of thy father's loins!

Thou rag of honour! thou detested —

Rich.   Margaret.

Q. Marg.   Richard!

Rich.   Ha!

Q. Marg.   I call thee not.

Rich. I cry thee mercy then; for I did think

That thou hadst call'd me all these bitter names.

Q. Marg. Why, so I did, but look'd for no
reply.

O, let me make the period to my curse!

Rich. 'Tis done by me, and ends in 'Margaret.'

Queen. Thus have you breath'd your curse
against yourself.   240

Q. Marg. Poor painted queen, vain flourish
of my fortune!

Why strew'st thou sugar on that bottled spider

Whose deadly web ensnareth thee about?

Fool, fool! thou whet'st a knife to kill thyself.

The day will come that thou shalt wish for me

To help thee curse this poisonous bunch-back'd
toad.   246

Hast. False-boding woman, end thy frantic
curse,

Lest to thy harm thou move our patience.

327

Q. Marg. Foul shame upon you! You have all mov'd mine.

Riv. Were you well serv'd, you would be taught your duty. 250

Q. Marg. To serve me well, you all should do me duty,
Teach me to be your queen, and you my subjects.
O, serve me well, and teach yourselves that duty!

Dor. Dispute not with her; she is lunatic.

Q. Marg. Peace, Master Marquess, you are malapert. 255
Your fire-new stamp of honour is scarce current.
O that your young nobility could judge
What 'twere to lose it and be miserable!
They that stand high have many blasts to shake them,
And if they fall, they dash themselves to pieces.

Rich. Good counsel, marry! Learn it, learn it, Marquess. 261

Dor. It touches you, my lord, as much as me.

Rich. Ay, and much more; but I was born so high:
Our aëry buildeth in the cedar's top
And dallies with the wind and scorns the sun.

Q. Marg. And turns the sun to shade — alas! alas! 266
Witness my son, now in the shade of death,
Whose bright outshining beams thy cloudy wrath
Hath in eternal darkness folded up.
Your aëry buildeth in our aëry's nest. 270
O God, that seest it, do not suffer it!
As it is won with blood, lost be it so!

Buck. Peace, peace, for shame, if not for charity.

Q. Marg. Urge neither charity nor shame to me.
Uncharitably with me have you dealt, 275
And shamefully my hopes by you are butcher'd.
My charity is outrage, life my shame,
And in that shame still live my sorrow's rage!

Buck. Have done, have done.

Q. Marg. O princely Buckingham, I'll kiss thy hand 280
In sign of league and amity with thee.
Now fair befall thee and thy noble house!
Thy garments are not spotted with our blood,
Nor thou within the compass of my curse.

Buck. Nor no one here; for curses never pass 285
The lips of those that breathe them in the air.

Q. Marg. I will not think but they ascend the sky

And there awake God's gentle-sleeping peace.
O Buckingham, take heed of yonder dog!
Look, when he fawns he bites; and when he bites, 290
His venom tooth will rankle to the death.
Have not to do with him, beware of him;
Sin, death, and hell have set their marks on him,
And all their ministers attend on him.

Rich. What doth she say, my Lord of Buckingham? 295

Buck. Nothing that I respect, my gracious lord.

Q. Marg. What, dost thou scorn me for my gentle counsel
And soothe the devil that I warn thee from?
O, but remember this another day, 299
When he shall split thy very heart with sorrow,
And say poor Margaret was a prophetess!
Live each of you the subjects to his hate,
And he to yours, and all of you to God's! *Exit.*

Hast. My hair doth stand an end to hear her curses.

Riv. And so doth mine. I muse why she's at liberty. 305

Rich. I cannot blame her. By God's holy Mother,
She hath had too much wrong, and I repent
My part thereof that I have done to her.

Queen. I never did her any to my knowledge.

Rich. Yet you have all the vantage of her wrong. 310
I was too hot to do somebody good
That is too cold in thinking of it now.
Marry, as for Clarence, he is well repaid;
He is frank'd up to fatting for his pains —
God pardon them that are the cause thereof!

Riv. A virtuous and a Christianlike conclusion — 316
To pray for them that have done scath to us.

Rich. So do I ever — (*speaks to himself*) being well advis'd;
For had I curs'd now, I had curs'd myself.

Enter *Catesby.*

Cates. Madam, his Majesty doth call for you; 320
And for your Grace; and you, my noble lords.

Queen. Catesby, I come. Lords, will you go with me?

Riv. We wait upon your Grace. *Exeunt all but Gloucester.*

Rich. I do the wrong, and first begin to brawl.
The secret mischiefs that I set abroach 325
I lay unto the grievous charge of others.

Clarence, whom I indeed have cast in darkness,
I do beweep to many simple gulls —
Namely, to Derby, Hastings, Buckingham —
And tell them 'tis the Queen and her allies 330
That stir the King against the Duke my
  brother.
Now they believe it, and withal whet me
To be reveng'd on Rivers, Dorset, Grey.
But then I sigh, and, with a piece of Scripture,
Tell them that God bids us do good for evil;
And thus I clothe my naked villany 336
With odd old ends stol'n forth of holy writ,
And seem a saint when most I play the devil.

Enter two Murtherers.

But soft! Here come my executioners.
How now, my hardy, stout, resolved mates? 340
Are you now going to dispatch this thing?
  Villain. We are, my lord, and come to have
    the warrant,
That we may be admitted where he is.
  Rich. Well thought upon. I have it here
    about me: [*Gives the warrant.*]
When you have done, repair to Crosby Place.
But, sirs, be sudden in the execution; 346
Withal obdurate, do not hear him plead;
For Clarence is well-spoken, and perhaps
May move your hearts to pity if you mark him.
  Villain. Tut, tut, my lord! we will not stand
    to prate; 350
Talkers are no good doers. Be assur'd
We go to use our hands, and not our tongues.
  Rich. Your eyes drop millstones when fools'
    eyes fall tears.
I like you, lads. About your business straight.
Go, go, dispatch.
  Villain.   We will, my noble lord. 355
                              Exeunt.

Scene IV. [*London. The Tower.*]

Enter Clarence and Keeper.

  Keep. Why looks your Grace so heavily
to-day?
  Clar. O, I have pass'd a miserable night,
So full of fearful dreams, of ugly sights,
That, as I am a Christian faithful man,
I would not spend another such a night 5
Though 'twere to buy a world of happy days —
So full of dismal terror was the time.
  Keep. What was your dream, my lord? I
pray you tell me.
  Clar. Methoughts that I had broken from
the Tower

And was embark'd to cross to Burgundy, 10
And in my company my brother Gloucester,
Who from my cabin tempted me to walk
Upon the hatches. Thence we look'd toward
  England
And cited up a thousand heavy times,
During the wars of York and Lancaster, 15
That had befall'n us. As we pac'd along
Upon the giddy footing of the hatches,
Methought that Gloucester stumbled, and in
  falling
Struck me (that thought to stay him) overboard
Into the tumbling billows of the main. 20
O Lord! methought what pain it was to drown!
What dreadful noise of water in mine ears!
What sights of ugly death within mine eyes!
Methoughts I saw a thousand fearful wracks;
A thousand men that fishes gnaw'd upon; 25
Wedges of gold, great anchors, heaps of pearl,
Inestimable stones, unvalued jewels,
All scatt'red in the bottom of the sea.
Some lay in dead men's skulls, and in the holes
Where eyes did once inhabit, there were crept
(As 'twere in scorn of eyes) reflecting gems, 31
That woo'd the slimy bottom of the deep
And mock'd the dead bones that lay scatt'red by.
  Keep. Had you such leisure in the time of
    death
To gaze upon these secrets of the deep? 35
  Clar. Methought I had; and often did I
    strive
To yield the ghost; but still the envious flood
Stopp'd in my soul, and would not let it forth
To find the empty, vast, and wand'ring air,
But smother'd it within my panting bulk, 40
Which almost burst to belch it in the sea.
  Keep. Awak'd you not in this sore agony?
  Clar. No, no, my dream was lengthen'd after
    life.
O, then began the tempest to my soul!
I pass'd (methought) the melancholy flood, 45
With that sour ferryman which poets write of,
Unto the kingdom of perpetual night.
The first that there did greet my stranger soul
Was my great father-in-law, renowned War-
  wick, 49
Who spake aloud 'What scourge for perjury
Can this dark monarchy afford false Clarence?'
And so he vanish'd. Then came wand'ring by
A shadow like an angel, with bright hair
Dabbled in blood, and he shriek'd out aloud
'Clarence is come — false, fleeting, perjur'd
  Clarence, 53
That stabb'd me in the field by Tewksbury.
Seize on him, Furies, take him unto torment!'

With that (methought) a legion of foul fiends
Environ'd me, and howled in mine ears
Such hideous cries that with the very noise 60
I trembling wak'd, and for a season after
Could not believe but that I was in hell,
Such terrible impression made my dream.

   Keep. No marvel, lord, though it affrighted
     you.
I am afraid (methinks) to hear you tell it. 65
   Clar. Ah, keeper, keeper, I have done these
     things
(That now give evidence against my soul)
For Edward's sake, and see how he requites me!
O God! if my deep pray'rs cannot appease thee,
But thou wilt be aveng'd on my misdeeds, 70
Yet execute thy wrath in me alone.
O, spare my guiltless wife and my poor children!
Keeper, I prithee sit by me awhile.
My soul is heavy, and I fain would sleep.
   Keep. I will, my lord. God give your Grace
     good rest! 75
                    [Clarence sleeps.]

     Enter *Brakenbury,* the *Lieutenant.*

   Brak. Sorrow breaks seasons and reposing
     hours,
Makes the night morning and the noontide
     night.
Princes have but their titles for their glories,
An outward honour for an inward toil;
And for unfelt imaginations 80
They often feel a world of restless cares;
So that between their titles and low name
There's nothing differs but the outward fame.

     Enter two *Murtherers.*

   1. Murd. Ho! who's here?
   Brak. What wouldst thou, fellow? and how
     cam'st thou hither? 85
   1. Murd. I would speak with Clarence, and
I came hither on my legs.
   Brak. What, so brief?
   2. Murd. 'Tis better, sir, than to be tedious.
Let him see our commission; and talk no more.
                [Brakenbury] reads it.
   Brak. I am, in this, commanded to deliver
The noble Duke of Clarence to your hands.
I will not reason what is meant hereby, 94
Because I will be guiltless from the meaning.
There lies the Duke asleep, and there the keys.
I'll to the King and signify to him
That thus I have resign'd to you my charge.
   1. Murd. You may, sir; 'tis a point of wis-
dom. Fare you well. 100
     Exit [Brakenbury with Keeper].

   2. Murd. What? Shall we stab him as he
sleeps?
   1. Murd. No. He'll say 'twas done cowardly
when he wakes.
   2. Murd. When he wakes? Why, fool, he
shall never wake until the great Judgment Day.
   1. Murd. Why, then he'll say we stabb'd
him sleeping.
   2. Murd. The urging of that word 'judgment' hath bred a kind of remorse in me. 110
   1. Murd. What? Art thou afraid?
   2. Murd. Not to kill him, having a warrant;
but to be damn'd for killing him, from the
which no warrant can defend me.
   1. Murd. I thought thou hadst been resolute.
   2. Murd. So I am, to let him live.
   1. Murd. I'll back to the Duke of Gloucester
and tell him so. 119
   2. Murd. Nay, I prithee stay a little. I hope
this passionate humour of mine will change. It
was wont to hold me but while one tells twenty.
   1. Murd. How dost thou feel thyself now?
   2. Murd. Faith, some certain dregs of conscience are yet within me. 125
   1. Murd. Remember our reward when the
deed's done.
   2. Murd. Zounds, he dies! I had forgot the
reward.
   1. Murd. Where's thy conscience now? 130
   2. Murd. O, in the Duke of Gloucester's
purse.
   1. Murd. So, when he opens his purse to give
us our reward, thy conscience flies out.
   2. Murd. 'Tis no matter; let it go. There's
few or none will entertain it. 135
   1. Murd. What if it come to thee again?
   2. Murd. I'll not meddle with it; it makes a
man a coward. A man cannot steal, but it ac-
cuseth him; a man cannot swear, but it checks
him; a man cannot lie with his neighbour's
wife, but it detects him. 'Tis a blushing shamefac'd spirit that mutinies in a man's bosom. It
fills a man full of obstacles. It made me once
restore a purse of gold that (by chance) I found.
It beggars any man that keeps it. It is turn'd
out of towns and cities for a dangerous thing,
and every man that means to live well endeavours to trust to himself and live without it.
   1. Murd. Zounds, it is even now at my elbow,
persuading me not to kill the Duke. 150
   2. Murd. Take the devil in thy mind, and
believe him not. He would insinuate with thee
but to make thee sigh.
   1. Murd. I am strong-fram'd; he cannot prevail with me. 155

2. Murd. Spoke like a tall man that respects
thy reputation. Come, shall we fall to work?

1. Murd. Take him on the costard with the
hilts of thy sword, and then throw him into the
malmsey butt in the next room.   161

2. Murd. O excellent device! and make a
sop of him.

1. Murd. Soft! he wakes.

2. Murd. Strike!

1. Murd. No, we'll reason with him.   165

Clar. Where art thou, keeper? Give me a
cup of wine.

1. Murd. You shall have wine enough, my
lord, anon.

Clar. In God's name, what art thou?

1. Murd. A man, as you are.

Clar. But not as I am, royal.   170

1. Murd. Nor you as we are, loyal.

Clar. Thy voice is thunder, but thy looks
are humble.

1. Murd. My voice is now the King's, my
looks mine own.

Clar. How darkly and how deadly dost thou
speak!   174
Your eyes do menace me. Why look you pale?
Who sent you hither? Wherefore do you come?

Both. To, to, to —

Clar. To murther me?

Both. Ay, ay.

Clar. You scarcely have the hearts to tell
me so,   180
And therefore cannot have the hearts to do
it.
Wherein, my friends, have I offended you?

1. Murd. Offended us you have not, but the
King.

Clar. I shall be reconcil'd to him again.

2. Murd. Never, my lord; therefore prepare
to die.   185

Clar. Are you drawn forth among a world
of men
To slay the innocent? What is my offence?
Where is the evidence that doth accuse me?
What lawful quest have given their verdict up
Unto the frowning judge? or who pronounc'd
The bitter sentence of poor Clarence' death?
Before I be convict by course of law
To threaten me with death is most unlawful.
I charge you, as you hope to have redemption
By Christ's dear blood shed for our grievous
sins,   195
That you depart, and lay no hands on me.
The deed you undertake is damnable.

1. Murd. What we will do, we do upon
command.

2. Murd. And he that hath commanded is
our king.

Clar. Erroneous vassals! the great King of
Kings   200
Hath in the table of his law commanded
That thou shalt do no murther. Will you then
Spurn at his edict, and fulfil a man's?
Take heed; for he holds vengeance in his hand
To hurl upon their heads that break his law.

2. Murd. And that same vengeance doth he
hurl on thee   206
For false forswearing and for murther too.
Thou didst receive the sacrament to fight
In quarrel of the house of Lancaster.

1. Murd. And like a traitor to the name of
God   210
Didst break that vow, and with thy treacherous
blade
Unrip'dst the bowels of thy sov'reign's son.

2. Murd. Whom thou wast sworn to cherish
and defend.

1. Murd. How canst thou urge God's dreadful law to us   214
When thou hast broke it in such dear degree?

Clar. Alas! for whose sake did I that ill
deed?
For Edward, for my brother, for his sake.
He sends you not to murther me for this,
For in that sin he is as deep as I.
If God will be avenged for the deed,   220
O, know you yet he doth it publicly!
Take not the quarrel from his pow'rful arm.
He needs no indirect or lawless course
To cut off those that have offended him.

1. Murd. Who made thee then a bloody
minister   225
When gallant-springing brave Plantagenet,
That princely novice, was struck dead by thee?

Clar. My brother's love, the devil, and my
rage.

1. Murd. Thy brother's love, our duty, and
thy faults
Provoke us hither now to slaughter thee. 230

Clar. If you do love my brother, hate not me:
I am his brother, and I love him well.
If you are hir'd for meed, go back again,
And I will send you to my brother Gloucester,
Who shall reward you better for my life   235
Than Edward will for tidings of my death.

2. Murd. You are deceiv'd. Your brother
Gloucester hates you.

Clar. O, no, he loves me and he holds me
dear.
Go you to him from me.

1. Murd.   Ay, so we will.

Clar. Tell him, when that our princely father
York   240
Bless'd his three sons with his victorious arm
And charg'd us from his soul to love each other,
He little thought of this divided friendship.
Bid Gloucester think on this, and he will weep.
   1. Murd. Ay, millstones, as he lessoned us to
      weep.   245
   Clar. O, do not slander him, for he is kind.
   1. Murd. Right,
As snow in harvest. Come, you deceive your-
self.
'Tis he that sends us to destroy you here.
   Clar. It cannot be, for he bewept my for-
      tune,   250
And hugg'd me in his arms, and swore with sobs
That he would labour my delivery.
   1. Murd. Why, so he doth when he delivers
      you
From this earth's thraldom to the joys of
      heaven.
   2. Murd. Make peace with God, for you
      must die, my lord.   255
   Clar. Have you that holy feeling in your souls
To counsel me to make my peace with God,
And are you yet to your own souls so blind
That you will war with God by murd'ring me?
O sirs, consider, they that set you on   260
To do this deed will hate you for the deed.
   2. Murd. What shall we do?
   Clar.   Relent, and save your souls.
   1. Murd. Relent? 'tis cowardly and woman-
      ish.
   Clar. Not to relent is beastly, savage, devilish.
Which of you, if you were a prince's son,   265

Being pent from liberty, as I am now,
If two such murtherers as yourselves came to
      you,
Would not entreat for life?
My friend, I spy some pity in thy looks.
O, if thine eye be not a flatterer,   270
Come thou on my side, and entreat for me
As you would beg, were you in my distress.
A begging prince what beggar pities not?
   2. Murd. Look behind you, my lord!
   1. Murd. Take that! and that! (*Stabs him.*)
      If all this will not do,   275
I'll drown you in the malmsey butt within.
                          Exit [*with the body*].
   2. Murd. A bloody deed, and desperately
      dispatch'd!
How fain (like Pilate) would I wash my hands
Of this most grievous guilty murther!

Enter *First Murtherer*.

   1. Murd. How now? What mean'st thou
      that thou help'st me not?   280
By heaven, the Duke shall know how slack you
      have been.
   2. Murd. I would he knew that I had sav'd
      his brother!
Take thou the fee and tell him what I say,
For I repent me that the Duke is slain. *Exit.*
   1. Murd. So do not I. Go, coward as thou
      art.   285
Well, I'll go hide the body in some hole
Till that the Duke give order for his burial;
And when I have my meed, I will away,
For this will out, and then I must not stay.
                                          Exit.

ACT II. Scene I. [*London. The Palace.*]

Flourish. Enter the *King,* [*Edward,*] sick, the
*Queen, Lord Marquess Dorset, Rivers, Hastings,
Catesby, Buckingham,* [*Grey,* and others*].

   King. Why, so! Now have I done a good
      day's work.
You peers, continue this united league.
I every day expect an embassage
From my Redeemer to redeem me hence;   4
And more in peace my soul shall part to heaven,
Since I have made my friends at peace on earth.
Rivers and Hastings, take each other's hand;
Dissemble not your hatred, swear your love.
   Riv. By heaven, my soul is purg'd from
      grudging hate,   9
And with my hand I seal my true heart's love.

   Hast. So thrive I as I truly swear the like!
   King. Take heed you dally not before your
      king,
Lest he that is the supreme King of Kings
Confound your hidden falsehood and award
Either of you to be the other's end.   15
   Hast. So prosper I as I swear perfect love!
   Riv. And I as I love Hastings with my
      heart!
   King. Madam, yourself are not exempt from
      this;
Nor you, son Dorset; Buckingham, nor you·
You have been factious one against the other.
Wife, love Lord Hastings, let him kiss your
      hand,   21
And what you do, do it unfeignedly.

Queen. There, Hastings. I will never more
remember
Our former hatred, so thrive I and mine!
King. Dorset, embrace him; Hastings, love
Lord Marquess.   25
Dor. This interchange of love, I here protest,
Upon my part shall be inviolable.
Hast. And so swear I.
                              [*They embrace.*]
King. Now, princely Buckingham, seal thou
this league
With thy embracements to my wive's allies, 30
And make me happy in your unity.
Buck. [*to the Queen*] Whenever Buckingham
doth turn his hate
Upon your Grace, but with all duteous love
Doth cherish you and yours, God punish me
With hate in those where I expect most love!
When I have most need to employ a friend, 36
And most assured that he is a friend,
Deep, hollow, treacherous, and full of guile
Be he unto me! This do I beg of heaven,
When I am cold in love to you or yours.   40
                              Embrace.
King. A pleasing cordial, princely Buck-
ingham,
Is this thy vow unto my sickly heart.
There wanteth now our brother Gloucester here
To make the blessed period of this peace.

Enter *Gloucester.*

Buck. And in good time here comes the
noble Duke.   45
Rich. Good morrow to my sovereign King
and Queen
And princely peers. A happy time of day!
King. Happy indeed, as we have spent the
day.
Gloucester, we have done deeds of charity,
Made peace of enmity, fair love of hate,   50
Between these swelling wrong-incensed peers.
Rich. A blessed labour, my most sovereign
lord.
Among this princely heap, if any here
By false intelligence or wrong surmise
Hold me a foe —   55
If I unwittingly, or in my rage,
Have aught committed that is hardly borne
By any in this presence, I desire
To reconcile me to his friendly peace.
'Tis death to me to be at enmity: 60
I hate it, and desire all good men's love.
First, madam, I entreat true peace of you,
Which I will purchase with my duteous service;
Of you, my noble cousin Buckingham,

If ever any grudge were lodg'd between us; 65
Of you, Lord Rivers, and, Lord Grey, of you,
That all without desert have frown'd on me;
Dukes, earls, lords, gentlemen — indeed, of all.
I do not know that Englishman alive
With whom my soul is any jot at odds   70
More than the infant that is born to-night.
I thank my God for my humility.
Queen. A holy day shall this be kept here-
after.
I would to God all strifes were well compounded.
My sovereign lord, I do beseech your Highness
To take our brother Clarence to your grace. 76
Rich. Why, madam, have I off'red love for
this,
To be so flouted in this royal presence?
Who knows not that the gentle duke is dead?
                              They all start.
You do him injury to scorn his corse.   80
King. Who knows not he is dead? Who
knows he is?
Queen. All-seeing heaven, what a world is
this!
Buck. Look I so pale, Lord Dorset, as the
rest?
Dor. Ay, my good lord; and no man in the
presence
But his red colour hath forsook his cheeks. 85
King. Is Clarence dead? The order was re-
vers'd.
Rich. But he (poor soul) by your first order
died,
And that a winged Mercury did bear.
Some tardy cripple bore the countermand,
That came too lag to see him buried.   90
God grant that some, less noble and less loyal,
Nearer in bloody thoughts, but not in blood,
Deserve not worse than wretched Clarence did,
And yet go current from suspicion!

Enter *Derby.*

Der. A boon, my sovereign, for my service
done!   [*Kneels.*]
King. I prithee peace. My soul is full of
sorrow.   96
Der. I will not rise unless your Highness
hear me.
King. Then say at once what is it thou re-
quests.
Der. The forfeit, sovereign, of my servant's
life,
Who slew to-day a riotous gentleman   100
Lately attendant on the Duke of Norfolk.
King. Have I a tongue to doom my broth-
er's death

And shall that tongue give pardon to a slave?
My brother kill'd no man: his fault was
  thought,
And yet his punishment was bitter death. 105
Who sued to me for him? Who (in my wrath)
Kneel'd at my feet and bid me be advis'd?
Who spoke of brotherhood? Who spoke of
  love?
Who told me how the poor soul did forsake
The mighty Warwick and did fight for me? 110
Who told me, in the field at Tewksbury,
When Oxford had me down, he rescued me
And said, 'Dear brother, live, and be a king'?
Who told me, when we both lay in the field
Frozen (almost) to death, how he did lap me 116
Even in his garments, and did give himself
(All thin and naked) to the numb cold night?
All this from my remembrance brutish wrath
Sinfully pluck'd, and not a man of you
Had so much grace to put it in my mind. 120
But when your carters or your waiting vassals
Have done a drunken slaughter and defac'd
The precious image of our dear Redeemer,
You straight are on your knees for pardon,
  pardon;
And I (unjustly too) must grant it you. 125
                    [*Derby rises.*]
But for my brother not a man would speak,
Nor I (ungracious) speak unto myself
For him, poor soul! The proudest of you all
Have been beholding to him in his life;
Yet none of you would once beg for his life. 130
O God, I fear thy justice will take hold
On me and you, and mine and yours, for this!
Come, Hastings, help me to my closet. Ah,
  poor Clarence!
      Exeunt some with King and Queen.
  Rich. This is the fruit of rashness! Mark'd
  you not
How that the guilty kindred of the Queen 135
Look'd pale when they did hear of Clarence'
  death?
O, they did urge it still unto the King!
God will revenge it. Come, lords, will you go
To comfort Edward with our company? 139
  Buck. We wait upon your Grace. *Exeunt.*

Scene II. [*London. The Palace.*]

Enter the old *Duchess of York*, with the two
  Children of *Clarence.*

  Boy. Good grandam, tell us, is our father
  dead?
  Duch. No, boy.

  Daughter. Why do you weep so oft, and beat
  your breast,
And cry 'O Clarence, my unhappy son'?
  Boy. Why do you look on us, and shake your
  head, 5
And call us orphans, wretches, castaways,
If that our noble father were alive?
  Duch. My pretty cousins, you mistake me
  both.
I do lament the sickness of the King, 9
As loath to lose him, not your father's death.
It were lost sorrow to wail one that's lost.
  Boy. Then you conclude, my grandam, he
  is dead.
The King mine uncle is to blame for this.
God will revenge it, whom I will importune
With earnest prayers all to that effect. 15
  Daughter. And so will I.
  Duch. Peace, children, peace! The King
  doth love you well.
Incapable and shallow innocents,
You cannot guess who caus'd your father's
  death.
  Boy. Grandam, we can; for my good uncle
  Gloucester 20
Told me the King, provok'd to it by the Queen,
Devis'd impeachments to imprison him;
And when my uncle told me so, he wept,
And pitied me, and kindly kiss'd my cheek;
Bade me rely on him as on my father, 25
And he would love me dearly as a child.
  Duch. Ah, that deceit should steal such
  gentle shape
And with a virtuous visor hide deep vice!
He is my son — ay, and therein my shame;
Yet from my dugs he drew not this deceit. 30
  Boy. Think you my uncle did dissemble,
  grandam?
  Duch. Ay, boy.
  Boy. I cannot think it. Hark! What noise
  is this?

Enter *Queen* [*Elizabeth*] with her hair about her
  ears, *Rivers* and *Dorset* after her.

  Queen. Ah, who shall hinder me to wail and
  weep,
To chide my fortune, and torment myself? 35
I'll join with black despair against my soul
And to myself become an enemy.
  Duch. What means this scene of rude im-
  patience?
  Queen. To make an act of tragic violence.
Edward, my lord, thy son, our king, is dead! 40
Why grow the branches when the root is gone?
Why wither not the leaves that want their sap?

If you will live, lament; if die, be brief,
That our swift-winged souls may catch the
    King's,
Or like obedient subjects follow him   45
To his new kingdom of ne'er-changing night.
    Duch. Ah, so much interest have I in thy
    sorrow
As I had title in thy noble husband.
I have bewept a worthy husband's death,
And liv'd with looking on his images;   50
But now two mirrors of his princely semblance
Are crack'd in pieces by malignant death,
And I for comfort have but one false glass
That grieves me when I see my shame in him.
Thou art a widow; yet thou art a mother   55
And hast the comfort of thy children left;
But death hath snatch'd my husband from
    mine arms
And pluck'd two crutches from my feeble hands,
Clarence and Edward. O, what cause have I
(Thine being but a moiety of my moan)   60
To overgo thy woes and drown thy cries!
    Boy. Good aunt, you wept not for our fa-
    ther's death.
How can we aid you with our kindred tears?
    Daughter. Our fatherless distress was left un-
    moan'd.
Your widow-dolour likewise be unwept!   65
    Queen. Give me no help in lamentation;
I am not barren to bring forth complaints.
All springs reduce their currents to mine eyes,
That I, being govern'd by the watery moon,
May send forth plenteous tears to drown the
    world.   70
Ah for my husband, for my dear lord Edward!
    Children. Ah for our father, for our dear lord
    Clarence!
    Duch. Alas for both, both mine, Edward and
    Clarence!
    Queen. What stay had I but Edward? and
    he's gone.
    Children. What stay had we but Clarence?
    and he's gone.   75
    Duch. What stays had I but they? and
    they are gone.
    Queen. Was never widow had so dear a loss.
    Children. Were never orphans had so dear a
    loss.
    Duch. Was never mother had so dear a loss.
Alas, I am the mother of these griefs!   80
Their woes are parcell'd, mine is general.
She for an Edward weeps, and so do I;
I for a Clarence weep, so doth not she:
These babes for Clarence weep, and so do I;
I for an Edward weep, so do not they.   85

Alas, you three on me, threefold distress'd,
Pour all your tears! I am your sorrow's nurse,
And I will pamper it with lamentation.
    Dor. Comfort, dear mother. God is much
    displeas'd
That you take with unthankfulness his doing.
In common worldly things 'tis call'd ungrate-
    ful   91
With dull unwillingness to repay a debt
Which with a bounteous hand was kindly lent;
Much more to be thus opposite with heaven
For it requires the royal debt it lent you.   95
    Riv. Madam, bethink you like a careful
    mother
Of the young Prince your son. Send straight
    for him;
Let him be crown'd; in him your comfort lives.
Drown desperate sorrow in dead Edward's
    grave   99
And plant your joys in living Edward's throne.

Enter *Richard, Buckingham, Derby, Hastings,*
    and *Ratcliff.*

    Rich. Sister, have comfort. All of us have
    cause
To wail the dimming of our shining star;
But none can help our harms by wailing them.
Madam, my mother, I do cry you mercy;
I did not see your Grace. Humbly on my knee
I crave your blessing.   106
    Duch. God bless thee, and put meekness in
    thy breast,
Love, charity, obedience, and true duty!
    Rich. Amen! — [*aside*] and make me die a
    good old man!
That is the butt end of a mother's blessing. 110
I marvel that her Grace did leave it out.
    Buck. You cloudy princes and heart-
    sorrowing peers
That bear this heavy mutual load of moan,
Now cheer each other in each other's love.
Though we have spent our harvest of this king,
We are to reap the harvest of his son.   116
The broken rancour of your high-swol'n hates,
But lately splinter'd, knit, and join'd together,
Must gently be preserv'd, cherish'd, and kept.
Me seemeth good that with some little train 120
Forthwith from Ludlow the young Prince be fet
Hither to London, to be crown'd our king.
    Riv. Why with some little train, my Lord of
    Buckingham?
    Buck. Marry, my lord, lest by a multitude
The new-heal'd wound of malice should break
    out,   125
Which would be so much the more dangerous

By how much the estate is green and yet un-
govern'd.
Where every horse bears his commanding rein
And may direct his course as please himself,
As well the fear of harm as harm apparent, 130
In my opinion, ought to be prevented.
  Rich. I hope the King made peace with all
    of us;
And the compact is firm and true in me.
  Riv. And so in me; and so (I think) in all.
Yet, since it is but green, it should be put 135
To no apparent likelihood of breach,
Which haply by much company might be urg'd.
Therefore I say with noble Buckingham
That it is meet so few should fetch the Prince.
  Hast. And so say I.   140
  Rich. Then be it so; and go we to determine
Who they shall be that straight shall post to
  Ludlow.
Madam, and you, my sister, will you go
To give your censures in this business?
  Both. With all our hearts.   145
    Exeunt. Manent Buckingham and Richard.
  Buck. My lord, whoever journeys to the
    Prince,
For God's sake let not us two stay at home;
For by the way I'll sort occasion,
As index to the story we late talk'd of,
To part the Queen's proud kindred from the
    Prince.   150
  Rich. My other self, my counsel's consistory,
My oracle, my prophet, my dear cousin,
I, as a child, will go by thy direction.
Toward Ludlow then, for we'll not stay behind.
                                        Exeunt.

Scene III. [*London. A street.*]

Enter one *Citizen* at one door and another at
    the other.

  1. Cit. Good morrow, neighbour. Whither
    away so fast?
  2. Cit. I promise you I scarcely know myself.
Hear you the news abroad?
  1. Cit.   Yes, that the King is dead.
  2. Cit. Ill news, by'r Lady. Seldom comes
    the better.
I fear, I fear 'twill prove a giddy world.   5

Enter another *Citizen.*

  3. Cit. Neighbours, God speed!
  1. Cit.   Give you good morrow, sir.
  3. Cit. Doth the news hold of good King
    Edward's death?

  2. Cit. Ay, sir, it is too true. God help the
    while!
  3. Cit. Then, masters, look to see a troublous
    world.
  1. Cit. No, no! By God's good grace his son
    shall reign.   10
  3. Cit. Woe to that land that's govern'd by
    a child!
  2. Cit. In him there is a hope of government,
That, in his nonage, council under him,
And, in his full and ripened years, himself,
No doubt shall then, and till then, govern well.
  1. Cit. So stood the state when Henry the
    Sixth   16
Was crown'd in Paris but at nine months old.
  3. Cit. Stood the state so? No, no, good
    friends, God wot!
For then this land was famously enrich'd
With politic grave counsel; then the King 20
Had virtuous uncles to protect his Grace.
  1. Cit. Why, so hath this, both by his father
    and mother.
  3. Cit. Better it were they all came by his
    father,
Or by his father there were none at all;
For emulation who shall now be nearest   25
Will touch us all too near, if God prevent not.
O, full of danger is the Duke of Gloucester,
And the Queen's sons and brothers haught and
    proud;
And were they to be rul'd, and not to rule,
This sickly land might solace as before.   30
  1. Cit. Come, come, we fear the worst. All
    will be well.
  3. Cit. When clouds are seen, wise men put
    on their cloaks;
When great leaves fall, then winter is at hand;
When the sun sets, who doth not look for night?
Untimely storms make men expect a dearth. 35
All may be well; but if God sort it so,
'Tis more than we deserve or I expect.
  2. Cit. Truly, the hearts of men are full of
    fear.
You cannot reason (almost) with a man
That looks not heavily and full of dread.   40
  3. Cit. Before the days of change, still is it
    so.
By a divine instinct men's minds mistrust
Ensuing danger; as by proof we see
The water swell before a boist'rous storm.
But leave it all to God. Whither away?   45
  2. Cit. Marry, we were sent for to the jus-
    tices.
  3. Cit. And so was I. I'll bear you company
                                        Exeunt.

Scene IV. [*London. The Palace.*]

Enter [the] *Archbishop* [*of York*], [the] young
[*Duke of*] *York, Queen* [*Elizabeth*], and the
Duchess of York.

Arch. Last night, I hear, they lay at North-
ampton;
At Stony Stratford they do rest to-night;
To-morrow or next day they will be here.
   Duch. I long with all my heart to see the
Prince.
I hope he is much grown since last I saw him. 5
   Queen. But I hear no. They say my son of
York
Has almost overta'en him in his growth.
   York. Ay, mother; but I would not have
it so.
   Duch. Why, my young cousin, it is good to
grow.
   York. Grandam, one night as we did sit at
supper, 10
My uncle Rivers talk'd how I did grow
More than my brother. 'Ay,' quoth my uncle
Gloucester,
'Small herbs have grace; great weeds do grow
apace.'
And since, methinks, I would not grow so fast,
Because sweet flow'rs are slow and weeds make
haste. 15
   Duch. Good faith, good faith, the saying did
not hold
In him that did object the same to thee.
He was the wretched'st thing when he was
young,
So long a-growing and so leisurely
That. if his rule were true, he should be gracious.
   Arch. And so no doubt he is, my gracious
madam. 21
   Duch. I hope he is; but yet let mothers
doubt.
   York. Now, by my troth, if I had been re-
memb'red,
I could have given my uncle's Grace a flout
To touch his growth nearer than he touch'd
mine. 25
   Duch. How, my young York? I prithee let
me hear it.
   York. Marry, they say my uncle grew so fast
That he could gnaw a crust at two hours old.
'Twas full two years ere I could get a tooth.
Grandam, this would have been a biting jest.
   Duch. I prithee, pretty York, who told thee
this? 31
   York. Grandam, his nurse.

   Duch. His nurse? Why, she was dead ere
thou wast born.
   York. If 'twere not she, I cannot tell who
told me.
   Queen. A parlous boy! Go to, you are too
shrewd. 35
   Duch. Good madam, be not angry with the
child.
   Queen. Pitchers have ears.

Enter a *Messenger.*

   Arch. Here comes a messenger. What news?
   Mess. Such news, my lord, as grieves me to
report.
   Queen. How doth the Prince?
   Mess.   Well, madam, and in health. 40
   Duch. What is thy news then?
   Mess. Lord Rivers and Lord Grey are sent
to Pomfret,
With them Sir Thomas Vaughan, prisoners.
   Duch. Who hath committed them?
   Mess.   The mighty Dukes,
Gloucester and Buckingham.
   Arch.   For what offence? 45
   Mess. The sum of all I can I have disclos'd.
Why or for what the nobles were committed
Is all unknown to me, my gracious lord.
   Queen. Ay me! I see the ruin of our house.
The tiger now hath seiz'd the gentle hind; 50
Insulting tyranny begins to jut
Upon the innocent and aweless throne.
Welcome destruction, blood, and massacre!
I see (as in a map) the end of all.
   Duch. Accursed and unquiet wrangling days,
How many of you have mine eyes beheld! 56
My husband lost his life to get the crown,
And often up and down my sons were toss'd
For me to joy and weep their gain and loss;
And being seated, and domestic broils 60
Clean overblown, themselves the conquerors
Make war upon themselves, brother to brother,
Blood to blood, self against self. O preposterous
And frantic outrage, end thy damned spleen,
Or let me die, to look on death no more! 65
   Queen. Come, come, my boy; we will to
sanctuary.
Madam, farewell.
   Duch.   Stay, I will go with you.
   Queen. You have no cause.
   Arch. [*to the Queen*] My gracious lady, go,
And thither bear your treasure and your goods.
For my part, I'll resign unto your Grace 70
The seal I keep; and so betide to me
As well I tender you and all of yours!
Go, I'll conduct you to the sanctuary. *Exeunt.*

ACT III. Scene I. [*London. A street.*]

The trumpets sound. Enter young *Prince*, the *Dukes of Gloucester* and *Buckingham Lord Cardinal* [*Bourchier, Catesby*,] with ~ners.

Buck. Welcome, sweet Prince, to London, to your chamber.

Rich. Welcome, dear cousin, my thoughts' sovereign.

The weary way hath made you melancholy.

Prince. No, uncle; but our crosses on the way

Have made it tedious, wearisome, and heavy.

I want more uncles here to welcome me.   6

Rich. Sweet Prince, the untainted virtue ʌf your years

Hath not yet div'd into the world's deceit.

No more can you distinguish of a man

Than of his outward show; which, God he knows,   10

Seldom or never jumpeth with the heart.

Those uncles which you want were dangerous.

Your Grace attended to their sug'red words

But look'd not on the poison of their hearts:

God keep you from them, and from such false friends!   15

Prince. God keep me from false friends! But they were none.

Rich. My lord, the Mayor of London comes to greet you.

Enter *Lord Mayor* [and his *Train*].

L. May. God bless your Grace with health and happy days!

Prince. I thank you, good my lord, and thank you all.

[*Mayor and his Train retire.*]

I thought my mother and my brother York   20

Would long ere this have met us on the way.

Fie, what a slug is Hastings that he comes not

To tell us whether they will come or no!

Enter *Lord Hastings*.

Buck. And, in good time, here comes the sweating lord.

Prince. Welcome, my lord. What, will our mother come?   25

Hast. On what occasion God he knows, not I,

The Queen your mother and your brother York

Have taken sanctuary. The tender Prince

Would fain have come with me to meet your Grace,

But by his mother was perforce withheld.   30

Buck. Fie, what an indirect and peevish course

Is this of hers! Lord Cardinal, will your Grace

Persuade the Queen to send the Duke of York

Unto his princely brother presently?

If she d·. y, Lord Hastings, go with him   35

And froɪ her jealous arms pluck him perforce.

Card. ᴧy Lord of Buckingham, if my weak oratory

Can from his mother win the Duke of York,

Anon expect him here; but if she be obdurate

To mild entreaties, God in heaven forbid   40

We should infringe the holy privilege

Of blessed sanctuary! Not for all this land

Would I be guilty of so great a sin.

Buck. You are too senseless-obstinate, my lord,

Too ceremonious and traditional.   45

Weigh it but with the grossness of his age,

You break not sanctuary in seizing him.

The benefit thereof is always granted

To those whose dealings have deserv'd the place

And those who have the wit to claim the place.

This prince hath neither claim'd it nor deserv'd it,   51

And therefore, in mine opinion, cannot have it.

Then, taking him from thence that is not there,

You break no privilege nor charter there.

Oft have I heard of sanctuary men,   55

But sanctuary children ne'er till now.

Card. My lord, you shall o'errule my mind for once.

Come on, Lord Hastings, will you go with me?

Hast. I go, my lord.

Prince. Good lords, make all the speedy haste you may.   60

Exeunt Cardinal and Hastings.

Say, uncle Gloucester, if our brother come,

Where shall we sojourn till our coronation?

Rich. Where it think'st best unto your royal self.

If I may counsel you, some day or two

Your Highness shall repose you at the Tower;

Then where you please, and shall be thought most fit   66

For your best health and recreation.

Prince. I do not like the Tower, of any place.

Did Julius Cæsar build that place, my lord?

Buck. He did, my gracious lord, begin that place,   70

Which, since, succeeding ages have re-edified.

338

Prince. Is it upon record, or else reported
Successively from age to age, he built it?
Buck. Upon record, my gracious lord.
Prince. But say, my lord, it were not regis-   75
t'red,
Methinks the truth should live from age to age,
As 'twere retail'd to all posterity,
Even to the general all-ending day.
Rich. [*aside*] So wise so young, they say do
   never live long.
Prince. What say you, uncle?   80
Rich. I say, without characters fame lives
long.
[*Aside*] Thus, like the formal vice, Iniquity,
I moralize two meanings in one word.
Prince. That Julius Cæsar was a famous
   man.
With what his valour did enrich his wit,   85
His wit set down to make his valour live.
Death makes no conquest of this conqueror,
For now he lives in fame, though not in life.
I'll tell you what, my cousin Buckingham —
Buck. What, my gracious lord?   90
Prince. An if I live until I be a man,
I'll win our ancient right in France again
Or die a soldier as I liv'd a king.
Rich. [*aside*] Short summers lightly have a
   forward spring.

Enter young York, Hastings, *and* Cardinal.

Buck. Now in good time, here comes the
   Duke of York.   95
Prince. Richard of York, how fares our
   noble brother?
York. Well, my dread lord — so must I call
   you now.
Prince. Ay, brother — to our grief, as it is
   yours.
Too late he died that might have kept that title,
Which by his death hath lost much majesty.
Rich. How fares our cousin, noble Lord of
   York?   101
York. I thank you, gentle uncle. O, my lord,
You said that idle weeds are fast in growth.
The Prince my brother hath outgrown me far.
Rich. He hath, my lord.
York.   And therefore is he idle? 105
Rich. O my fair cousin, I must not say so.
York. Then he is more beholding to you
   than I.
Rich. He may command me as my sovereign,
But you have power in me as in a kinsman.
York. I pray you, uncle, give me this dagger.
Rich. My dagger, little cousin? With all my
   heart.   111

Prince. A beggar, brother?
York. Of my kind uncle, that I know will
   give,
And being but a toy, which is no grief to
   give.
Rich. A greater gift than that I'll give my
   cousin.   115
York. A greater gift? O, that's the sword
   to it.
Rich. Ay, gentle cousin, were it light
   enough.
York. O, then I see you will part but with
   light gifts!
In weightier things you'll say a beggar nay.
Rich. It is too weighty for your Grace to
   wear.   120
York. I weigh it lightly, were it heavier.
Rich. What, would you have my weapon,
   little lord?
York. I would, that I might thank you as
   you call me.
Rich. How?
York. Little.   125
Prince. My Lord of York will still be cross
   in talk.
Uncle, your Grace knows how to bear with him.
York. You mean, to bear me, not to bear
   with me.
Uncle, my brother mocks both you and me:
Because that I am little, like an ape,   130
He thinks that you should bear me on your
   shoulders.
Buck. [*aside to Hastings*] With what a sharp-
   provided wit he reasons!
To mitigate the scorn he gives his uncle,
He prettily and aptly taunts himself.
So cunning, and so young, is wonderful.   135
Rich. My lord, will 't please you pass along?
Myself and my good cousin Buckingham
Will to your mother, to entreat of her
To meet you at the Tower and welcome you.
York. What, will you go unto the Tower,
   my lord?   140
Prince. My Lord Protector needs will have
   it so.
York. I shall not sleep in quiet at the
   Tower.
Rich. Why, what should you fear?
York. Marry, my uncle Clarence' angry
   ghost.
My grandam told me he was murther'd there.
Prince. I fear no uncles dead.   146
Rich. Nor none that live, I hope.
Prince. An if they live, I hope I need not
   fear.

But come, my lord; and with a heavy heart,
Thinking on them, go I unto the Tower.   150
   A sennet. Exeunt Prince, York, Hastings,
    [Cardinal, and others]. Manent Richard,
    Buckingham, and Catesby.
  Buck. Think you, my lord, this little prating
    York
Was not incensed by his subtile mother
To taunt and scorn you thus opprobriously?
  Rich. No doubt, no doubt. O, 'tis a parlous
    boy,
Bold, quick, ingenious, forward, capable.   155
He is all the mother's, from the top to toe.
  Buck. Well, let them rest. Come hither,
    Catesby.
Thou art sworn as deeply to effect what we
    intend
As closely to conceal what we impart.   159
Thou know'st our reasons urg'd upon the way.
What think'st thou? Is it not an easy matter
To make William Lord Hastings of our mind
For the instalment of this noble Duke
In the seat royal of this famous isle?
  Cates. He for his father's sake so loves the
    Prince   165
That he will not be won to aught against him.
  Buck. What think'st thou then of Stanley?
    Will not he?
  Cates. He will do all in all as Hastings doth.
  Buck. Well then, no more but this: go,
    gentle Catesby,
And, as it were far off, sound thou Lord
    Hastings   170
How he doth stand affected to our purpose,
And summon him to-morrow to the Tower
To sit about the coronation.
If thou dost find him tractable to us,   174
Encourage him, and tell him all our reasons:
If he be leaden, icy, cold, unwilling,
Be thou so too, and so break off the talk,
And give us notice of his inclination;
For we to-morrow hold divided councils,
Wherein thyself shalt highly be employ'd.   180
  Rich. Commend me to Lord William. Tell
    him, Catesby,
His ancient knot of dangerous adversaries
To-morrow are let blood at Pomfret Castle,
And bid my lord, for joy of this good news,
Give Mistress Shore one gentle kiss the more.
  Buck. Good Catesby, go effect this business
    soundly.   186
  Cates. My good lords both, with all the heed
    I can.
  Rich. Shall we hear from you, Catesby, ere
    we sleep?

  Cates. You shall, my lord.
  Rich. At Crosby House, there shall you find
    us both.   190
                Exit Catesby.
  Buck. Now, my lord, what shall we do if we
    perceive
Lord Hastings will not yield to our complots?
  Rich. Chop off his head! Something we will
    determine.
And look, when I am King, claim thou of me
The earldom of Hereford and all the moveables
Whereof the King my brother was possess'd.   196
  Buck. I'll claim that promise at your Grace's
    hand.
  Rich. And look to have it yielded with all
    kindness.
Come, let us sup betimes, that afterwards
We may digest our complots in some form.   200
                   Exeunt.

Scene II. [*Before the house of* Lord Hastings.]

Enter a Messenger *to the door of* Hastings.

  Mess. My lord! my lord!
  Hast. [*within*] Who knocks?
  Mess. One from the Lord Stanley.
  Hast. [*within*] What is't o'clock?
  Mess. Upon the stroke of four.   5

Enter Lord Hastings.

  Hast. Cannot my Lord Stanley sleep these
    tedious nights?
  Mess. So it appears by that I have to say.
First, he commends him to your noble self.
  Hast. What then?
  Mess. Then certifies your lordship that this
    night   10
He dreamt the boar had rased off his helm.
Besides, he says there are two councils kept;
And that may be determin'd at the one
Which may make you and him to rue at
    th' other.
Therefore he sends to know your lordship's
    pleasure,   15
If you will presently take horse with him
And with all speed post with him toward the
    North
To shun the danger that his soul divines.
  Hast. Go, fellow, go, return unto thy lord;
Bid him not fear the separated councils.   20
His Honour and myself are at the one,
And at the other is my good friend Catesby;

Where nothing can proceed that toucheth us
Whereof I shall not have intelligence.   24
Tell him his fears are shallow, without instance;
And for his dreams, I wonder he's so simple
To trust the mock'ry of unquiet slumbers.
To fly the boar before the boar pursues
Were to incense the boar to follow us
And make pursuit where he did mean no chase.
Go, bid thy master rise and come to me,   31
And we will both together to the Tower,
Where he shall see the boar will use us kindly.
   Mess. I'll go, my lord, and tell him what you
   say.   *Exit.*

Enter *Catesby.*

   Cates. Many good morrows to my noble
   lord!   35
   Hast. Good morrow, Catesby; you are early
   stirring.
What news, what news, in this our tott'ring
   state?
   Cates. It is a reeling world indeed, my lord,
And I believe will never stand upright
Till Richard wear the garland of the realm.   40
   Hast. How? wear the garland? Dost thou
   mean the crown?
   Cates. Ay, my good lord.
   Hast. I'll have this crown of mine cut from
   my shoulders
Before I'll see the crown so foul misplac'd.
But canst thou guess that he doth aim at it?
   Cates. Ay, on my life; and hopes to find you
   forward   46
Upon his party for the gain thereof;
And thereupon he sends you this good news,
That this same very day your enemies,
The kindred of the Queen, must die at Pom-
   fret.   50
   Hast. Indeed I am no mourner for that news,
Because they have been still my adversaries;
But that I'll give my voice on Richard's side
To bar my master's heirs in true descent —
God knows I will not do it, to the death!   55
   Cates. God keep your lordship in that gra-
   cious mind!
   Hast. But I shall laugh at this a twelve-
   month hence,
That they which brought me in my master's
   hate,
I live to look upon their tragedy.   59
Well, Catesby, ere a fortnight make me older,
I'll send some packing that yet think not on't.
   Cates. 'Tis a vile thing to die, my gracious
   lord,
When men are unprepar'd and look not for it.

   Hast. O monstrous. monstrous! and so falls
   it out
With Rivers, Vaughan, Grey; and so 'twill do
With some men else, that think themselves as
   safe   66
As thou and I, who (as thou know'st) are dear
To princely Richard and to Buckingham.
   Cates. The Princes both make high account
   of you —
[*Aside*] For they account his head upon the
   bridge.   70
   Hast. I know they do, and I have well de-
   serv'd it.

Enter *Lord Stanley.*

Come on, come on! Where is your boar-spear,
   man?
Fear you the boar, and go so unprovided?
   Stan. My lord, good morrow. Good mor-
   row, Catesby.
You may jest on, but, by the Holy Rood,   75
I do not like these several councils, I.
   Hast. My lord,
I hold my life as dear as you do yours,
And never in my days, I do protest,
Was it so precious to me as 'tis now.   80
Think you, but that I know our state secure,
I would be so triumphant as I am?
   Stan. The lords at Pomfret, when they rode
   from London,
Were jocund and suppos'd their states were
   sure,
And they indeed had no cause to mistrust;   85
But yet you see how soon the day o'ercast.
This sudden stab of rancour I misdoubt.
Pray God, I say, I prove a needless coward!
What, shall we toward the Tower? The day is
   spent.
   Hast. Come, come, have with you. Wot
   you what, my lord?   90
To-day the lords you talk of are beheaded.
   Stan. They, for their truth, might better
   wear their heads
Than some that have accus'd them wear their
   hats.
But come, my lord, let us away.

Enter a *Pursuivant.*

   Hast. Go on before. I'll talk with this good
   fellow.   95
                  Exeunt Lord Stanley and Catesby.
How now, sirrah? How goes the world with
   thee?
   Purs. The better that your lordship please
   to ask.

Hast. I tell thee, man, 'tis better with me now
Than when thou met'st me last where now we meet.
Then was I going prisoner to the Tower   100
By the suggestion of the Queen's allies;
But now I tell thee (keep it to thyself)
This day those enemies are put to death,
And I in better state than e'er I was.
  Purs. God hold it, to your Honour's good content!   105
  Hast. Gramercy, fellow. There, drink that for me.   *Throws him his purse.*
  Purs. God save your lordship!   *Exit.*

Enter a *Priest.*

Priest. Well met, my lord. I am glad to see your Honour.
Hast. I thank thee, good Sir John, with all my heart.
I am in your debt for your last exercise;   110
Come the next Sabbath, and I will content you.
            He whispers in his ear.

Enter *Buckingham.*

Buck. What, talking with a priest, Lord Chamberlain?
Your friends at Pomfret, they do need the priest;
You Honour hath no shriving work in hand.
Hast. Good faith, and when I met this holy man,   115
The men you talk of came into my mind.
What, go you toward the Tower?
Buck. I do, my lord, but long I cannot stay there.
I shall return before your lordship thence.
Hast. Nay, like enough, for I stay dinner there.   120
Buck. [aside] And supper too, although thou know'st it not.—
Come, will you go?
Hast. I'll wait upon your lordship. *Exeunt.*

Scene III. [*Pomfret Castle.*]

Enter *Sir Richard Ratcliff*, with *Halberds*, carrying the *Nobles, Rivers, Grey*, and *Vaughan*, to death at Pomfret.

Riv. Sir Richard Ratcliff, let me tell thee this:
To-day shalt thou behold a subject die
For truth, for duty, and for loyalty.

Grey. God bless the Prince from all the pack of you!
A knot you are of damned bloodsuckers.   5
  Vaugh. You live that shall cry woe for this hereafter.
  Rat. Dispatch! The limit of your lives is out.
  Riv. O Pomfret, Pomfret! O thou bloody prison,
Fatal and ominous to noble peers!
Within the guilty closure of thy walls   10
Richard the Second here was hack'd to death;
And, for more slander to thy dismal seat,
We give to thee our guiltless blood to drink.
  Grey. Now Margaret's curse is fall'n upon our heads,   14
When she exclaim'd on Hastings, you, and I,
For standing by when Richard stabb'd her son.
  Riv. Then curs'd she Richard, then curs'd she Buckingham,
Then curs'd she Hastings. O, remember, God,
To hear her prayer for them, as now for us!
And for my sister and her princely sons,   20
Be satisfied, dear God, with our true blood,
Which, as thou know'st, unjustly must be spilt.
  Rat. Make haste. The hour of death is expiate.
  Riv. Come, Grey; come, Vaughan; let us here embrace.
Farewell, until we meet again in heaven.   25
            Exeunt.

Scene IV. [*London. The Tower.*]

Enter *Buckingham, Derby, Hastings, Bishop of Ely, Norfolk, Ratcliff, Lovel*, with others, at a table; [*Officers of the Council* attending].

Hast. Now, noble peers, the cause why we are met
Is to determine of the coronation.
In God's name, speak. When is the royal day?
  Buck. Is all things ready for that royal time?
  Der. It is, and wants but nomination.   5
  Ely. To-morrow then I judge a happy day.
  Buck. Who knows the Lord Protector's mind herein?
Who is most inward with the noble Duke?
  Ely. Your Grace, we think, should soonest know his mind.
  Buck. We know each other's faces; for our hearts,   10
He knows no more of mine than I of yours;
Nor I of his, my lord, than you of mine.
Lord Hastings, you and he are near in love.

Hast. I thank his Grace, I know he loves me
well;
But, for his purpose in the coronation,   15
I have not sounded him, nor he deliver'd
His gracious pleasure any way therein;
But you, my honourable lords, may name the
time,
And in the Duke's behalf I'll give my voice,
Which, I presume, he'll take in gentle part. 20

Enter [*Richard, Duke of*] *Gloucester.*

Ely. In happy time, here comes the Duke
himself.
Rich. My noble lords and cousins all, good
morrow.
I have been long a sleeper; but I trust
My absence doth neglect no great design
Which by my presence might have been con-
cluded.   25
Buck. Had you not come upon your cue, my
lord,
William Lord Hastings had pronounc'd your
part —
I mean, your voice for crowning of the King.
Rich. Than my Lord Hastings no man might
be bolder.   29
His lordship knows me well, and loves me well.
My Lord of Ely, when I was last in Holborn
I saw good strawberries in your garden there.
I do beseech you send for some of them.
Ely. Marry and will, my lord, with all my
heart.   *Exit.*
Rich. Cousin of Buckingham, a word with
you.   [*Takes him aside.*]
Catesby hath sounded Hastings in our business
And finds the testy gentleman so hot
That he will lose his head ere give consent
His master's child, as worshipfully he terms
it,
Shall lose the royalty of England's throne. 40
Buck. Withdraw yourself awhile. I'll go
with you.
Exeunt Gloucester [*and Buckingham*].
Der. We have not yet set down this day of
triumph.
To-morrow, in my judgment, is too sudden;
For I myself am not so well provided
As else I would be, were the day prolong'd. 45

Enter the *Bishop of Ely.*

Ely. Where is my lord the Duke of Gloucester? I have sent for these strawberries.
Hast. His Grace looks cheerfully and smooth
this morning;
There's some conceit or other likes him well

When that he bids good morrow with such
spirit.   50
I think there's never a man in Christendom
Can lesser hide his love or hate than he,
For by his face straight shall you know his
heart.
Der. What of his heart perceive you in his face
By any likelihood he show'd to-day?   55
Hast. Marry, that with no man here he is
offended;
For were he, he had shown it in his looks.

Enter *Richard* and *Buckingham.*

Rich. I pray you all, tell me what they
deserve
That do conspire my death with devilish plots
Of damned witchcraft, and that have prevail'd
Upon my body with their hellish charms. 61
Hast. The tender love I bear your Grace, my
lord,
Makes me most forward in this princely
presence
To doom th' offenders, whosoe'er they be.
I say, my lord, they have deserved death. 65
Rich. Then be your eyes the witness of their
evil.
Look how I am bewitch'd. Behold, mine arm
Is like a blasted sapling, wither'd up;
And this is Edward's wife, that monstrous
witch,
Consorted with that harlot strumpet Shore, 70
That by their witchcraft thus have marked me.
Hast. If they have done this deed, my noble
lord —
Rich. If? Thou protector of this damned
strumpet,
Talk'st thou to me of if's? Thou art a traitor.
Off with his head! Now by Saint Paul I swear
I will not dine until I see the same.   76
Lovel and Ratcliff, look that it be done.
The rest that love me, rise and follow me.
*Exeunt. Manent Lovel and Ratcliff, with
the Lord Hastings.*
Hast. Woe, woe for England, not a whit
for me!
For I, too fond, might have prevented this. 80
Stanley did dream the boar did rase his helm;
But I did scorn it, and disdain to fly.
Three times to-day my footcloth horse did
stumble,
And startled when he look'd upon the Tower,
As loath to bear me to the slaughterhouse. 85
O, now I need the priest that spake to me!
I now repent I told the pursuivant,
As too triumphing, how mine enemies

To-day at Pomfret bloodily were butcher'd,
And I myself secure, in grace and favour.　90
O Margaret, Margaret, now thy heavy curse
Is lighted on poor Hastings' wretched head!
　Rat. Come, come, dispatch! The Duke
would be at dinner.
Make a short shrift; he longs to see your head.
　Hast. O momentary grace of mortal men,
Which we more hunt for than the grace of God!
Who builds his hope in air of your good looks
Lives like a drunken sailor on a mast,
Ready with every nod to tumble down
Into the fatal bowels of the deep.　100
　Lov. Come, come, dispatch! 'Tis bootless to
exclaim.
　Hast. O bloody Richard! Miserable England,
I prophesy the fearfull'st time to thee
That ever wretched age hath look'd upon.　104
Come, lead me to the block; bear him my head.
They smile at me who shortly shall be dead.
　　　　　　　　　　　　　　　Exeunt.

[Scene V. *London. The Tower walls.*]

Enter *Richard* and *Buckingham*, in rotten
　armour, marvellous ill-favoured.

　Rich. Come, cousin, canst thou quake and
change thy colour,
Murther thy breath in middle of a word,
And then again begin, and stop again,
As if thou wert distraught and mad with terror?
　Buck. Tut, I can counterfeit the deep tra-
gedian,　5
Speak and look back, and pry on every side,
Tremble and start at wagging of a straw,
Intending deep suspicion. Ghastly looks
Are at my service, like enforced smiles;
And both are ready in their offices,　10
At any time to grace my stratagems.
But what, is Catesby gone?
　Rich. He is; and see, he brings the Mayor
along.

Enter the [*Lord*] *Mayor* and *Catesby.*

　Buck. Lord Mayor —
　Rich. Look to the drawbridge there!　15
　Buck. Hark! a drum.
　Rich. Catesby, o'erlook the walls.
　Buck. Lord Mayor, the reason we have
sent —
　Rich. Look back! defend thee! Here are
enemies!
　Buck. God and our innocency defend and
guard us!　20

Enter *Lovel* and *Ratcliff*, with *Hastings'* head.

　Rich. Be patient, they are friends — Ratcliff
and Lovel.
　Lov. Here is the head of that ignoble traitor,
The dangerous and unsuspected Hastings.
　Rich. So dear I lov'd the man that I must
weep.　24
I took him for the plainest harmless creature
That breath'd upon the earth a Christian;
Made him my book, wherein my soul recorded
The history of all her secret thoughts.
So smooth he daub'd his vice with show of
virtue
That, his apparent open guilt omitted —　30
I mean, his conversation with Shore's wife —
He liv'd from all attainder of suspect.
　Buck. Well, well, he was the covert'st shel-
t'red traitor
That ever lived. Look ye, my Lord Mayor.
Would you imagine, or almost believe,　35
Were't not that by great preservation
We live to tell it, that the subtile traitor
This day had plotted, in the Council House
To murther me and my good Lord of Glouces-
ter?
　May. Had he done so?　40
　Rich. What? Think you we are Turks or
infidels?
Or that we would, against the form of law,
Proceed thus rashly in the villain's death
But that the extreme peril of the case,　44
The peace of England, and our persons' safety
Enforc'd us to this execution?
　May. Now fair befall you! He deserv'd his
death,
And your good Graces both have well proceeded
To warn false traitors from the like attempts.
I never look'd for better at his hands　50
After he once fell in with Mistress Shore.
　Buck. Yet had we not determin'd he should
die
Until your lordship came to see his end,
Which now the loving haste of these our friends,
Something against our meanings, have pre-
vented;　55
Because, my lord, we would have had you
heard
The traitor speak, and timorously confess
The manner and the purpose of his treasons,
That you might well have signified the same
Unto the citizens, who haply may　60
Misconster us in him and wail his death.
　May. But, my good lord, your Grace's word
shall serve,

THE TRAGEDY
OF
KING
RICHARD III

PHOTOGRAPHS BY JOHN VICKERS
PRODUCED BY THE OLD VIC COMPANY

Laurence Olivier in the role of the villainous
monster, King Richard III

Though hunch-backed, Richard is a valiant
warrior, and is skilled in the use of arms

"Anointed let me be with deadly venom; and die, ere men can say 'God save the queen!' " Anne (Joyce Redman) regrets her destiny as Richard's queen (Act IV, Scene I)

"And if thy poor devoted servant may but beg one favour at thy gracious hand, thou dost confirm his happiness for ever." Richard's wooing of Anne (Act I, Scene II)

Queen Margaret (Sybil Thorndike) prophesies against Elizabeth (Margaret Leighton) (Act I, Scene III)

"Our brother is imprison'd by your means, myself disgrac'd, and the nobility held in contempt." Richard accuses Elizabeth of working against him and his brother (Act I, Scene III)

Above: "And he shriek'd out aloud, ' . . . false, fleeting, perjur'd Clarence.' " Clarence (George Relph) tells Brakenbury (Humphrey Heathcote) of his tormented dream (Act I, Scene IV)

Left: "Come, Hastings, help me to my closet." In his last hours, King Edward (Harcourt Williams) is aided by Hastings (Michael Warre) and Queen Elizabeth (Act II, Scene I)

"My other self .. my oracle, my prophet!" Richard welcomes the support of Buckingham (Nicholas Hannen) (Act II, Scene II)

"Richard of York! how fares our loving brother?" The two young princes meet after the death of their father (Act III, Scene I)

"I pray you, uncle, give me this dagger." The young duke asks Richard for an ominous gift (Act III, Scene I)

"Look how I am bewitch'd; behold mine arm is like a blasted sapling, wither'd up." In order to destroy Hastings, Richard blames him for bewitching and deforming him (*Act III, Scene IV*)

"So dear I lov'd the man, that I must weep." Richard affects distress after having Hastings executed (*Act III, Scene V*)

"O Margaret, Margaret! now thy heavy curse is lighted on poor Hastings' wretched head." On his way to his death, Hastings recalls Margaret's prophecy (*Act III, Scene IV*)

"See, a book of prayer in his hand; true ornament to know a holy man." Richard assumes a pious pose while Buckingham lauds him to the people *(Act III, Scene VII)*

"Then I salute you with this royal title: Long live King Richard, England's worthy king!" Buckingham salutes the new king *(Act III, Scene VII)*

"Poor heart, adieu! I pity thy complaining." On her way to visit her two sons, imprisoned by Richard, Elizabeth commiserates with Queen Anne, whom Richard has widowed (*Act IV, Scene I*)

Laurence Olivier as Richard, "that bottled spider, that foul bunch-backed toad"

"I am not in the giving vein to-day." Richard is irritated by Buckingham's reminder that he has been promised an earldom (*Act IV, Scene II*)

Richmond (Ralph Richardson) and King Richard III meet on Bosworth Field (Act V, Scene IV)

"God and your arms be prais'd, victorious friends; the day is ours, the bloody dog is dead." Richmond announces Richard's death (Act V, Scene IV)

As well as I had seen, and heard him speak;
And do not doubt, right noble princes both,
But I'll acquaint our duteous citizens   65
With all your just proceedings in this case.
  Rich. And to that end we wish'd your lord-
    ship here,
T' avoid the censures of the carping world.
  Buck. But since you come too late of our
    intent,
Yet witness what you hear we did intend.   70
And so, my good Lord Mayor, we bid farewell.
                    Exit Mayor.
  Rich. Go after, after, cousin Buckingham.
The Mayor towards Guildhall hies him in all
    post.
There, at your meetest vantage of the time,
Infer the bastardy of Edward's children.   75
Tell them how Edward put to death a citizen
Only for saying he would make his son
Heir to the Crown, meaning indeed his house,
Which by the sign thereof was termed so.
Moreover, urge his hateful luxury   80
And bestial appetite in change of lust,
Which stretch'd unto their servants, daughters,
    wives,
Even where his raging eye or savage heart,
Without control, lusted to make a prey.   84
Nay, for a need, thus far come near my person:
Tell them, when that my mother went with child
Of that insatiate Edward, noble York,
My princely father, then had wars in France,
And by true computation of the time
Found that the issue was not his begot;   90
Which well appeared in his lineaments,
Being nothing like the noble Duke my father.
Yet touch this sparingly, as 'twere far off,
Because, my lord, you know my mother lives.
  Buck. Doubt not, my lord, I'll play the
    orator   95
As if the golden fee for which I plead
Were for myself — and so, my lord, adieu.
  Rich. If you thrive well, bring them to
    Baynard's Castle,
Where you shall find me well accompanied
With reverend fathers and well-learned bishops.
  Buck. I go; and towards three or four
    o'clock   101
Look for the news that the Guildhall affords.
                    Exit.
  Rich. Go, Lovel, with all speed to Doctor
    Shaw —
[*To Catesby*] Go thou to Friar Penker. — Bid
    them both   104
Meet me within this hour at Baynard's Castle.
    Exeunt [Lovel, Catesby, and Ratcliff].

Now will I go, to take some privy order
To draw the brats of Clarence out of sight,
And to give order that no manner person
Have any time recourse unto the Princes.
                    Exit.

[Scene VI. *London. A street.*]

Enter a *Scrivener* with a paper in his hand.

  Scriv. Here is the indictment of the good
    Lord Hastings,
Which in a set hand fairly is engross'd
That it may be to-day read o'er in Paul's.
And mark how well the sequel hangs together:
Eleven hours I have spent to write it over,   5
For yesternight by Catesby was it sent me;
The precedent was full as long a-doing,
And yet within these five hours Hastings liv'd,
Untainted, unexamin'd, free, at liberty.   9
Here's a good world the while! Who is so gross
That cannot see this palpable device?
Yet who so bold but says he sees it not?
Bad is the world, and all will come to naught
When such ill dealing must be seen in thought.
                    Exit.

[Scene VII. *London. Baynard's Castle.*]

Enter *Richard* and *Buckingham* at several doors.

  Rich. How now, how now? What say the
    citizens?
  Buck. Now, by the holy Mother of our Lord,
The citizens are mum, say not a word.
  Rich. Touch'd you the bastardy of Edward's
    children?
  Buck. I did, with his contract with Lady
    Lucy   5
And his contract by deputy in France;
Th' insatiate greediness of his desire
And his enforcement of the city wives;
His tyranny for trifles; his own bastardy,
As being got, your father then in France,   10
And his resemblance, being not like the Duke.
Withal I did infer your lineaments,
Being the right idea of your father
Both in your form and nobleness of mind;
Laid open all your victories in Scotland,   15
Your discipline in war, wisdom in peace,
Your bounty, virtue, fair humility;
Indeed, left nothing fitting for your purpose
Untouch'd, or slightly handled in discourse;

345

And when my oratory drew toward end,   20
I bid them that did love their country's good
Cry, 'God save Richard, England's royal
    King!'
    Rich. And did they so?
    Buck. No, so God help me, they spake not a
    word,
But, like dumb statuës or breathing stones,   25
Star'd each on other, and look'd deadly pale.
Which when I saw, I reprehended them
And ask'd the Mayor what meant this wilful
    silence.
His answer was, the people were not us'd
To be spoke to but by the Recorder.   30
Then he was urg'd to tell my tale again:
'Thus saith the Duke, thus hath the Duke
    inferr'd,' —
But nothing spake in warrant from himself.
When he had done, some followers of mine own,
At lower end of the hall, hurl'd up their
    caps,   35
And some ten voices cried 'God save King
    Richard!'
And thus I took the vantage of those few: —
'Thanks, gentle citizens and friends,' quoth I.
'This general applause and cheerful shout
Argues your wisdom and your love to Richard,'
And even here brake off and came away.   41
    Rich. What tongueless blocks were they!
    Would they not speak?
    Buck. No, by my troth, my lord.
    Rich. Will not the Mayor then and his
    brethren come?
    Buck. The Mayor is here at hand. Intend
    some fear;   45
Be not you spoke with but by mighty suit;
And look you get a prayer book in your hand
And stand between two churchmen, good my
    lord,
For on that ground I'll make a holy descant;
And be not easily won to our requests.   50
Play the maid's part: still answer nay, and
    take it.
    Rich. I go; and if you plead as well for
    them
As I can say nay to thee for myself,
No doubt we bring it to a happy issue.
    Buck. Go, go up to the leads! The Lord
    Mayor knocks.   55
        Exit [Richard].

Enter the [*Lord*] *Mayor*, [*Aldermen,*]
    and *Citizens.*

Welcome, my lord. I dance attendance here.
I think the Duke will not be spoke withal.

Enter *Catesby.*

Now, Catesby, what says your lord to my
    request?
    Cates. He doth entreat your Grace, my noble
    lord,
To visit him to-morrow or next day.   60
He is within, with two right reverend fathers,
Divinely bent to meditation,
And in no worldly suits would he be mov'd
To draw him from his holy exercise.
    Buck. Return, good Catesby, to the gracious
    Duke.   65
Tell him, myself, the Mayor and Aldermen,
In deep designs, in matter of great moment,
No less importing than our general good,
Are come to have some conference with his
    Grace.   69
    Cates. I'll signify so much unto him straight.
        Exit
    Buck. Aha, my lord! this prince is not an
    Edward.
He is not lulling on a lewd love-bed,
But on his knees at meditation;
Not dallying with a brace of courtesans,
But meditating with two deep divines;   75
Not sleeping, to engross his idle body,
But praying, to enrich his watchful soul.
Happy were England, would this virtuous
    prince
Take on his Grace the sovereignty thereof;
But sure I fear we shall not win him to it.   80
    May. Marry, God defend his Grace should
    say us nay!
    Buck. I fear he will. Here Catesby comes
    again.

Enter *Catesby.*

Now, Catesby, what says his Grace?
    Cates.   My lord
He wonders to what end you have assembled
Such troops of citizens to come to him,   85
His Grace not being warn'd thereof before.
He fears, my lord, you mean no good to
    him.
    Buck. Sorry I am my noble cousin should
Suspect me that I mean no good to him.
By heaven, we come to him in perfect love;   90
And so once more return and tell his Grace.
        Exit Catesby
When holy and devout religious men
Are at their beads, 'tis much to draw them
    thence,
So sweet is zealous contemplation.

Enter *Richard* aloft, between two *Bishops.*
[*Catesby* returns.]

May. See where his Grace stands, 'tween
  two clergymen.   95
Buck. Two props of virtue for a Christian
  prince,
To stay him from the fall of vanity;
And see, a book of prayer in his hand,
True ornaments to know a holy man.
Famous Plantagenet, most gracious prince, 100
Lend favourable ear to our requests,
And pardon us the interruption
Of thy devotion and right Christian zeal.
Rich. My lord, there needs no such apology.
I do beseech your Grace to pardon me,   105
Who, earnest in the service of my God,
Deferr'd the visitation of my friends.
But, leaving this, what is your Grace's pleasure?
Buck. Even that (I hope) which pleaseth
  God above
And all good men of this ungovern'd isle.   110
Rich. I do suspect I have done some offence
That seems disgracious in the city's eye,
And that you come to reprehend my ignorance.
Buck. You have, my lord. Would it might
  please your Grace,
On our entreaties, to amend your fault!   115
Rich. Else wherefore breathe I in a Christian
  land?
Buck. Know then it is your fault that you
  resign
The supreme seat, the throne majestical,
The scept'red office of your ancestors,
Your state of fortune and your due of birth,
The lineal glory of your royal house,   121
To the corruption of a blemish'd stock;
Whiles, in the mildness of your sleepy thoughts,
Which here we waken to our country's good,
The noble isle doth want his proper limbs;   125
His face defac'd with scars of infamy,
His royal stock graft with ignoble plants,
And almost should'red in the swallowing gulf
Of dark forgetfulness and deep oblivion.
Which to recure, we heartily solicit   130
Your gracious self to take on you the charge
And kingly government of this your land;
Not as Protector, steward, substitute,
Or lowly factor for another's gain;
But as successively, from blood to blood,   135
Your right of birth, your empery, your own.
For this, consorted with the citizens,
Your very worshipful and loving friends,
And by their vehement instigation,   139
In this just cause come I to move your Grace.

Rich. I cannot tell if to depart in silence,
Or bitterly to speak in your reproof,
Best fitteth my degree or your condition.
If not to answer, you might haply think   144
Tongue-tied ambition, not replying, yielded
To bear the golden yoke of sovereignty
Which fondly you would here impose on me.
If to reprove you for this suit of yours,
So season'd with your faithful love to me,   149
Then, on the other side, I check'd my friends.
Therefore — to speak, and to avoid the first,
And then, in speaking, not to incur the last —
Definitively thus I answer you.
Your love deserves my thanks, but my desert
Unmeritable shuns your high request.   155
First, if all obstacles were cut away,
And that my path were even to the crown
As the ripe revenue and due of birth,
Yet so much is my poverty of spirit,
So mighty and so many my defects,   160
That I would rather hide me from my greatness,
Being a bark to brook no mighty sea,
Than in my greatness covet to be hid
And in the vapour of my glory smother'd.   164
But, God be thank'd, there is no need of me,
And much I need to help you, were there need.
The royal tree hath left us royal fruit,
Which, mellow'd by the stealing hours of time,
Will well become the seat of majesty   169
And make (no doubt) us happy by his reign.
On him I lay that you would lay on me,
The right and fortune of his happy stars,
Which God defend that I should wring from
  him!
Buck. My lord, this argues conscience in
  your Grace,
But the respects thereof are nice and trivial,
All circumstances well considered.   176
You say that Edward is your brother's son.
So say we too, but not by Edward's wife;
For first was he contract to Lady Lucy —
Your mother lives a witness to his vow —   180
And afterward by substitute betroth'd
To Bona, sister to the King of France.
These both put off, a poor petitioner,
A care-craz'd mother to a many sons,
A beauty-waning and distressed widow,   185
Even in the afternoon of her best days,
Made prize and purchase of his wanton eye,
Seduc'd the pitch and height of his degree
To base declension and loath'd bigamy.
By her, in his unlawful bed, he got   190
This Edward, whom our manners call the
  Prince.
More bitterly could I expostulate

Save that, for reverence to some alive,
I give a sparing limit to my tongue.   194
Then, good my lord, take to your royal self
This proffer'd benefit of dignity;
If not to bless us and the land withal,
Yet to draw forth your noble ancestry
From the corruption of abusing times
Unto a lineal true-derived course.   200
    May. Do, good my lord. Your citizens entreat you.
    Buck. Refuse not, mighty lord, this proffer'd love.
    Cates. O, make them joyful, grant their lawful suit!
    Rich. Alas, why would you heap this care on me?
I am unfit for state and majesty.   205
I do beseech you take it not amiss,
I cannot nor I will not yield to you.
    Buck. If you refuse it — as, in love and zeal,
Loath to depose the child, your brother's son;
As well we know your tenderness of heart   210
And gentle, kind, effeminate remorse,
Which we have noted in you to your kindred
And egally indeed to all estates —
Yet know, whe'r you accept our suit or no,
Your brother's son shall never reign our king,
But we will plant some other in the throne   216
To the disgrace and downfall of your house;
And in this resolution here we leave you.
Come, citizens. Zounds, I'll entreat no more!
    Rich. O, do not swear, my lord of Buckingham.   220
    Exeunt [Buckingham, Mayor, Aldermen, and Citizens].
    Cates. Call him again, sweet prince, accept their suit.
If you deny them, all the land will rue it.

    Rich. Will you enforce me to a world of cares?
Call them again. I am not made of stone,
But penetrable to your kind entreaties,   225
Albeit against my conscience and my soul.

    Enter Buckingham and the rest.

Cousin of Buckingham, and sage grave men,
Since you will buckle fortune on my back,
To bear her burthen, whe'r I will or no,
I must have patience to endure the load;   230
But if black scandal or foul-fac'd reproach
Attend the sequel of your imposition,
Your mere enforcement shall acquittance me
From all the impure blots and stains thereof;
For God doth know, and you may partly see,
How far I am from the desire of this.   236
    May. God bless your Grace! We see it and will say it.
    Rich. In saying so you shall but say the truth.
    Buck. Then I salute you with this royal title —
Long live King Richard, England's worthy King!   240
    All. Amen.
    Buck. To-morrow may it please you to be crown'd?
    Rich. Even when you please, for you will have it so.
    Buck. To-morrow then we will attend your Grace,
And so most joyfully we take our leave.   245
    Rich. [*to the Bishops*] Come, let us to our holy work again. —
Farewell, my cousin; farewell, gentle friends.
        Exeunt.

ACT IV. Scene I. [*London. Before the Tower.*]

Enter the Queen [*Elizabeth*], Duchess of York, *and* Marquess Dorset, *at one door;* Anne Duchess of Gloucester, [*leading* Lady Margaret Plantagenet, Clarence's *young daughter,*] *at another door.*

    Duch. York. Who meets us here? My niece Plantagenet,
Led in the hand of her kind aunt of Gloucester?
Now, for my life, she's wand'ring to the Tower,

On pure heart's love, to greet the tender Prince.
Daughter, well met.
    Anne.   God give your Graces both   5
A happy and a joyful time of day!
    Queen. As much to you, good sister. Whither away?
    Anne. No farther than the Tower, and, as I guess,
Upon the like devotion as yourselves,
To gratulate the gentle Princes there.   10
    Queen. Kind sister, thanks. We'll enter all together;

Enter the *Lieutenant* [*Brakenbury*].

And in good time, here the Lieutenant comes.
Master Lieutenant, pray you, by your leave,
How doth the Prince, and my young son of
York?
Lieut. Right well, dear madam. By your
patience,   15
I may not suffer you to visit them;
The King hath strictly charg'd the contrary.
Queen. The King? Who's that?
Lieut. I cry you mercy! I mean the Lord
Protector.
Queen. The Lord protect him from that
kingly title!   20
Hath he set bounds between their love and me?
I am their mother. Who shall bar me from
them?
Duch. York. I am their father's mother. I
will see them.
Anne. Their aunt I am in law, in love their
mother.
Then bring me to their sights. I'll bear thy
blame   25
And take thy office from thee on my peril.
Lieut. No, madam, no! I may not leave it so.
I am bound by oath, and therefore pardon me.
Exit.

Enter *Stanley*.

Stan. Let me but meet you, ladies, one hour
hence,
And I'll salute your Grace of York as mother
And reverend looker-on of two fair queens. 31
[*To Anne*] Come, madam, you must straight to
Westminster,
There to be crowned Richard's royal queen.
Queen. Ah, cut my lace asunder,
That my pent heart may have some scope to
beat,   35
Or else I swoon with this dead-killing news!
Anne. Despiteful tidings! O unpleasing
news!
Dor. Be of good cheer. Mother, how fares
your Grace?
Queen. O Dorset, speak not to me, get thee
gone!
Death and destruction dogs thee at thy heels;
Thy mother's name is ominous to children. 41
If thou wilt outstrip death, go cross the seas,
And live with Richmond, from the reach of hell.
Go hie thee, hie thee from this slaughterhouse,
Lest thou increase the number of the dead 45
And make me die the thrall of Margaret's curse,
Nor mother, wife, nor England's counted
Queen.

Stan. Full of wise care is this your counsel,
madam.
Take all the swift advantage of the hours.
You shall have letters from me to my son 50
In your behalf, to meet you on the way.
Be not ta'en tardy by unwise delay.
Duch. York. O ill-dispersing wind of misery!
O my accursed womb, the bed of death!
A cockatrice hast thou hatch'd to the world,
Whose unavoided eye is murtherous.   56
Stan. Come, madam, come! I in all haste
was sent.
Anne. And I with all unwillingness will go.
O, would to God that the inclusive verge
Of golden metal that must round my brow   60
Were redhot steel, to sear me to the brains!
Anointed let me be with deadly venom,
And die ere men can say 'God save the Queen!'
Queen. Go, go, poor soul! I envy not thy
glory.
To feed my humour wish thyself no harm.   65
Anne. No? Why! when he that is my hus-
band now
Came to me as I follow'd Henry's corse,
When scarce the blood was well wash'd from
his hands
Which issued from my other angel husband
And that dear saint which then I weeping fol-
low'd —   70
O, when, I say, I look'd on Richard's face,
This was my wish: 'Be thou,' quoth I, 'ac-
curs'd
For making me, so young, so old a widow!
And when thou wed'st, let sorrow haunt thy
bed;
And be thy wife, if any be so mad,   75
More miserable by the life of thee
Than thou hast made me by my dear lord's
death!'
Lo, ere I can repeat this curse again,
Within so small a time, my woman's heart
Grossly grew captive to his honey words   80
And prov'd the subject of mine own soul's curse,
Which hitherto hath held mine eyes from rest;
For never yet one hour in his bed
Did I enjoy the golden dew of sleep,   84
But with his timorous dreams was still awak'd.
Besides, he hates me for my father Warwick,
And will (no doubt) shortly be rid of me.
Queen. Poor heart, adieu! I pity thy com-
plaining.
Anne. No more than with my soul I mourn
for yours.
Queen. Farewell, thou woful welcomer of
glory.   90

Anne. Adieu, poor soul, that tak'st thy leave of it.

Duch. York. [*to Dorset*] Go thou to Richmond, and good fortune guide thee!

[*To Anne*] Go thou to Richard, and good angels tend thee!

[*To Queen Elizabeth*] Go thou to sanctuary, and good thoughts possess thee!

I to my grave, where peace and rest lie with me!
Eighty odd years of sorrow have I seen,   96
And each hour's joy wrack'd with a week of teen.

Queen. Stay, yet look back with me unto the Tower.
Pity, you ancient stones, those tender babes
Whom envy hath immur'd within your walls —
Rough cradle for such little pretty ones!   101
Rude ragged nurse, old sullen playfellow
For tender princes — use my babies well!
So foolish sorrow bids your stones farewell.
                                         Exeunt.

Scene II. [*London. The Palace.*]

Sound a sennet. Enter Richard, in pomp, Buckingham, Catesby, Ratcliff, Lovel, [a Page, and others].

Rich. Stand all apart. Cousin of Buckingham —

Buck. My gracious sovereign?

Rich. Give me thy hand.

Sound. Here he ascendeth the throne.
                        Thus high, by thy advice
And thy assistance, is King Richard seated.
But shall we wear these glories for a day?   5
Or shall they last, and we rejoice in them?

Buck. Still live they, and for ever let them last!

Rich. Ah, Buckingham, now do I play the touch,
To try if thou be current gold indeed.
Young Edward lives. Think now what I would speak.   10

Buck. Say on, my loving lord.

Rich. Why, Buckingham, I say I would be king.

Buck. Why, so you are, my thrice-renowned liege.

Rich. Ha! Am I king? 'Tis so. But Edward lives.

Buck. True, noble prince.

Rich.   O bitter consequence,   15
That Edward still should live true noble prince!
Cousin, thou wast not wont to be so dull.

Shall I be plain? I wish the bastards dead,
And I would have it suddenly perform'd.
What say'st thou now? Speak suddenly, b
brief.   2

Buck. Your Grace may do your pleasure.

Rich. Tut, tut, thou art all ice; thy kindnes freezes.
Say, have I thy consent that they shall die?

Buck. Give me some little breath, som pause, dear lord,
Before I positively speak in this.   2
I will resolve you herein presently.   *Exi*

Cates. [*aside to another*] The King is angry
See, he gnaws his lip.

Rich. I will converse with iron-witted fool
                        [*Descends from the throne.*
And unrespective boys. None are for me
That look into me with considerate eyes.   3
High-reaching Buckingham grows circumspect
Boy!

Page. My lord?

Rich. Know'st thou not any whom corrupt
ing gold
Will tempt unto a close exploit of death?   3

Page. I know a discontented gentleman
Whose humble means match not his haughty spirit.
Gold were as good as twenty orators,
And will, no doubt, tempt him to anything.

Rich. What is his name?

Page.   His name, my lord, is Tyrrel.   4

Rich. I partly know the man. Go call him hither.

                                  Exit [*Page*]
The deep-revolving witty Buckingham
No more shall be the neighbour to my counsels
Hath he so long held out with me, untir'd,
And stops he now for breath? Well, be it so.   4

Enter Stanley.

How now, Lord Stanley? What's the new with you?

Stan. My lord, I hear the Marquess Dorset fled
To Richmond, in those parts beyond the seas
Where he abides.   [*Stands aside.*

Rich. Come hither, Catesby. Rumour i abroad   5
That Anne my wife is very grievous sick.
I will take order for her keeping close.
Inquire me out some mean poor gentleman,
Whom I will marry straight to Clarence daughter.
The boy is foolish, and I fear not him.   5
Look how thou dream'st! I say again, give ou

That Anne, my queen, is sick and like to die.
About it! for it stands me much upon
To stop all hopes whose growth may damage
me.
               [Exit Catesby.]
I must be married to my brother's daughter, 60
Or else my kingdom stands on brittle glass.
Murther her brothers, and then marry her —
Uncertain way of gain! But I am in
So far in blood that sin will pluck on sin.
Tear-falling pity dwells not in this eye. 65

    Enter [*Page*, with] *Tyrrel*.

Is thy name Tyrrel?
  Tyr. James Tyrrel, and your most obedient
    subject.
  Rich. Art thou indeed?
  Tyr.   Prove me, my gracious lord.
  Rich. Dar'st thou resolve to kill a friend of
    mine?
  Tyr. Please you; 70
But I had rather kill two enemies.
  Rich. Why, there thou hast it! Two deep
    enemies,
Foes to my rest and my sweet sleep's disturbers,
Are they that I would have thee deal upon.
Tyrrel, I mean those bastards in the Tower. 75
  Tyr. Let me have open means to come to
    them,
And soon I'll rid you from the fear of them.
  Rich. Thou sing'st sweet music. Hark, come
    hither, Tyrrel.
Go, by this token. Rise, and lend thine ear.
                    Whispers.
There is no more but so: say it is done, 80
And I will love thee and prefer thee for it.
  Tyr. I will dispatch it straight.
  Rich. Shall we hear from thee, Tyrrel, ere we
    sleep?
  Tyr. Ye shall, my lord.   *Exit.*

    Enter *Buckingham*.

  Buck. My lord, I have consider'd in my mind
The late request that you did sound me in. 86
  Rich. Well, let that rest. Dorset is fled to
    Richmond.
  Buck. I hear the news, my lord.
  Rich. Stanley, he is your wive's son. Well,
    look unto it.
  Buck. My lord, I claim the gift, my due by
    promise, 90
For which your honour and your faith is
    pawn'd:
Th' earldom of Hereford and the moveables
Which you have promised I shall possess.

  Rich. Stanley, look to your wife. If she
    convey
Letters to Richmond, you shall answer it. 95
  Buck. What says your Highness to my just
    request?
  Rich. I do remember me Henry the Sixth
Did prophesy that Richmond should be King
When Richmond was a little peevish boy.
A king! — perhaps — perhaps — 100
  Buck. My lord —
  Rich. How chance the prophet could not at
    that time
Have told me, I being by, that I should kill him?
  Buck. My lord, your promise for the earldom!
  Rich. Richmond! When last I was at Exeter,
The Mayor in courtesy show'd me the castle,
And call'd it Rouge-mount; at which name I
    started,
Because a bard of Ireland told me once
I should not live long after I saw Richmond.
  Buck. My lord —   110
  Rich. Ay, what's o'clock?
  Buck. I am thus bold to put your Grace in
    mind
Of what you promis'd me.
  Rich.   Well, but what's o'clock?
  Buck. Upon the stroke of ten.
  Rich.   Well, let it strike.
  Buck. Why let it strike? 115
  Rich. Because that like a Jack thou keep'st
    the stroke
Betwixt thy begging and my meditation.
I am not in the giving vein to-day.
  Buck. May it please you to resolve me in my
    suit.
  Rich. Thou troublest me; I am not in the
    vein. 120
          Exeunt [all but Buckingham].
  Buck. And is it thus? Repays he my deep
    service
With such contempt? Made I him King for
    this?
O, let me think on Hastings, and be gone
To Brecknock while my fearful head is on!
                     Exit.

  [Scene III. *London. The Palace.***]**

    Enter *Tyrrel*.

  Tyr. The tyrannous and bloody act is done,
The most arch deed of piteous massacre
That ever yet this land was guilty of.
Dighton and Forrest, whom I did suborn

To do this piece of ruthful butchery,   5
Albeit they were flesh'd villains, bloody dogs,
Melted with tenderness and mild compassion,
Wept like two children in their death's sad story.
'Lo, thus,' quoth Dighton, 'lay the gentle
   babes.'
'Thus, thus,' quoth Forrest, 'girdling one an-
   other   10
Within their alablaster innocent arms.
Their lips were four red roses on a stalk,
And in their summer beauty kiss'd each other.
A book of prayers on their pillow lay,
Which once,' quoth Forrest, 'almost chang'd
   my mind;   15
But O! the devil' — there the villain stopp'd;
When Dighton thus told on — 'We smothered
The most replenished sweet work of nature
That from the prime creation e'er she fram'd.'
Hence both are gone with conscience and re-
   morse   20
They could not speak; and so I left them both,
To bear this tidings to the bloody King.

Enter Richard.

And here he comes. All health, my sovereign
   lord!
Rich. Kind Tyrrel, am I happy in thy news?
Tyr. If to have done the thing you gave in
   charge   25
Beget your happiness, be happy then,
For it is done.
Rich.   But didst thou see them dead?
Tyr. I did, my lord.
Rich.   And buried, gentle Tyrrel?
Tyr. The chaplain of the Tower hath buried
   them;
But where (to say the truth) I do not know. 30
Rich. Come to me, Tyrrel, soon at after
   supper,
When thou shalt tell the process of their death.
Meantime, but think how I may do thee good,
And be inheritor of thy desire.   34
Farewell till then.
Tyr.   I humbly take my leave. *Exit.*
Rich. The son of Clarence have I pent up
   close,
His daughter meanly have I match'd in mar-
   riage,
The sons of Edward sleep in Abraham's bosom,
And Anne my wife hath bid this world good
   night.
Now, for I know the Britain Richmond aims   40
At young Elizabeth, my brother's daughter,
And by that knot looks proudly on the crown,
To her go I, a jolly thriving wooer.

Enter Ratcliff.

Rat. My lord —
Rich. Good or bad news, that thou com'st in
   so bluntly?   45
Rat. Bad news, my lord. Morton is fled to
   Richmond,
And Buckingham, back'd with the hardy
   Welshmen,
Is in the field, and still his power increaseth.
Rich. Ely with Richmond troubles me more
   near   49
Than Buckingham and his rash-levied strength.
Come! I have learn'd that fearful commenting
Is leaden servitor to dull delay;
Delay leads impotent and snail-pac'd beggary.
Then fiery expedition be my wing,
Jove's Mercury, and herald for a king!   55
Go muster men. My counsel is my shield.
We must be brief when traitors brave the field.
      Exeunt.

Scene [IV. *London. Before the Palace.*]

Enter old Queen Margaret.

Q. Marg. So now prosperity begins to mellow
And drop into the rotten mouth of death.
Here in these confines slily have I lurk'd
To watch the waning of mine enemies.
A dire induction am I witness to,   5
And will to France, hoping the consequence
Will prove as bitter, black, and tragical.
Withdraw thee, wretched Margaret! Who
   comes here?   [*Retires.*]

Enter Duchess of York and Queen [Elizabeth].

Queen. Ah, my poor princes! ah, my tender
   babes!
My unblown flowers, new-appearing sweets!   10
If yet your gentle souls fly in the air
And be not fix'd in doom perpetual,
Hover about me with your airy wings
And hear your mother's lamentation!
Q. Marg. [*aside*] Hover about her. Say that
   right for right   15
Hath dimm'd your infant morn to aged night.
Duch. So many miseries have craz'd my
   voice
That my woe-wearied tongue is still and mute.
Edward Plantagenet, why art thou dead?
Q. Marg. [*aside*] Plantagenet doth quit
   Plantagenet;   20
Edward for Edward pays a dying debt.

Queen. Wilt thou, O God, fly from such
    gentle lambs
And throw them in the entrails of the wolf?
When didst thou sleep when such a deed was
    done?
Q. Marg. [*aside*] When holy Harry died, and
    my sweet son.   25
Duch. Dead life, blind sight, poor mortal
    living ghost,
Woe's scene, world's shame, grave's due by life
    usurp'd,
Brief abstract and record of tedious days,
Rest thy unrest on England's lawful earth,
                         [*Sits down.*]
Unlawfully made drunk with innocent blood!
Queen. Ah that thou wouldst as soon afford
    a grave   31
As thou canst yield a melancholy seat!
Then would I hide my bones, not rest them here.
Ah, who hath any cause to mourn but we?
                     [*Sits down by her.*]
Q. Marg. [*comes forward*] If ancient sorrow
    be most reverent,   35
Give mine the benefit of seignory
And let my griefs frown on the upper hand.
If sorrow can admit society,
               [*Sits down with them.*]
Tell o'er your woes again by viewing mine.
I had an Edward, till a Richard kill'd him; 40
I had a Harry, till a Richard kill'd him:
Thou hadst an Edward, till a Richard kill'd
    him;
Thou hadst a Richard, till a Richard kill'd him.
Duch. I had a Richard too, and thou didst
    kill him;   44
I had a Rutland too, thou holp'st to kill him.
Q. Marg. Thou hadst a Clarence too, and
    Richard kill'd him.
From forth the kennel of thy womb hath crept
A hellhound that doth hunt us all to death.
That dog, that had his teeth before his eyes,
To worry lambs and lap their gentle blood, 50
That foul defacer of God's handiwork,
That excellent grand tyrant of the earth
That reigns in galled eyes of weeping souls,
Thy womb let loose to chase us to our graves.
O upright, just, and true-disposing God,   55
How do I thank thee that this carnal cur
Preys on the issue of his mother's body
And makes her pew-fellow with others' moan!
Duch. O Harry's wife, triumph not in my
    woes!   59
God witness with me I have wept for thine.
Q. Marg. Bear with me! I am hungry for
    revenge

And now I cloy me with beholding it.
Thy Edward he is dead, that kill'd my Edward;
Thy other Edward dead, to quit my Edward;
Young York he is but boot, because both they
Match'd not the high perfection of my loss. 66
Thy Clarence he is dead that stabb'd my
    Edward,
And the beholders of this frantic play,
Th' adulterate Hastings, Rivers, Vaughan,
    Grey,
Untimely smother'd in their dusky graves. 70
Richard yet lives, hell's black intelligencer;
Only reserv'd their factor to buy souls
And send them thither. But at hand, at hand,
Ensues his piteous and unpitied end.
Earth gapes, hell burns, fiends roar, saints pray,
To have him suddenly convey'd from hence. 76
Cancel his bond of life, dear God, I pray,
That I may live to say, 'The dog is dead.'
Queen. O, thou didst prophesy the time
    would come   79
That I should wish for thee to help me curse
That bottled spider, that foul bunch-back'd
    toad!
Q. Marg. I call'd thee then vain flourish of
    my fortune;
I call'd thee then poor shadow, painted queen,
The presentation of but what I was,
The flattering index of a direful pageant, 85
One heav'd a-high to be hurl'd down below,
A mother only mock'd with two fair babes,
A dream of what thou wast, a garish flag,
To be the aim of every dangerous shot;
A sign of dignity, a breath, a bubble,   90
A queen in jest, only to fill the scene.
Where is thy husband now? Where be thy
    brothers?
Where be thy two sons? Wherein dost thou
    joy?
Who sues and kneels and says 'God save the
    Queen'?   94
Where be the bending peers that flattered thee?
Where be the thronging troops that followed
    thee?
Decline all this, and see what now thou art:
For happy wife, a most distressed widow; 98
For joyful mother, one that wails the name;
For queen, a very caitiff crown'd with care;
For one being su'd to, one that humbly sues;
For she that scorn'd at me, now scorn'd of me;
For she being fear'd of all, now fearing one;
For she commanding all, obey'd of none.
Thus hath the course of justice whirl'd about
And left thee but a very prey to time, 106
Having no more but thought of what thou wast,

To torture thee the more, being what thou art.
Thou didst usurp my place, and dost thou not
Usurp the just proportion of my sorrow? 110
Now thy proud neck bears half my burthen'd
yoke,
From which even here I slip my wearied head
And leave the burthen of it all on thee.
Farewell, York's wife and queen of sad mis-
chance!
These English woes shall make me smile in
France. 115
  Queen. O thou well skill'd in curses, stay
awhile
And teach me how to curse mine enemies!
  Q. Marg. Forbear to sleep the night, and fast
the day;
Compare dead happiness with living woe;
Think that thy babes were sweeter than they
were 120
And he that slew them fouler than he is.
Bett'ring thy loss makes the bad causer worse;
Revolving this will teach thee how to curse.
  Queen. My words are dull. O, quicken them
with thine! 124
  Q. Marg. Thy woes will make them sharp
and pierce like mine. *Exit.*
  Duch. Why should calamity be full of words?
  Queen. Windy attorneys to their client woes,
Airy succeeders of intestate joys,
Poor breathing orators of miseries,
Let them have scope! Though what they will
impart 130
Help nothing else, yet do they ease the heart.
  Duch. If so, then be not tongue-tied. Go
with me,
And in the breath of bitter words let's smother
My damned son that thy two sweet sons
smother'd.
                [Trumpet within.]
The trumpet sounds. Be copious in exclaims.

Enter *King Richard* and his *Train*, marching,
  with *Drums* and *Trumpets.*

  Rich. Who intercepts me in my expedition?
  Duch. O, she that might have intercepted
thee,
By strangling thee in her accursed womb,
From all the slaughters (wretch!) that thou
hast done!
  Queen. Hid'st thou that forehead with a
golden crown 140
Where should be branded, if that right were
right,
The slaughter of the prince that ow'd that
crown

And the dire death of my poor sons and
brothers?
Tell me, thou villain-slave, where are my
children?
  Duch. Thou toad, thou toad, where is thy
brother Clarence? 145
And little Ned Plantagenet, his son?
  Queen. Where is the gentle Rivers, Vaughan,
Grey?
  Duch. Where is kind Hastings?
  Rich. A flourish, trumpets! Strike alarum,
drums! 149
Let not the heavens hear these telltale women
Rail on the Lord's anointed. Strike, I say!
              Flourish. Alarums.
Either be patient and entreat me fair,
Or with the clamorous report of war
Thus will I drown your exclamations.
  Duch. Art thou my son? 155
  Rich. Ay, I thank God, my father, and
yourself.
  Duch. Then patiently hear my impatience.
  Rich. Madam, I have a touch of your con-
dition
That cannot brook the accent of reproof.
  Duch. O, let me speak!
  Rich.   Do then, but I'll not hear. 160
  Duch. I will be mild and gentle in my words.
  Rich. And brief, good mother, for I am in
haste.
  Duch. Art thou so hasty? I have stay'd for
thee
(God knows) in torment and in agony.
  Rich. And came I not at last to comfort
you? 165
  Duch. No, by the holy rood, thou know'st it
well,
Thou cam'st on earth to make the earth my
hell.
A grievous burthen was thy birth to me;
Tetchy and wayward was thy infancy;
Thy schooldays frightful, desp'rate, wild, and
furious; 170
Thy prime of manhood daring, bold, and ven-
turous;
Thy age confirm'd, proud, subtle, sly, and
bloody,
More mild, but yet more harmful — kind in
hatred.
What comfortable hour canst thou name
That ever grac'd me with thy company? 175
  Rich. Faith, none, but Humphrey Hour, that
call'd your Grace
To breakfast once, forth of my company.
If I be so disgracious in your eye,

Let me march on and not offend you, madam.
Strike up the drum.
    Duch.   I prithee hear me speak. 180
    Rich. You speak too bitterly.
    Duch.   Hear me a word;
For I shall never speak to thee again.
    Rich. So.
    Duch. Either thou wilt die by God's just
    ordinance
Ere from this war thou turn a conqueror, 185
Or I with grief and extreme age shall perish
And never more behold thy face again.
Therefore take with thee my most grievous
    curse,
Which in the day of battle tire thee more 189
Than all the complete armour that thou wear'st!
My prayers on the adverse party fight,
And there the little souls of Edward's children
Whisper the spirits of thine enemies
And promise them success and victory!
Bloody thou art, bloody will be thy end; 195
Shame serves thy life and doth thy death
    attend.   *Exit.*
    Queen. Though far more cause, yet much
    less spirit to curse
Abides in me. I say amen to her.
    Rich. Stay, madam. I must talk a word with
    you.
    Queen. I have no more sons of the royal
    blood   200
For thee to slaughter. For my daughters,
    Richard,
They shall be praying nuns, not weeping queens;
And therefore level not to hit their lives.
    Rich. You have a daughter call'd Elizabeth,
Virtuous and fair, royal and gracious. 205
    Queen. And must she die for this? O, let
    her live,
And I'll corrupt her manners, stain her beauty,
Slander myself as false to Edward's bed,
Throw over her the veil of infamy. 209
So she may live unscarr'd of bleeding slaughter,
I will confess she was not Edward's daughter.
    Rich. Wrong not her birth. She is a royal
    princess.
    Queen. To save her life, I'll say she is not
    so.
    Rich. Her life is safest only in her birth.
    Queen. And only in that safety died her
    brothers.   215
    Rich. Lo, at their birth good stars were
    opposite.
    Queen. No, to their lives ill friends were
    contrary.
    Rich. All unavoided is the doom of destiny.

    Queen. True, when avoided grace makes
    destiny.
My babes were destin'd to a fairer death 220
If grace had bless'd thee with a fairer life.
    Rich. You speak as if that I had slain my
    cousins.
    Queen. Cousins indeed, and by their uncle
    cozen'd
Of comfort, kingdom, kindred, freedom, life.
Whose hand soever lanch'd their tender hearts,
Thy head (all indirectly) gave direction. 226
No doubt the murd'rous knife was dull and
    blunt
Till it was whetted on thy stone-hard heart
To revel in the entrails of my lambs.
But that still use of grief makes wild grief
    tame,   230
My tongue should to thy ears not name my
    boys
Till that my nails were anchor'd in thine eyes;
And I, in such a desp'rate bay of death,
Like a poor bark of sails and tackling reft,
Rush all to pieces on thy rocky bosom. 235
    Rich. Madam, so thrive I in my enterprise
And dangerous success of bloody wars
As I intend more good to you and yours
Than ever you and yours by me were harm'd!
    Queen. What good is cover'd with the face
    of heaven,   240
To be discovered, that can do me good?
    Rich. Th' advancement of your children,
    gentle lady.
    Queen. Up to some scaffold, there to lose
    their heads!
    Rich. Unto the dignity and height of for-
    tune,   244
The high imperial type of this earth's glory.
    Queen. Flatter my sorrow with report of it.
Tell me, what state, what dignity, what honour
Canst thou demise to any child of mine?
    Rich. Even all I have — ay, and myself and
    all —
Will I withal endow a child of thine, 250
So in the Lethe of thy angry soul
Thou drown the sad remembrance of those
    wrongs
Which thou supposest I have done to thee.
    Queen. Be brief, lest that the process of thy
    kindness
Last longer telling than thy kindness' date. 255
    Rich. Then know that from my soul I love
    thy daughter.
    Queen. My daughter's mother thinks it with
    her soul.
    Rich. What do you think?

Queen. That thou dost love my daughter
from thy soul.
So from thy soul's love didst thou love her
brothers,   260
And from my heart's love I do thank thee for it.
Rich. Be not so hasty to confound my
meaning.
I mean that with my soul I love thy daughter
And do intend to make her Queen of England.
Queen. Well then, who dost thou mean shall
be her king?   265
Rich. Even he that makes her Queen. Who
else should be?
Queen. What, thou?
Rich.   Even so. How think you
of it, madam?
Queen. How canst thou woo her?
Rich.   That I would learn of you,
As one being best acquainted with her humour.
Queen. And wilt thou learn of me?
Rich.   Madam, with all my heart.   270
Queen. Send to her by the man that slew
her brothers
A pair of bleeding hearts; thereon engrave
'Edward' and 'York.' Then haply will she
weep.
Therefore present to her — as sometime Mar-
garet   274
Did to thy father, steep'd in Rutland's blood —
A handkerchief, which say to her did drain
The purple sap from her sweet brother's body,
And bid her wipe her weeping eyes withal.
If this inducement move her not to love,
Send her a letter of thy noble deeds: 280
Tell her thou mad'st away her uncle Clarence,
Her uncle Rivers; ay (and for her sake!),
Mad'st quick conveyance with her good aunt
Anne.
Rich. You mock me, madam. This is not
the way
To win your daughter.
Queen.   There is no other way,   285
Unless thou couldst put on some other shape,
And not be Richard that hath done all this.
Rich. Say that I did all this for love of her.
Queen. Nay, then indeed she cannot choose
but hate thee,   289
Having bought love with such a bloody spoil.
Rich. Look, what is done cannot be now
amended.
Men shall deal unadvisedly sometimes,
Which after-hours gives leisure to repent.
If I did take the kingdom from your sons,
To make amends I'll give it to your daughter.
It I have kill'd the issue of your womb,   296

To quicken your increase I will beget
Mine issue of your blood upon your daughter.
A grandam's name is little less in love
Than is the doting title of a mother.   300
They are as children but one step below,
Even of your metal, of your very blood,
Of all one pain, save for a night of groans
Endur'd of her for whom you bid like sorrow.
Your children were vexation to your youth,
But mine shall be a comfort to your age.   306
The loss you have is but a son being king,
And by that loss your daughter is made queen.
I cannot make you what amends I would;
Therefore accept such kindness as I can.   310
Dorset your son, that with a fearful soul
Leads discontented steps in foreign soil,
This fair alliance quickly shall call home
To high promotions and great dignity.
The King, that calls your beauteous daughter
wife,   315
Familiarly shall call thy Dorset brother.
Again shall you be mother to a king,
And all the ruins of distressful times
Repair'd with double riches of content.
What, we have many goodly days to see.   320
The liquid drops of tears that you have shed
Shall come again, transform'd to orient pearl,
Advantaging their loan with interest
Of ten times double gain of happiness.
Go then, my mother; to thy daughter go;   325
Make bold her bashful years with your ex-
perience;
Prepare her ears to hear a wooer's tale;
Put in her tender heart th' aspiring flame
Of golden sovereignty; acquaint the princess
With the sweet silent hours of marriage joys;
And when this arm of mine hath chastised   331
The petty rebel, dull-brain'd Buckingham,
Bound with triumphant garlands will I come
And lead thy daughter to a conqueror's bed;
To whom I will retail my conquest won,   335
And she shall be sole victoress, Cæsar's Cæsar.
Queen. What were I best to say? Her
father's brother
Would be her lord? Or shall I say her uncle?
Or he that slew her brothers and her uncles?
Under what title shall I woo for thee   340
That God, the law, my honour, and her love
Can make seem pleasing to her tender years?
Rich. Infer fair England's peace by this
alliance.
Queen. Which she shall purchase with still-
lasting war.
Rich. Tell her the King, that may command,
entreats.   345

356

Queen. That at her hands which the King's King forbids.

Rich. Say she shall be a high and mighty queen.

Queen. To wail the title, as her mother doth.

Rich. Say I will love her everlastingly.

Queen. But how long shall that title 'ever' last? 350

Rich. Sweetly in force unto her fair live's end.

Queen. But how long fairly shall her sweet life last?

Rich. As long as heaven and nature lengthens it.

Queen. As long as hell and Richard likes of it.

Rich. Say I, her sovereign, am her subject low. 355

Queen. But she, your subject, loathes such sovereignty.

Rich. Be eloquent in my behalf to her.

Queen. An honest tale speeds best being plainly told.

Rich. Then plainly to her tell my loving tale.

Queen. Plain and not honest is too harsh a style. 360

Rich. Your reasons are too shallow and too quick.

Queen. O no, my reasons are too deep and dead —
Too deep and dead (poor infants) in their graves.

Rich. Harp not on that string, madam; that is past.

Queen. Harp on it still shall I till heart-strings break. 365

Rich. Now, by my George, my garter, and my crown —

Queen. Profan'd, dishonour'd, and the third usurp'd.

Rich. I swear —

Queen. By nothing, for this is no oath.
Thy George, profan'd, hath lost his lordly honour;
Thy garter, blemish'd, pawn'd his knightly virtue; 370
Thy crown, usurp'd, disgrac'd his kingly glory.
If something thou wouldst swear to be believ'd,
Swear then by something that thou hast not wrong'd.

Rich. Now by the world —

Queen. 'Tis full of thy foul wrongs.

Rich. My father's death —

Queen. Thy life hath that dishonour'd. 375

Rich. Then by myself —

Queen. Thyself is self-misus'd.

Rich. Why then, by God, —

Queen. God's wrong is most of all.
If thou didst fear to break an oath by him,
The unity the King my husband made
Thou hadst not broken, nor my brothers died.
If thou hadst fear'd to break an oath by him, 381
Th' imperial metal, circling now thy head,
Had grac'd the tender temples of my child,
And both the Princes had been breathing here,
Which now, two tender bedfellows for dust,
Thy broken faith hath made the prey for worms. 386
What canst thou swear by now?

Rich. The time to come.

Queen. That thou hast wronged in the time o'erpast;
For I myself have many tears to wash 389
Hereafter time, for time past wrong'd by thee.
The children live whose fathers thou hast slaughter'd,
Ungovern'd youth, to wail it with their age;
The parents live whose children thou hast butcher'd,
Old barren plants, to wail it with their age.
Swear not by time to come, for that thou hast 395
Misus'd ere us'd, by times ill-us'd o'erpast.

Rich. As I intend to prosper and repent,
So thrive I in my dangerous affairs
Of hostile arms! Myself myself confound!
Heaven and fortune bar me happy hours! 400
Day, yield me not thy light, nor, night, thy rest!
Be opposite all planets of good luck
To my proceeding if, with dear heart's love,
Immaculate devotion, holy thoughts, 404
I tender not thy beauteous princely daughter!
In her consists my happiness and thine;
Without her, follows to myself and thee,
Herself, the land, and many a Christian soul,
Death, desolation, ruin, and decay.
It cannot be avoided but by this; 410
It will not be avoided but by this.
Therefore, dear mother (I must call you so),
Be the attorney of my love to her.
Plead what I will be, not what I have been;
Not my deserts, but what I will deserve. 415
Urge the necessity and state of times,
And be not peevish-fond in great designs.

Queen. Shall I be tempted of the devil thus?

Rich. Ay, if the devil tempt you to do good.

Queen. Shall I forget myself to be myself?

Rich. Ay, if yourself's remembrance wrong
  yourself.   421
Queen. Yet thou didst kill my children.
Rich. But in your daughter's womb I bury
  them,
Where, in that nest of spicery, they will breed
Selves of themselves, to your recomforture. 425
Queen. Shall I go win my daughter to thy
  will?
Rich. And be a happy mother by the deed.
Queen. I go. Write to me very shortly,
And you shall understand from me her mind.
Rich. Bear her my true love's kiss; and so
  farewell —   430
                    Exit Queen [Elizabeth].
Relenting fool, and shallow, changing woman!

  Enter *Ratcliff*, [*Catesby* following].

How now? What news?
Rat. Most mighty sovereign, on the western
  coast
Rideth a puissant navy; to our shores   434
Throng many doubtful hollow-hearted friends,
Unarm'd, and unresolv'd to beat them back.
'Tis thought that Richmond is their admiral;
And there they hull, expecting but the aid
Of Buckingham to welcome them ashore.
Rich. Some light-foot friend post to the
  Duke of Norfolk.   440
Ratcliff, thyself — or Catesby — where is he?
Cates. Here, my good lord.
Rich.   Catesby, fly to the Duke.
Cates. I will, my lord, with all convenient
  haste.
Rich. Ratcliff, come hither. Post to Salisbury.
When thou com'st thither —[*To Catesby*] Dull
  unmindful villain,   445
Why stay'st thou here and go'st not to the
  Duke?
Cates. First, mighty liege, tell me your High-
  ness' pleasure,
What from your Grace I shall deliver to him.
Rich. O, true, good Catesby. Bid him levy
  straight
The greatest strength and power that he can
  make   450
And meet me suddenly at Salisbury.
Cates. I go.   *Exit.*
Rat. What, may it please you, shall I do at
  Salisbury?
Rich. Why, what wouldst thou do there be-
  fore I go?
Rat. Your Highness told me I should post
  before.   455
Rich. My mind is chang'd.

  Enter *Lord Stanley.*

              Stanley, what news with you?
Stan. None good, my liege, to please you
  with the hearing,
Nor none so bad but well may be reported.
Rich. Hoyday, a riddle! Neither good nor
  bad!   459
What need'st thou run so many miles about
When thou mayst tell thy tale the nearest way?
Once more, what news?
Stan.   Richmond is on the seas.
Rich. There let him sink, and be the seas
  on him!
White-liver'd runagate! what doth he there?
Stan. I know not, mighty sovereign, but by
  guess.   465
Rich. Well, as you guess?
Stan. Stirr'd up by Dorset, Buckingham,
  and Morton,
He makes for England, here to claim the crown.
Rich. Is the chair empty? Is the sword
  unsway'd?   469
Is the King dead? the empire unpossess'd?
What heir of York is there alive but we?
And who is England's king but great York's
  heir?
Then tell me, what makes he upon the seas?
Stan. Unless for that, my liege, I cannot
  guess.   474
Rich. Unless for that he comes to be your liege
You cannot guess wherefore the Welshman
  comes.
Thou wilt revolt and fly to him, I fear.
Stan. No, my good lord. Therefore mistrust
  me not.
Rich. Where is thy power then to beat him
  back?
Where be thy tenants and thy followers?   480
Are they not now upon the western shore,
Safe-conducting the rebels from their ships?
Stan. No, my good lord, my friends are in
  the North.
Rich. Cold friends to me! What do they in
  the North
When they should serve their sovereign in the
  West?   485
Stan. They have not been commanded,
  mighty king.
Pleaseth your Majesty to give me leave,
I'll muster up my friends and meet your Grace
Where and what time your Majesty shall please.
Rich. Ay, ay, thou wouldst be gone to join
  with Richmond.   490
But I'll not trust you, sir.

Stan.　　　　　　　Most mighty sovereign,
You have no cause to hold my friendship
　doubtful.
I never was nor never will be false.
　Rich. Go then and muster men. But leave
　behind
Your son, George Stanley. Look your heart
　be firm,　　　　　　　　　　　　　495
Or else his head's assurance is but frail.
　Stan. So deal with him as I prove true to
　you.　　　　　　　　　　　　　*Exit.*

Enter a Messenger.

　Mess. My gracious sovereign, now in Devon-
　shire,
As I by friends am well advertised,　　499
Sir Edward Courtney and the haughty prelate,
Bishop of Exeter, his elder brother,
With many moe confederates, are in arms.

Enter another Messenger.

　Mess. In Kent, my liege, the Guildfords are
　in arms,
And every hour more competitors
Flock to the rebels, and their power grows
　strong.　　　　　　　　　　　　505

Enter another Messenger.

　Mess. My lord, the army of great Buck-
　ingham —
　Rich. Out on ye, owls! Nothing but songs
　of death?　　　　　　　　*He striketh him.*
There, take thou that, till thou bring better
　news.
　Mess. The news I have to tell your Majesty
Is that by sudden floods and fall of waters　510
Buckingham's army is dispers'd and scatter'd,
And he himself wand'red away alone,
No man knows whither.
　Rich.　　　　　　I cry thee mercy.
There is my purse to cure that blow of thine.
Hath any well-advised friend proclaim'd　515
Reward to him that brings the traitor in?
　Mess. Such proclamation hath been made,
　my lord.

Enter another Messenger.

　Mess. Sir Thomas Lovel and Lord Marquess
　Dorset,
'Tis said, my liege, in Yorkshire are in arms.
But this good comfort bring I to your Highness:
The Britain navy is dispers'd by tempest.　521
Richmond in Dorsetshire sent out a boat
Unto the shore to ask those on the banks
If they were his assistants, yea or no;
Who answer'd him they came from Buckingham
Upon his party. He, mistrusting them,　　526
Hois'd sail, and made his course again for
　Britain.
　Rich. March on, march on, since we are up
　in arms;
If not to fight with foreign enemies,
Yet to beat down these rebels here at home.　530

Enter Catesby.

　Cates. My liege, the Duke of Buckingham
　is taken.
That is the best news. That the Earl of
　Richmond
Is with a mighty power landed at Milford
Is colder news, but yet they must be told.
　Rich. Away towards Salisbury! While we
　reason here,　　　　　　　　　　　535
A royal battle might be won and lost.
Some one take order Buckingham be brought
To Salisbury; the rest march on with me.
　　　　　　　　　　　Flourish. Exeunt.

Scene [V. Lord Derby's *house*.]

Enter Derby and Sir Christopher [Urswick].

　Der. Sir Christopher, tell Richmond this
　from me:
That in the sty of the most deadly boar
My son George Stanley is frank'd up in hold;
If I revolt, off goes young George's head;
The fear of that holds off my present aid.　5
So get thee gone. Commend me to thy lord.
Withal say that the Queen hath heartily con-
　sented
He should espouse Elizabeth her daughter.
But tell me, where is princely Richmond now?
　Chris. At Pembroke, or at Ha'rford-West in
　Wales.　　　　　　　　　　　　10
　Der. What men of name resort to him?
　Chris. Sir Walter Herbert, a renowned sol-
　dier,
Sir Gilbert Talbot, Sir William Stanley,
Oxford, redoubted Pembroke, Sir James Blunt,
And Rice ap Thomas, with a valiant crew,　15
And many other of great name and worth;
And towards London do they bend their power,
If by the way they be not fought withal.
　Der. Well, hie thee to thy lord. I kiss his
　hand.　　　　　　　　　　　　19
My letter will resolve him of my mind.
　　　　　　　　　　　　[Gives letter.]
Farewell.　　　　　　　　　　*Exeunt.*

ACT V. Scene I. [*Salisbury. An open place.*]

Enter *Buckingham* with *Halberds* [and the *Sheriff*], led to execution.

Buck. Will not King Richard let me speak with him?

Sher. No, my good lord. Therefore be patient.

Buck. Hastings, and Edward's children, Grey and Rivers,
Holy King Henry and thy fair son Edward,
Vaughan and all that have miscarried   5
By underhand corrupted foul injustice,
If that your moody discontented souls
Do through the clouds behold this present hour,
Even for revenge mock my destruction!
This is All Souls' day, fellow, is it not?   10

Sher. It is, my lord.

Buck. Why, then All Souls' day is my body's doomsday.
This is the day which in King Edward's time
I wish'd might fall on me when I was found
False to his children and his wife's allies;   15
This is the day wherein I wish'd to fall
By the false faith of him whom most I trusted.
This, this All Souls' day to my fearful soul
Is the determin'd respite of my wrongs.
That high All-seer which I dallied with   20
Hath turn'd my feigned prayer on my head
And given in earnest what I begg'd in jest.
Thus doth he force the swords of wicked men
To turn their own points in their masters' bosoms.   24
Thus Margaret's curse falls heavy on my neck.
'When he,' quoth she, 'shall split thy heart with sorrow,
Remember Margaret was a prophetess.' —
Come lead me, officers, to the block of shame.
Wrong hath but wrong, and blame the due of blame.   *Exit with officers.*

Scene II. [*Camp near Tamworth.*]

Enter *Richmond, Oxford,* [*Sir James*] *Blunt,* [*Sir Walter*] *Herbert,* and others, with *Drum* and *Colours.*

Richm. Fellows in arms, and my most loving friends,
Bruis'd underneath the yoke of tyranny,
Thus far into the bowels of the land

Have we march'd on without impediment;
And here receive we from our father Stanley   5
Lines of fair comfort and encouragement.
The wretched, bloody, and usurping boar,
That spoil'd your summer fields and fruitful vines,
Swills your warm blood like wash, and makes his trough   9
In your embowell'd bosoms — this foul swine
Lies now even in the centre of this isle,
Near to the town of Leicester, as we learn.
From Tamworth thither is but one day's march.
In God's name cheerly on, courageous friends,
To reap the harvest of perpetual peace   15
By this one bloody trial of sharp war.

Oxf. Every man's conscience is a thousand men,
To fight against this guilty homicide.

Herb. I doubt not but his friends will turn to us.

Blunt. He hath no friends but what are friends for fear,   20
Which in his dearest need will fly from him.

Richm. All for our vantage. Then in God's name march!
True hope is swift and flies with swallow's wings;
Kings it makes gods, and meaner creatures kings.   *Exeunt.*

[Scene III. *Bosworth Field.*]

Enter *King Richard* in arms, with *Norfolk, Ratcliff,* the *Earl of Surrey,* [and *Soldiers*].

Rich. Here pitch our tent, even here in Bosworth field.
My Lord of Surrey, why look you so sad?

Sur. My heart is ten times lighter than my looks.

Rich. My Lord of Norfolk —

Nor.   Here, most gracious liege.

Rich. Norfolk, we must have knocks. Ha! must we not?   5

Nor. We must both give and take, my loving lord.

Rich. Up with my tent! Here will I lie to-night;
  [*Soldiers begin to set up the King's tent.*]

360

But where to-morrow? Well, all's one for that.
Who hath descried the number of the traitors?

  Nor. Six or seven thousand is their utmost
    power.   10
  Rich. Why, our battalia trebles that account.
Besides, the King's name is a tower of strength,
Which they upon the adverse faction want.
Up with the tent! Come, noble gentlemen,
Let us survey the vantage of the ground.   15
Call for some men of sound direction.
Let's lack no discipline, make no delay,
For, lords, to-morrow is a busy day.   *Exeunt.*

*Enter Richmond, Sir William Brandon, Oxford,
Dorset, Herbert, and Blunt. [Some of the Soldiers pitch Richmond's tent.]*

  Richm. The weary sun hath made a golden
    set
And by the bright tract of his fiery car   20
Gives token of a goodly day to-morrow.
Sir William Brandon, you shall bear my stand-
  ard.
Give me some ink and paper in my tent.
I'll draw the form and model of our battle,
Limit each leader to his several charge,   25
And part in just proportion our small power.
My Lord of Oxford, — you, Sir William
  Brandon, —
And you, Sir Walter Herbert — stay with me.
The Earl of Pembroke keeps his regiment.
Good Captain Blunt, bear my good-night to
  him,   30
And by the second hour in the morning
Desire the Earl to see me in my tent.
Yet one thing more, good Captain, do for
  me.
Where is Lord Stanley quarter'd, do you know?

  Blunt. Unless I have mista'en his colours
    much   35
(Which well I am assur'd I have not done),
His regiment lies half a mile at least
South from the mighty power of the King.

  Richm. If without peril it be possible,
Sweet Blunt, make some good means to speak
  with him   40
And give him from me this most needful
  note.

  Blunt. Upon my life, my lord, I'll undertake
  it;
And so God give you quiet rest to-night!

  Richm. Good night, good Captain Blunt.
    [*Exit Blunt.*] Come, gentlemen,
Let us consult upon to-morrow's business.   45
Into my tent; the dew is raw and cold.
               They withdraw into the tent.

*Enter, [to his tent,] Richard, Ratcliff, Norfolk,
and Catesby.*

  Rich. What is't o'clock?
  Cates.   It's supper time, my lord;
It's nine o'clock.
  Rich.   I will not sup to-night.
Give me some ink and paper.
What, is my beaver easier than it was,   50
And all my armour laid into my tent?
  Cates. It is, my liege; and all things are in
    readiness.
  Rich. Good Norfolk, hie thee to thy charge;
Use careful watch, choose trusty sentinels.
  Nor. I go, my lord.   55
  Rich. Stir with the lark to-morrow, gentle
    Norfolk.
  Nor. I warrant you, my lord.   *Exit.*
  Rich. Catesby!
  Cates. My lord?
  Rich.   Send out a pursuivant-at-arms
To Stanley's regiment. Bid him bring his
  power   60
Before sunrising, lest his son George fall
Into the blind cave of eternal night.
                       [Exit Catesby.]
Fill me a bowl of wine. Give me a watch.
Saddle white Surrey for the field to-morrow.
Look that my staves be sound and not too
  heavy.   65
Ratcliff!
  Rat. My lord?
  Rich. Saw'st thou the melancholy Lord
    Northumberland?
  Rat. Thomas the Earl of Surrey and him-
    self,
Much about cockshut time, from troop to
  troop   70
Went through the army, cheering up the sol-
  diers.
  Rich. So, I am satisfied. Give me a bowl of
  wine.
I have not that alacrity of spirit
Nor cheer of mind that I was wont to have.
                     [Wine brought.]
Set it down. Is ink and paper ready?   75
  Rat. It is, my lord.
  Rich. Bid my guard watch. Leave me.
    Ratcliff,
About the mid of night come to my tent
And help to arm me. Leave me, I say.
                Exit Ratcliff [with others].
    *[King Richard retires into his tent, and
                            sleeps.]*

Enter *Derby* to *Richmond* in his tent.

Der. Fortune and victory sit on thy helm!

Richm. All comfort that the dark night can afford   81
Be to thy person, noble father-in-law!
Tell me, how fares our loving mother?

Der. I, by attorney, bless thee from thy mother,   84
Who prays continually for Richmond's good.
So much for that. The silent hours steal on
And flaky darkness breaks within the east.
In brief, for so the season bids us be,
Prepare thy battle early in the morning
And put thy fortune to th' arbitrement   90
Of bloody strokes and mortal-staring war.
I, as I may, — that which I would I cannot, —
With best advantage will deceive the time
And aid thee in this doubtful shock of arms.
But on thy side I may not be too forward,   95
Lest, being seen, thy brother, tender George,
Be executed in his father's sight.
Farewell. The leisure and the fearful time
Cuts off the ceremonious vows of love
And ample interchange of sweet discourse   100
Which so long sund'red friends should dwell upon.
God give us leisure for these rites of love!
Once more adieu. Be valiant, and speed well!

Richm. Good lords, conduct him to his regiment.   104
I'll strive with troubled noise, to take a nap,
Lest leaden slumber peise me down to-morrow
When I should mount with wings of victory.
Once more, good night, kind lords and gentlemen.

                 Exeunt. Manet Richmond.
O thou whose captain I account myself,
Look on my forces with a gracious eye.   110
Put in their hands thy bruising irons of wrath,
That they may crush down with a heavy fall
Th' usurping helmets of our adversaries.
Make us thy ministers of chastisement,
That we may praise thee in thy victory.   115
To thee I do commend my watchful soul
Ere I let fall the windows of mine eyes.
Sleeping and waking, O defend me still!

                        Sleeps.

Enter the *Ghost of Prince Edward*, son to *Henry the Sixth.*

Ghost. (*to Richard*) Let me sit heavy in thy soul to-morrow!
Think how thou stab'dst me in my prime of youth   120
At Tewksbury. Despair, therefore, and die!

(*To Richmond*) Be cheerful, Richmond; for the wronged souls
Of butcher'd princes fight in thy behalf.
King Henry's issue, Richmond, comforts thee.

Enter the *Ghost of Henry the Sixth.*

Ghost. (*to Richard*) When I was mortal, my anointed body   125
By thee was punched full of deadly holes.
Think on the Tower, and me. Despair and die!
Harry the Sixth bids thee despair and die!
(*To Richmond*) Virtuous and holy, be thou conqueror!   129
Harry, that prophesied thou shouldst be King,
Doth comfort thee in sleep. Live and flourish!

Enter the *Ghost of Clarence.*

Ghost. [*to Richard*] Let me sit heavy in thy soul to-morrow —
I that was wash'd to death with fulsome wine,
Poor Clarence by thy guile betray'd to death!
To-morrow in the battle think on me,   135
And fall thy edgeless sword. Despair and die!
(*To Richmond*) Thou offspring of the house of Lancaster,
The wronged heirs of York do pray for thee.
Good angels guard thy battle! Live and flourish!

Enter the *Ghosts* of *Rivers, Grey,* and *Vaughan.*

Riv. [*to Richard*] Let me sit heavy in thy soul to-morrow,   140
Rivers, that died at Pomfret! Despair and die!

Grey. Think upon Grey, and let thy soul despair!

Vaugh. Think upon Vaughan and with guilty fear
Let fall thy lance. Despair and die!

All. (*to Richmond*) Awake, and think our wrongs in Richard's bosom   145
Will conquer him! Awake and win the day!

Enter the *Ghost* of *Lord Hastings.*

Ghost. [*to Richard*] Bloody and guilty, guiltily awake
And in a bloody battle end thy days!
Think on Lord Hastings. Despair and die!
(*To Richmond*) Quiet untroubled soul, awake, awake!   150
Arm, fight, and conquer, for fair England's sake!

Enter the *Ghosts* of the two young *Princes.*

Ghosts. (*to Richard*) Dream on thy cousins smothered in the Tower.
Let us be lead within thy bosom, Richard.

And weigh thee down to ruin, shame, and
    death!   154
Thy nephews' souls bid thee despair and die!
(*To Richmond*) Sleep, Richmond, sleep in peace
    and wake in joy.
Good angels guard thee from the boar's annoy!
Live, and beget a happy race of kings!
Edward's unhappy sons do bid thee flourish.

      Enter the *Ghost* of *Anne*, his wife.

  Ghost. (*to Richard*) Richard, thy wife, that
    wretched Anne thy wife,   160
That never slept a quiet hour with thee,
Now fills thy sleep with perturbations.
To-morrow in the battle think on me,
And fall thy edgeless sword. Despair and die!
(*To Richmond*) Thou quiet soul, sleep thou a
    quiet sleep.   65
Dream of success and happy victory!
Thy adversary's wife doth pray for thee.

     Enter the *Ghost* of *Buckingham.*

  Ghost. (*to Richard*) The first was I that help'd
    thee to the crown;
The last was I that felt thy tyranny.
O, in the battle think on Buckingham,   170
And die in terror of thy guiltiness!
Dream on, dream on, of bloody deeds and
    death.
Fainting, despair; despairing, yield thy breath!
(*To Richmond*) I died for hope ere I could lend
    thee aid.   174
But cheer thy heart and be thou not dismay'd.
God and good angels fight on Richmond's side,
And Richard fall in height of all his pride!

    [*The Ghosts vanish.*] *Richard starts out of*
        his dream.

  Rich. Give me another horse! Bind up my
    wounds!
Have mercy, Jesu! Soft! I did but dream.   179
O coward conscience, how dost thou afflict me!
The lights burn blue. It is now dead midnight.
Cold fearful drops stand on my trembling flesh.
What do I fear? Myself? There's none else
    by.
Richard loves Richard: that is, I am I.   184
Is there a murtherer here? No. Yes, I am.
Then fly. What, from myself? Great reason
    why —
Lest I revenge myself upon myself?
Alack, I love myself. Wherefore? For any good
That I myself have done unto myself?
O no! Alas, I rather hate myself   190

For hateful deeds committed by myself.
I am a villain. Yet I lie, I am not.
Fool, of thyself speak well. Fool, do not flat-
    ter.
My conscience hath a thousand several tongues,
And every tongue brings in a several tale,   195
And every tale condemns me for a villain.
Perjury, perjury, in the high'st degree,
Murther, stern murther, in the dir'st degree,
All several sins, all us'd in each degree,   199
Throng to the bar, crying all 'Guilty! guilty!'
I shall despair. There is no creature loves
    me;
And if I die, no soul shall pity me.
Nay, wherefore should they, since that I myself
Find in myself no pity to myself?
Methought the souls of all that I had murther'd
Came to my tent, and every one did threat   206
To-morrow's vengeance on the head of Richard.

        Enter *Ratcliff.*

  Rat. My lord!
  Rich. Zounds, who's there?
  Rat. My lord, 'tis I. The early village cock
Hath twice done salutation to the morn.   211
Your friends are up and buckle on their armour.
  Rich. O Ratcliff, I have dream'd a fearful
    dream!
What thinkest thou? Will our friends prove
    all true?
  Rat. No doubt, my lord.
  Rich.   O Ratcliff, I fear, I fear! 215
  Rat. Nay, good my lord, be not afraid of
    shadows.
  Rich. By the apostle Paul, shadows to-night
Have struck more terror to the soul of Richard
Than can the substance of ten thousand soldiers
Armed in proof and led by shallow Richmond.
It is not yet near day. Come, go with me.   221
Under our tents I'll play the easedropper,
To hear if any mean to shrink from me.
        Exeunt Richard and Ratcliff.

    Enter the *Lords*, to *Richmond* sitting in
        his tent.

  Lords. Good morrow, Richmond.
  Richm. Cry mercy, lords and watchful gen-
    tlemen,   225
That you have ta'en a tardy sluggard here.
  Lords. How have you slept, my lord?
  Richm. The sweetest sleep, and fairest-
    boding dreams
That ever ent'red in a drowsy head
Have I since your departure had, my lords.   230

Methought their souls whose bodies Richard
   murther'd
Came to my tent and cried on 'Victory.'
I promise you my heart is very jocund
In the remembrance of so fair a dream.
How far into the morning is it, lords?   235
  Lords. Upon the stroke of four.
  Richm. Why, then 'tis time to arm and give
   direction.

His Oration to his Soldiers.

More than I have said, loving countrymen,
The leisure and enforcement of the time   239
Forbids to dwell upon. Yet remember this:
God and our good cause fight upon our side;
The prayers of holy saints and wronged souls,
Like high-rear'd bulwarks, stand before our
   faces.
Richard except, those whom we fight against
Had rather have us win than him they follow.
For what is he they follow? Truly, gentlemen,
A bloody tyrant and a homicide;
One rais'd in blood and one in blood establish'd;
One that made means to come by what he hath,
And slaughter'd those that were the means to
   help him;   250
A base foul stone, made precious by the foil
Of England's chair, where he is falsely set;
One that hath ever been God's enemy.
Then if you fight against God's enemy,
God will in justice ward you as his soldiers.   255
If you do sweat to put a tyrant down,
You sleep in peace, the tyrant being slain.
If you do fight against your country's foes,
Your country's fat shall pay your pains the hire.
If you do fight in safeguard of your wives,   260
Your wives shall welcome home the conquerors.
If you do free your children from the sword,
Your children's children quit it in your age.
Then in the name of God and all these rights,
Advance your standards, draw your willing
   swords.   265
For me, the ransom of my bold attempt
Shall be this cold corpse on the earth's cold face.
But if I thrive, the gain of my attempt
The least of you shall share his part thereof.
Sound drums and trumpets boldly and cheer-
   fully.   270
God and Saint George! Richmond and victory!
            [Exeunt.]

Enter King Richard, Ratcliff, etc.

  Rich. What said Northumberland as touching Richmond?
  Rat. That he was never trained up in arms.

  Rich. He said the truth. And what said
   Surrey then?
  Rat. He smil'd and said, 'The better for our
   purpose.'   275
  Rich. He was in the right, and so indeed it is.
             Clock strikes.
Tell the clock there. Give me a calendar.
Who saw the sun to-day?
  Rat.   Not I, my lord.
  Rich. Then he disdains to shine; for by the
   book
He should have brav'd the East an hour ago.
A black day will it be to somebody.   281
Ratcliff!
  Rat. My lord?
  Rich.   The sun will not be seen to-day;
The sky doth frown and low'r upon our army.
I would these dewy tears were from the ground.
Not shine to-day? Why, what is that to me
More than to Richmond? For the selfsame
   heaven   287
That frowns on me looks sadly upon him.

Enter Norfolk.

  Nor. Arm, arm, my lord! The foe vaunts in
   the field.
  Rich. Come, bustle, bustle! Caparison my
   horse!   290
Call up Lord Stanley, bid him bring his power.
I will lead forth my soldiers to the plain,
And thus my battle shall be ordered:
My foreward shall be drawn out all in length,
Consisting equally of horse and foot;   295
Our archers shall be placed in the midst;
John Duke of Norfolk, Thomas Earl of Surrey,
Shall have the leading of the foot and horse.
They thus directed, we ourself will follow
In the main battle, whose puissance on either
   side   300
Shall be well-winged with our chiefest horse.
This, and Saint George to boot! What think'st
   thou, Norfolk?
  Nor. A good direction, warlike sovereign.
This found I on my tent this morning.
          He showeth him a paper.

  Jockey of Norfolk, be not so bold,   305
  For Dickon thy master is bought and sold.

  Rich. A thing devised by the enemy.
Go, gentlemen, every man to his charge.
Let not our babbling dreams affright our souls;
For conscience is a word that cowards use,   310
Devis'd at first to keep the strong in awe.
Our strong arms be our conscience, swords our
   law!

March on, join bravely, let us to't pell-mell,
If not to heaven, then hand in hand to hell.

His Oration to his Army.

What shall I say more than I have inferr'd?
Remember whom you are to cope withal —
A sort of vagabonds, rascals, and runaways,
A scum of Britons and base lackey peasants,
Whom their o'ercloyed country vomits forth
To desperate adventures and assur'd destruc-
    tion.   320
You sleeping safe, they bring to you unrest;
You having lands, and bless'd with beauteous
    wives,
They would restrain the one, distain the other.
And who doth lead them but a paltry fellow,
Long kept in Britain at our mother's cost, 325
A milksop, one that never in his life
Felt so much cold as over shoes in snow?
Let's whip these stragglers o'er the seas again,
Lash hence these overweening rags of France,
These famish'd beggars, weary of their lives,
Who (but for dreaming on this fond exploit)
For want of means (poor rats) had hang'd
    themselves.
If we be conquered, let men conquer us,
And not these bastard Britons, whom our fa-
    thers
Have in their own land beaten, bobb'd, and
    thump'd,   335
And, on record, left them the heirs of shame.
Shall these enjoy our lands? lie with our wives?
Ravish our daughters? (*Drum afar off.*) Hark!
    I hear their drum.
Fight, gentlemen of England! Fight, bold
    yeomen!   339
Draw, archers, draw your arrows to the head!
Spur your proud horses hard, and ride in blood!
Amaze the welkin with your broken staves!

Enter a *Messenger.*

What says Lord Stanley? Will he bring his
    power?
Mess. My lord, he doth deny to come.
Rich. Off with his son George's head!   345
Nor. My lord, the enemy is past the marsh.
After the battle let George Stanley die.
Rich. A thousand hearts are great within my
    bosom.
Advance our standards, set upon our foes.
Our ancient word of courage, fair Saint George,
Inspire us with the spleen of fiery dragons! 351
Upon them! Victory sits on our helms.
                   Exeunt.

[Scene IV. *Another part of the field.*]

Alarum; excursions. Enter [*Norfolk and
    Forces;* to him] *Catesby.*

  Cates. Rescue, my Lord of Norfolk, rescue,
    rescue!
The King enacts more wonders than a man,
Daring an opposite to every danger.
His horse is slain, and all on foot he fights,
Seeking for Richmond in the throat of death. 5
Rescue, fair lord, or else the day is lost!

    Alarums. Enter *Richard.*

  Rich. A horse! a horse! my kingdom for a
    horse!
  Cates. Withdraw, my lord. I'll help you to a
    horse.
  Rich. Slave, I have set my life upon a cast
And I will stand the hazard of the die.   10
I think there be six Richmonds in the field;
Five have I slain to-day instead of him.
A horse! a horse! my kingdom for a horse!
                    [Exeunt.]

[Scene V. *Another part of the field.*]

Alarum. Enter *Richard* and *Richmond*;
    they fight; *Richard* is slain.

Retreat and flourish. Enter *Richmond, Derby*
bearing the crown, with *divers other Lords.*

  Richm. God and your arms be prais'd, vic-
    torious friends!
The day is ours; the bloody dog is dead.
  Der. Courageous Richmond, well hast thou
    acquit thee.
Lo, here these long usurped royalties
From the dead temples of this bloody wretch 5
Have I pluck'd off, to grace thy brows withal.
Wear it, enjoy it, and make much of it.
  Richm. Great God of heaven, say amen to
    all!
But tell me, is young George Stanley living?
  Der. He is, my lord, and safe in Leicester
    town,   10
Whither, if it please you, we may now with-
    draw us.
  Richm. What men of name are slain on
    either side?
  Der. John Duke of Norfolk, Walter Lord
    Ferrers,
Sir Robert Brakenbury, and Sir William
    Brandon.

Richm. Inter their bodies as become their
births.   15
Proclaim a pardon to the soldiers fled
That in submission will return to us;
And then, as we have ta'en the sacrament,
We will unite the White Rose and the Red.
Smile heaven upon this fair conjunction,   20
That long have frown'd upon their enmity!
What traitor hears me, and says not amen?
England hath long been mad and scarr'd her-
self;
The brother blindly shed the brother's blood;
The father rashly slaughtered his own son;   25
The son, compell'd, been butcher to the sire.
All this divided York and Lancaster,
Divided in their dire division,
O, now let Richmond and Elizabeth,

The true succeeders of each royal house,   30
By God's fair ordinance conjoin together!
And let their heirs (God, if thy will be so)
Enrich the time to come with smooth-fac'd
peace,
With smiling plenty, and fair prosperous days!
Abate the edge of traitors, gracious Lord,   35
That would reduce these bloody days again
And make poor England weep in streams of
blood!
Let them not live to taste this land's increase
That would with treason wound this fair land's
peace!   39
Now civil wounds are stopp'd, peace lives again:
That she may long live here, God say amen!
Exeunt.

KING HENRY THE EIGHTH

KING HENRY THE EIGHTH was first printed in the Folio of 1623, which is therefore the sole authority for the text.

The date of composition must be shortly before June 29, 1613, for on that day, during a performance of KING HENRY THE EIGHTH, then a new play, the Globe theatre caught fire from the cannon salute that marks the king's approach (i, 4, 49) and was burned down. Sir Henry Wotton gave a lively account of the accident in a letter to his nephew Sir Edmund Bacon written a few days later (July 2):

> Now, to let matters of state sleep, I will entertain you at the present with what has happened this week at the Bank's side. The King's players had a new play, called *All is True*, representing some principal pieces of the reign of Henry VIII, which was set forth with many extraordinary circumstances of pomp and majesty, even to the matting of the stage; the Knights of the Order with their Georges and garters, the Guards with their embroidered coats, and the like: sufficient in truth within a while to make greatness very familiar, if not ridiculous. Now, King Henry making a masque at the Cardinal Wolsey's house, and certain chambers being shot off at his entry, some of the paper, or other stuff, wherewith one of them was stopped, did light on the thatch, where being thought at first but an idle smoke, and their eyes more attentive to the show, it kindled inwardly, and ran round like a train, consuming within less than an hour the whole house to the very grounds. This was the fatal period of that virtuous fabric, wherein yet nothing did perish but wood and straw, and a few forsaken cloaks; only one man had his breeches set on fire, that would perhaps have broiled him, if he had not by the benefit of a provident wit put it out with bottle ale.

That the 'new play' that Wotton mentions was HENRY VIII — though he gives it a different title — is certain, not only from his description but from other testimony.' Thus Thomas Lorkin, in a letter written on June 30, says that the fire occurred 'yesterday, while Burbage's company were acting at the Globe the play of HENRY VIII, and there shooting off certain chambers [i.e. short cannon, standing upright] in way of triumph.' *All is True* was doubtless an alternative title. The Prologue of KING HENRY THE EIGHTH insists that the play is 'our chosen truth,' and a contemporary ballad 'upon the pittifal burneing of the Globe playhowse' has 'all this is true' in the refrain. The style and metre of the Shakespearean part of the drama accord with a late date.

That the greater part of KING HENRY THE EIGHTH is not Shakespeare's is certain. His share, except for a possible touch now and then, seems to comprise only scenes 1 and 2 of Act i, scenes 3 and 4 of Act ii, the first 203 lines of scene 2 in Act iii, and scene 1 in Act v. The rest is proved — to all intents and purposes — by style and manner, and especially by metre, to be the work of John Fletcher, though no direct evidence connects his name with the play. Such evidence, however, does exist for his association with Shakespeare in *The Two Noble Kinsmen*, which must be of about the same date (see p. 1409). The allotment gives Fletcher the two most famous passages in the drama — Wolsey's farewell to greatness and his advice to Cromwell (iii, 2, 351–372, 428–457). But Shakespeare can spare them, and they are not beyond Fletcher's powers. There is no reason to detect a third hand (Beaumont or another) in the play or to ascribe the Shakespearean scenes to Massinger.

That some of Shakespeare's scenes (v, 1, for instance) have been touched up by Fletcher is of course possible. Whether there was intimate collaboration, or whether Fletcher completed an unfinished Shakespearean play, cannot be determined by any tests beyond those of editorial imagination. What Fletcher did, however, he must have done by Shakespeare's authority, for HENRY THE EIGHTH was prepared for Shakespeare's company, and it was accepted by his partners — Heminge and Condell — as sufficiently his to be included in their edition, the Folio of 1623.

For history, the authors went to Holinshed's *Chronicle*. For the Cranmer episode (v, 1–3), however, both Shakespeare and Fletcher, whether they worked in concert or not, had recourse to Foxe's *Book of Martyrs*, phrases from which appear frequently in the text of both. Henry's remark in v, 3, 174-6, for example, simply versifies Foxe's words: 'It came into a common prouerbe: "Do vnto my Lord of Canterbury displeasure or a shrewed turne, and then you may be sure to haue him your frend whiles he lyueth."' Queen Katherine's speech at the Blackfriar's trial (ii, 4, 13–57) is versified from Holinshed with very little change. At least two lines of the blank verse are taken word for word from the prose chronicle. The whole may be compared with Hermione's defence in *The Winter's Tale* (iii, 2).

Chronology is sacrificed, as usual, to dramatic convenience, but without doing violence to the title *All is True*. Thus Queen Katherine's petition in behalf of the commons overwhelmed by the sixth-part tax (i, 2) comes immediately after the arrest of Buckingham (i, 1) and before his trial and conviction (ii, 1). In fact, he was arrested in April, 1521, and convicted on May 13, 1521; whereas the exaction of 'the sixth part of every man's substance' was not decreed until 1525. Wolsey died in 1530; Elizabeth was born in 1533; Queen Katherine died in 1536. In the play, Queen Katherine's death precedes Elizabeth's birth, and Wolsey's death is told the Queen just before her own takes place. The accusation of Cranmer before the Council (v, 3) was not until after 1540 (probably in 1544). In the play, however, it precedes the christening of Elizabeth (1533).

In 1605 was published a play by Samuel Rowley entitled 'When you see me, You know me. Or the famous Chronicle Historie of King Henry the eight, with the birth and vertuous life of Edward Prince of Wales.' It was probably known to the authors of HENRY THE EIGHTH, but they owe it nothing. Had they borrowed from this random-roaming play, their procedure would have merited what Rowley makes Patch, the Cardinal's fool, say to Will Sommers: 'Wee haue but little wit betweene vs already, and so we should haue none at all!'

THE FAMOUS HISTORY OF THE LIFE OF
KING HENRY THE EIGHTH

[Dramatis Personæ.

King Henry the Eighth.
Cardinal Wolsey.
Cardinal Campeius.
Capucius, Ambassador from the Emperor Charles V.
Cranmer, Archbishop of Canterbury.
Duke of Norfolk.
Duke of Buckingham.
Duke of Suffolk.
Earl of Surrey.
Lord Chamberlain.
Lord Chancellor.
Gardiner, King's Secretary, afterwards Bishop of Winchester.
Bishop of Lincoln.
Lord Abergavenny.
Lord Sandys (also styled *Sir William Sandys*).
Sir Henry Guildford.
Sir Thomas Lovell.
Sir Anthony Denny.
Sir Nicholas Vaux.
Cromwell, servant to *Wolsey.*
Secretaries to *Wolsey.*

Griffith, Gentleman Usher to *Queen Katherine.*
Three Gentlemen.
Doctor Butts, Physician to the *King.*
Garter King-at-Arms.
Surveyor to the *Duke of Buckingham.*
Brandon, and a Sergeant-at-Arms.
Doorkeeper of the Council Chamber.
Porter, and his Man.
Page to *Gardiner.*
A Crier.

Queen Katherine, wife to *King Henry,* afterwards divorced.
Anne Bullen, her Maid of Honour, afterwards Queen.
An old Lady, friend to *Anne Bullen.*
Patience, woman to *Queen Katherine.*

Spirits.

Several Bishops, Lords, and Ladies in the Dumb Shows; Women attending upon the Queen; Scribes, Officers, Guards, and other Attendants.

SCENE. — *London; Westminster; Kimbolton.*]

THE PROLOGUE.

I come no more to make you laugh. Things now
That bear a weighty and a serious brow,
Sad, high, and working, full of state and woe,
Such noble scenes as draw the eye to flow,   4
We now present. Those that can pity, here
May (if they think it well) let fall a tear:
The subject will deserve it. Such as give
Their money out of hope they may believe,
May here find truth too. Those that come to see
Only a show or two and so agree   10
The play may pass — if they be still and willing,
I'll undertake may see away their shilling
Richly in two short hours. Only they
That come to hear a merry bawdy play,
A noise of targets, or to see a fellow   15
In a long motley coat guarded with yellow,
Will be deceiv'd. For, gentle hearers, know,
To rank our chosen truth with such a show
As fool and fight is, beside forfeiting
Our own brains and the opinion that we bring   20
To make that only true we now intend,
Will leave us never an understanding friend.
Therefore, for goodness sake, and as you are known
The first and happiest hearers of the town,
Be sad, as we would make ye. Think ye see   25
The very persons of our noble story
As they were living. Think you see them great,
And follow'd with the general throng, and sweat
Of thousand friends. Then, in a moment, see
How soon this mightiness meets misery.   30
And if you can be merry then, I'll say
A man may weep upon his wedding day.

369

ACT I. Scene I. [*London. An antechamber in the Palace.*]

Enter the *Duke of Norfolk* at one door; at the other, the *Duke of Buckingham* and the *Lord Abergavenny.*

Buck. Good morrow and well met. How have ye done
Since last we saw in France?
Nor.   I thank your Grace:
Healthful, and ever since a fresh admirer
Of what I saw there.
Buck.   An untimely ague
Stay'd me a prisoner in my chamber when 5
Those suns of glory, those two lights of men,
Met in the vale of Andren.
Nor.   'Twixt Guynes and Arde.
I was then present, saw them salute on horseback;
Beheld them when they lighted, how they clung
In their embracement, as they grew together;
Which had they, what four thron'd ones could have weigh'd 11
Such a compounded one?
Buck.   All the whole time
I was my chamber's prisoner.
Nor.   Then you lost
The view of earthly glory. Men might say,
Till this time pomp was single, but now married
To one above itself. Each following day 16
Became the next day's master, till the last
Made former wonders its. To-day the French,
All clinquant, all in gold, like heathen gods, 19
Shone down the English; and to-morrow they
Made Britain India — every man that stood
Show'd like a mine. Their dwarfish pages were
As cherubins, all gilt. The madams too,
Not us'd to toil, did almost sweat to bear
The pride upon them, that their very labour 25
Was to them as a painting. Now this masque
Was cried incomparable; and th' ensuing night
Made it a fool and beggar. The two kings,
Equal in lustre, were now best, now worst,
As presence did present them — him in eye 30
Still him in praise; and being present both,
'Twas said they saw but one, and no discerner
Durst wag his tongue in censure. When these suns
(For so they phrase 'em) by their heralds challeng'd 34
The noble spirits to arms, they did perform
Beyond thought's compass, that former fabulous story,

Being now seen possible enough, got credit,
That Bevis was believ'd.
Buck.   O, you go far!
Nor. As I belong to worship and affect
In honour honesty, the tract of ev'ry thing 40
Would by a good discourser lose some life
Which action's self was tongue to. All was royal.
To the disposing of it naught rebell'd;
Order gave each thing view. The office did
Distinctly his full function.
Buck.   Who did guide — 45
I mean, who set the body and the limbs
Of this great sport together, as you guess?
Nor. One, certes, that promises no element
In such a business.
Buck.   I pray you, who, my lord?
Nor. All this was ord'red by the good discretion 50
Of the right reverend Cardinal of York.
Buck. The devil speed him! No man's pie is freed
From his ambitious finger. What had he
To do in these fierce vanities? I wonder
That such a keech can with his very bulk 55
Take up the rays o' th' beneficial sun
And keep it from the earth.
Nor.   Surely, sir,
There's in him stuff that puts him to these ends;
For, being not propp'd by ancestry, whose grace
Chalks successors their way, nor call'd upon 60
For high feats done to th' crown, neither allied
To eminent assistants, but spiderlike
Out of his self-drawing web, 'a gives us note
The force of his own merit makes his way —
A gift that heaven gives for him, which buys
A place next to the King.
Aber.   I cannot tell 66
What heaven hath given him. Let some graver eye
Pierce into that; but I can see his pride
Peep through each part of him. Whence has he that?
If not from hell, the devil is a niggard, 70
Or has given all before and he begins
A new hell in himself.
Buck.   Why the devil,
Upon this French going out, took he upon him
(Without the privity o' th' King) t' appoint
Who should attend on him? He makes up the file 75

Of all the gentry; for the most part such
To whom as great a charge as little honour
He meant to lay upon; and his own letter,
The Honourable Board of Council out,
Must fetch him in he papers.
 Aber.   I do know 80
Kinsmen of mine, three at the least, that have
By this so sicken'd their estates that never
They shall abound as formerly.
 Buck.   O, many
Have broke their backs with laying manors
 on 'em 84
For this great journey. What did this vanity
But minister communication of
A most poor issue?
 Nor.   Grievingly I think
The peace between the French and us not
 values
The cost that did conclude it.
 Buck.   Every man,
After the hideous storm that follow'd, was 90
A thing inspir'd, and, not consulting, broke
Into a general prophecy — that this tempest,
Dashing the garment of this peace, aboded
The sudden breach on't.
 Nor.   Which is budded out;
For France hath flaw'd the league and hath
 attach'd 95
Our merchants' goods at Bordeaux.
 Aber.   Is it therefore
Th' ambassador is silenc'd?
 Nor.   Marry is't!
 Aber. A proper title of a peace, and pur-
 chas'd
At a superfluous rate!
 Buck.   Why, all this business
Our reverend Cardinal carried.
 Nor.   Like it your Grace, 100
The state takes notice of the private difference
Betwixt you and the Cardinal. I advise you
(And take it from a heart that wishes towards
 you
Honour and plenteous safety) that you read
The Cardinal's malice and his potency 105
Together; to consider further, that
What his high hatred would effect wants not
A minister in his power. You know his nature,
That he's revengeful; and I know his sword
Hath a sharp edge; it's long, and 't may be
 said 110
It reaches far, and where 'twill not extend,
Thither he darts it. Bosom up my counsel;
You'll find it wholesome. Lo, where comes that
 rock
That I advise your shunning.

Enter *Cardinal Wolsey*, the purse borne before
him, certain of the *Guard*, and two *Secretaries*
with papers. The *Cardinal* in his passage fixeth
his eye on *Buckingham*, and *Buckingham* on
 him, both full of disdain.

 Car. The Duke of Buckingham's surveyor?
 Ha! 115
Where's his examination?
 Secr.   Here, so please you.
 Car. Is he in person ready?
 Secr.   Ay, please your Grace.
 Car. Well, we shall then know more, and
 Buckingham
Shall lessen this big look.
     Exeunt Cardinal and his Train.
 Buck. This butcher's cur is venom-mouth'd,
 and I 120
Have not the power to muzzle him; therefore
 best
Not wake him in his slumber. A beggar's book
Outworths a noble's blood.
 Nor.   What, are you chaf'd?
Ask God for temp'rance. That's th' appliance
 only
Which your disease requires.
 Buck.   I read in's looks 125
Matter against me, and his eye revil'd
Me as his abject object. At this instant
He bores me with some trick. He's gone to
 th' King.
I'll follow and outstare him.
 Nor.   Stay, my lord, 129
And let your reason with your choler question
What 'tis you go about. To climb steep hills
Requires slow pace at first. Anger is like
A full hot horse, who being allow'd his way,
Self-mettle tires him. Not a man in England
Can advise me like you. Be to yourself 135
As you would to your friend.
 Buck.   I'll to the King
And from a mouth of honour quite cry down
This Ipswich fellow's insolence, or proclaim
There's difference in no persons.
 Nor.   Be advis'd.
Heat not a furnace for your foe so hot 140
That it do singe yourself. We may outrun
By violent swiftness that which we run at,
And lose by overrunning. Know you not
The fire that mounts the liquor till 't run o'er
In seeming to augment it wastes it? Be advis'd.
I say again there is no English soul 146
More stronger to direct you than yourself,
If with the sap of reason you would quench,
Or but allay, the fire of passion.

Buck. Sir,
I am thankful to you, and I'll go along 150
By your prescription. But this top-proud
fellow —
Whom from the flow of gall I name not, but
From sincere motions, by intelligence,
And proofs as clear as founts in July when
We see each grain of gravel — I do know 155
To be corrupt and treasonous.
Nor. Say not treasonous.
Buck. To th' King I'll say't and make my
vouch as strong
As shore of rock. Attend. This holy fox,
Or wolf, or both (for he is equal rav'nous
As he is subtile, and as prone to mischief 160
As able to perform't, his mind and place
Infecting one another, yea, reciprocally),
Only to show his pomp as well in France
As here at home, suggests the King our master
To this last costly treaty, th' interview 165
That swallowed so much treasure and like a
glass
Did break i' th' wrenching.
Nor. Faith, and so it did.
Buck. Pray give me favour, sir. This cun-
ning Cardinal
The articles o' th' combination drew
As himself pleas'd; and they were ratified 170
As he cried 'Thus let be!' to as much end
As give a crutch to th' dead. But our Count-
Cardinal
Has done this, and 'tis well; for worthy
Wolsey
(Who cannot err) he did it. Now this follows
(Which, as I take it, is a kind of puppy 175
To th' old dam, treason), Charles the Emperor,
Under pretence to see the Queen his aunt
(For 'twas indeed his colour, but he came
To whisper Wolsey), here makes visitation.
His fears were that the interview betwixt 180
England and France might through their amity
Breed him some prejudice; for from this league
Peep'd harms that menac'd him. He privily
Deals with our Cardinal; and, as I trow —
Which I do well, for I am sure the Emperor 185
Paid ere he promis'd; whereby his suit was
granted
Ere it was ask'd — but when the way was made,
And pav'd with gold, the Emperor thus desir'd,
That he would please to alter the King's course
And break the foresaid peace. Let the King
know 190
(As soon he shall by me) that thus the Cardinal
Does buy and sell his honour as he pleases,
And for his own advantage.

Nor. I am sorry
To hear this of him, and could wish he were
Something mistaken in't.
Buck. No, not a syllable. 195
I do pronounce him in that very shape
He shall appear in proof.

*Enter Brandon, a Sergeant-at-arms before him,
and two or three of the Guard.*

Bran. Your office, sergeant; execute it.
Serg. Sir,
My lord the Duke of Buckingham and Earl
Of Hereford, Stafford, and Northampton, I 200
Arrest thee of high treason, in the name
Of our most sovereign King.
Buck. Lo you, my lord,
The net has fall'n upon me! I shall perish
Under device and practice.
Bran. I am sorry
To see you ta'en from liberty, to look on 205
The business present. 'Tis his Highness' pleas-
ure
You shall to th' Tower.
Buck. It will help me nothing
To plead mine innocence, for that dye is on me
Which makes my whit'st part black. The will
of heav'n
Be done in this and all things! I obey. 210
O my Lord Aberga'ny, fare you well!
Bran. Nay, he must bear you company. [*To
Abergavenny*] The King
Is pleas'd you shall to th' Tower till you know
How he determines further.
Aber. As the Duke said,
The will of heaven be done, and the King's
pleasure 215
By me obey'd!
Bran. Here is a warrant from
The King t' attach Lord Montacute and the
bodies
Of the Duke's confessor, John de la Car,
One Gilbert Peck, his chancellor —
Buck. So, so! 219
These are the limbs o' th' plot. No more, I hope.
Bran. A monk o' th' Chartreux.
Buck. O, Nicholas Hopkins?
Bran. He.
Buck. My surveyor is false. The o'er-great
Cardinal
Hath show'd him gold; my life is spann'd
already.
I am the shadow of poor Buckingham, 224
Whose figure even this instant cloud puts on
By dark'ning my clear sun. My lord, farewell.
Exeunt.

Scene II. [*London. The Council Chamber.*]

Cornets. Enter *King Henry*, leaning on the
Cardinal's shoulder, the *Nobles*, and *Sir Thomas
Lovell* [with others]. The *Cardinal* places him-
self under the *King's* feet on his right side.

King. My life itself, and the best heart of it,
Thanks you for this great care. I stood i' th'
    level
Of a full-charg'd confederacy, and give thanks
To you that chok'd it. Let be call'd before us
That gentleman of Buckingham's. In person
I'll hear him his confessions justify,   6
And point by point the treasons of his master
He shall again relate.

A noise within, crying 'Room for the Queen!'
Enter the *Queen* [*Katherine*], usher'd by the
Dukes of Norfolk and *Suffolk*. She kneels. The
*King riseth from his state, takes her up, kisses
    and placeth her by him.*

Queen. Nay, we must longer kneel. I am a
    suitor.
King. Arise and take place by us. Half your
    suit   10
Never name to us; you have half our power.
The other moiety ere you ask is given.
Repeat your will, and take it.
Queen.   Thank your Majesty.
That you would love yourself, and in that love
Not unconsidered leave your honour nor   15
The dignity of your office, is the point
Of my petition.
King.   Lady mine, proceed.
Queen. I am solicited, not by a few,
And those of true condition, that your subjects
Are in great grievance. There have been com-
    missions   20
Sent down among 'em, which hath flaw'd the
    heart
Of all their loyalties; wherein, although,
My good Lord Cardinal, they vent reproaches
Most bitterly on you as putter-on   24
Of these exactions, yet the King our master,
Whose honour heaven shield from soil! — even
    he escapes not
Language unmannerly; yea, such which breaks
The sides of loyalty and almost appears
In loud rebellion.
Nor.   Not almost appears —
It doth appear! for, upon these taxations,   30
The clothiers all, not able to maintain
The many to them 'longing, have put off
The spinsters, carders, fullers, weavers, who,

Unfit for other life, compell'd by hunger   34
And lack of other means, in desperate manner
Daring th' event to th' teeth, are all in uproar,
And danger serves among them.
King.   Taxation?
Wherein? and what taxation? My Lord
    Cardinal,
You that are blam'd for it alike with us,
Know you of this taxation?
Card.   Please you, sir,   40
I know but of a single part in aught
Pertains to th' state, and front but in that file
Where others tell steps with me.
Queen.   No, my lord;
You know no more than others! But you frame
Things that are known alike, which are not
    wholesome   45
To those which would not know them and yet
    must
Perforce be their acquaintance. These exactions
(Whereof my sovereign would have note) —
    they are
Most pestilent to th' hearing; and, to bear 'em,
The back is sacrifice to th' load. They say   50
They are devis'd by you, or else you suffer
Too hard an exclamation.
King.   Still exaction!
The nature of it? In what kind, let's know,
Is this exaction?
Queen.   I am much too venturous
In tempting of your patience, but am bold'ned
Under your promis'd pardon. The subject's
    grief   56
Comes through commissions, which compels
    from each
The sixth part of his substance, to be levied
Without delay; and the pretence for this
Is nam'd, your wars in France. This makes
    bold mouths.   60
Tongues spit their duties out, and cold hearts
    freeze
Allegiance in them. Their curses now
Live where their prayers did; and it's come to
    pass
This tractable obedience is a slave
To each incensed will. I would your Highness
Would give it quick consideration, for   66
There is no primer business.
King.   By my life,
This is against our pleasure.
Card.   And for me,
I have no further gone in this than by
A single voice, and that not pass'd me but   70
By learned approbation of the judges. If I
    am

Traduc'd by ignorant tongues, which neither
know
My faculties nor person yet will be
The chronicles of my doing, let me say   74
'Tis but the fate of place and the rough brake
That virtue must go through. We must not
stint
Our necessary actions in the fear
To cope malicious censurers, which ever,
As rav'nous fishes, do a vessel follow
That is new-trimm'd, but benefit no further 80
Than vainly longing. What we oft do best,
By sick interpreters (once weak ones) is
Not ours, or not allow'd; what worst, as oft,
Hitting a grosser quality, is cried up
For our best action. If we shall stand still, 85
In fear our motion will be mock'd or carp'd at,
We should take root here where we sit, or sit
State-statues only.
    King.   Things done well
And with a care exempt themselves from fear;
Things done without example, in their issue 90
Are to be fear'd. Have you a precedent
Of this commission? I believe, not any.
We must not rend our subjects from our laws
And stick them in our will. Sixth part of each?
A trembling contribution! Why, we take 95
From every tree lop, bark, and part o' th'
timber;
And though we leave it with a root, thus hack'd,
The air will drink the sap. To every county
Where this is question'd send our letters with
Free pardon to each man that has denied 100
The force of this commission. Pray look to't.
I put it to your care.
    Card. [*aside to the Secretary*] A word with
you.
Let there be letters writ to every shire
Of the King's grace and pardon. The grieved
commons
Hardly conceive of me. Let it be nois'd 105
That through our intercession this revokement
And pardon comes. I shall anon advise you
Further in the proceeding.
                                Exit Secretary.

            Enter *Surveyor.*

    Queen. I am sorry that the Duke of Buck-
ingham
Is run in your displeasure.
    King.   It grieves many. 110
The gentleman is learn'd and a most rare
speaker,
To nature none more bound; his training such
That he may furnish and instruct great teachers

And never seek for aid out of himself. Yet see,
When these so noble benefits shall prove 115
Not well dispos'd, the mind growing once
corrupt,
They turn to vicious forms, ten times more ugly
Than ever they were fair. This man so com-
plete,
Who was enroll'd 'mongst wonders, and when
we,   119
Almost with ravish'd list'ning, could not find
His hour of speech a minute — he, my lady,
Hath into monstrous habits put the graces
That once were his and is become as black
As if besmear'd in hell. Sit by us; you shall
hear
(This was his gentleman in trust) of him 125
Things to strike honour sad. Bid him recount
The fore-recited practices, whereof
We cannot feel too little, hear too much.
    Card. Stand forth and with bold spirit relate
what you,
Most like a careful subject, have collected 130
Out of the Duke of Buckingham.
    King.   Speak freely.
    Surv. First, it was usual with him — every
day
It would infect his speech — that if the King
Should without issue die, he'll carry it so
To make the sceptre his. These very words 135
I've heard him utter to his son-in-law,
Lord Aberga'ny, to whom by oath he menac'd
Revenge upon the Cardinal.
    Card.   Please your Highness note
His dangerous conception in this point.
Not friended by his wish, to your high person
His will is most malignant, and it stretches 141
Beyond you to your friends.
    Queen.   My learn'd Lord Cardinal,
Deliver all with charity.
    King.   Speak on.
How grounded he his title to the crown
Upon our fail? To this point hast thou heard
him   145
At any time speak aught?
    Surv.   He was brought to this
By a vain prophecy of Nicholas Hopkins.
    King. What was that Hopkins?
    Surv.   Sir, a Chartreux friar,
His confessor, who fed him every minute
With words of sovereignty.
    King.   How know'st thou this? 150
    Surv. Not long before your Highness sped to
France,
The Duke being at the Rose, within the parish
Saint Lawrence Poultney, did of me demand

What was the speech among the Londoners
Concerning the French journey. I replied 155
Men fear'd the French would prove perfidious,
To the King's danger. Presently the Duke
Said 'twas the fear indeed, and that he doubted
'Twould prove the verity of certain words
Spoke by a holy monk 'that oft,' says he, 160
'Hath sent to me, wishing me to permit
John de la Car, my chaplain, a choice hour
To hear from him a matter of some moment;
Whom after under the confession's seal
He solemnly had sworn that what he spoke 165
My chaplain to no creature living but
To me should utter, with demure confidence
This pausingly ensu'd: "Neither the King nor 's
heirs
(Tell you the Duke) shall prosper. Bid him
strive
To gain the love o' th' commonalty. The Duke
Shall govern England."'
   Queen.   If I know you well, 171
You were the Duke's surveyor and lost your
office
On the complaint o' th' tenants. Take good
heed
You charge not in your spleen a noble person
And spoil your nobler soul. I say, take heed;
Yes, heartily beseech you.
   King.   Let him on. 176
Go forward.
   Surv.   On my soul, I'll speak but truth.
I told my lord the Duke, by th' devil's illusions
The monk might be deceiv'd; and that 'twas
dangerous for him
To ruminate on this so far until   180
It forg'd him some design, which, being believ'd,
It was much like to do. He answer'd 'Tush,
It can do me no damage!' adding further
That, had the King in his last sickness fail'd,
The Cardinal's and Sir Thomas Lovell's heads
Should have gone off.
   King.   Ha! What? so rank? Aha!
There's mischief in this man. Canst thou say
further?
   Surv. I can, my liege.
   King.   Proceed.
   Surv.   Being at Greenwich,
After your Highness had reprov'd the Duke
About Sir William Bulmer —
   King.   I remember 190
Of such a time. Being my sworn servant,
The Duke retain'd him his. But on! What
hence?
   Surv. 'If,' quoth he, 'I for this had been
committed,

As to the Tower I thought, I would have play'd
The part my father meant to act upon 195
Th' usurper Richard, who, being at Salisbury,
Made suit to come in's presence, which if
granted,
As he made semblance of his duty, would
Have put his knife into him.'
   King.   A giant traitor!
   Card. Now, madam, may his Highness live
in freedom,   200
And this man out of prison?
   Queen.   God mend all!
   King. There's something more would out of
thee. What say'st?
   Surv. After 'the Duke his father,' with the
'knife,'
He stretch'd him, and, with one hand on his
dagger,   204
Another spread on 's breast, mounting his eyes,
He did discharge a horrible oath, whose tenour
Was, were he evil us'd, he would outgo
His father by as much as a performance
Does an irresolute purpose.
   King.   There's his period,
To sheathe his knife in us. He is attach'd. 210
Call him to present trial. If he may
Find mercy in the law, 'tis his; if none,
Let him not seek't of us. By day and night,
He's traitor to the height!   *Exeunt.*

Scene III. [*London. An antechamber
in the Palace.*]

Enter *Lord Chamberlain* and *Lord Sandys.*

   L. Cham. Is't possible the spells of France
should juggle
Men into such strange mysteries?
   L. Sandys.   New customs,
Though they be never so ridiculous
(Nay, let 'em be unmanly), yet are follow'd.
   L. Cham. As far as I see, all the good our
English   5
Have got by the late voyage is but merely
A fit or two o' th' face; but they are shrewd
ones;
For when they hold 'em, you would swear
directly
Their very noses had been councillors
To Pepin or Clotharius, they keep state so. 10
   L. Sandys. They have all new legs, and lame
ones. One would take it,
That never saw 'em pace before, the spavin
Or springhalt reign'd among 'em.

L. Cham.   Death, my lord!
Their clothes are after such a pagan cut to't
That sure th' have worn out Christendom.

Enter *Sir Thomas Lovell.*

                              How now? 15
What news, Sir Thomas Lovell?
    Lov.   Faith, my lord,
I hear of none but the new proclamation
That's clapp'd upon the court gate.
    L. Cham.   What is't for?
    Lov. The reformation of our travell'd gal-
lants
That fill the court with quarrels, talk, and
    tailors.   20
    L. Cham. I'm glad 'tis there. Now I would
    pray our monsieurs
To think an English courtier may be wise
And never see the Louvre.
    Lov.   They must either
(For so run the conditions) leave those rem-
    nants
Of fool and feather that they got in France, 25
With all their honourable points of igno-
    rance
Pertaining thereunto, — as fights and fire-
    works;
Abusing better men than they can be,
Out of a foreign wisdom, — renouncing clean
The faith they have in tennis and tall stock-
    ings,   30
Short blist'red breeches, and those types of
    travel,
And understand again like honest men,
Or pack to their old playfellows. There, I take
    it,
They may *cum privilegio* wear away
The lag-end of their lewdness and be laugh'd
    at.   35
    L. Sandys. 'Tis time to give 'em physic, their
    diseases
Are grown so catching.
    L. Cham.   What a loss our ladies
Will have of these trim vanities!
    Lov.   Ay, marry,
There will be woe indeed, lords. The sly
    whoresons   39
Have got a speeding trick to lay down ladies.
A French song and a fiddle has no fellow.
    L. Sandys. The devil fiddle 'em! I am glad
    they are going,
For sure there's no converting of 'em. Now
An honest country lord, as I am, beaten
A long time out of play, may bring his plain-
    song   45

And have an hour of hearing, and, by'r Lady,
Held current music too.
    L. Cham.   Well said, Lord Sandys.
Your colt's tooth is not cast yet.
    L. Sandys.   No, my lord,
Nor shall not while I have a stump.
    L. Cham.   Sir Thomas,
Whither were you a-going?
    Lov.   To the Cardinal's. 50
Your lordship is a guest too.
    L. Cham.   O, 'tis true.
This night he makes a supper, and a great
    one,
To many lords and ladies. There will be
The beauty of this kingdom, I'll assure you.
    Lov. That churchman bears a bounteous
    mind indeed,   55
A hand as fruitful as the land that feeds us;
His dews fall everywhere.
    L. Cham.   No doubt he's noble.
He had a black mouth that said other of
    him.
    L. Sandys. He may, my lord; has where-
    withal. In him
Sparing would show a worse sin than ill doc-
    trine.   60
Men of his way should be most liberal;
They are set here for examples.
    L. Cham.   True, they are so;
But few now give so great ones. My barge
    stays;
Your lordship shall along. Come, good Sir
    Thomas,
We shall be late else; which I would not be, 65
For I was spoke to, with Sir Henry Guildford,
This night to be comptrollers.
    L. Sandys.   I am your lordship's.
                                 Exeunt.

Scene IV. [*Westminster. The presence
        chamber in York Place.*]

*Hautboys. A small table under a state for the
Cardinal, a longer table for the guests.* Then
enter *Anne Bullen* and divers other *Ladies* and
Gentlemen, as guests at one door; at another
    door enter *Sir Henry Guildford.*

    Sir H. Guild. Ladies, a general welcome from
        his Grace
Salutes ye all. This night he dedicates
To fair content and you. None here, he hopes,
In all this noble bevy, has brought with her
One care abroad. He would have all as merry

Paul Rogers playing the part of the portly, uxorious English sovereign, Henry VIII

THE FAMOUS STORY OF THE LIFE
OF
KING HENRY VIII

PHOTOGRAPHS BY HOUSTON ROGERS
PRODUCED BY THE OLD VIC COMPANY

"Lo you, my lord, the net has fall'n upon me." Arrested on a charge of treason, Buckingham despairs of escaping (*Act I, Scene I*)

Leo Genn as the ill-fated Buckingham, victim of the intrigues of Cardinal Wolsey

At the order of Wolsey (Alexander Fox), the Duke of Buckingham's surveyor (Wolfe Morris) testifies against him before Henry and Katharine (Gwen Ffrangcon Davies) (*Act I, Scene II*)

Gwen Ffrangcon Davies as Henry's queen, Katharine, divorced by Henry on the grounds she had been married to his brother

Alexander Knox as Wolsey, who destroys Buckingham, but is himself overturned through his double dealings with Henry.

Henry drinks a toast to Anne Bullen at the masque (*Act I, Scene IV*)

Below: Lord Sands (James Ottaway) in dalliance with Anne Bullen (Jeannette Sterke) and another woman of the court

An old woman (Wynne Clarke) jests with Anne Bullen about King Henry's interest (Act II, Scene III)

The ecclesiastical hearing on the marriage of Henry and Katharine (Act II, Scene IV)

Campeius and Wolsey seek to persuade Queen Katharine to accept an annulment of her marriage with Henry (Act III, Scene I)

The King dismisses Wolsey and Campeius, the hearing having been adjourned (Act II, Scene IV)

"Read o'er this: and after, this: and then to breakfast with what appetite you have." The king presents Wolsey with the evidence of his malfeasance (Act III, Scene II)

Wolsey bids his secretary Cromwell (Timothy Bateson) to profit by his example. "Had I but served my God with half the zeal I served my king, he would not in mine age have left me naked to mine enemies" (Act III, Scene II)

"Be of good cheer; they shall no more prevail than we give way to." Henry assures Cranmer (William Squire) that he will support him against the unfriendly primates (Act V, Scene I)

King Henry honours Cranmer, Archbishop of Canterbury, in the Council (Act V, Scene III)

While Katharine lies ill at Kimbolton, her steward Griffith (Wolfe Morris) tells of the fall of Wolsey (*Act IV, Scene II*)

A porter (Newton Blick) and his man making preparations for the christening of Elizabeth (*Act V, Scene IV*)

Below: James Ottaway, Robert Hardy, and Newton Blick as three gentlemen watching the coronation (*Act IV, Scene I*)

Cranmer presides at the christening of the infant Princess Elizabeth (*Act V, Scene V*)

As, first, good company, good wine, good welcome   6
Can make good people.

Enter *Lord Chamberlain, Lord Sandys,* and
 [*Sir Thomas*] *Lovell.*

        O my lord, y'are tardy!
The very thought of this fair company
Clapp'd wings to me.
 Cham. You are young, Sir Harry Guildford.
 Sandys. Sir Thomas Lovell, had the Cardinal
But half my lay thoughts in him, some of
 these   11
Should find a running banquet ere they rested
I think would better please 'em. By my life,
They are a sweet society of fair ones.
 Lov. O that your lordship were but now
 confessor   15
To one or two of these!
 Sandys.   I would I were.
They should find easy penance.
 Lov.   Faith, how easy?
 Sandys. As easy as a down bed would afford
 it.
 Cham. Sweet ladies, will it please you sit?
 Sir Harry,
Place you that side; I'll take the charge of
 this.   20
His Grace is ent'ring. Nay, you must not
 freeze!
Two women plac'd together makes cold
 weather.
My Lord Sandys, you are one will keep 'em
 waking.
Pray sit between these ladies.
 Sandys.   By my faith,
And thank your lordship. By your leave, sweet
 ladies.   25

 [*Seats himself between Anne Bullen and
   another Lady.*]

If I chance to talk a little wild, forgive me.
I had it from my father.
 Anne B.   Was he mad, sir?
 Sandys. O, very mad, exceeding mad, in
 love too.
But he would bite none. Just as I do now,
He would kiss you twenty with a breath.
         [*Kisses her.*]
 Cham.   Well said, my lord. 30
So, now y'are fairly seated. Gentlemen,
The penance lies on you if these fair ladies
Pass away frowning.
 Sandys.   For my little cure,
Let me alone.

Hautboys. Enter *Cardinal Wolsey,* [attended]
 and takes his state.

 Card. Y'are welcome, my fair guests. That
 noble lady   35
Or gentleman that is not freely merry
Is not my friend. This to confirm my welcome;
And to you all, good health. [*Drinks.*]
 Sandys.   Your Grace is noble.
Let me have such a bowl may hold my thanks
And save me so much talking.
 Card.   My Lord Sandys, 40
I am beholding to you. Cheer your neighbours.
Ladies, you are not merry. Gentlemen,
Whose fault is this?
 Sandys.   The red wine first must rise
In their fair cheeks, my lord; then we shall
 have 'em
Talk us to silence.
 Anne B. You are a merry gamester, 45
My Lord Sandys.
 Sandys. Yes, if I make my play.
Here's to your ladyship; and pledge it, madam,
For 'tis to such a thing —
 Anne B.   You cannot show me.
 Sandys. I told your Grace they would talk
 anon.
  Drum and trumpet. Chambers discharg'd.
 Card.   What's that?
 Cham. Look out there, some of ye.
        [*Exit a Servant.*]
 Card.   What warlike voice, 50
And to what end, is this? Nay, ladies, fear not.
By all the laws of war y'are privileg'd.

     Enter a *Servant.*

 Cham. How now? What is't?
 Serv.   A noble troop of strangers,
For so they seem. Th' have left their barge and
 landed,
And hither make, as great ambassadors 55
From foreign princes.
 Card.   Good Lord Chamberlain,
Go, give 'em welcome; you can speak the
 French tongue;
And pray receive 'em nobly and conduct 'em
Into our presence, where this heaven of beauty
Shall shine at full upon them. Some attend
 him.   60
 [*Exit Chamberlain, attended.*] *All rise, and
         tables remov'd.*
You have now a broken banquet; but we'll
 mend it.
A good digestion to you all! and once more
I show'r a welcome on ye. Welcome all.

Hautboys. Enter *King* and others, as Maskers, habited like shepherds, usher'd by the *Lord Chamberlain.* They pass directly before the *Cardinal* and gracefully salute him.

A noble company! What are their pleasures?

Cham. Because they speak no English, thus they pray'd   65
To tell your Grace: that, having heard by fame
Of this so noble and so fair assembly
This night to meet here, they could do no less
(Out of the great respect they bear to beauty)
But leave their flocks and, under your fair conduct,   70
Crave leave to view these ladies and entreat
An hour of revels with 'em.

Card.   Say, Lord Chamberlain,
They have done my poor house grace; for which I pay 'em
A thousand thanks and pray 'em take their pleasures.

    Choose ladies. King and Anne Bullen.

King. The fairest hand I ever touch'd! O beauty,   75
Till now I never knew thee!

    Music. Dance.

Card. My lord!

Cham.   Your Grace?

Card.   Pray tell 'em thus much from me:
There should be one amongst 'em, by his person,
More worthy this place than myself; to whom,
If I but knew him, with my love and duty   80
I would surrender it.

Cham.   I will, my lord.

    Whisper [with the Maskers].

Card. What say they?

Cham.   Such a one they all confess
There is indeed, which they would have your Grace
Find out, and he will take it.

Card.   Let me see then.

    [Comes from his state.]

By all your good leaves, gentlemen, here I'll make   85
My royal choice.

King.   *[unmasks]* Ye have found him Cardinal.
You hold a fair assembly. You do well, lord
You are a churchman, or, I'll tell you, Cardinal,
I should judge now unhappily.

Card.   I am glad
Your Grace is grown so pleasant.

King.   My Lord Chamberlain,   90
Prithee come hither. What fair lady's that?

Cham. An't please your Grace, Sir Thomas Bullen's daughter,
The Viscount Rochford, one of her Highness' women.

King. By heaven, she is a dainty one Sweetheart,
I were unmannerly to take you out   95
And not to kiss you. [*Kisses her.*] A health gentlemen!
Let it go round.

Card. Sir Thomas Lovell, is the banquet ready
I' th' privy chamber?

Lov.   Yes, my lord.

Card.   Your Grace
I fear, with dancing is a little heated.   100

King. I fear, too much.

Card.   There's fresher air, my lord
In the next chamber.

King. Lead in your ladies, ev'ry one. Sweet partner,
I must not yet forsake you. Let's be merry.
Good my Lord Cardinal, I have half a dozen healths   105
To drink to these fair ladies and a measure
To lead 'em once again; and then let's dream
Who's best in favour. Let the music knock it.

    Exeunt with Trumpets

ACT II. Scene I. [*Westminster. A street.*]

Enter two *Gentlemen* at several doors.

1. Gent. Whither away so fast?

2. Gent.   O, God save ye!
Ev'n to the Hall, to hear what shall become
Of the great Duke of Buckingham.

1. Gent.   I'll save you
That labour, sir. All's now done but the ceremony
Of bringing back the prisoner.

2. Gent.   Were you there?

1. Gent. Yes indeed was I.

2. Gent.   Pray speak what has happen'd

1. Gent. You may guess quickly what.

2. Gent.   Is he found guilty?

1. Gent. Yes, truly is he, and condemn'd upon't.

2. Gent. I am sorry for't.

1. Gent.   So are a number more

2. Gent. But pray how pass'd it?   1

1. Gent. I'll tell you in a little. The great
          Duke
Came to the bar; where to his accusations
He pleaded still not guilty and alleg'd
Many sharp reasons to defeat the law.
The King's Attorney, on the contrary,   15
Urg'd on the examinations, proofs, confessions
Of divers witnesses, which the Duke desir'd
To have brought *viva voce* to his face;
At which appear'd against him his surveyor,
Sir Gilbert Peck his chancellor, and John Car,
Confessor to him, with that devil monk,   21
Hopkins, that made this mischief.
2. Gent.   That was he
That fed him with his prophecies.
1. Gent.   The same.
All these accus'd him strongly, which he fain
Would have flung from him, but indeed he
          could not;   25
And so his peers upon this evidence
Have found him guilty of high treason. Much
He spoke, and learnedly, for life, but all
Was either pitied in him or forgotten.
2. Gent. After all this how did he bear
          himself?   30
1. Gent. When he was brought again to th'
          bar to hear
His knell rung out, his judgment, he was
          stirr'd
With such an agony he sweat extremely
And something spoke in choler, ill and hasty;
But he fell to himself again and sweetly   35
In all the rest show'd a most noble patience.
2. Gent. I do not think he fears death.
1. Gent.   Sure he does not;
He never was so womanish. The cause
He may a little grieve at.
2. Gent.   Certainly
The Cardinal is the end of this.
1. Gent.   'Tis likely   40
By all conjectures: first, Kildare's attainder,
Then Deputy of Ireland, who remov'd,
Earl Surrey was sent thither, and in haste
          too,
Lest he should help his father.
2. Gent.   That trick of state
Was a deep envious one.
1. Gent.   At his return   45
No doubt he will requite it. This is noted
(And generally), whoever the King favours
The Cardinal instantly will find employment,
And far enough from court too.
2. Gent.   All the commons
Hate him perniciously and, o' my conscience,
Wish him ten fadom deep. This duke as much

They love and dote on, call him bounteous
          Buckingham,
The mirror of all courtesy —

Enter *Buckingham* from his arraignment;
Tipstaves before him; the axe with the edge
towards him; *Halberds* on each side; accompanied with *Sir Thomas Lovell, Sir Nicholas
Vaux, Sir William Sandys,* and *common
          people,* &c.

1. Gent.   Stay there, sir,
And see the noble ruin'd man you speak of.
2. Gent. Let's stand close and behold him.
Buck.   All good people,   55
You that thus far have come to pity me,
Hear what I say and then go home and lose
          me.
I have this day receiv'd a traitor's judgment
And by that name must die. Yet heaven bear
          witness,
And if I have a conscience, let it sink me   60
Even as the axe falls, if I be not faithful!
The law I bear no malice for my death:
'T has done, upon the premises, but justice.
But those that sought it I could wish more
          Christians.
Be what they will, I heartily forgive 'em.   65
Yet let 'em look they glory not in mischief
Nor build their evils on the graves of great men;
For then my guiltless blood must cry against
          'em.
For further life in this world I ne'er hope,   69
Nor will I sue, although the King have mercies
More than I dare make faults. You few that
          lov'd me
And dare be bold to weep for Buckingham,
His noble friends and fellows, whom to leave
Is only bitter to him, only dying,
Go with me like good angels to my end;   75
And, as the long divorce of steel falls on me,
Make of your prayers one sweet sacrifice
And lift my soul to heaven. Lead on, a God's
          name!
Lov. I do beseech your Grace, for charity,
If ever any malice in your heart   80
Were hid against me, now to forgive me frankly.
Buck. Sir Thomas Lovell, I as free forgive
          you
As I would be forgiven. I forgive all.
There cannot be those numberless offences
'Gainst me that I cannot take peace with. No
          black envy   85
Shall mark my grave. Commend me to his
          Grace;
And if he speak of Buckingham, pray tell him

You met him half in heaven. My vows and
    prayers
Yet are the King's and, till my soul forsake me,
Shall cry for blessings on him. May he live 90
Longer than I have time to tell his years!
Ever belov'd and loving may his rule be!
And when old time shall lead him to his end,
Goodness and he fill up one monument!

  Lov. To th' waterside I must conduct your
    Grace; 95
Then give my charge up to Sir Nicholas Vaux,
Who undertakes you to your end.

  Vaux. Prepare there;
The Duke is coming. See the barge be ready
And fit it with such furniture as suits
The greatness of his person.

  Buck. Nay, Sir Nicholas, 100
Let it alone. My state now will but mock me.
When I came hither, I was Lord High Constable
And Duke of Buckingham; now, poor Edward
    Bohun.
Yet I am richer than my base accusers,
That never knew what truth meant. I now
    seal it; 105
And with that blood will make 'em one day
    groan for't.
My noble father, Henry of Buckingham,
Who first rais'd head against usurping Richard,
Flying for succour to his servant Banister, 109
Being distress'd, was by that wretch betray'd
And without trial fell. God's peace be with him!
Henry the Seventh succeeding, truly pitying
My father's loss, like a most royal prince
Restor'd me to my honours and out of ruins
Made my name once more noble. Now his son,
Henry the Eighth, life, honour, name, and all
That made me happy, at one stroke has taken
For ever from the world. I had my trial,
And must needs say a noble one; which makes
    me
A little happier than my wretched father. 120
Yet thus far we are one in fortunes: both
Fell by our servants, by those men we lov'd
    most —
A most unnatural and faithless service!
Heaven has an end in all. Yet, you that hear
    me,
This from a dying man receive as certain: 125
Where you are liberal of your loves and counsels
Be sure you be not loose; for those you make
    friends
And give your hearts to, when they once per-
    ceive
The least rub in your fortunes, fall away
Like water from ye, never found again 130

But where they mean to sink ye. All good
    people,
Pray for me! I must now forsake ye. The last
    hour
Of my long weary life is come upon me.
Farewell! 134
And when you would say something that is sad,
Speak how I fell. I have done; and God for-
    give me! *Exeunt Duke and Train.*

  1. Gent. O, this is full of pity! Sir, it calls,
I fear, too many curses on their heads
That were the authors.

  2. Gent. If the Duke be guiltless,
'Tis full of woe. Yet I can give you inkling 140
Of an ensuing evil, if it fall,
Greater than this.

  1. Gent. Good angels keep it from us!
What may it be? You do not doubt my faith,
    sir?

  2. Gent. This secret is so weighty 'twill
    require
A strong faith to conceal it.

  1. Gent. Let me have it. 145
I do not talk much.

  2. Gent. I am confident.
You shall, sir. Did you not of late days hear
A buzzing of a separation
Between the King and Katherine?

  1. Gent. Yes, but it held not;
For when the King once heard it, out of anger
He sent command to the Lord Mayor straight
To stop the rumour and allay those tongues
That durst disperse it.

  2. Gent. But that slander, sir,
Is found a truth now; for it grows again 154
Fresher than e'er it was, and held for certain
The King will venture at it. Either the Car-
    dinal,
Or some about him near, have out of malice
To the good Queen possess'd him with a scruple
That will undo her. To confirm this too,
Cardinal Campeius is arriv'd, and lately; 160
As all think, for this business.

  1. Gent. 'Tis the Cardinal;
And merely to revenge him on the Emperor
For not bestowing on him at his asking
The archbishopric of Toledo, this is purpos'd.

  2. Gent. I think you have hit the mark. But
    is't not cruel 165
That she should feel the smart of this? The
    Cardinal
Will have his will, and she must fall.

  1. Gent. 'Tis woful.
We are too open here to argue this.
Let's think in private more. *Exeunt.*

Scene II. [*London.   An antechamber
in the Palace.*]

Enter Lord Chamberlain, reading this letter.

Cham. 'My Lord, — The horses your lordship
sent for, with all the care I had, I saw well chosen,
ridden, and furnish'd. They were young and handsome and of the best breed in the North. When
they were ready to set out for London, a man of my
Lord Cardinal's by commission and main power
took 'em from me, with this reason — his master
would be serv'd before a subject, if not before the
King; which stopp'd our mouths, sir.'   10

I fear he will indeed. Well, let him have them.
He will have all, I think.

*Enter to the Lord Chamberlain the Dukes
of Norfolk and Suffolk.*

Nor. Well met, my Lord Chamberlain.
Cham. Good day to both your Graces.
Suf. How is the King employ'd?
Cham.   I left him private,   15
Full of sad thoughts and troubles.
Nor.   What's the cause?
Cham. It seems the marriage with his
brother's wife
Has crept too near his conscience.
Suf.   No, his conscience
Has crept too near another lady.
Nor.   'Tis so.
This is the Cardinal's doing, the King-Car-
dinal!   20
That blind priest, like the eldest son of For-
tune,
Turns what he list. The King will know him
one day.
Suf. Pray God he do! He'll never know
himself else.
Nor. How holily he works in all his business
And with what zeal! for, now he has crack'd
the league   25
Between us and the Emperor, the Queen's
great nephew,
He dives into the King's soul, and there
scatters
Dangers, doubts, wringing of the conscience,
Fears, and despairs — and all these for his
marriage.
And out of all these to restore the King,   30
He counsels a divorce, a loss of her
That like a jewel has hung twenty years
About his neck, yet never lost her lustre;
Of her that loves him with that excellence   34
That angels love good men with; even of her

That, when the greatest stroke of fortune falls,
Will bless the King: — and is not this course
pious?
Cham. Heaven keep me from such counsel!
'Tis most true
These news are everywhere, every tongue
speaks 'em,
And every true heart weeps for't. All that dare
Look into these affairs see this main end —   41
The French King's sister. Heaven will one
day open
The King's eyes that so long have slept upon
This bold bad man.
Suf.   And free us from his slavery.
Nor. We had need pray,   45
And heartily, for our deliverance,
Or this imperious man will work us all
From princes into pages. All men's honours
Lie like one lump before him, to be fashion'd
Into what pitch he please.
Suf.   For me, my lords,   50
I love him not, nor fear him. There's my creed.
As I am made without him, so I'll stand,
If the King please. His curses and his bless-
ings
Touch me alike; th' are breath I not believe
in.
I knew him, and I know him; so I leave him
To him that made him proud, the Pope.
Nor.   Let's in   56
And with some other business put the King
From these sad thoughts that work too much
upon him.
My lord, you'll bear us company?
Cham.   Excuse me.
The King has sent me otherwhere. Besides,   60
You'll find a most unfit time to disturb him.
Health to your lordships!
Nor. Thanks, my good Lord Chamberlain.
*Exit Lord Chamberlain; and the King draws
the curtain and sits reading pensively.*
Suf. How sad he looks! Sure he is much
afflicted.
King. Who's there, ha?
Nor.   Pray God he be not angry.
King. Who's there, I say? How dare you
thrust yourselves   65
Into my private meditations?
Who am I? ha?
Nor. A gracious king, that pardons all
offences
Malice ne'er meant. Our breach of duty this
way
Is business of estate; in which we come   70
To know your royal pleasure.

King.   Ye are too bold.
Go to! I'll make ye know your times of
business.
Is this an hour for temporal affairs? ha?

Enter [*Cardinals*] *Wolsey* and *Campeius*
with a commission.

Who's there? My good Lord Cardinal? O my
Wolsey,
The quiet of my wounded conscience!   75
Thou art a cure fit for a king. [*To Campeius*]
You're welcome,
Most learned reverend sir, into our kingdom.
Use us and it. [*To Wolsey*] My good lord, have
great care
I be not found a talker.
Wol.   Sir, you cannot.   79
I would your Grace would give us but an hour
Of private conference.
King.   [*to Norfolk and Suffolk*] We are
busy. Go.
Nor. [*aside to Suffolk*] This priest has no
pride in him!
Suf.   [*aside to Norfolk*] Not to speak of.
I would not be so sick though for his place.
But this cannot continue.
Nor.   [*aside to Suffolk*] If it do,
I'll venture one have-at-him.
Suf. [*aside to Norfolk*] I another.   85
                Exeunt Norfolk and Suffolk.
Wol. Your Grace has given a precedent of
wisdom
Above all princes in committing freely
Your scruple to the voice of Christendom.
Who can be angry now? what envy reach you?
The Spaniard, tied by blood and favour to her
Must now confess, if they have any goodness,
The trial just and noble. All the clerks
(I mean the learned ones) in Christian king-
doms
Have their free voices. Rome, the nurse of
judgment,
Invited by your noble self, hath sent   95
One general tongue unto us, this good man,
This just and learned priest, Cardinal Cam-
peius,
Whom once more I present unto your Highness.
King. And once more in mine arms I bid
him welcome
And thank the holy conclave for their loves.
They have sent me such a man I would have
wish'd for.   101
Camp. Your Grace must needs deserve all
strangers' loves,
You are so noble. To your Highness' hand

I tender my commission; by whose virtue,
The Court of Rome commanding, you, my Lord
Cardinal of York, are join'd with me their
servant   106
In the unpartial judging of this business.
King. Two equal men. The Queen shall be
acquainted
Forthwith for what you come. Where's Gar-
diner?
Wol. I know your Majesty has always lov'd
her   110
So dear in heart not to deny her that
A woman of less place might ask by law —
Scholars allow'd freely to argue for her.
King. Ay, and the best she shall have; and
my favour
To him that does best. God forbid else. Car-
dinal,   115
Prithee call Gardiner to me, my new Secretary.
I find him a fit fellow.
                        [*Exit Wolsey.*]

Enter [*Wolsey*, with] *Gardiner.*

Wol. [*aside to Gardiner*] Give me your hand.
Much joy and favour to you!
You are the King's now.
Gard.   [*aside to Wolsey*] But to be com-
manded
For ever by your Grace, whose hand has rais'd
me.   120
King. Come hither, Gardiner.
                        Walks and whispers.
Camp. My Lord of York, was not one Doctor
Pace
In this man's place before him?
Wol.   Yes, he was.
Camp. Was he not held a learned man?
Wol.   Yes, surely.
Camp. Believe me, there's an ill opinion
spread then,   125
Even of yourself, Lord Cardinal.
Wol.   How? of me?
Camp. They will not stick to say you envied
him,
And fearing he would rise (he was so virtuous),
Kept him a foreign man still, which so griev'd
him
That he ran mad and died.
Wol.   Heav'n's peace be with him!   130
That's Christian care enough. For living mur-
murers
There's places of rebuke. He was a fool,
For he would needs be virtuous. That good
fellow,
If I command him, follows my appointment.

I will have none so near else. Learn this,
    brother,   135
We live not to be grip'd by meaner persons.
    King. Deliver this with modesty to th'
    Queen.
                                        Exit Gardiner.
The most convenient place that I can think of
For such receipt of learning is Blackfriars.
There ye shall meet about this weighty business.
My Wolsey, see it furnish'd. O my lord,   141
Would it not grieve an able man to leave
So sweet a bedfellow? But, conscience, con-
    science!
O, 'tis a tender place! and I must leave her.
                                        Exeunt.

Scene III. [*London. An antechamber
in the* Queen's *apartments.*]

Enter *Anne Bullen* and an *Old Lady.*

Anne. Not for that neither! Here's the pang
    that pinches:
His Highness having liv'd so long with her, and
    she
So good a lady that no tongue could ever
Pronounce dishonour of her — by my life,
She never knew harm-doing! — O, now, after 5
So many courses of the sun enthroned,
Still growing in a majesty and pomp, the which
To leave a thousandfold more bitter than
'Tis sweet at first t' acquire — after this process
To give her the avaunt, it is a pity   10
Would move a monster.
    Old L.   Hearts of most hard temper
Melt and lament for her.
    Anne.   O, God's will! much better
She ne'er had known pomp. Though't be tem-
    poral,
Yet, if that quarrel, fortune, do divorce
It from the bearer, 'tis a sufferance panging 15
As soul and body's severing.
    Old. L.   Alas, poor lady!
She's a stranger now again.
    Anne.   So much the more
Must pity drop upon her. Verily
I swear 'tis better to be lowly born
And range with humble livers in content   20
Than to be perk'd up in a glist'ring grief
And wear a golden sorrow.
    Old L.   Our content
Is our best having.
    Anne.   By my troth and maidenhead,
I would not be a queen.

    Old L.   Beshrew me, I would,
And venture maidenhead for't! and so would
    you,   25
For all this spice of your hypocrisy.
You that have so fair parts of woman on you
Have, too, a woman's heart, which ever yet
Affected eminence, wealth, sovereignty;
Which, to say sooth, are blessings, and which
    gifts   30
(Saving your mincing) the capacity
Of your soft chiveril conscience would receive,
If you might please to stretch it.
    Anne.   Nay, good troth!
    Old L. Yes, troth, and troth! You would not
    be a queen?   34
    Anne. No, not for all the riches under heaven.
    Old L. 'Tis strange! A threepence bow'd
    would hire me,
Old as I am, to queen it. But I pray you,
What think you of a duchess? Have you limbs
To bear that load of title?
    Anne.   No, in truth.
    Old L. Then you are weakly made. Pluck off
    a little.   40
I would not be a young count in your way
For more than blushing comes to. If your back
Cannot vouchsafe this burthen, 'tis too weak
Ever to get a boy.
    Anne.   How you do talk!
I swear again, I would not be a queen   45
For all the world.
    Old L.   In faith, for little England
You'ld venture an emballing. I myself
Would for Carnarvonshire, although there
    'long'd
No more to th' crown but that. Lo, who comes
    here?

Enter *Lord Chamberlain.*

    Cham. Good morrow, ladies. What were't
    worth to know   50
The secret of your conference?
    Anne.   My good lord,
Not your demand; it values not your asking.
Our mistress' sorrows we were pitying.
    Cham. It was a gentle business and becoming
The action of good women. There is hope   55
All will be well.
    Anne.   Now I pray God, amen!
    Cham. You bear a gentle mind, and heav'nly
    blessings
Follow such creatures. That you may, fair lady,
Perceive I speak sincerely and high note's
Ta'en of your many virtues, the King's Majesty
Commends his good opinion of you, and   61

Does purpose honour to you no less flowing
Than Marchioness of Pembroke; to which title
A thousand pound a year, annual support,
Out of his grace he adds.
 Anne.   I do not know 65
What kind of my obedience I should tender.
More than my all is nothing; nor my prayers
Are not words duly hallowed; nor my wishes
More worth than empty vanities. Yet prayers
 and wishes 69
Are all I can return. Beseech your lordship,
Vouchsafe to speak my thanks and my obe-
 dience,
As from a blushing handmaid, to his Highness;
Whose health and royalty I pray for.
 Cham.   Lady,
I shall not fail t' approve the fair conceit
The King hath of you. [*Aside*] I have perus'd
 her well. 75
Beauty and honour in her are so mingled
That they have caught the King; and who
 knows yet
But from this lady may proceed a gem
To lighten all this isle? — I'll to the King
And say I spoke with you.
 Anne.   My honour'd lord! 80
       Exit Lord Chamberlain.
 Old L. Why, this it is! See, see!
I have been begging sixteen years in court
(Am yet a courtier beggarly) nor could
Come pat betwixt too early and too late
For any suit of pounds; and you (O fate!), 85
A very fresh fish here — fie, fie, fie upon
This compell'd fortune! — have your mouth
 fill'd up
Before you open it.
 Anne.   This is strange to me.
 Old L. How tastes it? Is it bitter? Forty
 pence, no.
There was a lady once ('tis an old story) 90
That would not be a queen, that would she not,
For all the mud in Egypt. Have you heard it?
 Anne. Come, you are pleasant.
 Old L.   With your theme I could
O'ermount the lark. The Marchioness of
 Pembroke?
A thousand pounds a year, for pure respect?
No other obligation? By my life, 96
That promises moe thousands! Honour's train
Is longer than his foreskirt. By this time
I know your back will bear a duchess. Say,
Are you not stronger than you were?
 Anne.   Good lady, 100
Make yourself mirth with your particular fancy
And leave me out on't. Would I had no being

If this salute my blood a jot! It faints me
To think what follows.
The Queen is comfortless, and we forgetful 105
In our long absence. Pray do not deliver
What here y'have heard to her.
 Old L.   What do you think me?
          Exeunt.

Scene IV. [*London. A hall in Blackfriars.*]

Trumpets, sennet, and cornets. Enter two
Vergers, with short silver wands; next them,
two *Scribes,* in the habit of Doctors; after
them, the [*Arch*]*bishop of Canterbury* alone;
after him, the *Bishops of Lincoln, Ely, Rochester,* and *Saint Asaph*; next them, with some
small distance, follows a *Gentleman* bearing the
purse, with the great seal, and a Cardinal's hat;
then two *Priests,* bearing each a silver cross;
then a *Gentleman Usher* bareheaded, accompanied with a *Sergeant-at-arms* bearing a silver
mace; then two *Gentlemen* bearing two great
silver pillars; after them, side by side, the two
Cardinals, [*Wolsey* and *Campeius,*] two *Noblemen* with the sword and mace. The *King* takes
place under the cloth of state; the two *Cardinals* sit under him as Judges. The *Queen* takes
place some distance from the *King.* The
Bishops place themselves on each side the
court, in manner of a consistory; below them,
the *Scribes.* The *Lords* sit next the *Bishops.
The rest of the Attendants stand in convenient
order about the stage*

 Wol. Whilst our commission from Rome is
 read,
Let silence be commanded.
 King.   What's the need?
It hath already publicly been read,
And on all sides th' authority allow'd.
You may then spare that time.
 Wol.   Be't so. Proceed. 5
 Scribe. Say, 'Henry King of England, come
into the court.'
 Crier. Henry King of England, &c.
 King. Here.
 Scribe. Say, 'Katherine Queen of England
come into the court.' 11
 Crier. Katherine Queen of England, &c.
  *The Queen makes no answer, rises out of her
  chair, goes about the court, comes to the
  King, and kneels at his feet; then speaks.*
 Queen. Sir, I desire you do me right and
 justice

384

And to bestow your pity on me; for
I am a most poor woman and a stranger,   15
Born out of your dominions, having here
No judge indifferent, nor no more assurance
Of equal friendship and proceeding. Alas, sir,
In what have I offended you? What cause   19
Hath my behaviour given to your displeasure
That thus you should proceed to put me off
And take your good grace from me? Heaven
    witness
I have been to you a true and humble wife,
At all times to your will conformable,
Ever in fear to kindle your dislike,   25
Yea, subject to your countenance — glad or
    sorry
As I saw it inclin'd. When was the hour
I ever contradicted your desire
Or made it not mine too? Or which of your
    friends   29
Have I not strove to love, although I knew
He were mine enemy? What friend of mine
That had to him deriv'd your anger did I
Continue in my liking? nay, gave notice
He was from thence discharg'd? Sir, call to
    mind   34
That I have been your wife in this obedience
Upward of twenty years and have been blest
With many children by you. If in the course
And process of this time you can report,
And prove it too, against mine honour aught,
My bond to wedlock, or my love and duty,   40
Against your sacred person, in God's name
Turn me away, and let the foul'st contempt
Shut door upon me, and so give me up
To the sharp'st kind of justice. Please you, sir,
The King your father was reputed for   45
A prince most prudent, of an excellent
And unmatch'd wit and judgment. Ferdinand,
My father, King of Spain, was reckon'd one
The wisest prince that there had reign'd by
    many
A year before. It is not to be question'd   50
That they had gather'd a wise council to them
Of every realm, that did debate this business,
Who deem'd our marriage lawful. Wherefore I
    humbly
Beseech you, sir, to spare me till I may
Be by my friends in Spain advis'd, whose
    counsel   55
I will implore. If not, i' th' name of God,
Your pleasure be fulfill'd!
    Wol.   You have here, lady
(And of your choice), these reverend fathers,
    men
Of singular integrity and learning,   59

Yea, the elect o' th' land, who are assembled
To plead your cause. It shall be therefore
    bootless
That longer you defer the court, as well
For your own quiet as to rectify
What is unsettled in the King.
    Camp.   His Grace
Hath spoken well and justly. Therefore,
    madam,   65
It's fit this royal session do proceed
And that (without delay) their arguments
Be now produc'd and heard.
    Queen.   Lord Cardinal,
To you I speak.
    Wol.   Your pleasure, madam?
    Queen.   Sir,
I am about to weep; but, thinking that   70
We are a queen (or long have dream'd so),
    certain
The daughter of a king, my drops of tears
I'll turn to sparks of fire.
    Wol.   Be patient yet.
    Queen. I will, when you are humble; nay,
    before,
Or God will punish me. I do believe   75
(Induc'd by potent circumstances) that
You are mine enemy; and make my challenge
You shall not be my judge; for it is you
Have blown this coal betwixt my lord and me —
Which God's dew quench! Therefore I say
    again   80
I utterly abhor, yea, from my soul
Refuse you for my judge, whom yet once more
I hold my most malicious foe and think not
At all a friend to truth.
    Wol.   I do profess
You speak not like yourself, who ever yet   85
Have stood to charity and display'd th' effects
Of disposition gentle and of wisdom
O'ertopping woman's pow'r. Madam, you do
    me wrong.
I have no spleen against you, nor injustice
For you or any. How far I have proceeded,
Or how far further shall, is warranted   91
By a commission from the Consistory,
Yea, the whole Consistory of Rome. You
    charge me
That I have blown this coal. I do deny it.
The King is present. If it be known to him   95
That I gainsay my deed, how may he wound,
And worthily, my falsehood! Yea, as much
As you have done my truth. If he know
That I am free of your report, he knows
I am not of your wrong. Therefore in him   100
It lies to cure me, and the cure is to

Remove these thoughts from you; the which
before
His Highness shall speak in, I do beseech
You, gracious madam, to unthink your speaking
And to say so no more.
  Queen.   My lord, my lord,   105
I am a simple woman, much too weak
T' oppose your cunning. Y'are meek and
    humble-mouth'd;
You sign your place and calling, in full seem-
    ing,
With meekness and humility; but your heart
Is cramm'd with arrogancy, spleen, and pride.
You have, by fortune and his Highness' favours,
Gone slightly o'er low steps and now are
    mounted
Where pow'rs are your retainers and your words
(Domestics to you) serve your will as't please
Yourself pronounce their office. I must tell you
You tender more your person's honour than   116
Your high profession spiritual; that again
I do refuse you for my judge and here,
Before you all, appeal unto the Pope,
To bring my whole cause fore his Holiness   120
And to be judg'd by him.
    She curtsies to the King and offers to depart.
  Camp.   The Queen is obstinate,
Stubborn to justice, apt to accuse it, and
Disdainful to be tried by't. 'Tis not well.
She's going away.
  King. Call her again.   125
  Crier. Katherine Queen of England, come
into the court.
  Gent. Usher. Madam, you are call'd back.
  Queen. What need you note it? Pray you
keep your way.
When you are call'd, return. Now the Lord
help!
They vex me past my patience. Pray you pass
on.   130
I will not tarry; no, nor ever more
Upon this business my appearance make
In any of their courts.
    Exeunt Queen and her Attendants.
  King.   Go thy ways, Kate.
That man i' th' world who shall report he has
A better wife, let him in naught be trusted   135
For speaking false in that. Thou art, alone
(If thy rare qualities, sweet gentleness,
Thy meekness saintlike, wifelike government,
Obeying in commanding, and thy parts   139
Sovereign and pious else, could speak thee out)
The queen of earthly queens. She's noble born,
And like her true nobility she has
Carried herself towards me.

  Wol.   Most gracious sir,
In humblest manner I require your Highness
That it shall please you to declare in hearing
Of all these ears (for where I am robb'd and
    bound,   146
There must I be unloos'd, although not there
At once and fully satisfied) whether ever I
Did broach this business to your Highness, or
Laid any scruple in your way which might   150
Induce you to the question on't, or ever
Have to you, but with thanks to God for such
A royal lady, spake one the least word that
    might
Be to the prejudice of her present state
Or touch of her good person.
  King.   My Lord Cardinal,   155
I do excuse you; yea, upon mine honour,
I free you from't. You are not to be taught
That you have many enemies that know not
Why they are so, but, like to village curs,   159
Bark when their fellows do. By some of these
The Queen is put in anger. Y'are excus'd.
But will you be more justified? You ever
Have wish'd the sleeping of this business; never
Desir'd it to be stirr'd; but oft have hind'red,
    oft,   164
The passages made toward it. On my honour,
I speak my good Lord Cardinal to this point,
And thus far clear him. Now, what mov'd me
    to't,
I will be bold with time and your attention.
Then mark th' inducement. Thus it came;
    give heed to't.
My conscience first receiv'd a tenderness,   170
Scruple, and prick on certain speeches utter'd
By th' Bishop of Bayonne, then French am-
    bassador,
Who had been hither sent on the debating
A marriage 'twixt the Duke of Orleans and
Our daughter Mary. I' th' progress of this
    business,   175
Ere a determinate resolution, he
(I mean the Bishop) did require a respite
Wherein he might the King his lord advertise
Whether our daughter were legitimate,   179
Respecting this our marriage with the dowager,
Sometimes our brother's wife. This respite
    shook
The bottom of my conscience, enter'd me,
Yea, with a splitting power and made to tremble
The region of my breast, which forc'd such way
That many maz'd considerings did throng   185
And press'd in with this caution. First, me-
    thought
I stood not in the smile of heaven, who had

Commanded nature that my lady's womb,
If it conceiv'd a male child by me, should
Do no more offices of life to't than   190
The grave does to th' dead; for her male issue
Or died where they were made or shortly after
This world had air'd them. Hence I took a
    thought
This was a judgment on me, that my kingdom
(Well worthy the best heir o' th' world) should
    not   195
Be gladded in't by me. Then follows that
I weigh'd the danger which my realms stood in
By this my issue's fail, and that gave to me
Many a groaning throe. Thus hulling in
The wild sea of my conscience, I did steer 200
Toward this remedy whereupon we are
Now present here together. That's to say
I meant to rectify my conscience, which
I then did feel full sick, and yet not well,
By all the reverend fathers of the land   205
And doctors learn'd. First I began in private
With you, my Lord of Lincoln. You remember
How under my oppression I did reek
When I first mov'd you.

B. Linc.   Very well, my liege.

King. I have spoke long. Be pleas'd your-
    self to say   210
How far you satisfied me.

B. Linc.   So please your Highness,
The question did at first so stagger me,
Bearing a state of mighty moment in't
And consequence of dread, that I committed

The daring'st counsel which I had to doubt 215
And did entreat your Highness to this course
Which you are running here.

King.   I then mov'd you,
My Lord of Canterbury, and got your leave
To make this present summons. Unsolicited
I left no reverend person in this court,   220
But by particular consent proceeded
Under your hands and seals. Therefore go on;
For no dislike i' th' world against the person
Of the good Queen, but the sharp thorny points
Of my alleged reasons, drives this forward. 225
Prove but our marriage lawful, by my life
And kingly dignity, we are contented
To wear our mortal state to come with her,
Katherine our queen, before the primest
    creature
That's paragon'd o' th' world.

Camp.   So please your Highness, 230
The Queen being absent, 'tis a needful fitness
That we adjourn this court till further day.
Meanwhile must be an earnest motion
Made to the Queen to call back her appeal
She intends unto his Holiness.

King.   [*aside*] I may perceive 235
These Cardinals trifle with me. I abhor
This dilatory sloth and tricks of Rome.
My learn'd and well-beloved servant Cranmer,
Prithee return. With thy approach I know
My comfort comes along. — Break up the
    court.   240
I say, set on. *Exeunt in manner as they enter'd.*

ACT III. Scene I. [*London. A room in the* Queen's *apartments.*]

Enter the *Queen* and her *Women,* as at work.

Queen. Take thy lute, wench. My soul grows
    sad with troubles.
Sing, and disperse 'em if thou canst. Leave
working.

Song.

Orpheus with his lute made trees
And the mountain tops that freeze
    Bow themselves when he did sing.   5
To his music plants and flowers
Ever sprung, as sun and showers
    There had made a lasting spring.

Everything that heard him play,
Even the billows of the sea,   10
    Hung their heads, and then lay by.
In sweet music is such art
Killing care and grief of heart
    Fall asleep, or hearing, die.

Enter a *Gentleman.*

Queen. How now?   15
Gent. An't please your Grace, the two great
    Cardinals
Wait in the presence.
Queen.   Would they speak with
    me?
Gent. They will'd me say so, madam.
Queen.   Pray their Graces
To come near. [*Exit Gent.*] What can be their
    business
With me, a poor weak woman, fall'n from
    favour?   20
I do not like their coming. Now I think
    on't,
They should be good men, their affairs as
    righteous;
But all hoods make not monks.

Enter the two *Cardinals, Wolsey* and *Campeius.*

Wol.   Peace to your Highness!

Queen. Your Graces find me here part of a
  housewife   24
(I would be all) against the worst may happen.
What are your pleasures with me, reverend
  lords?

Wol. May it please you, noble madam, to
  withdraw
Into your private chamber, we shall give you
The full cause of our coming.

Queen.   Speak it here.
There's nothing I have done yet, o' my con-
  science,   30
Deserves a corner. Would all other women
Could speak this with as free a soul as I do!
My lords, I care not (so much I am happy
Above a number) if my actions   34
Were tried by ev'ry tongue, ev'ry eye saw 'em,
Envy and base opinion set against 'em,
I know my life so even. If your business
Seek me out, and that way I am wife in,
Out with it boldly. Truth loves open dealing.

Wol. Tanta est erga te mentis integritas,
regina serenissima —   41

Queen. O, good my lord, no Latin!
I am not such a truant since my coming
As not to know the language I have liv'd in.
A strange tongue makes my cause more strange,
  suspicious.   45
Pray speak in English. Here are some will
  thank you,
If you speak truth, for their poor mistress' sake.
Believe me, she has had much wrong. Lord
  Cardinal,
The willing'st sin I ever yet committed
May be absolv'd in English.

Wol.   Noble lady,   50
I am sorry my integrity should breed
(And service to his Majesty and you)
So deep suspicion where all faith was meant.
We come not by the way of accusation   54
To taint that honour every good tongue blesses,
Nor to betray you any way to sorrow —
You have too much, good lady — but to know
How you stand minded in the weighty differ-
  ence
Between the King and you, and to deliver   59
(Like free and honest men) our just opinions
And comforts to your cause.

Camp.   Most honour'd madam,
My Lord of York, out of his noble nature,
Zeal and obedience he still bore your Grace,
Forgetting (like a good man) your late censure

Both of his truth and him (which was too far),
Offers, as I do, in a sign of peace,   66
His service and his counsel.

Queen.   [*aside*] To betray me. —
My lords, I thank you both for your good wills.
Ye speak like honest men (pray God ye prove
  so!).
But how to make ye suddenly an answer   70
In such a point of weight, so near mine honour
(More near my life, I fear), with my weak
  wit,
And to such men of gravity and learning,
In truth I know not. I was set at work
Among my maids, full little (God knows)
  looking   75
Either for such men or such business.
For her sake that I have been — for I feel
The last fit of my greatness — good your
  Graces,
Let me have time and counsel for my cause.
Alas, I am a woman friendless, hopeless!   80

Wol. Madam, you wrong the King's love
  with these fears.
Your hopes and friends are infinite.

Queen.   In England
But little for my profit. Can you think, lords,
That any Englishman dare give me counsel?
Or be a known friend 'gainst his highness'
  pleasure   85
(Though he be grown so desperate to be honest)
And live a subject? Nay forsooth, my friends,
They that must weigh out my afflictions,
They that my trust must grow to, live not here.
They are (as all my other comforts) far hence,
In mine own country, lords.

Camp.   I would your Grace   91
Would leave your griefs and take my counsel.

Queen.   How, sir?

Camp. Put your main cause into the King's
  protection.
He's loving and most gracious. 'Twill be much
Both for your honour better and your cause;
For if the trial of the law o'ertake ye,   96
You'll part away disgrac'd.

Wol.   He tells you rightly.

Queen. Ye tell me what ye wish for both —
  my ruin.
Is this your Christian counsel? Out upon ye!
Heaven is above all yet. There sits a judge 100
That no king can corrupt.

Camp.   Your rage mistakes us.

Queen. The more shame for ye! Holy men
  I thought ye,
Upon my soul, two reverend cardinal virtues;
But cardinal sins and hollow hearts I fear ye.

Mend 'em for shame, my lords! Is this your
   comfort?   105
The cordial that ye bring a wretched lady?
A woman lost among ye, laugh'd at, scorn'd?
I will not wish ye half my miseries;
I have more charity. But say I warn'd ye.
Take heed, for heaven's sake take heed, lest at
   once   110
The burthen of my sorrows fall upon ye.
   Wol. Madam, this is a mere distraction.
You turn the good we offer into envy.
   Queen. Ye turn me into nothing. Woe upon
   ye
And all such false professors! Would you have
   me   115
(If you have any justice, any pity,
If ye be anything but churchmen's habits)
Put my sick cause into his hands that hates
   me?
Alas, has banish'd me his bed already,
His love, too long ago! I am old, my lords, 120
And all the fellowship I hold now with him
Is only my obedience. What can happen
To me above this wretchedness? All your
   studies
Make me a curse like this!
   Camp.   Your fears are worse.
   Queen. Have I liv'd thus long (let me speak
   myself,   125
Since virtue finds no friends) a wife, a true
   one?
A woman (I dare say, without vainglory)
Never yet branded with suspicion?
Have I with all my full affections
Still met the King? lov'd him next heav'n?
   obey'd him?   130
Been (out of fondness) superstitious to him?
Almost forgot my prayers to content him?
And am I thus rewarded? 'Tis not well,
   lords.
Bring me a constant woman to her husband,
One that ne'er dream'd a joy beyond his
   pleasure,   135
And to that woman (when she has done most)
Yet will I add an honour — a great patience.
   Wol. Madam, you wander from the good
   we aim at.
   Queen. My lord, I dare not make myself so
   guilty
To give up willingly that noble title   140
Your master wed me to. Nothing but death
Shall e'er divorce my dignities.
   Wol.   Pray hear me.
   Queen. Would I had never trod this English
   earth

Or felt the flatteries that grow upon it!
Ye have angels' faces, but heaven knows your
   hearts.   145
What will become of me now, wretched lady?
I am the most unhappy woman living.
[*To her Women*] Alas, poor wenches, where are
   now your fortunes?
Shipwrack'd upon a kingdom where no pity,
No friends, no hope, no kindred weep for me,
Almost no grave allow'd me! Like the lily 151
That once was mistress of the field and flour-
   ish'd,
I'll hang my head and perish.
   Wol.   If your Grace
Could but be brought to know our ends are
   honest,
You'd feel more comfort. Why should we,
   good lady,   155
Upon what cause, wrong you? Alas, our places,
The way of our profession is against it.
We are to cure such sorrows, not to sow 'em.
For goodness sake, consider what you do;
How you may hurt yourself, ay, utterly   160
Grow from the King's acquaintance, by this
   carriage.
The hearts of princes kiss obedience,
So much they love it; but to stubborn spirits
They swell and grow as terrible as storms.
I know you have a gentle, noble temper,   165
A soul as even as a calm. Pray think us
Those we profess — peacemakers, friends, and
   servants.
   Camp. Madam, you'll find it so. You wrong
   your virtues
With these weak women's fears. A noble spirit,
As yours was put into you, ever casts   170
Such doubts as false coin from it. The King
   loves you.
Beware you lose it not. For us, if you please
To trust us in your business, we are ready
To use our utmost studies in your service.
   Queen. Do what ye will, my lords; and pray
   forgive me   175
If I have us'd myself unmannerly.
You know I am a woman, lacking wit
To make a seemly answer to such persons.
Pray do my service to his Majesty.
He has my heart yet and shall have my
   prayers   180
While I shall have my life. Come, reverend
   fathers,
Bestow your counsels on me. She now begs
That little thought, when she set footing here,
She should have bought her dignities so dear.
                                 Exeunt.

Scene II. [*London. Antechamber to the King's apartment.*]

Enter the *Duke of Norfolk, Duke of Suffolk, Lord Surrey,* and *Lord Chamberlain.*

Nor. If you will now unite in your complaints
And force them with a constancy, the Cardinal
Cannot stand under them. If you omit
The offer of this time, I cannot promise   4
But that you shall sustain moe new disgraces
With these you bear already.

Sur.   I am joyful
To meet the least occasion that may give me
Remembrance of my father-in-law, the Duke,
To be reveng'd on him.

Suf.   Which of the peers
Have uncontemn'd gone by him, or at least   10
Strangely neglected? When did he regard
The stamp of nobleness in any person
Out of himself?

Cham. My lords, you speak your pleasures.
What he deserves of you and me I know.   14
What we can do to him (though now the time
Gives way to us) I much fear. If you cannot
Bar his access to th' King, never attempt
Anything on him; for he hath a witchcraft
Over the King in's tongue.

Nor.   O, fear him not!
His spell in that is out. The King hath found
Matter against him that for ever mars   21
The honey of his language. No, he's settled
(Not to come off) in his displeasure.

Sur.   Sir,
I should be glad to hear such news as this
Once every hour.

Nor.   Believe it, this is true.   25
In the divorce his contrary proceedings
Are all unfolded; wherein he appears
As I would wish mine enemy.

Sur.   How came
His practices to light?

Suf.   Most strangely.

Sur.   O, how? how?

Suf. The Cardinal's letters to the Pope
miscarried   30
And came to th' eye o' th' King, wherein was
read
How that the Cardinal did entreat his Holiness
To stay the judgment o' th' divorce; for if
It did take place, 'I do,' quoth he, 'perceive
My king is tangled in affection to   35
A creature of the Queen's, Lady Anne Bullen.'

Sur. Has the King this?

Suf.   Believe it.

Sur.   Will this work?

Cham. The King in this perceives him, how
he coasts
And hedges his own way. But in this point
All his tricks founder and he brings his physic
After his patient's death: the King already   41
Hath married the fair lady.

Sur.   Would he had!

Suf. May you be happy in your wish, my
lord!
For I profess you have it.

Sur.   Now all my joy
Trace the conjunction!

Suf.   My amen to't!

Nor.   All men's!   45

Suf. There's order given for her coronation.
Marry, this is yet but young and may be left
To some ears unrecounted. But, my lords,
She is a gallant creature and complete
In mind and feature. I persuade me, from
her   50
Will fall some blessing to this land which shall
In it be memoriz'd.

Sur.   But will the King
Digest this letter of the Cardinal's?
The Lord forbid!

Nor.   Marry amen!

Suf.   No, no!   54
There be moe wasps that buzz about his nose
Will make this sting the sooner. Cardinal
Campeius
Is stol'n away to Rome, hath ta'en no leave,
Has left the cause o' th' King unhandled, and
Is posted as the agent of our Cardinal
To second all his plot. I do assure you   60
The King cried 'Ha!' at this.

Cham.   Now God incense him
And let him cry 'Ha!' louder!

Nor.   But, my lord,
When returns Cranmer?

Suf. He is return'd in his opinions, which
Have satisfied the King for his divorce,   65
Together with all famous colleges
Almost in Christendom. Shortly, I believe,
His second marriage shall be publish'd and
Her coronation. Katherine no more
Shall be call'd Queen, but Princess Dowager   70
And widow to Prince Arthur.

Nor.   This same Cranmer's
A worthy fellow and hath ta'en much pain
In the King's business.

Suf.   He has, and we shall see him
For it an archbishop.

Nor.   So I hear.

Suf.   'Tis so.

Enter [*Cardinal*] *Wolsey* and *Cromwell*.
The Cardinal!
  Nor.   Observe, observe! He's moody. 75
  Card. The packet, Cromwell,
Gave't you the King?
  Crom.   To his own hand, in 's bedchamber.
  Card. Look'd he o' th' inside of the papers?
  Crom.   Presently
He did unseal them; and the first he view'd,
He did it with a serious mind; a heed   80
Was in his countenance. You he bade
Attend him here this morning.
  Card.   Is he ready
To come abroad?
  Crom.   I think by this he is.
  Wol. Leave me awhile.
               Exit Cromwell.
[*Aside*] It shall be to the Duchess of Alençon,
The French king's sister. He shall marry her.
Anne Bullen? No! I'll no Anne Bullens for
him.
There's more in 't than fair visage. Bullen?
No, we'll no Bullens! Speedily I wish
To hear from Rome. The Marchioness of
   Pembroke?   90
  Nor. He's discontented.
  Suf.   May be he hears the King
Does whet his anger to him.
  Sur.   Sharp enough,
Lord, for thy justice!
  Wol. [*aside*] The late Queen's gentlewoman,
   a knight's daughter,
To be her mistress' mistress? the Queen's
   queen?   95
This candle burns not clear. 'Tis I must
   snuff it.
Then out it goes! What though I know her
   virtuous
And well deserving? Yet I know her for
A spleeny Lutheran, and not wholesome to 99
Our cause that she should lie i' th' bosom of
Our hard-rul'd king. Again, there is sprung up
An heretic, an arch one — Cranmer, one
Hath crawl'd into the favour of the King
And is his oracle.
  Nor.   He is vex'd at something.

Enter *King*, reading of a schedule, [and *Lovell*].

  Sur. I would 'twere something that would
   fret the string,   105
The master-cord on 's heart!
  Suf.   The King, the King!
  King. What piles of wealth hath he accumu-
   lated

To his own portion! and what expense by
   th' hour
Seems to flow from him! How i' th' name of
   thrift   109
Does he rake this together? — Now, my lords,
Saw you the Cardinal?
  Nor.   My lord, we have
Stood here observing him. Some strange com-
   motion
Is in his brain. He bites his lip and starts,
Stops on a sudden, looks upon the ground,   114
Then lays his finger on his temple; straight
Springs out into fast gait, then stops again,
Strikes his breast hard, and anon he casts
His eye against the moon. In most strange
   postures
We have seen him set himself.
  King.   It may well be;
There is a mutiny in 's mind. This morning 120
Papers of state he sent me to peruse,
As I requir'd; and wot you what I found
There — on my conscience, put unwittingly?
Forsooth, an inventory, thus importing,   124
The several parcels of his plate, his treasure,
Rich stuffs and ornaments of household; which
I find at such proud rate that it outspeaks
Possession of a subject.
  Nor.   It's heaven's will.
Some spirit put this paper in the packet
To bless your eye withal.
  King.   If we did think 130
His contemplation were above the earth
And fix'd on spiritual object, he should still
Dwell in his musings; but I am afraid
His thinkings are below the moon, not worth
His serious considering.
    King takes his seat; whispers Lovell, who
               goes to the Cardinal.
  Card.   Heaven forgive me! 135
Ever God bless your Highness!
  King.   Good my lord,
You are full of heavenly stuff and bear the in-
   ventory
Of your best graces in your mind; the which
You were now running o'er. You have scarce
   time
To steal from spiritual leisure a brief span 140
To keep your earthly audit. Sure, in that
I deem you an ill husband, and am glad
To have you therein my companion.
  Card.   Sir,
For holy offices I have a time; a time
To think upon the part of business which   145
I bear i' th' state; and nature does require
Her times of preservation, which perforce

I, her frail son, amongst my brethren mortal,
Must give my tendance to.
    King.   You have said well.
    Card. And ever may your Highness yoke
    together   150
(As I will lend you cause) my doing well
With my well saying!
    King.   'Tis well said again,
And 'tis a kind of good deed to say well;
And yet words are no deeds. My father lov'd
    you;   154
He said he did, and with his deed did crown
His word upon you. Since I had my office,
I have kept you next my heart; have not
    alone
Employ'd you where high profits might come
    home,
But par'd my present havings to bestow
My bounties upon you.
    Card. [*aside*] What should this mean? 160
    Sur. [*aside*] The Lord increase this business!
    King.   Have I not made you
The prime man of the state? I pray you tell
    me
If what I now pronounce you have found true;
And if you may confess it, say withal   164
If you are bound to us or no. What say you?
    Card. My sovereign, I confess your royal
    graces,
Show'r'd on me daily, have been more than
    could
My studied purposes requite, which went
Beyond all man's endeavours. My endeavours
Have ever come too short of my desires, 170
Yet fil'd with my abilities. Mine own ends
Have been mine so that evermore they pointed
To th' good of your most sacred person and
The profit of the state. For your great graces
Heap'd upon me (poor undeserver) I   175
Can nothing render but allegiant thanks,
My pray'rs to heaven for you, my loyalty,
Which ever has and ever shall be growing
Till death (that winter) kill it.
    King.   Fairly answer'd!
A loyal and obedient subject is   180
Therein illustrated. The honour of it
Does pay the act of it, as, i' th' contrary,
The foulness is the punishment. I presume
That, as my hand has open'd bounty to you,
My heart dropp'd love, my pow'r rain'd hon-
    our, more   185
On you than any, so your hand and heart,
Your brain, and every function of your power
Should, notwithstanding that your bond of
    duty,

As 'twere in love's particular, be more
To me, your friend, than any.
    Card.   I do profess 190
That for your Highness' good I ever labour'd
More than mine own; that am, have, and will
    be —
Though all the world should crack their duty
    to you
And throw it from their soul; though perils did
Abound as thick as thought could make 'em and
Appear in forms more horrid — yet my duty,
As doth a rock against the chiding flood,
Should the approach of this wild river break
And stand unshaken yours.
    King.   'Tis nobly spoken.
Take notice, lords, he has a loyal breast, 200
For you have seen him open't. Read o'er this;
                     [*Gives him papers.*]
And after, this; and then to breakfast with
What appetite you have.
    Exit King frowning upon the Cardinal. The
    Nobles throng after him, smiling and
    whispering.
    Card.   What should this mean?
What sudden anger's this? How have I reap'd
    it?
He parted frowning from me, as if ruin   205
Leap'd from his eyes. So looks the chafed lion
Upon the daring huntsman that has gall'd him;
Then makes him nothing. I must read this
    paper;
I fear, the story of his anger. 'Tis so!   209
This paper has undone me. 'Tis th' accompt
Of all that world of wealth I have drawn to-
    gether
For mine own ends; indeed, to gain the pope-
    dom
And fee my friends in Rome. O negligence
Fit for a fool to fall by! What cross devil 214
Made me put this main secret in the packet
I sent the King? Is there no way to cure
    this?
No new device to beat this from his brains?
I know 'twill stir him strongly; yet I know
A way, if it take right, in spite of fortune,
Will bring me off again. What's this? 'To
    th' Pope'?   220
The letter (as I live!) with all the business
I writ to's Holiness! Nay then, farewell!
I have touch'd the highest point of all my great-
    ness,
And from that full meridian of my glory
I haste now to my setting. I shall fall   225
Like a bright exhalation in the evening,
And no man see me more.

Enter to *Wolsey* the *Dukes of Norfolk* and *Suffolk*, the *Earl of Surrey*, and the *Lord Chamberlain*.

Nor. Hear the King's pleasure, Cardinal,
  who commands you
To render up the great seal presently
Into our hands and to confine yourself   230
To Asher House, my Lord of Winchester's,
Till you hear further from his Highness.
  Card.   Stay.
Where's your commission, lords? Words cannot carry
Authority so weighty.
  Suf.   Who dares cross 'em,
Bearing the King's will from his mouth expressly?   235
  Card. Till I find more than will or words
  to do it
(I mean your malice), know, officious lords,
I dare and must deny it. Now I feel
Of what coarse metal ye are moulded — envy;
How eagerly ye follow my disgraces,   240
As if it fed ye! and how sleek and wanton
Ye appear in everything may bring my ruin!
Follow your envious courses, men of malice.
You have Christian warrant for 'em, and no
  doubt   244
In time will find their fit rewards. That seal
You ask with such a violence, the King
(Mine and your master) with his own hand
  gave me;
Bade me enjoy it, with the place and honours,
During my life, and to confirm his goodness
Tied it by letters patents. Now who'll take
  it?   250
  Sur. The King, that gave it.
  Card.   It must be himself then.
  Sur. Thou art a proud traitor, priest.
  Card.   Proud lord, thou liest!
Within these forty hours Surrey durst better
Have burnt that tongue than said so.
  Sur.   Thy ambition
(Thou scarlet sin) robb'd this bewailing land
Of noble Buckingham, my father-in-law.   256
The heads of all thy brother cardinals
(With thee and all thy best parts bound
  together)
Weigh'd not a hair of his. Plague of your
  policy!
You sent me Deputy for Ireland;   260
Far from his succour, from the King, from
  all
That might have mercy on the fault thou
  gav'st him;

Whilst your great goodness, out of holy pity,
Absolv'd him with an axe.
  Wol.   This, and all else
This talking lord can lay upon my credit,   265
I answer is most false. The Duke by law
Found his deserts. How innocent I was
From any private malice in his end,
His noble jury and foul cause can witness.
If I lov'd many words, lord, I should tell
  you   270
You have as little honesty as honour,
That in the way of loyalty and truth
Toward the King, my ever royal master,
Dare mate a sounder man than Surrey can
  be
And all that love his follies.
  Sur.   By my soul,   275
Your long coat, priest, protects you! Thou
  shouldst feel
My sword i' th' lifeblood of thee else. My
  lords,
Can ye endure to hear this arrogance?
And from this fellow? If we live thus tamely,
To be thus jaded by a piece of scarlet,   280
Farewell nobility! let his Grace go forward
And dare us with his cap, like larks!
  Card.   All goodness
Is poison to thy stomach.
  Sur.   Yes, that goodness
Of gleaning all the land's wealth into one,   284
Into your own hands, Cardinal, by extortion;
The goodness of your intercepted packets
You writ to th' Pope against the King. Your
  goodness,
Since you provoke me, shall be most notorious.
My Lord of Norfolk, — as you are truly noble,
As you respect the common good, the state   290
Of our despis'd nobility, our issues
(Who, if he live, will scarce be gentlemen), —
Produce the grand sum of his sins, the articles
Collected from his life. I'll startle you
Worse than the sacring bell when the brown
  wench   295
Lay kissing in your arms, Lord Cardinal.
  Card. How much, methinks, I could despise
  this man
But that I am bound in charity against it!
  Nor. Those articles, my lord, are in the
  King's hand;
But thus much — they are foul ones.
  Wol.   So much fairer   300
And spotless shall mine innocence arise
When the King knows my truth.
  Sur.   This cannot save you.
I thank my memory, I yet remember

Some of these articles, and out they shall! 304
Now if you can blush and cry guilty, Cardinal,
You'll show a little honesty.
Wol. Speak on, sir.
I dare your worst objections. If I blush,
It is to see a nobleman want manners.
Sur. I had rather want those than my head.
Have at you!
First, that without the King's assent or know-
    ledge 310
You wrought to be a legate, by which power
You maim'd the jurisdiction of all bishops.
Nor. Then, that in all you writ to Rome, or
    else
To foreign princes, 'Ego et Rex meus'
Was still inscrib'd; in which you brought the
    King 315
To be your servant.
Suf. Then, that without the knowledge
Either of King or Council, when you went
Ambassador to the Emperor, you made bold
To carry into Flanders the great seal.
Sur. Item, you sent a large commission 320
To Gregory de Cassado to conclude,
Without the King's will or the state's allowance,
A league between his Highness and Ferrara.
Suf. That out of mere ambition you have
    caus'd
Your holy hat to be stamp'd on the King's
    coin. 325
Sur. Then, that you have sent innumerable
    substance
(By what means got, I leave to your own con-
    science)
To furnish Rome and to prepare the ways
You have for dignities, to the mere undoing
Of all the kingdom. Many more there are, 330
Which, since they are of you, and odious,
I will not taint my mouth with.
Cham. O my lord,
Press not a falling man too far! 'Tis virtue.
His faults lie open to the laws; let them,
Not you, correct him. My heart weeps to see
    him 335
So little of his great self.
Sur. I forgive him.
Suf. Lord Cardinal, the King's further
    pleasure is —
Because all those things you have done of late
By your power legatine within this kingdom
Fall into th' compass of a præmunire — 340
That therefore such a writ be sued against you,
To forfeit all your goods, lands, tenements,
Chattels, and whatsoever, and to be
Out of the King's protection. This is my charge.

Nor. And so we'll leave you to your medi-
    tations 345
How to live better. For your stubborn answer
About the giving back the great seal to us,
The King shall know it, and (no doubt) shall
    thank you.
So fare you well, my little good Lord Cardinal.
          Exeunt all but Wolsey.
Wol. So farewell to the little good you bear
    me! 350
Farewell, a long farewell, to all my greatness!
This is the state of man: to-day he puts forth
The tender leaves of hopes; to-morrow blos-
    soms
And bears his blushing honours thick upon him;
The third day comes a frost, a killing frost, 355
And when he thinks, good easy man, full surely
His greatness is a-ripening, nips his root,
And then he falls, as I do. I have ventur'd,
Like little wanton boys that swim on bladders,
This many summers in a sea of glory; 360
But far beyond my depth. My high-blown
    pride
At length broke under me, and now has left me,
Weary and old with service, to the mercy
Of a rude stream that must for ever hide me.
Vain pomp and glory of this world, I hate
    ye! 365
I feel my heart new open'd. O, how wretched
Is that poor man that hangs on princes' fa-
    vours!
There is betwixt that smile we would aspire to,
That sweet aspect of princes, and their ruin
More pangs and fears than wars or women
    have; 370
And when he falls, he falls like Lucifer,
Never to hope again.

        Enter *Cromwell*, standing amazed.

            Why, how now, Cromwell!
Crom. I have no power to speak, sir.
Card. What, amaz'd
At my misfortunes? Can thy spirit wonder
A great man should decline? Nay, an you
    weep, 375
I am fall'n indeed.
Crom. How does your Grace?
Card. Why, well;
Never so truly happy, my good Cromwell.
I know myself now, and I feel within me
A peace above all earthly dignities,
A still and quiet conscience. The King has
    cur'd me — 380
I humbly thank his Grace — and from these
    shoulders,

These ruin'd pillars, out of pity taken
A load would sink a navy — too much honour.
O 'tis a burden, Cromwell, 'tis a burden			384
Too heavy for a man that hopes for heaven!
  Crom. I am glad your Grace has made that
    right use of it.
  Card. I hope I have. I am able now, me-
thinks,
Out of a fortitude of soul I feel,
To endure more miseries and greater far
Than my weak-hearted enemies dare offer.	390
What news abroad?
  Crom.				The heaviest and the worst
Is your displeasure with the King.
  Card.					God bless him!
  Crom. The next is that Sir Thomas More is
    chosen
Lord Chancellor in your place.
  Card.				That's somewhat sudden.
But he's a learned man. May he continue	395
Long in his Highness' favour and do justice
For truth's sake and his conscience; that his
    bones,
When he has run his course and sleeps in
    blessings,
May have a tomb of orphans' tears wept on
    him!
What more?
  Crom.		That Cranmer is return'd with
    welcome,						400
Install'd Lord Archbishop of Canterbury.
  Card. That's news indeed.
  Crom.			Last, that the Lady Anne,
Whom the King hath in secrecy long married,
This day has view'd in open as his queen,
Going to chapel; and the voice is now		405
Only about her coronation.
  Card. There was the weight that pull'd me
    down. O Cromwell,
The King has gone beyond me! All my glories
In that one woman I have lost for ever.
No sun shall ever usher forth mine honours	410
Or gild again the noble troops that waited
Upon my smiles. Go get thee from me, Crom-
    well!
I am a poor fall'n man, unworthy now
To be thy lord and master. Seek the King.
That sun, I pray, may never set! I have told
    him							415
What and how true thou art. He will advance
    thee.
Some little memory of me will stir him
(I know his noble nature) not to let
Thy hopeful service perish too. Good Crom-
    well,							419

Neglect him not; make use now, and provide
For thine own future safety.
  Crom.				O my lord,
Must I then leave you? Must I needs forgo
So good, so noble, and so true a master?
Bear witness, all that have not hearts of iron,
With what a sorrow Cromwell leaves his lord.
The King shall have my service, but my pray'rs
For ever and for ever shall be yours.
  Card. Cromwell, I did not think to shed a
    tear
In all my miseries; but thou hast forc'd me
(Out of thy honest truth) to play the woman.
Let's dry our eyes; and thus far hear me,
    Cromwell,					431
And when I am forgotten, as I shall be,
And sleep in dull cold marble, where no mention
Of me more must be heard of, say I taught
    thee —						434
Say Wolsey, that once trod the ways of glory
And sounded all the depths and shoals of hon-
    our,
Found thee a way (out of his wrack) to rise
    in —
A sure and safe one, though thy master miss'd
    it.
Mark but my fall and that that ruin'd me.	439
Cromwell, I charge thee, fling away ambition!
By that sin fell the angels. How can man
    then
(The image of his Maker) hope to win by
    it?
Love thyself last. Cherish those hearts that
    hate thee;
Corruption wins not more than honesty.
Still in thy right hand carry gentle peace	445
To silence envious tongues. Be just, and fear
    not.
Let all the ends thou aim'st at be thy country's,
Thy God's, and truth's. Then if thou fall'st, O
    Cromwell,
Thou fall'st a blessed martyr. Serve the King.
And prithee lead me in.					450
There take an inventory of all I have
To the last penny. 'Tis the King's. My robe,
And my integrity to heaven, is all
I dare now call mine own. O Cromwell, Crom-
    well!						454
Had I but serv'd my God with half the zeal
I serv'd my king, he would not in mine age
Have left me naked to mine enemies.
  Crom. Good sir, have patience.
  Card.				So I have. Farewell
The hopes of court! My hopes in heaven do
    dwell.						*Exeunt.*

ACT IV. Scene I. [*A street in Westminster.*]

Enter two *Gentlemen*, meeting one another.

1. Gent. Y'are well met once again.

2. Gent.   So are you.

1. Gent. You come to take your stand here
and behold
The Lady Anne pass from her coronation?

2. Gent. 'Tis all my business. At our last
encounter   4
The Duke of Buckingham came from his trial.

1. Gent. 'Tis very true; but that time offer'd
sorrow;
This, general joy.

2. Gent.   'Tis well. The citizens
I am sure have shown at full their royal minds—
As, let 'em have their rights, they are ever
forward —
In celebration of this day with shows,   10
Pageants, and sights of honour.

1. Gent.   Never greater,
Nor, I'll assure you, better taken, sir.

2. Gent. May I be bold to ask what that
contains,
That paper in your hand?

1. Gent.   Yes. 'Tis the list
Of those that claim their offices this day   15
By custom of the coronation.
The Duke of Suffolk is the first, and claims
To be High Steward; next, the Duke of Nor-
folk,
He to be Earl Marshal. You may read the rest.

2. Gent. I thank you, sir. Had I not known
those customs,   20
I should have been beholding to your paper.
But, I beseech you, what's become of Katherine,
The Princess Dowager? How goes her busi-
ness?

1. Gent. That I can tell you too. The Arch-
bishop
Of Canterbury, accompanied with other   25
Learned and reverend fathers of his order,
Held a late court at Dunstable, six miles off
From Ampthill, where the Princess lay, to
which
She was often cited by them, but appear'd not;
And, to be short, for not appearance and   30
The King's late scruple, by the main assent
Of all these learned men she was divorc'd
And the late marriage made of none effect;
Since which she was remov'd to Kimbolton,
Where she remains now sick.

2. Gent.   Alas, good lady!   35
                                                        [*Trumpets.*]
The trumpets sound. Stand close! The Queen
is coming.   *Hautboys.*

THE ORDER OF THE CORONATION.

1. A lively flourish of trumpets.
2. Then two *Judges.*
3. *Lord Chancellor*, with purse and mace before
   him.
4. *Choristers* singing.   *Music.*
5. *Mayor of London*, bearing the mace. Then
   Garter, in his coat of arms, and on his head
   he wore a gilt copper crown.
6. *Marquess Dorset*, bearing a sceptre of gold,
   on his head a demi-coronal of gold. With
   him the *Earl of Surrey*, bearing the rod of
   silver with the dove, crowned with an
   earl's coronet. Collars of Esses.
7. *Duke of Suffolk*, in his robe of estate, his
   coronet on his head, bearing a long white
   wand, as High Steward. With him the
   Duke of Norfolk, with the rod of marshal-
   ship, a coronet on his head. Collars of.
   Esses.
8. A canopy borne by four of the *Cinque Ports*;
   under it, the *Queen* in her robe, in her
   hair, richly adorned with pearl, crowned.
   On each side her the *Bishops of London*
   and *Winchester.*
9. The old *Duchess of Norfolk*, in a coronal of
   gold, wrought with flowers, bearing the
   Queen's train.
10. Certain *Ladies* or *Countesses*, with plain
    circlets of gold without flowers.
    *Exeunt, first passing over the stage in order
    and state, and then a great flourish of
    trumpets.*

2. Gent. A royal train, believe me. These I
know.
Who's that that bears the sceptre?

1. Gent.   Marquess Dorset;
And that the Earl of Surrey with the rod.

2. Gent. A bold brave gentleman. That
should be   40
The Duke of Suffolk.

1. Gent.   'Tis the same: High Steward.

2. Gent. And that my Lord of Norfolk?

1. Gent.   Yes.

2. Gent.   [*looks on the Queen*] Heaven
    bless thee!
Thou hast the sweetest face I ever look'd on.
Sir, as I have a soul, she is an angel!
Our king has all the Indies in his arms,   45
And more, and richer, when he strains that lady.
I cannot blame his conscience.
    1. Gent.   They that bear
The cloth of honour over her are four Barons
Of the Cinque Ports.
    2. Gent. Those men are happy, and so are
    all are near her.   50
I take it, she that carries up the train
Is that old noble lady, Duchess of Norfolk.
    1. Gent. It is, and all the rest are countesses.
    2. Gent. Their coronets say so. These are
    stars indeed,
And sometimes falling ones.
    1. Gent.   No more of that.   55
                        [*Exit procession.*]

        Enter a third *Gentleman.*

God save you, sir! Where have you been
    broiling?
    3. Gent. Among the crowd i' th' Abbey, where
    a finger
Could not be wedg'd in more. I am stifled
With the mere rankness of their joy.
    2. Gent.   You saw
The ceremony?
    3. Gent.   That I did.
    1. Gent.   How was it?   60
    3. Gent. Well worth the seeing.
    2. Gent.   Good sir, speak it to us.
    3. Gent. As well as I am able. The rich stream
Of lords and ladies, having brought the Queen
To a prepar'd place in the choir, fell off   64
A distance from her, while her Grace sat down
To rest awhile, some half an hour or so,
In a rich chair of state, opposing freely
The beauty of her person to the people.
Believe me, sir, she is the goodliest woman
That ever lay by man; which when the people
Had the full view of, such a noise arose   71
As the shrouds make at sea in a stiff tempest,
As loud, and to as many tunes. Hats, cloaks
(Doublets, I think) flew up; and had their faces
Been loose, this day they had been lost. Such joy
I never saw before. Great-bellied women   76
That had not half a week to go, like rams
In the old time of war, would shake the press
And make 'em reel before 'em. No man living
Could say 'This is my wife' there, all were
    woven   80
So strangely in one piece.

    2. Gent.   But what follow'd?
    3. Gent. At length her Grace rose and with
    modest paces
Came to the altar, where she kneel'd and
    saintlike
Cast her fair eyes to heaven and pray'd de-
    voutly;   84
Then rose again and bow'd her to the people;
When by the Archbishop of Canterbury
She had all the royal makings of a queen;
As holy oil, Edward Confessor's crown,
The rod, and bird of peace, and all such
    emblems,
Laid nobly on her; which perform'd, the choir
With all the choicest music of the kingdom   91
Together sung 'Te Deum.' So she parted
And with the same full state pac'd back again
To York Place, where the feast is held.
    1. Gent.   Sir,
You must no more call it York Place. That's
    past;   95
For since the Cardinal fell that title's lost.
'Tis now the King's, and call'd Whitehall.
    3. Gent.   I know it;
But 'tis so lately alter'd that the old name
Is fresh about me.
    2. Gent.   What two reverend bishops
Were those that went on each side of the Queen?
    3. Gent. Stokesly and Gardiner; the one of
    Winchester,   101
Newly preferr'd from the King's Secretary,
The other, London.
    2. Gent.   He of Winchester
Is held no great good lover of the Archbishop's,
The virtuous Cranmer.
    3. Gent.   All the land knows that.   105
However, yet there is no great breach. When
    it comes,
Cranmer will find a friend will not shrink from
    him.
    2. Gent. Who may that be, I pray you?
    3. Gent.   Thomas Cromwell,
A man in much esteem with th' King, and truly
A worthy friend. The King has made him
    Master   110
O' th' Jewel House
And one, already, of the Privy Council.
    2. Gent. He will deserve more.
    3. Gent.   Yes, without all doubt.
Come, gentlemen, ye shall go my way, which
Is to th' court, and there ye shall be my guests.
Something I can command. As I walk thither,
I'll tell ye more.
    Both.   You may command us, sir.
                        Exeunt.

Scene II. [*Kimbolton.*]

Enter *Katherine*, Dowager, sick; led between
Griffith (her *Gentleman Usher*) and *Patience*
(her *Woman*).

Grif. How does your Grace?
Kath.   O Griffith, sick to death!
My legs like loaden branches bow to th' earth,
Willing to leave their burthen. Reach a chair.
So. Now, methinks, I feel a little ease.
Didst thou not tell me, Griffith, as thou led'st
    me,   5
That the great child of honour, Cardinal
    Wolsey,
Was dead?
Grif. Yes, madam; but I think your Grace,
Out of the pain you suffer'd, gave no ear to't.
Kath. Prithee, good Griffith, tell me how he
    died.
If well, he stepp'd before me happily   10
For my example.
Grif.   Well, the voice goes, madam;
For after the stout Earl Northumberland
Arrested him at York and brought him forward,
As a man sorely tainted, to his answer,
He fell sick suddenly and grew so ill   15
He could not sit his mule.
Kath.   Alas, poor man!
Grif. At last, with easy roads, he came to
    Leicester,
Lodg'd in the abbey; where the reverend
    Abbot,
With all his covent, honourably receiv'd him;
To whom he gave these words: 'O Father
    Abbot,   20
An old man, broken with the storms of state,
Is come to lay his weary bones among ye.
Give him a little earth for charity!'
So went to bed; where eagerly his sickness   24
Pursu'd him still; and three nights after this,
After the hour of eight, which he himself
Foretold should be his last, full of repentance,
Continual meditations, tears, and sorrows,
He gave his honours to the world again,   29
His blessed part to heaven, and slept in peace.
Kath. So may he rest! His faults lie gently
    on him!
Yet thus far, Griffith, give me leave to speak
    him,
And yet with charity. He was a man
Of an unbounded stomach, ever ranking   34
Himself with princes; one that by suggestion
Tied all the kingdom. Simony was fair play;
His own opinion was his law. I' th' presence

He would say untruths, and be ever double
Both in his words and meaning. He was never
(But where he meant to ruin) pitiful.   40
His promises were, as he then was, mighty;
But his performance, as he is now, nothing.
Of his own body he was ill, and gave
The clergy ill example.
Grif.   Noble madam,   44
Men's evil manners live in brass; their virtues
We write in water. May it please your High-
    ness
To hear me speak his good now?
Kath.   Yes, good Griffith.
I were malicious else.
Grif.   This Cardinal,
Though from an humble stock, undoubtedly
Was fashion'd to much honour from his cradle.
He was a scholar, and a ripe and good one;   51
Exceeding wise, fair-spoken, and persuading;
Lofty and sour to them that lov'd him not,
But to those men that sought him sweet as
    summer.
And though he were unsatisfied in getting   55
(Which was a sin), yet in bestowing, madam,
He was most princely. Ever witness for him
Those twins of learning that he rais'd in you,
Ipswich and Oxford; one of which fell with
    him,
Unwilling to outlive the good that did it;   60
The other, though unfinish'd, yet so famous,
So excellent in art, and still so rising,
That Christendom shall ever speak his virtue.
His overthrow heap'd happiness upon him;
For then, and not till then, he felt himself   65
And found the blessedness of being little.
And, to add greater honours to his age
Than man could give him, he died fearing
    God.
Kath. After my death I wish no other herald,
No other speaker of my living actions   70
To keep mine honour from corruption,
But such an honest chronicler as Griffith,
Whom I most hated living, thou hast made
    me,
With thy religious truth and modesty,   74
Now, in his ashes, honour. Peace be with him!
Patience, be near me still, and set me lower.
I have not long to trouble thee. Good Griffith,
Cause the musicians play me that sad note
I nam'd my knell, whilst I sit meditating,
On that celestial harmony I go to.   80
                Sad and solemn music.
Grif. She is asleep. Good wench, let's sit
    down quiet
For fear we wake her. Softly, gentle Patience.

The Vision.

Enter, solemnly tripping one after another, six
personages clad in white robes, wearing on their
heads garlands of bays, and golden vizards on
their faces; branches of bays or palm in their
hands. They first congee unto her, then dance;
and, at certain changes, the first two hold a
spare garland over her head; at which the
other four make reverent curtsies. Then the
two that held the garland deliver the same to
the other next two, who observe the same order
in their changes and holding the garland over
her head; which done, they deliver the same
garland to the last two, who likewise observe
the same order; at which (as it were by inspiration) she makes (in her sleep) signs of rejoicing
and holdeth up her hands to heaven. And so in
their dancing vanish, carrying the garland with
them. *The music continues.*

Kath. Spirits of peace, where are ye? Are
    ye all gone
And leave me here in wretchedness behind ye?
Grif. Madam, we are here.
Kath.   It is not you I call for. 85
Saw ye none enter since I slept?
Grif.   None, madam.
Kath. No? Saw you not even now a blessed
    troop
Invite me to a banquet, whose bright faces
Cast thousand beams upon me like the sun?
They promis'd me eternal happiness 90
And brought me garlands, Griffith, which I feel
I am not worthy yet to wear. I shall, assuredly.
Grif. I am most joyful, madam, such good
    dreams
Possess your fancy.
Kath.   Bid the music leave.
They are harsh and heavy to me.
                     Music ceases.
Pat.   Do you note 95
How much her Grace is alter'd on the sudden?
How long her face is drawn? how pale she
    looks,
And of an earthy colour? Mark her eyes!
Grif. She is going, wench. Pray, pray!
Pat.   Heaven comfort her!

Enter a *Messenger.*

Mess. An't like your Grace —
Kath.   You are a saucy fellow. 100
Deserve we no more reverence?
Grif.   You are to blame,
Knowing she will not lose her wonted greatness,
To use so rude behaviour. Go to, kneel!

Mess. I humbly do entreat your Highness'
    pardon.
My haste made me unmannerly. There is
    staying 105
A gentleman, sent from the King, to see you.
Kath. Admit him entrance, Griffith. But
    this fellow
Let me ne'er see again.
                  Exit Messenger.

Enter *Lord Capucius.*

                If my sight fail not,
You should be Lord Ambassador from the
    Emperor, 109
My royal nephew, and your name Capucius.
Cap. Madam, the same — your servant.
Kath.   O my lord,
The times and titles now are alter'd strangely
With me since first you knew me. But I pray
    you,
What is your pleasure with me?
Cap.   Noble lady,
First mine own service to your Grace; the next,
The King's request that I would visit you, 116
Who grieves much for your weakness and by
    me
Sends you his princely commendations
And heartily entreats you take good comfort.
Kath. O my good lord, that comfort comes
    too late! 120
'Tis like a pardon after execution.
That gentle physic, given in time, had cur'd me;
But now I am past all comforts here but prayers.
How does his Highness?
Cap.   Madam, in good health.
Kath. So may he ever do! and ever flourish
When I shall dwell with worms, and my poor
    name 126
Banish'd the kingdom! Patience, is that letter
I caus'd you write yet sent away?
Pat.   No, madam.
            [Gives it to Katherine.]
Kath. Sir, I most humbly pray you to de-
    liver
This to my lord the King.
Cap.   Most willing, madam. 130
Kath. In which I have commended to his
    goodness
The model of our chaste loves, his young
    daughter —
The dews of heaven fall thick in blessings on
    her! —
Beseeching him to give her virtuous breeding —
She is young and of a noble modest nature; 135
I hope she will deserve well — and a little

To love her for her mother's sake, that lov'd
  him,
Heaven knows how dearly. My next poor
  petition
Is that his noble Grace would have some pity
Upon my wretched women, that so long   140
Have follow'd both my fortunes faithfully;
Of which there is not one, I dare avow
(And now I should not lie), but will deserve,
For virtue and true beauty of the soul,
For honesty and decent carriage,   145
A right good husband — let him be a noble;
And sure those men are happy that shall have
  'em.
The last is for my men — they are the poorest
(But poverty could never draw 'em from me) —
That they may have their wages duly paid 'em,
And something over to remember me by.   151
If heaven had pleas'd to have given me longer
  life
And able means, we had not parted thus.
These are the whole contents; and, good my
  lord,   154
By that you love the dearest in this world,

As you wish Christian peace to souls departed,
Stand these poor people's friend and urge the
  King
To do me this last right.
   Cap.   By heaven, I will,
Or let me lose the fashion of a man!
   Kath. I thank you, honest lord. Remember
  me   160
In all humility unto his Highness.
Say his long trouble now is passing
Out of this world. Tell him in death I bless'd
  him,
For so I will. Mine eyes grow dim. Farewell,
My lord. Griffith, farewell. Nay, Patience, 165
You must not leave me yet. I must to bed;
Call in more women. When I am dead, good
  wench,
Let me be us'd with honour. Strew me over
With maiden flowers, that all the world may
  know   169
I was a chaste wife to my grave. Embalm me,
Then lay me forth. Although unqueen'd, yet like
A queen, and daughter to a king, inter me.
I can no more.   *Exeunt, leading Katherine.*

ACT V. Scene I. [*London. A gallery in the Palace.*]

Enter *Gardiner, Bishop of Winchester,* a *Page*
with a torch before him, met by *Sir Thomas
Lovell.*

   Gard. It's one o'clock, boy, is't not?
   Boy.   It hath struck.
   Gard. These should be hours for necessities,
Not for delights; times to repair our nature
With comforting repose, and not for us
To waste these times. Good hour of night, Sir
  Thomas!   5
Whither so late?
   Lov.   Came you from the King, my lord?
   Gard. I did, Sir Thomas, and left him at
  primero
With the Duke of Suffolk.
   Lov.   I must to him too,
Before he go to bed. I'll take my leave.
   Gard. Not yet, Sir Thomas Lovell. What's
  the matter?   10
It seems you are in haste. An if there be
No great offence belongs to't, give your friend
Some touch of your late business. Affairs that
  walk
(As they say spirits do) at midnight have
In them a wilder nature than the business   15
That seeks dispatch by day.

   Lov.   My lord, I love you,
And durst commend a secret to your ear
Much weightier than this work. The Queen's
  in labour,
They say in great extremity, and fear'd
She'll with the labour end.
   Gard.   The fruit she goes with 20
I pray for heartily, that it may find
Good time, and live; but for the stock, Sir
  Thomas,
I wish it grubb'd up now.
   Lov.   Methinks I could
Cry the amen; and yet my conscience says
She's a good creature, and, sweet lady, does 25
Deserve our better wishes.
   Gard.   But, sir, sir!
Hear me, Sir Thomas! Y'are a gentleman
Of mine own way. I know you wise, religious;
And let me tell you it will ne'er be well — 29
'Twill not, Sir Thomas Lovell, take't of me —
Till Cranmer, Cromwell, her two hands, and she
Sleep in their graves.
   Lov.   Now, sir, you speak of two
The most remark'd i' th' kingdom. As for
  Cromwell,
Beside that of the Jewel House, is made
  Master

O' th' Rolls and the King's Secretary; further,
    sir,   35
Stands in the gap and trade of moe preferments,
With which the time will load him. Th' Arch-
    bishop
Is the King's hand and tongue; and who dare
    speak
One syllable against him?
    Gard.   Yes, yes, Sir Thomas,
There are that dare, and I myself have ven-
    tur'd   40
To speak my mind of him; and indeed this day
(Sir I may tell it you, I think) I have
Incens'd the lords o' th' Council that he is
(For so I know he is, they know he is)
A most arch-heretic, a pestilence   45
That does infect the land; with which they
    mov'd
Have broken with the King, who hath so far
Given ear to our complaint — of his great grace
And princely care, foreseeing those fell mischiefs
Our reasons laid before him — hath com-
    manded   50
To-morrow morning to the Council board
He be convented. He's a rank weed, Sir
    Thomas,
And we must root him out. From your affairs
I hinder you too long. Good night, Sir Thomas.
    Lov. Many good nights, my lord! I rest
        your servant.   55
                Exeunt Gardiner and Page.

            Enter *King* and *Suffolk.*

King. Charles, I will play no more to-night;
My mind's not on't; you are too hard for
    me.
Suf. Sir, I did never win of you before.
King. But little, Charles,
Nor shall not when my fancy's on my play.   60
Now, Lovell, from the Queen what is the news?
Lov. I could not personally deliver to her
What you commanded me, but by her woman
I sent your message, who return'd her thanks
In the great'st humbleness and desir'd your
    Highness   65
Most heartily to pray for her.
King.   What say'st thou? Ha?
To pray for her? What, is she crying out?
Lov. So said her woman, and that her suf-
    f'rance made
Almost each pang a death.
King.   Alas, good lady!
Suf. God safely quit her of her burthen and
With gentle travail, to the gladding of   71
Your Highness with an heir!

King.   'Tis midnight, Charles.
Prithee to bed, and in thy pray'rs remember
Th' estate of my poor queen. Leave me alone,
For I must think of that which company   75
Would not be friendly to.
Suf.   I wish your Highness
A quiet night and my good mistress will
Remember in my prayers.
King.   Charles, good night.
                    Exit Suffolk.

            Enter *Sir Anthony Denny.*

Well, sir, what follows?
Den. Sir, I have brought my lord the Arch-
    bishop,   80
As you commanded me.
King.   Ha? Canterbury?
Den. Ay, my good lord.
King.   'Tis true. Where is he, Denny?
Den. He attends your Highness' pleasure.
King.   Bring him to us.
                    [Exit Denny.]
Lov. [aside] This is about that which the
    Bishop spake.
I am happily come hither.   85

            Enter *Cranmer* and *Denny.*

King. Avoid the gallery. (*Lovell seems to
    stay.*) Ha! I have said. Be gone.
What!
                Exeunt Lovell and Denny.
Cran.   [aside] I am fearful. Wherefore
    frowns he thus?
'Tis his aspect of terror. All's not well.
King. How now, my lord? You do desire
    to know
Wherefore I sent for you?
Cran.   [kneels] It is my duty   90
T' attend your Highness' pleasure.
King.   Pray you arise,
My good and gracious Lord of Canterbury.
Come, you and I must walk a turn together.
I have news to tell you. Come, come, give me
    your hand.
Ah, my good lord, I grieve at what I speak   95
And am right sorry to repeat what follows.
I have, and most unwillingly, of late
Heard many grievous — I do say, my lord,
Grievous complaints of you; which, being
    consider'd,   99
Have mov'd us and our Council that you shall
This morning come before us; where I know
You cannot with such freedom purge yourself
But that, till further trial in those charges
Which will require your answer, you must take

                        401

Your patience to you and be well contented
To make your house our Tow'r. You a brother
   of us,   106
It fits we thus proceed, or else no witness
Would come against you.

   Cran.   I humbly thank your Highness,
And am right glad to catch this good occasion
Most throughly to be winnowed where my chaff
And corn shall fly asunder; for I know   111
There's none stands under more calumnious
   tongues
Than I myself, poor man.

   King.   Stand up, good Canterbury.
Thy truth and thy integrity is rooted
In us, thy friend. Give me thy hand, stand up.
                             [*Cranmer rises.*]
Prithee let's walk. Now by my holidame, 116
What manner of man are you? My lord, I
   look'd
You would have given me your petition that
I should have ta'en some pains to bring together
Yourself and your accusers and to have heard
   you   120
Without indurance further.

   Cran.   Most dread liege,
The good I stand on is my truth and honesty.
If they shall fail, I with mine enemies
Will triumph o'er my person, which I weigh
   not,
Being of those virtues vacant. I fear nothing
What can be said against me.

   King.   Know you not 126
How your state stands i' th' world, with the
   whole world?
Your enemies are many and not small; their
   practices
Must bear the same proportion; and not ever
The justice and the truth o' th' question carries
The due o' th' verdict with it. At what ease
Might corrupt minds procure knaves as corrupt
To swear against you! Such things have been
   done.
You are potently oppos'd, and with a malice
Of as great size. Ween you of better luck, 135
I mean in perjur'd witness, than your Master,
Whose minister you are, whiles here he liv'd
Upon this naughty earth? Go to, go to!
You take a precipice for no leap of danger
And woo your own destruction.

   Cran.   God and your Majesty 140
Protect mine innocence, or I fall into
The trap is laid for me!

   King.   Be of good cheer.
They shall no more prevail than we give way
   to.
Keep comfort to you, and this morning see
You do appear before them. If they shall
   chance,   145
In charging you with matters, to commit you,
The best persuasions to the contrary
Fail not to use, and with what vehemency
Th' occasion shall instruct you. If entreaties
Will render you no remedy, this ring   150
Deliver them and your appeal to us
There make before them. Look, the good man
   weeps!
He's honest, on mine honour. God's blest
   Mother!
I swear he is true-hearted, and a soul
None better in my kingdom. Get you gone 155
And do as I have bid you. (*Exit Cranmer.*) He
   has strangled
His language in his tears.

                Enter *Old Lady.*

   Gent. (*within*) Come back! What mean you?

   Lady. I'll not come back. The tidings that
   I bring
Will make my boldness manners. Now good
   angels   159
Fly o'er thy royal head and shade thy person
Under their blessed wings!

   King.   Now by thy looks
I guess thy message. Is the Queen deliver'd?
Say ay, and of a boy.

   Lady.   Ay, ay, my liege!
And of a lovely boy. The God of heaven
Both now and ever bless her! 'Tis a girl 165
Promises boys hereafter. Sir, your queen
Desires your visitation, and to be
Acquainted with this stranger. 'Tis as like
   you
As cherry is to cherry.

   King.   Lovell!

                [Enter *Lovell.*]

   Lov.   Sir?

   King. Give her an hundred marks. I'll to
   the Queen.   *Exit*

   Lady. An hundred marks? By this light,
   I'll ha' more!   171
An ordinary groom is for such payment.
I will have more or scold it out of him.
Said I for this the girl was like to him?
I will have more or else unsay 't, and now, 175
While it is hot, I'll put it to the issue.

                         Exeunt.

Scene II. [*Lobby before the Council Chamber.*]

[*Pursuivants and others in waiting.*]

Enter *Cranmer, Archbishop of Canterbury.*

Cran. I hope I am not too late; and yet the gentleman
That was sent to me from the Council pray'd me
To make great haste. All fast? What means this? Ho!
Who waits there? Sure you know me?

Enter *Keeper.*

Keep.   Yes, my lord.
But yet I cannot help you.   5
Cran. Why?
Keep. Your Grace must wait till you be call'd for.

Enter *Doctor Butts.*

Cran.   So.
Butts. [*aside*] This is a piece of malice. I am glad
I came this way so happily. The King
Shall understand it presently.   *Exit.*
Cran.   'Tis Butts, 10
The King's physician. As he pass'd along,
How earnestly he cast his eyes upon me!
Pray heaven he sound not my disgrace! For certain,
This is of purpose laid by some that hate me
(God turn their hearts! I never sought their malice)   15
To quench mine honour. They would shame to make me
Wait else at door, a fellow councillor,
'Mong boys, grooms, and lackeys. But their pleasures
Must be fulfill'd, and I attend with patience.

Enter the *King* and *Butts* at a window above.

Butts. I'll show your Grace the strangest sight —
King.   What's that, Butts?   20
Butts. I think your Highness saw this many a day.
King. Body o' me, where is it?
Butts.   There, my lord:
The high promotion of his Grace of Canterbury,
Who holds his state at door 'mongst pursuivants,
Pages, and footboys.

King.   Ha? 'Tis he indeed. 25
Is this the honour they do one another?
'Tis well there's one above 'em yet. I had thought
They had parted so much honesty among 'em —
At least, good manners — as not thus to suffer
A man of his place and so near our favour 30
To dance attendance on their lordships' pleasures,
And at the door too, like a post with packets.
By holy Mary, Butts, there's knavery!
Let 'em alone, and draw the curtain close. 34
We shall hear more anon.   [*Exeunt.*]

[Scene III. *The Council Chamber.*]

A Council table brought in, with chairs and stools, and placed under the state. Enter *Lord Chancellor*, places himself at the upper end of the table on the left hand, a seat being left void above him, as for *Canterbury's* seat. *Duke of Suffolk, Duke of Norfolk, Surrey, Lord Chamberlain, Gardiner* seat themselves in order on each side; *Cromwell* at lower end, as Secretary.
[*Keeper at the door.*]

Chan. Speak to the business, Master Secretary.
Why are we met in Council?
Crom.   Please your Honours,
The chief cause concerns his Grace of Canterbury.
Gard. Has he had knowledge of it?
Crom.   Yes.
Nor.   Who waits there?
Keep. Without, my noble lords?
Gard.   Yes.
Keep.   My Lord Archbishop, 5
And has done half an hour to know your pleasures.
Chan. Let him come in.
Keep.   Your Grace may enter now.
Cranmer approaches the Council table.
Chan. My good Lord Archbishop, I'm very sorry
To sit here at this present and behold 9
That chair stand empty; but we all are men,
In our own natures frail and capable
Of our flesh; few are angels; out of which frailty
And want of wisdom, you, that best should teach us,
Have misdemean'd yourself, and not a little:
Toward the King first, then his laws, in filling

The whole realm by your teaching and your
   chaplains   16
(For so we are inform'd) with new opinions,
Divers and dangerous; which are heresies,
And, not reform'd, may prove pernicious.
   Gard. Which reformation must be sudden
   too,   20
My noble lords; for those that tame wild horses
Pace 'em not in their hands to make 'em
   gentle,
But stop their mouths with stubborn bits and
   spur 'em
Till they obey the manage. If we suffer,
Out of our easiness and childish pity   25
To one man's honour, this contagious sickness,
Farewell all physic! And what follows then?
Commotions, uproars, with a general taint
Of the whole state, as of late days our neigh-
   bours,
The upper Germany, can dearly witness,   30
Yet freshly pitied in our memories.
   Cran. My good lords, hitherto, in all the
   progress
Both of my life and office, I have labour'd,
And with no little study, that my teaching
And the strong course of my authority   35
Might go one way, and safely; and the end
Was ever to do well; nor is there living
(I speak it with a single heart, my lords)
A man that more detests, more stirs against,
Both in his private conscience and his place,
Defacers of a public peace than I do.   41
Pray heaven the King may never find a heart
With less allegiance in it! Men that make
Envy and crooked malice nourishment
Dare bite the best. I do beseech your lord-
   ships   45
That in this case of justice my accusers,
Be what they will, may stand forth face to
   face
And freely urge against me.
   Suf.   Nay, my lord,
That cannot be. You are a Councillor,   49
And by that virtue no man dare accuse you.
   Gard. My lord, because we have business of
   more moment,
We will be short with you. 'Tis his Highness'
   pleasure
And our consent, for better trial of you,
From hence you be committed to the Tower,
Where, being but a private man again,   55
You shall know many dare accuse you boldly,
More than, I fear, you are provided for.
   Cran. Ah, my good Lord of Winchester, I
   thank you.

You are always my good friend. If your will
   pass,
I shall both find your lordship judge and juror,
You are so merciful. I see your end —   61
'Tis my undoing. Love and meekness. lord,
Become a churchman better than ambition;
Win straying souls with modesty again,   64
Cast none away. That I shall clear myself,
Lay all the weight ye can upon my patience,
I make as little doubt as you do conscience
In doing daily wrongs. I could say more,
But reverence to your calling makes me modest.
   Gard. My lord, my lord, you are a sectary!
That's the plain truth. Your painted gloss
   discovers,   71
To men that understand you, words and weak-
   ness.
   Crom. My Lord of Winchester, you are a
   little,
By your good favour, too sharp. Men so noble,
However faulty, yet should find respect   75
For what they have been. 'Tis a cruelty
To load a falling man.
   Gard.   Good Master Secretary,
I cry your Honour mercy. You may worst
Of all this table say so.
   Crom.   Why, my lord?
   Gard. Do not I know you for a favourer   80
Of this new sect? Ye are not sound.
   Crom.   Not sound?
   Gard. Not sound, I say.
   Crom.   Would you were half so honest!
Men's prayers then would seek you, not their
   fears.
   Gard. I shall remember this bold language.
   Crom.   Do.
Remember your bold life too.
   Chan.   This is too much.   85
Forbear for shame, my lords.
   Gard.   I have done.
   Crom.   And I.
   Chan. Then thus for you, my lord: it stands
   agreed,
I take it, by all voices, that forthwith
You be convey'd to th' Tower a prisoner,
There to remain till the King's further pleas-
   ure   90
Be known unto us. Are you all agreed, lords?
   All. We are.
   Cran.   Is there no other way of mercy
But I must needs to th' Tower, my lords?
   Gard.   What other
Would you expect? You are strangely trouble-
   some.
Let some o' th' guard be ready there!

404

Enter the *Guard.*

Cran. For me? 95
Must I go like a traitor thither?

Gard. Receive him
And see him safe i' th' Tower.

Cran. Stay, good my lords.
I have a little yet to say. Look there, my lords.
[*Shows ring.*]
By virtue of that ring I take my cause
Out of the gripes of cruel men and give it 100
To a most noble judge, the King my master.

Chan. This is the King's ring.

Sur. 'Tis no counterfeit.

Suf. 'Tis the right ring, by heav'n! I told
ye all,
When we first put this dangerous stone a-rolling,
'Twould fall upon ourselves.

Nor. Do you think, my lords, 105
The King will suffer but the little finger
Of this man to be vex'd?

Chan. 'Tis now too certain.
How much more is his life in value with him!
Would I were fairly out on't!

Crom. My mind gave me,
In seeking tales and informations 110
Against this man — whose honesty the devil
And his disciples only envy at —
Ye blew the fire that burns ye. Now have at ye!

Enter *King,* frowning on them; *takes his seat.*

Gard. Dread sovereign, how much are we
bound to heaven 114
In daily thanks, that gave us such a prince,
Not only good and wise but most religious;
One that in all obedience makes the Church
The chief aim of his honour, and, to strengthen
That holy duty, out of dear respect,
His royal self in judgment comes to hear 120
The cause betwixt her and this great offender.

King. You were ever good at sudden com-
mendations,
Bishop of Winchester. But know I come not
To hear such flattery now, and in my presence.
They are too thin and bare to hide offences.
To me you cannot reach you play the spaniel
And think with wagging of your tongue to
win me.
But whatsoe'er thou tak'st me for, I'm sure
Thou hast a cruel nature and a bloody.
[*To Cranmer*] Good man, sit down. Now let me
see the proudest, 130
He that dares most, but wag his finger at thee.
By all that's holy, he had better starve
Than but once think this place becomes thee
not.

Sur. May it please your Grace —

King. No, sir, it does not please me.
I had thought I had had men of some under-
standing 135
And wisdom of my Council; but I find none.
Was it discretion, lords, to let this man,
This good man (few of you deserve that title),
This honest man, wait like a lousy footboy 139
At chamber door? and one as great as you are?
Why, what a shame was this! Did my com-
mission
Bid ye so far forget yourselves? I gave ye
Power as he was a Councillor to try him,
Not as a groom. There's some of ye, I see,
More out of malice than integrity, 145
Would try him to the utmost, had ye mean;
Which ye shall never have while I live.

Chan. Thus far,
My most dread sovereign, may it like your
Grace
To let my tongue excuse all. What was pur-
pos'd
Concerning his imprisonment was rather 150
(If there be faith in men) meant for his trial
And fair purgation to the world than malice,
I'm sure, in me.

King. Well, well, my lords, respect him.
Take him, and use him well; he's worthy of it.
I will say thus much for him — if a prince 155
May be beholding to a subject, I
Am for his love and service so to him.
Make me no more ado, but all embrace him.
Be friends for shame, my lords! My Lord of
Canterbury, 159
I have a suit which you must not deny me.
That is, a fair young maid that yet wants
baptism,
You must be godfather and answer for her.

Cran. The greatest monarch now alive may
glory
In such an honour. How may I deserve it
That am a poor and humble subject to you?

King. Come, come, my lord, you'd spare
your spoons! You shall have 166
Two noble partners with you, the old Duchess
of Norfolk
And Lady Marquess Dorset. Will these please
you?
Once more, my Lord of Winchester, I charge
you
Embrace and love this man.

Gard. With a true heart 170
And brother's love I do it.

Cran. And let heaven
Witness how dear I hold this confirmation.

King. Good man, those joyful tears show
thy true heart.
The common voice I see is verified
Of thee, which says thus: 'Do my Lord of
Canterbury   175
A shrewd turn, and he's your friend for ever.'
Come, lords, we trifle time away. I long
To have this young one made a Christian.
As I have made ye one, lords, one remain;
So I grow stronger, you more honour gain. 180
Exeunt.

Scene [IV. *The Palace Yard.*]

Noise and tumult within. Enter *Porter*
and his *Man.*

Port. You'll leave your noise anon, ye rascals! Do you take the court for Parish Garden?
Ye rude slaves, leave your gaping!
(*Within*) Good Master Porter, I belong to
th' larder.   5
Port. Belong to th' gallows and be hang'd,
ye rogue! Is this a place to roar in? Fetch me
a dozen crabtree staves, and strong ones. These
are but switches to 'em. I'll scratch your heads.
You must be seeing christenings! Do you look
for ale and cakes here, you rude rascals?   11
Man. Pray, sir, be patient! 'Tis as much
impossible,
Unless we sweep 'em from the door with
cannons,
To scatter 'em as 'tis to make 'em sleep
On May Day morning, which will never be. 15
We may as well push against Powl's as stir 'em.
Port. How got they in, and be hang'd?
Man. Alas, I know not. How gets the tide
in?
As much as one sound cudgel of four foot 19
(You see the poor remainder) could distribute,
I made no spare, sir.
Port.   You did nothing, sir.
Man. I am not Samson, nor Sir Guy, nor
Colebrand,
To mow 'em down before me; but if I spar'd
any
That had a head to hit, either young or old,
He or she, cuckold or cuckold-maker,   25
Let me ne'er hope to see a chine again;
And that I would not for a cow, God save her!
(*Within*) Do you hear, Master Porter?
Port. I shall be with you presently, good
Master Puppy!
Keep the door close, sirrah.   30
Man. What would you have me do?

Port. What should you do but knock 'em
down by th' dozens? Is this Moorfields to
muster in? Or have we some strange Indian
with the great tool come to court, the women so
besiege us? Bless me, what a fry of fornication
is at door! On my Christian conscience, this
one christening will beget a thousand; here will
be father, godfather, and all together.   39
Man. The spoons will be the bigger, sir.
There is a fellow somewhat near the door; he
should be a brazier by his face, for, o' my conscience, twenty of the dogdays now reign in's
nose. All that stand about him are under the
Line; they need no other penance. That fire-
drake did I hit three times on the head, and
three times was his nose discharged against me.
He stands there like a mortar-piece to blow us.
There was a haberdasher's wife of small wit
near him, that rail'd upon me till her pink'd
porringer fell off her head, for kindling such a
combustion in the state. I miss'd the meteor
once and hit that woman, who cried out
'Clubs!' when I might see from far some forty
truncheoners draw to her succour, which were
the hope o' th' Strond, where she was quar-
tered. They fell on; I made good my place.
At length they came to th' broomstaff to me.
I defied 'em still; when suddenly a file of boys
behind 'em, loose shot, deliver'd such a show'r
of pebbles that I was fain to draw mine honour
in and let 'em win the work. The devil was
amongst 'em, I think surely.   62
Port. These are the youths that thunder at a
playhouse and fight for bitten apples; that no
audience but the tribulation of Tower Hill or
the limbs of Limehouse, their dear brothers, are
able to endure. I have some of 'em in Limbo
Patrum, and there they are like to dance these
three days, besides the running banquet of two
beadles that is to come.   70

Enter *Lord Chamberlain.*

Cham. Mercy o' me, what a multitude are
here!
They grow still too; from all parts they are
coming
As if we kept a fair here! Where are these
porters,
These lazy knaves? Y'have made a fine hand,
fellows!
There's a trim rabble let in. Are all these 75
Your faithful friends o' th' suburbs? We shall
have
Great store of room, no doubt, left for the ladies
When they pass back from the christening.

406

Port.   An't please your Honour,
We are but men; and what so many may do,
Not being torn a-pieces, we have done.   80
An army cannot rule 'em.

Cham.   As I live,
If the King blame me for't, I'll lay ye all
By th' heels, and suddenly, and on your heads
Clap round fines for neglect. Y'are lazy knaves,
And here ye lie baiting of bombards when   85
Ye should do service. Hark! the trumpets
    sound!
Th'are come already from the christening.
Go break among the press and find a way out
To let the troop pass fairly, or I'll find
A Marshalsea shall hold ye play these two
    months.   90

Port. Make way there for the Princess!

Man.   You great fellow,
Stand close up, or I'll make your head ache!

Port. You i' th' chamblet,
Get up o' th' rail. I'll peck you o'er the pales
    else!   *Exeunt.*

Scene V. [*The Palace.*]

Enter *Trumpets*, sounding; then two *Aldermen,*
Lord Mayor, Garter, Cranmer, Duke of Norfolk
with his Marshal's staff, *Duke of Suffolk,* two
Noblemen bearing great standing bowls for the
christening gifts; then four *Noblemen* bearing a
canopy, under which the *Duchess of Norfolk,*
godmother, bearing the child richly habited in a
mantle, &c., train borne by a *Lady;* then follows the *Marchioness Dorset,* the other godmother, and *Ladies.* The troop pass once about
the stage, and *Garter* speaks.

Gart. Heaven, from thy endless goodness
send prosperous life, long, and ever happy, to
the high and mighty Princess of England,
Elizabeth!

Flourish. Enter *King* and *Guard.*

Cran. [*kneels*] And to your royal Grace and
    the good Queen!   5
My noble partners and myself thus pray
All comfort, joy, in this most gracious lady,
Heaven ever laid up to make parents happy,
May hourly fall upon ye!

King. Thank you, good Lord Archbishop:
What is her name?

Cran.   Elizabeth.

King.   Stand up, lord.   10
    [*Cranmer rises. The King kisses the child.*]

With this kiss take my blessing. God protect
    thee!
Into whose hand I give thy life.

Cran.   Amen.

King. My noble gossips, y'have been too
    prodigal.
I thank ye heartily. So shall this lady,
When she has so much English.

Cran.   Let me speak, sir,   15
For heaven now bids me; and the words I utter
Let none think flattery, for they'll find 'em
    truth.
This royal infant — heaven still move about
    her! —
Though in her cradle, yet now promises   19
Upon this land a thousand thousand blessings,
Which time shall bring to ripeness. She shall be
(But few now living can behold that goodness)
A pattern to all princes living with her
And all that shall succeed. Saba was never
More covetous of wisdom and fair virtue   25
Than this pure soul shall be. All princely graces
That mould up such a mighty piece as this is,
With all the virtues that attend the good,
Shall still be doubled on her. Truth shall nurse
    her,   29
Holy and heavenly thoughts still counsel her.
She shall be lov'd and fear'd. Her own shall
    bless her;
Her foes shake like a field of beaten corn
And hang their heads with sorrow. Good grows
    with her.
In her days every man shall eat in safety   34
Under his own vine what he plants, and sing
The merry songs of peace to all his neighbours.
God shall be truly known, and those about her
From her shall read the perfect ways of honour
And by those claim their greatness, not by
    blood.
Nor shall this peace sleep with her; but as
    when   40
The bird of wonder dies, the maiden phœnix,
Her ashes new create another heir
As great in admiration as herself,
So shall she leave her blessedness to one
(When heaven shall call her from this cloud of
    darkness)   45
Who from the sacred ashes of her honour
Shall starlike rise, as great in fame as she was,
And so stand fix'd. Peace, plenty, love, truth,
    terror,
That were the servants to this chosen infant,
Shall then be his and like a vine grow to him.
Wherever the bright sun of heaven shall shine,
His honour and the greatness of his name

Shall be, and make new nations. He shall
flourish
And like a mountain cedar reach his branches
To all the plains about him. Our children's
children   55
Shall see this, and bless heaven.
   King.   Thou speakest wonders.
   Cran. She shall be, to the happiness of
England,
An aged princess; many days shall see her,
And yet no day without a deed to crown it.
Would I had known no more! But she must
die —   60
She must, the saints must have her — yet a
virgin,
A most unspotted lily, shall she pass
To th' ground, and all the world shall mourn
her.
   King. O Lord Archbishop,   64
Thou hast made me now a man! Never before
This happy child did I get anything.
This oracle of comfort has so pleas'd me
That when I am in heaven I shall desire
To see what this child does, and praise my
Maker.   69
I thank ye all. To you, my good Lord Mayor,
And your good brethren I am much beholding.

I have receiv'd much honour by your presence,
And ye shall find me thankful. Lead the way,
lords.
Ye must all see the Queen, and she must thank
ye;   74
She will be sick else. This day no man think
'Has business at his house; for all shall stay.
This little one shall make it holiday.
                         Exeunt.

THE EPILOGUE.

'Tis ten to one this play can never please
All that are here. Some come to take their
ease
And sleep an act or two; but those, we fear,
W'have frighted with our trumpets; so, 'tis
clear,   4
They'll say 'tis naught; others, to hear the city
Abus'd extremely, and to cry 'That's witty!'
Which we have not done neither; that, I fear,
All the expected good w'are like to hear
For this play at this time, is only in
The merciful construction of good women; 10
For such a one we show'd 'em. If they smile
And say 'twill do, I know within a while
All the best men are ours; for 'tis ill hap,
If they hold when their ladies bid 'em clap.

Poems

VENUS AND ADONIS AND LUCRECE

VENUS AND ADONIS was entered in the Stationers' Register by Richard Field on April 18, 1593, and the First Quarto was printed by him in the same year. This is the authority for the text. Nine other editions appeared before Shakespeare's death in 1616 and several others came out during the first half of the seventeenth century.

The poem was much admired. Meres who, in his *Palladis Tamia* (1598), praises Shakespeare for his comedies and tragedies (see p. 33, above), declares that 'the sweete wittie soule of *Ouid* liues in mellifluous & hony-tongued *Shakespeare*, witness his *Venus and Adonis*, his *Lucrece*, his sugred Sonnets among his priuate friends.' John Weever celebrates it (along with *Lucrece*, *Romeo and Juliet*, and '*Richard*') in an address to 'honie-tong'd Shakespeare' in his *Epigrammes* (1599). Gabriel Harvey testifies that 'the younger sort takes much delight in Shakespeares Venus, & Adonis: but his Lucrece, & his tragedie of Hamlet ... haue it in them, to please the wiser sort' (see p. 1145, above). 'I'le worshipp sweet Mr. Shakspeare,' says Gullio in the Cambridge play *The Return from Parnassus*, 'and to honoure him will lay his Venus and Adonis under my pillowe' (Part I: *ca.* 1599).

When the poem was written we do not know. In the dedication Shakespeare calls it 'the first heir of my invention,' but these words by no means imply that it was the first thing he had ever written. Before 1593 he had certainly done a good deal of dramatic composition (see p. 746). None of his work, however, had been published when VENUS AND ADONIS appeared. That the poem abounds in rural imagery is no proof that he wrote it before he left Stratford, for the scene is laid in the woods and fields. Probably it was written not long before the date of publication, perhaps in 1592.

Shakespeare undoubtedly read the story of Adonis at school, for Ovid's *Metamorphoses*, which tells it (x, 520–559, 705–739), was in every schoolboy's hand (cf. *Titus Andronicus*, iv, 1, 41–42). It is not necessary to appeal to Golding's English translation of the *Metamorphoses* (1567). The Latin motto in the title page of VENUS AND ADONIS comes from Ovid's *Amores* (i, 15, 35–36). The reluctance of Adonis is taken from Ovid's story of Hermaphroditus (iv, 316 ff.) and from that of Narcissus and Echo (iii, 356 ff.). In this feature perhaps Shakespeare was also influenced by Lodge's *Scilla's Metamorphosis* (1589), which has the same form of stanza as VENUS AND ADONIS. This stanza, however, was common at the time. Shakespeare uses it in *Love's Labour's Lost*, i, 1, 150–162. The story of Narcissus is mentioned in LUCRECE, 265–266.

The Quarto of LUCRECE, as the title page styles the poem, though the title heading is THE RAPE OF LUCRECE, came out in 1594. It had been registered on May 9 of that year. Four other editions appeared before 1616. The text of the Quarto is authoritative.

In the dedication to VENUS AND ADONIS, Shakespeare had 'vowed to take advantage of all idle hours' for 'some graver labour.' LUCRECE was the fulfilment of his pledge. It was probably written in 1593 or 1594. That it was regarded by contemporaries as indeed a graver and more solid piece of work is shown by Harvey's note (quoted above).

The seven-line stanza (known as 'rhyme royal') had long been a favourite form with English poets. Chaucer had used it in four of his *Canterbury Tales* and with extraordinary skill and variety in his *Troilus*, with which Shakespeare was familiar. Lydgate had adopted it for his *Falls of Princes*, once a highly esteemed performance. Sixteenth-century critics regarded this stanza as peculiarly fit 'for grave discourses.' Spenser adopted it for *The Ruines of Time* (1590) and Daniel for *The Complaint of Rosamond* (1592). There are some echoes of Daniel's phraseology in Shakespeare's poem, and Lucrece's study of the painting which figures the Trojan war (1366 ff.) may have been suggested by a similar incident in the *Rosamond*. In describing the picture Shakespeare doubtless had in mind the paintings on the walls of Dido's temple (Æneid, ii, 453 ff.).

The sources of LUCRECE were naturally Livy (i, 57–60) and Ovid (*Fasti*, ii, 721–852). Painter, in *The Palace of Pleasure* (1566) had published a rather close translation of Livy's story, but Shakespeare owes nothing to Painter. He could read Livy for himself. His version, indeed, serves to correct a mistake in Painter, whose 'from whence he [Brutus] should conceive that determination' is a blundering rendition of 'unde novum in Bruti pectore ingenium.' Shakespeare's words about Brutus's assumed idiocy (1807–1820) show that he understood the passage. It is possible that he had read the story in Belleforest's *Histoires Tragiques*, or in Bandello, whom Belleforest translated, but Livy (i, 56) and Ovid (ii, 717) gave him all information about Brutus's stratagem that he needed. Livy's description of Brutus as 'ludibrium verius quam comes' to the Tarquins is expanded in verses 1811–1813 of LUCRECE.

Livy's 'addit ad metum dedecus' appears in verse 516 as 'To kill thine honour with thy live's decay.' His 'Nec ulla deinde inpudica Lucretiae exemplo vivet' is rendered in verses 1714–1715 by

> 'No, no!' quoth she. 'No dame hereafter living
> By my excuse shall claim excuse's giving.'

Cf. also with verses 1619–1621 Livy's 'Vestigia viri alieni, Conlatine, in lecto sunt tuo.' Many suggestions are also taken from Ovid. The first stanza reflects one of his elegiac couplets (761–762):

> Interea iuvenis furiales regius ignis
> Concipit et caeco raptus amore furit.

Brutus's oath 'by chaste Lucrece' soul' (1839) is Ovid's 'per tuos manes' (842). His 'Ter conata loqui, ter destitit' (823) appears in verses 1604–1605. The metaphor of the wolf and the lamb (677) comes from Ovid (799–800). The long and eloquent passage describing Tarquin's revulsion of feeling (689 ff.) may have been suggested by Ovid (811–812):

> Quid, victor, gaudes? Haec te victoria perdet.
> Heu quanto regnis nox stetit una tuis!

It is altogether probable that Shakespeare knew Chaucer's *Legend of Good Women*, in which the story of Lucretia is told in strict accordance with Ovid's *Fasti*; but LUCRECE owes nothing to Chaucer.

VENUS AND ADONIS

Vilia miretur vulgus: mihi flavus Apollo
Pocula Castalia plena ministret aqua.

TO THE

RIGHT HONOURABLE HENRY WRIOTHESLEY,

EARL OF SOUTHAMPTON, AND BARON OF TITCHFIELD.

RIGHT HONOURABLE,

  I know not how I shall offend in dedicating
my unpolish'd lines to your Lordship, nor how the
world will censure me for choosing so strong a prop
to support so weak a burthen; only, if your Honour seem but pleased, I account myself highly
praised, and vow to take advantage of all idle
hours till I have honoured you with some graver
labour. But if the first heir of my invention prove
deformed, I shall be sorry it had so noble a godfather, and never after ear so barren a land, for
fear it yield me still so bad a harvest. I leave it to
your honourable survey, and your Honour to your
heart's content; which I wish may always answer
your own wish and the world's hopeful expectation.

Your Honour's in all duty,

WILLIAM SHAKESPEARE.

Even as the sun with purple-colour'd face
Had ta'en his last leave of the weeping morn,
Rose-cheek'd Adonis hied him to the chase.
Hunting he lov'd, but love he laugh'd to scorn.
 Sick-thoughted Venus makes amain unto him
 And like a bold-fac'd suitor gins to woo him.

'Thrice fairer than myself,' thus she began,
'The field's chief flower, sweet above compare,
Stain to all nymphs, more lovely than a man,
More white and red than doves or roses are, 10
 Nature that made thee, with herself at strife,
 Saith that the world hath ending with thy life.

'Vouchsafe, thou wonder, to alight thy steed
And rein his proud head to the saddlebow.
If thou wilt deign this favour, for thy meed 15
A thousand honey secrets shalt thou know.
 Here come and sit, where never serpent hisses,
 And being set, I'll smother thee with kisses,

'And yet not cloy thy lips with loath'd satiety,
But rather famish them amid their plenty, 20

Making them red and pale with fresh variety —
Ten kisses short as one, one long as twenty.
 A summer's day will seem an hour but short,
 Being wasted in such time-beguiling sport.'

With this she seizeth on his sweating palm, 25
The precedent of pith and livelihood,
And, trembling in her passion, calls it balm,
Earth's sovereign salve to do a goddess good.
 Being so enrag'd, desire doth lend her force
 Courageously to pluck him from his horse. 30

Over one arm the lusty courser's rein,
Under her other was the tender boy,
Who blush'd and pouted in a dull disdain,
With leaden appetite, unapt to toy;
 She red and hot as coals of glowing fire, 35
 He red for shame, but frosty in desire.

The studded bridle on a ragged bough
Nimbly she fastens. O, how quick is love!
The steed is stalled up, and even now
To tie the rider she begins to prove. 40
 Backward she push'd him, as she would be
  thrust,
 And govern'd him in strength, though not in
  lust.

So soon was she along as he was down,
Each leaning on their elbows and their hips.
Now doth she stroke his cheek, now doth he
 frown   45
And gins to chide; but soon she stops his lips
 And kissing speaks, with lustful language
  broken:
 'If thou wilt chide, thy lips shall never open.'

He burns with bashful shame; she with hei
 tears
Doth quench the maiden burning of his cheeks.
Then with her windy sighs and golden hairs 51
To fan and blow them dry again she seeks.
 He saith she is immodest, blames her miss;
 What follows more she murthers with a kiss.

Even as an empty eagle, sharp by fast, 55
Tires with her beak on feathers, flesh, and bone,
Shaking her wings, devouring all in haste,
Till either gorge be stuff'd or prey be gone —

413

Even so she kiss'd his brow, his cheek, his
  chin,
And where she ends she doth anew begin. 60

Forc'd to content, but never to obey,
Panting he lies and breatheth in her face.
She feedeth on the steam as on a prey
And calls it heavenly moisture, air of grace;
  Wishing her cheeks were gardens full of
    flowers, 65
  So they were dew'd with such distilling
    showers.

Look how a bird lies tangled in a net,
So fast'ned in her arms Adonis lies.
Pure shame and aw'd resistance made him fret,
Which bred more beauty in his angry eyes. 70
  Rain added to a river that is rank
  Perforce will force it overflow the bank.

Still she entreats, and prettily entreats,
For to a pretty ear she tunes her tale.
Still is he sullen, still he low'rs and frets, 75
'Twixt crimson shame and anger ashy-pale.
  Being red, she loves him best; and being
    white,
  Her best is better'd with a more delight.

Look how he can, she cannot choose but love;
And by her fair immortal hand she swears 80
From his soft bosom never to remove
Till he take truce with her contending tears,
  Which long have rain'd, making her cheeks
    all wet;
  And one sweet kiss shall pay this comptless
    debt.

Upon this promise did he raise his chin, 85
Like a divedapper peering through a wave,
Who, being look'd on, ducks as quickly in.
So offers he to give what she did crave;
  But when her lips were ready for his pay,
  He winks and turns his lips another way. 90

Never did passenger in summer's heat
More thirst for drink than she for this good turn.
Her help she sees, but help she cannot get:
She bathes in water, yet her fire must burn.
  'O, pity,' gan she cry, 'flint-hearted boy! 95
  'Tis but a kiss I beg. Why art thou coy?

'I have been wooed, as I entreat thee now,
Even by the stern and direful god of war,
Whose sinewy neck in battle ne'er did bow,
Who conquers where he comes in every jar; 100

Yet hath he been my captive and my slave
And begg'd for that which thou unask'd
  shalt have.

'Over my altars hath he hung his lance,
His batt'red shield, his uncontrolled crest,
And for my sake hath learn'd to sport and
  dance, 105
To toy, to wanton, dally, smile, and jest,
  Scorning his churlish drum and ensign red,
  Making my arms his field, his tent my bed.

'Thus he that overrul'd I overswayed,
Leading him prisoner in a red-rose chain. 110
Strong-temper'd steel his stronger strength
  obeyed;
Yet was he servile to my coy disdain.
  O, be not proud, nor brag not of thy might,
  For mast'ring her that foil'd the god of fight!

'Touch but my lips with those fair lips of thine—
Though mine be not so fair, yet are they red —
The kiss shall be thine own as well as mine.
What see'st thou in the ground? Hold up thy
  head.
  Look in mine eyeballs; there thy beauty lies.
  Then why not lips on lips, since eyes in eyes?

'Art thou asham'd to kiss? Then wink again,
And I will wink. So shall the day seem night.
Love keeps his revels where there are but twain.
Be bold to play; our sport is not in sight.
  These blue-vein'd violets whereon we lean 125
  Never can blab, nor know not what we mean.

'The tender spring upon thy tempting lip
Shows thee unripe; yet mayst thou well be
  tasted.
Make use of time, let not advantage slip:
Beauty within itself should not be wasted. 130
  Fair flowers that are not gath'red in their
    prime
  Rot and consume themselves in little time.

'Were I hard-favour'd, foul, or wrinkled old,
Ill-nurtur'd, crooked, churlish, harsh in voice,
O'erworn, despised, rheumatic, and cold, 135
Thick-sighted, barren, lean and lacking juice,
  Then mightst thou pause, for then I were not
    for thee;
  But having no defects, why dost abhor me?

'Thou canst not see one wrinkle in my brow;
Mine eyes are grey and bright and quick in
  turning; 140

414

My beauty as the spring doth yearly grow,
My flesh is soft and plump, my marrow burn-
ing;
  My smooth moist hand, were it with thy
    hand felt,
  Would in thy palm dissolve or seem to melt.

'Bid me discourse, I will enchant thine ear, 145
Or, like a fairy, trip upon the green,
Or, like a nymph, with long dishevelled hair,
Dance on the sands, and yet no footing seen.
  Love is a spirit all compact of fire, 149
  Not gross to sink, but light, and will aspire.

'Witness this primrose bank whereon I lie;
These forceless flowers like sturdy trees sup-
  port me.
Two strengthless doves will draw me through
  the sky
From morn till night, even where I list to sport
  me.
  Is love so light, sweet boy, and may it be 155
  That thou should think it heavy unto thee?

'Is thine own heart to thine own face affected?
Can thy right hand seize love upon thy left?
Then woo thyself, be of thyself rejected:
Steal thine own freedom, and complain on
  theft. 160
  Narcissus so himself himself forsook,
  And died to kiss his shadow in the brook.

'Torches are made to light, jewels to wear,
Dainties to taste, fresh beauty for the use,
Herbs for their smell, and sappy plants to bear.
Things growing to themselves are growth's
  abuse. 166
  Seeds spring from seeds, and beauty breed-
    eth beauty.
  Thou wast begot; to get it is thy duty.

'Upon the earth's increase why shouldst thou
  feed
Unless the earth with thy increase be fed? 170
By law of nature thou art bound to breed,
That thine may live when thou thyself art dead;
  And so, in spite of death, thou dost survive,
  In that thy likeness still is left alive.'

By this, the lovesick queen began to sweat, 175
For where they lay the shadow had forsook
  them,
And Titan, tired in the midday heat,
With burning eye did hotly overlook them,
  Wishing Adonis had his team to guide,
  So he were like him, and by Venus' side. 180

And now Adonis, with a lazy sprite,
And with a heavy, dark, disliking eye,
His low'ring brows o'erwhelming his fair sight,
Like misty vapours when they blot the sky,
  Souring his cheeks, cries, 'Fie, no more of
    love! 185
  The sun doth burn my face. I must remove.'

'Ay me!' quoth Venus, 'young, and so unkind?
What bare excuses mak'st thou to be gone!
I'll sigh celestial breath, whose gentle wind
Shall cool the heat of this descending sun. 190
  I'll make a shadow for thee of my hairs.
  If they burn too, I'll quench them with my
    tears.

'The sun that shines from heaven shines but
  warm;
And, lo, I lie between that sun and thee. 194
The heat I have from thence doth little harm;
Thine eye darts forth the fire that burneth me,
  And were I not immortal, life were done
  Between this heavenly and earthly sun.

'Art thou obdurate, flinty, hard as steel?
Nay, more than flint, for stone at rain re-
  lenteth. 200
Art thou a woman's son, and canst not feel
What 'tis to love? how want of love tor-
  menteth?
  O, had thy mother borne so hard a mind,
  She had not brought forth thee, but died
    unkind!

'What am I that thou shouldst contemn me
  this? 205
Or what great danger dwells upon my suit?
What were thy lips the worse for one poor kiss?
Speak, fair! but speak fair words, or else be
  mute.
  Give me one kiss, I'll give it thee again,
  And one for int'rest, if thou wilt have twain.

'Fie, liveless picture, cold and senseless stone,
Well-painted idol, image dull and dead,
Statue contenting but the eye alone,
Thing like a man, but of no woman bred!
  Thou art no man, though of a man's com-
    plexion, 215
  For men will kiss even by their own direction.'

This said, impatience chokes her pleading
  tongue,
And swelling passion doth provoke a pause;
Red cheeks and fiery eyes blaze forth her wrong;
Being judge in love, she cannot right her cause.

And now she weeps, and now she fain would
  speak,   221
And now her sobs do her intendments break.

Sometime she shakes her head, and then his
  hand;
Now gazeth she on him, now on the ground;
Sometime her arms infold him like a band —
She would, he will not in her arms be bound;
  And when from thence he struggles to be gone,
  She locks her lily fingers one in one.

'Fondling,' she saith, 'since I have hemm'd thee
  here
Within the circuit of this ivory pale,   230
I'll be a park, and thou shalt be my deer;
Feed where thou wilt, on mountain or in dale;
  Graze on my lips; and if those hills be dry,
  Stray lower, where the pleasant fountains lie.

'Within this limit is relief enough,   235
Sweet bottom-grass, and high delightful plain,
Round rising hillocks, brakes obscure and rough,
To shelter thee from tempest and from rain.
  Then be my deer, since I am such a park.
  No dog shall rouse thee, though a thousand
    bark.'   240

At this Adonis smiles as in disdain,
That in each cheek appears a pretty dimple.
Love made those hollows, if himself were slain,
He might be buried in a tomb so simple,
  Foreknowing well, if there he came to lie, 245
  Why, there Love liv'd, and there he could
    not die.

These lovely caves, these round enchanting pits,
Open'd their mouths to swallow Venus' liking.
Being mad before, how doth she now for wits?
Struck dead at first, what needs a second strik-
  ing?   250
  Poor queen of love, in thine own law forlorn,
  To love a cheek that smiles at thee in scorn!

Now which way shall she turn? what shall she
  say?
Her words are done, her woes the more in-
  creasing;
The time is spent, her object will away,   255
And from her twining arms doth urge releasing.
  'Pity!' she cries, 'some favour, some re-
    morse!'
  Away he springs and hasteth to his horse.

But, lo, from forth a copse that neighbours by
A breeding jennet, lusty, young, and proud, 260

Adonis' trampling courser doth espy,
And forth she rushes, snorts, and neighs aloud.
  The strong-neck'd steed, being tied unto a tree,
  Breaketh his rein, and to her straight goes he.

Imperiously he leaps, he neighs, he bounds, 265
And now his woven girths he breaks asunder;
The bearing earth with his hard hoof he wounds,
Whose hollow womb resounds like heaven's
  thunder;
  The iron bit he crusheth 'tween his teeth,
  Controlling what he was controlled with. 270

His ears up-prick'd; his braided hanging mane
Upon his compass'd crest now stand on end;
His nostrils drink the air, and forth again,
As from a furnace, vapours doth he send;
  His eye, which scornfully glisters like fire, 275
  Shows his hot courage and his high desire.

Sometime he trots, as if he told the steps,
With gentle majesty and modest pride;
Anon he rears upright, curvets, and leaps,
As who should say, 'Lo, thus my strength is
  tried,   280
  And this I do to captivate the eye
  Of the fair breeder that is standing by.'

What recketh he his rider's angry stir,
His flattering 'Holla' or his 'Stand, I say'?
What cares he now for curb or pricking spur?
For rich caparisons or trappings gay?   286
  He sees his love, and nothing else he sees,
  For nothing else with his proud sight agrees.

Look, when a painter would surpass the life
In limning out a well-proportioned steed, 290
His art with nature's workmanship at strife,
As if the dead the living should exceed —
  So did this horse excel a common one
  In shape, in courage, colour, pace, and bone.

Round-hoof'd, short-jointed, fetlocks shag and
  long,   295
Broad breast, full eye, small head, and nostril
  wide,
High crest, short ears, straight legs and passing
  strong,
Thin mane, thick tail, broad buttock, tender
  hide:
  Look, what a horse should have he did not
    lack,
  Save a proud rider on so proud a back. 300

Sometime he scuds far off, and there he stares;
Anon he starts at stirring of a feather;

To bid the wind a base he now prepares,
And whe'r he run or fly they know not whether,
  For through his mane and tail the high wind
    sings, 305
  Fanning the hairs, who wave like feath'red
    wings.

He looks upon his love and neighs unto her;
She answers him, as if she knew his mind.
Being proud, as females are, to see him woo her,
She puts on outward strangeness, seems un-
    kind, 310
  Spurns at his love and scorns the heat he feels,
  Beating his kind embracements with her heels.

Then, like a melancholy malcontent,
He vails his tail, that, like a falling plume,
Cool shadow to his melting buttock lent; 315
He stamps, and bites the poor flies in his fume.
  His love, perceiving how he is enrag'd,
  Grew kinder, and his fury was assuag'd.

His testy master goeth about to take him,
When, lo, the unback'd breeder, full of fear, 320
Jealous of catching, swiftly doth forsake him,
With her the horse, and left Adonis there.
  As they were mad, unto the wood they hie
    them,
  Outstripping crows that strive to overfly
    them.

All swol'n with chafing, down Adonis sits, 325
Banning his boist'rous and unruly beast;
And now the happy season once more fits
That lovesick Love by pleading may be blest;
  For lovers say the heart hath treble wrong
  When it is barr'd the aidance of the tongue.

An oven that is stopp'd, or river stay'd, 331
Burneth more hotly, swelleth with more rage;
So of concealed sorrow may be said:
Free vent of words love's fire doth assuage;
  But when the heart's attorney once is mute,
  The client breaks, as desperate in his suit.

He sees her coming and begins to glow,
Even as a dying coal revives with wind,
And with his bonnet hides his angry brow,
Looks on the dull earth with disturbed mind,
  Taking no notice that she is so nigh, 341
  For all askance he holds her in his eye.

O, what a sight it was, wistly to view
How she came stealing to the wayward boy!
To note the fighting conflict of her hue, 345
How white and red each other did destroy!

But now her cheek was pale, and by-and-by
It flash'd forth fire, as lightning from the sky.

Now was she just before him as he sat,
And like a lowly lover down she kneels; 350
With one fair hand she heaveth up his hat,
Her other tender hand his fair cheek feels.
  His tend'rer cheek receives her soft hand's
    print
  As apt as new-fall'n snow takes any dint.

O, what a war of looks was then between them,
Her eyes petitioners to his eyes suing! 356
His eyes saw her eyes as they had not seen
    them;
Her eyes wooed still, his eyes disdain'd the
    wooing;
  And all this dumb play had his acts made
    plain
  With tears which chorus-like her eyes did rain.

Full gently now she takes him by the hand,
A lily prison'd in a jail of snow,
Or ivory in an alablaster band —
So white a friend engirts so white a foe.
  This beauteous combat, wilful and unwilling,
  Showed like two silver doves that sit a-billing.

Once more the engine of her thoughts began:
'O fairest mover on this mortal round,
Would thou wert as I am, and I a man,
My heart all whole as thine, thy heart my
    wound! 370
  For one sweet look thy help I would assure
    thee,
  Though nothing but my body's bane would
    cure thee.'

'Give me my hand!' saith he. 'Why dost thou
    feel it?'
'Give me my heart,' saith she, 'and thou shalt
    have it.
O, give it me, lest thy hard heart do steel it,
And being steel'd, soft sighs can never grave it.
  Then love's deep groans I never shall regard,
  Because Adonis' heart hath made mine hard.'

'For shame!' he cries. 'Let go, and let me go!
My day's delight is past, my horse is gone, 380
And 'tis your fault I am bereft him so.
I pray you hence, and leave me here alone;
  For all my mind, my thought, my busy care
  Is how to get my palfrey from the mare.'

Thus she replies: 'Thy palfrey, as he should,
Welcomes the warm approach of sweet desire.

Affection is a coal that must be cool'd;
Else, suffer'd, it will set the heart on fire.
  The sea hath bounds, but deep desire hath
    none;
  Therefore no marvel though thy horse be gone.

'How like a jade he stood, tied to the tree,
Servilely master'd with a leathern rein!
But when he saw his love, his youth's fair fee,
He held such petty bondage in disdain,
  Throwing the base thong from his bending
    crest,   395
  Enfranchising his mouth, his back, his breast.

'Who sees his true-love in her naked bed,
Teaching the sheets a whiter hue than white,
But, when his glutton eye so full hath fed,
His other agents aim at like delight?   400
  Who is so faint that dares not be so bold
  To touch the fire, the weather being cold?

'Let me excuse thy courser, gentle boy;
And learn of him, I heartily beseech thee,
To take advantage on presented joy.   405
Though I were dumb, yet his proceedings teach
    thee.
  O, learn to love! The lesson is but plain,
  And once made perfect, never lost again.'

'I know not love,' quoth he, 'nor will not know
    it,
Unless it be a boar, and then I chase it.   410
'Tis much to borrow, and I will not owe it.
My love to love is love but to disgrace it;
  For I have heard it is a life in death,
  That laughs, and weeps, and all but with a
    breath.

'Who wears a garment shapeless and unfin-
    ish'd?   415
Who plucks the bud before one leaf put forth?
If springing things be any jot diminish'd,
They wither in their prime, prove nothing
    worth.
  The colt that's back'd and burthen'd being
    young   419
  Loseth his pride and never waxeth strong.

'You hurt my hand with wringing. Let us part,
And leave this idle theme, this bootless chat.
Remove your siege from my unyielding heart;
To love's alarms it will not ope the gate.
  Dismiss your vows, your feigned tears, your
    flatt'ry;   425
  For where a heart is hard they make no
    batt'ry.'

'What! canst thou talk?' quoth she. 'Hast
    thou a tongue?
O, would thou hadst not, or I had no hearing!
Thy mermaid's voice hath done me double
    wrong;   429
I had my load before, now press'd with bearing:
  Melodious discord, heavenly tune harsh
    sounding,
  Ear's deep-sweet music, and heart's deep-
    sore wounding.

'Had I no eyes but ears, my ears would love
That inward beauty and invisible;   434
Or were I deaf, thy outward parts would move
Each part in me that were but sensible.
  Though neither eyes nor ears, to hear nor
    see,
  Yet should I be in love by touching thee.

'Say that the sense of feeling were bereft me,
And that I could not see, nor hear, nor touch,
And nothing but the very smell were left me,
Yet would my love to thee be still as much;
  For from the stillitory of thy face excelling
  Comes breath perfum'd that breedeth love
    by smelling.

'But, O, what banquet wert thou to the taste,
Being nurse and feeder of the other four! 446
Would they not wish the feast might ever last
And bid Suspicion double-lock the door,
  Lest Jealousy, that sour unwelcome guest,
  Should by his stealing in disturb the feast?'

Once more the ruby-colour'd portal open'd 451
Which to his speech did honey passage yield;
Like a red morn, that ever yet betoken'd
Wrack to the seaman, tempest to the field,
  Sorrow to shepherds, woe unto the birds, 455
  Gusts and foul flaws to herdmen and to herds.

This ill presage advisedly she marketh.
Even as the wind is hush'd before it raineth,
Or as the wolf doth grin before he barketh,
Or as the berry breaks before it staineth, 460
  Or like the deadly bullet of a gun,
  His meaning struck her ere his words begun.

And at his look she flatly falleth down,
For looks kill love, and love by looks reviveth;
A smile recures the wounding of a frown. 465
But blessed bankrout that by love so thriveth!
  The silly boy, believing she is dead,
  Claps her pale cheek till clapping makes it
    red,

And all amaz'd brake off his late intent,
For sharply he did think to reprehend her, 470
Which cunning love did wittily prevent.
Fair fall the wit that can so well defend her!
  For on the grass she lies as she were slain
  Till his breath breatheth life in her again.

He wrings her nose, he strikes her on the
    cheeks, 475
He bends her fingers, holds her pulses hard,
He chafes her lips; a thousand ways he seeks
To mend the hurt that his unkindness marr'd.
  He kisses her; and she, by her good will,
  Will never rise, so he will kiss her still. 480

The night of sorrow now is turn'd to day:
Her two blue windows faintly she upheaveth,
Like the fair sun when in his fresh array
He cheers the morn and all the earth relieveth;
  And as the bright sun glorifies the sky, 485
  So is her face illumin'd with her eye;

Whose beams upon his hairless face are fix'd,
As if from thence they borrowed all their shine.
Were never four such lamps together mix'd,
Had not his clouded with his brow's repine; 490
  But hers, which through the crystal tears
      gave light,
  Shone like the moon in water seen by night.

'O, where am I?' quoth she, 'in earth or
    heaven,
Or in the ocean drench'd, or in the fire?
What hour is this? or morn or weary even? 495
Do I delight to die, or life desire?
  But now I liv'd, and life was death's annoy;
  But now I died, and death was lively joy.

'O, thou didst kill me! Kill me once again!
Thy eyes' shrowd tutor, that hard heart of
    thine, 500
Hath taught them scornful tricks, and such
    disdain
That they have mur'dred this poor heart of
    mine;
  And these mine eyes, true leaders to their
      queen,
  But for thy piteous lips no more had seen.

'Long may they kiss each other, for this cure!
O, never let their crimson liveries wear! 506
And as they last, their verdure still endure,
To drive infection from the dangerous year!
  That the stargazers, having writ on death,
  May say the plague is banish'd by thy breath.

'Pure lips, sweet seals in my soft lips imprinted,
What bargains may I make, still to be sealing?
To sell myself I can be well contented,
So thou wilt buy, and pay, and use good deal-
    ing; 514
  Which purchase if thou make, for fear of slips
  Set thy seal manual on my wax-red lips.

'A thousand kisses buys my heart from me;
And pay them at thy leisure, one by one.
What is ten hundred touches unto thee? 519
Are they not quickly told and quickly gone?
  Say for nonpayment that the debt should
      double,
  Is twenty hundred kisses such a trouble?'

'Fair queen,' quoth he, 'if any love you owe me,
Measure my strangeness with my unripe years.
Before I know myself, seek not to know me.
No fisher but the ungrown fry forbears. 526
  The mellow plum doth fall, the green sticks
      fast,
  Or being early pluck'd is sour to taste.

'Look, the world's comforter, with weary gait,
His day's hot task hath ended in the West; 530
The owl, night's herald, shrieks; 'tis very late;
The sheep are gone to fold, birds to their nest,
  And coal-black clouds that shadow heaven's
      light
  Do summon us to part and bid good night.

'Now let me say "Good night," and so say you.
If you will say so, you shall have a kiss.' 536
'Good night,' quoth she; and, ere he says
    'Adieu,'
The honey fee of parting tend'red is:
  Her arms do lend his neck a sweet embrace;
  Incorporate then they seem; face grows to
      face; 540

Till breathless he disjoin'd, and backward drew
The heavenly moisture, that sweet coral mouth,
Whose precious taste her thirsty lips well knew,
Whereon they surfeit, yet complain on drouth.
  He with her plenty press'd, she faint with
      dearth, 545
  Their lips together glu'd, fall to the earth.

Now quick desire hath caught the yielding prey,
And glutton-like she feeds, yet never filleth.
Her lips are conquerors, his lips obey,
Paying what ransom the insulter willeth; 550
  Whose vulture thought doth pitch the price
      so high
  That she will draw his lips' rich treasure dry.

And having felt the sweetness of the spoil,
With blindfold fury she begins to forage.
Her face doth reek and smoke, her blood doth
boil,   555
And careless lust stirs up a desperate courage,
Planting oblivion, beating reason back,
Forgetting shame's pure blush and honour's
wrack.

Hot, faint, and weary with her hard embracing,
Like a wild bird being tam'd with too much
handling,   560
Or as the fleet-foot roe that's tir'd with chasing,
Or like the froward infant still'd with dandling,
He now obeys and now no more resisteth,
While she takes all she can, not all she listeth.

What wax so frozen but dissolves with tem-
p'ring   565
And yields at last to every light impression?
Things out of hope are compass'd oft with
vent'ring,
Chiefly in love, whose leave exceeds commission.
Affection faints not like a pale-fac'd coward,
But then wooes best when most his choice is
froward.   570

When he did frown, O, had she then gave over,
Such nectar from his lips she had not suck'd.
Foul words and frowns must not repel a lover.
What though the rose have prickles, yet 'tis
pluck'd.
Were beauty under twenty locks kept fast,
Yet love breaks through and picks them all
at last.   576

For pity now she can no more detain him.
The poor fool prays her that he may depart.
She is resolv'd no longer to restrain him;   579
Bids him farewell, and look well to her heart,
The which, by Cupid's bow she doth protest,
He carries thence incaged in his breast.

'Sweet boy,' she says, 'this night I'll waste in
sorrow,
For my sick heart commands mine eyes to
watch.
Tell me, love's master, shall we meet to-
morrow?   585
Say, shall we? shall we? wilt thou make the
match?'
He tells her no; to-morrow he intends
To hunt the boar with certain of his friends.

'The boar!' quoth she; whereat a sudden pale,
Like lawn being spread upon the blushing rose,

Usurps her cheek; she trembles at his tale,   591
And on his neck her yoking arms she throws;
She sinketh down, still hanging by his neck,
He on her belly falls, she on her back.

Now is she in the very lists of love,   595
Her champion mounted for the hot encounter.
All is imaginary she doth prove,
He will not manage her, although he mount her;
That worse than Tantalus' is her annoy,
To clip Elysium and to lack her joy.   600

Even so poor birds, deceiv'd with painted
grapes,
Do surfeit by the eye and pine the maw;
Even so she languisheth in her mishaps
As those poor birds that helpless berries saw.
The warm effects which she in him finds
missing   605
She seeks to kindle with continual kissing.

But all in vain. Good queen, it will not be!
She hath assay'd as much as may be prov'd.
Her pleading hath deserv'd a greater fee: 609
She's Love, she loves, and yet she is not lov'd.
'Fie, fie!' he says. 'You crush me; let me go!
You have no reason to withhold me so.'

'Thou hadst been gone,' quoth she, 'sweet boy,
ere this,
But that thou told'st me thou wouldst hunt the
boar.
O, be advis'd! Thou know'st not what it is   615
With javelin's point a churlish swine to gore,
Whose tushes never sheath'd he whetteth still,
Like to a mortal butcher bent to kill.

'On his bow-back he hath a battle set
Of bristly pikes that ever threat his foes;   620
His eyes like glowworms shine when he doth
fret;
His snout digs sepulchres where'er he goes;
Being mov'd, he strikes whate'er is in his way,
And whom he strikes his crooked tushes slay.

'His brawny sides, with hairy bristles armed,
Are better proof than thy spear's point can
enter;   626
His short thick neck cannot be easily harmed;
Being ireful, on the lion he will venter.
The thorny brambles and embracing bushes,
As fearful of him, part; through whom he
rushes.   630

'Alas, he naught esteems that face of thine,
To which Love's eyes pays tributary gazes;

Nor thy soft hands, sweet lips, and crystal eyne,
Whose full perfection all the world amazes;
But having thee at vantage (wondrous
    dread!),   635
Would root these beauties as he roots the
    mead.

'O, let him keep his loathsome cabin still!
Beauty hath naught to do with such foul fiends.
Come not within his danger by thy will.
They that thrive well take counsel of their
    friends.   640
When thou didst name the boar, not to dis-
    semble,
I fear'd thy fortune, and my joints did
    tremble.

'Didst thou not mark my face? Was it not
    white?
Sawest thou not signs of fear lurk in mine eye?
Grew I not faint? and fell I not downright?
Within my bosom, whereon thou dost lie, 646
My boding heart pants, beats, and takes no
    rest,
But, like an earthquake, shakes thee on my
    breast.

'For where Love reigns, disturbing Jealousy
Doth call himself Affection's sentinel,   650
Gives false alarms, suggesteth mutiny,
And in a peaceful hour doth cry "Kill, kill!"
Distemp'ring gentle Love in his desire,
As air and water do abate the fire.

'This sour informer, this bate-breeding spy, 655
This canker that eats up Love's tender spring,
This carry-tale, dissentious Jealousy,
That sometime true news, sometime false doth
    bring,
Knocks at my heart, and whispers in mine ear
That if I love thee, I thy death should fear;

'And more than so, presenteth to mine eye
The picture of an angry chafing boar,
Under whose sharp fangs on his back doth lie
An image like thyself, all stain'd with gore;
Whose blood upon the fresh flowers being
    shed   665
Doth make them droop with grief and hang
    the head.

'What should I do, seeing thee so indeed,
That tremble at th' imagination?
The thought of it doth make my faint heart
    bleed,
And fear doth teach it divination.   670

I prophesy thy death, my living sorrow,
If thou encounter with the boar to-morrow.

'But if thou needs wilt hunt, be rul'd by me;
Uncouple at the timorous flying hare,
Or at the fox which lives by subtlety,   675
Or at the roe which no encounter dare.
Pursue these fearful creatures o'er the downs,
And on thy well-breath'd horse keep with
    thy hounds.

'And when thou hast on foot the purblind hare,
Mark the poor wretch, to overshoot his troubles,
How he outruns the wind, and with what care
He cranks and crosses with a thousand doubles.
The many musits through the which he goes
Are like a labyrinth to amaze his foes.

'Sometime he runs among a flock of sheep, 685
To make the cunning hounds mistake their
    smell,
And sometime where earth-delving conies keep,
To stop the loud pursuers in their yell;
And sometime sorteth with a herd of deer.
Danger deviseth shifts; wit waits on fear;

'For there his smell with others being mingled,
The hot scent-snuffing hounds are driven to
    doubt,
Ceasing their clamorous cry till they have
    singled
With much ado the cold fault cleanly out.
Then do they spend their mouths; echo re-
    plies,   695
As if another chase were in the skies.

'By this, poor Wat, far off upon a hill,
Stands on his hinder legs with list'ning ear,
To hearken if his foes pursue him still.
Anon their loud alarums he doth hear,   700
And now his grief may be compared well
To one sore sick that hears the passing bell.

'Then shalt thou see the dew-bedabbled wretch
Turn and return, indenting with the way. 704
Each envious brier his weary legs do scratch;
Each shadow makes him stop, each murmur
    stay;
For misery is trodden on by many
And, being low, never reliev'd by ar y.

'Lie quietly and hear a little more.   709
Nay, do not struggle, for thou shalt not rise.
To make thee hate the hunting of the boar,
Unlike myself thou hear'st me moralize,

Applying this to that, and so to so;
For love can comment upon every woe.

'Where did I leave?' 'No matter where,'
  quoth he.   715
'Leave me, and then the story aptly ends.
The night is spent.' 'Why, what of that?'
  quoth she.
'I am,' quoth he, 'expected of my friends;
  And now 'tis dark, and going I shall fall.'
  'In night,' quoth she, 'desire sees best of all.'

'But if thou fall, O, then imagine this:
The earth, in love with thee, thy footing trips,
And all is but to rob thee of a kiss.
Rich preys make true men thieves. So do thy
  lips
  Make modest Dian cloudy and forlorn, 725
  Lest she should steal a kiss and die forsworn.

'Now of this dark night I perceive the reason:
Cynthia for shame obscures her silver shine,
Till forging Nature be condemn'd of treason
For stealing moulds from heaven that were
  divine;   730
  Wherein she fram'd thee, in high heaven's
    despite,
  To shame the sun by day, and her by night.

'And therefore hath she brib'd the Destinies
To cross the curious workmanship of Nature,
To mingle beauty with infirmities   735
And pure perfection with impure defeature,
  Making it subject to the tyranny
  Of mad mischances and much misery;

'As burning fevers, agues pale and faint,
Life-poisoning pestilence, and frenzies wood,
The marrow-eating sickness whose attaint 741
Disorder breeds by heating of the blood,
  Surfeits, imposthumes, grief, and damn'd
    despair
  Swear Nature's death for framing thee so fair.

'And not the least of all these maladies 745
But in one minute's fight brings beauty under.
Both favour, savour, hue, and qualities,
Whereat th' impartial gazer late did wonder,
  Are on the sudden wasted, thaw'd, and done,
  As mountain snow melts with the midday
    sun.   750

'Therefore, despite of fruitless chastity,
Love-lacking vestals, and self-loving nuns,
That on the earth would breed a scarcity
And barren dearth of daughters and of sons,

Be prodigal. The lamp that burns by night
Dries up his oil to lend the world his light.

'What is thy body but a swallowing grave,
Seeming to bury that posterity
Which by the rights of time thou needs must
  have   759
If thou destroy them not in dark obscurity?
  If so, the world will hold thee in disdain,
  Sith in thy pride so fair a hope is slain.

'So in thyself thyself art made away —
A mischief worse than civil home-bred strife,
Or theirs whose desperate hands themselves do
  slay,   765
Or butcher sire that reaves his son of life.
  Foul cank'ring rust the hidden treasure frets,
  But gold that's put to use more gold begets.'

'Nay, then,' quoth Adon, 'you will fall again
Into your idle over-handled theme.   770
The kiss I gave you is bestow'd in vain,
And all in vain you strive against the stream;
  For, by this black-fac'd night, desire's foul
    nurse,
  Your treatise makes me like you worse and
    worse.   774

'If love have lent you twenty thousand tongues,
And every tongue more moving than your own,
Bewitching like the wanton mermaid's songs,
Yet from mine ear the tempting tune is blown;
  For know, my heart stands armed in mine ear
  And will not let a false sound enter there,

'Lest the deceiving harmony should run 781
Into the quiet closure of my breast;
And then my little heart were quite undone,
In his bedchamber to be barr'd of rest.   784
  No, lady, no! My heart longs not to groan,
  But soundly sleeps while now it sleeps alone.

'What have you urg'd that I cannot reprove?
The path is smooth that leadeth on to danger.
I hate not love, but your device in love, 789
That lends embracements unto every stranger.
  You do it for increase. O strange excuse,
  When reason is the bawd to lust's abuse!

'Call it not love, for Love to heaven is fled
Since sweating Lust on earth usurp'd his name;
Under whose simple semblance he hath fed 795
Upon fresh beauty, blotting it with blame;
  Which the hot tyrant stains and soon be-
    reaves,
  As caterpillars do the tender leaves.

'Love comforteth like sunshine after rain,
But Lust's effect is tempest after sun.   800
Love's gentle spring doth always fresh remain;
Lust's winter comes ere summer half be done.
  Love surfeits not, Lust like a glutton dies;
  Love is all truth, Lust full of forged lies.

'More I could tell, but more I dare not say:
The text is old, the orator too green.   806
Therefore in sadness now I will away.
My face is full of shame, my heart of teen;
  Mine ears, that to your wanton talk attended,
  Do burn themselves for having so offended.'

With this he breaketh from the sweet embrace
Of those fair arms which bound him to her
      breast
And homeward through the dark laund runs
      apace;
Leaves Love upon her back, deeply distress'd;
  Look how a bright star shooteth from the
      sky —   815
  So glides he in the night from Venus' eye;

Which after him she darts, as one on shore
Gazing upon a late-embarked friend
Till the wild waves will have him seen no more,
Whose ridges with the meeting clouds contend.
  So did the merciless and pitchy night   821
  Fold in the object that did feed her sight.

Whereat amaz'd, as one that unaware
Hath dropp'd a precious jewel in the flood,
Or stonish'd as night-wand'rers often are,   825
Their light blown out in some mistrustful
      wood —
  Even so confounded in the dark she lay,
  Having lost the fair discovery of her way.

And now she beats her heart, whereat it groans,
That all the neighbour caves, as seeming
      troubled,   830
Make verbal repetition of her moans.
Passion on passion deeply is redoubled:
  'Ay me!' she cries, and twenty times, 'Woe,
      woe!'
  And twenty echoes twenty times cry so.

She, marking them, begins a wailing note   835
And sings extemporally a woful ditty —
How love makes young men thrall, and old men
      dote;
How love is wise in folly, foolish-witty.
  Her heavy anthem still concludes in woe,
  And still the choir of echoes answer so.   840

Her song was tedious and outwore the night,
For lovers' hours are long, though seeming
      short.
If pleas'd themselves, others, they think, delight
In such-like circumstance, with such-like sport.
  Their copious stories, oftentimes begun,   845
  End without audience and are never done.

For who hath she to spend the night withal
But idle sounds resembling parasits,
Like shrill-tongu'd tapsters answering every
      call,
Soothing the humour of fantastic wits?   850
  She says ''Tis so.' They answer all, ''Tis so!'
  And would say after her if she said 'No.'

Lo, here the gentle lark, weary of rest,
From his moist cabinet mounts up on high
And wakes the morning, from whose silver
      breast   855
The sun ariseth in his majesty;
  Who doth the world so gloriously behold
  That cedar tops and hills seem burnish'd gold.

Venus salutes him with this fair good-morrow:
'O thou clear god, and patron of all light,   860
From whom each lamp and shining star doth
      borrow
The beauteous influence that makes him bright,
  There lives a son that suck'd an earthly
      mother
  May lend thee light, as thou dost lend to
      other.'

This said, she hasteth to a myrtle grove,   865
Musing the morning is so much o'erworn
And yet she hears no tidings of her love.
She hearkens for his hounds and for his horn.
  Anon she hears them chant it lustily,
  And all in haste she coasteth to the cry;   870

And as she runs, the bushes in the way
Some catch her by the neck, some kiss her face,
Some twine about her thigh to make her stay.
She wildly breaketh from their strict embrace,
  Like a milch doe whose swelling dugs do ache
  Hasting to feed her fawn hid in some brake.

By this, she hears the hounds are at a bay;
Whereat she starts, like one that spies an adder
Wreath'd up in fatal folds just in his way,
The fear whereof doth make him shake and
      shudder.   880
  Even so the timorous yelping of the hounds
  Appals her senses and her spirit confounds.

For now she knows it is no gentle chase,
But the blunt boar, rough bear, or lion proud,
Because the cry remaineth in one place,   885
Where fearfully the dogs exclaim aloud..
  Finding their enemy to be so curst,
  They all strain court'sy who shall cope him
    first.

This dismal cry rings sadly in her ear,
Through which it enters to surprise her heart,
Who, overcome by doubt and bloodless fear,   891
With cold-pale weakness numbs each feeling
    part:
  Like soldiers when their captain once doth
    yield,
  They basely fly and dare not stay the field.

Thus stands she in a trembling ecstasy;   895
Till, cheering up her senses all dismay'd,
She tells them 'tis a causeless fantasy,
And childish error that they are afraid;
  Bids them leave quaking, bids them fear no
    more;
  And with that word she spied the hunted
    boar,   900

Whose frothy mouth, bepainted all with red,
Like milk and blood being mingled both to-
    gither,
A second fear through all her sinews spread,
Which madly hurries her she knows not whither.
  This way she runs, and now she will no
    further,   905
  But back retires to rate the boar for murther.

A thousand spleens bear her a thousand ways;
She treads the path that she untreads again;
Her more than haste is mated with delays,
Like the proceedings of a drunken brain,   910
  Full of respects, yet naught at all respecting,
  In hand with all things, naught at all effect-
    ing.

Here kennell'd in a brake she finds a hound
And asks the weary caitiff for his master;
And there another licking of his wound,   915
'Gainst venom'd sores the only sovereign plas-
    ter;
  And here she meets another sadly scowling,
  To whom she speaks, and he replies with
    howling.

When he hath ceas'd his ill-resounding noise,
Another flap-mouth'd mourner, black and grim,
Against the welkin volleys out his voice.   921
Another and another answer him,

Clapping their proud tails to the ground
    below,
Shaking their scratch'd ears, bleeding as they
    go.

Look how the world's poor people are amazed
At apparitions, signs, and prodigies,   926
Whereon with fearful eyes they long have gazed,
Infusing them with dreadful prophecies:
  So she at these sad signs draws up her breath
  And, sighing it again, exclaims on Death.   930

'Hard-favour'd tyrant, ugly, meagre, lean,
Hateful divorce of love!' (thus chides she
    Death) —
'Grim-grinning ghost, earth's worm, what dost
    thou mean
To stifle beauty and to steal his breath
  Who, when he liv'd, his breath and beauty set
  Gloss on the rose, smell to the violet?   936

'If he be dead — O no, it cannot be,
Seeing his beauty, thou shouldst strike at it!
O yes, it may! Thou hast no eyes to see,
But hatefully at randon dost thou hit.   940
  Thy mark is feeble age; but thy false dart
  Mistakes that aim and cleaves an infant's
    heart.

'Hadst thou but bid beware, then he had spoke,
And, hearing him, thy power had lost his power.
The Destinies will curse thee for this stroke. 945
They bid thee crop a weed; thou pluck'st a
    flower.
  Love's golden arrow at him should have fled,
  And not Death's ebon dart to strike him dead.

'Dost thou drink tears, that thou provok'st
    such weeping?
What may a heavy groan advantage thee?   950
Why hast thou cast into eternal sleeping
Those eyes that taught all other eyes to see?
  Now Nature cares not for thy mortal vigour,
  Since her best work is ruin'd with thy rigour.'

Here overcome, as one full of despair,   955
She vail'd her eyelids, who, like sluices, stopp'd
The crystal tide that from her two cheeks fair
In the sweet channel of her bosom dropp'd;
  But through the floodgates breaks the silver
    rain   959
  And with his strong course opens them again.

O, how her eyes and tears did lend and borrow,
Her eyes seen in the tears, tears in her eye!

Both crystals, where they view'd each other's
   sorrow —
Sorrow that friendly sighs sought still to dry;
  But like a stormy day, now wind, now rain,
  Sighs dry her cheeks, tears make them wet
    again.   966

Variable passions throng her constant woe,
As striving who should best become her grief.
All entertain'd, each passion labours so
That every present sorrow seemeth chief, 970
  But none is best. Then join they all together,
  Like many clouds consulting for foul weather.

By this, far off she hears some hunstman
   halloa.
A nurse's song ne'er pleas'd her babe so well.
The dire imagination she did follow   975
This sound of hope doth labour to expel;
  For now reviving joy bids her rejoice
  And flatters her it is Adonis' voice.

Whereat her tears began to turn their tide,
Being prison'd in her eye like pearls in glass;
Yet sometimes falls an orient drop beside, 981
Which her cheek melts, as scorning it should
   pass
  To wash the foul face of the sluttish ground,
  Who is but drunken when she seemeth
   drown'd.

O hard-believing love, how strange it seems 985
Not to believe, and yet too credulous!
Thy weal and woe are both of them extremes;
Despair and hope makes thee ridiculous:
  The one doth flatter thee in thoughts un-
   likely,   989
  In likely thoughts the other kills thee quickly.

Now she unweaves the web that she hath
   wrought:
Adonis lives, and Death is not to blame;
It was not she that call'd him all to naught.
Now she adds honours to his hateful name:
  She clepes him king of graves, and grave for
   kings,   995
  Imperious supreme of all mortal things.

'No, no!' quoth she. 'Sweet Death, I did but
   jest.
Yet pardon me I felt a kind of fear
When as I met the boar, that bloody beast
Which knows no pity but is still severe.   1000
  Then, gentle shadow (truth I must confess),
  I rail'd on thee, fearing my love's decesse.

''Tis not my fault. The boar provok'd my
   tongue.
Be wreak'd on him, invisible commander.
'Tis he, foul creature, that hath done thee
   wrong.   1005
I did but act; he's author of thy slander.
  Grief hath two tongues, and never woman
   yet
  Could rule them both without ten women's
   wit.'

Thus hoping that Adonis is alive,
Her rash suspect she doth extenuate;   1010
And that his beauty may the better thrive,
With Death she humbly doth insinuate;
  Tells him of trophies, statues, tombs, and
   stories,
  His victories, his triumphs, and his glories.

'O Jove,' quoth she, 'how much a fool was I
To be of such a weak and silly mind   1016
To wail his death who lives, and must not die
Till mutual overthrow of mortal kind!
  For he being dead, with him is beauty slain,
  And, beauty dead, black chaos comes again.

'Fie, fie, fond love, thou art so full of fear 1021
As one with treasure laden hemm'd with thieves.
Trifles, unwitnessed with eye or ear,
Thy coward heart with false bethinking grieves.'
  Even at this word she hears a merry horn,
  Whereat she leaps that was but late forlorn.

As falcons to the lure, away she flies.
The grass stoops not, she treads on it so light;
And in her haste unfortunately spies
The foul boar's conquest on her fair delight;
  Which seen, her eyes, as murd'red with the
   view,   1031
  Like stars asham'd of day, themselves with-
   drew;

Or as the snail, whose tender horns being hit,
Shrinks backward in his shelly cave with pain,
And there, all smooth'red up, in shade doth sit,
Long after fearing to creep forth again;   1036
  So at his bloody view her eyes are fled
  Into the deep-dark cabins of her head;

Where they resign their office and their light
To the disposing of her troubled brain;   1040
Who bids them still consort with ugly night
And never wound the heart with looks again;
  Who, like a king perplexed in his throne,
  By their suggestion gives a deadly groan,

Whereat each tributary subject quakes, 1045
As when the wind, imprison'd in the ground,
Struggling for passage, earth's foundation shakes,
Which with cold terror doth men's minds confound.
  This mutiny each part doth so surprise
  That from their dark beds once more leap her eyes, 1050

And, being open'd, threw unwilling light
Upon the wide wound that the boar had trench'd
In his soft flank; whose wonted lily white
With purple tears that his wound wept was drench'd.
  No flow'r was nigh, no grass, herb, leaf, or weed, 1055
  But stole his blood and seem'd with him to bleed.

This solemn sympathy poor Venus noteth.
Over one shoulder doth she hang her head.
Dumbly she passions, franticly she doteth:
She thinks he could not die, he is not dead; 1060
  Her voice is stopp'd, her joints forget to bow;
  Her eyes are mad that they have wept till now.

Upon his hurt she looks so steadfastly
That her sight dazzling makes the wound seem three;
And then she reprehends her mangling eye,
That makes more gashes where no breach should be.
  His face seems twain, each several limb is doubled;
  For oft the eye mistakes, the brain being troubled.

'My tongue cannot express my grief for one,
And yet,' quoth she, 'behold two Adons dead!
My sighs are blown away, my salt tears gone,
Mine eyes are turn'd to fire, my heart to lead.
  Heavy heart's lead, melt at mine eyes' red fire!
  So shall I die by drops of hot desire.

'Alas, poor world, what treasure hast thou lost!
What face remains alive that's worth the viewing? 1076
Whose tongue is music now? What canst thou boast
Of things long since, or any thing ensuing?

The flowers are sweet, their colours fresh and trim;
But true-sweet beauty liv'd and died with him. 1080

'Bonnet nor veil henceforth no creature wear!
Nor sun nor wind will ever strive to kiss you.
Having no fair to lose, you need not fear.
The sun doth scorn you, and the wind doth hiss you; 1084
  But when Adonis liv'd, sun and sharp air
  Lurk'd like two thieves, to rob him of his fair;

'And therefore would he put his bonnet on,
Under whose brim the gaudy sun would peep;
The wind would blow it off, and, being gone,
Play with his locks. Then would Adonis weep,
  And straight, in pity of his tender years, 1091
  They both would strive who first should dry his tears.

'To see his face the lion walk'd along
Behind some hedge, because he would not fear him.
To recreate himself when he hath song, 1095
The tiger would be tame, and gently hear him.
  If he had spoke, the wolf would leave his prey
  And never fright the silly lamb that day.

'When he beheld his shadow in the brook,
The fishes spread on it their golden gills. 1100
When he was by, the birds such pleasure took
That some would sing, some other in their bills
  Would bring him mulberries and ripe-red cherries:
  He fed them with his sight, they him with berries.

'But this foul, grim, and urchin-snouted boar,
Whose downward eye still looketh for a grave,
Ne'er saw the beauteous livery that he wore:
Witness the entertainment that he gave.
  If he did see his face, why then I know
  He thought to kiss him, and hath kill'd him so. 1110

''Tis true, 'tis true! thus was Adonis slain:
He ran upon the boar with his sharp spear,
Who did not whet his teeth at him again,
But by a kiss thought to persuade him there;
  And nuzzling in his flank, the loving swine
  Sheath'd unaware the tusk in his soft groin.

'Had I been tooth'd like him, I must confess,
With kissing him I should have kill'd him first;
But he is dead, and never did he bless   1119
My youth with his — the more am I accurst.'
   With this, she falleth in the place she stood
   And stains her face with his congealed blood.

She looks upon his lips, and they are pale;
She takes him by the hand, and that is cold;
She whispers in his ears a heavy tale,   1125
As if they heard the woful words she told;
   She lifts the coffer-lids that close his eyes,
   Where, lo, two lamps burnt out in darkness
   lies;

Two glasses, where herself herself beheld
A thousand times, and now no more reflect,
Their virtue lost wherein they late excell'd,
And every beauty robb'd of his effect.
   'Wonder of time,' quoth she, 'this is my spite,
   That, thou being dead, the day should yet
   be light.

'Since thou art dead, lo, here I prophesy   1135
Sorrow on love hereafter shall attend.
It shall be waited on with jealousy,
Find sweet beginning, but unsavoury end,
   Ne'er settled equally, but high or low,
   That all love's pleasure shall not match his
   woe.   1140

'It shall be fickle, false, and full of fraud,
Bud and be blasted in a breathing while,
The bottom poison, and the top o'erstraw'd
With sweets that shall the truest sight beguile.
   The strongest body shall it make most weak,
   Strike the wise dumb, and teach the fool to
   speak.   1146

'It shall be sparing, and too full of riot,
Teaching decrepit age to tread the measures;
The staring ruffian shall it keep in quiet,
Pluck down the rich, enrich the poor with
   treasures;   1150
   It shall be raging mad and silly mild,
   Make the young old, the old become a child.

'It shall suspect where is no cause of fear;
It shall not fear where it should most mistrust;
It shall be merciful, and too severe,   1155
And most deceiving when it seems most just;
   Perverse it shall be where it shows most
   toward,
   Put fear to valour, courage to the coward.

'It shall be cause of war and dire events
And set dissension 'twixt the son and sire,   1160
Subject and servile to all discontents,
As dry combustious matter is to fire.
   Sith in his prime death doth my love destroy,
   They that love best their loves shall not
   enjoy.'

By this, the boy that by her side lay kill'd   1165
Was melted like a vapour from her sight,
And in his blood, that on the ground lay spill'd,
A purple flower sprung up, check'red with
   white,
   Resembling well his pale cheeks and the
   blood
   Which in round drops upon their whiteness
   stood.   1170

She bows her head the new-sprung flower to
   smell,
Comparing it to her Adonis' breath,
And says within her bosom it shall dwell,
Since he himself is reft from her by death;
   She crops the stalk, and in the breach appears
   Green-dropping sap, which she compares to
   tears.   1176

'Poor flow'r,' quoth she, 'this was thy father's
   guise —
Sweet issue of a more sweet-smelling sire —
For every little grief to wet his eyes.
To grow unto himself was his desire,   1180
   And so 'tis thine; but know, it is as good
   To wither in my breast as in his blood.

'Here was thy father's bed, here in my breast;
Thou art the next of blood, and 'tis thy
   right.
Lo, in this hollow cradle take thy rest;   1185
My throbbing heart shall rock thee day and
   night.
   There shall not be one minute in an hour
   Wherein I will not kiss my sweet love's
   flow'r.'

Thus weary of the world, away she hies
And yokes her silver doves, by whose swift
   aid   1190
Their mistress, mounted, through the empty
   skies
In her light chariot quickly is convey'd,
   Holding their course to Paphos, where their
   queen
   Means to immure herself and not be seen.

THE RAPE OF LUCRECE

TO THE

RIGHT HONOURABLE HENRY WRIOTHESLEY,

EARL OF SOUTHAMPTON, AND BARON OF TITCHFIELD.

The love I dedicate to your Lordship is without
end; whereof this pamphlet without beginning is
but a superfluous moiety. The warrant I have of
your honourable disposition, not the worth of my
untutor'd lines, makes it assured of acceptance.
What I have done is yours; what I have to do is
yours; being part in all I have, devoted yours.
Were my worth greater, my duty would show
greater; meantime, as it is, it is bound to your
Lordship, to whom I wish long life still length'ned
with all happiness.

Your Lordship's in all duty,

WILLIAM SHAKESPEARE.

THE ARGUMENT.

Lucius Tarquinius (for his excessive pride surnamed Superbus), after he had caused his own
father-in-law Servius Tullius to be cruelly mur-
d'red, and, contrary to the Roman laws and customs, not requiring or staying for the people's
suffrages, had possessed himself of the kingdom,
went, accompanied with his sons and other noblemen of Rome, to besiege Ardea; during which
siege the principal men of the army meeting one
evening at the tent of Sextus Tarquinius, the
King's son, in their discourses after supper every
one commended the virtues of his own wife;
among whom Collatinus extolled the incomparable
chastity of his wife Lucretia. In that pleasant
humour they all posted to Rome; and intending
by their secret and sudden arrival to make trial
of that which every one had before avouched, only
Collatinus finds his wife (though it were late in the
night) spinning amongst her maids; the other
ladies were all found dancing and revelling, or in
several disports. Whereupon the noblemen yielded
Collatinus the victory, and his wife the fame. At
that time Sextus Tarquinius being inflamed with
Lucrece' beauty, yet smoothering his passions for
the present, departed with the rest back to the
camp; from whence he shortly after privily withdrew himself, and was (according to his estate)
royally entertained and lodged by Lucrece at Collatium. The same night he treacherously stealeth
into her chamber, violently ravish'd her, and early
in the morning speedeth away. Lucrece, in this
lamentable plight, hastily dispatcheth messengers,
one to Rome for her father, another to the camp
for Collatine. They came, the one accompanied
with Junius Brutus, the other with Publius Va-
lerius; and finding Lucrece attired in mourning
habit, demanded the cause of her sorrow. She,
first taking an oath of them for her revenge, re-
vealed the actor and whole manner of his dealing,
and withal suddenly stabbed herself. Which done,
with one consent they all vowed to root out the
whole hated family of the Tarquins; and bearing
the dead body to Rome, Brutus acquainted the
people with the doer and manner of the vile deed,
with a bitter invective against the tyranny of the
King; wherewith the people were so moved that
with one consent and a general acclamation the
Tarquins were all exiled, and the state government
changed from kings to consuls.

From the besieged Ardea all in post,
Borne by the trustless wings of false desire,
Lust-breathed Tarquin leaves the Roman host
And to Collatium bears the lightless fire
Which, in pale embers hid, lurks to aspire   5
    And girdle with embracing flames the waist
    Of Collatine's fair love, Lucrece the chaste.

Haply that name of 'chaste' unhap'ly set
This bateless edge on his keen appetite;
When Collatine unwisely did not let   10
To praise the clear unmatched red and white
Which triumph'd in that sky of his delight,
    Where mortal stars, as bright as heaven's
        beauties,
    With pure aspects did him peculiar duties.

For he the night before, in Tarquin's tent,   15
Unlock'd the treasure of his happy state:
What priceless wealth the heavens had him lent
In the possession of his beauteous mate;
Reck'ning his fortune at such high proud rate
    That kings might be espoused to more fame,
    But king nor peer to such a peerless dame.

O happiness enjoy'd but of a few,
And, if possess'd, as soon decay'd and done
As is the morning's silver-melting dew
Against the golden splendour of the sun!   25
An expir'd date, cancell'd ere well begun.
    Honour and beauty, in the owner's arms,
    Are weakly fortress'd from a world of harms.

428

Beauty itself doth of itself persuade
The eyes of men without an orator.   30
What needeth then apology be made
To set forth that which is so singular?
Or why is Collatine the publisher
    Of that rich jewel he should keep unknown
    From thievish ears, because it is his own?   35

Perchance his boast of Lucrece' sov'reignty
Suggested this proud issue of a king;
For by our ears our hearts oft tainted be.
Perchance that envy of so rich a thing
Braving compare, disdainfully did sting   40
    His high-pitch'd thoughts that meaner men
        should vaunt
    That golden hap which their superiors want.

But some untimely thought did instigate
His all too timeless speed, if none of those.
His honour, his affairs, his friends, his state,
Neglected all, with swift intent he goes   46
To quench the coal which in his liver glows.
    O rash false heat, wrapp'd in repentant
        cold,
    Thy hasty spring still blasts and ne'er grows
        old!

When at Collatium this false lord arrived,   50
Well was he welcom'd by the Roman dame,
Within whose face Beauty and Virtue strived
Which of them both should underprop her
        fame.
When Virtue bragg'd, Beauty would blush for
        shame;
    When Beauty boasted blushes, in despite 55
    Virtue would stain that o'er with silver white.

But Beauty, in that white entituled,
From Venus' doves doth challenge that fair
        field.
Then Virtue claims from Beauty Beauty's red,
Which Virtue gave the Golden Age to gild   60
Their silver cheeks, and call'd it then their
        shield,
    Teaching them thus to use it in the fight,
    When shame assail'd, the red should fence
        the white.

This heraldry in Lucrece' face was seen,
Argued by Beauty's red and Virtue's white. 65
Of either's colour was the other queen,
Proving from world's minority their right.
Yet their ambition makes them still to fight,
    The sovereignty of either being so great   69
    That oft they interchange each other's seat.

This silent war of lilies and of roses
Which Tarquin view'd in her fair face's field,
In their pure ranks his traitor eye encloses;
Where, lest between them both it should be
        kill'd,
The coward captive vanquished doth yield   75
    To those two armies that would let him go
    Rather than triumph in so false a foe.

Now thinks he that her husband's shallow
        tongue,
The niggard prodigal that prais'd her so,
In that high task hath done her beauty wrong,
Which far exceeds his barren skill to show. 81
Therefore that praise which Collatine doth owe
    Enchanted Tarquin answers with surmise,
    In silent wonder of still-gazing eyes.

This earthly saint, adored by this devil,   85
Little suspecteth the false worshipper;
For unstain'd thoughts do seldom dream on evil;
Birds never lim'd no secret bushes fear.
So guiltless she securely gives good cheer   89
    And reverend welcome to her princely guest,
    Whose inward ill no outward harm express'd;

For that he colour'd with his high estate,
Hiding base sin in pleats of majesty;
That nothing in him seem'd inordinate,
Save sometime too much wonder of his eye, 95
Which, having all, all could not satisfy;
    But, poorly rich, so wanteth in his store
    That, cloy'd with much, he pineth still for
        more.

But she, that never cop'd with stranger eyes,
Could pick no meaning from their parling looks,
Nor read the subtle-shining secrecies   101
Writ in the glassy margents of such books.
She touch'd no unknown baits, nor fear'd no
        hooks;
    Nor could she moralize his wanton sight,
    More than his eyes were open'd to the light.

He stories to her ears her husband's fame,
Won in the fields of fruitful Italy;
And decks with praises Collatine's high name,
Made glorious by his manly chivalry,
With bruised arms and wreaths of victory. 110
    Her joy with heav'd-up hand she doth express,
    And wordless so greets heaven for his success.

Far from the purpose of his coming thither
He makes excuses for his being there.
No cloudy show of stormy blust'ring weather

Doth yet in his fair welkin once appear,   116
Till sable Night, mother of dread and fear,
  Upon the world dim darkness doth display
  And in her vaulty prison stows the day.

For then is Tarquin brought unto his bed, 120
Intending weariness with heavy sprite;
For, after supper, long he questioned
With modest Lucrece, and wore out the night.
Now leaden slumber with live's strength doth
    fight,
  And every one to rest themselves betake, 125
  Save thieves, and cares, and troubled minds
    that wake.

As one of which doth Tarquin lie revolving
The sundry dangers of his will's obtaining;
Yet ever to obtain his will resolving,
Though weak-built hopes persuade him to ab-
    staining.   130
Despair to gain doth traffic oft for gaining;
  And when great treasure is the meed pro-
    posed,
  Though death be adjunct, there's no death
    supposed.

Those that much covet are with gain so fond
For what they have not, that which they pos-
    sess,   135
They scatter and unloose it from their bond,
And so, by hoping more, they have but less;
Or, gaining more, the profit of excess
  Is but to surfeit, and such griefs sustain
  That they prove bankrout in this poor rich
    gain.   140

The aim of all is but to nurse the life
With honour, wealth, and ease in waning age;
And in this aim there is such thwarting strife
That one for all, or all for one we gaģe:
As life for honour in fell battle's rage;   145
  Honour for wealth; and oft that wealth doth
    cost
  The death of all, and all together lost;

So that in vent'ring ill we leave to be
The things we are for that which we expect;
And this ambitious foul infirmity,   150
In having much, torments us with defect
Of that we have: so then we do neglect
  The thing we have; and, all for want of wit,
  Make something nothing by augmenting it.

Such hazard now must doting Tarquin make,
Pawning his honour to obtain his lust: 156

And for himself himself he must forsake.
Then where is truth, if there be no self-trust?
When shall he think to find a stranger just
  When he himself himself confounds, betrays
  To sland'rous tongues and wretched hateful
    days?   161

Now stole upon the time the dead of night,
When heavy sleep had clos'd up mortal eyes.
No comfortable star did lend his light,
No noise but owls' and wolves' death-boding
    cries.   165
Now serves the season that they may surprise
  The silly lambs. Pure thoughts are dead and
    still,
  While lust and murder wakes to stain and kill.

And now this lustful lord leapt from his bed,
Throwing his mantle rudely o'er his arm;   170
Is madly toss'd between desire and dread:
Th' one sweetly flatters, th' other feareth harm;
But honest fear, bewitch'd with lust's foul
    charm,
  Doth too too oft betake him to retire,
  Beaten away by brainsick rude desire,   175

His falchion on a flint he softly smiteth,
That from the cold stone sparks of fire do fly;
Whereat a waxen torch forthwith he lighteth,
Which must be lodestar to his lustful eye;
And to the flame thus speaks advisedly: 180
  'As from this cold flint I enforc'd this fire,
  So Lucrece must I force to my desire.'

Here pale with fear he doth premeditate
The dangers of his loathsome enterprise,
And in his inward mind he doth debate   185
What following sorrow may on this arise;
Then looking scornfully, he doth despise
  His naked armour of still-slaughtered lust
  And justly thus controls his thoughts unjust:

'Fair torch, burn out thy light, and lend it not
To darken her whose light excelleth thine! 191
And die, unhallowed thoughts, before you blot
With your uncleanness that which is divine!
Offer pure incense to so pure a shrine.
  Let fair humanity abhor the deed   195
  That spots and stains love's modest snow-
    white weed.

'O shame to knighthood and to shining arms!
O foul dishonour to my household's grave!
O impious act including all foul harms!
A martial man to be soft fancy's slave!   200

True valour still a true respect should have;
   Then my digression is so vile, so base,
   That it will live engraven in my face.

'Yea, though I die, the scandal will survive
And be an eyesore in my golden coat.   205
Some loathsome dash the herald will contrive
To cipher me how fondly I did dote;
   That my posterity, sham'd with the note,
   Shall curse my bones, and hold it for no sin
   To wish that I their father had not been. 210

'What win I if I gain the thing I seek?
A dream, a breath, a froth of fleeting joy.
Who buys a minute's mirth to wail a week?
Or sells eternity to get a toy?   214
For one sweet grape who will the vine destroy?
   Or what fond beggar, but to touch the crown,
   Would with the sceptre straight be stroken
      down?

'If Collatinus dream of my intent,
Will he not wake, and in a desp'rate rage
Post hither this vile purpose to prevent — 220
This siege that hath engirt his marriage,
This blur to youth, this sorrow to the sage,
   This dying virtue, this surviving shame,
   Whose crime will bear an ever-during blame?

'O, what excuse can my invention make   225
When thou shalt charge me with so black a
      deed?
Will not my tongue be mute, my frail joints
      shake,
Mine eyes forgo their light, my false heart
      bleed?
   The guilt being great, the fear doth still exceed;
   And extreme fear can neither fight nor fly,
   But coward-like with trembling terror die.

'Had Collatinus kill'd my son or sire,
Or lain in ambush to betray my life,
Or were he not my dear friend, this desire
Might have excuse to work upon his wife,   235
As in revenge or quittal of such strife;
   But as he is my kinsman, my dear friend,
   The shame and fault finds no excuse nor end.

'Shameful it is. Ay, if the fact be known.
Hateful it is. There is no hate in loving. 240
I'll beg her love. But she is not her own.
The worst is but denial and reproving.
   My will is strong, past reason's weak removing.
   Who fears a sentence or an old man's saw
   Shall by a painted cloth be kept in awe.' 245

Thus graceless holds he disputation
'Tween frozen conscience and hot-burning will,
And with good thoughts makes dispensation,
Urging the worser sense for vantage still;
Which in a moment doth confound and kill 250
   All pure effects, and doth so far proceed
   That what is vile shows like a virtuous deed.

Quoth he, 'She took me kindly by the hand
And gaz'd for tidings in my eager eyes,
Fearing some hard news from the warlike band
Where her beloved Collatinus lies.   256
O, how her fear did make her colour rise!
   First red as roses that on lawn we lay,
   Then white as lawn, the roses took away.

'And how her hand, in my hand being lock'd,
Forc'd it to tremble with her loyal fear! 261
Which struck her sad, and then it faster rock'd
Until her husband's welfare she did hear;
Whereat she smiled with so sweet a cheer
   That, had Narcissus seen her as she stood, 265
   Self-love had never drown'd him in the flood.

'Why hunt I then for colour or excuses?
All orators are dumb when beauty pleadeth;
Poor wretches have remorse in poor abuses;
Love thrives not in the heart that shadows
      dreadeth.   270
Affection is my captain, and he leadeth;
   And when his gaudy banner is display'd,
   The coward fights and will not be dismay'd.

'Then childish fear avaunt! debating die!
Respect and reason wait on wrinkled age!   275
My heart shall never countermand mine eye.
Sad pause and deep regard beseems the sage;
My part is youth, and beats these from the
      stage.
   Desire my pilot is, beauty my prize;
   Then who fears sinking where such treasure
      lies?'   280

As corn o'ergrown by weeds, so heedful fear
Is almost chok'd by unresisted lust.
Away he steals with open list'ning ear,
Full of foul hope and full of fond mistrust;
Both which, as servitors to the unjust,   285
   So cross him with their opposite persuasion
   That now he vows a league, and now inva-
      sion.

Within his thought her heavenly image sits,
And in the selfsame seat sits Collatine.   289
That eye which looks on her confounds his wits;

That eye which him beholds, as more divine,
Unto a view so false will not incline;
  But with a pure appeal seeks to the heart,
  Which once corrupted takes the worser part;

And therein heartens up his servile powers,
Who, flatt'red by their leader's jocund show,
Stuff up his lust, as minutes fill up hours;
And as their captain, so their pride doth grow,
Paying more slavish tribute than they owe.
  By reprobate desire thus madly led,   300
  The Roman lord marcheth to Lucrece' bed.

The locks between her chamber and his will,
Each one by him enforc'd retires his ward;
But, as they open, they all rate his ill,   304
Which drives the creeping thief to some regard.
The threshold grates the door to have him
    heard;
  Night-wand'ring weasels shriek to see him
    there;
  They fright him, yet he still pursues his fear.

As each unwilling portal yields him way,   309
Through little vents and crannies of the place
The wind wars with his torch to make him stay,
And blows the smoke of it into his face,
Extinguishing his conduct in this case;
  But his hot heart, which fond desire doth
    scorch,   314
  Puffs forth another wind that fires the torch;

And being lighted, by the light he spies
Lucretia's glove, wherein her needle sticks.
He takes it from the rushes where it lies,
And griping it, the needle his finger pricks,
As who should say, 'This glove to wanton tricks
  Is not inur'd. Return again in haste!   321
  Thou see'st our mistress' ornaments are
    chaste.'

But all these poor forbiddings could not stay
    him;
He in the worst sense consters their denial:
The doors, the wind, the glove, that did delay
    him,   325
He takes for accidental things of trial;
  Or as those bars which stop the hourly dial,
  Who with a ling'ring stay his course doth let
  Till every minute pays the hour his debt.

'So, so,' quoth he, 'these lets attend the time,
Like little frosts that sometime threat the spring
To add a more rejoicing to the prime
And give the sneaped birds more cause to sing.

Pain pays the income of each precious thing:
  Huge rocks, high winds, strong pirates,
    shelves and sands,   335
  The merchant fears ere rich at home he lands.'

Now is he come unto the chamber door
That shuts him from the heaven of his thought,
Which with a yielding latch, and with no more,
Hath barr'd him from the blessed thing he
    sought.   340
So from himself impiety hath wrought
  That for his prey to pray he doth begin,
  As if the heavens should countenance his sin.

But in the midst of his unfruitful prayer,
Having solicited th' eternal power   345
That his foul thoughts might compass his fair
    fair,
And they would stand auspicious to the hour,
Even there he starts. Quoth he, 'I must de-
    flow'r.
  The powers to whom I pray abhor this fact;
  How can they then assist me in the act?   350

'Then Love and Fortune be my gods, my guide!
My will is back'd with resolution.
Thoughts are but dreams till their effects be
    tried;
The blackest sin is clear'd with absolution;   354
Against love's fire fear's frost hath dissolution.
  The eye of heaven is out, and misty night
  Covers the shame that follows sweet delight.'

This said, his guilty hand pluck'd up the latch,
And with his knee the door he opens wide.
The dove sleeps fast that this night owl will
    catch.   360
Thus treason works ere traitors be espied.
Who sees the lurking serpent steps aside;
  But she, sound sleeping, fearing no such
    thing,
  Lies at the mercy of his mortal sting.

Into the chamber wickedly he stalks   365
And gazeth on her yet unstained bed.
The curtains being close, about he walks,
Rolling his greedy eyeballs in his head.
By their high treason is his heart misled,
  Which gives the watchword to his hand full
    soon   370
  To draw the cloud that hides the silver moon.

Look, as the fair and fiery-pointed sun,
Rushing from forth a cloud, bereaves our sight,
Even so, the curtain drawn, his eyes begun

To wink, being blinded with a greater light;
Whether it is that she reflects so bright   376
    That dazzleth them, or else some shame sup-
        posed —
    But blind they are, and keep themselves
        enclosed.

O, had they in that darksome prison died,
Then had they seen the period of their ill!   380
Then Collatine again, by Lucrece' side,
In his clear bed might have reposed still!
But they must ope, this blessed league to kill,
    And holy-thoughted Lucrece to their sight
    Must sell her joy, her life, her world's delight.

Her lily hand her rosy cheek lies under,   386
Coz'ning the pillow of a lawful kiss;
Who, therefore angry, seems to part in sunder,
Swelling on either side to want his bliss;
Between whose hills her head entombed is;   390
    Where like a virtuous monument she lies,
    To be admir'd of lewd unhallowed eyes.

Without the bed her other fair hand was,
On the green coverlet; whose perfect white
Show'd like an April daisy on the grass,   395
With pearly sweat resembling dew of night.
Her eyes, like marigolds, had sheath'd their
        light,
    And canopied in darkness sweetly lay
    Till they might open to adorn the day.

Her hair like golden threads play'd with her
        breath   400
O modest wantons! wanton modesty!
Showing life's triumph in the map of death,
And death's dim look in life's mortality.
Each in her sleep themselves so beautify
    As if between them twain there were no
        strife,   405
    But that life liv'd in death, and death in life.

Her breasts like ivory globes circled with blue,
A pair of maiden worlds unconquered,
Save of their lord no bearing yoke they knew,
And him by oath they truly honoured.   410
These worlds in Tarquin new ambition bred,
    Who like a foul usurper went about
    From this fair throne to heave the owner out.

What could he see but mightily he noted?
What did he note but strongly he desired?   415
What he beheld, on that he firmly doted,
And in his will his wilful eye he tired.
With more than admiration he admired

Her azure veins, her alablaster skin,   419
Her coral lips, her snow-white dimpled chin.

As the grim lion fawneth o'er his prey,
Sharp hunger by the conquest satisfied,
So o'er this sleeping soul doth Tarquin stay,
His rage of lust by gazing qualified;
Slack'd, not suppress'd; for, standing by her
        side,   425
    His eye, which late this mutiny restrains,
    Unto a greater uproar tempts his veins;

And they, like straggling slaves for pillage
        fighting,
Obdurate vassals fell exploits effecting,
In bloody death and ravishment delighting,   430
Nor children's tears nor mothers' groans re-
        specting,
    Swell in their pride, the onset still expecting.
    Anon his beating heart, alarum striking,
    Gives the hot charge and bids them do their
        liking.

His drumming heart cheers up his burning eye,
His eye commends the leading to his hand;   436
His hand, as proud of such a dignity,
Smoking with pride, march'd on to make his
        stand
On her bare breast, the heart of all her land;
    Whose ranks of blue veins, as his hand did
        scale,   440
    Left their round turrets destitute and pale.

They, must'ring to the quiet cabinet
Where their dear governess and lady lies,
Do tell her she is dreadfully beset   444
And fright her with confusion of their cries.
She, much amaz'd, breaks ope her lock'd-up
        eyes,
    Who, peeping forth this tumult to behold,
    Are by his flaming torch dimm'd and con-
        troll'd.

Imagine her as one in dead of night,   449
From forth dull sleep by dreadful fancy waking,
That thinks she hath beheld some ghastly
        sprite,
Whose grim aspect sets every joint a-shaking.
What terror 'tis! but she, in worser taking,
    From sleep disturbed, heedfully doth view
    The sight which makes supposed terror true.

Wrapp'd and confounded in a thousand fears,
Like to a new-kill'd bird she trembling lies.
She dares not look; yet, winking, there appears

433

Quick-shifting antics ugly in her eyes.   459
Such shadows are the weak brain's forgeries,
  Who, angry that the eyes fly from their lights,
  In darkness daunts them with more dreadful
    sights.

His hand, that yet remains upon her breast
(Rude ram, to batter such an ivory wall!)
May feel her heart (poor citizen!) distress'd,
Wounding itself to death, rise up and fall,
Beating her bulk, that his hand shakes withal.
  This moves in him more rage and lesser pity,
  To make the breach and enter this sweet city.

First like a trumpet doth his tongue begin   470
To sound a parley to his heartless foe;
Who o'er the white sheet peers her whiter chin,
The reason of this rash alarm to know,
Which he by dumb demeanour seeks to show;
  But she with vehement prayers urgeth still
  Under what colour he commits this ill.   476

Thus he replies: 'The colour in thy face,
That even for anger makes the lily pale
And the red rose blush at her own disgrace,
Shall plead for me and tell my loving tale.   480
Under that colour am I come to scale
Thy never-conquered fort. The fault is thine,
For those thine eyes betray thee unto mine.

'Thus I forestall thee, if thou mean to chide:
Thy beauty hath ensnar'd thee to this night,
Where thou with patience must my will abide—
My will, that marks thee for my earth's delight,
Which I to conquer sought with all my might;
  But as reproof and reason beat it dead,
  By thy bright beauty was it newly bred.   490

'I see what crosses my attempt will bring;
I know what thorns the growing rose defends;
I think the honey guarded with a sting;
All this beforehand counsel comprehends;
But Will is deaf and hears no heedful friends;
  Only he hath an eye to gaze on Beauty,   496
  And dotes on what he looks, 'gainst law or
    duty.

'I have debated even in my soul
What wrong, what shame, what sorrow I shall
    breed;
But nothing can affection's course control   500
Or stop the headlong fury of his speed.
I know repentant tears ensue the deed
  Reproach, disdain, and deadly enmity;
  Yet strive I to embrace mine infamy.'

This said, he shakes aloft his Roman blade,   505
Which, like a falcon tow'ring in the skies,
Coucheth the fowl below with his wings' shade,
Whose crooked beak threats if he mount he
    dies.
So under his insulting falchion lies
  Harmless Lucretia, marking what he tells   510
  With trembling fear, as fowl hear falcons'
    bells.

'Lucrece,' quoth he, 'this night I must enjoy
    thee.
If thou deny, then force must work my way;
For in thy bed I purpose to destroy thee.
That done, some worthless slave of thine I'll
    slay,   515
To kill thine honour with thy live's decay;
  And in thy dead arms do I mean to place him,
  Swearing I slew him, seeing thee embrace him.

'So thy surviving husband shall remain
The scornful mark of every open eye;   520
Thy kinsmen hang their heads at this disdain,
Thy issue blurr'd with nameless bastardy;
And thou, the author of their obloquy,
  Shalt have thy trespass cited up in rhymes
  And sung by children in succeeding times.   525

'But if thou yield, I rest thy secret friend:
The fault unknown is as a thought unacted.
A little harm done to a great good end
For lawful policy remains enacted.   529
The poisonous simple sometime is compacted
  In a pure compound; being so applied,
  His venom in effect is purified.

'Then, for thy husband and thy children's sake,
Tender my suit. Bequeath not to their lot
The shame that from them no device can take,
The blemish that will never be forgot;   536
Worse than a slavish wipe or birth-hour's blot;
  For marks descried in men's nativity
  Are nature's faults, not their own infamy.'

Here with a cockatrice' dead-killing eye   540
He rouseth up himself and makes a pause;
While she, the picture of pure piety,
Like a white hind under the gripe's sharp claws,
Pleads, in a wilderness where are no laws,
  To the rough beast that knows no gentle right
  Nor aught obeys but his foul appetite.   546

But when a black-fac'd cloud the world doth
    threat,
In his dim mist th' aspiring mountains hiding,

From earth's dark womb some gentle gust doth
    get,
Which blows these pitchy vapours from their
    biding,   550
Hind'ring their present fall by this dividing —
  So his unhallowed haste her words delays,
  And moody Pluto winks while Orpheus plays.

Yet, foul night-waking cat, he doth but dally,
While in his hold-fast foot the weak mouse
    panteth.   555
Her sad behaviour feeds his vulture folly,
A swallowing gulf that even in plenty wanteth.
His ear her prayers admits, but his heart
    granteth
  No penetrable entrance to her plaining.
  Tears harden lust, though marble wear with
    raining.   560

Her pity-pleading eyes are sadly fixed
In the remorseless wrinkles of his face.
Her modest eloquence with sighs is mixed,
Which to her oratory adds more grace.
She puts the period often from his place,   565
  And midst the sentence so her accent breaks
  That twice she doth begin ere once she speaks.

She conjures him by high almighty Jove,
By knighthood, gentry, and sweet friendship's
    oath,
By her untimely tears, her husband's love,   570
By holy human law and common troth,
By heaven and earth, and all the power of both,
  That to his borrowed bed he make retire
  And stoop to honour, not to foul desire.

Quoth she, 'Reward not hospitality   575
With such black payment as thou hast pre-
    tended;
Mud not the fountain that gave drink to thee;
Mar not the thing that cannot be amended.
End thy ill aim before thy shoot be ended.
  He is no woodman that doth bend his bow
  To strike a poor unseasonable doe.   581

'My husband is thy friend — for his sake spare
    me;
Thyself art mighty — for thine own sake leave
    me;
Myself a weakling — do not then ensnare me;
Thou look'st not like deceit — do not deceive
    me.   585
My sighs like whirlwinds labour hence to heave
    thee.
  If ever man were mov'd with woman's moans,
  Be moved with my tears, my sighs, my groans;

'All which together, like a troubled ocean,
Beat at thy rocky and wrack-threat'ning heart,
To soften it with their continual motion;   591
For stones dissolv'd to water do convert.
O, if no harder than a stone thou art,
  Melt at my tears and be compassionate!
  Soft pity enters at an iron gate.   595

'In Tarquin's likeness I did entertain thee:
Hast thou put on his shape to do him shame?
To all the host of heaven I complain me:
Thou wrong'st his honour, wound'st his princely
    name.
Thou art not what thou seem'st; and if the
    same,   600
  Thou seem'st not what thou art, a god, a king;
  For kings like gods should govern everything.

'How will thy shame be seeded in thine age
When thus thy vices bud before thy spring?
If in thy hope thou dar'st do such outrage,   605
What dar'st thou not when once thou art a king?
O, be rememb'red, no outrageous thing
  From vassal actors can be wip'd away:
  Then kings' misdeeds cannot be hid in clay.

'This deed will make thee only lov'd for fear;
But happy monarchs still are fear'd for love. 611
With foul offenders thou perforce must bear
When they in thee the like offences prove.
If but for fear of this, thy will remove;
  For princes are the glass, the school, the book,
  Where subjects' eyes do learn, do read, do
    look.   616

'And wilt thou be the school where Lust shall
    learn?
Must he in thee read lectures of such shame?
Wilt thou be glass wherein it shall discern
Authority for sin, warrant for blame,   620
To privilege dishonour in thy name?
  Thou back'st reproach against long-living
    laud
  And mak'st fair reputation but a bawd.

'Hast thou command? By him that gave it
    thee,
From a pure heart command thy rebel will! 625
Draw not thy sword to guard iniquity,
For it was lent thee all that brood to kill.
Thy princely office how canst thou fulfil
  When, pattern'd by thy fault, foul Sin may
    say,
  He learn'd to sin, and thou didst teach the
    way?   630

'Think but how vile a spectacle it were
To view thy present trespass in another.
Men's faults do seldom to themselves appear;
Their own transgressions partially they smother:
This guilt would seem death-worthy in thy
    brother.   635
    O, how are they wrapp'd in with infamies
    That from their own misdeeds askaunce
    their eyes!

'To thee, to thee, my heav'd-up hands appeal,
Not to seducing lust, thy rash relier!
I sue for exil'd majesty's repeal;   640
Let him return, and flatt'ring thoughts retire.
His true respect will prison false desire
    And wipe the dim mist from thy doting eyne,
    That thou shalt see thy state, and pity mine.'

'Have done,' quoth he. 'My uncontrolled tide
Turns not, but swells the higher by this let. 646
Small lights are soon blown out; huge fires
    abide
And with the wind in greater fury fret.
The petty streams that pay a daily debt
    To their salt sovereign with their fresh falls'
    haste,   650
    Add to his flow, but alter not his taste.'

'Thou art,' quoth she, 'a sea, a sovereign king;
And, lo, there falls into thy boundless flood
Black lust, dishonour, shame, misgoverning,
Who seek to stain the ocean of thy blood. 655
If all these petty ills shall change thy good,
    Thy sea within a puddle's womb is hearsed,
    And not the puddle in thy sea dispersed.

'So shall these slaves be king, and thou their
    slave;
Thou nobly base, they basely dignified; 660
Thou their fair life, and they thy fouler grave;
Thou loathed in their shame, they in thy pride.
The lesser thing should not the greater hide.
    The cedar stoops not to the base shrub's
    foot,
    But low shrubs wither at the cedar's root. 665

'So let thy thoughts, low vassals to thy state'—
'No more,' quoth he. 'By heaven, I will not
    hear thee!
Yield to my love; if not, enforced hate,
Instead of love's coy touch, shall rudely tear
    thee.
That done, despitefully I mean to bear thee 670
    Unto the base bed of some rascal groom,
    To be thy partner in this shameful doom.'

This said, he sets his foot upon the light,
For light and lust are deadly enemies;
Shame folded up in blind concealing night, 675
When most unseen, then most doth tyrannize.
The wolf hath seiz'd his prey; the poor lamb
    cries,
    Till with her own white fleece her voice
    controll'd
    Entombs her outcry in her lips' sweet fold;

For with the nightly linen that she wears 680
He pens her piteous clamours in her head,
Cooling his hot face in the chastest tears
That ever modest eyes with sorrow shed.
O, that prone lust should stain so pure a bed!
    The spots whereof could weeping purify, 685
    Her tears should drop on them perpetually.

But she hath lost a dearer thing than life,
And he hath won what he would lose again.
This forced league doth force a further strife;
This momentary joy breeds months of pain;
This hot desire converts to cold disdain; 691
    Pure Chastity is rifled of her store,
    And Lust, the thief, far poorer than before.

Look, as the full-fed hound or gorged hawk,
Unapt for tender smell or speedy flight, 695
Make slow pursuit, or altogether balk
The prey wherein by nature they delight,
So surfeit-taking Tarquin fares this night:
    His taste delicious, in digestion souring, 699
    Devours his will, that liv'd by foul devouring.

O, deeper sin than bottomless conceit
Can comprehend in still imagination!
Drunken Desire must vomit his receipt
Ere he can see his own abomination.
While Lust is in his pride, no exclamation 705
    Can curb his heat or rein his rash desire
    Till, like a jade, Self-will himself doth tire.

And then with lank and lean discolour'd cheek,
With heavy eye, knit brow, and strengthless
    pace,   709
Feeble Desire, all recreant, poor, and meek,
Like to a bankrout beggar wails his case.
The flesh being proud, Desire doth fight with
    Grace,
    For there it revels; and when that decays,
    The guilty rebel for remission prays.

So fares it with this fault-full lord of Rome, 715
Who this accomplishment so hotly chased;
For now against himself he sounds this doom

That through the length of times he stands dis-
    graced.
Besides, his soul's fair temple is defaced;   719
  To whose weak ruins muster troops of cares,
  To ask the spotted princess how she fares.

She says her subjects with foul insurrection
Have batter'd down her consecrated wall,
And by their mortal fault brought in subjection
Her immortality and made her thrall   725
To living death and pain perpetual;
  Which in her prescience she controlled still,
  But her foresight could not forestall their
    will.

Ev'n in this thought through the dark night he
    stealeth,
A captive victor that hath lost in gain;   730
Bearing away the wound that nothing healeth,
The scar that will despite of cure remain;
Leaving his spoil perplex'd in greater pain.
  She bears the load of lust he left behind,
  And he the burthen of a guilty mind.   735

He like a thievish dog creeps sadly thence;
She like a wearied lamb lies panting there.
He scowls, and hates himself for his offence;
She desperate with her nails her flesh doth tear.
He faintly flies, sweating with guilty fear;   740
  She stays, exclaiming on the direful night;
  He runs, and chides his vanish'd loath'd
    delight.

He thence departs a heavy convertite;
She there remains a hopeless castaway.   744
He in his speed looks for the morning light;
She prays she never may behold the day,
'For day,' quoth she, 'night's scapes doth open
    lay,
  And my true eyes have never practis'd how
  To cloak offences with a cunning brow.

'They think not but that every eye can see   750
The same disgrace which they themselves be-
    hold;
And therefore would they still in darkness be,
To have their unseen sin remain untold;
For they their guilt with weeping will unfold
  And grave, like water that doth eat in steel,
  Upon my cheeks what helpless shame I feel.'

Here she exclaims against repose and rest
And bids her eyes hereafter still be blind.
She wakes her heart by beating on her breast
And bids it leap from thence, where it may find

Some purer chest to close so pure a mind.   761
  Frantic with grief thus breathes she forth her
    spite
  Against the unseen secrecy of night:

'O comfort-killing Night, image of hell!
Dim register and notary of shame!   765
Black stage for tragedies and murthers fell!
Vast sin-concealing chaos! nurse of blame!
Blind muffled bawd! dark harbour for defame!
  Grim cave of death! whisp'ring conspirator
  With close-tongu'd treason and the ravisher!

'O hateful, vaporous, and foggy Night!   771
Since thou art guilty of my cureless crime,
Muster thy mists to meet the Eastern light,
Make war against proportion'd course of time;
Or if thou wilt permit the sun to climb   775
  His wonted height, yet ere he go to bed,
  Knit poisonous clouds about his golden head.

'With rotten damps ravish the morning air;
Let their exhal'd unwholesome breaths make
    sick
The life of purity, the supreme fair,   780
Ere he arrive his weary noontide prick;
And let thy musty vapours march so thick
  That in their smoky ranks his smoth'red light
  May set at noon and make perpetual night.

'Were Tarquin Night, as he is but Night's child,
The silver-shining queen he would distain;   786
Her twinkling handmaids too, by him defil'd,
Through Night's black bosom should not peep
    again.
So should I have copartners in my pain;
  And fellowship in woe doth woe assuage,   790
  As palmers' chat makes short their pilgrim-
    age;

'Where now I have no one to blush with me,
To cross their arms and hang their heads with
    mine,
To mask their brows and hide their infamy;
But I alone, alone must sit and pine,   795
Seasoning the earth with show'rs of silver brine,
  Mingling my talk with tears, my grief with
    groans,
  Poor wasting monuments of lasting moans.

'O Night, thou furnace of foul reeking smoke,
Let not the jealous Day behold that face   800
Which underneath thy black all-hiding cloak
Immodestly lies martyr'd with disgrace!
  Keep still possession of thy gloomy place,

That all the faults which in thy reign are made
May likewise be sepulcher'd in thy shade!

'Make me not object to the telltale Day! 806
The light will show, character'd in my brow,
The story of sweet chastity's decay,
The impious breach of holy wedlock vow.
Yea, the illiterate, that know not how 810
　To cipher what is writ in learned books,
　Will quote my loathsome trespass in my
　　looks.

'The nurse, to still her child, will tell my story
And fright her crying babe with Tarquin's
　name.
The orator, to deck his oratory, 815
Will couple my reproach to Tarquin's shame.
Feast-finding minstrels, tuning my defame,
　Will tie the hearers to attend each line,
　How Tarquin wronged me, I Collatine. 819

'Let my good name, that senseless reputation,
For Collatine's dear love be kept unspotted.
If that be made a theme for disputation,
The branches of another root are rotted,
And undeserv'd reproach to him allotted
　That is as clear from this attaint of mine 825
　As I ere this was pure to Collatine.

'O unseen shame! invisible disgrace!
O unfelt sore! crest-wounding private scar!
Reproach is stamp'd in Collatinus' face,
And Tarquin's eye may read the mot afar, 830
How he in peace is wounded, not in war.
　Alas, how many bear such shameful blows
　Which not themselves, but he that gives
　　them knows!

'If, Collatine, thine honour lay in me,
From me by strong assault it is bereft: 835
My honey lost, and I, a drone-like bee,
Have no perfection of my summer left,
But robb'd and ransack'd by injurious theft.
　In thy weak hive a wand'ring wasp hath crept
　And suck'd the honey which thy chaste bee
　　kept. 840

'Yet am I guilty of thy honour's wrack;
Yet for thy honour did I entertain him.
Coming from thee, I could not put him back,
For it had been dishonour to disdain him.
Besides, of weariness he did complain him 845
　And talk'd of virtue — O unlook'd-for evil
　When virtue is profan'd in such a devil!

'Why should the worm intrude the maiden
　bud?
Or hateful cuckoos hatch in sparrows' nests?
Or toads infect fair founts with venom mud?
Or tyrant folly lurk in gentle breasts? 851
Or kings be breakers of their own behests?
　But no perfection is so absolute
　That some impurity doth not pollute.

'The aged man that coffers up his gold 855
Is plagu'd with cramps and gouts and painful
　fits,
And scarce hath eyes his treasure to behold,
But like still-pining Tantalus he sits
And useless barns the harvest of his wits,
　Having no other pleasure of his gain 860
　But torment that it cannot cure his pain.

'So then he hath it when he cannot use it,
And leaves it to be mast'red by his young,
Who in their pride do presently abuse it. 864
Their father was too weak, and they too strong,
To hold their cursed-blessed fortune long.
　The sweets we wish for turn to loathed sours
　Even in the moment that we call them ours.

'Unruly blasts wait on the tender spring;
Unwholesome weeds take root with precious
　flow'rs; 870
The adder hisses where the sweet birds sing;
What virtue breeds iniquity devours.
We have no good that we can say is ours,
　But ill-annexed opportunity
　Or kills his life or else his quality. 875

'O Opportunity, thy guilt is great!
'Tis thou that execut'st the traitor's treason;
Thou sets the wolf where he the lamb may get;
Whoever plots the sin, thou point'st the season.
'Tis thou that spurn'st at right, at law, at
　reason; 880
　And in thy shady cell, where none may spy
　　him,
　Sits Sin, to seize the souls that wander by
　　him.

'Thou makest the vestal violate her oath;
Thou blowest the fire when temperance is
　thaw'd;
Thou smother'st honesty, thou murth'rest
　troth, 885
Thou foul abettor! thou notorious bawd!
Thou plantest scandal and displacest laud.
　Thou ravisher, thou traitor, thou false thief!
　Thy honey turns to gall, thy joy to grief.

'Thy secret pleasure turns to open shame, 890
Thy private feasting to a public fast,
Thy smoothing titles to a ragged name,
Thy sug'red tongue to bitter wormwood taste:
Thy violent vanities can never last.
 How comes it then, vile Opportunity, 895
 Being so bad, such numbers seek for thee?

'When wilt thou be the humble suppliant's
 friend
And bring him where his suit may be obtained?
When wilt thou sort an hour great strifes to
 end?
Or free that soul which wretchedness hath
 chained? 900
Give physic to the sick, ease to the pained?
 The poor, lame, blind, halt, creep, cry out for
 thee;
 But they ne'er meet with Opportunity.

'The patient dies while the physician sleeps;
The orphan pines while the oppressor feeds; 905
Justice is feasting while the widow weeps;
Advice is sporting while infection breeds.
Thou grant'st no time for charitable deeds:
 Wrath, envy, treason, rape, and murther's
 rages,
 Thy heinous hours wait on them as their
 pages. 910

'When Truth and Virtue have to do with thee,
A thousand crosses keep them from thy aid.
They buy thy help; but Sin ne'er gives a fee,
He gratis comes; and thou art well apaid
As well to hear as grant what he hath said. 915
 My Collatine would else have come to me
 When Tarquin did, but he was stay'd by
 thee.

'Guilty thou art of murther and of theft,
Guilty of perjury and subornation,
Guilty of treason, forgery, and shift, 920
Guilty of incest, that abomination —
An accessary by thine inclination
 To all sins past and all that are to come,
 From the creation to the general doom.

'Misshapen Time, copesmate of ugly Night,
Swift subtle post, carrier of grisly care, 926
Eater of youth, false slave to false delight,
Base watch of woes, sin's packhorse, virtue's
 snare!
Thou nursest all, and murth'rest all that are.
 O, hear me then, injurious, shifting Time!
 Be guilty of my death, since of my crime.

'Why hath thy servant Opportunity
Betray'd the hours thou gav'st me to repose?
Cancell'd my fortunes, and enchained me
To endless date of never-ending woes? 935
Time's office is to fine the hate of foes,
 To eat up errors by opinion bred,
 Not spend the dowry of a lawful bed.

'Time's glory is to calm contending kings, 939
To unmask falsehood and bring truth to light,
To stamp the seal of time in aged things,
To wake the morn and sentinel the night,
To wrong the wronger till he render right,
 To ruinate proud buildings with thy hours,
 And smear with dust their glitt'ring golden
 tow'rs; 945

'To fill with wormholes stately monuments,
To feed oblivion with decay of things,
To blot old books and alter their contents,
To pluck the quills from ancient ravens' wings
To dry the old oak's sap and cherish springs,
 To spoil antiquities of hammer'd steel 951
 And turn the giddy round of Fortune's wheel;

'To show the beldame daughters of her daugh-
 ter,
To make the child a man, the man a child,
To slay the tiger that doth live by slaughter,
To tame the unicorn and lion wild, 956
To mock the subtle in themselves beguil'd,
 To cheer the ploughman with increaseful
 crops
 And waste huge stones with little water-
 drops. 959

'Why work'st thou mischief in thy pilgrimage,
Unless thou couldst return to make amends?
One poor retiring minute in an age
Would purchase thee a thousand thousand
 friends,
Lending him wit that to bad debtors lends.
 O this dread night, wouldst thou one hour
 come back, 965
 I could prevent this storm and shun thy
 wrack!

'Thou ceaseless lackey to Eternity,
With some mischance cross Tarquin in his
 flight.
Devise extremes beyond extremity 969
To make him curse this cursed crimeful night.
Let ghastly shadows his lewd eyes affright,
 And the dire thought of his committed evil
 Shape every bush a hideous shapeless devil.

'Disturb his hours of rest with restless trances;
Afflict him in his bed with bedrid groans; 975
Let there bechance him pitiful mischances
To make him moan, but pity not his moans.
Stone him with hard'ned hearts harder than
  stones,
  And let mild women to him lose their mild-
    ness, 979
  Wilder to him than tigers in their wildness.

'Let him have time to tear his curled hair,
Let him have time against himself to rave,
Let him have time of Time's help to despair,
Let him have time to live a loathed slave,
Let him have time a beggar's orts to crave, 985
  And time to see one that by alms doth live
  Disdain to him disdained scraps to give.

'Let him have time to see his friends his foes
And merry fools to mock at him resort;
Let him have time to mark how slow time
  goes 990
In time of sorrow, and how swift and short
His time of folly and his time of sport;
  And ever let his unrecalling crime
  Have time to wail th' abusing of his time.

'O Time, thou tutor both to good and bad, 995
Teach me to curse him that thou taught'st this
  ill!
At his own shadow let the thief run mad,
Himself himself seek every hour to kill!
Such wretched hands such wretched blood
  should spill; 999
  For who so base would such an office have
  As sland'rous deathsman to so base a slave?

'The baser is he, coming from a king,
To shame his hope with deeds degenerate.
The mightier man, the mightier is the thing
That makes him honour'd or begets him hate;
For greatest scandal waits on greatest state.
  The moon being clouded presently is miss'd,
  But little stars may hide them when they
    list.

'The crow may bathe his coal-black wings in
  mire
And unperceiv'd fly with the filth away; 1010
But if the like the snow-white swan desire,
The stain upon his silver down will stay.
Poor grooms are sightless night, kings glorious
  day:
  Gnats are unnoted wheresoe'er they fly,
  But eagles gaz'd upon with every eye. 1015

'Out, idle words, servants to shallow fools!
Unprofitable sounds, weak arbitrators!
Busy yourselves in skill-contending schools;
Debate where leisure serves with dull debaters;
To trembling clients be you mediators: 1020
  For me, I force not argument a straw,
  Since that my case is past the help of law.

'In vain I rail at Opportunity,
At Time, at Tarquin, and uncheerful Night;
In vain I cavil with mine infamy; 1025
In vain I spurn at my confirm'd despite:
This helpless smoke of words doth me no right.
  The remedy indeed to do me good
  Is to let forth my foul defiled blood.

'Poor hand, why quiver'st thou at this decree?
Honour thyself to rid me of this shame; 1031
For if I die, my honour lives in thee;
But if I live, thou liv'st in my defame.
Since thou couldst not defend thy loyal dame
  And wast afeard to scratch her wicked foe,
  Kill both thyself and her for yielding so.'

This said, from her betumbled couch she start-
  eth
To find some desp'rate instrument of death;
But this no slaughterhouse no tool imparteth
To make more vent for passage of her breath;
Which, thronging through her lips, so vanisheth
  As smoke from Ætna that in air consumes
  Or that which from discharged cannon fumes.

'In vain,' quoth she, 'I live, and seek in vain
Some happy mean to end a hapless life. 1045
I fear'd by Tarquin's falchion to be slain,
Yet for the selfsame purpose seek a knife;
But when I fear'd I was a loyal wife.
  So am I now. — O no, that cannot be! 1049
  Of that true type hath Tarquin rifled me.

'O, that is gone for which I sought to live,
And therefore now I need not fear to die.
To clear this spot by death, at least I give
A badge of fame to slander's livery,
A dying life to living infamy. 1055
  Poor helpless help, the treasure stol'n away,
  To burn the guiltless casket where it lay!

'Well, well, dear Collatine, thou shalt not know
The stained taste of violated troth.
I will not wrong thy true affection so, 1060
To flatter thee with an infringed oath.
This bastard graff shall never come to growth:
  He shall not boast who did thy stock pollute
  That thou art doting father of his fruit. 1064

'Nor shall he smile at thee in secret thought,
Nor laugh with his companions at thy state;
But thou shalt know thy int'rest was not bought
Basely with gold, but stol'n from forth thy gate.
For me, I am the mistress of my fate, 1069
    And with my trespass never will dispense
    Till life to death acquit my forc'd offence.

'I will not poison thee with my attaint
Nor fold my fault in cleanly coin'd excuses;
My sable ground of sin I will not paint
To hide the truth of this false night's abuses.
My tongue shall utter all; mine eyes, like
    sluices, 1076
    As from a mountain spring that feeds a dale,
    Shall gush pure streams to purge my impure
    tale.'

By this, lamenting Philomele had ended 1079
The well-tun'd warble of her nightly sorrow,
And solemn night with slow sad gait descended
To ugly hell; when, lo, the blushing morrow
Lends light to all fair eyes that light will
    borrow;
    But cloudy Lucrece shames herself to see
    And therefore still in night would cloist'red
    be. 1085

Revealing day through every cranny spies
And seems to point her out where she sits
    weeping;
To whom she sobbing speaks: 'O eye of eyes,
Why pry'st thou through my window? Leave
    thy peeping.
Mock with thy tickling beams eyes that are
    sleeping. 1090
    Brand not my forehead with thy piercing
    light,
    For day hath naught to do what's done by
    night.'

Thus cavils she with everything she sees.
True grief is fond and testy as a child,
Who wayward once, his mood with naught
    agrees. 1095
Old woes, not infant sorrows, bear them mild:
Continuance tames the one; the other wild,
    Like an unpractis'd swimmer plunging still,
    With too much labour drowns for want of
    skill.

So she, deep drenched in a sea of care, 1100
Holds disputation with each thing she views
And to herself all sorrow doth compare;
No object but her passion's strength renews;

And as one shifts, another straight ensues.
    Sometime her grief is dumb and hath no
    words; 1105
    Sometime 'tis mad and too much talk affords.

The little birds that tune their morning's joy
Make her moans mad with their sweet melody:
For mirth doth search the bottom of annoy;
Sad souls are slain in merry company; 1110
Grief best is pleas'd with grief's society;
    True sorrow then is feelingly suffic'd
    When with like semblance it is sympathiz'd.

'Tis double death to drown in ken of shore;
He ten times pines that pines beholding food;
To see the salve doth make the wound ache
    more; 1116
Great grief grieves most at that would do it
    good;
Deep woes roll forward like a gentle flood,
    Who, being stopp'd, the bounding banks
    o'erflows;
    Grief dallied with nor law nor limit knows.

'You mocking birds,' quoth she, 'your tunes
    entomb 1121
Within your hollow-swelling feathered breasts,
And in my hearing be you mute and dumb;
My restless discord loves no stops nor rests —
A woful hostess brooks not merry guests. 1125
    Relish your nimble notes to pleasing ears;
    Distress likes dumps when time is kept with
    tears.

'Come, Philomele, that sing'st of ravishment,
Make thy sad grove in my dishevell'd hair.
As the dank earth weeps at thy languishment,
So I at each sad strain will strain a tear 1131
And with deep groans the diapason bear;
    For burthen-wise I'll hum on Tarquin still,
    While thou on Tereus descants better skill;

'And whiles against a thorn thou bear'st thy
    part 1135
To keep thy sharp woes waking, wretched I,
To imitate thee well, against my heart
Will fix a sharp knife to affright mine eye;
Who, if it wink, shall thereon fall and die.
    These means, as frets upon an instrument,
    Shall tune our heartstrings to true languish-
    ment. 1141

'And for, poor bird, thou sing'st not in the day,
As shaming any eye should thee behold,
Some dark deep desert, seated from the way,

That knows not parching heat nor freezing cold,
Will we find out; and there we will unfold 1146
  To creatures stern sad tunes, to change their
  kinds.
  Since men prove beasts, let beasts bear gentle
  minds.'

As the poor frighted deer that stands at gaze,
Wildly determining which way to fly, 1150
Or one encompass'd with a winding maze
That cannot tread the way out readily,
So with herself is she in mutiny,
  To live or die which of the twain were better
  When life is sham'd and death reproach's
  debtor. 1155

'To kill myself,' quoth she, 'alack, what were it
But with my body my poor soul's pollution?
They that lose half with greater patience bear it
Than they whose whole is swallowed in con-
  fusion.
That mother tries a merciless conclusion 1160
  Who, having two sweet babes, when death
  takes one,
  Will slay the other and be nurse to none.

'My body or my soul, which was the dearer
When the one pure, the other made divine?
Whose love of either to myself was nearer 1165
When both were kept for heaven and Collatine?
Ay me! the bark pil'd from the lofty pine,
  His leaves will wither and his sap decay.
  So must my soul, her bark being pil'd away.

'Her house is sack'd, her quiet interrupted, 1170
Her mansion batter'd by the enemy;
Her sacred temple spotted, spoil'd, corrupted,
Grossly engirt with daring infamy.
Then let it not be call'd impiety
  If in this blemish'd fort I make some hole
  Through which I may convey this troubled
  soul. 1176

'Yet die I will not till my Collatine
Have heard the cause of my untimely death;
That he may vow, in that sad hour of mine,
Revenge on him that made me stop my breath.
My stained blood to Tarquin I'll bequeath, 1181
  Which, by him tainted, shall for him be spent
  And as his due writ in my testament.

'My honour I'll bequeath unto the knife
That wounds my body so dishonoured. 1185
'Tis honour to deprive dishonour'd life:
  The one will live, the other being dead.

So of shame's ashes shall my fame be bred,
  For in my death I murther shameful scorn;
  My shame so dead, mine honour is new born.

'Dear lord of that dear jewel I have lost, 1191
What legacy shall I bequeath to thee?
My resolution, love, shall be thy boast,
By whose example thou reveng'd mayst be.
How Tarquin must be us'd, read it in me: 1195
  Myself thy friend will kill myself thy foe,
  And for my sake serve thou false Tarquin so.

'This brief abridgment of my will I make:
My soul and body to the skies and ground;
My resolution, husband, do thou take; 1200
Mine honour be the knife's that makes my
  wound;
  My shame be his that did my fame confound
  And all my fame that lives disbursed be
  To those that live and think no shame of me.

'Thou, Collatine, shalt oversee this will. 1205
How was I overseen that thou shalt see it!
My blood shall wash the slander of mine ill;
My live's foul deed, my life's fair end shall free
  it.
Faint not, faint heart, but stoutly say, "So
  be it."
  Yield to my hand; my hand shall conquer
  thee: 1210
  Thou dead, both die, and both shall victor
  be.'

This plot of death when sadly she had laid
And wip'd the brinish pearl from her bright
  eyes,
With untun'd tongue she hoarsely calls her
  maid,
Whose swift obedience to her mistress hies; 1215
For swift-wing'd duty with thought's feathers
  flies.
  Poor Lucrece' cheeks unto her maid seem so
  As winter meads when sun doth melt their
  snow.

Her mistress she doth give demure good-morrow
With soft-slow tongue, true mark of modesty
And sorts a sad look to her lady's sorrow, 1221
For-why her face wore sorrow's livery;
But durst not ask of her audaciously
  Why her two suns were cloud-eclipsed so,
  Nor why her fair cheeks overwash'd with woe.

But as the earth doth weep, the sun being set,
Each flower moist'ned like a melting eye,

Even so the maid with swelling drops gan wet
Her circled eyne, enforc'd by sympathy
Of those fair suns set in her mistress' sky, 1230
 Who in a salt-wav'd ocean quench their light,
 Which makes the maid weep like the dewy
  night.

A pretty while these pretty creatures stand,
Like ivory conduits coral cisterns filling.
One justly weeps; the other takes in hand 1235
No cause, but company, of her drops spilling.
Their gentle sex to weep are often willing,
 Grieving themselves to guess at others'
  smarts,
 And then they drown their eyes or break
  their hearts. 1239

For men have marble, women waxen minds,
And therefore are they form'd as marble will.
The weak oppress'd, th' impression of strange
 kinds
Is form'd in them by force, by fraud, or skill.
Then call them not the authors of their ill,
 No more than wax shall be accounted evil
 Wherein is stamp'd the semblance of a devil.

Their smoothness, like a goodly champain
 plain,
Lays open all the little worms that creep;
In men, as in a rough-grown grove, remain
Cave-keeping evils that obscurely sleep. 1250
Through crystal walls each little mote will peep.
 Though men can cover crimes with bold stern
  looks,
 Poor women's faces are their own faults'
  books.

No man inveigh against the withered flow'r,
But chide rough winter that the flow'r hath
 kill'd. 1255
Not that devour'd, but that which doth devour,
Is worthy blame. O, let it not be hild
Poor women's faults that they are so fulfill'd
 With men's abuses: those proud lords to
  blame
 Make weak-made women tenants to their
  shame. 1260

The precedent whereof in Lucrece view,
Assail'd by night with circumstances strong
Of present death, and shame that might ensue
By that her death, to do her husband wrong.
Such danger to resistance did belong 1265
 That dying fear through all her body spread;
 And who cannot abuse a body dead?

By this, mild patience bid fair Lucrece speak
To the poor counterfeit of her complaining.
'My girl,' quoth she, 'on what occasion break
Those tears from thee that down thy cheeks
 are raining? 1271
If thou dost weep for grief of my sustaining,
 Know, gentle wench, it small avails my mood.
 If tears could help, mine own would do me
  good.

'But tell me, girl, when went' (and there she
 stay'd 1275
Till after a deep groan) 'Tarquin from hence?'
'Madam, ere I was up,' replied the maid,
'The more to blame my sluggard negligence.
Yet with the fault I thus far can dispense:
 Myself was stirring ere the break of day, 1280
 And ere I rose was Tarquin gone away.

'But, lady, if your maid may be so bold,
She would request to know your heaviness.'
'O, peace!' quoth Lucrece. 'If it should be
 told,
The repetition cannot make it less; 1285
For more it is than I can well express,
 And that deep torture may be call'd a hell
 When more is felt than one hath power to tell.

'Go get me hither paper, ink, and pen.
Yet save that labour, for I have them here. 1290
What should I say? One of my husband's men
Bid thou be ready, by-and-by, to bear
A letter to my lord, my love, my dear.
 Bid him with speed prepare to carry it;
 The cause craves haste, and it will soon be
  writ.' 1295

Her maid is gone, and she prepares to write,
First hovering o'er the paper with her quill.
Conceit and grief an eager combat fight;
What wit sets down is blotted straight with
 will.
This is too curious good, this blunt and ill: 1300
 Much like a press of people at a door,
 Throng her inventions, which shall go before.

At last she thus begins: 'Thou worthy lord
Of that unworthy wife that greeteth thee,
Health to thy person! Next vouchsafe t' af-
 ford 1305
(If ever, love, thy Lucrece thou wilt see)
Some present speed to come and visit me.
 So I commend me, from our house in grief.
 My woes are tedious, though my words are
  brief.'

443

Here folds she up the tenure of her woe, 1310
Her certain sorrow writ uncertainly.
By this short schedule Collatine may know
Her grief, but not her grief's true quality.
She dares not thereof make discovery,
    Lest he should hold it her own gross abuse
    Ere she with blood had stain'd her stain'd
    excuse. 1316

Besides, the life and feeling of her passion
She hoards, to spend when he is by to hear her,
When sighs and groans and tears may grace the
    fashion
Of her disgrace, the better so to clear her 1320
From that suspicion which the world might
    bear her.
    To shun this blot, she would not blot the
    letter
    With words till action might become them
    better.

To see sad sights moves more than hear them
    told;
For then the eye interprets to the ear 1325
The heavy motion that it doth behold,
When every part a part of woe doth bear.
'Tis but a part of sorrow that we hear:
    Deep sounds make lesser noise than shallow
    fords,
    And sorrow ebbs, being blown with wind of
    words. 1330

Her letter now is seal'd, and on it writ,
'At Ardea to my lord with more than haste.'
The post attends, and she delivers it,
Charging the sour-fac'd groom to hie as fast
As lagging fowls before the Northern blast. 1335
    Speed more than speed but dull and slow she
    deems:
    Extremity still urgeth such extremes.

The homely villain cursies to her low;
And, blushing on her, with a steadfast eye
Receives the scroll without or yea or no 1340
And forth with bashful innocence doth hie.
But they whose guilt within their bosoms lie
    Imagine every eye beholds their blame;
    For Lucrece thought he blush'd to see her
    shame,

When, seely groom! God wot, it was defect
Of spirit, life, and bold audacity. 1346
Such harmless creatures have a true respect
To talk in deeds, while others saucily
Promise more speed, but do it leisurely.

Even so this pattern of the worn-out age 1350
Pawn'd honest looks, but laid no words to
    gage.

His kindled duty kindled her mistrust,
That two red fires in both their faces blazed.
She thought he blush'd as knowing Tarquin's
    lust, 1354
And, blushing with him, wistly on him gazed;
Her earnest eye did make him more amazed.
    The more she saw the blood his cheeks re-
    plenish,
    The more she thought he spied in her some
    blemish.

But long she thinks till he return again,
And yet the duteous vassal scarce is gone. 1360
The weary time she cannot entertain,
For now 'tis stale to sigh, to weep and groan.
So woe hath wearied woe, moan tired moan,
    That she her plaints a little while doth stay,
    Pausing for means to mourn some newer way.

At last she calls to mind where hangs a piece
Of skilful painting, made for Priam's Troy,
Before the which is drawn the power of Greece,
For Helen's rape the city to destroy, 1369
Threat'ning cloud-kissing Ilion with annoy;
    Which the conceited painter drew so proud
    As heaven, it seem'd, to kiss the turrets bow'd.

A thousand lamentable objects there,
In scorn of nature, art gave liveless life.
Many a dry drop seem'd a weeping tear 1375
Shed for the slaught'red husband by the wife.
The red blood reek'd, to show the painter's
    strife;
    And dying eyes gleam'd forth their ashy
    lights,
    Like dying coals burnt out in tedious nights.

There might you see the labouring pioner 1380
Begrim'd with sweat, and smeared all with dust;
And from the tow'rs of Troy there would appear
The very eyes of men through loopholes thrust,
Gazing upon the Greeks with little lust. 1384
    Such sweet observance in this work was had
    That one might see those far-off eyes look
    sad.

In great commanders grace and majesty
You might behold triumphing in their faces;
In youth, quick bearing and dexterity;
And here and there the painter interlaces 1390
Pale cowards marching on with trembling paces,

444

Which heartless peasants did so well resemble
That one would swear he saw them quake and
   tremble.

In Ajax and Ulysses, O, what art
Of physiognomy might one behold!   1395
The face of either cipher'd either's heart;
Their face their manners most expressly told:
In Ajax' eyes blunt rage and rigour roll'd;
   But the mild glance that sly Ulysses lent
   Show'd deep regard and smiling government.

There pleading might you see grave Nestor
   stand,   1401
As 'twere encouraging the Greeks to fight,
Making such sober action with his hand
That it beguil'd attention, charm'd the sight.
In speech it seem'd his beard, all silver white,
   Wagg'd up and down, and from his lips did
     fly   1406
   Thin winding breath, which purl'd up to the
     sky.

About him were a press of gaping faces
Which seem'd to swallow up his sound advice,
All jointly list'ning, but with several graces,
As if some mermaid did their ears entice,   1411
Some high, some low — the painter was so nice.
   The scalps of many, almost hid behind,
   To jump up higher seem'd, to mock the mind.

Here one man's hand lean'd on another's head,
His nose being shadowed by his neighbour's ear;
Here one, being throng'd, bears back, all boll'n
   and red;
Another, smother'd, seems to pelt and swear;
And in their rage such signs of rage they bear
   As, but for loss of Nestor's golden words,   1420
   It seem'd they would debate with angry
     swords.

For much imaginary work was there;
Conceit deceitful, so compact, so kind,
That for Achilles' image stood his spear,
Grip'd in an armed hand; himself behind   1425
Was left unseen, save to the eye of mind:
   A hand, a foot, a face, a leg, a head
   Stood for the whole to be imagined.

And from the walls of strong-besieged Troy
When their brave hope, bold Hector, march'd
   to field,   1430
Stood many Troyan mothers, sharing joy
To see their youthful sons bright weapons
   wield;

And to their hope they such odd action yield
   That through their light joy seemed to ap-
     pear
   (Like bright things stain'd) a kind of heavy
     fear.   1435

And from the strond of Dardan, where they
   fought,
To Simois' reedy banks the red blood ran,
Whose waves to imitate the battle sought
With swelling ridges; and their ranks began
To break upon the galled shore, and than   1440
   Retire again, till, meeting greater ranks,
   They join, and shoot their foam at Simois'
     banks.

To this well-painted piece is Lucrece come,
To find a face where all distress is stell'd.   1444
Many she sees where cares have carved some,
But none where all distress and dolour dwell'd
Till she despairing Hecuba beheld,
   Staring on Priam's wounds with her old eyes,
   Which bleeding under Pyrrhus' proud foot
     lies.

In her the painter had anatomiz'd   1450
Time's ruin, beauty's wrack, and grim care's
   reign;
Her cheeks with chops and wrinkles were dis-
   guis'd;
Of what she was no semblance did remain.
Her blue blood, chang'd to black in every
   vein,
   Wanting the spring that those shrunk pipes
     had fed,   1455
   Show'd life imprison'd in a body dead.

On this sad shadow Lucrece spends her eyes
And shapes her sorrow to the beldame's woes,
Who nothing wants to answer her but cries
And bitter words to ban her cruel foes.   1460
The painter was no god to lend her those;
   And therefore Lucrece swears he did her
     wrong
   To give her so much grief and not a tongue.

'Poor instrument,' quoth she, 'without a sound!
I'll tune thy woes with my lamenting tongue,
And drop sweet balm in Priam's painted wound,
And rail on Pyrrhus that hath done him wrong,
And with my tears quench Troy that burns so
   long,
   And with my knife scratch out the angry
     eyes
   Of all the Greeks that are thine enemies.   1470

445

'Show me the strumpet that began this stir,
That with my nails her beauty I may tear.
Thy heat of lust, fond Paris, did incur
This load of wrath that burning Troy doth bear.
Thy eye kindled the fire that burneth here, 1475
    And here in Troy, for trespass of thine eye,
    The sire, the son, the dame and daughter die.

'Why should the private pleasure of some one
Become the public plague of many moe?
Let sin, alone committed, light alone   1480
Upon his head that hath transgressed so;
Let guiltless souls be freed from guilty woe.
    For one's offence why should so many fall,
    To plague a private sin in general?

'Lo, here weeps Hecuba, here Priam dies, 1485
Here manly Hector faints, here Troilus sounds,
Here friend by friend in bloody channel lies,
And friend to friend gives unadvised wounds,
And one man's lust these many lives confounds.
    Had doting Priam check'd his son's desire,
    Troy had been bright with fame, and not
        with fire.'   1491

Here feelingly she weeps Troy's painted woes:
For sorrow, like a heavy hanging bell,
Once set on ringing, with his own weight goes;
Then little strength rings out the doleful knell.
So Lucrece, set awork, sad tales doth tell 1496
    To pencill'd pensiveness and colour'd sorrow:
    She lends them words, and she their looks
        doth borrow.

She throws her eyes about the painting round,
And who she finds forlorn she doth lament. 1500
At last she sees a wretched image bound
That piteous looks to Phrygian shepherds lent.
His face, though full of cares, yet show'd content;
    Onward to Troy with the blunt swains he goes,
    So mild that Patience seem'd to scorn his
        woes.   1505

In him the painter labour'd with his skill
To hide deceit, and give the harmless show
An humble gait, calm looks, eyes wailing still,
A brow unbent that seem'd to welcome woe,
Cheeks neither red nor pale, but mingled so
    That blushing red no guilty instance gave
    Nor ashy pale the fear that false hearts have;

But, like a constant and confirmed devil,
He entertain'd a show so seeming just,
And therein so ensconc'd his secret evil, 1515

That jealousy itself could not mistrust
False creeping craft and perjury should thrust
    Into so bright a day such black-fac'd storms
    Or blot with hell-born sin such saintlike
        forms.   1519

The well-skill'd workman this mild image drew
For perjur'd Sinon, whose enchanting story
The credulous old Priam after slew;
Whose words like wildfire burnt the shining
    glory
Of rich-built Ilion, that the skies were sorry,
    And little stars shot from their fixed places
    When their glass fell wherein they view'd
        their faces.   1526

This picture she advisedly perus'd
And chid the painter for his wondrous skill,
Saying, some shape in Sinon's was abus'd;
So fair a form lodg'd not a mind so ill.   1530
And still on him she gaz'd, and gazing still,
    Such signs of truth in his plain face she spied
    That she concludes the picture was belied.

'It cannot be,' quoth she, 'that so much
    guile' —   1534
She would have said 'can lurk in such a look';
But Tarquin's shape came in her mind the while
And from her tongue 'can lurk' from 'cannot'
    took.
'It cannot be' she in that sense forsook
    And turn'd it thus: 'It cannot be, I find,
    But such a face should bear a wicked mind;

'For even as subtile Sinon here is painted, 1541
So sober-sad, so weary, and so mild —
As if with grief or travail he had fainted —
To me came Tarquin armed; so beguil'd
With outward honesty, but yet defil'd   1545
    With inward vice. As Priam him did cherish,
    So did I Tarquin; so my Troy did perish.

'Look, look, how list'ning Priam wets his eyes
To see those borrowed tears that Sinon sheeds!
Priam, why art thou old, and yet not wise?
For every tear he falls a Troyan bleeds.   1551
His eye drops fire, no water thence proceeds.
    Those round clear pearls of his that move thy
        pity
    Are balls of quenchless fire to burn thy city.

'Such devils steal effects from lightless hell;
For Sinon in his fire doth quake with cold
And in that cold hot burning fire doth dwell.
These contraries such unity do hold

446

Only to flatter fools and make them bold.
  So Priam's trust false Sinon's tears doth
    flatter   1560
  That he finds means to burn his Troy with
    water.'

Here, all enrag'd, such passion her assails
That patience is quite beaten from her breast.
She tears the senseless Sinon with her nails,
Comparing him to that unhappy guest   1565
Whose deed hath made herself herself detest.
  At last she smilingly with this gives o'er:
  'Fool, fool!' quoth she, 'His wounds will not
    be sore.'

Thus ebbs and flows the current of her sor-
    row,
And time doth weary time with her complain-
    ing.   1570
She looks for night, and then she longs for
    morrow,
And both she thinks too long with her remain-
    ing.
Short time seems long in sorrow's sharp sus-
    taining;
  Though woe be heavy, yet it seldom sleeps,
  And they that watch see time how slow it
    creeps;   1575

Which all this time hath overslipp'd her thought
That she with painted images hath spent,
Being from the feeling of her own grief brought
By deep surmise of others' detriment.   1580
  Losing her woes in shows of discontent.
  It easeth some, though none it ever cured,
  To think their dolour others have endured.

But now the mindful messenger, come back,
Brings home his lord and other company;
Who finds his Lucrece clad in mourning black,
And round about her tear-distained eye   1586
Blue circles stream'd, like rainbows in the
    sky.
  These water-galls in her dim element
  Foretell new storms to those already spent.

Which when her sad-beholding husband saw,
Amazedly in her sad face he stares.   1591
Her eyes, though sod in tears, look'd red and
    raw,
Her lively colour kill'd with deadly cares.
He hath no power to ask her how she fares;
  But stood, like old acquaintance in a trance,
  Met far from home, wond'ring each other's
    chance.   1596

At last he takes her by the bloodless hand
And thus begins: 'What uncouth ill event
Hath thee befall'n, that thou dost trembling
    stand?
Sweet love, what spite hath thy fair colour
    spent?   1600
Why art thou thus attir'd in discontent?
  Unmask, dear dear, this moody heaviness
  And tell thy grief, that we may give redress.'

Three times with sighs she gives her sorrow fire
Ere once she can discharge one word of woe.
At length address'd to answer his desire,   1606
She modestly prepares to let them know
Her honour is ta'en prisoner by the foe,
  While Collatine and his consorted lords 1609
  With sad attention long to hear her words.

And now this pale swan in her wat'ry nest
Begins the sad dirge of her certain ending:
'Few words,' quoth she, 'shall fit the trespass
    best
Where no excuse can give the fault amending.
In me moe woes than words are now depending,
  And my laments would be drawn out too long
  To tell them all with one poor tired tongue.

'Then be this all the task it hath to say:
Dear husband, in the interest of thy bed
A stranger came and on that pillow lay   1620
Where thou wast wont to rest thy weary head;
And what wrong else may be imagined
  By foul enforcement might be done to me,
  From that, alas, thy Lucrece is not free.   1624

'For in the dreadful dead of dark midnight
With shining falchion in my chamber came
A creeping creature with a flaming light
And softly cried, "Awake, thou Roman dame,
And entertain my love; else lasting shame
  On thee and thine this night I will inflict,
  If thou my love's desire do contradict.   1631

'"For some hard-favour'd groom of thine,'
    quoth he,
"Unless thou yoke thy liking to my will,
I'll murther straight, and then I'll slaughter
    thee
And swear I found you where you did fulfil 1635
The loathsome act of lust, and so did kill
  The lechers in their deed. This act will be
  My fame and thy perpetual infamy."

'With this I did begin to start and cry;
And then against my heart he set his sword,

Swearing, unless I took all patiently,   1641
I should not live to speak another word.
So should my shame still rest upon record,
　And never be forgot in mighty Rome
　Th' adulterate death of Lucrece and her
　　groom.   1645

'Mine enemy was strong, my poor self weak —
And far the weaker with so strong a fear.
My bloody judge forbode my tongue to speak;
No rightful plea might plead for justice there.
His scarlet lust came evidence to swear   1650
　That my poor beauty had purloin'd his eyes;
　And when the judge is robb'd, the prisoner
　　dies.

'O, teach me how to make mine own excuse!
Or (at the least) this refuge let me find:
Though my gross blood be stain'd with this
　　abuse,   1655
Immaculate and spotless is my mind;
That was not forc'd; that never was inclin'd
　To accessary yieldings, but still pure
　Doth in her poison'd closet yet endure.'

Lo, here, the hopeless merchant of this loss,   1660
With head declin'd and voice damm'd up with
　　woe,
With sad-set eyes and wreathed arms across,
From lips new waxen pale begins to blow
The grief away that stops his answer so.
　But, wretched as he is, he strives in vain;
　What he breathes out his breath drinks up
　　again.   1666

As through an arch the violent roaring tide
Outruns the eye that doth behold his haste,
Yet in the eddy boundeth in his pride   1669
Back to the strait that forc'd him on so fast;
In rage sent out, recall'd in rage being past:
　Even so his sighs, his sorrows, make a saw,
　To push grief on, and back the same grief
　　draw.

Which speechless woe of his poor she attendeth
And his untimely frenzy thus awaketh: 1675
'Dear lord, thy sorrow to my sorrow lendeth
Another power. No flood by raining slaketh.
My woe too sensible thy passion maketh
　More feeling-painful. Let it then suffice   1679
　To drown one woe, one pair of weeping eyes.

'And for my sake when I might charm thee so,
For she that was thy Lucrece — now attend me.

Be suddenly revenged on my foe,
Thine, mine, his own. Suppose thou dost de-
　fend me
From what is past. The help that thou shalt
　lend me   1685
　Comes all too late, yet let the traitor die;
　For sparing justice feeds iniquity.

'But ere I name him, you fair lords,' quoth
　she,
Speaking to those that came with Collatine,
'Shall plight your honourable faiths to me   1690
With swift pursuit to venge this wrong of
　mine;
For 'tis a meritorious fair design
　To chase injustice with revengeful arms.
　Knights by their oaths should right poor
　　ladies' harms.'

At this request, with noble disposition   1695
Each present lord began to promise aid,
As bound in knighthood to her imposition,
Longing to hear the hateful foe bewray'd.
But she, that yet her sad task hath not said,
　The protestation stops. 'O, speak!' quoth
　　she,   1700
　'How may this forced stain be wip'd from me?

'What is the quality of my offence,
Being constrain'd with dreadful circumstance?
May my pure mind with the foul act dispense,
My low-declined honour to advance?   1705
May any terms acquit me from this chance?
　The poisoned fountain clears itself again;
　And why not I from this compelled stain?'

With this they all at once began to say,
Her body's stain her mind untainted clears;
While with a joyless smile she turns away   1711
The face, that map which deep impression bears
Of hard misfortune, carv'd in it with tears.
　'No, no!' quoth she, 'No dame hereafter
　　living   1714
　By my excuse shall claim excuse's giving.'

Here with a sigh as if her heart would break
She throws forth Tarquin's name: 'He, he!'
　she says,
But more than 'he' her poor tongue could not
　speak,
Till after many accents and delays,   1719
Untimely breathings, sick and short assays,
　She utters this: 'He, he! fair lords, 'tis he
　That guides this hand to give this wound to
　　me.'

Even here she sheathed in her harmless breast
A harmful knife, that thence her soul un-
  sheathed.
That blow did bail it from the deep unrest 1725
Of that polluted prison where it breathed.
Her contrite sighs unto the clouds bequeathed
  Her winged sprite, and through her wounds
    doth fly
  Live's lasting date from cancell'd destiny.

Stone-still, astonish'd with this deadly deed,
Stood Collatine and all his lordly crew,   1731
Till Lucrece' father, that beholds her bleed,
Himself on her self-slaught'red body threw,
And from the purple fountain Brutus drew
  The murd'rous knife, and, as it left the place,
  Her blood, in poor revenge, held it in chase;

And bubbling from her breast, it doth divide
In two slow rivers, that the crimson blood
Circles her body in on every side,
Who, like a late-sack'd island, vastly stood 1740
Bare and unpeopled in this fearful flood.
  Some of her blood still pure and red remain'd,
  And some look'd black, and that false Tar-
    quin stain'd.

About the mourning and congealed face
Of that black blood a wat'ry rigoll goes,   1745
Which seems to weep upon the tainted place;
And ever since, as pitying Lucrece' woes,
Corrupted blood some watery token shows,
  And blood untainted still doth red abide,
  Blushing at that which is so putrefied.   1750

'Daughter, dear daughter!' old Lucretius cries,
'That life was mine which thou hast here de-
    prived.
If in the child the father's image lies,
Where shall I live now Lucrece is unlived?
Thou wast not to this end from me derived.
  If children predecease progenitors,   1756
  We are their offspring, and they none of ours.

'Poor broken glass, I often did behold
In thy sweet semblance my old age new born;
But now that fresh fair mirror, dim and old,
Shows me a bare-bon'd death by time outworn.
O, from thy cheeks my image thou hast torn
  And shiver'd all the beauty of my glass,
  That I no more can see what once I was.

'O time, cease thou thy course, and last no
    longer,   1765
If they surcease to be that should survive.

Shall rotten death make conquest of the
    stronger
And leave the falt'ring feeble souls alive?
The old bees die, the young possess their hive.
  Then live, sweet Lucrece, live again and see
  Thy father die, and not thy father thee.' 1771

By this, starts Collatine as from a dream
And bids Lucretius give his sorrow place;
And then in key-cold Lucrece' bleeding stream
He falls, and bathes the pale fear in his face,
And counterfeits to die with her a space; 1776
  Till manly shame bids him possess his breath
  And live to be revenged on her death.

The deep vexation of his inward soul   1779
Hath serv'd a dumb arrest upon his tongue;
Who, mad that sorrow should his use control,
Or keep him from heart-easing words so long,
Begins to talk; but through his lips do throng
  Weak words, so thick come in his poor heart's
    aid   1784
  That no man could distinguish what he said.

Yet sometime 'Tarquin' was pronounced plain,
But through his teeth, as if the name he tore.
This windy tempest, till it blow up rain,
Held back his sorrow's tide, to make it more.
At last it rains, and busy winds give o'er; 1790
  Then son and father weep with equal strife
  Who should weep most, for daughter or for
    wife.

The one doth call her his, the other his;
Yet neither may possess the claim they lay.
The father says 'She's mine.' 'O, mine she is!'
Replies her husband. 'Do not take away 1796
My sorrow's interest. Let no mourner say
  He weeps for her; for she was only mine,
  And only must be wail'd by Collatine.'

'O,' quoth Lucretius, 'I did give that life 1800
Which she too early and too late hath spill'd.'
'Woe, woe!' quoth Collatine. 'She was my
    wife,
I owed her, and 'tis mine that she hath kill'd.'
'My daughter' and 'my wife' with clamours
    fill'd
  The dispers'd air, who, holding Lucrece' life,
  Answer'd their cries, 'my daughter' and 'my
    wife.'   1806

Brutus, who pluck'd the knife from Lucrece'
    side,
Seeing such emulation in their woe,

449

Began to clothe his wit in state and pride,
Burying in Lucrece' wound his folly's show.
He with the Romans was esteemed so   1811
  As seely jeering idiots are with kings,
    For sportive words and utt'ring foolish things;

But now he throws that shallow habit by
Wherein deep policy did him disguise,   1815
And arm'd his long-hid wits advisedly
To check the tears in Collatinus' eyes.
'Thou wronged lord of Rome,' quoth he, 'arise!
  Let my unsounded self, suppos'd a fool,   1819
  Now set thy long-experienc'd wit to school.

'Why, Collatine, is woe the cure for woe?
Do wounds help wounds, or grief help grievous
    deeds?
Is it revenge to give thyself a blow
For his foul act by whom thy fair wife bleeds?
Such childish humour from weak minds pro-
    ceeds.   1825
  Thy wretched wife mistook the matter so,
  To slay herself that should have slain her
    foe.

'Courageous Roman, do not steep thy heart
In such relenting dew of lamentations;
But kneel with me, and help to bear thy
    part   1830
To rouse our Roman gods with invocations
That they will suffer these abominations

(Since Rome herself in them doth stand dis-
    graced)
By our strong arms from forth her fair streets
    chased.

'Now, by the Capitol that we adore,   1835
And by this chaste blood so unjustly stained,
By heaven's fair sun that breeds the fat earth's
    store,
By all our country rights in Rome maintained,
And by chaste Lucrece' soul that late com-
    plained   1839
  Her wrongs to us, and by this bloody knife,
  We will revenge the death of this true wife.'

This said, he struck his hand upon his breast
And kiss'd the fatal knife to end his vow;
And to his protestation urg'd the rest,
Who, wond'ring at him, did his words allow.
Then jointly to the ground their knees they
    bow;   1846
  And that deep vow which Brutus made be-
    fore
  He doth again repeat, and that they swore.

When they had sworn to this advised doom,
They did conclude to bear dead Lucrece thence,
To show her bleeding body thorough Rome,
And so to publish Tarquin's foul offence;
Which being done with speedy diligence,
  The Romans plausibly did give consent
  To Tarquin's everlasting banishment.   1855

SONNETS AND OTHER POEMS

On May 20, 1609, Thomas Thorpe registered 'A Booke called Shakespeares sonnettes.' This came out in quarto in that same year: 'Shake-speares Sonnets. Neuer before Imprinted.' The same Quarto contains A LOVER's COMPLAINT, which follows the SONNETS and is ascribed to 'William Shake-speare' in the title heading. His authorship of this curious poem is very doubtful. Two of the sonnets in Thorpe's collection (cxxxviii, cxliv) had already been published in THE PASSIONATE PILGRIM (1599); cvii seems to refer to the death of Elizabeth and the accession of James I in 1603. The dates of the rest are not to be determined. They must have been written at different times and on miscellaneous occasions throughout Shakespeare's literary life from *ca.* 1592 to 1609. Though the Quarto was not, apparently, an authorized edition, and although it was carelessly printed, the text of the SONNETS is reasonably good. Numerous misprints have proved easy to correct. About a score of passages are still doubtful, but in most of these the sense is clear enough.

It is customary to regard Sonnets i-cxxvi as a continuous series and to assume that they are all addressed to the same person — some young man of noble birth. This idea takes it for granted that Thorpe's arrangement is Shakespeare's. That, however, is a pure assumption. Nor does it follow, even if the arrangement is admitted to be canonical, that the same person is addressed in all the hundred and twenty-six. *A priori* such unity of dedication is not very likely, and unprepossessed reading confirms the antecedent improbability. The first seventeen sonnets form a group by themselves. They sound like merely fanciful variations on the theme of *Venus and Adonis*, verses 129-132, 163-174, 751-768 (cf. *Romeo and Juliet*, i, 1, 215-231; *All's Well*, i, 1, 137-162; *Twelfth Night*, i, 5, 259-261). Nos. xxv, xxvi, xxxviii, might have been sent to a noble and friendly patron; in tone and manner they are very like the dedication to *Lucrece*. Nos. xxx-xxxii might be addressed to the same patron or to some friend of more nearly the poet's own rank. No. cviii can hardly have been sent to that patron or friend. In any case, this sonnet, if compared with lxx, is enough to destroy the theory of a continuous and orderly series (i-cxxvi); for cviii calls the recipient 'sweet boy,' and lxx is addressed to some one who has 'pass'd by the ambush of young days.' Several sonnets of the supposed series are manifestly addressed to a woman; and several of the others (e.g., xx, xxi, xlviii, lvi, lxvi, lxix, lxxiii-lxxv, cxviii, cxix, cxxvi) cannot reasonably be supposed to have been offered to a great nobleman. The young man thought to be addressed in i-cxxvi has been identified with the Earl of Southampton and the Earl of Pembroke. These interpretations are more or less mixed up with Thorpe's mysterious 'Mr. W. H.,' to whom he dedicated the book. 'W. H.' would fit Pembroke, whose name was William Herbert; he became Earl in 1601. 'W. H.' (reversed) would fit Southampton (Henry Wriothesley), to whom Shakespeare dedicated both *Venus and Adonis* and *Lucrece*. Southampton is the favourite claimant; but his title is no stronger than Pembroke's, perhaps not so strong. Neither case is at all demonstrated or demonstrable. Nos. lxxviii, lxxx, lxxxii-lxxxvi raise the vexed question of the Rival Poet. He has been identified with more than a dozen poets of the time — including Spenser, Marlowe, Barnabe Barnes, Ben Jonson, John Davies, Chapman, and Daniel. Chapman is the most popular candidate, but his popularity is waning.

Whatever one may think of the continuity of i-cxxvi, it is quite clear that the remaining sonnets (cxxvii-cliv) do not make an orderly sequence. The Dark Lady who haunts them may be a real person who played a sinister rôle in Shakespeare's life, but she is somehow connected with the dark Rosaline of *Love's Labour's Lost*. Some of the sonnets that concern her are not more serious in autobiographical significance than Berowne's paradox (iv, 3, 248–265; cf. v, 2, 32 ff.). If she is to be identified with the stolen mistress of xl-xlii, that is further disproof of the continuity and completeness of the supposed first cycle. To identify her with Mary Fitton is impossible. She must remain a mystery.

In treating the SONNETS as material for Shakespeare's biography, we should not forget that we are dealing with the supreme dramatist — with that extraordinary genius who, beyond all others, could put himself in the place of any human being, man or woman, and then could make that person express thoughts and feelings and passions as he or she would have uttered them if endowed with superhuman power of expression. In a sonnet, both from its very nature and from the conventions that attend it, the author must seem to 'unlock his heart.' He must either refrain or run the risk of a literal (that is, a personal) interpretation. Nothing, therefore, can prove that Shakespeare's sonnets are, or are not, autobiographical except the discovery of outside evidence that they accord, or do not accord, with facts of his life; and no such evidence is forthcoming. It is idle to talk of 'sincerity' in this regard. Hamlet's soliloquies are sincere, and Iago's cynical revelations of his code, and Macbeth's poetic imaginings that visualize to the brink of delirium. The testimony of the SONNETS must remain ambiguous.

'THE PASSIONATE PILGRIME. *By W. Shakespeare*,' a tiny octavo, was printed for William Jaggard in 1599. The title is simply the publisher's fancy. The book contains twenty short poems. Nos. xv-xx, however, have a separate title page ('Sonnets To sundry notes of Musicke'), which does not claim the poems for Shakespeare. Nos. i and ii are Sonnets cxxxviii and cxliv (see pp. 1516, 1517); iii, v, and xvi are from *Love's Labour's Lost* (iv, 3, 60–73; iv, 2, 109–122; iv, 3, 101–120 (see pp. 209, 211)); xii is usually accepted as Shakespeare's. None of the other poems can be ascribed to Shakespeare with any confidence. Nos. xv and xix are certainly not his, and are therefore omitted in the present edition. Nos. iv, vi, ix, and xi may be by Bartholomew Griffin. They resemble each other strongly, and No. xi is contained in his *Fidessa* (1596). Nos. viii and xx are found in Richard Barnfield's *Poems: in Divers Humours* (1598), and xvii may also be his, though part of it is printed in Thomas Weelkes's *Madrigals* (1597). Probably Weelkes wrote the music only. This leaves vii, x, xiii, xiv, and xviii. Their right to be regarded as Shakespeare's is far from strong, but no other poet claims them.

THE PHŒNIX AND TURTLE is unquestionably genuine. It is printed, with Shakespeare's signature (as one of 'some new compositions of seuerall moderne Writers whose names are subscribed'), in Robert Chester's 'Loves Martyr: Or, Rosalins Complaint. Allegorically shadowing the truth of Loue, in the constant Fate of the Phoenix and Turtle' (1601). The volume also contains signed poems by Jonson, Chapman, and Marston.

SONNETS

I

From fairest creatures we desire increase,
That thereby beauty's rose might never die,
But as the riper should by time decease,
His tender heir might bear his memory;
But thou, contracted to thine own bright eyes,
Feed'st thy light's flame with self-substantial
    fuel,   6
Making a famine where abundance lies,
Thyself thy foe, to thy sweet self too cruel.
Thou that art now the world's fresh ornament
And only herald to the gaudy spring,   10
Within thine own bud buriest thy content
And, tender churl, mak'st waste in niggarding.
    Pity the world, or else this glutton be,
    To eat the world's due, by the grave and thee.

II

When forty winters shall besiege thy brow
And dig deep trenches in thy beauty's field,
Thy youth's proud livery, so gaz'd on now,
Will be a tatter'd weed of small worth held.
Then being ask'd where all thy beauty lies,   5
Where all the treasure of thy lusty days,
To say, within thine own deep-sunken eyes
Were an all-eating shame and thriftless praise.
How much more praise deserv'd thy beauty's
    use   9
If thou couldst answer, 'This fair child of mine
Shall sum my count and make my old excuse,'
Proving his beauty by succession thine!
    This were to be new made when thou art old
    And see thy blood warm when thou feel'st it
        cold.

III

Look in thy glass and tell the face thou viewest
Now is the time that face should form another,
Whose fresh repair if now thou not renewest,
Thou dost beguile the world, unbless some
    mother.
For where is she so fair whose unear'd womb 5
Disdains the tillage of thy husbandry?
Or who is he so fond will be the tomb
Of his self-love, to stop posterity?
Thou art thy mother's glass, and she in thee
Calls back the lovely April of her prime.   10
So thou through windows of thine age shalt
    see,
Despite of wrinkles, this thy golden time.
    But if thou live remem'bred not to be,
    Die single, and thine image dies with thee.

IV

Unthrifty loveliness, why dost thou spend
Upon thyself thy beauty's legacy?
Nature's bequest gives nothing, but doth lend,
And, being frank, she lends to those are free. 4
Then, beauteous niggard, why dost thou abuse
The bounteous largess given thee to give?
Profitless usurer, why dost thou use
So great a sum of sums, yet canst not live?
For, having traffic with thyself alone,
Thou of thyself thy sweet self dost deceive. 10
Then how, when nature calls thee to be gone,
What acceptable audit canst thou leave?
    Thy unus'd beauty must be tomb'd with
        thee,
    Which, used, lives th' executor to be.

V

Those hours that with gentle work did frame
The lovely gaze where every eye doth dwell,
Will play the tyrants to the very same
And that unfair which fairly doth excel;
For never-resting time leads summer on   5
To hideous winter and confounds him there,
Sap check'd with frost and lusty leaves quite
    gone,
Beauty o'ersnow'd and bareness everywhere.
Then, were not summer's distillation left
A liquid prisoner pent in walls of glass,   10
Beauty's effect with beauty were bereft —
Nor it, nor no remembrance what it was;

But flowers distill'd, though they with winter
meet,
Leese but their show — their substance still
lives sweet.

VI

Then let not winter's ragged hand deface
In thee thy summer ere thou be distill'd.
Make sweet some vial; treasure thou some
place
With beauty's treasure ere it be self-kill'd.
That use is not forbidden usury   5
Which happies those that pay the willing loan:
That's for thyself to breed another thee,
Or ten times happier, be it ten for one.
Ten times thyself were happier than thou art,
If ten of thine ten times refigur'd thee.   10
Then what could death do if thou shouldst
depart,
Leaving thee living in posterity?
  Be not self-will'd, for thou art much too fair
  To be death's conquest and make worms
  thine heir.

VII

Lo, in the Orient when the gracious light
Lifts up his burning head, each under eye
Doth homage to his new-appearing sight,
Serving with looks his sacred majesty;
And having climb'd the steep-up heavenly hill,
Resembling strong youth in his middle age, 6
Yet mortal looks adore his beauty still,
Attending on his golden pilgrimage;
But when from highmost pitch, with weary car,
Like feeble age he reeleth from the day,   10
The eyes (fore duteous) now converted are
From his low tract and look another way.
  So thou, thyself outgoing in thy noon,
  Unlook'd on diest unless thou get a son.

VIII

Music to hear, why hear'st thou music sadly?
Sweets with sweets war not, joy delights in joy.
Why lov'st thou that which thou receiv'st not
gladly,
Or else receiv'st with pleasure thine annoy?
If the true concord of well-tuned sounds, 5
By unions married, do offend thine ear,
They do but sweetly chide thee, who confounds
In singleness the parts that thou shouldst bear.
Mark how one string, sweet husband to another,
Strikes each in each by mutual ordering;   10
Resembling sire and child and happy mother,
Who. all in one. one pleasing note do sing;

Whose speechless song, being many, seeming
one,
Sings this to thee: 'Thou single wilt prove
none.'

IX

Is it for fear to wet a widow's eye
That thou consum'st thyself in single life?
Ah! if thou issueless shalt hap to die,
The world will wail thee like a makeless wife;
The world will be thy widow, and still weep 5
That thou no form of thee hast left behind
When every private widow well may keep,
By children's eyes, her husband's shape in mind.
Look, what an unthrift in the world doth spend
Shifts but his place, for still the world enjoys
it;   10
But beauty's waste hath in the world an end,
And kept unus'd, the user so destroys it.
  No love toward others in that bosom sits
  That on himself such murd'rous shame com-
  mits.

X

For shame! Deny that thou bear'st love to
any,
Who for thyself art so unprovident.
Grant, if thou wilt, thou art belov'd of many,
But that thou none lov'st is most evident;
For thou art so possess'd with murd'rous hate 5
That 'gainst thyself thou stick'st not to con-
spire,
Seeking that beauteous roof to ruinate
Which to repair should be thy chief desire.
O, change thy thought, that I may change my
mind!
Shall hate be fairer lodg'd than gentle love? 10
Be as thy presence is, gracious and kind,
Or to thyself at least kind-hearted prove.
  Make thee another self for love of me,
  That beauty still may live in thine or thee.

XI

As fast as thou shalt wane, so fast thou grow'st
In one of thine, from that which thou departest;
And that fresh blood which youngly thou be-
stow'st
Thou mayst call thine when thou from youth
convertest.
Herein lives wisdom, beauty, and increase; 5
Without this, folly, age, and cold decay.
If all were minded so, the times should cease,
And threescore year would make the world
away.

Let those whom Nature hath not made for
store,
Harsh, featureless, and rude, barrenly perish.
Look, whom she best endow'd she gave the
more,   11
Which bounteous gift thou shouldst in bounty
cherish.
   She carv'd thee for her seal, and meant
thereby
   Thou shouldst print more, not let that copy
die.

XII

When I do count the clock that tells the time
And see the brave day sunk in hideous night,
When I behold the violet past prime
And sable curls all silver'd o'er with white,
When lofty trees I see barren of leaves,   5
Which erst from heat did canopy the herd,
And summer's green all girded up in sheaves
Borne on the bier with white and bristly beard—
Then of thy beauty do I question make
That thou among the wastes of time must
go,   10
Since sweets and beauties do themselves forsake
And die as fast as they see others grow,
   And nothing 'gainst Time's scythe can make
defence
   Save breed, to brave him when he takes thee
hence.

XIII

O, that you were yourself! but, love, you are
No longer yours than you yourself here live.
Against this coming end you should prepare
And your sweet semblance to some other give.
So should that beauty which you hold in lease
Find no determination; then you were   6
Yourself again after yourself's decease
When your sweet issue your sweet form should
bear.
Who lets so fair a house fall to decay,
Which husbandry in honour might uphold   10
Against the stormy gusts of winter's day
And barren rage of death's eternal cold?
   O, none but unthrifts! Dear my love, you
know
   You had a father — let your son say so.

XIV

Not from the stars do I my judgment pluck,
And yet methinks I have astronomy;
But not to tell of good or evil luck,
Of plagues, of dearths, or seasons' quality;

Nor can I fortune to brief minutes tell,   5
Pointing to each his thunder, rain, and wind,
Or say with princes if it shall go well
By oft predict that I in heaven find;
But from thine eyes my knowledge I derive,
And, constant stars, in them I read such art   10
As truth and beauty shall together thrive
If from thyself to store thou wouldst convert;
   Or else of thee this I prognosticate:
   Thy end is truth's and beauty's doom and
date.

XV

When I consider every thing that grows
Holds in perfection but a little moment,
That this huge stage presenteth naught but
shows
Whereon the stars in secret influence comment;
When I perceive that men as plants increase,   5
Cheered and check'd even by the selfsame sky,
Vaunt in their youthful sap, at height decrease,
And wear their brave state out of memory:
Then the conceit of this inconstant stay
Sets you most rich in youth before my sight,   10
Where wasteful Time debateth with Decay
To change your day of youth to sullied night
   And, all in war with Time for love of you,
   As he takes from you, I ingraft you new.

XVI

But wherefore do not you a mightier way
Make war upon this bloody tyrant, Time?
And fortify yourself in your decay
With means more blessed than my barren
rhyme?
Now stand you on the top of happy hours;   5
And many maiden gardens, yet unset,
With virtuous wish would bear your living flow-
ers,
Much liker than your painted counterfeit.
So should the lines of life that life repair
Which this time's pencil, or my pupil pen,   10
Neither in inward worth nor outward fair
Can make you live yourself in eyes of men.
   To give away yourself keeps yourself still,
   And you must live, drawn by your own sweet
skill.

XVII

Who will believe my verse in time to come
If it were fill'd with your most high deserts?
Though yet, heaven knows, it is but as a tomb
Which hides your life and shows not half your
parts.

If I could write the beauty of your eyes   5
And in fresh numbers number all your graces,
The age to come would say, 'This poet lies!
Such heavenly touches ne'er touch'd earthly
faces.'
So should my papers (yellowed with their age)
Be scorn'd, like old men of less truth than
tongue,   10
And your true rights be term'd a poet's rage
And stretched metre of an antique song.
But were some child of yours alive that time,
You should live twice — in it, and in my
rhyme.

XVIII

Shall I compare thee to a summer's day?
Thou art more lovely and more temperate.
Rough winds do shake the darling buds of
May,
And summer's lease hath all too short a date.
Sometime too hot the eye of heaven shines,   5
And often is his gold complexion dimm'd;
And every fair from fair sometime declines,
By chance, or nature's changing course, un-
trimm'd;
But thy eternal summer shall not fade
Nor lose possession of that fair thou ow'st,   10
Nor shall Death brag thou wand'rest in his
shade
When in eternal lines to time thou grow'st.
So long as men can breathe or eyes can
see,
So long lives this, and this gives life to thee.

XIX

Devouring Time, blunt thou the lion's paws
And make the earth devour her own sweet
brood;
Pluck the keen teeth from the fierce tiger's
jaws
And burn the long-liv'd phœnix in her blood;
Make glad and sorry seasons as thou fleets,   5
And do whate'er thou wilt, swift-footed Time,
To the wide world and all her fading sweets;
But I forbid thee one most heinous crime:
O, carve not with thy hours my love's fair
brow,
Nor draw no lines there with thine antique
pen!   10
Him in thy course untainted do allow
For beauty's pattern to succeeding men.
Yet do thy worst, old Time! Despite thy
wrong,
My love shall in my verse ever live young.

XX

A woman's face, with Nature's own hand
painted,
Hast thou, the master mistress of my passion;
A woman's gentle heart, but not acquainted
With shifting change, as is false women's fash-
ion;
An eye more bright than theirs, less false in
rolling,   5
Gilding the object whereupon it gazeth;
A man in hue all hues in his controlling,
Which steals men's eyes and women's souls
amazeth.
And for a woman wert thou first created,
Till Nature as she wrought thee fell a-doting   10
And by addition me of thee defeated
By adding one thing to my purpose nothing.
But since she prick'd thee out for women's
pleasure,
Mine be thy love, and thy love's use their
treasure.

XXI

So is it not with me as with that Muse
Stirr'd by a painted beauty to his verse,
Who heaven itself for ornament doth use
And every fair with his fair doth rehearse;
Making a couplement of proud compare   5
With sun and moon, with earth and sea's rich
gems,
With April's first-born flowers, and all things
rare
That heaven's air in this huge rondure hems.
O, let me, true in love, but truly write,
And then believe me, my love is as fair   10
As any mother's child, though not so bright
As those gold candles fix'd in heaven's air.
Let them say more that like of hearsay well;
I will not praise that purpose not to sell.

XXII

My glass shall not persuade me I am old
So long as youth and thou are of one date;
But when in thee time's furrows I behold,
Then look I death my days should expiate.
For all that beauty that doth cover thee   5
Is but the seemly raiment of my heart,
Which in thy breast doth live, as thine in me.
How can I then be elder than thou art?
O, therefore, love, be of thyself so wary
As I, not for myself, but for thee will,   10
Bearing thy heart, which I will keep so chary
As tender nurse her babe from faring ill.

Presume not on thy heart when mine is slain:
Thou gav'st me thine, not to give back again.

XXIII

As an unperfect actor on the stage
Who with his fear is put besides his part,
Or some fierce thing replete with too much rage,
Whose strength's abundance weakens his own
  heart;
So I, for fear of trust, forget to say   5
The perfect ceremony of love's rite,
And in mine own love's strength seem to decay,
O'ercharg'd with burthen of mine own love's
  might.
O, let my looks be then the eloquence
And dumb presagers of my speaking breast, 10
Who plead for love, and look for recompense,
More than that tongue that more hath more
  express'd.
O, learn to read what silent love hath writ!
To hear with eyes belongs to love's fine wit.

XXIV

Mine eye hath play'd the painter and hath
  stell'd
Thy beauty's form in table of my heart;
My body is the frame wherein 'tis held,
And perspective it is best painter's art.
For through the painter must you see his skill
To find where your true image pictur'd lies. 6
Which in my bosom's shop is hanging still,
That hath his windows glazed with thine eyes.
Now see what good turns eyes for eyes have
  done:
Mine eyes have drawn thy shape, and thine for
  me   10
Are windows to my breast, wherethrough the
  sun
Delights to peep, to gaze therein on thee.
  Yet eyes this cunning want to grace their
    art —
  They draw but what they see, know not the
    heart.

XXV

Let those who are in favour with their stars
Of public honour and proud titles boast,
Whilst I, whom fortune of such triumph bars,
Unlook'd for joy in that I honour most.
Great princes' favourites their fair leaves spread
But as the marigold at the sun's eye;   6
And in themselves their pride lies buried,
For at a frown they in their glory die.

The painful warrior famoused for fight,
After a thousand victories once foil'd,   10
Is from the book of honour rased quite,
And all the rest forgot for which he toil'd.
  Then happy I, that love and am beloved
  Where I may not remove nor be removed.

XXVI

Lord of my love, to whom in vassalage
Thy merit hath my duty strongly knit,
To thee I send this written embassage,
To witness duty, not to show my wit:
Duty so great, which wit so poor as mine   5
May make seem bare, in wanting words to
  show it,
But that I hope some good conceit of thine
In thy soul's thought (all naked) will bestow it;
Till whatsoever star that guides my moving
Points on me graciously with fair aspect,   10
And puts apparel on my tattered loving
To show me worthy of thy sweet respect.
  Then may I dare to boast how I do love
    thee;
  Till then not show my head where thou mayst
    prove me.

XXVII

Weary with toil, I haste me to my bed,
The dear repose for limbs with travel tired;
But then begins a journey in my head
To work my mind when body's work's expired.
For then my thoughts, from far where I abide,
Intend a zealous pilgrimage to thee,   6
And keep my drooping eyelids open wide,
Looking on darkness which the blind do see;
Save that my soul's imaginary sight
Presents thy shadow to my sightless view, 10
Which, like a jewel hung in ghastly night,
Makes black night beauteous and her old face
  new.
  Lo, thus, by day my limbs, by night my
    mind,
  For thee, and for myself, no quiet find.

XXVIII

How can I then return in happy plight
That am debarr'd the benefit of rest,
When day's oppression is not eas'd by night,
But day by night and night by day oppress'd,
And each, though enemies to either's reign, 5
Do in consent shake hands to torture me,
The one by toil, the other to complain
How far I toil, still farther off from thee?

I tell the day, to please him, thou art bright
And dost him grace when clouds do blot the
    heaven;   10
So flatter I the swart-complexion'd night,
When sparkling stars twire not, thou gild'st
    the even.
  But day doth daily draw my sorrows longer,
  And night doth nightly make grief's strength
    seem stronger.

XXIX

When, in disgrace with Fortune and men's eyes,
I all alone beweep my outcast state,
And trouble deaf heaven with my bootless cries,
And look upon myself and curse my fate,
Wishing me like to one more rich in hope, 5
Featur'd like him, like him with friends pos-
    sess'd,
Desiring this man's art, and that man's scope,
With what I most enjoy contented least;
Yet in these thoughts myself almost despising,
Haply I think on thee, and then my state, 10
Like to the lark at break of day arising
From sullen earth, sings hymns at heaven's
    gate;
  For thy sweet love rememb'red such wealth
    brings
  That then I scorn to change my state with
    kings.

XXX

When to the sessions of sweet silent thought
I summon up remembrance of things past,
I sigh the lack of many a thing I sought
And with old woes new wail my dear time's
    waste.
Then can I drown an eye (unus'd to flow) 5
For precious friends hid in death's dateless
    night,
And weep afresh love's long since cancell'd woe,
And moan th' expense of many a vanish'd sight.
Then can I grieve at grievances foregone,
And heavily from woe to woe tell o'er 10
The sad account of fore-bemoaned moan,
Which I new pay as if not paid before.
  But if the while I think on thee, dear friend,
  All losses are restor'd and sorrows end.

XXXI

Thy bosom is endeared with all hearts
Which I by lacking have supposed dead;
And there reigns love, and all love's loving
    parts,
And all those friends which I thought buried.

How many a holy and obsequious tear 5
Hath dear religious love stol'n from mine eye,
As interest of the dead, which now appear
But things remov'd that hidden in thee lie!
Thou art the grave where buried love doth
    live,
Hung with the trophies of my lovers gone, 10
Who all their parts of me to thee did give:
That due of many now is thine alone.
  Their images I lov'd I view in thee,
  And thou (all they) hast all the all of me.

XXXII

If thou survive my well-contented day
When that churl Death my bones with dust
    shall cover,
And shalt by fortune once more resurvey
These poor rude lines of thy deceased lover, 4
Compare them with the bett'ring of the time,
And though they be outstripp'd by every pen,
Reserve them for my love not for their rhyme,
Exceeded by the height of happier men.
O, then vouchsafe me but this loving thought:
'Had my friend's Muse grown with this grow-
    ing age, 10
A dearer birth than this his love had brought,
To march in ranks of better equipage;
  But since he died, and poets better prove,
  Theirs for their style I'll read, his for his love.'

XXXIII

Full many a glorious morning have I seen
Flatter the mountain tops with sovereign eye,
Kissing with golden face the meadows green,
Gilding pale streams with heavenly alchemy;
Anon permit the basest clouds to ride 5
With ugly rack on his celestial face
And from the forlorn world his visage hide,
Stealing unseen to West with this disgrace.
Even so my sun one early morn did shine
With all triumphant splendour on my brow;
But, out alack! he was but one hour mine, 11
The region cloud hath mask'd him from me
    now.
  Yet him for this my love no whit disdaineth;
  Suns of the world may stain when heaven's
    sun staineth.

XXXIV

Why didst thou promise such a beauteous day
And make me travel forth without my cloak,
To let base clouds o'ertake me in my way,
Hiding thy brav'ry in their rotten smoke?

Sonnets

'Tis not enough that through the cloud thou
break   5
To dry the rain on my storm-beaten face,
For no man well of such a salve can speak
That heals the wound, and cures not the dis-
grace:
Nor can thy shame give physic to my grief;
Though thou repent, yet I have still the loss.
Th' offender's sorrow lends but weak relief   11
To him that bears the strong offence's cross.
  Ah, but those tears are pearl which thy love
    sheeds,
  And they are rich and ransom all ill deeds.

XXXV

No more be griev'd at that which thou hast done:
Roses have thorns, and silver fountains mud;
Clouds and eclipses stain both moon and sun,
And loathsome canker lives in sweetest bud.
All men make faults, and even I in this,   5
Authorizing thy trespass with compare,
Myself corrupting, salving thy amiss,
Excusing thy sins more than thy sins are;
For to thy sensual fault I bring in sense —
Thy adverse party is thy advocate —   10
And 'gainst myself a lawful plea commence.
Such civil war is in my love and hate
  That I an accessary needs must be
  To that sweet thief which sourly robs from
    me.

XXXVI

Let me confess that we two must be twain,
Although our undivided loves are one.
So shall those blots that do with me remain,
Without thy help by me be borne alone.
In our two loves there is but one respect,   5
Though in our lives a separable spite,
Which though it alter not love's sole effect,
Yet doth it steal sweet hours from love's
    delight.
I may not evermore acknowledge thee,   9
Lest my bewailed guilt should do thee shame;
Nor thou with public kindness honour me,
Unless thou take that honour from thy name.
  But do not so. I love thee in such sort
  As, thou being mine, mine is thy good report.

XXXVII

As a decrepit father takes delight
To see his active child do deeds of youth,
So I, made lame by Fortune's dearest spite,
Take all my comfort of thy worth and truth;

For whether beauty, birth, or wealth, or wit, 5
Or any of these all, or all, or more,
Entitled in thy parts do crowned sit,
I make my love engrafted to this store.
So then I am not lame, poor, nor despis'd
Whilst that this shadow doth such substance
    give   10
That I in thy abundance am suffic'd
And by a part of all thy glory live.
  Look what is best — that best I wish in
    thee.
  This wish I have; then ten times happy me :

XXXVIII

How can my Muse want subject to invent
While thou dost breathe, that pour'st into my
    verse
Thine own sweet argument, too excellent
For every vulgar paper to rehearse?
O, give thyself the thanks if aught in me   5
Worthy perusal stand against thy sight;
For who's so dumb that cannot write to
    thee,
When thou thyself dost give invention light?
Be thou the tenth Muse, ten times more in
    worth   9
Than those old nine which rhymers invocate;
And he that calls on thee, let him bring forth
Eternal numbers to outlive long date.
  If my slight Muse do please these curious
    days,
  The pain be mine, but thine shall be the
    praise.

XXXIX

O, how thy worth with manners may I sing
When thou art all the better part of me?
What can mine own praise to mine own self
    bring?
And what is't but mine own when I praise
    thee?
Even for this let us divided live   5
And our dear love lose name of single one,
That by this separation I may give
That due to thee which thou deserv'st alone.
O absence, what a torment wouldst thou prove,
Were it not thy sour leisure gave sweet leave
To entertain the time with thoughts of love,
Which time and thoughts so sweetly doth
    deceive,
  And that thou teachest how to make one
    twain —
  By praising him here who doth hence re-
    main!

459

XL

Take all my loves, my love, yea, take them all!
What hast thou then more than thou hadst
 before?
No love, my love, that thou mayst true love
 call;
All mine was thine before thou hadst this more.
Then, if for my love thou my love receivest, 5
I cannot blame thee for my love thou usest;
But yet be blam'd if thou thyself deceivest
By wilful taste of what thyself refusest.
I do forgive thy robb'ry, gentle thief,
Although thou steal thee all my poverty; 10
And yet love knows it is a greater grief
To bear love's wrong than hate's known injury.
 Lascivious grace, in whom all ill well shows,
 Kill me with spites; yet we must not be foes.

XLI

Those pretty wrongs that liberty commits
When I am sometime absent from thy heart,
Thy beauty and thy years full well befits,
For still temptation follows where thou art.
Gentle thou art, and therefore to be won; 5
Beauteous thou art, therefore to be assailed;
And when a woman wooes, what woman's son
Will sourly leave her till she have prevailed?
Ay me! but yet thou mightst my seat forbear,
And chide thy beauty and thy straying youth,
Who lead thee in their riot even there 11
Where thou art forc'd to break a twofold
 truth —
 Hers, by thy beauty tempting her to thee,
 Thine, by thy beauty being false to me.

XLII

That thou hast her, it is not all my grief,
And yet it may be said I lov'd her dearly;
That she hath thee is of my wailing chief,
A loss in love that touches me more nearly.
Loving offenders, thus I will excuse ye: 5
Thou dost love her because thou know'st I
 love her,
And for my sake even so doth she abuse me,
Suff'ring my friend for my sake to approve her.
If I lose thee, my loss is my love's gain,
And losing her, my friend hath found that loss:
Both find each other, and I lose both twain, 11
And both for my sake lay on me this cross.
 But here's the joy — my friend and I are
 one.
 Sweet flattery! then she loves but me alone.

XLIII

When most I wink, then do mine eyes best see,
For all the day they view things unrespected,
But when I sleep, in dreams they look on thee
And, darkly bright, are bright in dark directed.
Then thou, whose shadow shadows doth make
 bright, 5
How would thy shadow's form form happy show
To the clear day with thy much clearer light
When to unseeing eyes thy shade shines so!
How would, I say, mine eyes be blessed made
By looking on thee in the living day, 10
When in dead night thy fair imperfect shade
Through heavy sleep on sightless eyes doth
 stay!
 All days are nights to see till I see thee,
 And nights bright days when dreams do
 show thee me.

XLIV

If the dull substance of my flesh were thought,
Injurious distance should not stop my way;
For then, despite of space, I would be brought,
From limits far remote, where thou dost stay.
No matter then although my foot did stand 5
Upon the farthest earth remov'd from thee;
For nimble thought can jump both sea and land
As soon as think the place where he would be.
But, ah, thought kills me that I am not thought,
To leap large lengths of miles when thou art
 gone, 10
But that, so much of earth and water wrought,
I must attend time's leisure with my moan,
 Receiving naught by elements so slow
 But heavy tears, badges of either's woe.

XLV

The other two, slight air and purging fire,
Are both with thee, wherever I abide;
The first my thought, the other my desire,
These present-absent with swift motion slide.
For when these quicker elements are gone 5
In tender embassy of love to thee,
My life, being made of four, with two alone
Sinks down to death, oppress'd with melan-
 choly;
Until live's composition be recured 9
By those swift messengers return'd from thee,
Who even but now come back again, assured
Of thy fair health, recounting it to me.
 This told, I joy; but then no longer glad,
 I send them back again and straight grow
 sad.

Sonnets

XLVI

Mine eye and heart are at a mortal war
How to divide the conquest of thy sight;
Mine eye my heart thy picture's sight would
    bar,
My heart mine eye the freedom of that right.
My heart doth plead that thou in him dost lie
(A closet never pierc'd with crystal eyes) ; 6
But the defendant doth that plea deny
And says in him thy fair appearance lies.
To 'cide this title is impanneled
A quest of thoughts, all tenants to the heart,
And by their verdict is determined 11
The clear eye's moiety and the dear heart's
    part:
    As thus — mine eye's due is thy outward part,
    And my heart's right thy inward love of
    heart.

XLVII

Betwixt mine eye and heart a league is took,
And each doth good turns now unto the other.
When that mine eye is famish'd for a look,
Or heart in love with sighs himself doth smother,
With my love's picture then my eye doth feast
And to the painted banquet bids my heart. 6
Another time mine eye is my heart's guest
And in his thoughts of love doth share a part.
So, either by thy picture or my love,
Thyself away art present still with me; 10
For thou not farther than my thoughts canst
    move,
And I am still with them, and they with thee;
    Or, if they sleep, thy picture in my sight
    Awakes my heart to heart's and eye's delight.

XLVIII

How careful was I, when I took my way,
Each trifle under truest bars to thrust,
That to my use it might unused stay
From hands of falsehood, in sure wards of trust!
But thou, to whom my jewels trifles are, 5
Most worthy comfort, now my greatest grief,
Thou, best of dearest, and mine only care,
Art left the prey of every vulgar thief.
Thee have I not lock'd up in any chest,
Save where thou art not, though I feel thou
    art, 10
Within the gentle closure of my breast,
From whence at pleasure thou mayst come and
    part;
    And even thence thou wilt be stol'n, I fear,
    For truth proves thievish for a prize so dear.

XLIX

Against that time (if ever that time come)
When I shall see thee frown on my defects,
When as thy love hath cast his utmost sum,
Call'd to that audit by advis'd respects; 4
Against that time when thou shalt strangely pass
And scarcely greet me with that sun, thine eye,
When love, converted from the thing it was,
Shall reasons find of settled gravity —
Against that time do I ensconce me here
Within the knowledge of mine own desart, 10
And this my hand against myself uprear,
To guard the lawful reasons on thy part.
    To leave poor me thou hast the strength of
    laws,
    Since why to love I can allege no cause.

L

How heavy do I journey on the way
When what I seek (my weary travel's end)
Doth teach that ease and that repose to say,
'Thus far the miles are measur'd from thy
    friend !'
The beast that bears me, tired with my woe, 5
Plods dully on, to bear that weight in me,
As if by some instinct the wretch did know
His rider lov'd not speed, being made from thee.
The bloody spur cannot provoke him on
That sometimes anger thrusts into his hide; 10
Which heavily he answers with a groan,
More sharp to me than spurring to his side;
    For that same groan doth put this in my
    mind —
    My grief lies onward and my joy behind.

LI

Thus can my love excuse the slow offence
Of my dull bearer when from thee I speed:
From where thou art, why should I haste me
    thence?
Till I return, of posting is no need.
O, what excuse will my poor beast then find 5
When swift extremity can seem but slow?
Then should I spur, though mounted on the
    wind,
In winged speed no motion shall I know.
Then can no horse with my desire keep pace;
Therefore desire, of perfect'st love being made,
Shall neigh (no dull flesh) in his fiery race; 11
But love, for love, thus shall excuse my jade —
    Since from thee going he went wilful slow,
    Towards thee I'll run and give him leave to go.

LII

So am I as the rich whose blessed key
Can bring him to his sweet up-locked treasure,
The which he will not ev'ry hour survey,
For blunting the fine point of seldom pleasure.
Therefore are feasts so solemn and so rare, 5
Since, seldom coming, in the long year set,
Like stones of worth they thinly placed are,
Or captain jewels in the carcanet.
So is the time that keeps you as my chest,
Or as the wardrobe which the robe doth hide,
To make some special instant special blest 11
By new unfolding his imprison'd pride.
  Blessed are you, whose worthiness gives scope,
  Being had, to triumph, being lack'd, to hope.

LIII

What is your substance, whereof are you made,
That millions of strange shadows on you tend?
Since every one hath, every one, one shade,
And you, but one, can every shadow lend.
Describe Adonis, and the counterfeit 5
Is poorly imitated after you.
On Helen's cheek all art of beauty set,
And you in Grecian tires are painted new.
Speak of the spring, and foison of the year:
The one doth shadow of your beauty show, 10
The other as your bounty doth appear,
And you in every blessed shape we know.
  In all external grace you have some part,
  But you like none, none you, for constant heart.

LIV

O, how much more doth beauty beauteous seem
By that sweet ornament which truth doth give!
The rose looks fair, but fairer we it deem
For that sweet odour which doth in it live.
The canker blooms have full as deep a dye 5
As the perfumed tincture of the roses,
Hang on such thorns, and play as wantonly
When summer's breath their masked buds discloses;
But, for their virtue only is their show,
They live unwoo'd and unrespected fade, 10
Die to themselves. Sweet roses do not so:
Of their sweet deaths are sweetest odours made.
  And so of you, beauteous and lovely youth,
  When that shall vade, by verse distills your truth.

LV

Not marble nor the gilded monuments
Of princes shall outlive this pow'rful rhyme;
But you shall shine more bright in these contents
Than unswept stone, besmear'd with sluttish time.
When wasteful war shall statues overturn, 5
And broils root out the work of masonry,
Nor Mars his sword nor war's quick fire shall burn
The living record of your memory.
'Gainst death and all-oblivious enmity
Shall you pace forth; your praise shall still find room 10
Even in the eyes of all posterity
That wear this world out to the ending doom.
  So, till the judgment that yourself arise,
  You live in this, and dwell in lovers' eyes.

LVI

Sweet love, renew thy force; be it not said
Thy edge should blunter be than appetite,
Which but to-day by feeding is allay'd,
To-morrow sharp'ned in his former might.
So, love, be thou: although to-day thou fill 5
Thy hungry eyes even till they wink with fulness,
To-morrow see again, and do not kill
The spirit of love with a perpetual dulness.
Let this sad int'rim like the ocean be
Which parts the shore where two contracted new
Come daily to the banks, that, when they see
Return of love, more blest may be the view;
  Or call it winter, which, being full of care,
  Makes summer's welcome thrice more wish'd, more rare.

LVII

Being your slave, what should I do but tend
Upon the hours and times of your desire?
I have no precious time at all to spend,
Nor services to do, till you require.
Nor dare I chide the world-without-end hour 5
Whilst I, my sovereign, watch the clock for you,
Nor think the bitterness of absence sour
When you have bid your servant once adieu.
Nor dare I question with my jealous thought
Where you may be, or your affairs suppose, 10
But, like a sad slave, stay and think of nought
Save where you are how happy you make those.
  So true a fool is love that in your will,
  Though you do anything, he thinks no ill.

Sonnets

LVIII

That god forbid that made me first your slave
I should in thought control your times of
    pleasure,
Or at your hand th' account of hours to crave,
Being your vassal bound to stay your leisure!
O, let me suffer (being at your beck)   5
Th' imprison'd absence of your liberty;
And patience, tame to sufferance, bide each
    check
Without accusing you of injury.
Be where you list; your charter is so strong
That you yourself may privilege your time   10
To what you will; to you it doth belong
Yourself to pardon of self-doing crime.
    I am to wait, though waiting so be hell;
    Not blame your pleasure, be it ill or well.

LIX

If there be nothing new, but that which is
Hath been before, how are our brains beguil'd,
Which, labouring for invention, bear amiss
The second burthen of a former child!
O that record could with a backward look,   5
Even of five hundreth courses of the sun,
Show me your image in some antique book,
Since mind at first in character was done!
That I might see what the old world could say
To this composed wonder of your frame;   10
Whether we are mended, or whe'r better they,
Or whether revolution be the same.
    O, sure I am the wits of former days
    To subjects worse have given admiring praise.

LX

Like as the waves make towards the pebbled
    shore,
So do our minutes hasten to their end;
Each changing place with that which goes be-
    fore,
In sequent toil all forwards do contend.
Nativity, once in the main of light,   5
Crawls to maturity, wherewith being crown'd,
Crooked eclipses 'gainst his glory fight,
And Time that gave doth now his gift confound.
Time doth transfix the flourish set on youth
And delves the parallels in beauty's brow,   10
Feeds on the rarities of nature's truth,
And nothing stands but for his scythe to mow;
    And yet to times in hope my verse shall
        stand,
    Praising thy worth, despite his cruel hand.

LXI

Is it thy will thy image should keep open
My heavy eyelids to the weary night?
Dost thou desire my slumbers should be broken
While shadows like to thee do mock my sight?
Is it thy spirit that thou send'st from thee   5
So far from home into my deeds to pry,
To find out shames and idle hours in me,
The scope and tenure of thy jealousy?
O, no! thy love, though much, is not so great.
It is my love that keeps mine eye awake;   10
Mine own true love that doth my rest defeat,
To play the watchman ever for thy sake.
    For thee watch I whilst thou dost wake else-
        where,
    From me far off, with others all too near.

LXII

Sin of self-love possesseth all mine eye
And all my soul and all my every part;
And for this sin there is no remedy,
It is so grounded inward in my heart.
Methinks no face so gracious is as mine,   5
No shape so true, no truth of such account,
And for myself mine own worth do define
As I all other in all worths surmount.
But when my glass shows me myself indeed,
Beated and chopt with tann'd antiquity,   10
Mine own self-love quite contrary I read;
Self so self-loving were iniquity.
    'Tis thee (myself) that for myself I praise,
    Painting my age with beauty of thy days.

LXIII

Against my love shall be as I am now,
With Time's injurious hand crush'd and o'er-
    worn;
When hours have drain'd his blood, and fill'd
    his brow
With lines and wrinkles; when his youthful
    morn
Hath travell'd on to age's steepy night,   5
And all those beauties whereof now he's king
Are vanishing, or vanish'd out of sight,
Stealing away the treasure of his spring —
For such a time do I now fortify
Against confounding age's cruel knife,   10
That he shall never cut from memory
My sweet love's beauty, though my lover's life
    His beauty shall in these black lines be seen,
    And they shall live, and he in them still
        green.

LXIV

When I have seen by Time's fell hand defaced
The rich proud cost of outworn buried age;
When sometime lofty towers I see down rased,
And brass eternal slave to mortal rage;
When I have seen the hungry ocean gain   5
Advantage on the kingdom of the shore,
And the firm soil win of the wat'ry main,
Increasing store with loss, and loss with store;
When I have seen such interchange of state,
Or state itself confounded, to decay;   10
Ruin hath taught me thus to ruminate,
That Time will come and take my love away.
 This thought is as a death, which cannot
   choose
 But weep to have that which it fears to lose.

LXV

Since brass, nor stone, nor earth, nor boundless
   sea,
But sad mortality o'ersways their power,
How with this rage shall beauty hold a plea,
Whose action is no stronger than a flower?
O, how shall summer's honey breath hold out 5
Against the wrackful siege of batt'ring days,
When rocks impregnable are not so stout,
Nor gates of steel so strong, but Time decays?
O fearful meditation! Where, alack,
Shall Time's best jewel from Time's chest lie
   hid?   10
Or what strong hand can hold his swift foot
   back?
Or who his spoil of beauty can forbid?
 O, none! unless this miracle have might,
 That in black ink my love may still shine
   bright.

LXVI

Tir'd with all these, for restful death I cry:
As, to behold desert a beggar born,
And needy nothing trimm'd in jollity,
And purest faith unhappily forsworn,
And gilded honour shamefully misplac'd,   5
And maiden virtue rudely strumpeted,
And right perfection wrongfully disgrac'd,
And strength by limping sway disabled,
And art made tongue-tied by authority,
And folly (doctor-like) controlling skill,   10
And simple truth miscall'd simplicity,
And captive good attending captain ill.
 Tir'd with all these, from these would I be
   gone,
 Save that, to die, I leave my love alone.

LXVII

Ah, wherefore with infection should he live
And with his presence grace impiety,
That sin by him advantage should achieve
And lace itself with his society?
Why should false painting imitate his cheek 5
And steal dead seeing of his living hue?
Why should poor beauty indirectly seek
Roses of shadow, since his rose is true?
Why should he live, now Nature bankrout is,
Beggar'd of blood to blush through lively veins?
For she hath no exchequer now but his,   11
And, proud of many, lives upon his gains.
 O, him she stores, to show what wealth she
   had
 In days long since, before these last so bad.

LXVIII

Thus is his cheek the map of days outworn,
When beauty liv'd and died as flowers do now,
Before these bastard signs of fair were born
Or durst inhabit on a living brow;
Before the golden tresses of the dead,   5
The right of sepulchres, were shorn away
To live a second life on second head;
Ere beauty's dead fleece made another gay.
In him those holy antique hours are seen,
Without all ornament, itself and true,   10
Making no summer of another's green,
Robbing no old to dress his beauty new;
 And him as for a map doth Nature store,
 To show false Art what beauty was of yore.

LXIX

Those parts of thee that the world's eye doth
   view
Want nothing that the thought of hearts can
   mend.
All tongues (the voice of souls) give thee that
   due,
Utt'ring bare truth, even so as foes commend.
Thy outward thus with outward praise is
   crown'd;   5
But those same tongues that give thee so thine
   own
In other accents do this praise confound
By seeing farther than the eye hath shown.
They look into the beauty of thy mind,
And that in guess they measure by thy deeds;
Then, churls, their thoughts (although their
   eyes were kind)
To thy fair flower add the rank smell of weeds,

But why thy odour matcheth not thy show,
The soil is this — that thou dost common
  grow.

LXX

That thou art blam'd shall not be thy defect,
For slander's mark was ever yet the fair;
The ornament of beauty is suspect,
A crow that flies in heaven's sweetest air.
So thou be good, slander doth but approve 5
Thy worth the greater, being woo'd of time;
For canker vice the sweetest buds doth love,
And thou present'st a pure unstained prime.
Thou hast pass'd by the ambush of young days,
Either not assail'd, or victor being charg'd; 10
Yet this thy praise cannot be so thy praise
To tie up envy, evermore enlarg'd.
  If some suspect of ill mask'd not thy show,
  Then thou alone kingdoms of hearts shouldst
    owe.

LXXI

No longer mourn for me when I am dead
Than you shall hear the surly sullen bell
Give warning to the world that I am fled
From this vile world, with vilest worms to dwell.
Nay, if you read this line, remember not 5
The hand that writ it; for I love you so
That I in your sweet thoughts would be forgot
If thinking on me then should make you woe.
O, if, I say, you look upon this verse
When I, perhaps, compounded am with clay, 10
Do not so much as my poor name rehearse,
But let your love even with my life decay,
  Lest the wise world should look into your
    moan
  And mock you with me after I am gone.

LXXII

O, lest the world should task you to recite
What merit liv'd in me, that you should love
After my death, dear love, forget me quite,
For you in me can nothing worthy prove;
Unless you would devise some virtuous lie, 5
To do more for me than mine own desert
And hang more praise upon deceased I
Than niggard truth would willingly impart.
O, lest your true love may seem false in this,
That you for love speak well of me untrue, 10
My name be buried where my body is,
And live no more to shame nor me nor you!
  For I am sham'd by that which I bring forth,
  And so should you, to love things nothing
    worth.

LXXIII

That time of year thou mayst in me behold
When yellow leaves, or none, or few, do hang
Upon those boughs which shake against the cold,
Bare ruin'd choirs where late the sweet birds
  sang.
In me thou see'st the twilight of such day 5
As after sunset fadeth in the West,
Which by-and-by black night doth take away,
Death's second self, that seals up all in rest.
In me thou see'st the glowing of such fire
That on the ashes of his youth doth lie, 10
As the deathbed whereon it must expire,
Consum'd with that which it was nourish'd
  by.
  This thou perceiv'st, which makes thy love
    more strong,
  To love that well which thou must leave ere
    long.

LXXIV

But be contented. When that fell arrest
Without all bail shall carry me away,
My life hath in this line some interest,
Which for memorial still with thee shall stay.
When thou reviewest this, thou dost review 5
The very part was consecrate to thee.
The earth can have but earth, which is his
  due;
My spirit is thine, the better part of me.
So then thou hast but lost the dregs of life,
The prey of worms, my body being dead — 10
The coward conquest of a wretch's knife,
Too base of thee to be remembered.
  The worth of that is that which it contains,
  And that is this, and this with thee remains.

LXXV

So are you to my thoughts as food to life,
Or as sweet-season'd showers are to the ground;
And for the peace of you I hold such strife
As 'twixt a miser and his wealth is found:
Now proud as an enjoyer, and anon 5
Doubting the filching age will steal his treasure;
Now counting best to be with you alone,
Then better'd that the world may see my pleas-
  ure;
Sometime all full with feasting on your sight,
And by-and-by clean starved for a look; 10
Possessing or pursuing no delight
Save what is had or must from you be took.
  Thus do I pine and surfeit day by day,
  Or gluttoning on all, or all away.

LXXVI

Why is my verse so barren of new pride?
So far from variation or quick change?
Why, with the time, do I not glance aside
To new-found methods and to compounds
   strange?
Why write I still all one, ever the same, 5
And keep invention in a noted weed,
That every word doth almost tell my name,
Showing their birth, and where they did pro-
   ceed?
O, know, sweet love, I always write of you,
And you and love are still my argument: 10
So all my best is dressing old words new,
Spending again what is already spent;
   For as the sun is daily new and old,
   So is my love still telling what is told.

LXXVII

Thy glass will show thee how thy beauties
   wear,
Thy dial how thy precious minutes waste.
The vacant leaves thy mind's imprint will bear,
And of this book this learning mayst thou taste.
The wrinkles which thy glass will truly show, 5
Of mouthed graves will give thee memory.
Thou by thy dial's shady stealth mayst know
Time's thievish progress to eternity.
Look, what thy memory cannot contain,
Commit to these waste blanks, and thou shalt
   find 10
Those children nurs'd, deliver'd from thy brain,
To take a new acquaintance of thy mind.
   These offices, so oft as thou wilt look,
   Shall profit thee and much enrich thy book.

LXXVIII

So oft have I invok'd thee for my Muse
And found such fair assistance in my verse
As every alien pen hath got my use
And under thee their poesy disperse.
Thine eyes, that taught the dumb on high to
   sing 5
And heavy ignorance aloft to fly,
Have added feathers to the learned's wing
And given grace a double majesty.
Yet be most proud of that which I compile,
Whose influence is thine, and born of thee. 10
In others' works thou dost but mend the style,
And arts with thy sweet graces graced be;
   But thou art all my art and dost advance
   As high as learning my rude ignorance.

LXXIX

Whilst I alone did call upon thy aid,
My verse alone had all thy gentle grace;
But now my gracious numbers are decay'd,
And my sick Muse doth give another place.
I grant, sweet love, thy lovely argument 5
Deserves the travail of a worthier pen;
Yet what of thee thy poet doth invent
He robs thee of, and pays it thee again.
He lends thee virtue, and he stole that word
From thy behaviour. Beauty doth he give, 10
And found it in thy cheek. He can afford
No praise to thee but what in thee doth live.
   Then thank him not for that which he doth
    say,
   Since what he owes thee thou thyself dost pay.

LXXX

O, how I faint when I of you do write,
Knowing a better spirit doth use your name
And in the praise thereof spends all his might
To make me tongue-tied, speaking of your fame!
But since your worth, wide as the ocean is, 5
The humble as the proudest sail doth bear,
My saucy bark, inferior far to his,
On your broad main doth wilfully appear.
Your shallowest help will hold me up afloat
Whilst he upon your soundless deep doth ride;
Or, being wrack'd, I am a worthless boat, 11
He of tall building and of goodly pride.
   Then if he thrive, and I be cast away,
   The worst was this: my love was my decay.

LXXXI

Or I shall live your epitaph to make,
Or you survive when I in earth am rotten.
From hence your memory death cannot take,
Although in me each part will be forgotten. 4
Your name from hence immortal life shall have,
Though I, once gone, to all the world must
   die.
The earth can yield me but a common grave
When you entombed in men's eyes shall lie.
Your monument shall be my gentle verse,
Which eyes not yet created shall o'erread; 10
And tongues to be your being shall rehearse
When all the breathers of this world are
   dead.
   You still shall live (such virtue hath my
    pen)
   Where breath most breathes, even in the
    mouths of men.

Sonnets

LXXXII

I grant thou wert not married to my Muse
And therefore mayst without attaint o'erlook
The dedicated words which writers use
Of their fair subject, blessing every book.
Thou art as fair in knowledge as in hue, 5
Finding thy worth a limit past my praise;
And therefore art enforc'd to seek anew
Some fresher stamp of the time-bettering days.
And do so, love; yet when they have devis'd
What strained touches rhetoric can lend, 10
Thou, truly fair, wert truly sympathiz'd
In true plain words by thy true-telling friend;
 And their gross painting might be better us'd
 Where cheeks need blood; in thee it is abus'd.

LXXXIII

I never saw that you did painting need,
And therefore to your fair no painting set;
I found (or thought I found) you did exceed
The barren tender of a poet's debt;
And therefore have I slept in your report, 5
That you yourself, being extant, well might
 show
How far a modern quill doth come too short,
Speaking of worth, what worth in you doth
 grow.
This silence for my sin you did impute,
Which shall be most my glory, being dumb; 10
For I impair not beauty, being mute,
When others would give life, and bring a tomb.
 There lives more life in one of your fair
  eyes
 Than both your poets can in praise devise.

LXXXIV

Who is it that says most which can say more
Than this rich praise — that you alone are you?
In whose confine immured is the store
Which should example where your equal grew.
Lean penury within that pen doth dwell 5
That to his subject lends not some small
 glory;
But he that writes of you, if he can tell
That you are you, so dignifies his story.
Let him but copy what in you is writ,
Not making worse what nature made so clear,
And such a counterpart shall fame his wit, 11
Making his style admired everywhere.
 You to your beauteous blessings add a curse,
 Being fond on praise, which makes your
  praises worse.

LXXXV

My tongue-tied Muse in manners holds her still
While comments of your praise, richly compil'd,
Reserve their character with golden quill
And precious phrase by all the Muses fil'd.
I think good thoughts whilst other write good
 words, 5
And, like unlettered clerk, still cry 'Amen'
To every hymn that able spirit affords
In polish'd form of well-refined pen.
Hearing you prais'd, I say ''Tis so, 'tis true!'
And to the most of praise add something more;
But that is in my thought, whose love to you,
Though words come hindmost, holds his rank
 before.
 Then others for the breath of words respect;
 Me for my dumb thoughts, speaking in effect.

LXXXVI

Was it the proud full sail of his great verse,
Bound for the prize of all-too-precious you,
That did my ripe thoughts in my brain inhearse,
Making their tomb the womb wherein they
 grew?
Was it his spirit, by spirits taught to write 5
Above a mortal pitch, that struck me dead?
No, neither he, nor his compeers by night
Giving him aid, my verse astonished.
He, nor that affable familiar ghost
Which nightly gulls him with intelligence, 10
As victors, of my silence cannot boast —
I was not sick of any fear from thence;
 But when your countenance fill'd up his line,
 Then lack'd I matter; that enfeebled mine.

LXXXVII

Farewell! thou art too dear for my possessing,
And like enough thou know'st thy estimate.
The charter of thy worth gives thee releasing;
My bonds in thee are all determinate.
For how do I hold thee but by thy granting, 5
And for that riches where is my deserving?
The cause of this fair gift in me is wanting,
And so my patent back again is swerving.
Thyself thou gav'st, thy own worth then not
 knowing,
Or me, to whom thou gav'st it, else mistaking:
So thy great gift, upon misprision growing, 11
Comes home again, on better judgment making.
 Thus have I had thee as a dream doth flat-
  ter —
 In sleep a king, but waking no such matter.

LXXXVIII

When thou shalt be dispos'd to set me light
And place my merit in the eye of scorn,
Upon thy side against myself I'll fight
And prove thee virtuous, though thou art for-
    sworn.   4
With mine own weakness being best acquainted,
Upon thy part I can set down a story
Of faults conceal'd wherein I am attainted,
That thou, in losing me, shalt win much glory.
And I by this will be a gainer too;   9
For, bending all my loving thoughts on thee,
The injuries that to myself I do,
Doing thee vantage, double vantage me.
   Such is my love, to thee I so belong,
   That for thy right myself will bear all wrong.

LXXXIX

Say that thou didst forsake me for some fault,
And I will comment upon that offence.
Speak of my lameness, and I straight will halt,
Against thy reasons making no defence.
Thou canst not, love, disgrace me half so ill, 5
To set a form upon desired change,
As I'll myself disgrace, knowing thy will.
I will acquaintance strangle and look strange,
Be absent from thy walks, and in my tongue
Thy sweet beloved name no more shall dwell,
Lest I (too much profane) should do it wrong
And haply of our old acquaintance tell.
   For thee, against myself I'll vow debate,
   For I must ne'er love him whom thou dost
   hate.

XC

Then hate me when thou wilt! if ever, now!
Now, while the world is bent my deeds to
   cross,
Join with the spite of fortune, make me bow,
And do not drop in for an after-loss.
Ah, do not, when my heart hath scap'd this
   sorrow,   5
Come in the rearward of a conquer'd woe;
Give not a windy night a rainy morrow,
To linger out a purpos'd overthrow.
If thou wilt leave me, do not leave me last, 9
When other petty griefs have done their spite,
But in the onset come. So shall I taste
At first the very worst of fortune's might;
   And other strains of woe, which now seem
   woe,
   Compar'd with loss of thee will not seem
   so.

XCI

Some glory in their birth, some in their skill,
Some in their wealth, some in their body's force;
Some in their garments, though newfangled ill;
Some in their hawks and hounds, some in their
   horse;   4
And every humour hath his adjunct pleasure,
Wherein it finds a joy above the rest;
But these particulars are not my measure:
All these I better in one general best.
Thy love is better than high birth to me,
Richer than wealth, prouder than garments'
   cost,   10
Of more delight than hawks or horses be,
And having thee, of all men's pride I boast —
   Wretched in this alone, that thou mayst take
   All this away and me most wretched make.

XCII

But do thy worst to steal thyself away,
For term of life thou art assured mine;
And life no longer than thy love will stay,
For it depends upon that love of thine.
Then need I not to fear the worst of wrongs 5
When in the least of them my life hath end.
I see a better state to me belongs
Than that which on thy humour doth depend.
Thou canst not vex me with inconstant mind,
Since that my life on thy revolt doth lie.   10
O, what a happy title do I find,
Happy to have thy love, happy to die!
   But what's so blessed-fair that fears no blot?
   Thou mayst be false, and yet I know it not.

XCIII

So shall I live, supposing thou art true,
Like a deceived husband; so love's face
May still seem love to me, though alter'd new —
Thy looks with me, thy heart in other place.
For there can live no hatred in thine eye; 5
Therefore in that I cannot know thy change.
In many's looks the false heart's history
Is writ in moods and frowns and wrinkles
   strange;
But heaven in thy creation did decree   9
That in thy face sweet love should ever dwell;
Whate'er thy thoughts or thy heart's workings
   be,
Thy looks should nothing thence but sweetness
   tell.
   How like Eve's apple doth thy beauty grow
   If thy sweet virtue answer not thy show!

XCIV

They that have pow'r to hurt and will do none,
That do not do the thing they most do show,
Who, moving others, are themselves as stone,
Unmoved, cold, and to temptation slow —
They rightly do inherit heaven's graces 5
And husband nature's riches from expense;
They are the lords and owners of their faces,
Others but stewards of their excellence.
The summer's flow'r is to the summer sweet,
Though to itself it only live and die; 10
But if that flow'r with base infection meet,
The basest weed outbraves his dignity:
  For sweetest things turn sourest by their
    deeds;
  Lilies that fester smell far worse than weeds.

XCV

How sweet and lovely dost thou make the
    shame
Which, like a canker in the fragrant rose,
Doth spot the beauty of thy budding name!
O, in what sweets dost thou thy sins enclose!
That tongue that tells the story of thy days 5
(Making lascivious comments on thy sport)
Cannot dispraise but in a kind of praise:
Naming thy name blesses an ill report.
O, what a mansion have those vices got
Which for their habitation chose out thee, 10
Where beauty's veil doth cover every blot
And all things turns to fair that eyes can see!
  Take heed, dear heart, of this large privilege.
  The hardest knife ill us'd doth lose his edge.

XCVI

Some say thy fault is youth, some wanton-
    ness;
Some say thy grace is youth and gentle sport.
Both grace and faults are lov'd of more and
    less;
Thou mak'st faults graces that to thee resort.
As on the finger of a throned queen 5
The basest jewel will be well esteem'd,
So are those errors that in thee are seen
To truths translated and for true things deem'd.
How many lambs might the stern wolf betray
If like a lamb he could his looks translate! 10
How many gazers mightst thou lead away
If thou wouldst use the strength of all thy
    state!
  But do not so. I love thee in such sort
  As, thou being mine, mine is thy good report.

XCVII

How like a winter hath my absence been
From thee, the pleasure of the fleeting year!
What freezings have I felt, what dark days
    seen!
What old December's bareness everywhere!
And yet this time remov'd was summer's time,
The teeming autumn, big with rich increase, 6
Bearing the wanton burthen of the prime,
Like widowed wombs after their lords' decease;
Yet this abundant issue seem'd to me
But hope of orphans and unfathered fruit; 10
For summer and his pleasures wait on thee,
And, thou away, the very birds are mute;
  Or, if they sing, 'tis with so dull a cheer
  That leaves look pale, dreading the winter's
    near.

XCVIII

From you have I been absent in the spring,
When proud-pied April, dress'd in all his trim,
Hath put a spirit of youth in everything,
That heavy Saturn laugh'd and leapt with him,
Yet nor the lays of birds, nor the sweet smell 5
Of different flowers in odour and in hue,
Could make me any summer's story tell,
Or from their proud lap pluck them where they
    grew;
Nor did I wonder at the lily's white,
Nor praise the deep vermilion in the rose: 10
They were but sweet, but figures of delight,
Drawn after you, you pattern of all those.
  Yet seem'd it winter still, and, you away,
  As with your shadow I with these did play.

XCIX

The forward violet thus did I chide:
Sweet thief, whence didst thou steal thy sweet
    that smells,
If not from my love's breath? The purple
    pride
Which on thy soft cheek for complexion dwells
In my love's veins thou hast too grossly dy'd. 5
The lily I condemned for thy hand;
And buds of marjoram had stol'n thy hair.
The roses fearfully on thorns did stand,
One blushing shame, another white despair;
A third, nor red nor white, had stol'n of both,
And to his robb'ry had annex'd thy breath; 11
But, for his theft, in pride of all his growth
A vengeful canker eat him up to death.
  More flowers I noted, yet I none could see
  But sweet or colour it had stol'n from thee.

C

Where art thou, Muse, that thou forget'st so long
To speak of that which gives thee all thy might?
Spend'st thou thy fury on some worthless song,
Dark'ning thy pow'r to lend base subjects light?
Return, forgetful Muse, and straight redeem 5
In gentle numbers time so idly spent.
Sing to the ear that doth thy lays esteem
And gives thy pen both skill and argument.
Rise, resty Muse, my love's sweet face survey,
If Time have any wrinkle graven there. 10
If any, be a satire to decay
And make Time's spoils despised everywhere.
  Give my love fame faster than Time wastes
    life:
  So thou prevent'st his scythe and crooked
    knife.

CI

O truant Muse, what shall be thy amends
For thy neglect of truth in beauty dy'd?
Both truth and beauty on my love depends;
So dost thou too, and therein dignified.
Make answer, Muse. Wilt thou not haply say,
'Truth needs no colour, with his colour fix'd; 6
Beauty no pencil, beauty's truth to lay;
But best is best, if never intermix'd'?
Because he needs no praise, wilt thou be dumb?
Excuse not silence so; for't lies in thee 10
To make him much outlive a gilded tomb
And to be prais'd of ages yet to be.
  Then do thy office, Muse. I teach thee how
  To make him seem, long hence, as he shows
    now.

CII

My love is strength'ned, though more weak in
    seeming;
I love not less, though less the show appear.
That love is merchandiz'd whose rich esteeming
The owner's tongue doth publish everywhere.
Our love was new, and then but in the spring, 5
When I was wont to greet it with my lays,
As Philomel in summer's front doth sing
And stops her pipe in growth of riper days;
Not tha⁺ the summer is less pleasant now
Than when her mournful hymns did hush the
    night, 10
But that wild music burthens every bough,
And sweets grown common lose their dear
    delight.
  Therefore, like her, I sometime hold my
    tongue,
  Because I would not dull you with my song.

CIII

Alack, what poverty my Muse brings forth,
That, having such a scope to show her pride,
The argument all bare is of more worth
Than when it hath my added praise beside!
O, blame me not if I no more can write! 5
Look in your glass, and there appears a face
That overgoes my blunt invention quite,
Dulling my lines and doing me disgrace.
Were it not sinful then, striving to mend,
To mar the subject that before was well? 10
For to no other pass my verses tend
Than of your graces and your gifts to tell;
  And more, much more, than in my verse can
    sit
  Your own glass shows you when you look in it.

CIV

To me, fair friend, you never can be old,
For as you were when first your eye I ey'd,
Such seems your beauty still. Three winters cold
Have from the forests shook three summers'
    pride,
Three beauteous springs to yellow autumn
    turn'd 5
In process of the seasons have I seen,
Three April perfumes in three hot Junes burn'd,
Since first I saw you fresh, which yet are green.
Ah, yet doth beauty, like a dial hand, 9
Steal from his figure, and no pace perceiv'd!
So your sweet hue, which methinks still doth
    stand,
Hath motion, and mine eye may be deceiv'd;
  For fear of which, hear this, thou age unbred:
  Ere you were born was beauty's summer
    dead.

CV

Let not my love be call'd idolatry
Nor my beloved as an idol show,
Since all alike my songs and praises be
To one, of one, still such, and ever so.
Kind is my love to-day, to-morrow kind. 5
Still constant in a wondrous excellence;
Therefore my verse, to constancy confin'd,
One thing expressing, leaves out difference.
'Fair, kind, and true,' is all my argument,
'Fair, kind, and true,' varying to other words;
And in this change is my invention spent,
Three themes in one, which wondrous scope
    affords.
  Fair, kind, and true have often liv'd alone,
  Which three till now never kept seat in one.

CVI

When in the chronicle of wasted time
I see descriptions of the fairest wights,
And beauty making beautiful old rhyme
In praise of ladies dead and lovely knights,
Then, in the blazon of sweet beauty's best, 5
Of hand, of foot, of lip, of eye, of brow,
I see their antique pen would have express'd
Even such a beauty as you master now.
So all their praises are but prophecies
Of this our time, all you prefiguring; 10
And, for they look'd but with divining eyes,
They had not skill enough your worth to sing;
  For we, which now behold these present days,
  Have eyes to wonder, but lack tongues to praise.

CVII

Not mine own fears, nor the prophetic soul
Of the wide world, dreaming on things to come,
Can yet the lease of my true love control,
Suppos'd as forfeit to a confin'd doom.
The mortal moon hath her eclipse endur'd, 5
And the sad augurs mock their own presage;
Incertainties now crown themselves assur'd,
And peace proclaims olives of endless age.
Now with the drops of this most balmy time
My love looks fresh, and Death to me subscribes, 10
Since, spite of him, I'll live in this poor rhyme
While he insults o'er dull and speechless tribes;
  And thou in this shalt find thy monument
  When tyrants' crests and tombs of brass are spent.

CVIII

What's in the brain that ink may character
Which hath not figur'd to thee my true spirit?
What's new to speak, what new to register,
That may express my love or thy dear merit?
Nothing, sweet boy; but yet, like prayers divine, 5
I must each day say o'er the very same;
Counting no old thing old, thou mine, I thine,
Even as when first I hallowed thy fair name.
So that eternal love in love's fresh case
Weighs not the dust and injury of age, 10
Nor gives to necessary wrinkles place,
But makes antiquity for aye his page,
  Finding the first conceit of love there bred
  Where time and outward form would show it dead.

CIX

O, never say that I was false of heart,
Though absence seem'd my flame to qualify!
As easy might I from myself depart
As from my soul, which in thy breast doth lie.
That is my home of love. If I have rang'd, 5
Like him that travels I return again,
Just to the time, not with the time exchang'd,
So that myself bring water for my stain.
Never believe, though in my nature reign'd
All frailties that besiege all kinds of blood, 10
That it could so preposterously be stain'd
To leave for nothing all thy sum of good;
  For nothing this wide universe I call
  Save thou, my rose; in it thou art my all.

CX

Alas, 'tis true I have gone here and there
And made myself a motley to the view,
Gor'd mine own thoughts, sold cheap what is most dear,
Made old offences of affections new.
Most true it is that I have look'd on truth 5
Askance and strangely; but, by all above,
These blenches gave my heart another youth,
And worse essays prov'd thee my best of love.
Now all is done, have what shall have no end!
Mine appetite I never more will grind 10
On newer proof, to try an older friend,
A god in love, to whom I am confin'd.
  Then give me welcome, next my heaven the best,
  Even to thy pure and most most loving breast.

CXI

O, for my sake do you with Fortune chide,
The guilty goddess of my harmful deeds,
That did not better for my life provide
Than public means which public manners breeds.
Thence comes it that my name receives a brand; 5
And almost thence my nature is subdu'd
To what it works in, like the dyer's hand.
Pity me then, and wish I were renew'd;
Whilst, like a willing patient, I will drink
Potions of eysell 'gainst my strong infection; 10
No bitterness that I will bitter think,
Nor double penance, to correct correction.
  Pity me, then, dear friend, and I assure ye
  Even that your pity is enough to cure me.

CXII

Your love and pity doth th' impression fill
Which vulgar scandal stamp'd upon my brow;
For what care I who calls me well or ill,
So you o'er-green my bad, my good allow?
You are my all the world, and I must strive 5
To know my shames and praises from your
    tongue —
None else to me, nor I to none alive,
That my steel'd sense or changes right or wrong.
In so profound abysm I throw all care
Of others' voices that my adder's sense 10
To critic and to flatterer stopped are.
Mark how with my neglect I do dispense:
  You are so strongly in my purpose bred
  That all the world besides methinks are dead.

CXIII

Since I left you, mine eye is in my mind;
And that which governs me to go about
Doth part his function and is partly blind,
Seems seeing, but effectually is out;
For it no form delivers to the heart 5
Of bird, of flow'r, or shape which it doth
    latch;
Of his quick objects hath the mind no part,
Nor his own vision holds what it doth catch;
For if it see the rud'st or gentlest sight,
The most sweet favour or deformed'st creature,
The mountain or the sea, the day or night, 11
The crow or dove, it shapes them to your fea-
    ture.
  Incapable of more, replete with you,
  My most true mind thus mak'th mine eye
    untrue.

CXIV

Or whether doth my mind, being crown'd with
    you,
Drink up the monarch's plague, this flattery?
Or whether shall I say mine eye saith true,
And that your love taught it this alchemy,
To make of monsters and things indigest 5
Such cherubins as your sweet self resemble,
Creating every bad a perfect best
As fast as objects to his beams assemble?
O, 'tis the first! 'Tis flatt'ry in my seeing,
And my great mind most kingly drinks it up.
Mine eye well knows what with his gust is
    greeing, 11
And to his palate doth prepare the cup.
  If it be poison'd, 'tis the lesser sin
  That mine eye loves it and doth first begin.

CXV

Those lines that I before have writ do lie,
Even those that said I could not love you
    dearer.
Yet then my judgment knew no reason why
My most full flame should afterwards burn
    clearer.
But reckoning Time, whose million'd accidents
Creep in 'twixt vows and change decrees of
    kings, 6
Tan sacred beauty, blunt the sharp'st in-
    tents,
Divert strong minds to th' course of alt'ring
    things —
Alas, why, fearing of Time's tyranny,
Might I not then say 'Now I love you best' 10
When I was certain o'er incertainty,
Crowning the present, doubting of the rest?
  Love is a babe. Then might I not say so,
  To give full growth to that which still doth
    grow.

CXVI

Let me not to the marriage of true minds
Admit impediments. Love is not love
Which alters when it alteration finds
Or bends with the remover to remove.
O, no! it is an ever-fixed mark 5
That looks on tempes.s and is never shaken;
It is the star to every wand'ring bark,
Whose worth's unknown, although his highth
    be taken.
Love's not Time's fool, though rosy lips and
    cheeks
Within his bending sickle's compass come. 10
Love alters not with his brief hours and
    weeks,
But bears it out even to the edge of doom.
  If this be error, and upon me proved,
  I never writ, nor no man ever loved.

CXVII

Accuse me thus: that I have scanted all
Wherein I should your great deserts repay;
Forgot upon your dearest love to call,
Whereto all bonds do tie me day by day;
That I have frequent been with unknown
    minds 5
And given to time your own dear-purchas'd
    right;
That I have hoisted sail to all the winds
Which should transport me farthest from your
    sight.

Book both my wilfulness and errors down,
And on just proof surmise accumulate; 10
Bring me within the level of your frown,
But shoot not at me in your wakened hate;
   Since my appeal says I did strive to prove
   The constancy and virtue of your love.

CXVIII

Like as, to make our appetites more keen,
With eager compounds we our palate urge;
As, to prevent our maladies unseen,
We sicken to shun sickness when we purge:
Even so, being full of your ne'er-cloying sweet-
   ness, 5
To bitter sauces did I frame my feeding;
And, sick of welfare, found a kind of meet-
   ness
To be diseas'd ere that there was true need-
   ing.
Thus policy in love, t' anticipate
The ills that were not, grew to faults assured,
And brought to medicine a healthful state, 11
Which, rank of goodness, would by ill be
   cured.
   But thence I learn, and find the lesson true,
   Drugs poison him that so fell sick of you.

CXIX

What potions have I drunk of Siren tears,
Distill'd from limbecks foul as hell within,
Applying fears to hopes and hopes to fears,
Still losing when I saw myself to win!
What wretched errors hath my heart commit-
   ted 5
Whilst it hath thought itself so blessed never!
How have mine eyes out of their spheres been
   fitted
In the distraction of this madding fever!
O benefit of ill! Now I find true
That better is by evil still made better; 10
And ruin'd love, when it is built anew,
Grows fairer than at first, more strong, far
   greater.
   So I return rebuk'd to my content,
   And gain by ills thrice more than I have
   spent.

CXX

That you were once unkind befriends me now,
And for that sorrow which I then did feel
Needs must I under my transgression bow,
Unless my nerves were brass or hammered
   steel.

For if you were by my unkindness shaken, 5
As I by yours, y'have pass'd a hell of time,
And I, a tyrant, have no leisure taken
To weigh how once I suffered in your crime.
O that our night of woe might have rememb'red
My deepest sense how hard true sorrow hits, 10
And soon to you, as you to me then, tend'red
The humble salve which wounded bosoms fits!
   But that your trespass now becomes a fee;
   Mine ransoms yours, and yours must ran-
   som me.

CXXI

'Tis better to be vile than vile esteemed
When not to be receives reproach of being,
And the just pleasure lost, which is so deemed
Not by our feeling but by others' seeing.
For why should others' false adulterate eyes 5
Give salutation to my sportive blood?
Or on my frailties why are frailer spies,
Which in their wills count bad what I think
   good?
No, I am that I am; and they that level
At my abuses reckon up their own. 10
I may be straight though they themselves be
   bevel;
By their rank thoughts my deeds must not be
   shown,
   Unless this general evil they maintain —
   All men are bad and in their badness reign.

CXXII

Thy gift, thy tables, are within my brain
Full character'd with lasting memory,
Which shall above that idle rank remain
Beyond all date, even to eternity;
Or, at the least, so long as brain and heart 5
Have faculty by nature to subsist,
Till each to raz'd oblivion yield his part
Of thee, thy record never can be miss'd.
That poor retention could not so much hold,
Nor need I tallies thy dear love to score. 10
Therefore to give them from me was I bold,
To trust those tables that receive thee more.
   To keep an adjunct to remember thee
   Were to import forgetfulness in me.

CXXIII

No, Time, thou shalt not boast that I do
   change!
Thy pyramids built up with newer might
To me are nothing novel, nothing strange;
They are but dressings of a former sight.

Our dates are brief, and therefore we admire 5
What thou dost foist upon us that is old,
And rather make them born to our desire
Than think that we before have heard them
    told.
Thy registers and thee I both defy,
Not wond'ring at the present nor the past; 10
For thy records and what we see doth lie,
Made more or less by thy continual haste.
    This I do vow, and this shall ever be —
    I will be true, despite thy scythe and thee.

CXXIV

If my dear love were but the child of state,
It might for Fortune's bastard be unfather'd,
As subject to Time's love or to Time's hate,
Weeds among weeds, or flowers with flowers
    gather'd.
No, it was builded far from accident; 5
It suffers not in smiling pomp, nor falls
Under the blow of thralled discontent,
Whereto th' inviting time our fashion calls.
It fears not Policy, that heretic
Which works on leases of short-numb'red hours,
But all alone stands hugely politic, 11
That it nor grows with heat nor drowns with
    show'rs.
    To this I witness call the fools of time,
    Which die for goodness, who have liv'd for
    crime.

CXXV

Were't aught to me I bore the canopy,
With my extern the outward honouring,
Or laid great bases for eternity,
Which prove more short than waste or ruining?
Have I not seen dwellers on form and favour 5
Lose all, and more, by paying too much rent,
For compound sweet forgoing simple savour —
Pitiful thrivers, in their gazing spent?
No, let me be obsequious in thy heart,
And take thou my oblation, poor but free, 10
Which is not mix'd with seconds, knows no
    art
But mutual render, only me for thee.
    Hence, thou suborn'd informer! A true soul
    When most impeach'd stands least in thy
    control.

CXXVI

O thou, my lovely boy, who in thy power
Dost hold Time's fickle glass, his sickle hour;
Who hast by waning grown, and therein show'st
Thy lovers withering as thy sweet self grow'st —

If Nature (sovereign mistress over wrack), 5
As thou goest onwards, still will pluck thee
    back,
She keeps thee to this purpose, that her skill
May time disgrace, and wretched minutes kill.
Yet fear her, O thou minion of her pleasure!
She may detain, but not still keep, her treasure;
    Her audit, though delay'd, answer'd must be,
    And her quietus is to render thee.

CXXVII

In the old age black was not counted fair,
Or if it were, it bore not beauty's name;
But now is black beauty's successive heir,
And beauty slander'd with a bastard shame;
For since each hand hath put on nature's
    power, 5
Fairing the foul with art's false borrow'd face,
Sweet beauty hath no name, no holy bower,
But is profan'd, if not lives in disgrace.
Therefore my mistress' brows are raven black,
Her eyes so suited, and they mourners seem 10
At such who, not born fair, no beauty lack,
Sland'ring creation with a false esteem.
    Yet so they mourn, becoming of their woe,
    That every tongue says beauty should look so.

CXXVIII

How oft, when thou, my music, music play'st
Upon that blessed wood whose motion sounds
With thy sweet fingers when thou gently sway'st
The wiry concord that mine ear confounds,
Do I envy those jacks that nimble leap 5
To kiss the tender inward of thy hand,
Whilst my poor lips, which should that harvest
    reap,
At the wood's boldness by thee blushing
    stand!
To be so tickled, they would change their
    state
And situation with those dancing chips 10
O'er whom thy fingers walk with gentle gait,
Making dead wood more blest than living
    lips.
    Since saucy jacks so happy are in this,
    Give them thy fingers, me thy lips to kiss.

CXXIX

Th' expense of spirit in a waste of shame
Is lust in action; and till action, lust
Is perjur'd, murd'rous, bloody, full of blame,
Savage, extreme, rude, cruel, not to trust;

Enjoy'd no sooner but despised straight; 5
Past reason hunted, and no sooner had,
Past reason hated, as a swallowed bait
On purpose laid to make the taker mad;
Mad in pursuit, and in possession so; 9
Had, having, and in quest to have, extreme;
A bliss in proof — and prov'd, a very woe;
Before, a joy propos'd; behind, a dream.
  All this the world well knows; yet none
    knows well
  To shun the heaven that leads men to this
    hell.

CXXX

My mistress' eyes are nothing like the sun;
Coral is far more red than her lips' red;
If snow be white, why then her breasts are dun;
If hairs be wires, black wires grow on her head.
I have seen roses damask'd, red and white, 5
But no such roses see I in her cheeks;
And in some perfumes is there more delight
Than in the breath that from my mistress reeks.
I love to hear her speak; yet well I know
That music hath a far more pleasing sound. 10
I grant I never saw a goddess go:
My mistress, when she walks, treads on the
    ground.
  And yet, by heaven, I think my love as rare
  As any she belied with false compare.

CXXXI

Thou art as tyrannous, so as thou art,
As those whose beauties proudly make them
    cruel;
For well thou know'st to my dear-doting heart
Thou art the fairest and most precious jewel.
Yet, in good faith, some say that thee behold,
Thy face hath not the power to make love
    groan. 6
To say they err I dare not be so bold,
Although I swear it to myself alone.
And, to be sure that is not false I swear,
A thousand groans, but thinking on thy face,
One on another's neck, do witness bear 11
Thy black is fairest in my judgment's place.
  In nothing art thou black save in thy deeds,
  And thence this slander, as I think, proceeds.

CXXXII

Thine eyes I love, and they, as pitying me,
Knowing thy heart torments me with disdain,
Have put on black and loving mourners be,
Looking with pretty ruth upon my pain.

And truly not the morning sun of heaven 5
Better becomes the grey cheeks of the East,
Nor that full star that ushers in the even
Doth half that glory to the sober West,
As those two mourning eyes become thy face.
O, let it then as well beseem thy heart 10
To mourn for me, since mourning doth thee
    grace,
And suit thy pity like in every part.
  Then will I swear beauty herself is black
  And all they foul that thy complexion lack.

CXXXIII

Beshrew that heart that makes my heart to
    groan
For that deep wound it gives my friend and me!
Is't not enough to torture me alone
But slave to slavery my sweet'st friend must
    be?
Me from myself thy cruel eye hath taken, 5
And my next self thou harder hast engrossed.
Of him, myself, and thee I am forsaken —
A torment thrice threefold thus to be crossed.
Prison my heart in thy steel bosom's ward;
But then my friend's heart let my poor heart
    bail; 10
Whoe'er keeps me, let my heart be his guard:
Thou canst not then use rigour in my jail.
  And yet thou wilt; for I, being pent in thee,
  Perforce am thine, and all that is in me.

CXXXIV

So, now I have confess'd that he is thine
And I myself am mortgag'd to thy will,
Myself I'll forfeit, so that other mine
Thou wilt restore to be my comfort still.
But thou wilt not, nor he will not be free, 5
For thou art covetous, and he is kind;
He learn'd but surety-like to write for me
Under that bond that him as fast doth bind.
The statute of thy beauty thou wilt take,
Thou usurer that put'st forth all to use, 10
And sue a friend came debtor for my sake:
So him I lose through my unkind abuse.
  Him have I lost, thou hast both him and me
  He pays the whole, and yet am I not free.

CXXXV

Whoever hath her wish, thou hast thy Will,
And Will to boot, and Will in overplus.
More than enough am I that vex thee still,
To thy sweet will making addition thus.

Wilt thou, whose will is large and spacious, 5
Not once vouchsafe to hide my will in thine?
Shall will in others seem right gracious
And in my will no fair acceptance shine?
The sea, all water, yet receives rain still
And in abundance addeth to his store; 10
So thou, being rich in Will, add to thy Will
One will of mine to make thy large Will
    more.
  Let no unkind no fair beseechers kill;
  Think all but one, and me in that one Will.

CXXXVI

If thy soul check thee that I come so near,
Swear to thy blind soul that I was thy Will,
And will, thy soul knows, is admitted there:
Thus far for love my love-suit, sweet, fulfil.
Will will fulfil the treasure of thy love, 5
Ay, fill it full with wills, and my will one.
In things of great receipt with ease we prove
Among a number one is reckon'd none.
Then in the number let me pass untold,
Though in thy store's account I one must
    be; 10
For nothing hold me, so it please thee hold
That nothing me, a something, sweet, to
    thee.
  Make but my name thy love, and love that
    still,
  And then thou lovest me, for my name is Will.

CXXXVII

Thou blind fool, Love, what dost thou to mine
    eyes
That they behold, and see not what they
    see?
They know what beauty is, see where it lies,
Yet what the best is take the worst to be.
If eyes, corrupt by over-partial looks, 5
Be anchor'd in the bay where all men ride,
Why of eyes' falsehood hast thou forged hooks,
Whereto the judgment of my heart is tied?
Why should my heart think that a several
    plot
Which my heart knows the wide world's com-
    mon place? 10
Or mine eyes seeing this, say this is not,
To put fair truth upon so foul a face?
  In things right true my heart and eyes have
    erred,
  And to this false plague are they now trans-
    ferred.

CXXXVIII

When my love swears that she is made of truth
I do believe her, though I know she lies,
That she might think me some untutor'd youth,
Unlearned in the world's false subtilties.
Thus vainly thinking that she thinks me young,
Although she knows my days are past the best,
Simply I credit her false-speaking tongue:
On both sides thus is simple truth suppress'd.
But wherefore says she not she is unjust?
And wherefore say not I that I am old? 10
O, love's best habit is in seeming trust,
And age in love loves not to have years told.
  Therefore I lie with her and she with me,
  And in our faults by lies we flattered be.

CXXXIX

O, call not me to justify the wrong
That thy unkindness lays upon my heart!
Wound me not with thine eye, but with thy
    tongue;
Use power with power, and slay me not by art!
Tell me thou lov'st elsewhere; but in my sight,
Dear heart, forbear to glance thine eye aside. 6
What need'st thou wound with cunning when
    thy might
Is more than my o'erpress'd defence can bide?
Let me excuse thee: — Ah, my love well knows
Her pretty looks have been mine enemies; 10
And therefore from my face she turns my foes,
That they elsewhere might dart their injuries.
  Yet do not so; but since I am near slain,
  Kill me outright with looks and rid my pain.

CXL

Be wise as thou art cruel; do not press
My tongue-tied patience with too much dis-
    dain;
Lest sorrow lend me words, and words express
The manner of my pity-wanting pain.
If I might teach thee wit, better it were, 5
Though not to love, yet, love, to tell me so;
As testy sick men, when their deaths be near,
No news but health from their physicians know.
For if I should despair, I should grow mad,
And in my madness might speak ill of thee. 10
Now this ill-wresting world is grown so bad
Mad slanderers by mad ears believed be.
  That I may not be so, nor thou belied,
  Bear thine eyes straight, though thy proud
    heart go wide.

CXLI

In faith, I do not love thee with mine eyes,
For they in thee a thousand errors note;
But 'tis my heart that loves what they despise,
Who in despite of view is pleas'd to dote.
Nor are mine ears with thy tongue's tune de-
  lighted;   5
Nor tender feeling to base touches prone,
Nor taste, nor smell, desire to be invited
To any sensual feast with thee alone;
But my five wits nor my five senses can
Dissuade one foolish heart from serving thee, 10
Who leaves unsway'd the likeness of a man,
Thy proud heart's slave and vassal wretch to
  be.
    Only my plague thus far I count my gain,
    That she that makes me sin awards me pain.

CXLII

Love is my sin, and thy dear virtue hate,
Hate of my sin, grounded on sinful loving.
O, but with mine compare thou thine own state,
And thou shalt find it merits not reproving!
Or if it do, not from those lips of thine,   5
That have profan'd their scarlet ornaments
And seal'd false bonds of love as oft as mine,
Robb'd others' beds' revenues of their rents.
Be it lawful I love thee as thou lov'st those
Whom thine eyes woo as mine importune thee.
Root pity in thy heart, that, when it grows, 11
Thy pity may deserve to pitied be.
    If thou dost seek to have what thou dost
    hide,
    By self-example mayst thou be denied!

CXLIII

Lo, as a careful housewife runs to catch
One of her feathered creatures broke away,
Sets down her babe, and makes all swift dis-
  patch
In pursuit of the thing she would have stay;
Whilst her neglected child holds her in chase, 5
Cries to catch her whose busy care is bent
To follow that which flies before her face,
Not prizing her poor infant's discontent —
So runn'st thou after that which flies from thee,
Whilst I thy babe chase thee afar behind; 10
But if thou catch thy hope, turn back to me
And play the mother's part, kiss me, be kind.
    So will I pray that thou mayst have thy Will,
    If thou turn back and my loud crying still.

CXLIV

Two loves I have, of comfort and despair,
Which like two spirits do suggest me still.
The better angel is a man right fair,
The worser spirit a woman colour'd ill.
To win me soon to hell, my female evil   5
Tempteth my better angel from my side,
And would corrupt my saint to be a devil,
Wooing his purity with her foul pride.
And whether that my angel be turn'd fiend
Suspect I may, yet not directly tell;   10
But being both from me, both to each friend,
I guess one angel in another's hell.
    Yet this shall I ne'er know, but live in
    doubt,
    Till my bad angel fire my good one out.

CXLV

Those lips that Love's own hand did make
Breath'd forth the sound that said 'I hate'
To me that languish'd for her sake;
But when she saw my woful state,
Straight in her heart did mercy come,   5
Chiding that tongue that ever sweet
Was us'd in giving gentle doom,
And taught it thus anew to greet:
'I hate' she alter'd with an end
That follow'd it as gentle day   10
Doth follow night, who, like a fiend,
From heaven to hell is flown away.
    'I hate' from hate away she threw,
    And sav'd my life, saying 'not you.'

CXLVI

Poor soul, the centre of my sinful earth,
. . . these rebel pow'rs that thee array,
Why dost thou pine within and suffer dearth,
Painting thy outward walls so costly gay?
Why so large cost, having so short a lease, 5
Dost thou upon thy fading mansion spend?
Shall worms, inheritors of this excess,
Eat up thy charge? Is this thy body's end?
Then, soul, live thou upon thy servant's
  loss,
And let that pine to aggravate thy store; 10
Buy terms divine in selling hours of dross;
Within be fed, without be rich no more.
    So shalt thou feed on Death, that feeds on
    men,
    And Death once dead, there's no more dying
    then.

CXLVII

My love is as a fever, longing still
For that which longer nurseth the disease;
Feeding on that which doth preserve the ill,
Th' uncertain sickly appetite to please.
My Reason, the physician to my Love,   5
Angry that his prescriptions are not kept,
Hath left me, and I desperate now approve
Desire is death, which physic did except.
Past cure I am, now reason is past care,
And frantic-mad with evermore unrest;   10
My thoughts and my discourse as madmen's are,
At randon from the truth vainly express'd;
  For I have sworn thee fair, and thought thee bright,
  Who art as black as hell, as dark as night.

CXLVIII

O me, what eyes hath Love put in my head,
Which have no correspondence with true sight!
Or, if they have, where is my judgment fled,
That censures falsely what they see aright?
If that be fair whereon my false eyes dote,   5
What means the world to say it is not so?
If it be not, then love doth well denote
Love's eye is not so true as all men's no.
How can it? O, how can Love's eye be true,
That is so vex'd with watching and with tears?
No marvel then though I mistake my view: 11
The sun itself sees not till heaven clears.
  O cunning Love! with tears thou keep'st me blind,
  Lest eyes well-seeing thy foul faults should find.

CXLIX

Canst thou, O cruel! say I love thee not
When I against myself with thee partake?
Do I not think on thee when I forgot
Am of myself, all tyrant for thy sake?
Who hateth thee that I do call my friend?   5
On whom frown'st thou that I do fawn upon?
Nay, if thou low'r'st on me, do I not spend
Revenge upon myself with present moan?
What merit do I in myself respect
That is so proud thy service to despise,   10
When all my best doth worship thy defect,
Commanded by the motion of thine eyes?
  But, love, hate on, for now I know thy mind:
  Those that can see thou lov'st, and I am blind.

CL

O, from what pow'r hast thou this pow'rful might
With insufficiency my heart to sway?
To make me give the lie to my true sight
And swear that brightness doth not grace the day?   4
Whence hast thou this becoming of things ill,
That in the very refuse of thy deeds
There is such strength and warrantise of skill
That in my mind thy worst all best exceeds?
Who taught thee how to make me love thee more,   9
The more I hear and see just cause of hate?
O, though I love what others do abhor,
With others thou shouldst not abhor my state!
  If thy unworthiness rais'd love in me,
  More worthy I to be belov'd of thee.

CLI

Love is too young to know what conscience is;
Yet who knows not conscience is born of love?
Then, gentle cheater, urge not my amiss,
Lest guilty of my faults thy sweet self prove.
For, thou betraying me, I do betray   5
My nobler part to my gross body's treason;
My soul doth tell my body that he may
Triumph in love; flesh stays no farther reason,
But, rising at thy name, doth point out thee   9
As his triumphant prize. Proud of this pride,
He is contented thy poor drudge to be,
To stand in thy affairs, fall by thy side.
  No want of conscience hold it that I call
  Her 'love' for whose dear love I rise and fall.

CLII

In loving thee thou know'st I am forsworn,
But thou art twice forsworn, to me love swearing;
In act thy bed-vow broke, and new faith torn
In vowing new hate after new love bearing.
But why of two oaths' breach do I accuse thee
When I break twenty? I am perjur'd most;   6
For all my vows are oaths but to misuse thee,
And all my honest faith in thee is lost;
For I have sworn deep oaths of thy deep kindness,
Oaths of thy love, thy truth, thy constancy;   10
And, to enlighten thee, gave eyes to blindness,
Or made them swear against the thing they see;
  For I have sworn thee fair — more perjur'd I,
  To swear against the truth so foul a lie!

CLIII

Cupid laid by his brand and fell asleep.
A maid of Dian's this advantage found
And his love-kindling fire did quickly steep
In a cold valley-fountain of that ground;
Which borrow'd from this holy fire of Love   5
A dateless lively heat, still to endure,
And grew a seething bath, which yet men prove
Against strange maladies a sovereign cure.
But at my mistress' eye Love's brand new fired,
The boy for trial needs would touch my breast.
I, sick withal, the help of bath desired   11
And thither hied, a sad distemper'd guest,
  But found no cure. The bath for my help lies
  Where Cupid got new fire — my mistress' eyes.

CLIV

The little Love-god, lying once asleep,
Laid by his side his heart-inflaming brand,
Whilst many nymphs that vow'd chaste life to keep
Came tripping by; but in her maiden hand
The fairest votary took up that fire   5
Which many legions of true hearts had warm'd;
And so the general of hot desire
Was sleeping by a virgin hand disarm'd.
This brand she quenched in a cool well by,
Which from Love's fire took heat perpetual,
Growing a bath and healthful remedy   11
For men diseas'd; but I, my mistress' thrall,
  Came there for cure, and this by that I prove —
  Love's fire heats water, water cools not love.

A LOVER'S COMPLAINT

From off a hill whose concave womb reworded
A plaintful story from a sist'ring vale,
My spirits t' attend this double voice accorded,
And down I laid to list the sad-tun'd tale;
Ere long espied a fickle maid full pale, 5
Tearing of papers, breaking rings atwain,
Storming her world with sorrow's wind and rain.

Upon her head a platted hive of straw,
Which fortified her visage from the sun,
Whereon the thought might think sometime it
    saw 10
The carcass of a beauty spent and done.
Time had not scythed all that youth begun,
Nor youth all quit; but, spite of heaven's fell
    rage,
Some beauty peep'd through lattice of sear'd
    age.

Oft did she heave her napkin to her eyne, 15
Which on it had conceited characters,
Laund'ring the silken figures in the brine
That seasoned woe had pelleted in tears,
And often reading what contents it bears;
As often shrieking undistinguish'd woe 20
In clamours of all size, both high and low.

Sometimes her levell'd eyes their carriage ride,
As they did batt'ry to the spheres intend;
Sometime diverted their poor balls are tied
To th' orbed earth; sometimes they do extend
Their view right on; anon their gazes lend 26
To every place at once, and, nowhere fix'd,
The mind and sight distractedly commix'd.

Her hair, nor loose nor tied in formal plat,
Proclaim'd in her a careless hand of pride; 30
For some, untuck'd, descended her sheav'd hat,
Hanging her pale and pined cheek beside;
Some in her threaden fillet still did bide
And, true to bondage, would not break from
    thence,
Though slackly braided in loose negligence. 35

A thousand favours from a maund she drew
Of amber, crystal, and of beaded jet,
Which one by one she in a river threw,
Upon whose weeping margent she was set;
Like usury, applying wet to wet, 40
Or monarch's hands that lets not bounty fall
Where want cries some but where excess begs all.

Of folded schedules had she many a one,
Which she perus'd, sigh'd, tore, and gave the
    flood;
Crack'd many a ring of posied gold and
    bone, 45
Bidding them find their sepulchres in mud;
Found yet moe letters sadly penn'd in blood,
With sleided silk feat and affectedly
Enswath'd and seal'd to curious secrecy.

These often bath'd she in her fluxive eyes, 50
And often kiss'd, and often gan to tear;
Cried, 'O false blood, thou register of lies,
What unapproved witness dost thou bear!
Ink would have seem'd more black and damned
    here!'
This said, in top of rage the lines she rents, 55
Big discontent so breaking their contents.

A reverend man that graz'd his cattle nigh —
Sometime a blusterer that the ruffle knew
Of court, of city, and had let go by
The swiftest hours, observed as they flew — 60
Towards this afflicted fancy fastly drew,
And, privileg'd by age, desires to know
In brief the grounds and motives of her woe.

So slides he down upon his grained bat,
And comely distant sits he by her side; 65
When he again desires her, being sat,
Her grievance with his hearing to divide.
If that from him there may be aught applied
Which may her suffering ecstasy assuage,
'Tis promis'd in the charity of age. 70

'Father,' she says, 'though in me you behold
The injury of many a blasting hour,
Let it not tell your judgment I am old.
Not age, but sorrow, over me hath power. 74
I might as yet have been a spreading flower,
Fresh to myself, if I had self-applied
Love to myself, and to no love beside.

'But woe is me! too early I attended
A youthful suit — it was to gain my grace —
Of one by nature's outwards so commended 80
That maidens' eyes stuck over all his face.
Love lack'd a dwelling and made him her
    place;
And when in his fair parts she did abide,
She was new lodg'd and newly deified.

'His browny locks did hang in crooked curls,
And every light occasion of the wind   86
Upon his lips their silken parcels hurls.
What's sweet to do, to do will aptly find:
Each eye that saw him did enchant the mind;
For on his visage was in little drawn   90
What largeness thinks in Paradise was sawn.

'Small show of man was yet upon his chin;
His phœnix down began but to appear,
Like unshorn velvet, on that termless skin,
Whose bare out-bragg'd the web it seem'd to
    wear.   95
Yet show'd his visage by that cost more dear;
And nice affections wavering stood in doubt
If best were as it was, or best without.

'His qualities were beauteous as his form,   99
For maiden-tongu'd he was, and thereof free;
Yet, if men mov'd him, was he such a storm
As oft 'twixt May and April is to see,
When winds breathe sweet, unruly though they
    be.
His rudeness so with his authoriz'd youth
Did livery falseness in a pride of truth.   105

'Well could he ride, and often men would say,
"That horse his mettle from his rider takes.
Proud of subjection, noble by the sway,
What rounds, what bounds, what course, what
    stop he makes!"
And controversy hence a question takes,   110
Whether the horse by him became his deed,
Or he his manage by th' well-doing steed.

'But quickly on this side the verdict went:
His real habitude gave life and grace
To appertainings and to ornament,   115
Accomplish'd in himself, not in his case.
All aids, themselves made fairer by their place,
Came for additions; yet their purpos'd trim
Piec'd not his grace but were all grac'd by him.

'So on the tip of his subduing tongue   120
All kind of arguments and question deep,
All replication prompt and reason strong,
For his advantage still did wake and sleep.
To make the weeper laugh, the laugher weep,
He had the dialect and different skill,   125
Catching all passions in his craft of will;

'That he did in the general bosom reign
Of young, of old, and sexes both enchanted,
To dwell with him in thoughts, or to remain   129
In personal duty, following where he haunted.
Consents bewitch'd, ere he desire, have granted,

And dialogu'd for him what he would say,
Ask'd their own wills and made their wills
    obey.

'Many there were that did his picture get,   134
To serve their eyes, and in it put their mind;
Like fools that in th' imagination set
The goodly objects which abroad they find
Of lands and mansions, theirs in thought as-
    sign'd,
And labouring in moe pleasures to bestow them
Than the true gouty landlord which doth owe
    them.   140

'So many have, that never touch'd his hand,
Sweetly suppos'd them mistress of his heart.
My woful self, that did in freedom stand
And was my own fee-simple, not in part,
What with his art in youth and youth in art,
Threw my affections in his charmed power,   146
Reserv'd the stalk and gave him all my flower.

'Yet did I not, as some my equals did,
Demand of him, nor being desired yielded.
Finding myself in honour so forbid,   150
With safest distance I mine honour shielded.
Experience for me many bulwarks builded
Of proofs new-bleeding, which remain'd the
    foil
Of this false jewel, and his amorous spoil.

'But, ah, who ever shunn'd by precedent   155
The destin'd ill she must herself assay?
Or forc'd examples, 'gainst her own content,
To put the by-past perils in her way?
Counsel may stop awhile what will not stay;
For when we rage, advice is often seen   160
By blunting us to make our wits more keen.

'Nor gives it satisfaction to our blood
That we must curb it upon others' proof,
To be forbod the sweets that seem so good
For fear of harms that preach in our behoof.
O appetite, from judgment stand aloof!   166
The one a palate hath that needs will taste,
Though Reason weep and cry "It is thy last."

'For further I could say, "This man's untrue,"
And knew the patterns of his foul beguiling;
Heard where his plants in others' orchards
    grew;   171
Saw how deceits were gilded in his smiling;
Knew vows were ever brokers to defiling;
Thought characters and words merely but art,
And bastards of his foul adulterate heart.   175

481

'And long upon these terms I held my city,
Till thus he gan besiege me: "Gentle maid,
Have of my suffering youth some feeling pity
And be not of my holy vows afraid.
That's to ye sworn to none was ever said;   180
For feasts of love I have been call'd unto,
Till now did ne'er invite nor never woo.

'"All my offences that abroad you see
Are errors of the blood, none of the mind.
Love made them not. With acture they may
      be,   185
Where neither party is nor true nor kind.
They sought their shame that so their shame did
      find;
And so much less of shame in me remains
By how much of me their reproach contains.

'"Among the many that mine eyes have seen,
Not one whose flame my heart so much as
      warmed,   191
Or my affection put to th' smallest teen,
Or any of my leisures ever charmed.
Harm have I done to them, but ne'er was
      harmed;
Kept hearts in liveries, but mine own was free
And reign'd commanding in his monarchy. 196

'"Look here what tributes wounded fancies
      sent me
Of pallid pearls and rubies red as blood,
Figuring that they their passions likewise lent
      me
Of grief and blushes, aptly understood   200
In bloodless white and the encrimson'd mood —
Effects of terror and dear modesty,
Encamp'd in hearts, but fighting outwardly.

'"And, lo, behold these talents of their hair,
With twisted metal amorously empleach'd, 205
I have receiv'd from many a several fair,
Their kind acceptance weepingly beseech'd,
With the annexions of fair gems enrich'd,
And deep-brain'd sonnets that did amplify
Each stone's dear nature, worth, and quality.

'"The diamond — why, 'twas beautiful and
      hard,   211
Whereto his invis'd properties did tend;
The deep-green em'rald, in whose fresh regard
Weak sights their sickly radiance do amend;
The heaven-hu'd sapphire, and the opal blend
With objects manifold: each several stone, 216
With wit well blazon'd, smil'd or made some
moan.

'"Lo, all these trophies of affections hot,
Of pensiv'd and subdu'd desires the tender,
Nature hath charg'd me that I hoard them
      not,   220
But yield them up where I myself must ren-
      der:
That is, to you, my origin and ender;
For these of force must your oblations be,
Since I their altar, you enpatron me.

'"O, then, advance of yours that phraseless
      hand   225
Whose white weighs down the airy scale of
      praise!
Take all these similes to your own command,
Hallowed with sighs that burning lungs did
      raise.
What me, your minister, for you obeys,
Works under you; and to your audit comes
Their distract parcels in combined sums. 231

'"Lo, this device was sent me from a nun,
Or sister sanctified, of holiest note,
Which late her noble suit in court did shun,
Whose rarest havings made the blossoms dote;
For she was sought by spirits of richest coat,
But kept cold distance, and did thence re-
      move
To spend her living in eternal love.

'"But, O my sweet, what labour is't to leave
The thing we have not, mast'ring what not
      strives,   240
Paling the place which did no form receive,
Playing patient sports in unconstrained gyves?
She that her fame so to herself contrives,
The scars of battle scapeth by the flight   244
And makes her absence valiant, not her might.

'"O, pardon me, in that my boast is true!
The accident which brought me to her eye
Upon the moment did her force subdue,
And now she would the caged cloister fly.
Religious love put out religion's eye.   250
Not to be tempted, would she be immur'd,
And now, to tempt all, liberty procur'd.

'"How mighty then you are, O, hear me tell!
The broken bosoms that to me belong   254
Have emptied all their fountains in my well,
And mine I pour your ocean all among.
I strong o'er them, and you o'er me being
      strong,
Must for your victory us all congest,
As compound love to physic your cold breast.

'"My parts had pow'r to charm a sacred nun,
Who, disciplin'd, ay, dieted in grace,   261
Believ'd her eyes when they t' assail begun,
All vows and consecrations giving place.
O most potential love! vow, bond, nor space
In thee hath neither sting, knot, nor confine,
For thou art all, and all things else are thine.

'"When thou impressest, what are precepts
          worth
Of stale example? When thou wilt inflame,
How coldly those impediments stand forth
Of wealth, of filial fear, law, kindred, fame!   270
Love's arms are peace, 'gainst rule, 'gainst
          sense, 'gainst shame;
And sweetens, in the suff'ring pangs it bears,
The aloes of all forces, shocks, and fears.

'"Now all these hearts that do on mine depend,
Feeling it break, with bleeding groans they
          pine;   275
And supplicant their sighs to you extend,
To leave the batt'ry that you make 'gainst mine,
Lending soft audience to my sweet design,
And credent soul to that strong-bonded oath
That shall prefer and undertake my troth."   280

'This said, his wat'ry eyes he did dismount,
Whose sights till then were levell'd on my face;
Each cheek a river running from a fount
With brinish current downward flow'd apace.
O, how the channel to the stream gave grace!
Who glaz'd with crystal gate the glowing roses
That flame through water which their hue en-
          closes.

'O father, what a hell of witchcraft lies
In the small orb of one particular tear!
But with the inundation of the eyes   290
What rocky heart to water will not wear?
What breast so cold that is not warmed here?
O cleft effect! cold modesty, hot wrath,
Both fire from hence and chill extincture hath.

'For, lo, his passion, but an art of craft,   295
Even there resolv'd my reason into tears;
There my white stole of chastity I daff'd,
Shook off my sober guards and civil fears;
Appear to him as he to me appears,
All melting; though our drops this diff'rence
          bore —   300
His poison'd me, and mine did him restore.

'In him a plenitude of subtle matter,
Applied to cautels, all strange forms receives,
Of burning blushes, or of weeping water,   304
Or sounding paleness; and he takes and leaves,
In either's aptness, as it best deceives —
To blush at speeches rank, to weep at woes,
Or to turn white and sound at tragic shows;

'That not a heart which in his level came
Could scape the hail of his all-hurting aim, 310
Showing fair nature is both kind and tame;
And, veil'd in them, did win whom he would
          maim.
Against the thing he sought he would exclaim:
When he most burn'd in heart-wish'd luxury,
He preach'd pure maid and prais'd cold chas-
          tity.   315

'Thus merely with the garment of a Grace
The naked and concealed fiend he cover'd;
That th' unexperient gave the tempter place,
Which, like a cherubin, above them hover'd.
Who, young and simple, would not be so lov-
          er'd?   320
Ay me! I fell; and yet do question make
What I should do again for such a sake.

'O, that infected moisture of his eye,
O, that false fire which in his cheek so glow'd,
O, that forc'd thunder from his heart did fly,
O, that sad breath his spongy lungs bestow'd,
O, all that borrowed motion seeming ow'd,
Would yet again betray the fore-betray'd
And new pervert a reconciled maid!'

THE PASSIONATE PILGRIM

IV

Sweet Cytherea, sitting by a brook
With young Adonis, lovely, fresh, and green,
Did court the lad with many a lovely look,
Such looks as none could look but beauty's
    queen.
She told him stories to delight his ear;   5
She show'd him favours to allure his eye;
To win his heart she touch'd him here and
    there —
Touches so soft still conquer chastity.
But whether unripe years did want conceit,
Or he refus'd to take her figured proffer,   10
The tender nibbler would not touch the bait,
But smile and jest at every gentle offer.
    Then fell she on her back, fair queen, and
      toward.
    He rose and ran away. Ah, fool too froward!

VI

Scarce had the sun dried up the dewy morn,
And scarce the herd gone to the hedge for shade,
When Cytherea, all in love forlorn,
A longing tarriance for Adonis made
Under an osier growing by a brook,   5
A brook where Adon us'd to cool his spleen.
Hot was the day; she hotter that did look
For his approach that often there had been.
Anon he comes, and throws his mantle by,
And stood stark naked on the brook's green
    brim.   10
The sun look'd on the world with glorious eye,
Yet not so wistly as this queen on him.
    He, spying her, bounc'd in whereas he stood.
    'O Jove,' quoth she, 'why was not I a flood?'

VII

Fair is my love, but not so fair as fickle;
Mild as a dove, but neither true nor trusty;
Brighter than glass, and yet as glass is brittle;
Softer than wax, and yet as iron rusty;
    A lily pale, with damask dye to grace her: 5
    None fairer, nor none falser to deface her.

Her lips to mine how often hath she joined,
Between each kiss her oaths of true love swear-
    ing!

How many tales to please me hath she coined,
Dreading my love, the loss whereof still fearing!
    Yet, in the midst of all her pure protestings,
    Her faith, her oaths, her tears, and all were
    jestings.

She burnt with love, as straw with fire flameth;
She burnt out love, as soon as straw outburneth;
She fram'd the love, and yet she foil'd the
    framing;   15
She bade love last, and yet she fell a-turning.
    Was this a lover, or a lecher whether?
    Bad in the best, though excellent in neither.

VIII

If music and sweet poetry agree,
As they must needs (the sister and the brother),
Then must the love be great 'twixt thee and me,
Because thou lov'st the one, and I the other.
Dowland to thee is dear, whose heavenly touch
Upon the lute doth ravish human sense;   6
Spenser to me, whose deep conceit is such
As, passing all conceit, needs no defence.
Thou lov'st to hear the sweet melodious sound
That Phœbus' lute (the queen of music) makes;
And I in deep delight am chiefly drown'd   11
When as himself to singing he betakes.
    One god is god of both, as poets feign;
    One knight loves both, and both in thee
    remain.

IX

Fair was the morn when the fair queen of love,
*   *   *   *   *   *   *   *   *
Paler for sorrow than her milk-white dove,
For Adon's sake, a youngster proud and wild,
Her stand she takes upon a steep-up hill.   5
Anon Adonis comes with horn and hounds.
She, silly queen, with more than love's good will,
Forbade the boy he should not pass those
    grounds.
'Once,' quoth she, 'did I see a fair sweet youth
Here in these brakes deep wounded with a boar,
Deep in the thigh, a spectacle of ruth!   11
See, in my thigh,' quoth she, 'here was the sore.'
    She showed hers; he saw more wounds than
    one,
    And blushing fled and left her all alone.

1524

484

X

Sweet rose, fair flower, untimely pluck'd, soon
 vaded,
Pluck'd in the bud, and vaded in the spring!
Bright orient pearl, alack, too timely shaded!
Fair creature, kill'd too soon by death's sharp
 sting!
 Like a green plum that hangs upon a tree, 5
 And falls, through wind, before the fall
  should be.

I weep for thee, and yet no cause I have;
For why, thou lefts me nothing in thy will:
And yet thou lefts me more than I did crave;
For why, I craved nothing of thee still.   10
 O yes, dear friend, I pardon crave of thee!
 Thy discontent thou didst bequeath to me.

XI

Venus, with young Adonis sitting by her
Under a myrtle shade, began to woo him.
She told the youngling how god Mars did try
 her,
And as he fell to her, so fell she to him.
'Even thus,' quoth she, 'the warlike god em-
 brac'd me,'   5
And then she clipp'd Adonis in her arms.
'Even thus,' quoth she, 'the warlike god un-
 lac'd me,'
As if the boy should use like loving charms.
'Even thus,' quoth she, 'he seized on my lips,'
And with her lips on his did act the seizure; 10
And as she fetched breath, away he skips,
And would not take her meaning nor her pleas-
 ure.
 Ah, that I had my lady at this bay,
 To kiss and clip me till I run away!

XII

Crabbed age and youth cannot live together:
Youth is full of pleasance, age is full of care;
Youth like summer morn, age like winter
 weather;
Youth like summer brave, age like winter bare.
Youth is full of sport, age's breath is short; 5
Youth is nimble, age is lame;
Youth is hot and bold, age is weak and cold;
Youth is wild, and age is tame.
Age, I do abhor thee; youth, I do adore thee.
O, my love, my love is young!   10
Age, I do defy thee.
O sweet shepherd, hie thee,
For methinks thou stays too long.

XIII

Beauty is but a vain and doubtful good;
A shining gloss that vadeth suddenly;
A flower that dies when first it gins to bud;
A brittle glass that's broken presently;
 A doubtful good, a gloss, a glass, a flower, 5
 Lost, vaded, broken, dead within an hour.

And as goods lost are seld or never found,
As vaded gloss no rubbing will refresh,
As flowers dead lie withered on the ground,
As broken glass no cement can redress: 10
 So beauty blemish'd once, for ever lost,
 In spite of physic, painting, pain, and cost.

XIV

Good night, good rest. Ah, neither be my share!
She bade good night that kept my rest away,
And daff'd me to a cabin hang'd with care
To descant on the doubts of my decay.
 'Farewell,' quoth she, 'and come again to-
  morrow.'   5
 Fare well I could not, for I supp'd with
  sorrow.

Yet at my parting sweetly did she smile,
In scorn or friendship, nill I conster whether.
'T may be she joy'd to jest at my exile;   9
'T may be again, to make me wander thither:
 'Wander'— a word for shadows like my-
  self
 As take the pain but cannot pluck the pelf.

Lord, how mine eyes throw gazes to the East![1]
My heart doth charge the watch; the morning
 rise
Doth cite each moving sense from idle rest,
Not daring trust the office of mine eyes.
 While Philomela sits and sings, I sit and
  mark,   5
 And wish her lays were tuned like the lark;

For she doth welcome daylight with her ditty
And drives away dark dreaming night.
The night so pack'd, I post unto my pretty;
Heart hath his hope, and eyes their wished
 sight;   10
 Sorrow chang'd to solace and solace mix'd
  with sorrow;
 For why, she sigh'd and bade me come to-
  morrow.

[1] The next three stanzas are in many editions
printed as a separate poem.

Were I with her, the night would post too
  soon,
But now are minutes added to the hours;
To spite me now, each minute seems a
  moon;   15
Yet not for me, shine sun to succour flowers!
  Pack night, peep day! Good day, of night
    now borrow.
  Short, night, to-night, and length thyself
    to-morrow.

XVII

My flocks feed not,
My ewes breed not,
My rams speed not,
  All is amiss:
Love's denying,   5
Faith's defying,
Heart's renying,
  Causer of this.
All my merry jigs are quite forgot,
All my lady's love is lost, God wot.   10
Where her faith was firmly fix'd in love,
There a nay is plac'd without remove.
One silly cross
Wrought all my loss.
  O frowning Fortune, cursed fickle dame! 15
For now I see
Inconstancy
  More in women than in men remain.

In black mourn I,
All fears scorn I,   20
Love hath forlorn me,
  Living in thrall.
Heart is bleeding,
All help needing —
O cruel speeding,   25
  Fraughted with gall!
My shepherd's pipe can sound no deal;
My wether's bell rings doleful knell;
My curtail dog, that wont to have play'd,
Plays not at all, but seems afraid.   30
My sighs so deep
Procure to weep,
  In howling wise, to see my doleful plight.
How sighs resound
Through heartless ground,   35
  Like a thousand vanquish'd men in bloody
    fight!

Clear wells spring not,
Sweet birds sing not,
Green plants bring not
  Forth their dye.   40

Herds stand weeping,
Flocks all sleeping,
Nymphs back peeping
  Fearfully.
All our pleasure known to us poor swains, 45
All our merry meetings on the plains,
All our evening sport from us is fled,
All our love is lost, for Love is dead.
Farewell, sweet lass!
Thy like ne'er was   50
  For a sweet content, the cause of all my
    moan.
Poor Corydon
Must live alone.
  Other help for him I see that there is none.

XVIII

When as thine eye hath chose the dame
And stall'd the deer that thou shouldst strike,
Let reason rule things worthy blame,
As well as fancy, partial might;
  Take counsel of some wiser head,   5
  Neither too young nor yet unwed.

And when thou com'st thy tale to tell,
Smooth not thy tongue with filed talk,
Lest she some subtile practice smell —
A cripple soon can find a halt;   10
  But plainly say thou lov'st her well,
  And set thy person forth to sell.

What though her frowning brows be bent,
Her cloudy looks will calm ere night;
And then too late she will repent   15
That thus dissembled her delight,
  And twice desire, ere it be day,
  That which with scorn she put away.

What though she strive to try her strength,
And ban and brawl and say thee nay?   20
Her feeble force will yield at length,
When craft hath taught her thus to say:
  'Had women been so strong as men,
  In faith, you had not had it then.'

And to her will frame all thy ways.   25
Spare not to spend, and chiefly there
Where thy desert may merit praise
By ringing in thy lady's ear.
  The strongest castle, tower, and town,
  The golden bullet beats it down.   30

Serve always with assured trust
And in thy suit be humble-true.

Unless thy lady prove unjust,
Press never thou to choose a new.
  When time shall serve, be thou not slack 35
  To proffer, though she put thee back.

The wiles and guiles that women work,
Dissembled with an outward show,
The tricks and toys that in them lurk,
The cock that treads them shall not know. 40
  Have you not heard it said full oft,
  A woman's nay doth stand for naught?

Think women still to strive with men
To sin, and never for to saint.
There is no heaven: be holy then 45
When time with age shall them attaint.
  Were kisses all the joys in bed,
  One woman would another wed.

But, soft! enough! — too much, I fear;
Lest that my mistress hear my song. 50
She will not stick to round me on th' ear,
To teach my tongue to be so long.
  Yet will she blush, here be it said,
  To hear her secrets so bewray'd.

XX

As it fell upon a day
In the merry month of May,
Sitting in a pleasant shade
Which a grove of myrtles made,
Beasts did leap and birds did sing, 5
Trees did grow and plants did spring;
Everything did banish moan,
Save the nightingale alone.
She, poor bird, as all forlorn,
Lean'd her breast up-till a thorn 10
And there sung the dolefull'st ditty,
That to hear it was great pity.
'Fie, fie, fie!' now would she cry;
'Tereu, tereu!' by-and-by;

That to hear her so complain 15
Scarce I could from tears refrain;
For her griefs, so lively shown,
Made me think upon mine own.
'Ah,' thought I, 'thou mourn'st in vain!
None takes pity on thy pain. 20
Senseless trees they cannot hear thee;
Ruthless beasts they will not cheer thee.
King Pandion, he is dead;
All thy friends are lapp'd in lead;
All thy fellow birds do sing, 25
Careless of thy sorrowing.
Even so, poor bird, like thee,
None alive will pity me.
Whilst as fickle Fortune smil'd,
Thou and I were both beguil'd.' 30
  Every one that flatters thee
Is no friend in misery.
Words are easy, like the wind;
Faithful friends are hard to find.
Every man will be thy friend 35
Whilst thou hast wherewith to spend;
But if store of crowns be scant,
No man will supply thy want.
If that one be prodigal,
Bountiful they will him call, 40
And with such-like flattering,
'Pity but he were a king.'
If he be addict to vice,
Quickly him they will entice.
If to women he be bent, 45
They have at commandëment.
But if Fortune once do frown,
Then farewell his great renown!
They that fawn'd on him before
Use his company no more. 50
He that is thy friend indeed,
He will help thee in thy need.
If thou sorrow, he will weep;
If thou wake, he cannot sleep.
Thus of every grief in heart 55
He with thee doth bear a part.
These are certain signs to know
Faithful friend from flatt'ring foe.

The PHŒNIX and TURTLE

Let the bird of loudest lay,
On the sole Arabian tree,
Herald sad and trumpet be,
To whose sound chaste wings obey.

But thou shrieking harbinger,   5
Foul precurrer of the fiend,
Augur of the fever's end,
To this troop come thou not near!

From this session interdict
Every fowl of tyrant wing,   10
Save the eagle, feath'red king:
Keep the obsequy so strict.

Let the priest in surplice white,
That defunctive music can,
Be the death-divining swan,   15
Lest the requiem lack his right.

And thou treble-dated crow,
That thy sable gender mak'st
With the breath thou giv'st and tak'st,
'Mongst our mourners shalt thou go.   20

Here the anthem doth commence:
Love and constancy is dead,
Phœnix and the turtle fled
In a mutual flame from hence.

So they lov'd as love in twain   25
Had the essence but in one;
Two distincts, division none:
Number there in love was slain.

Hearts remote, yet not asunder;
Distance, and no space was seen   30
'Twixt this turtle and his queen;
But in them it were a wonder.

So between them love did shine
That the turtle saw his right
Flaming in the phœnix' sight: 35
Either was the other's mine.

Property was thus appalled,
That the self was not the same;
Single nature's double name
Neither two nor one was called.   40

Reason, in itself confounded,
Saw division grow together,
To themselves yet either neither,
Simple were so well compounded;

That it cried, 'How true a twain   45
Seemeth this concordant one!
Love hath reason, reason none,
If what parts can so remain.'

Whereupon it made this threne
To the phœnix and the dove,   50
Co-supremes and stars of love,
As chorus to their tragic scene.

THRENOS.

Beauty, truth, and rarity,
Grace in all simplicity,
Here enclos'd in cinders lie.   55

Death is now the phœnix' nest;
And the turtle's loyal breast
To eternity doth rest,

Leaving no posterity:
'Twas not their infirmity,   60
It was married chastity.

Truth may seem, but cannot be;
Beauty brag, but 'tis not she:
Truth and Beauty buried be.

To this urn let those repair   65
That are either true or fair;
For these dead birds sigh a prayer.